THE OXFORD HANDBOOK OF

U.S. ENVIRONMENTAL POLICY

THE OXFORD HANDBOOK OF

U.S. ENVIRONMENTAL POLICY

Edited by

SHELDON KAMIENIECKI

and

MICHAEL E. KRAFT

OXFORD

UNIVERSITY PRESS

Oxford University Press is a department of the University of Oxford.
It furthers the University's objective of excellence in research, scholarship,
and education by publishing worldwide.

Oxford   New York
Auckland   Cape Town   Dar es Salaam   Hong Kong   Karachi
Kuala Lumpur   Madrid   Melbourne   Mexico City   Nairobi
New Delhi   Shanghai   Taipei   Toronto

With offices in
Argentina   Austria   Brazil   Chile   Czech Republic   France   Greece
Guatemala   Hungary   Italy   Japan   Poland   Portugal   Singapore
South Korea   Switzerland   Thailand   Turkey   Ukraine   Vietnam

Published in the United States of America by
Oxford University Press
198 Madison Avenue, New York, NY 10016

Library of Congress Cataloging-in-Publication Data
The Oxford handbook of U.S. environmental policy / edited by
Sheldon Kamieniecki and Michael E. Kraft.
p. cm.
Includes bibliographical references and index
ISBN 978–0–19–974467–1
1. Environmental policy—United States—History.   2. Environmentalism—
United States—History.   I. Kamieniecki, Sheldon.   II. Kraft, Michael E.
GE180O94 2013
333.70973—dc23
2012005632

ISBN 978–0–19–974467–1

1 3 5 7 9 8 6 4 2
Printed in the United States of America
on acid-free paper

To Lisa and Sandy,
for their love and support

CONTENTS

....

PART IV   GOVERNMENT INSTITUTIONS AND POLICY MAKING

PART V   THE ROLE OF INFORMAL POLITICAL ACTORS

PART VI   POLICY APPROACHES AND ANALYTIC TOOLS

PART VII   CONCLUSION

PREFACE

....

The study of environmental policy and politics has advanced greatly over the past four decades as governments have begun to take seriously the wide array of contemporary environmental and natural resource challenges facing the world. In this volume the contributing authors take stock of what we know and do not know about American environmental policy and politics, from broad questions about governance of common pool resources in the twenty-first century to the well-established role of key institutions such as Congress, the courts, and the presidency, and the influence of interest groups, political parties, and public opinion on policy choices. We leave to others the tasks of reviewing comparable research in other fields of political science such as comparative and international environmental policy and politics, and political theory.

As the United States and other nations struggle today to respond to third-generation environmental problems such as climate change and loss of biological diversity, it is essential to ask what government has done to date in developing and implementing environmental policies, what those policies have achieved and where they have fallen short, and the strengths and weaknesses of various policy approaches that have been used and might be used in the future. It is equally important to ask about the conditions for successful policy action, and the capacity to formulate and adopt effective, efficient, equitable, and politically acceptable solutions in the future as the United States and other nations seek to integrate the policy concerns of the past with the broader agenda of sustainable development for the rest of this century.

Our introductory chapter sets out these purposes in more detail, reviews key policy developments and research over time, and tries to place the study of environmental policy and politics within the larger disciplinary debate over research needs and approaches within political science and policy studies as well as within the larger context of interdisciplinary research on the environment. The chapter also introduces the topics addressed in the book and the rationale for including them.

We asked the contributing authors to explain and evaluate the evolution of studies conducted in their fields of expertise. In doing so, they sought to integrate a large body of scholarship on a variety of substantive environmental problems, from pollution control to the use of public lands and energy resources. Each contributing chapter offers a concise overview of the topic, reviews the most important research to date, discusses the major agreements and disagreements among scholars, and sets out fresh questions for future exploration. Taken together, we hope that the chapters provide a valuable resource for those entering the field as well as a useful retrospective for those who have long studied environmental policy and politics, whether in the U.S. political system or in other nations.

We chose to emphasize governing capacity, major theoretical ideas, political processes and institutions, and policy approaches and analytic methods as the most appropriate way to conduct such a review and synthesis of disciplinary knowledge. Yet we encouraged contributors to illustrate their arguments with examples of substantive policy issues as they deemed appropriate. We hope the result is a clear and comprehensive summary of key environmental policy developments over time as well as a thorough assessment of scholarly work on U.S. environmental policy and politics.

We thank the contributing authors for their cooperation and expeditious responses to our many requests for revisions. A volume like this is possible only because our contributors agreed with us that it served a valuable purpose and they were willing to devote considerable time to the project. It has been a pleasure to work with such a talented and dedicated group of colleagues. We also want to acknowledge support from the University of California, Santa Cruz (UCSC), and the University of Wisconsin–Green Bay. We are particularly grateful for the invaluable assistance provided by Andrea Cohen at UCSC. For more than two years she worked hard communicating with the book's contributors on a regular basis, gathering important information from them, and assisting us in assembling the book's chapters. Duran Fiack, a Ph.D. student in the Environmental Studies Department at UCSC, did a marvelous job assembling the index, and we are grateful for his efforts. Finally, we want to thank the staff of Oxford University Press and Newgen North America for their splendid editorial work and overall management of the project: Amy Whitmer, Molly Morrison, Christi Stanforth, Caelyn Cobb, and David McBride. As always, we take responsibility for any errors or omissions that have escaped our notice during the extended period of writing, editing, and production.

About the Contributors

Richard N. L. Andrews is Professor of Environmental Policy in the Department of Public Policy and in the Department of Environmental Sciences & Engineering of the Gillings School of Global Public Health, University of North Carolina, Chapel Hill.

William Ascher is Professor of Government and Economics, Claremont McKenna College.

Walter F. Baber is Professor and Director of the Graduate Center for Public Policy and Administration, California State University, Long Beach.

Robert V. Bartlett is Gund Professor of Liberal Arts in the Political Science Department, University of Vermont.

Amy Below is Assistant Professor of Political Science in the School of Public Policy, Oregon State University.

Lori S. Bennear is Assistant Professor of Environmental Economics and Policy in the Nicholas School of the Environment, Duke University.

Christopher J. Bosso is Professor of Public Policy and Associate Dean of the School of Public Policy and Urban Affairs, Northeastern University.

Cary Coglianese is the Edward B. Shils Professor of Law, Professor of Political Science, and Director of the Penn Program on Regulation, University of Pennsylvania.

Steven Cohen is the Executive Director of The Earth Institute, Professor in the Practice of Public Affairs, Director of Master of Public Administration Program in Environmental Science and Policy & Energy and Environmental Policy Concentration in the School of International and Public Affairs, and Director of the Master of Science in Sustainability Management in the School of Continuing Education, Columbia University.

Dorothy M. Daley is Associate Professor in the Department of Political Science and in the Environmental Studies Program, University of Kansas.

David P. Daniels is a graduate student in the Department of Political Science, Stanford University.

Elizabeth R. DeSombre is Frost Professor of Environmental Studies and Director of the Environmental Studies Program, Wellesley College.

Timothy P. Duane is Professor of Environmental Studies, University of California, Santa Cruz, and Associate Professor of Law, Vermont Law School.

Robert J. Duffy is Professor of Political Science, Colorado State University.

Daniel J. Fiorino is Director of the Center for Environmental Policy in the School of Public Affairs, American University.

Scott R. Furlong is Dean of the College of Liberal Arts and Sciences and Professor of Public and Environmental Affairs and Political Science, University of Wisconsin–Green Bay.

Andrea K. Gerlak is Director of Academic Development with the International Studies Association, Visiting Professor in the Department of Political Science, and Senior Policy Associate with the Udall Center for Studies in Public Policy, University of Arizona.

Deborah Lynn Guber is Associate Professor of Political Science, University of Vermont.

Tanya Heikkila is Associate Professor, School of Public Affairs, University of Colorado at Denver.

Lamont C. Hempel is Hedco Professor of Environmental Studies, University of Redlands.

Sheldon Kamieniecki is the Dean of the Division of Social Sciences and Professor of Environmental Studies, University of California, Santa Cruz.

Michael E. Kraft is the Herbert Fisk Johnson Professor of Environmental Studies Emeritus and Professor Emeritus, Political Science and Public and Environmental Affairs, University of Wisconsin–Green Bay.

Jon A. Krosnick is Professor of Political Science, Communication, and Psychology, Frederic O. Glover Professor in Humanities and Social Sciences, and Senior Fellow at Woods Institute, Stanford University.

Judith A. Layzer is Professor of Environmental Policy in the Department of Urban Studies and Planning, Massachusetts Institute of Technology.

Mark Lubell is a Professor in the Department of Environmental Science and Policy, University of California, Davis.

Richard A. Matthew is Professor of Environmental Politics and International Relations in the Schools of Social Ecology and Social Science and Director of the Center for Unconventional Security Affairs, University of California, Irvine.

Daniel A. Mazmanian is Professor and Bedrosian Chair in Governance and the Director of the Judith and John Bedrosian Center on Governance and the Public Enterprise, Sol Price School of Public Policy, University of Southern California.

Laurie Kaye Nijaki is a Postdoctoral Fellow at the School of Natural Resources and the Environment at the University of Michigan.

Sheila M. Olmstead is a Fellow at Resources for the Future, Washington, D.C.

Kate O'Neill is an Associate Professor in the Department of Environmental Science, Policy and Management, University of California, Berkeley.

Robert C. Paehlke is Professor Emeritus of Political Studies and Environmental and Resource Studies, Trent University, Peterborough, Ontario, Canada.

Sara R. Rinfret is Assistant Professor in the Department of Political Science, Hartwick College, Oneonta, New York.

Walter A. Rosenbaum is Director Emeritus, Bob Graham Center for Public Service, University of Florida, and Professor of Political Science, Emeritus, University of Florida.

Denise Scheberle is the Herbert Fisk Johnson Professor of Environmental Studies Emeritus and Professor Emeritus, Political Science and Public and Environmental Affairs, University of Wisconsin–Green Bay.

Alexis Schulman is a Ph.D. candidate in the Department of Urban Studies and Planning, Massachusetts Institute of Technology.

Henrik Selin is Associate Professor in the Department of International Relations, Boston University.

Toddi A. Steelman is Professor of Environmental and Natural Resource Policy in the Department of Forestry and Environmental Resources, North Carolina State University.

Lawrence Susskind is Ford Professor of Urban and Environmental Planning, Massachusetts Institute of Technology, and Vice Chair of the Program on Negotiation, Harvard Law School.

Craig W. Thomas is Professor of Public Affairs at the Daniel J. Evans School of Public Affairs, University of Washington.

Michael P. Tichy is the Urgent Care Program Manager, Southeast Incorporated, Columbus, Ohio.

Trevor Tompson is the Global Director of Polling for the Associated Press.

Stacy D. VanDeveer is Associate Professor of Political Science, University of New Hampshire, and 2011–2012 Senior Fellow, Transatlantic Academy, German Marshall Fund of the United States.

Norman J. Vig is Winifred and Atherton Bean Professor of Science, Technology and Society, Emeritus, Carleton College.

THE OXFORD HANDBOOK OF

U.S. ENVIRONMENTAL POLICY

PART I

INTRODUCTION

CHAPTER 1

....

THE EVOLUTION OF RESEARCH ON U.S. ENVIRONMENTAL POLICY

....

SHELDON KAMIENIECKI AND MICHAEL E. KRAFT

ENVIRONMENTAL policy and politics today are clearly important for society's well-being even if policy choices and their impacts generate considerable disagreement and controversy. Despite elaborate efforts by government and industry to control pollution emissions and conserve natural resources over the past 40-plus years, the United States and other countries face serious and in many ways growing environmental challenges in the twenty-first century. These range from protection of the nation's and the world's biodiversity to action on energy use, climate change, and the imperative of sustainable development. Proposed solutions have long been of concern to social scientists, policy analysts, business leaders, and policy makers because of their cost and impacts on society. As a result, we now have a thriving literature on the strengths, weaknesses, and promise of policy alternatives. This is particularly the case for environmental protection policy, long dominated by conventional regulation, where analysts have proposed and studied alternatives such as the use of market incentives, flexible regulation, public-private partnerships, and stakeholder collaboration (e.g., Cohen, Kamieniecki, and Cahn 2005; Durant, Fiorino, and O'Leary 2004; Eisner 2007; Fiorino 2006; Kraft, Stephan, and Abel 2011; Press and Mazmanian 2013; Rosenau 2000). Much the same is true for natural resource policy, where new approaches have been praised and, at least to some extent, have become the object of scholarly analysis (Fairfax et al. 2005; Layzer 2008; Lubell and Segee 2013; Sabatier et al. 2005; Weber 2003; Whiteley, Ingram, and Perry 2008).

Since the first Earth Day in April 1970, federal, state, and local governments have adopted dozens of major laws and hundreds of regulations intended to control pollution, protect natural resources, and foster sustainable approaches to economic development. New institutions, such as the U.S. Environmental Protection Agency (EPA), have been created, and governments have assumed a wide range of new responsibilities. Social scientists, particularly political scientists and policy scholars, have written a large body of work that explores the various aspects of the environmental policy-making process and the role of a diverse set of policy actors and institutions—from organized interest groups and the media to government policy makers and the role of both natural and social scientists in the policy process (e.g., Durant, Fiorino, and O'Leary 2004; Klyza and Sousa 2008; Kraft 2011; Miller 2002; Vig and Kraft 2013). Respected scholarship traces the history and impact of environmental ideas and how they have been integrated with other social movements (Andrews 2006). An interdisciplinary literature similarly assesses the capacity of policy analysis methods and various public policy tools to address the environmental, energy, and resource problems facing governments at all levels and in different countries (e.g., Axelrod, VanDeveer, and Downie 2010; Bartlett 1989; Knaap and Kim 1998; Susskind, Jain, and Martyniuk 2001).

While most of the literature deals with environmental politics and policy at the federal level, increasingly research concerns state and local issues, policy processes, and institutions as well. Although not a primary focus of this book, global environmental problems (most notably, protection of the ozone layer, climate change, and common pool resources) and comparative analyses of politics and policy making between developing and developed nations (e.g., Harrison and Sundstrom 2010; Kamieniecki 1993; Selin and VanDeveer 2009; Steinberg and VanDeveer 2012; Tobin 2013) have also received much more attention in recent years.

This book takes stock of the environmental policy field and provides a broad and comprehensive review and assessment of the literature on U.S. environmental politics and policy. The field has grown substantially from its beginnings in the late 1960s, when it built on a rich but limited tradition of earlier analyses of conservation and natural resource policy (Caldwell 1970; Foss 1960; Ingram and Mann 1983; McConnell 1966; Smith 1966). With the expansion of government policies in the 1960s and 1970s and increasing interest in contemporary environmental challenges, from pollution control to forest management, political scientists and policy scholars have greatly expanded the scope and sophistication of research, and they have increasingly relied on major theoretical concepts and analytic frameworks from the discipline (for example, those related to agenda setting, interest group lobbying, policy-making processes, and compliance behavior) and have used the full range of social science research methods commonly employed today. Yet there is no single volume, encyclopedia, or edited collection that authoritatively brings together this impressive body of work in a way that can alert those entering the field to the most important topics that have been addressed, the most significant scholarship that has been produced, and the priorities for future research.

The modest efforts made in the 1980s and 1990s, such as the second edition of James Lester's edited volume, *Environmental Politics and Policy: Theories and Evidence* (1995a), cover only a narrow set of these topics and are now sadly dated. The major goal of this book is to fill that gap by providing a comprehensive, in-depth investigation of the central research issues and concerns in environmental politics and policy, primarily within the U.S. political system. Another major objective is to provide researchers and policy makers with an extensive and rich source of the most current information available that can contribute to their knowledge and help guide their work in key areas of interest.

In selecting the topics to be covered in this book, we have identified the most important research areas in the literature and have solicited contributions from distinguished scholars. As a clear sign that such a work like this is desperately needed, nearly every researcher we invited agreed to contribute a chapter to this volume. Moreover, we are fortunate in being able to draw from our own scholarship in the field and from work over the past decade in coediting a prominent book series at MIT Press titled American and Comparative Environmental Policy. Although Oxford University Press was generous in affording us considerable latitude in determining the size of the volume, we are aware that we have not covered every area of research interest in the literature and that some readers may be somewhat disappointed as a result. For instance, much work has been done in the fields of political theory, comparative politics, and international relations that is not covered here due to space limitations. Future Oxford volumes may explore scholarship in the fields that we have omitted from the book. Most students of American environmental policy, however, will find this book extremely useful in their research on environmental policy issues in the United States.

As noted, the research areas identified here reflect a strong desire on the editors' part to produce a book that will be helpful to scholars and students conducting research on U.S. environmental politics and policy. In an effort to meet this goal, contributors were asked to explain and evaluate the evolution of research in their fields of expertise. Specifically, we asked contributors to review the literature within their specified areas, assess its strengths and weaknesses, provide insights on the major agreements and disagreements among scholars, and identify gaps in the research that future analysts should fill. We hope that the end product is the most authoritative volume on the U.S. environmental politics and policy literature published thus far. Due to the critical nature of the topics selected within the literature, we believe this book will become the universal starting point for those embarking on research on U.S. environmental policy making.

This introductory chapter establishes a foundation for the book. We begin the discussion by analyzing the varying phases and contexts of U.S. environmental policy and the literature. The chapter then turns to addressing certain problematic approaches in the literature. The organization of the book is presented at the conclusion of the discussion.

1. VARYING PHASES AND CONTEXTS OF U.S. ENVIRONMENTAL POLICY AND THE LITERATURE

In order to understand fully the modern evolution of the literature on U.S. environmental politics and policy, one needs to take into account the political and policy contexts in which major studies were conducted. In most cases, the literature has sought to analyze particular environmental problems and policy issues and explain why major changes did or did not take place in environmental policy at a given point in time. Thus, a brief review of the political times in which studies were conducted contributes to a better explanation of how the literature developed. Since many studies were conducted in response to the adoption of environmental policies, we first examine the evolution of U.S. environmental policy over time prior to discussing how the literature developed. Mazmanian and Kraft (2009) have provided a useful way to outline the various epochs of environmental policy development, and we use that framework here.

In what is generally considered to be the first generation of modern environmental policy actions, in the late 1960s and early 1970s the federal government greatly expanded its role in the regulation of air, water, and land, supplanting what was widely recognized as highly variable and ineffective state regulation (Davies and Davies 1975; Ingram and Mann 1983; Mazmanian and Kraft 2009). The new style of federal command-and-control regulation was most evident in the Clean Air Act Amendments of 1970 and the Clean Water Act of 1972, both of which set the tone for further advances in environmental protection legislation throughout the 1970s (Vig and Kraft 2013). The prevailing belief at the time was that pollution was caused primarily by callous and unthinking businesses whose behavior was predominantly guided by the profit motive and could be changed only through federal regulation that would compel environmentally appropriate actions under the threat of severe penalties for noncompliance (Mazmanian and Kraft 2009).

The spurt of legislative initiatives, from the Safe Drinking Water Act of 1974 to the Comprehensive Environmental Response, Compensation, and Liability Act (Superfund) of 1980, was driven by a sharp increase in public concern about environmental threats, as well as by expanded media coverage and extensive lobbying by newly organized environmental groups (Bosso 2005; Cohen, Kamieniecki, and Cahn 2005; Kraft 2011). While public health continued to be important, Americans were now beginning to become increasingly alarmed by the damage that was being done to the natural environment as well as the rapid exploitation of the nation's (and the world's) natural resources. Industry groups were unable to prevent these legislative enactments at either the federal or state level, although they did manage to limit their impact somewhat through provisions that required agencies to thoroughly justify their environmental quality standards and regulations and that permitted court challenges to such agency decisions. In some early cases, it was actually less costly to ignore the law and be fined than to comply with the regulation. This problem was soon corrected by legislators and regulators.

One consequence of the "environmental decade" of the 1970s was that business groups and their political allies mounted a vigorous and persistent campaign over the next twenty years to reform the regulatory process—in particular, to reduce the burdens and costs these new laws had imposed on industry. In Mazmanian and Kraft's (2009) view, the second epoch has been characterized by efficiency-based regulatory reform and flexibility in environmental policy making. This second epoch of environmental policy began in the late 1970s but was most notable during Ronald Reagan's presidency as the White House sought to curtail implementation actions by the U.S. Environmental Protection Agency (EPA), sharply reduce the agency's budget, and impose new cost-benefit tests for regulations, among other actions (also see Vig and Kraft 1984 and 2013 as well as Vig's chapter in this book). But the regulatory reform agenda did not disappear with Reagan's departure from the presidency. It was equally visible during George H. W. Bush's presidency and during the 1990s as Bill Clinton pursued a range of reform measures, such as the EPA's Common Sense Initiative and Project XL, to head off even stronger action favored by Congress. As Kraft (chapter 13, this volume) observes, the Republican takeover of Congress after the 1994 elections, the election of George W. Bush in 2000 and 2004, and the Republican success in recapturing the House of Representatives in the 2010 elections strongly suggested that regulatory reform would remain a contentious issue for years to come.

Yet the legacy of some 30 years of regulatory reform efforts has been decidedly mixed. The centralized command-and-control policies of the 1970s remain largely intact despite the many experiments in regulatory flexibility, collaborative decision making, public-private partnerships, use of market incentives, and voluntary pollution control (Coglianese and Nash 2006; Dietz and Stern 2003; John 1994; Mazmanian and Kraft 2009; Press and Mazmanian 2013; Rosenau 2000; Vogel 2005). While the EPA under the Barack Obama administration increased controls on automobile emissions under the Clean Air Act, Congress once again failed to adopt a climate change policy directed at control of greenhouse gas emissions despite strong action on climate change within the states (Rabe 2004, 2010). As Below points out in her chapter, unprecedented levels of partisanship in Congress before and during the Obama presidency, however, prevented both the Democrats and the Republicans from changing previous major environmental and energy policy to satisfy their strongest interest group supporters and campaign contributors (Bafumi and Herron 2010; Klyza and Sousa 2008; Kraft 2011). Clearly, insufficient political consensus at the national level has prohibited any major alteration of the first generation of environmental policies. Even the worst economic crisis since the Great Depression at the end of the Bush administration and during the Obama administration failed to produce significant rollbacks in what many argue are costly environmental regulation and policy. The result is that a new layer of reform measures has been built on the foundation of the first generation of environmental (and resource) policies without substantially changing their goals or the means used to achieve them.

For this reason, business interests remain dissatisfied and continue to seek further reforms even as a third generation of environmental policies grounded in the concepts of sustainable development and sustainable communities has emerged (Kamieniecki 2006; Kraft and Kamieniecki 2007). This latest policy agenda encompasses a wide variety of private sector actions that are often described as voluntary "greening" of the corporation, although scholars are divided over the degree to which such voluntary measures have worked or are likely to work in the future (Cohen, Kamieniecki, and Cahn 2005; Harrison and Antweiler 2003; Kamieniecki 2006; Kraft and Kamieniecki 2007; Kraft, Stephan, and Abel 2011; Mazmanian and Kraft 2009; Potoski and Prakash 2005; Press and Mazmanian 2013).

In this third era we have begun to see and will continue to see movement toward "a more enduring and sustainable epoch in which concerns for the natural environment and how it relates to all other aspects of our economic and social worlds will play a far more pronounced role in policymaking" (Mazmanian and Kraft 2009, 11). Mazmanian and Kraft believe that "the transition will occur at widely varying rates and in different forms from one region of the nation to another and across communities" (2009, 11). Few would expect otherwise, even if environmentalists prefer a more consistent and coherent agenda for pursuit of sustainability. It is apparent, for example, that the term "sustainable development" has taken on many different interpretations and meanings in order to fit and often bolster a particular perspective or position.

Mazmanian and Kraft's (2009) work categorizes the various phases of environmental policy development. Most of the literature parallels their three described epochs and reflects the evolution of environmental policy by including studies that anticipate policy development, analyze policy change, or investigate the economic and environmental impacts of policy change within a particular time period. Within this context Lester (1995b) reviews the historical evolution of the environmental politics and policy literature in the introductory chapter of his edited volume. He divides the literature into three periods of theoretical development: early work (1960–1977), growing maturity (1978–1985), and the contemporary period (1986–present).

According to Lester (1995b), the earliest phase of the literature was basically devoted to "consciousness raising" among those interested in environmental protection. He believes most of the writings during this era were "descriptive in nature" and included major works by natural scientists, such as *Silent Spring* by Rachel Carson (1962), *The Closing Circle* by Barry Commoner (1970), and *The Population Bomb* by Paul Ehrlich (1968). These and similar publications raised awareness among students and the public about the plight of the environment. Lester correctly observes that only a handful of political scientists and policy scholars contributed actively to the literature during this time period, although some of this early work clearly went beyond merely describing the problems to an increasingly concerned public. This was also a time when the subfield of environmental politics and policy was being defined and research needs set out (Ingram and Mann 1983; Nagel 1974), the first texts appeared (Davies and Davies 1975; Rosenbaum 1973), some of the earliest empirical work was being conducted and published (e.g., Jones

1975), and analyses of sustainability (Ophuls 1977; Pirages 1977) and population policy (Kraft and Schneider 1978) began to appear.

Lester (1995b) argues that during this era a major debate took place over the appropriate role of political scientists involved in the study of environmental issues. Some contended that political scientists should analyze environmental problems principally because of their serious threats to the global ecosystem and society at large and because solutions would require an understanding of the role of politics and government. Engaging environmental issues in this way would require political scientists to redefine the traditional boundaries of their discipline and also to develop at least some expertise in other disciplines related to environmental study, such as ecology or environmental science. However, others argued that political scientists should take every step to avoid blurring the boundaries of their field of investigation and seek instead to contribute to the growth of disciplinary knowledge. Many who advocated this position believed that political science researchers should strive to employ only scientific and professional goals and standards when analyzing environmental policies. As Lester (1995b) observes, this debate eventually shaped the next generation of research, which was primarily concerned with developing greater empirical understanding of environmental issues and policy-making processes through the use of disciplinary theories and methods of study. Nonetheless, even as scholarship turned increasingly to theoretically informed empirical studies, much of the expanding literature on environmental policy and politics sought to inform society's continuing struggle to address mounting environmental problems. By 1978 political scientists had begun to contribute to a reservoir of accumulated knowledge of political attitudes and behavior, the functioning of governmental institutions, and policy formulation and implementation involving environmental and natural resource issues. This second generation of research was empirical (and less frequently descriptive) in nature, and it provided an increased understanding of the determinants of U.S. environmental policy (Lester 1995b). In addition, the focus of environmental concern broadened from air and water pollution and pesticide regulation to toxic waste and solid waste management, ocean dumping, and land use planning. However, while researchers acquired a deeper and broader comprehension of the empirical foundation of environmental politics, they tended not to explore the normative implications of institutional and regulatory failures in environmental policy making, with some notable exceptions (e.g., Ophuls 1977). Among other things, this became a major driver behind the third generation of the environmental policy literature.

According to Lester (1995b), after 1986 political scientists turned their attention to normative concerns associated with U.S. environmental politics and policy. During this time researchers were attempting to define the essence of the "environmental problematique" and, based on what they found, prescribed the appropriate solution (e.g., Milbrath 1989). In this vein, Michael Kraft (1992) argued at the time that this literature focused on "such basic questions as the nature and viability of modern industrial society, the structure of political and economic institutions and the effectiveness of their decision making mechanism, the ways in which political ideologies and paradigms affect our capacity to recognize and act on ecological problems, and how an environmental ideology or ethic might alter both personal and political decision making" (713). Paehlke's contribution to this volume (chapter 5) explores the latter phenomenon in some depth.

Since the publication of Lester's (1995b) book, the literature on environmental policy has continued to evolve and expand in various ways. For instance, while interest in federal environmental policy continues to flourish, there is now a greater focus on local and state governments and their approaches to improving air and water quality, acting on energy and climate change issues, and promoting sustainable communities (e.g., Betsill and Rabe 2009; Mazmanian and Kraft 2009; Mullin 2009; Portney 2012; Rabe 2004). At the same time, there is much more being written about environmental and natural resource issues in developing and developed nations, global challenges such as the depletion of the ozone layer and climate change, biodiversity, preservation of marine life in the oceans, forest conservation, and the development of sustainable societies (e.g., Axelrod, VanDeveer, and Downie 2010; Desai, 2002; DeSombre 2000; Harrison and Sundstrom 2010; Selin and VanDeveer 2009; Steinberg and VanDeveer 2012; Vig and Faure 2004; Young 2010).

Beyond these developments, studies at all levels of government have employed disciplinary theories and models in increasingly creative ways and have become more and more empirical, often incorporating highly sophisticated quantitative techniques in addressing current and alternative approaches to direct or command-and-control regulation (e.g., Kraft, Stephan, and Abel 2011; Sabatier et al. 2005). The field of environmental and natural resource economics also has quickly expanded and has significantly contributed to the policy literature (e.g., Cole 2002; Driesen 2010; Portney and Stavins 2000; Rothenberg 2002; Toman 2001). More generally, ideas and concepts related to governing capacity (see chapter 9 in this volume), government institutions (chapter 15), science and policy making (chapter 29), agenda building (chapter 20), citizen and interest group involvement and collaboration (chapter 23), environmental security (chapter 6), government regulation versus private markets (chapter 25), and assessment of various policy tools and approaches (chapter 28) are being closely studied by political scientists and policy analysts (e.g., Adger and Jordan 2009; Ascher, Steelman, and Healy 2010; Cohen, Kamieniecki, and Cahn 2005; Harrison and Bryner 2004; Kamieniecki 2006; Kamieniecki and Below 2008; Keller 2009; Kettl 2002; Kraft and Kamieniecki 2007; Kraft, Stephan, and Abel 2011; Layzer 2008; Matthew 2013; Miller 2002).

2. PROBLEMATIC APPROACHES IN THE LITERATURE

Although the literature now includes more studies that tend to be objective and balanced than ever before, with major goals of data collection, theory testing, knowledge accumulation, and learning, what might be called a bias of environmentalism still exists in many research approaches and publications. This kind of bias persists in various areas of study, from research on the role of business and elites in shaping environmental policy to analyses of the virtue of voluntary environmental regulation to investigations that assume that science and policy analysis should drive environmental policy choices. In many cases, scholars begin their work with a specific conclusion and frame their research in such a way, intentionally or not, that their results support that conclusion. Such writings may sometimes be entertaining to read and offer useful perspectives, but they also can fall short in describing the problem and what works and what does not in policy development and implementation.

One example of this phenomenon can be seen in the literature on "environmental justice." A number of researchers, representing various disciplines in the social sciences, have studied the implementation of Superfund, the operation of the Toxics Release Inventory, and other environmental programs from an environmental justice perspective. Some of these scholars (e.g., Bryant and Mohai 1992; Bullard 1983, 1993, 1994a, 1994b) have been affiliated with the environmental justice movement and seek to demonstrate how private industry is more likely to expose people of color (i.e., African Americans, Hispanics, and other ethnic groups) than white people to dangerous pollutants. They also have argued that government tends to delay pollution control and cleanup actions in minority areas. Unfortunately, Bullard (1994a), a sociologist and a major figure in the environmental justice movement, and some other environmental justice researchers at times have purposely selected cases or presented other types of subjective evidence that support such conclusions: that is, they report that people of color are disproportionately exposed to toxic waste or toxic chemicals in every part of the country (Kamieniecki and Steckenrider 1997).

A number of the early studies on environmental justice also contained serious methodological flaws (Hird 1994; Kamieniecki and Below 2008; Kamieniecki and Steckenrider 1997; Ringquist 2006). Analyses by Bullard and some others, for example, tended to rely on isolated case studies based on anecdotal accounts of environmental racism, and they failed to present solid empirical evidence to demonstrate the existence of an intentional policy to expose minorities disproportionately at the local, state, or national level. In some cases the methodological flaws included failing to consider and correct for varying population densities (Lavelle and Coyle 1992). Merely conveying the percentage of minority residents in a particular community does not tell us how many citizens are actually exposed to environmental threats, let alone whether those threats were already present before large numbers of minority citizens moved into a given locality (Kamieniecki and Below 2008; Kamieniecki and Steckenrider 1997). In addition, many studies defined affected locations in geographic terms that are too large to permit careful examination of exposure to toxic substances. Previous studies based on state (e.g., Lester, Allen, and Lauer 1994), county (e.g., Allen, Lester, and Hill 1995), municipal (e.g., Greenberg 1994), or zip code areas (e.g., United Church of Christ 1987) were likely to contain "aggregation errors," which can conceal exposure patterns. Using census tracts is better, since doing so provides more precision in determining location of people and hazardous waste sites.

Finally, a number of environmental justice studies have relied only on aggregate data to draw conclusions about individual behavior. Researchers who incorrectly generalize from one unit of analysis (e.g., state or county) to another (the individual) are said by statisticians to have committed an "ecological fallacy" (Kamieniecki and Steckenrider 1997). Attitudinal and epidemiological surveys based on scientific random sampling techniques and employing proper measurement procedures, although not without their problems, are a valuable source of information and should be employed to supplement aggregate data analysis.

Today scholars are expected to put aside their personal agendas and use the best theories and methodologies available to study environmental politics, policy, and outcomes without bias as to preferred results. Investigators are being strongly encouraged to select those theories and methodologies that most directly address central research questions and hypotheses. Nevertheless, although generally the field has matured and expectations now reflect the perspectives of scholars in the larger discipline, some studies continue to include various biases, and some are simply not as rigorous as others. The challenge looking ahead is to analyze critically important issues in environmental politics and policy by making the most appropriate use of theory and methods. In the end, such studies may offer more reliable knowledge than was previously available and thus might become more influential in informing policy decisions.

Partly because of such concerns, expectations and research standards today are much higher than in the 1970s even as a diversity of scholarly approaches are used. Some studies lend themselves well to rigorous study because pertinent databases and/or a sufficient number of different case studies are available. Yet there is still great value in using qualitative methods, particularly when the questions being explored are new and important and where little empirical data exist. Many important topics need fresh vision and exploration even if they cannot be studied rigorously. These include questions of new governance arrangements, proposals of new policy ideas, and descriptions of some new and intriguing developments, such as innovative policy making and implementation at the state and local level or new ways to promote stakeholder collaboration. Where a particular topic lends itself well to empirical inquiry, however, scholars need to employ the best methods possible and move beyond summary accounts and descriptive studies, and certainly beyond personal biases and political agendas.

3. The Organization of the Book

We have divided the book into seven distinct parts. The first contains the introductory chapter, and the last includes the concluding chapter. That chapter returns to the themes set out in this introduction, summarizes the contributions outlined in the various chapters, and reviews a number of key research directions for the future mentioned by contributors.

Part 2 addresses the evolution of environmental policy and covers major concepts, theoretical ideas, and policy changes that have been analyzed in the literature. The chapters provide a historical overview of the environmental movement and the development of public policies. They address the rise of green ideas in relation to politics and governing, including environmental ethics, environmental justice, sustainability, and environmental security. This section links these ideas to policy development through an overview of empirical studies on agenda setting, issue framing, and political discourse.

Part 3 includes chapters on a set of macro-level questions about governing capacity in relation to the magnitude and urgency of global environmental challenges, particularly those concerning a third generation of environmental problems, such as climate change and the quest for sustainable development. An advisory committee to the National Science Foundation (NSF) recently presented the challenges this way: "The world is at a crossroads. The global footprint of humans is such that we are stressing natural and social systems beyond their capacities. We must address these complex environmental challenges and mitigate global scale environmental change or accept likely all-pervasive disruptions" (Advisory Committee for Environmental Research and Education 2009, 6). The writings in this section present a broad discussion of how governments can respond and have responded to these challenges at the appropriate scale and in a timely manner. Contributors also examine how governments have addressed sustainability challenges, and what we know and what we need to learn about such challenges. Finally, within this context, the chapters offer an assessment of the U.S. leadership role past and present, notable actions and challenges, and the factors that affect U.S. policy making on global environmental issues. What can political science and public policy studies contribute either alone or as a component of interdisciplinary research to discussions and analyses concerning the major global problems we face during the new century?

Part 4 examines U.S. political institutions and policy-making processes, with special attention paid to institutional capacity, institutional development and adaptation over time, and policy innovation. More specifically, the chapters in this segment of the volume analyze Congress and environmental policy, including distinctive legislative processes and actors, and constraints and opportunities for policy making; the American presidency, leadership, and environmental policy; the courts, legal analysis, and environmental policy; the bureaucracy and environmental and natural resource policy; rule-making processes and public management, including deregulation and its effects on regulatory reform; state and local government and federalism; and multilevel governance and collaborative decision making.

The fifth part of the book evaluates the role of informal political actors, especially in regard to their participation in policy making and public education. Thus, contributors analyze the role of public opinion, public participation, interest groups, and campaigns, elections, and the media in educating Americans and in the policy-making process. Here, too, attention is paid to the implications for governing capacity and conflict resolution.

Part 6 provides an in-depth examination of a diversity of policy approaches and analytic tools and determines their potential contributions to policy making. The same advisory committee to NSF noted above urged the adoption of an integrated and interdisciplinary approach to achieve a better understanding of the complex and rapidly changing environmental systems and human activities that push them toward sometimes irreversible tipping points. The report also called for a new set of tools that can improve our understanding of these natural-human systems and help to communicate findings to the public and policy makers as public policies are developed (Advisory Committee for Environmental Research and Education 2009). As these tools continue to evolve, they merit careful appraisal in relation to governing capacity, their contribution to understanding the consequences of policy choices, and their capacity to address questions of policy effectiveness, efficiency, and equity. In response to this challenge, the chapters in this portion of the book address the role of science, political economy, market incentives, ecosystem management and restoration, environmental planning and impact assessments, and privatization, self-regulation, information disclosure, and other voluntary programs in environmental policy making. The use of quantitative economic analysis in the environmental policy literature is not covered in this volume because of its unique nature and because the subject demands much more attention than space allows. However, several individual chapters in this and other sections do draw on this literature.

In every case in the book, contributors were asked to explain and evaluate the evolution of studies conducted in their fields of expertise. In writing on these topics contributors were able to integrate a large body of scholarship that deals with a variety of substantive environmental problems, from pollution control and public lands to energy and renewable resources. We emphasize governing capacity, major theoretical ideas, political processes and institutions, and policy approaches and analytic methods as the best way to identify fruitful areas of scholarship within the discipline. At the same time, we encouraged contributors to illustrate their arguments with examples of substantive policy issues at appropriate points in their chapters. We hope that readers will agree that our approach to the difficult task of selecting the most critical topics and organizing the vast literature in this field has allowed us to produce a clear, comprehensive, and valuable assessment of important previous research on U.S. environmental politics and policy as well as opportunities to expand this research in new directions in the years ahead.

REFERENCES

Adger, W. N., and A. Jordan, eds. 2009. *Governing Sustainability*. Cambridge: Cambridge University Press.

Advisory Committee for Environmental Research and Education. 2009. *Transitions and Tipping Points in Complex Environmental Systems*. Washington, DC: National Science Foundation.

Allen, D. W., J. P. Lester, and K. M. Hill. 1995. "Prejudice, Profits, and Power: Assessing the Eco-Racism Thesis at the County Level." Paper presented at the Annual Meeting of the Western Political Science Association, Portland, OR, March 16–18.

Andrews, R. N. L. 2006. *Managing the Environment, Managing Ourselves: A History of American Environmental Policy*. 2nd ed. New Haven: Yale University Press.

Ascher, W., T. Steelman, and R. Healy. 2010. *Knowledge and Environmental Policy: Re-Imagining the Boundaries of Science and Politics*. Cambridge, MA: MIT Press.

Axelrod, R. S., S. D. VanDeveer, and D. L. Downie, eds. 2010. *The Global Environment: Institutions, Law, and Policy*. 3rd ed. Washington, DC: CQ Press.

Bafumi, J., and M. C. Herron. 2010. "Leapfrog Representation and Extremism: A Study of American Voters and Their Members in Congress." *American Political Science Review* 104 (3): 519–542.

Bartlett, R. V., ed. 1989. *Policy through Impact Assessment: Institutionalized Analysis as a Policy Strategy*. New York: Greenwood.

Betsill, M. M., and B. G. Rabe. 2009. "Climate Change and Multilevel Governance: The Evolving State and Local Roles." In *Toward Sustainable Communities: Transition and Transformations in Environmental Policy*, 2nd ed., ed. D. A. Mazmanian and M. E. Kraft. Cambridge, MA: MIT Press.

Bosso, C. J. 2005. *Environment, Inc.: From Grassroots to Beltway*. Lawrence: University Press of Kansas.

Bryant, B., and P. Mohai, eds. 1992. *Race and the Incidence of Environmental Hazards: A Time for Disclosure*. Boulder: Westview.

Bullard, R. D. 1983. "Solid Waste Sites and the Black Houston Community." *Sociological Inquiry* 53 (spring): 273–288.

Bullard, R. D., ed. 1993. *Confronting Environmental Racism: Voices from the Grassroots*. Boston: South End.

Bullard, R. D. 1994a. *Dumping in Dixie: Race, Class, and Environmental Quality*. 2nd ed. Boulder: Westview.

Bullard, R. D., ed. 1994b. *Unequal Protection: Environmental Justice and Communities of Color*. San Francisco: Sierra Club Books.

Caldwell, L. K. 1970. *Environment: A Challenge for Modern Society*. Garden City, NY: Natural History Press.

Carson, R. 1962. *Silent Spring*. New York: Houghton Mifflin.

Coglianese, C., and J. Nash, eds. 2006. *Leveraging the Private Sector: Management-Based Strategies for Improving Environmental Performance*. Washington, DC: Resources for the Future.

Cohen, S., S. Kamieniecki, and M. A. Cahn. 2005. *Strategic Planning in Environmental Regulation: A Policy Approach That Works*. Cambridge, MA: MIT Press.

Cole, D. H. 2002. *Pollution and Property: Comparing Ownership Institutions for Environmental Protection*. Cambridge: Cambridge University Press.

Commoner, B. 1970. *The Closing Circle: Nature, Man and Technology*. New York: Alfred Knopf.

Davies, J. C., and B. S. Davies. 1975. *The Politics of Pollution*. 2nd ed. Indianapolis: Pegasus.

Desai, U., ed. 2002. *Environmental Politics and Policy in Industrialized Countries.* Cambridge, MA: MIT Press.

DeSombre, E. R. 2000. *Domestic Sources of International Environmental Policy: Industry, Environmentalists, and U.S. Power.* Cambridge, MA: MIT Press.

Dietz, T., and P. C. Stern, eds. 2003. *New Tools for Environmental Protection: Education, Information, and Voluntary Measures.* Washington, DC: National Academy Press.

Driesen, D. M., ed. 2010. *Economic Thought and U.S. Climate Change Policy.* Cambridge, MA: MIT Press.

Durant, R. F., D. J. Fiorino, and R. O'Leary, eds. 2004. *Environmental Governance Reconsidered: Challenges, Choices, and Opportunities.* Cambridge, MA: MIT Press.

Ehrlich, P. 1968. *The Population Bomb.* New York: Ballantine.

Eisner, M. A. 2007. *Governing the Environment: The Transformation of Environmental Regulation.* Boulder: Lynne Rienner.

Fairfax, S. K., L. Gwin, M. A. King, L. Raymond, and L. A. Watt. 2005. *Buying Nature: The Limits of Land Acquisition as a Conservation Strategy: 1780–2004.* Cambridge, MA: MIT Press.

Fiorino, D. J., 2006. *The New Environmental Regulation.* Cambridge, MA: MIT Press.

Foss, P. 1960. *Politics and Grass: The Administration of Grazing on the Public Domain.* Seattle: University of Washington Press.

Greenberg, M. R. 1994. "Separate and Not Equal: Health-Environmental Risk and Economic-Social Impacts in Remediating Hazardous Waste Sites." In *Environmental Contaminants and Health*, ed. S. Majumdar, F. J. Brenner, E. W. Miller, and L. M. Rosenfeld. Philadelphia: Pennsylvania Academy of Science.

Harrison, K., and W. Antweiler. 2003. "Incentives for Pollution Abatement: Regulation, Regulatory Threats, and Non-Governmental Pressures." *Journal of Policy Analysis and Management* 22 (3): 361–382.

Harrison, K., and L. M. Sundstrom, eds. 2010. *Global Commons, Domestic Decisions: The Comparative Politics of Climate Change.* Cambridge, MA: MIT Press.

Harrison, N. E., and G. C. Bryner, eds. 2004. *Science and Politics in the International Environment.* Lanham, Md.: Rowman and Littlefield.

Hird, J. A. 1994. *Superfund: The Political Economy of Environmental Risk.* Baltimore: Johns Hopkins University Press.

Ingram, H., and D. Mann. 1983. "Environmental Protection Policy." In *Encyclopedia of Policy Studies*, ed. S. S. Nagel. New York: Marcel Dekker.

John, D. 1994. *Civic Environmentalism: Alternatives to Regulation in States and Communities.* Washington, DC: CQ Press.

Jones, C. A. 1975. *Clean Air: The Policies and Politics of Pollution Control.* Pittsburgh: University of Pittsburgh Press.

Kamieniecki, S., ed. 1993. *Environmental Politics in the International Arena: Movements, Parties, Organizations, and Policy.* Albany: SUNY Press.

Kamieniecki, S. 2006. *Corporate America and Environmental Policy: How Often Does Business Get Its Way?* Palo Alto: Stanford University Press.

Kamieniecki, S., and A. Below. 2008. "Ethical Issues in Storm Water Policy Implementation: Disparities in Financial Burdens and Overall Benefits." In *Water, Place, and Equity*, ed. J. M. Whiteley, H. Ingram, and R. W. Perry. Cambridge, MA: MIT Press.

Kamieniecki, S., and J. Steckenrider. 1997. "Two Faces of Equity in Superfund Implementation." In *Flashpoints in Environmental Policymaking: Controversies in Achieving Sustainability*, ed. S. Kamieniecki, G. A. Gonzalez, and R. O. Vos. Albany: SUNY Press.

Keller, A. C. 2009. *Science in Environmental Policy: The Politics of Objective Advice*. Cambridge, MA: MIT Press.

Kettl, D. F., ed. 2002. *Environmental Governance: A Report on the Next Generation of Environmental Policy*. Washington, DC: Brookings Institution Press.

Klyza, C. M., and D. Sousa. 2008. *American Environmental Policy, 1990–2006: Beyond Gridlock*. Cambridge, MA: MIT Press.

Knaap, G. J., and T. J. Kim, eds. 1998. *Environmental Program Evaluation: A Primer*. Urbana: University of Illinois Press.

Kraft, M. E. 1992. "Ecology and Political Theory: Broadening the Scope of Environmental Politics." *Policy Studies Journal* 20 (4): 712–718.

Kraft, M. E. 2011. *Environmental Policy and Politics*. 5th ed. New York: Pearson Longman.

Kraft, M. E., and S. Kamieniecki, eds. 2007. *Business and Environmental Policy: Corporate Interests in the American Political System*. Cambridge, MA: MIT Press.

Kraft, M. E., and M. Schneider, eds. 1978. *Population Policy Analysis: Issues in American Politics*. Lexington: Lexington Books.

Kraft, M. E., M. Stephan, and T. D. Abel. 2011. *Coming Clean: Information Disclosure and Environmental Performance*. Cambridge, MA: MIT Press.

Lavelle, M., and M. Coyle. 1992. "Unequal Protection: The Racial Divide in Environmental Law." *National Law Journal* (September 21): S1–S12.

Layzer, J. A. 2008. *Natural Experiments: Ecosystem-Based Management and the Environment*. Cambridge, MA: MIT Press.

Lester, J. P., ed. 1995a. *Environmental Politics and Policy: Theories and Evidence*. 2nd ed. Durham, NC: Duke University Press.

Lester, J. P. 1995b. "Introduction." In *Environmental Politics and Policy: Theories and Evidence*, 2nd ed., ed. J. P. Lester. Durham, NC: Duke University Press.

Lester, J. P., D. W. Allen, and D. A. Lauer. 1994. "Race, Class, and Environmental Quality: An Examination of Environmental Racism in the American States." Paper presented at the Annual Meeting of the Western Political Science Association, Albuquerque, NM, March 10–12.

Lubell, M., and B. Segee. 2013. "Conflict and Cooperation in Natural Resource Management." In *Environmental Policy: New Directions for the Twenty-First Century*, 8th ed., ed. N. Vig and M. E. Kraft. Washington, DC: CQ Press.

Matthew, R. A. 2013. "Environmental Security." In *Environmental Policy: New Directions for the Twenty-First Century*, 8th ed., ed. N. Vig and M. E. Kraft. Washington, DC: CQ Press.

Mazmanian, D. A., and M. E. Kraft. 2009. "The Three Epochs of the Environmental Movement." In *Toward Sustainable Communities: Transition and Transformation in Environmental Policy*, 2nd ed., ed. D. A. Mazmanian and M. E. Kraft. Cambridge, MA: MIT Press.

McConnell, Grant. 1966. *Private Power and American Democracy*. New York: Knopf.

Milbrath, L. W. 1989. *Envisioning a Sustainable Society: Learning Our Way Out*. Albany: SUNY Press.

Miller, N. 2002. *Environmental Politics: Interest Groups, the Media, and the Making of Policy*. Boca Raton: Lewis.

Mullin, M. 2009. *Governing the Tap: Special District Governance and the New Local Politics of Water*. Cambridge, MA: MIT Press.

Nagel, S. S., ed. 1974. *Environmental Politics*. New York: Praeger.

Ophuls, W. 1977. *Ecology and the Politics of Scarcity: Prologue to a Political Theory of the Steady State*. San Francisco: W. H. Freeman.

Pirages, D. C., ed. 1977. *The Sustainable Society: Implications for Limited Growth*. New York: Praeger.

Portney, K. E. 2012. *Taking Sustainable Cities Seriously: Economic Development, the Environment, and Livability in American Cities*. Cambridge, MA: MIT Press.

Portney, P. R., and R. N. Stavins, eds. 2000. *Public Policies for Environmental Protection*. 2nd ed. Washington, DC: Resources for the Future.

Potoski, M., and A. Prakash. 2005. "Green Clubs and Voluntary Governance: ISO 14001 and Firms' Regulatory Compliance." *American Journal of Political Science* 49 (2): 235–248.

Press, D., and D. A. Mazmanian. 2013. "Toward Sustainable Production: Finding Workable Strategies for Government and Industry." In *Environmental Policy: New Directions for the Twenty-First Century*, 8th ed., ed. N. Vig and M. E. Kraft. Washington, DC: CQ Press.

Rabe, B. 2004. *Statehouse and Greenhouse: The Emerging Politics of American Climate Change Policy*. Washington, DC: Brookings Institution Press.

Rabe, B., ed. 2010. *Greenhouse Governance: Addressing Climate Change in America*. Washington, DC: Brookings Institution Press.

Ringquist, E. J. 2006. "Environmental Justice: Normative Concerns, Empirical Evidence, and Government Action." In *Environmental Policy: New Directions for the Twenty-First Century*, 6th ed., ed. N. Vig and M. E. Kraft. Washington, DC: CQ Press.

Rosenau, P. V. 2000. *Public-Private Policy Partnerships*. Cambridge, MA: MIT Press.

Rosenbaum, W. A. 1973. *The Politics of Environmental Concern*. New York: Praeger.

Rothenberg, L. S. 2002. *Environmental Choices: Policy Responses to Green Demands*. Washington, DC: CQ Press.

Sabatier, P. A., W. Focht, M. Lubell, Z. Trachtenberg, A. Vedlitz, and M. Matlock, eds. 2005. *Swimming Upstream: Collaborative Approaches to Watershed Management*. Cambridge, MA: MIT Press.

Selin, H., and S. D. VanDeveer, eds. 2009. *Changing Climates in North American Politics: Institutions, Policymaking, and Multilevel Governance*. Cambridge, MA: MIT Press.

Smith, Frank E. 1966. *The Politics of Conservation*. New York: Harper and Row.

Steinberg, P. F., and S. D. VanDeveer, eds. 2012. *Comparative Environmental Politics*. Cambridge, MA: MIT Press.

Susskind, L. E., R. K. Jain, and A. O. Martyniuk. 2001. *Better Environmental Policy Studies: How to Design and Conduct More Effective Analyses*. Washington, DC: Island Press.

Tobin, R. J. 2013. "Environment, Population, and the Developing World." In *Environmental Policy: New Directions for the Twenty-First Century*, 8th ed., ed. N. Vig and M. E. Kraft. Washington, DC: CQ Press.

Toman, M. A. 2001. *Climate Change Economics and Policy*. Washington, DC: Resources for the Future.

United Church of Christ, Commission for Racial Justice. 1987. *Toxic Wastes and Race in the United States*. New York: United Church of Christ.

Vig, N. J., and M. G. Faure, eds. 2004. *Green Giants?: Environmental Policies of the United States and the European Union*. Cambridge, MA: MIT Press.

Vig, N.J., and M. E. Kraft, eds. 1984. *Environmental Policy in the 1980s: Reagan's New Agenda*. Washington, DC: CQ Press.

Vig, N. J., and M. E. Kraft, eds. 2013. *Environmental Policy: New Directions for the Twenty- First Century*. 8th ed. Washington, DC: CQ Press.

Vogel, D. 2005. *The Market for Virtue: The Potential and Limits of Corporate Social Responsibility*. Washington, DC: Brookings Institution Press.

Young, O. R. 2010. *Institutional Dynamics: Emergent Patterns in International Environmental Governance*. Cambridge, MA: MIT Press.

Weber, E. P. 2003. *Bringing Society Back In: Grassroots Ecosystem Management, Accountability, and Sustainable Communities*. Cambridge, MA: MIT Press.

Whiteley, J. M., H. Ingram, and R. W. Perry, eds. 2008. *Water, Place, and Equity*. Cambridge, MA: MIT Press.

PART II

THE EVOLUTION OF ENVIRONMENTAL POLICY: MAJOR CONCEPTS, IDEAS, AND MOVEMENTS

CHAPTER 2

.....

ENVIRONMENTAL POLITICS AND POLICY IN HISTORICAL PERSPECTIVE

.....

RICHARD N. L. ANDREWS

1. FRAMING THE HISTORICAL SUBJECT MATTER OF ENVIRONMENTAL POLITICS AND POLICY

.....

THE unifying label of "environmental" policy was not coined until the 1960s (Caldwell 1963). In reality, however, the use of public policies to shape human use of the natural world, as well as the political pressures associated with the creation, implementation, and evolution of those policies, extends back to the earliest years of the American nation and to the colonial period that preceded it. Countless policies over 400-plus years have purposely influenced human use of the natural environment, from land and water and air to wildlife, minerals, and other natural resources and the ecosystems that sustain them. What counts, then, as "environmental" politics and policy?

The scope of environmental politics and policy logically includes all actions by government that were consciously intended to influence human interactions with nature, including but not limited to those intended to conserve or protect nature and to protect human health from environmental hazards. It also includes conscious decisions by government *not* to intervene and thus to allow certain uses of nature to proceed unconstrained by government control or management (Crenson 1971). Many of these earlier actions laid the foundations, precedents, and constraints for modern environmental politics and policies.

The historical development of environmental policies also shows strong path dependence. Early environmental problems led to policies responsive to the politics, priorities, and environmental perceptions of their times, but in the process also set the stage for future environmental problems and bounded the opportunities for solving them. Examples include policies privatizing large portions of the nation's land and resource use rights, promoting cheap industrial extraction of minerals and fossil fuels, subsidizing large-scale agricultural production, facilitating the spread of low-density, automobile-dependent patterns of urban development, and, more recently, promoting both a domestic and a global economy dependent on high rates of worldwide trade and consumption of environmental goods and services.

Public policies were not the sole determinants of these patterns of environmental change: technological innovations, economic opportunities, and demographic choices were also important factors. But public policies were essential drivers and constraints on these patterns and significantly influenced both their intended and their unanticipated environmental consequences.

This chapter provides a historical overview of the foundations and evolution of U.S. environmental politics and policy over time, and of research on them, from their early foundations through the parallel and intersecting histories of natural resource development and conservation, environmental health, and other policies that ultimately have shaped contemporary environmental policy issues. It also suggests potential lessons from history about the U.S. political system and policy change over time and about research needs for the future.

2. FOUNDATIONS

The basic foundations of U.S. environmental politics and policy lie in two sources: in distinctive principles of property rights—who has rights to do what to the natural environment and its resources (land, water, plants, minerals, wildlife, etc.)—and in key provisions of the U.S. Constitution, which established the powers and limitations of government to enact policies affecting private and public management of the environment. Both have evolved over time, but both also bear enduring marks of their origins that distinguish them from those of other countries.

The most fundamental environmental policies determine who has the right to do what to the environment: who owns the land, water, wildlife, and other natural resources, and what rights are associated with ownership (Andrews 2006, 34–50). Colonial American policies were distinctive in their establishment of a predominantly freehold system of landownership, such that rights not specifically reserved or regulated by the government lie with the individual owner, including rights to extract, commercialize, subdivide, and otherwise transform the environment and its ecosystems (Cronon 1983). Rights to land generally included rights to its surface resources, as well as to exclude, subdivide, and develop it as a commodity. Water rights in the eastern U.S. generally followed the riparian principle that they are shared by all riparian owners "undiminished in quantity and quality" by the uses of others. This principle was significantly weakened in the late nineteenth century by court decisions allowing "reasonable use," including industrial waste discharges; and these precedents, in turn, were partially superseded by modern statutes regulating wastewater discharges from point sources and limiting discharges to a "total maximum daily load."

Western water use rights, in contrast, are owned separately from the land under the prior appropriation system and may be bought and sold subject to the constraints of water availability and of reserved water rights for Native American tribes and government stewardship of instream flows for fisheries. Subsurface mineral rights also may be owned separately from surface landownership, and fish and wildlife may be owned by capture ("taking") subject to federal and state regulation to sustain viable populations of them.

The core of these policies is that most of the primary rights to use or transform the environment lie with private individuals and businesses, for individual economic gain or personal preference; and the burden of proof legally is on advocates of government regulation to demonstrate a compelling public justification to restrict them.

The second essential foundation for U.S. environmental policy is the federal Constitution, which established both the powers and the limitations of American government as well as the processes of its operation (Andrews 2006, 51–70). All government powers to impose and enforce environmental policies must be derived from constitutional authority. Most environmental regulatory policies are derived from a broad interpretation of the federal government's constitutional power to regulate interstate commerce; management of the public lands and their resources derives from its authority to manage government property; imposition of federal environmental policies on the states derives largely from the supremacy and treaty-making clauses.

The Fifth Amendment (and its extension to the states in the Fourteenth Amendment) established two of the most powerful limitations on federal environmental policy making. One stated that no one shall be deprived of property by government—including, for instance, rights to use of the environment—without "due process" of law. This process was spelled out in detail by the Administrative Procedure Act of 1946, which placed a clear burden on government to justify proposed regulations through notice and comment, hearings, constitutional and statutory authority, a reviewable record, and "substantial evidence," to demonstrate that they are not "arbitrary and capricious." The courts were empowered to enforce these principles by judicial review and remand of proposed administrative actions.

The second strong limitation was that no property may be "taken for public use" without just compensation. "Property" in this case has been taken to mean not only physical property but also environmental use rights and the rights of property owners to derive economic benefit from their use of the environment ("regulatory takings"). This provision thus exists in constant tension with the government's police powers to regulate public nuisances and other damages to other parties and to the public without compensation: when can government legitimately regulate individuals and businesses to protect against environmental damages, and when must it buy out the rights of private users for a "public purpose"? Other constitutional provisions shaping environmental policy include the powers to tax and to regulate interstate compacts, among others.

3. Natural Resources for Economic Development

From colonial times through much of the nineteenth century, the dominant U.S. environmental policy was to encourage the settlement, privatization, and extraction of natural resources from the environment for economic development. This thread of environmental policy began with the colonial and mercantile policies of Britain and other European colonial powers, dominated U.S. policy through the early-nineteenth-century laws promoting land privatization (sales for settlement, and land grants for "internal improvements" such as canals and railroads for transportation infrastructure), and continues as a powerful thread up through the present, in tension with subsequent policies intended to conserve and protect nature against the damaging impacts of unrestrained exploitation. Benjamin Hibbard (1924) describes public land in the nineteenth century as a "balance wheel," a public resource that could be allocated by policy as needed to pay soldiers, to generate government revenues (and thus lower reliance on import tariffs and other taxes), to encourage economic democracy through settlement and property ownership, to finance transportation infrastructures (and thus promote economic development), to develop internal markets (and thus reduce U.S. dependence on European empires), to reserve for public schools and colleges and other public needs, and for other purposes as they arose. These purposes were frequently in conflict—for instance, individual settlers competed for control over land with land and railroad companies —and the course of nineteenth-century land "disposal" policy was consequently chaotic, messy, and often contradictory or even fraudulent. Overall, however, its course reflected a gradual shift toward policies favoring individual settlers over large land companies (the Preemption and Homestead Acts, for instance); and toward policies leveraging the "free" asset of public land to finance transportation infrastructure investments (canals and then railroads), thus benefiting the development of a strong national economy with mutually supportive internal markets, but also subsidizing the development of the vast private and corporate fortunes of late-nineteenth-century American capitalism (Hibbard 1924; Engelbert 1950; Andrews 2006, 71–108).

The results included both the growth of the U.S. economy to the stature of a global powerhouse, and, concurrently, a vast increase in commercial exploitation of the continent's natural resources, accompanied by considerable environmental destruction. Important voices in literature and art spoke out for nature's more spiritual values during this period—for instance, Thoreau extolled the benefits of nature and simplicity, Emerson wrote about the possibility of spiritual transcendence in nature, and the artists John James Audubon and George Catlin cataloged and celebrated nature in their works—but their efforts had little impact on policy until later generations. Only in the latter half of the nineteenth century did large-scale environmental conflicts and consequences begin to rise to the level of environmental policy: George Perkins Marsh's powerful book on the lessons of environmental destruction by the great ancient civilizations (Marsh 1864); the 1872 investigation by the American Association for the Advancement of Science into the drying up of the Erie Canal (and the subsequent New York constitutional provision declaring the Adirondacks "forever wild"); public fears of a "timber famine" after the stripping of the Midwest's forests to build and fuel the railroads; the degradation of the Yosemite Valley (then a state park), which galvanized the formation of the Sierra Club; and the severe droughts of the late 1880s. These events paved the way for the rise of the conservation movement during the era of President Theodore Roosevelt.

4. Environmental Health Policy: Sanitation as the First Environmental Movement

As cities and towns grew in the nineteenth century, their environmental hazards—disease, fire, squalor—produced a parallel movement, first in England and then in the United States, for improving public health by improving sanitary conditions in cities (Andrews 2006, 109–135; Duffy 1990; Rosen 1958; Smillie 1955; Winslow 1923). The sanitation movement was arguably the first grassroots environmental movement, composed of broad-based alliances among business, professional, and medical leaders and urban reformers promoting public infrastructures and local and state health departments to clean up the cities. Most of the resulting policies began at the local level and did not lead to national action until the early twentieth century, but they laid the foundations for subsequent environmental health politics and policies, such as the City Beautiful and urban cleanliness movements of the Progressive Era, and key elements of the modern environmental movement (the modern Environmental Protection Agency even today is primarily an environmental health regulatory agency). Their initial solutions also laid the foundations for later environmental problems: piping in water from clean but distant sources without sewers to remove it, then treating drinking water supplies but not wastewater discharges, thus increasing risks of waterborne disease downstream (Tarr 1985). Wastewater discharges were not seriously addressed in most places until more than half a century later, with strict federal regulations and subsidies for municipal and industrial wastewater treatment under the 1972 Clean Water Act.

The reliance of the sanitation movement on the theory of miasmas—disease causation by noxious vapors from waste material—led to its eventual marginalization, as the discoveries of bacteriology by Louis Pasteur, Joseph Lister, and others in the 1880s shifted the blame for disease from environmental conditions to microbes and shifted the focus of public health professionals from environmental cleanup to pasteurization, vaccination, and other interventions targeted at individuals, leaving the broader task of environmental sanitation as a mere nuisance to be managed by public works departments. The rise and fall of the sanitation movement thus provides an early forerunner of conflicts common to modern environmental politics over the use of science to justify environmental policy, and over the demand for proof of risk rather than merely administrative judgments of prudence before regulating.

5. PUBLIC ENVIRONMENTAL MANAGEMENT: PROGRESSIVE CONSERVATION, PRESERVATION, AND SCIENTIFIC MANAGEMENT

A major turning point in American environmental policy was the rise of public management of the environment, prominently by Theodore Roosevelt's Progressive administration in the early twentieth century, but before that by late-nineteenth-century policies that differentiated and classified public lands for particular uses, and in some cases reserved them from other claims for permanent public management (Andrews 2006, 94–108; Miller 1973). These developments, in turn, required the creation and professionalization of government agencies to administer them: the Army Corps of Engineers and Agriculture Department (already in existence); the U.S. Geological Survey; later the Reclamation Service, Forest Service, and National Park Service; and eventually other federal environmental management agencies.

The Progressive philosophy of utilitarian scientific management of the environment for efficient economic use, both of public lands and waters, and the contemporaneous local socialization of waste management by municipal governments, dominated much of U.S. environmental policy for the first two-thirds of the twentieth century. It articulated a powerful new set of principles: that natural resources were a public asset to be used for the greatest good of the greatest number of Americans rather than merely for private profit and that government—populated by scientifically trained, politically neutral professionals—could manage the nation's public lands and waters more efficiently for multiple uses than could private businesses and markets alone (Andrews 2006, 136–153; Hays 1959; Lacey 1979; Melosi 1980; Pinchot 1910). Among other policy innovations, the Progressive Era gave birth to the Bureau of Reclamation to develop and manage multiple-use projects for western water (irrigation, hydropower, water supply, recreation, navigation, and others), financed by a revolving loan fund, and to the National Forest Service to manage multiple uses of large areas of the federal lands (timber, grazing, mining, wildlife, recreation, and others).

The Progressive Era also laid the foundations for market-oriented environmental policy tools such as user fees for timber and grazing rights, and auctioning of lease rights for fossil fuel extraction (rather than outright land claims); and for national environmental health regulatory policies, including the federal meat inspection program (following publication of Upton Sinclair's 1906 exposé *The Jungle)*, the Public Health Service, and national regulatory authority over drinking water standards for interstate transport carriers (precursor and precedent for EPA's Safe Drinking Water Act half a century later).

Roosevelt's and Pinchot's Progressive vision for environmental management remained in continuing tension, however, both with congressional, conservative, and self-interested business opponents of strong executive government and administrative discretion, and with the rising movement led by John Muir and the Sierra Club for preservation of public lands for their inspirational beauty rather than for extractive use. These tensions led on the one hand to congressional revocation of presidential powers to reserve national forests, in 1906, and on the other hand, to the creation in 1916 of a separate National Park Service whose primary mission was preservation rather than multiple use; and they continue as fundamental threads of modern environmental politics and policy. The decade after World War I is most widely remembered for the Teapot Dome oil scandal rather than for environmental policy initiatives; the Progressive vision largely went into decline under a series of conservative presidents, with the exception of Herbert Hoover's support for multipurpose water management and some federal-state cooperative programs for forest management (Swain 1963).

6. PUBLIC INVESTMENT, SUBSIDIES, AND STAKEHOLDERS: NEW DEAL CONSERVATION AND WARTIME PLANNING

The Great Depression and World War II marked both the apex of government dominance in environmental management and its limits. Facing the concurrent and interconnected crises of economic collapse and environmental disasters (drought followed by vast dust storms and then devastating floods), Franklin Roosevelt's New Deal policies used massive public investments, subsidies, innovative programs, and government planning not only to create jobs and "prime the pump" of economic recovery but concurrently to achieve environmental restoration, infrastructure improvements, and agricultural stabilization, and even to seek comprehensive watershed-based and national environmental planning (Andrews 2005; Andrews 2006, 154–178; Owens 1983). The Civilian Conservation Corps, Public Works Administration, and Works Progress Administration provided jobs for the unemployed, replanting and restoring eroded lands and creating vast amounts of new public infrastructure. Federally subsidized dams, justified by benefit-cost analysis, in turn, would tame the floods and create from them a new resource of stored water for multiple uses and economic development. The Tennessee Valley Authority (TVA) was envisioned as a macro-watershed-scale example of the Progressive vision of multiple-purpose watershed management, coupling ecological restoration and soil conservation with agricultural modernization and urban and industrial development, powered by cheap hydroelectricity and managed by a public corporation. Agricultural soil conservation and price stabilization programs would revitalize the nation's farms both economically and environmentally, making minimum returns predictable while retiring the most erodible acres from production. Earmarked user fees from taxes on hunting and fishing and their equipment would provide a permanent source of funding for fish and wildlife management, protected from marginalization in the overall federal budget process. Large areas of land in the eastern United States, often cut over and eroded or abandoned by owners unwilling or unable to pay the taxes on them, were brought back into federal ownership and replanted and restored as eastern national forests and parks. Rural electrification brought modernization and economic progress to the rural hinterlands of the United States.

The New Deal thus stands out for its use of public expenditures to finance ecological restoration and repurchase of lands for restoration, management, and protection; for its use of major public investments to develop infrastructures for productive use of the environment, both for economic development and for outdoor recreation; and for the serious attempt, though ultimately unsuccessful, to create integrated executive-level policy making and long-term planning institutions for the use of national natural and economic resources. Roosevelt sought but failed to secure congressional authority for ongoing executive-level environmental planning and policy coordination (a National Resource Planning Board, a Department of Conservation). In his water management and dam-building programs he achieved some of the great dreams of Theodore Roosevelt's Progressivism, and while the New Deal did not return the nation to full employment and economic prosperity until wartime, it did rescue capitalism from collapse and in the process used public employment programs to repair ecological devastation and build wide-ranging infrastructures for environmental services that remain as assets today.

Unlike the Progressives, however, Franklin Roosevelt came to rely not just on apolitical expert administrators but also on stakeholder alliances with beneficiary interest groups, such as soil and water conservation districts controlled by farmers, grazing districts dominated by ranchers, fish and wildlife conservation programs dominated by hunters and fishermen, and water projects promoted by pork-barrel congressional power brokers. The TVA quickly abandoned its visionary ideals in order to accommodate stakeholder interests (Selznick 1949), and it became more exclusively a major public power utility, eventually relying far more heavily on strip-mined coal and nuclear power than on environmentally more benign hydropower. Agricultural stabilization endured long beyond its immediate need, as a subsidy program for large-scale agribusinesses in a few commodity crops at the expense of taxpayers, consumers, small farmers, poorer countries, and the environment. In short, the environmental policy ideals of apolitical Progressive utilitarianism gradually evolved into a "broker state" of "iron triangles" dominated by economic beneficiary interests, their congressional patrons, and the captured agencies whose decisions would benefit or hinder their interests (Graham 1976).

One concurrent phenomenon not usually associated with the New Deal was the widespread discovery and competitive extraction of U.S. petroleum resources, driven both by the rise in petroleum-powered military transport during World War I and the rapid growth of civilian motor vehicle use after the war, and by the "tragedy of the commons," motivating property owners above common pools of oil to extract it as rapidly as possible before their neighbors did so. The result was vast overproduction, which drove prices down to unsustainably low levels, used up U.S. domestic oil resources (U.S. domestic oil production peaked in the 1970s and has declined ever since), and at the same time encouraged patterns of U.S. economic growth and investment that were structurally dependent on the permanent availability of cheap oil: energy-inefficient buildings and industries, and low-density suburban and commercial development that was increasingly dependent on gasoline- and diesel-powered motor vehicles. The "hot oil" act of 1935 partially stabilized this overproduction but did no more to manage the larger influence of cheap oil; and the demands of World War II, as well as the pent-up consumer demand for the "American dream" of more affluent suburban lifestyles that followed it, embedded for at least half a century the almost unquestionable policy presumption that U.S. economic progress depended on continued access to cheap oil, first from offshore drilling and then from the Middle East once the United States took over the former geopolitical dominance of the British and French empires in that oil-rich region (Andrews 2006, 158–59, 295–301; Carley 2011).

7. POSTWAR POLICIES AND THE RISE OF THE MODERN ENVIRONMENTAL MOVEMENT

The modern environmental movement and the policies it produced were born in the period from the late 1940s to 1970, a period of profound transformation and unique mass affluence in the U.S. economy and polity (Andrews 2006, 179–226; Richardson 1973; Sundquist 1968).

The policy imperatives of World War II triggered all-out industrialization and vast increases in material and energy extraction, as well as wartime economic controls and enforced savings and federal defense funding to mobilize and allocate environmental resources for wartime priorities. Unlike previous wars, which were followed by economic demobilization, military-driven industrialization continued amid Cold War fears; civilian production vastly expanded as well, to keep the factories humming, serve pent-up consumer demand and newfound mass affluence, and open new global markets in exchange for raw material imports. Even public investments in dams and other infrastructures continued, despite economic prosperity, first to ward off fears of a postwar return to recession, and then to serve the interests of the congressional districts that benefited from them. Nuclear weapons and then civilian nuclear power also created a wholly new set of environmental concerns, both promoted and significantly underwritten by public policies.

In short, the United States became both superpower and supermarket, driven by wartime savings, the postwar "baby boom," mass suburbanization, and the rise of mass-media television advertising of convenience consumerism (Jackson 1985). As members of a newly affluent middle class satisfied initial yearnings for housing, automobiles, and appliances, however, they also developed widespread demands for outdoor recreation and preservation of natural beauty, demands that were inherently in tension with industrial extractive uses; and even as the mass media promoted increased material consumption, they also spread a national awareness of previously localized environmental controversies and of environmental health hazards—radiation and pesticides, for instance—that had previously been overlooked or tolerated.

Environmental policy also was transformed by dramatic changes in political representation, driven by congressional reapportionment from rural areas to the rapidly growing cities and suburbs. It was further reshaped by a discrediting of the Progressive faith in scientific management by government experts, first from the right—postwar conservatism produced the Administrative Procedure Act of 1946, which spelled out the due process mandate of the Constitution and imposed a heavier and more explicit burden on government to justify its actions—and by the 1960s from the left as well, as environmental groups used first public demonstrations and then environmental litigation—in addition to traditional lobbying—as tactics for demanding environmental policy change. In particular, Joseph Sax (1971) articulated the theory of environmental resources as a public trust that agencies were duty-bound to protect. He proposed that citizens be empowered by law to act as "citizen attorneys general" by giving them standing in the courts—leveling the playing field with business interests—not just to assert their personal interests, but also to compel the agencies to fulfill their environmental protection duties to the general public.

8. THE "ENVIRONMENTAL ERA": NATIONALIZATION AND REGULATION OF ENVIRONMENTAL PROTECTION

In 1963 political scientist Lynton Caldwell proposed that "environment" be considered a new integrative focus for public policy (Caldwell 1963), and by the end of the 1960s many previously disparate groups advocating for environmental health protection, ecological conservation, and nature preservation coalesced into a loosely coordinated network under the label of the "environmental movement." These organizations shared common interests, deferred to each other as lead organizations on particular issues, and attracted a broad and (at least for a decade) significantly bipartisan base of public support.

These processes culminated in enactment of the National Environmental Policy Act of 1969 (NEPA); in the vast public participation in the first Earth Day in April 1970, the largest mass demonstrations since the victory celebrations at the end of World War II; in the creation of the Environmental Protection Agency, by President Richard Nixon; and in the enactment of nearly a dozen sweeping new regulatory statutes for environmental protection, passed by bipartisan majorities and most of them signed by Republican presidents, during the 1970s. The Clean Air and Clean Water Acts, Safe Drinking Water Act, pesticide and toxic substances acts, endangered species and marine mammal protection acts, and laws regulating the disposal of solid and hazardous waste and the cleanup of contaminated sites from past disposal: all were passed in this single decade, along with the occupational safety and health and consumer product safety statutes and several new statutes for management of the public lands. Together they represented an unprecedented and broadly popular expansion of federal authority to protect the environment and public health and safety through regulation (Andrews 2006, 227–254; Jones 1975; Lazarus 2004).

For those charged to implement these mandates, they represented an equally unprecedented challenge. The EPA was created almost overnight in 1970 by presidential reorganization plan, putting together subunits from disparate agencies—the Public Health Service, Agriculture, Interior, and the Atomic Energy Commission—and their existing statutory authorities, but with no new overall statutory mandate or "organic act" to authorize integration or priority-setting among them. Then and ever since, the EPA's programs have remained substantially separate from one another, authorized by different statutes, and its priorities have largely been set more by the annual appropriations process than by integrated management.

The Clean Air, Clean Water, and solid and hazardous waste acts each directed the EPA to set technology-based standards for pollutant discharges to air, water, or land, respectively, for each industrial sector and for municipalities. Much of the implementation and enforcement was delegated to the states, an important area of study in itself ("environmental federalism"); and industries and municipalities themselves must then invest in separate compliance technologies for each medium. Ultimately, these policies were highly effective within the limits of their goals—pollution discharges from industrial and municipal point sources were significantly reduced, and solid and hazardous wastes were far more safely and professionally managed—but they were far less than fully successful in improving ambient air and water quality, since nonpoint sources of water pollution remained unregulated and new emissions sources added pollution even with the best available technology. While emission rates from new motor vehicles were radically improved, the number of vehicles as well as their annual miles traveled continued to increase (Davies and Mazurek 1998).

The drinking water, pesticide, and toxic substance statutes, meanwhile, as well as the provisions controlling hazardous air pollutants and toxic water pollutants, required the EPA to address vastly more chemicals on a substance-by-substance basis. These statutory authorities themselves were based not on "best available technology" but on demonstrating that the risks and the benefits of controlling them exceeded the costs of control. This required the EPA to satisfy a far higher burden of proof to justify proposed regulations, for substances potentially numbering in the thousands, using science that was inevitably subject to uncertainties and economic analyses that were always arguable. The EPA was never funded at a level sufficient to fulfill these mandates, and substance-by-substance regulation in itself was arguably a far less effective policy than, say, reducing exposures of populations that were at greatest risk from multiple hazards (Hornstein 1993; for EPA budget figures see also Vig and Kraft 2010, 378). These statutes thus were far less effective than the simpler though crude technology-based mandates: few potentially hazardous chemicals were ever fully reviewed and regulated, and far more effort was devoted, both by the EPA and by the affected industries, to perennial legal conflicts over the scientific and economic analyses than to actually reducing exposures. The courts, accordingly, became a far more significant venue for environmental politics and policy beginning in this period, and have continued so (O'Leary 2010; Stewart 1975).

A parallel set of conflicts over management of the public lands and ecological conservation more generally, meanwhile, also became increasingly contentious. The Wilderness Act of 1964 established a process for permanently protecting large areas of the national forests and other public lands from extractive use, giving increased influence to environmental groups at the expense of the forest and mining industries and even of intensive recreational-use businesses. The National

Forest Management Act of 1976 authorized industrial-scale clear-cutting on the national forests, but with significant restrictions and significantly increased voice for environmental groups in forest management decisions. The Federal Lands Policy and Management Act of 1976 for the first time formally authorized permanent and active management of the public lands by the Bureau of Land Management, superseding nearly two centuries of de facto dominance over these lands by western extractive industries, ranchers, and off-road recreational vehicle users. Finally, the Endangered Species Act of 1973 established for the first time a "bright line," enforceable in the courts, against any damage to endangered species or their critical habitat even on privately owned lands, creating simultaneously both the most powerful legal weapon for advocates of ecosystem protection and the most contentious challenge yet to the balance between legitimate use of regulation under government's police powers and the constitutional requirement of compensation for any "taking" of property for public use.

By the end of the 1970s, as the EPA and the public land agencies neared completion of their initial implementation of these statutes, two important new developments began to take shape. The first was an organized counterattack by business conservatives and a western "Sagebrush Rebellion," which reframed the issues from environmental protection to government overregulation. This political mobilization contributed significantly to the election of Ronald Reagan in 1980 and to the fracture of bipartisan support for national environmental policy into sharp and continuing ideologically based partisan conflict. The second new development, in contrast, was a new argument articulated by some leading businesses and consultants that "pollution prevention *pays*." From a business perspective, pollution is not only a social nuisance but also an economic waste of materials and energy that the business itself has paid for as inputs to production. Pollution reduction, therefore, is consistent with best business practices if businesses were given flexible incentives to seek the most cost-effective ways to prevent pollution in the first place rather than merely saddled with the costs of end-of-pipe compliance technologies (Royston 1979).

9. MARKET-ORIENTED POLICY INNOVATIONS

The 1980s began with a concerted attempt by the first Reagan administration not simply to reform but to reverse the 1970s legacy of federal environmental regulation. Domestically, Reagan initiated a series of radical, unilateral policy changes by administrative fiat to "deregulate, de-fund, and devolve" environmental policy from the federal government to the states. Internationally, Reagan withdrew U.S. participation from negotiation of the major environmental treaty of his era, the Law of the Sea Treaty, which had been initiated and championed by Richard Nixon (Andrews 2006, 255–283; Durant 1992; Vig and Kraft 1984).

This series of policy reversals was arguably one of the most unfortunate lost opportunities in the modern history of environmental policy. The initial statutes of the environmental era needed refinement, both to make them more effective and to reduce their burdens, and a constructive Republican administration could conceivably have built a valuable and enduring legacy on reforms already proposed. By attempting instead to undermine and radically reverse the regulatory policies of the 1970s, the Reagan administration poisoned the well of trust necessary for any bipartisan reform of environmental policy, polarized the issue into a lasting partisan and ideological conflict over the role of government, and severely underestimated the continuing public support for environmental protection as a national responsibility. By 1983 Reagan was forced to fire nearly all of his top 30 appointees to the EPA, as well as Interior Secretary James Watt. The number and membership of environmental advocacy groups rebounded dramatically, with a far more adversarial and partisan perspective; the Democrats regained control of the Congress in 1984; and the new Congress enacted a series of aggressive deadlines and "hammer" clauses aimed at compelling executive implementation and enforcement of environmental laws (Andrews 2006, 255–283).

A positive policy change during the 1980s, however, was a newfound receptiveness to market-oriented policy incentives as tools for achieving environmental protection. Chief among these were tools such as emissions trading programs, which set a mandatory overall performance outcome but allowed businesses to decide themselves how to allocate emission reductions among their facilities. Examples included EPA's "bubble," emissions trading, and banking policies, the trading of production phasedown quotas for leaded gasoline and CFCs, wetlands mitigation trading and banking programs, the landmark cap-and-trade program for sulfur and nitrogen oxides under the Clean Air Act Amendments of 1990, the subsequent adoption of greenhouse gas cap-and-trade programs by nations that were parties to the Kyoto Protocol (despite the United States' nonparticipation), and a series of U.S. legislative proposals for greenhouse gas trading (though none had been enacted as of 2012). From a business perspective these tools were more flexible and cost-efficient than technology-based regulations, although participation in emissions trading markets required new skills and imposed new risks. From an environmental perspective, they could in some cases be far more effective, such as the Clean Air Act sulfur trading program, and less vulnerable to endless litigation challenging the scientific justification for regulations.

A second type of market-oriented policy was an expansion of disclosure and documentation requirements. Full disclosure of information was justified by mainstream economic principles and could potentially have more pervasive and self-enforcing market consequences than new regulatory proposals, which were increasingly constrained by insufficient funding, legal challenges, and the burden of proof on the EPA to justify them. Economic benefit-cost analysis had been used since the 1940s as a check on pork-barrel funding of federal water projects, and under President Reagan it was mandated by executive order for environmental regulatory proposals as well (Andrews 1984). The environmental impact statements

(EISs) required by the National Environmental Policy Act were another of the major expansions of information disclosure requirements, along with the more general Freedom of Information Act, but like benefit-cost analysis, these applied only to government actions. By the 1980s the courts had largely limited EISs to a procedural requirement for documentation and disclosure rather than a substantive mandate for environmentally favorable decisions (see chapters 25 and 26 in this volume).

In the wake of the Bhopal industrial disaster in 1985, however, a series of state "right-to-know" statutes culminated in the 1986 federal Emergency Planning and Community Right to Know Act, which established a Toxics Release Inventory requiring public disclosure by all major industrial chemical users of the annual quantities of toxic chemicals released to the environment. This policy had some success in motivating reduction of toxic chemical use and releases, and it led to interest in other forms of information disclosure policy tools, either voluntary or required, such as energy efficiency labeling ("Energy Star"), sustainability certification and labeling for fish and forest products, and "carbon footprint" labeling for consumer products more generally (Cashore, Auld, and Newsom 2004; Hadden 1986, 1989; Kraft, Stephan, and Abel 2011).

10. Contemporary Environmental Politics and Policy

In the late 1980s President George H. W. Bush attempted to define his presidency as a moderate, market-oriented but pro-environmental form of Republicanism, recalling the less partisan environmental politics of the 1970s. President Reagan in his later years had signed, and the Senate had ratified, the Montreal Protocol on reducing damage to the stratospheric ozone layer, with support from both the business community and environmental advocacy groups. Bush went further, with policies calling for no net loss of wetlands, the extraordinarily innovative and successful cap-and-trade program for industrial air pollution established by the 1990 Clean Air Act Amendments, and the landmark (though weakened) 1992 UN Framework Convention on Climate Change, which the Senate also ratified.

Bush's defeat in 1992 by Bill Clinton and his ardent environmentalist vice president Al Gore, however, solidified Republican strategists' conclusion—a concern articulated as early as Nixon in his later years (Flippen 2000)—that Democrats would always defeat Republican candidates on environmental issues and that Republicans' hope thus lay in appealing to business and libertarian constituencies by reframing these issues and campaigning against them as excesses of "big government." With the "Gingrich revolution" of the 1994 congressional elections, and subsequently the election of George W. Bush in 2000, U.S. national environmental politics and policy settled into a state of prolonged gridlock. With rare exceptions, Republican congressional majorities and Bush as president sought to weaken environmental protection policies and the influence of environmental advocacy organizations, while Democrats remained strong enough to forestall most of these attempts but not strong enough to pass significant new laws or even reforms of existing ones (Andrews 2006, 350–395; Klyza and Sousa 2008; Lazarus 2003). This stalemate continued into the Obama years, with Republican senators using the constant threat of filibusters to block action on environmental legislative proposals that could not muster a 60-vote supermajority in the Senate.

Several major consequences followed from this pattern. One was that many serious environmental problems remained unsolved, including even some from which many businesses as well as concerned citizens could have benefited from policy reforms and better solutions. A prominent example was the failure of any form of pricing or cap-and-trade legislation for greenhouse gas emissions, an outcome sought in some form even by many businesses (though by no means all) as a more flexible and market-oriented alternative to EPA regulation, a signal of regulatory clarity for firms that must make new long-term capital investments, and an opportunity for U.S. firms to participate in emerging global carbon markets.

A second consequence was that most national environmental policy making was conducted by administrative initiatives of the White House and executive branch agencies and swung back and forth in its emphasis with the politics of each administration (Andrews 2006, 350–395; Vig 2010). Democratic President Bill Clinton, for instance, initially championed multi-stakeholder negotiations to solve contentious environmental problems, such as the Everglades and endangered species habitat in the northwestern forests, and successfully introduced an innovative environmental "side agreement" into the NAFTA trade treaty. Faced with a hostile Republican Congress beginning in 1994, however, he resorted to unilateral executive actions to regulate and enforce aggressively against pollution, to preserve vast areas of the public lands from extractive uses as national monuments and roadless areas, and to promote a binding international treaty on global climate change. Republican president George W. Bush, like President Reagan in his first term, used unilateral executive actions to reduce regulatory enforcement, to open the western public lands as rapidly as possible to accelerated permitting of oil and gas extraction, and to withdraw U.S. participation from multilateral environmental treaty negotiations. Democratic president Barack Obama, in turn, used large-scale economic stimulus funding both to try to revive the economy and to redirect it toward renewable energy production, and once again pursued aggressive environmental regulation and enforcement while supporting international and federal proposals to reduce greenhouse gases by cap-and-trade legislation. Ultimately, however, these legislative proposals were thwarted by near-unanimous Republican political opposition. An even more hostile Republican-dominated House of Representatives elected in 2010 threatened to try to reduce or defund EPA's regulatory authority as well.

A third consequence of the ideological polarization of environmental politics was that the courts became more and more frequently the arbiters of the legality of these executive initiatives and of challenges to them both by businesses and by environmental advocacy groups (Glicksman and Schroeder 1991; Lazarus 1991). This process began as early as the late 1960s, with the rise of "public interest environmental law" organizations such as the Environmental Defense Fund and Natural Resources Defense Council—building on Joseph Sax's arguments for the "public trust" doctrine enforced by "citizen attorneys general" (Sax 1971) —and expanded with the proliferation of similarly constituted but more conservative law groups challenging environmental laws and regulations, along with more traditional business lawsuits. The outcomes of these lawsuits did not always favor environmental protection advocates: some served to limit the effectiveness of NEPA's environmental impact statements, for instance, and others imposed a far more burdensome standard of proof on EPA to justify its regulations. Yet overall the courts became and remained an important force in maintaining the effectiveness of environmental protection laws and regulations against attempts to weaken them by unilateral executive action and by business and conservative litigation (Lazarus 2003; O'Leary 2010).

Finally, in the face of continuing gridlock at the federal level, state governments became increasingly active in initiating their own environmental policy innovations—particularly for greenhouse gas reduction and renewable energy promotion, but also for air pollution and other environmental issues—at least until they were overwhelmed by the economic crisis of 2008. Over half of the states, for instance, enacted innovative new incentives for energy efficiency and renewable energy production, several groups of states established regional carbon emissions trading programs, and more than a few pioneered policy innovations to address other environmental issues (Rabe 2004, 2010). Whether these initiatives will be successful, sustained, more widely adopted, and not eventually superseded by national models remains to be seen (Carley 2009, 2011; Ringquist 1993).

11. LESSONS AND RESEARCH ISSUES

The examination of environmental politics and policy from a historical perspective offers important insights for consideration and for further research. First, this chapter has offered only the barest glimpse of some of the most important patterns and highlights: there is far more for the serious scholar to unearth and examine, including both longitudinal histories of particular environmental issues and cross-sectional histories relating environmental policy developments to other issues during particular periods. The history of public lands policy, for instance, is the subject of a sizable literature in itself (U.S. Public Land Law Review Commission 1968), as is constitutional reinterpretation of the Commerce Clause and the Fifth

Amendment over time, histories of some particular issues (e.g., Faeth 1989; Melosi 1981; Tarr 1985; Worster 1985), and histories of key agencies such as the Army Corps of Engineers (Maass 1951), Forest Service (Dana and Fairfax 1980; Hirt 1994), Bureau of Land Management (Foss 1960; Klyza 1996), Soil Conservation Service (Morgan 1965), and National Park Service (Foresta 1985; Lowry 2009), though not of others that still deserve definitive histories, such as the EPA. Similarly, full understanding of the environmental policies of Theodore or Franklin Roosevelt or Richard Nixon or other presidents requires cross-cutting examination of the other contemporaneous issues and pressures that interacted with environmental policy making during their administrations. And the realm of U.S. international policies affecting the environment—international environmental agreements per se as well as trade, security, and other foreign policies affecting the environment—is a large and important area for environmental policy research in its own right, beyond the scope of this chapter (see, e.g., Andrews 2006, 317–349; DeSombre 2000; Paarlberg 1999; Speth 2004; Susman 2004).

Second, the history of environmental policies reveals a rich range of policy instruments that have been used at different times and to address different problems: not just regulation, as is so commonly assumed by policy makers and the public today, but also land grants and sales, taxes and charges and user fees, public investments, subsidies, liability and insurance requirements, revolving loan funds, information disclosure and public reporting requirements, direct public management of environmental resources and services, government procurement policies, and others. Each of these has had successes, failures, and unforeseen consequences. As a group they represent a rich range of research opportunities, both for historical understanding and for potential adaptation (or cautionary examples) to address contemporary environmental challenges (Andrews 2006; Eisner 2007; Hatch 2005; U.S. EPA 2001).

Third, the history of U.S. environmental policy is suffused with complex research questions of administrative discretion and environmental federalism. How much discretionary authority should federal agencies have to prevent serious hazards, based on their scientific expertise and prudent judgment rather than on advance proof of consequences? And how should policies be designed to utilize the best features of multilevel governance and avoid their worst side effects, in the context of cooperation, delegation, and/or conflict between federal environmental policy making and the policies of state and local governments? On the one hand, modern federal environmental regulation relies heavily on state and local implementation, supported in some cases by federal subsidies (Andrews 2006, 227–228, 249–250, 275–277; U.S. Congress 2008). On the other hand, large areas of environmental policy making remain open to or even dominated by state and local powers (Rabe 2010). With continuing partisan gridlock at the federal level, many states are forging ahead on their own, with results that may ultimately provide models for national legislation or may produce approaches that are inconsistent, imperfect, ineffective, costly, and/or competing (Keeler 2007; Wiener 2007). This, too, is an important and under-researched topic.

Fourth, the history of environmental policy is strongly path-dependent. Today's environmental problems are deeply influenced by the policies that have and have not been chosen to address past issues, and choices for the future in principle require either layering additional new policies on top of old ones, or reforming or abolishing past policies whose consequences have become anachronistic. All environmental policies today remain profoundly influenced by distinctively American concepts of environmental property rights that emerged in the colonial era and by constitutional doctrines of the powers and limitations of government. Many policies from the distant past also still exist today—for example, cheap mining royalties from the 1870s, agricultural commodity subsidies from the 1930s, and policies since at least the 1930s promoting continued economic dependence on cheap fossil fuels rather than energy efficiency and renewable energy alternatives. Perversely, layering new policies or regulatory restraints on top of old ones is politically easier to accomplish but less effective (and in many cases, arguably less efficient) than reforming past policies whose consequences have become perverse but which have organized constituencies with vested interests in their continuation. This is an important topic for further research, including the need for creative options capable of overcoming the political inertia of past policies and their beneficiaries.

Finally, the history of environmental policy cannot be held up as a triumphalist story of progress and gradual victory of environmental sustainability over past practices (Dowie 1995). The policies of the 1970s achieved major reductions in pollution from industrial and municipal point sources and in unsafe waste management, but even more serious environmental damage continues, both domestically and in particular worldwide: global climate change, air and water pollution from unmanaged sources, deforestation and loss of biodiversity, loss of the world's wild fisheries, and overuse of increasingly scarce water resources, among others. Environmental transmission of disease also continues to raise serious threats despite temporary victories, as pathogens evolve resistance to pesticides and medications.

In reality, U.S. environmental policy to date is more a story of perennial conflicts among organized advocates of various specific commercial or appreciative uses of natural assets, often pitting short-term private extractive benefits against damage to long-term ecological sustainability. These interests wage trench warfare in legislatures, administrative proceedings, and courts, augmented by direct private and voluntary initiatives (both positive and negative) and public opinion and punctuated by temporary "republican moments" of mobilized mass public pressure such as the 1970s (Farber 1992, 59, 66; Lazarus 2003). Serious consideration of environmental policy solutions has been reduced to two competing political framing narratives: on the environmentalists' side, by the idealistic vision of an affluent but environmentally sustainable society coupled with the Progressive Era morality tale demonizing big business as the root source of all environmental damage, and, on the business/conservative side, by the centuries-old American narrative idealizing unfettered free-market capitalism and demonizing the bogeymen of big government and distant bureaucrats armed with unaccountable discretionary powers.

- and now at the intu'l level
w/ global governance, Paris Ag't

Behind this reality, however, lies a deeper one. The political battle lines in national environmental politics are often portrayed as environmental advocacy groups versus businesses and property owners, liberals versus conservatives, "blue states" versus "red states," "elitists" versus "common people." In fact, however, the key fault lines in environmental politics and policy run not so much between these constituencies but within each of them, dividing each between those who see their interests and values aligned with long-term ecological and community sustainability and those aligned with short-term, self-serving outcomes at the expense of longer-term shared values. Businesses themselves are deeply divided between those within each sector that seek to modernize and innovate, often reducing environmental impacts, and those that seek policies allowing them to continue environmentally damaging processes and products (National Research Council 2005). Some entire business sectors have significant interests in stronger environmental protection, such as insurance companies' exposures to the risks of environmental hazards such as climate change, while others depend on maintaining the status quo. Many red-state ranchers and forest managers are deeply committed to long-term land and wildlife conservation, and are troubled by the impacts of mining and oil and gas extraction. Conversely, environmental advocacy groups include many individuals who are open to the concerns of these other constituencies, but also some who are so zealously dedicated to their own agendas, so indiscriminately hostile to business, so contemptuous of property owners or rural producers, or so self-righteously certain of the superiority of their own knowledge and values, that they are poorly prepared to help build broader coalitions (Andrews 2006, 407–410).

Effective solutions to environmental policy problems are stalemated by the political dominance of these frames and of the half-truths that they each contain in the hands of political opinion leaders on each side (see chapter 20 in this volume). Understanding these political forces warrants careful reading of the insights of key political theorists, most of whom were writing not specifically about environmental politics but more generally, such as Mancur Olson (1965), Hugh Heclo (1978), and John Kingdon (1984), as well as Anthony Downs (1972) and the rich body of research that now exists on the tragedies and management of open-access resources (Ostrom et al. 2002). There also needs to be far more research on the social and behavioral influences driving individual and business behavior that affects the environment and on how different policy incentives affect the external barriers (costs, availability, etc.) and the internal barriers (values, attitudes, beliefs, assumptions, social norms) that drive behavioral choices both favorable and harmful to the environment (e.g., Dietz et al. 2009; Maibach et al. 2011; National Research Council 2002; Stern 2000).

The central issue for future environmental policy is how to achieve an environmentally sustainable civilization that is resilient to the increasing pressures and threats to it, both at the micro level of individuals and businesses and at the macro level of aggregate extraction of materials and energy from the environment and aggregate transformation of ecosystems. Achieving such a civilization will require more integrated, enduring, and adaptable policy-making institutions and political commitment, at all levels of governance, than has yet been achieved. It also will require far more research aimed at documenting and transforming both production and consumption and the public policies—and lack of policies—that shape them (see, e.g., Adger 2009; Mazmanian and Kraft 2009; Rockström et al. 2009; United Nations Environment Programme 2007; United Nations Millennium Project 2005; and chapter 9 in this volume).

REFERENCES

Adger, W. N., and A. Jordan, eds. 2009. *Governing Sustainability*. Cambridge: Cambridge University Press.

Andrews, R. N. L. 1984. "Economics and Environmental Decisions, Past and Present." In *Environmental Policy under Reagan's Executive Order: The Role of Benefit-Cost Analysis*, ed. V. Kerry Smith. Chapel Hill: University of North Carolina Press.

———. 2005. "Recovering the Environmental Legacy of FDR." In *FDR and the Environment*, ed. Henry L. Henderson and David B. Woolner. New York: St. Martin's.

———. 2006. *Managing the Environment, Managing Ourselves: A History of American Environmental Policy*. 2nd ed. New Haven, CT: Yale University Press.

Caldwell, L. 1963. "Environment: A New Focus for Public Policy?" *Public Administration Review* 22: 132–139.

Carley, S. 2009. "State Renewable Energy Electricity Policies: An Empirical Evaluation of Effectiveness." *Energy Policy* 37: 3071–3081.

———. 2011a. "Decarbonization of the U.S. Electricity Sector: Are State Energy Policy Portfolios the Answer?" *Energy Economics* 33: 1004–1023.

———. 2011b. "Historical Analysis of U.S. Energy Markets: Reassessing Carbon Lock-In." *Energy Policy* 39: 720–732.

Cashore, B., G. Auld, and D. Newsom. 2004. *Governing through Markets: Forest Certification and the Emergence of Non-State Authority*. New Haven, CT: Yale University Press.

Crenson, M. A. 1971. *The Un-Politics of Air Pollution: A Study of Non-Decisionmaking in the Cities*. Baltimore: Johns Hopkins University Press.

Cronon, W. 1983. *Changes in the Land: Indians, Colonists, and the Ecology of New England*. New York: Hill and Wang.

Dana, S. T., and S. K. Fairfax. 1980 [1956]. *Forest and Range Policy*. New York: McGraw-Hill.

Davies, J. C., and J. Mazurek. 1998. *Pollution Control in the United States: Evaluating the System*. Washington, DC: Resources for the Future Press.

DeSombre, E. 2000. *Domestic Sources of International Environmental Policy: Industry, Environmentalists, and U.S. Power*. Cambridge, MA: MIT Press.

Dietz, T., G. T. Gardner, J. Gilligan, P. C. Stern, and M. P. Vandenbergh. 2009. "Household Actions Can Provide a Behavioral Wedge to Rapidly Reduce U.S. Carbon Emissions." *Proceedings of the National Academy of Sciences* 106: 18452–18456.

Dowie, M. 1995. *Losing Ground: American Environmentalism at the Close of the Twentieth Century.* Cambridge, MA: MIT Press.

Downs, A. 1972. "Up and Down with Ecology: The Issue-Attention Cycle." *Public Interest,* no. 28 (Summer): 38–50.

Duffy, J. 1990. *The Sanitarians: A History of American Public Health.* Urbana: University of Illinois Press.

Durant, R. F. 1992. *The Administrative Presidency Revisited: Public Lands, the BLM, and the Reagan Revolution.* Albany: State University of New York Press.

Eisner, M. A. 2007. *Governing the Environment: The Transformation of Environmental Regulation.* Boulder, CO: Lynne Rienner.

Engelbert, E. A. 1950. "American Policy for Natural Resources: An Historical Survey to 1862." PhD diss., Harvard University.

Faeth, P. et al. 1989. *Paying the Farm Bill: U.S. Agricultural Policy and the Transition to Sustainable Agriculture.* Washington, DC: World Resources Institute.

Farber, D. A. 1992. "Politics and Procedure in Environmental Law." *Journal of Law, Economics and Organizations* 8: 59, 66 (quoting James G. Pope, "Republican Moments: The Role of Direct Popular Power in the American Constitutional Order," *University of Pennsylvania Law Review* 139 [1990]: 287, 292).

Flippen, J. B. 2000. *Nixon and the Environment.* Albuquerque: University of New Mexico Press.

Foresta, R. A. 1985. *America's National Parks and Their Keepers.* Washington: Resources for the Future Press.

Foss, P. 1960. *Politics and Grass.* Seattle: University of Washington Press.

Glicksman, R., and C. Schroeder. 1991. "EPA and the Courts: Twenty Years of Law and Politics." *Law and Contemporary Problems* 54 (4): 249–309.

Graham, O. L., Jr. 1976. *Toward a Planned Society: From Roosevelt to Nixon.* New York: Oxford University Press.

Hadden, S. G. 1986. *Read the Label: Reducing Risk by Providing Information.* Boulder, CO: Westview.

———. 1989. *A Citizen's Right to Know: Risk Communication and Public Policy.* Boulder, CO: Westview.

Hatch, M. T., ed. 2005. *Environmental Policymaking: Assessing the Use of Alternative Policy Instruments.* Albany: State University of New York Press.

Hays, S. P. 1959. *Conservation and the Gospel of Efficiency: The Progressive Conservation Movement, 1980–1920.* Cambridge, MA: Harvard University Press.

Heclo, H. 1978. "Issue Networks and the Executive Establishment." In *The New American Political System,* ed. Anthony King. Washington, DC: American Enterprise Institute.

Hibbard, B. H. 1924. *A History of the Public Land Policies.* New York: Macmillan.

Hirt, P. W. 1994. *A Conspiracy of Optimism: Management of the National Forests since World War Two.* Lincoln: University of Nebraska Press.

Hornstein, D. 1993. "Lessons from Federal Pesticide Regulation on the Paradigms and Politics of Environmental Law Reform." *Yale Journal on Regulation* 10: 369–446.

Jackson, K. T. 1985. *Crabgrass Frontier: The Suburbanization of the United States.* New York: Oxford University Press.

Jones, C. O. 1975. *Clean Air: The Policies and Politics of Pollution Control.* Pittsburgh: University of Pittsburgh Press.

Keeler, A. 2007. "State Greenhouse Gas Reduction Policies: A Move in the Right Direction?" *Policy Sciences* 40: 353–365.

Kingdon, J. W. 1984. *Agendas, Alternatives, and Public Policies.* Boston: Little, Brown.

Klyza, C. M. 1996. *Who Controls the Public Lands?* Chapel Hill: University of North Carolina Press.

Klyza, C. M., and D. J. Sousa. 2008. *American Environmental Policy, 1990–2006: Beyond Gridlock.* Cambridge, MA: MIT Press.

Kraft, M. E., M. Stephan, and T. D. Abel. 2011. *Coming Clean: Information Disclosure and Environmental Performance.* Cambridge, MA: MIT Press.

Lacey, M. J. 1979. "The Mysteries of Earth-Making Dissolve: A Study of Washington's Intellectual Community and the Origins of American Environmentalism in the Late Nineteenth Century." PhD diss., George Washington University.

Lazarus, R. J. 1991. "The Tragedy of Distrust in the Implementation of Federal Environmental Law." *Law and Contemporary Problems* 54 (4): 311–374.

———. 2003. "A Different Kind of 'Republican Moment' in Environmental Law." *Minnesota Law Review* 87: 999–1035.

———. 2004. *The Making of Environmental Law.* Chicago: University of Chicago Press.

Leiserowitz, A., Maibach, E., and Roser-Renouf, C. 2009. *Global Warming's Six Americas: An Audience Segmentation Analysis.* Yale University and George Mason University. New Haven, CT: Yale University Project on Climate Change. Available online at: http://environment.yale.edu/climate/files/climatechange-6americas.pdf

Lowry, W. R. 2009. *Repairing Paradise: The Restoration of Nature in America's National Parks.* Washington, DC: Brookings Institution.

Maass, A. 1951. *Muddy Waters: The Army Engineers and the Nation's Rivers.* Cambridge, MA: Harvard University Press.

Maibach, E., Leiserowitz, A., Roser-Renouf, C., and Mertz, C. K. 2011. Identifying Like-Minded Audiences for Global Warming Public Engagement Campaigns: An Audience Segmentation Analysis and Tool Development. *PLoS ONE* 6: e17571.

Marsh, G. P. 1965 [1864]. *Man and Nature: Or, Physical Geography as Modified by Human Action.* Cambridge, MA: Harvard University Press.

Mazmanian, D. A., and M. E. Kraft. 2009. *Toward Sustainable Communities: Transition and Transformations in Environmental Policy.* 2nd ed. Cambridge, MA: MIT Press.

Melosi, M., ed. 1980. *Pollution and Reform in American Cities, 1870–1930.* Austin: University of Texas Press.

———. 1981. *Garbage in the Cities: Refuse, Reform, and the Environment, 1880–1980.* Chicago: Dorsey Press.

Miller, J. A. 1973. "Congress and the Origins of Conservation: Natural Resource Policies, 1865–1900." PhD diss., University of Minnesota.

Morgan, R. J. 1965. *Governing Soil Conservation: Thirty Years of the New Decentralization.* Baltimore: Johns Hopkins University Press.

National Research Council. 2002. *New Tools for Environmental Protection: Education, Information, and Voluntary Measures.* Washington, DC: National Academy Press.

———. 2005. *Decision Making for the Environment: Social and Behavioral Science Research Priorities.* Washington, DC: National Academy Press.

O'Leary, R. 2010. "Environmental Policy in the Courts." In *Environmental Policy: New Directions for the Twenty-First Century,* 7th ed., ed. N. J. Vig and M. E. Kraft. Washington, DC: CQ Press.

Olson, M. 1965. *The Logic of Collective Action.* Cambridge, MA: Harvard University Press.

Ostrom, E., et al., eds. 2002. *The Drama of the Commons*. Washington, DC: National Academies Press.

Owen, A. L. R. 1983. *Conservation under F.D.R.* New York: Praeger.

Paarlberg, R. 1999. "Lapsed Leadership: U.S. International Environmental Policy since Rio." In *The Global Environment: Institutions, Law, and Policy*, ed. N. J. Vig and R. S. Axelrod. Washington, DC: CQ Press.

Pinchot, G. 1967 [1910]. *The Fight for Conservation*. Seattle: University of Washington Press.

Rabe, B. 2004. *Statehouse and Greenhouse: The Emerging Politics of American Climate Change Policy*. Washington, DC: Brookings Institution.

———. 2010. "Racing to the Top, the Middle, or the Bottom of the Pack? The Evolving State Government Role in Environmental Protection." In *Environmental Policy: New Directions for the Twenty-First Century*, 7th ed., ed. N. J. Vig and M. E. Kraft. Washington, DC: CQ Press.

Richardson, E. 1973. *Dams, Parks and Politics: Resource Development and Preservation in the Truman-Eisenhower Era*. Lexington: University Press of Kentucky.

Ringquist, E. 1993. *Environmental Protection at the State Level: Politics and Progress in Controlling Pollution*. Armonk, NY: M. E. Sharpe.

Rockström, J., et al. 2009. "A Safe Operating Space for Humanity." *Nature* 461: 472–475.

Rosen, G. 1958. *A History of Public Health*. New York: MD Publications.

Royston, M. 1979. *Pollution Prevention Pays*. London: Pergamon.

Sax, J. L. 1971. *Defending the Environment*. New York: Knopf.

Selznick, P. 1949. *TVA and the Grass Roots*. Berkeley: University of California Press.

Smillie, W. G. 1955. *Public Health: Its Promise for the Future, 1607–1914*. New York: Macmillan.

Speth, J. G. 2004. "First Attempt at Global Environmental Governance" and "Anatomy of Failure." In *Red Sky at Morning: America and the Crisis of the Global Environment*. New Haven, CT: Yale University Press.

Stern, P. C. 2000. "Toward a Coherent Theory of Environmentally Significant Behavior." *Journal of Social Issues* 56 (3): 407–424.

Stewart, R. B. 1975. "The Reformation of American Administrative Law." *Harvard Law Review* 88: 1667–1815.

Sundquist, J. L. 1968. *Politics and Policy: The Eisenhower, Kennedy, and Johnson Years*. Washington, DC: Brookings Institution.

Susman, G. 2004. "The USA and Global Environmental Policy: Domestic Constraints on Effective Leadership." *International Political Science Review* 5: 349–369.

Swain, D. 1963. *Federal Conservation Policy 1921–1933*. Publications in History, vol. 76. Berkeley: University of California Press.

Tarr, J. 1985. "The Search for the Ultimate Sink: Urban Air, Land and Water Pollution in Historical Perspective." In *Environmental History: Critical Issues in Comparative Perspective*, ed. K. Bailes. New York: University Press of America.

United Nations Environment Program. 2007. *Global Environment Outlook 4 (GEO4): Environment for Development*. Malta: Progress Press.

United Nations Millennium Project. 2005. *Environment and Human Well-Being: A Practical Strategy*. Report of the Task Force on Environmental Sustainability. London: Earthscan.

U.S. Congress. House of Representatives. Committee on Energy and Commerce. 2008. *Climate Change Legislation Design White Paper: Appropriate Roles for Different Levels of Government.* Prepared by the Committee on Energy and Commerce staff, February.

U.S. Environmental Protection Agency. 2001. *The United States' Experience with Economic Incentives for Protecting the Environment.* Report No. EPA-240-R-01–001, January.

U.S. Public Land Law Review Commission. 1968. *History of Public Land Law Development.* Washington, DC: Government Printing Office.

Vig, N. J. 2010. "Presidential Powers and Environmental Policy." In *Environmental Policy: New Directions for the Twenty-First Century,* 7th ed., ed. N. J. Vig and M. E. Kraft. Washington, DC: CQ Press.

Vig, N. J., and M. E. Kraft, eds. 1984. *Environmental Policy in the 1980s: Reagan's New Agenda.* Washington, DC: CQ Press.

———. 2010. *Environmental Policy: New Directions for the Twenty-First Century,* 7th ed. Washington, DC: CQ Press.

Wiener, J. 2007. "Think Globally, Act Globally: The Limits of Local Climate Policies." *University of Pennsylvania Law Review* 155: 1961–1979.

Winslow, C. E. A. 1923. *The Evolution and Significance of the Modern Public Health Campaign.* New Haven, CT: Yale University Press.

Worster, D. M. 1985. *Rivers of Empire: Water, Aridity, and the Growth of the American West.* New York: Pantheon.

CHAPTER 3

GREEN POLITICAL IDEAS AND ENVIRONMENTAL POLICY

WALTER F. BABER AND ROBERT V. BARTLETT

1. INTRODUCTION

POLITICAL movements always give rise to distinct discourses that are (in the first instance, at least) stories that a movement tells to itself, about itself. These stories describe, interpret, and evaluate the ideas of the movement from a particular point of view, searching for the most intelligible and compelling account of what is important within each discourse. Different discourses also offer ideas about how a movement might and should change the world and, as such, are any movement's political currency. There have been at least six such collections of ideas that have powerfully influenced the development of environmental policy thinking and action in the United States from the mid-nineteenth century to the present. All six—ecological perspectives, notions about knowledge and rationality, participatory politics, economic principles, environmental justice, and organizational structure—continue to affect ongoing policy, policy debates, and policy initiatives, sometimes in conflict with each other. Antecedents for all of these ideas can be found that predate the emergence of the environmental movement, and each of these clusters of ideas has had at least one major political "moment in the sun" in the decades since. Early efforts to explain environmentalism tended to pit ultimate values against one another (e.g., conservation versus preservation; economic values versus environmental protection) by calling out particular elements of reality thought to be problematic from an environmental perspective but without providing analytical constructs for resolving the tensions between those values. Contemporary environmental thought shows a certain progressive development inasmuch as later discourses do tend to organize environmental thinking along identifiable dimensions while attempting to integrate, or at least accommodate, other discourses.

In this chapter we provide a brief overview of these six sets of ideas as they have appeared in the research literature and have (or have not) influenced environmental politics and policy development in the United States. Somewhat surprisingly, political theory and political philosophy have made few contributions to these discourses or sets of ideas. We conclude the chapter with a brief analysis and speculation on why political theory and political philosophy have not been, and are not soon likely to be, significant contributors to the pool of influential green political ideas shaping American environmental politics and policy.

2. CONSERVATION, PRESERVATION, AND ECOLOGY

Resource conservation as an environmental concept can trace its lineage to some of the first regulatory actions of both colonial governments and the early Republic (see chapter 2 in this volume). Concerns over the continued availability of wild game and the increasing deforestation of the continent lay behind both state and local statutes for resource conservation and the development of the national park system. Game protection initiatives (both private and public) and basic statutory schemes to conserve timber resources coalesced in a viewpoint that is an obvious precursor of today's ecosystem management (Andrews 1999). From its earliest beginnings, the conservation movement was characterized by a focus on management that viewed nature as a resource to be used to meet human needs. Its objective, as described by Gifford Pinchot, was to ensure that natural resources were used rationally and efficiently to benefit the present generation, avoiding waste and the unjust enrichment of the privileged (Hays 1959). While this may sound woefully inadequate to modern ears, the idea of conservation was remarkably progressive for its time and provided conceptual material that serves the environmental movement to this day. For instance, without the conservationist's faith in the ability of humans to manage the consequences of their own choices, the logic of environmental impact assessment would be entirely unpersuasive. Conservationists' own confidence in their ability to manage the environment gave rise to the second hallmark idea of early green thought—preservation.

The preservation movement is more than just a reaction to the technocratic quality of the idea of conservation. Preservationists posit a profound relationship between humans and nature—sometimes psychological, sometimes spiritual. This relationship is evidence of the intrinsic value of unspoiled wilderness, nature untouched by humankind. Some preservationists such as John Muir were led to a more comprehensive critique of human culture in general, which they viewed as superficial, tawdry, or downright evil. Although most preservationists have never embraced this more radical critique of industrialized civilization, it was an antecedent for subsequent holistic views of environmental challenges that emphasize the comprehensive nature of environmental problems, their integration with other policy problems, and the necessity for anticipatory and preventive policy approaches (Buhrs and Bartlett 1993; Caldwell 1995, 1963). For preservationists, protecting the environment entails far more than ensuring a continued flow of environmental goods. Rather, it is, in large part, a matter of weaning ourselves away from that flow.

The dialogue between preservationists and conservationists largely defined American green political thought in its early years—identifying the features of the world that were the subjects of environmental ideas, determining how those subjects were defined, and explaining how changes in the condition of those subjects came about. Beginning in the nineteenth century and continuing to the present day, the ideas of conservation and preservation have been major influences on many American policy developments at all levels, ranging from the creation of parks and reserves (National Forests; National Wildlife Refuges; national, state, and local parks) to the creation of innumerable nongovernmental organizations (Sierra Club, National Audubon Society, National Wildlife Federation) and networks to the establishment of new government institutions, responsibilities, and processes (Wilderness Act, Soil Conservation Service, Fish and Wildlife Service).

The institutionalization of conservation and preservationist ideas, inside and outside government, positioned these ideas and their advocates in the 1950s and 1960s to embrace and dominate environmentalism as it emerged as a distinct social movement in the 1960s, when ideas from ecology and ecological theory offered a way of integrating and building on their own earlier ideas (and social movements) and those of public health, consumerism, outdoor recreation, public beauty, and planning. Ideas from ecological theory were tremendously influential in the development of environmental policy. Ecological theory itself has evolved considerably in the last half century, partly in response to increased resources and attention and partly in reflexive reconsideration of the potential for and limits to how ecological knowledge can contribute to environmental social learning and action (Kingsland 2005). Conservation and preservation ideas were blended together with ecological ones to influence a dramatic investment in new programs, laws, and agencies at all levels of government, including many that mainly addressed traditional conservation and preservation concerns (Endangered Species Act, Surface Mining Control and Reclamation Act) and others that were primarily public health oriented (pollution control agencies, Clean Air Act) but often with significant conservationist and preservationist aspects (zero discharge, prevention of significant deterioration). This strong influence of conservationist and preservationist thought in the United States continues to be the characteristic that most distinguishes U.S. environmentalism and environmental policy from what has developed in most other countries since the 1960s (Dryzek et al. 2003; Ruha 2000; Schreurs 2002).

3. Economics and the Environment

Efficiency and waste control have been core ideas of environmentalism from the beginning, having been directly imported from the earlier resource conservation movement (Hays 1959). More recently, significant developments in public and resource economics, promoted by think tanks such as Resources for the Future, as well as the development of public choice (rational choice) theorizing, have been deeply influential in environmental policy thinking. Particularly since the late 1970s, politicians and policy reformers have become increasingly concerned with finding less costly, more flexible, and more efficient ways to achieve environmental goals (see chapters 25 and 26 in this volume). Initially controversial experiments with such ideas as tradable pollution permits in the 1990 amendments to the Clean Air Act have worked so well that many who at first opposed the idea have become advocates. At the same time, policy entrepreneurs have continued to try to figure out how to reconcile environmental imperatives with the worldwide commitment of most politicians, nearly all businesspeople, and an overwhelming majority of the public to continued wealth generation (development). Such ideas as sustainable development (see chapters 4 and 9 in this volume) and industrial ecology (Allenby 1999) have come to dominate symbolic debates over environmental policy, although they have had less practical influence on U.S. environmental policy than in other countries and on international policy development.

A discourse that encompasses most of these concerns in wealthier countries could be characterized as ecological modernization, although this set of ideas has had relatively little direct political influence in the United States. This wholehearted embrace of modernity recognizes equity issues of access to and allocation of environmental goods. But it takes the solution to these problems, as well as the depletion of natural resources generally, to consist in the reduction of waste and improved efficiency made possible by technological innovation and the streamlining and rationalization of organizational processes. Overcoming the supposed evils of materialism and consumerism is no part of this discourse. Where access to environmental goods is flawed, more perfect markets are the solution. And where environmental goods (and bads) are inappropriately allocated, the existing set of incentives within which individuals make their decisions can be reformed. The objective throughout is to achieve forms of sustainable development that allow for continued economic growth while reducing or mitigating environmental impacts.

A competing discourse on the economy and the environment that embraces each of these topics is the citizen-worker movement (Mayer 2008, 2009; Mayer, Brown, and Morello-Frosch 2010). Originally an outgrowth of the NIMBY (not in my backyard) and occupational health and safety movements, the citizen-worker movement tends to be rather peripatetic (Foster 2007). Its attention tends to wander from one specific issue to another, often following the latest headlines. Its focus tends to remain constant, however, insofar as it is concerned with the failures of markets to incorporate all of the costs of economic growth into the price of the goods produced (Jahn 1993). Every manifestation of production generates its own forms of negative externalities, the distribution of which rarely mirrors the distribution of benefits. Citizen-worker activists evidence a deep skepticism about whether this sort of problem can be adequately addressed through the manipulation of markets and the improvement of incentives (Krajnc 2000). Their solution is to substitute bureaucracy (in the form of regulatory action by politically responsive agencies) for markets as the guiding force in these areas of collective life.

While the citizen-worker movement does contest much of the sustainable development discourse, it is not an exercise in direct opposition. For the citizen-worker activist, the problem with materialism and consumerism is not so much that they are unsustainable ecologically as that they are irrational economically because their costs are not accurately calculated. For this reason, no comprehensive critique of capitalism and its impact on the environment is necessary; all that is required is a political decision that capitalism requires adult supervision.

Another discourse in the economics category is that of ecological economics, founded on a set of ideas developed by academic political economists. Early theorists such as Kenneth Boulding and Herman Daly developed the basic, radical idea that, over a longer term of centuries if not decades, economic systems can only flourish within and must be consistent with the basic conservation laws of thermodynamics and fundamental principles of ecosystem behavior. Ignoring natural capital and assuming the fungibility of all physical resources undermine the foundations of traditional economic analysis (Costanza 1991). The idea of "steady-state economics," in line with the ideas prominent in the 1970s of "limits to growth" and "zero growth," challenged the commitment of conventional economics to perpetual growth (Daly 1977). Daly argued that it was impossible to extend the high-consumption economy of the United States to the world population; hence the (necessary but utopic) solution was for wealthy societies to reduce consumption, while poor societies slowed population growth and in some cases raised consumption to the new, "reduced" level of the wealthy nations. More recent thinking about accounting for natural capital and ecosystem services raises questions about whether much of the traditional development project necessarily results in an actual net increase in either wealth or well-being (Costanza et al. 1997; Prugh et al. 1999). Some of those societies thought of as poor and underdeveloped may be, in terms of access to important ecosystem services, much richer than those held by traditional accounting, whereas others may be more impoverished—and likewise for those labeled as affluent. Although ecological economics is now a well-established field (with its own scholarly journal, *Ecological Economics*) emphasizing policy-relevant research and outreach to activists and policy makers (through, among other means, a journal-magazine called *Solutions*), its impact on national—as well as nearly all state and local—environmental policy debates and choices continues to be nearly imperceptible.

4. Knowledge and Rationality in Environmental Policy

Ecological theory is only one of many fields of knowledge crucial to environmentalism and to environmental policy. Many environmental problems cannot even be perceived without a great deal of scientific information and technological sophistication (Caldwell 1990; Paehlke 1989). Given the limits of the sciences, the science-dependent character of environmentalism means that there will always be a degree of uncertainty about the true nature and severity of environmental problems (Alm, Burkhart, and Simon 2010; Kirkman 2002). This uncertainty is exacerbated by tensions that are inherent in the relationship between science, environmental values, and risk. Moreover, these perspectives on the environment do not necessarily trump, and are seldom easily reconciled with, perspectives anchored in the rationalities of technology, economics, law, or politics (Baber and Bartlett 2005, 2009). Much environmental policy innovation has resulted from insights into how different kinds of knowledge can be created, collected, integrated, and applied in the cause of environmental understanding and protection (Ascher, Steelman, and Healy 2010; Keller 2009; Layzer 2008).

The problem of relating knowledge and rational decision making to environmental protection is well expressed in the discourse of reform environmentalism (Brulle 2000; Dryzek 2005; Dryzek and Schlosberg 2005). Grounded in the natural sciences, but dedicated to the notion that humanity exists as part of the Earth's ecosystem, reform environmentalism is pragmatic in character. Coming of age in an era of urbanization and industrialization, it is a movement that saw no inherent conflict between protection of the environment and promotion of human interest (properly understood). Concerned in the early twentieth century with issues such as urban sanitation and air quality, reform environmentalism adapted easily to campaigns against pesticides after the publication of *Silent Spring* (Carson 1962) and efforts to impose "limits to growth" after the first Earth Day.

In fact, reform environmentalism's science-based and pragmatic nature has made it an extremely durable theoretical perspective. It has accommodated itself easily to an era in which risk assessment and management has threatened to eclipse environmental protection as the dominant theme of green thought. Its tendency to accommodate and its substantial influence on American policy development are precisely the characteristics that most clearly distinguish it from the competing discourse of deep ecology.

Deep ecology, as a way of relating knowledge to decision, is fundamentally intuitive. The confrontation of reform environmentalism by deep ecologists highlights a question that is essentially normative: can nature be properly regarded as a resource to sustain human existence, or does nature bear an independent right of existence quite apart from any value that humans might attach to it or any of its constituent parts (Dryzek 2005; Foreman 1998)? If nature is a rights bearer, it makes no sense to trade off damage to the environment for human benefit. Deep ecology does not reject scientific knowledge and rational decision making, but it turns those concepts in a very different direction by problematizing their use to advance human technology and economic growth. It advocates, instead, the use of science and reason to go beyond wilderness preservation—to restore a fully functioning biosphere in which nature's varied ecosystems can evolve free of anthropomorphic distortion and debasement.

The debate between those advocating reform environmentalism and deep ecology ranges over the entire terrain of human knowledge and the role that it plays in environmental policy. In reform environmentalism, knowledge is the very stuff of environmental action. All environmental questions are, at their base, dependent on questions of fact. Unlike many other areas of policy discourse, environmental problems have distinctly better and worse solutions because they relate directly to an independent world composed of protons and electrons that is what it is, quite apart from what humans think about it. For the deep ecologist, however, matters are not so simple. Deep ecology would focus our attention on the unavoidably ethical relationship between human beings and the natural environment. It expands the boundaries of both ethics and nature in the direction of one another. Recognizing nature and its elements as components of the same community in which humans interact and accept mutual responsibilities, deep ecology "moralizes" nature at the same time that it "naturalizes" humankind by drawing us into the framework of the environment. That it does so without positing elemental particles constituting the moral world—"morons," in Ronald Dworkin's (2011) formulation—suggests clearly that deep ecology has a view of knowledge that is fundamentally antirealistic. Accordingly, it has room in its canon for both prose and poetry, and both explanation and exhortation (though it often emphasizes the second member of each of these pairings).

Along with this confrontation over the character and role of knowledge come consequent disagreements (of an unavoidably moral nature) over rationality, science, and technology. Reform environmentalists tend to reason in pragmatic ways. They are environmental problem solvers, not indifferent to the ethical big picture but not concerned with it as their initial point of departure. They embrace the sciences on their own terms, mining the various disciplines for practical solutions to discrete ecological problems. They celebrate technological innovations that improve our ability to reconcile the exploitation of natural resources with their conservation over the long term. They view as entirely legitimate the practice of risk assessment and management as a methodology for balancing the pros and cons of modern life and its environmental consequences. Deep ecology and other radical green discourses such as bioregionalism, ecocentrism, social ecology, ecosocialism, ecofeminism, ecotheology, and animal liberation (Dryzek 2005), however, problematize all that reform environmentalists embrace. These radical green discourses typically view modern forms of rationality as hubris, science as a method of distancing ourselves from moral responsibility for the environment, and technological fixes as the planet-wrecking consequences of living at that distance from nature. Risk assessment and management, for radical environmentalists, is arrogance raised to a form of art—virtually a form of human self-worship. All of these elements of human modernity are seen as camouflage for a relationship between humans and nature that defiles and ultimately destroys the living essence of both. Except for occasionally at the local level or in referenda campaigns, radical environmentalism has had little direct policy impact in the United States.

5. DEMOCRACY AND THE ENVIRONMENT

William Ophuls (1977, 2011), among others, views the relationship between democracy and the environment as deeply problematic, suggesting that popular government is incapable of responding to expert opinion and taking the difficult decisions that are necessary to avert ecological disaster. After all, popular government assumes that the views and interests of citizens are "givens" from a political point of view. In a democracy, government officials cater to popular preferences for resource consumption; they do not try to alter or frustrate them.

Others have argued that democracy is an essential element of environmental rationality and sustainable public policy (Baber and Bartlett 2005, 2009; Dryzek and Stevenson 2010; Lafferty and Meadowcroft 1996; Paehlke 2003, 2005). After all, it is difficult to understand how policies that are politically unsustainable (which in the modern world is true of policies imposed undemocratically) could be anything other than ecologically unsustainable as well. Innumerable environmental policies and programs have been adopted in the United States since the 1960s that have attempted to import more democratic practices into policy making (Beirle and Cayford 2002) and to experiment with participatory governance arrangements (Mazmanian and Kraft 2009; Weber 2003).

Policies based on nothing more than commenting, testifying, or voting cannot capture public preferences in all of their complexity, much less change them for the better. The environmental discourses already mentioned highlight this failure of aggregative politics. Aggregative forms of democracy leave dominant preferences unchallenged, allowing citizens to ignore the underlying science of environmentalism, impose inequitable distributions on minorities, and neglect the concerns of the disenfranchised if they so choose. This suggests a need to incorporate deliberative elements into environmental policy making, practices that will use the complexity and diversity of existing public opinion to allow citizens to develop more sophisticated and (ultimately) more environmentally friendly public policies.

Associated with the rise of less hierarchical and more participatory forms of governance, deliberative environmentalism focuses our attention on the value of thoughtful and discursive public participation in environmental decision making (Baber and Bartlett 2005; Dryzek and Stevenson 2010; Smith 2003). Rather than focusing on voting, interest aggregation, or the assertion of individual rights, deliberative environmentalism emphasizes the transformative potential of allowing groups of citizens to develop solutions to environmental challenges through uncoerced discussion of the available policy alternatives. The assumption is that appropriately structured social relations will allow citizens to evaluate critically their own views and the views of others in ways that will recognize consensus where it exists and promote its development in areas where it has yet to emerge. But deliberative democracy does not presume that fundamental moral disagreements such as are common in environmental politics will simply dissolve in the presence of sufficient deliberation. Rather, deliberative democracy fits with the imperatives of environmental politics especially well because "the greatest strength of deliberative democracy is not to solve deep moral disagreements...but to politicize and initiate reflection about beliefs, policies and institutions that are uncritically accepted by most people, and hence not discussed at all" (Rostbøll 2008, 220).

While deliberative environmentalism posits new and more directly participatory forms of environmental citizenship (Dobson 2003; Dobson 2009; Dobson and Bell 2006), it also broadens the discussion of environmental governance. It directs our attention to the complex (and potentially fruitful) interactions between governmental organizations and processes and the institutions of civil society in which most interactions between citizens actually occur.

An assumption underlying deliberative environmentalism is that ordinary citizens are not victims of some systemic form of false consciousness or that, if they are, an appropriately structured interaction among themselves is sufficient to free them from it. A discourse that problematizes this assumption is critical ecology. Grounded in the literature of the Frankfurt School, critical ecology employs the themes of domination and liberation to understand the relationship between humans and nature. Often viewing itself as a master discourse within which deep ecology, socialist ecology, environmental justice, and ecofeminism exist as subsidiary conversations, critical ecology views the ancient forms of individualism, scientific reasoning, and the domination of nature by humans as the foundational elements of modernity (Merchant 2008). While paying tribute to Marxist insights into the ecological costs of capitalism, critical ecologists rely on Max Horkheimer and Theodor Adorno for their critique of the Enlightenment myth of progress through the exploitation of nature—something that Marx and Engels were unable to escape (Eckersley 1992). They view this central economic logic as pervading every aspect of modern society, from the psychological and spiritual development of the individual to the institutional structure of law and government and the content of popular culture. Thus modern social relations, citizenship, and civil society are constitutionally incapable of being anything other than destructive of nature. Only a liberation ideology (or theology?) can successfully confront modernity's project of subjecting nature to the total domination of humans. Nature must be converted from an object to a subject, on the same plane of existence occupied by humans, through a process of reenchantment—allowing humans to regain the mystical understanding of nature that was typical of premodern societies.

6. Justice and the Environment

It is through ideas of environmental justice that political philosophy and theory has contributed most to American environmental politics and policy, drawing as it has on well-developed concepts of political liberalism (Schlosberg 2009). In the 1980s, contemporary green thought began prominently to feature concerns related to the roles played by people of color, indigenous populations, and women in environmental decision making. Both the epistemic validity and the political legitimacy of environmental policies can be subjected to criticism from the perspective of "difference democrats" who advocate a more inclusive form of environmental discourse than has existed heretofore. This emerging relationship between environmentalists and human rights advocates has brought attention to problems of distributional justice in both the allocation of environmental risks and the exploitation of natural resources. Locally undesirable land uses show a geographic distribution (both within individual nations and internationally) that imposes greater burdens on the poor and people of color than on others. The consumption of natural resources by the world's most developed countries far exceeds levels that would be predicted based on their population, posing challenges for advocates of sustainable development.

The best-known and most widely discussed form of this kind of environmentalism is the environmental justice movement. It is based on the demonstrable relationship between the distribution of environmental risks across various communities and the racial diversity of the residents in those communities. The "people of color" environmental movement involved not so much the birth of new groups and the creation of new discourses as the convergence of existing environmental and civil rights organizations (most often at the local level) and the exploration of their shared concerns. Until the 1980s, this was a little-noticed and nearly unexplored frontier of environmental thought. In the 1960s and 1970s, when civil rights activists thought about the environment at all, it was likely that they regarded it as a distraction from the far more pressing concerns that animated their movement.

During that same period, environmental organizations tended to be populated almost entirely by middle-class whites. Beginning in the mid- to late 1970s, however, a number of environmental policy entrepreneurs began to produce and promote research that bore out what many civil rights workers at the local level already knew instinctively—that the burdens of environmental pollutants and locally undesirable land uses fall disproportionately on people of color. Eventually spreading to Native American as well as indigenous populations outside the United States, this new discourse on environmental racism advocated the cessation of the production and dumping of toxins, hazardous wastes, and radioactive materials in politically disenfranchised and economically vulnerable communities and the enforcement of strict accountability on the producers of such materials for the consequences of their actions.

Another expression of difference and diversity in environmentalism is ecofeminism (Merchant 2008). Ecofeminism is a viewpoint grounded in the connection of the emergence of patriarchal forms of society and their domination of women by men with the domination of nature by humankind. In this view, both women and nature have come to be treated as objects to be possessed and exploited rather than as the subjects of a cooperative relationship. Male-dominated society, in both its early agricultural and later industrial forms, exploited nature and women in the same heedless ways. The solution is a new egalitarianism brought about through a cultural revolution. Once the cultural forms of patriarchy are overthrown, the feminine psyche, grounded in empathy for and identification with the nonhuman and an innate concern for future generations, will be able to assert itself. The result will be a new environmental ethic that is attentive to the voice of the feminine in a way that modern society, with its Enlightenment epistemology, can never be. The voice of the feminine, it is argued, will be able to work a fundamental socioeconomic change that other forces are incapable of producing. So far, feminist green political thought has probably had more influence on international development policy (Bhavnani, Foran, and Kurian 2003; Kurian 2000) than on any domestic U.S. environmental policy.

7. ORGANIZATION AND THE ENVIRONMENT

The environmental discourses arising within the clusters of ideas relating ecology to democracy, distribution, and difference all have at least one thing in common: they pose a fundamental structural question that political theorists would characterize as the problem of decentralization. If environmental policy needs to be more participatory, more just, and more inclusive, it would seem to require a radically decentralized form of governing. But the scope of environmental challenges faced by humankind would seem to suggest national and international solutions. Moreover, the need to incorporate deliberative elements and critical perspectives into environmental policy making also adds a procedural dimension to the structural challenges of decentralization.

One entrée to discourses concerned with organization and the environment is the literature on globalization. Globalization has distinctive economic and political elements. Its economic dimension can be documented by the apparent triumph of the so-called Washington consensus. This phrase most commonly refers to an orientation toward free-market policies that has been highly influential among mainstream economists, politicians, and journalists since about 1980 and underlies the policies of global institutions like the International Monetary Fund and the World Bank. In general, the term refers to market-friendly policies recommended for both advanced and emerging economies. When directed more narrowly to emerging economies, it refers to economic reforms that include the reduction of government deficits, the liberalization and deregulation of international trade and cross-investment, and the pursuit of export-led economic growth. The parallel political aspects of globalization involve changes in the nature of the state itself. Generally speaking, globalization results in a decline in the capacity of Westphalian nation-states freely to determine their own policies with regard to economic growth, trade and investment, and environmental regulation. Both because these challenges are now global in character and because state actors are more constrained in their responses to them, the institutions that states had previously employed are not as effective as they once were. Two distinctive discourses have emerged to inform our thinking about globalization. They can be referred to as the new institutionalism and cosmopolitanism.

New institutionalism (or neo-institutionalism) is an intellectual tradition concerned with developing a sociological view of institutions, the ways they interact with each other, and the ways they affect social processes generally. It provides a perspective for viewing institutions outside the traditional views of economics by explaining why so many organizations end up having the same structure even though they evolved in different ways, and how institutions shape the behavior of individual members. In the context of globalization, neo-institutionalism emphasizes the potential of regulatory bureaucracies and other organs of government administration to compensate for the increasing weakness of traditional nation-states by supplying policy coordination through the interaction of specialists in policy networks. These policy networks—spanning the boundaries between local, regional, national, and international governments—can provide environmental governance where actual government may lack sufficient capacity or may not even exist.

The discourse of cosmopolitanism takes a different approach to the problem of reconciling democracy's demand for decentralization with the environmental need for coordinated action. Cosmopolitanism is an ideological commitment to the view that all human ethnic groups belong to a single category based on a shared sense of morality. When contrasted with nationalism (the most nearly antonymous concept), cosmopolitanism advocates some sort of world government with a direct relationship to the global population, unmediated by national officials. Less concretely, it may be used to refer to more inclusive moral, economic, and political relationships between nations or individuals of different nations or (most loosely) a less parochial attitude on the part of one people toward the rest of humanity.

Less elitist and (perhaps) more idealistic than the new institutionalism, cosmo-politanism lends itself to an environmentalism that attaches greater importance to the development of a widely shared environmental ethic than to the crafting of a transnational web of environmental actors.

Another important discourse in American environmental politics and policy has been that of privatization. The idea that the environment can best be managed by the private sector is one that has influenced much theorizing and many reform pro-posals. Much but by no means all of this discourse originates from different places on the political right, from libertarian antigovernment free-market environmental-ism espoused by the Cato Institute and the Foundation for Research on Economics and the Environment (Baden and Noonan 1998; Goklany 2007), to the philosophi-cal underpinnings of the conservation land trust movement (Fairfax et al. 2005), to the regular calls from politicians and the frequent initiatives by regulatory agencies seeking voluntary environmental actions by corporations, other governments, civil society, and citizens (Coglianese and Nash 2006; Dietz and Stern 2002; Kamieniecki 2006; Khana and Brouhle 2009; Kraft and Kamieniecki 2007; Potoski and Prakash 2005; Press and Mazmanian 2010; Vogel 2005). A large number of such private sec-tor voluntary programs have been tried and evaluated since the 1960s; assessment of their success and potential has yielded decidedly mixed results.

All of these organizational discourses—decentralization, globalization, new institutionalism, cosmopolitanism, and privatization—are increasingly understood to be part of and contributing to use of the conceptual language of governance in discussions of environmental politics and policy. "Governance" is used to describe all patterns of rule or governing (Bevir 2009), and "environmental governance" can be defined as "the formal and informal institutions, policies, rules, and prac-tices that shape how humans interact with the environment at all levels of social organization" (Hendricks et al. 2009, 1). Governance is increasingly the language used and perspective taken by transnational and global research on environmental programs, collaborative arrangements, regulatory codes, management schemes, law, regimes, practices, markets, and civil society politics (Adger and Jordan 2009; Biermann et al. 2009; Demas and Young 2009), and it is also a vibrant perspective on the complexity of environmental governing in the United States (Eisner 2007).

8. WHITHER POLITICAL THEORY AND POLITICAL PHILOSOPHY IN GREEN POLITICAL THOUGHT?

The roots of green political ideas reviewed here can be found in pragmatic activ-ist politics as well as in, among others, the literatures of economics, science (both social and natural), engineering, design, aesthetics, organizational theory, and even religion. Perhaps the most remarkable divination offered by this review of green political ideas is the limited degree to which those sets of ideas, particularly the ones that have had the greatest influence on American politics and policy, have derived from political theory or political philosophy. Insight into why this should be so is provided by Dobson (2007, 2), who distinguishes between "ecologism and its more visible cousin environmentalism." Environmentalism, according to Dobson, "argues for a managerial approach to environmental problems, secure in the belief that they can be solved without fundamental changes in present values or patterns of production and consumption," whereas ecologism "holds that a sustainable and fulfilling existence presupposes radical changes in our relationship with the non-human natural world, and in our mode of social and political life" (Dobson 2007, 2–3). Political philosophers and political theorists drawing on the traditions of pragmatism have had some influence on American policy debates (e.g., Norton 2005; Sagoff 2007), but most to the extent they have considered the environmental problematique at all, have focused entirely on intellectually and ideologically satisfying analyses of improbable alternatives and of tabula rasa social and political design, investing little energy in thinking about how to get there from here (Bartlett 2005, 48).

These efforts to theorize our relationship with the environment have always tended to lurch off course in one of two distinctly unproductive directions. The first of these is the tendency to think that the natural world has intrinsic value—a value independent of what humans think about its value. The second is a tendency toward ethical monism—the view that our objective is to find a single, comprehensive ethical orientation that will determine all of our interactions with the nonhuman world (Smith 2003). It would be bad enough if these two mistakes were merely conceptual culs-de-sac. But they are worse than that. Each of these mistakes is characteristic of a skepticism toward human achievement (and artifice more generally) that can be traced back to treatises written by Jean-Jacques Rousseau in the eighteenth century, attacking civilization and applauding nature. This skepticism contributes to an estrangement of environmental ethics and political philosophizing from most of normative political philosophy, which by and large follows Immanuel Kant in its confidence that human inventiveness and social cooperation can ultimately chart a successful and democratic course for humankind (Wolfe 2010). The result is that green political thought is impoverished and political philosophy is blinded, each to an extent that neither need be.

The mistake in thinking that nature has intrinsic value is easy to spot, if not always to avoid. Environmentalists as different in their thinking as Aldo Leopold and Gifford Pinchot recognized that only human beings have values. In other words, only human beings make self-conscious judgments such as "This is good" or "This is valuable" (Sagoff 2007). To believe otherwise is a mistake because it obscures the fact that the primary reason we theorize about our relationship to the environment is so that we may evaluate and, where necessary, alter the institutions we use to govern that relationship (Biermann 2008). That objective is ultimately defeated if the normative framework it relies on becomes unbounded and indeterminate through the introduction of a new cluster of "values" that are by their very nature ineffable. The contributions that mainstream political theory might offer are liable to be held hostage to diversionary discourses, such as those regarding animal "rights," causing philosophers who might have been helpful (like John Rawls) to shy away from environmental subject matter altogether (Baber and Bartlett 2005). The problem is that both the world of contemporary political theory and the universe of Western political discourse more generally are both implicitly and avowedly Kantian. Rousseau may touch our hearts, but Kant describes our world. Placing humankind in that world and charting a course through it are what politics, policy, and political philosophy have been and will continue to be about. When green theorists forget that, in their zeal to avoid anthropocentrism, sexism, placism, materialism, or any of the other -isms that gnaw on the green conscience, they ultimately make themselves irrelevant.

The mistake involved in ethical monism is a bit harder to identify. This is because ethical monism in environmentalism can take one of two forms. First, it can manifest itself as an assumption that somewhere there is a "single ethic to guide our interventions in the non-human worlds" (Smith 2003, 18). This is the assumption of compatibility—that all values related to the environment are ultimately understood and justified in terms of a master value that transcends human interests and intentions—which is, of course, a more abstract version of the "intrinsic value of nature" error and subject to the same general criticisms. To admit nature into our normative framework is to confound our analysis beyond any hope of easy resolution, because although humans as behaving creatures are actually rather simple, they have the capacity to reflect all of the complexity of nature in their decision making (Simon 1996).

Second, ethical monism in environmentalism can appear in the form of an assumption that there must be a single theoretical framework that "can explain all of our interactions, both those between humans and between human and non-human worlds" (Smith 2003, 18). This is the assumption of commensurability—that there is some principle or decision rule against which incompatible values can be evaluated. To make the counterargument, the argument for the incommensurability of values, is easier in one way and more difficult in another. It is easier because apparent evidence for the incommensurability of values lies strewn around the political landscape, like the broken weapons and warriors of an endless ideological battle. But it is more difficult because giving up on the idea of commensurability seems equivalent to giving up on rationality, on philosophy, and on the very idea of theorizing.

But this difficulty is really challenging only for those who aspire to the role of a cultural overseer, one who would know everyone's common ground or at least what that common ground should be. Pretenders to the throne of environmental philosopher-king must know what everybody else is doing and why (whether everybody else knows or not) because they must understand the ultimate context within which all values become commensurable. So these aspiring monarchs could never allow themselves even to entertain the notion that environmental values might be incommensurable. There is, however, a less demanding way to theorize the relationship between humans and nature. It is to concede the incommensurability of environmental values and to focus instead on building environmental policies and a future green politics based on the richest possible understanding of the best ideas that are animated by those values. This envisions the green theorist not as a philosopher-king but as a "polypragmatic, Socratic intermediary between various discourses" (Rorty 1979, 317)—an intermediary who seeks to provide a ground on which the Kantian perspectives of political philosophy may reenter the many ongoing environmental politics dialogues embedded in those six broad sets of ideas, surveyed in this chapter, that continue powerfully to influence the development of environmental policy and action in the United States.

REFERENCES

Adger, W. N., and A. Jordan, eds. 2009. *Governing Sustainability.* New York: Cambridge University Press.

Allenby, B. 1999. *Industrial Ecology: Policy Framework and Implementation.* Upper Saddle River, NJ: Prentice Hall.

Alm, L. R., R. E. Burkhart, and M. V. Simon. 2010. *Turmoil in American Public Policy: Science, Democracy, and the Environment.* Santa Barbara, CA: Praeger.

Andrews, R. N. L. 1999. *Managing the Environment, Managing Ourselves: A History of American Environmental Policy.* New Haven, CT: Yale University Press.

Ascher, W., T. Steelman, and R. Healy. 2010. *Knowledge and Environmental Policy: Re-Imagining the Boundaries of Science and Politics.* Cambridge, MA: MIT Press.

Baber, W. F., and R. V. Bartlett. 2005. *Deliberative Environmental Politics: Democracy and Ecological Rationality.* Cambridge, MA: MIT Press.

———. 2009. *Global Democracy and Sustainable Jurisprudence: Deliberative Environmental Law.* Cambridge, MA: MIT Press.

Baden, J. A., and D. S. Noonan, eds. 1998. *Managing the Commons.* 2nd ed. Bloomington: Indiana University Press.

Bartlett, R. V. 2005. "Ecological Reason in Administration: Environmental Impact Assessment and Green Politics." In *Managing Leviathan: Environmental Politics and the Administrative State*, ed. R. Paehlke and D. Torgerson. Peterborough, ON: Broadview.

Beirle, T. C., and J. Cayford. 2002. *Democracy in Practice: Public Participation in Environmental Decisions.* Washington, DC: RFF Press.

Bevir, M. 2009. *Key Concepts in Governance.* Thousand Oaks, CA: Sage.

Bhavnani, K., J. Foran, and P. A. Kurian. 2003. *Feminist Futures: Re-imagining Women, Culture, and Development.* New York: Zed Books.

Biermann, F. 2008. "Earth System Governance: A Research Agenda." In *Institutions and Environmental Change: Principal Findings, Applications, and Research Frontiers*, ed. O. R. Young, L. A. King, and H. Schroeder. Cambridge, MA: MIT Press.

Biermann, F., M. M. Betsill, J. Gupta, N. Kanie, L. Lebel, K. Liverman, H. Schroeder, and B. Siebenhuner. 2009. *Earth System Governance: People, Places, and the Planet.* Earth System Implementation Plan of the Earth System Governance Project. Bonn, Germany: Earth System Governance Project.

Brulle, R. J. 2000. *Agency, Democracy, and Nature: The U.S. Environmental Movement from a Critical Theory Perspective*. Cambridge, MA: MIT Press.

Buhrs, T., and R. V. Bartlett. 1993. *Environmental Policy in New Zealand: The Politics of Clean and Green?* New York: Oxford University Press.

Caldwell, L. K. 1963. "Environment: A New Focus for Public Policy?" *Public Administration Review* 23: 132–139.

———. 1990. *Between Two Worlds: Science, the Environmental Movement, and Policy Choice*. Cambridge: Cambridge University Press.

———. 1995. *Environment as a Focus for Public Policy*. College Station: Texas A&M University Press.

Carson, R. 1962. *Silent Spring*. Boston: Houghton Mifflin.

Coglianese, C., and J. Nash. 2006. *Leveraging the Private Sector: Management-Based Strategies for Improving Environmental Performance*. Washington, DC: Resources for the Future.

Costanza, R. ed. 1991. *Ecological Economics: The Science and Management of Sustainability*. New York: Columbia University Press.

Costanza, R., J. H. Cumberland, H. Daly, R. Goodland, and R. B. Norgaard. 1997. *An Introduction to Ecological Economics*. Boca Raton, FL: CRC Press.

Daly, H. 1977. *Steady-State Economics*. San Francisco: W. H. Freeman.

Demas, M. A., and O. R. Young, eds. 2009. *Governance for the Environment: New Perspectives*. New York: Cambridge University Press.

Dietz, T., and P. C. Stern, eds. 2002. *New Tools for Environmental Protection: Education, Information, and Voluntary Measures*. Washington, DC: National Academy Press.

Dobson, A. 2003. *Citizenship and the Environment*. New York: Oxford University Press.

———. 2007. *Green Political Thought*. 4th ed. New York: Routledge.

———. 2009. "Citizens, Citizenship, and Governance for Sustainability." In *Governing Sustainability*, ed. W. N. Adger and A. Jordan. New York: Cambridge University Press.

Dobson, A., and D. Bell, eds. 2006. *Environmental Citizenship*. Cambridge, MA: MIT Press.

Dryzek, J. S. 2005. *The Politics of the Earth: Environmental Discourses*. 2nd ed. New York: Oxford University Press.

Dryzek, J. S., D. Downes, C. Hunold, and D. Schlosberg. 2003. *Green States and Social Movements: Environmentalism in the United States, United Kingdom, Germany, and Norway*. New York: Oxford University Press.

Dryzek, J. S., and D. Schlosberg, eds. 2005. *Debating the Earth: The Environmental Politics Reader*. 2nd ed. New York: Oxford University Press.

Dryzek, J. S., and H. Stevenson. 2010. "Democracy and Earth System Governance." In *Earth System Governance Working Paper*. Lund and Amsterdam: Earth System Governance Project.

Dworkin, R. 2011. *Justice for Hedgehogs*. Cambridge, MA: Belknap Press of Harvard University Press.

Eckersley, R. 1992. *Environmentalism and Political Theory*. Albany: State University of New York Press.

Eisner, M. A. 2007. *Governing the Environment: The Transformation of Environmental Regulation*. Boulder, CO: Lynne Rienner.

Fairfax, S. K., L. Gwin, M. A. King, L. Raymond, and L. A. Watt. 2005. *Buying Nature: The Limits of Land Acquisition as a Conservation Strategy, 1780–2004.* Cambridge, MA: MIT Press.

Foreman, D. 1998. "Wilderness Areas for Real." In *The Great New Wilderness Debate*, ed. J. B. Callicott and M. P. Nelson. Athens: University of Georgia Press.

Foster, D. 2007. "Steel Magnolias: Labor Allies with the Environmental Movement." *New Labor Forum* 16 (1): 59–67.

Goklany, I. M. 2007. *The Improving State of the World: Why We're Living Longer, Healthier, and More Comfortable Lives on a Cleaner Planet.* Washington, DC: Cato Institute.

Hays, S. P. 1959. *Conservation and the Gospel of Efficiency: The Progressive Conservation Movement, 1890–1920.* Cambridge, MA: Harvard University Press.

Hendricks, P., M. Betsell, T. Cheng, and P. Taylor. 2009. "The Landscape of Environmental Goverance Research." Fort Collins: Environmental Governance Working Group, Colorado State University.

Jahn, D. 1993. "Environmentalist!!: Challenging the Societal Consensus between Labour and Capital?" *Innovation in Social Sciences Research* 6 (4): 499–517.

Kamieniecki, S. 2006. *Corporate America and Environmental Policy: How Often Does Business Get Its Way?* Palo Alto, CA: Stanford University Press.

Keller, A. C. 2009. *Science in Environmental Policy: The Politics of Objective Advice.* Cambridge, MA: MIT Press.

Khana, M., and K. Brouhle. 2009. "The Effectiveness of Voluntary Environmental Initiatives." In *Governance for the Environment: New Perspectives*, ed. M. A. Delmas and O. R. Young. New York: Cambridge University Press.

Kingsland, S. E. 2005. *The Evolution of American Ecology, 1890–2000.* Baltimore: Johns Hopkins University Press.

Kirkman, R. 2002. *Skeptical Environmentalism: The Limits of Philosophy and Science.* Bloomington: Indiana University Press.

Kraft, M. E., and S. Kamieniecki, eds. 2007. *Business and Environmental Policy: Corporate Interests in the American Political System.* Cambridge, MA: MIT Press.

Krajnc, A. 2000. "Popular Environmental Education: Lessons from the Labor and Civil Rights Movements." *New Political Science* 22 (3): 341–360.

Kurian, P. A. 2000. *Engendering the Environment? Gender in the World Bank's Environmental Policies.* Aldershot, UK: Ashgate.

Lafferty, W. M., and J. Meadowcroft, eds. 1996. *Democracy and the Environment: Problems and Prospects.* Cheltenham, UK: Edward Elgar.

Layzer, J. A. 2008. *Natural Experiments: Ecosystem-Based Management and the Environment.* Cambridge, MA: MIT Press.

Mayer, B. 2008. *Blue-Green Coalitions: Fighting for Save Workplaces and Healthy Communities.* Ithaca, NY: Cornell University Press.

———. 2009. "Cross-Movement Coalition Formation: Bridging the Labor-Environment Divide." *Sociological Inquiry* 79 (2): 219–239.

Mayer, B., P. Brown, and R. Morello-Frosch. 2010. "Labor-Environmental Coalition Formation: Framing and the Right to Know." *Sociological Forum* 25 (4): 746–768.

Mazmanian, D. A., and M. E. Kraft, eds. 2009. *Toward Sustainable Communities: Transitions and Transformations in Environmental Policy.* 2nd ed. Cambridge, MA: MIT Press.

Merchant, C., ed. 2008. *Ecology, Key Concepts in Critical Theory.* Amherst, NY: Humanity Books.

Norton, B. G. 2005. *Sustainability: A Philosophy of Adaptive Ecosystem Management.* Chicago: University of Chicago Press.

Ophuls, W. 1977. *Ecology and the Politics of Scarcity.* San Francisco: W. H. Freeman.

———. 2011. *Plato's Revenge: Politics in the Age of Ecology.* Cambridge, MA: MIT Press.

Paehlke, R. C. 1989. *Environmentalism and the Future of Progressive Politics.* New Haven, CT: Yale University Press.

———. 2003. *Democracy's Dilemma: Environment, Social Equity, and the Global Economy.* Cambridge, MA: MIT Press.

———. 2005. "Democracy and Environmentalism: Opening a Door to the Administrative State?" In *Managing Leviathan: Environmental Politics and the Administrative State*, ed. R. C. Paehlke and D. Torgerson. Peterborough, ON: Broadview.

Potoski, M., and A. Prakash. 2005. "Green Clubs and Voluntary Governance: ISO 14001 and Firms' Regulatory Compliance." *American Journal of Political Science* 49 (2): 235–248.

Press, D., and D. A. Mazmanian. 2010. "Toward Sustainable Production: Finding Workable Strategies for Government and Industry." In *Environmental Policy: New Directions for the Twenty-First Century*, ed. M. E. Kraft and N. J. Vig. Washington, DC: CQ Press.

Prugh, T., H. Daly, R. Goodland, and J. H. Cumberland. 1999. *Natural Capital and Human Economic Survival.* Boca Raton, FL: CRC Press.

Rorty, R. 1979. *Philosophy and the Mirror of Nature.* Princeton, NJ: Princeton University Press.

Rostbøll, C. F. 2008. *Deliberative Freedom: Deliberative Democracy as Critical Theory.* Albany: State University of New York Press.

Ruha, R. 2000. *Environmentalism: A Global History.* New York: Longman.

Sagoff, M. 2007. *The Economy of the Earth: Philosophy, Law, and the Environment.* 2nd ed. New York: Cambridge University Press.

Schlosberg, D. 2009. *Defining Environmental Justice: Theories, Movements, and Nature.* New York: Oxford University Press.

Schreurs, M. A. 2002. *Environmental Politics in Japan, Germany, and the United States.* New York: Cambridge University Press.

Simon, H. A. 1996. *The Sciences of the Artificial.* 3rd ed. Cambridge, MA: MIT Press.

Smith, G. 2003. *Deliberative Democracy and the Environment.* New York: Routledge.

Vogel, D. 2005. *The Market for Virtue: The Potential and Limits of Corporate Social Responsibility.* Washington, DC: Brookings Institution Press.

Weber, E. P. 2003. *Bringing Society Back In: Grassroots Ecosystem Management, Accountability, and Sustainable Communities.* Cambridge, MA: MIT Press.

Wolfe, A. 2010. *The Future of Liberalism.* New York: Vintage.

CHAPTER 4

EVOLVING CONCEPTS OF SUSTAINABILITY IN ENVIRONMENTAL POLICY

LAMONT C. HEMPEL

A public policy, in its broadest sense, is a statement about the future (Tugwell 1973). Public policy making in democratic polities can be viewed as a struggle to create and legitimize statements about the future in ways that persuade the attentive public, or at least secure its acquiescence. Sustainability involves a particular kind of statement about the future—for example, that communities of life continue to flourish in the long term—while the questions of what exactly is to be sustained or allowed to flourish, and for how long, are usually left unanswered. Most sustainability concepts promote an intergenerational perspective that requires integration of environmental, social, and economic quality of life across both spatial and temporal dimensions of existence.

Anthropocentric notions of sustainability envision a future that "will indefinitely support human security, wellbeing, and health" (McMichael, Butler, and Folke 2003). A middle view holds that human welfare is a necessary but not sufficient condition for achieving sustainability; the welfare of all species must be considered. In many versions, ecological integrity, social equity, and economic vitality are combined as the three "pillars" of sustainability, with humans as the core beneficiaries but with the added recognition that human welfare depends on the welfare of many other species (Marshall and Toffel 2005). Although there is significant disagreement about what constitutes the core of sustainability, the concept has become influential in environmental politics and offers an intriguing but operationally challenging ideal to guide public policy design and evaluation.

Sustainability makes normative claims on policy and directs attention to political constituencies not yet born. While moralistic overtones are clearly evident in the rhetoric of sustainability, some advocates prefer to emphasize sustainability *science*, or at least testable principles of sustainable design. Most, however, acknowledge an ethical core that sometimes makes it difficult to distinguish policy debates about sustainability from those taking place under the rubric of "environmental justice." The explicit inclusion of values statements and concerns about intergenerational equity are no doubt responsible for some of the resistance to the concept exhibited by many policy analysts and decision makers, who remain uncomfortable with overtly normative approaches to policy making.

The standard definition of sustainability is the one provided by the Brundtland Commission: "[meeting] the needs of the present without compromising the ability of future generations to meet their own needs" (WCED 1987, 8). Such a definition benefits from the use of strategic ambiguity about timescales and capacities to anticipate the needs and abilities of future generations. Such ambiguity was critical for the successful integration of the terms "sustainable" and "development" into public policies promoted at the first Earth Summit, the United Nations Conference on Environment and Development (United Nations 1993), and has subsequently dominated much of the international environmental policy agenda.

Critics point out that these political strengths are intellectual weaknesses. The Brundtland definition invites serious questions about the specification of *needs* and determination of future *abilities*, not to mention the precise nature of policies or practices that might be *compromising*. Many analysts argue that present generations cannot reliably forecast needs of future generations or their capabilities, especially those developed through unforeseeable advances in science and technology (Barraclough 2005). Nor can they possibly know to what degree their own actions might compromise the ability of future generations to act. Why, then, should present generations be held strictly responsible for preserving resources and opportunities for future generations?

In practice, sustainability has become a "sponge" word that absorbs multiple meanings and interpretations, many of which simultaneously expand its appeal yet undermine its integrative power. Much has been written about the vagueness of the sustainability concept (Lele 1991) and the difficulty in applying it to non-overlapping future generations (Sachs 1993). Perhaps the strongest criticism has been directed at its allegedly "hidden" political agenda. This is particularly troublesome when the word "sustainable" is paired with the word "development." Many see the phrase as an oxymoron (Sachs 1993 and 1999), rife for misappropriation by governments and corporations bent on promoting business-as-usual growth while using the rhetoric of environmental and social responsibility. For some, sustainable development is a self-serving justification by rich countries for imposing "limits to growth" constraints on developing countries with which they compete for scarce resources

(Banerjee 2003). Others see the real objective as controlling population growth in developing countries (Anderson 2002; Aguirre 2002). A few see the concept as the spearhead of an effort to impose world government or to establish a new and dangerous anti-Western ideology that threatens America's reputation and its dominant position in world affairs (Wood 2009).

Defenders of sustainability ideas are quick to point out that our society's most precious concepts—for instance, democracy, freedom, faith, justice, critical thinking—appear elusive when subjected to rigorous analysis. In fact, it appears that most powerful ideas resist precise definition. Sustainable development, for many supporters, represents a politically expedient compromise among corporate capitalists, social justice activists, and environmentalists. By harnessing the power of strategic ambiguity, sustainable development makes possible environmental action that would not be achievable using environmental rhetoric alone (Hempel 1996). From a political perspective, the term is an enabler for coalition formation and compromise, an outcome that seems increasingly important in an era of "play to the base" politics (Frum 2007). But there is also a deeply held belief among supporters that sustainability invokes fundamental principles that, if taken seriously, will greatly improve the quality and legitimacy of public policy making across the board.

With that objective in mind, this chapter explores the evolution and application of sustainability concepts in environmental politics and policy, paying particular attention to the challenges of operationalizing and measuring sustainability in the highly dynamic environment of twenty-first-century politics and policy. After surveying the concept's historical roots, the chapter examines the struggle to refine and apply the concept in contemporary policy analysis. It reviews the key policy initiatives that have incorporated sustainability language or contributed to its development within each branch of government. Attention is then focused on the pragmatic adoption of sustainability principles in policy making, culminating in a discussion of future directions and research needs.

1. CONCEPTUAL EVOLUTION AND HISTORICAL INTEGRATION

In order to appreciate the power and insights provided by sustainability discourses, it is important to understand their historical development and social context. Like tributaries of a vast river system, the ideas that carry sustainability forward flow from many different sources, some deep and powerful, others shallow and sometimes underground. Unfortunately, achieving consensus about the nature and boundaries of this intellectual "watershed" is very difficult. The study of concept evolution is typically fraught with hazards of interpretation and social construction. Hence, this chapter surveys the intellectual roots of sustainability in a state of deep humility about what is known and how it influences environmental policy today.

There have been previous attempts to map a detailed intellectual history of sustainability, usually in the form of a time line,[1] but as is usually the case, influential voices from the past are often missed or, at the other extreme, granted undue prominence. Both types of errors will be difficult to avoid in the brief overview that follows.

1.1 Early Conceptual Tributaries

The evolution of sustainability concepts can be traced back to at least the fifth century BC, starting with Plato, and probably earlier. Long before the language of sustainability appeared in U.S. literature and policy, non-English terms for "sustainability" were being employed in Europe and in certain African and Asian countries (Du Pisani 2006), perhaps most prominently in the early literature about German forestry. Hans Carl von Carlowitz wrote about sustainable forestry practices in 1713, using the term *nachhaltende Nutzung*, which can be translated as "sustainable use" (Du Pisani 2006, 85).

Strong intimations of the concept are clearly present in some of the writings of America's founding fathers. Writing to Madison in 1789, Thomas Jefferson argued that the environment "belongs in usufruct to the living." By using the legal concept of "usufruct"—the temporary right of stewards of the land to use the environment in benign ways—Jefferson called for intergenerational equity in development of natural resources, so as not to allow "one generation of men to bind another" (Ball 2000). Jefferson was merely invoking long-standing stewardship principles found in the Bible and in Locke's notion of the environment as a commons that should be accessible across generations.

During this period, Malthus was writing his *Essay on the Principle of Population* (1798), warning of both social and environmental disruption from overpopulation. The condition of overshoot described by Malthus was based on an immutable mathematical logic but offered very little of what today we would call insights about human behavior from social science or notions of resilience and substitutability. Whether his conclusions were wrong or simply premature, the impact of his deterministic ideas helped spawn research on the concept of carrying capacity, which later influenced debates about sustainability.

---

1. See, for example, the timeline of the history of sustainability concepts available at www.archis.org/history-of-sustainability/(originally published in *Volume #18–After Zero* published by Archis.org). A similar timeline, but with an American focus, is available at sustainableleadership.info/SustainableTimeline.pdf.

1.2 Nineteenth-Century Streams of Thought

Carrying this debate forward in the nineteenth century were two peripheral and occasionally interwoven streams of thought: American transcendentalism and anti-industrialism. As expressed in the writings of George Ripley (1802–1880), Ralph Waldo Emerson (1803–1882), Margaret Fuller (1810–1850), Henry David Thoreau (1817–1862), John Ruskin (1819–1900), and many others, securing the future meant finding a balance in nature, spirit, development, and community that allowed individuals, through direct experience, to develop "an original relation to the universe" (Emerson 1990, 3). Implicit in much of their idealism was the notion of a sustainable civilization that operated far above the imperatives of biological survival. Similarly, the anti-industrial themes prominent in many of these writers called for a concept of community that rested on values and goals more fundamental than technological innovation and economic growth. Some of these sustainability-friendly ideas have helped to fuel the "degrowth" and "transition towns" movements today.

John Stuart Mill's writings about formation of a just "stationary state" helped buttress these ideas with philosophical observations about the political economy of sustainability. In *Principles of Political Economy* (1848, book IV, chapter 6), Mill combines arguments about economic growth and population growth in ways that anticipate many contemporary debates about sustainability (O'Connor 1997).

Other important contributions flowed from the pens of naturalists and environmental defenders of the mid- to late nineteenth century. George Perkins Marsh, echoing Jefferson's use in 1789 of the term "usufruct," explored sustainability themes through his experience as a Vermont conservationist, concerned about forests and grasslands in many different parts of the world. In *Man and Nature* (1864), he writes, "Man has long forgotten that the earth was given to him for usufruct alone, not for consumption, still less for profligate waste" (Marsh 1965, 36).

Similar arguments can be found in the writings of John Muir, John Wesley Powell, and a host of other Victorian Era writers in Europe and the United States, many of whom strongly asserted that human welfare and improvements in the distribution of wealth need not result in a loss of nature (Lumley 2004). Interwoven in these arguments was the notion that what many today call "sustainability" was a matter of moral duty, not simply a means for sustaining human welfare or social progress. Like the anti-industrialists, they often tied issues of sustainability to ideals about flourishing communities.

1.3 Twentieth-Century Watersheds

Toward the end of the nineteenth century, sustainability concepts began to branch more visibly, with one major stream influencing the early development of professional natural resource management, as associated with Gifford Pinchot, and the other stream emerging as part of urban reform and progressive thought, as exemplified by the Garden City movement, which took much of its impetus from

Ebenezer Howard's (1898) publication *Tomorrow: A Peaceful Path to Real Reform*. This latter branch served to facilitate development of what is today referred to as the "sustainable community" or "smart growth" movement. Thinkers from Patrick Geddes to Lewis Mumford helped determine the direction, tone, and depth of this movement, with much of the progress measured in the planning and design features of new urban forms and settlement patterns (Hempel 2009, 38).

The stream carrying elements of natural resource management policy emerged most forcefully in the views of Gifford Pinchot, following a course set nearly 200 years earlier by the German forester von Carlowitz. Pinchot saw conservation struggles in terms remarkably similar to those used by the Brundtland Commission to define sustainable development:

> the right of the present generation to use what it needs and all it needs of the natural resources now available, but…equally our obligation so to use what we need that our descendents shall not be deprived of what they need. (Pinchot 1910, 80)

Amplifying Pinchot's views was President Theodore Roosevelt's effort to preserve for future generations large areas of forest and scenic lands as national monuments and parks. In a 1910 speech entitled "The New Nationalism," Roosevelt used sustainable development arguments to temper his growing reputation in conservation with related concerns about development and intergenerational equity:

> Conservation means development as much as it does protection. I recognize the right and duty of this generation to develop and use the natural resources of our land; but I do not recognize the right to waste them, or to rob, by wasteful use, the generations that come after us. (Roosevelt 1910)

Closely aligned with this form of presidential activism was President Franklin Roosevelt's New Deal, which included explicit goals to integrate economic recovery with social improvement and environmental conservation, using programs such as the Civilian Conservation Corps. Aldo Leopold's land ethic (1948) extended the conservation idea by expanding the meaning of community, thereby providing an important frame for later development of sustainability concepts.

Following World War II, ideas about sustainability appear to have temporarily receded in public debate, although not without provoking strong warnings from pioneers of the modern environmental movement. Publications that nicely capture some of the sustainability concerns beginning to emerge during this period include Fairfield Osborn's *Our Plundered Planet* (1948), William Vogt's *Road to Survival* (1948), the Paley Commission's *Resources for Freedom* (1952), Harrison Brown's *The Challenge of Man's Future* (1956), Murray Bookchin's (a.k.a. Lewis Herber's) *Our Synthetic Environment* (1962), Rachel Carson's *Silent Spring* (1962), Paul Ehrlich's *The Population Bomb* (1968), and Barry Commoner's *The Closing Circle* (1971). In the late 1960s and early 1970s, the convergence of concerns about environmental protection, social welfare, and economic development accelerated, and for the first time the concept of sustainable development was elevated to the status of an organizing principle for both national and international policy. Perhaps the first international forum to discuss the power of this concept was the Intergovernmental Conference for Rational Use and Conservation of Biosphere, convened by UNESCO in 1968.

Shortly after the meeting, Barbara Ward popularized the concept, using the language of "sustainable development" in a book coauthored with Rene Dubos, *Only One Earth: The Care and Maintenance of a Small Planet* (1972). The concept was further developed in the Stockholm Declaration on the Human Environment (1972), which incorporated the concept of sustainable development in its call for the integration of environmental, social, and economic components of development.

Serving to energize sustainable development ideas at the Stockholm Conference and give them added academic and scientific support was the release in 1972 of the book *Limits to Growth* (Meadows, Randers, and Meadows), the first report to the Club of Rome. This controversial report essentially galvanized the systems-level thinking needed for analyzing sustainability objectives on university campuses and in think tanks around the world. Despite its weaknesses, *Limits to Growth* provided the first highly visible test for operationalizing the concept of sustainability using dynamic systems modeling.

Parallel research on entropy by economist Nicholas Georgescu-Roegen (1971), and on resilience by C. S. Holling (1973) and other ecologists, also contributed important new scientific perspectives on sustainability. These writers and others helped to create novel perspectives that propelled sustainability concepts in the direction of intellectually defensible and operational uses.

It was only a short time before the language of sustainability began appearing in many different disciplines and publishing venues, ranging from influential essays by E. F. Schumacher (1973) to major environmental reports, such as the *World Conservation Strategy* (IUCN 1980), as well as in the titles of popular books, such as Lester Brown's *Building a Sustainable Society* (1981). During this period, academic disciplines were beginning to undertake research on sustainability, often pushed by radical ecologists, such as Edward Goldsmith, and skeptical economists, such as Robert Solow (1974). This was followed by work conducted by social scientists trying to gauge the attitudinal and policy implications of value changes associated with this growing phenomenon—see, for example, Ronald Inglehart's theory of postmaterial value change (1977).

By the time the Brundtland Commission published its widely influential definition of sustainable development (1987), the ground had already been very well prepared for the public emergence of the concept. During the ensuing two decades, widespread adoption took place under the guise of *environmental* sustainability. It is only in recent years that a comprehensive, integrated concept of sustainability that transcends ecology has begun to flourish, although it remains to be seen whether this expanded concept will be embraced by the environmental policy community.

2. Expansion and Convergence

In thinking about the influence of sustainability on environmental policy making, it is important to recognize how young this field of study is in relation to most other lines of scholarship. Almost all of the specialized academic analyses of environmental policy and politics have appeared in the last four decades. It can be nicely characterized by the evolutionary stages—the three "generations"—presented in chapter 1. With the exceptions noted in the previous section, sustainability has only two decades of organized scholarship behind it and consequently stands in relation to environmental policy in much the same way as a baby to a toddler. Despite dozens of books and hundreds of published articles, the integration of scholarship about environmental policy and sustainability is very much in its infancy.

2.1 The Operational Challenge

Sustainability concepts have made inroads in policy dialogue and analysis partly because conventional environmental policy and regulation has increasingly been viewed as a domain of special interest politics—one that seems hostile to development interests and economic growth. The perceived legitimacy of environmental policies that reach beyond narrowly defined goals for protecting human health appears to have declined as political polarization has increased. Although the tendency in the past has been to equate sustainability with *ecological* sustainability, the growing attention to social and economic dimensions has opened the concept to wider dialogue about policy integration and synergy, potentially enlarging the ideological space needed for bipartisan efforts to emerge. At the same time, however, the continuing emphasis that policy analysts place on the quantification of environmental risks and costs may discourage efforts to reconceptualize environmental issues within the broader and more qualitative terms of sustainability.

For nearly three decades, the U.S. EPA has relied on risk frameworks for improving environmental policy and management. In the summer of 2011 recommendations were developed by the National Research Council (NRC) to assist the EPA in incorporating sustainability concepts formally in its goals and practices (U.S. National Research Council 2011). Known as the "Green Book," the NRC report marks a potentially major transition from the era of risk management to one more loosely based on sustainability. A closely related study, "Sustainability Linkages in the Federal Government" (U.S. NRC 2011), attempts to address the sustainability potential for federal agencies in general. A challenge for the authors of both reports was the implicit need for sustainability indicators and scientific measures that could be used in operationalizing sustainability concepts, ideally in accord with rigorous quantitative standards.

Herein lies the crux of a dilemma that faces policy makers and analysts interested in sustainability. A practical implication of the sustainability revolution is that environmental specialists will be encouraged to replace the familiar quantitative risk framework with a qualitative one derived from cross-cutting ideals of sustainability. But most of these specialists appear to favor environmental frameworks that lend themselves to quantification, ordinal ranking, and legal sufficiency tests based on narrow precedents. Sustainability frameworks tend to be qualitative, normative, and sometimes metaphysical. Operationalizing sustainability almost invariably means narrowing its usual definitions and applying it reductively to measurable subsystems of human and natural systems. It cannot be easily and simultaneously applied to both in ways that meet the test of scientific rigor. Moreover, it pulls environmental policy analysts in transdisciplinary directions that seem to devalue their expertise.

Sustainability objectives require optimization across multiple policy domains, implying high levels of synthetic research and integrative understanding—a difficult challenge for policy communities comprised mostly of disciplinary microspecialists, each working in one of many very narrow policy subfields. Further complicating efforts to incorporate sustainability are the demands it places on futures modeling and forecasting. Anticipation of social and ecological feedback processes is a vital requirement for policy communities concerned with sustainability. Anticipating the net aggregated results of simultaneous feedback from the economy, social systems, and the natural environment is a forecasting challenge that few if any policy organizations are prepared to meet with a high degree of competence.

There is also the question of dilution of policy aims and content due to sustainability's requirement for expanded objectives and target groups. Sustainability, having evolved to include social justice and economic claims that cannot be trumped or ignored by environmental claimants, threatens to undermine policies based almost exclusively on environmental concerns. The very legitimacy of "environment only" approaches is called into question. Even laws that in a sense seem radical in their sustainability aims, such as the Endangered Species Act, could conceivably become vulnerable to weakening amendments and reinterpretation under a broad and mostly anthropocentric notion of sustainability.

Remaking environmental policy with the language of sustainability implies a loss of environmental primacy. It may even suggest a devaluation of environmental policy itself. Sustainability adherents can argue with justification that changes in certain nonenvironmental policies (e.g., campaign finance reform) may have greater influence on valued environmental outcomes than policies explicitly aimed at environmental protection. Following the integrative logic of sustainability arguments, environmental policy targets may be seen as lower priorities in situations in which changes in finance policy or tax equity may be more urgently needed for enabling lasting improvements in ecosystems, economies, and social justice. Moreover, a truly balanced sustainability "portfolio" (e.g., optimal shares of environment, economy, equity) would seem to require a deemphasis of environmental concerns in current discussions about sustainability.

Because sustainability issues historically have been foremost about environmental matters, even sustainability advocates may be uncomfortable with agendas dominated by economic welfare and social equity issues. For reasons of entrained thought, the sustainability movement has seldom emphasized equity concerns or

issues of economic regulation as appropriate priorities in policy design for sustainability. For example, very few sustainability advocates would regard Elizabeth
Warren, a well-known consumer financial protection advocate, as a leading figure
in the sustainability movement. But a closer inquiry into the environmental implications of banking policy and the financial dimensions of sustainability might
suggest that such reform efforts are indispensable to the movement's ultimate aims
and constitute one of the most critical challenges for sustainability advocates of
this era.

2.2 Economic Perspectives

The closest thing we have to a self-confident institutional basis for optimization
and operational assessment is provided by economics, but many professionals
and academics outside this field dismiss its claims as acts of hubris. Critics from
ecologists to ethicists argue that the "devil" can be found in the assumptions of
economists. Economists tend to reduce sustainability ideas to issues of dynamic
efficiency and intergenerational equity (Stavins 2003), defining the objective as
merely "non-declining utility" in the long run. Having largely dismissed the "limits to growth" arguments of the 1970s (Nordhaus 1992), most economists have not
embraced sustainability themes with great enthusiasm.

One might expect exceptions in the case of environmental economists, but a
perusal of the relevant literature suggests a general lack of enthusiasm for efforts
to refine the concept in operational terms. Support for sustainability ideas in economics is likely to rest on a distinction between *ecological* and environmental
economists. Environmental economists are heavily invested in theories of market failure for explaining unsustainable environmental practices. Socially optimal
policies are simply those that yield long-term net benefits without reducing the
productivity of natural systems (unless comparable artificial substitutes are available). Sustainability simply adds the proviso that the "long term" should extend
to nonoverlapping future generations and across national markets, provided that
people in the future continue to value the protections sustainability policies afford,
as evidenced by their willingness to pay for their continuation.

Ecological economists, such as Kenneth Boulding, Herman Daly, and Robert
Costanza, are more comfortable with the language of sustainability and its potential for practical application. In their view, differences between present and future
welfare reflect deeply seated assumptions about discounting and self-serving methods for making intertemporal comparisons. As Bromley argues, "Environmental
policy that is consistent with achieving sustainability must consider the present
in terms of the future. In contrast, the [current process] fails precisely because it
considers the future in terms of the present" (2007, 679).

Very few conventional economists subscribe to the view held by ecological economists and sustainability advocates, in general, that increasing limits

on carrying capacity are likely to affect human welfare. Many would agree with Martin Weitzman that "the historical record is full of past hurdles to growth that were overcome by substitution and technological progress" (1992, 53). Indeed, the historical support for this view is strong; the question is whether the past will continue to be prologue.

For policy analysts trained in economics, arguments about past and prologue appear unproductive. They tend to focus, instead, on the ability to operationalize sustainability principles in ways that allow analysts reliably to measure policy inputs, outputs, and long-term outcomes (Howarth 2007). Some economists note that sustainability arguments, regardless of their merit, are unlikely to have a major influence on policy making as long as they are treated as dichotomous choices, bound by inflexible notions of "either/or"—that is, sustainable or unsustainable outcomes. Economist Robert Solow, for example, offers an "almost practical step" toward the incorporation of sustainability into policy debates:

> In a complex world, populated by people with diverse interests and tastes, and enmeshed in uncertainty about the future (not to mention the past), there is a lot to be gained by transforming questions of yes-or-no into questions of more-or-less. Yes-or-no lends itself to stalemate and confrontation; more-or-less lends itself to trade-offs. The trick is to understand more of what and less of what. (1993, 172)

2.3 Idealists and Pragmatists

The utility of sustainability concepts for achieving effective environmental protection depends on whether sustainability is conceived as an end or a means. While some embrace sustainability as an ethic, others view it as a form of strategic optimization—that is, managing the inevitable trade-offs involved in simultaneously addressing social, economic, and environmental imperatives. Sustainability as an ethic can go far, perhaps, in motivating and strengthening support for environmental measures. But only when sustainability is conceived in terms of large-scale optimization is it likely to have far-reaching effects on policy content.

Given the central importance of economic arguments in policy debates involving optimization, it seems clear that the future role of sustainability in environmental policy may depend in important ways on developments in the fields of ecological economics and, perhaps, in a reconceptualization of welfare economics. But beyond that, it will depend on progress in quantifying and accounting for sustainability practices in ways that provide financial and scientific credibility. Toward that end, much of the policy future may turn on developments in sustainability science (e.g., Kates et al. 2001) and accounting (e.g., ISO 14000). To date, progress in these fields has not been particularly visible outside associated centers of research. Hence, the search for precision and reliability in defining and measuring sustainability still appears to have a long way to go. Ambitious research in this area may include not only efforts to reinvent the science of choice, presently ruled by neoclassical economists, but to reinvent science itself in the service of sustainability. Such research is likely to encounter strong resistance but, if successful, lead to revolutions in normal science, triggered perhaps by the rise of Kuhnian anomalies in the old paradigm.

With these operational limitations in mind, it is helpful to examine some of the actual policy initiatives of the present and recent past that attempt to infuse sustainability principles in environmental protection. By identifying the origins and tracing the influence of these principles in particular initiatives, the promise and limitations of sustainability in environmental policy become clearer, even as the concept continues to evolve.

3. POLICY INITIATIVES

The National Environmental Policy Act (NEPA 1969) contains language that is very close in meaning to that commonly used today to define sustainability. In the first paragraph of Title 1 (Section 101a), the Act calls for the creation and maintenance of human and natural systems that "exist in productive harmony, and fulfill the social, economic and other requirements of present and future generations of Americans." The Act goes on to declare that it is the responsibility of each generation to be a "trustee" for future generations (Section 101b1). There is even a call for interdisciplinarity, a hallmark of sustainability thinking, in the Act's provisions for design and implementation. Section 102(a) of the Act directs all federal agencies to "utilize a systematic, interdisciplinary approach which will insure the integrated use of the natural and social sciences and the environmental design arts in planning and in decision-making which may have an impact on man's environment."

Although the appearance of sustainability concepts in federal law predates NEPA, it is common to view NEPA as the enabling legislation for nearly all subsequent U.S. policy initiatives seeking to promote sustainability. Initiatives and partnerships at the international level that have utilized NEPA principles include U.S. positions at the Stockholm Conference on the Human Environment (1972), the Earth Summit in Rio (1992), and the World Summit on Sustainable Development in Johannesburg (2002). Of special significance were 27 core principles, including the precautionary principle adopted at the Earth Summit and given expression as parts of Agenda 21, the Framework Convention on Climate Change, and the Convention on Biological Diversity.[2]

Domestic policy initiatives developed under the influence of NEPA are extensive and varied. They are addressed in what follows as part of an effort to summarize some of the major milestones in U.S. sustainability policy, organized by branch and level of government.

3.1 Presidential Leadership

White House leadership on sustainability extends back at least 100 years, although the resulting policies, if any, have usually been weakly designed and implemented. Beginning with Jefferson's views on usufruct and the aforementioned efforts of Presidents Teddy Roosevelt and Franklin Roosevelt to incorporate sustainable development principles into natural resource conservation policy, evidence of early presidential leadership on sustainability is reasonably strong with respect to agenda setting and, on occasion, policy formation.

George H. W. Bush took the first opportunity as president to endorse a policy explicitly calling for sustainable development: Agenda 21 (signed at the first Earth Summit in June 1992). But it was President Clinton who became the first chief executive actively to promote the term "sustainable development" as administration policy (EO 12852 and 13141) and to link it indirectly to initiatives for environmental justice (EO 12898). By establishing the President's Council on Sustainable Development in 1993, Clinton provided an important venue for policy discussion and analysis of sustainability concepts. The second Bush administration included sustainability language in some of its programs and executive orders (e.g., EO 13423) as well, and accepted "promotion of sustainable development" as an explicit goal of the Trade Promotion Act of 2002 (19 USC § 3803–3805). President Obama has continued the trend of inserting sustainability language and goals into a number of policy initiatives and executive orders (e.g., EO 13584). In the eyes of some observers, the use of sustainability rhetoric by presidents and other government leaders has now become almost perfunctory, although the repeated use of phrases such as "sustainable growth" may call into question the level of understanding behind the rhetoric.

3.2 Congressional Leadership

Legislative initiatives, like those of the executive and judicial branches, are spread across many decades of policy history and sometimes have their origins in state and local initiatives. In the U.S. Congress, however, the development of sustainability policies has proceeded with more mixed results and failed outcomes, as exemplified, arguably, by the Senate's resounding rejection of the Kyoto Protocol in 1997. Although many sustainability-related initiatives have appeared since then, most retain the singular design and focus of energy, transportation, health, and environmental policies from past eras.[3] The NEPA, as noted earlier, remains the foundation for most sustainability initiatives to date. However, the Endangered Species Act of 1973 (ESA) probably represents the most far-reaching step taken by Congress

2. The 27 principles are listed in the "Report of the U.N. Conference on Environment and Development," Annex I, available at http://www.un.org/documents/ga/conf151/aconf15126–1annex1.htm.

on behalf of sustainability, foreshadowed to some extent by prior conservation acts, such as the Lacey Act of 1900 and the Migratory Bird Treaty (1918).

Sustainability policy in the 111th and 112th Congress, as of this writing, has shown little progress. In fact, the demise of legislation on climate protection and green energy in 2010 and the highly polarized budget battles of 2011 suggest that sustainability initiatives may have lost ground in contemporary American politics. Despite extensive lip service, actual legislative commitments on behalf of sustainability in the first decade of the twenty-first century have been at best meager and disappointing in the eyes of most sustainability advocates (see chapter 13 in this volume).

3.3 Judicial Leadership

In the case of the judicial branch, most efforts to incorporate sustainability principles and rhetoric in court rulings and judicial policy have predictably occurred in piecemeal and ad hoc fashion. Probably the earliest court rulings with strong sustainability overtones arose with the Federal Power Act and related Supreme Court cases of *Scenic Hudson Preservation v. Federal Power Commission* and *Udall v. Federal Power Commission* (Hodas 1998). Beyond that, a flurry of lawsuits involving air and water pollution in the 1960s and 1970s helped focus attention on the trade-offs involved in environmental protection and economic development and may have steered future policy in directions conducive to multicriteria and integrated decision making. Subsequent judicial interpretations of the Clean Air Act, Clean Water Act, and many other major legislative initiatives may have invited shifts in policy strategy from single-media, command-and-control regulatory frameworks to broader, multimedia approaches that were much more amenable to the language and concepts of sustainability. But it was in cases involving the Endangered Species Act of 1973 (ESA) and issues of legal standing—for example, *Sierra Club v. Morton*, 405 U.S. 727 (1972)—that the biggest implications for policy development emerged with respect to sustainability.

Perhaps the high point in recent Supreme Court rulings came in a 5–4 ruling in 2007 (*Massachusetts v. Environmental Protection Agency*) in which the Court declared that the EPA had authority to regulate greenhouse gas emissions from automobiles and trucks under the Clean Air Act. The implications of this decision are potentially enormous for climate protection and the EPA's future, but resistance by Republicans and some Democrats in the 112th Congress has been strong. Whatever its long-term impacts, however, this decision has not signaled a major rise in judicial sympathy for sustainability arguments. James May, writing about the Supreme Court under Justice Roberts, finds little evidence that sustainability is faring well within the highest level of the judiciary: "In sum, the Court seems at

3. See, for example, initiatives compiled by Smart Growth America's Leadership Institute: "Initiative for Sustainable Communities and States," available on line at http://www. sustainablecommunitiesandstates.org/.

worst hostile to, at best agnostic about, and most likely ignorant of sustainability as a governing principle" (May 2009, 29).

3.4 Local and State Government Leadership

Agenda 21 provided a potentially strong foundation on which to build local and state initiatives in sustainability. For one thing, the document calls for "delegating planning and management responsibilities to the lowest level of public authority consistent with effective action" (UNCED, Agenda 21, UN Doc A/CONF.151.26 paragraph 20.1). It also explicitly encourages development of local versions of Agenda 21, expanding on the 27 principles for sustainable development offered in the original document. In the United States, much of the actual policy development at the local level has occurred under labels such as "smart growth" and "livable communities."

At the state level, policy development has emphasized either climate change issues, as in California, or better statewide integrated land use planning, such as that in Oregon. A few states, such as Hawaii, have language in their constitutions that incorporates sustainability goals and decision criteria. One of the most strongly worded sustainability efforts at the state level can be found in the Oregon Sustainability Act (HB 3948) and subsequent executive orders by Oregon governors John Kitzhaber (EO 00–07) and Theodore Kulongoski (EO 03–03 and EO 06–02).

Many of these state, regional, and local sustainability initiatives have developed greater traction than their federal counterparts, especially in the case of the expanding sustainable communities movement (Mazmanian and Kraft 2009), a subject to which we shall return in the final sections of this chapter.

4. THE PRAGMATIC EMBRACE OF SUSTAINABILITY

Sustainability is viewed in policy circles less as an attainable goal than as a "process of constant improvement" (Faber 2005, 27–28), preferably with measurable baselines and milestones. Because the ideal of sustainability faces serious challenges of scientific uncertainty, poorly integrated governance, single-issue politics, corporate capitalism, and soft enforcement, the policy community is unlikely to adopt it unchanged. What started out as an all-encompassing, nonincremental policy ideal has predictably become incremental and contingent. Rather than talk about an entity that is sustainable, in any final sense, it is preferable to talk about an entity that is sustainable *in relation to* another entity of similar function or purpose (Faber 2005, 5). The dynamics of the concept preclude rigid definition or interpretation. Moreover, they limit the use of the term as a metaconcept that can be applied to anything and everything. For policy analysts, sustainability needs to have operational objectives and useful evaluation criteria if it is to have any widespread application beyond political and rhetorical appeal (Howarth 2007). But therein lies the split between pragmatists and idealists. Embracing sustainability as the organizing principle for all future policy initiatives—environmental and non-environmental—lies at the core of idealists' belief systems, but it is likely to strike many policy pragmatists as something more akin to religion than to a reasoned outcome of collective action in the political arena.

For many policy analysts, sustainability is merely one more criterion to be added to a list of considerations in policy design, adoption, implementation, and evaluation. The following is a list of key criteria commonly employed in policy analysis and evaluation, with sustainability representing the newest addition:

1. **Effectiveness**—does the policy or program accomplish its goals and objectives?
2. **Cost-effectiveness/efficiency**—is the ratio of valued inputs to valued outputs and outcomes less than 1.0? And are resources employed at the Pareto optimal level?
3. **Priority responsiveness**—are the problems addressed by the policy or program the most significant and urgent ones?
4. **Equity**—is the distribution of costs and benefits from implementation perceived by stakeholders as fair?
5. **Sustainability**—are the policy outcomes conducive to living sustainably within the means of nature, justice, and economic resilience?

Note that many of the criteria above are employed within a framework of individualistic utility maximization. They are appropriate for treating public policy as a collective action problem that seeks to reconcile competing claims of individuals. However, the addition of sustainability as a criterion challenges the individualistic frame of analysis, especially if sustainability is understood to be fundamentally concerned with the relationships between communities, both present and future, both human and nonhuman. For that reason, it may be more appropriate to think in terms of *sustainability* policy, as distinct from *environmental* policy.

4.1 Sustainability Policy versus Environmental Policy

Sustainability is not a new category of environmental policy but, rather, a new way of understanding and combining existing categories by way of integration with social and economic concerns. That is to say, sustainability provides a new and broader way of framing what was previously viewed largely as natural resource policy or environmental regulation. Many sustainability advocates argue that environmental policy is best understood as a subcategory of sustainability. They are careful to distinguish between environmental policy and "sustainability policy" (Pezzey 2004), arguing that the terms cannot be used interchangeably without unacceptable distortion.

Although many distinctions between environmental policy and sustainability policy involve semantics more than substance, there are at least two important respects in which the two seem to differ fundamentally. On the one hand, sustainability implies a values commitment that is inflexible and indivisible—an "all or nothing" goal. Environmental policy, on the other hand, can accomplish 99 percent of what is needed to preserve habitat, protect human health, or minimize environmental risk and thereby receive lavish praise for good design and effectiveness. Sustainability does not offer that luxury. A hard-driven set of policies and behaviors that make a system *almost* sustainable are nevertheless failures in terms of the only criterion that ultimately matters. As policy analyst Richard Nelson (1977) observed, these kinds of policies involve indivisible ends and means. In theory, achieving sustainability, like going to the moon, ultimately allows no room for near misses or missions "almost accomplished."

The second distinction is even more fundamental to a proper understanding of the concept. Although it is widely assumed that *environmental* sustainability is the first and prime imperative of sustainability in its broadest sense, scholars have begun to turn this logic on its head (e.g., Agyeman 2003). They note, invoking a very common argument, that people living in absolute poverty or in deeply oppressive societies are in no position to put environmental needs first. Basic food, justice, and other human needs must be met before environmental concerns can emerge. This notion of nested imperatives has helped propel efforts to define sustainability as a *primary* concept—one that cannot be reduced to separate core components. Sustainability as a concept and practice transcends environmental applications. Strictly speaking, there is no such thing as *environmental* sustainability, only *sustainability*—an irreducible synergy of social justice, ecological integrity, and economic vitality, applied across present and future generations. Although the health of our ecological life-support system is logically prior to and dominant among sustainability imperatives, maintaining the health of ecosystems on a human-dominated planet requires achievements in social health and economic vitality that are imperatives in their own right, and not just for environmental protection. While securing the life-support system seems a logical first priority, creating a healthy economy and social system in the short term may be a logical prerequisite for addressing that long-term fact. Efforts to avoid infinite regress in such arguments are futile. Hence, *sustainability* as a primary concept cannot be coherently reduced to its environmental, social, and economic components. It is the synergy of all three that constitutes the essence of the concept.

4.2 Policy Dilemmas

Many sustainability advocates believe that there is no room to compromise on objectives. The indivisible means and ends previously discussed drive sustainability's true believers in radical directions. Sustainability, after all, is both the goal and the criterion for measuring success. Hence, champions of sustainability policy will often be regarded as politically weak, since they lack any significant capacity to bargain about ends within the policy-making process.

Paradoxically, pragmatic supporters of sustainability may be drawn to the concept in large part because they believe its application increases the potential for successful bargaining and coalition formation. This was the key insight of those who planned the Earth Summit (United Nations 1993): to employ the term "sustainable development" as a negotiating bridge between environmental and economic development interests.

As sustainability has gained more and more pragmatic adherents in environmental policy, a question has arisen that closely parallels the previous discussion of sustainability as an ethic. Advocates want to know whether the growing use of sustainability language represents primarily a strategic approach to environmental politics or an ethical commitment to a new policy paradigm. While both motivations may be found in the same individual, the perceived legitimacy of sustainability policies may rest increasingly on their ethical appeal for paradigm change. "Business as usual" environmental policy is profoundly inadequate in the view of many environmentalists and sustainability advocates alike. Increasingly, they fear that even perfect compliance with all existing environmental rules and regulations, fully implemented and enforced, would merely delay, not prevent, ecological ruin and serious threats to human health and well-being. Consequently, the politics-versus-ethics dichotomy, while simplistic, operates as a useful litmus test for "true believers" in sustainability policy. They demand qualitatively new "frames," constructed from the core principles of sustainability and accompanied by quantum leaps in the rate and magnitude of policy changes based on those principles.

5. Rethinking Environmental Sustainability

An oversimplified, yet potentially useful, three-word characterization of the history of U.S. environmental policy might label the three generations introduced in chapter 1 as "conservation," "risk," and "sustainability." A similar attempt to characterize the historical evolution of sustainability might distinguish four generations and employ four different terms of emphasis: "usufruct," "carrying capacity," "development," and "community."

As mentioned previously, the sustainability generation that is most associated with the current evolutionary stage of environmental policy may not represent the most highly evolved form of sustainability available. In fact, the environmental policy perspective on sustainability continues, not surprisingly, to focus more on older generations of approaches, involving carrying capacity and the environmental costs of development—that is, *environmental* sustainability. Merely to use the term *environmental policy* today implies that notions of sustainability as an irreducible primary concept are not yet in vogue. Quite understandably, most environmental policy makers and analysts are not yet ready or able to subsume their interests and expertise in policy domains that are inherently *synthetic*, in the best sense of that word, and inseparable from issues of social justice, economic vitality, and other considerations that lie outside core environmental concerns.

Replacing the old dichotomy of environmentalist versus developer with that of sustainable versus unsustainable development has obvious political appeal, but if sustainability is just another word for environmental protection, the improvement may be cosmetic. The rhetoric of sustainable development, viewed within the frame of environmental problem solving, is really just a variation on carrying capacity arguments. The ecological footprint concept, for example, would be more practical and helpful in such situations than the broader notion of sustainability.

5.1 Panarchy

Given the implications of sustainability as a primary concept, many in the environmental policy community may find the concept of "panarchy" (Holling 2000) more alluring than the latest generation of sustainability thought. While the two have considerable overlap, panarchy has more to offer environmental specialists in terms of ecological focus and a language that resonates among ecologists. Holling defines panarchy as

> the structure in which systems of nature (e.g., forests, grasslands, lakes, rivers, and seas), of humans (e.g., systems of governance, tribes, and cultures), as well as combined human–nature systems (e.g., agencies that control natural resource use), are interlinked in never-ending adaptive cycles of growth, accumulation, restructuring, and renewal. These transformational cycles take place in nested sets at scales ranging, for example, from a leaf to the biosphere, over periods from days to geologic epochs. (2000, 7)

Such a conceptual framework, based in ecology, seems to require much less emphasis on, say, poverty eradication or banking regulation than does the latest thinking about sustainability, which gives increasing attention to properties of social and economic resilience while focusing on the enduring life of interactive communities as a single complex adaptive system.

Downplaying the environmental prominence of earlier phases of sustainability thought is now viewed as a necessary step in reclaiming sustainability as an organizing principle for public policy design and implementation everywhere. Simply stated, sustainability concepts have been so closely associated with environmental ends in the past that their continued conceptual evolution may depend on efforts to transcend their "green" connotations and to elevate and blend social and economic concerns seamlessly with those of ecological substance.

Unfortunately, this more inclusive idea of sustainability strikes many environmental policy specialists as a transcendental exercise in overreach and imprecision. It runs counter to the reductionist tendencies of modern policy analysis and the microspecialization that characterizes the education and training of analysts. Although attempts to compartmentalize sustainability in ways that retain an environmental focus may appeal to many in the environmental community, the urge to compartmentalize is clearly incompatible with the evolving meaning of sustainability. The concept has outgrown its home in environmentalism.

Perhaps the only way to rescue sustainability from the fate of becoming too big to apply analytically is to pair it with other concepts, such as *design* or *community*, thereby providing greater specificity and focus. The notion of *sustainable community* is particularly appealing as a way to harness the environmental, social, and economic synergies implicit in both concepts.

5.2 Sustainable Communities

From the perspectives of both policy utility and moral credibility, the most frequent and best use of sustainability concepts may be in conjunction with concepts of community. (For instance, see chapter 9 in this volume.) Sustainable communities do not face the widespread criticism reserved for sustainable *development*, viewed by many to be an oxymoron. Moreover, community ideas resonate deeply in both the worlds of ecology and human affairs.

In fact, the essence of sustainability could be defined as preserving the life of community (human and nonhuman) for purposes that include happiness, spiritual growth, and progress toward unfulfilled potential, perhaps in the form of evolving standards of human decency and accountability. Ultimately, sustainability requires the societal investment and collective self-restraint necessary for the survival of our species. But its highest objective is not species survival, at least not as *Homo sapiens* or "*Homo colossus*" (Catton 1982, 170). Instead, it is primarily about securing the great web of life and the nonliving systems that support development of *Homo humanus*—a creative, intellectually curious, spiritual, and empathic being that justifies continuation of life beyond mere biological existence. It is premised on the idea that human potential is sufficiently great to privilege our species with a special claim on continued existence, but only under conditions in which stable populations of enlightened humans cooperate to protect and preserve ecological and social life-support systems for purposes beyond our own existence. As such, the objective of sustainability is *preserving the opportunity* to discover our connection to something greater than ourselves. It is the precondition for achieving a sense of community that outlives us as individuals. When sustainability and community are linked in this way, the object of sustainability is specified in a way that is broad enough to encompass the aspirations of *Homo humanus*, yet narrow enough to permit policy design that is concrete, locally bounded, and applicable across time and space.

Sustainable communities ideally have levels of pollution, consumption, and population size that are in keeping with regional and global carrying capacity; their members share an ethic of responsibility to each other and to future generations; they provide decent livelihoods and health, safety, and lifelong education services for all who need them; the price of their goods and services reflect the full social and environmental costs of their provision and disposal; their poorest members are protected from the impacts of full-cost pricing by equity mitigation measures; their systems of governance, education, and civic leadership encourage informed democratic deliberation; and their design of markets, transport, land use, and architecture enhances community livability and preserves ecological integrity.

Clearly, these objectives represent "soft" policy targets, in the sense that ideas such as "regional carrying capacity," "decent livelihoods," and "full-cost pricing" are, like sustainability itself, difficult to operationalize. In summary form, as provided here, many of them appear hopelessly idealistic and values-driven. Yet it is difficult to imagine any concept of sustainable community worth embracing that can be fully captured in a detailed model, econometric analysis, or conventional policy design. Box 4.1 provides a sample of criteria that could be used as initial guidelines for policy development, but it is far from being either comprehensive or operational in any clear way. The policy community is confronted with a trade-off between future policy responsiveness and present methodological rigor, in much the same way that past policy making has sometimes pitted legal sufficiency against efficiency and problem-solving effectiveness.

Box 4.1 Criteria for Assessing Sustainability Objectives and Practices in Public Policy

---

Does a proposed policy or program:
General Objectives (ideals)

1. Advance the welfare of people and ecosystems, coevolving through time?
2. Provide economic vitality and security for those most in need?
3. Stop the export of problems to other peoples, places, or times?
4. Strike a balance between national pride, global citizenship, and local self-reliance ("glocal" thinking)?
5. Reform financial incentive structures that enable greed, domination, and exploitation?
6. Promote just, participatory, prosperous, and peaceful institutions and livelihoods?
7. Reflect whole systems thinking and informed, democratic decision making?
8. Redefine progress in ways that emphasize art and learning over technology?
9. Help build a green economy that operates with efficiency, within a culture of sufficiency?
10. Restore damaged people, communities, cultures, and natural areas to life with dignity?
11. Avoid making by-products, waste, or pollution that exceeds nature's assimilative capacity?
12. Encourage glocal connections and local solutions that harness the power of diversity?

13. Recognize the resilience, and limitations of resilience, in natural systems?
14. Recognize the resilience, and limitations of resilience, in human social systems?
15. Communicate knowledge, skills, and values necessary for a sustainable way of life?
16. Leave a legacy or bequest to future generations that help us feel good about ourselves?
17. Create opportunities and values that help us discover the purpose of our lives?

Specific Objectives

18. Increase the Earth's tree cover and enlarge and strengthen protected natural areas?
19. Champion efforts to achieve equity in gender, race, and social background?
20. Help to voluntarily stabilize human population and promote small, happy families?
21. Aid development of wholesome food production systems at appropriate scales for a stabilized population?
22. Accelerate the transition to clean and renewable energy sources and systems?
23. Support the aims of living wage and progressive tax and tax-shifting reforms?
24. Secure for future generations the opportunity to experience wildlife in their native habitat?
25. Conserve and provide access to freshwater, topsoil, and other essential natural resources through land reform and protection of common property?
26. Reinvigorate participatory democracy through campaign finance reform and fair redistricting?
27. Encourage appropriate use of durable, recycled, and reusable materials?
28. Defend coral reefs and contribute to the recovery of a healthy ocean?
29. Prepare communities for adaptation to climate disruption and extreme weather events?
30. Maintain or enhance biodiversity and the value of unpriced ecosystem services?
31. Preserve wild space, open space, and the common heritage of outer space?
32. Address the concentration of wealth and power in financial institutions and industries that benefit greatly from unsustainable practices and products?

6. CONCLUSION

Sustainability as a primary concept has major implications for policy specialists in environmental, social welfare, and economic development areas. In effect, policy specialists from each of the three knowledge domains would be expected to transcend their narrow interest and training for the sake of an integrative and synergistic idea. Environmental analysts would have to probe the social and economic meaning of environmental policies over an indefinite period of time and across a transjurisdictional range of space. This is not only demanding and daunting but also suggests to many policy specialists that depth of knowledge must be sacrificed for breadth. In essence, a focus on sustainability tends to reduce the power and authority of specialists and the long-standing political, academic, and professional organizations that support them.

To be sure, an army of specialists will be required to achieve major improvements in sustainability. The point is that achieving such progress will demand increasing amounts of transdisciplinary knowledge and skills, and leadership from broad-gauged, integrative thought leaders. Their agendas will necessarily require familiarity with a wide range of interlocking social, economic, and environmental issues. Synthesis will become as important as analysis.

Within the environmental policy community, calculating the value added, if any, of sustainability approaches over those of traditional environmental policy is largely a matter of paradigm change and framing environmental issues in new ways. The credibility and effectiveness of emerging sustainability policy initiatives will take decades to assess properly. By elevating nonenvironmental objectives of social and economic welfare, sustainability policy calls for far-reaching equity measures and investment strategies that may compete with conventional environmental policy objectives designed to internalize externalities through emissions taxes, resource subsidies, and command-and-control regulation (Pezzey 2004). As a result, sustainability approaches are likely to continue to be viewed by many in the environmental policy community as "soft" and even counterproductive.

Production of good research under the rubric of sustainability science will help with credibility issues, but some of the most valuable research is likely to emerge from highly applied fields of investigation, such as geospatial decision support systems, integrated sensor networks for monitoring ecosystems, and regional governance design. Systems dynamics software for use in modeling and responding to sustainability challenges at the local level may be particularly helpful for moving policy analysis to higher levels of integration and specificity. So will advances in green accounting practices.

Research that advances sustainability science, spatial analysis, local modeling, and accounting practices will be important for hastening the adoption of sustainability policies. But so will value changes that hold policy making to higher ethical standards. Progress in both areas, in turn, may facilitate needed changes in the structure of today's consumption-driven economies, designed in an era of cheap oil and planned obsolescence. Ultimately, any lasting shift to sustainability policy implies a wholesale transformation of the incentive structures that drive economic and social development. The ways in which those incentives are designed to serve the interests of rich and powerful political actors should provide sobering reflections about just how difficult such a transformation will be. In the short run, at least, sustainability arguments are more likely to provide rhetorical and political cover than policy substance.

Is that a justification for inaction? Probably not, if one accepts the view that environmental policy, as presently conceived, is failing to halt the rapid decline of ecosystem health and massive overexploitation of natural resources. A new consensus is needed, one that starts with some very basic insights: a world that works for everyone will be green, profitable, fair, and "glocal." It will encourage lifelong learning. And it will *not* be based on models of governance, development, or education that prevailed in the nineteenth and twentieth centuries.

Sustainability, as a primary concept, offers a promising model for policy development in an emerging era of integrative systems thinking, but it may also undermine important policies from the tunnel-visioned past. It promises to improve moral legitimacy, but not necessarily economic efficiency, environmental effectiveness, or short-term social harmony. Fundamentally, sustainability is about our collective bequest: what we leave future generations in the way of healthy ecosystems, strong economies, great art, vibrant communities, adaptive management systems, and challenges worthy of a highly educated society. Sustainability, as a unifying philosophy that is grounded in the life of community, might just satisfy the disparate needs of people today and those who will follow, and might warrant the serious risk taking that all big ideas demand.

REFERENCES

Aguirre, M. S. 2002. "Sustainable Development: Why the Focus on Population?" *International Journal of Social Economics* 29 (12): 923–945.

Agyeman, J., R. Bullard, and B. Evans, eds. 2003. *Just Sustainabilities: Development in an Unequal World.* Cambridge, MA: MIT Press.

Anderson, M. J. 2002. *Sustainable Development.* WFF Voices, 17, 1 Online Edition, available at www.wf-f.org/02–1-UNSustainableDev.html (accessed May 8, 2012).

Ball, T. 2000. "The Earth Belongs to the Living: Thomas Jefferson and the Problem of Intergenerational Relations." *Environmental Politics* 9 (2): 61–77.

Banerjee, A. V. 2003."Contracting Constraints, Credit Markets and Economic Development." In *Advances in Economics and Econometrics: Theory and Applications, Eighth World Congress, Vol. III,* ed. L. Hansen, M. Dewatripont, and S. Turnovsky. Cambridge, UK: Cambridge University Press.

Barraclough, S. 2005. "In Quest of Sustainable Development." Paper 4. Geneva, Switzerland: United Nations Research Institute for Social Development (UNRISD).

Catton, W. R. 1982. *Overshoot: The Ecological Basis of Revolutionary Change.* Chicago: Illini Books.

Du Pisani, J.A. 2006. "Sustainable Development: Historical Roots of the Concept." *Environmental Sciences* 3, 2 (June): 83 – 96.

Emerson, R. W. 1990. *Ralph Waldo Emerson.* Ed. Richard Poirier. Oxford: Oxford University Press.

Faber, N., R. Jorna, and J. van Engelen. 2005. "The Sustainability of 'Sustainability'—A Study into the Conceptual Foundations of the Notion of 'Sustainability.'" *Journal of Environmental Assessment Policy and Management* 7 (1): 1–33.

Frum, D. 2007. "Building a Coalition; Forgetting to Rule." *New York Times,* August 14.

Georgescu-Roegen, N. 1971. *The Entropy Law and the Economic Process.* Cambridge, MA: Harvard University Press.

Hempel, L. C. 1996. *Environmental Governance: The Global Challenge.* Washington, DC: Island Press.

———. 2009. "Conceptual and Analytical Challenges in Building Sustainable Communities." In *Toward Sustainable Communities: Transition and*

Transformations in Environmental Policy, 2nd ed., ed. D. A. Mazmanian and M. E. Kraft. Cambridge, MA: MIT Press.

Hodas, David R. 1998. "The Role of Law in Defining Sustainable Development: NEPA Reconsidered."*Widener Law Symposium Journal* 3,1 (1998): 1–60.

Holling, C. S. 1973. "Resilience and Stability of Ecological Systems." *Annual Review of Ecology and Systematics* 4: 1–24.

———. 2000. "Theories for Sustainable Futures." *Conservation Ecology* 4 (2): 7.

Howarth, R. B. 2007. "Towards an Operational Sustainability Criterion." *Ecological Economics* 63: 656–663.

International Union for Conservation of Nature (IUCN), United Nations Environment Program, and World Wildlife Fund. 1980. *World Conservation Strategy*. Gland, Switzerland: IUCN.

Kates, R., et al. 2001. "Sustainability Science." *Science* 292 (5517): 641–642.

Lele, S. M. 1991. "Sustainable Development: A Critical Review." *World Development* 19 (6): 607–621.

Lumley, S., and P. Armstrong. 2004. "Some of the Nineteenth Century Origins of the Sustainability Concept." *Environment, Development and Sustainability* 6 (3): 367–378.

McMichael. A. J., C.D. Butler, and C. Folke. 2003. "New Visions for Addressing Sustainability." *Science* 302 (December 12, 2003): 1919–1920.

Marsh, G. P. 1965. *Man and Nature*, ed. David Lowenthal. Cambridge, MA: Belknap Press of Harvard University Press.

Marshall, J. D., and M. W. Toffel. 2005. "Framing the Elusive Concept of Sustainability: A Sustainability Hierarchy." *Environmental Science and Technology* 39 (3): 673–682.

Mazmanian, D. A., and M. E. Kraft, eds. 2009. *Toward Sustainable Communities: Transition and Transformations in Environmental Policy*. 2nd ed. Cambridge, MA: MIT Press.

National Environmental Policy Act. 1969. 42 U.S.C. 4321 et seq. Washington, DC: U.S. Government Printing Office. Available at epw.senate.gov/nepa69.pdf.

Nordhaus, W. 1992. "Lethal Model 2: The Limits to Growth Revisited." *Brookings Papers on Economic Activity* 2: 1–43.

O'Connor, M. 1997. "John Stuart Mill's Utilitarianism and the Social Ethics of Sustainable Development." *European Journal of the History of Economic Thought* 4 (3): 478–506.

Pezzey, J. 2004 "Sustainability Policy and Environmental Policy." *Scandinavian Journal of Economics* 106 (2): 339–359.

Pinchot, G. 1910. *The Fight for Conservation*. New York: Doubleday, Page & Company.

Roosevelt, T. 1910. "The New Nationalism." Speech at Osawatomie, Kansas, August 31, available at www.presidentialrhetoric.com/historicspeeches/roosevelt_theodore/newnationalism.html (accessed December 14, 2010).

Sachs, W., ed. 1993. *Global Ecology: A New Arena of Political Conflict*. London: Zed Books.

———. 1999. "Sustainable Development and the Crisis of Nature: On the Political Anatomy of an Oxymoron." In *Living with Nature: Environmental Politics as Cultural Discourse*, ed. F. Fischer and H. A. Maarten. New York: Oxford University Press.

Schumacher, E. F. 1973. *Small Is Beautiful: A Study of Economics as if People Mattered*. London: Blond and Briggs.

Solow, R. M. 1974. "Intergenerational Equity and Exhaustible Resources." *Review of Economic Studies* 41: 29–46.

Stavins, R. N., A. F. Wagner, and G. Wagner. 2003. "Interpreting Sustainability in Economic Terms: Dynamic Efficiency Plus Intergenerational Equity." *Economics Letters* 79 (3): 339–343.

Tugwell, F. 1973. *Search for Alternatives: Public Policy and the Study of the Future.* Cambridge, MA: Winthrop.

United Nations. 1993. *Agenda 21: The United Nations Programme of Action from Rio.* New York: United Nations.

U.S. National Research Council. 2011. "Incorporating Sustainability in the U.S. Environmental Protection Agency." Report commissioned by EPA (ORD). Washington, DC: National Academy of Sciences.

Wood, P. 2009. "The Sustainability Movement in the American University." Princeton, NJ: National Association of Scholars, July 27, available at www.nas.org/articles/The_Sustainability_Movement_in_the_American_University (accessed May 8, 2012).

World Commission on Environment and Development (WCED). 1987. *Our Common Future.* New York: Oxford University Press.

CHAPTER 5

....

ETHICAL CHALLENGES IN ENVIRONMENTAL POLICY

....

ROBERT C. PAEHLKE

ANY broad assessment of environmental politics and policy, such as what this volume attempts to provide, also needs to consider many related ethical concerns and debates. This chapter seeks to do that. It begins with a brief look at the historical links between environmental policy and environmental ethics. It then goes on to examine some of the ethical issues associated with protecting wild nature and wilderness. It discusses the idea of environmental rights, including the possibility that there is a right to a clean environment. From that discussion it moves to a close look at the ethical dimensions of the relationship between social inequality and environmental protection: how can we assure that the opportunities to utilize and to enjoy and be sustained by nature are fairly distributed among humans? I then discuss ethical concerns raised in debates over environmental aspects of using private and common property. The chapter closes with a discussion of the ethical aspects of emerging environmental policy concerns, including genetically modified organisms and climate change.

1. ENVIRONMENTAL ETHICS AND ENVIRONMENTAL POLICY: EARLY HISTORY

....

Contemporary environmental ethics might well have begun with the work of Aldo Leopold, who in 1949 argued that the roots of an ecological crisis were philosophical in nature. Others, including Lynn White Jr. (1967) and Garrett Hardin (1968), added to our understanding of the ethical underpinnings of human impositions on nature, but the formal academic study of environmental ethics dates to the 1970s: the journal *Environmental Ethics* commenced publication in 1979.

Environmental policy has always had ethical dimensions. The act of protecting nature through governance implicitly asks: what obligations do humans hold regarding nonhuman species and whole ecosystems? Since humans can alter nature in ways that no other species can and can almost always survive and prosper in alternative ways without imposing on nature in particular ways, are we not then obliged to alter our collective activities accordingly in thoughtful ways? We cannot avoid having some impacts, but how and where do we draw the line regarding which impacts are acceptable and which are not?

Even the earliest environmental policies, long prior to the academic study of environmental ethics or environmental policy as a concept, had implicit ethical dimensions. An early complaint about air pollution by John Evelyn dates to 1661, but even ineffective laws were not passed by the Parliament of Great Britain until the mid-nineteenth century. Regarding water pollution in the Thames, the Reverend Benjamin Armstrong wrote in 1855: "The ride on the water was refreshing except for the stench. What a pity this noble river should be made a common sewer" (Paehlke 1989, 23; Armstrong 1963). In 1866 and 1872 there were cholera outbreaks in London as a result, and in 1876 the Benjamin Disraeli government passed the Rivers Pollution Prevention Act.

Urban concentrations of human population accelerated as a result of early industrialization, a process that in the earliest days benefited only the owners of industries. Workers flocking to cities following the Enclosure Acts had been, for the most part, far better off on agricultural smallholdings, and even as serfs, where they had fresh air and water and, most of the time, enough to eat. The least well-off of industrial workers faced the greatest threats to health in crowded slums and in coal mines. The inequality and misery chronicled by so many were, in part, a matter of environmental ethics—who had access to clean air and water and who did not and why. Income was not the only thing that was unfairly distributed.

Two other dimensions of environmental ethics were implicit as well in the writing of the Reverend Armstrong: in speaking of the noble Thames he at least implied that, being noble, nature itself might have rights, as might future generations of humans who wished to enjoy nature. Similarly, many early monarchs, especially in France, preserved vast tracks of forest and protected the wildlife therein for future hunters and for future supplies of wood. Without such protections, and benefiting from a seemingly limitless frontier, forests in North America were cleared on a massive scale. Early in the nineteenth century John James Audubon raised questions about wildlife habitat and the protection of America's forests. He expressed this concern succinctly when he wrote: "The greedy mills told the sad tale, that in a century the noble forests...should exist no more" (Herrick 2006, 9–10). Again, in his text Audubon clearly raised questions regarding the rights of nature and of future generations, both human and nonhuman.

Later, American conservationists built these concerns into political movements, beginning with the first mass conservation movement, which led to the
world's first national parks, as well as the more contemporary advances in environmental policy in the late 1960s and 1970s.

2. Ethics and the Protection of Wilderness and Habitat

The nineteenth-century arguments for the protection of nature and wilderness in
North America had two distinct ethical roots. One argument was rooted in the
prudent avoidance of waste and in a respect for nature's complexity in relation to
a human capacity to alter the landscape irretrievably. The second ethically based
argument emerged from a stronger sense of reverence for and devotion to nature's
glories—nature as it exists with minimal human interference. The former led
toward a desire for "wise use" and scientific management of renewable nature. The
latter led to a case for the preservation of nature's greatest settings and spaces and
for only a very modest human presence within those places.

In both cases these ideas arose well before the accelerated capacity to alter
nature that emerged with full-blown industrialization, motorized vehicles,
and appropriately named earth-moving machinery. George Perkins Marsh, an
American designer, lawyer, and naturalist writing in the mid-nineteenth century,
cataloged human alterations to geography and nature, including erosion associated with deforestation, and various effects of mining and agricultural activities
throughout the world. He contributed enormously to the beginnings of an awareness of the unintended consequences of human economic activities (Marsh 1965).
The landscape and its alteration was for Marsh primarily a human responsibility. Humans were charged with moral responsibility for nature and disruptions to
nature. This understanding was essential to the later adoption of scientific forestry
and improved agricultural practices.

Henry David Thoreau and John Muir created the beginnings of a deeper, more
reverential basis for environmental ethics and the protection of nature. Both rel-
ished life as witnesses to and participants in relatively untouched wilderness. Hiking
and living within wild nature was an essential part of their lives; Thoreau hiked
through New England and Muir across the continent. They saw wilderness as an
essential part and parcel of what it was to be human. Thoreau (1851) wrote that "in
Wildness is the preservation of the World." Muir turned that ethical assertion into
a political movement for the preservation of vast tracts of glorious natural landscapes within national parks. His campaign was not about husbanding resources
to use another day; it was about avoiding all impositions on nature's splendor. Muir
admired North America's native people because, in his view, they "walk softly and

hurt the landscape hardly more than the birds or squirrels, and their brush and bark huts last hardly longer than woodrats" (Teale 1954, 117). He was horrified by the damming of watercourses and the scars on the landscape inflicted previously by the California gold rush.

This ethical tradition lies behind public policies that set rules regarding the protection of nature and seek to preserve its greatest treasures from human impositions beyond visiting, studying, and admiring—"Take only photographs, leave only footprints." Through his writing Muir created a mass following for the protection of the stunning beauty of the American West. Needless to say, there were and are very real limits to this preservationist vision within the political and policy realm. Human settlement and human industry are voracious. Nature's glories are also seen by powerful interests, and implicitly by all who lead modern lives—seen in terms of tons, barrels, and board-feet. There are policy-making struggles inherent in these differing ethical perspectives, and the ensuing policy differences are still very much alive today.

The so-called wise use of resources, embraced by Gifford Pinchot, the head of the U.S. Forest Service from 1898 to 1910 and later governor of Pennsylvania, was a blending of these intense ethically based disagreements. Scientific management of resource extraction, in Pinchot's view, would allow for the protection of nature and for the long-term use of renewable resources like forests. Pinchot opposed excessive cutting and supported replanting efforts and the protection of watersheds. The ethical basis for his resource management policies was rooted in a belief that resources could be harvested in perpetuity if harvested prudently and that government could play a central role in protecting the long-term public interest (Miller 2004). His views are carried forward today within the concept of sustainable development, an attempt to accommodate economic and environmental interests simultaneously.

Preservation and wise use came to be used as guides to policy and practice, the former within an expanding system of national parks, the latter on public and some private land. In 1960 this mixed approach was further codified in the Multiple Use–Sustained Yield Act, which asserted that "the National Forests are established and shall be administered for outdoor recreation, range, timber, watershed and wildlife and fish purposes" (Andrews 1999, 196). Whether logging was to be the leading priority was left to local administrators. In the Reagan years, commercially oriented users of public lands were ascendant and sought expansion of resource extraction on protected lands. Many protections were rolled back, but the most radical proposals were defeated by internal divisions and a resurgent environmental movement. Even today debates over intensified resource extraction on public lands are far from over, and new ethical issues regarding the protection of nature have emerged.

Expanding ecological knowledge in the twentieth century led to new policy debates as well as to new policies and regulations. As ecologists came to understand the habitat needs of more species, it became clear that existing protected wilderness areas were not always adequate. This was and is especially true of the habitat needs of top predators, including grizzly bears, mountain lions and other large cats, and wolves, which of necessity often range far beyond the boundaries of national parks or other protected areas. In some cases species survival in a region may depend on protecting animals within corridors that extend onto private lands and even across national borders. Ethical dilemmas and policy conflicts arise when human settlements encroach on the spaces utilized by these species. In India, where land is scarce, humans are not easily moved to other locations and can be at risk, though attacks by tigers are rare. Domesticated herds are also at risk in the North American West, and as grizzly populations have been restored from low levels, more grizzlies have been lost to hunting, often in defense of domesticated herds.

Advancing ecological understanding has also led to other land management policy conflicts. Many species require very distinctive habitats. Woodpeckers require standing dead trees, and so do a number of bird, animal, and insect species that live in hollowed-out cores. Other species require fallen trees or underbrush of various kinds for food and shelter. Some species of animals and insects and birds depend on particular or a small number of particular plant species. Replanted forests are typically same age, same species, to maximize future wood resources and to allow for future simultaneous clear-cuts. In such "tree farms" there are no dead and fallen trees and little plant variety, and thus little ecological diversity; some have called replanted forests ecological deserts—trees, but not a forest. Cutting rules now may mandate so-called sloppy cuts, where dead trees are left standing and litter is left on the ground.

The spotted owl controversy symbolized this shifting apprehension of land management. The spotted owl and many other species only thrive in old-growth forest settings (Yaffee 1994). When it was declared to be endangered under the Endangered Species Act, some forests that might have been logged were protected. In broader terms, replanting logged areas became less an act of environmental responsibility than a grossly inadequate approach to ecological management. Yes, replanting helped to prevent erosion and produced more lumber or pulp per acre per decade, but if widely used it also will threaten biodiversity and the ecological richness of forests (Maser 1990). The Parks Service, the Forest Service, the Bureau of Land Management, private industries, and parallel agencies in other nations have had to rethink many related policies and regulations.

3. Ecological Science and the Protection of Nature

Other ethical issues have arisen out of advancing ecological knowledge combined with interventions intent on undoing negative actions of the past. The emerging field of restoration ecology has, for example, led to a number of policy challenges. For example, to what extent is it ethically appropriate to restore natural landscapes to how they were prior to human imposition rather than the form they would take if nature was left alone from this point forward? Do we reintroduce only the species that were present prior to the damage caused by mining or other human activities? In other settings, do we remove exotic species that have been introduced accidentally, or deliberately, by humans? And what of destruction that might have occurred had humans not prevented it? Some plant species (jack pine, for example) require fire to propagate effectively, but preventing or fighting forest fires may alter that pattern (Pyne 2001). What is the correct policy—do we mimic nature or "save it from itself"?

The great irony is that many of the policies that we have adopted and many of the spaces and species that we protect may soon be threatened by a new danger of human origin: climate change. We protect many specific places for ecological reasons, but ecological conditions within those places may be altered by rising temperatures or changing patterns of precipitation—sometimes for the better, for some wild species and some human crops, and sometimes for the worse. In addition, some fish species thrive only within a very narrow range of water temperatures, and some streams may become too warm. More dramatically, as glaciers retreat or if snow levels decline at high altitudes, water supplies may be reduced, affecting every species, including humans. And while the possibility of forest growth may move north in Canada, some forests in British Columbia are already ravaged by insects at higher altitudes than previously would have been the case had average temperatures not risen. As climate change advances, all habitats will be altered, and the ecology of places we have set aside in perpetuity may be radically altered and could turn out to be the wrong places to have set aside.

We are thus still a very long way from reliably and consistently implementing Leopold's land ethic. This was evidenced most recently in President Obama's 2010 approval for expanded offshore drilling, which was followed almost immediately by a massive explosion and oil gusher in British Petroleum's offshore drilling rig. Before approving expansion seeking to undercut incessant Republican and industry demands, he might well have recalled Leopold's words: "People should quit thinking about decent land-use as solely an economic problem. Examine each question in terms of what is ethically and esthetically right, as well as what is economically expedient. A thing is right when it tends to preserve the integrity, stability, and beauty of the biotic community. It is wrong when it tends otherwise" (Andrews 1999, 195).

4. ENVIRONMENTAL RIGHTS

There has been much discussion among environmental ethicists regarding the concept of environmental rights. Can animals be said to have rights? Is there a human right to clean air or water? How and where might such rights be enshrined?

Is there a basic right to some minimum share or even an equal share of the planet's resources? Do future generations not have a right at least to continued existence and some hope of prosperity comparable to that which present generations enjoy? In this case there have been only limited policy developments flowing from the extended academic discussion.

Many discussions of the rights of animals or the rights of nature have included doubts as to whether nonsentient beings or places or ecosystems could be said to have rights. The debates regarding the rights of nature or animal rights have had only very limited impact on public policy. Some nations have signed antiwhaling treaties, some tuna cans are labeled dolphin safe, and dolphin bycatches and other wasteful practices have been reduced. There have also been some changes in practices regarding the treatment of domestic animals, more people are vegetarians, and free-range chicken and grass-fed beef are sought out by some consumers, but many of these changes involve shifts in habits more than alterations in policy.

There are, however, a wide variety of conflicts between rights that could be assigned to nature and human opportunities for economic well-being and cultural fulfillment, a deep ethical dilemma at times. Risks increase for villagers in crowded India if tiger habitat expands. Some cultures (the Japanese and the Sami and Inuit peoples, for example) are heavily invested in hunting whales even in the face of depleted numbers and strong opposition from some conservation groups. Other indigenous people's cultural costumes and ceremonies require eagle feathers, and again, there is resistance to hunting eagles since populations have been depleted by pesticide exposures and other threats.

The issue of assigning rights to animals or nature, however, captures only a small part of the policy potential associated with a consideration of environmental rights. Environmental rights might better be seen as an extension of human rights—a human right to access to the essentials of life, of the right to life as in the right to "life, liberty and the pursuit of happiness." Without clean water and air there is no life. All humans, if they are to survive and to pursue happiness, need assured access to these common property resources.

The African Charter of Human and Peoples' Rights (1981), in Article 24, asserts that "all peoples shall have the right to a general satisfactory environment favorable to their development." This article is palpably vague and does not include what many have advocated such as an individual human right to clean water, a right that might well place great burdens on governments both in terms of protecting water quality and obtaining adequate supplies.

In 2008, major Canadian environmental organizations presented model legislation for a Canadian Environmental Bill of Rights, a statutory (as opposed to a constitutional) right to a healthy environment that would not guarantee provision, but would empower Canadians and Canadian environmental organizations to press for the enforcement of environmental legislation through the courts. Legislation in this spirit, an Environmental Bill of Rights creating an Environmental Commissioner and taking other citizen empowering initiatives, was legislated in Ontario in 1993.

Several laws in the United States empower citizens to use the courts to press government to enforce environmental laws. In addition, many pieces of federal environmental legislation in the 1970s opened administrative processes to public participation in the development of regulations. These include the Clean Air Act Amendments of 1970 and 1977, the 1972 amendments to the Federal Water Pollution Control Act, the Toxic Substances Control Act of 1976, the Resource Conservation and Recovery Act of 1976, and the Comprehensive Environmental Response, Compensation, and Liability Act of 1980 (Superfund) (Paehlke 1990; O'Leary 2010). In the United States at several levels of government there has also been environmental right-to-know legislation regarding the transportation, storage, disposal, and emission of toxic substances. Fire and emergency workers long before the attacks of September 11 demanded such information should they ever have to enter facilities where there was a high risk of having to deal with toxic or explosive substances. It seems plain, too, that individuals and communities have a right to know that they live near such risks. This ethical principle was recognized in law with the passage of numerous state right-to-know laws and with the Emergency Planning and Community Right to Know Act, which required that communities and emergency workers be informed of dangerous stored substances (Adams 1983; Kraft, Stephan, and Abel 2011). Right-to-know rules can be seen as one type of basic environmental rights and should be seen much more broadly. Should there not be, for example, a mandatory calculation regarding the external (often environmental) costs of any major proposal, action, or policy? A right to an estimate and public statement regarding possible unintended consequences would seem reasonable. Some of this intent is part of environmental assessment procedures under the National Environmental Policy Act (NEPA), but these are far from consistently applied. This is essentially a call for more comprehensive accounting procedures for both government and industry.

Some have also argued that an environmental right to know should be extended internationally so that citizens of poor nations know, for example, whether hazardous wastes are being imported into their nations. Ethically, the practice of exporting hazardous wastes to jurisdictions with little capacity to detect or remedy environmental hazards is reprehensible. The Basel Convention was signed in 1989 and was ratified by enough nations by 1992 to come into force. This Convention sought to reduce or eliminate the shipping of hazardous wastes to poorer nations in Africa, the Caribbean, Asia, Eastern Europe, and elsewhere. After 1992 shippers made the claim that such wastes were exported not for disposal but for "recycling." Only with a 1995 amendment to close this loophole was shipping toxic wastes from rich countries to poor significantly reduced (Clapp 2010).

Some analysts have taken environmental rights much further and have argued that a *right to a clean environment* should be constitutionally enshrined. Tim Hayward (2005) argues that there is a fundamental right to an adequate environment and that this right ought to be provided in the constitution of any modern democratic state. Hayward makes a case that such a right adds to existing human rights and environmental protections and would help to assure environmental justice. Environmental protections, it might also be argued, are otherwise less likely to be available to the least wealthy, minorities, and those living in poor and powerless regions.

5. ENVIRONMENTAL RIGHTS AND GLOBAL INEQUALITY

On a global scale, inequalities in terms of environmental protection are perhaps even more dramatic than those within nations. If such principles were somehow enshrined in international law, those suffering the effects of pollutants originating outside of their own nations might have recourse. Such situations include, for example, those in the far north who suffer the effects of persistent organic pollutants that are emitted thousands of miles from where they live. Even if they could not bring a case against a polluter in another jurisdiction, if their own nation had a constitutional right to a healthy environment, they could force compensation in their national courts and thereby pressure their own nation to act more forcefully in the international sphere. Even more significant than transboundary chemical pollution might be the differential effects of climate change within nations that have contributed only negligibly to the problem. This will be discussed further below. Resource sustainability issues, especially regarding oil and freshwater, raise another possible aspect of environmental rights on the international level. Carley and Spapens (1998, 57) discuss at length the implications of coming to terms with the earth's biophysical limits, arguing for nothing less than "global equity of access to the Earth's resources by all nations and all peoples." This is obviously a very radical proposal. As these authors explain, "The equity principle states that each person in the world has the same right (but not obligation) to use an equal amount of global resources, now and in the future. In advocating the equity principle, the environmental space approach parts company with much thinking on sustainable development, which either ignores the issue of distribution or, like the Brundtland Commission, overtly assumes that Northern consumption would remain far in excess of Southern consumption for the foreseeable future" (Carley and Spapens 1998, 66).

On its face, this perspective seems unlikely to be implemented—it is at odds with some of the practices and principles of capitalist economic systems. Those systems are much better at driving goods production and wealth concentration forward than they are at accommodating or adapting to ethical considerations related to either social equity or resource sustainability. This does not refute, however, the fact that the planet may well not have sufficient biophysical capacity to allow the whole of the world to produce and consume in a pattern anything like the recent historical norm in North America or Western Europe. Unless wealthy nations alter their consumption patterns and habits, much of the rest of the world will soon adopt them. This is not sustainable (Tobin 2010). This possible future, of course, is partially self-correcting. Resource prices are rising inexorably, and new, less resource- and energy-intensive products and consumption patterns are emerging and will continue to emerge. It is not clear, however, whether this new pattern will emerge quickly enough to avoid severe environmental damage, sufficient access in poor counties to a minimum of essential resources, or resource-based economic disruptions in China (or, for that matter, in the United States). The basic question is, can we depend on markets alone to sort everything out, or should there be some collective effort, perhaps through an assured minimum right to shared access to resources, to accelerate the move to a more sustainable global economy?

Again, the discussion of environmental rights has not resulted in great policy change thus far, but it may well alter the way we think about rights. Legal and political rights were followed in some nations and internationally by human rights as well as social rights (Marshall and Bottomore 1992). The twenty-first century may bring about the development and evolution of environmental rights.

6. Ethics, Environmental Protection, and Inequality

From the beginning of the environmental movement in the 1960s there have been clear links between environmental protection and social equity. Environmentalists were accused by opponents of environmental protection of being elitists, of being more concerned about protecting obscure species or improving the scenery at the expense of the jobs of loggers or factory workers. The accusation was often ethically dubious for at least three reasons. First, the environmentalism of the day was moving from a central concern with wilderness to more urban-centric concerns like pollution, including industrial toxic exposures and improved public transit. Second, industrial communities are exposed to higher levels of pollution than are the elites environmentalists were accused of being. Third, environmentally friendly ways of doing things are often more, not less, labor-intensive—in most cases they create more jobs, not fewer. Nonetheless, the accusations had political resonance in some circles. Protecting the environment may add to the cost of production for some industries at least temporarily, even if they grow the economy in net terms. In addition, those jurisdictions that avoid effective environmental regulations may attract certain industries to the benefit of some. There are also real differences within those few industries that are utterly eclipsed by strong environmental concerns: the clear-cutting of old-growth forests or the production of electricity from coal, especially in older plants.

There thus may be clear ethical dilemmas in a small number of particular contexts—a stark choice between social equity and employment opportunities, on the one hand, and clean air or ecological protection, on the other. Again, these are out-of-the-ordinary situations. Most problems can be resolved by changing technologies, and those changes add jobs more often than they reduce them, as in the case of expanded public transit, the addition of pollution abatement or increased energy efficiency, or the expansion of the provision of cleaner energy from renewable sources (Paehlke 1998). Even in the more ethically charged contexts, policy intervention can ameliorate negative employment impacts, either partially offsetting the cost of pollution abatement or retraining workers displaced in the name of environmental protection.

Interestingly, there has been a dramatic shift over the past four decades regarding the environment/jobs ethical tension. In the 1970s environmentalists often flatly opposed the existence of dirty industries and reflected on the "limits to growth" and on the possibility and desirability of zero economic growth. In 1987 the Brundtland Commission Report (World Commission on Environment and Development 1987) helped to shift the discourse on this issue by identifying some of the ways that poverty also has significant negative environmental consequences. In the face of being unable to feed their families, no one would be concerned about the ecological effects of overgrazing or of clearing a forest, and if a mining or industrial enterprise proposed to create jobs, almost no one would ask questions about the possible effects on water quality.

In the face of poverty, longer-term preferences regarding nature, both practical and ethical, give way readily to short-term considerations regarding human survival. Prosperity and the environment are clearly not a simple matter of either/or. From the 1990s forward, green products became increasingly visible to consumers in wealthy nations. Some of these were self-identified hype, but many were products created with a dramatically different level of environmental impact throughout the product life cycle, from production through use to disposal (Paehlke 1999). More fuel-efficient vehicles, paper made from 100 percent postconsumer waste, rooftop solar panels, and even products whose environmental benefits are not hyped (e.g., an MP3 device that replaces a stereo and a very large stack of CDs) can make a measurable difference in terms of environmental impact.

Indeed, the jobs/environment ethical tensions of the past have dissipated to the point that following the 2008 financial meltdown spreading outward from the United States, many nations used so-called green stimulus initiatives, attempting to create jobs and revive their economies by expanding investment in wind energy, solar, public transit, and other green initiatives. Van Jones, in his widely read book *The Green Collar Economy*, argued that green investment was the best way to address America's two leading problems (ecological damage and economic inequality): we could resolve them simultaneously, he wrote, by putting the unemployed and underemployed to work insulating homes, installing new energy-efficient lighting, and building improved public transit (Jones 2009).

There are, however, other ethical issues associated with the tension between social equity and environmental protection. One set of ethical issues of this sort arose in the 1980s and early 1990s, when debt-for-nature swaps were frequently used to protect wild nature in poor, heavily indebted nations. Debt from these nations was purchased by conservation organizations in wealthy nations, often for pennies on the dollar, and lands within the indebted nation were protected using public money freed from debt-servicing costs. In some cases these transactions had positive impacts, but often successes were limited because the poor nations lacked an effective land protection infrastructure and popular support for the initiatives (Visser and Mendoza 1994). Also, ethnic minorities were sometimes denied continued access to lands that had once sustained them.

Another ethically charged social-environmental linkage point is environmental justice, the differential impact of pollution and other environmental impacts on minorities and the poor. Beginning in the early 1980s minority communities launched campaigns regarding the differential exposure of minorities to polluted land, air, and water. The first such campaign was waged in 1982 in opposition to a proposed hazardous waste landfill in rural Warren County, North Carolina, slated to receive 30,000 cubic yards of PCB-laden soil. Soon thereafter it was shown that hazardous industries and hazardous waste treatment facilities and disposal sites were more likely to be located near minority communities than would be suggested by the local proportion of minorities in the larger population (Bullard 2000). Uranium mines were disproportionately on Native lands, dirty industries and landfills disproportionately near African American and Hispanic communities in Texas and elsewhere, and so forth. Hundreds of local environmental justice organizations sprang up.

Some scholars showed that this pattern was not always the result of prejudicial siting processes. That is, in at least some cases the environmentally problematic facility was there first, and lower property values and housing prices made the neighborhood more affordable for low-income minority populations (Hurley 1997). Even these cases are ethically problematic, even if not a result of deliberate decisions regarding facility location by corporations or elected representatives. These outcomes are but another example of how poverty contributes to ongoing environmental damage. Until the environmental justice movement raised these issues, minority communities did not have sufficient political clout to demand the mitigation or elimination of impacts.

In 1992 the Office of Environmental Justice was created within the Environmental Protection Agency. In 1994 President Clinton issued Executive Order 12898, which directed federal agencies to consider environmental factors that negatively affected minority populations (Ringquist 1997). There were some improvements in performance in this regard, but many notable problems, including differential impacts related to the petrochemical industry in Louisiana, were not resolved. During the administration of George W. Bush, funding for the Office of Environmental Justice was significantly reduced, but increased consciousness regarding differential impacts on minority communities still makes placing problematic facilities less easy to accomplish.

The environmental justice movement was important because it helped to broaden the political appeal of environmental protection and to make it more difficult to hide environmental problems in minority communities or other jurisdictions of lesser political influence. When mobilized, some communities were able to press for effective cleanups instead of lower-cost "solutions" that were really just a matter of hiding problems away in lower-income neighborhoods. The environmental justice movement also brought about changes in the hiring policies of major environmental organizations—there was a significant increase in minority hiring within environmental movement organizations from about 1990 onward.

The debate regarding environmental justice has broadened since the early campaigns and analysis of the 1980s. More recently, David Schlosberg has sorted out four definitions of environmental justice. The first and doubtless most central concerns the equitable distribution of environmental risks and benefits. The second is about fair and meaningful participation in environmental decision making (which would include, for example, a right to know, as discussed above, and to contribute to policy and regulatory decision making). The third focuses on a recognition of community ways of life, local knowledge, and cultural difference. The fourth emphasizes protecting and enhancing community and individual capability to function and flourish in society (Schlosberg 2009). Another simple typology might divide environmental justice issues into local, regional, international, and global issues.

In all cases environmental justice focuses on fairness regarding access to the benefits and avoidance of the harms that flow from resources and the environment. In the early days the focus was primarily on possible harms, especially harms at the local level. As environmental justice moved to the global scale, the focus at first remained on harms, such as the long-range transport of pollutants: peoples whose health was negatively affected by these polluting industrial processes had no share whatever in the profits or jobs, or even the products associated with the processes. In poorer nations there were also many issues raised regarding the survival of ways of life when vast tracts of tropical forest were destroyed or dams were built, eliminating the forest-based livelihoods of local peoples.

The policy implications of these campaigns were considerable, especially in nations where corruption was rife at the national level and/or where economic growth was so relentlessly pursued that environmental considerations were all but ignored. Typical of these issues were the Three Gorges Dam project in China and the multiple dams on the Narmada River in India. In both cases the projects proceeded with some additional efforts to resettle peoples whose homes were flooded by the projects and, in the case of India, to plant new trees to replace lost forested land. In recent years some tropical forests have been protected as a result of the purchase of carbon credits by industries in developed nations or as a result of fund-raising by global environmental organizations.

Other aspects of environmental justice also deserve mention. These matters reflect the continuing broadening of the scope of environmental justice in that they are associated with access to environmental benefits rather than the avoidance of harms. Robert Bullard (1997), one of the leading interpreters of the environmental justice movement, has argued that improved access to public transit is an important part of environmental justice. When more government funding is spent on automobile transportation rather than public transit, it not only harms the environment but also disproportionately harms less wealthy urban residents relative to more wealthy suburban and rural residents. Improved transit funding serves both the environment and social justice. The public subsidies to automobile transportation in the United States are significantly disproportionate on a per capita basis. Bicycles and walking too (which account for perhaps 10 percent of trips to work in urban areas) get less funding than automobiles (Newman and Kenworthy 1989).

Finally there is the issue of local food and disproportionate access to healthy food (especially fresh, organic fruits and vegetables). Alice Waters, the noted California chef who first worked hand in hand with local farmers to procure fresh, organic produce for her Berkeley restaurant, began working with local schools, often in poorer neighborhoods, to teach children how to produce their own fresh, organic vegetables (McNamee 2008). This expanded into a national movement for healthier foods served in schools. Also, many community groups in poor urban neighborhoods protested the existence of "food deserts"—neighborhoods where fresh produce was simply unavailable. More recently, some poor urban neighborhoods have organized to produce fresh food themselves or have attracted farmers from outlying areas to sell it directly in downtown open-air markets.

These efforts have not always been seen as part of the environmental justice movement but could well be understood as such. Locally produced foods that make up the now widely noted "100-mile menu" are fresher, require no preservatives, and use far less energy for processing or transportation (a normal North American food item travels on average 1,000 miles or more). The environmental benefits are obvious, as are the health benefits of fresh produce for the urban poor. These efforts have gained a very significant boost from First Lady Michelle Obama, whose White House garden involved local Washington children and produced a great variety of fresh, organic produce in a highly visible way. Sustainable agriculture is very much a part of a contemporary conception of environmental justice.

7. COMMON PROPERTY, PRIVATE PROPERTY, AND ENVIRONMENTAL ETHICS

Garrett Hardin's insights regarding common property resources and the tragedy of the commons were conceptually important to the early environmental movement. The idea that individuals who grazed their flocks on shared or public common lands could, with relatively innocent motivations, collectively destroy the resource on which they all depended helped us understand the dilemma we face. Each participant in the destruction would want to maximize his herd faster than each other participant, and together they would overgraze the land. The same motivations may also apply to the pollution of the air and the water. These are also common property resources, as are ocean fisheries, which if unregulated are frequently overfished, to the long-term detriment of all concerned.

Some analysts and economists have concluded that the solution to the problems associated with common property resources is private ownership, which vests a long-term economic interest in the future of the resource. That is, overcutting of forests or an unwillingness to replant forests would in this view be lessened if forest companies owned the forests or held very long-term leases and cattlemen owned the land on which their herds grazed. Corporations could own bodies of freshwater as well. It is more difficult, of course, to assign property rights in air. Indeed, even for forests, perhaps the easiest common property resource to put into private hands, there are potential problems with the theory. What is to prevent a "forest" company from turning a quick profit on lumber and going into another business altogether after selling the land to developers or farmers?

At the same time, there are many cases where private holdings of forest lands are carefully managed for the long term, in some cases quite thoughtfully with regard to ecological impacts (and in some cases only with regard to long-term lumber production). There are, however, several other ways to organize the management of common property resources. One is public ownership (applicable to forests, as is commonplace in Canada, for example). Another is government regulation (of air and water quality or emissions, for example) or international treaty-based regulation or resource management (ocean fisheries). Regulations by single governments or several governments cooperating to enforce common standards each on their own territory have been effective in many instances, but international regimes regarding ocean fisheries generally have not. A third alternative option is producer-based, cooperative self-management. At its roots this debate is about ethics and about competing views of human nature. Are human beings primarily motivated by short-term individual gains, or are they social creatures that can cooperate in the best interests of their communities over the long term? Nothing could be more fundamental. The answer, of course, is not a simple one. The answer depends on how the humans in question have organized themselves—are they indeed a community, or for that matter a nation, inclined to cooperate with the world?—and it depends on scientific or traditional knowledge. Many a commons has been destroyed without anyone knowing that they were destroying it, believing that next year's crops would grow like last year's, that there were more animals to hunt over the next hill, or that there were more fish than those that were caught last week.

Elinor Ostrom devoted much of her life to researching resource-based communities and the conditions under which they adopt sustainability-oriented behaviors. One factor in determining success is the character of the resource on which the people in question depend. Success is more likely if the resource has definable boundaries—a predetermined amount of common land, for example. Second, the community in question must be resource-dependent, the threat to the resource must be perceptible (not an anomalous surprise), and there must be few available substitutes for the resource. Third, the community must in fact be a small, stable community with strong social networks and shared norms. Fourth, there must be enforced community-based rules and procedures that provide incentives for responsible use and punishments for overuse of the shared resource (Ostrom 1990; Ostrom and Hess 2006).

Many of these conditions are not widely influential within modern industrial societies. Most people live in cities and even many rural communities are not stable and do not have shared norms, at least norms that are collectively enforced by the community itself. More important, perhaps, few communities either share their resources cooperatively or would acknowledge that they could not find alternative means of support. Most imagine that they could lure a new industry to town or attract tourists. Most important, economies are organized on a basis that is much wider than the community, and people are individually responsible to "find another job" if what they are doing is no longer viable. Most resource extraction and consumption is organized on a national or global basis.

Accordingly, while Ostrom has shown that humans can manage resources in sustainable ways within communities under the right circumstances, in today's global economy we need to do so on a much larger local level and a regional, national, and global scale, a much more challenging undertaking. Nonetheless, global-scale solutions must be designed for varying resources, varying cultural contexts, and varying circumstances. The solutions may utilize the rights and obligations of ownership, incorporate an appropriate role for government, and/or mobilize those who use the resources in question or whose behaviors affect those resources. Changing behaviors to a focus on the long term is particularly challenging when such considerations can negatively affect immediate survival—that is, when immediate survival all but requires overgrazing, overfishing, or poaching endangered species.

They are also challenging within political cultures that tilt the balance of decision making toward the rights of private property owners to the point where they limit government's capacity to regulate in the common interest. The Fifth Amendment to the United States Constitution states: "nor shall private property be taken for public use, without just compensation." After the 1922 decision of the Supreme Court in *State of Pennsylvania v. Mahon* the concept of "regulatory takings" became far more significant. That is, compensation may be owed to owners whose property is reduced in value by the passage of laws designed, among other things, to protect the environment. In this particular case, the state of Pennsylvania was seeking to reduce incidences of land subsidence and sinkholes as a result of coal mining, a problem that still exists today within the state.

Since that case was decided, the courts have tried to interpret the concept of regulatory takings in a balanced way, but there are currents in U.S. political culture that would greatly limit the power of the government to interfere with private property rights in any way beyond the protection of lives and limitations on criminal activities. Fortunately, there has been a long-standing evolution in terms of legal precedents, and there is a complex of entrenched habits of interaction between the public and private sectors regarding environmental damage within communities. These patterns can be built upon as new environmental problems arise. Leigh Raymond's (2003) discussion of the uses of licensed private rights of access to, short of ownership of, public resources is instructive in this regard. These market approaches might be applied, for example, through cap-and-trade systems that create markets in pollutants, including shares in total allowable carbon dioxide emissions.

Such approaches combine the two broad patterns of human motivation: community-mindedness and the self-protection of private interests. One hopes that such combined motivations can be adapted to a global scale. Market-based approaches do not exclude other policy approaches, including stringent regulation of emissions or taxation. Nor do they exclude ethically minded actions at the individual or community level. Given the scale of the problems we face and the lack of success in addressing such things as climate change thus far, the simultaneous use of all approaches are likely to prove necessary.

8. Emerging Issues in Environmental Ethics and Policy: GMOs and Climate Change

There are two environmental policy issues of relatively recent origin, each with an array of ethical dimensions. One concerns the implications of biotechnology, genetically modified organisms (GMOs), especially genetically modified (GM) food crops. The second is climate change. The deep ethical implications of climate change were not widely considered before the late 1980s, perhaps later than that. The extensive discussion of ethical issues related to GMOs is also recent and fraught with challenges.

Genetic modification has considerable potential for improving food and fiber outputs, producing pharmaceuticals, and many other uses. Some oppose all such initiatives; others are simply wary about the potential for unintended side effects in the absence of careful regulation. I will only address the ethics of genetic modification as applied to agriculture, by far its most common use to date. Some object to eating foods that have been genetically modified, concerned that we do not really know whether they are different from other foods in terms of their potential effects on human health. The industry argues that food from GM plants is the same as food that is produced from seeds that are selectively bred in other ways.

Another concern is the possible effects of GM crops on the natural word. There is some evidence, for example, that some insect-resistant GM crops can harm butterflies as well as other insects. Generally, there are also questions as to whether introduced traits can, in some cases, spread into the wild within other, related plant species. It is clear that GM crops can intermingle with non-GM crops in adjacent fields.

This latter fact has very great ethical implications, since to the extent that this is the case it becomes very difficult to label accurately GM versus GM-free foods such as grains or soybeans. Is there a right to know regarding the consumption of GM crops? Should foods be labeled as GMO free? Does such labeling not seem appropriate even if one assumes that there is no health implication associated with human consumption? That is, do people concerned about possible environmental effects of GMOs not have a right as consumers to avoid consuming and thereby supporting the production of such crops (see Andree 2008)?

There has been stronger opposition to GMOs in Europe than in the United States, and this has in turn led to trade disputes regarding the importation of potentially "contaminated" (intermingled) crops. There is perhaps even stronger opposition to the genetic modification of animals, especially those that could readily escape into the wild, such as farmed fish genetically modified to grow rapidly and to a larger size. At the same time, many argue for the potential of genetic modification, especially of crop plants, in order to create plants that are more tolerant of heat or drought (which may increase with climate change) or what are increasingly common saline growing conditions that have resulted from irrigation practices. Clearly, these issues pose considerable challenges for both ethicists and regulators.

There are at least three ethical dilemmas related to climate change. The first is that the worst impacts of climate change fall on nations that did not contribute significantly to creating the problem. These include low-lying nations like Bangladesh, small island-nations faced with rising sea levels, the far North, and dry regions, including North Africa. Second, there is an ongoing tension between the need for economic growth in poor nations, nations where millions remain hungry, and the need to reduce the consumption of fossil fuels globally. Third is the question of how to fairly determine appropriate greenhouse gas emissions for each nation—should only current and future current per capita emissions be considered, or should historical total emissions be taken into account, and, if the latter, how? Historical emitters did not know the problem they were creating at the time they created it, but they did benefit economically in ways that carry forward to today.

Vanderheiden, in his discussion of the moral elements of resolving global climate change, describes two possible methods for determining the obligations of those whose past per capita emissions have been low. One way to resolve this dilemma is to determine a safe level of total emissions, including historical emissions, per capita, and allocate that amount globally to nations based on population. A second method would calculate a basic minimum a person would be "allowed to emit in order to meet their basic human needs and to which all persons would therefore be entitled as a matter of basic rights, even if the world's population producing GHGs at this rate would still contribute to the increasing atmospheric concentrations that cause climate change" (Vanderheiden 2008, 72).

Clearly, however the matter is resolved, lower historical emissions should not determine current emissions if the formula is impossible for high historical emitters to meet in a timely enough way to avoid catastrophic outcomes. The rate of increase of emissions in nations like China, India, and other fast-growing economies suggests that that could be the case. It is little wonder that global cooperation on climate change has been limited thus far and will not be easily achieved in the future. It will not be easy to find emissions allocation rules that are both sufficient and fair—but finding the ethically and practically best approximation is essential and urgent.

9. SUMMARY AND CONCLUSION

Public policy is about advancing some human values and limiting others. We cannot avoid making such choices, even if we are not fully aware of the many ways in which public policy initiatives (or the lack thereof) cause us to make them. It is a basic premise of democracy that the prospects of outcomes that are preferred by more people are advanced by discussions that face up to an open consideration of both facts and the core values of concerned citizens. Environmental policy, in particular, needs to be thought of and discussed in terms of ethical choices.

This chapter has argued that from the very beginnings of environmental policy ethical issues have been front and center, beginning at first with consideration of the human need for wilderness and the survival needs of nonhuman species. Such concerns have become more complex as ecological science has advanced. As environmental ethics has developed and become more widely debated policy, discussions have proceeded to a consideration of environmental rights and the relationship between such rights and such fundamental matters as global inequality, environmental justice, and rights to property, both common and private. Finally, in recent years a new focus has developed around the ethical dimensions of two very important emerging environmental policy issues: climate change and genetically modified organisms.

Achieving environmental protection through public policy is essential to human well-being, but there are possible costs in terms of other human values. The best way to maximize protection, while minimizing those costs, is to think carefully about what we value most and why.

REFERENCES

Adams, M. L. 1983. "Right to Know: A Summary." *Alternatives: Perspectives on Society and Environment* 11 (3/4): 29–36.

African Charter of Human and Peoples' Rights. 1981. Available at www.hrcr.org/docs/Banjul/afrhr.html; accessed April 25, 2012.

Andree, P. 2008. *Genetically Modified Diplomacy: The Global Politics of Agricultural Biotechnology and the Environment.* Seattle: University of Washington Press.

Andrews, R. N. L. 1999. *Managing the Environment, Managing Ourselves.* New Haven, CT: Yale University Press.

Armstrong, H. B. J., ed. 1963. *Armstrong's Norfolk Diary.* London: Hodder & Stoughton.

Bullard, R. 1997. *Just Transportation: Dismantling Race and Class Barriers to Mobility.* Gabriola Island, BC: New Society.

———. 2000. *Dumping in Dixie: Race, Class and Environmental Quality.* Boulder: Westview.

Carley, M., and P. Spapens. 1998. *Sharing the World: Sustainable Living and Global Equity in the 21st Century.* London: Earthscan.

Clapp, J. 2010. *Toxic Exports: The Transfer of Hazardous Wastes from Rich to Poor Nations.* Ithaca, NY: Cornell University Press.

Hardin, G. 1968. "The Tragedy of the Commons." *Science* 162 (859): 1243–1248.

Hayward, T. 2005. *Constitutional Environmental Rights.* New York: Oxford University Press.

Herrick, F. H., ed. 2006. *John James Audubon: Delineations of American Scenery and Character.* Whitefish, MT: Kessinger.

Hurley, A. 1997. "Fiasco at Wagner Electric: Environmental Justice and Urban Geography in St. Louis." *Environmental History* 2: 460–481.

Jones, V. 2009. *The Green Collar Economy: How One Solution Can Fix Our Two Biggest Problems.* New York: HarperOne.

Kraft, M. E., M. Stephan, and T. D. Abel. 2011. *Coming Clean: Information Disclosure and Environmental Performance.* Cambridge, MA: MIT Press.

Marsh, G. P. 1965. *Man and Nature: Physical Geography as Modified by Human Action.* Cambridge, MA: Harvard University Press.

Marshall, T. H., and T. Bottomore. 1992. *Citizenship and Social Class.* London: Pluto.

Maser, C. 1990. *The Redesigned Forest.* Toronto: Stoddart.

McNamee, T. 2008. *Alice Waters and Chez Panisse.* New York: Penguin.

Miller, C. 2004. *Gifford Pinchot and the Making of Modern Environmentalism.* Washington, DC: Island.

Newman, P., and J. Kenworthy. 1989. *Cities and Automobile Dependence: An International Sourcebook.* Hants, UK: Gower.

O'Leary, R. 2010. "Environmental Policy in the Courts." In *Environmental Policy: New Directions for the Twenty-First Century,* ed. M. E. Kraft and N. J. Vig., 125–146. Washington, DC: CQ Press.

Ostrom, E. 1990. *Governing the Commons: The Evolution of Institutions for Collective Action.* New York: Cambridge University Press.

Ostrom, E., and C. Hess, eds. 2006. *Understanding Knowledge as a Commons: From Theory to Practice.* Cambridge, MA: MIT Press.

Paehlke, R. 1989. *Environmentalism and the Future of Progressive Politics.* New Haven, CT: Yale University Press.

———. 1990. "Democracy and Environmentalism: Opening a Door to the Administrative State." In *Managing Leviathan: Environmental Politics and the Administrative State,* ed. R. Paehlke and D. Torgerson, 35–55. Peterborough, ON: Broadview.

———. 1998. "Work in a Sustainable Society." In *Political Ecology: Global and Local,* ed. R. Keil, D. V. J. Bell, P. Penz, and L. Fawcett, 272–291. New York: Routledge.

————. 1999. "Towards Defining, Measuring and Achieving Sustainability: Tools and Strategies for Environmental Valuation." In *Sustainability and the Social Sciences*, ed. E. Becker and T. Jahn, 243–263. New York: Zed Books.

Pyne, S. J. 2001. *Fire: A Brief History.* Seattle: University of Washington Press.

Raymond, L. 2003. *Private Rights in Public Resources: Equity and Property Allocation in Market-Based Environmental Policy.* Washington, DC: Resources for the Future.

Ringquist, E. J. 1997. "Environmental Justice: Normative Concerns and Empirical Evidence." In *Environmental Policy in the 1990s*, ed. N. J. Vig and M. E. Kraft, 231–254. Washington, DC: CQ Press.

Schlosberg, D. 2009. *Defining Environmental Justice: Themes, Movements and Nature.* New York: Oxford University Press.

Teale, E. W., ed. 1954. *The Wilderness World of John Muir.* Boston: Houghton Mifflin.

Thoreau, H. D. 1851. "The Wild: Lecture Given at the Concord Lyceum." April 23. Available at www.thoreau.eserver.org/walking.html (accessed April 26, 2012).

Tobin, R. J. 2010. "Environment, Population and the Developing World." In *Environmental Policy: New Directions for the Twenty-First Century*, ed. M. E. Kraft and N. J. Vig, 286–307. Washington, DC: CQ Press.

Vanderheiden, S. 2008. *Atmospheric Justice: A Political Theory of Climate Change.* New York: Oxford University Press.

Visser, D. R., and G. A. Mendoza 1994. "Debt-for-Nature Swaps in Latin America." *Journal of Forestry* 92 (6): 13–16.

White, L. 1967. "The Historic Roots of Our Ecologic Crisis." *Science* 155: 1203–1207.

World Commission on Environment and Development. 1987. *Our Common Future.* New York: Oxford University Press.

Yaffee, S. L. 1994. *The Wisdom of the Spotted Owl: Policy Lessons for a New Century.* Washington, DC: Island.

CHAPTER 6

ENVIRONMENTAL SECURITY AND U.S. POLITICS

RICHARD A. MATTHEW

IN the context of international relations, the term "security" denotes a distinctive domain of theory and practice. Throughout the twentieth century there was broad agreement in the United States that at the core of this domain were the paramount issues of war and the use of military power, an agreement virtually guaranteed insofar as security studies had emerged as a field of intellectual inquiry and policy support in direct response to the unprecedented scale of damage and suffering that occurred during World War I and again in World War II. However, as is the case with many domains of theory and practice, from the outset the boundaries of "security studies" were contested.

For example, Barry Buzan (1983) inspired the so-called Copenhagen School of Security Studies to develop around his argument for integrating issues such as poverty and pollution into the field of security studies. The rationale behind this suggestion was that there are many things that threaten people and states, and all of these should be studied as security issues. Moreover, for Buzan, the way governments attach themselves to certain threats, and the ways in which fear and secrecy can be used to mobilize financial and political support for specific defense and foreign policies, are also important issues for the field to address. Buzan's work exemplifies a vibrant tradition of critique of the dominant understanding of the purpose of "security studies."

This type of critique engendered many thoughtful responses. For example, in his influential 1991 review of the evolution of security studies, Stephen Walt endorsed the conventional or "realist" view of the field as the study of war and military power. He argued for limiting its expansion to issues such as "arms control" and "crisis management" that "are clearly relevant to the main focus of the field, because they bear directly on the likelihood and character of war" (Walt 1991, 213). While acknowledging that poverty and pollution are indeed among the many forces that threaten human well-being and survival, Walt counters that "defining the [academic] field in this way would destroy its intellectual coherence and make it more difficult to devise solutions to any of these important problems" (1991, 213). For Walt, a narrow definition creates the conditions for high-quality, cumulative research. Of course, critics of the narrow perspective can in turn argue that realist scholarship could be viewed as often little more than a well-rewarded endorsement of defense policy.

How security is defined has important implications. For example, realists are fully aware that war and the use of military power are matters of great importance to state governments. In the United States, defense spending has been a significant percentage of gross domestic product (GDP) for the past century; in 2010, for example, it was about 6.7 percent. This type of economic leverage translates into considerable support for research in the field of security studies, and it also creates significant employment opportunities in government and consulting firms for PhDs with a security focus. Moreover, the availability of public research funding and the opportunities to consult or spend some time in government also create powerful incentives to carry out research that can be applied, distinguishing this domain from most other arts and social science disciplines and subfields. The narrow definition preferred by Walt and others facilitates and reinforces this close and rewarding relationship; the critical approach of Buzan poses more of a challenge to it. There are costs and benefits associated with both perspectives, which may be why they persist.

Environmental security has emerged in the context of this perennial debate and has come to embody it. Some of its critics raise concerns about the potential risks of linking the environment to the high politics of war, military power, and secrecy (Deudney 1990). They would prefer strengthening linkages to the low politics of economic cooperation, to the epistemic communities forged by natural science, to emerging issues of justice and ethics, to development theory and practice, and to questions about group identity and behavior. Other critics of the term believe introducing the language of environmental change could weaken the intellectual platform that realist scholars have carefully crafted since World War I, a platform that they believe has brought greater methodological rigor and a clearer theoretical identity into the field (Walt 1991).

In contrast, advocates of the term "environmental security" tend to agree with the sentiment of Buzan that security studies should focus on the various forces that truly endanger people at different levels of social organization, and scholars should also examine how understandings of threat are generated, funded, and operationalized throughout the world. Further, some environmental security experts are worried that certain modalities of global environmental change, such as biodiversity loss and climate change, may actually be, or at least have the potential to become, existential threats to countries and even possibly to humankind itself. For these analysts, reproducing a twentieth-century worldview that in some grave sense is out of sync with twenty-first-century world reality is rather sentimental, unproductive, and even irresponsible. Put simply, they believe we need more research support for and policy attention to the emerging threat of climate change than to the diminishing threat of world war.

This chapter provides a brief overview of the multifaceted subfield of "environmental security." I discuss the historical factors driving the consolidation and growth of this subfield, summarize some of its key findings, assess its policy impact, and outline areas of future research productivity. As appropriate, I summarize major criticisms of the field. My principal focus throughout is on research and policy activity in the United States.

As noted in the introduction to this volume, "In order to understand fully the modern evolution of the literature on U.S. environmental politics and policy, one needs to take into account the political and policy contexts in which major studies were conducted." The consolidation of the subfield of "environmental security," the policy activity that scholars in this subfield have examined and often endorsed, and the concerns that have been raised about the risks of situating environmental change in the context of security have in large measure been a response to the convergence of the Rio worldview and the end of the Cold War in the early 1990s. Scholars and policy makers working at this intersection of a dramatic rethinking of both our relationship to the natural environment and our understandings of security that were so robust in the decades after World War II, have very explicitly sought to define a worldview appropriate to the post–Cold War era. For the United States, this task has had a particular urgency as it has sought to redefine its role in world affairs. While the literature has many imperfections, it also has much vitality and vision and is likely to continue to be a critical part of discussions about security and security policy in the years ahead.

1. The Roots of Environmental Security

Just as the boundaries around fields of inquiry are often unstable and contested, so are the histories of these fields open to debate and disagreement. In *The Upside of Down* (2006), Thomas Homer-Dixon makes a compelling case for explaining the dramatic collapse of Rome in the fifth century BC in terms of energy scarcity. As classical Rome grew, he argues, it required more energy, especially in the forms of food, fodder, and slaves, all of which it had to import. The cost of importing energy mounted steadily as the Romans had to search farther and farther afield, and the time arrived when the abundant, cheap, and reliable energy imports a large and bustling Rome required ceased to be available. Its weaknesses soon became evident to the hinterland peoples it had been exploiting, and it suddenly became the target of their anger, was invaded and sacked, and collapsed into ruins. For Homer-Dixon, the rise and fall of societies often is closely tied to their access to energy. Hence, in today's world, in which the demand for energy threatens to move beyond affordable supplies, and high prices could have dramatic effects in large parts of Africa, the Middle East, and South Asia that are struggling to develop economically, we might soon see societal breakdowns around the planet (see also Diamond 1994, 2004).

The roots of environmental security can be found in past events such as the collapse of Rome. They also can be found in the writings of thinkers stretching back over millennia. Both Thucydides's *The Peloponnesian War* and Plato's *Republic*, for example, can be interpreted as discussions about the relative strengths and weaknesses of societies living within their limits, like Sparta, compared to those that must draw in resources from abroad, like Athens (Matthew 2002). In both cases, the authors conclude that self-sufficient, minimalist societies may be less dramatic and exciting but are better suited to longevity and stability. One could trace this line of thinking through the ages, lingering on thinkers such as the eighteenth-century demographer Thomas Malthus, who argued that human populations would grow faster than their agricultural output, leading to a host of negative social outcomes such as famines, epidemics, and wars.

Deep roots confer on ideas a certain type of credibility that is much valued in social science, and this type of historicization of a concept can be both educational and entertaining. At the same time, it is important to note that the collapse of Rome and the writings of Plato and Thucydides have been interpreted in many different ways. There is always the risk that we see in the past what we want to see in the past. It is sufficient for the purposes of this chapter, however, simply to note that both analyses of past events and past scholarship have suggested that forms of environmental stress may well have had important security implications throughout human history. But, while perhaps partly indebted to the insights and experiences of earlier generations, the large and growing body of research on environmental security that has been carried out over the past two decades has been shaped in large measure by recent trends and events. It can be organized into three waves (Levy 1995a).

1.1 Wave One

The first wave of environmental security thinking emerged in the 1960s and 1970s in response to concerns about population growth and pollution, about the control of oil prices by the Organization of the Petroleum Exporting Countries (OPEC), and about the military use of defoliants and herbicides such as Agent Orange and the even more unsettling prospect of a nuclear winter. The writings of people like Rachel Carson (*Silent Spring*, 1962), Lynn White Jr. ("The Historical Roots of Our

Ecological Crisis," 1967), Garrett Hardin ("The Tragedy of the Commons," 1968), Paul Ehrlich (*The Population Bomb*, 1968), and Donella Meadows et al. (*The Limits to Growth*, 1972), combined to produce a compelling Malthusian worldview. The government response in the United States was to establish the Environmental Protection Agency and enact legislation to ensure clean air, both in 1970, and then to enact the Clean Water Act in 1972. Also in 1972, over 100 countries gathered in Stockholm for the first UN Conference on the Human Environment, and the United States agreed to provide funds to create the UN Environment Programme in Nairobi, Kenya.

Environmental concerns became explicitly linked to national security following OPEC's decision in 1973 to impose an oil embargo in response to U.S. support for Israel during the Yom Kippur War. During this period, a different type of security concern emerged as evidence of the effects of using Agent Orange in Vietnam became public. By the late 1970s Lester Brown (1977) was describing environmental degradation as a security issue, and Richard Ullman (1983) argued for a broadening of the concept of security to include issues like pollution. These largely conceptual and pioneering arguments occupied the fringes of the field of security studies, which through the 1980s remained focused on the Cold War and the possibility of a nuclear exchange.

1.2 Wave Two

A second wave of environmental security thinking was driven by two overlapping events. First, during the period 1987–1992, the publication of *Our Common Future* (1987) and the subsequent Rio Summit on Environment and Development, held in 1992, made the case for a global commitment to sustainable development as the most viable pathway for harmonizing economic goals and environmental limits. The Malthusian view of the late 1960s was reiterated, with more scientific support, as the likely consequence of expanding economic development that plundered and destroyed the natural environment. Chernobyl was seen by many as a case of unbridled development leading to massive environmental damage. Second, at the same time as global concern for environmental change mounted dramatically, the Cold War came to an end, and by the early 1990s the U.S. security community was focused on identifying the likely threats and vulnerabilities of the post–Cold War era.

This second wave of environmental security thinking developed along three distinct but interactive trajectories. One group of scholars worked on redefining the term "security," seeking to replace the definition of security that was dominant during the twentieth century and focused on communist expansion and a nuclear world war with something more reflective of the threats to survival and well-being that people and states faced now (Barnett 2001; Deudney and Matthew 1999; Matthew, Halle and Switzer 2002; Myers 1993; United Nations Development Programme [UNDP] 1994). The rationale for integrating concern about environmental change into a modified understanding of security was facilitated by the Rio Summit, which mobilized world attention around climate change, biodiversity loss, and deforestation; emphasized the importance of developing conservation strategies at all levels of human organization; and introduced the world-transformative paradigm of sustainable development. This also dovetailed perfectly with the effort of the security community itself to determine whether the twin threats of nuclear war and communist expansion had diminished enough to allow for a reconfiguring of national security strategy—and perhaps for the reallocation of some defense funds to other issue areas. This line of inquiry was reinforced by evidence that interstate war was declining and that, at the close of the twentieth century, violent conflict was typically a form of civil war that often was long-lasting and difficult to end decisively, even with high levels of military power (Collier 2000a, b, 2007). Some analysts began to expand their understanding of threat to include variables such as economic crisis and infectious disease, and even devised and developed alternative frameworks for thinking about security, such as the UNDP's 1994 concept of "human security" (Matthew et al. 2010; UNDP 1994).

Another group of scholars who shaped the second wave of environmental security was less concerned with rethinking security and, instead, examined ways in which environmental change might contribute to traditional security issues such as war (Bannon and Collier 2003; de Soysa and Gleditsch 1999; Diamond 1994; Gleick 1993; Homer-Dixon 1991, 1999; Kahl 2006; Klare 2001; World Commission on Environment and Development 1987). These neo-Malthusian scholars are perhaps less conceptual and more empirical, employing large-N and case study methodologies to make their arguments. Through this work, they have described processes through which both scarce (water, farmland) and high-value (diamonds, oil) natural resources may become important variables in social outcomes such as government corruption, underdevelopment, population displacement, and violent conflict.

A third group of researchers seized on the access to information enabled by the end of the Cold War to measure the ecological footprints of war and other military activities, to assess the toxic legacy of the Cold War, and to promote base cleanup, respect for national and international environmental laws, military-to-military collaboration in decommissioning nuclear facilities and disposing of nuclear materials, and environmentally sensitive land management by the military (Butts 1993, 1994, 1996).

1.3 Wave Three

Finally, a third wave of environmental security thinking has appeared in the past few years as a response to climate science, and especially to the 2007 Intergovernmental Panel on Climate Change (IPCC) reports. Climate scientists have observed significant changes in the distribution of water across the planet's surface, increases in the intensity of storms and other severe weather events, longer heat waves and droughts, gradual sea-level rise, and, related to this, aggressive flooding. Some prominent climate scientists have voiced a concern that if the current trend in climate change is not modified, the planet might breach critical thresholds, triggering rare and extreme phenomena, or "black swan" events, such as massive gas releases, rapid glaciation, and microbial explosions. In response, social scientists have imagined many ways in which climate change might generate threats to human and national security (Barnett and Adger 2007; Buhaug et al. 2008; Brown et al. 2007; Campbell 2008; CNA 2007; Maas and Taenzler 2009; Matthew 2011; Matthew and Hammill 2012; Raleigh and Urdal 2007; Sachs 2005; Smith 2004; Smith and Vivekananda 2007; Stern 2007; Urdal 2008; Walt 2009).

2. RESEARCH FINDINGS

What insights have been generated by five decades of research? In this section I organize the field of environmental security under distinct subheadings and discuss the research findings within each area.

2.1 Environment and Violent Conflict

The research that has captured the attention of the largest audience has been carried out over the last twenty years. The best-known work has focused on the ways in which environmental variables might contribute to traditional security concerns such as violent conflict. In particular, the work of Homer-Dixon (1991, 1999, 2000, 2006) gained considerable attention during the 1990s, when he led a team of researchers that studied the social effects of scarcities of water, cropland, and pasture. This research tested the theory that when vital natural resources become scarce in developing countries, the social effects may be very violent. Homer-Dixon identified two negative social effects: resource capture, in which one group seizes control of a resource on which others depend, and ecological marginalization, in which some people are displaced into resource-poor lands. Both of these outcomes may trigger, amplify, or prolong violent conflict. Research by Colin Kahl (2006) developed this theory further by linking resource scarcity to state failure (the collapse of functional capacity and social cohesion) and to state exploitation (when a collapsing state acts to preserve itself by giving greater access to natural resources to groups it believes can prop it up).

A related concern explores ways in which environmental stress might affect adversely elements of national power. National power is usually understood as the product of several variables, including geography and resource endowment; military assets; intelligence-gathering and analysis capacity; population size and cohesiveness; regime type; and the size and productivity of the national economy. Environmental change has the potential to affect adversely any of the basic elements of national power. As I observe elsewhere, "For example, militaries may be less effective at projecting and exercising power if they have to operate in flooded terrain or during a heat wave. Warming that affects land cover could reduce a country's renewable resource base. Intelligence is difficult to gather and analyze in a domain marked by uncertainty about social effects" (Matthew 2011, 55).

Another dimension of this research strand has focused on what happens to the environment during war. This issue has two dimensions: first, natural resources are often plundered during a war to enrich people willing to benefit from lawless conditions or to fund combatants, either of which can extend the war; and second, the environment can be damaged by the war itself. This includes direct damage such as the burning of plantations, the poisoning of water sources and laying of land mines, and indirect damage due to a disruption of environmental data gathering and government enforcement, or the displacement of people into protected or fragile environments (United National Environment Programme [UNEP] 2009). Important work has been carried out by organizations such as Global Witness, which provides reliable case-by-case information about how resources such as diamonds, timber, ivory, and gold have been exploited illegally during wars and also used to fund war itself. In regard to environmental damage caused by war, UNEP's Post-Conflict and Disasters Branch has conducted over thirty assessments since the early 1990s, when it undertook its first assessment in Bosnia, and it has become the world's primary source of this type of data.

Finally, important work has also explored the ways in which conservation practices could contribute to conflict. Based on extensive research in the Great Lakes region of Africa, Anne Hammill and her coauthors argue that conservation and conflict are closely linked, and they identify three ways in which conservation can contribute to conflict: (1) by restricting access to key livelihood resources—for example, creating a protected area where people once had access to natural resources; (2) by introducing economic burdens and risks into a community—for example, protecting wild animals that might eat nearby crops; and (3) by leading to an unequal distribution of the benefits of conservation—for example, hiring a few local people to work in protected areas (2009, 3).

Not all analysts are persuaded that these arguments and findings are compelling or typical, and Homer-Dixon in particular has been criticized on methodological grounds (Levy 1995b). But the arguments of Homer-Dixon, Kahl, and others have stimulated considerable research activity, found strong support among some social scientists, and informed policy activity (Hanson et al. 2011; Hauge and Ellingsen 1998). For example, twenty years after Homer-Dixon's first article, Thor Hanson and his coauthors argued that "over 90 percent of the major armed conflicts between 1950 and 2000 occurred within countries containing biodiversity hotspots, and more than 80 percent took place directly within hotspot areas" (2011, 578).

2.2 Environment and Human Security

Inspired by the UNDP's 1994 annual report, research has been undertaken around the world on how environmental change affects human security. In the UNDP report, human security "was said to have two main aspects. It means, first, safety from such chronic threats as hunger, disease and repression. And second, it means protection from sudden and harmful disruptions in the patterns of daily life" (1994, 23). The authors of the report described four key dimensions of human security: it is universal, its components are interdependent, it is easier to protect through prevention than intervention, and it is people-centered (1994, 22). In response to this report, in 1997 a group of scholars established the Global Environmental Change and Human Security program. Led by Stephen Lonergan, they defined human security "as something that is achieved when and where individuals and communities have the options necessary to end, mitigate or adapt to threats to their human, environmental and social rights; have the capacity and freedom to exercise these options; and actively participate in pursuing these options" (GECHS Science Plan 1999, 29).

Many of the findings generated through this program were included in *Global Environmental Change and Human Security* (Matthew et al. 2010). In that volume, for example, Mike Brklacich, May Chazan, Hans-Georg Bohle, and Victoria Basolo examine the ways in which environmental change can increase the vulnerability of certain communities to natural disasters. Bryan McDonald makes a similar argument about vulnerability to infectious disease. Karen O'Brien, Robin Leichenko, Laura Little, and Chris Cocklin explore the relationships between equity and vulnerability to the adverse effects of global environmental change. Jon Barnett and Neil Adger argue that environmental change can increase human insecurity, which in turn can increase the likelihood of violent conflict. The analytical perspective that unifies this body of work is grounded in a concern for the differential way in which global environmental change, which is largely a product of the consumption patterns of the wealthiest quintile of humankind, filters through a web of inequality evident in institutions and practices around the world, to affect adversely the poor and the marginalized—those who often are least responsible for the global scale of the problem, and least able to adapt and respond to its impacts.

2.3 Environment and Peace

At the end of the Cold War, the United Nations developed the concept and practice of "peacebuilding." Today it is typically thought of as a 5- to 10-year process designed and implemented after the peacemaking (i.e., diplomatic efforts to broker a peace agreement) and peacekeeping (i.e., the dispatch of military forces to monitor and implement a peace agreement) missions, although the boundaries separating the three phases of the peace process are not in any sense inflexible and tend to overlap. During the peacebuilding phase, the United Nations focuses on building capacity in areas that are critical to sustainable peace and development, where it has expertise, and that are not being carried out by another organization such as the World Bank or the U.S. Agency for International Development (USAID). UN peace-building activities might include providing basic security; building the capacity of the national government and civil society; encouraging socioeconomic recovery and growth; and addressing the conditions, attitudes, and actions that drive violent conflict, in order to prevent its recurrence (OECD 2007; UNEP 2009).

Peacebuilding is about both identifying and addressing immediate needs, developing a plan for national reconstruction, and generating the technical and other capacities needed to achieve this. In recent years, natural resources have been identified as critical to many aspects of the peacebuilding process (Conca and Dabelko 2002; UNEP 2009; Weinthal 2004). They are needed to support economic recovery and to serve as the platform for sustainable livelihoods. Their management can contribute to multiple forms of dialogue, cooperation, and confidence building (UNEP 2009, 13). Considerable empirical evidence suggests that failing to integrate natural resource management (and perhaps climate change adaptation) into peace-building operations and national reconstruction plans can undermine security and development efforts and exacerbate conditions that contribute to violent conflict. It is therefore critical that postconflict societies, which typically have resource-based economies, acquire the technical and legal capacity to manage natural resources sustainably and cope with the additional stress of climate change impacts.

Since the 2009 UNEP report, natural resource management has been formally integrated into peacebuilding operations in Sierra Leone and is poised to become a critical feature of all future peacebuilding operations. Guidance on integrating environmental factors into peacekeeping, and climate change adaptation and miti-gation into peacebuilding, are in preparation. Finally, another promising dimen-sion of the relationship between the environment and peace focuses on the benefits of establishing peace parks in areas of conflict (Ali 2007).

2.4 Climate Change and Security

Research linking environmental change to national and human security has served as a platform for exploring the security implications of climate change, especially since the publication of the 2007 IPCC working group reports. Climate science has identified statistically significant changes in the distribution of fresh-water, increases in the frequency and intensity of severe weather events, longer heat waves, longer droughts, and sea-level rise and flooding (IPCC 2007a). Some scientists have predicted that climate change will move the planet across critical thresholds, causing events such as sudden extinctions (IPCC 2007b; Wilson 1999).

In terms of threats to human security, the 2009 report of the International Federation of the Red Cross and Red Crescent Societies (IFRC 2009) argues that

> the threat of disaster resulting from climate change is twofold. First, individual extreme events will devastate vulnerable communities in their path. If population

growth is factored in, many more people may be at significant risk. Together, these events add up to potentially the most significant threat to human progress that the world has seen. Second, climate change will compound the already complex problems of poor countries, and could contribute to a downward development spiral for millions of people, even greater than has already been experienced. (2009: 95)

Existential threats are also emerging for the Maldives and some 40 other island states that could disappear under rising seas. Glacial outburst floods could cause similar devastation in countries such as Nepal and Bhutan, and a change in the ocean conveyer could even cause developed countries such as the United Kingdom to disappear under several feet of ice within a few years.

Against this backdrop, many experts have argued that climate change could amplify the environment-conflict linkage identified by Homer-Dixon and others. In 2006, for example, Sir Nicholas Stern estimated that as many as 200 million people could be displaced by rising sea levels, massive flooding, and droughts by the middle of the twenty-first century. The authors of the CNA Corporation's publication *National Security and the Threat of Climate Change* concluded that "climate change acts as a threat multiplier for instability in some of the most volatile regions of the world" (2007, 6). Further, they predicted that "projected climate change will add to tensions even in stable regions of the world" (2007, 7). Similarly, the German Advisory Council on Global Change's report *World in Transition: Climate Change as a Security Risk* argued that "climate change will overstretch many societies' adaptive capacities within the coming decades" (2008, 1). Analysts throughout North America and Europe have worried that climate change will add enormous stress to states that are already fragile, bolster violent conflict, increase population displacement, heighten vulnerability to disasters, and undermine development and poverty alleviation programs (Campbell 2008). Most at risk, these experts contend, are countries in South Asia, the Middle East, and sub-Saharan Africa, where vast populations of poor people and their shaky governments are ill-equipped to manage the effects of flood and drought. Of course, there has also been some well-conceived criticism of these hastily assembled, headline-grabbing claims. Henrik Urdal, for example, contends that the "potential for and challenges related to migration spurred by climate change should be acknowledged, but not overemphasized. Some forms of environmental change associated with climate change like extreme weather and flooding may cause substantial and acute, but mostly temporal, displacement of people. However, the most dramatic form of change expected to affect human settlements, sea-level rise, is likely to happen gradually, as are processes of soil and freshwater degradation" (2008, 5).

3. ENVIRONMENTAL SECURITY AND U.S. POLICY

The three waves of environmental security research can be linked to three distinct periods of policy activity.

3.1 Wave One: Strong U.S. Leadership

As noted earlier, in the 1960s and 1970s environmental change was linked to security in the writings by Paul Ehrlich, Garrett Hardin, Donella Meadows, and others. The policy response to these bleak assessments and Malthusian predictions
was remarkably forceful and in many ways created models that were emulated
throughout the world, such as the U.S. Environmental Protection Agency and the
Clean Air Act and Clean Water Act.

   Another important stream of policy emerged in response to concerns about military management of land, military use of defoliants and herbicides, and estimates of
the environmental impact of nuclear war. Department of Defense (DOD) Directive
5100.50, "Protection and Enhancement of Environmental Quality," was issued in 1973.
The United States also signed and ratified two important international agreements:
the Additional Protocol I to the 1949 Geneva Convention on the Protection of Victims
of International Armed Conflicts (1977) and the Convention on the Prohibition of
Military or Any Other Hostile Use of Environmental Modification Techniques (1977).
During the Reagan administration, Congress established the Defense Environmental
Restoration Account to help cover the costs of decontaminating military sites. In general, however, the high level of policy attention given to the environment in the 1970s,
driven to some degree by security concerns, diminished dramatically in the 1980s.
Nonetheless, a very strong platform for environmental assessment, rescue, and management was created during this period of American leadership.

3.2 Wave Two: Strong Start, Weak Finish in the Early Post–
Cold War Era

When President Bill Clinton assumed office in January 1993, security policy
experts were thinking through the implications of the end of the Cold War and
digesting the voluminous output from the Rio Earth Summit—which included the
Rio Declaration, *Agenda 21*, the Framework Convention on Climate Change, and
the Convention on Biological Diversity. (See also chapters 10 and 11 in this book.)
At that time President Clinton, as well as Vice President Al Gore, appeared very
supportive of the promise of Rio and made concern for the environment a priority
of their administration. Moreover, as they sought to make sense of, and orient U.S.
policy on, the first post–Cold War crises, such as Somalia, Haiti, and Rwanda, they
were influenced by the emerging literature linking environmental stress to violent
conflict and state failure (this is discussed in Durant 2007 and Floyd 2010).

   The end of the Cold War created an obvious need to rethink security policy and
defense spending. Part of the Clinton-Gore response to this need was to scale up the
integration of environment and national security around the arguments of thinkers like Homer-Dixon. To assist with this integration, Eileen Claussen, former head
of atmospheric programs at the EPA, was appointed special assistant to the president for global environmental affairs at the National Security Council. Claussen

assisted Secretary of Defense Les Aspin, and later Secretary of Defense William Perry, in creating four new offices at the undersecretary level. One of these was the Undersecretary of Defense for Acquisition and Technology (USDAT), which included the new Office of the Deputy Undersecretary of Defense for Environmental Security (DUSDES), headed by Sherri Goodman. It was in this office that concerns about environmental stress and national security were articulated and promoted.

Robert Durant has described Goodman's objective as "to align corporate structures, processes, and procedures better with greening strategies by enhancing civilian ENR [environmental and natural resources] control, by redressing inadequate management systems critical to greening, and by creating parallel decision structures to ensure a role for greening proponents in readiness and weapons system decisions" (2007, 69). This focus on civilian participation, however, upset many military professionals, who quickly found ways to work around or undermine Goodman's office (Durant 2007, 73). It also found advocates within the military who saw this linkage as offering opportunities to develop new forms of military-to-military collaboration, improve DOD's public image by speeding up base cleanup and improving land management, and become conversant with an unprecedented threat system (Butts 1993, 1994, 1996).

Results were generally mixed. Here, one can see the gridlock created when opposing perspectives clash inside the Beltway. For example, on the issue of base cleanup, DOD battled with the White House and Congress on issues of assessment and funding, so progress remained slow. However, some new initiatives were quite successful. For example, Secretary of Defense Perry's doctrine of "preventative defense" included using environmental security to expand military-to-military contact programs and hence to promote regional security through cooperation. DOD worked with Russian counterparts on decommissioning nuclear subs and disposing of nuclear materials, and it worked with Sweden to develop environmental standards for military training and operations.

Vice President Gore took the lead on several related initiatives, such as establishing the Medea Group under the National Intelligence Council (NIC) in 1992, to explore how archived satellite images collected by the intelligence community might be of value to environmental experts. The Director of Central Intelligence Environmental Center was created as a bridge between the two. Gore also commissioned the State Failure Task Force and requested that it focus particular attention on environmental factors.

The Clinton administration also acted to integrate the concept of environmental security into the Department of State. In April 1996, Secretary of State Warren Christopher announced that "the environment has a profound impact on our national interests in two ways: First, environmental forces transcend borders and oceans to threaten directly the health, prosperity and jobs of American citizens. Second, addressing natural resource issues is frequently critical to achieving political and economic stability, and to pursuing our strategic goals around the world." He added that "environmental initiatives can be important, low-cost, high-impact tools in promoting our national security interests" and set up an elaborate architecture of Environmental Opportunity Hubs around the world to support this vision (1998, 417).

Many of these new initiatives were overturned by President George Bush. The 2002 *National Security Strategy*, for example, was focused mainly on the threat of terrorism and made no mention of environmental security. There was a slight shift in response to Hurricane Katrina, however, and in 2006 the *National Security Strategy of the United States* contained a list of new challenges related to globalization that included *"environmental destruction, whether caused by human behavior or cataclysmic mega-disasters such as floods, hurricanes, earthquakes, or tsunamis. Problems of this scope may overwhelm the capacity of local authorities to respond, and may even overtax national militaries, requiring a larger international response....* These challenges are not traditional national security concerns, such as the conflict of arms or ideologies. But if left unaddressed they can threaten national security" (National Security Council 2006, 47, emphasis in original).

3.3 Wave Three: Policy Silence in Response to the 2007 IPCC Reports

As noted in a preceding section, the 2007 IPCC reports galvanized considerable speculation on the security implications of climate change. This has ranged from Stern's estimate of 200 million climate-displaced people by 2050, through the CNA Corporation's contention that "climate change acts as a threat multiplier for instability in some of the most volatile regions of the world" (2007: 6), to the German Advisory Council on Global Change's claim that "climate change will overstretch many societies' adaptive capacities within the coming decades" (2008: 1). These reports also galvanized considerable policy activity in many countries and in the United Nations. In the United Kingdom, for example, the Royal United Services Institute "has engaged with traditional security actors to increase their understanding of the implications of climate change for security. This dialogue has focused specifically on the potential for climate change to impact the geopolitical landscape and the types of operational responses that will be required from the Defence Community" (RUSI website 2011). Addressing security risks associated with climate change has become a priority of the United Kingdom's Department for International Development.

Similarly, the United Nations has taken the issue very seriously. In 2007, the United Nations Security Council (UNSC) discussed the potential impact of climate change on global peace and security. In July 2011, the UNSC devoted a special meeting to this issue at Germany's request. At this time (August 2011), the outcomes from this session are unclear: there appears to be agreement with the idea, but challenges in coordinating a common response. In 2009, the UN General Assembly adopted Resolution A/63/281, *Climate Change and Its Possible Security Implications*, as proposed by the Pacific Small Island Developing States. Also in 2009, the secretary general of the United Nations presented a report of the same name to the UN General Assembly. This report identified five potential links between climate change and security: (1) increasing human vulnerability; (2) slowing down, possibly reversing, economic and social development; (3) triggering responses that may increase risks of conflict; (4) causing statelessness; and (5) straining mechanisms of international cooperation. It also suggested that climate change adaptation and mitigation should be viewed as threat minimizers. Moreover, every agency in the United Nations has developed an assessment of the security implications of climate change in relation to its activities. UNEP is currently in the process of developing a guidance note for integrating climate change adaptation and mitigation into peacebuilding operations.

So far, however, there has been no policy movement on this front in the United States, apart from verbal support to the UN initiatives, a call for a clean energy standard in the 2011 State of the Nation address, and the March 2011 release of a document entitled *Blueprint for a Secure Energy Future*. Most analysts contend that little will happen as long as Congress, which authorizes funding, remains deeply divided on how to respond to climate change. Finally, the Obama administration also has not acted to restore any of the environmental security initiatives of the Clinton administration.

4. CONCLUSIONS

Is there a path forward for environmental security? I would suggest that four variables are important in this regard.

4.1 Public Perception

The first factor is public perception. The median American is concerned by the scientific data about environmental degradation and climate change, but she or he does not perceive an immediate threat on this front (Matthew et al. 2010). Political scientists often study the policy preferences of the median voter, and it appears that it is difficult for policy makers to deviate very far from median preferences (Matthew and Shambaugh 2005b). We know that the perceptions and preferences of the median voter can be empirically false (e.g., perceptions of increasing crime often are not supported by data) or at least tenuous, but this does not mean that they can be ignored. For those voters who regard environmental stress and climate change as slow-onset issues that rarely affect them directly and are very costly to redirect, the language of environmental security is unlikely to be very resonant with their fears and aspirations (Matthew and Shambaugh 2005a, 2005b). Perhaps a higher level of public proficiency in earth systems science would reduce this number, but the trend here is not encouraging.

4.2 Research Findings

More research can certainly improve understanding of the relationships between ecological and human systems, and can identify friction points and feedback loops.

Research on these relationships tends to have a disciplinary focus, and there is thus a great need to deepen the dialogue between the natural and social sciences. Without this, our understanding of the interactions between the two systems, of how they adapt or fail to adapt to changes in themselves and each other, will continue to be crude and of limited predictive value. Modeling techniques and quantitative research can help us assess the explanatory value of an environmental variable as opposed to a social one vis-à-vis a dependent variable such as violent conflict. More qualitative research helps us to trace processes in specific cases and, in its more philosophical expressions, may help us to pose important new questions or examine the world in important new ways. More research may assist us in understanding the entry points and leverage factors that have the potential to transform complex systems from conditions conducive to crisis and breakdown toward conditions of resilience, innovation, and sustainability. The conditions under which research findings catalyze behavioral change or policy innovation are quite opaque and also require further study. Areas where research could be productive and of interest to the broader practitioner community include

- A deepening of the work on the implications of climate change for security, including historical research and better use of science data.
- Work that integrates environmental security with other fields—some closely linked, such as humanitarian relief and disaster warning/response, and others much broader in focus, such as security and conflict studies.
- Research that better integrates local expertise from the areas—for example, sub-Saharan Africa—that are the focus of much of this subfield.
- More research on environment and natural resource issues in relation to other global threats such as terrorism, crime, and disease—these connections are remarkably understudied.
- More research on the real impacts of integrating natural resource management and climate change adaptation into peacebuilding.
- Better early warning/early response systems research, which is important as the world faces the growing challenge of natural disasters in a crowded, urbanized, and climate-stressed planet.
- The potential role of information technology in this area—much information technology may have considerable capacity to make these large, complex, and long-term challenges more manageable for policy makers.
- The development of training modules that take the best research and make it accessible to practitioners in multiple fields.

4.3 Political Leadership

Currently, there is no leadership on the issue of climate change and security in the United States. However, the evidence of the past two decades suggests strongly that (a) the vitality of the U.S. economy, and hence our national power and national security, depends on how efficiently we use energy, water, and other resources, and (b) research on security at all levels (human, national, and global) and in different nations is showing links to the management of natural resources, adaptation to climate change, building resilience and stability in weak and failed states, and promoting sustainability and sustainable development. This implies that our political leadership needs to focus on core issues such as water, food, and energy both at home and abroad. We need to consider carefully the real and potential changes in the geopolitics of South Asia, sub-Saharan Africa, the Middle East, and possibly the Arctic that could be generated by climate change and other large-scale forms of environmental degradation and stress.

To some extent, our stature in the world as a leader depends on how we address the ethical, technical, and political dimensions of environmental challenges. Moreover, economic growth over the next several decades will take place mainly in the emerging markets of countries such as China and India. There is a vast and growing market in the global middle class and bottom billion for goods and services that solve real needs for things like energy, water, housing, food, and transportation. For some time, these will need to be affordable, easy to maintain, and efficient. The United States will lose position in this emerging market if it cannot compete with countries like China and India that are attuned to its environmental stresses and needs. Losing global market share could weaken national power and hence compromise security.

Against this background, American political leaders should carefully consider the long-term security benefits that might accrue from initiating transformations in key areas such as:

- Greening public procurement
- Addressing unsustainable incentive structures such as current subsidies in energy and agriculture
- Investing in environmental education and research
- Developing a foreign policy focused on stability and sustainability, and empowering the U.S. Department of State and USAID to lead and collaborate along these fronts
- Developing a deeper appreciation of how other emerging market countries such as Brazil, China, and India are approaching these issues

4.4 Transformative Events

Public pressure, compelling research, and political leadership could revive and improve the orientation of the early post-Rio/post–Cold War period. A key issue, of course, is, can this process organize itself, or will it require the trigger of transformative, catastrophic events? Events such as the Chernobyl meltdown, Hurricane Katrina, the BP oil spill in the Gulf, and the tsunami and subsequent nuclear reactor problems in Japan have been serious and have generated policy responses, but given the steep climb in the cost and frequency of disasters, this would appear to be a fairly violent pathway to transformation. But there are many authors (e.g.,

Homer-Dixon 2006) who are highly skeptical that key groups such as political and business leaders will take farsighted actions in the near future, and they argue that the world needs to think about how it will reemerge from the breakdowns of the early twenty-first century.

REFERENCES

Ali, S. ed. 2007. *Peace Parks: Conservation and Conflict Resolution.* Cambridge, MA: MIT Press.

Bannon, I., and P. Collier, eds. 2003. *Natural Resources and Violent Conflict Options and Actions.* Washington, DC: World Bank.

Barnett, J. 2001. *The Meaning of Environmental Security: Ecological Politics and Policy in the New Security Era.* London: Zed Books.

Barnett, J., and W. N. Adger. 2007. "Climate Change, Human Security and Violent Conflict." *Political Geography* 26: 639–655.

Brown, L. 1977. *Redefining National Security.* Worldwatch Paper, No. 14. Washington, DC: Worldwatch.

Brown, O., A. Hammill, and R. McLeman. 2007. "Climate Change as the 'New' Security Threat: Implications for Africa." *International Affairs* 83 (6): 1141–1154.

Buhaug, H., N. Gleditsch, and O. Magnus Theisen. 2008. *The Implications of Climate Change for Armed Conflict.* Washington, DC: World Bank Group.

Butts, K. 1993. *Environmental Security: What Is DoD's Role?* Occasional Paper. Carlisle Barracks, PA: Strategic Studies Institute, Army War College.

———. 1994. "Why the Military Is Good for the Environment." In *Green Security or Militarized Environment*, ed. J. Kakonen. New York: Brookfield.

———. 1996. "National Security, the Environment, and DOD." *Environmental Change and Security Project Report* 2: 22–27.

Buzan, B. 1983. *People, States, and Fear: The National Security Problem in International Relations.* Chapel Hill: University of North Carolina Press.

Campbell, K. 2008. *Climatic Cataclysm: The Foreign Policy and National Security Implications of Climate Change.* Washington, DC: Brookings Institution Press.

Carson, R. 1962. *Silent Spring.* New York: Houghton Mifflin.

Christopher, W. 1998. *In the Stream of History: Shaping Foreign Policy for a New Era.* Stanford: Stanford University Press.

CNA. 2007. *National Security and the Threat of Climate Change.* Alexandria. VA: CNA Corp. Available at http://www.cna.org/sites/default/files/news/FlipBooks/Climate%20Change%20web/flipviewerxpress.html (accessed May 7, 2012).

Collier, P. 2000a. "Doing Well Out of War: An Economic Perspective." In *Greed and Grievance: Economic Agendas in Civil Wars*, ed. M. Berdal and D. Malone, 91–111. Boulder, CO: Lynne Rienner.

———. 2000b. *Economic Causes of Civil Conflict and Their Implications for Policy.* Washington, DC: World Bank Group. Available at http://people.umass.edu/educ870/PostConflict/resources/CausesofConflict-CollierWB.pdf (accessed May 7, 2012).

———. 2007. *The Bottom Billion.* Oxford: Oxford University Press.

Conca, K., and G. Dabelko. 2002. *Environmental Peacemaking.* Washington, DC: Woodrow Wilson Center Press.

De Soysa, I., and N. Gleditsch. 1999. *To Cultivate Peace: Agriculture in a World of Conflict*. Oslo, Norway: PRIO Report.

Deudney, D. 1990. "The Case against Linking Environmental Degradation and National Security." *Millennium: Journal of International Studies* 19: 461–476.

Deudney, D., and R. Matthew, eds. 1999. *Contested Grounds: Security and Conflict in the New Environmental Politics*. New York: State University of New York Press.

Diamond, J. 1994. "Ecological Collapse of Past Civilizations." *Proceedings of the American Philosophical Society* 138: 363–370.

———. 2004. *Collapse: How Societies Choose to Fail or Succeed*. New York: Viking.

Durant, R. 2007. *The Greening of the U.S. Military: Environmental Policy, National Security, and Organizational Change*. Washington, DC: Georgetown University Press.

Ehrlich, P. 1968. *The Population Bomb*. New York: Ballantine.

Floyd, R. 2010. *Security and the Environment: Securitisation Theory and U.S. Environmental Security Policy*. Cambridge: Cambridge University Press.

GECHS. 1999. *Global Environmental Change and Human Security Science Plan*. International Human Dimensions Programme on Global Environmental Change (IHDP) Report 11. Bonn: IHDP. Available at www.ihdp.unu.edu/file/get/8548.

German Advisory Council on Global Change. 2008. *World in Transition: Climate Change as a Security Risk*. London: Earthscan.

Gleick, P. 1993. "Water and Conflict: Fresh Water Resources and International Security." *International Security* 18: 79–112.

Hanson, T., et al. 2011. "Warfare in Biodiversity Hotspots." *Conservation Biology* 23 (3): 578–587.

Hardin, G. 1968. "Tragedy of the Commons." *Science* 162: 1243–1248.

Hauge, W., and T. Ellingsen.1998. "Beyond Environmental Scarcity: Causal Pathways to Conflict." *Journal of Peace Research* 35 (3): 299–317.

Homer-Dixon, T. 1991. "On the Threshold: Environmental Changes as Causes of Acute Conflict." *International Security* 16 (2): 76–116.

———. 1999. *Environment, Scarcity and Violence*. Princeton, NJ: Princeton University Press.

———. 2000. *The Ingenuity Gap*. New York: Alfred A. Knopf.

———. 2006. *The Upside of Down: Catastrophe, Creativity, and the Renewal of Civilization*. Washington, DC: Island.

IFRC. 2009. *World Disasters Report 2009*. Geneva: IFRC. Available at http://www.ifrc.org/Global/WDR2009-full.pdf (accessed May 7, 2012).

Intergovernmental Panel on Climate Change (IPCC). 2007a. *Working Group II Report: Climate Change Impacts, Adaptation, and Vulnerability*. Cambridge: Cambridge University Press. Available at http://www.ipcc.ch/publications_and_data/publications_ipcc_fourth_assessment_report_wg2_report_impacts_adaptation_and_vulnerability.htm (accessed May 7, 2012).

IPCC. 2007b. *Working Group III Report: Mitigation of Climate Change*. Cambridge: Cambridge University Press. Available at http://www.ipcc.ch/publications_and_data/ar4/wg3/en/contents.html (accessed May 7, 2012).

Kahl, C. 2006. *States, Scarcity, and Civil Strife in the Developing World*. Princeton, NJ: Princeton University Press.

Klare, M. 2001. *Resource Wars: The New Landscape of Global Conflict*. New York: Henry Holt and Company.

Levy, M. 1995a. "Time for a Third Wave of Environment and Security Scholarship?" *Environmental Change and Security Project Report* 1: 44–46.

———. 1995b. "Is the Environment a National Security Issue?" *International Security* 20 (2): 36–62.

Maas, A., and D. Taenzler. 2009, January. *Regional Security Implications of Climate Change: A Synopsis.* Berlin: Adelphi Consult.

Matthew, R. 2002. *Dichotomy of Power: Nation versus State in World Politics.* Lanham, MD: Lexington.

———. 2011. "Is Climate Change a National Security Issue?" *Issues in Science and Technology* 27 (3): 49–60.

Matthew, R., J. Barnett, B. McDonald, and K. O'Brien, eds. 2009. *Global Environmental Change and Human Security.* Cambridge, MA: MIT Press.

Matthew, R., M. Halle, and J. Switzer, eds. 2002. *Conserving the Peace: Resources, Livelihoods, and Security.* Geneva: IISD.

Matthew, R., and A. Hammill. 2010. "Peacebuilding and Climate Change Adaptation." *St. Antony's International Review* 5 (2): 89–112.

Matthew, R., R. Sexton, M. Beevers, H. Mann, and M. van Eeden. 2010. *Sierra Leone: Environment, Conflict and Peacebuilding Assessment.* Geneva: United Nations Environment Programme.

Matthew, R., and G. Shambaugh. 2005a. "The Limits of Terrorism: A Network Perspective." *International Studies Review* 7: 617–627.

———. 2005b. "The Pendulum Effect: Explaining Shifts in the Democratic Response to Terrorism." *Analyses of Social Issues and Public Policies* 5 (1): 223–233.

Matthew, R., G. Shambaugh, R. Silver, B. McDonald, M. Poulin, and S. Blum. 2010. "Public Perceptions of Traumatic Events and Policy Preferences during the George W. Bush Administration: A Portrait of America in Turbulent Times." *Studies in Conflict and Terrorism* 33 (1): 55–90.

Meadows, D., and D. Meadows. 1972. *The Limits to Growth: A Report for the Club of Rome's Project on the Predicament of Mankind.* New York: Universe Books.

Myers, N. 1993. *Ultimate Security: The Environmental Basis of Political Stability.* New York: Norton.

National Security Council. 2006, March. *National Security Strategy.* Washington, DC: Government Printing Office. Available at http://georgewbush-whitehouse. archives.gov/nsc/nss/2006/ (accessed May 7, 2012). .

OECD. 2007. "Capacity Development." In *Glossary of Statistical Terms.* Available at stats.oecd.org/glossary/detail.asp?ID=7230 (accessed May 7, 2012).

Raleigh, C., and H. Urdal. 2007. "Climate Change, Environmental Degradation and Armed Conflict." *Political Geography* 26 (6): 674–694.

RUSI website. 2011. Available at www.rusi.org (accessed May 7, 2012).

Sachs, J. 2005. "Climate Change and War." Available at http://www.tompaine.com/ print/climate_change_and_war.php (accessed May 7, 2012).

Smith, D., et al. 2004. *Utstein Peace Building Study.* Available at http://www.prio.no/ Research-and-Publications/Project/?oid=92706 (accessed May 7, 2012).

Smith, D., and J. Vivekananda. 2007, November. *A Climate of Conflict: The Links between Climate Change, Peace and War.* London: International Alert. Available at http://reliefweb.int/node/22990 (accessed May 7, 2012).

Stern, N. 2007. *The Economics of Climate Change.* Cambridge: Cambridge University Press. Available at http://webarchive.nationalarchives.gov.uk and www. hm-treasury.gov.uk/sternreview_index.htm (accessed May 7, 2012).

Ullman, R. 1983. "Redefining Security." *International Security* 8 (1): 129–153.

United Nations Development Programme (UNDP). 1994. *Human Development Report 1994*. Oxford: Oxford University Press.

United Nations Environment Programme (UNEP). 2009. *From Conflict to Peacebuilding: The Role of Natural Resources and the Environment*. Geneva: UNEP.

Urdal, H. 2008, January. *Demographic Aspects of Climate Change, Environmental Degradation and Armed Conflict*. New York: United Nations Expert Group Meeting on Population Distribution, Urbanization, Internal Migration and Development.

Walt, S. 1991. "The Renaissance of Security Studies." *International Studies Quarterly* 35: 211–239.

———. 2009. "National Security Heats Up?" *Foreign Policy*. Available at walt.foreignpolicy.com/posts/2009/08/10/national_security_heats_up.

Weinthal, E. 2004. "From Environmental Peacemaking to Environmental Peacekeeping." *Environmental Change and Security Project Report* 10: 19–23.

White, L. 1967. "The Historical Roots of Our Ecologic Crisis." *Science* 10: 1203–1207.

Wilson, E. O. 1999. *The Diversity of Life*. New York: W. W. Norton.

World Commission on Environment and Development (WCED). 1987. *Our Common Future*. Oxford: Oxford University Press.

PART III

GOVERNING CAPACITY AND ENVIRONMENTAL CHALLENGES

CHAPTER 7

....

CAPACITY FOR GOVERNANCE

INNOVATION AND THE
CHALLENGE OF THE THIRD ERA

....

WALTER A. ROSENBAUM

In the councils of a state, the question is not so much
"What ought to be done?" as "What can be done?"

French proverb

AMERICANS have witnessed a vast expansion of the domestic Environmental Era of
the 1970s to global proportions and the rapid domestic evolution of numerous new,
often unprecedented, domestic environmental laws, governmental institutions, and
technological innovations. Much of what today is considered ordinary in environmental governance is, in fact, a historic innovation. Almost half of all Americans
living today were born into a nation without an Environmental Protection Agency,
effective national air and water pollution laws, automobile fuel efficiency standards,
endangered species protection, and pollution prevention programs—in short, a
nation without a coherent national structure of environmental governance. During
the first several decades following Earth Day 1970, the United States was the global
leader in environmental governance, and many domestic innovations, like the
National Environmental Policy Act (NEPA), have become models or inspirations
for evolving environmental governance internationally. This chapter concerns four

of the most significant domestic innovations in environmental governance since that first Earth Day. The discussion begins by placing these important innovations in the context of major challenges posed to domestic environmental governance by the Third Environmental Era. The narrative then turns to the research significance of these innovations and examines important research issues now posed by continuing experience with this domestic governance. This chapter illustrates the broad purpose of this volume to provide a comprehensive review and assessment of the literature of environmental politics and policy by examining the important current literature about environmental governance and its implications for a future research agenda, issues fundamental to any discussion of environmental politics and policy, past and future.

Perhaps the most singular aspect of modern environmental governance is the remarkable rapidity of its development. Virtually all the nation's major new environmental laws and governmental institutions, for instance, were created in a single decade following the first Earth Day. These include the EPA, the National Oceanographic and Atmospheric Administration (NOAA), the Clean Air and Clean Water Acts, the Toxic Substances Control Act, the Endangered Species Act, "Superfund," and much more—in all, nineteen major new federal environmental laws and institutions (Ashford and Caldart 2008).

A generation of Americans has now grown up with this constellation of national environmental laws and institutions so familiar that they may appear firmly embedded in American civic culture and government. Governance change is not necessarily progress, however, and familiarity can be deceptive. Behind the facade of firmly founded institutions and laws lies a constant competition between stability and change, a collision between efforts to create order and predictability essential to effective environmental management and the relentless pressure to innovate and adapt to change. In many ways, the most fundamental challenge to the American Environmental Era has been, and remains, finding a way to confront this inevitable domestic and global change continually and successfully, so that environmental laws and institutions become environmental *governance*. This challenge to governance has become especially formidable at the outset of the twenty-first century, in the face of turbulence nurtured by national and global forces new or formidably transformed from those confronting the generation that first witnessed the first Earth Day.

Certainly, no matter relating to effective domestic environmental management has been more essential yet politically contentious than the economic and political structure of governance. From the first Earth Day, the administrative design, policy goals, and scientific foundations of current domestic environmental regulation have also been contested, especially by political and economic conservatives, often allied with dissenting scientists. This persisting contention continues to be a potent policy flashpoint, creating contested issues and adding further to the significant governance challenges in the Third Environmental Generation (Dressler and Parsons 2010; Durant, Fiorino, and O'Leary 2004; Layzer 2011 Lomborg 2001; Manheim 2011; Ravesz and Stavins 2004).

1. THE CHALLENGE OF ENVIRONMENTALISM'S THIRD GENERATION

Discussions of domestic and global environmental governance are rich, with a multitude of different implications and nuances. However, several qualities are commonly understood as fundamental to most conceptions of governance. Essentially, governance comprehends the laws, institutions, administrators, public officials, and other governmental organizations or activities concerned with national environmental protection or improvement. This is often discussed as government capacity, resources, or structures for environmental protection or regulation (Weidner and Janicke 2002). The original fourteenth-century meaning of "govern" was "to steer," and that understanding is still relevant in the sense that "governance involves regulating, guiding, and mediating the actions and interactions of people and things so that they follow along a course and pathway; in this instance, a path toward environmental management" (Latham 2006).

A second implication is that governance usually implies *good*, or *effective*, or *successful* governance—"governance that works"—and it is this sense of the term that prevails in subsequent discussion. The challenge of effective governance is the most profound, ultimate test of environmental quality. The essential requisites for national ecological conservation or improvement never alone assure even sufficient environmental protection. These are, at best, the raw materials of governance. The challenge of environmental *governance* is to craft laws and institutions that actually solve environmental problems and promote environmental quality and do not, as Ronald Reagan once complained of government, tend less "to solve problems than to rearrange them." All of the necessary foundation for environmental management—grand intentions accompanied by laws and institutions, the political weight of an environmentally conscious and concerned public, committed public officials supported by a competent, professional bureaucracy—must ultimately work as intended, with reasonable compatibility. And this must be resilient governance capable of sustained effectiveness (Paddock 2008). The challenge of effective governance is now especially formidable because many of the environmental problems currently commanding national attention—climate change, modified organisms, or nanotechnology, for instance—are unprecedented, arising amid a relentless transformation of global science, society, and politics (Najam, Papa, and Taiyab 2007).

Additionally, environmental governance in our domestic discourse implies that environmental management should be not only ecologically sound but also *politically acceptable*. The process of policy making in this perspective should be at least inherently transparent, accountable, reliable, participatory, and responsive to public opinion—all qualities traditionally associated with democratic societies— but also alert and receptive to sound scientific research and debate.

As Kamieniecki and Kraft note in chapter 1, domestic environmental governance has now entered a Third Generation involving a different agenda of environmental policy priorities, a rapidly transforming domestic and global context of policy making, and a steadily evolving and expanding body of scientific research (Durant, Fiorino, and O'Leary 2004; Kettl 2002; and see chapter 9 in this volume). The American generation that experienced the onset of the second millennium has already passed the threshold of this Third Generation (Mazmanian and Kraft 2009a). This new generation's unprecedented issues have become another defining challenge for domestic and global ecological protection.

1.1 Governance and Sustainability

Sustainability, described in depth by Mazmanian and Kraft (2009b), has become a signature of Third Generation environmentalism. Governance is now increasingly associated with sustainability in the sense that an essential quality of governance is, or should be, the capacity to create and maintain at least an ecologically benign society with a capability to anticipate and enhance its own environmental future without dangerously degrading future global ecological quality. Numerous chapters in this handbook demonstrate that the definition of "sustainability" is anything but settled. Nonetheless, a global preoccupation with sustainability— albeit often differently conceived—is slowly evolving in the civic discourse of nations, and in the United States the practical consequences have often been to permeate civic discussion of environmental governance with relatively new associations, such as the implications for long-term species evolution or sustained energy consumption, and, especially, to frame discussion of contemporary environmental policy making in terms of the implications for the ecological vitality of future generations (Mazmanian and Kraft 2009b). The creation and visibility of the President's Council on Sustainable Development, chaired by Vice President Al Gore between 1994 and 1999, suggests how successfully the idea of sustainability has acquired political potency in American civic discussion. While the council itself proved nonsustainable, it exemplified a slow but continuing diffusion of sustainability planning and study groups among state and local governments (Saha and Paterson 2010; Salking 2009), colleges, think tanks, business organizations, and churches. For example, the International Council for Local Environmental Initiatives (ICELI—Local Governments for Sustainability), an international organization promoting community sustainability, lists 600 communities and advocacy groups in its U.S. roster (ICLEI 2011).

As the idea of sustainability permeates differing scales of domestic government, it is proving adaptable as a conceptual setting used by many state and local communities to promote the integration of otherwise disparate environmental planning programs and administrative entities into a coherent regime of environmental management. A practical example is the framing of climate change planning—itself an increasingly compelling governance issue—in a broader perspective of multiple policy issues and policy integration. These early experiments in planning for adaption to the impacts of climate change often have approached climate change adaptation not as a narrow infrastructure or emergency preparedness assignment of traditional disaster planning, but as an opportunity for broad-based participation by a wide range of stakeholders. Either as an initial objective or as an outcome of the participative process, these experiments have framed adaptation as an element of community or regional resilience or sustainability, related to current development stresses as well as longer term projections of climate change. In many cases, in fact, climate change has become the catalyst for more integrated attention to sustainability issues beyond climate change alone. (Wilbanks and Kates 2010, 721–722)

Whether sustainability ultimately proves practical or durable in facilitating the integration of environmental policy planning among state and local governments will remain problematic. It is, however, among the most potentially valuable policy innovations to emerge during the Third Era of environmental governance (National Research Council Committee on the Challenge of Developing Sustainable Urban Systems, 2010).

1.2 Governance, Globalism, and Transboundary Issues

In August 2004, a World Wide Web search for references to "global governance" produced about 184,000 pages. By 2011, a similar search yields about 5,330,000 citations. Globalism now assumes an increasingly prominent presence in domestic environmental affairs. Increasing economic, cultural, and political interdependence among nations—powerfully driven by the diffusion of mass media, especially through the rapid expansion of telecommunications—increasingly tests the resilience of domestic environmental institutions in several ways. One important source of globally driven pressures is the proliferation of regional and international political agreements and institutions with which the United States must often negotiate, or assume the initiative to create, including especially global environmental frameworks (GEFs), multilateral environmental agreements (MEAs), and nongovernmental organizations (NGOs). Global environmental issues are explored in this volume in chapters 10 and 11.

Peter Haas notes that one of the most conspicuous attributes of current environmentalism is the "proliferation of new political actors and the diffusion of political authority over major governmental functions, particularly in the environmental sphere. These new actors include NGOs, MNCs, organized scientific networks…global policy networks, and selective international institutions that are capable of exercising discretionary behavior independently of the wishes of the dominant member states" (Haas 2004, 4). Globalization also creates an increasing international flow of scientific information, compelling domestic environmental institutions and actors to conceive domestic environmental policy, often initially focused on purely domestic problems, in an increasingly broad regional and global context (Young 2010). The political cost of recasting policy in such broader perspective is often high. A globalizing world, observes Haas, requires "more holistic or comprehensive policies to address environmental externalities...and to support Sustainable Development" (2004, 6). However, most international and national institutions "were designed historically to address discrete problems, whereas the current globalized agenda consists of intertwined...issues whose effective management requires procedures for responsible agencies to think how their actions will affect the responsibilities of other autonomous agencies and how their policy domain may be affected by decisions taken in or by other bodies" (ibid.).

This impact of globalization on American environmental governance has been acute because scientific research and practical governing experience reveal that almost all environmental problems, often initially conceived in largely domestic terms, are transboundary issues whose resolution requires multistate, regional, or international governance (Speth and Haas 2007; Woodrow Wilson International Center for Scholars 2010). The most conspicuous contemporary example for Americans has been the contentious, decades-long domestic conflict over global climate policy, in which all policy options must take account of global climate change and the related policies of the world's other industrialized and industrializing nations. Thomas Wilbanks and Robert Kates (2010, 722) illustrate how deeply a transboundary issue like climate change has permeated American civic life: "States, cities, and towns recognize that climate change is only one of many driving forces for global change that shape the sustainability of localities, regions, and nations. Its importance is wrapped up in how it interacts with other driving forces such as demographic change, global economic change, technological change, and institutional change." The rapid globalization of environmental science, governance, and policy discourse has opened up a vast and still-growing agenda for globally derived research in virtually all aspects of environmental management (Delmas and Young 2009; Mol 2006; Mol and Spaargaren 2006; Spaargaren, Mol and Butel 2006).

1.3 Governance and Social Integration

Modern environmental management increasingly now requires a broad integration of social structures domestically as well as internationally (Levi-Faur 2005). Environmental governance entails increasingly broad collateral social and economic impacts that require social collaboration on an increasing scale—partially because, until the onset of the Environmental Era, domestic environmental institutions and policy makers had practically no experience with national environmental governance to demonstrate the extensive social depth and breadth of the impact (Durant 2007; Jasanoff and Martello 2004; Matthew 2010).

In February 1972, for example, one of the earliest domestic air pollution regulations appeared when the EPA announced that all domestic gasoline stations would be required to carry unleaded gasoline. American petroleum refiners and the entire domestic automobile industry reacted, reluctantly and slowly. At the time, the EPA had existed for little more than a year, and practically no national arrangements existed for long-term, socially encompassing discussion and planning for the impact for the new lead standard or for virtually any other federal air quality regulation. In contrast, now domestic air pollution standards are understood to affect not only air quality but also automobile development, community planning, toxic waste management, and international trade. Since the first decade of the Environmental Era, a whole generation of new regulatory, business, environmental, and intergovernmental organizations have also evolved to influence, implement, and in many instances to predict and assess the expected impact of regulation in practically every aspect of domestic society, not excluding religion, the arts, recreation, and food supply (Wilbanks and Stern 2003).

1.4 New Scientific Information

The scientific information to be interpreted and integrated into domestic environmental policy making persistently increases in quality and volume. One result has been to sustain, often to intensify, competing claims on the information that should inform policy making (e.g., Ascher, Steelman, and Healy 2010; Keller 2009; Lomborg 2001; McGarity and Wagner 2008). Another consequence is a paradox: improving data diversity and reliability may vastly enrich the scientific foundation for environmental policy making but also can unsettle existing governance by compelling a critical rethinking and revision of existing policy, or a confrontation with new, politically and technically difficult issues. An example is the impact of new atmospheric research compelling the EPA to initiate in 1997 and again in 2006, amid considerable political controversy, new regulatory rules tightening the air quality standard for small particulates, a common automobile and industrial air pollutant, more than twenty years after the existing standards had been mandated (Esworthy 2010). The new standard is predicted to improve public health significantly, but it also compels automobile manufacturers and major U.S. industries to install costly new pollution emission controls. As legal scholar Bradley Karkkainen (2002) suggests, the increasing capacity of environmental data to characterize the environment holistically—to be sensible to its complexity—inevitably changes the conceptual foundations of environmental governance. "What is new," he suggests, "is our growing recognition of the implications of [a] conception of ecosystems as complex, dynamic, non-linear, human-influenced systems for environmental law and policy" (Karkkanien 2002, 8).

Much of this evolving science results from rapid technological innovation such as satellite monitoring, improved computer hardware, integrated regional and global data networks, and refinements of Geographic Information System (GIS) technology. These developing technologies, in turn, create opportunities for greater understanding and prediction of environmental conditions (National Research Council 2010). The creation of increasingly complex computer models capable of statistically and mathematically integrating vast amounts of environmental data has evolved to the extent that modeling is now a routine basis for much EPA policy making. Like many other federal agencies concerned with environmental protection and health, "EPA uses a wide variety of computational models to support the scientific analyses that inform our decisions and policies....Frequently, these models become the basis for environmental cleanup, protection, or regulation. Models therefore underlie how the Agency chooses to address a multitude of environmental questions" (U.S. EPA 2011; National Research Council 2007). Perhaps the best-known and fiercely debated example of contemporary, model-based governance is created by the general climate models (GCM) used by the Intergovernmental Panel of Climate Change (IPCC) to predict the magnitude and impact of future global climate change. The most ambitious environmental modeling enables environmental scientists and policy makers to envision and forecast environmental change and the entailed policy issues on an unprecedented temporal and geographic scale. In effect, these transformations are subtly but persistently reframing the terms of environmental law and civic discourse into an increasingly future-driven conception of governance (Schiffries 2005).

1.5 Governance and Scale

No aspect of Third Generation environmental management has become more apparent than the inexorable, intricate, and growing interconnection of almost all environmental problems in both their science and their governance scale (Karkkainen, 2002; Young 2002). For example, increasingly comprehensive research about contemporary U.S. water pollution and species protection—issues that might initially seem to differ substantially—are similar in that they both require effective management on many different geographic levels simultaneously, embracing communities, states, regions, the nation, and ultimately other nations. Effective environmental governance, then, increasingly involves discovering how to create laws and institutions on scales appropriate to the character of the issues they confront—for instance, to create state or local governance institutions or laws to deal with unique local or regional air pollution or species declines rather than attempt to make and enforce governance from Washington (Betsill and Rabe 2009; Selin and VanDeveer 2009).

2. Confronting the Third Generation: Evaluating Governance Response and Innovation in Four Perspectives

Among the multitude of institutions, laws, and other components associated with Third Era environmental management, research and related literature concerning four governance issues has been especially important. These issues focus on four of the most important innovations in national environmental management, illuminate frequently effective governance, and epitomize the governance challenges posed by the Third Era.

2.1 An Enduring Innovation: NEPA and the EIS

Perhaps no single creation in domestic environmental governance has proven more durable, or traveled farther internationally, than the National Environmental Policy Act (NEPA) of 1970 (Pub. L. 91–190). NEPA's unprecedented declaration of a national commitment to environmental protection and, especially, its complementary creation of the Environmental Impact Statement (EIS) mandated for all federal government agencies has been termed "the world's first comprehensive statement of environmental policy" and remains perhaps the single most internationally widespread governance model created by the United States (Weiner 2009, 10675). For example, Article 4, §1(f), of the United Nations Framework Convention on Climate Change, ratified by the United States in 1992, specifically cites environmental impact assessment as an important tool for considering and reducing climate impacts (Gerrard 2009). A global network of consultation about the development and implementation of EISs has been institutionalized through numerous multinational arrangements, such as the International Network for Environmental Compliance and Enforcement and the EPA's own International Programs Office. Domestically, NEPA is often esteemed by environmental policy researchers and practitioners to be among the most important, perhaps the most important, environmental governance innovation (Environmental Law Institute 2010). Every state now has created some version of NEPA and an EIS. NEPA's robustness is especially remarkable because the entire statute, at only five and a half pages long, is the shortest major U.S. environmental law since Earth Day I. Few legacies from that historic gathering on the Washington Mall have also been more extensively documented and appraised. Because NEPA's required EIS process compels *all* federal agencies to perform a careful, detailed, multistage evaluation of *any* policies or projects likely to have significant environmental impacts, the EIS process itself has produced an enormous volume of policy analysis, scientific literature, litigation, legal scholarship, and public debate and remains a matter of continual research. After more than four decades, experience with NEPA and the EIS suggests that the impact of the EIS on domestic environmental governance has been significant, occasionally profound, but often disappointing and ambiguous (Anderson 2011; Caldwell 1999).

The EIS has fulfilled at least some of its ambitious intent. It has often educated administrative agencies to the environmental implications of their policy making and, in the process, compelled public and media attention to environmentally relevant policies and their impacts. The EIS often becomes a domestic "early warning system," calling public and media attention to the implications of agency programs that might otherwise be unrecognized or obscure—a particularly valuable diffusion of information to environmental advocacy organizations—thus setting the stage for an open public debate and discourse on environmental consequences of agency actions. Equally important, the EIS mandate has brought the courts and judges extensively into environmental governance and created an important judicial oversight, and sometimes an essential judicial restraint, on environmental agency decision making. EISs have often compelled important, environmentally protective changes in administrative environmental plans and programs still in the development stage. The EIS process has also promoted greater coordination between federal, regional, state, and local environmental management agencies. The EIS has also been important as a powerful incentive for new research concerning the ecological consequences of governmental action and tracing the often complex web of impacts across governmental levels and ecological domains.

The EIS process has undoubtedly permeated the whole of federal environmental governance and been deeply diffused across all levels of state and local governance, often as its creators intended. But its legislative intent has often been blunted, and its mandate for a deliberate, alert, and environmentally sensitive process of governmental decision making has often been reduced from reality to ritual (Lindstrom and Smith 2003). Considerable research has revealed a number of widely acknowledged deficiencies of the matured EIS process. Perhaps most important, the federal courts have held almost from its inception that NEPA and the EIS process compel federal agencies to follow meticulously the *procedures* for preparing and reviewing an EIS and then must *consider* the environmental information disclosed, but—contrary to the intent of NEPA's creators—NEPA does not compel revision or rejection of agency programs or projects even if an EIS reveals serious and possibly preventable environmental impacts. In short, the EIS has been a judicially construed procedural requirement, not, as originally intended, a *substantive* mandate that agencies not only consider the implications of the EIS but also follow the most environmentally benign policy options it proposes.

Thus, agencies may have to create an EIS, but they do not have to like it or allow it to deflect the mission fixation so often dominating governmental agencies. "After 40 years," observes legal scholar George Mannina, "NEPA is seen by many federal agencies as yet another mountain to climb in the path to project implementation rather than as a tool to aid and improve decision making" (2009, 10660). Whether intentionally or not, agencies frequently produced bloated, massively documented, technically dense, and highly expensive EISs more fogbound than transparent for the public. The EIS process has often been short-circuited, moreover, by the creation of various administrative improvisations such as categorical exclusions, scoping, findings of no significant environmental impact (FONSIs), and other procedures which, however unintentionally, often obscure or ignore important environmental aspects of proposed policies in the name of facilitating decisions and reducing paperwork (Mandelker 2009). Finally, the EIS process often does not encourage continuing oversight and evaluation of agency actions intended to mitigate potentially undesirable environmental impacts revealed by an EIS process after agencies have taken initial precautionary measures as required by NEPA. The decades of experience with NEPA and the EIS have also produced a significant agenda for continuing research and policy reform (Bolig 2009; Council on Environmental Quality 1997; Farber 2009; Mannina 2009; NEPA Task Force 2003; Wishnie 2008).

2.2 Governance and Managing Common Pool Resources

The award of the 2010 Nobel Prize in Economics to Elinor Ostrom, an American political scientist and the first woman to become a Nobel laureate in economics, exemplified the rise of common resource governance to an issue of global proportions and, especially, the contribution of imaginative domestic U.S. policy research to innovative international environmental management (Sabatier et al. 2005). "Common pool resources" are significant natural resources, such as forests, fisheries, irrigation systems, rivers, or lakes—any natural resource and its infrastructure—widely shared among dependent populations vulnerable to severe consequences should the resource be mismanaged or destroyed. Ostrom is prominent among numerous international policy scholars and practitioners concerned with designing resilient governance institutions that will manage common resources effectively and prevent an ecosystem collapse (Koontz and Thomas 2006; Singh 1994; Weber 2003). Much of Ostrom's research and writing has focused on community management of common pool resources in developing countries throughout Africa and Asia, emphasizing the importance of creative, locally based governance arrangements, an alert sensibility to the value of local institutions and actors in designing governance, and a rejection of prescriptive, single-resource management models (e.g., Brentwood and Robar 2004; O'Rourke 2004).

Among her most important governance prescriptions are eight "design principles" that are, or should be, characteristic of effective local common resource management (Ostrom 1990, 1993; Ostrom and the National Research Council 2002):

1. Clearly defined boundaries (effective exclusion of external unentitled parties).
2. Rules regarding the appropriation and provision of common resources are adapted to local conditions.
3. Collective-choice arrangements allow most resource appropriators to participate in the decision-making process.
4. Effective monitoring by monitors who are part of or accountable to the appropriators.
5. A scale of graduated sanctions for resource appropriators who violate community rules.
6. Mechanisms of conflict resolution that are cheap and easy to access.
7. Community self-determination recognized by higher-level authorities.
8. Organization of large common pool resources (CPRs) in the form of multiple layers of nested enterprises, with small local CPRs at the base level.

Like Ostrom, many of her contemporaries initially focused primarily on common resource problems in underdeveloped and developing nations, but the empirical and theoretical foundations of their research, together with a growing, more recent literature concerned with common pool resources in industrialized nations, have proven highly relevant to the United States (Ghate, Narpat, and Mukhodadhyay 2008; Ostrom 2005, 2008; Ostrom et al. 2002).

Ostrom and her contemporaries have insisted on the importance of matching the scale of governance with the character of the resource to be managed, so that the scale becomes appropriate and responsive to the qualities of the resource and the experience of those who depend on it. Among the most important implications of the research conducted by Ostrom and other scholars is a recognition that community-created traditions and collaborative community action, often assisted by NGOs, is a viable complement or substitute—often a more effective strategy altogether—for commons management than centralized, top-down governance that relies on bureaucracies remote from local community experience and management traditions. Especially where

> government regulators have been losing both their power and resources, others, including communities and NGOs have begun to fill the regulatory space they previously occupied. Community-based environmental protection has gained increasing attention as either a complement or a substitute for traditional direct regulation. At least in principle it can deliver both procedural and outcome benefits. Such an approach also fosters environmental awareness in the community, which in turn can lead the community to mobilize in ways that result in improvements in environmental performance at a local level. (Gunningham 2009, 196)

Ostrom and others' shared belief in the efficacy of locally inspired, community-based institutions for common resource management implicitly challenge the validity of a pervasive assumption among many resource scholars and policy practitioners that when common resources are collectively owned and managed they will inevitably be degraded—the "tragedy of the commons," most famously argued by Garrett Hardin. The rejection of an inevitable "tragedy of the commons" also becomes a potent challenge to economic theories of resource management based on a conviction that privatization of common resources is the best way, perhaps the only way, to conserve common resources with economically efficient management.

Much of the evidence supporting the efficacy of locally based, frequently informal common resource governance originates from research in Africa or Asia, from global examples involving comparatively small geographic resource domains, and from experience over relatively short time periods (Ostrom, Schroeder, and Wyannne 1993). A major question remains concerning the durability and resilience of the community-based governance studied by Ostrom and related policy scholars and practitioners. Another salient issue concerns whether these creative, local arrangements can become governance models for management of much larger, globally pervasive common resources such as fisheries and geographically sprawling resources such as whole forest systems.

2.3 Atmospheric Governance: The Clean Air Act

When the Aspen Institute, an internationally recognized center for public policy research and advocacy, celebrated the 40th anniversary of the EPA in 2010 by citing ten ways in which EPA "had strengthened America," four policies, embracing the largest environmental domain among all Aspen's selections, concerned air pollution, and all in some way originated with the Clean Air Act (CAA) of 1970. The CAA is frequently cited by both environmental advocacy organizations and environmental historians as the most potent symbol and contemporary achievement of the Environmental Era, the strategic and political foundation of the nation's environmental governance evolving since 1970.

The CAA defines virtually all of the major governance institutions for contemporary national air pollution control. These include the first comprehensive federal standards for ambient air pollutants (National Ambient Air Quality Standards), and the first mandated national regulatory program to control existing and future air pollution emissions and to replace a multitude of differing, often nonexistent state air pollution control laws with a comprehensive federal governance structure implemented through the states. Other major provisions include mandated emission standards for both stationary and mobile sources of air pollution, standards for the definition and regulation of toxic air emissions, requirements of state plans to implement and enforce the federally mandated pollution regulations, and provision for states to create air quality standards exceeding the minimum federal requirements. Amendments to the original CAA in 1977 and 1990 further amplified the scope and impact of the 1970 legislation. These amendments provided the opportunity for states to create emissions trading as a supplement, or alternative, to conventional emissions regulation, added provisions for the reduction of acid rain and tropospheric ozone depletion, and established new automobile gasoline formulation requirements. After the creation of the 1970 legislation, state and local governments have continued to refine and extend the CAA's scope in response to local air pollution circumstances.

Despite its elephantine size (it is the longest, largest, most complex federal regulatory legislation), and notwithstanding the expansive controversy attending almost all of its major provisions, the CAA has become a successful governance model in numerous, significant ways. It has demonstrated that the standards-and-enforcement design of environmental regulation *can* significantly reduce or virtually eliminate many of the nation's most troublesome air pollutants, such as ambient lead, and inhibit the growth of others, including sulfur oxides and particulates. The CAA has proven responsive to continuing scientific research and innovation through provisions requiring EPA to periodically review and revise existing air quality standards in light of continuing research and new pollution technology developments. It has expanded citizen access to environmental governance: the CAA is the first federal environmental regulatory program specifically allowing citizen suits against federal, state, or local governments for failure to implement its regulatory requirements—in effect, creating within the federal

pollution regulatory process greater public transparency and active citizen engagement. Its provision for reduction of acid precipitation and atmospheric ozone
depletion has been framed so as to encourage the development of transboundary
governance through multistate and regional regulatory authorities. In confronting
the inevitable challenge of crafting institutional arrangements to different regulatory scales within the federal structure, the CAA permits considerable negotiation
and administrative support for the states in creating and enforcing their required
State Implementation Plans in response to such differing state characteristics as
their economies, geographical and environmental settings, civic cultures, and
administrative resources for regulation.

The CAA also possess, in generous measure, not only desirable qualities inherent to standards-and-enforcement regulation but also many of the problematic and
controversial elements challenging policy scholars and practitioners to continued
critical appraisal and research (National Research Council 2004). Perhaps the most
vigorous debate and sustained research among policy scholars and economists
concerns the comparative economic cost and efficiency of standards and enforcement governance as a regulatory strategy exemplified by the CAA in comparison
to so-called market approaches, which depend primarily on the use of economic
incentives such as emission charges, tradable or marketable pollution rights (sometimes called "cap-and-trade"), or tax subsidies to create pollution emission controls (Gayer and Horowitz 20). Since its inception, legislative and administrative
revisions of the CAA, supplemented by some state initiatives, have nudged the
CAA regulatory style toward greater efforts at collaboration rather than confrontation and litigation between regulated industries and regulators in developing and
implementing emission controls (Fiorino 2006). The economic and environmental
impacts of what is sometimes called this "new" regulatory approach have become
important continuing issues on the regulatory agenda.

The U.S. experience with market-based air pollution control is still limited, but
increasing. The economic performance of the existing markets has been inconclu-
sive. The CAA's important Title IV (Acid Deposition Control) provisions allowing
the establishment of state and regional markets in tradable sulfur oxide emissions
is generally considered successful, and the few state-based experiments in tradable
emission rights for other pollutants, such as the Illinois trading program for volatile
organic compounds, have proven successful enough to encourage further research.
As national and international concern about the impact and management of global
climate change steadily intensifies, the development of cap-and-trade strategies for
CO_2 emissions control has become a compelling issue.

Among the most important currently innovative approaches to climate governance has been the development of interstate and cross-national cap-and-trade
markets for CO_2 emissions, an emerging experiment in transboundary governance. The U.S. currently participates in three of these innovative early transboundary markets (the Regional Greenhouse Gas Initiative, the Western Climate
Initiative, and the Midwestern Climate Initiative), and their development will be a
major focus of continuing research, debate, and critical appraisal. The evolution of

these closely watched, potentially important alternative strategies for air pollution management is likely to have a critical impact on future U.S. air pollution regulation. If market-based and transboundary governance models prove durable both politically and economically, they are likely to be increasingly adopted on all scales of environmental management.

A final matter of continuing importance to air pollution governance—in fact, an issue embedded in practically all pollution control arrangements—concerns the quality of the science on which pollution standards are established. Two seminal science issues have become inseparable from the establishment of air quality standards used in both standards-and-enforcement regulation and market-oriented management strategies: the reliability of the data used as a basis for setting air quality standards and the risk analysis process used to calculate the safe limits of environmental exposure to air pollutants. Controversy over both these volatile issues seems predestined for practically all governance strategies for diminishing air pollution. In essence, the reliability issues persist because new data about human and animal exposures to air pollutants, and the precision of methods used to assemble the data, continually improve. The CAA, like all air pollution law, is based on these exposure data—especially human exposure—and the CAA requires the EPA to periodically reevaluate its existing air quality standards in light of this ongoing research. Continuing scientific research and mandated review of existing standards guarantee seemingly unremitting controversy among all stakeholders in existing pollution governance concerning whether new data require a revision of existing air quality standards. The risk analysis issue concerns the process used to determine when human exposure to air pollutants, especially the risk of cancer, exceeds acceptable limits. Debate persists concerning whether the animal experiments used in setting most standards for human exposure to pollutants are reliable and whether the limit of "acceptable risk" from human pollutant exposure is sufficiently rigorous (National Research Council Committee on Improving Risk Analysis Used by the EPA 2009). From the inception of the CAA, research, advocacy, and critical appraisal of air pollution science has been a growth industry and will continue to accompany almost all aspects of air pollution governance in one way or another.

2.4 Governance and Information-Based Public Engagement

No transformation in the nation's environmental governance has been more pervasive since Earth Day 1970 than the constantly increasing volume and variety of public environmental information, together with rapidly evolving communication technologies that facilitate public access and interpretation of the information. Information-based public engagement is, among other objectives, intended to fortify the political foundation of governance by promoting transparency, citizen involvement, accountability, and responsiveness.

One consequence has been a continuing diffusion of publicly available and accessible environmental data, progressively permeating all scales of government. This amplification of ecological information creates unprecedented opportunities for citizen environmental education and civic engagement (Cohen 2000; Mol 2006). Advocacy groups have successfully exploited this cascade of data for political capital and strategic advantage in the competition for governmental access and policy influence. Publicly available environmental data, especially environmental monitoring, research reports, records of administrative decisions, and public hearings, have become a potent political resource for environmental advocacy organizations (especially for smaller, community-based organizations), helping them to mobilize their own membership and to improve the quality and impact of their policy discourse. Equally important, the proliferation of available information has become a catalyst for the creation and development of new advocacy organizations and a powerful stimulus to the expansion of political activism among scientists and science-based interest groups.

This information-based engagement has evolved from a diverse array of federal, state, and local governmental statutes, administrative determination, and judicial rulings (Dietz and Stern 2008; Guber and Bosso 2010). Many of the laws sustaining this civic engagement, such as the federal Freedom of Information Act (1966), were not initially conceived in the context of environmental policy making, although they immediately became relevant following the first Earth Day as new federal, state, and community environmental laws were instituted.[1] In the aftermath of Earth Day, these numerous enactments created a multitude of additional, different pathways for public access to information concerning environmental regulation, agency policy making and rule making, scientific research, environmental monitoring, and related activities (Case 2001; Esty 2004; Mol 2006; National Academy of Engineering 2001; Wright, Duncan, and Lach 2009).

Virtually all major federal environmental legislation since 1970 contains a mandate that the relevant regulatory agencies and departments facilitate public access to information about their environmental decision making and—especially important—to the scientific and technical data supporting regulatory policies, which is otherwise seldom easily available, if at all, to the public. The impact of this information revolution on federal environmental agencies has been amplified by complementary statutory and administrative provisions guaranteeing a public right to be informed and to participate in some manner in agency policy making—as, for example, in provisions of the Clean Water Act specifying that the EPA and state agencies implementing the legislation must provide for, encourage,

---

[1]. Especially important, in 1996 the Freedom of Information Act definition of "records" was amended to include digital files and to require federal agencies to create Internet "electronic reading rooms" where the public could access and download frequently requested information without filing a formal request.

and assist public participation in promulgating and enforcing agency regulations (Dietz and Stern 2008).

Perhaps the most comprehensive example of these requirements is the Emergency Planning and Right-to-Know Act of 1986 (Title III of Superfund Amendments and Reauthorization), which mandates a national reporting of toxic and hazardous chemical production, use, and community storage. To assist the public in interpretation of its regulatory data, the EPA, like many other agencies, has created multiple formats for public access to virtually all of its regulatory information bases, such as the Toxic Releases Inventory (TRI), Hazardous Waste Violations and Permits, the Toxic Substances Control Acts (TSCAs) Chemical Substance Inventory, "Superfund" toxic waste sites, and much more. Additionally, numerous other federal agencies also make this information available through web-based information gateways such as Data.gov, which consolidate public identification and access to data from multiple federal environmental entities.

The proliferation of computer technology and the Internet has substantially improved public availability and interpretation of environmental information in several significant ways (OMB Watch 2011). The information gateways are generally user-friendly, highly flexible, and interactive. Many databases are comprehensively coded in a manner that enables users to relate information to their specific communities, often to their own neighborhood. The Toxic Release Inventory, for example, has coded data by geography (zip code, county, state, nation), chemical, industry, sector, or year. Users can choose alternative formats, such as trend data. The agency's *EnviroMapper* program uses an interactive geographic information system (GIS) allowing point-and-click selection of specific locations and then an array of multiple pollution control databases, including water quality, air quality, and hazardous waste. Increasingly, these integrated data gateways also aggregate federal, state, and community data. For example:

> One important and widely used mechanism for making pollution-control compliance and enforcement information publicly available is the Enforcement and Compliance History Online (ECHO). ECHO is a Web-based source of such information for approximately 800,000 facilities around the nation that have permits issued by the U.S. Environmental Protection Agency (USEPA). These include facilities owned by U.S. enterprises and by foreign enterprises doing business in the United States. Anyone in the world can use ECHO to determine whether environmental compliance inspections have been conducted by USEPA, state, or local government, and whether violations were detected, enforcement actions taken, and penalties assessed. (United Nations Environment Programme 2011)

As the TRI illustrates, the rapid evolution of GIS has accelerated both the growth of environmental data bases and the variety of ways in which the data can be disaggregated for public use. "The spread of digital technology," the National Academy of Engineering noted early in its development, has also increased the demand for real-time information....GISs, which enable the collation, manipulation, and integration of spatial environmental information in ways not envisioned before, are being demanded by industry, government, and the public. This type of information can be used to show people the impact of releases from a facility or group of facilities. The GIS enables a visual map of an affected area to be overlain with a street map of the immediate area to give the public information about public risk (National Academy of Engineering 2001, 176–177)

In recent years the Environmental Protection Agency (EPA) has integrated databases in its "Envirofacts" data warehouse. With the advent of the Internet, the user interface for selecting information has become highly flexible and interactive.

As environmental data outlets increase, the variety of nongovernmental mega-data websites, sponsored by private interest groups that aggregate multiple information outlets, classify information, and facilitate public access, have grown into a satellite information industry. A typical example is the web-based Right-to-Know Network (www.rtknet.org), which provides users with numerous links to environmental information and complimentary news. And like the Environmental Impact Statements discussed in section 1.1, information gateways and public involvement mandates have gradually been diffused to virtually all governmental scales within the federal system.[2]

---

2. An immense amount of scholarship, policy debate, and critical appraisal has accompanied this rapidly enlarging supply of publicly available information (Kraft, Stephan, and Abel 2011). Among the numerous policy-related issues sustained by the information revolution, several constitute a core of generic issues on which most related governance research is grounded. In the several decades following Earth Day 1970, research focused on issues related to the early quality and impact of the increased information flow, especially (1) whether information is publicly accessible and relevant to agency decision making; (2) which interests use this information and for what purpose; (3) which interests are advantaged or disadvantaged by access to this information; (4) in what manner the use of this information influences governance decisions; and (5) whether the availability of various forms of information improves the quality of public knowledge and discourse about environmental governance. Virtually all the agenda has now been recast in the context of publicly proliferating computer technology and the Internet's pervasive impact on mass communication. Thus, future research agendas will predictably give increasing attention to characterizing how—or *whether*—computers and the Internet, in particular, are changing conclusions about these fundamental issues. With onrushing globalization, research is also turning increasingly toward issues related to how globally available and disseminated information, and the entities that produce it, may influence domestic environmental governance. Communication technology now implies an accelerating pace of innovation, so that both policy researchers and practitioners will be closely following the implications of emergent new technologies for civic environmental engagement.

3. CONCLUSION

The four governance innovations that dominate this narrative are deep currents in a vaster sea. The political tide of the American environmentalism that broke so memorably upon a largely unsuspecting and unprepared national political leadership on Earth Day 1970 continues to move broadly and deeply across *all* governmental institutions, testing their ability to adapt to a rapidly transforming political culture in which environmental significance increasingly permeates almost all domains of public policy, and investing issues with an environmental relevance previously unimagined—the fate of dishwashing liquid, for instance, or the purchase of new mail trucks for the post office, or the location of a military installation. In this broad perspective, environmental governance is an enduring issue, constantly emerging at the strategic core of all environmental policy research, and continually compelling because environmental governance is inherently vulnerable to unexpected social change and new scientific information. As the National Research Council has repeatedly emphasized in its discussions of environmental governance, "No governance structure works best for all situations; rather the critical task is to find the arrangement that is most appropriate for particular governance problems" (Brewer and Sterns 2006, 4).

Many of the significant challenges confronting the nation's environmental governance have become readily apparent, some are still implicit, and both constitute a priority list for continuing policy research and policy innovation. These are especially relevant for the four governance institutions previously discussed because these institutions are a vital institutional foundation for current environmental policy making.

3.1 Improving NEPA

After more than four decades, it is widely recognized that NEPA, and particularly its EIS process, have been both successful and problematic; both are historically vital environmental institutions requiring innovative redesign. The most imperative research issues commonly identified in the current EIS process include (1) improving the extent to which federal agencies introduce the results of the EIS process early in their strategic planning; (2) encouraging greater public involvement, and especially more participation by frequently unengaged minorities, in the EIS process; (3) facilitating greater exchange of EIS-relevant information between agencies; (4) promoting more science-based monitoring of EIS implementation—for example, mitigation of adverse program environmental impacts—by agencies; (5) creating more concise, less complicated, and more readily comprehensible EIS documents; and (6) including climate change within the scope of issues in EIS substantive requirements (Bolig 2009; Council on Environmental Quality 1997; Gerrard 2008; Mannina 2009; NEPA Task Force 2003; Wishnie 2008). In all these respects, comparative research involving the growing experience of other national venues, especially the European

Union, with NEPA-like procedures and also an evaluation of the consequences of state and local "little NEPAs" (Weiner 2009) will be very useful.

3.2 A National Perspective on Common Pool Resources

As interest in sustainability continues to grow in American civic culture, an especially important agenda for future research about common pool resources (CPRs) includes attention to how CPRs can be applied in domestic community and regional settings and integrated with other evolving state, regional, and community development strategies such as sustainability or its near relatives, like "smart growth" (Ostrom 2008). In this respect, comparative studies of CPR planning within U.S. venues and between the United States and other Western nations, such as the European Union, can be highly informative about circumstances that promote or inhibit the development of CPR planning. Studies of CPRs in both non-Western and Western settings also suggest that CPR planning confronts a number of implementation problems likely to require attention within the United States as well. Among the most important of these implementation issues are problems of infrastructure development, including the management of crowding and overuse, lack of continuing investment in infrastructure, lack of robustness in institutional durability, and changing social expectations concerning CPR performance (Bots and Kunneke 2008; Schlager and Heikkila 2011). As ecosystem management becomes a more frequent consideration in domestic environmental policy, the adaptability of CPR strategies for ecosystem-based planning also becomes an important research challenge (Brewer and Stern 2006).

In addition, discourse and advocacy of CPR institutions must now be placed in the context of emerging global concern about climate change and evolving climate change science (National Research Council, Panel on Advancing the Science of Climate Change 2010). While the climate change issue has been recognized domestically as especially relevant to domestic water basin and watershed management, the climate issue clearly relates to broader concerns with all forms of community planning. Research is particularly imperative concerning which domestic venues are most vulnerable to prospective near-term climate impacts—such as coastal and riverine communities—and what CPR strategies might be applied in these venues.

The adaptability of CPR arrangements to collaborative state-federal management, or to public-private hybrid governance, is a particularly salient issue within the U.S. constitutional system. Not least important, the development of appropriate monitoring and indicators for CPR institutions will be a compelling concern for many decades.

3.3 The Clean Air Act Reconsidered

Perhaps the most profound research issues now posed by the Clean Air Act (CAA) concern its relevance to global climate change and its capacity to create an appropriate regulatory response. The unprecedented challenges posed by climate change are particularly formidable because climate change management entails many scientific, political, and economic assumptions quite unlike the premises on which the CAA was conceived and its regulatory strategies crafted (Leber 2009; National Research Council, Panel on Advancing the Science of Climate Change 2010). The most compelling research priorities now include (1) creation of scientifically credible and administratively practical methods for characterizing the human health impacts of climate change in terms relevant to the regulatory criteria required by the CAA; (2) creation of procedures for characterizing the domestic ecological and socioeconomic impacts consequences of climate warming in terms relevant for the CAA; (3) development and evaluation of alternative regulatory strategies to address the predicted national impact of climate change; and (4) assessment of current institutional capacities for regulatory management of climate change across domestic governmental scales and an investigation of alternative and innovative approaches to multilevel governance.

Growing concern about the CAA's capacity to create effective regulatory governance in an era of global change (U.S. Government Accountability Office 2009) compounds the existing imperative for continuing research on alternative governance models for regulating conventional air pollutants that improve on current models economically, scientifically, and administratively. Current regulatory strategies involve the CAA's original standards-and-enforcement regulatory design, cap-and-trade market-based schemes, and hybrid models combining market-based and traditional nonmarket regulation. The comparative economic and environmental advantage of these existing regulatory approaches requires continuing monitoring and evaluation. Newer, innovative regulatory models merit continuing evaluation, especially strategies that effectively integrate federal, state, and local regulation and adapt regulatory governance to differing scales of environmental pollution—for instance, models that effectively link subnational institutions to regulatory objectives established nationally or internationally.

As experience with the CAA grows, it has also become increasingly apparent that the content and quality of the Regulatory Impact Analysis (RIA) and its entailed Benefit-Cost Analysis (BCA)—processes inherent to current CAA regulatory rule making—urgently require reform. Research is particularly needed, for example, to improve the technical quality and both RIAs and BCAs, to promote earlier and more comprehensive consideration of these documents in agency decision making, and to clarify the distributional impacts of proposed regulations (Harrington, Heinzerling, and Morgenstern 2009).

3.4 Enhancing Sustainability Policy Making

Few environmental policies are more globally advocated and conceptually elusive than "sustainability." Not surprisingly, concluded a National Academy of Science panel, it is in operationally defining and clarifying the practical policy implications of sustainability that the research community "can play a particularly crucial role" (Brewer and Stern 2004, 4). The agenda for research about domestic sustainability policy making should give high priority to issues that promote the translation of sustainability into terms relevant to policy makers and stakeholders at all governmental levels. Among the most salient issues is the development of practical planning guidelines for policy makers. This includes (1) identification of indicators for sustainability that create baselines, planning goals, and criteria for evaluating the implementation of sustainability policies; (2) comparative studies of sustainability policy implementation in different governmental settings to identify factors that facilitate or inhibit sustainability planning; (3) development of comprehensive ecological measures for sustainability planning, such as "ecological footprint analysis," enabling integration of natural sciences with economic and social research; (4) creation of institutions for monitoring sustainability plans and facilitating adaptive management; and (5) development of institutions linking and integrating governments across scales of sustainability planning.

A second set of salient issues concern the involvement of the public, and especially stakeholders, in sustainability plans. Important concerns include how to (1) promote citizen education and engagement in sustainability planning; (2) identify appropriate and useful means of governmental intervention when collaborative public-private planning for sustainability falters; (3) define environmental justice and create procedures for resolving the equity, distributive, and environmental justice implications of sustainability plans; and (4) achieve continuing public involvement in monitoring sustainability plans (Hempel 1999, 43–74; Mazmanian and Kraft 2009, 286–311).

Finally, sustainability planning ultimately depends on the active, informed engagement and appropriate education of elective public officials and professional administrators at all governmental levels. Continuing research focused on the creation and inclusion of sustainability curricula in the education of both public officials and administrators is an important concern if future sustainability planning is to remain robust.

REFERENCES

Anderson, F. R. 2011. *NEPA in the Courts: A Legal Analysis of the National Environmental Policy Act*. Washington, DC: Resources for the Future Press.
Asher, W., T. Steelman, and R. Healy. 2010. *Knowledge and Environmental Policy: Re-Imagining the Boundaries of Science and Politics*. Cambridge, MA: MIT Press.
Ashford, N. A., and C. C. Caldart. 2008. *Environmental Law, Policy and Economics: Reclaiming the Environmental Agenda*. Cambridge, MA: MIT Press.
Betsill, M. M., and B. G. Rabe. 2009. "Climate Change and Multilevel Governance: The Evolving State and Local Roles." In *Toward Sustainable Communities:*

Transition and Transformations in Environmental Policy, ed. D. A. Mazmanian and M. E. Kraft. Cambridge, MA: MIT Press.

Bolig, E. A. 2009. "Toward a Better NEPA Process for Decisionmakers." *Environmental Law Reporter* 39: 10656–10663.

Bots, P., and R. Kunneke. 2008. *Understanding Common-Pool Resource Problems in Infrastructures: Exploring Analogies with Natural Resource Systems.* Available at esd.mit.edu/symp09/presentations/day3.session3c.bots.pdf (accessed May 4, 2012).

Brentwood, M., and S. Robar, eds. 2004. *Managing Common Pool Groundwater Resources: An International Perspective.* New York: Praeger.

Brewer, G. D., and P. C. Stern, eds. Panel on Social and Behavioral Science Research Priorities for Environmental Decision Making. 2006. *Decision Making on the Environment: Social and Behavioral Science Research Priorities.* Washington, DC: National Academies Press.

Caldwell, L. K. 1999. *The National Environmental Policy Act: An Agenda for the Future.* Bloomington: Indiana University Press.

Case, D. W. 2001. "The Law and Economics of Environmental Information as Regulation." *Environmental Law Reporter* 31: 10773–10789.

Cohen, M. A. 2000. *Information as a Policy Instrument in Protecting the Environment: What Have We Learned?* Washington, DC: Environmental Defense Fund. Available at http://sitemason.vanderbilt.edu/files/ehxkf6/elr_published_april_20011.pdf (accessed May 6, 2012).

Council on Environmental Quality. 1997. *The National Environmental Policy Act: A Study of Its Effectiveness after Twenty-five Years.* Washington, DC: Council on Environmental Quality.

Delmas, M. A., and O. R. Young, eds. 2009. *Governance for the Environment: New Perspectives.* New York: Cambridge University Press.

Dessler, A. E., and E. A. Parson. 2010. *The Science and Politics of Climate Change: A Guide to the Debate.* 2nd ed. Cambridge: Cambridge University Press.

Dietz, T., and P. C. Stern, eds. 2008. *New Tools for Environmental Protection: Education, Information, and Voluntary Measures.* Washington, DC: National Academies Press.

———. 2008. *Public Participation in Environmental Assessment and Decision Making.* Washington, DC: National Academies Press.

Durant, R. F. 2007. *The Greening of the U.S. Military: Environmental Policy, National Security, and Organizational Change.* Washington, DC: Georgetown University Press.

Durant, R. F., D. J. Fiorino, and R. O'Leary, eds. 2004. *Environmental Governance Reconsidered: Challenges, Choices, and Opportunities.* Cambridge, MA: MIT Press.

Environmental Law Institute. 2010. *NEPA Success Stories: Celebrating 40 Years of Transparency and Open Government.* Washington, DC: Environmental Law Institute. At www.eli.org.

Esty, Daniel C. 2004. "Environmental Protection in the Information Age." Yale University Faculty Scholarship Series, Paper 431. Available at digitalcommons.law.yale.edu/fss_papers/431 (accessed February 10, 2012).

Esworthy, R. 2010. *National Ambient Air Quality Standards (NAAQS) for Fine Particulate Matter (PM2.5): Designating Nonattainment Areas. Report No. R40096.* Washington, DC: Congressional Research Service.

Farber, D. A. 2009. "Adaptation Planning and Climate Impact Assessments: Learning from NEPA's Flaws." *Environmental Law Reporter* 39: 10605.

Fiorino, D. J. 2006. *The New Environmental Regulation*. Cambridge, MA: MIT Press.

Freedom of Information Act. 1966. Public Law 110–175.

Gayer, T., and J. K. Horowitz. 2006. "Market-Based Approaches to Environmental Regulation." *Foundations and Trends in Microeconomics* 1 (4): 3–35.

Gerrard, M. B. 2008. "Climate Change and the Environmental Impact Review Process." *Natural Resources and the Environment* 22 (3): 20–24.

———. 2009. "The Effect of NEPA outside the Courtroom." *Environmental Law Reporter* 35: 10615–10631.

Ghate, R., J. Narpat, and P. Mukhopadhyay, eds. 2008. *Promise, Trust and Evolution: Managing the Commons in South Asia*. New York: Oxford University Press.

Guber, D., and C. J. Bosso. 2010. "Past the Tipping Point? Public Discourse and the Role of the Environmental Movement in a Post-Bush Era." In *Environmental Policy*, 7th ed., ed. N. J. Vig and M. E. Kraft, 51–74. Washington, DC: CQ Press.

Gunningham, N. 2009. "Environment Law, Regulation and Governance: Shifting Architectures." *Journal of Environmental Law* 21 (2): 179–212.

Haas, P. M. 2004. "Addressing Global Governance Deficit." *Global Environmental Politics* 4 (4): 1–15.

Harrington, W., L. Heinzerling, and R. D. Morgenstern, eds. 2009. *Reforming Regulatory Impact Analysis*. Washington, DC: Resources for the Future.

Hempel, L. C. 1999. "Conceptual and Analytical Challenges in Building Sustainable Communities." In *Toward Sustainable Communities: Transition and Transformation*, ed. D. Mazmanian and M. E. Kraft, 43–74. Cambridge, MA: MIT Press.

ICLEI Local Governments for Sustainability. *Members*. Available at http://www.iclei.org/index.php?id=global-members (accessed May 5, 2012).

Jasanoff, S., and M. Martello. 2004. *Earthly Politics: Local and Global in Environmental Governance*. Cambridge, MA: MIT Press.

Karkkainen, B. C. 2002. "Collaborative Ecosystem Governance: Scale, Complexity, and Dynamism." *Virginia Environmental Law Journal* 21 (1): 189–244.

Keller, A. C. 2009. *Science in Environmental Policy: The Politics of Objective Advice*. Cambridge, MA: MIT Press.

Kettl, D. F., ed. 2002. *Environmental Governance: A Report on the Next Generation of Environmental Policy*. Washington, DC: Brookings Institution Press.

Koontz, T. M., and C. W. Thomas. 2006. "What Do We Know and Need to Know about the Environmental Outcomes of Collaborative Management?" *Public Administration Review* 66 (6): 111–121.

Korten, F. 2011. "Elinor Ostrom Wins Nobel for Common(s) Sense." *Yes! Magazine.* www.yesmagazine.org/. Available at http://www.yesmagazine.org/issues/america-the-remix/elinor-ostrom-wins-nobel-for-common-s-sense (accessed May 7, 2012).

Kraft, M. E., M. Stephan,, and T. D. Abel. 2011. *Coming Clean: Information Disclosure and Environmental Performance*. Cambridge, MA: MIT Press.

Latham, R. 2006. "Knowledge and Governance in the Digital Age: The Politics of Monitoring Planetary Life." *First Monday* 11 (9). At firstmonday.org/issues/issue11_9/latham/index.html.

Layzer, J. A. 2011. *The Environmental Case: Translating Values into Policy*. 3rd ed. Washington, DC: CQ Press.

Leber, J. 2009. "Can NEPA Pass Tests Posed by Climate-Related Projects?" *New York Times*, March 26.

Levi-Faur, D. 2005. "The Global Diffusion of Regulatory Capitalism." *Annals of the American Academy of Political and Social Science*, vol. 528: *The Global Diffusion of a New Order* 32 (March): 12–32.

Lindstrom, M. J., and Z. A. Smith. 2003. *The National Environmental Policy Act: Judicial Misconstruction, Legislative Indifference, and Executive Neglect.* College Station: Texas A&M University Press.

Lomborg, B. 2001. *The Skeptical Environmentalist.* Rev. ed. Cambridge: Cambridge University Press.

Mandelker, D. R. 2009. "Thoughts on NEPA at 40." *Environmental Law Reporter* 39: 10640–10641.

Manheim, F. T. 2011. *The Conflict over Environmental Regulation in the United States: Origins, Outcomes, and Comparisons with the EU and Other Regions.* New York: Springer.

Mannina, G. J., Jr. 2009. "NEPA at 40." *Environmental Law Reporter* 39: 10660–10662.

Matthew, R. A. 2010. "Environmental Security." In *Environmental Policy: New Directions for the Twenty-First Century*, 7th ed., ed. N. Vig and M. E. Kraft. Washington, DC: CQ Press.

Mazmanian, D. A., and M. E. Kraft. 2009a. "The Three Epochs of the Environmental Movement." In *Toward Sustainable Communities: Transition and Transformations in Environmental Policy*, 2nd ed., ed. D. A. Mazmanian and M. E. Kraft. Cambridge, MA: MIT Press.

——— 2009b. *Toward Sustainable Communities: Transition and Transformations in Environmental Policy.* 2nd ed. Cambridge, MA: MIT Press.

McGarity, T. O., and W. Wagner. 2008. *Bending Science: How Special Interests Corrupt Public Health Research.* Cambridge, MA: Harvard University Press.Mol, A. P. J. 2006. "Environmental Governance in the Information Age." *Environment and Planning C: Government and Policy* 24 (3): 497–514.

Mol, A. P. J., and G. Spaargaren. 2006. "Towards a Sociology of Environmental Flows: A New Agenda for 21st Century Environmental Sociology." In *Governing Environmental Flows: Global Challenges for Social Theory*, ed. G. Spaargaren, A. P. J. Mol, and F. H. Buttel, 39–83. Cambridge, MA: MIT Press.

Najam, A., M. Papa, and N. Taiyab. 2007. "Global Environmental Governance: Key Challenges to Effective Global Governance." In *Encyclopedia of the Earth.* Washington, DC: National Council for Science and the Environment. Available at www.eoearth.org/article/Global_Environmental_Governance_Key Challenges_to_Effective_Global_Environmental_Governance.

National Academy of Engineering. 2001. *Information Systems and the Environment.* Ed. Richards, D. J., R. A. Braden, and W. D. Compton. Washington D. C.: National Academies Press.

National Research Council, Committee on Air Quality Management in the United States. 2004. "Transforming the Nation's AQM System to Meet the Challenges of the Coming Decades." In *Air Quality Management in the United States.* Washington, DC: National Academies Press.

National Research Council, Committee on the Challenge of Developing Sustainable Urban Systems. 2010. *Pathways to Sustainability.* Washington, DC: National Academies Press.

National Research Council, Committee on Improving Risk Analysis Used by the EPA. 2009. *Science and Decisions: Advancing Risk Assessment.* Washington, DC: National Academies Press.

National Research Council, Committee on Indicators for Understanding Global
    Climate Change. 2010. *Monitoring Climate Change Impacts: Metrics at the Intersection
    of the Human and Earth Systems*. Washington, DC: National Research Council.
National Research Council, Committee on Models in the Regulatory Process. 2007.
    Models in Environmental Regulatory Decision Making. Washington, DC: National
    Academies Press.
National Research Council, Panel on Advancing the Science of Climate Change.
    2010. *America's Climate Choices*. Washington, DC: National Academies Press.
NEPA Task Force. 2003. *Modernizing NEPA Implementation: Report to the Council
    on Environmental Quality*. Washington, DC: Council on Environmental Quality.
OMB Watch. 2011. www.rtknet.org.
O'Rourke, D. 2004. *Community-Driven Regulation: Balancing Development and the
    Environment in Vietnam*. Cambridge, MA: MIT Press.
Ostrom, E. 1990. *Governing the Commons: The Evolution of Institutions for Collective
    Action*. New York: Cambridge University Press.
———. 2005. *Understanding Institutional Diversity*. Princeton, NJ: Princeton
    University Press.
———. 2008. "The Challenge of Common Pool Resources." *Environment Magazine*
    50 (4): 8–21.
Ostrom, E., L. Schroeder, and S. Wyanne. 1993. *Institutional Incentives and
    Sustainable Development: Infrastructure Policies in Perspective*. Boulder, CO:
    Westview.
Ostrom, E., and National Research Council Committee on the Human Dimensions
    of Global Change, eds. 2002. *The Drama of the Commons*. Washington, DC:
    National Academy Press.
Paddock, L. C. 2008. "Building the Competencies Necessary for Effective
    Environmental Management." *Environmental Law Reporter* 38: 10609–10642.
Ravesz, R. L., and R. Stavins. 2004. "Environmental Law and Public Policy." In
    Environmental Law and Policy, vol. 1, ed. A. M. Polinsky and S. Shavell, 499–571.
    Washington, DC: RFF Press;
Sabatier, P. A., W. Focht, M. Lubell, Z. Trachtenberg, A. Vedlitz, and M. Matlock,
    eds. 2005. *Swimming Upstream: Collaborative Approaches to Watershed
    Management*. Cambridge, MA: MIT Press.
Saha, D., and R. G. Paterson. 2010. "Local Government Efforts to Promote the 'Three
    Es' of Sustainable Development: A Survey of Medium to Large Cities in the United
    States." *Journal of Planning Education and Research* 28 (1): 21–37.
Salking, P. E. 2009. "Sustainability and Land Use Planning: Greening State and
    Local Land Use Plans and Regulations to Address Climate Change Challenges and
    Preserve Resources for the Future." *William and Mary Environmental Law and
    Policy Journal* 34 (1): 121–170.
Schiffries, C., ed. 2005. *Forecasting Environmental Changes: A Report of the Fifth
    National Conference on Science, Policy and the Environment*. Washington, DC:
    National Council for Science and Environment.
Schlager, E., and T. Heikkila. 2011. "Left High and Dry? Climate Change, Common
    Pool Resource Theory, and the Adaptability of Western Water Compacts." *Public
    Administration Review* 71 (3): 461–470.
Selin, H., and S. D. VanDeveer, eds. 2009. *Changing Climates in North American
    Politics: Institutions, Policymaking, and Multilevel Governance*. Cambridge, MA:
    MIT Press.

Singh, K. 1994. *Managing Common Pool Resources: Principles and Studies*. New York: Cambridge University Press.

Spaargaren, G., A. J. P. Mol, and F. H. Buttel. 2006. *Governing Environmental Flows: Global Challenges for Social Theory*. Cambridge, MA: MIT Press.

Speth, J. G., and P. M. Haas. 2007. *Global Environmental Governance*. New York: Island.

United Nations Environment Programme. 2011. *Environment for Development: Freedom of Access to Environmental Information in the United States*. Available at www.unep.org/dec/onlinemanual/Enforcement/InstitutionalFrameworks/PublicAccesstoInformation/Resource/tabid/975/Default.aspx (accessed May 4, 2012).

U.S. Environmental Protection Agency, International Programs. *Environmental Governance*. Available at www.epa.gov/oia/regions/Asia/india/environmental_governance.html (accessed May 3, 2012).

U.S. Government Accountability Office. 2009. *Environmental Protection Agency: Major Management Challenges*. Report No. 09–434. Washington, DC: Government Printing Office.

Weber, E. P. 2003. *Bringing Society Back In: Grassroots Ecosystem Management, Accountability, and Sustainable Communities*. Cambridge, MA: MIT Press.

Weidner, H., and M. Janicke. 2002. *Capacity Building in National Environmental Policy*. Berlin: Springer-Verlag.

Weiner, K. S. 2009. "NEPA and State NEPAs: Learning from the Past, Foresight for the Future." *Environmental Law Reporter* 39: 10675–10687.

Wilbanks, T. J., and R. W. Kates. 2010. "Beyond Adapting to Climate Change: Embedding Adaptation in Responses to Multiple Threats and Stresses." *Annals of the Association of American Geographers* 100 (4): 719–728.

Wilbanks, T. J., and P. C. Stern. 2003. "New Tools for Environmental Protection: What We Know and Need to Know." In *New Tools for Environmental Protection: Education, Information, and Voluntary Measures*, ed. T. Dietz and P. C. Stern, 337–348. Washington, DC: National Academies Press.

Wishnie, L. G. 2008. "NEPA for a New Century: Change and Reform of the National Environmental Policy Act." *NYU Environmental Law Journal* 16 (2): 628–654.

Woodrow Wilson International Center for Scholars, Environmental Change and Security Program. 2010. *Report, Issue 13*. Washington, DC: Wilson Center.

Wright, D. J., S. L. Duncan, and D. Lach. 2009. "Social Power and GIS Technology: A Review and Assessment of Approaches to Natural Resource Management." *Annals of the Association of American Geographers* 99 (2): 254–272.

Young, O. R. 2002. *The Institutional Dimensions of Environmental Change: Fit, Interplay, and Scale*. Cambridge, MA: MIT Press.

———. 2010. *Institutional Dynamics: Emergent Patterns in International Environmental Governance*. Cambridge, MA: MIT Press.

CHAPTER 8

....

U.S. CLIMATE CHANGE POLITICS

FEDERALISM AND COMPLEXITY

....

HENRIK SELIN AND
STACY D. VANDEVEER

CLIMATE change politics in the United States cannot be analyzed without attention to the country's fragmentation of powers and the tradition of environmental federalism, in which many environmental policies are first developed and enacted in states (and sometimes in cities) before taken up by the federal government (Kelemen 2004; Selin and VanDeveer 2009). U.S. climate change policy making includes interactions of public, private, and civil society actors within and across different governance levels as well as beyond the country's borders. National politics is shaped by global institutions as well as policymaking at federal, state, and municipal levels, as each domestic governance level is connected to institutions and actors in other jurisdictions (Rabe 2010, 2011; chapter 18 in this volume; Selin and VanDeveer 2012; Steinberg and VanDeveer 2012). Consequently, it is necessary to take both domestic and international aspects of the issue into consideration when examining U.S. climate change politics and policymaking.

Global efforts on climate change mitigation are also highly dependent on U.S. measures to reduce its emissions of greenhouse gases (GHGs). The United States remains the world's largest GHG emitter in historical, cumulative terms, but China surpassed the United States as the leading annual national GHG emitter during the mid-2000s. U.S. GHG emissions increased by 17 percent between 1990 and 2007;

per capita emissions reached to an amount equivalent to about 24 tons of carbon dioxide (CO_2) equivalent. By comparison, per capita emissions in much of Europe are less than half of this figure, and those of countries such as China and India are much smaller still. In fact, GHG emissions of many U.S. states are equivalent to entire industrial or developing countries. Consequently, without substantial emissions cuts in the United States, it will be impossible to reduce global emissions to levels in line with adopted policy goals.

But the United States is often identified as a laggard on climate change policymaking and efforts to control GHG emissions. It is true that presidential leadership on climate change over successive administrations has tended to be weak, or even explicitly hostile to direct emission regulations and other measures to tackle CO_2 and other GHGs. Multiple U.S. Congresses since the 1990s have also repeatedly rejected calls for mandatory controls on GHGs. However, despite this significant resistance at the national level, many U.S. states and municipalities have enacted a wide range of climate change measures that go well beyond federal mandates (Koehn 2010; Rabe 2010; Selin and VanDeveer 2009). These bottom-up dynamics of policy making follow a similar trend of past subnational leadership in other major environmental issue areas, including air pollution abatement and hazardous waste management.

This chapter analyzes federal and international aspects of U.S. climate change politics and policy making. It begins with a discussion of a few key aspects of U.S. federalism and the governance complexity of addressing climate change as a prime example of a third-generation environmental problem, as described in the introductory chapter of this book. This is followed by an examination of American climate change politics at federal and subnational governance levels, involving a multitude of legal and political activities and interactions by a large number of public, private, and civil society sector actors. Next, the chapter discusses U.S. global and transnational engagement around climate change mitigation and adaptation issues, before offering a few concluding remarks about the future of U.S. climate change governance. In addition, the chapter identifies some priority areas for continuing empirical research and more in-depth analysis.

1. U.S. Federalism and Complexity

Multilevel governance involves public and private sector actors operating across different levels of social organization and jurisdictional authority. Such governance, whether in North America, Europe, or elsewhere, is typically characterized by horizontal and vertical linkages. Horizontal linkages involve interactions within the same governance level. In the United States, this includes relationships between different branches of the federal government and federal agencies as well as among states or among cities. U.S. vertical linkages involve interactions across governance levels, such as those between federal agencies and state and municipal governments. In this context of multilevel governance, Selin and VanDeveer (2009) introduce the notion of "complex multilevel coordination" as a way to think about developing climate change governance, as public, private, and civil society actors cooperate and compete to enact and implement climate change policies for adaptation and mitigation across and among different governance levels.

As the United States is a federal state, much of its domestic politics, policy making, and implementation are characterized by extensive multilevel governance involving a large number of jurisdictions protective of their authority. Bednar (2009, 18–19) specifies requirements for "robust federation," including firm boundaries of territory and authority that cannot be unilaterally abolished by the constituent states and national government. U.S. federalist governance, however, is dynamic over time, as some of the rules for division of authority and responsibility change as new areas of policy, such as climate change, are added to the system. Federal climate change law and politics involves much debate and controversy about legal and regulatory authority—who has the right to decide which specific issues and who is responsible for their implementation and enforcement—both within and across governance scales. That is, issues of authority are addressed simultaneously as a multitude of public and private sector actors interact at the federal and local levels both in support of and in opposition to ambitious climate change policy.

"Ideal" federal systems are said to be characterized by "cooperative federalism," where political actors at different governance levels cooperate and support each other toward the fulfillment of shared goals. Here all levels within a federal system act in a complementary manner. However, Derthick (2010) argues that U.S. climate change politics can be better described as "compensatory federalism," where subnational entities take actions to compensate for a lack of action by the federal government. Similarly, many observers have noted that U.S. domestic climate change politics has been characterized by bottom-up dynamics, with subnational jurisdictions moving beyond lagging federal standards and requirements (Lutsey and Sperling 2008; Rabe 2004, 2010; Selin and VanDeveer 2007, 2009). As the U.S. federal government has been largely inactive, sometimes even working actively against state and local efforts to set GHG regulations, subnational entities—states and municipalities—have stepped into the policy vacuum left by the federal government and developed their own plethora of climate change policies and standards.

U.S. states organize responsibilities quite differently as they allocate environmental authority and tasks to local agencies (Woods and Potoski 2010). So do municipalities: many—from small towns to large metropolises—are very active in climate change mitigation and adaptation policy making, often involving networks designed to facilitate and enhance their actions (Gore and Robinson 2009; Hoffmann 2011). Further complicating governance, climate change is a preeminent example of so-called third-generation environmental issues, shaping politics and creating significant policy-making challenges. Whereas first-generation (conservation of species and land) and second-generation (pollution and natural resources) environmental issues can also give rise to contentious politics, third-generation issues are characterized by a much greater combination of scientific and technical complexity and broad social, economic, and political complexity and uncertainty. They entail long-term timescales, large numbers of stakeholders with varying interests, and (usually) transjurisdictional or transnational dimensions (Mazmanian and Kraft 2009).

Achieving societal consensus on third-generation policy issues can be extremely challenging. Such issues also typically require adaptable governance structures and varying capacities at different levels of governance authority (from global to regional, national and local). Furthermore, U.S. climate change politics is shaped by fierce debate about the definition and role of science in public policy and society, and how scientific knowledge is created, manipulated, and used (or not used) in making laws, regulations, judicial decisions, and investments (Ascher, Steelman, and Healy 2010; Farrell and Jager 2006). Finally, climate change is much more than "just" an environmental issue; it connects to the energy, economic, and social issues foundational to U.S. society and politics. American wealth, power, and social relations rest, in part, on generations of relatively inexpensive fossil fuels and the expectation of growing demand and supply of such energy. The nation's economy and major aspects of its social structure were built on these foundations. Climate change is therefore ultimately a sustainable development issue, demonstrating complexity in abundance (see chapter 9 in this volume).

2. National Climate Change Governance at Multiple Levels

While discussions of federalist dynamics often focus on the federal and state levels (Rabe 2004, 2010; Selin and VanDeveer 2012), U.S. climate change politics is shaped by events and actors from local levels to Washington, DC (and beyond). Thus, U.S. multilevel climate change politics are influenced by actions and outcomes at both federal and subnational levels, involving a multitude of horizontal and vertical linkages within and across jurisdictions and governance scales.

2.1 Federal Level

All three branches of the federal government—executive, legislative, and judicial—engage with and shape climate change politics. Furthermore, interaction within and among the branches is often characterized by controversy. While some federal actors work to expand climate change policy-making authority and leadership, actors within other branches have worked to obstruct action.

Presidential leadership in the *executive branch* has been an important factor shaping U.S. climate change politics since the Reagan administration (1981–1989) (see chapter 14 in this volume). Climate change was not a salient topic during the Reagan era, although this was the time during which scientists began expressing public concerns about growing emissions and atmospheric concentrations of carbon dioxide and other GHGs (Weart 2008). Congress held hearings about climate change; many of them involving Al Gore, who was then a senator. It was during the Reagan administration that the United States and other countries, through the United Nations Environment Programme (UNEP) and the World Meteorological Organization (WMO), established the Intergovernmental Panel on Climate Change (IPCC). The IPCC provides assessments on the current state of scientific knowledge of climate change and its potential environmental and socioeconomic impacts; it has issued a series of high-profile reports since 1990. The Reagan administration was characterized by a deregulation agenda, including in the area of environmental policy.

Climate change gained greater prominence during the George H. W. Bush administration (1989–1993). Following a presidential initiative in 1989, Congress established the U.S. Global Change Research Program (USGCRP), which involved 13 departments and agencies and was charged with coordinating federal research on changes in the global environment and their implications for society, including climate change. Since the 1990s, the federal government—through the National Science Foundation, the Department of Energy, and the National Aeronautics and Space Administration, among others—has been the leading global funder of scientific research related to climate change, the products of which feed into national and international assessments, including by the IPCC. Together with most other world leaders, President Bush signed the United Nations Framework Convention on Climate Change (UNFCCC) on June 12, 1992, at the Rio Earth Summit. Following a speedy Senate ratification and final presidential approval on October 13, 1992, the United States was among the first to ratify the UNFCCC. However, the George H. W. Bush administration did not initiate any national GHG regulations.

Climate change became increasingly controversial in the United States during the Clinton administration (1993–2001). Within the UNFCCC process, the United States was very active during the negotiation of the 1997 Kyoto Protocol, the follow-up agreement to the UNFCCC. Vice President Al Gore signed the Kyoto Protocol for the United States, having flown to Kyoto to help broker a final agreement on the treaty. President Clinton, knowing that the protocol lacked congressional support, never submitted it for Senate ratification. Even as Al Gore and other administration officials expressed support for ambitious climate change policy, the Environmental Protection Agency (EPA) in 1999 rejected a petition from environmental groups to set CO_2 emissions standards for vehicles on the grounds that it did not believe that the Clean Air Act provided authority for such controls. During the 1990s and the 2000s presidential elections, major U.S. firms and trade associations led private sector opposition to the introduction of mandatory GHG emission reductions, including extensive lobbying of public officials and a well-funded mass media advertising campaign (Levy 2005).

George W. Bush ran for president in 2000 pledging support for regulating CO_2 emissions, but after he was elected his administration (2001–2009) staunchly opposed mandatory controls of GHGs as well as the ratification of the Kyoto Protocol. Administration officials downplayed the importance of climate change, expressed skepticism about climate change science, and decried the economic damage they argued would be caused by GHG regulations. Rather, federal policy during the 2000s focused on voluntary programs aimed at reducing the economy's GHG "intensity," as measured by GHG emissions per unit of gross domestic product. Absolute increases in U.S. GHG emissions continued. Federal agencies funded extensive scientific study of climate change and the development of emissions-reducing technologies, in part drawing on work by the previously established USGCRP. However, the administration's political appointees repeatedly discouraged executive branch officials from speaking or writing publicly about the growing scientific evidence of human-induced climate change.

The arrival of the Obama administration (2009) brought a significant shift in the executive branch's attitudes toward climate change science and policy. During the election campaign and after taking office in January 2009, President Obama supported the goal of returning U.S. GHG emissions to 1990 levels by 2020—a position translating into an emissions cut of about 17 percent from 2005 levels. The Obama administration urged Congress to pass comprehensive climate change and energy legislation, which only the House of Representatives accomplished. The Obama administration also took administrative initiatives to regulate GHGs under the Clean Air Act, including issuing an EPA "endangerment finding" in 2009 stating that the current and projected atmospheric concentrations of carbon dioxide (CO_2), methane (CH_4), nitrous oxide (N_2O), hydrofluorocarbons (HFCs), perfluorocarbons (PFCs), and sulfur hexafluoride (SF_6) threaten the public health and welfare of current and future generations. Following this endangerment finding, the EPA began to explore options for developing GHG controls through administrative and regulatory means.

The *legislative branch* has consistently rejected the need for legally binding regulations on GHGs. While there have been advocates for serious legislation since the 1980s, they have remained a minority. Congressional critics have questioned the science of human-induced climate change and argued that costs of climate change policy action would be too high. Senators and representatives have shaped U.S. domestic climate change action and global climate change politics largely via their refusal to enact policies intended to reduce GHG or to foster adaptation. The Senate also responded differently to the two main climate change treaties. It quickly ratified the UNFCCC in 1992, which imposed few domestic commitments or burdens. However, a 1997 "Sense of the Senate" resolution passed 95–0 prior to the final negotiations of the Kyoto Protocol, declaring the body's opposition to agreements that "could result in serious harm to the United States economy, including significant job loss, trade disadvantages, increased energy and consumer costs, or any combination thereof." The Kyoto Protocol lists the United States in Annex I with other developed countries. U.S. negotiators agreed to a 7 percent

GHG reduction target from 1990 levels by 2012, but the agreement was never submitted to the Senate for consideration.

Senator James Inhofe (R-OK), former chair of the Senate Committee on Environment and Public Works, famously described global warming as "the greatest hoax ever perpetrated on the American people" (Kolbert 2006). Particularly strong congressional opposition came from congressional Republicans from 1994 onward. Opposition to domestic and international efforts to reduce GHG emissions has been shaped by the general desire to reduce the role of government and decrease regulation, while some congressional opposition is linked to the natural resource base and energy uses of the states that House and Senate members represent (Fisher 2006). Both Republican and Democratic members from states with large resource extraction industries, particularly coal and oil, tend to side with industrial lobbies against reducing fossil fuel subsidies and regulating GHG emissions. Similarly, members from states with heavy manufacturing—especially automobiles and other energy-intensive production industries—have resisted efforts to price CO_2 emissions, fearing local economic (and political) impacts of higher energy costs.

Some congressional members proposed many climate change-related bills in the late 1990s and 2000s, but most never got a hearing in committee, much less were put to a full vote (Rabe 2010). The Energy Independence and Security Act of 2007, however, raised the national Corporate Average Fuel Economy (CAFE) standards for vehicles for the first time in over thirty years. The act also included new product energy efficiency standards as well as subsidies and mandates intended to increase the use of ethanol and biofuels. In 2009, the Obama administration raised the CAFE standards to 35.5 mpg by 2016 (42 mpg for automobiles and 26 mpg for light trucks). In 2011, the EPA proposed additional increases for the years 2017–2025, pushing overall requirements to over 54 miles per gallon by 2025. This effort was followed by rules to increase efficiency standards for heavy trucks by 20 percent by 2018. In addition, the EPA is reviewing existing rules for pollutants like sulfur dioxide, nitrogen oxide, and ground-level ozone. While these regulations are not aimed explicitly at reducing GHG emissions, some are expected to also do so if fully implemented.

Regarding legislation designed to regulate GHGs specifically during the 111th Congress (2009–2011), the House of Representatives in 2009 narrowly passed the American Clean Energy and Security Act by a vote of 219 to 212. This Act, also known as the Waxman-Markey bill after its two main sponsors, sought to reduce national GHG emissions through a host of measures. It called for a 17 percent cut in GHG emissions from 2005 levels by 2020, to be increased to an approximate 80 percent reduction by 2050. A core component of the bill was the proposed creation of a national cap-and-trade scheme. However, neither this bill nor any other that regulates GHG emissions was brought to a vote on the Senate floor during the 111th Congress. In both chambers, Republican opposition was nearly unanimous, as Democrats struggled to reach agreement on the various proposals. The 112th Congress (2011–2013) seems unlikely to pass any kind of climate change legislation, as some members also introduced attempts to either delay or strip the EPA's authority to control GHGs under the Clean Air Act.

Closely linked with initiatives in the other two branches of the federal government, U.S. climate change policy making is also shaped by the *judicial branch* (Doran 2008; Engel 2010; O'Leary 2010). The regulation of GHGs has been repeatedly addressed in federal courts, bringing the judicial branch into the center of much climate change politics. As courts rule for or against the authority of different jurisdictions to regulate GHG emissions from mobile and stationary sources, these rulings are met with loud praise and criticism from presidential administrations and executive branch agencies, congressional members, and a broad array of industrial and civil society actors, depending on their stands on climate change and other regulatory issues. Major legal debates about the domestic regulation of GHG emissions date back to the 1990s. In 1999, for example, several leading environmental groups petitioned the EPA to set CO_2 emissions standards for vehicles. The Clinton administration EPA, however, rejected this request on the grounds that the agency did not believe the Clean Air Act provided authority for such controls.

Consistent with the bottom-up development of much U.S. climate change politics, subnational policy leaders, with the support of environmental advocacy groups, continued to challenge the EPA. Deeply frustrated by federal recalcitrance, Attorneys General from 12 states (California, Connecticut, Illinois, Maine, Massachusetts, New Jersey, New Mexico, New York, Oregon, Rhode Island, Vermont, and Washington) filed suit in federal court in 2003, challenging this decision and demanding that the EPA's authority to regulate carbon be clarified by the court. Following a long and much-watched legal process through the federal court system—with the George W. Bush administration, several other states, and the automobile industry among the suit's many opponents—in 2007 the U.S. Supreme Court, in a 5–4 ruling (in *Massachusetts v. EPA*), stated that CO_2 can be classified as a pollutant under the Clean Air Act. This major decision cleared one significant legal hurdle and provided supporters of more aggressive climate change policy with a new set of political tools for controlling GHGs.

In the wake of *Massachusetts v. EPA*, Obama administration officials and other advocates of GHG-related legislation attempted to use administrative regulation by the EPA to spur congressional action. Policy advocates argued that if Congress wanted to shape GHG regulation, it should enact law directing the EPA's activities. However, in 2011 the U.S. Supreme Court, in an 8–0 ruling (in *American Electric Power Co. v. Connecticut*), blocked a federal lawsuit by a few leader states and advocacy groups who sought to force cuts in GHG emissions from power plants and expressed disappointment with the slow progress by federal authorities following the 2007 decision. In their 2011 ruling, the justices stated that the authority to reduce GHG emission rested with the EPA, not with federal judges. In addition, federal and state courts have played important roles in shaping subnational climate change and energy laws and standards across the country, including in California. As subnational policy efforts accelerated in the 2000s, legal challenges to such efforts also increased, illustrating federalist contestation across governance levels and branches of government.

2.2 Subnational Level

While the three branches of the federal government failed to formulate a serious and coherent national climate change policy, many states acted (Burke and Ferguson 2010; Posner 2010; Rabe 2004, 2010; Selin and VanDeveer 2007, 2009). Since the early 2000s, leader states have initiated a growing number of policy initiatives, individually and in groups. Many state initiatives subsequently diffuse to other states through the influence of networks of civil servants, elected officials, and nongovernmental organizations (NGOs). State leadership, and federal responses to it, fit into a much broader pattern of federalist contestation between states and federal authority, illustrating the institutionalization of environmental policy expertise and action at the state level over the past three decades. Posner (2010) argues that both horizontal and vertical diffusion of environmental policies are shaped by characteristics of U.S. federalism, as the nature of American federalism offers state-based pathways for environmental leadership even as federal actors choose how to respond to state action. By sustaining room for state action, U.S. federalism also encourages policy learning and diffusion among states.

Certainly, subnational climate change policy making is not without controversy. While some states enact policies declaring their disappointment with the federal government, others side with opponents in Washington and reject the need for GHG controls. Also, because climate change politics is so expansive in its coverage and its connections to other issues—including energy, agriculture, transportation, and construction—patterns of political conflict are quite complex at the state level. For example, it may not be surprising to find traditional environmental leaders such as California, Oregon, and Massachusetts leading on climate change, but it may be more surprising to find Texas among the leaders on renewable energy development or Nebraska leading on climate-friendly land use policies (Rabe 2004). The latter two states, however, remain hostile to capping GHG emissions, even if they are energy and agricultural production states into which some forms of clean energy fit well. In these instances, however, actors pushing lower-carbon energy or agricultural practices remain unlikely to frame their policy proposals in terms of climate change.

Since the 1990s, a growing number of states have initiated a diverse set of measures. The Pew Center on Global Climate Change tracks the adoption of 21 different policies. Half of all states have adopted individual GHG reduction targets, ranging from modest to quite ambitious. Almost 30 states established renewable portfolio standards requiring electricity providers within a state to obtain a minimum percentage of power from renewable sources. Many states set mandates and incentives for ethanol production, while an expanding number follow California in setting vehicle emission standards higher than those mandated by the federal government. In addition, many state agencies adopt green building standards, expand investments in energy efficiency programs, and mandate the sale of increasingly efficient appliances and electronic equipment. Furthermore, some state initiatives are producing substantive emissions reductions. For example, by 2010 Massachusetts was on track to reduce its CO_2 emissions by at least 18 percent below 1990 levels by 2020 (Massachusetts 2010). However, while many states on the West Coast and in the Northeast enacted 18 to 21 of the 21 policies tracked, many states in the South and the Great Plains engaged only three to six of the listed initiatives as their GHG emissions continue to grow.

California emerged in the 2000s as the foremost policy leader among U.S. states, building on its long tradition of leadership on both air pollution and energy efficiency (Farrell and Hanemann 2009; Urpelainen 2009). As in the case with other state leaders, California policy making is often framed in terms of climate change action aimed at reducing GHG emissions and also linked to debates about "smart growth" and the creation of "green jobs." California's legislative and gubernatorial leadership led the enactment of a large suit of laws and regulations aimed at capping and reducing state CO_2 emissions, expanding renewable energy production, launching a carbon cap-and-trade system, increasing automobile fuel efficiency, and pushing the expansion of low- and zero-emissions vehicles, reducing the carbon content of fuels, and increasing energy efficiency standards for buildings and products. Because of these expansive efforts, California now ranks among the world's most aggressive jurisdictions in its development of climate change policy. California and other frontrunner states are also pushing federal authorities to recognize their actions under their developing rule-making processes.

Beyond individual state initiatives, leaders also collaborate. Multistate cooperation is intended to strengthen states' collective position vis-à-vis the federal government and laggard states as well as to take advantage of efficiency gains. Some such initiatives also include Canadian provinces and/or Mexican states. An early example: in 2000 the Conference of New England Governors (Maine, New Hampshire, Vermont, Massachusetts, Rhode Island, and Connecticut) and Eastern Canadian Premiers (Nova Scotia, Newfoundland and Labrador, Prince Edward Island, New Brunswick, and Quebec) adopted a resolution that recognized climate change as a joint concern that affected local environments and economies. This resolution eventually produced a 2001 Climate Change Action Plan. Under this action plan, states and provinces pledged to reduce their GHGs to 1990 levels by 2010 and 10 percent below 1990 levels by 2020. They ultimately agreed to decrease emissions to levels that do not pose a threat to the climate, which according to an official estimate would require a 75 to 85 percent reduction from 2001 emission levels.

The Regional Greenhouse Gas Initiative (RGGI), North America's first publicly run GHG emissions trading scheme, is a multistate initiative. Launched in 2009, RGGI is a mandatory cap-and-trade scheme for CO_2 emissions from power plants in the participating states: Maryland, Maine, Vermont, New Hampshire,

Massachusetts, Rhode Island, Connecticut, New York, and Delaware. RGGI seeks to stabilize CO_2 emissions from the region's power sector between 2009 and 2015. After that, each state's annual CO_2 emissions budget is scheduled to decline by 2.5 percent per year, achieving a total 10 percent reduction by 2019. While RGGI goals are modest, the trading scheme's development constitutes an important first in North America. The scheme also allocates most emissions permits to firms via auction, rather than giveaways, in contrast to most other such schemes in the world. The RGGI states have asked the EPA to let them use RGGI to comply with any future federal rules for the utility sector.

Even if interest in GHG emissions trading among members of the U.S. Congress waned in the late 2000s, other subnational actors have continued to explore the possible enactment of their own GHG emissions trading policies as they seek to draw lessons from RGGI and experiences from other individual state initiatives. Such discussions include groups of states around the Great Lakes and the West Coast through the Western Climate Initiative. These efforts include plans to establish a joint carbon cap-and-trade system among several U.S. states and Canadian provinces, and/or linking up with other regional systems like RGGI. Opposition from some industrial interests and from many Republican officials slowed or reversed this work in many midwestern and some western states after the 2010 elections, but California and a small set of other states and Canadian provinces continued to plan for a second regional cap-and-trade scheme through the Western Climate Initiative.

State initiatives, individually and collectively, also draw from The Climate Registry, a regional initiative involving a large group of U.S. states as well as Mexican and Canadian jurisdictions. By 2010, The Climate Registry had 61 member states, provinces, and tribes from all three North American countries (41 U.S. states, the District of Columbia, nine Canadian provinces, six Mexican states, and four native tribes). Launched in 2007, The Climate Registry seeks to develop a common system for private and public entities to calculate and report GHG emissions, allowing for consistent measurement verification and the reporting of emissions. This is yet another example of the kind of bottom-up climate change action common in North America; because federal actors and institutions have not established common techniques and standards for GHG measurement, verification, and reporting, states and provinces attempt to do so. This may not be considered high politics, but these kinds of standard-setting exercises can shape much state-level action as well as future federal policy making.

Paralleling the expansion of state-level climate change action, since early 2000s a growing number of U.S. municipalities have enacted serious climate change policies (although municipal action is often developed separate from state-level initiatives). Many municipalities participate in domestic and international organizations and networks that disseminate policy ideas and lessons on climate change-related issues across cities that may not otherwise interact (Betsill and Bulkeley 2006; Bulkeley and Betsill 2003; Gore and Robinson 2009). These fora include the U.S. Conference of Mayors Climate Protection Center, which oversees the U.S. Conference of Mayors Climate Protection Agreement. More than 1,000 mayors from all 50 states signed this agreement. Signatories strive to meet or beat the U.S. Kyoto Protocol target for GHG reductions in their own communities (i.e., a 7 percent reduction from 1990 levels by 2012), push for state governments to enact GHG reduction policies, and urge Congress to pass bipartisan legislation establishing a national GHG emissions trading system.

In another major example of municipal activities, over 150 U.S. cities are members of the International Council for Local Environmental Initiatives (ICLEI) and its Cities for Climate Protection (CCP) program (most members of which have also signed the Mayors Climate Protection Agreement). Members of the CCP program commit to a five-step process for addressing climate change: (1) creating a GHG emissions inventory and forecast; (2) setting an emissions reductions plan; (3) developing a local action plan; (4) implementing the local action plan; and (5) monitoring progress and reporting results. A few major cities, such as Philadelphia, New York City, Houston, Los Angeles, and Chicago, are also members of the C40 network partnering with the Clinton Foundation to promote ways of reducing GHG emissions and improve energy efficiency. While the GHG impacts of many municipal climate change programs are modest to date, a few cities (such as Portland, Oregon) promoting urban sustainability more broadly have achieved noteworthy results as they engage in policy experimentations of different kinds (Gore and Robinson 2009; Hoffmann 2011).

State and municipal leadership, however, is not without its opponents. Critics in many state legislatures and governors' offices have defeated various proposals and initiatives. Between 2008 and 2011, opposition grew vocal and active. Republican electoral gains at every level of government in 2010 further emboldened and empowered opponents of climate change action. By 2011, state legislatures and governors in several states were working to reverse early climate change and renewable energy policies; for example, several withdrew, or were considering withdrawal, from RGGI and the Western Governors Initiative. A majority of the midwestern states that agreed in 2007 to launch their own cap-and-trade scheme officially abandoned the idea in 2011. Although California voters affirmed the state's commitment to reducing GHG emissions in a 2010 referendum, and California officials are moving toward implementation of their state's suite of aggressive GHG reduction initiatives, legal challenges to the policies mount in state and federal courts, raising uncertainty about proposed rules and deadlines.

As the discussion above makes clear, the structure of U.S. federalism and the ways it shapes political action at different levels of government have substantial impacts on policy outcomes. Less well understood are similarities and differences of climate change and energy lobbying at separate governance levels and jurisdictions, including across different states and local communities. Similarly, it is clear that the development of a staunch antiregulation agenda since the 1980s, one that includes hostility toward much environmental policy, has had significant influence on national- and state-level debates. Less well explained, however, is which specific political and economic factors have shaped the broad Republican and conservative opposition from advocacy groups and office holders to most forms of climate change policy (as well as possible similarities and differences in these factors in different parts of the country). Finally, it is not yet clear why U.S. climate change politics show much more pronounced bottom-up dynamics than many other countries (including federalist ones). In all these areas, more research remains to be done.

3. The U.S. in Global and Transnational Climate Change Politics

Much of the U.S. national and local debate about climate change and the initiation of possible mitigation and adaptation measures is predominantly domestic in nature, as elected officials and stakeholder groups focus on specific conditions and interests of particular regions, states, and municipalities. However, U.S. climate change politics is also deeply connected with international issues and governance. Global outcomes of mitigation efforts also are greatly dependent on the United States, since this one country emits a significant proportion of humanity's GHG emissions. Alongside the development of domestic climate change politics, U.S. representatives interact with officials from other countries and international organizations in a growing number of international fora. This includes—but is not limited to—the UN-sponsored system of global cooperation around climate change. The United States has also been a very active member of the IPCC since its creation in 1988. Numerous Americans have participated in the multiple rounds of assessments and writings of scientific and socioeconomic reports.

Both as a party to the UNFCCC and as one of the world's largest economies and GHG emitters, the United States, through the federal government, is central to any efforts to design a global approach to climate change mitigation and adaptation. The UNFCCC establishes the principle of "common but differentiated responsibilities" as a guide for countries working together (Article 3). This means that all countries share an obligation to act, but wealthier countries such as the United States have more responsibility to lead in reducing GHG emissions because of their great wealth and contributions to the problem. Through the 1992 Senate ratification of the UNFCCC, the United States committed to the treaty's policy goals and principles. In response to mounting scientific evidence about human-induced climate change and to growing concern about the negative economic and social effects of climate change, UNFCCC parties negotiated the Kyoto Protocol between 1995 and 1997. The Kyoto Protocol regulates six GHGs: carbon dioxide (CO_2), methane (CH_4), nitrous oxide (N_2O), perfluorocarbons (PFCs), hydrofluorocarbons (HFCs), and sulfur hexafluoride (SF_6). These are the same GHGs identified by the U.S. EPA in its 2009 endangerment finding.

Under the Kyoto Protocol, U.S. representatives from the Clinton administration agreed to a target of a 7 percent reduction in GHG emissions, but (as discussed above) it was never ratified by the U.S. Senate. Because the Kyoto Protocol commitment period expires in 2012, interest in negotiating a follow-up agreement grew among climate policy advocates over the second half of the 2000s. In 2007, the United States and other UNFCCC parties launched a political process designed to negotiate a follow-up agreement to the Kyoto Protocol, with the goal of adopting a new agreement in 2009. The 2009 Copenhagen meeting, however, failed to reach a legally binding agreement satisfactory to leading industrialized and developing countries. Instead, following chaotic last-minute negotiations, delegates from a small group of countries, including the United States (led by President Obama), agreed on the Copenhagen Accord (Dimitrov 2010). This accord calls for countries to set voluntary GHG reduction goals. In response, the Obama administration reported a target of "in the range of" 17 percent reduction below 2005 levels by 2020.

Global climate change negotiations include a daunting set of challenges. One key issue to the United States and other countries concerns the setting of collective and individual targets and timetables for emission controls, building on those reported under the Copenhagen Accord. Negotiators are struggling to find agreement around targets that are both aggressive enough to make a real difference and politically, economically, and technically feasible. This is also one area where the refusal of Congress to set national GHG controls is closely linked with global politics. On the one hand, it is very difficult for the federal government (currently the Obama administration) to agree on binding international targets without first having set domestic ones. There is also very little chance that the Senate will ratify a treaty with mandatory targets if no domestic ones exist first. On the other hand, senators and the federal government have repeatedly refused to accept any binding targets for the United States without similar targets set for other major emitters, including those in the developing world. Developing countries like China and Brazil, however, argue that this violates the principle of common but differentiated responsibilities.

Discussions around targets and timetables are linked with debates on financing, capacity building, and technology transfer. This includes how international efforts should support capacity building and economic and political changes around the world, including financing and technology transfer to developing countries. The Copenhagen Accord noted that industrialized countries will try to mobilize jointly $100 billion a year by 2020. The Copenhagen Accord calls for the establishment of a Green Climate Fund to raise resources for mitigation and adaptation projects in developing countries. Agreement to set up this fund and begin developing distribution rules was reached in Cancun in 2010, but fund-raising was off to a slow start. From a global equity perspective, this situation gives rise to critical justice issues. Annex II of the UNFCCC lists 23 countries and the EU that have committed to provide "new and additional financial resources" to developing countries for addressing climate change issues (Article 4). As global negotiators seek to design and implement political agreements and technical and scientific programs—and U.S. officials seek to shape these efforts—developing country representatives raise critical capacity issues as they express concerns about a perceived lack of resources.

As global climate change politics is developing simultaneously in a multitude of fora, some analysts have started to talk about the emergence of a dense "regime complex" for climate change (Keohane and Victor 2011). This involves the dispersion of international political, scientific, and technical activities across a growing number of venues in addition to the UNFCCC-centered process. The United States, in part, contributed to this development, as it has engaged other countries in an expanding number of venues. As the George W. Bush administration rejected the Kyoto Protocol and the idea of mandatory GHG reductions both at home and abroad, it sought to build alliances and find alternative bilateral and multilateral forums to pursue its interests in nonbinding approaches and support for technical solutions that required minimal behavioral changes. The Obama administration stepped up engagement under the UNFCCC when taking office in 2009, but only agreed to voluntary goals under the Copenhagen Accord. It also continued parallel discussions in forums such as the G20. Many of these discussions have involved other leading industrialized countries as well as major developing countries.

Furthermore, not all international climate change politics relevant to the United States and domestic activities involve formal discussions between national governments. There has also been a sharp growth in a different kind of international climate change politics and policy experimentation since the 1990s (Hoffmann 2011). An important part of both U.S. federalism and transnational politics of climate change is the growing interaction of U.S. states and municipalities with foreign counterparts, apart from the international discussions led by the federal government. For example, as U.S. leader states such as California, New York, and Massachusetts expand policy on transportation, renewable energy, and energy conservation, they also are looking for inspirations and partners outside the country's borders. Examples of this include the previously discussed collaborative efforts between the New England Governors and the Eastern Canadian Premiers under the auspices of a joint action plan, as well as the Western Climate Initiative involving partners and observers from the United States, Canada, and Mexico. In both of these cases, joint activities serve to blur the line between domestic and international climate change politics.

In another example of how contemporary transnational climate change politics is rapidly moving beyond the exclusive scope of national governments, the International Carbon Action Partnership was created in 2007 to share best practices in designing and implementing GHG cap-and-trade systems (Selin and VanDeveer 2010). Founding members include the European Commission, several EU member states, and a multitude of U.S. states working on emissions trading issues under RGGI and the Western Climate Initiative. U.S. states are also developing memoranda of understanding with European countries. Governors from, for example, California, Florida, Wisconsin, and Michigan have signed memoranda of understanding with countries. These are not legally binding—U.S. states are constitutionally prohibited from entering into treaties with foreign jurisdictions—but they are designed to exchange policy experiences and best practices, promoting public awareness, collaborating on research and technology development, and facilitating trade in low-carbon technologies. Similarly, cities are expanding collaboration under both old and new forums such as ICLEI and the C40 Cities program.

Recent research in the area of global climate change politics has expanded outside an early focus on the UNFCCC and the Kyoto Protocol to include both other political, scientific, and technical fora and a much broader set of actors beyond national governments. There is, however, still room for much more detailed study of the different kinds of roles that U.S. public, private, and civil society actors play internationally, as well as how global politics and policy outcomes influence these domestic actors and their interests and strategies. Furthermore, in terms of research on comparative climate change politics, from which insights about important characteristics of U.S. politics and policy making might be gleaned, there is a dearth of such research beyond the transatlantic space. Opportunities for expanded North American regional policy action on climate change has been noted (Selin and VanDeveer 2011), but systematic comparative analysis of U.S. and North American policy making with political processes and actors in other countries and regions remains relatively rare (Harrison and Sundstrom 2010).

4. CONCLUSION

The U.S. federalist structure as well as the interests and strategies of a large number of policy actors shape climate change policy processes and outcomes. Over time, a complex case of multilevel governance has emerged where compensatory federalism and bottom-up policy making are dominating forces. Going forward, this raises important questions about the future direction of both federal and subnational politics. In many issue areas, federal authorities have established minimum standards with which public and private subnational actors must comply. Subnational authorities can also be allowed (or even encouraged) to exceed at least some federal standards, as federal action establishes policy "floors." This would leave room for more ambitious action by states, cities, and firms to pursue. At the same time, it is unclear how far subnational policy leaders are able or willing to go in the absence of more stringent federal standards and levels of federal support.

The national growth in GHG emissions and the inability to formulate a coherent domestic approach to climate change mitigation and adaptation give rise to critical questions about the ability of the United States to address this issue in both short-term and long-term ways. Proactive states and municipalities since the 1990s have used legal, political, and technical measures to try to push lagging subnational jurisdictions and federal policy makers to act, but they have little to show for it. At the same time, there remains considerable opposition from some state and municipal policy makers against GHG controls. Even if there is more private sector support in the early 2010s than in the 1990s, there is also much well-organized and well-funded private sector opposition from firms and conservative and free-market think tanks attacking regulations on both political and economic grounds while continuing to reject the science behind human-induced climate change (Jacques, Dunlap, and Freeman 2008; Jones and Levy 2009). At the same time, environmental advocacy groups have failed to have a significant impact on federal policy making, even if they have been more influential in some local-level debates.

Many polls show that Americans are generally concerned about climate change and its impacts. However, the issue has a relatively low priority compared to other economic and social concerns (the individual effects of which are often more immediate). Also, many who profess concern about climate change tell pollsters they are not willing to pay very much for policy responses and that they have changed few of their behaviors in response to their concern (Borick 2010; IEEP/NRDC 2008; Lehmann 2011). The public is also divided along partisan lines: self-described Democrats and Independents are generally more supportive of policy action, while Republicans are more opposed (Dunlap and McCright 2008). This suggests that years of criticism of climate change science by conservative and industry groups have been successful at undermining public confidence in climate change science (and scientists) even as the research community has grown more confident and expanded its consensus about the causes, trends, and threats posed by climate change (see chapters 20 and 21 in this volume) (McCright and Dunlap 2010, 2011).

In an attempt to promote policy progress, some analysts and environmental activists have attempted to shift public and policy-maker views of climate change and energy issues by framing them in terms of "security." The climate change and security links have been the subject of intellectual and policy-maker debate since the 1990s, when Al Gore was vice president and academic attention turned to such topics. Climate change issues have been framed in terms of U.S. national security concerns in terms of energy independence and energy security and the more expansive and humanitarian-focused "human security" agenda, much of which has focused on Arctic conditions and populations (Matthew et al. 2009; Moran 2011; Paskal 2010). While these different kinds of climate and security debates show little evidence of influencing public opinion or public debate, they have been discussed in the U.S. Department of Defense, the National Intelligence Council, the CIA and among a host of Washington-based security-related think tanks.

As U.S. climate change politics proceeds in a slow and messy fashion, there are many areas ripe for further research and analysis. This includes ongoing struggles over policy-making and standard-setting authority between federal and subnational authorities and how outcomes of these struggles will influence future climate change action. More systematic and comparative research into the interests and strategies of domestic policy actors—either advocating for aggressive climate change policy or lobbying against such measures—could shed needed light on factors that shape policy processes and outcomes within and across jurisdictions from small towns to Washington, DC, and global political fora. In addition, there are many opportunities for expanded study of possibilities and limitations of multi-jurisdictional climate change action stretching from domestic groups of cities and states to transnational collaborations between subnational and national governments. In these and other ways, U.S. climate change policy promises to be a major area of both multifaceted political action and exciting academic research for many decades to come.

REFERENCES

Ascher, W., T. Steelman, and R. Healy. 2010. *Knowledge and Environmental Policy: Re-Imagining the Boundaries of Science and Politics.* Cambridge, MA: MIT Press.

Bednar, J. 2009. *The Robust Federation: Principles of Design.* Cambridge: Cambridge University Press.

Betsill, M. M., and H. Bulkeley. 2006. "Cities and Multilevel Governance of Climate Change." *Global Governance* 12 (2): 141–159.

Borick, C. P. 2010. "American Public Opinion and Climate Change." In *Greenhouse Governance: Addressing Climate Change in America*, ed. B. G. Rabe. Washington, DC: Brookings Institution Press.

Bulkeley, H., and M. M. Betsill. 2003. *Cities and Climate Change: Urban Sustainability and Global Environmental Governance.* New York: Routledge.

Burke, B., and M. Ferguson. 2010. "Going Alone or Moving Together: Canadian and American Middle Tier Strategies on Climate Change." *Publius: The Journal of Federalism* 40 (3): 436–459.

Derthick, M. 2010. "Compensatory Federalism." In *Greenhouse Governance: Addressing Climate Change in America*, ed. B. G. Rabe. Washington, DC: Brookings Institution Press.

Dimitrov, R. S. 2010. "Inside UN Climate Change Negotiations: The Copenhagen Conference." *Review of Policy Research* 27 (6): 795–821.

Doran, K. L. 2008. "U.S. Sub-Federal Climate Change Initiatives: An Irrational Means to a Rational End." *Virginia Environmental Law Journal* 26 (1): 181–217.

Dunlap, R. E., and A. M. McCright. 2008. "A Widening Gap: Republican and Democratic Views on Climate Change." *Environment* 50 (5): 26–35.

Engel, K. H. 2010. "Courts and Climate Policy: Now and in the Future." In *Greenhouse Governance: Addressing Climate Change in America*, ed. B. G. Rabe. Washington, DC: Brookings Institution Press.

Farrell, A. E., and M. J. Hanemann. 2009. "Field Notes on the Political Economy of California Climate Policy." In *Changing Climates in North American Politics: Institutions, Policymaking, and Multilevel Governance*, ed. H. Selin and S. D. VanDeveer. Cambridge, MA: MIT Press.

Farrell, A. E., and J. Jager. 2006. *Assessments of Regional and Global Environmental Risks: Designing Processes for the Effective Use of Science in Decisionmaking.* Washington, DC: RFF.

Fisher, D. 2006. "Bringing the Material Back In: Understanding the United States Position on Climate Change." *Sociological Forum* 21 (3): 467–494.

Harrison, K., and L. M. Sundstrom, eds. 2010. *Global Commons, Domestic Decisions: The Comparative Politics of Climate Change.* Cambridge, MA: MIT Press.

Hoffmann, M. J. 2011. *Climate Governance at the Crossroads: Experimenting with a Global Response after Kyoto.* Oxford: Oxford University Press.

Gore, C., and P. Robinson. 2009. "Local government response to climate change: Our last, best hope" in *Changing Climates in North American Politics: Institutions, Policymaking and Multilevel Governance.* ed. H. Selin and S.D. VanDeveer. Cambridge, MA: MIT Press.

IEEP/NRDC.2008. "Climate Change and Sustainable Energy Policies in Europe and the United States." Institute for European Environmental Policy and Natural Resources Defense Council, Brussels.

Jacques, P. J., R. E. Dunlap, and M. Freeman. 2008. "The Organization of Denial: Conservative Think Tanks and Environmental Skepticism." *Environmental Politics* 17 (3): 349–385.

Jones, C. A., and D. L. Levy. 2009. "Business Strategies and Climate Change." In *Changing Climates in North American Politics: Institutions, Policymaking, and Multilevel Governance,* ed. H. Selin and S. D. VanDeveer. Cambridge, MA: MIT Press.

Kelemen, R. D. 2004. *The Rules of Federalism: Institutions and Regulatory Politics in the EU and Beyond.* Cambridge, MA: Harvard University Press.

Keohane, R. O., and D. G. Victor. 2011. "The Regime Complex for Climate Change." *Perspectives on Politics* 9 (1): 7–23.

Koehn, P. 2010. "Climate Policy and Action 'underneath' Kyoto and Copenhagen: China and the United States." *Wiley Interdisciplinary Reviews: Climate Change* 1 (3): 405–417.

Kolbert, E. 2006. *Field Notes from a Catastrophe: Man, Nature, and Climate Change.* New York: Bloomsbury

Lehmann, E. 2011. "Public Opinion: In Mass., Belief in Climate Change Stronger Than Action to Prevent It." *ClimateWire,* April 19.

Levy, D. L. 2005. "Business and the Evolution of the Climate Regime: The Dynamics of Corporate Strategies." In *The Business of Global Environmental Governance,* ed. D. L. Levy and P. J. Newell. Cambridge, MA: MIT Press.

Lutsey, N., and D. Sperling. 2008. "America's Bottom-Up Climate Change Mitigation Policy." *Energy Policy* 36 (2): 673–685.

Massachusetts. 2010. *Massachusetts Clean Energy and Climate Plan for 2020: Executive Summary.* Boston: Commonwealth of Massachusetts.

Matthew, R., J. Barnett, B. McDonald, and K. O'Brien, eds. 2009. *Global Environmental Change and Human Security.* Cambridge, MA: MIT Press.

Mazmanian, D. A., and M. E. Kraft. 2009. "The Three Epochs of the Environmental Movement." In *Toward Sustainable Communities: Transition and Transformation in Environmental Policy,* 2nd ed., ed. D. A. Mazmanian and M. E. Kraft. Cambridge, MA: MIT Press.

McCright, A., and R. E. Dunlap. 2010. "Anti-Reflexivity: The American Conservative Movement's Success in Undermining Climate Science and Policy." *Theory, Culture & Society* 27 (2–3): 100–133.

———. 2011. "Politicization of Climate Change and Polarization in the American Public's Views of Global Warming, 2000–2010." *Sociological Quarterly* 52 (2): 155–194.

Moran, D. 2011. *Climate Change and National Security*. Washington, DC:
  Georgetown University Press.
O'Leary, R. 2010. "Environmental Policy in the Courts." In *Environmental Policy:
  New Directions for the Twenty-First Century*, ed. N. J. Vig and M. E. Kraft.
  Washington, DC: CQ Press.
Paskal, C. 2010. *Global Warring: How Environmental, Economic, and Political Crisis
  Will Redraw the World Map*. New York: Palgrave Macmillan.
Posner, P. L. 2010. "The Politics of Vertical Diffusion: The States and Climate
  Change." In *Greenhouse Governance: Addressing Climate Change in America*, ed.
  B. G. Rabe. Washington, DC: Brookings Institution Press.
Rabe, B. G. 2004. *Statehouse and Greenhouse: The Emerging Politics of American
  Climate Change Policy*. Washington, DC: Brookings Institution Press.
———, ed. 2010. *Greenhouse Governance: Addressing American Climate Change
  Policy*. Washington, DC: Brookings Institution Press.
———. 2011. "Contested Federalism and American Climate Policy." *Publius: The
  Journal of Federalism* 41 (3): 494–521.
Selin, H., and S. D. VanDeveer. 2007. "Political Science and Prediction: What's Next
  for U.S. Climate Change Policy?" *Review of Policy Research* 24 (1): 1–27.
———, eds. 2009. *Changing Climates in North American Politics: Institutions,
  Policymaking and Multilevel Governance*. Cambridge, MA: MIT Press.
———. 2010. "Multilevel Governance and Transatlantic Climate Change Politics." In
  Greenhouse Governance: Addressing Climate Change in America, ed. B. G. Rabe.
  Washington, DC: Brookings Institution Press.
———. 2011. "Climate Change Regionalism in North America." *Review of Policy
  Research* 28 (3): 295–304.
———. 2012. "Federalism, Multilevel Governance and Climate Change Politics across
  the Atlantic." In *Comparative Environmental Politics*, ed. P. F. Steinberg and S. D.
  VanDeveer. Cambridge, MA: MIT Press.
Steinberg, P., and S.D. VanDeveer, eds. 2012. *Comparative Environmental Politics*.
  Cambridge, MA: MIT Press.
Urpelainen, J. 2009. "Explaining the Schwarzenegger Phenomenon: Local
  Frontrunners in Climate Policy." *Global Environmental Politics* 9 (3): 82–105.
Weart, S. R. 2008. *The Discovery of Global Warming*. 2nd ed. Cambridge, MA:
  Harvard University Press.
Woods, N. D., and M. Potoski. 2010. "Environmental Federalism Revisited:
  Second-Order Devolution in Air Quality Regulation." *Review of Policy Research*
  27 (6): 721–739.

CHAPTER 9

....

SUSTAINABLE DEVELOPMENT AND GOVERNANCE

....

DANIEL A. MAZMANIAN AND LAURIE KAYE NIJAKI

SUSTAINABLE development merges into a single guiding principle two concepts that had been considered contradictory and even incompatible only a few short decades ago. It is based on the idea that development is possible without further depleting the world's stock of natural resources and exacerbating the harmful human health and environmental effects of industrialization and, moreover, that development can be harmonious with both the environment and equity. This characterization of sustainability was first introduced into professional policy, planning, and environmental circles with the 1980 release of the *World Conservation Strategy* (IUCN 1980). Policy makers worldwide embraced the concept with the release of the UN's Brundtland Commission Report of 1987 and with the Earth Summit of 1992. Since then it has become the primary path through which governments—from the very local to the global—can and should reconcile their development ambitions in view of their environmental challenges (Hempel 2009).

Although the vision has been widely accepted, significant questions remain about how societies rooted so deeply in the past can embrace sustainability values and design institutions that enable their realization. One central concern is that while ecological problems seldom respect political boundaries, governments at all levels, from local communities, states, nations, and around the globe, have by and large maintained their traditional geographic boundaries, administrative structures, and decision-making practices. Individual wants, deeply held beliefs, and cultures of consumption—which are often problematic for, if not incompatible with, ecological and social sustainability—are slow to adapt to the requisites of a new order. The principles of neoclassical economics and emphasis on short-term profits that guide most of the world's business and industry today are proving equally difficult to change.

How can and should environmental and economic resources be governed, given the objectives of sustainability? The answer is not simple, although we are beginning to see efforts at reaching across the three Es of equity, environmental, and economically driven values that will underlie any governing system worthy of the label "governance commensurate with sustainable development." To appreciate what this entails, we begin with a brief overview of the rationale for sustainability. This is followed by the requisite features of society and governance system in a sustainability epoch, along with recognition of several critical barriers to attaining it today. Finally, we turn to several of the major features or criteria of governing in an epoch of sustainable development that we believe are prerequisites and indicative of the changes to come, which we believe helps to identify critical research needs as we all go forward.

Also of importance, our discussion focuses on sustainable development efforts at the community and local level of governance. While the discussion of policy changes is being conducted in international forums and at the national and state level—as indicated elsewhere throughout this volume—action inevitably comes down to what individuals and local communities are willing and prepared to embrace. Those behind the emerging paradigm of sustainable development recognize the many unknowns and uncertainties about how to transform society. They argue that experimentation and policy entrepreneurship should be undertaken at the community and local level and that we can all learn from it. In fact, as we show, this is precisely what is occurring.

Interestingly, building from the local community up is in stark contrast to the philosophy dominant in the first environmental epoch, the 1970s—as outlined in chapter 1 and elaborated on below—where the prevailing belief was that stringent pollution requirements would need to be imposed on local governments, and their businesses and citizens, by the national government.

1. GOVERNANCE AS A DIMENSION OF SUSTAINABLE DEVELOPMENT

Granting the compelling vision of a sustainable future, attention has begun to shift to the social values, economic principles, and governing strategies, institutions, and public policies that achieving the vision will require. We recognize that we are in the early stages of ferreting out the best answers. What we address in this chapter is an exploration of the most probable contextual and governing characteristics of the path forward. We arrive at these by identifying the critical features of the three epochs of the modern environmental movement, including sustainability, the one evolving today. The clearest picture of the future comes from understanding the path charted in addressing environmental problems in the past epoch. Unfortunately, some of the solutions devised and institutions created to address past challenges have emerged as barriers to be overcome in transitioning to sustainability.

1.1. The Historical Trajectory of Sustainability

The roots of today's environmental protection practices can be found in the modern environmental movement of the past 40 years.[1] As noted in the introductory chapter, this began with the epoch of clean air, water, waste, and land use environmental protection policies enacted at the outset of the 1970s. The profound difference between this first epoch and today is evident in the dominant political beliefs and values of the period, how policy was formulated, what implementation strategies were utilized, and how "success" was measured. The changes in attitude, policies, and other features of the movement have in many ways been incremental in their unfolding—evolving policy by policy, place by place, over the course of many years—but when one considers them across the last four decades, three major periods come into view (see Table 9.1, left-hand column, for the eight key characteristics of an environmental epoch).

This can be seen clearly in the United States, a leader in setting the pace and tone of the first environmental epoch, which extended from 1970 to 1990 and was characterized by an emphasis on "regulation for environmental protection." The second epoch, from the 1980s to the 2000s, was defined by the push for "efficiency-based regulatory reform and flexibility." The third, the one we are now entering, is characterized by the drive toward "sustainable communities," and its intellectual roots and central ideas reach back to the early 1990s.

Each epoch is distinguished by a dominant way of framing and defining the environmental problem that needs be addressed in both scientific and normative terms. This produces a set of policy goals, the use of different implementation strategies, and other features that must be taken together to capture the essence of the epoch (Mazmanian and Kraft 2009). Each epoch has its distinctive set of characteristics—which eventually overshadow, but can never fully replace, those of prior epochs—resulting at times in confusion and contradiction.

First, the regulatory epoch was based on growing concerns about environmental pollution, catapulted forward politically in the United States by the Santa Barbara oil spill (1969) and the first Earth Day (1970). It was a period of zero-sum politics between the proponents of change and defenders of the status quo, weighted in favor of proponents of change and symbolized by the establishment of a new national regulatory agency, the U.S. Environmental Protection Agency (EPA),

[1] This section draws heavily on the discussion of the evolution to sustainability in "The Three Epochs of the Environmental Movement" (Mazmanian and Kraft 2009, 1–32).

Table 9.1 Dimensions of an Environmental Epoch and Features of the Sustainability Epoch

Dimensions of an Environmental Epoch	Features of the Sustainability Epoch (the third epoch of the modern environmental movement)
Problem Identification and Policy Objectives	• Bring into harmony human and natural systems on a sustainable basis around the three Es (economy, environment, equity) • Bring into balance the long-term societal and natural system needs through system design and adaptive management • Emphasize resource and energy conservation • Halt diminution of biodiversity
Implementation Philosophy	• Embrace an ecocentric ethic • Develop new mechanisms and institutions that balance the needs of human and natural systems • Emphasize consensus building and education over command-and-control • Concentrate on outcomes and performance measures
Points of Intervention	• Work on societal-level needs assessment and goal prioritization • Pay attention at industry level to product design, materials selection, and environmental strategic planning • Employ community-level action and experimentation • Emphasize individual behavior and lifestyle choices
Policy Approaches and "Tools"	• Undertake comprehensive sustainability visioning at all levels • Develop local and regional sustainability plans and guidelines • Foster Total Quality Environmental Management (TQEM) and life-cycle-design practice in industry • Remain open to various experiments with new ways of changing/guiding sustainability efforts
Information and Data Management Needs	• Develop sustainability criteria and indicators, including ecological footprint and projections of climate change effect • Identify eco-human support system thresholds • Understand region/community/global interaction effects (e.g., regarding CO_2 emissions and depletion of ozone layer) • Adopt material and energy "flow-through" inventories and accounting methods • Develop computer modeling of human-natural systems interactions

(continued)

Table 9.1 *(Continued)*

Predominant Political/Institutional Context	• Build legitimacy and political support at all levels, with initial emphasis on building from the bottom up • Provide extensive governmental support for community sustainability visioning, capacity building, and consensus building • Develop mechanisms of coordination and cooperation around sustainability goals among levels of government and sectors of society • Emphasize "beneficiary pays" principles in funding sustainability initiatives • Establish mechanisms for addressing issues of equity within and across generations
Key Triggering and Signaling Events	• Brundtland Commission report, Our Common Future • Earth Summit (UNCED) • Montreal Protocol on CFCs • Kyoto Protocol • Intergovernmental Panel on Climate Change (series of reports) • Hurricane Katrina • COP 15 • BP oil spill in the Gulf • Tsunami and resultant nuclear power crisis in Japan

Adapted from Mazmanian and Kraft 2009, Table 1.1.

that had significant enforcement powers and implemented a bevy of new national environmental policies, including the Clean Air and Clean Water Acts. Pollution was attributed to industrial production and a business climate devoid of corporate responsibility when it came to environmental protection. The governing strategy of the epoch was based on establishing national goals to clean up the environment and the regulatory apparatus to implement them. Significantly, the regulations developed aimed at reducing pollution at the end of the production pipeline, the wastewater stream, the tailpipe of the internal combustion engine automobile, and the industrial smokestack. Left unaddressed was the need for fundamental change in the modes of production and in the nature and quantity of what was being produced. Policy in this period was driven by the federal government through command-and-control, along with substantial federal investment into emissions reduction technologies and methods of reducing pollutants harmful to human health.

The second epoch is characterized most distinctively by a shift in implementation strategy. While pollution reduction goals were mostly unchanged, regulations were to be submitted to a cost-effectiveness test, and implementation flexibility would be provided to ease the burden on business and industry. The second epoch paralleled the presidency of Ronald Reagan and the ascendency of Republicans to national power. Extending through the 1990s, it represented a political back-lash to the real and perceived shortcomings of the stringent regulatory goals and enforcement of the first epoch. Only in response to major toxic pollution episodes and chemical spills was regulatory policy coverage expanded to include toxic and chemical waste. Meanwhile, many oversight and enforcement responsibilities were decentralized and shifted from federal to state and local agencies.

The third epoch, toward sustainable communities, emerged from the recognition that for all the effort and resources expended in the first two epochs, the challenges to environmental and natural resources protection are worsening when viewed in total and around the globe. Brought to the forefront in framing the issue was the interdependence of human and natural systems and limitation of the Earth's ability to sustain infinitely expanding human populations and levels of material consumption. Equally profound, the epoch is characterized by the conviction that the development-environment conflict of the prior epochs can be resolved, albeit only through strategies of economic development that are environmentally friendly and equitable across human populations. With the third sustainability epoch has come recognition that solving environment and natural resources problems presents a myriad of challenges, the solutions to which require complex system thinking, comprehensive and multimedia policy and management strategies, and inspired leadership, which can only be attained within an environment-development-justice framework of thought and action. And it is at the local and community level that the needed action is most likely to occur and is in fact being initiated today.

Understanding the elements of the first two epochs and the lessons learned about what has and has not worked and about how addressing today's challenges requires addressing simultaneously all three of the three Es is the basis of the transformation in thinking that frames the sustainability epoch.[2]

1.2. Governance as a Dimension of the Third Environmental Epoch

The sustainability epoch differs from the preceding two along all seven critical dimensions, from problem identification to triggering events. Table 9.1 provides a summary of how the dimensions are defined and comprise the distinctive features of an epoch.

2. For a full elaboration, see Mazmanian and Kraft 2009. We want to emphasize that the moving into the second and third the environmental epochs has not meant the disappearance of but only the reframing and in many instances subordination of the first, with its focus on command-and-control regulation. Most environmental policy scholars and practitioners recognize that the federally driven regulatory policies of the first epoch continue to dominate governmental environmental protection activities on the ground. Moreover, the case has been made that the continuance of some level of stringent regulation is essential for other more collaborative and voluntary approaches of the second and now third epochs to be effective—such as regulatory flexibility, the use of market incentives, and the adoption of life-cycle-design practices in industry (Fiorino 2006).

The political framing of an epoch is revealed in the problem identification and policy objectives. In the regulatory epoch the problem was defined as the pollution caused by callous and unthinking business and industry. The implementation philosophy was based on the assumption that addressing the problem required the imposition of strict top-down national regulatory standards. This was tempered in the second epoch of efficiency-based regulation and flexibility, where the focus shifted from allegations of callous behavior to how to incentivize environmental protection through market-based mechanisms and professional training. In the sustainability epoch the problem's definition has changed rather dramatically: it now focuses on establishing harmony among economic, social, and natural systems through balancing long-term societal and natural system needs. This is most likely to be accomplished by embracing a philosophy and decision-making practices that gives priority to comprehensive and integrated design and adaptive management decisions, across sectors and at all levels of society.

Whereas the point of intervention in the regulatory epoch was at the "end of the pipe," in the sustainability epoch the focus has shifted to substantially reducing, if not eliminating, pollution and unwanted side effects *at the source*. The goal is to design products and production processes that avoid the release of "wasted" energy and harmful pollutants entirely, along with the resulting air, water, and other environmental and human health effects. New and different incentive programs, technologies, and industrial policies and approaches are being devised to achieve this. Additionally, it is argued that there is no universal or quick fix and that the transformation is most likely to be realized by shifting away from centrally developed prescriptive standards of the regulatory epoch to comprehensive, participatory, long-range, community-based visioning and planning processes, on the one hand, and the incorporation of life-cycle-design-type practices in industry and commerce, on the other.

In the sustainability epoch, a precursor to comprehensive planning and decision making is effective measurement and modeling, which has emerged as a major focus of researchers and professionals today and into the foreseeable future. We need better methods of large data-set management to understand more precisely how natural and human systems behave and interact and to develop analytical techniques to match the comprehensive, systemic, and integrated economic, social, and ecological thinking and planning under way. It is worth recalling that when environmentalism burst on the scene in the early 1970s, there was little questioning of the severity and implications of the problems. One did not need to be an expert to realize that many waterways were polluted to the point of killing off fish and no longer suitable for drinking and swimming. Urban smog was a very visible eyesore—literally—in most major industrial centers, especially in the hot and dry climates, where the city of Los Angeles, California, epitomized the phenomenon. By contrast, today the problems need to be understood at the level of the minute particles, on the one hand, and the stratosphere, on the other.

In the first two epochs, proposed solutions could be addressed within the existing patterns of politics and top-down government. Contending interests mobilized, petitioned the public for support, and lobbied policy makers. Administrative capacity to carry out the policies enacted during these epochs was needed, as with the U.S. EPA, but this could be accomplished within the well-established principles of the twentieth-century administrative state. Setting the sustainability epoch apart is that management and coordination need to reach well beyond establishing another new or umbrella entity to rethinking and redesigning a host of special-purpose administrative agencies, departments, commissions, and other bodies built up over the earlier epochs, across all levels of government. This in turn necessitates new policy tools and implementing capacity, played against a backdrop of public support. In essence, sustainability necessitates that the requisite conditions in each of the seven dimensions be in sync. Without a commitment on the part of political leaders to comprehensive and forward-looking policies, and methods of implementation that overcome barriers to change, little of significant substance should be expected.

2. BARRIERS IN TRANSITIONING TO SUSTAINABLE GOVERNANCE

Drawing on both theory and practice, this section highlights one key question. What uniquely characterizes *environmental governance* in the sustainability epoch? Absent a theory of governance that speaks to the relationship between citizens and leaders, that prescribes the broad purposes of a government and its substantive and procedural responsibilities and, in the context of sustainable development, the responsibilities of nation-states to the collective provision of the three Es around the globe, it is difficult to know with certainty whether we are moving in the right direction. Of course, we have no such well-thought-out theory. In the contemporary efforts to address the challenges of sustainability, however, several characteristics of the needed theory are becoming evident, and these we can address. In effect, we argue that there is a path forward being charted of which we can take stock, even though its ultimate form and viability are still uncertain. First, we turn to several past ways of framing environmental and pollution problems and the solutions to them that are barriers or, stated more constructively, puzzles to be solved in the new epoch. We begin with the three conceptual challenges identified by Scott Campbell (1996) in his "contradictions of sustainable development," followed by what experience has shown to be governance mismatches that are impeding progress in addressing the environmental and social problems of the new epoch that will need to be overcome to achieve sustainability effectively.

2.1. Campbell's Contradictions

In assessing the vision of sustainable development articulated in the World Conservation Strategy, few have illuminated as well as Scott Campbell (1996) the contradictions and governing challenges embedded in the vision as we move into the third environmental epoch. His thesis is presented in terms of the prospects of the greening of cities and addressed explicitly to planners, but it is applicable to all efforts at guiding society on the path to sustainability. He reminds us that societies that want to reproduce themselves indefinitely must reconcile not just two but three perennial issues: delivering economic growth while providing *both* environmental protection and social justice (the three Es). Moreover, he makes the case that the three values must be understood in terms of a "triangle of conflicting goals" that cannot simply be wished away through synoptic thinking and comprehensive visioning but must be resolved through politics and planning. These are the conflicts that arise when past neoclassical economic strategies of growth result in growing inequality among the rich and poor (*the property conflict*); between the aspirations and moral "right" of developing nations to industrialize in the face of the environmental degradation and resource depletion that results (*the development conflict*); and between worldwide propensity toward economic growth for both rich and poor nations and the environmental degradation and depletion of the limited stock of the Earth's natural assets that results as the human population grows from 6.9 billion today to 9 billion by midcentury (*the resource conflict*).

The challenge of sustainability requires resolving the three bilateral challenges along each of the axis of the triangle of conflicts in a comprehensive manner. The point is that solutions need to reach beyond the conventional framings of the three conflicts. This means finding methods of mediating if not resolving the current conflicts within and across nations, between the wants and ambitions of developing nations and resources depletion globally, and between the continued production, consumption, and resource depletion within all nations. In addition, methods must be found to resolve the issue of unequal consumption levels within and across developed and developing nations.

There have been myriad forums, conferences, and discussions on how to reconcile the three "contradictions," yet so far even the most promising efforts have failed to address more than two of the three conflicts. There are growing signs that important interest groups and governments have begun to pair up the values of environment and the economy, the environment and equity, and the economy and equity. For example, labor and business/industry are united by a common interest in economic growth, and, in the instance of green economic growth, in green buildings, green manufacturing, and renewable energy, all of which generate green jobs. In addition, labor brings to the discussion its long-standing commitment in assuring equity in addition to their fundamental economic concerns.

The potential linkages between business and labor can be seen in the recent movement toward green manufacturing initiatives, including the newly established Green Urban Manufacturing Initiative in Los Angeles, and the development of other "clean tech" and "eco-industrial" parks in various cities domestically and internationally (Wheeler 2000). Likewise, some environmental and labor groups are beginning to find common ground in focusing on jobs and the environment, and there is some evidence that this can be (and is being) extended to the third dimension of equity as well, resulting in the reshaping of the environmental justice movement (Pastor et al. 2009). This is aptly demonstrated by the new "green-collar" jobs movement, which seeks to provide opportunities in environmental remediation in comparatively low-skilled blue-collar occupations, potentially creating opportunities directly for environmental justice communities in cleaning up environmental blight. For example, along with the advocacy group Green For All, the nationally focused Apollo Alliance is a prominent interest group composed of environmental, business, and labor interests that popularized the notion of green-collar jobs and has developed a variety of policy proposals largely aimed at jobs in energy-related industries. Many efforts originating from this uncommon alliance include opportunities in employment in the retrofit of buildings (Apollo Alliance 2007).

Finally, environment and industry have been able to come together around some mix of environmental and economic interests through profitable business approaches to pollution prevention (e.g., in non–fossil fuel energy production) and resources protection (e.g., in fair trade coffee and sustainable yield in forestry and fishing). Green industry associations and local chambers of commerce increasingly seek to work toward locating employment opportunities in green industries, as evidenced by organizations such as the National Resources Defense Council's E2 program and the Environmental Defense Fund's Corporate Partnerships. Both directly engage the business community and often focus on large corporations on an individual level. Similarly, the workforce development community at both the state and the national level, including the Bureau of Labor Statistics and the state of California, are conducting surveys to identify occupational and industry-based opportunities in green jobs that, in the end, will identify specific business opportunities that are largely palatable to environmental interest groups (Rivkin 2010). Similar efforts are being conducted at the municipal level through green jobs business plans in the city of Berkeley and elsewhere. Additionally, cities such as Santa Monica have encouraged the use of such products and created business opportunities through the integration of green purchasing programs for municipal services and products (Worrell and Nijaki 2010). Once again, though, if the vision of sustainability is to be realized, the reconciliation will need to bridge all three dimensions, as Campbell (1996) reminds us.

2.2. Governing Mismatches

In addition to the contradictions identified by Campbell (1996), there are institutional barriers to moving into the sustainable epoch. These barriers result from the institutions—federal, state, and local agencies and departments—and decision-making procedures and practices established in earlier eras to address the needs of the day and to solve environmental pollution problems that are less suited to addressing present sustainability challenges. Three main ones are illustrative and are summarized in Table 9.2.

Table 9.2 Sustainability Epoch: Governing and Policy Mismatches

Key Problem/Policy Mismatch	Environmental Challenge	Examples
Local versus Global Benefits and Costs	How can a local area be appropriately governed when local governmental quality is driven by environmental degradation that is global in scope?	Goods movement: Local environmental quality is driven by global trade of goods moving through communities. Climate change mitigation: For a community, state, or single nation to require significant mitigation is likely to place it at an economic disadvantage, at least in the near term.
Scope of Government Authority and Responsibility	How can government institutions be held accountable for effectively addressing either or both local and global dimensions of sustainability given the marble cake of multiple laws and jurisdictions, and the general lack of overall responsibility for addressing sustainability issues?	Transboundary air pollution: It is a common occurrence that air pollution generated in one location within and across national boundaries is beyond the control of the affected location. Fishing on the high seas: There is no effective governing regime to curtail the worldwide overfishing of consumable fish.
Temporal Concerns	How are nonrenewable natural resources as well as pollution burdens to be apportioned between haves and have-nots today, on the one hand, and current and future generations, on the other?	Climate change policy: Environmental justice advocates have concerns that using offsets as part of climate mitigation policy will lead to geographical shifts of copollutants to their already overburdened areas. Southern hemisphere nations are opposed to policies that will constrain their growth and the quality of life of their future generations relative to the developed nations.

2.2.1. Local Costs and Equity Concerns versus Larger-Area Benefits

An increasingly globalizing world presents new challenges to governance. How can a local or regional community govern itself effectively when environmental degradation emanates in other jurisdictions over which it has little or no control? How can any existing community effectively govern when issues are global in scale, as with the need to mitigate the effects of greenhouse gas emissions to address climate change? The expanded scope and scale of environmental problems today makes arriving at solutions increasingly difficult. At the same time, to the extent that effects are felt locally, local governments are motivated to fill gaps where there is an absence of larger governing institutions equal to the task, or a lack of governing institutions altogether.

This challenge can be illustrated by the Los Angeles region's struggle with managing the "externalities" of ambient air pollution, road congestion, and health and equity effects of the global flow of containerized goods passing through the Los Angeles basin. Extending from Asia to the Atlantic seaboard of the United States, and even on to Europe, goods that pass through the ports of Los Angeles and Long Beach together account for 40 percent of the nation's containerized traffic. As part of the national and global economy, and as such mostly governed by national and international bodies, there are environmental effects and costs that are left for local jurisdictions—effects such as blight and air pollution along the major goods movement corridors across the region, of which the resultant social and health impacts are borne by local, usually less-well-off populations. Establishing governing strategies and bodies that have as their mission balancing the local and concentrated "costs" with diffuse national and global "benefits" to trade and goods movement is essential in achieving sustainable development (Mazmanian 2009).

2.2.2. Locus of Authority and Responsibility in Multilayered Governing Systems

How can the numerous government institutions, established in prior environmental epochs and with a history of accomplishing important but ultimately unsustainable goals, be transformed in mission and brought together under the sustainability banner? Finding the right ways of doing so in theory and practice is a significant part of the challenge in the sustainability epoch.

Climate change, again, is a poignant and possibly the most important example of the mismatch between the scale of problem and governing institutions at which it is being addressed. The problem is global, yet the most impressive efforts to date in addressing it are being taken at the level of local governments, all around the globe (exemplified by ICLEI—Local Governments for Sustainability) (Layzer and Stern 2010), followed by some subnational government actors (such as in states in the United States and provinces in Canada), and some associations of nations, as with the European Union. However, adding up the pieces has not resulted in a policy equal to the challenge by any stretch of the imagination, nor has building from the bottom up resulted in generating sufficient political pressure on the leading nation-states of the world to agree on a comprehensive climate change mitigation strategy (Bertoill and Bulkeley 2006; Wheeler 2000).

2.2.3. *Equity within and across Generations*

Concern with equity underlies many of the governing challenges in achieving sustainable development. However, as illustrated in the Brundtland Commission report, concerns of equity have been primarily hinged on considerations of inter-generational equity (Batina 1999). Policy tools and mechanisms were expected to focus on long-term intergenerational economic, environmental, and equity costs and benefits. However, another and possibly even more pressing matter is the disproportionate effects of environmental degradation and harm on less-well-off populations within nations and between especially nations of the North and South today. Those affected have made it clear that the needs of current populations must be given priority over those of future populations, a point that underscores Campbell's (1996) contradiction of equity, which must be overcome if the vision is to be realized.

A key component of a successful sustainability strategy will be the assurance to the less-well-off that their situation will improve. The discussion around climate change presents an example of this tension. Namely, why should the less-well-off (or anyone else, for that matter) care about the effects of climate change on future inhabitants of the planet if they are worried about the pollution sources in their neighborhood that are having health and quality-of-life impacts on them today? Governing sustainably will necessitate governing through both inter- and intragenerational evaluations of policy strategies. While the "precautionary principle," which has become a tenet of the emerging sustainable paradigm, has been invoked to avoid exacerbating problems for the environment and human health in future generations (Myers and Raffensperger 2006), an equivalent principle has yet to be invoked for improving the position of the less-well-off as we go forward.

3. A PRELIMINARY ASSESSMENT OF GOVERNING FOR SUSTAINABLE DEVELOPMENT

Sustainability principles are beginning to permeate the mission and operation of many communities through the adoption of comprehensive environmental protection, smart growth, and sustainability policies and practices. They are mostly predicated on viewing the community (local, state, or nation) as an integrated and dynamic system. Cities and regions especially have begun to develop such strategies. Commonly employed strategies start with recycling, municipal procurement policies including alternative fuel fleets, land use policies that incorporate transit-oriented development and brownfields remediation, and alternative water and energy supply and use practices. Approaches can then expand to more comprehensive visions, plans, and commitments, bridging economic development and equity in new ways (Layzer and Stern 2010; Wheeler 2000; Zeemering 2009).

As noted, efforts have begun to address Campbell's contradictions, although none have yet successfully addressed all three. Thus, while the mismatches in actual planning and governing are recognized, overcoming them is proving difficult. Nonetheless, these attempts are shedding light on the features of a sustainable development epoch that are percolating up among communities that are pioneers in the new epoch along several of the dimensions identified in Table 9.1.

3.1. Problem Identification and Policy Objectives

Devising and implementing strategies for environmental preservation and sustainability begins with issue framing (see chapters 20, 21 and 24 in this volume) and coalition building (Baumgartner and Jones 1993; Schon and Rein 1994). Issue framing of environment and sustainability is paramount in motivating and laying the groundwork for working together across environmental preservation, economic growth, and social justice interests. The initial buy-in, the necessary first step in this process, has already proceeded quite far, as exemplified by the fact that more than 1,000 city mayors have signed the Mayor's Action Pledge for meeting Kyoto Protocol targets, there is good participation in the Cities for Climate Network, and over 90 cities have become members of the Urban Sustainability Directors Network (Layzer and Stern 2010). Many of these cities are beginning to move in the direction of sustainable communities, with ecocentric ethics guiding policy making and the adoption of policy tools for holistic planning and development.

Imagining what sustainable development can look and feel like is an important first step, though simply elevating the needed visioning process to the top of a community's political agenda is no easy feat. In a world of finite resources and pressing needs, policy makers often treat long-range planning as a luxury they can ill afford. Where sustainability thinking has been achieved, it has been the result of people coming together and crafting messages around the goals of economic development, equity, and environmental preservation.

3.2. Implementing Philosophy and Points of Intervention

Once issues are framed in terms of sustainable development, the question remains of who sees to the adoption and implementation of the requisite public policies. Absent an existing comprehensive governing framework for sustainability, the vast majority of sustainability policies and concrete actions taken have come through the agencies and programs established in prior epochs, such as around air pollution or water management strategies, or transportation and renewable energy planning, that build in two or more of the three Es. Given the newness of these initiatives, moreover, each has been the product of policy entrepreneurs, either elected leaders—particularly the mayors of cities (Sharp, Daley, and Lynch 2011)—or environmental or resource agency leaders. In a recent study examining the motivation of various municipal officials in fostering sustainability policies, Zeemering (2009) found that approaches varied widely in terms of how economic, environmental, and justice goals were intertwined with each other. Portland, Oregon, as an example, increased municipal sustainability through the expansion of public transportation options within the existing agency structure. Maryland, meanwhile, designated funding priority areas through the Smart Growth and Neighborhood Conservation programs, where sustainability measures were targeted within the existing infrastructure of the state.

3.3 Policy Approaches and Tools

To move beyond the institutions established in the first and second epochs, intergovernmental coordination is essential. Turning sustainability goals into action requires plans and a process that brings together interested actors from the public, nonprofit, and business sectors if for no other reason than to avoid either disjointed action or political and policy gridlock, a problem cited in chapter 28 in this volume. This is no simple task: as noted, environmental problems and their solutions do not often conform to existing governmental and institutional boundaries. But this is only the beginning. At the most basic level, a key impediment for implementing sustainability strategies is the overarching nature of sustainability itself—it goes beyond traditional governmental and organizational boundaries and capabilities in society today.

Transportation planning illustrates the need for coordination between and among an array of governmental and community actors and interests. We know that today's automobiles and trucks are responsible for substantial amounts of emissions of carbon, nitrogen oxide, sulfur dioxide, and particulate matter, among other noxious pollutants associated with significant health ailments (Hricko 2008). Scientific studies have largely reinforced the link. As noted by the United Nations (2003), a rapid increase in vehicle travel has negatively affected environmental quality in numerous ways. The growth of travel has degraded air quality and has increased traffic noise.

Transportation planning also affects the location of housing, the nexus between home and employment, and urban sprawl in ways that can and often does lead to unsustainable environmental outcomes in a city or a region. To rectify these situations, sustainability and environmental planning necessitates an interdisciplinary, interdepartmental understanding and cooperative relationship between traditionally disparate agencies and actors within a coordinated institutional structure. A sustainable transportation policy aimed at bolstering livability and reducing environmental impacts cannot be pursued in the absence of a housing strategy that incorporates an understanding of the travel behavior of individuals. Even within a city's general planning processes, there is a need to update the housing and transportation elements complementarily.

Complicating all this, as with transportation corridors, emissions do not readily conform to many (if not most) previously drawn and progressively counterproductive political boundaries. Particularly in megaregions, transportation throughout the area continually crosses city limits. Individuals' daily travels take them across political boundaries. They work in one city, play in another, and live in yet a third. Governing the externalities of this behavior in a world of congestion and heightened attention around greenhouse gas emissions is one more challenge that a sustainability approach must be designed to address.

3.4. Data, Information Management, and Assessment

Each successive environmental epoch has witnessed impressive increases in information about environmental pollutants and the health of natural resources and human communities, and the systematic linking of successful policy intervention, with measurable improvements. While good measurement and monitoring can never assure prompt and effective policy responsiveness, especially in the short term, absent good data and information dissemination, little if any policy response is likely to address a given environmental problem correctly and effectively. New data and understanding of the natural world and its connection to economic growth and equity is essential as both a political necessity and as a central foundational principle of sustainable development.

Measures are advancing that gauge the health of the environment, pollution levels, economic development, and equity, though no single measure or index yet captures the multiple dimensions needed to assess the overall sustainability of a community. Researchers are developing an array of useful instruments. However, Michael Toman (1994) has argued that to be useful a gauge of sustainability must be grounded in a fully developed and measurable definition of sustainability followed by persuasive empirical measures; this is a necessary precursor to empirical testing and the widespread adoption of sustainable policies. Fisher and Freudenburg (2004) gauge the improvement in environmental performance by the reduction in emissions. They find that measures of ecological efficiency are the strongest indicators of carbon emissions, leading them to view ecological efficiency in business and industry as a key component of transition to sustainability. Similarly, Abbasi (2009) argues for the development of a "Dow Jones index for climate change" that uses climate change as the central feature of sustainability but builds on Fisher and Freudenberg's (2004) approach by incorporating other measurable impacts in the environment and closely links environmental indicators with economic indicators. Robert Costanza and his colleagues (2009) take an important step forward through their sustainability indicator proxy, termed the Genuine Progress Indicator. This indicator incorporates pertinent sustainability values by extending the notion of a nation's welfare to take into account the cost of environmental degradation and a myriad of other values. And Boyd and Banzhaf (2005) use the conception of ecosystem services to incorporate a notion of sustainability based on how the end products of nature impact well-being. Finally, sustainability can be measured from an institutional, governance standpoint by assessing the efficacy of policy and programs aimed at environmental quality. Kent Portney (2009) measures sustainability through the presence of a whole range of policies and programs aimed at fostering sustainability at the municipal level.

In light of these efforts, municipalities and regions have begun to incorporate into their sustainability plans a number of metrics. Some states, likewise, have adopted metrics in their sustainability and climate change planning. As a result, in utilizing the emerging data and measuring techniques, climate and sustainability planning has become a formalized method through which governmental institutions are beginning to manage and monitor their environmental goals in a comprehensive manner. Table 9.3 thematically summarizes a range of environmental and sustainability indicators—each attempting to measure the success of sustainable governance—as they have evolved over the course of the three epochs of the environmental movement. Absent a full-blown theory, they nonetheless are tapping the dimensions that on their face appear reasonable dimensions to gauge and assess.

As indicated by the range and depth of these measuring schemes, there has been increasing sophistication in the ability to evaluate the sustainability of places generally and to quantify the degree and nature of environmental preservation or degradation within certain established geographical boundaries. Scholars have sought to define sustainability internationally, for example, through the development of countrywide indices such as the Environmental Performance Index. The EPI combines different environmental measures and provide opportunities to compare across different geographical or institutional boundaries. Likewise, Sustainlane.com rates the level of sustainability at the municipal level and ranks the largest cities in the United States in accordance with their environmental progress. This prompts cities to think through their progress in comparison with others and can provide the impetus to inspiring them to innovate new ways to manage their environmental resources. The more these measures come into use, the greater the probability of realizing sustainability.

The growing popularity of sustainability planning and of increasingly integrating environmental preservation as a function of municipal governance can be seen through the sheer number of municipal participants of ICLEI and other like associations, as noted above. Although some cities and states have become forerunners in terms of expressing and monitoring their sustainability intent, integrated sustainability planning is still in its incipient stages.

Table 9.3 Sustainable Development Epoch Measures and Indicators

General Indicator Type	Specific Measure(s)	Examples of Indicator Use
Single Parameter Measures of Sustainability	**Representative Indicators:** Provide a snapshot of conditions or trends overtime in a certain indicator (UNEP 2006)	**Measuring Indicator Species:** In an ecosystem, the presence or absence of a particular species indicates the presence or absence of certain environmental conditions associated with a healthy ecosystem. **Measuring Landscape Factors:** The health of an ecosystem is linked to landscape fragmentation and to watershed integrity (nitrogen, phosphorous, turbidity, temperature, and intragravel dissolved oxygen).
	Performance Indicators: Measure performance by gauging performance toward a benchmark or target (UNEP 2006)	**Environmental Benchmarks:** These benchmarks are scientifically determined thresholds that include the maximum level of a pollutant's concentration in the air or water deemed tolerable for human and environmental health. For example, "Urban Air Quality" is measured and benchmarked as the percentage of monitoring stations recording exceedances of the U.S. threshold for average ozone concentrations over an eight-hour period. **Environmental Targets:** These targets are normative policy goals. For example, national or regional indicators can use targets associated with international commitments or accords or with national policy goals. This may include a reference point such as an international target for the percentage of land to be set aside as a protected area.
Multiple Parameter Measures of Sustainability	**Aggregated Indices:** An overall picture of a system's performance, which can include a weighting scheme to even out the relationships among the disparate indicators and their dependence on subjective interpretation.	**The Living Planet Index Published by WWF:** Provides a trend line of the world's natural ecosystems by averaging three subindices measuring changes in abundance of terrestrial, freshwater, and marine species (see wwf.panda.org). **Ecological Footprint Analysis:** Measures environmental impact through resource use that can be as narrowly defined as resource use or footprint estimation at the individual household level (Ewing et al. 2010).

(continued)

Table 9.3 (*Continued*)

Comparative Indices:	Absolute Scores:
Compare multiple indicators among multiple subjects	*The Environmental Sustainability Index (ESI):* Measures environmental performance through 22 indicators to track the relative success of 146 counties (see epi.yale.edu).
	Global Climate Change Index: Measures atmospheric concentrations of greenhouse gases, average global temperature, length and intensity of extreme heat days, frequency and intensity of extreme weather events, extent and thickness of sea ice and glaciers, changes in ice sheet volume, rate of sea-level rise, incidence of climate-sensitive disease, ocean acidification, incidence of drought and flood, and extent of permafrost thawing (Abbasi 2009).

Rankings:

UNDP Human Development Index: See hdr.undp.org/en/

Taking Sustainable Cities Seriously Index: Ranks cities by presence of sustainability programs (Portney 2009)

Sustainlane City Rankings: Ranks cities by overall level of environmental sustainability (see Sustainlane.com)

3.5 Predominant Political Context

Governance requires the mobilization of interest and, in the case of sustainable development, new and different political alliances and networks (Gemmil and Bamidele-Izu 2009). Triple-bottom-lines solutions require uncommon alliances that reflect this new amalgamation of goals and considerations. This facilitates the information flow so that best practices can be translated and alliances can support appropriate projects and polices. Just as government needs to overcome silo effects, so too the nonprofit and community groups must overcome governance challenges. Business representatives and labor advocates likewise must become voices within the governance process of sustainable development. Widening the net of decision makers and voices can be effective for two primary reasons. First, these stakeholder groups can provide invaluable expertise and practical knowledge around the sustainability challenges that they face. Second, participation can help to avoid conflict during the policy-making process by enabling policy makers to identify and address potential points of disagreements.

4. FROM ENVIRONMENTAL PROTECTION TO SUSTAINABLE DEVELOPMENT

Over the course of the past several decades, environmental protection has been governed through a host of policies directed at water, air, waste, toxic substances, and resource and habitat protection. Each has evolved mainly within the specific arena. Still, significant strides in environmental cleanup, and to a lesser extent resource protection, have occurred. Even in their successes, in more instances than we like to admit, they have been pursued without sufficient attention to where they fit within a broader framework of sustainability, and especially with respect to their equity and justice implications for those most at risk from health and environmental harms. Consequently, the overall level of economic growth, patterns of human consumption, and resource and environmental degradation have together outpaced the positive steps in protecting the environment and human health over the past four decades (Holdren 2008). Continuing along the lines of 1970s-style centrally directed and regulatory approaches to environmental governance is now recognized as inadequate to the challenge sustainable development (Durant 2004; Fiorino 2006).

In this chapter we have identified the nature of governance concerns from the early regulatory epoch of environmental protection to the governing processes and needs of governance in an epoch of sustainable development. We find notable progress in terms of the embracing the idea of an epoch of sustainable development at the global and local level. Only at the local level, however, have significant strides been made to turn the vision into concrete policy goals, and even here, far more has been proposed than adopted and implemented. At the same time, the critical prerequisites of visioning and gauging the threats and challenges to almost all major transformative changes is evolving, and quite rapidly.

Before the sustainability movement expands beyond the pioneering efforts of today, advocates will need to demonstrate persuasively that conditions on the planet as a whole as well as within nations are deteriorating and will continue to deteriorate at an accelerating rate and that the policies being adopted particularly within cities and regions are guides to weaving together comprehensive strategies of economic growth, environmental and resource protection, and equity. They will need to argue persuasively that collaboration within the public sector and coordination across the public, nonprofit, and business sectors is the best if not the only viable path forward in governing the transition to sustainability.

Addressing environmental degradation and fostering a sense of sustainability in our cities and regions requires bringing together a multitude of urban policies—everything from housing and transportation planning to tourism and economic development—all of which have environmental consequences. For planners and policy makers, understanding the interconnectedness at the level of the city and the region will presumably show the way to doing the same at the state, nation, and, where necessary, the planet, to achieving the ultimate transformation to sustainable development.

How best to think about the governing system this will require? Our best assessment is that it will require nothing short of ecosystem-management-type approaches that assume complexity, a tiering of actors and arenas of activity from local up through global arenas, and an ability to adapt as the human and environmental conditions evolve over time. That is, we need to craft approaches that bring together dynamic "living" systems that incorporate economic, environmental, social, and cultural factors (Gemmil and Bamidele-Izu 2009). This begins with a reasoned understanding of the primary causes of environmental degradation and an evaluation of the cost and benefits of the myriad of possible policy approaches. Uncertainties around these costs and benefits are likewise assessed. The focus is on addressing problems comprehensively—taking environmental governance out of a vacuum in a manner that understands vital policy interconnections. As the third environmental epoch continues to see progress in this direction, ecosystems thinking and approaches will guide the way in which governmental entities understand their challenges and implementation of their plans, programs, and policies.

The prevailing strategy for moving to sustainability today—the concept of thinking globally while acting locally (Adger and Jordan 2009; Leuenberger and Bartle 2009)—builds on this approach. While the need for sustainability is global in scope, this approach recognizes that political and economic barriers to significant change among and within nation-states are problematic at best. It also reflects the reality that subnational political leaders and especially those in cities around the world are most visibly concerned and most willing to act. The need to act locally in the face of global environment and development challenges can be equally important when addressing the traditional needs of freshwater, clean air, resource and land management, the reduction of industrial pollution, and the creation of green jobs and a meaningful quality of life. Moreover, acting locally often includes mobilizing across traditional political and economic dividing lines.

What experience so far has suggested is that new coalitions and political and economic alignments are needed to overcome the limitations of a community's traditional political and economic arrangements. They must leverage their limited resources in order to address the ecological scale of today's problems. With this as a template, it is likely that building from the local and community up through an ecosystems approach is going to be the most viable path to greater regional, state, national, and eventually worldwide cooperation on sustainability. Even at the local level, though, ambition is far ahead of actual transformation. Only time will reveal the necessary governance brew for achieving sustainability outcomes across the board.

REFERENCES

Abbasi, D. 2009. "A Dow Jones for Climate: The Case for a Global Warming Index. *Yale Environment 360,* August 24.

Adger, W. N., and A. Jordan, eds. 2009. *Governing Sustainability.* Cambridge: Cambridge University Press.

Apollo Alliance. 2007. *New Energy for Cities: Energy-Saving and Job Creation Policies for Local Governments.* Washington, DC: Apollo Alliance.

Batina, R. G., and J. A. Kraemer. 1999. "On Sustainability and Intergenerational Transfers with a Renewable Resource." *Land Economics* 75 (2): 167–184.

Baumgartner, F. R., and B. D. Jones. 1993. *Agendas and Instability in American Politics.* Chicago: University of Chicago Press.

Bertoill, M., and H. Bulkeley. 2006. "Cities and Multilevel Governance of Global Climate Change." *Global Governance* 12 (2): 141–159.

Boyd, J. W., and H. S. Banzhaf. 2005. "Ecosystem Services and Government Accountability: The Need for a New Way of Judging Nature's Value." *Resources.* .158: 16–19.

Campbell, S. 1996. "Green Cities, Growing Cities, Just Cities? Urban Planning and the Contradictions of Sustainable Development." *APA Journal.* 62(3): 296–312.

Costanza, R., H. Hart, S. Posner, and J. Talberth. 2009. *Beyond GDP: Need for New Measures of Progress.* Boston: Boston University Pardee Center.

Daily, G. C., and P. R. Ehrlich. 1996. "Socioeconomic Equity, Sustainability and the Earth's Carrying Capacity." *Ecological Applications,* 6 (4): 991–1001.

Durant, R., Y. Chun, B. Kim, and S. Lee. 2004. "Toward a New Governance Paradigm for Environmental and Natural Resources Management in the 21st Century?" *Administration and Society* 35 (6): 643–682.

Ewing, B., D. Moore, S. Goldfinger, A. Oursler, A. Reed, and M. Wackernagel. 2010. *The Ecological Atlas 2010.* Oakland: Global Footprint Network.

Fiorino, D. J. 2006. *The New Environmental Regulation.* Cambridge, MA: MIT Press.

Fisher, D., and W. R. Freudenburg. 2004. "Postindustrialization and Environmental Quality: An Empirical Analysis of the Environmental State." *Social Forces* 83 (1): 157–188.

Gemmil, B. and A. Bamidele-Izu. 2009. *The Role of NGOs and Civil Society in Environmental Governance.* New Haven, CT: Yale University Center for Environmental Law and Policy.

Hempel, L. 2009. "Conceptual and Analytical Challenges in Building Sustainable Communities." In *Toward Sustainable Communities: Transition and Transformations in Environmental Policy,* 2nd ed., ed. D. A. Mazmanian and M. E. Kraft. Cambridge, MA: MIT Press.

Holdren, J. P. 2008. "Science and Technology for Sustainable Well-Being." *Science,* 319: 424–434.

Hricko, A. 2008. "Global Trade Comes Home: Community Impacts of Goods Movement." *Environmental Health Perspectives* 116: A78–A81.

IUCN. 1980. *World Conservation Strategy.* Switzerland: International Union of Conservation and Natural Resources.

Layzer, J., and S. B. Stern. 2010. "What Works and Why? Evaluating the Effectiveness of Cities Sustainability Initiatives." Paper presented at the American Political Science Association Meeting, Washington, DC, September 2–5.

Leuenberger, D. Z., and J. R. Bartle. 2009. *Sustainable Development for Public Administration.* New York: M. E. Sharpe.

Mazmanian, D. A. 2009. "Los Angeles' Clean Air Saga—Spanning the Three Epochs." In *Toward Sustainable Communities: Transition and Transformations in Environmental Policy,* 2nd ed., ed. D. A. Mazmanian and M. E. Kraft. Cambridge, MA: MIT Press.

Mazmanian, D. A., and M. E. Kraft, eds. 2009. *Toward Sustainable Communities: Transition and Transformations in Environmental Policy.* 2nd ed. Cambridge, MA: MIT Press.

Myer, N. J., and C. Raffensperger, eds. 2006. *Precautionary Tools for Reshaping Environmental Policy.* Cambridge, MA: MIT Press.

Pastor, M., G. Benner, and M. Matsuoka. 2009. *This Could Be the Start of Something Big: How Social Movements for Regional Equity Are Reshaping Metropolitan America.* Ithaca, NY: Cornell University Press.

Portney, K. 2009. "Sustainability in American Cities: A Comprehensive Look at What Cities Are Doing and Why." In *Toward Sustainable Communities: Transition and Transformations in Environmental Policy,* 2nd ed., ed. D. A. Mazmanian and M. E. Kraft. Cambridge, MA: MIT Press.

Rivkin, D., et al. 2010. *Greening the World of Work: Implications for ONET SOC and New and Merging Occupations.* Washington, DC: Bureau of Labor Statistics.

Schon, D., and M. Rein. 1994. *Frame Reflections: Toward the Resolution of Intractable Policy Controversies.* New York: Basic Books.

Sharp, E. B., D. M. Daley, and M. S. Lynch. 2011. "Understanding Local Adoption and Implementation of Climate Change Mitigation Policy." *Urban Affairs Review* 47 (3): 433–457.

Toman, M. 1994. "Economics and Sustainability: Balancing Trade-offs and Imperatives." *Land Economics* 70 (4): 399–419.

United Nations Environmental Programme (UNEP). 2006. *Environmental Indicators for North America.* Nairobi, Kenya: United Nations Environmental Programme.

United Nations University. 2003. *Defining an Ecosystem Approach to Urban Management and Policy Development.* Japan: Institute of Advanced Study.

Wheeler, S. M. 2000. "Planning for Metropolitan Sustainability." *Journal of Planning Education and Resource* 20 (2): 133–145.

Worrell, G., and L. K. Nijaki. 2010. "Buying Green." *Planning Magazine,* September/August.

Zeemering, E. 2009. "What Does Sustainability Mean to Sustainability Officials?" *Urban Affairs Review* 45 (2): 247–273.

CHAPTER 10

....

UNITED STATES INTERNATIONAL ENVIRONMENTAL POLICY

....

ELIZABETH R. DESOMBRE

WHEN Barack Obama was elected president of the United States, environmentalists around the world rejoiced. They envisioned an end to the U.S. international environmental isolationism of the George W. Bush presidency, in which the United States avoided signing or ratifying the major international environmental agreements negotiated and worked to undermine or weaken those negotiations.

But the early years of the Obama administration did not deliver the U.S. international environmental multilateralism many environmentalists—and scholars—envisioned. No ratifications of existing treaties were quickly forthcoming, and, although the United States did participate somewhat less reluctantly than previously in international climate negotiations, no major new agreements emerged. Determining the causes of U.S. behavior in international environmental policy is essential if one wants to understand this lack of dramatic change, account for U.S. behavior historically, and predict its international environmental tactics in the future.

The U.S. approach to international environmental policy has puzzled scholars for decades. Rather than a dramatic change from early leadership in the 1970s to active opposition in the 1990s, as is often presented (e.g., Brunnée 2004; Caron 2003), the United States has always exhibited a streak of reluctance about international environmental cooperation, sometimes taking on leadership roles but often resisting or actively hindering international action to address environmental problems. Hypotheses abound to account for U.S. behavior: a general U.S. suspicion of multilateralism that may be a manifestation of a belief in U.S. exceptionalism; the costliness of environmental regulation or special characteristics of the United States that make international environmental action more difficult on some issues than for other states; concern about international action that delivers benefits primarily to developing states at a cost to the United States; or even the existing uncertainty present in many international environmental issues.

On the whole, scholarship has done a good job of assessing potential determinants of U.S. international environmental policy empirically and theoretically. Some work is, of necessity, purely empirical, describing U.S. policy toward specific environmental problems. This close empiricism provides necessary case material for broader analysis. Similarly, efforts to understand broad approaches followed by the United States when deciding how to address international environmental problems make good use of theories of foreign policy making or international cooperation in suggesting commonalities across a wide range of seemingly divergent actions, even if these efforts sometimes disagree or rely on different case material for their analysis. It is in bringing together this empirical material with broader decision-making theories that an overall pattern can be ascertained. Ultimately, this chapter argues, the explanation is to be found in the structure of domestic politics within the United States, and, in particular, Congress.

1. WHY THE UNITED STATES MATTERS

The United States is arguably the most important potential participant in addressing problems of the global environment. Others may stake a claim: China and India are developing states with the fastest-growing populations; surely the way they choose to industrialize will affect the globe for centuries to come. The states of the European Union (EU), acting together, are responsible for the most advanced collective regulatory approaches to address environmental issues, and the continued growth of the EU brings new states under that regulatory umbrella. Some quick-growing oil-producing states in the Middle East (such as the United Arab Emirates) use resources and produce pollution at the most intensive per capita rate (Global Footprint Network 2010). But the United States has, by most measures, the population with the biggest ecological footprint (Brunnée 2004); it is also the country with the greatest economic wealth and power and encompasses the largest single-country market, with influence internationally.

The environmental impact, both currently and throughout history, of the United States cannot be denied. The country combines a large per capita output of substances like carbon dioxide, consumption of resources, and generation of waste, with a large population and a long history of high consumption and energy use. And as the only industrialized state with substantial population growth, the impact per person is magnified as the number of Americans affecting the environment grows.

U.S. power is also undisputed. By almost any measure the United States has the most powerful (and active) military, and the country has the largest gross domestic product (GDP), both aggregate and per capita. The market power of the United States is also nearly unparalleled; it is consistently among the top exporters and importers globally, and how it produces or consumes can thus help set the international agenda. It is among the largest providers of overseas development assistance (Shah 2010). Its influence in international negotiations is thus central, both because what it does domestically will affect the global environment (and its participation is thus necessary to address environmental problems to which it contributes) and because its international muscle can be used to influence what other states do.

2. U.S. LEADERSHIP

The early leadership of the United States in addressing international environmental issues is rightly trumpeted. Early international successes in protecting endangered species and mitigating ocean pollution can be attributed primarily to U.S. leadership. The United States also played an important, albeit changing, role in the negotiation of international agreements to protect the ozone layer. Scholarly work examining U.S. leadership on these issues rightly points to the importance of domestic action undertaken initially and the intersection between U.S. concerns and the necessity to pursue action internationally to address these problems successfully.

2.1. Species Protection

The United States was at the forefront of some of the earliest international conservation treaties, negotiating with Russia an informal agreement to protect seals in 1893, followed by the Convention for the Preservation and Protection of Fur Seals in 1911, which also included the United Kingdom and Japan. And the United States worked domestically to protect species protected elsewhere: the Lacey Act of 1900, among other provisions, disallowed trade in any species taken in contravention of domestic rules in their country of origin (16 USC 3372(a)(1)(1988)).

By the 1960s on the international level a new approach emerged: the concern to conserve species not for what could be considered sustainable use but, rather, for their protection, simply because they were endangered. Domestic interest in protecting endangered species for ethical reasons led to U.S. interest in working to protect species internationally at the same time that they were being protected in the

United States. The first of the global treaties to protect endangered species broadly was the Convention on International Trade in Endangered Species of Wild Fauna and Flora, or CITES (1973); the negotiations that led to this treaty were convened by the United States, which played a key role working toward agreement (Sand 1997, 6). The United States also contributed importantly to the negotiation process behind other protections of endangered species, such as the Ramsar Convention on Wetlands of International Importance Especially as Waterfowl Habitat (1972). And it was key to the creation of the commercial whaling moratorium within the regulatory process in the International Whaling Commission, shortly after U.S. domestic law mandated the protection of whales. Interestingly, however, the United States has remained apart from the Convention on Migratory Species (1979), suggesting that its role as a protector of species internationally is incomplete.

2.2. Ocean Pollution

U.S. leadership was also key in addressing some aspects of international regulation of ocean pollution, again led in part by using international efforts to tackle what the United States had already begun to address but could not successfully do alone. It was President Nixon who urged the negotiation of what became the Convention on the Prevention of Marine Pollution by Dumping of Wastes and Other Matter (1972), following a study by the U.S. Council on Environmental Quality which suggested that both domestic and international action were necessary to protect the oceans from intentional pollution. The United States began by implementing its own domestic rules, and it proposed the first negotiating text of the international agreement (Chasek 2001).

The United States also played an important role in the eventual negotiation of the International Convention for the Prevention of Pollution from Ships (MARPOL). A spate of subsequent oil spills in U.S. waters in the 1970s persuaded the United States to become more involved in oil pollution prevention. In an effort to assist in the adoption of MARPOL, which had not been ratified by enough states to enter into force, the United States pushed for the creation of an International Conference on Tanker Safety and Pollution Prevention (TSPP) to modify the original agreement. The United States played a clear role in advocating the most environmentally protective options throughout these negotiations (Chasek 2001). The new agreement entered into force as MARPOL 73/78.

2.3. Ozone Depletion

The role the United States played in initial negotiations to address ozone depletion in the 1980s was a bit more complicated (because of domestic businesses that sought to avoid costly regulation), but ultimately it was its leadership that can be credited with the international acceptance, and depth, of cooperation to phase out most ozone-depleting substances. Most of the initial research that showed ozone depletion to be a threat was conducted within the United States by U.S. scientists (Clark et al. 2001, 35). The United States was also ahead of the rest of the world in restricting the use domestically of some of the chemicals of concern, beginning with the 1977 Clean Air Act Amendments, which required the phaseout of chloro-fluorocarbons (CFCs) in nonessential aerosols (DeSombre 2000, 93). In addition, the United States hosted the first intergovernmental conference that same year to discuss action to address this potential problem.

U.S. leadership on the issue was not simple, however. Immediately following the 1977 International Conference on the Ozone Layer, the United States turned away from support for serious international action. The United States did, however, play a decisive role in the eventual negotiation of the 1987 Montreal Protocol on Substances That Deplete the Ozone Layer. And the country was willing to take action to hold states to ozone-reducing behavior even if the international negotiations failed. While international negotiations were ongoing, the U.S. Congress passed a set of regulations that would have held other countries to U.S. domestic standards on ozone-depleting substances in order to be allowed to trade in these substances with the United States (DeSombre 2000).

But the United States has become increasingly reluctant to accept the recent expansion of the list of controlled substances. In particular, it has opposed strengthening the phaseout of methyl bromide, and it has continued to use it in domestic agriculture under an essential use exemption. From the beginning of the negotiation of the methyl bromide provisions in the Montreal Protocol, the United States (regardless of political party of leadership) played a role in restricting the severity of the rules: initially, any exceptions for essential use were to be capped at 30 percent of a state's baseline use of the substance, but the United States urged the removal of that provision. In years following the new restrictions the United States took advantage of this more permissive option, asking for critical use exemptions above 30 percent of baseline (Gareau 2008). This recent reluctance should not over-shadow the important role the United States played in the development and adoption of this agreement, but it does point to the central role of domestic politics in determining U.S. action internationally, even regarding an issue on which it has generally exhibited international leadership.

3. U.S. Reluctance

Although the U.S. recalcitrance about international environmental cooperation may appear recent, in reality the United States has always had a complex approach to international environmental negotiation and has resisted multilateral action on a number of issues since the beginning of the era of major international action to

address environmental problems. Examining the issues on which the United States
has resisted participation in major international cooperation is key to understanding overall U.S. international environmental strategy and the role of domestic politics in determining international leadership. The major issues on which the United
States has worked to avoid or slow international action include the Law of the Sea,
issues of transboundary control of hazardous and toxic materials, protection of
biodiversity, efforts to address acid rain in North America, and, of course, mitigation of climate change, all issues on which U.S. domestic action has lagged behind
that of other countries in some respects, and all issues that demonstrate ideological
and material disagreements between the executive and legislative branches of U.S.
government.

3.1. Law of the Sea

The United Nations Convention on the Law of the Sea (UNCLOS) was negotiated intensively for nearly a decade and reached its final form in 1982. It was an
attempt to bring together all issues relating to ocean protection and regulation into
one enormous agreement. Many of the provisions in the agreement were ones the
United States favored and negotiated to include: an expansion of the area of the
ocean (newly named the Exclusive Economic Zone) in which states are allowed to
control access to resources, efforts to protect against ocean pollution, and important guarantees of navigational rights and innocent passage for both commercial
and military vessels.

    But some of the provisions were ones the United States opposed; most impor-
tant were the provisions for regulating deep-seabed mining. In particular, the
agreement contained redistributive elements, reserving access to some areas of the
seabed for mining by either an entity created by UNCLOS that would share the
benefits of the mining across all countries, or by developing countries in the future
(UNCLOS 1982, Annex III, Article 13). The United States was also concerned about
not being guaranteed a role in decisions on these issues: a council of states was
elected to fixed terms, and in some cases this council could make decisions that did
not need to be unanimous (UNCLOS 1982, Article 168(8)). The United States might
thus be outvoted or even be excluded from the decision making.

    Even after the agreement entered into force (without the official participa-
tion of the United States), U.S. policy makers worked to renegotiate parts of the
agreement to make it acceptable. Under the George H. W. Bush administration the
United States led the negotiation of the Agreement Relating to the Implementation
of Part XI of the Convention (1994), an annex to the agreement that modified the
seabed mining provisions. It ensures U.S. representation on the council and modi-
fies several aspects of voting and representation to increase the influence of the
United States in decision making in the International Seabed Authority and its
council. This agreement also removed the council's authority to make decisions

about whether a given proposed mining operation could be conducted; instead, permits would be allocated on a first-come, first-served basis.

With that interpretation in place, the United States was finally willing to sign the treaty in 2004, and George W. Bush submitted it to Congress for ratification. Such ratification has continued to be elusive, however. Although the Senate Foreign Relations Committee unanimously approved it, it was not brought up for a full Senate vote that year. The Bush administration tried again in 2007, and high-powered executive branch officials testified in the Senate in favor of ratification. The Senate Foreign Relations Committee voted 17–4 in favor of ratification, but the Senate leadership declined to bring it forward for a vote of the full Senate.

Bipartisan domestic pressure for ratification has continued to grow. Climate change provides a compelling reason for the United States to participate: new resources, such as sea routes and access to minerals, become accessible as polar sea ice melts, and the Law of the Sea creates the institutional context in which decisions about state claims to these types of resources will be decided. The treaty, for instance, allows states to claim access to mineral resources in continental shelf areas contiguous to their territory. Disputes about such claims are adjudicated by the governing process of the treaty, and only those states who have ratified can participate in that process. Moreover, only those who have ratified the agreement are able to claim an extended continental shelf, so the United States is excluded from this option unless it ratifies the agreement (Bellinger 2009).

Obama has urged the ratification of the treaty. He conferred with senators on the topic, but his ambitious—and controversial—domestic agenda seemed to dissuade Foreign Relations Committee chair John Kerry from deciding to bring ratification forward (Morello 2009). As of early 2012, no Senate action has been taken toward ratification.

3.2. Toxics Treaties

A second cluster of issues on which the United States has been a reluctant international participant is the set of negotiations relating to transboundary movement of toxics and hazards. The first of these issues to be the subject of international negotiation was the trade in hazardous waste. The United States is by far the largest generator of waste considered to be hazardous. Although most of that waste is disposed domestically, the less than 1 percent of it that is shipped across international borders is sufficient in quantity to make the United States among the largest sources of transboundary hazardous waste shipments (Tiemann 1998). The international framework for addressing this issue is the Basel Convention on the Transboundary Movement of Hazardous Wastes and Their Disposal (1989).

The United States participated in the negotiation of the Basel Convention, primarily in an effort to weaken the direction of international regulation on the issue (Chasek, Downie, and Brown 2006). The primary issue in the initial negotiation of the agreement was whether international trade in this kind of waste would be prohibited altogether (which many developing states advocated and to which European states were largely sympathetic). The United States led a coalition of other developed states that refused to participate if trade were prohibited altogether. Because of their recalcitrance, the eventual compromise reached was to create a system in which those states shipping hazardous waste need to give prior notification to receiving states so that they have the opportunity to decide not to accept it.

Although the United States signed the agreement, George H. W. Bush did not send it to the Senate for ratification. There has been domestic opposition to ratification on several fronts. The first is a general concern about new restrictions. Relatedly, the definition of hazardous waste in the treaty is broader than the domestic definition; the agreement would thus be seen as an expansion of the domestic framework for regulating hazardous waste (O'Neill 1999).

Developing countries continued to press for greater restrictions on trade once the agreement was up and running. Parties to the agreement eventually negotiated an amendment, known as the Basel Ban, that would put into practice the ban on trade between developed and developing states. The United States actively campaigned against the amendment as it was being negotiated and gave funding for international meetings designed to persuade states of the potential problems with such a ban (Puckett 1997). The Basel Ban amendment has been ratified (as of this writing) by 69 states (Basel Secretariat 2011), just shy of the number it needs to enter into force.

Two related issues are trade in hazardous pesticides and chemicals and in persistent organic pollutants. The first was addressed via the Rotterdam Convention on the Prior Informed Consent Procedure for Certain Hazardous Chemicals and Pesticides in International Trade (1998). This agreement created something akin to, but more stringent than, the Basel Convention's process for ensuring that states that received potentially hazardous substances had agreed in advance to do so. The substances for which this prior informed consent is required are those on a collective list, and the U.S. negotiators worked during the negotiations to increase the difficulty for including a substance on this list. The United States signed the resulting agreement but, despite the inclusion of U.S.-backed provisions, has not ratified the treaty.

The issue of international trade in persistent organic pollutants (certain types of pollutants that do not quickly degrade in the environment) was addressed with the Stockholm Convention on Persistent Organic Pollutants (2001). Although the United States signed and eventually ratified this agreement, it worked during negotiations to slow down the process of regulation, blocking a European proposal to begin immediate scientific review of chemicals that might be included in the regulations (Schafer 2005). Although U.S. action on this agreement had a better resolution, the negotiations involving toxic chemicals and waste show the United States resisting rather than leading on this issue. The United States has worked to slow or limit action even when it does support international cooperative efforts.

3.3. Biodiversity

A third issue the United States has been reluctant to support at the international level is the protection of biodiversity. Given the U.S. leadership on international efforts to protect endangered species, the resistance on this issue may seem surprising, but biodiversity is protected through a different regulatory process. The governing agreement is the Convention on Biological Diversity (CBD), negotiated as a part of the 1992 United Nations Conference on Environment and Development held in Rio de Janeiro. The United States did exhibit some leadership on this issue, initiating discussions in the late 1980s within the UNEP governing council (Chasek 2001). But as negotiations progressed, the U.S. negotiators worried that an agreement on this matter would require strengthening the U.S. Endangered Species Act at a time when the executive branch was trying to weaken the law.

In addition, the negotiations moved quickly to embrace the principle, favored by developing countries, of equitable sharing of the benefits of biodiversity. Those states with biodiversity resources feared the exploitation of these resources by businesses from rich countries that would reap all the benefits. If these states were going to undertake to protect biodiversity resources, they wanted to be sure that they would be able to share in the profits that derived from them.

U.S.-based biotechnology and pharmaceutical companies feared potential loss of access or profit with such principles in place (along with other fears about inadequate protections for intellectual property rights in any regime that prioritized sharing of resources) and worked to ensure that efforts to limit trade in genetically modified organisms or mention of the phrase "biosafety" was excluded from the negotiated draft (Raustiala 1997a). Despite its negotiating success, however, the United States announced just prior to the conference in Rio de Janeiro that it would not sign the agreement. President George H. W. Bush indicated, in particular, that he was concerned that the agreement would have a negative effect on jobs in the United States (Devroy 1992, A1).

Some businesses disagreed with U.S. opposition to the agreement. At the end of 1992, after the election of Bill Clinton to the presidency, a group of pharmaceutical and biotechnology firms (including major industry actors like Merck, Genetech, and WRI) concluded that the agreement would not have negative short-term economic ramifications and that in the long term it might be beneficial for the United States to be a part of the international regulatory process (Raustiala 1997b). Clinton signed the agreement in 1993 and sent it to the Senate for ratification. He included an interpretive letter favored by the industry group, suggesting that, under U.S. interpretation, the agreement would neither harm industrial innovation or research nor endanger existing patent protection. The Committee on Foreign Relations voted 16–3 to support ratification. But by this time 35 Republican senators (one more than needed to block ratification) had publicly indicated their intention to vote against ratification. They gave varying reasons for opposition, including concerns that the agreement would commit the United States to transferring technology and funding that would hinder U.S. business interests, or that the agreement was too vague or simply unnecessary (Paarlberg 1997). Ratification has not been attempted since then, but since President Obama's election, nongovernmental and intergovernmental organizations have stepped up efforts to persuade the United States to ratify the treaty.

3.4. Acid Rain

The case of acid rain is also illustrative. Although the United States—and Canada (as part of the United Nations Economic Commission for Europe, which negotiated the initial agreements in a broader effort toward Cold War cooperation)— signed and ratified the Convention on Long-Range Transboundary Air Pollution (LRTAP) in 1979, U.S. behavior on this issue took different shape when the issue of its actual emissions in North America came into question. Initially, in the late 1970s, efforts on acid rain were led in part by the U.S. Congress. The Canadian prime minister in 1977 had called for negotiations on the issue, but no negotiation immediately followed. The U.S. Senate then passed a "sense of the Senate" resolution in 1978 that asked the president to negotiate an agreement with Canada, driven in part by U.S. concerns about new construction of Canadian coal-burning power plants near the U.S.-Canadian border (Munton 1997). But the Canadian response pointed out the extent to which U.S. emissions led to acid rain in Canada, which decreased U.S. interest in pursuing the issue. After continued Canadian pressure the United States agreed in 1980 to a memorandum of intent (MOI). Negotiations began as intended, but they were suspended shortly thereafter. For the better part of the 1980s, Canada pushed but the United States resisted action, arguing that the problem was not serious enough to justify action and that more research was needed.

In 1989, after George Bush became U.S. president, Congress began revising the national Clean Air Act to include provisions to respond to acid rain domestically, because power plant emissions from the Midwest were creating acid rain damage in states in the East, creating a domestic reason for action. The executive branch proposed regulations in which SO_2 reductions would take place through creating a tradable permits system, which would make U.S. reductions less costly and more efficient and would work to diminish problems within the country from acid rain. These measures passed as the Clean Air Act Amendments of 1990, and the United States was once again willing to negotiate with Canada (Golich and Young 1993). The resulting agreement came 11 years after the official bilateral negotiations were initiated. While it committed both states to specific reductions of acidifying substances, the provisions did little beyond what the United States would already have done under the Clean Air Act amendments.

On the one hand, unlike the other examples in this section, this issue resulted in actual international commitment by the United States to address the environmental problem. On the other hand, the United States spent a decade attempting to avoid bilateral cooperation, and it agreed to international action only after it had already taken on the relevant obligations in domestic law. There also was a new president in office.

3.5. Climate Change

The other major issue on which the United States has remained aloof from international efforts is, perhaps most important, climate change (see chapter 8 in this volume). Again, the United States took an early leadership role in the underlying scientific discussion of the phenomenon of climate change. But from the point of international negotiations it moved quickly to obstructionism. In the negotiations leading up to what became the United Nations Framework Convention on Climate Change, the primary U.S. goal was the avoidance of binding targets and timetables for reductions of greenhouse gases, a goal in which it was successful.

Nevertheless, the framework convention does commit member states to some important principles, including the requirement that "developed country Parties should take the lead in combating climate change and the adverse effects thereof," and agreement on the objective of stabilizing the concentrations of greenhouse gases in the atmosphere "at a level that would prevent dangerous anthropogenic interference with the climate system" (Kyoto Protocol 1997, Articles 2 and 3). The United States signed this agreement and the Senate quickly ratified it.

Negotiations toward a protocol with binding emissions reductions obligations began shortly after the negotiation of the Framework Convention, and the U.S. executive branch participated constructively in this negotiation process; a U.S. negotiator suggested publicly that negotiations should work toward "a realistic, verifiable, and medium-term emissions target" (Grubb et al. 1999, 54). The initial U.S. proposal was for a freeze of emissions at 1990 levels by 2008, but the United States did eventually agree to accept a reduction of emissions (which were set differently for different developed states) at 7 percent below 1990 levels (Kyoto Protocol 1997, Annex B).

The Senate, however, felt differently. Prior to the negotiations it passed, by a vote of 95–0, what became known as the Byrd-Hagel Resolution. The statement indicated the Senate's refusal to ratify any climate agreement that required emissions reductions from developed countries if developing countries were also not granted emissions reduction obligations (U.S. Congress 1997, S8113–8138). This statement from the Senate had various causes. Some—like Senator Robert Byrd, who represented West Virginia, a major coal-producing region whose source of income would be hurt by a reduction in demand for greenhouse-gas-intensive fuels like coal, almost certainly intended the resolution to prevent U.S. action on climate altogether, rather than simply signal the necessity of involving developing states in emissions reductions. (The same may be true for Senator Chuck Hagel, from Nebraska, where industrial agriculture is heavily dependent on fossil fuel use.) Others may have been more legitimately concerned about the inability of U.S. action to address the problem without participation by those states with the fastest-growing greenhouse gas emissions, or simply the possibility of U.S. competition with states whose emissions were not regulated.

These concerns, though expressed before the negotiations ended, did not affect the negotiation process; provisions of the Framework Convention—which the United States had ratified—indicated the necessity of action by developed states before developing states would be required to take their own climate protection action; the Kyoto negotiations had been premised on not requiring developing states to reduce emissions. The Senate's vote, however, prevented any possibility of ratification. President Bill Clinton signed the agreement on behalf of the United States (something George W. Bush tried—unsuccessfully—to undo once he took office), but he knew that efforts at ratification would be fruitless.

Congress, moreover, took further steps to derail U.S. participation in international—or domestic—climate change efforts by defeating proposed legislation that would have encouraged behavior consistent with international obligations. One approach of legislative climate action opponents was to ensure that voluntary emissions reductions would not be allowed to be credited toward any eventual reductions that might be required in the future. The 105th and 106th Congresses also defeated several bills that would have encouraged voluntary reductions. Opponents of these bills argued that they would serve the same purpose as Kyoto and would encourage global regulation.

Other congressional recalcitrance went even further, with bills introduced to forbid any action to address or prevent climate change. More effective efforts against action on climate change came from successful legislative riders to appropriations bills in 2000 and 2001. Collectively, the set of defeated proposals to encourage action and proposed legislation to prohibit it is credited with discouraging domestic action to encourage voluntary emissions reduction behavior (Anderson 2002, 243).

The more recent story, however, is mixed. Senator Joseph Lieberman (initially D- and later I-CT) has repeatedly introduced—with different cosponsors—versions of legislation to cap and then reduce U.S. greenhouse gas emissions; support for this legislation increased annually from 2003 to 2008. The 2008 version, the Lieberman-Warner Climate Security Act, came closer than any previous measures to passing. Although it was subject to procedural jockeying and never received a full vote in the Senate, 54 Senators indicated their support for cap-and-trade measures for greenhouse gases (Pew Center 2008).

More important, in 2009, the House actually passed the American Clean Energy and Security Act, much more ambitious than legislation previously considered in the Senate, which included a cap-and-trade system to implement reductions of greenhouse gases by 17 percent by 2020 and by 83 percent by 2050 (Pew Center 2009). The Senate failed to act, however, when it became clear that the measure would not pass.

4. Reasons for U.S. Reluctance

The mixed record of U.S. leadership and resistance on international environmental cooperation suggests that the explanation is not straightforward. The United States has had moments in which it participates in strong international action and other moments in which it actively undermines international collective action. Some explanations can be easily dismissed: it is not the case that Democratic presidents lead the United States forward to multilateral environmental cooperation and Republican presidents resist. And although the U.S. resistance to international environmental action can realistically be described as increasing over time, it is not the case that the United States has gone from action to inaction or leadership to obstructionism in a clear trajectory.

Then what explains the pattern of U.S. behavior in international environmental politics? Scholars have a number of plausible, and competing, explanations worth evaluating. Prominent among them are a general U.S. suspicion of multilateralism, the domestic cost of international action, concern about the political implications of economic or technological transfers to developing countries, the uncertainty underlying environmental issues, or certain aspects of U.S. domestic politics, including strong economic interests. These explanations, however, ultimately do not account for the pattern of U.S. approaches to international environmental policy. Ultimately, the nature of domestic politics—divided government and the role and increasing polarization of the U.S. Congress—can best explain U.S. international environmental action or inaction.

The U.S. concern about multilateralism seems deep and, as an explanation for international behavior, has the advantage that it may account for U.S. attitudes even beyond the issue area of the environment. The United States has also resisted, especially in recent years, international cooperation in issue areas ranging from human rights to arms control. David Forsyth (1991) characterizes this unilateralist bent in U.S. policy as part of U.S. "exceptionalism."

On the face of it, the idea of U.S. suspicion of multilateralism, as an explanation for the U.S. approach to international environmental policy, seems unlikely: how can you use a constant to explain a variable? It may be, however, that some agreements are more multilateral than others in implementation, or that some international approaches challenge the U.S. tendency to isolationism more than others, or even that the avoidance of multilateralism has grown along with relative U.S. power in the post–Cold War world: the United States, as the most powerful state, does not need multilateral cooperation to accomplish what it desires.

Brunnée (2004) argues that multilateral environmental governance has grown more intrusive in the recent era. Where once a treaty simply outlined a set of obligations states agreed to take on, treaties now frequently create international organizations that oversee decision processes that none of the member states alone may be able to steer in their preferred directions. Whether or not this issue really is a clear trend, it is certainly true that many of the treaties contain these decision-making processes. The Senate expressed concern about precisely this element in the CBD; for instance, Senator Conrad Burns (R-MT) expressed fears that the treaty "could give a panel outside the United States the right to dictate what our environmental laws should say. That is wrong" (quoted in Brunnée 2004, 641). Other Republican Senators expressed similar concerns about this treaty.

This explanation, however, is lacking. It is difficult to ascertain a relative level of multilateralism in the agreements the U.S. adopts or avoids, but to the extent that one can be characterized, it does not seem to match U.S. involvement or lack thereof. If anything, the U.S.-supported Montreal Protocol (in which provisions can be adjusted with only a two-thirds majority vote, providing the decision is supported by a majority of both developed and developing states) would be considered among the most multilateral of agreements, and the U.S.-opposed CBD, in which states have few specific obligations and the treaty's decision-making body is extremely weak, would be among the least. Similarly, in the CITES, lists of protected species can be changed without unanimity (although states that are outvoted can opt out of implementation of the provisions), a fairly intrusive multilateral governance process in which the United States participates.

Environmental issues, moreover, would seem the least likely arena in which to pursue self-interested unilateralism: unlike most other environmental issues, the common-pool-resource nature of most environmental issues (Barkin and Shambaugh 1999) means that a single state, no matter how powerful, will be unable to address the issue alone, and one as powerful as the United States can undermine the beneficial environmental impact of the cooperation of others by its free riding. And as Brunnée (2004) observes, environmental multilateralism should pose less concern than trade multilateralism, which the United States generally embraces, for international action to affect domestic obligations. Regardless, as Andrew Moravcsik (2002) notes, identifying exceptionalism does not explain it.

A second possibility is that the United States considers the economic cost of international environmental action when deciding which issues to address on the international level. The United States is the wealthiest state no matter how the calculation is done, so this explanation would be unlikely to account for U.S. inaction compared to the action of other states. But it could nevertheless be the case that the United States prioritizes its own decisions about international action based on cost—or perhaps on some kind of cost-benefit analysis—and thereby chooses which environmental issues to address through international cooperation.

This approach would not be surprising. Detlef Sprinz and Tapani Vaahtoranta (1998) suggest that abatement costs play a role in determining whether states will become leaders in addressing international issues; those with the lowest costs will be willing to push for international action. That explanation is certainly plausible when one considers U.S. resistance to international climate policy. Sebastian Oberthür and Arther Ott (1999, 18) argue that the cost to the United States, the world's major producer of gas, oil, and coal, can explain its unwillingness to take on international climate protection action.

A more obvious way to look at cost is the relationship between the benefits and the costs from international action. Sprinz and Vaahtoranta's (1998) main argument is that state leadership on international environmental issues is primarily determined by the extent to which states are harmed by the environmental problem in question. They would predict U.S. action on the environmental problems that pose the greatest costs to the United States (and for which, therefore, the benefits of collective action would likely outweigh the costs). Cass Sunstein (2007), similarly, argues that a straight cost-benefit analysis explains the difference between U.S. action on ozone depletion and on climate change. Although action on climate change would certainly be expensive to the United States, agreements like UNCLOS would not be; however, lack of participation in climate change agreements may itself prove costly as the United States becomes unable to contribute to important distributive discussion in that process.

A related explanation is that the U.S. concern is not aggregate cost or benefit, per se, but who bears the costs or receives the benefits from international action. A standard domestic complaint about international cooperative efforts is the transfer of wealth, technology, or, more important, decision-making power they allocate to developing countries. U.S. opposition to these measures has frequently been framed as opposition to the distributional aspects of the relevant agreements. Harold K. Jacobson (2002, 428) argues that what the Law of the Sea, CBD, and Kyoto Protocol (three of the major issues on which the United States has resisted international cooperation) have in common is large-scale redistribution of benefits to developing countries. It was the regime to distribute benefits of deep-seabed mining to developing countries that drew U.S. opposition to the Law of the Sea; the provisions to required shared benefits from the exploitation of biodiversity resources caused concern on behalf of pharmaceutical and biotechnology companies in the CBD, and the Senate stated its unwillingness to ratify an agreement on climate change that contained obligations for developed countries if developing countries did not have to reduce their emissions. On the first two issues, the U.S. negotiators explicitly attempted to exclude such provisions from the agreements but failed. The high profile of these concerns in U.S. action suggests there may be something to this explanation.

There are some inconsistencies with this explanation, however. The United States participated wholeheartedly in the Kyoto Protocol negotiations despite the framing that ensured that the eventual agreement would impose no obligations on developing countries; the concern expressed about this issue was voiced only by the legislative branch, not by the executive. Other aspects of the Kyoto Protocol negotiations that the United States actively advocated—a variety of flexibility mechanisms that allowed states to gain credit for undertaking projects in other states, or allowed trading in credits—would likely provide redistributed benefits to developing countries.

It is also the case that some of the issues on which the United States has actively led—most prominently ozone depletion—had redistributive benefits, whereas others on which it resisted—such as the toxics treaties—did not. The international agreement to address ozone depletion was noteworthy and precedent-setting for the extent of differentiation between the obligations of developed and developing countries: even initial reduction obligations were delayed 10 years for developing country parties, during which time they were allowed to increase their use of ozone-depleting substances (Montreal Protocol 1987, Article 5). Moreover, a prominent part of the process involved the creation of the Multilateral Fund, which not only transferred funding from developed to developing countries for the purpose of supporting phaseout activities but also gave them as much of a say in determining its allocation as was given to the donor states, a dramatic departure from how international funding had previously been organized (DeSombre and Kauffman 1996). Although the toxics treaties were largely initiated by developing countries, they do not have the redistributive effects that other treaties the United States opposes do.

Environmental issues are rife with uncertainties, and the extent of uncertainty could be another determining factor for U.S. involvement in international efforts. U.S. reluctance to act on climate change has clearly been influenced by the increasing prominence of so-called climate skeptics, who question the extent to which climate change is happening, is caused by humans, or is even a problem (i.e., whether a changing climate would cause problems or might conversely even create benefits). If it is unclear whether an environmental problem is real, or the extent to which it will cause harm, it may be difficult to build the political capital to address it. It is here that a major difference between the parties has recently emerged, with Republicans (especially those in Congress) denying the human impact on the global climate system. Republicans in the House Energy and Commerce committee in March 2011 unanimously voted down three Democratic amendments to proposed amendments to the Clean Air Act that simply stated—without requiring any legislative action— that human activity is causing increased greenhouse gases to accumulate in the atmosphere, leading to global warming (Democrats Committee on Energy and Commerce 2011). A poll in late 2010 showed that 53 percent of Republicans (and 70 percent of those identifying themselves with the Tea Party) do not believe that climate change is real (Pew Research Center 2010). These trends, while important for the United States going forward on addressing climate change, are quite new and cannot account for previous U.S. inaction on the issue or reluctance on global environmental issues more broadly. It is likely that Republican distrust of the scientific consensus on climate change results from, rather than causes, reluctance to act to address the problem.

Perhaps it is not the uncertainty of an issue, per se, that influences international action, but instead national approaches to addressing uncertainty or risk. Sheila Jasanoff (1990), who has done comparative analysis of state approaches to regulation under conditions of uncertainty, points out that the United States approaches risk regulation differently than the more risk-averse European states. Bodansky (2003) agrees, arguing that the level of risk acceptance by the United States may make it more likely to approach uncertainty by avoiding regulation than is the case for European states. This explanation might account for U.S. inaction on international toxics regulation—the United States is more willing to accept risk, specifically from harmful substances, than are other states. Jasanoff (1990) also notes that actors resistant to environmental action in the United States may frame action as the risky option, given the uncertainty about the extent of the problem and the cost of changing behavior. It is also consistent with the lack of concern about biotechnology and, therefore, its lack of interest in the biosafety protocol to the CBD.

When one looks across international environmental issues, however, it is difficult to see uncertainty or risk acceptance as the primary obstacle to U.S. international action. The United States acted domestically (and then internationally) on ozone depletion long before uncertainty was resolved about the extent or effects of the problem, and it acknowledged the importance of addressing biodiversity, an effort in which it later refused to participate. Uncertainty may instead simply be a convenient excuse when behavior is determined by some other process. Lawrence Susskind (1994, 65) argues that once the United States has decided to avoid environmental action, it attacks "the available data as insufficient regardless of the strength of the worldwide scientific consensus."

5. THE ROLE OF DOMESTIC POLITICS: CONGRESS

The crux of the domestic politics argument for U.S. international environmental behavior is Congress. The difference between executive and legislative branch interests in international environmental politics is notable, and most U.S. reluctance on international environmental issues appears to come from the legislative side. The lack of U.S. participation in the Law of the Sea, the CBD, and the Kyoto Protocol, all of which the United States has signed, comes from lack of Senate ratification. Although the United States has not signed the Basel Convention, it has signed the Rotterdam Convention, and, again, the obstacle is Senate ratification. Clearly, it is lack of Senate support—or, in some cases, outright Senate opposition—that is behind the most egregious cases of U.S. international environmental reluctance. Although recently it is Republican recalcitrance that accounts for the bulk of that opposition (see Amy Below's chapter in this volume), the issue is much broader than a Republican/Democratic divide when examined across recent decades of congressional opposition to international environmental action.

What, then, explains congressional opposition to international environmental cooperation? There are a number of possible explanations, many of which probably work in conjunction with each other. One is the increasing polarization in Congress, especially the Senate, and the structural role that Congress is supposed to play in a federal system, with senators or representatives focusing on what is best for their states or districts rather than for the nation as a whole. A second hypothesis involves the politics of stalemate that has come to dominate the practice of two-party politics within the United States. Finally, the context in which this polarization actually comes into play is the state of the existing regulatory structure compared to potential international action. The decreasing attention in the country (and particularly its regulatory bodies) to environmental issues at the domestic level suggests that the United States will continue to fall behind on international environmental regulatory issues.

The broader scholarly context into which this analysis fits is the concept of "two-level games," the idea that international negotiators face two different audiences that may require different approaches and compromises: the group of states internationally with which formal negotiations take place, and the domestic constituency that ultimately needs to accept any international deal that has been struck (Putnam 1988). A state is constrained internationally by the set of options its domestic political process will find acceptable (and may even choose to use those domestic constraints for bargaining leverage internationally).

The hurdle for treaty ratification, requiring the positive vote of a supermajority (two-thirds) of the Senate, is—intentionally—a high bar for domestic acquiescence. Even for processes that do not require ratification, the current version of the filibuster rule requires consent of three-fifths of the Senate to move a measure forward to a vote. Although the routine use of this process has been rare historically, it has grown dramatically in recent decades, and it exploded during the beginning of Obama's time in office. Although most countries have a domestic ratification process for treaties, the one in the United States is particularly difficult because U.S. ratification requires not only a supermajority vote, but one in a completely separate branch of government, something that is not an issue for the majority of industrialized states with parliamentary systems. Oona Hathaway notes that the United States is one of only six states in the world requiring support of a supermajority of a separate legislative body for ratification, and one of only a few in which ratification automatically incorporates the international agreement into domestic law (Hathaway 2008).[1]

At the same time, congressional polarization has grown dramatically, with implications both for governing generally and for ratification or implementation of international agreements specifically, the step on which U.S. international environmental action seems to founder. The fact that Senate ratification is required is particularly relevant, because structurally the Senate is especially susceptible to pressure from domestic interest groups. Because senators are elected in statewide (rather than national) elections, they need to focus on the issues of concern to their state constituencies, rather than those of national interest, to be elected and reelected. The political polarization of the Senate means that cooperation would be needed from senators on dramatically different parts of the political spectrum to reach the two-thirds vote needed for ratification of treaties. Hathaway points out that if the senators in the 109th Congress were lined up on a political spectrum, the 67th senator is more than twice as conservative—on all issues—as the 51st (and the same analysis would hold in the liberal direction) (Hathaway 2008, 1310–1311). On issues where it might be possible to gain a simple majority vote, two-thirds majority agreement on anything is dramatically more difficult.

Along with the increasing polarization of the country and the Congress is the additional difficulty that occurs when a president advocating ratification is from

1. The others are Cyprus, Ethiopia, Mexico, Slovenia, and Tajikistan (Hathaway 2008, 1273).

a political party that does not control the Senate. These political disjunctures go a long way toward explaining recent difficulties with ratification. Seen in the context of two-level games, that difficulty can also play a role in the negotiation itself, with the executive branch unlikely to want to agree internationally to something it will not be able to implement domestically.

Within this context, one of the factors that might determine what the domestic political system will find acceptable is what it has already undertaken. Kal Raustiala (1997b) notes that states usually rely on existing domestic regulatory structures, rather than creating entirely new ones, to implement international environmental agreements. Peter Cowhey argues that "national politicians have been unlikely to accept any global regime that fails to reinforce the preferred domestic regime" (1990, 171). This explanation may intersect with the cost discussion above; if the United States has already acted on an issue, it may be less costly to undertake action than would be the case if it would have to create a new domestic regulatory structure, to say nothing of the new costs that might accrue to domestic industry actors. The extent of U.S. domestic action prior to international negotiation is the major determinant of what the United States will undertake internationally (DeSombre 2000).

This domestic action explanation gets us reasonably far. For most of the issues on which the United States has led internationally, most prominently those to protect endangered species and the ozone layer and protect the ocean from pollution, the country had already taken strong domestic action before it began to work internationally. Likewise, the United States has strongly resisted undertaking domestic climate regulatory measures, with weaker domestic climate regulation than almost any industrialized state. In this context, acid rain cooperation with Canada is especially noteworthy: the United States agreed to meaningful bilateral action only after it had essentially created the same rules on the domestic level. In some cases, such as ozone depletion, working for international action could actually further the competitiveness of U.S. businesses, as previously unregulated international competitors of already-regulated U.S. businesses now had to take on the same, more costly, restrictions.[2]

6. Future Leadership? Future Scholarship?

The lost U.S. leadership on many international environmental issues is problematic both for international cooperation on pressing issues that will, ultimately, affect the United States if they are not resolved, and for the country's competitive advantage

2. In addition, since many of the substitute chemicals for those that depleted the ozone layer were made by U.S. manufacturers, there was an advantage to having widely adopted regulation internationally.

on issues on which it has previously led. The recent decade is instructive, however, for understanding what is possible in a context of congressional recalcitrance on international environmental issues.

The participation of the United States is absolutely necessary for international environmental action. What can be done to increase its ability or willingness to lead, or at least not prevent, such action? The most important lesson for those within the United States is to "think globally, regulate locally" (DeSombre 2000). Perhaps because Congress is the most important determinant of international environmental action, what it has already decided to regulate domestically is what will get its acquiescence internationally. Its international action is not—nor need it be—altruistic. Often pressure for international action can come from domestic actors, already regulated, hoping to restrict the actions of their international competitors. But that incentive applies only if the domestic regulation comes first.

Understanding the domestic determinants of U.S. international leadership also explains the trend away from that leadership following an era of increased polarization and lack of domestic environmental action. Future research on determinants of domestic environmental action is thus the most important source of information for understanding U.S. international environmental action. The dramatic Republican recalcitrance on environmental issues and especially climate change prevention does not account for the overall record of U.S. action or inaction, but it may represent a shift in the direction of inaction generally and is thus worth understanding. A renewed focus domestically on meeting environmental challenges can lead to an era of increased U.S. leadership internationally and increased competitiveness internationally.

REFERENCES

Anderson, K. S. 2002. "The Climate Policy Debate in the U.S. Congress." In *Climate Change Policy*, ed. S. H. Schneider, A. Rosencranz, and J. O. Niles, 235–250. Washington, DC: Island.

Barkin, S., and G. Shambaugh, eds. 1999. *Anarchy and the Environment: The International Relations of Common Pool Resources*. Albany: State University of New York Press.

Basel Convention Secretariat. 2011. "Ratifications of the Ban Amendment." Available at www.basel.int/ratif/ban-alpha.htm (accessed January 28, 2011).

Bellinger, J. B., III. 2009. "The United States and the Law of the Sea Convention." *Berkeley Journal of International Law Publicist* 1 (2): 7–17.

Bodansky, D. 2003. "Transatlantic Environmental Relations." In *Europe, America and Bush: Transatlantic Relations in the Twenty-First Century*, ed. John Peterson and Mark Pollack, 58–68. London and New York: Routledge, pp. 58–68.

Brunnée, J. 2004. "The United States and International Environmental Law: Living with an Elephant." *European Journal of International Law* 15 (4): 617–649.

Caron, D. D. 2003. "Between Empire and Community: The United States and Multilateralism 2001–2003, an Assessment." *Berkeley Journal of International Law* 21 (3): 395–404.

Chasek, P. 2001. *Earth Negotiations: Analyzing Thirty Years of Environmental Diplomacy.* New York: United Nations University Press.

Chasek, P. S., D. L. Downie, and J. W. Brown. 2006. *Global Environmental Politics.* Cambridge, MA: Westview.

Clark, W. C., et al. 2001. "Acid Rain, Ozone Depletion, and Climate Change: An Historical Overview." In *Learning to Manage Global Environmental Risks*, vol. 1, ed. Social Learning Group. Cambridge, MA: MIT Press.

Cowhey, P. F. 1990. "International Telecommunications Regime: The Political Roots of Regimes for High Technology." *International Organization* 44 (2): 169–199.

Democrats Committee on Energy and Commerce, U.S. House of Representatives. 2011. Full Committee Markup on H.R. 910 (Continued). Available at http://democrats.energycommerce.house.gov/sites/default/files/image_uploads/031011%20EP%20Markup%20of%20HR%20910,%20Energy%20Tax%20Prevention%20Act%20of%202011.pdf

DeSombre, E. R. 2000. *Domestic Sources of International Environmental Policy: Industry, Environmentalists, and U.S. Power.* Cambridge, MA: MIT Press.

DeSombre, E., and Kauffman, J. 1996. "The Montreal Protocol Multilateral Fund: Partial Success Story." In *Institutions for Environmental Aid*, ed. Robert Keohane and Marc Levy, 89–126. Cambridge, MA: MIT Press.

Devroy, A. 1992. "President Affirms Biodiversity Stance; Citing Jobs, Bush Firmly Rejects Treaty." *Washington Post*, June 8, p. A1.

Forsythe, D. 1991. *The Internationalization of Human Rights.* Lexington, MA: Lexington Books.

Gareau, B. 2008. "Dangerous Holes in Global Environmental Governance: The Roles of Neoliberal Discourse, Science, and California Agriculture in the Montreal Protocol." *Antipode* 40 (1): 102–130.

Global Footprint Network. 2010. "Footprint for Nations." Available at www.footprintnetwork.org/en/index.php/GFN/page/footprint_for_nations/ (accessed March 23, 2011).

Golich, V. L., and T. F. Young. 1993. *United States–Canadian Negotiations for Acid Rain Control, Case 452.* Pew Case Studies in International Affairs. Washington, DC: Institute for the Study of Diplomacy, Pew Case Studies Center, Georgetown University.

Grubb, M., with C. Vrolijk and D. Brack. 1999. *The Kyoto Protocol.* London: Royal Institute of International Affairs.

Hathaway, O. A. 2008. "Treaties' End: The Past, Present, and Future of International Lawmaking in the United States." *Yale Law Journal* 117 (8): 1236–1372.

Jacobson, H. K. 2002. "Climate Change, Unilateralism, Realism, and Two-Level Games." In *Multilateralism and U.S. Foreign Policy: Ambivalent Engagement*, ed. S. Forman and P. Stewart, 415–434. Boulder, CO: Lynne Rienner.

Jasanoff, S. 1990. "American Exceptionalism and the Political Acknowledgment of Risk." *Daedalus* 19 (4): 395–406.

Kyoto Protocol to the United Nations Framework Convention on Climate Change. 1997.

Moravcsik, A. 2002. "Why Is U.S. Human Rights Policy So Unilateralist?" In *Multilateralism and U.S. Foreign Policy: Ambivalent Engagement*, ed. S. Forman and P. Stewart, 435–476. Boulder, CO: Lynne Rienner.

Morello, L. 2009. "U.S. Pushes for Law of the Sea Ratification as New Arctic Mapping Project Begins." *New York Times*, July 29; www.nytimes.com/cwire/20 09/07/29/29climatewire-us-pushes-for-law-of-the-sea-ratification-as-89174.html (accessed March 23, 2011).

Munton, D. 1997. "Acid Rain and Transboundary Air Quality in Canadian-American Relations." *American Review of Canadian* 27 (3): 327–355.

Oberthür, S., and A. Ott. 1999. *The Kyoto Protocol*. Berlin: Springer.

O'Neill, K. 1999. "Hazardous Waste Disposal." *Foreign Policy in Focus* 4 (1) (January); www.fpif.org (accessed January 31, 2011).

Paarlberg, R. L. 1997. "Earth in Abeyance: Explaining Weak Leadership in U.S. International Environmental Policy." In *Eagle Adrift: American Foreign Policy at the End of the Century*, ed. R. J. Lieber, 135–160. New York: Longman.

Pew Center on Global Climate Change. 2008. "Analysis of the Lieberman-Warner Climate Security Act of 2008." Available at www.pewclimate.org/analysis/l-w (accessed January 31, 2011).

———. 2009. "The American Clean Energy and Security Act (Waxman-Markey Bill)." Available at www.pewclimate.org/acesa (accessed January 31, 2011).

Pew Research Center. 2010. "Wide Partisan Divide over Global Warming." October 27; pewresearch.org/pubs/1780/poll-global-warming-scientists-energy-policies-off shore-drilling-tea-party.

Puckett, J. 1997. "The Basel Ban: A Triumph over Business-as-Usual." Available at www.ban.org/about_basel_ban/jims_article.html (accessed March 23, 2011).

Putnam, R. 1988. "Diplomacy and Domestic Politics: The Logic of Two-Level Games." *International Organization* 42 (3): 427–460.

Raustiala, K. 1997a. "The Domestic Politics of Global Biodiversity Protection in the United Kingdom and United States." In *The Internationalization of Environmental Protection*, ed. M. Schreurs and E. Economy, 42–73. Cambridge: Cambridge University Press.

———. 1997b. "Domestic Institutions and International Regulatory Cooperation: Comparative Responses to the Convention on Biological Diversity." *World Politics* 49 (4): 482–509.

Sand, P. H. 1997. "Whither CITES? The Evolution of a Treaty Regime in the Borderland of Trade and Environment." *European Journal of International Law* 8 (1): 29–58.

Schafer, K. S. 2005. "Ratifying Global Toxics Treaties: The U.S. Must Provide Leadership." *Foreign Policy in Focus*, October 5; www.fpif.org/articles/ratifying_global_toxics_treaties_the_us_must_provide_leadership (accessed March 23, 2011).

Shah, A. 2010. "Foreign Aid for Development Assistance." *Global Issues*. Available at www.globalissues.org/article/35/foreign-aid-development-assistance (accessed March 23, 2011).

Sprinz, D., and T. Vaahtoranta. 1998. "The Interest-Based Explanation of International Environmental Policy." *International Organization* 48 (1): 77–105.

Sunstein, C. R. 2007. "Montreal and Kyoto: A Tale of Two Protocols." *Harvard Environmental Law Review* 31: 1–65.

Supreme Court of the United States. 2007. Massachusetts et al. v. Environmental
   Protection Agency et al. No. 05–1120. Argued November 29, 2006; decided April 2,
   2007. Available at www.supremecourt.gov/opinions/06pdf/05–1120.pdf.
Susskind, L. E. 1994. *Environmental Diplomacy: Negotiating More Effective Global
   Agreements*. Oxford: Oxford University Press.
Tiemann, M. 1998. "Waste Trade and the Basel Convention: Background and
   Update." *CRS Report for Congress* 98–638 ENR, December 30.
U.S. Congress. 1997. *Congressional Record Daily Edition*, July 27, S8113–8138.

CHAPTER 11

....

GLOBAL ENVIRONMENTAL POLICY MAKING

KATE O'NEILL

....

THIS chapter addresses the emergence of the environment as a global policy issue and the ways in which the international community has responded to global environmental problems, focusing on the period since the first global conference on the environment, held in Stockholm, Sweden, in 1972. For most of that time, global environmental policy making has been dominated by the negotiation and implementation of intergovernmental agreements or regimes, which have drawn most, if not all, countries into taking some action to address global environmental degradation. More specifically, this chapter discusses the role of the United States in global environmental governance over this time period, as well as the impacts of global environmental policy on the country itself. It also traces the emergence and maturation of a distinct body of academic literature: global, or international, environmental politics. Beginning as a subfield of international relations theory, this literature has broadened into an interdisciplinary social science field of its own, addressing both the political causes of the global environmental crisis and the politics of global environmental governance.[1] In recent years the architecture of global environmental governance has changed considerably as new initiatives and new actors have emerged that challenge, but also address, some of the gaps and

---

1. In addition to the works cited in this chapter, the reader is referred to some of the leading journals in this field, such as *Global Environmental Politics*, *International Environmental Agreements*, and *Environmental Politics*, which have been founded or expanded significantly in the past 12 years.

weaknesses of the dominant mode of governance through interstate diplomacy. Likewise, it affords challenges, opportunities, and new avenues for future research for scholars in this critical field of study.

1. The Emergence of the Environment as a Global Policy Issue

Environmental problems are long-familiar accompaniments to human expansion and industrialization. From wilderness protection to addressing urban air pollution and providing clean drinking water, early environmental legislation focused on the visible, local impacts of environmental problems. But environmental degradation crosses national borders, and it has long been recognized that activities in one country can easily affect environmental quality in another, with effluents or emissions borne by winds, rivers, and ocean currents. In the 1950s and 1960s, scientists began serious work on the ways in which the Earth's atmosphere and biosphere were threatened by human activity, identifying climate change, ozone layer depletion, and the loss of biological diversity as three particular problems whose impacts could be huge. At the same time, there was growing popular awareness of problems such as acid rain, emanating from the United Kingdom and destroying forests in Northern Europe, major industrial pollution incidents in many countries, and the threats to particular "charismatic" species, such as panda bears and whales, and the Amazon rainforest. Questions of resource limits and population growth and its impacts began to cross over from academic debates to popular culture (Ehrlich 1968; Meadows 1972). This transition from seeing the environment as a "local" problem to one with "global" ramifications began to be reflected in political arenas, too, supported by a growing environmental movement, especially in industrialized countries.

The central problem for global environmental governance—as is the case with many global problems—is that some form of international cooperation is necessary for global environmental problems to be addressed. Activities within the borders of one country may affect environmental quality both in neighboring (and sometimes even distant) regions and in the global commons—the oceans and the atmosphere. Such cooperation is difficult for reasons related to the "anarchic" nature of the international system and to the complexities, uncertainties, and longtime horizons associated with many environmental problems. In other words, in the absence of a sovereign authority, states are unwilling to take on costly commitments that might not be matched by other states, generating serious collective action problems that impede effective cooperation. Nonetheless, by the late 1960s, there already existed a substantial, albeit somewhat ad hoc body of international environmental law—treaties and legal agreements around, for example, whaling and the protection of migratory species, and a patchwork of agreements around shared rivers or limiting emissions of power plants close to shared borders (see chapter 10 in this volume).

It took concerted action by the United Nations to place the environment squarely on the international political agenda and to attempt to build a coherent framework for global environmental cooperation. In the late 1960s, and in the face of scientific discoveries and new data about transboundary air pollution, ozone layer depletion, biodiversity loss, and climate change, and a growing awareness that population growth and economic expansion may, in fact, be limited by the Earth's resource base, the UN convened one of the first truly international summits of its kind. The UN Conference on Humans and the Environment (UNCHE) was held in Stockholm, Sweden, in 1972.[2]

The Stockholm Conference's main accomplishment was to establish the architecture of global environmental governance as we understand it today. Representatives from 114 countries attended the meeting, with the goals of setting environmental goals and priorities for the international community and establishing a coordinated legal and political framework through which to meet them. In essence, delegates at Stockholm ratified existing practices of global environmental governance: the negotiation and implementation by nation-states of multilateral environmental agreements on an issue-by-issue basis. More than that, however, they also established the United Nations Environment Programme (UNEP), whose mandate would be to convene and monitor processes of international environmental cooperation. The Stockholm Declaration codified 26 general principles of international environmental law, simultaneously protecting the sovereign right of states to use their own natural resources while recognizing an obligation not to affect other countries' environmental quality, and laying out a number of priorities for the international community.

In terms of the role of the United States at Stockholm, it is clear from contemporary and later accounts (Haas 2002; Ivanova 2007, 2010; Sohn 1973) that while America was not directly an instigator of the meeting, it was a key team player, brokering agreements at several points in negotiations over the creation of UNEP and the drafting of the Stockholm Principles, while still looking out for its own interests and the balance of costs. This stands in contrast to its more combative role 20 years later at the Rio Earth Summit (Gardner 1992). Both domestically and internationally, UNCHE came at a good moment in U.S. politics, as the federal government established the Environmental Protection Agency and was in the process of enacting critical framework legislation, and Cold War tensions had (temporarily) lessened (see chapters 7, 9, and 15 in this volume).

UNCHE thus marked the beginning of four decades, so far, of concerted international efforts to protect the global environment, providing a legal framework, goals, and policy tools to enable states to work together to meet shared environmental challenges. It also marks the start of an ongoing debate over how to balance

2. On global environmental conferences and their history, see Soroos 2011. For a discussion of UN megaconferences, see Friedman et al. 2005, chapter 1.

environmental protection and economic growth and development. This debate was sparked by the growing influence of countries of the global South, and their concern that their own development would be limited by environmental rules emanating from the wealthier North. This has become a critical theme in the theory and practice of global environmental governance. Over this time frame, too, we see the rise and—as some see it—the decline of multilateral environmental agreements (MEAs) as the central platform for global environmental governance. The next section charts the emergence and significance of MEAs. The following sections examine alternatives and current debates over the architecture of global environmental governance.

2. STATE-LED GLOBAL ENVIRONMENTAL GOVERNANCE, 1972–2010

Since 1972, the dominant model of global environmental governance has been the negotiation by nation-states of MEAs on an issue-by-issue basis. According to one estimate, over 140 MEAs have been created since 1920, and over half of these since 1973 (Haas 2001, 316). This number, in fact, underrepresents the complexity of international environmental diplomacy: most MEAs have several associated amendments, protocols, or annexes. Taking these into account, "three or more governments have agreed on legally binding commitments over 700 times" (Mitchell 2003, 434–435). In addition, many international agreements in other issue areas—trade being a prominent example—have environmental components. Highlights include binding agreements over ozone layer depletion, the protection of biological diversity, and agreements over hazardous substances, from trading in hazardous wastes to the phasing out of persistent organic pollutants (POPs). The most high-profile and contentious negotiating process has occurred over climate change, notably over the ratification of the 1997 Kyoto Protocol, with many staunch critics on both sides of the spectrum. This time period has also been punctuated by two more "Earth Summits": the UN Conference on Environment and Development, held in Rio de Janeiro in 1992, and the World Summit on Sustainable Development, held in Johannesburg in 2002.

In turn, the emergence of the environment as an arena of international political action has generated significant academic interest from scholars in a range of disciplines, from international relations to sociology to political ecology and science and technology studies.[3] Particularly relevant to the discussion of state-led global environmental governance is the application of regime theory to case studies of environmental diplomacy. Regime theory comes out of the discipline

---

3. For a lengthier discussion of these issues, see O'Neill 2009.

of international relations. It examines the emergence, durability, and impacts of international cooperation, recognizing that beyond the physical treaty (the "piece of paper"), international cooperation creates an entire web of "rules, norms, principles and decision-making procedures" that govern the expectations and behavior of actors involved in the regime, from government representatives to international bureaucrats to nonstate actors, such as environmental activist organizations (Krasner 1983, 3). Therefore, in international environmental politics, we refer to the ozone regime, the biodiversity regime, or the climate regime: all separate processes governing their own individual issue areas, anchored by one or more major treaties.

Scholars of global environmental politics thus have a rich set of cases for examining how environmental regimes emerge, why they take on particular forms, and the factors contributing to their success, or lack thereof.[4] They have also generated important critiques of this system, and discussed what should be done to make it work better.[5] We now look at each of these areas in turn.

3. Treaty Negotiation: Design and Characteristics of International Environmental Regimes

One of the fundamental challenges of global governance is to create arrangements that are acceptable to all signatory governments and that have some positive impact on the problems they are designed to solve. Studies of international cooperation all agree that developing ways to overcome collective action problems and reconciling competing national interests represents the critical challenge to effective solutions to global problems.

The system of international environmental diplomacy ratified at Stockholm was rooted in the pragmatic desire to bring on board, and maintain consensus among, as many nation-states as possible. This is not to say every MEA is a capitulation to the status quo, or the lowest common denominator. For example, the Stockholm Declaration puts strong emphasis on the role of science in creating shared understandings of the causes of problems and the need for action. And unlike other arenas of global governance, environmental negotiations have been open to the attendance and perspectives of nonstate actors, notably environmental activist organizations, but also business sector representatives, although only

---

4. See, for example, Axelrod et al. 2011; Haas, Keohane, and Levy 1993; Mitchell 2003; O'Neill 2009; Young 1994.
5. See, for example, Biermann et al. 2009; Conca 2005, 2006; Hoffmann 2011; Speth 2004; Wapner 2003.

state representatives can vote and make formal decisions. Not only has the presence of these civil society representatives provided an audience visible and present to negotiators, their involvement in providing information and helping forge solutions has also been an important part of global environmental negotiations (Betsill and Corell 2007). Also, many point to the role of certain lead negotiators—UNEP leaders, such as Mostafa Tolba or Tommy Koh—and some smaller states (the Scandinavian countries, for example) in creatively forging consensus, leading to stronger measures than might have been expected on several occasions (Skodvin and Andresen 2006; Young 1991).[6]

Most MEAs share common characteristics designed to bring as many signatory states as possible on board, while gradually committing them to actual behavioral change. First, one of UNEP's functions is agenda setting: raising concern about problems and framing them in a way that is conducive to international action. One way UNEP has accomplished this is by sponsoring scientific research and creating scientific organizations to generate and disseminate consensual knowledge. The best-known of these organizations is the Intergovernmental Panel on Climate Change (IPCC), established in 1988, whose function is to review, compile, and assess the state of global knowledge around climate change and its impacts. An influential approach to studying the role of scientists in international cooperation was developed by Peter Haas, who examined the influence of epistemic communities—transnational communities of scientists and experts who share causal opinions and normative beliefs and who are in a position to influence their governments—on negotiations (Haas 1990, 1992). Where such communities exist (as, arguably, in the case of the ozone regime), they are able to cut through political debates and push their respective delegates toward a stronger solution than is the case in their absence.

Second, negotiations are open to every nation-state that wishes to participate, and they are encouraged to do so. The rationale for this measure is that a broad, international consensus leads to stronger, legitimate agreements with which states are more likely to comply and that multilateral pressures will bring laggard states along. The main criticism of this approach is that it can lead to lowest-common-denominator bargaining, costing more for states with high stakes in the matter and precluding the possibility of stronger agreements limited to a smaller number of parties (Hoffmann 2005; Susskind 1994).

Third, and in order to balance universal participation, international environmental negotiations usually proceed in stages. In the first stage, states negotiate and sign a framework convention—usually a fairly general statement of the parameters of the problem and the courses of action that need to be taken in the future that does not obligate states to measures much more extensive than reporting and information requirements. The next stage involves the negotiation of more detailed agreements that do contain binding commitments, usually in the form of protocols

---

6. Studies of the 1979 Long-Range Transboundary Air Pollution Agreement (LRTAP) point to the way Scandinavian states upped the ante by pledging deeper commitments than other countries and challenging them to meet those commitments (Levy 1993).

or amendments to the framework convention. Treaty texts also contain specific requirements for entry into force, usually based on the ratification of the treaty by a given number of signatory states.[7] The intention is that once states have signed up to the first step, they will be amenable to taking further, more stringent steps down the road. Thus, many international environmental regimes consist of nested agreements. In the case of the climate change regime, the 1997 Kyoto Protocol, which commits signatory states to binding emissions reductions, follows directly on from the 1992 UN Framework Convention on Climate Change. While the strength of this system is that it allows reluctant states to commit themselves gradually, it does have the drawback of leading to very long time frames, which can fail to keep up with the pace of environmental change.

A fourth set of common characteristics across MEAs has to do with measures designed to share adjustment burdens equitably among rich and poor countries—the North and South. Many MEAs impose differential responsibilities on Northern and Southern countries. Under the ozone regime, for example, Southern countries were given an additional 10 years to phase out the use and production of CFCs. Under the climate regime, Southern countries currently have no greenhouse gas emissions reductions requirements—an issue that has been the source of some controversy, especially for the United States. In addition, many regimes have funding mechanisms that are designed to increase the capacity of Southern countries to meet their obligations. Many of these mechanisms work under the umbrella of the Global Environment Facility, whose function is to provide "additional" aid to projects that further the goals of specific international agreements.[8] Southern countries—often represented by the "Group of 77" less developed countries—have exercised considerable leverage at international negotiations, noting that as the North is actually responsible for much of the current predicament, they should be the ones to bear the primary cost burden (Najam 2011). Some Northern states counter that as Southern countries grow, they are likely to overtake the North in areas such as greenhouse gas emissions and should therefore be undertaking reduction measures now. For some, this "conflict" has been a primary reason why international environmental cooperation is so weak (Susskind 1994). Others see ways in which the "ongoing dialogue" between North and South has in fact strengthened environmental agreements, creating ones that are perceived as more equitable across the board, and that often it is not Northern but Southern countries taking the lead in environmental negotiations (Najam 2005; Wapner 2003). An early example of this phenomenon is the negotiations over the 2004 UN Convention to

---

7. In some cases, entry into force requires only a simple majority of signatories to ratify; in other cases, requirements are more complicated. The 1997 Kyoto Protocol required rich country parties representing at least 55 percent of global emissions to ratify first, which in part explains why it did not enter into force until 2005.
8. "Additionality" in this context refers to that part of a project that would carry broader global environmental benefits but would be too costly to add on in the absence of targeted aid. For an assessment of GEF, see Porter et al. 2008.

Combat Desertification, pushed for by the Southern countries most affected by land degradation (Najam 2004). Wapner (2003) notes the push made by the South at Johannesburg to define issues such as fresh water and wood fuel availability as critical to an agenda that links environmental quality to poverty remediation.

4. Major Multilateral Environmental Agreements: Stories from the Trenches

Table 11.1 summarizes some of the major MEAs currently in existence, from one of the earliest, the International Whaling Convention (1946), to the most recent, the Stockholm Convention on Persistent Organic Pollutants (2001). It shows the major protocols associated with framework conventions, where relevant, and when each entered into force after acquiring the relevant number of ratifications. It also shows that many MEAs have a wide membership, up to 196 member states (in the case of the ozone regime), making many of them close to universal. These numbers tend to trend upward over time: in early 2008, membership of the ozone regime stood at 191 states. Some of the later signatories, perhaps not surprisingly, include Afghanistan (2004) and Iraq (2008), who have been encouraged to rejoin the international community after periods of exile.

The role of the United States in the MEAs listed in Table 11.1 has varied extensively (see chapter 10 in this volume). While in some cases—whaling, the Convention on International Trade in Endangered Species (CITES), the Stockholm POPs convention, and the ozone regime—it has led or supported the eventual agreement, in other cases (the Basel Convention on hazardous waste trading, for example), it has never signed. In others—the Convention on Biological Diversity (CBD), for example, it has signed the convention but never ratified the treaty, often due to the inability to pull together the required two-thirds majority in the Senate, and a lack of political will thereafter. Still, as a signatory of the CBD, the United States led the opposition to the 2000 Cartagena Biosafety Protocol. After President George W. Bush withdrew the United States from the Kyoto Protocol in 2001, it has never rejoined, although as a UNFCCC signatory, it continues to play an ongoing role in climate negotiations.

There are many interesting stories behind the entries in this table that illustrate trends, successes, failures, and anomalies in global environmental diplomacy. Some of these regimes have proven to be very successful: the ozone regime is a case in point. It took only a few years from the start of negotiations for nation-states to actually agree to ban the production of chlorofluorocarbons (CFCs), the main ozone-depleting substance (but a very widely used chemical), in the wake of strong scientific evidence that their production and subsequent emission into the stratosphere was causing the hole in the ozone layer identified over the Arctic; the

Table 11.1 Major Multilateral Environmental Agreements

Agreement and Major Associated Legal Instruments	Purpose	Date Adopted/Entry into Force	No. of Parties (2012)
International Whaling Convention (IWC)	To provide for the proper conservation of whale stocks and thus make possible the orderly development of the whaling industry	1946/1946	89
Convention on International Trade in Endangered Species (CITES)	To ensure that the international trade in wild plant and animal species does not threaten their survival	1973/1975	175
International Convention for the Prevention of Pollution from Ships (MARPOL)	To prevent and minimize pollution from ships, both accidental and from routine operations	1973/1983 1978/1983	151 151
Protocol Related to MARPOL	*To strengthen regulations specific to oil tanker operations*		
UN Convention on the Law of the Seas (UNCLOS) *Agreement for the Implementation of UNCLOS related to the Conservation and Management of Straddling and Highly Migratory Fish Stocks*	To establish a comprehensive legal order to promote peaceful use of the oceans and seas, equitable and efficient utilization of their resources, and conservation of their living resources	1982/1994 1995/2001	162 78
Vienna Convention on Substances That Deplete the Ozone Layer *Montreal Protocol*	To protect human health and the environment from the effects of stratospheric ozone *To reduce and eventually eliminate emissions of man-made ozone-depleting substances*	1985/1988 1987/1989	197 197
Basel Convention on the Control and Transboundary Movements of Hazardous Wastes and Their Disposal	To ensure environmentally sound management of hazardous wastes by minimizing their generation, reducing their transboundary movement, and disposing of these wastes as close to their point of generation as possible	1989 1995/n.a.	179 73
Basel Ban Amendment (Decision III/1, COP 3)	*To ban the trade in hazardous wastes for disposal and recycling from OECD to non-OECD countries*		

(continued)

Agreement and Major Associated Legal Instruments	Purpose	Date Adopted/Entry into Force	No. of Parties (2012)
UN Framework Convention on Climate Change (UNFCCC)	To stabilize greenhouse gas concentrations in the atmosphere at a level preventing dangerous human-caused interference with the climate system	1992/1994 *1997/2005*	194 *192*
Kyoto Protocol	*To supplement the UNFCCC by establishing legally binding constraints on greenhouse gas emissions and encouraging economic and other incentives to reduce emissions*		
Convention on Biological Diversity (CBD)	To conserve biodiversity and promote its sustainable use and to encourage the equitable sharing of the benefits arising out of the use of genetic resources	1992/1993 *2000/2004*	193 *163*
Cartagena Biosafety Protocol	*To promote biosafety by establishing practical rules and procedures for the safe transfer, handling, and use of genetically modified organisms, especially as they move across national borders*		
UN Convention to Combat Desertification (UNCCD)	To combat desertification in order to mitigate the effects of drought and ensure the long-term productivity of dry lands	1994/1996	194
Stockholm Convention on Persistent Organic Pollutants (POPs)	To protect human health and the environment from POPs by eliminating or reducing their release into the environment	2001/2004	177

Adapted and updated from O'Neill 2009, Table 4.1.

(relatively few) large multinational chemical producers were able to shift quickly to using alternatives to CFCs (Parson 2003).

Turning to the conservation arena, CITES, too, is considered a strong agreement, with a lot of support, even though in the early 2000s debates over the inclusion or exclusion of particular species from export or import had generated controversy among member states (Gehring and Ruffing 2008). Its purpose is clear, it has wide support (including from the United States), and implementing it—through systems of permits, export controls, and border inspections—is relatively straightforward.

By contrast, the main conservation-related agreement, the 1992 Convention on Biological Diversity (CBD) has trodden a path more politically charged, and many would say less effective (Guruswamy 1998; McGraw 2002). Its architects, which included the NGO umbrella group the International Union for the Conservation of Nature (IUCN), initially intended it as an umbrella convention that would bring together and strengthen existing conservation-related agreements (including CITES, the 1975 Convention on Migratory Species, and the 1972 World Heritage Convention). These intentions were derailed early on in the course of preparatory negotiations, as Southern countries—not coincidentally the main repositories of much of the world's biological diversity—proclaimed they would not support an agreement that limited their access to their own resources in the interests of what they saw as largely Northern conservation values and goals. Ultimately, therefore, the CBD focused far more broadly on general biodiversity protection goals and the right of nations to manage their own resources and to limit or permit access as they saw fit. This outcome dissatisfied many in the conservation biology community, as did the first protocol of the CBD on biosafety, essentially seeking to control export of genetically modified organisms to Southern countries. In a broader context, the 2000 Cartagena protocol provided a valuable counterweight to negotiations under the auspices of the World Trade Organization that looked like it would open up those markets to genetically modified organisms. However, to some it seemed tangential at best to the overall goals of the CBD itself.

Worth mentioning in the conservation context, too, is the absence of an international forests convention. Although one was intended to be ready for signature at the 1992 Rio Summit, negotiations failed amid disagreements over the types of forests that should be covered and the objection by powerful Southern governments to accepting controls on their ability to extract and benefit from timber resources. As a result, global forest regulation has been relegated to fairly informal intergovernmental forums and has become a key arena of nonstate global environmental governance, discussed below (Gulbrandsen 2004; Humphreys 2003).

Turning to chemicals regulation at the global level, another illustrative story is that of the 1989 Basel Convention, which regulates the international trade in hazardous wastes (O'Neill 2001). First, it exemplifies how UNEP frames global environmental problems. Rather than focusing on the broader problem—overgeneration and improper disposal of hazardous wastes in developed countries—it targeted an issue that was clearly international: waste dumping from North to South. Initiated after a series of fairly egregious instances of waste dumping from rich to poor countries, in its initial form the Basel Convention sought primarily to regulate, rather than overtly restrict, such trade. This relatively weak outcome incensed many countries, who saw it as essentially ratifying the existing status quo. Therefore, in 1995 parties passed an amendment to the convention that would ban outright the export of hazardous wastes to Southern countries—both for final disposal and for recycling. However, that ban has yet to reach the required number of signatories to enter into force.[9] It faces strong opposition from relevant business groups and also from a number of Southern countries, such as India, who feel they should not be arbitrarily excluded from being able to import and recycle wastes. This opposition, in turn, may fuel a challenge to the Basel Ban as violating global trade rules (O'Neill and Burns 2005). A major issue now for Basel and other chemicals agreements—including the 2001 Stockholm Convention on Persistent Organic Pollutants—is the extent to which they could or should be integrated into one larger framework that would cover the entire chemicals lifecycle (Downie et al. 2005; Selin 2009). Informal discussions under way suggest that this innovative solution may eventually come into being.

Finally, a torturous and drawn-out negotiating process underlies the climate change regime (Betsill 2011; Hoffmann 2005; Prins and Rayner 2007). The framework convention, a very general document was, along with the CBD, opened for signature at the 1992 Earth Summit in Rio. The issue of climate change has proven incredibly problematic for the international community to address. For one, the issue itself is fraught with scientific uncertainties, and only in the early years of the twenty-first century was any sort of scientific consensus over the anthropogenic causes of climate change actually reached. For another, taking action to achieve concrete reductions in greenhouse gas emissions was going to prove costly, particularly for industrialized countries, including the United States. At the same time, Southern countries made it clear that they were not going to proceed with GHG emissions reductions without some form of support from Northern countries. These conflicts shaped the following 20 years of negotiations.

The 1997 Kyoto Protocol was a hard-fought compromise over emissions reductions and the creation of mechanisms that would enable Northern countries to meet their targets by funding projects in developing countries that pleased few scientists and others concerned about climate impacts. This politically charged situation was heightened over the ensuing years by a battle over ratification and entry into force of the Kyoto Protocol and President George W. Bush's withdrawal of the United States from the Protocol in early 2001. The Kyoto Protocol finally entered into force in 2005 after the European Union essentially bribed Russia into ratifying the agreement (and then promptly withdrew its "bribe," support for Russian entry into the World Trade Organization). With Kyoto due to expire in 2012, and with very few signatories meeting their targets, negotiations in the early 2000s made little headway despite the election of "friendlier" governments in the United States and Australia, both long-standing opponents of global climate rules. Conferences of the parties to the UNFCCC held in Copenhagen in 2009 and in Cancun in 2010 failed to make real headway in creating a new and binding post-Kyoto agreement (Victor 2011).

---

9. The Basel Ban Amendment requires that 75 percent of the parties accepting the amendment and actually present at the Third Conference where it was adopted must ratify before it enters into force.

5. IMPACTS OF STATE-LED GLOBAL ENVIRONMENTAL GOVERNANCE ON THE UNITED STATES

The above sections touch on the role that the United States has played at different times in international environmental negotiations. Less often discussed have been the impacts of engaging in global environmental diplomacy on America itself. Because the United States is a leading industrialized nation and has often been only a reluctant participant in multilateral negotiations, one assumes these impacts have been minimal. In fact, that has not been the case.

First, participation in global environmental governance has brought new issues and issue-framings into U.S. politics, such as ozone layer depletion, climate change, and biodiversity. While these problems have been addressed in domestic as well as in international legal measures, the global framing of and research into these problems have helped structure domestic politics around these issues. And as DeSombre notes in this volume, where the United States has signed on to multilateral environmental agreements, its record of compliance has generally been good. However, certain global environmental issues—notably climate change, but also domestic legislation around species protection—became a lightning-rod issue during the George W. Bush and Barack Obama administrations, bringing the legitimacy of scientific research front and center in U.S. policy debates (Jacques et al. 2008).

Second, it has also driven the creation of new political bodies—often agencies within agencies—and laws. For example, the Bureau of Oceans and International Environmental and Scientific Affairs, located within the U.S. State Department, was created in 1974 to advance U.S. foreign policy goals across a range of issue areas, including the environment. In a related development, environmental provisions are now routinely included in other sets of negotiations, notably regional trade agreements, where they were not previously mentioned. In part, this development relates to bitter disputes over the creation of the North American Free Trade Agreement (NAFTA) in the early 1990s (Audley 1997).

Engagement with global environmental governance has also brought the United States new overseas aid commitments. In 2009, it contributed $80 million to the Global Environmental Facility (GEF), with an additional $25 million to tropical forest conservation and to the World Bank Forest Carbon Partnership, with commitments to a wider range of international environmental programs set to rise substantially in subsequent years (Lattanzio 2010, 1). Since 1994, the United States has pledged a total of $1.61 billion to the GEF and has actually paid $1.36 billion of this total (Lattanzio 2010, 4). This is, of course, only a fraction of U.S. spending overseas, and lower as a percentage of GDP than the contribution of many other donor nations, but nonetheless represents a significant commitment, especially given its very open reservations about the lower obligations awarded to Southern countries under many environmental regimes.

Third, and just outside the halls of Congress, global environmental problems and governance efforts have led most leading U.S.-based environmental NGOs to incorporate international components in their campaigns. Further from the corridors of power, many grassroots environmental groups are embracing global issues such as climate change as part of their platforms (Dawson 2010). Likewise, we can see similar developments in the corporate sector, although not always in a pro-environmental fashion: the Global Climate Coalition (GCC, now disbanded) was a coalition of U.S. oil companies seeking to undermine global measures to combat climate change. More constructively, U.S. businesses have started to engage with climate issues (Jones and Levy 2009), partnerships between NGO and business interests around renewable energy and other climate-related issues are starting to thrive, and the U.S. venture capital sector is helping sponsor "clean-tech" innovation.

In addition, and well beyond the Beltway, many U.S. state governments (such as California and states in the Northeast) and cities are now seeking a role as direct players in combating global climate change. In part, this movement comes in reaction to the weak response of the federal government. Some state governments are working to enact strong GHG emissions reductions targets unilaterally. California's role is important here, given its track record of "ratcheting up" U.S. environmental policy (Vogel 1995). Other states in the Northeast are working together, and with Canadian provinces, to meet particular climate goals at a regional level (Betsill and Rabe 2009; Selin and VanDeveer 2009). Finally, U.S. cities are members of transnational municipal networks such as the International Council for Local Environmental Initiatives (ICLEI), which encourage action at the local level to meet global environmental goals (Gore and Robinson 2009).[10]

6. The Architecture of State-Led Global Environmental Governance: Effectiveness and Critiques

The decades since the early 1970s have marked a remarkable flowering of political initiatives designed to address global and transboundary environmental problems. The dominant mode of global environmental governance has been the negotiation and implementation by national governments of multilateral environmental agreements across a wide range of different issue areas: in other words, the creation of

---

10. Gore and Robinson (2009, 140) note that as of 2007, 152 U.S. cities and local governments were members of ICLEI's Cities for Climate Protection campaign. Another leading U.S.-based initiative, the U.S. Conference of Mayors Climate Protection Agreement, has, as of 2011, been signed by over 1,000 mayors, representing around 88 million Americans. See www.usmayors.org/climateprotection/agreement.htm.

international environmental regimes. These initiatives have been largely overseen and coordinated by UNEP and follow long-established practices and processes of international law. In sum, they comprise the architecture of the state-led model of global environmental governance.

The political impacts of this system of global environmental governance have been far-reaching, and in some ways surprising, with more durable and real inter-state cooperation than many observers of the international system might have thought possible. Ongoing environmental negotiations have engaged and empow-ered a wide range of actors, from NGOs to business groups. They have (perhaps more seriously than some other arenas of global governance) grappled with issues of distributional equity and differential responsibility within the global commu-nity and generated and encouraged scientific research and knowledge dissemina-tion around critical global problems. Further, these global governance processes and obligations have helped shape structures and content of environmental regula-tion in many countries, as the brief discussion of their impact on the United States in the above section demonstrates.

Despite this system's longevity and some of its positive political impacts, seri-ous questions have been raised about how effective the model of international envi-ronmental diplomacy has been in addressing the extent of the global environmental crisis. On the one hand, these concerns have given rise to an extensive literature on regime effectiveness and impacts: how to define and measure them, and which fac-tors improve effectiveness (Bernauer 1995; Mitchell 2001, 2003; Weiss and Jacobson 1998; Young 1994). On the other, they have given rise to calls for abandoning the state-led model (Speth 2004), for recognizing alternative ways of accomplishing global environmental governance (e.g., Conca 2005), and for greater diversity and experimentation in global environmental governance systems (Hoffmann 2011).

In one sense—the extent to which environmental regimes solve the problems they are designed to—the jury is very definitely out. The causal impacts of regimes on problem solving are hard to measure. For one, environmental regimes are sub-ject to exogenous impacts, ranging from an unanticipated change in the problem to economic fluctuations that alter countries' contributions to the problem. For another, often environmental data are available only after a long time lag, mak-ing it hard to identify direct causal connections within a reasonable time frame. Often, the correct question is not about "absolute" effectiveness but about counter-factuals: how much worse would the problem be in the absence of a regime? Some of the most successful agreements—ozone, LRTAP, or CITES, for example—have achieved success because solutions were fairly straightforward and available, and they elicited wide support from states and other affected actors. Some issues, such as climate or biodiversity, are seen as hamstrung by intergovernmental politics or a very weak agreement. Others, despite a rhetoric of failure, have accomplished more than might have been expected, often through normative force: even though the Basel Ban has yet to go into effect, North–South waste dumping has, by all accounts, dwindled significantly, and episodes that do occur are subject to pub-licity and swift retaliation. It is also possible to identify measures through which regime actors are able to learn and improve performance over time (Siebenhüner 2006): later rounds of negotiations provide such opportunities, as do assessment exercises and measures to incorporate new knowledge into regime development. The extent to which individual regimes can do this, however, varies considerably (Depledge 2006).

A more commonly used notion of effectiveness focuses on compliance: do signatory states actually fulfill their obligations under the terms of the regime? These obligations may range from reporting requirements to the enactment and implementation of new legislation. The evidence that states actually comply with agreements is reasonably strong (Weiss and Jacobson 1998). The problem, of course, with using compliance as a measure of regime effectiveness is that it does not control for the possibility that the regime requirements are relatively weak or that they effectively reinforce the existing status quo. Nonetheless, through identifying regime characteristics such as transparency, capacity building, and even (in some cases) punitive measures, this literature identifies important ways to improve willingness and ability of countries to comply with international environmental obligations.[11]

In sum, the issue of whether environmental regimes actually work is something of a "glass half full/half empty" question, the answer to which often depends on the analyst's perspective. By reforming existing political institutions and creating new ones, environmental regimes have outperformed expectations. From the point of view of actually achieving environmental goals, however, environmental regimes are falling short. Many observers (e.g., Susskind 1994) point out, for instance, the slow and cumbersome nature of environmental negotiations and their propensity to result in agreements that are far too weak in terms of their obligations. Moreover, they do not encompass the complexity of many global environmental problems (Conca 2006). And the sheer number of concurrent negotiation processes has led to what some term "summit fatigue" (VanDeveer 2003), as well as a very real case that legal processes of global environmental governance have "stalled" (Conca 2005). James Gustave Speth, former director of the World Resources Institute and former dean of Yale University's School of Forestry and Environmental Studies, offers a strong condemnation of this system:

> [The] rates of environmental degradation that stirred the international community continue essentially unabated today. The disturbing trends persist, and the problems have become deeper and truly urgent. The steps that governments took over the past two decades represent the first attempt at global environmental governance. It is an experiment that has largely failed. (2004, 1–2)

While the history of and experience with state-led global governance does not entirely bear out this grim assessment, recent examples suggest that innovative

---

11. See also Mitchell 2001, 1994. Mitchell's work on the evolution of MARPOL demonstrates how regimes can incorporate changes (in this case, replacing discharge limits with easier-to-verify vessel equipment standards).

solutions need to be added to the global environmental policy repertoire. For example, the 2002 World Summit on Sustainable Development, held in Johannesburg, suggested a departure from the MEA model. Unlike the 1992 Rio Earth Summit, no big new conventions were opened for signature, and the overall mood was one of searching for new options and focusing on smaller-scale, on-the-ground development projects around clean water, biodiversity, and pollutants. More recently, the climate negotiations, as witnessed at the Fifteenth Conference of the Parties held in Copenhagen in December 2009, have stalled, as countries have failed so far to produce a new, binding agreement that will replace the Kyoto Protocol after it expires in 2012. The next section discusses the changing shape of global environmental governance architecture, the ways that new and existing actors are establishing different ways to tackle global environmental problems, and the challenges and opportunities that currently exist in this political arena. It also identifies some of the important research questions that are emerging or remain to be addressed in the field of global environmental governance.

7. NEW DIRECTIONS IN GLOBAL ENVIRONMENTAL GOVERNANCE

The complexity of global environmental challenges and the difficulties of creating an effective global governance architecture solely through the negotiation of multilateral environmental agreements have led to a landscape of global environmental governance that started to change significantly in the first decade of the twenty-first century. These shifts reflect the complexity and diversity of a globalized political and economic system and the wider array of choices facing both state and nonstate actors in constructing and participating in governance initiatives. They are also generating a new wave of research that is both adding to our understanding of global environmental policy and generating new questions.

In individual issue areas, such as climate change or forest management, we see a sort of "fragmentation" (Biermann et al. 2009), with the emergence of different sorts of state-led agreements (often voluntary or informal) and of a vibrant sector of "nonstate" global environmental governance initiatives that are seen by many as a significant departure from the status quo (O'Neill 2009). Another way of framing this issue is the emergence of "regime complexes" in particular issue areas (Keohane and Victor 2011; Raustiala and Victor 2004), a framing that emphasizes that the entities within the complex are linked, albeit sometimes loosely.

At a macro level, the proliferation of environmental regimes, organizations, and institutions, along with increased overlap with international economic regimes, has led to calls for a rationalization or even centralization of global environmental governance. These two sets of pressures—decentralization (toward more and more diverse global environmental initiatives) and centralization (creating a more coherent governance system) —are not as incompatible as one might think, given the complexity of global problems and the range and number of actors engaged in this field. For the United States, several of these developments—especially in terms of decentralization—are politically more compatible with a market-oriented approach to environmental policy and reluctance to take on binding international commitments, especially around climate change.

The "fragmentation" of governance architectures refers to the "patchwork" of institutions, rules, and norms, often speaking to different constituencies and existing at multiple scales within particular policy domains (Biermann et al. 2009, 16). Such analysis spotlights, for example, the diversity of global regimes and initiatives that have emerged in the climate regime, from the UNFCCC process to privately run carbon markets to regional intergovernmental agreements, often voluntary in nature, such as the 2005 Asia-Pacific Partnership on Clean Development and Climate. Similar sorts of fragmentation can be seen across global chemicals and biodiversity-related regimes, although to a lesser extent. Diversity in institutional arrangements is matched by a diversity in regulatory tools for global governance, including the growth in the use of market-based and voluntary mechanisms as an alternative to mandatory targets and obligations.

In other issue areas as well, intergovernmental processes are complemented by a range of initiatives often established and managed by nonstate actors, or run as partnership arrangements between international agencies, civil society actors, and the private sector. The rise of "nonstate" global environmental governance has been recognized as a significant trend in this field (O'Neill 2009). Perhaps the most widely cited examples of nonstate governance are third-party certification schemes, whereby producers sign up to have an agreed-upon set of environmental and/or social standards certified by an independent organization. Eco-labels broadcast their compliance to investors, shareholders, and consumers. Transnational certification schemes exist across many different sectors, from forest management to fisheries, chemicals, agriculture, and tourism (Gulbrandsen 2005). Among the best-known is the Forest Stewardship Council, established by a coalition of NGOs, forest owners, and forest dwellers in 1993 (Cashore et al. 2004). FSC requires that its members meet quite an exhaustive set of standards, and it is now one of the two leading forest certification schemes in the world, with over 140 million hectares of certified forest in 81 countries at this point in time.

Many of these initiatives emerged in response to perceived failures of state-led global environmental governance: forest certification is a key example here, given the failure to negotiate a global forests treaty. They have also emerged as a result of the willingness of many corporate actors (often multinational corporations already under fire for environmental practices) to engage with environmental impacts and behaviors, whether as a way of preempting formal regulation or improving their image, or genuinely motivated by environmental concern. Likewise, over the last couple of decades NGOs have become more willing to partner directly with industry (Deutsch 2006).

Nonstate governance initiatives have some advantages over cumbersome state-led regimes. They are perceived as faster, more flexible, and more direct in terms of influencing purchasing decisions, such as in the case of certification schemes. Because they are voluntary, they elicit considerable industry support, and some analysts see them as the way of the future for global environmental governance (Speth 2004). Governments, too, often appreciate them for taking up some of the burdens they are unable or unwilling to shoulder. At the same time, they struggle with many of the same effectiveness issues as their intergovernmental counterparts. For example, their voluntary nature means that many of the worst-behaving actors are unlikely to join such initiatives. For many smaller firms, the cost of joining is prohibitively high, while studies demonstrate some confusion on the part of consumers about what these labels mean and question the price premiums they are actually willing to pay for certified goods (Brockmann et al. 1996; McCluskey and Loureiro 2003). More generally, there is some concern with the legitimacy and ultimate accountability of nonstate governance initiatives that exist without the checks and balances and constitutional backing of state-led governance (Cashore 2002; Vogler 2005).

Despite these challenges, it is quite clear that nonstate global environmental governance has become a fixture on the international policy scene. Further, there are signs that some initiatives are evolving over time to take on regime-like characteristics, in the sense that they demonstrate durability, their own sets of rules, norms, and decision-making procedures, as well as the ability to change and evolve in response to experience (Bernstein and Cashore 2007). Rather than displacing traditional state-led governance, the relatively new roles of nonstate actors as architects and full-fledged participants in global environmental governance appear to be generating a new and potentially complementary array of governance approaches.

Shifting to the macro level, global environmental architectures as a whole, it is impossible not to notice the growing density and numbers of international environmental agreements, rules, and organizational entities. This recognition has led to growing interest in how these regimes overlap and intersect, and the conflicts or inefficiencies or, alternatively, the potential for synergies that emerges from taking advantage of certain forms of overlap (Jinnah 2010; Selin and VanDeveer 2003; Young 1996).

There are multiple sources of regime linkages. Some have to do with the way that environmental problems intersect. Climate change and biodiversity loss, for example, are intrinsically linked, as climate change is a driver of biodiversity loss. However, some of the measures put forward to mitigate climate change, such as establishing tree plantations to store carbon, are also damaging for biodiversity. Likewise, the primary substitute for ozone-depleting CFCs is itself a potent greenhouse gas. These sorts of linkages make it imperative for these regimes to take into account impacts across different issue areas. A second source of linkage or overlap occurs across international environmental regimes in terms of the functions and activities of different institutions and agencies, such as convention secretariats (Jinnah 2008). Many (although not all) of these agencies already work together, and there is some impetus for formal consolidation, or clustering, of organizations and activities. One area of proposed consolidation is based on issue area: As mentioned above, some advocate bringing together the different chemicals- and waste-related agreements under a single umbrella convention to address more successfully the full life-cycle of toxic substances (Downie et al. 2005). Another could be functional—for example, the creation of a single international scientific agency that could supply expert knowledge and advice to different regimes (Von Moltke 2001). More comprehensive reorganization of international environmental regimes across the board, while probably more efficient from an organizational perspective, is far less politically feasible.

These questions of linkages, conflicts, and synergies become more politically charged when addressing linkages between environmental and other realms of global governance, notably the set of rules and practices that make up the international trade regime. Traditionally, global economic regimes were seen as operating in a political arena distinct from environmental concerns. Increasingly, however, they are emerging as sites of global environmental governance in their own right. The World Bank, for example, which came under fire for its funding of environmentally (and socially) damaging infrastructure projects, such as large dams, has established environmental assessment procedures, administers the GEF, and is starting to advocate smaller-scale or more sustainable development projects.

The relationship between the World Trade Organization (WTO), which administers the General Agreement on Tariffs and Trade (GATT), and a range of other trade-related agreements and environmental regulation has also come under a good deal of scrutiny. Trade liberalization, particularly under GATT rules, has been seen as environmentally problematic for a long time (Zaelke et al. 1993). Not only does expanded international trade carry with it greater environmental burdens (both through economic growth and resource use and through transportation externalities), but domestic environmental regulations can also be brought in front of WTO dispute panels as possible protectionist measures. The best-known of these was Mexico's dispute with the United States over its banning of imports of Mexican tuna caught without measures to protect dolphins. More recently, there has been significant concern that trade-related provisions of MEAs (such as bans on trade in recyclable hazardous wastes or genetically modified organisms) might violate WTO rules and be struck down in the event of a dispute (O'Neill and Burns 2005). The upshot of these concerns has been that the WTO has moved to emphasize its potential role in fostering sustainable development (as highlighted in the Doha Round of trade talks). UNEP has highlighted how trade liberalization can, in fact, enhance sustainable development goals, a perspective much in evidence at the 2002 Johannesburg summit. At a more basic level, representatives from both organizations have worked together to minimize potential for legal conflicts, which neither side wants (Jinnah 2010).

Taken together, the proliferation of issue-by-issue regimes and the recognition of linkages and the potential for conflict, not only among environmental regimes but across traditional "borders" of global governance, have generated calls for some form of centralization or rationalization of this system (Biermann and Bauer 2005). Such centralization could happen via clustering across issues or functions, or, at a higher level, through the creation of some form of World Environment Organization whose legal standing and enforcement capacity could potentially match that of the WTO, or at least that of the World Health Organization.[12] While the lack of international political support for a new global bureaucracy makes such a development unlikely (Najam 2003), the question of how state-led global environmental governance could strengthen its scientific, legal, and political capacity through some form of centralization or clustering remains current (Biermann 2007). While such centralization may seem to contradict support for diverse forms of global environmental governance, it could, in fact, provide a secure platform as well as a set of norms and principles endorsed across nation-states that could help support, not supplant, state, nonstate, and hybrid governance initiatives alike.

The new diversity of global environmental governance institutions, actors, and rules opens a range of questions for future research. As indicated above, questions of effectiveness and impacts of all forms of governance remain of paramount importance for research that seeks to be policy-relevant, as does the relative role of science and advocacy compared with national interests in determining policy outcomes. More research needs to be done on the interplay between local, national, and global scales in global environmental politics, as the above section on U.S. impacts demonstrates. It is important, too, despite the dominance of climate change as a pressing global issue, not to ignore other environmental problems, their political causes and impacts. Other potentially fruitful avenues of research address more analytical questions across the social sciences: how do we understand change and evolution in global environmental governance? Do these diverse institutions add up to something more than the sum of their parts, and do they have the potential to transform broader global interactions? What sorts of power dynamics shape the current system? Are states in fact being marginalized in the development of new, multi-stakeholder governance processes?

Finally, more research needs to be done into processes of institutional learning and interaction at the global level. In many ways, the global environmental politics field has been far ahead of international relations theory in generating research that is applied and that pushes on important political science questions, such as the effectiveness of international cooperation. Its unique perspective—combining theoretical and applied work—has the potential to provide significant and useful contributions to the theory and practice of global governance.

---

12. The World Health Organization gets its autonomy and enforcement powers from its status as a UN *agency*. UNEP, by contrast, as a *program*, does not have these strengths. Elevating UNEP to agency status would be a significant step in creating environmental regimes with greater enforcement capacity (Biermann 2001).

8. CONCLUSIONS

Global environmental policy making is a complex phenomenon that has evolved considerably over the nearly 40 years during which the environment has been formally recognized as an arena of global governance. The above sections chart the major characteristics of this system of governance and some of its achievements and challenges. Two "big picture" points emerge from this analysis. First, the practice of global environmental governance has generated substantial political impacts, both at the global level and at national levels. These political changes have, however, likely not been enough to keep up with the pace of global environmental degradation. Second, and perhaps contrary to some critiques of this system, it has in fact demonstrated considerable malleability in the face of pressures for change both within individual regimes and at the "metalevel" of governance architecture (O'Neill 2007). In the last 10 years, the proliferation of other sorts of governance initiatives, as outlined in this chapter, have been recognized in official and academic circles as part of a multifaceted, diverse system that we need to understand and acknowledge a full view of global environmental governance (Conca 2005; Wapner 2003). What we are likely to see over the next decades is that while some issues (often the pollution-oriented regimes, but also some components of the biodiversity regimes) are likely to continue squarely centered in state-led governance practices (and possibly in more formally clustered forms), others (notably climate change) will be governed through a far more fragmented system (Biermann et al. 2009; Keohane and Victor 2011). The challenge here will be one of coordination and ensuring that this diversity of approaches is subject to verification and accountability measures.

The role of the United States in the evolution of this system has varied considerably over time. Its leadership/supportive role at Stockholm and in the negotiation of key early agreements was supplanted at the 1992 Rio and 2002 Johannesburg Earth Summits by considerable intransigence over binding commitments and the leeway given to countries of the global South, an attitude that reached its apogee in the U.S. federal government's rejection of the Kyoto Protocol in 2001. Perhaps ironically, the recent emergence of market-driven policies in state-led governance initiatives, as well as voluntary forms of interstate partnerships and the rise of nonstate/hybrid initiatives, is more compatible with U.S. politics and foreign environmental policy in the 2000s and early 2010s. Not only do these initiatives fit with the dominant tone of domestic U.S. environmental policy and discourse over balancing environmental and economic concerns; they also provide ways for pro-environmental actors in U.S. policy, NGO, and other circles to bypass ongoing congressional hostility to formal environmental treaties. How this relationship evolves and changes over time and to what extent it helps resolve the global environmental crisis will be a fascinating object of study for years to come.

REFERENCES

Audley, J. J. 1997. *Green Politics and Global Trade: NAFTA and the Future of Environmental Politics*. Washington, DC: Georgetown University Press.

Axelrod, R. S., S. VanDeveer, and D. L. Downie, eds. 2011. *The Global Environment: Institutions, Law, and Policy*. 3rd ed. Washington, DC: CQ Press.

Bernauer, T. 1995. "The Effect of International Environmental Institutions: How We Might Learn More." *International Organization* 49 (2): 351–377.

Bernstein, S., and B. Cashore. 2007. "Can Non-State Global Governance Be Legitimate? An Analytical Framework." *Regulation and Governance* 1 (4): 347–371.

Betsill, M. M. 2011. "International Climate Change Policy: Toward the Multilevel Governance of Global Warming." In *The Global Environment: Institutions, Law, and Policy*, 3rd ed., ed. R. Axelrod, S. VanDeveer, and D. L. Downie. Washington, DC: CQ Press.

Betsill, M. M., and E. Corell, eds. 2007. *NGO Diplomacy: The Influence of Nongovernmental Organizations in International Environmental Negotiations*. Cambridge, MA: MIT Press.

Betsill, M. M., and B. G. Rabe. 2009. "Climate Change and Multilevel Governance." In *Toward Sustainable Communities: Transition and Transformations in Environmental Policy*, 2nd ed., ed. D. A. Mazmanian and M. E. Kraft. Cambridge, MA: MIT Press.

Biermann, F. 2001. "The Emerging Debate on the Need for a World Environment Organization: A Commentary." *Global Environmental Politics* 1 (1): 45–55.

———. 2007. "'Earth System Governance' as a Crosscutting Theme of Global Change Research." *Global Environmental Change* 17: 326–337.

Biermann, F., and S. Bauer, eds. 2005. *A World Environment Organization: Solution or Threat for Effective International Environmental Governance?* London: Ashgate.

Biermann, F., P. Pattberg, H. van Asselt, and F. Zelli. 2009. "The Fragmentation of Global Governance Architectures: A Framework for Analysis." *Global Environmental Politics* 9 (4): 14–40.

Brockmann, K. L., J. Hemmelskamp, and O. Hohmeyer. 1996. *Certified Tropical Timber and Consumer Behavior: The Impact of a Certification Scheme for Tropical Timber from Sustainable Forest Management on German Demand*. Heidelberg: Physica-Verlag.

Cashore, B. 2002. "Legitimacy and the Privatization of Environmental Governance: How Non-State Market Driven (NSMD) Governance Systems Gain Rule-Making Authority." *Governance: An International Journal of Policy and Administration* 15 (4): 503–529.

Cashore, B., G. Auld, and D. Newsom. 2004. *Governing through Markets: Forest Certification and the Emergence of Non-State Authority*. New Haven, CT: Yale University Press.

Conca, K. 2005. "Environmental Governance after Johannesburg: From Stalled Legalization to Environmental Human Rights?" *Journal of International Law and International Relations* 1 (1–2): 121–138.

———. 2006. *Governing Water: Contentious Transnational Politics and Global Institution Building*. Cambridge, MA: MIT Press.

Dawson, A. 2010. "Climate Justice: The Emerging Movement against Green Capitalism." *South Atlantic Quarterly* 109 (2): 313–338.

Depledge, J. 2006. "The Opposite of Learning: Ossification in the Climate Change Regime." *Global Environmental Politics* 6 (1): 1–22.

Deutsch, C. 2006. "Companies and Critics Try Collaboration." *New York Times*, May 17.

Downie, D., J. Krueger, J. and H. Selin. 2005. "Global Policy for Hazardous Chemicals." In *Global Environmental Politics*, 2nd ed., ed. N. J. Vig, R. S. Axelrod, and D. Downie. Washington, DC: CQ Press.

Ehrlich, P. R. 1968. *The Population Bomb.* New York: Ballantine Books.

Friedman, E. J., K. Hochstetler, and A. M. Clark. 2005. *Sovereignty, Democracy, and Global Civil Society.* Albany: State University of New York Press.

Gardner, R. N. 1992. *Negotiating Survival: Four Priorities after Rio.* New York: Council on Foreign Relations Press.

Gehring, T., and E. Ruffing. 2008. "When Arguments Prevail over Power: The CITES Procedure for the Listing of Endangered Species." *Global Environmental Politics* 8 (2): 123–148.

Gore, C., and P. Robinson. 2009. "Local Government Response to Climate Change: Our Last, Best Hope?" In *Changing Climates in North American Politics: Institutions, Policymaking and Multilevel Governance*, ed. H. Selin and S. VanDeveer. Cambridge, MA: MIT Press.

Gulbrandsen, L. H. 2004. "Overlapping Public and Private Governance: Can Forest Certification Fill the Gaps in the Global Forest Regime?" *Global Environmental Politics* 4 (2): 75–99.

———. 2005. "Mark of Sustainability? Challenges for Fishery and Forestry Eco-Labeling." *Environment* 47 (5): 8–23.

Guruswamy, L. D. 1998. "The Convention on Biological Diversity: A Polemic." In *Protection of Global Biodiversity: Converging Strategies*, ed. L. D. Guruswamy and J. A. McNeely. Durham, NC: Duke University Press.

Haas, P. M. 1990. *Saving the Mediterranean: The Politics of International Environmental Cooperation.* New York: Columbia University Press.

———. 1992. "Introduction: Epistemic Communities and International Policy Coordination." *International Organization* 46 (1): 1–35.

———. 2001. "Environment: Pollution." In *Managing Global Issues: Lessons Learned*, ed. C. d. J. Oudraat, P. J. Simmons, and J. T. Matthews. Washington, DC: Carnegie Endowment for International Peace.

———. 2002. "UN Conferences and Constructivist Governance of the Environment." *Global Governance* 8 (1): 73–91.

Haas, P. M., R. O. Keohane, and M. A. Levy, eds. 1993. *Institutions for the Earth: Sources of Effective International Environmental Protection.* Cambridge, MA: MIT Press.

Hoffmann, M. J. 2005. *Ozone Depletion and Climate Change: Constructing a Global Response.* Albany: State University of New York Press.

———. 2011. *Climate Governance at the Crossroads: Experimenting with a Global Response after Kyoto.* Oxford: Oxford University Press.

Humphreys, D. 2003. "Life Protective or Carcinogenic Challenge? Global Forests Governance under Advanced Capitalism." *Global Environmental Politics* 3 (2): 40–55.

Ivanova, M. 2007. "Designing the United Nations Environment Programme: A Story of Compromise and Confrontation." *International Environmental Agreements* 7: 337–361.

————. 2010. "UNEP in Global Environmental Governance: Design, Leadership, Location." *Global Environmental Politics* 10 (1): 30–59.

Jacques, P. J., R. E. Dunlap, and M. Freeman. 2008. "The Organization of Denial: Conservative Think Tanks and Environmental Skepticism." *Environmental Politics* 17 (3): 349–385.

Jinnah, S. 2008. "Who's in Charge? International Bureaucracies and the Management of Global Governance." PhD diss., University of California at Berkeley.

————. 2010. "Overlap Management in the World Trade Organization: Secretariat Influence on Trade-Environment Politics." *Global Environmental Politics* 10 (2): 54–79.

Jones, C. A., and D. L. Levy. 2009. "Business Strategies and Climate Change." In *Changing Climates in North American Politics: Institutions, Policymaking, and Multilevel Governance*, ed. H. Selin and S. VanDeveer. Cambridge, MA: MIT Press.

Keohane, R. O., and D. G. Victor. 2011. "The Regime Complex for Climate Change." *Perspectives on Politics* 9 (1): 7–23.

Krasner, S. D., ed. 1983. *International Regimes*. Ithaca, NY: Cornell University Press.

Lattanzio, R. K. 2010. "Global Environment Facility (GEF): An Overview." *CRS Report for Congress*. Washington, DC: Congressional Research Service.

Levy, M. A. 1993. "European Acid Rain: The Power of Tote-Board Diplomacy." In *Institutions for the Earth: Sources of Effective International Environmental Protection*, ed. P. M. Haas, R. O. Keohane, and M. A. Levy. Cambridge, MA: MIT Press.

McCluskey, J. J., and M. L. Loureiro. 2003. "Consumer Preferences and Willingness to Pay for Food Labeling: A Discussion of Empirical Studies." *Journal of Food Distribution Research* 34 (1): 95–102.

McGraw, D. M. 2002. "The CBD—Key Characteristics and Implications for Implementation." *RECIEL* 11 (1): 17–28.

Meadows, D. H. 1972. *Limits to Growth: A Report for the Club of Rome's Project on the Predicament of Mankind*. New York: Universe Books.

Mitchell, R. B. 1994. *Intentional Oil Pollution at Sea: Environmental Policy and Treaty Compliance*. Cambridge, MA: MIT Press.

————. 2001. "Institutional Aspects of Implementation, Compliance and Effectiveness." In *International Relations and Climate Change*, ed. U. Luterbacher and D. F. Sprinz. Cambridge, MA: MIT Press.

————. 2003. "International Environmental Agreements: A Survey of Their Features, Formation and Effects." *Annual Review of Environment and Resources* 28: 429–461.

Najam, A. 2003. "The Case against a New International Environmental Organization." *Global Governance* 9: 367–384.

————. 2004. "Dynamics of the Southern Collective: Developing Countries in Desertification Negotiations." *Global Environmental Politics* 4 (3): 128–154.

————. 2005. "Developing Countries and Global Environmental Governance: From Contestation to Participation to Engagement." *International Environmental Agreements* 5: 303–321.

————. 2011. "The View from the South: Developing Countries in Global Environmental Politics." In *The Global Environment: Institutions, Law and Policy*, 3rd ed., ed. R. Axelrod, S. VanDeveer, and D. L. Downie. Washington, DC: CQ Press.

O'Neill, K. 2001. "The Changing Nature of Global Waste Management for the 21st Century: A Mixed Blessing?" *Global Environmental Politics* 1 (1): 77–98.

———. 2007. "From Stockholm to Johannesburg and Beyond: The Evolving Meta-Regime for Global Environmental Governance." Paper presented at the Amsterdam Conference on the Human Dimensions of Global Environmental Change, May 24–26, 2007.

———. 2009. *The Environment and International Relations.* Cambridge: Cambridge University Press.

O'Neill, K., and W. C. G. Burns. 2005. "Trade Liberalization and Global Environmental Governance: The Potential for Conflict." In *Handbook of Global Environmental Governance,* ed. P. Dauvergne. Cheltenham, UK: Edward Elgar.

Parson, E. A. 2003. *Protecting the Ozone Layer: Science and Strategy.* Oxford: Oxford University Press.

Porter, G., N. Bird, N. Kaur, and L. Peskott. 2008. *New Finance for Climate Change and the Environment.* Report published by the World Wildlife Foundation and the Heinrich Böll Foundation. Available at www.odi.org.uk/resources/download/2980.pdf.

Prins, G., and S. Rayner. 2007. "Time to Ditch Kyoto." *Nature* 449 (25): 973–975.

Raustiala, K., and D. G. Victor. 2004. "The Regime Complex for Plant Genetic Resources." *International Organization* 58 (2): 277–309.

Selin, H. (2009). "Managing Hazardous Chemicals: Longer-Range Challenges." *The Pardee Papers,* vol. 5. Boston: Frederick S. Pardee Center for the Study of the Longer-Range Future, Boston University. Available at www.bu.edu/pardee/.

Selin, H., and S. D. VanDeveer, eds. 2009. *Changing Climates in North American Politics: Institutions, Policymaking, and Multilevel Governance.* Cambridge, MA: MIT Press.

———. 2003. "Mapping Institutional Linkages in European Air Pollution Politics." *Global Environmental Politics* 3 (3): 14–46.

Siebenhüner, B. 2006. "Can Assessments Learn, and If So, How? A Study of the IPCC." In *Assessments of Regional and Global Environmental Risks: Designing Processes for the Effective Use of Science in Decisionmaking,* ed. A. E. Farrell and J. Jäger. Cambridge, MA: MIT Press.

Skodvin, T., and S. Andresen. 2006. "Leadership Revisited." *Global Environmental Politics* 6 (3): 13–27.

Sohn, L. B. 1973. "The Stockholm Declaration on the Human Environment." *Harvard International Law Journal* 14: 423–515.

Soroos, M. S. 2011. "Global Institutions and the Environment: An Evolutionary Perspective." In *The Global Environment: Institutions, Law, and Policy,* 3rd ed., ed. R. Axelrod, S. VanDeveer, and D. L. Downie. Washington, DC: CQ Press.

Speth, J. G. 2004. *Red Sky at Morning: America and the Crisis of the Global Environment.* New Haven, CT: Yale University Press.

Susskind, L. E. 1994. *Environmental Diplomacy: Negotiating More Effective Global Environmental Agreements.* Oxford: Oxford University Press.

VanDeveer, S. 2003. "Green Fatigue." *Wilson Quarterly,* Autumn Issue: 55–59.

Victor, D. G. 2011. "Why the UN Can Never Stop Climate Change." *Guardian* (London), April 4.

Vogel, D. 1995. *Trading Up: Consumer and Environmental Regulation in a Global Economy.* Cambridge, MA: Harvard University Press.

Vogler, J. 2005. "In Defense of International Environmental Cooperation." In *The State and the Global Ecological Crisis,* ed. J. Barry and R. Eckersley. Cambridge, MA: MIT Press.

von Moltke, K. 2001. "The Organization of the Impossible." *Global Environmental Politics* 1 (1): 23–28.

Wapner, P. 2003. "World Summit on Sustainable Development: Toward a Post-Jo'burg Environmentalism." *Global Environmental Politics* 3 (1): 1–10.

Weiss, E. B., and H. K. Jacobson, eds. 1998. *Engaging Countries: Strengthening Compliance with International Environmental Accords*. Cambridge, MA: MIT Press.

Young, O. R. 1991. "Political Leadership and Regime Formation: On the Development of Institutions in International Society." *International Organization* 45 (3): 281–308.

———. 1994. *International Governance: Protecting the Environment in a Stateless Society*. Ithaca, NY: Cornell University Press.

———. 1996. "Institutional Linkages in International Society: Polar Perspectives." *Global Governance* 2 (1): 1–24.

Zaelke, D., P. Orbuch, and R. F. Housman, eds. 1993. *Trade and the Environment: Law, Economics, and Policy*. Washington, DC: Island.

PART IV

GOVERNMENT INSTITUTIONS AND POLICY MAKING

CHAPTER 12

....

COURTS, LEGAL ANALYSIS, AND ENVIRONMENTAL POLICY

....

TIMOTHY P. DUANE

1. INTRODUCTION

....

THE American legal system is distinctive in several ways, and those distinctions mean that U.S. environmental policy is formulated and implemented through different institutional structures than many other policy systems. In particular, the structure of the U.S. system gives the courts a prominent role in resolving both legal and political disputes about U.S. environmental policy. The result is a complex, dynamic system of policy development that shifts among a wide range of institutional actors (Lazarus 2004). As Alexis de Tocqueville noted nearly two centuries ago, "Scarcely any political question arises in the United States that is not resolved, sooner or later, into a judicial question" (1835, book 1, chap. 16). This remains true for U.S. environmental policy today, and it is likely to remain true given the U.S. constitutional system.

This chapter reviews the role of the courts and legal analysis in relationship to U.S. environmental policy. The key theme is that the courts play a vital and distinctive role in the dynamic development of U.S. environmental policy that directly affects both the power relationships among key policy stakeholders and the substantive outcomes of both legislative and regulatory processes. Distinctive features of environmental policy making and how those features have challenged the judicial system are also addressed. I emphasize the structural features of the American judicial system and how that structure influences the dynamics of environmental policy making and implementation. I summarize those features and briefly describe the most important constitutional provisions and cases driving those dynamics across a wide range of substantive issues. Other chapters in this volume offer more detailed discussion of nonjudicial processes that are prescribed in part by the courts (e.g., public participation [chapter 22], rule making [chapter 17], and bureaucratic implementation [chapter 15]). Chapter 17 is particularly relevant to the role of the courts.

The literature on the role of the courts in U.S. environmental policy reflects two very different approaches to scholarship: a political science literature that often takes a quantitative, empirical approach to analyze the factors driving outcomes for large data sets of court cases (Kamieniecki 2006; O'Leary 1993, 2010; Wenner 1982); and narrower legal analyses that tend to focus on seminal cases and the doctrinal ramifications of specific judicial decisions. The latter is very case-specific and dominates legal scholarship even if quantitative empirical legal scholarship is increasingly common.

The quantitative studies clearly demonstrate the influence of the courts on U.S. environmental policy. For example, Wenner reviewed and coded 1,900 federal court cases from 1971 to 1979 to characterize the relationship between the status of the parties (e.g., the EPA as litigant or defendant; environmental groups versus industry as plaintiff), the institutional setting for the litigation (e.g., district versus circuit versus Supreme Court; differences among the circuit courts); the role of political affiliations (e.g., between circuit court judges and U.S. senators in the states within a given circuit), and similar factors. Wenner found that the role of the courts shifted during the decade of the 1970s and that the legislative branch responded dynamically to judicial action in the environmental arena: "Although the environmental decade began with environmental groups initiating a preponderance of the requests for judicial action, by the midpoint of the decade, industry and the executive branch of government were making an increasing percentage of the inputs to courts. It is clear that all sides of this important policy issue felt that the due process concerns of the judicial system could benefit their interest" (Wenner 1982, 170). Environmentalists initially used the courts to delay implementation of government projects that might harm the environment. As environmental legislation became institutionalized through rule making, however, industry responded by turning to the courts to delay regulation. Industry and government also turned to the legislative branch to thwart environmental successes in the courts: "Eventually the legislative branch simply overturned that action through the passage of another law, which effectively eliminated the procedural niceties on which that delay rested" (Wenner 1982, 170). As Wenner notes, "The potential for this type of outcome was always present" (ibid.); indeed, it is a central element of American constitutional design. This dynamic interaction between the courts and the legislative and executive branches is a key theme of this chapter.

O'Leary surveyed over 2,000 court decisions from 1972 to 1992 and studied 1,400 of them in further depth. Her study period therefore extended through the Reagan and first Bush administrations. She found that "federal court decisions have affected the administration of the EPA in several ways: Prompting a redistribution of budgetary and staff resources within the EPA, reducing the discretion and autonomy of EPA administrators, increasing the power of the EPA legal staff, decreasing the power and authority of EPA scientists, and selectively empowering certain organizational units within the EPA. In addition, court decisions have yielded an increase in external power and authority of the EPA as a whole" (O'Leary 1993, 160). Moreover, "perhaps the most significant impact of federal court decisions on the EPA has been on policy.... Compliance with court orders has become one of the agency's top priorities, at times overtaking congressional mandates. The courts have dictated which issues get attention at the EPA" (ibid., 168). This remains true today, as the EPA's budget is being sharply reduced and court-ordered actions have become the agency's de facto priorities. Litigation by environmental groups can therefore achieve—through court orders to the EPA—what the EPA may not be able to achieve itself through budget negotiations with Congress. Strategic alliances between the EPA and litigating parties are therefore a critical determinant of the substantive outcomes of legislated environmental policy. Moreover, litigation settlements between the EPA and litigants may set the terms of policy debates through the courts in ways that tie the hands of Congress—which raises important questions about transparency and participation. Whether and how the EPA chooses to defend itself in court is an important policy decision.

The most recent empirical study of the role of the courts in EPA policy is by Kamieniecki (2006), who examined litigation by business interests in the DC Circuit Court from 1995 to 2002 (from the middle of the Clinton administration into the first years of the second Bush administration). Kamieniecki found that business groups' success varied as a function of the statute: industry had more success under CERCLA and the Toxic Substances Control Act, while the EPA was more successful with appeals under RCRA and the Clean Air Act. (The EPA and industry each won about half of the Clean Water Act appeals.)

Weiland (2007) notes that business is not monolithic and that many environmental cases involve conflicts between different business interests. Stricter air quality regulations may favor newer facilities, for example, giving those competitors an advantage over older facilities facing costly retrofits; stronger coal emissions regulations make natural-gas-fueled power plants more cost-competitive. Business interests, therefore, use the courts strategically against each other for competitive purposes. Given these complex motivations and relationships among participants in the judicial process, it is very difficult to code and analyze large data sets of court cases—federal agencies are not monolithic either within administrations (e.g., the Corps of Engineers and the Fish and Wildlife Service) or across administrations (e.g., Bush vs. Obama appointees), environmental groups have different goals and litigation strategies when challenging federal agencies, and companies will use environmental litigation to impose costs on their competitors.

Each of these studies affirms, however, that the courts play an important and distinctive role in U.S. environmental policy. The importance of that role is by design: the American constitutional system has evolved to make the courts an important arbiter of political conflict. It is therefore important to understand that structure and how it establishes a dynamic law-making process that is continually in motion.

2. THE STRUCTURE OF THE AMERICAN LEGAL SYSTEM

Three features define the structure of the American legal system: (1) *separation of powers,* where both the federal government and state governments divide power and responsibilities among the legislative, executive, and judicial branches of government; (2) *federalism,* where the national (federal) government is one of "limited and enumerated powers" under the U.S. Constitution and all other powers are reserved to the states; and (3) a *common law* (rather than civil law) tradition, which makes nonstatutory law relevant to both the types of policies that can be implemented through legislative action and the actors who may play a role in challenging or supporting such policy action.

All three of these features contribute to fragmented decision making, limited and sometimes ephemeral authority for policy implementation, and shifting power relationships among key environmental policy actors. These conditions have a direct bearing on the character of the politics of U.S. environmental policy as well as the capacity of key organizations charged with implementing such policy. Moreover, U.S. policy making is characterized by what Kagan has called "adversarial legalism" (Kagan 1991, 2001), which contrasts sharply with the corporatist approaches to policy development common in some other nations. This adversarial legalism sees its greatest manifestation through the judicial system.

Despite repeated cries about fragmented authority, "gridlock" among the political parties, and excessive litigation, however, it is important to bear in mind that this structure is *by design.* The framers of the U.S. Constitution did not want a strong, effective, coherent central government; indeed, the American nation was forged from deep mistrust of such authority. Moreover, the ultimate form of the U.S. Constitution (and, equally important, its interpretation) reflected political compromises that retained some avenues for judicial redress that have made the courts increasingly important to the resolution of what are often inherently political questions. We should therefore expect to see a continuing and growing role for the courts in U.S. policy (McSpadden 2007; Weiland 2007).

3. SEPARATION OF POWERS

The U.S. Constitution divides governmental authority among three branches: the legislative (Article I), executive (Article II), and judicial (Article III). No bill can become a law under the U.S. Constitution unless both the House and the Senate pass the bill in identical form (bicameralism) and then present it to the president (present-ment). Achieving the first (approval in both legislative houses) is difficult even when one political party controls both houses (due in no small part to Senate rules, which are not to be found in the Constitution, requiring 60 votes for cloture to stop a fili-buster); it is nearly impossible when different political parties control the House and the Senate. This problem of "divided government" is exacerbated when the president is from a party other than the one controlling one or both houses of the legisla-tive branch. The president has the authority to veto legislation presented to him by Congress, and Congress can only override that veto with a two-thirds majority in *both* houses of Congress. Giving the president such veto power has a dramatic affect on the political dynamics of U.S. environmental policy making—especially when one party controls the Congress and another party occupies the White House.

Article III is the focus of this chapter: it establishes that "[t]he judicial Power of the United States shall be vested in one supreme Court, and in such inferior Courts as the Congress may from time to time ordain and establish" (U.S. Constitution, Art. III, sec. 1). Article III also states that "[t]he judicial Power shall extend to all Cases, in Law and Equity, arising under this Constitution, the Laws of the United States, and Treaties made, or which shall be made, under their Authority"; more-over, such power extends to "Controversies...between Citizens of different States," establishing federal court jurisdiction over any cases in "diversity" (i.e., involving citizens of diverse states).

Although the Constitution does not specify that the judicial branch shall have the last word on conflicts among the branches, it has been established (and accepted) since *Marbury v. Madison* in 1803 that the courts are the final arbiter of such disputes.

Federal courts, then, have authority over a wide range of matters: anyone chal-lenging the constitutionality of a federal (or, following the FourteenthAmendment, state) law; how a federal agency has interpreted or applied a federal statute; or in any conflicts (including those that do not involve any federal law whatsoever) involv-ing parties in diversity. Moreover, the remedies available to such federal courts lie in both "law" (i.e., the awarding of monetary damages) and "equity" (i.e., through injunctive relief and other remedies that do not involve monetary damages). Federal litigation regarding environmental policy often involves a request for equitable relief either to enjoin or compel implementation of some federal statute (sometimes based on arguments about the nonconstitutionality of the statute). However, common law diversity claims under *state* common law (discussed below) are also heard by federal courts, and many of those may be suits for damages at law.

4. CONSTITUTIONAL CONSIDERATIONS

The U.S. Constitution not only establishes the *structure* of the federal govern-ment, of course; it also establishes the *substantive scope* of its authority. Three clauses of the Constitution are particularly relevant to U.S. environmental policy:[1] (1) the Commerce Clause, which states, "The Congress shall have the Power...To regulate Commerce with foreign Nations, and among the several States, and with the Indian Tribes" (Art. I, sec. 8); (2) the Due Process Clause, which states, "No person shall...be deprived of life, liberty, or property without due process of law" (Amend. V); and (3) the Takings Clause, which adds (immediately after the Due Process Clause), "nor shall private property be taken for public use, without just compensation" (Amend. V). These restrictions originally applied only to the federal government, but their reach was extended to state governments (and the civil subdivisions of state governments, including cities, counties, and special districts) with the Fourteenth Amendment in 1868 ("nor shall any State deprive any person of life, liberty, or property, without due process of law").

Constitutional challenges to federal environmental law and policy usually take one of three forms: (1) a challenge to the constitutionality of the statute itself on the grounds that it involves federal reach into an issue reserved for the states (often challenging the statute as violating the Commerce Clause); (2) a challenge to the authority of the federal agency implementing the statute on the grounds that the Congress has delegated too much authority to the agency (under the Nondelegation Doctrine); or (3) a challenge to implementation of the statute by the agency on the grounds that it violates either the Due Process Clause or the Takings Clause. The latter category of Takings Clause claims often involves state or local agencies under the Fourteenth Amendment.

Federal courts also hear cases and controversies about whether the statutory language has been interpreted correctly by federal agencies. Indeed, these types of claims dominate administrative law and judicial decisions and seem to reflect two primary concerns: *due process* and *separation of powers*. In the first, the courts are concerned with whether citizens have been given adequate opportunity to seek redress from administrative agencies before those agencies take actions that may affect the citizens' "life, liberty, or property." Prominent examples involve welfare payments, tax decisions, and the like. In the second category, the courts are concerned with whether the administrative agencies are going beyond the authority delegated to them by Congress to implement a statute. Environmental cases have played a prominent role in this jurisprudence, but the degree of deference that a court will give an agency has also been determined by a series of cases that do not involve environmental matters. Administrative law is therefore a complex field that involves many substantive matters and agencies unrelated to environmental policy. In essence, it is part of a bigger debate about how to structure government (Lazarus 2004; see chapter 17 in this volume).

---

1. The Property Clause is also important regarding the federal lands and waters, but it is not central to most environmental litigation involving regulation on private property.

5. THE COMMERCE CLAUSE

The U.S. Supreme Court has waxed and waned on important constitutional questions, with a broad interpretation of Congress's powers under the Commerce Clause serving as the primary rationale for federal adoption of many environmental statutes. (A similar approach to Commerce Clause jurisprudence was the foundation for many of the civil rights rulings of the 1950s and 1960s, which laid the foundation for the broad reach of Congress into the environmental arena in the late 1960s and through the 1980s.) More recently, however, the Court has begun to limit Congress's reach by invalidating some federal statutes as being inconsistent with the Commerce Clause. (The most important nonenvironmental decisions in this regard were *Lopez* in 1995 [invalidating a federal statute making handgun possession close to public schools a federal crime] and *Morrison* in 2000 [invalidating a federal statute making domestic violence a federal crime].) The key cases reflecting this shift in the environmental field have focused on the Clean Water Act and the question of whether certain wetlands are within the Corps of Engineers' jurisdiction under section 404 to require a federal permit before filling or altering such wetlands. The Court accepted broad jurisdiction for the Corps in *Riverside Bayview* in 1985, but then narrowed the jurisdiction in *Solid Waste Agency of Cook County (SWANCC)* in 2001 to exclude some intrastate waters. More recently, the Court's split 4–1–4 opinion in *Rapanos* in 2006 has increased ambiguity about the reach of the Act and raised broader questions about whether federal environmental law will continue to be comprehensive in scope and territorial jurisdiction or be constrained in cases involving only intrastate resources and or impacts.

On its surface, the Court has never addressed the question of the constitutionality of the Clean Water Act for intrastate waters (i.e., those not directly involved in interstate commerce); instead, the Court has focused on the question of whether or not the Corps' regulations are consistent with the statute passed by Congress. As the Court states in *SWANCC*, however, the constitutional question is never far from the surface: the *SWANCC* Court suggests that there may be a shifting standard of judicial review as Congress comes closer to the Court's perceived limits of the federal government's authority under the Commerce Clause. The constitutional question is laid bare even more starkly in *Rapanos*, where Justice Scalia's opinion directly challenges any regulatory interpretation of the statute that does not have a direct connection to navigability and, therefore, a clear Commerce Clause source of federal jurisdictional authority to regulate wetlands and other "waters of the United States." This issue has also been raised regarding endangered species that may have the ecological misfortune of living only within one state, for their lack of interstate activity could conceivably limit the federal government's authority under the Endangered Species Act (ESA).

Commerce Clause challenges go to the question of whether the federal government has authority to regulate at all; in contrast, Due Process Clause and Takings Clause challenges go to the question of how the federal (and, through the Fourteenth Amendment, state) government actually implements such regulation.

There is a complex body of jurisprudence in this area, and the Supreme Court itself has acknowledged that it has sometimes conflated Due Process Clause analysis with Takings Clause analysis (effectively eliminating the former as a primary theoretical basis for such challenges in the *Lingle* decision in 2005, when the Court expressly overturned its precedent from *Agins* in 1980). I therefore focus here on the principles of Takings Clause analysis.

6. THE TAKINGS CLAUSE

The Takings Clause has just 12 words: "nor shall private property be taken for public use, without just compensation" (U.S. Constitution, Amend. V). These words serve as a potential constraint on any regulatory scheme that might result in "inverse condemnation," or an effective "taking" of private property through regulation (rather than through eminent domain or physical occupation of the private property, both of which clearly require "just compensation"). Four questions arise in a Takings Clause inquiry: (1) What is the "private property" in question? (2) At what level of regulatory restriction is such private property "taken"? (3) What is a "public use"? and (4) What is "just compensation"? In essence, the Court's attempt to clarify these questions has generated a great deal of confusion and a great deal of controversy.

The general rule under the *Penn Central* case of 1978 is that a three-part "balancing test" is to be applied to the "parcel in the whole" to determine if a "taking" has occurred; when this rule is applied, courts rarely find a taking. Two categorical takings also exist: when there is a physical occupation of the property (under *Loretto* in 1982) or when there is a complete diminution in the value of the property (under *Lucas* in 1992). Moreover, negotiated "exactions" (where conditions are imposed in exchange for granting a permit) must demonstrate both a "nexus" between the permit condition and the mitigated harm (under *Nollan* in 1987) and "rough proportionality" between the burden placed on the landowner and the mitigated harm (under *Dolan* in 1994).

Regulatory agencies must therefore be attentive in some circumstances to the effect of their regulations on the economic value of private property subject to such regulation. This is true for federal and state environmental regulators (e.g., the Corps of Engineers under the CWA, the Fish and Wildlife Service under the ESA), regional entities (e.g., state coastal regulators), and local governments (e.g., cities and counties establishing zoning regulations that limit potential development or in issuing permits with "exactions"). The cost to the agency of affecting a "taking" is to pay "just compensation" for the "taking"; it is not sufficient simply to invalidate the regulation (under *First English* in 1987). The prospect of having to pay potential takings claims, therefore, constraints some regulators. Judicial interpretation and application of takings analysis thus plays an important role in the extent to which environmental policy affects action by private property owners.

Takings concerns can also be translated through legislative action: in the wake of the *Kelo* case in 2005 (validating a high level of deference to local legislative bodies in determining a broad interpretation of the "public use" standard), many state legislatures adopted restrictions on cities and redevelopment agencies designed to limit such agencies beyond the degree to which the U.S. Constitution limited them. Moreover, some states have passed legislation and/or initiatives (notably Oregon's Measure 37 in 2004, which was then substantially modified through Measure 49 in 2007) that call for either invalidation of regulations or compensation for a wide range of economic effects from regulation (even if such regulations would not be deemed a taking under the U.S. Constitution). These state limits may be either statutory or through state constitutional amendments; in either case, they constrain regulatory action.

Lake Tahoe has been the site of several important takings cases. The lake straddles the California-Nevada border and is especially sensitive to pollution, so the two states established the Tahoe Regional Planning Agency (TRPA) through a bistate compact that was ratified by Congress in 1969 and modified in 1980. The TRPA adopted a long-range regional plan in 1984 that significantly restricts the development allowed on private lands throughout the Tahoe basin; concomitantly, public land acquisition has returned much of the land to public ownership to limit both development and legal conflict over application of TRPA's strict regulations. Some private landowners have sued the TRPA for a violation of the Takings Clause, however, and two of those cases have reached the U.S. Supreme Court: the *Suitum* case in 1997 and the *Tahoe-Sierra Preservation Council (TSPC)* case in 2002. In both cases, landowners asserted that their property rights had been taken because the amount of development allowable on their lands had been severely reduced by the TRPA land use regulations (in some cases, no development was allowed on the land under the TRPA regulations)—but, unlike in the *Lucas* case, TRPA allowed a "transfer of development rights" (TDR) scheme that was similar to that upheld in the *Penn Central* case under New York City's land use regulations. The two cases illustrate the complexity of takings jurisprudence and why "the search for the Holy Grail" of a simple takings rule has proved so elusive for the Court: *Suitum* focused on the question of whether or not the case was "ripe for adjudication" (the Court found that it was ripe, even though Suitum had not applied to sell TDRs to another parcel), while *TSPC* addressed the issue of whether a "temporary taking" had occurred under the rule laid down in *First English* (the Court found that TRPA's temporary building moratorium had not been of sufficient duration to constitute a temporary taking). Takings jurisprudence remains a muddled, ad hoc inquiry in all but the simplest cases.

7. Judicial Review

Even when there is no constitutional question, however, the role of the courts in affecting U.S. environmental policy often comes down to a single, recurring question for the courts: how much deference should the courts give the agency charged with implementing a federal statute in its interpretation and application of the statute? This is the bread-and-butter of administrative law, where the twin constitutional concerns about due process and separation of powers cast a shadow over what the proper "standard of review" should be. In essence, the standard of review often determines who wins a case: a weak standard of review, granting judicial deference to the agency, will generally mean that the agency's decisions will be able to withstand challenge by those who disagree with agency decisions; in contrast, a strict standard of review, where the court does not grant much deference to the agency's decisions, will more likely result in successful challenges to agency decisions. As many legal analysts remark, "If you tell me the standard of review, I can probably tell you who will win the case." The standard of review is therefore the key to understanding the (shifting) role of the courts in influencing U.S. environmental policy.

As a constitutional matter, the issue of how much deference to afford executive branch (and so-called independent) agencies involves the Nondelegation Doctrine: because Article I of the Constitution establishes that "[a]ll legislative Powers herein granted shall be vested in a Congress of the United States" (Art. I, sec. 1), agencies are not supposed to legislate—instead, they must execute or administer the implementation of legislation that comes from the Congress. In many cases, however, Congress prefers to delegate some discretionary authority to agencies that appears to be legislative in character—either because the technical complexity of the problem is beyond the expertise of Congress or because such delegation will push any politically difficult decisions onto nameless, faceless bureaucrats who can then be blamed if there is political fallout for implementing new environmental policy. Through 2011, the U.S. Supreme Court has invalidated congressional legislation only twice (on any matter) under the Nondelegation Doctrine, however, so it is not a serious threat to agency discretion. Indeed, the most recent major case on the issue (*American Trucking* in 2001) upheld broad discretion for the U.S. Environmental Protection Agency's adoption of rules regarding environmental standards for expanded trucking entries into the United States under the North American Free Trade Agreement (NAFTA).

Instead, nondelegation concerns are usually addressed *indirectly* through the question of judicial deference during judicial review. It is important to note that any judicial review of agency implementation of a congressional statute also usually involves the Administrative Procedure Act of 1946 (APA), which applies to a wide range of agency actions. (See chapter 17 in this volume for a detailed discussion of the rulemaking process under the APA.) Review standards under the APA are well developed, but they may be trumped by more specific standards embodied in a particular statute: the Clean Air Act or the Clean Water Act, for example, might establish different standards of review than the Endangered Species Act. Violation of some provision of the APA is nevertheless nearly always invoked in litigation challenging federal agency action. In particular, section 706(2)(A) of the APA calls for a court to overturn agency action that is "arbitrary, capricious, an abuse of discretion, or otherwise not in accordance with law."

Judicial review under this provision has developed what is known as the "hard look" doctrine, which has two distinct meanings: (1) the *court* should take a "hard look" at the agency's decision-making process to determine if it meets both the statutory requirements of the APA and avoids conflict with constitutional concerns about due process, and (2) in taking that "hard look" at the agency's decision-making process, the court may examine the substance of the agency decision to determine whether the *agency* took a "hard look" at the evidence before it and whether the agency's decision is supported by adequate evidence. The first meaning emphasizes *process*, which is widely recognized as a legal requirement under case law since *Scenic Hudson* in 1965 and *Overton Park* in 1971. The second meaning, which actually gets to the *substance* of agency decisions and the relationship between the agency's decisions and the evidence before the agency, has been the subject of much more debate (see subsequent discussion in *Mead, Brand X, Gonzales*, and *Long Island Care* cases below). Courts vary widely in their actual practice—but they have generally been more deferential to agency decisions since the U.S. Supreme Court decisions in *State Farm* in 1983 and *Chevron* in 1984.

The U.S. Supreme Court established the basic parameters of judicial review in the *Chevron* case in 1984. The case involved the question of whether EPA's "bubble policy" of regulating a single permitted facility under the Clean Air Act was allowable or if every individual emissions stack in a facility had to be regulated as a separate "source." The *Chevron* Doctrine calls for a two-part test: (1) is the statute *ambiguous?*, and, if the court determines that it is ambiguous, (2) is the agency's interpretation of that ambiguity—its attempt to fill any "gap" in the statute left by Congress—either *permissible* or *reasonable?* The *Chevron* test is only applied in situations where the agency has been charged by Congress with implementing a particular statute, so this threshold question (as to whether or not the *Chevron* two-step test should be applied by a court to a particular challenge to agency action) is sometimes referred to as "*Chevron* Step Zero."

The *Chevron* test, not surprisingly, has generally meant that agency actions usually survive judicial review. Moreover, the second step in the "*Chevron* two-step" is very easy to meet: an agency action would survive challenge as long as any "reasonable" person *could* have reached the interpretation reached by the agency. Therefore, plaintiffs rarely win in a challenge to agency action if a court finds the statute is ambiguous. Perhaps the very fact that the parties are in court disputing the meaning of the statute suggests that *any* statute before a court in such a proceeding is probably ambiguous enough to be found to be ambiguous by a court that is so inclined. This was the outcome in *Chevron*. The Supreme Court found that Congress had been ambiguous, leaving a "gap" in the Clean Air Act to be filled by the EPA's expertise ("*Chevron* step 1"); the EPA's construction of the statute through its regulations was also "permissible" and "reasonable" ("*Chevron* step 2"), so the Court deferred to the EPA's construction. (The EPA met the "Chevron step 0" test in that Congress had delegated authority to the EPA to implement the Clean

Air Act; similar deference would not have been given, though, to EPA's interpretation of a statute that Congress had assigned to another agency.)

Chevron has become canonical; it is the second most widely cited case
in American judicial history.[2] However, the Court has been chipping away at
Chevron's high level of deference over the past decade in a series of cases (*Mead*
in 2001, *Brand X* in 2005, *Gonzales* in 2006, and *Long Island Care* in 2007) that
have now reduced the level of judicial deference for certain types of agency action.[3]
This general trend toward lesser judicial deference to agencies played a prominent
role in the seminal *Massachusetts v. EPA* in 2007 (where the Court did *not* defer to
EPA's interpretation of the Clean Air Act that carbon dioxide did not qualify as an
"air pollutant"; instead, the Court held that there was no ambiguity or "gap" in the
act and therefore the EPA was obligated to regulate it under the act unless the EPA
could demonstrate specific findings to show that carbon dioxide was not an "air
pollutant" under the act). Broadly deferential judicial review would have meant
that EPA would have survived that challenge; instead, a stricter standard of judicial
review—where the Court did not find any ambiguity in the meaning of the terms
of the act (*Chevron* step 1)—constrained agency discretion.

8. STANDING

The *Massachusetts v. EPA* case raises another important issue regarding the role of
the courts in relationship to the broader ecosystem of U.S. environmental policy:
whether or not parties have standing to bring suit in federal court in the first place.
In many cases, U.S. environmental statutes explicitly give all citizens standing
to take an agency to court under that statute. Where such broad standing is not
explicitly conferred by a statute, however, the Court has developed both constitutional and prudential rationales for limiting access to the federal courts. Broad
standing doctrine means that many parties may challenge an agency decision; narrower standing doctrine means that agency decisions are more likely to avoid any
lawsuits by unhappy parties. Standing doctrine reached a high point (i.e., broad
access) in the 1970s, but the Court then generally tightened standing doctrine in
the 1990s with *Lujan* in 1992.

The three basic elements of standing today are (1) injury-in-fact (i.e., the party
suing must be able to demonstrate injury from the agency's actions), (2) causation

---

2. The most-cited case is *Erie Railroad v. Tompkins*, which established in 1938 that federal
   courts were to apply *state* common law when deciding matters of state law in diversity
   cases.
3. Moving the standard in some situations more toward the approach articulated in
   Skidmore in 1944—where an agency's interpretation may carry some greater weight and
   can be persuasive, but it is not presumptively valid against challengers' interpretations.

(i.e., the party must show that the agency caused the injury), and (3) redressability (i.e., the party must show that the party's injury will be redressed by the court's action in the case). Many of the prominent standing cases have involved environmental matters, and much of the *Massachusetts v. EPA* decision revolved around the issue of standing. Many more cases result in dismissal of the litigation on procedural grounds (without ever getting to the substance of the claim against the agency) because the plaintiffs lack standing. The exception is when an environmental statute itself establishes standing (e.g., any "citizen" can sue to enforce the Clean Water Act): such statutory specificity trumps the generalized constitutional and prudential standards for standing. Weiland (2007) offers a useful overview of the procedural considerations that may affect whether a party will turn to the federal courts to achieve its purposes for environmental policy.

9. FEDERALISM AND PREEMPTION

As noted, the U.S. Constitution is a document reflecting a complex set of compromises between the desire to have a competent federal authority and the desire by the states to retain as much power as possible (see chapter 18 in this volume). It therefore reserves for the states all powers that have not been granted through the Constitution to the federal government; moreover, only those realms in which the federal government actually "occupies the field" are preempted from state action. The states, however, have plenary power as sovereigns that can be exercised through the Police Power. State power to occupy a field is constrained by only two considerations: (1) whether the Constitution grants authority for the field to the federal government *and* the federal government has exercised such authority to occupy that field; and (2) if either the state or federal Constitution provides protections for a state's citizens against the particular means by which a state may exercise its Police Power (e.g., through the federal Due Process, Equal Protection, or Takings Clauses as applied to the states through the Fourteenth Amendment).

Environmental policy was therefore largely the responsibility of the states (and, through them, local governments and special districts) until the wave of federal legislation and regulation of the late 1960s through the 1970s. The federal government did not impose national ambient air quality standards or water effluent technology standards on the states or their industries; instead, each state was free to regulate those topics as it saw fit. California, for example, had begun to tackle severe air quality problems in Southern California (under its sovereign Police Power) and therefore had a much stricter regulatory regime than any other state or the federal government. State mobile-source tailpipe emissions regulations or stationary-source (e.g., power plant, refinery) emissions regulations to achieve state and local air quality standards were "legal" then because they were not (yet) preempted by the federal government.

That situation changed dramatically when the federal Clean Air Act of 1970 and the Federal Water Pollution Control Act (Clean Water Act) of 1972 were adopted. The federal government, utilizing its authority under the Commerce Clause (as interpreted by the Supreme Court at the time), was now occupying the field of air and water quality protection—thereby preempting any state schemes that might conflict with Congress's attempt to establish a national regime. Congress created a special waiver provision for California when it came to air quality, however, allowing California to continue to have stricter standards despite the economic impact of such standards on the then-largely-domestic automobile industry. The 1990 Clean Air Act Amendments then further extended the policy-forcing power of California regulators by allowing other states to adopt *either* the national standards *or* the California standards. States wishing to adopt stricter standards were preempted by the statute from adopting their own standards, but Congress was willing to have two standards for automobile and light truck tailpipe emissions.

Other areas of environmental policy also reflect this balancing act between a goal of establishing national standards and allowing some state and local discretion to accommodate the different economic, social, and environmental conditions among the states.[4] Federal air pollutant emission regulations for automobiles (with the exception of California and any states adopting the California regulations) give way to state-by-state regulation of stationary air pollution sources through State Implementation Plans (SIPs) under the Clean Air Act. The SIPs are developed by the states but must then be approved by the federal EPA; if an SIP is deemed inadequate, the act gives EPA the authority to develop a Federal Implementation Plan (FIP) to achieve national goals. Similarly, water quality standards under the Clean Water Act allow for both state determination of total maximum daily load (TMDL) levels for individual pollutants and state allocation of responsibilities for meeting those TMDL standards.

This system gives states the discretion to trade off economic and environmental goals under the oversight of federal agency officials who must ensure that some nationally mandated minimum level of environmental protection is achieved (or, as the statutes often actually require, is *to be* achieved under a *plan* required under the statute). The federal agency cannot simply look the other way, however, for many environmental statutes include citizen suit provisions that allow any citizen to bring suit to compel the agency to enforce the law. This invariably brings the courts into the picture: the agency need not be concerned about a law if the courts have strict standing criteria, loose standards of review, and high levels of judicial deference to agencies and fail to take a "hard look" at whether an agency has taken

---

4. The goal of national standards is driven by both an efficiency rationale, in that such standards allow industry to avoid having to develop products that respond to a fifty-state regulatory maze, and by equity concerns, in that all Americans ostensibly have the same air and water quality standards under a uniform system of national environmental regulation.

a "hard look." How the courts approach their role of judicial review, therefore, has a direct effect on the substance of environmental policy.

The federal government has largely "occupied the field" of environmental policy (with the prominent exception of land use regulation, which remains primarily a state prerogative that is generally exercised through local government regulation), forcing state regulators to work within the federal statutory scheme rather than through independent state law. Some states have parallel state structures, however, designed to ensure a "backstop" of adequate regulation in case recurring calls for weakened federal regulation result in gaps. The *SWANCC* and *Rapanos* decisions had the effect of strengthening some state wetland protection statutes, for example, as environmental advocates and political actors feared that wetlands associated with intrastate waters (under *SWANCC*) or those not adequately linked to navigable waters (under the Scalia and Kennedy opinions in *Rapanos*) would no longer be protected by the federal government under the federal Clean Water Act (as they had clearly been within its jurisdiction under *Riverside Bayview*). Many states also have parallel (and sometimes stricter) state Endangered Species Acts, for example, or environmental review statutes modeled on the federal National Environmental Policy Act (NEPA).

The California Environmental Quality Act (CEQA), adopted in 1970 as a "little NEPA," illustrates how the judicial role can be quite different under a state statute than a federal statute. The California Supreme Court extended CEQA's reach (which originally called for an environmental impact report [EIR] to be prepared for any state "project") to include all discretionary local governmental land use permitting decisions in the 1972 *Friends of Mammoth* decision. There is no central state agency charged with assuring agency compliance with CEQA, so citizen suits are the primary means of assuring compliance. The result has been a plethora of case law on every nuance of CEQA while dramatically increasing the time and cost necessary to get a project approved.

The CEQA case law has therefore changed the power relations among key actors in local land use decisions (and therefore environmental policy) in California: local activist groups can threaten to sue local governments that do not exhaustively review controversial projects, thereby exposing the consequences of such project to public review (as well as to delays that increase the likelihood of electing a new city council or board or supervisors before a final vote is taken on a project). Unlike NEPA, CEQA also has a *substantive* requirement (in the absence of specific findings of "overriding considerations") not to approve any project unless all of its likely environmental impacts are reduced to a less than "significant" level (a level that has been litigated in nearly all of its forms—for traffic, air quality, water quality, visual aesthetics, noise, etc.). The role of the courts in establishing the scope of CEQA and enforcing its provisions (both procedural and substantive), therefore, has a direct effect on the design of projects, the likelihood of them being permitted, the mitigation measures that may be attached to such permits, and their timing and cost. This would simply not have occurred without strong judicial review.

10. COMMON LAW

The American legal system was first built on the common law, yet our contemporary understanding of it from civics classes and the news media is focused on legislative statutes and the administrative law of government agencies. Common law is law that has developed through case-by-case application of competing judicial principles: rather than being formally articulated by a legislature, it is the law that emerges from a series of judicial decisions addressing the similarities and differences between cases addressing a common set of concerns (Holmes 1881). It is, therefore, an antecedent to the modern administrative state. In some cases, common law doctrines and claims have been incorporated directly into statutory schemes; in others, the statutory scheme has expressly displaced the common law. In most cases, however, common law claims—which vary from state to state—continue to coexist with federal statutes and administrative law to implement such statutes. The result is a very complex system of environmental law that may vary substantively from one state to another.

For example, the federal Clean Air Act establishes a complex system of National Ambient Air Quality Standards (NAAQS) for six "criteria pollutants" and the federal EPA must approve SIPs before states are able to issue permits allowing specified technologies and/or levels of emissions, but it also expressly maintains the right of citizens to make state common law claims against polluters. A power plant may therefore have a valid permit from a state regulatory agency that was issued under a SIP approved by the EPA—but that power plant owner may still face a lawsuit in state or federal court under a state common law doctrine of nuisance or trespass. Indeed, such claims have been a critical factor driving some of the politics of climate change legislation: some greenhouse gas (GHG) emitters would prefer to have federal GHG regulation than to face an unpredictable set of juries in state courts at common law.

The standard law school curriculum, which has been in place since Harvard Law School Dean Christopher Columbus Langdell established it in the late nineteenth century, emphasizes common law courses in the first year: contracts, property, torts, criminal law, and civil procedure typically comprise the bulk of the first-year curriculum, along with constitutional law. In some cases, the common law principles of a field have been codified through statutes (e.g., the Uniform Commercial Code for some aspects of contracts; incorporating the Doctrine of Habitability from property into California's Code; state or federal adoption of tort or criminal law standards for awarding or limiting either judgments or sanctions for specific behavior). Traditionally, the problem of environmental pollution was handled primarily by tort and property law; the common law was ultimately deemed ineffective by the U.S. Congress, however, due in part to problems of demonstrating causation or harm as well as the high transactions costs associated with litigating hundreds of common law tort and property claims against a complex set of polluters. Similarly, many problems associated with natural resources management (e.g., forests, wildlife, water) were originally addressed through property law; again, property law was deemed unable to meet the task without some legislative assistance. Torts and property law remain the most important areas of common law for U.S. environmental policy, but other areas of common law also have relevance to how both legislatures and the courts ultimately address a given policy challenge. All action is therefore conducted in the shadow of the common law.[5]

One interesting way in which state common law may play an unusual role is in Takings Clause cases. In *Lucas* (1992), the Court said that regulation was valid if it restricted the use of private property in ways that otherwise would have been restricted anyway by "background principles of the state's property and nuisance" law. There has been a heated debate since then about whether statutes and regulations are included in such "background principles," but there is no doubt that Justice Scalia included common law doctrines from property and nuisance in his reference. Because common law often varies by state, however, this means that *state* common law can be the basis for determining whether a *federal* regulation has affected a *federal* taking under the *federal* Constitution. A standard approach to federal environmental policy could therefore conceivably be unconstitutional when applied in one state but constitutional when applied in another state that had different "background principles" establishing private property rights.

State common law plays an especially important role regarding water rights: the federal government has not preempted state water rights under the Reclamation Act of 1902, the Federal Power Acts of 1920 and 1935, or the Clean Water Act.[6] State water rights systems are often a complex amalgamation of common law, constitutional, statutory, and administrative law—so the common law continues to play a role even where the legislature has adopted a formal statutory scheme with administrative duties delegated to a state engineer or water board. California water rights appropriations must be consistent with the Public Trust Doctrine articulated in the *National Audubon Society (Mono Lake)* decision of 1983, for example, which then makes the Public Trust Doctrine a background principle under *Lucas* that should then apply to any analysis of whether or not "property" has been taken under the Takings Clause.[7]

The common law, in short, continues to live and breathe through such statutory and administrative law to the extent that those charged with interpreting statutes and regulations are steeped in the common law. Nearly all judges and

---

5. Courts have recently rejected several common law claims regarding climate change, however, on the grounds that the statutory scheme enacted by Congress through the Clean Air Act—which the Supreme Court determined in *Massachusetts v. EPA* (2007) applies to carbon dioxide emissions—has preempted federal (but not state) common law claims. *See AEP v. Connecticut* (2011) and *Comer v. Murphy Oil* (2010, 2009).

6. However, see *Jefferson County PUD* from 1993 regarding the complex role of state implementation of the Clean Water Act for purposes of certifying standards under the Federal Power Act.

7. For a complex illustration of this issue, see the *Casitas* case (2011, 2008), where this issue is central: the plaintiff claimed that a federal requirement to divert water down

certainly all attorneys are fed a steady diet of common law meals from their first day of law school, so common law doctrines and a fundamental trust in the common law is a central part of American legal culture. Common law therefore influences all aspects of law through the cultural conceptions of those who occupy the courtroom.

11. CONCLUSIONS

This chapter has been only a cursory introduction to a few of the ways in which the courts and legal analysis influence U.S. environmental policy. The U.S. Constitution establishes structural conditions that give the courts a specific role in relationship to the legislative and executive branches, and that role has evolved into one in which both access to the courts and the stringency of judicial review of both statutes and administrative action are often determinative of substantive policy outcomes. The U.S. Constitution also establishes substantive limits to the role of the federal government in relationship to both the states and the citizenry, and those limits either do (under the Takings Clause) or could (under the Commerce Clause) play a critical role in constraining U.S. environmental policy. At the same time, the retention of both state prerogatives and common law causes of action have helped to reinvigorate federal environmental policy by allowing innovation by states and through the courts: gridlock in the U.S. Congress cannot completely freeze the U.S. environmental policy regime. (See chapter 13 in this volume.)

The courts, therefore, are a vital element in U.S. environmental policy: without them, the classic civics textbook sequence of legislation followed by administrative implementation would tend to favor both elite interests and stagnation. Instead, access to the courts and a willingness by the judiciary to hold agencies accountable to legislative requirements have helped to move U.S. environmental policy in new directions (either positive or negative, depending on one's point of view) despite relatively few major legislative changes over the past two decades. Indeed, one could argue that the focus of U.S. environmental policy is now at the state level and in the courts. That new focal point for policy innovation is likely to be maintained unless and until a major breakthrough happens in the U.S. Congress.

---

a fish ladder in order to protect an endangered species is a physical taking of its water (where Lucas would apply to the entire amount of water that has been "taken"), while the state and federal governments argued that the there can be no "taking" of private property because the property interest under California's "background principles" includes a duty to protect fish (under both the Public Trust Doctrine and state common law). A similar federal restriction under the ESA in another state—where such a duty to protect fish downstream of a diversion was not one of the "background principles" of state water law—could therefore lead to a different conclusion as to whether there is a taking.

Courts and legal analysis will therefore continue to shape the dynamic evolution of U.S. environmental policy.

There is much that we still need to learn, however, about the specific ways in which the American judicial system influences that evolution. The studies to date have generally been either quite broad and quantitative or very narrow and qualitative. What is needed is an intermediate inquiry, where a set of factors identified through studies to date are used to parse the large data sets into a meaningful set of cases that can be studied with more nuance. Moreover, the courts influence much more than the cases they see: they also influence power relationships that determine who will enter the courtroom, whether parties will seek legislative or executive action, and what the substance of any negotiations in those other fora will yield. The reach of our scholarship must therefore extend beyond what is formally processed by the judicial system. This is where systematic study of political conflicts over environmental policy issues can move to an intermediate level of inquiry. For example, when there is split government and the executive branch is controlled by Republicans, how does standing doctrine affect the settlement of disputes in the Congress over funding enforcement of specific environmental programs? Does that differ from when there is unified Democratic control of the Congress and the executive? Does standing doctrine lead businesses to use the courts more or less often, or is party control of the executive more important? What are the substantive differences in settlement outcomes under the different conditions above? It is clear that the courts influence U.S. environmental policy in powerful ways; the question for scholars now is how and when and in what specific ways that happens.

REFERENCES

De Tocqueville, A. 1835. *Democracy in America, Part 1.* Available at www.gutenberg. org (accessed May 2, 2012).

Holmes, O. W. 1881. *The Common Law.* Available at www.gutenberg.org (accessed May 2, 2012).

Kagan, R. A. 1991. "Adversarial Legalism and American Government." *Journal of Policy Analysis and Management* 10: 369–406.

———. 2001. *Adversarial Legalism: The American Way of Law.* Cambridge, MA: Harvard University Press.

Kamieniecki, S. 2006. *Corporate America and Environmental Policy: How Often Does Business Get Its Way?* Palo Alto, CA: Stanford University Press.

Lazarus, R. J. 2004. *The Making of Environmental Law.* Chicago: University of Chicago Press.

McSpadden, L. 2007. "Industry's Use of the Courts." In *Business and Environmental Policy: Corporate Interests and the American Political System,* ed. M. E. Kraft and S. M. Kamieniecki, 232–262. Cambridge, MA: MIT Press.

O'Leary, R. 1993. *Environmental Change: Federal Courts and the EPA.* Philadelphia: Temple University Press.

———. 2010. "Environmental Policy in the Courts." In *Environmental Policy: New Directions for the Twenty-First Century*, 7th ed., ed. N. K Vig and M. E. Kraft, 125–146. Washington, DC: CQ Press.

Weiland, P. S. 2007. "Business and Environmental Policy in the Federal Courts." In *Business and Environmental Policy: Corporate Interests and the American Political System*, ed. M. E. Kraft and S. M. Kamieniecki, 213–232. Cambridge, MA: MIT Press.

Wenner, L. M. 1982. *The Environmental Decade in the Courts*. Bloomington: Indiana University Press.

Cases Cited

Agins v. City of Tiburon, 447 U.S. 255 (1980).

American Electric Power (AEP) v. Connecticut, 131 S. Ct. 2527 (2011).

American Trucking: Whitman v. American Trucking Associations, Inc., 531 U.S. 457 (2001).

Brand X: National Cable and Telecommunications Ass'n v. Brand X Internet Services, 546 U.S. 967 (2005).

Casitas Municipal Water District. v. U.S., 102 Fed. Cl. 443 (2011), 543 F.3d 1276 (2008).

Chevron U.S.A., Inc. v. Natural Resources Defense Council, Inc., 467 U.S. 837 (1984).

Comer v. Murphy Oil U.S.A., 607 F. 3d 1049 (2010), 585 F. 3d 855 (2009).

Dolan v. City of Tigard, 512 U.S. 374 (1994).

Erie Railroad Co. v. Tompkins, 304 U.S. 64 (1938).

First English Evangelical Lutheran Church v. Los Angeles County, 482 U.S. 304 (1987).

Friends of Mammoth v. Board of Supervisors of Mono County, 8 Cal.3d 247, 502 P.2d 1049 (1972).

Gonzales v. Oregon, 546 U.S. 243 (2006).

Jefferson County PUD: PUD No. 1 of Jefferson County v. Washington Dep't of Ecology, 511 U.S. 700 (1994).

Kelo v. City of New London, 545 U.S. 469 (2005).

Lingle v. Chevron U.S.A., Inc., 544 U.S. 528 (2005).

Long Island Care at Home, Ltd. v. Coke, 127 S.Ct. 2339 (2007).

Lopez: United States v. Alfonso Lopez, Jr., 514 U.S. 549 (1995).

Loretto v. Teleprompter Manhattan CATV Corp., 458 U.S. 419 (1982).

Lucas v. South Carolina Coastal Council, 505 U.S. 1003 (1992).

Lujan v. Defenders of Wildlife, 504 U.S. 555 (1992).

Marbury v. Madison, 5 U.S. (1 Cranch) 137 (1803).

Massachusetts v. Environmental Protection Agency, 549 U.S. 497 (2007).

Mead: United States v. Mead Corp., 533 U.S. 218 (2001).

Morrison: United States v. Morrison, 529 U.S. 598 (2000).

National Audubon Society v. Superior Court of Alpine County, 33 Cal.3d 419 (1983).

Nollan v. California Coastal Comm'n, 483 U.S. 625 (1987).

Overton Park: Citizens to Preserve Overton Park, Inc. v. Volpe, 401 U.S. 402 (1971).

Penn Central Transportation Co. v. New York City, 438 U.S. 104 (1978).

Rapanos v. United States, 547 U.S. 715 (2006).

Riverside Bayview: United States v. Riverside Bayview Homes, Inc., 474 U.S. 121 (1985).

Scenic Hudson Preservation Conference v. FPC, 354 F.2d 608 (2d Cir. 1965).

Skidmore v. Swift & Co., 323 U.S. 134 (1944).

State Farm: Motor Vehicle Manufacturers' Association v. State Farm Mutual Automobile Insurance Co., 463 U.S. 29 (1983).

Suitum v. Tahoe Regional Planning Agency, 520 U.S. 725 (1997).

SWANCC: Solid Waste Agency of Cook County (SWANCC) v. U.S. Army Corps of Engineers, 531 U.S. 159 (2001).

TSPC: Tahoe-Sierra Preservation Council, Inc. v. Tahoe Regional Planning Agency, 535 U.S. 302 (2002).

CHAPTER 13

··

CONGRESS AND ENVIRONMENTAL POLICY

··

MICHAEL E. KRAFT

ANY observer of American environmental policy and politics can readily under-stand the critical importance of the U.S. Congress. As other chapters in this vol-ume have noted well, over time Congress has put its firm stamp on environmental policy, from the Clean Air Act and Clean Water Act to the Endangered Species Act, setting highly ambitious goals and directing administrative agencies to employ a variety of policy tools to meet them. Arguably, Congress has had more influence on both environmental protection and natural resource policy than the White House, the courts, or the executive agencies have had (Andrews 2006; Cooley and Wandesforde-Smith 1970; Davies and Davies 1975; Kraft 1973, 1995; Smith 1966). It is equally clear that Congress will be similarly influential in the future, whether the decisions concern pursuit of long-term goals of sustainable development or addressing short-term demands, for example, by critics of environmental policy for reduction of regulatory burdens and costs.

Yet the increasing partisan divisions within Congress guarantee that envi-ronmental policy change in the future will not come easily despite widespread calls by scholars and policy analysts for redesigning policy goals and means to meet twenty-first-century challenges such as climate change and the need for sustainable economic development (Eisner 2007; Fiorino 2006; Klyza and Sousa 2008; Mazmanian and Kraft 2009). Some of the obstacles to bipartisan coopera-tion in a reformulation of policy were made clear during 2011 when the House of Representatives made repeated efforts to weaken environmental policy. For example, House Republicans sought to curtail the power of the U.S. Environmental Protection Agency (EPA) to regulate greenhouse gases, block a number of proposed EPA regulations on air quality, and constrain the EPA and other environmental agencies through dozens of appropriation bill riders favored by Tea Party backers and other conservatives, even though most observers anticipated that such legislation had little chance of gaining Senate or White House approval (Kaufman 2011).[1] The gulf between the two major parties evident in these disputes has widened in recent years, possibly ushering in a prolonged period of partisan bickering and legislative gridlock rather than a cooperative search for more effective and efficient environmental policy.

As is the case with other chapters in the book, my purpose here is to describe Congress and both the internal and external policy actors who affect its policy decisions. I also review and assess the institution's distinctive features that affect its actions on environmental policy and related issues. Given its roles in setting the direction of U.S. environmental policy, political scientists and other policy scholars need to explore both the constraints and opportunities for policy making in the years ahead, particularly the conditions for overcoming the policy stalemate that has been so prominent on Capitol Hill during the 1990s and 2000s (Binder 2003; Kraft 2013; Klyza and Sousa 2008). As a representative legislature, Congress is a microcosm of the U.S. political system, reflecting not only the views of the American public but also the positions and activities of myriad organized interests and competing political institutions that vie to affect policy making. Hence, many of the insights offered in other chapters on the presidency, political parties, interest groups, public opinion, and issue framing and agenda setting are pertinent here as well.[2]

Despite its obvious importance, there has been relatively little systematic research on Congress and environmental policy over the past four decades. At the same time we have seen robust growth of a well-developed political science literature on Congress in general, much of it reflecting rigorous and theoretically

---

1. The House majority leader, Rep. Eric Cantor (R-VA), announced a series of environmental votes to be taken in the House in the fall of 2011 and winter of 2012 to block what he and his Republican colleagues viewed as "job-killing" or "job-destroying" environmental regulations. See his comments to colleagues on the 10 most destructive federal regulations identified by House committee chairs in 2011 (many of which deal with environmental regulation) at majority leader.gov/blog/2011/08/memo-on-upcoming-jobs-agenda.html (accessed April 2012). The votes and other actions anticipated in the House were all tied to a "job-creation" agenda that the Republicans found to be political appealing in 2011 because of high and persistent unemployment and a stagnant U.S. economy.

2. I wrote a similar review of political science research on Congress and environmental policy in 1995 that describes some of the older research that might be of interest to some readers of this chapter. See Kraft 1995. As Kamieniecki and I indicate in chapter 1 of this volume, the earlier collection of such review essays by James P. Lester (1995) was a uniquely valuable resource for those seeking an introduction to scholarship on environmental policy and politics, particularly within the discipline of political science.

informed empirical research. One conclusion is that anyone interested in how Congress affects environmental policy should look to this wider body of work on the institution and its politics (e.g., Carson 2012; Dodd and Oppenheimer 2009; Loomis 2012; Schickler and Lee 2011).[3] I will highlight some of the best of this work below while also taking stock of research that deals directly with environmental policy and politics in Congress. Consistent with the purpose of chapters in this part of the book, I give special attention to Congress's institutional capacity to act on the most challenging environmental issues of the twenty-first century.

1. CONGRESS'S AUTHORITY FOR POLICY MAKING AND IMPLEMENTATION

Under the U.S. Constitution, Congress shares authority with the president for federal policy making on the environment, and its reach is exceptionally broad. Every year members of both the Senate and House of Representatives make critical decisions on hundreds of legislative, administrative, and appropriation measures that affect the environment, from renewing or revising key statutes and funding the operations of the EPA and other agencies to acting on bills dealing with highways and mass transit, forestry, farming, oil and gas exploration, energy research and development, creation of new wilderness areas, and international population and development assistance. Most of what Congress does requires agreement between the House and Senate. Indeed, to become law, all bills must be passed by both houses in identical form and signed by the president. Yet each chamber also has distinctive authority granted by the Constitution and can act independently of the other and of the White House. For example, either house can hold committee hearings and approve resolutions without regard to what the other chooses to do (particularly likely under divided partisan control). The Senate also has independent authority to act on presidential nominations and treaties. All of these congressional decisions can have significant impacts on environmental protection and sustainable development in the United States and around the world. Most of them are not well publicized, and they are largely out of sight for most of the public and the media, which does not, however, diminish their importance.

It is common to distinguish congressional actions in several different stages of the policy process: agenda setting, formulation and adoption of policies, and implementation of them in executive agencies. There is little question that presidents have greater opportunities than Congress to set the political or policy agenda, that

---

3. Equally valuable are some of the leading texts on Congress, which include descriptions of the major research findings, from elections and voter behavior to committee decision making and party leadership. See, for example, Davidson, Oleszek, and Lee 2012; Quirk and Binder 2005; and Smith, Roberts, and Vander Wielen 2009.

is, to call attention to specific problems and define the terms of debate (Kingdon 1995; Vig 2013 and chapter 14). Nonetheless, members of Congress can have a major impact on the agenda through legislative and oversight hearings as well as through the many opportunities they have for introducing bills, requesting and publicizing studies and reports, making speeches in Washington or at home, issuing policy statements, and voting in committee and on the floor (Davidson, Oleszek, and Lee 2012; Kamieniecki 2006; Kraft 1995, 2013).

As Guber and Bosso note well in their chapter on agenda setting and issue framing (chapter 20), all of these actions can assist members in framing issues in a way that promotes their preferred policy solutions, whether they do so on the campaign trail or in a variety of legislative venues, from committee hearing rooms to party policy committees. Holding hearings on climate change to question the consensus in the scientific community, as the House Energy and Commerce Committee did in 2011, is one example, but there is no shortage of similar agenda-setting and issue-framing actions in Congress (e.g., see Guber and Bosso 2007 and Layzer 2007). Well before the modern environmental era was fully established, members of Congress who clearly fit the category of "policy entrepreneurs" (Kingdon 1995) were adept at using these opportunities to highlight, define, and promote issues as diverse as U.S. and global population growth, threats to air and water quality, concerns over nuclear energy, and a diversity of natural resource and ecological challenges. They included most notably Senators Henry ("Scoop") Jackson (D-WA), Edmund Muskie (D-ME), Ernest Gruening (D-AK), and Gaylord Nelson (D-WI), and Representatives Paul Rogers (D-FL), John Saylor (R-PA), Paul ("Pete") McCloskey (R-CA), George Brown (D-CA), Henry Reuss (D-WI), Morris Udall (D-AZ), John Blatnik (D-MN), and John Dingell (D-MI), among many others (Baumgartner and Jones 1993; Cooley and Wandesforde-Smith 1970; Davies and Davies 1975; Jones 1975; Kraft 1973, 1994).

Under the Constitution Congress shares authority with the president for policy adoption, and, as noted, historically Congress has been equally if not more active than the president in formulating major environmental and natural resource policies. It is well equipped as an institution for doing so, particularly through its committee system, well staffed with knowledgeable and experienced professionals, and assisted by very capable legislative support agencies. Particularly important among these are the nonpartisan Congressional Research Service (CRS), the Government Accountability Office (GAO), the Congressional Budget Office (CBO), and, prior to 1995 when a Republican Congress eliminated it, the Office of Technology Assessment (OTA). Taken together, the number of people employed on Capitol Hill as either personal office staff of members, committee staff, party leadership staff, or support agency personnel total nearly 20,000 individuals, forming a bedrock of Congress's impressive capability to act on legislative issues.[4] Members of Congress draw as well from the thousands of think tanks and interest groups in Washington

---

4. The numbers are compiled regularly by C-SPAN and are available at the organization's website, www.c-span.org.

and elsewhere that seek to inform and influence the full spectrum of environmental policy decisions. The White House and executive agencies add to this profusion of policy studies available to members of Congress with their own program evaluations and assessments of policy needs.

Because they have such extensive executive powers, presidents also can dominate the process of policy implementation in the agencies (see chapters 14 and 15). Here too, however, Congress can substantially affect agency actions, through its budgetary decisions, its keen and persistent attention to agency rulemaking (see chapter 17), and the Senate's authority to act on presidential nominations to top executive positions. Every federal agency must have its budget approved annually, and congressional consideration of budget requests is often accompanied by inquiries into agency performance and spending patterns, especially for any decisions that become controversial because of their costs and other impacts. Environmental organizations as well as those representing business and industry regularly make their views known to members of Congress during the budgetary process and at other times. These congressional powers translate into an influential and continuing role of overseeing, and often criticizing, actions in executive agencies such as the EPA, Department of Energy, Geological Survey, Fish and Wildlife Service, Bureau of Land Management, and Forest Service (Lubell and Segee 2013; Rosenbaum 2013).

As one example, in late 2008 and early 2009 congressional Democrats closely followed a series of regulatory changes affecting environmental and natural resource policies that were proposed in the last few months of the Bush administration, seeking ways to overturn them in the 111th Congress, when they could expect support from President Obama (Lubell and Segee 2013; Savage 2009). When Republicans assumed control of the House following the 2010 elections, the tables were turned. House Republicans launched repeated oversight investigations into the operations of the EPA and other environmental agencies (Kaufman 2011; Maron 2011). In one prominent illustration of the change, in September 2011 Republican members of a House Energy and Commerce subcommittee on oversight and investigations criticized the Obama administration's decision to offer loan guarantees to solar industry manufacturers, part of its much-touted "green jobs" initiatives, after one of the firms that received a sizable loan, Solyndra, declared bankruptcy (Lipton and Broder 2011; Wald 2011).[5]

As stated earlier, the Republican House in the 112th Congress was determined to use its budgetary powers to seek major cuts in environmental agency spending

5. There are many sources for following environmental policy actions in Congress, from newspapers such as the *New York Times* and *Washington Post* to policy newsletters such as the Natural Resources Defense Council's *Legislative Watch* (www.nrdc.org/legislation/legwatch.asp and available by email), among similar reports issued by environmental groups, industry groups such as trade associations, and policy research institutes. Among the best of the nonpartisan journalistic accounts is *CQ Weekly*, a longtime publication of Congressional Quarterly, which offers detailed and objective reporting on activities in Congress on environmental, energy, and other natural resource issues. It is available at most college and university libraries.

that went well beyond what might have been expected as part of the larger federal deficit-reduction efforts that were so prominent and contentious during 2011— about 18 percent for the EPA and 7 percent for the Department of Interior (Broder 2011a; Kaufman 2011). At the same time, anti-EPA rhetoric flourished on the campaign trail as Republican candidates seeking the party's presidential nomination found the agency a favorite target and an irresistible example of what they characterized as regulatory excess, particularly for the EPA's initial efforts to limit greenhouse gas emissions; the same rhetoric echoed in the halls of Congress (Broder 2011b; Broder and Galbraith 2011). Similar budget cutting efforts took place during Ronald Reagan's presidency and the George W. Bush administration (Vig 2013), although they were somewhat muted by political support for the EPA in Congress. Similarly, during Bill Clinton's presidency a Republican Congress sought to cut EPA's budget sharply but was constrained by Clinton's veto of the budget bill. As was the case in 2011, Congress frequently has turned to the use of riders, or legislative stipulations in appropriation bills, to prevent funds from being used to implement laws that were out of favor in Congress at the moment (Kraft 2003, 2013).

Through its constitutional power to advise and consent on presidential nominations, the Senate has a unique role in approving or blocking a president's choice to fill critical positions in the top layers of the federal bureaucracy and on the federal courts (see chapters 12, 14, and 15 in this volume, Binder and Maltzman 2009). It almost always approves presidential nominees when the same party controls both institutions. As a headline of one article in early 2009 stated, "Obama's Choice for EPA Chief Meets Little Criticism on Capitol Hill"; at that time Democrats controlled both the House and Senate. Following the 2010 elections, when Republicans took control of the House and narrowed the Democratic margin in the Senate to a few votes, Republicans were able to challenge many Obama administration nominees and slow the approval process considerably (Appelbaum 2011). Much of the power of the minority party in the Senate to delay or disapprove a nomination or a legislative proposal derives from that body's increasing use of, or threat to employ, the filibuster. The result is that almost all controversial action today requires a minimum of 60 votes in the Senate, which is often impossible at a time of narrow partisan control of that body (Davidson, Oleszek, and Lee 2012).

Even if it cannot compete on an equal footing with the president in some of these agenda setting and policy-making activities, historically Congress has been highly influential in the formulation and adoption of environmental policies (Andrews 2006; Davies and Davies 1975; Lazarus 2004). In addition, for much of the modern environmental era prior to the mid-1990s, it operated with bipartisan cooperation on the issues, even if the parties diverged in their preferred policy positions. For example, President Richard Nixon created the U.S. EPA by executive order and signed the Clean Air Act Amendments of 1970, and President George H. W. Bush strongly backed the Clean Air Act's amendment in 1990, which set new directions for clean air policy (Bryner 1995, 2007).

However, such bipartisanship on environmental issues largely disappeared after the 1994 elections, which gave the Republicans control of the House for the first time in 40 years, and ushered in a prolonged period of anti-environmental actions under the guise of "regulatory reform" and led to bitter relations between the two parties on a wide range of environmental policy issues that in many ways continued through the 2000s (Eisner 2007; Klyza and Sousa 2008; Kraft 2003). Among the legislative "reform" efforts that Congress approved during this period were the Unfunded Mandates Reform Act of 1995, Small Business Regulatory Enforcement Fairness Act of 1996, and Data Quality Act of 2000. The last of these was approved as an appropriations rider (27 lines buried in a massive budget bill that President Clinton had to sign) that received no direct consideration by Congress and yet became the basis for frequent legal challenges mounted against regulatory actions believed to be a burden to business (Kraft 2011, 155–156; Raeburn 2006). Even during this period, however, the parties occasionally found themselves in agreement on key actions when both benefited politically. Cases in point are the revision of pesticide policy in the Food Quality Protection Act of 1996, reauthorization of the Safe Drinking Water Act, also in 1996, and a major expansion of wilderness protection approved in 2009 as the Omnibus Public Lands Management Act (Kraft 1995, 2013).

As this brief historical review indicates, the way in which Congress exercises its formidable policy-making powers is shaped by several critical variables. Among them are the saliency of the issues (which is typically quite low), public sentiment on them (historically favorable to environmental protection but less solidly so in recent years), the influence of organized interest groups, and which party controls the House and Senate and by what margins. The way Congress appraises the president and his agenda is also a significant factor, particularly when partisan control of the White House and Congress is divided. Other chapters in this volume speak to each of these factors (see also Kraft and Kamieniecki 2007b; Vig and Kraft 2013).

2. POLICY CONSEQUENCES OF CONGRESS'S INSTITUTIONAL CHARACTERISTICS

The Constitution grants an impressive array of powers to Congress, and yet its actions on the environment also reflect its dualistic nature as a political institution. It serves, of course, as the national lawmaking body, and in that capacity it is widely considered by students of legislative politics to be the most powerful legislature in the world at a time when the executive dominates policy making and implementation in most nations (Davidson, Oleszek, and Lee 2012).

Yet Congress is simultaneously a representative assembly whose elected officials seek to reflect the views and demands of politically disparate House districts and states. Not surprisingly, members seek to represent local and regional concerns and interests as they act on national policy, and this can put them at odds with the president or their own party leaders. Indeed, as students of congressional politics have observed for decades, members of Congress have powerful electoral incentives that induce them to think as much about local and regional impacts of environmental policies (particularly short-term and highly visible impacts such as job losses and other costs linked to regulation) as they do about the larger national interest (Davidson, Oleszek, and Lee 2012; Jacobson 2009; Mayhew 1974).

These kinds of political pressures led members in the early 2000s to drive up the cost of President George W. Bush's energy proposals with what one journalist called an "abundance of pet projects, subsidies and tax breaks" to specific industries in their districts and states. Much the same occurred with congressional approval of the Energy Policy Act of 2005, where one journalist referred to its provisions as "spectacular giveaways" in tax credits and other subsidies to energy producers such as the oil and gas industry (Kraft 2011, 175–176; Oppenheimer 2012). This overwhelming concern with local and state impacts of national policy, especially short-term impacts, is also a prime reason why Congress has been unable to approve national climate change policy (see chapter 8 in this volume).

Another distinctive institutional characteristic concerns the structure of decision making within Congress, particularly reliance on an elaborate system of House and Senate standing committees, where most policy decisions take place. Congress has long operated with such a committee system to divide the workload and promote specialization among its members, particularly in the House (Davidson, Oleszek, and Lee 2012). Yet the committee system sometimes seems to defy organizational logic and it has proven to be intensely resistant to reform. One key result of this system is that Congress relies on dozens of committees and subcommittees for environmental and natural resource policies, with overlapping jurisdictions and periodic battles over committees' legislative authority (Kenski and Kenski 1981; Kraft 2011, 2013). Occasionally, the House Speaker and other party leaders may cajole the committee leaders to push the party agenda through the House, as Speaker Newt Gingrich did in the mid-1990s. But more often than not the committees continue to operate with considerable autonomy (Aldrich and Rohde 2009; Pearson and Schickler 2009).

The outcomes of specific legislative battles may turn on which members sit on and control particular committees, and the extent to which they respond to organized constituencies. Historically, for example, committees dealing with natural resource issues have attracted members with narrow district or state interests in public lands, energy exploration and extraction, agriculture, mining, ranching, and forestry, among other concerns, contributing to the classic description of natural resource subgovernments. In such cases, members are said to work cooperatively with agency officials and key external constituency groups (e.g., the oil and natural gas industry) to shape policy decisions, typically far out of the public eye (Clarke and McCool 1996; McConnell 1966; McCool 1990; McCurdy 1990; Murphy 1974). Critics assert that these patterns help to explain why natural resource policies so often benefit such narrow constituencies rather than a larger public interest, and why some of the policies, such as the Mining Law of 1872, have been so difficult to reform (Lowry 2006; Kraft and Kamieniecki 2007a; Vig and Kraft 2013).

Taken together, these congressional characteristics have important implications for environmental policy. First, building policy consensus in Congress is rarely easy because of the diversity of members and interests whose concerns need to be met and the conflicts that can arise among committees and leaders, between the majority and minority party, or between the House and Senate. Hence legislative gridlock is common (Binder 2003; Kraft 2013), and when policy change does come, it is often piecemeal and incremental, and with a carefully crafted mix of substantive and symbolic actions in an effort to satisfy diverse constituents and groups.

Second, policy compromises invariably reflect members' preoccupation with local and regional impacts of environmental decisions, and their assessment of short-term economic and political consequences, such as how climate change policy will affect businesses, energy use, and homeowners in their states and districts. Such congressional policy appraisals often differ from those of the president and White House staff, environmental policy advocates, and the scientific community, all of whom tend to emphasize longer-term, more comprehensive, and national perspectives on the problems. These kinds of legislative perspectives can create significant institutional barriers to acting on third-generation environmental and resource challenges such as climate change and loss of biodiversity.

Third, White House leadership matters a great deal in agenda setting and formulation—for example, in how the issues are defined or framed and the way in which the president and Congress cooperate in trying to make policy decisions acceptable to the pertinent interests. Yet the president's influence is limited by the highly independent political calculations members make on Capitol Hill as well as the pervasive partisan disputes that affect so many policy decisions today. Reviews of recent presidential actions on environmental policy underscore the imperative of securing Congress's approval to make much headway, and the difficulty of gaining that congressional support (Bryner 1995; Daynes and Sussman 2010; Soden 1999; Vig 2013).

The rest of this chapter is devoted to a selected review of major topics in the study of Congress and environmental policy and some of the key research needs in this area, with special attention to patterns of institutional behavior and policy making and the capacity of Congress and its members to engage in effective policy action in the decades ahead in light of widespread concern over its seeming inability to address both persistent flaws in U.S. environmental policy as well as mounting challenges presented by third-generation environmental issues such as climate change.

3. CAMPAIGNS, ELECTIONS, AND REPRESENTATION

As a representative legislature, Congress's action on environmental policy reflects the views of its 535 voting members, who in turn are strongly motivated to attend to electoral incentives. The short (two-year) term of House members makes them particularly sensitive to electoral forces, including general public opinion and the perspectives and political clout of key constituencies and interest groups, especially those whose political and financial support may be instrumental in their success at the polls. For example, Republicans may depend on the support of business groups, agricultural interests, and energy producers more than Democrats do, and Democrats are eager to have the support of environmental advocacy organizations that only rarely support Republicans. Democrats from energy-producing regions of the nation, however (e.g., West Virginia, Louisiana, and Texas), are equally interested in the support of the energy industry and its employees. There is a well-developed literature on congressional campaigns and elections, representation, and voting behavior, most of which applies to the politics of environmental policy in Congress (e.g., Davidson, Oleszek, and Lee 2012; Erikson and Wright 2009; Jacobson 2009; Kingdon 1989; Mayhew 1974).

Amy Below's chapter in this volume (chapter 24) reviews much of what we know about differences between the two parties in voting behavior and other electoral issues, as do previous reviews of literature on partisan and ideological differences that have long been evident in studies of roll-call voting in Congress and state legislatures (Dunlap, Xiao, and McCright 2001; Kamieniecki 1995). As Shipan and Lowry (2001) show so well in their study of partisan differences in Congress as measured by League of Conservation Voters scores, the two parties have diverged increasingly over time in member voting on environmental issues, a trend that appears to have continued since they conducted their study.[6] Looking at a wider set of issues in a roll-call voting analysis that is nonetheless instructive, McCarty, Poole, and Rosenthal (2006) report that ideological differences between the parties in Congress are at the highest level in some 120 years, chiefly because Republican members have moved so far to the right (see also Davidson, Oleszek, and Lee 2012, chap. 9). One major reason for this trend of ideological polarization, especially in the House, is that most congressional districts are now heavily Democratic or Republican rather than closely divided between the two parties.

Even though public opinion has generally favored environmental policy actions (Dunlap 1995; Guber 2003; and chapter 21 in this volume), much depends on the saliency of the issue, how the public appraises the consequences, and the relative success of environmental groups and their opponents in framing the issues and shaping public views of them. For a variety of reasons, the public today is less strongly favorable toward environmental policy actions than previously the

---

6. League of Conservation Voters (LCV) roll-call voting scores have been available since 1970s, but as the case with other group scorecards for members of Congress, their use in research is not without complications, as most scholars acknowledge. Still, given the period of time over which the group has selected issues for scoring, it is a unique and valuable source of information on member voting on environmental issues. Other databases that could prove useful include the American National Election Studies, campaign finance records available from the Federal Election Commission, and committee voting records.

case. Moreover, the public's position on the issues has less to do with the scientific facts and more to how the issues are framed. Members of Congress in both political parties are well attuned to the need to use framing language to garner support for their initiatives, evident, for example, when Republicans characterize environmental regulation as "job killing" and Democrats try to link energy and climate change legislation to "security" concerns (chapters 20 and 23 in this volume; Layzer 2007).

When issues are not salient for the general public, members of Congress tend to look to more specialized constituencies, such as organized interest groups, or to their own policy preferences, for clues on how to vote (Kingdon 1989). As Richard Fenno (1978) has aptly observed, there is not one constituency for members of Congress but rather several that overlap as concentric circles: the geographical constituency that is the district (or state), the reelection constituency that is supportive during campaigns and elections, the primary constituency of strongest supporters, and finally, the personal constituency of key individuals with whom the members maintains close contact. In much the same way, many election analysts also distinguish the general public or even the party supporters from the attentive public or the "core" constituencies within each party. Core constituents are much more likely to hold strong views on the issues like environmental policy and are more likely to vote in both primary and general elections.

In a related vein, Sarah Anderson (2011) studied "complex constituencies" for members of Congress to measure the degree to which organized environmental groups in House districts in two Congresses (the 105th and 109th) influenced member voting. By measuring environmental group membership in the district as a "subconstituency," she was able to show a strong link exists between the strength of environmental groups in House districts and member voting. Members of the House representing districts with more environmental group members were more likely to vote in a pro-environmental manner than their colleagues. Both Democrats and Republicans were equally responsive to this special constituency interest.

One similar line of research analyzes campaign promises on environmental and other issues, and the likelihood that members vote and otherwise act in accordance with such promises once in office. Tracy Sulkin (2009) finds that they do so on a range of issues, and rather than relying on the traditional measure of roll-call voting, she looks to the many other kinds of activities in which members engage, particularly agenda setting, such as introducing or cosponsoring resolutions or legislation as an indicator of how members choose to spend their time once in office. In a parallel effort that focuses on environmental issues, Ringquist and Dasse (2004, 417) find that members of Congress do vote in a way that is consistent with campaign promises they made, although they also find that Republicans are "far more likely to break their campaign promises," and that pro-environmental campaign promises are more likely to be broken than others are (ibid.). The explanation for such findings is likely found in the need for Republicans to express support for popular environmental policy activities (e.g., government regulations to keep the air and water clean) even though philosophically they are inclined to support deregulatory legislation. In short, it is politically imperative to campaign in favor of the environment, but also easy to break such promises after the election because the issues are rarely salient to voters.

Scholars also have devoted much effort to understanding the influence of organized interest groups on environmental policy (see chapter 23 in this volume and Ingram, Colnic, and Mann 1995). At least some of these studies focus on group influence within Congress, and they speak to the kinds of research methods that are appropriate for what has long been a difficult subject to study. We have studies of the activities in which groups engage, including lobbying members of Congress, and we have a great deal of case study research that addresses what groups try to do and how successful they are at getting their way. Kraft and Kamieniecki (2007a) survey both the general literature on group influence and research that deals directly with the influence of business on environmental policy, and offer a number of suggestions for fruitful research in the future, as Kamieniecki does in *Corporate America and Environmental Policy* (2006). Several chapters in *Business and Environmental Policy* (Kraft and Kamieniecki 2007b) explore the role of business groups in lobbying Congress, in part through studies of issue framing and agenda setting on climate change (Layzer 2007) and in part through an assessment of lobbying efforts and their effects over time in the case of the Clean Air Act (Bryner 2007).

These and similar studies acknowledge the phenomenal growth of interest groups and lobbying activities in Washington since the 1960s (Berry and Wilcox 2009). While public interest groups, including environmental organizations, have grown in number and have attracted hundreds of thousands of members, generally they are less well endowed financially than business groups (Baumgartner and Jones 1993, 189; Bosso 2005; Duffy 2003). It is no surprise, therefore, that studies of group influence in Congress often point to the dominance of business interests in policy making (Clauson, Neustadt, and Weller 1998; Hacker and Pierson 2010; Kraft and Kamieniecki 2007a; Maisel and Berry 2011; Schlozman and Tierney 1986). Although business clearly does not always gets its way (e.g., Smith 2000), it can be particularly influential when the issues are low in saliency, media coverage is minimal, and lawmakers are unlikely to hear much from the general public (Kraft and Kamieniecki 2007b).

Business groups may be especially influential when the Republican Party controls one or both houses of Congress. As discussed earlier, for example, Republicans in the House in 2011 frequently sought to constrain the EPA's regulatory activities, citing the negative impact of regulations on business and job creation. Some business groups, including the U.S. Chamber of Commerce and the fossil fuels industry, have been especially active in lobbying against cap-and-trade proposals and regulatory action on climate change (Layzer 2007; Rabe 2010). The access of business groups, such as energy producers and chemical companies, to members of Congress can be explained in part by their capacity to contribute substantial funds to reelection campaigns of members, and in part by their level of staffing, access to members, and other advantages that enable them to make their case on Capitol Hill very effectively.

In light of these apparent advantages, further studies of how business and other interest groups lobby members of Congress would be of great interest. For example, how much money do the groups contribute to congressional election campaigns? Which ones have contributed the most? How do the contributions by business groups compare to those by environmental organizations that have been heavily involved in election campaigns, such as the League of Conservation Voters and the Sierra Club? While we have many anecdotal accounts and case studies of interest group lobbying as well as of their involvement in campaigns, a more systematic and nuanced accounting of group activities could address many of the questions about business and environmental group influence that remain unanswered.[7]

4. Congressional Structure and Environmental Policy

As discussed earlier, the way in which Congress organizes itself has important implications for its decisions on environmental policy. This is particularly the case with the committee system and political party leadership, which have been the objects of intensive scholarly interest for years (Davidson, Oleszek, and Lee 2012; Deering and Smith 1997; Fenno 1973), including most recently the unusual ways in which policy making takes place through creative use of special procedures despite the many obstacles to decision making presented by the structure of Congress and the usual rules and procedures that must be followed (Sinclair 2011).

4.1 The Committee System and Party Leaders

The committee system that lies at the heart of congressional policy making contributes to the dispersion of power in the House and Senate, and often to a fragmented or piecemeal approach to public policy, an outcome that often is said to fall short of the need for integrated or holistic policy. Environmental policy is no exception (e.g., Ingram and Mann 1983; Mann 1986; Ophuls and Boyan 1992). Yet some scholars have argued that there are also many virtues in a congressional system of dispersed power, among them the increased opportunities for committees and subcommittees to engage in agenda-setting activities and oversight of administrative agencies; such a decentralized or pluralistic system also creates additional

---

7. As one example, Baumgartner et al.'s *Lobbying and Policy Change* (2009) offer a data-rich study of lobbying and policy change in Congress that relies on extensive interviews with lobbyists as well as publicly available information such as lobbying disclosure reports and sets high standards for future research.

venues for the representation of constituencies that otherwise might not find a ready acceptance on Capitol Hill (Davidson 1981; Ingram and Ullery 1980; Kenski and Kenski 1981; Kingdon 1995).

In light of the contemporary role of committees in shaping environmental policy, additional research on their activities would be welcome. Although committee jurisdiction over environmental policy is widely shared, several committees in each house of Congress play a dominant role (e.g., Energy and Commerce, and Natural Resources in the House and Energy and Natural Resources and Environment and Public Works in the Senate). Studies of one or more of these committees could illuminate how they operate. How are major environmental issues acted on by the committees, and with what involvement by the committee staff, party leaders, informal congressional caucuses, or outside interest groups? What makes the most difference in the policies adopted or the oversight investigations the committees choose to undertake? One interesting question is what conditions lead the parties to cooperate on environmental policy (even if rare today), and what conditions tend to foster further polarization and gridlock? In particular, what might be done through the committees (or the party leadership) to encourage the conduct and use of policy analysis by committee and legislative support agency staff, especially studies that might encourage members to give more attention to long-term national and global environmental problems and the need for an integrated approach to sustainable development (see chapter 9)?

Only a few scholars have carefully studied how policy analysis and science are viewed and used by members of the committees (Ascher, Steelman, and Healy 2010; Bryner 1992, 1995; Keller 2009; Whiteman 1985, 1995), but well-crafted case studies of policy making could shed light on the way the committees and party leadership tackle environmental issues and the extent to which studies by the National Academy of Sciences or other scientific bodies make a difference. One case that comes to mind is the successful effort by the House to enact climate change legislation, the American Clean Energy and Security Act of 2009, even though the Senate later declined to take up similar legislation despite strong White House backing for it. Other recent cases include the Energy Policy Act of 2005 and the Energy Independence and Security Act of 2007, both of which involved sharp partisan and regional splits among members and extensive lobbying by the energy industry and environmental groups but which nevertheless were approved (Kraft 2011; Oppenheimer 2012).

Other major legislative actions of special interest because of unusual bipartisan cooperation in their approval include the Clean Air Act Amendments of 1990 (see Bryner 1995, 2007), the Safe Drinking Water Act Amendments of 1996, the Food Quality Protection Act of 1996, the Healthy Forests Restoration Act of 2003, and the Omnibus Public Lands Management Act of 2009. It also would be interesting after 40-plus years to revisit congressional consideration of the landmark legislation of the 1960s and 1970s (e.g., the National Environmental Policy Act of 1969, the Clean Air Act Amendments of 1970, the Clean Water Act of 1972, and the Endangered Species Act of 1973) to ask similar questions about how these far-reaching policies were formulated and adopted at that time. Recent studies of the impact of business groups on environmental policy making point to how such research on congressional decision making might be framed and conducted (Kamieniecki 2006; Kraft and Kamieniecki 2007b).

4.2. The Role of Technical Support Agencies and Policy Analysis

Despite a very large research literature on Congress, we have very few studies of the legislative support agencies, in particular, the CRS, CBO, and GAO, and in earlier years, the OTA (e.g., Bryner 1992). The support staffs contribute in many ways to the policy-making process, but the nature of their relationship to the committees and key policy makers could be clearer. For example, how are studies requested of the GAO or CRS, and how are they used once they are completed and delivered to members of Congress? How do CBO analyses of budgetary issues (Joyce 2011) help to inform member policy choices? These are a subset of the fascinating question of how knowledge or science affects policy decisions (Ascher, Steelman, and Healy 2010; Keller 2009). Does this unique congressional capacity for policy analysis and evaluation make much difference in environmental policy making, and if so, how?

As Gary Bryner noted in his collection of studies on the OTA, the challenge confronting policy makers "was clearly not a lack of information." The question is what kinds of information members of Congress find to be most useful—concise, timely, trustworthy, related to specific policy alternatives, and economically and politically realistic (Bryner 1992, 229). Much of the information provided by technical studies of environmental problems often fails to meet such expectations, and it is also very likely to be filtered by political and ideological values, as has been the case, for example, with climate science. In one of the systematic studies of how OTA reports were used by congressional committees, David Whiteman found that "strategic" use of the reports was the most common. This is where analytic information is used in a "supportive capacity," such as when it reinforces existing positions or is used to advocate them (Whiteman 1985) to reinforce and advocate existing positions. Yet Whiteman also found evidence of what he called "substantive" use (where no previous policy commitment had been made) as well as of "elaborative" use (where the information is used to extend or refine previously established policy positions).

The legislative support agencies might well be more important in the future as a source of information and analysis that could allow members to deal with complex and sometimes conflicting scientific information, for example, on climate change, biodiversity loss, the promise of new energy technologies, the health effects of toxic chemicals, or the costs of policy action in a variety of areas. In light of the imposing nature of third-generation environmental issues, does Congress have sufficient capacity to study the problems and consider policy responses to them? What else might be needed to do so?

Although they receive considerably less attention by scholars, the informal legislative caucuses that have proliferated in recent decades merit study as well (Hammond 1998). To illustrate, there have been caucuses on topics as diverse as electronic waste (e-waste), biofuels, passenger rail, sustainable energy and the environment, international conservation, forests, coastal issues, agricultural energy use, climate change, coal, green jobs, peak oil, and children's environmental health, among others. What do these caucuses do, and what impact do they have on agenda setting and policy making? What role do they play in policy innovation or in building advocacy coalitions for policy change?

Similarly, it would be useful to know more about the way agency or White House assessments (e.g., by the Office of Management and Budget, Council on Environmental Quality, or the Office of Information and Regulatory Affairs) are used on Capitol Hill. Formal environmental program evaluations are somewhat rare, and studies of their impact on policy making are equally unusual, and yet we know much about the general factors that shape the use of such studies (Knapp and Kim 1998; Susskind, Jain, and Martyniuk 2001). They may become more important for members of Congress in the future as they try to determine where to invest scarce budgetary dollars.

4.3. Committee Oversight of Administrative Agencies

Among the most important activities of congressional committees are the conduct of oversight investigations that seek to learn how well authorized programs are working and what effects they have produced. Congressional oversight is commonly listed among the key functions of the modern Congress, and it is closely linked to Congress's role in policy implementation. Yet students of the legislative process nearly always conclude that it is both less frequent than might be expected and less rigorous than desirable. The reasons have much to do with insufficient incentives for members to take oversight seriously in comparison to the rewards that accompany less demanding but more politically rewarding actions, such as taking positions on issues, taking credit for particular benefits conveyed to the state or district, and advertising oneself in various media venues (Mayhew 1974). As Joel Aberbach (1990) concluded, oversight is likely to increase under conditions of divided government (split partisan control of the presidency and at least one house of Congress), when Congress needs to respond to outside groups to which the White House has been insufficiently responsive, when Congress seeks to protect favored agencies, when staff resources are available, and when there is publicity over and evidence of malfeasance in the agencies. A recent example of the last condition occurred when lawmakers questioned Interior Department supervision of offshore oil drilling following the massive Deepwater Horizon oil spill in the Gulf of Mexico in 2010.

Oversight can be a time-consuming and difficult process, and not surprisingly members and committees tend to engage in the activity when the anticipated rewards are high, as Aberbach suggested. Students of congressional oversight also distinguish between different qualities of oversight, particularly"fire alarm" oversight, where committees seek to respond opportunistically to a particular event or decision that will draw the media to a hearing (such as the Obama administration clean energy investments discussed earlier), and "police patrol" oversight, which would be more frequent, direct, regular, and systematic. Fire alarm oversight is far more common than police patrol oversight because it is politically rewarding but involves a minimum investment of time and resources (Aberbach 1990; Davidson, Oleszek, and Lee 2012; Foreman 1988).

A classic example of Congress responding to a prominent set of events took place in the early 1980s, when the Reagan administration EPA came under frequent media scrutiny. Between May 1981 (when she was confirmed) and December 1982, the EPA administrator Anne Burford testified 15 times before congressional committees. In all, EPA officials appeared more than 70 times before congressional committees between October 1981 and July 1982 (Cook and Davidson 1985). Comparing the 96th Congress (1979–1980) and the 97th Congress (1981–1982), Cook and Davidson (1985) found that the House Agriculture, Energy and Commerce, and Interior Committees all significantly increased their oversight, as did the Senate Environment and Public Works Committee.

Baumgartner and Jones (1993) found a similar increase in committee oversight of the nuclear energy industry as the issues rose in saliency in the 1970s, and a dramatic shift took place, reflecting increasing public skepticism toward nuclear energy. Between 1945 and 1987, Baumgartner and Jones identified 1,237 hearings in Congress on civilian nuclear power and coded them as positive, negative, or neutral in tone. The early years told a tale of a nuclear subgovernment, with a small number of committees examining the subject, few hearings held, and a very positive stance on nuclear power. By the 1970s, however, the picture changed significantly. By that time congressional committees competed with one another to put the industry's feet to the fire, and eventually the old nuclear power subgovernment completely disappeared, "as two dozen different committees or subcommittees of the Congress held hearings on some aspect of the civilian nuclear program in a typical year" (Baumgartner and Jones 1993, 74). The consequences for the nuclear industry were distinctly unfavorable, ushering in a prolonged era of decline as no new power plants were proposed. Only by the late 2000s did the industry resume interest in promoting new U.S. plants as concern over the nation's dependence on fossil fuels and climate change sparked a modest rebound in its fortunes.

Similarly, in one of the most thorough studies of such activities, James Thurber (1991) examined congressional oversight of the Department of Energy's high-level nuclear waste disposal and environmental restoration programs, including analysis of over 800 congressional hearings and other documents. He concluded that Congress's oversight ranged from "benign neglect" to "micromanagement," but that typically it involved mutual cooperation and comanagement of program implementation.[8] That pattern likely applies to many other subject areas as well.

5. Congressional Relationships with the Presidency and the Courts

Other chapters in this volume examine in detail the role of the presidency (chapter 14) and the courts (chapter 12). Both speak to the relationship of Congress to the presidency and the court system. As noted earlier, Congress has the constitutional authority to cooperate with or to compete with the president in policy making. The latter is an increasingly common pattern under divided government that leads many commentators within the discipline and outside of it to describe a "dysfunctional" Congress mired in partisan gridlock and seemingly incapable of dealing with environmental policy and many other contemporary challenges (Klyza and Sousa 2008; Loomis 2012; Mann and Ornstein 2006).

There is little question that Congress jealously guards and frequently uses its legislative oversight and budgetary authority to compete with the White House, even when the two branches are controlled by the same party. The level of competition and distrust can increase markedly under conditions of divided government, particularly in light of the contemporary partisan disagreements over the size and role of government and federal spending, and the extent of regulation, all of which are common points of contention in environmental policy.

Although less well appreciated, Congress also has considerable authority to shape the court system through the Senate's role in considering nominations to the federal bench and through its ability to rewrite environmental laws to respond to judicial decisions with which it disagrees. For example, following the Supreme Court's decision in *Massachusetts v. EPA* (2007) on the power of the EPA to regulate greenhouse gases under authority granted by the Clean Air Act, House Republicans on the Energy and Commerce Committee sought in early 2011 to rewrite the act to negate the Court's ruling. The committee's bill, the Energy Tax Prevention Act, sought to exclude greenhouse gases from being characterized as pollutants under the language of the Clean Air Act. As a reminder of the authority of Congress to

---

8. As Thurber's study and the others highlighted here make clear, there are invaluable data sources for such analysis, including verbatim transcripts of all congressional hearings accessible online via the Lexis-Nexis congressional database (available through most university libraries) and the elaborate database that Baumgartner and Jones have established for analysis of agenda setting in an "ambitious attempt to provide truly comparable measures of policy changes in the United States since the Second World War." See the Policy Agendas Project's website: www.policyagendas.org, from which the quotation is taken.

take this approach, one member of the committee, Rep. Ed Whitfield (R-KY), said such action would "properly reassert Congress' authority" over climate change issues (Hogue 2011). In April 2011 the House voted 255 to 172, largely along party lines, to approve the bill, although it had little chance of becoming law (Broder 2011a).

There is a substantial political science literature on the relationship between the White House and Congress, and a smaller though important one on the nature of this relationship with respect to environmental issues (Binder and Maltzman 2009; Daynes and Sussman 2010; Vig 2013; chapter 14 in this volume). That relationship is explored in many studies of environmental policy making, such as analysis of clean air politics (Bryner 1995, 2007; Jones 1975), pesticide regulation (Bosso 1987), energy (Kraft 1981, 1992; Oppenheimer 2012), and population policy (Kraft 1994), among others.

Much of this literature adopts a case study approach to both describe and explain the nature of presidential-congressional relationships, although at least some of the research has been guided by rich theoretical frameworks such as agenda-setting theory, including punctuated equilibrium and multiple streams models (Baumgartner and Jones 1993; Kingdon 1995) and advocacy coalition theory (Sabatier 2007; Sabatier and Jenkins-Smith 1993). Some of the best research on policy formulation and adoption has not made explicit use of such theories and yet has yielded valuable insights into the factors that shape environmental policy formulation, adoption, and implementation. For example, Charles Jones's early account of the formation of clean air policy in *Clean Air* (1975) is particularly notable for its careful assessment of the congressional role in the policy process and its emphasis on congressional incentives for taking action in response to new public demands for a dramatic "escalation" in clear air policy that deviated markedly from the norm of incremental policy making. Ultimately, Jones faulted Congress's "speculative augmentation" in air quality policy for creating what he termed "policy beyond capability," that is, policy that could not be easily implemented.

In what direction should research head? As highlighted throughout this chapter, there is no shortage of interesting and pertinent topics to investigate. In light of the overall purpose of this volume and the current state of affairs in U.S. environmental policy, however, more research could be directed to the seeming limited capacity of Congress to work with the White House to fashion a more comprehensive and coordinated approach to environmental challenges that is of central concern in the era of sustainability (Mazmanian and Kraft 2009; chapter 9 in this volume). What are the fundamental obstacles to such cooperation, and what conditions need to be met to overcome them?

6. CONCLUSIONS

We know much about how Congress acts on public policy, including environmental policy. As the literature reviewed in this chapter makes clear, however, a number of important questions remain unanswered and could be the focus of future research. Beyond what has been suggested throughout the chapter, it would be useful to build on what has been studied previously to further refine our understanding of congressional processes, and to take on some of the more challenging topics of how the U.S. political system, and Congress in particular, can adapt to twenty-first-century needs for environmental policy. As many students of American politics have argued in recent years, incremental and modest changes in existing policy will not suffice at a time when the nation and world need to make more significant progress in designing effective and politically acceptable paths toward sustainability (Mazmanian and Kraft 2009). There are no simple solutions, but Congress clearly will play a major role in searching for and legitimizing solutions through the legislative process.

In light of those overarching needs, new research that can speak to congressional capacity to act on important environmental challenges, such as climate change, and how that capacity might be strengthened, would be particularly of value. As noted at the beginning of the chapter, Congress is unique among national legislatures in the world. It remains a strong, well-equipped, and highly independent legislature that is well positioned to study and prepare for action on a wide range of contemporary environmental problems. Yet too often it falls victim to ideological and partisan bickering and limits itself to reactive policy making that meets short-term political needs at the expense of long-term problem solving.

From this perspective, Congress needs to be much more proactive in addressing emerging environmental problems and to find a way to resolve its partisan differences. The public seems to agree on that score. As many recent surveys have indicated, there is little trust or confidence in Congress and its members today, with pollsters finding record low approval ratings (Cohen 2011; Zeleny and Thee-Brenan 2011). Moreover, what the public has long found particularly disturbing is the seeming inability of Congress to act sensibly to solve public problems. This pattern has been evident for well over a decade (e.g., Hibbing and Theiss-Morse 1995, 2002), and in light of continued partisan gridlock in Congress, there is little reason to expect a change in the public's assessment of Congress anytime soon. Members of Congress would be wise to take notice of the public's disapproval of their work and to search for viable ways for the two parties to work together to chart a more productive path to the future.

REFERENCES

Aberbach, J. D. 1990. *Keeping a Watchful Eye: The Politics of Congressional Oversight.* Washington, DC: Brookings Institution Press.

Aldrich, J. H., and D. W. Rohde. 2009. "Congressional Committees in a Continuing Partisan Era." In *Congress Reconsidered*, 9th ed., ed. L. C. Dodd and B. I. Oppenheimer, 217–240. Washington, DC: CQ Press.

Anderson, S. A. 2011. "Complex Constituencies: Intense Environmentalists and Representation." *Environmental Politics* 20 (4): 547–565.

Andrews, R. N. L. 2006. *Managing the Environment, Managing Ourselves: A History of American Environmental Policy*, 2nd ed. New Haven, CT: Yale University Press.

Appelbaum, B. 2011. "Nominees at Standstill as G.O.P. Flexes Its Muscle." *New York Times*, June 19.

Ascher, W., T. Steelman, and R. Healy. 2010. *Knowledge and Environmental Policy: Re-Imagining the Boundaries of Science and Politics.* Cambridge, MA: MIT Press.

Baumgartner, F. R., J. M. Berry, M. Hojnacki, D. C. Kimball, and B. L. Leach. 2009. *Lobbying and Policy Change: Who Wins, Who Loses, and Why.* Chicago: University of Chicago Press.

Baumgartner, F. R., and B. D. Jones. 1993. *Agendas and Instability in American Politics.* Chicago: University of Chicago Press.

Berry, J. M., and C. Wilcox. 2009. *The Interest Group Society.* 5th ed. New York: Longman.

Binder, S. A. 2003. *Stalemate: Causes and Consequences of Legislative Gridlock.* Washington, DC: Brookings Institution Press.

Binder, S. A., and F. Maltzman. 2009. "The Politics of Advice and Consent: Putting Judges on the Federal Bench." In *Congress Reconsidered*, 9th ed., ed. L. C. Dodd and B. I. Oppenheimer, 241–261. Washington, DC: CQ Press.

Bosso, C. J. 1987. *Pesticides and Politics: The Life Cycle of a Public Issue.* Pittsburgh: University of Pittsburgh Press.

———. 2005. *Environment, Inc.: From Grassroots to Beltway.* Lawrence: University Press of Kansas.

Broder, J. M. 2011a. "House Votes to Bar E.P.A. from Regulating Industrial Emissions." *New York Times*, April 7.

———. 2011b. "Bashing E.P.A. Is New Theme in G.O.P. Race." *New York Times*, August 17.

Broder, J. M., and K. Galbraith. 2011. "For Perry, the E.P.A. Has Long Been a Favorite Target." *New York Times*, September 29.

Bryner, G. C. 1992. *Science, Technology, and Politics: Policy Analysis in Congress.* Boulder, CO: Westview.

———. 1995. *Blue Skies, Green Politics: The Clean Air Act of 1990.* 2nd ed. Washington, DC: CQ Press.

———. 2007. "Congress and Clean Air." In *Business and Environmental Policy: Corporate Interests in the American Political System*, ed. M. E. Kraft and S. Kamieniecki, 127–151. Cambridge, MA: MIT Press.

Carson, J. L., ed. 2012. *New Directions in Congressional Politics.* New York: Routledge.

Clarke, J. N., and D. McCool. 1996. *Taking Out the Terrain: Power and Performance among Natural Resource Agencies*, 2nd ed. Albany: State University of New York Press.

Clauson, D., A. Neustadt, and M. Weller. 1998. *Dollars and Votes: How Business Campaign Contributions Subvert Democracy.* Philadelphia: Temple University Press.

Cohen, J. 2011. "Poll: Majority of Public Has Lost Faith in Government Ability to Fix Economy." *Washington Post*, August 10.

Cook, M. E., and R. H. Davidson. 1985. "Deferral Politics: Congressional Decision Making on Environmental Issues in the 1980s." In *Public Policy and the Natural Environment*, ed. H. M. Ingram and R. K. Godwin. Greenwich, CT: JAI Press.

Cooley, R. A., and G. Wandesforde-Smith, eds. 1970. *Congress and the Environment.* Seattle: University of Washington Press.

Davidson, R. H. 1981. "Subcommittee Government: New Channels for Policy Making." In *The New Congress*, ed. T. E. Mann and N. J. Ornstein. Washington, DC: American Enterprise Institute.

Davidson, R. H., W. J. Oleszek, and F. Lee. 2012. *Congress and Its Members*. 13th ed. Washington, DC: CQ Press.

Davies, J. C., and B. S. Davies. 1975. *The Politics of Pollution*. 2nd ed. Indianapolis: Bobbs-Merrill.

Daynes, B. and Sussman, G. 2010. *White House Politics and the Environment: Franklin D. Roosevelt to George W. Bush*. College Station: Texas A&M University Press.

Deering, C. P., and S. S. Smith. 1997. *Congressmen in Committees*. Washington, DC: CQ Press.

Dodd, L.C., and B. I. Oppenheimer, eds. 2009. *Congress Reconsidered*. 9th ed. Washington, DC: CQ Press.

Duffy, R. J. 2003. *The Green Agenda in American Politics: New Strategies for the Twenty-First Century*. Lawrence: University of Kansas Press.

Dunlap, R. E. 1995. "Public Opinion and Environmental Policy." In *Environmental Politics and Policy: Theories and Evidence*, 2nd ed., ed. J. P. Lester, 63–114. Durham, NC: Duke University Press.

Dunlap, R. E., C. Xiao, and A. M. McCright. 2001. "Politics and Environment in America: Partisan and Ideological Cleavages in Public Support for Environmentalism." *Environmental Politics* 10(4): 23–48.

Eisner, M. A. 2007. *Governing the Environment: The Transformation of Environmental Regulation*. Boulder, CO: Lynne Rienner.

Erikson, R. S., and G. C. Wright. 2009. "Voters, Candidates, and Issues in Congressional Elections." In *Congress Reconsidered*, 9th ed., ed. L. C. Dodd and B. I. Oppenheimer, 71–95. Washington, DC: CQ Press.

Fenno, R. F., Jr. 1973. *Congressmen in Committees*. Boston: Little, Brown.

———. 1978. *Home Style: House Members in Their Districts*. Boston: Little, Brown.

Fiorino, D. J. 2006. *The New Environmental Regulation*. Cambridge, MA: MIT Press.

Foreman, C. H., Jr. 1988. *Signals from the Hill: Congressional Oversight and the Challenge of Social Regulation*. New Haven, CT: Yale University Press.

Guber, D. L. 2003. *The Grassroots of a Green Revolution: Polling American on the Environment*. Cambridge, MA: MIT Press.

Guber, D. L., and C. J. Bosso. 2007. "Framing ANWR: Citizens, Consumers, and the Privileged Position of Business." In *Business and Environmental Policy: Corporate Interests in the American Political System*, ed. M. E. Kraft and S. Kamieniecki, 35–39. Cambridge, MA: MIT Press.

Hacker, J. S., and P. Pierson. 2010. *Winner-Take-All Politics: How Washington Made the Rich Richer—and Turned Its Back on the Middle Class*. New York: Simon and Schuster.

Hammond, S. W. 1998. *Congressional Caucuses in National Policymaking*. Baltimore: Johns Hopkins University Press.

Hibbing, J. R., and E. Theiss-Morse. 1995. *Congress as Public Enemy: Public Attitudes toward American Political Institutions*. New York: Cambridge University Press.

———. 2002. *Stealth Democracy: Americans' Beliefs about How Government Should Work*. New York: Cambridge University Press.

Hogue, C. 2011. "Congress: Draft Bill Would Take Away Agency's Authority to Regulate Greenhouse Gases." *Chemical and Engineering News* 89 (7): 5, February 14.

Ingram, H. M., D. H. Colnic, and D. E. Mann. 1995. "Interest Groups and Environmental Policy." In *Environmental Politics and Policy: Theories and Evidence*, 2nd ed., ed. J. P. Lester, 115–145. Durham, NC: Duke University Press.

Ingram, H. M., and D. E. Mann. 1983. "Environmental Protection Policy." In *Encyclopedia of Policy Studies*, ed. S. Nagel, 687–725. New York: Marcel Dekker.

Ingram, H. M., and S. Ullery. 1980. "Policy Innovation and Institutional Fragmentation." *Policy Studies Journal* 8(5): 664–682.

Jacobson, G.C. 2009. *The Politics of Congressional Elections.* 7th ed. New York: Pearson Longman.

Jones, C. O. 1975. *Clean Air: The Policies and Politics of Pollution Control.* Pittsburgh: University of Pittsburgh Press.

Joyce, P. G. 2011. *The Congressional Budget Office: Honest Numbers, Power, and Policymaking.* Washington, DC: Georgetown University Press.

Kamieniecki, S. 1995. "Political Parties and Environmental Policy." In *Environmental Politics and Policy: Theories and Evidence*, 2nd ed., ed. J. P. Lester, 146–167. Durham, NC: Duke University Press.

———. 2006. *Corporate America and Environmental Policy: How Much Does Business Get Its Way?* Palo Alto, CA: Stanford University Press.

Kaufman, L. 2011. "Republicans Seek Big Cuts in Environmental Rules." *New York Times*, July 27.

Keller, A. C. 2009. *Science in Environmental Policy: The Politics of Objective Advice.* Cambridge, MA: MIT Press.

Kenski, H. C., and M. C. Kenski. 1981. "Partnership, Ideology, and Constituency Differences on Environmental Issues in the U.S. House of Representatives and Senate: 1973–1978." In *Environmental Policy Formation: The Impact of Values, Ideology, and Standards.* Lexington, MA: Lexington Books.

Kingdon, J. W. 1989. *Congressmen's Voting Decisions.* 3rd ed. Ann Arbor: University of Michigan Press.

———. 1995. *Agendas, Alternatives, and Public Policies.* 2nd ed. New York: Longman.

Klyza, C. M., and D. Sousa. 2008. *American Environmental Policy, 1990–2006: Beyond Gridlock.* Cambridge, MA: MIT Press.

Knapp, G. J., and T. J. Kim, eds. 1998. *Environmental Program Evaluation: A Primer.* Champaign: University of Illinois Press.

Kraft, M.E. 1973. "Congressional Attitudes toward the Environment: Attention and Issue Orientation in Ecological Politics." PhD diss., Yale University.

———. 1981. "Congress and National Energy Policy: Assessing the Policymaking Process." In *Environment, Energy, Public Policy*, ed. R. S. Axelrod. Lexington, MA: Lexington Books.

———. 1994. "Population Policy." In *Encyclopedia of Policy Studies*, 2nd ed., ed. S. S. Nagel, 617–642. New York: Marcel Dekker.

———. 1995. "Congress and Environmental Policy." In *Environmental Politics and Policy: Theories and Evidence*, 2nd ed., ed. J. P. Lester, 168–205. Durham, NC: Duke University Press.

———. 2003. "Environmental Policy in Congress: From Consensus to Gridlock." In *Environmental Policy*, 5th ed., ed. N. J. Vig and M. E. Kraft, 1270–150. Washington, DC: CQ Press.

———. 2011. *Environmental Policy and Politics.* 5th ed. New York: Pearson-Longman

———. 2013. "Environmental Policy in Congress." In *Environmental Policy*, 8th ed., ed. N. J. Vig and M. E. Kraft, 109–134. Washington, DC: CQ Press.

Kraft, M. E., and S. Kamieniecki. 2007a. "Analyzing the Role of Business in Environmental Policy." In *Business and Environmental Policy: Corporate Interests in the American Political System*, ed. M. E. Kraft and S. Kamieniecki, 3–31. Cambridge, MA: MIT Press.

———, eds. 2007b. *Business and Environmental Policy: Corporate Interests in the American Political System*. Cambridge, MA: MIT Press.

Layzer, J. A. 2007. "Deep Freeze: How Business Has Shaped the Global Warming Debate in Congress." In *Business and Environmental Policy: Corporate Interests in the American Political System*, ed. M. E. Kraft and S. Kamieniecki, 93–125. Cambridge, MA: MIT Press.

Lazarus, R. J. 2004. *The Making of Environmental Law*. Chicago: University of Chicago Press.

Lipton, E., and J. M. Broder. 2011. "In Rush to Assist Solyndra, U.S. Missed Warning Signs." *New York Times*, September 22.

Loomis, B., ed. 2012. *The U.S. Senate: From Deliberation to Dysfunction*. Washington, DC: CQ Press.

Lowry, W. R. 2006. "A Return to Traditional Priorities in Natural Resource Policies." In *Environmental Policy*, 6th ed., ed. N. J. Vig and M. E. Kraft, 311–332. Washington, DC: CQ Press.

Lubell, M., and B. Segee. 2013. "Conflict and Cooperation in Natural Resource Management." In *Environmental Policy*, 8th ed., ed. N. J. Vig and M. E. Kraft, 185–205. Washington, DC: CQ Press.

Maisel, L. S., and J. M. Berry, eds. 2011. *The Oxford Handbook of American Political Parties and Interest Groups*. New York: Oxford University Press.

Mann, D. E. 1986. "Democratic Politics and Environmental Policy." In *Controversies in Environmental Policy*, ed. S. Kamieniecki, R. O'Brien, and M. Clarke. Albany: State University of New York Press.

Mann, T. E., and N. J. Ornstein. 2006. *The Broken Branch: How Congress Is Failing America and How to Get It Back on Track*. New York: Oxford University Press.

Maron, D. F. 2011. "New Anti-EPA Bill Aims to 'Rein in' Agency's Climate Rules Permanently." *New York Times*, March 4.

Mayhew, D. R. 1974: *Congress: The Electoral Connection*. New Haven, CT: Yale University Press.

Mazmanian, D. A., and M. E. Kraft, eds. 2009. *Toward Sustainable Communities: Transition and Transformations in Environmental Policy*. 2nd ed. Cambridge, MA: MIT Press.

McCarty, N., K. Poole, and H. Rosenthal. 2006. *Polarized America: The Dance of Ideology and Unequal Riches*. Cambridge, MA: MIT Press.

McConnell, G. 1966. *Private Power and American Democracy*. New York: Knopf.

McCool, D. 1990. "Subgovernments as Determinants of Political Viability." *Political Science Quarterly* 105 (Summer): 269–293.

McCurdy, K. M. 1990. "Environmental Legislation as Viewed from Different Committees: A Comparison of Committee Membership and Decisions." Paper presented at the annual meeting of the Midwest Political Science Association, Chicago, IL, April.

Murphy, J. T. 1974. "Political Parties and the Porkbarrel: Party Conflict and Cooperation in House Public Works Committee Decision Making." *American Political Science Review* 68: 169–185.

Ophuls, W., and A. S. Boyan Jr. 1992. *Ecology and the Politics of Scarcity Revisited.* New York: W. H. Freeman.

Oppenheimer, B. I. 2012. "Congress and Energy Policy, 1960–2010." In *The U.S. Senate: From Deliberation to Dysfunction*, ed. B. Loomis. Washington, DC: CQ Press.

Pearson, K., and E. Schickler. 2009. "The Transition to Democratic Leadership in a Polarized House." In *Congress Reconsidered*, 9th ed., ed. L. C. Dodd and B. I. Oppenheimer, 165–188. Washington, DC: CQ Press.

Quirk, P. J., and S. A. Binder, eds. 2005. *The Legislative Branch.* New York: Oxford University Press.

Rabe, B. G. 2010. *Greenhouse Governance: Addressing Climate Change in America.* Washington, DC: Brookings Institution Press.

Raeburn, P. 2006. "A Regulation on Regulations." *Scientific American* 295 (July): 18–19.

Ringquist, E. J., and C. Dasse. 2004. "Lies, Damned Lies, and Campaign Promises? Environmental Legislation in the 105th Congress." *Social Science Quarterly* 85 (June): 400–419.

Rosenbaum, W.A. 2013. "Science, Politics, and Policy at the EPA." In *Environmental Policy*, 8th ed., ed. N. J. Vig and M. E. Kraft, 158–184. Washington, DC: CQ Press.

Sabatier, P.A., ed. 2007. *Theories of the Policy Process.* 2nd ed. Boulder, CO: Westview.

Sabatier, P. A., and H. C. Jenkins-Smith, eds. 1993. *Policy Change and Learning: An Advocacy Coalition Approach.* Boulder, CO: Westview.

Savage, C. 2009. "Democrats Look for Ways to Undo Late Bush-Era Rules by Agencies." *New York Times*, January 2.

Schickler, E., and F. E. Lee, eds. 2011. *The Oxford Handbook of the American Congress.* New York: Oxford University Press.

Schlozman, K. L., and J. T. Tierney. 1986. *Organized Interests and American Democracy.* New York: Harper and Row.

Shipan, C. R., and W. R. Lowry. 2001. "Environmental Policy and Party Divergence in Congress." *Political Research Quarterly* 54 (June): 245–263.

Sinclair, B. 2011. *Unorthodox Lawmaking: New Legislative Processes in the U.S. Congress.* 4th ed. Washington, DC: CQ Press.

Smith, F. E. 1966. *The Politics of Conservation.* New York: Harper and Row.

Smith, M. A. 2000. *American Business and Political Power: Public Opinion, Elections, and Democracy.* Chicago: University of Chicago Press.

Smith, S.S., J. M. Roberts, and R. J. Vander Wielen. 2009. *The American Congress.* 6th ed. New York: Cambridge University Press.

Soden, D., ed. 1999. *The Environmental Presidency.* Albany: State University of New York Press.

Sulkin, T. 2009. "Promises Made and Promises Kept." In *Congress Reconsidered*, 9th ed., ed. L. C. Dodd and B. I. Oppenheimer, 119–139. Washington, DC: CQ Press.

Susskind, L., R. K. Jain, and A. O. Martyniuk. 2001. *Better Environmental Policy Studies: How to Design and Conduct More Effective Analyses.* Washington, DC: Island.

Thurber, J. 1991. "Congressional Oversight of High-Level Nuclear Waste Disposal Policy: The DOE Weapons Complex Clean-Up Contribution." *Political Science*, no. 283, 121–139. Reprinted in E. B. Herzik and A. H. Mushkatel, eds., *Problems and Prospects in Nuclear Waste Disposal Policy* (Westport, CT: Greenwood, 1993).

Vig, N. J. 2013. "Presidential Powers and Environmental Policy." In *Environmental Policy*, 8th ed., ed. N. J. Vig and M. E. Kraft, 84–108. Washington, DC: CQ Press.

Vig, N.J., and M.E. Kraft, eds. 2013. *Environmental Policy: New Directions for the Twenty-First Century*. 8th ed. Washington, DC: CQ Press.

Wald, M. L. 2011. "Republicans Suggest White House Rushed Solar Company's Loans."*New York Times*, September 14.

Whiteman, D. 1985. "The Fate of Policy Analysis in Congressional Decision Making: Three Types of Use in Committees." *Western Political Quarterly* 38:294–311.

———. 1995. *Communication in Congress: Members, Staff, and the Search for Information*. Lawrence: University Press of Kansas.

Zeleny, J., and M. Thee-Brenan. 2011. "New Poll Finds a Deep Distrust of Government." *New York Times*, October 25.

CHAPTER 14

THE AMERICAN PRESIDENCY AND ENVIRONMENTAL POLICY

NORMAN J. VIG

Of all the questions which can come before this
nation...there is none which compares in importance with
the great central task of leaving this land even a better land
for our descendants than it is for us, and training them into
a better race to inhabit the land and pass it on. Conservation
is a great moral issue, for it involves the patriotic duty of
insuring the safety and continuance of the nation.

—Theodore Roosevelt

IN the century since Teddy Roosevelt's declaration, no president has devoted as
much time and energy to environmental preservation as he did. Nor has any president exercised such expansive presidential powers in this domain, with the possible
exception of Franklin Roosevelt (Brinkley 2009; Cutright 1956, 1985; Daynes and
Sussman 2010; Gould 1991; Roosevelt 1972). Yet most recent presidents have used
their powers to shape environmental policies, for better or worse. In the period
since 1970, Presidents Richard Nixon, Jimmy Carter, George H. W. Bush, and Bill
Clinton have made significant advances in environmental policy, while Gerald

Ford, Ronald Reagan, and George W. Bush attempted to slow or reverse the actions of their predecessors.

A large environmental policy literature has developed over the past four decades, as summarized in this volume. At the same time, presidential studies have emerged as a major subfield in political science (Moe 2009). Yet there are still very limited overlaps between the two literatures. Few presidential scholars have devoted much attention to environmental policy, and conversely, environmental policy scholars have been slow to integrate the increasingly sophisticated literature on the presidency into their analyses. When the first academic conference on the "environmental presidency" was held in 2000, only a handful of political scientists had published in the field.[1] Nevertheless, since the mid-1980s a new focus on use of presidential powers in this area has slowly emerged. The following section traces some of these developments. Subsequent sections discuss the use of presidential powers in more detail. In keeping with the purpose of this volume, the conclusion summarizes emerging perspectives on the president's role in environmental policy making and suggests further avenues for research.

1. DEVELOPMENT OF THE FIELD

There is now a vast body of research on the presidency that cannot be fully summarized here (for recent overviews see Edwards and Howell 2009; Edwards and Wayne 2010; Nelson 2010). For decades after Richard Neustadt first published his classic *Presidential Power* in 1960, scholars focused on individual presidents' use of informal political and bargaining skills to *persuade* other actors in the system to follow their lead since their institutional position was essentially one of weakness. Much of the subsequent focus has been on the constitutional and institutional limits of the presidency in our system of "separate institutions sharing powers" (Jones 2005; Neustadt 1990). Despite the growth of the "institutional presidency" since the 1930s—that is, a large White House staff and the Executive Office of the President—occupants of the Oval Office are seen as having to mobilize a wide array of political resources to overcome systemic structural constraints (Burke 2010). This has often involved efforts to *centralize* power in the White House and *politicize* the bureaucracy in order to control policy making through use of executive powers rather than by legislation (Moe 1985). Presidential studies have thus focused increasingly on the rational exercise of administrative powers, especially during periods of divided government, gridlock in Congress, and national emergency (Howell 2003, 2009b; Mayer 2009; Moe and Howell 1999; Waterman 2009).

---

1. Fifth Annual Stegner Center Symposium, titled "The Presidency and the Environment," University of Utah, Salt Lake City, March 30–31, 2000. The author was a participant.

Publication of Richard Nathan's seminal work, *The Administrative Presidency*, in 1983 set the stage for much of the new research, particularly in regard to environmental policy. Nathan argued that Richard Nixon and Ronald Reagan both followed an "administrative presidency strategy" to pursue their domestic policy agendas through tight management and control of the bureaucracy rather than through legislation. Under Reagan this strategy involved appointment of cabinet councils to oversee executive agencies (including one for natural resources and the environment chaired by Interior Secretary James Watt); rigorous screening of all agency appointments to ensure loyalty to the president's ideology and agenda; targeted budgetary and personnel reductions to weaken regulatory agencies; reduced enforcement of environmental laws; and enhanced oversight of all regulatory decision making, including strict requirements for cost-benefit analysis of proposed environmental regulations (Eads and Fix 1984; Smith 1984).

The first book-length study of a recent president's environmental policies, *Environmental Policy in the 1980s: Reagan's New Agenda*, edited by Vig and Kraft (1984), drew heavily on Nathan's work. Vig and Kraft argued that in its "regulatory reform" strategy the Reagan administration had gone much too far in unilaterally altering the intent of environmental laws, thus undermining the political legitimacy, bureaucratic competence, and technical rationality necessary for implementing their policies (see also Kraft and Vig 1984). The forced resignations of James Watt and EPA administrator Anne Burford in 1983 were the result. Other contributors to the Vig and Kraft volume traced the deleterious impacts of Reagan's strategy on different environmental institutions and programs. Congressional, judicial, and public opinion reactions to these policies forced the president to modify or abandon many of his initiatives in his second term (Vig and Kraft 1990).[2]

Two books published by political scientists in 1992 also focused on Reagan's administrative presidency. Robert A. Shanley's *Presidential Influence and Environmental Policy* dissected Reagan's use of executive orders, control of regulatory risk analysis, and legal enforcement record in greater detail. Shanley also compared Reagan's administrative strategy to those of other recent presidents, concluding that an overly aggressive, confrontational strategy was likely to be counterproductive (see also Wood 1988; Wood and Waterman 1994). Robert F. Durant's *The Administrative Presidency Revisited* (1992) traced the actual results of Reagan's natural resource policies in still greater depth, using implementation of Bureau of Land Management (BLM) policies in New Mexico as evidence. He demonstrated that bureaucratic responses to the administrative presidency varied widely across issue items and offices, in many cases modifying or negating presidential initiatives. Building on these findings, he developed a rigorous theoretical framework for studying policy implementation processes and outcomes. His research was thus a valuable corrective to previous presidential research that had focused primarily on administrative actions or *outputs* rather than on substantive *outcomes*.

---

2. Vig and Kraft have updated their analyses of presidential administrations in seven new editions since 1990; see, most recently, Vig and Kraft 2013.

The Environmental Presidency (1999), edited by Dennis L. Soden, broadened the field beyond the administrative presidency model. Soden organized his volume around five traditional roles of the president: as commander in chief, chief diplomat, chief executive, legislative leader, and opinion/party leader. Although historically these powers have ranked in descending order of importance, in the contemporary world of environmental politics (including global issues) all of them are critical. While executive powers have often been most important in domestic policy development, role dependence varies among presidents and issues. Nor is it certain that presidents will fully exercise their powers. Thus, the book set out two hypotheses for analyzing the "environmental presidency" across administrations:

> First, the president's abilities to take advantage of the power resources at his disposal places him in a stronger position . . . than other actors in the policy process, *although presidents do not necessarily use their resources to maximize the potential of the office.* Thus, the roles of the president may take on different patterns based on how resources are used and the particular policy under question. Thus we ask: *within the environmental policy arena has the use of power resources been weak or underutilized in comparison to other policy domains and historical patterns?* (Soden 1999, 7; italics in original)

The authors are thus able to evaluate presidents since Truman according to how passive or active they were and as to whether they exercised their powers in a positive or negative fashion regarding environmental protection. For example, Truman and Eisenhower are classified as passively negative, Nixon as actively positive, and Reagan as actively negative (Soden 1999, 339). The book broke new ground in analyzing presidential opinion leadership and in considering environmental foreign policy and national defense issues and also contained an insightful early assessment of Bill Clinton's presidency (Daynes 1999).

The effort to rank the environmental policy performance of presidents longitudinally was continued and expanded by two of the Soden volume's contributors, Byron Daynes and Glen Sussman. In *White House Politics and the Environment* (2010), they have evaluated the environmental records of all 12 presidents since Franklin Roosevelt based on four qualitative factors: political communication, legislative leadership, administrative actions, and environmental diplomacy. Ultimately, presidents are rated normatively according to their positive or negative impacts on the environment, yielding a "continuum of greenness" (Daynes and Sussman 2010, 210–215). Seven presidents are classified as having a positive impact on the environment (Roosevelt, Truman, Kennedy, Johnson, Nixon, Carter, and Clinton), three as having mixed impacts (Eisenhower, Ford, and G. H. W. Bush), and two as having negative impacts (Reagan and G. W. Bush). Interestingly, Roosevelt and Nixon rank as the "greenist."

I have classified presidents somewhat differently into three categories, based primarily on their environmental policy agendas and relative success in achieving them (Vig 2013).[3] *Opportunistic leaders* (Nixon and George H. W. Bush) came

---

3. Gerald Ford's presidency is not considered in this analysis.

to office with relatively weak environmental records and agendas but were driven by surges of public environmental concern to exert leadership in the passage of major legislation (see Bryner 1995; Jones 1975). However, they both adopted hostile stances toward environmental regulation later in their terms. By contrast, *frustrated underachievers* (Carter and Clinton) came to power with strong policy agendas but ebbing public and congressional support. Hence, they were unable to enact much of their program into law and turned, instead, to reliance on executive powers to salvage their agendas (as pointed out below, they both left huge public land legacies at the end of their terms). The third category, *rollback advocates*, consists of those presidents who entered office with antiregulatory agendas that sought to soften or repeal environmental policies that they saw as unnecessarily burdensome on business and economic growth (Reagan and George W. Bush). However, neither of these presidents succeeded in altering major environmental statutes, and many of their efforts to politicize the bureaucracy proved counterproductive. At this writing it is too early to tell how President Obama will be classified, but so far he appears to fit the pattern of Carter and Clinton.

In the following section I discuss the nature of presidential powers in more detail. Space does not permit an examination of all of the president's roles; thus I will focus on the exercise of executive powers to shape domestic environmental policies. Examples of how these powers have been used over the past four decades are given, with references to the relevant environmental policy and presidential studies literatures. Other important powers, such as the president's role in environmental diplomacy and in making (or blocking) adoption of international environmental treaties and agreements, will not be covered here (see chapters 10 and 11 in this volume).

2. Presidential Powers

The powers conferred on the president in Article II of the Constitution are few and broadly stated. The president shall exercise the "executive power" and "take care that the laws be faithfully executed." The Constitution also authorizes the president to nominate and appoint certain officials, report to Congress on the state of the union, veto legislation, make international treaties and agreements (with the advice and consent of the Senate), and serve as commander in chief of the armed forces. The practical authority implied by these powers has varied greatly over time, and all presidents have had to decide exactly how to exploit the office. For the most part, presidential power has expanded over the past century.

The chief executive now presides over 15 cabinet departments and more than 50 noncabinet agencies, boards, and corporations. The Executive Office of the President (EOP) alone has some 1,800 employees scattered among 16 offices and councils, including the White House Office and the Office of Management and Budget (OMB), which attempt to coordinate the activities and budgets of the rest of the federal bureaucracy. Needless to say, the president has relatively little time to devote to any one policy arena unless it is a matter of top priority.

Environmental policy has sometimes been a high priority for recent presidents, but for the most part it has not been. Presidents Nixon, Carter, and G. H. W. Bush devoted considerable time and political capital to the passage of environmental legislation. Other presidents have relied more heavily on administrative strategies to change policies through control of the bureaucracy, as noted above. But given the exigencies of foreign policy, national security, economic growth, and other necessary priorities, environmental policy has only rarely achieved even second-tier status on the president's agenda (Soden 1999, 344). Still, presidents and their appointees set the general tone and direction of actions throughout the government, and they do have multiple specific powers that can influence environmental policies directly or contextually.

3. CONTEXTUAL POWERS

"Contextual powers" are those that indirectly shape the direction of presidential policies by establishing the context within which decisions are made. For our purposes, these include agenda setting and policy framing, appointments, budgeting, and reorganization. "Unilateral powers" are those that the president can exercise alone or through surrogates to influence directly policy decisions. These include legislative vetoes and signing statements, executive orders and proclamations, regulatory review of rule making, and control of information. Unilateral powers appeared to reach a new level of importance during the George W. Bush administration as the president embraced a theory of "unitary executive" that allowed him to claim virtually unlimited prerogatives to control the executive branch (Mayer 2009; Waterman 2009).

3.1. Agenda Setting and Policy Framing

All presidents come to power with broad policy prescriptions and themes. Set out in campaign speeches, platform documents, press conferences, and major occasions such as inaugural and State of the Union addresses, they signal what the president's priorities are and often presage major legislative proposals (Wayne 2009; Wood 2009). The "bully pulpit" can be used to rally public support behind these proposals, especially during the president's first year in office. These initial themes are often abandoned or modified due to uncontrollable events or changing political circumstances as the term wears on. Nevertheless, it matters greatly how the president initially frames issues such as energy and environmental policy. For example, in the Reagan administration (and to a lesser extent in the George W. Bush administration), environmental policy was largely defined in terms of regulatory relief to promote resource development and economic growth. Environmental protection itself was thus reduced to a residual or third-tier issue. By contrast, the Clinton and Obama administrations framed environmental protection and clean energy development in positive terms as priority investments that would yield new generations of "green jobs" and ensure "sustainable" economic growth. They have also attempted to reframe energy and environmental problems such as climate change as national security issues—thus far with limited success (Matthew 2013 and chapter 6 of this volume).

Presidents can define themselves as "pro-" or "anti-"environmental. Richard Nixon redefined his mission in 1970 by proclaiming the "environmental decade," addressing a joint session of Congress on the urgent need for antipollution legislation, outbidding congressional proposals for a strong Clean Air Act (Jones 1975), and establishing the Environmental Protection Agency (EPA) by executive order. Although his motives and rhetoric have been questioned, Nixon helped to create a context in which most of the major contemporary environmental legislation was enacted (Train 1996; Vickery 2004).[4] Jimmy Carter, on the other hand, came to office with strong environmental credentials but saw his image tarnished by repeated compromises with Congress (Stine 1998).

Following eight years of increasingly unpopular Reagan administration initiatives to weaken environmental policies, George H. W. Bush proclaimed in the midst of his electoral campaign that he would be an "environmental president" in the Teddy Roosevelt tradition. He recast the need for Clean Air Act amendments to control acid precipitation, toxic air pollutants, and urban smog in positive, market-friendly terms. As a result, the new cap-and-trade program for reducing acid rain precursors passed in 1990 with bipartisan support (Bryner 1995). By contrast, George W. Bush was unsuccessful in rebranding proposals from Vice President Dick Cheney's energy policy task force for easing regulations on power plants as his "Clear Skies Initiative" (Eisner 2007; Klyza and Sousa 2008). Presidential rhetoric can backfire if it is not credible.

3.2. Appointments

Another obvious way in which presidents try to impose their agenda is through White House and agency appointments. More than 3,200 officials are political appointees, including cabinet secretaries and their deputies and assistants, agency and bureau chiefs and their top assistants, and some Executive Office staff. Most of the important agency and departmental appointees (more than 1,000 in all) require Senate confirmation: for example, the administrator and office heads at EPA; the director of OMB and the Office of Information and Regulatory Affairs (OIRA), which oversees regulation; and the heads of the U.S. Fish and Wildlife Service and the U.S. Forest Service. By selecting individuals whose ideology and policy views coincide with his own, or whose prior records reveal their stance on critical issues, the president can tilt policy implementation toward his own goals (Durant and Resh 2009).

---

4. For a list of major environmental laws passed since 1969, see Vig and Kraft 2013, Appendix I.

There is lively debate among presidency scholars over how effective such "politi-cization" strategies are (Lewis 2008, 2009). Those appointed for patronage or ideo-logical reasons may lack substantive expertise and managerial competence. If they are too controversial, they might not be confirmed by the Senate, or may become lightning rods for opposition attacks (as, for example, in the case of James Watt). But presidents do usually signal their intentions regarding environmental policy by key appointments such as secretaries of the interior and energy and the EPA admin-istrator. A good example is the elder President Bush's appointment of William Reilly, the respected president of the World Wildlife Fund and the Conservation Foundation, to head the EPA to dramatize his break with Reagan administration policies. However, appointments do not necessarily indicate how officials will be allowed to operate. Reilly was often stymied by opposition from White House Chief of Staff John Sununu and other administration heavyweights. Some appointments are almost purely symbolic. George W. Bush's selection of former New Jersey gov-ernor Christine Todd Whitman to head the EPA is a clear example: Whitman was countermanded by Vice President Cheney, Interior Secretary Gale Norton, and other conservatives on matters relating to clean air regulation and climate change, lead-ing to her early departure in 2003. Bush's subcabinet appointees were heavily drawn from regulated industries and conservative law firms and think tanks, and they con-sciously tried to "implant their DNA throughout the government" (Allen 2004).

Bill Clinton and Barack Obama won praise for their selection of environ-mentalist "green teams" to carry out their policies. Clinton chose Al Gore as vice president, former Gore Senate aides Carol Browner to head EPA and Kathleen McGinty to lead a new Office of Environmental Policy in the White House, and Bruce Babbitt, president of the League of Conservation Voters, as secretary of the interior; and he appointed several other environmental leaders to high positions. President Obama's appointments were perhaps even more impressive, including Browner as White House energy and climate change "czar"; Lisa Jackson, a chemi-cal engineer, as EPA administrator; Steven Chu, a Nobel Prize–winning physicist, as energy secretary; Senator Ken Salazar as interior secretary; and John Holdren, a Harvard physics professor and climate expert, as White House science adviser. These appointees have moved many of Obama's policies forward at the agency and departmental levels. Even so, their success was blunted by failure to enact climate change legislation and mishandling of the BP Deepwater Horizon Oil spill in 2010. And Browner announced her departure from the White House in early 2011.

3.3. Budgeting

Presidents clearly signal their priorities through the annual budgets they transmit to Congress and in their longer-term spending projections.[5] Even though Congress

---

5. Budgets and projections for all federal agencies and departments since 1976 can be found at www.gpoaccess.gov/usbudget/hist.html.

rarely accepts these budget proposals without change, they carry great weight. Budgets and other financial legislation can make draconian policy changes. The most dramatic example was Ronald Reagan's Economic Recovery Tax Act and Omnibus Budget Reconciliation Act of 1981, which reduced income taxes by 25 percent and cut deeply into government programs. Environmental agencies and programs were especially targeted in subsequent budgets (Bartlett 1984). The EPA lost one-third of its operating budget and about one-fifth of its employees. After first trying to abolish the Council on Environmental Quality (CEQ), Reagan cut almost all of its budget and staff so that it barely continued to function. In the Interior Department funds were shifted from conservation activities to those promoting development. The net result was a substantial setback for environmental programs established in the previous decade.

Presidents George H. W. Bush and Bill Clinton restored funding for environmental programs in the 1990s. George W. Bush's first budget proposal, for FY 2002, called for a modest 4 percent increase in overall domestic discretionary spending, but an 8 percent reduction in funding for natural resource and environmental protection programs (the largest cut for any sector). The EPA's budget was to be slashed by 6.4 percent. In this case Congress rejected the cuts and actually *increased* EPA funding. However, in real terms (adjusted for inflation) the EPA's operating budget remained flat during the 2000–2008 period (see Vig and Kraft 2013). By contrast, Barack Obama signaled his intention to give higher priority to EPA by requesting 48 percent more for the agency in FY 2010 than Bush had proposed in his final budget (Vig 2013, 100). The Democratic majorities in Congress largely obliged, though Obama reduced EPA funding in his proposed 2012 budget and House Republicans sought to cut the agency's budget more severely. Budget deficits are likely to limit all environmental funding in coming years.

3.4. Reorganization

The final contextual change presidents can make is reorganizing institutions and processes to increase their policy leverage. Reorganizations may require legislative approval, but many do not. Richard Nixon established the EPA in 1970 by executive order after his reorganization plan had been debated and approved by Congress. By regrouping pollution control functions from several departments into one agency reporting to him, Nixon sought to increase White House control over implementation of the emerging policies. The institutionalization of regulatory review processes, starting with Nixon's "Quality of Life" reviews, also became a powerful tool for centralization of control (see below).

All presidents reorganize White House staff functions and procedures. Some presidents like Reagan and George W. Bush delegate responsibilities through tight hierarchical structures, while others like Carter and Clinton follow much looser procedures (Burke 2009). Reagan instituted a system of cabinet councils through which policies were monitored and coordinated across departments and agencies (including natural resources and environmental regulation), but it did not survive his first term. He also established a Task Force on Regulatory Relief chaired by Vice President George H. W. Bush to propose regulatory changes sought by business interests. When Bush became president, he instituted a similar body called the Council on Competitiveness headed by Vice President Dan Quayle.

Bill Clinton was the most active recent president in terms of organizational change. Upon taking office he abolished the Competitiveness Council and created a new Office of Environmental Policy in the White House. This body was later folded into the CEQ, but environmental interests clearly had a more central presence than in the previous administrations. Clinton also established a new President's Council on Sustainable Development and proposed that the EPA be converted to a Cabinet department (legislation including this provision died in Congress). He also supported passage of the Government Performance and Results Act (GPRA) in 1993, which required federal agencies (including EPA) to develop long-term plans for measuring and improving their performance. Under the rubric of "reinventing environmental regulation," the president and vice president launched a well-publicized initiative in 1995 that included creation of more than 50 new programs at the EPA. These programs, such as Project XL, the Common Sense Initiative, and the National Environmental Partnership Performance System (NEPPS), were intended to promote new forms of voluntary collaboration between the EPA and regulated businesses, industrial sectors, and states through flexible application of regulations and rewards for achieving results "beyond compliance." All of these innovations were based on administrative actions rather than on changes in the underlying pollution control statutes and in the end left little in the way of lasting policies and institutions (Fiorino 2006, 213; see also chapter 15 in this volume).

George W. Bush made no major organizational changes in environmental administration, preferring instead to influence policies and regulatory processes through direct White House intervention. For example, much of his new energy and environmental agenda was developed by a secret "task force" chaired by Vice President Dick Cheney; most of the 106 proposals that resulted were carried out through administrative channels. Bush, like Reagan, relied heavily on OMB to monitor and control agency rule making and attempted to extend political controls further down into the regulatory agencies. Vice President Cheney often intervened directly in agency decision making (Gellman 2008). Bush also used White House agencies such as CEQ as organs of information control (see below). Unfortunately, we have few detailed studies of White House–agency relationships in this area.

4. UNILATERAL POWERS

Although the distinction between contextual and unilateral powers is not always clear, the president can act alone or through immediate surrogates to control certain policy decisions. Some of these unilateral powers are essentially informal, exercised behind the scenes through Neustadt's "power of persuasion." For example, Bill Clinton convened a "timber summit" in Portland in 1993 to work out compromises for protecting old-growth forests and endangered species such as the spotted owl in the Pacific Northwest. He also experimented with a broad range of other "collaborative" policy making approaches, including negotiated agreements among stakeholders to preserve the Florida Everglades and to establish "habitat conservation plans" for hundreds of smaller areas (Klyza and Sousa 2008, 195–246). However, I will focus here on some of the formal tools for influencing policy decisions.

4.1. Legislative Vetoes and Signing Statements

Perhaps the president's most specific constitutional power is the right to veto laws passed by Congress. Vetoes can be overridden by a two-thirds majority in both Houses, but this rarely happens. It did, however, occur more often during the Nixon, Ford, and Reagan administrations. President Nixon's veto of the Federal Water Pollution Control Act (Clean Water Act) Amendments of 1972 was overridden, as were almost one in five of Gerald Ford's vetoes (Daynes and Sussman 2010, 148). Congress passed several important environmental bills against Ronald Reagan's opposition, including the Superfund Amendments and Reauthorization Act of 1986, the Clean Water Act Amendments of 1987, and the Nuclear Waste Policy Act of 1987. No vetoes of major environmental bills have occurred since the 1980s, but Bill Clinton used the veto power effectively against certain (but not all) anti-environmental riders to appropriation bills in 1995, leading to a partial government shutdown (Klyza and Sousa 2008, 63–83; Wayne 2009, 322–323). He continued to threaten vetoes when the Republicans in Congress attached further riders to legislation, resulting in the removal of most of them from final budget and appropriation bills. This is a tactic that President Obama is likely to use if the Republican House majority elected in 2010 attempts to block implementation of greenhouse gas emission controls and other regulation through riders or amendments to budget bills.

Even if presidents sign legislation they may attempt to negate parts of the resulting laws by attaching "signing statements" to them. Such statements usually claim congressional infringement of executive powers or other constitutional reasons for refusing to implement certain provisions (Kelley and Marshall 2008). George W. Bush established the modern record for signing statements, issuing more than 1,100 in his two terms (mostly claiming executive prerogatives as commander in chief). Many critics objected that such extensive use of signing statements amounted to an unconstitutional exercise of a line-item veto to thwart the will of Congress (Cooper 2005; Savage 2007). Barack Obama criticized the practice during his campaign for the presidency and vowed to use the power sparingly (Savage 2009). He issued only 13 such statements during his first two years in office. However, in April 2011

Obama made it clear that he would employ signing statements to block implementation of budget riders that unduly restricted his powers (Risen 2011).

4.2. Executive Orders and Proclamations

One of the president's most direct policy tools is the authority to issue executive orders, proclamations, and other policy directives (Mayer 2001, 2009; Warber 2006; Waterman 2009). Executive orders (EOs) have the force of law unless Congress overrides them—something that has only rarely happened—or until another president amends or rescinds them. Although they are not as permanent as legislation, they can give the president a decisive advantage as "first mover" by changing the policy status quo when Congress is unable to act (Howell 2003; Lewis and Moe 2010). EOs have been used by all presidents since Theodore Roosevelt to shape environmental policies. Richard Nixon issued 46 EOs dealing with the environment and natural resources, Carter 48, and Clinton 45 (Klyza and Sousa 2008, 102; West and Sussman 1999, 79–90). They have been used less since the Clinton administration. George W. Bush issued a total of 291 EOs, about 15 of which pertained to energy, the environment, or regulation. In his first two years, Barack Obama issued 72 EOs, only five of which dealt with the environment (two of them on the Gulf Oil spill). Thus, in the decade 2001–2010 only about 5.5 percent of EOs concerned environmental, energy, or related regulatory policies.[6] However, Obama made greater use of EOs during the second half of his term, including several on the environment (Savage 2012; Vig 2013, 101–102).

Most executive orders deal with administrative organization and procedures. Perhaps the most important EO of this kind for environmental policy was Nixon's order establishing the EPA in December 1970 (following congressional approval). Another critical change was implemented by Ronald Reagan's EO12291 in 1981 requiring cost-benefit analysis of environmental regulations and EO 12498 ordering agencies to submit regulatory calendars in advance to OMB. Clinton replaced these orders with one of his own, and George W. Bush added further political controls over regulation (see next section).

EOs have been used to introduce other new policies as well. In 1970 Nixon invoked the Refuse Act of 1899 to issue an order requiring permits for all industrial discharges into navigable waters; this program laid the basis for the National Pollution Discharge Elimination System (NPDES) established by the 1972 water pollution amendments (Train 1996). Bill Clinton's EO 12898, issued in 1994, required all federal agencies to adopt "environmental justice" as part of their missions "by identifying and addressing...disproportionately high and adverse human health or environmental effects of its programs...on minority populations and low

---

6. Executive orders are available at www.archives.gov/federal-register/executive-orders. html. Some judgment is involved in determining which orders significantly promote environmental quality.

income populations" (West and Sussman 1999, 89). Another important set of executive orders and directives during the Clinton administration dealt with "greening" the military through guidance for reducing fuel consumption, reduced use and disposal of toxic materials, protection of air and water on military bases and training facilities, and strategic planning for environmental threats such as climate change. Many of these initiatives were consolidated into Clinton's EO 13148 of 1999, "Greening the Government through Leadership in Environmental Management." Several new offices were also created for strategic planning. Although some of these reforms met strong bureaucratic resistance and were never fully implemented or funded, many positive changes resulted (Durant 2007, 2009). However, some of these initiatives were allowed to lapse during the "war on terrorism" after September 2001 (Matthew 2013).

Of the 20 most relevant EOs issued during 2001–2010, four created new executive bodies (an interagency task force on the Great Lakes, an Ocean Policy advisory committee, a national commission on the BP Deepwater Horizon Oil Spill, and a Gulf Coast Ecosystem Restoration task force). Several others during the Bush years were to expedite energy and transportation projects by "streamlining" or eliminating environmental reviews. Following his 2006 State of the Union address calling for ending our "addiction to oil" and request the following year for massive increases in ethanol and other alternative fuel production, Bush issued EO 13423, which required federal agencies to reduce petroleum fuel use by 2 percent annually and to increase use of alternative fuels by 10 percent a year. EO 13432 further directed agencies to cooperate in reducing greenhouse gas emissions from motor vehicles and from off-road vehicles and engines. But the most controversial order issued by Bush was EO 13422 of January 2007, "Regulatory Planning and Review," which required that regulatory review officers in all executive agencies be political appointees, thus further politicizing the process. Barack Obama rescinded this order in January 2009, reinstating the process established by President Clinton in 1993; but in January 2011 he issued a new order of his own on regulatory review (see below). In other actions, Obama issued a sweeping EO (13534) titled "Federal Leadership in Environmental, Energy, and Economic Performance" requiring federal agencies to meet a broad range of "sustainability" goals, including greenhouse gas emission targets, and launched a new effort to protect and restore Chesapeake Bay (EO 13508).

Since Teddy Roosevelt most presidents have made use of the Antiquities Act of 1906 to protect public lands. This law allows presidents to designate areas of unique scenic, scientific, or historical value as national monuments by executive proclamations. Recent presidents have often used this authority when Congress was unable or unwilling to act on pending land preservation issues. Perhaps the best example was Jimmy Carter's designation of 17 national monuments covering 56 million acres of Alaska in December 1978, which forced Congress to resolve its differences and enact the Alaska National Interest Lands Conservation Act two years later (Stine 1998). In 1996 Clinton announced the creation of the Grand Staircase–Escalante National Monument in Utah while the Senate was still debating long-awaited but weaker legislation to protect the area. Clinton went on to issue proclamations establishing 18 other national monuments and enlarging three others at the end of his term (Klyza and Sousa 2008, 109–122). George W. Bush made little use of the law to protect land areas but established four large marine reserves around the Hawaiian Islands and American territories in the Pacific Ocean during his last two years in office.

4.3. Rule Making and Regulatory Oversight

Environmental laws such as the Clean Air Act and Clean Water Act delegate authority to implementing agencies (in this case the EPA) to issue detailed rules and regulations to achieve the goals of the legislation, often by a certain date. These rules usually have to be made according to requirements of the Administrative Procedure Act of 1946, which mandates such things as publication of proposed actions in the *Federal Register*, holding of hearings and comment periods, and publication and review of evidence on which decisions are based (see chapter 17 in this volume). Federal courts also review most environmental rules if they are challenged and can overturn them or remand them to the issuing agency for reconsideration (see chapter 12 in this volume). However, courts tend to defer to agency discretion if proper procedures are followed and it is not easy for subsequent presidents to undo regulations once they are in place. To cite one dramatic example, Bill Clinton issued a long-awaited "Roadless Area Rule" just before he left office in 2001. This rule would give added protection to nearly 60 million acres of national forest land by prohibiting construction of new roads, thus limiting such activities as logging and mining. On taking office, George W. Bush postponed all pending rules including the Roadless Rule for 60 days. But because the rule had been adopted after a lengthy and careful process, he could not simply reject it. Instead, the administration encouraged legal challenges to the rule and refused to defend it in court, and then attempted to substitute a new rule of its own giving governors much greater control over roadless decisions. However, in September 2006 a federal district court judge struck down the proposed rule and reinstated the Clinton rule (see Klyza and Sousa 2008, 122–134).

There would thus seem to be many checks to prevent agencies and presidents from acting arbitrarily or capriciously. Nevertheless, beginning with President Nixon, all presidents have attempted to establish tighter central control over agency rule making through regulatory oversight. Perhaps more than any other power, this development lay at the heart of the "administrative presidency" model.

The rise of regulatory oversight and clearance has been analyzed by numerous scholars (Durant and Resh 2009; Eads and Fix 1984; Eisner 2007; Lewis and Moe 2010; Moe 1985; Shanley 1992; Smith 1984). Although all presidents since Nixon (and well before) have tried to control bureaucratic decision making through central clearance procedures, Ronald Reagan took the biggest step forward by issuing EO

12291 in February 1981. This order transferred authority to review proposed environmental (and other) regulations to a little-known body in OMB created by Jimmy Carter—the Office of Information and Regulatory Affairs (OIRA)—and mandated rigorous cost-benefit analysis of all major regulations (those with impacts of over $100 million) along with evaluations of alternative approaches. "In a departure from past practice, OMB now allowed agencies to issue rules only when the benefits exceeded the costs; it also required them to choose among possible rules so as to maximize the net benefits to society as a whole. Moreover, OMB now asserted the right to delay proposed rules indefinitely while review was pending" (Lewis and Moe 2010, 390). Reagan later issued a second order (12498) requiring agencies to give OIRA advance notice of their upcoming regulatory calendars. These review processes were clearly aimed at controlling environmental and health and safety rule making. The main effect was to slow down or halt the issuance of many new regulations and to force agencies such as the EPA to revise existing regulations that the administration targeted. According to one source, OIRA resubmitted or killed an average of 85 rules a year during the Reagan presidency (Durant and Resh 2009, 584). Congress responded by writing increasingly detailed regulatory mandates into revisions of environmental laws in the 1980s in an attempt to limit the EPA's (and thus the administration's) discretionary authority, but there is no doubt that the number of new environmental rules declined sharply (Eisner 2007, 80–85).

Bill Clinton replaced Reagan's EO 12291 with a new one of his own, EO 12866, in 1993. The new order restored regulatory oversight to OIRA, but allowed more flexibility in measuring costs and considering benefits:

> In deciding whether and how to regulate, agencies should assess all costs and benefits of available regulatory alternatives, including the alternative of not regulating. Costs and benefits shall be understood to include both quantifiable measures (to the fullest extent that these can be usefully estimated) and qualitative measures of costs and benefits that are difficult to quantify, but nevertheless essential to consider. Further, in choosing among alternative regulatory approaches, agencies should select those approaches that maximize net benefits (including potential economic, environmental, public health and safety, and other advantages; distributive impacts; and equity), unless a statute requires another regulatory approach. (Eisner 2007, 88)

This guidance and its application were definitely more conducive to environmental rule making. Although Clinton also experimented with many new forms of flexible, results-based regulation as discussed earlier, the EPA issued a number of important new rules. Among these were tighter standards for ozone and airborne particulates in 1997 and for arsenic in drinking water in 2000.

President George W. Bush left Clinton's executive order in place, but appointed conservative OIRA directors (John Graham and Susan Dudley) who were far more hostile to regulation (Lewis and Moe 2010, 393). Upon taking office Bush suspended a number of last-minute Clinton regulations pending further review, including the new arsenic standard. After an uproar from environmentalists and members of Congress, the administration commissioned a further review of scientific evidence by the National Research Council, whose findings broadly supported the Clinton standard. Shortly after the report was released, EPA administrator Whitman announced that it would reinstate the Clinton rule (Rosenbaum 2006, 179–182). However, the Bush administration attempted to impose other rules that fell considerably short of what EPA and other scientists recommended. When Bush's "Clear Skies" bill stalled in Congress, the administration attempted to alter the Clean Air Act's requirements for "new source performance standards" (mainly for construction of new power plants and expansion of existing ones) and to establish emission standards for mercury and other air pollutants that were more lenient than those advocated by many scientists at EPA. These efforts resulted in the so-called Interstate Rule (covering conventional air pollutants in 28 eastern states) and a proposed cap-and-trade program for mercury, both of which failed to survive in the courts (see Klyza and Sousa 2008, 135–147).

Perhaps out of frustration, in January 2007 Bush issued EO 13422, which required every regulatory agency to have a regulatory review officer who is a presidential (political) appointee. The order also granted OIRA new authority to review and edit "agency guidance documents," which could include agency opinions, scientific documents, or memoranda; required agencies to identify in writing what market failure warranted the new regulation; and required that agencies provide estimates of the cumulative regulatory costs and benefits of rules they expected to publish in the coming year in order to set regulatory priorities. A Congressional Research Service report concluded, "The changes made by this executive order represent a clear expansion of presidential authority over rule-making agencies. In that regard, EO 13422 can be viewed as part of a broader statement of presidential authority presented throughout the Bush Administration—from declining to provide access to executive branch documents and information to presidential signing statements indicating that certain statutory provisions will be interpreted consistent with the President's view of the 'unitary executive'" (Copeland 2007a, 14; Copeland 2007b). Shortly before leaving office, the Bush administration issued a series of rules that opened new areas to oil and gas drilling, made it easier to dispose of mountaintop mining wastes under the Clean Water Act, and freed federal agencies from the obligation to consult independent scientists under the Endangered Species Act before approving projects that might harm endangered wildlife.

President Obama promptly revoked EO 13422 in January 2009 and restored the Clinton order. His administration has clearly been more favorable to environmental regulation, including EPA regulation of greenhouse gases. However, following loss of the House of Representatives to Republicans in the 2010 midterm elections, Obama attempted to "reset" his administration to be more friendly to business and job creation. On January 18, 2011, he issued EO 13563, which reaffirmed the principles of Clinton's order but called on agencies to review all existing regulations and eliminate any that are duplicative or unnecessary to protect public health and the environment. It appeared that the Obama administration was prepared to take a softer stance on air pollution than initially proposed. In September 2011 the president rejected an EPA proposal to tighten ozone standards, citing economic costs (Broder 2011).

4.4. Secrecy and Information Control

All presidents claim executive privilege, which allows them to keep various kinds of advice and policy information confidential. In matters of national security these prerogatives generally extend further. It is also not unusual for the White House and agency principals to require some form of clearance for important statements and publications. However, some recent presidents—including Reagan, Clinton, and George W. Bush—have claimed broader rights to classify or otherwise conceal routine information from Congress and the public (Rudalevige 2006; Savage 2007). Bush extended these powers further through executive orders restricting access to presidential records and allowing the vice president as well as the president to classify virtually any document. By this time the administration had claimed executive privilege in several cases, including Vice President Cheney's secret meetings with industry representatives to formulate energy and environmental policies (Rudalevige 2006, 189–192).

The most serious charges of information control in the Bush administration concerned manipulation or suppression of intelligence data and scientific documents (Pfiffner 2007; Savage 2007). The latter charge was especially notable in regard to evidence concerning climate change, endangered species, and other environmental issues. In 2002 and 2003 the *New York Times* revealed that Philip Cooney, chief of staff to James Connaughton, who was then chairman of the Council on Environmental Quality, extensively edited reports on global warming, in some cases to the point of deleting entire sections on the issue (Revkin 2002; Revkin and Seelye 2003). This was part of a broader strategy by the Bush-Cheney administration to deny the validity of climate science. In 2007 the House Oversight and Government Reform Committee held hearings and concluded after reviewing 27,000 pages of documents that there had been a systematic effort by the administration to "manipulate climate science and mislead policymakers and the public about the dangers of global warming" (US House of Representatives, Committee on Oversignt and Government Reform 2007; see also Biello 2009). In December 2008 the inspector general of the Interior Department issued a report finding that officials at the U.S. Fish and Wildlife Service had altered scientific evidence regarding endangered species in at least 15 cases (Savage 2008). Finally, a survey by the Union of Concerned Scientists released that year found that 889 of nearly 1,600 staff scientists at EPA reported that they had experienced political interference in their work in the previous five years (Union of Concerned Scientists 2008).

In his campaign and his inaugural address Barack Obama promised greater transparency and to "restore science to its rightful place" at the EPA and other government agencies. On March 9, 2009, he issued a Memorandum on Scientific

Integrity to the heads of executive departments and agencies. The memorandum stated:

> The public must be able to trust the science and scientific process informing public policy decisions. Political officials should not suppress or alter scientific or technological findings and conclusions. If scientific and technological information is developed and used by the Federal Government, it should ordinarily be made available to the public. To the extent permitted by law, there should be transparency in the preparation, identification, and use of scientific and technological information in policymaking.

The memo set out six principles to achieve this goal and gave science adviser John Holdren, as director of the Office of Science and Technology Policy, the responsibility for carrying them out. After a delay of nearly two years, Holdren issued detailed guidance to departments for implementing the new policies in December 2010. The Interior Department was the first agency to adopt the guidelines in January 2011. It remains to be seen how effective they will be, but it can be hoped that scientific evidence will be used more responsibly and effectively in the future (see Keller 2009).

5. WHITHER THE PRESIDENCY?

It is clear that presidents will play a central role in the future of American environmental policy—though not necessarily a dominant one. During the first two decades of the contemporary environmental era (1970–1990), a bipartisan majority in Congress passed virtually all of the current environmental legislation and could be said to dominate environmental policy making (by contrast, Congress proved incapable of enacting national energy policies). But since passage of the Clean Air Act Amendments of 1990, Congress has been gridlocked and unable to enact new environmental laws (with the exception of the Food Quality Act and Safe Drinking Water Amendments of 1996, both of which were supported by Republicans as well as Democrats). Hence, it has been argued by Christopher Klyza and David Sousa (2008, 100) that unilateral actions of the president have become one of the principal "alternative pathways" for advancing environmental policies in an era of political stalemate—along with the courts, states, and various new forms of local collaborative decision making (see chapters 12, 13, 18, and 19 in this volume). However, given the antigovernment majority elected to the House of Representatives in 2010, that role may primarily be one of defending existing environmental policies and institutions rather than advancing new ones.

It can certainly still be argued with Richard Neustadt that in our fragmented and polarized political system, characterized by so many points of access and influence, the president remains vulnerable: "*weak* remains the word with which to start" (Neustadt 1990, xix). But presidential studies over the past two decades have painted a different picture, one of growing ability by presidents of both parties to seize prerogatives such as those discussed in this chapter and assert unilateral powers to shift the status quo. Thus, what was earlier seen by many as a novel and illegitimate model of presidential control—the "administrative presidency"—is now viewed as a normal part of the *office*. That is, no matter who holds the presidency the incumbent will try to maximize control over what is already a very large *regulatory state*.

In this context, we need to know a great deal more about policy implementation. How are executive orders carried out? How much bureaucratic resistance is there? How many and what kinds of proposed regulations are blocked by OIRA, and on what grounds? How much political control is there over scientific research and analysis used in policy making? How has the use of presidential policy instruments changed over time? Is the administrative presidency model still useful, or is it more productive to focus on the larger context of policy making, including the role of public opinion and the media? Should we pay more attention to presidential rhetoric (Peterson 2004)? How has the growing polarization between parties over environmental issues in the past two decades affected the scope for presidential action?

Robert Durant (2009) has suggested the need for detailed longitudinal case studies to trace administrative policy dynamics. His studies of implementation processes reveal the pitfalls of the administrative presidency strategy better than any other. Considerable progress has been made in measuring policy outputs, for example, in studies of executive orders and appointments (Howell 2003, 2009a; Lewis 2008; Mayer 2001; Rudalevige 2010; Warber 2006). However, we also need more quantitative analysis of actual policy *outcomes*. Our models for evaluating presidential performance and ranking presidential contributions to environmental policy are still largely qualitative and normative (see section 1 above).

One more positive approach might be to focus on how regulatory reforms empower certain interests and exclude others, rather than characterizing them as pro- or antiregulatory (Shapiro 2007). Another approach advocated by rational choice and "new institutionalism" scholars would pay more attention to past policy commitments and the growth of a thickly institutionalized "green state" that structures the opportunities available to presidents (Klyza and Sousa 2008, 8; Moe 2009). Given the relatively limited research on the "environmental presidency" to date, a variety of middle-range theoretical models should be explored.

REFERENCES

Allen, M. 2004. "Bush to Change Economic Team." *Washington Post*, November 29.
Bartlett, R. V. 1984. "The Budgetary Process and Environmental Policy." In *Environmental Policy in the 1980s*, ed. N. J. Vig and M. E. Kraft, 121–141. Washington, DC: CQ Press.

Biello, D. 2009. "Editing Scientists: Science Policy and the White House." *Scientific American*, October 22.

Brinkley, D. 2009. *The Wilderness Warrior: Theodore Roosevelt and the Crusade for America*. New York: HarperCollins.

Broder, J. 2011. "Obama Abandons a Stricter Limit on Air Pollution." *New York Times*, September 3.

Bryner, G. C. 1995. *Blue Skies, Green Politics: The Clean Air Act of 1990 and Its Implementation*. 2nd ed. Washington, DC: CQ Press.

Burke, J. P. 2009. "Organizational Structure and Presidential Decision Making." In *Oxford Handbook of the American Presidency*, ed. G. C. Edwards III and W. G. Howell, 501–527. Oxford: Oxford University Press.

——. 2010. "The Institutional Presidency." In *The Presidecy and the Political System*, 9th ed., ed. M. Nelson, 341–366. Washington, DC: CQ Press.

Cooper, P. J. 2005. "George W. Bush, Edgar Allan Poe and the Use and Abuse of Presidential Signing Statements." *Presidential Studies Quarterly* 35: 517–532.

Copeland, C. W. 2007a. *CRS Report for Congress: Changes to the OMB Regulatory Process by Executive Order 13422*, February 5. Washington, DC: Congressional Research Service.

——. 2007b. "The Law: Executive Order 13422: An Expansion of Presidential Influence in the Rulemaking Process." *Presidential Studies Quarterly* 37: 531–544.

Cutright, P. R. 1956. *Theodore Roosevelt the Naturalist*. New York: Harper.

——. 1985. *Theodore Roosevelt: The Making of a Conservationist*. Urbana: University of Illinois Press.

Daynes, B. 1999. "Bill Clinton: Environmental President." In *The Environmental Presidency*, ed. D. L. Soden, 259–312. Albany, NY: State University of New York Press.

Daynes, B., and G. Sussman. 2010. *White House Politics and the Environment: Franklin D. Roosevelt to George W. Bush*. College Station: Texas A&M University Press.

Durant, R. F. 1992. *The Administrative Presidency Revisited: Public Lands, the BLM, and the Reagan Revolution*. Albany, NY: State University of New York Press.

——. 2007. *The Greening of the U.S. Military: Environmental Policy, National Security, and Organizational Change*. Washington, DC: Georgetown University Press.

——. 2009. "Back to the Future? Toward Revitalizing the Study of the Administrative Presidency." *Presidential Studies Quarterly* 39: 89–110.

Durant, R. F., and W. G. Resh. 2009. "Presidential Agendas, Administrative Strategies, and the Bureaucracy." In *Oxford Handbook of the American Presidency*, ed. G. C. Edwards III and W. G. Howell, 577–600. Oxford: Oxford University Press.

——. 2010. "'Presidentializing' the Bureaucracy." In *Oxford Handbook of American Bureaucracy*, ed. R. F. Durant and G. C. Edwards III. Oxford: Oxford University Press.

Eads, G. C., and M. Fix, ed. 1984. *The Reagan Regulatory Strategy: An Assessment*. Washington, DC: Urban Institute Press.

Edwards, G. C., III, and W. G. Howell, ed. 2009. *Oxford Handbook of the American Presidency*. Oxford: Oxford University Press.

Edwards, G. C., III, and S. J. Wayne. 2010. *Presidential Leadership: Politics and Policy Making*. 8th ed. Boston: Cengage Wadsworth.

Eisner, M. A. 2007. *Governing the Environment: The Transformation of Environmental Regulation*. Boulder, CO: Lynne Rienner.

Fiorino, D. J. 2006. *The New Environmental Regulation*. Cambridge, MA: MIT Press.

Gellman, B. 2008. *Angler: The Cheney Vice Presidency*. New York: Penguin.

Gould, L. L. 1991. *The Presidency of Theodore Roosevelt*. Lawrence: University Press of Kansas.

Howell, W. G. 2003. *Power without Persuasion: The Politics of Direct Presidential Action*. Princeton, NJ: Princeton University Press.

———. 2009a. "Quantitative Approaches to Studying the Presidency." In *Oxford Handbook of the American Presidency*, ed. G. C. Edwards III and W. G. Howell, 9–29. Oxford: Oxford University Press.

———. 2009b. "Unilateral Powers: A Brief Overview." *Presidential Studies Quarterly* 35: 417–439.

Jones, C. O. 1975. *Clean Air: The Policy and Politics of Pollution Control*. Pittsburgh: University of Pittsburgh Press.

———. 2005. *The Presidency in a Separated System*. 2nd ed. Washington, DC: Brookings Institution Press.

Keller, A. C. 2009. *Science in Environmental Policy: The Politics of Objective Advice*. Cambridge, MA: MIT Press.

Kelley, C. S., and B. W. Marshall. 2008. "The Last Word: Presidential Power and the Role of Signing Statements." *Presidential Studies Quarterly* 38: 248–297.

Klyza, C. M., and D. J. Sousa. 2008. *American Environmental Policy, 1990–2006: Beyond Gridlock*. Cambridge, MA: MIT Press.

Kraft, M. E., and N. J. Vig. 1984. "Environmental Policy in the Reagan Presidency." *Political Science Quarterly* 99: 415–439.

Lewis, D. E. 2008. *The Politics of Presidential Appointments: Political Control and Bureaucratic Performance*. Princeton, NJ: Princeton University Press.

———. 2009. "Revisiting the Administrative Presidency: Policy, Patronage, and Agency Competence." *Presidential Studies Quarterly* 39: 60–73.

Lewis, D. E., and T. M. Moe. 2010. "The Presidency and the Bureaucracy: The Levers of Presidential Control." In *The Presidency and the Political System*, 9th ed., ed. M. Nelson, 367–400. Washington, DC: CQ Press

Matthew, R. A. 2013. "Environmental Security." In *Environmental Policy*, 8th ed., ed. N. J. Vig and M. E. Kraft, 344–367. Washington, DC: CQ Press.

Mayer, K. R. 2001. *With the Stroke of a Pen: Executive Orders and Presidential Power*. Princeton, NJ: Princeton University Press.

———. 2009. "Going Alone: The Presidential Power of Unilateral Action." In *Oxford Handbook of the American* Presidency, ed. G. C. Edwards III and W.G. Howell, 427–454. Oxford: Oxford University Press.

Moe, T. M. 1985. "The Politicized Presidency." In *The New Direction in American Politics*, ed. J. E. Chubb and P. E. Peterson. Washington, DC: Brookings Institution Press.

———. 2009. "The Revolution in Presidential Studies." *Presidential Studies Quarterly* 39: 701–724.

Moe, T. M., and W. G. Howell. 1999. "Unilateral Action and Presidential Power: A Theory." *Presidential Studies Quarterly* 29: 850–872.

Nathan, R. P. 1983. *The Administrative Presidency*. New York: John Wiley.

Nelson, M., ed. 2010. *The Presidency and the Political System*. 9th ed. Washington, DC: CQ Press.

Neustadt, R. E. 1990. *Presidential Power and the Modern Presidents: The Politics of Leadership from Roosevelt to Reagan*. New York: Free Press.

Peterson, T. R., ed. 2004. *Green Talk in the White House: The Rhetorical Presidency Encounters Ecology*. College Station: Texas A&M University Press.

Pfiffner, J. P. 2007. "Intelligence and Decision Making before the War in Iraq." In *The Polarized Presidency of George W. Bush*, ed. G. C. Edwards III and D. S. King, 213–242. Oxford: Oxford University Press.

Revkin, A. C. 2002. "With White House Approval, E.P.A. Pollution Report Omits Global Warming Section." *New York Times*, September 15.

Revkin, A. C., and K. Q. Seelye. 2003. "Report by the E.P.A. Leaves out Data on Climate Change." *New York Times*, June 19.

Risen, J. 2011. "Obama Takes on Congress over Policy Czar Positions." *New York Times*, April 16.

Roosevelt, F. D. 1972. *Franklin D. Roosevelt and Conservation: 1911–1945: Use and Abuse of America's Natural Resources*. Comp. and ed. by E. B. Nixon. New York: Arno.

Rosenbaum, W. A. 2006. "Improving Environmental Regulation at the EPA: The Challenge in Balancing Politics, Policy, and Science." In *Environmental Policy*, 6th ed., ed. N. J. Vig and M. E. Kraft, 169–192. Washington, DC: CQ Press.

Rudalevige, A. 2006. *The New Imperial Presidency: Renewing Presidential Power after Watergate*. Ann Arbor: University of Michigan Press.

——. 2010. "The Presidency and Unilateral Powers: A Taxonomy." In *The Presidency and the Political* System, 9th ed., ed. M. Nelson, 463–488. Washington, DC: CQ Press.

Savage, C. 2007. *Takeover: The Return of the Imperial Presidency and the Subversion of American Democracy*. New York: Little, Brown.

——. 2008. "Report Finds Manipulation of Interior Department Actions." *New York Times*, December 16.

——. 2009. "Obama Vows Sparing Use of Signing Statements." *New York Times*, March 10.

——. 2012. "Shift on Executive Power Lets Obama Bypass Rivals." *New York Times*, April 23.

Shanley, R. A. 1992. *Presidential Influence and Environmental Policy*. Westport, CT: Greenwood.

Shapiro, S. 2007. "An Evaluation of the Bush Administration Reforms to the Regulatory Process." *Presidential Studies Quarterly* 37: 270–290.

Smith, V. K., ed. 1984. *Environmental Policy under Reagan's Executive Order: The Role of Benefit-Cost Analysis*. Chapel Hill: University of North Carolina Press.

Soden, D. L., ed. 1999. *The Environmental Presidency*. Albany: State University of New York Press.

Stine, J. K. 1998. "Environmental Policy during the Carter Presidency." In *The Carter Presidency: Policy Choices in the Post-New Deal Era*, ed. G. M. Fink and H. D. Graham, 179–201. Lawrence: University of Kansas Press.

Train, R. E. 1996. "The Environmental Record of the Nixon Administration." *Presidential Studies Quarterly* 26: 185–196.

Union of Concerned Scientists. 2008. "Hundreds of EPA Scientists Report Political Interference over Last Five Years." Available at http://www.ucsusa.org/news/press_release/hundreds-of-epa-scientists-0112.html.

US House of Representatives, Committee on Oversight and Government Reform. 2007. "Political Interference with Climate Change Science Under the

Bush Administration." Available at http://www.lpl.arizona.edu/resources/
globalwarming/documents/political-interference.pdf.

Vickery, M. R. 2004. "Conservative Politics and the Politics of Conservation: Richard
Nixon and the Environmental Protection Agency." In *Green Talk in the White
House*, ed. T. R. Peterson, 113–131. College Station, Texas: Texas A&M University
Press.

Vig, N. J. 2013. "Presidential Powers and Environmental Policy." In Environmental
Policy, 8th ed., ed. N.J. Vig and M.E. Kraft, 84–108. Washington, DC: CQ Press.

Vig, N. J., and M. E. Kraft, eds. 1984. *Environmental Policy in the 1980s: Reagan's New
Agenda*. Washington, DC: CQ Press.

———.1990. *Environmental Policy in the 1990s*. Washington, DC: CQ Press.

———.2013. *Environmental Policy: New Directions for the Twenty-First Century*. 8th
ed. Washington, DC: CQ Press.

Warber, A. L. 2006. *Executive Orders and the Modern Presidency: Legislating from the
Oval Office*. Boulder, CO: Lynne Rienner.

Waterman, R. W. 2009. "Assessing the Unilateral Presidency." In *Oxford Handbook
of the American Presidency, ed. G. C.* Edwards III and W. G. Howell, 477–499.
Oxford: Oxford University Press.

Wayne, S. J. 2009. "Legislative Skills." In *Oxford Handbook of the American
Presidency, ed. G. C. Edwards III and W. G. Howell . Oxford: Oxford University
Press.

West, J. P., and G. Sussman. 1999. "Implementation of Environmental Policy: The
Chief Executive." In *The Environmental Presidency*, ed. D. L. Soden. Albany, NY:
State University of New York Press.

Wood, B. D. 1988. "Principals, Bureaucrats and Responsiveness in Clean Air Act
Enforcements." *American Political Science Review* 82: 213–234.

———.2009. "Presidents and the Political Agenda." In *Oxford Handbook of the
American* Presidency, ed. G. C. Edwards III and W. G. Howell. Oxford: Oxford
University Press.

Wood, B. D., and R.W. Waterman. 1994. *Bureaucratic Dynamics*. Boulder, CO:
Westview.

CHAPTER 15

ENVIRONMENTAL BUREAUCRACIES

THE ENVIRONMENTAL PROTECTION AGENCY

DANIEL J. FIORINO

IN the first week of December 2010, a series of events in Washington, DC, marked the 40th anniversary of the founding of the U.S. Environmental Protection Agency (EPA). The first such event was a conversation with EPA administrator Lisa Jackson, held at the Aspen Institute in Washington. The main topic was a list that the EPA and the institute were releasing of the agency's top 10 achievements over four decades. It included the removal of lead from the air, a ban on DDT, gains in water quality, controls on toxic chemicals, vehicle efficiency and emissions controls, expansion of community right-to-know laws, and awareness of inequities in environmental protection for minority and low-income groups. Although other experts might select different issues for a top 10, it was generally accepted that the EPA could take credit for many achievements (Aspen Institute 2010).

Beyond the list, however, were general statements about the agency and its role. Among these was the assertion that the EPA had shifted from "a concept of cleanup after the fact to a culture of innovation" that "helped to make many American businesses competitive in areas where they might not have been otherwise." The report contended that "a culture of innovation and cooperation has made the EPA a model for regulatory agencies around the world" (Aspen Institute 2010, 7–8). Over the last 40 years, the document further stated, the EPA has evolved from a notion of cleaning up the environment "to a more nuanced understanding of the innate talent of the American people for technological ingenuity and innovation" (p. 6). These are sweeping claims that would have drawn less agreement than the list of accomplishments, even among strong supporters of environmental programs.

This 40th anniversary document illustrates many contradictions in the EPA's history. On the one hand, its efforts under the Clean Air Act, Clean Water Act, and other statutes have led to gains for health, quality of life, and ecosystem protection. That the quality of the environment in the United States is better, probably markedly so, than it would have been without the EPA and its panoply of regulatory laws is generally accepted. At the same time, there has always been debate about its role and approach. Critics claim that EPA has been adversarial, inflexible, and intolerant of new approaches; in the eyes of many observers, the shift to a culture of innovation and partnerships has barely begun (e.g., Davies and Mazurek 1998; Eisner 2006; Larson 1998; NAPA 2000). The EPA's defenders would respond that the rough-and-tumble of U.S. environmental politics and opposition of industry interests leaves little choice but to rely on confrontational strategies that force change on its own terms.

This chapter presents a guide to and analysis of the EPA as perhaps the world's foremost environmental bureaucracy. By design, the EPA does conform in most respects to the ideal type of a bureaucracy that Max Weber famously outlined more than a century ago. In this respect, it is not fundamentally different from environmental agencies that were established in other nations, many at about the same time as the EPA (Schreurs 2002). It relies heavily on expert knowledge, an array of rules, hierarchical organization, a complex division of labor, career staff, and some insulation from political influence (Rosenbaum 1995). It also reflects a typically American model of administrative policy making, in which Congress delegates authority to agencies under regulatory statutes, the president appoints top officials and oversees implementation, and the courts hear challenges to agency actions. The EPA also operates in a federal system that involves complex relationships with state agencies. In sum, the EPA exemplifies bureaucracy, American style.

The chapter begins with a brief history of the agency and its evolution over four decades, and then analyzes its organization and decision making. Following that is an analysis of the EPA and the administrative and policy literature associated with it under three headings: relationships with state agencies; the role of economic and risk analysis in decision making; and the capacity for innovation. The final section considers the extent to which the EPA's past should define its future and that of U.S. environmental policy. Consistent with the overall themes of this volume, the chapter gives special attention to the EPA's institutional capacity, its development and adaptation over the last four decades, and its potential for policy innovation. It aims to present a guide to the agency as an environmental bureaucracy, assess the literature, and suggest priorities for future research.

1. ORIGINS AND EVOLUTION

The American republic functioned for almost 200 years before creating a national environmental protection agency. Before 1970, the now-EPA functions that existed within the federal government were scattered among a dozen agencies. Authority for air pollution was housed in the former Department of Health, Education, and Welfare. Water quality, pesticides, and radiation lay with the Interior and Agriculture Departments and the Atomic Energy Commission. More important, Washington's role in pollution control and environmental protection was limited. Laws that existed before 1970 defined a federal role focused on guidelines, research, and assistance. Authority for air and water pollution control rested with the states, but few had chosen to act. As concern with pollution grew in the late 1960s, and many states did not or could not respond, federal policy makers stepped in to fill the gap (Davies 1970; Davies and Davies 1975; Graham 1999).

Two events in 1970 dramatically and permanently changed the landscape of U.S. environmental policy. First, President Richard Nixon signed the executive order creating the EPA. In doing so, he adopted the advice of the Ash Council on Executive Organization to establish an independent agency, outside the cabinet, to consolidate pollution control and related functions across the government. The second event was the passage of the Clean Air Act (CAA) of 1970. The CAA was as critical to the future of the EPA as the creation of the agency itself. The executive order served only to collect previously scattered functions that provided limited national authority; it did not define any new powers for the EPA. The pathbreaking CAA invested the EPA administrator with substantial authority to set national air quality goals; determine legally binding, technology-forcing emission standards for industrial sources and vehicles; require and approve state air quality plans aimed at meeting the national goals; and perform several other functions.

Following on the National Environmental Policy Act of 1969, these two events set the stage for a remarkable decade of policy innovation (Lazarus 2004; Portney and Stavins 2000). In 1972, the Federal Water Pollution Control Act granted the EPA administrator authority comparable to that in the CAA over industrial and municipal sources of water pollution. Over the next eight years, Congress enacted the Safe Drinking Water Act, Toxic Substances Control Act, Resource Conservation and Recovery Act, Comprehensive Environmental Response, Compensation, and Liability (Superfund) Act, and Endangered Species Act (although the last was not assigned to the EPA). By adding to the authority in the order creating the EPA, such as for pesticides and radiation issues, this "environmental decade" made it the most powerful and visible pollution control agency in the world (Vogel 1993). As a result, the United States was widely viewed as a leader in environmental protection and pollution policy in these early years.

Many publications exist regarding the EPA's history since its founding and the 40th anniversary celebration in December 2010. Some provide general overviews of its actions or of the legal framework in which it operates. Others examine specific aspects of policies or factors that affect its decisions. It is worth noting, however, that no definitive, general, in-depth history and analysis of the EPA exists. This is a significant gap in the literature, given the obvious importance of the agency in U.S. public policy. For a time, the agency employed an official historian whose efforts were drawn upon for this chapter, but that position ended in 1995.[1] The conclusion to this chapter recommends topics that should form the basis for future research on the EPA, its role, and its policies.

William Ruckelshaus, the first and fifth EPA administrator, once analogized the cycles of U.S. environmental policy to a pendulum, moving from aggressive to lax regulation and back again over time (Ruckelshaus 1996). As one looks at the EPA's four decades, the strength of the analogy is apparent. As the first administrator, Ruckelshaus thought it important to move quickly to establish an enforcement presence and actively use the authority Congress had granted. The programs the EPA had inherited from other agencies remained largely intact. Despite concerns from the White House about the EPA being too forceful in these early days, Ruckelshaus and his successor, Russell Train, established the EPA as a credible regulatory agency. This pattern continued in the 1970s, although the twin challenges of a sluggish economy and energy crisis in the late 1970s forced the EPA under Administrator Douglas Costle, Jimmy Carter's appointee, to give greater attention to economic analysis and stimulated proposals for regulatory reform.

The environmental decade of the 1970s and period of relative consensus came to an abrupt end in 1981 with the administration of Ronald Reagan. Having campaigned for smaller government and less regulation, Reagan viewed the EPA as a prime target for reductions in authority, budgets, and economic impacts. With efforts to change the laws blocked by a Democratic Congress, Administrator Anne Gorsuch set out to reduce the EPA's enforcement presence, cut staff and resources, emphasize cost over environmental concerns, and devolve authority to states under the rubric of a "New Federalism," although "devolution" in this case was little more than an excuse for defunding and weakening programs established in the previous decade (Andrews 1999, 257–281).

The response from Capitol Hill was to pass prescriptive laws that would force the EPA to fulfill its regulatory obligations (Durant 1993). Indeed, the pendulum effect that Ruckelshaus observed was firmly established in these partisan struggles. Rather than take a middle ground on program reform, the administration adopted a deregulatory stance that was unsupportable politically. The effect was to mobilize the opposition. The membership and budgets of national environmental advocacy groups, for example, increased dramatically in the 1980s (Bosso 2000), This pattern of Republican efforts to reduce the stringency of programs and Democratic efforts to defend them was repeated in the actions of a conservative 106th Congress in 1995 and George W. Bush in the early 2000s (Kraft 2010; Rosenbaum 2003). The pendulum clearly was in full swing.

---

1. The products of the history office at EPA may be found at http://www.epa.gov/history. These include oral history interviews with several EPA Administrators.

The Reagan strategy failed. In 1983, Reagan persuaded Ruckelshaus to return as EPA administrator. He was given control over personnel and some latitude on policy. In addition to recruiting outstanding appointees, he worked to restore the EPA's credibility and defuse some of the political controversy by adopting risk as a conceptual foundation for the EPA's policies (Landy et al. 1990, 1993). Central to this strategy was a distinction proposed by the National Academy of Sciences between risk management and assessment (National Academy of Sciences 1983). EPA policies moved back toward the middle. Ruckelshaus's successor, Lee Thomas, continued the restoration of EPA and its programs, although with less political clout than his predecessor had been able to bring to the job.

The first two years of the George H. W. Bush administration may be seen today as a period of relative bipartisanship in U.S. environmental policy. The new administrator, William Reilly, was a respected environmentalist and head of the World Wildlife Fund. In these first two years, Bush adopted a moderate stance on environmental issues, to the extent of working with Senate Majority Leader George Mitchell (D-ME) to pass the Clean Air Act Amendments of 1990, perhaps the most significant regulatory law in U.S. history.

Reilly also presided over a period of policy innovation that began under his two predecessors. In the mid- and late 1980s, the EPA made progress on several new policies and strategies, such as risk-based planning, emissions trading, information-based regulation, and cross-program coordination. Although some of these were more durable than others, it was a period in which many new ideas were incorporated into the policy framework. Among these were the use of risk as a priority-setting tool, appreciation of the global environment, more attention to collaborative processes (O'Leary and Raines 2001), and tools other than regulation for defining the agency's role. Reilly led a major expansion in the EPA's capacity for international engagement, frustrated to some extent by the administration's refusal at the 1992 Earth Summit in Rio de Janeiro to commit to global agreements on climate change and biodiversity. Indeed, by the 1992 election, President Bush was considerably less green than he had been in the first few years. Criticism from major business interests and promarket, small-government advocates within his party pushed Bush back toward a more conservative environmental agenda.

President Bush's return to his conservative base in 1992 set the stage for another pendulum swing when Carol Browner took over as Bill Clinton's EPA administrator. As an aide to Senator Al Gore and former head of Florida's environmental agency, Browner brought strong credentials to the job. She would move the agency back in the direction of more stringent air quality standards, aggressive enforcement, and a degree of skepticism toward cost-benefit and risk-based analysis. The EPA shifted from industry to environmental groups as a source of ideas and political support. This was tempered somewhat by the takeover of the House by conservative Republicans in 1995. Although deregulation failed, as it had in the early 1980s, it stimulated a period of program assessment and regulatory streamlining that coincided with the government reinvention movement of the 1990s (Fiorino 2006; Rosenbaum 2000).

The EPA's fourth decade has reinforced the validity of the pendulum analogy. From 2001 to 2009, the Bush administration pushed for several changes in pollution policy, particularly on issues affecting the fossil fuel industry, and stalled on greenhouse gases (Rosenbaum 2003 and 2010b). Bush's first EPA administrator, Christine Todd Whitman, left after two years, due particularly to the administration's position on climate change. Her successors, Michael Leavitt and Stephen Johnson, largely carried out administration policies, which did include new diesel standards, more stringent ozone and particulate goals, and other achievements. The overall stance of the administration on many issues, however, such as mercury from utility emissions and climate change, and an alleged softness on enforcement, paved the way for another noticeable pendulum swing in 2009 (Rosenbaum 2010b). Lisa Jackson, President Obama's choice at the EPA, stressed in no uncertain terms that the EPA as a tough enforcer and regulator was back, and collaboration with industry would be suspect (Hobson 2009). The administration was forced to moderate its stance on many issues after the 2010 midterm elections, when the Republicans returned as a majority in the House of Representatives and made gains in the Senate as well. On such issues as greenhouse gases, mountaintop mining, and nonpoint source water, the House majority, reflecting a strong antigovernment mood, called for drastic budget cuts and program changes. Ideological and interparty polarization was more marked than ever, and the EPA was caught in the middle (see, for example, Fears 2011).

These partisan shifts have consequences for the EPA. First, they make it difficult to establish continuity over time (see Gaertner, Gaertner, and Devine 1983 on the Reagan transition). Even good ideas and initiatives under one administration may be dropped by the next one. Not only is the change in EPA leadership a source of discontinuity, partisan shifts in Congress and in committee and subcommittee chairs are disruptive. Changes in House control to Democrats in 2007 and back to Republicans in 2011 provide a recent example. Second, these partisan swings reinforce the "adversarial legalism" many scholars associate with environmental policy in the United States, by causing each side to lock in policies that cannot easily be undone (Kagan 1995; Wallace 1995). When the fight is over the simple dichotomy of having more or less regulation, it is difficult to seek a middle ground that leads to better policies. This was the point Ruckelshaus made with the pendulum analogy; the highly charged atmosphere following the Republican takeover of the House in 2011 has only reinforced validity of the Ruckelshaus analogy.

An alternative way of viewing the EPA's history is by identifying different periods in its 40-year evolution. One such formulation is Daniel Mazmanian and Michael Kraft's (2009) demarcation of three epochs in U.S. environmental policy.[2] The first, *regulating for environmental protection* (1970–1990), focused on creating the legal instruments, scientific capabilities, and bureaucratic infrastructure needed to control major pollution sources. A second epoch of *efficiency-based regulatory reform and flexibility* (1980–2000s) modified the regulatory structure

---

2. For a similar interpretation of the evolution of EPA in terms of types of learning see Fiorino 2001.

by incorporating market-based approaches, methods for preventing pollution, information disclosure tools, collaborative relationships, and greater attention to cost-effectiveness and cost-benefit analysis. The third epoch, a transition to *sustainable development*, began in the 1990s and is still at an early stage. It is concerned with the need to balance relationships among the economic, environmental, and social systems and of not foreclosing choices for future generations.

The transition to the third, sustainability epoch is still emerging. The EPA and its work are defined by the first epoch, regulating for environmental protection, with some progress into the second. The transition to sustainable development remains more a challenge than a reality. Given the EPA's limited control over many of the environmental components of sustainability—among them energy, resources management, transportation, agriculture, and urban development—this transition must be achieved by the federal government as a whole, not just the EPA. The question at this point is whether American political institutions are prepared to make a sustainability transition possible.

2. ORGANIZATION AND DECISION MAKING

EPA's organization was determined by the process that created it and the framework of laws it administers. As the first administrator, Ruckelshaus considered alternative structures but decided that reorganization would be disruptive and distract from the critical task of establishing the agency and its role (Marcus 1980a, 1980b, 1991).

As a result, the EPA's organization today is roughly what it was after its founding in the early 1970s (Fiorino 1995). It reflects the architecture of laws it administers and the congressional committees and subcommittees that oversee it. At the core of the EPA of today are the four national program offices for air, water, waste, and chemicals issues. These are the Office of Air (air quality, including climate mitigation, and radiation); the Office of Water (water quality, water habitat, drinking water); the Office of Solid Waste and Emergency Response (waste and materials; waste cleanup); and the Office of Chemical Safety and Pollution Prevention (chemicals regulation, including pesticides, and pollution prevention). Their work is defined by the laws they administer. Corresponding to these are committees and subcommittees in the Senate and House of Representatives that oversee the EPA; this oversight is especially intense when different parties control Congress and the White House. The effects of this oversight are discussed below.

The rest of the EPA is structured along functional and geographic lines. Organized by function are offices for enforcement and compliance, research and development, international affairs, information policy, and legal counsel. Like the four program offices, these are led by an assistant administrator who is appointed by the president and confirmed by the Senate. These offices work closely with the programs, although historically there have been concerns about how well such functions as research and development respond to program needs. Ten regional offices link Washington with state environmental agencies and oversee implementation (Crotty 1988). The largest are those for the Southeast, based in Atlanta, and the Midwest, based in Chicago. Of nearly 18,000 employees in 2010, some two-thirds were located outside Washington in regional offices and research labs around the country.

The EPA's decision making occurs in a contested and often politicized setting. Two fundamental tensions define this setting. One is that the EPA is both a science agency and a regulator. Scientific expertise is a foundation of its legitimacy and a reason for its existence (on use of science, see MacBeth and Marchant 2008; Powell 1999). In a classic model of administrative rationality, an environmental agency would first establish the factual premises for its decisions and then decide what policies should be adopted based on those premises. In practice, however, agencies like the EPA typically confront scientific uncertainty that cannot be resolved before making policy decisions. Recently, even conclusions for which there is overwhelming scientific consensus, such as estimates of climate change, are challenged politically. Critics on both sides of the debate, for and against stricter regulation, point not just to uncertainties in the science behind decisions but also to efforts to modify assessments for political ends (see Rosenbaum 2010b).

The second tension is that the EPA is expected to protect the environment without imposing economic harm or interfering with growth. Indeed, although the precise terms differ, the pollution control laws instruct the EPA to prescribe some version of best available technology balanced against economic feasibility, affordability, or social benefits. Only in a few instances, such as in setting National Ambient Air Quality Standards based only on health considerations, are the instructions one-sided (Fraas 1991; Morgenstern 1997). In most cases, the EPA must decide where to draw the line between environmental and economic objectives. The swings of the pendulum described by Ruckelshaus have turned, more than anything else, on this economic issue. As a result, the EPA is criticized at any one time for being an overbearing job-killer that undermines national prosperity and as a lackey of industry that places profit over public health. The recent politics of climate change illustrate this tension perfectly.

Science has been both a source of legitimacy and vulnerability for the EPA. Like most science-based agencies, it established a Science Advisory Board (SAB) to advise on technical issues, such as scientific analyses that underpin air quality standards (Jasanoff 1990). Board members are selected on the basis of technical expertise rather than interest group affiliations. The theory behind an expert advisory group such as the SAB is that political neutrality will allow members to apply their technical expertise to the science underlying decisions. The process has not always worked as smoothly as this theory suggests; values enter into interpretation and evaluation of scientific assessments. Having a politically balanced and technically expert advisory group, however, has been a source of credibility for agencies, helping to assure the public of the science behind decisions. The SAB and similar advisory bodies are central to the EPA's decision making.

The EPA's organization, combined with the external pressures discussed in the next section, has led to a complex process for developing regulations. Thomas McGarity has described the EPA as having "one of the most highly developed internal procedures for generating rules of any agency in the federal government" (1991, 70; see also Coglianese 2007; Fiorino 1995; Furlong 2007). The challenge historically has been to coordinate the multiple perspectives (program, technical, legal, economic, scientific) that define various parts of the agency; make needed links across programs, contaminants, and problems; and balance national goals against regional and local priorities. The result has been a largely team-oriented, bottom-up model in which staff-level work groups build consensus and recommend policies to higher levels in the agency. Although there is more top-down engagement by senior managers on high-profile, controversial issues, this bottom-up team model still defines most of the EPA's regulatory decision making.

A fact of life for the EPA over the years has been the constraints of its budget. The largest in its history was the $10.3 billion Congress authorized in FY 2010, although that included $3.0 billion in spending under the American Reinvestment and Recovery Act of 2009 for the stimulus. A better indication of funds available for running EPA programs is its operating budget, which excludes grants, loan funds, and other resources passed on to state and local government or others. Between 2004 and 2009, the operating budget averaged some $3.2 billion annually, then increased to $3.9 billion in 2010 (EPA 2010a).

In real terms, the operating budget in 2009 was roughly what it was in 1980, despite a major expansion in responsibilities. In 1980, the EPA did not have to contend with greenhouse gases, a long list of air toxics, bio- and nanoengineered materials, radon in homes, ozone-depleting substances, small-quantity hazardous waste generators, threats to homeland security, and a host of other issues. If anything, the burdens of scientific and legal proof underlying its decisions have grown over the four decades. Like most federal domestic agencies, the EPA budget is not likely to increase in coming years. The disparity between what it is expected to do and what it realistically may accomplish grows every year. This "implementation gap" raises questions not only about resource levels but implementation strategies (Davies and Mazurek 1998; Rosenbaum 2010a). The success of future problem solving may depend more on changing those strategies on environmental innovation—than in hoping for budget increases that are unlikely at best.

3. EXTERNAL INFLUENCES: THE EPA'S POLITICAL ENVIRONMENT

Few federal agencies operate in as political and controversial an environment as the EPA. Its responsibilities reveal many of the fundamental fault lines of American politics, among them the role of government, the demands for economic growth, the efficiency and fairness of markets, and the validity of science. Moreover, the EPA is by definition a *regulator*; it achieves its goals by constraining the behavior of others in society. It is neither a distributor of benefits nor a pure science agency. As a result, nearly every EPA decision is the subject of conflicts among interests and values in society.

Given this reality, the EPA is influenced strongly by external forces. Much of the literature has focused on the effects of the presidency, Congress, courts, other agencies, and different levels of government on the EPA. These forces define a context in which advocates of competing interests—business and environmental groups in particular—attempt to influence policy in desired directions. Rather than discuss the strategies and views of these interests groups here, a topic that is covered elsewhere in this volume, this section sets out the effects of external institutional forces as they influence the EPA.

Any analysis of external institutions would have to begin with Congress (Kraft 1995, 2000, 2010). After all, much of the early leadership for national programs came from policy entrepreneurs such as Senator Edmund Muskie, who was instrumental in the passage of the air and water laws. Through the 1990s, it was Congress that generally took the lead in setting out the legal infrastructure for environmental programs. Similarly, during the Reagan administration assault of the early 1980s, a Democratic majority in Congress resisted statutory change while also inserting action-forcing mechanisms in reauthorized laws. At the same time, it should be noted that it was the executive branch that protected environmental programs from the attempts to eviscerate the implementation of environmental laws by the newly conservative, Republican House of Representatives in 1995. A similar pattern occurred in 2011, when a House majority chose the EPA as a target for major reductions and challenged its authority in several areas, especially for regulating greenhouse gases. In sum, the role of Congress has been to initiate action as well as to offset the power of the White House, depending on the distribution of power within the government.

The literature on Congress focuses on the three critical roles it plays for the EPA: as statutory enabler, appropriator of funds, and overseer of implementation. In terms of enabling laws, policy entrepreneurs in Congress have often taken the lead in enacting major environmental laws. In two major instances—the FWPCA of 1972 and Clean Water Act of 1987—Congress passed key legislation over a president's veto. At other times, presidential and congressional leadership combined to enact major change. The best example occurred over two decades ago, when President George H. W. Bush and Senator George Mitchell worked together to pass the 1990 Clean Air Act Amendments. In appropriations, a typical role for Congress has been to increase the EPA's funding after it is cut by Republican presidents. Democratic control of one or both houses of Congress has offset the budgetary swings that result from changes of party control of the White House. Similarly, Republicans would point out that their party's oversight moderates the excessive zeal that defines the EPA's regulatory policies in Democratic administrations.

Much of the literature on Congress and the EPA has focused on legislative oversight. Common themes in this literature are fragmentation and inconsistency. Michael Kraft has written that "the congressional committee system is the embodiment of structural fragmentation and dispersal of influence in American government" (1995, 178). In the Senate, Kraft counts 14 committees and 20 subcommittees with jurisdiction over the EPA; the comparable House numbers are 18 and 38 (in 1994), respectively. Although two committees are the most central to the EPA—Environment and Public Works in the Senate and Energy and Commerce in the House—they rely heavily on specialized subcommittees. In both houses, the appropriations and general oversight and investigations subcommittees further carve up EPA oversight.

This oversight structure has several consequences. An obvious one is difficulty in coordinating, let alone integrating, policy across statutory and program boundaries. The oversight structure mirrors and thus reinforces the EPA's fragmented statutory framework, with separate laws for air, water, waste, chemicals, and other issues (Fiorino 1995, 32–36; Ruckelshaus 1996). This structure similarly is reflected in the EPA's internal organization and that of state agencies. In the past, this structure has raised concerns about the EPA's ability to address issues holistically and consider cross-media environmental impacts (Fiorino 2001; NAPA 1995). More recently, it may be argued, this oversight system constrains the EPA's ability to promote environmental sustainability.

Another consequence of this oversight structure and legal framework is that it limits the EPA's ability to think and act strategically. Like all agencies, it prepares a five-year strategic plan under the Government Performance and Results Act of 1993 (EPA 2010b). The EPA's strategic goals are Clean Air and Global Climate Change (some 12 percent of the budget); Clean and Safe Water (46 percent); Land Preservation and Restoration (18 percent); Healthy Communities and Ecosystems (17 percent); and Compliance and Environmental Stewardship (8 percent). To be truly strategic, an agency should have discretion to allocate resources based on the seriousness of problems and the likely return on investments. It should have some flexibility in tailoring program strategies to the issues. This is difficult when there are many laws and diverse oversight authorities (Davies and Mazurek 1998; NAPA 1995).

The president and executive office influence the EPA in many ways (Vig 2000). These include appointing the administrator and other top officials, recommending budgets to Congress, setting priorities, and reviewing regulations. The regulatory review authority has been controversial and a recurring challenge for the EPA, especially but not only under Republican administrations (Percival 1991). Some kind of executive office review, almost always by OMB, has been part of the EPA's decision making from the beginning. Within the Nixon White House, concern over the economic impacts of the newly constituted EPA led to "Quality of Life" reviews by the Commerce Department and OMB in 1971. Later in the decade, President Gerald Ford not only continued this practice but added "Inflation Impact Statements" overseen by the Council on Wage and Price Stability.

In 1978, Jimmy Carter's order "Improving Government Regulations" required a cost-benefit analysis of major regulations, among other measures. A major step up in White House oversight came in 1981 with Reagan's Executive Order 12291 (Smith 1984). It directed agencies to submit proposed and final rules to OMB and only adopt those for which, to the extent permitted by law, the benefits exceeded the costs. This order set the stage for executive-legislative conflict in the 1980s, as a Republican White House and largely Democratic Congress struggled to control the EPA.

The federal courts also have been a major influence on the EPA and its decisions (O'Leary 1993; Weiland 2007). Under the Administrative Procedure Act of 1946, any party that is adversely affected by a federal administrative decision may take the issue to the U.S. Courts of Appeals. Given the high stakes, EPA decisions are challenged regularly in court. Rosemary O'Leary (2010) describes five effects that courts have on the agency. They determine access to the courts by defining who has *standing* to make an appeal; determine the *ripeness* or readiness of issues for review; define the *standard of review* to apply; *interpret environmental statues* and the EPA's conformity with them; and *choose remedies* for carrying out rulings. For regulators, courts are a constant presence. The Office of the General Counsel participates actively in decision making, and the anticipated reactions from courts greatly influence policy deliberations and outcomes.

A small number of EPA decisions may eventually reach the U.S. Supreme Court. Two such decisions, one issued in 2001 and the other in 2007, illustrate the effects the Court may have on the EPA (O'Leary 2010). In the 2001 case, *Whitman v. American Trucking Association*, the Court upheld the more stringent National Ambient Air Quality Standards the EPA had set for ozone and particulate matter in 1997 under Administrator Carol Browner. Rejecting the claims of the Trucking Association and a long list of other business groups, the Court held that the EPA's authority under the Clean Air Act was not unconstitutionally vague and that the agency did not have to conduct a cost-benefit analysis of the standard in issuing it. In the 2007 case, *Massachusetts v. EPA*, the Court accepted the argument of several states that the EPA had authority under the Clean Air Act to regulate carbon dioxide (CO_2) as a pollutant. Indeed, if the EPA were to determine that (CO_2) endangers public health and welfare, which the agency later did, it had a legal obligation to regulate it. In both cases, the Court took a pro-environmental stance, based on its reading of the law. In the first, this meant upholding the agency; in the second, it meant pushing the agency toward action despite the Bush administration's refusal to act.

The literature on the EPA's external political environment and the effects on decision making are substantial, and it covers many topics covered elsewhere in this volume. Most of the political science literature focuses on the executive and legislative branches, with some attention to the courts (Lester 1995a). A far more extensive treatment of the decisions of the federal courts and their effects on the agency may be found in the legal scholarship. The sources cited here and the discussions and references in other chapters provide a more detailed and extensive guide to the literature on external influences.

4. Cross-Cutting Issues for Understanding the EPA

The chapter so far has considered the history and evolution of the EPA, its internal organization and decision making, and external influences. This section expands on our analysis of the EPA and the relevant literature by examining three cross-cutting issues: relationships among levels of government, or federalism; the role of economic and risk analysis; and the EPA's capacity for environmental and program innovation.

4.1. Relationships among Levels of Government

One of the most distinctive characteristics of environmental policy in the United States is federalism. Policy making occurs in the context of complex and often confusing divisions of labor between the national, state, and local governments. On some issues, such as land use or solid waste management, state and local authorities assume primary responsibility. On others, such as air and water pollution control, drinking water quality, and hazardous waste management, responsibilities are shared, although with the federal EPA having substantial authority. Especially for new sources of air and water pollution and drinking water contaminants, the agency takes the lead. For other issues, such as toxic substances, pesticides, and vehicles, the EPA makes nearly all the major policy decisions.

This complex relationship is based on three principles, at least for the issues in which authority is shared. First, the EPA generally has responsibility for setting goals and issuing standards, and the states are charged with implementing them. On the one hand, states perform over 90 percent of the inspections, handle over 90 percent of permitting, and collect 95 percent of the data for the EPA on regulated sources. The EPA, on the other hand, sets national air quality goals and approves state water goals, determines technology standards for new sources of air and water pollution, issues standards for drinking water contaminants, and prescribes rules for managing, treating, and disposing of hazardous wastes. The EPA focuses on policy; states are primary implementers (on state workloads, see NAPA 1995 and 1997; Rabe 2010).

Second, national laws preempt state action. Justified constitutionally under the Commerce Clause, the Clean Air Act and other laws replace state with national authority (Lazarus 2004). However, the EPA then hands back much of that authority through a process of delegation, but with strings attached. States must demonstrate that they have the legal authority, resources, and implementing mechanisms in place to be able to exercise authority to administer environmental programs within their boundaries.

The third principle is that state environmental standards may be more but not less stringent than federal ones. Part of the justification for having a national EPA is that certain minimum levels of environmental quality should exist regardless of the state. Some states, notably California and its air quality programs, have often adopted stricter higher standards than the EPA's. More recently, states like New Jersey have passed laws blocking the Department of Environmental Protection from exceeding EPA standards. An exception to this principle is limits on vehicle emissions. They affect products sold nationally, so states are required to obtain a waiver from EPA to set stricter emission limits. These waivers were granted routinely to California until 2007, when EPA administrator Stephen Johnson denied the state's request to set stricter CO_2 limits than federal ones (a decision that was quickly reversed when the Obama administration took over in 2009).

The EPA's history consists in large part of shifting patterns of centralization and devolution in national-state relations (Scheberle 2004a and 2004b). The EPA was formed in the first place and empowered by environmental statutes because states were seen as being inadequate for dealing with pollution. Among the particular concerns were that state policy makers would not stand up to powerful economic interests, that states would compete for economic development in a "race to the bottom," and that only a federal agency could address regional pollution. The 1970s consisted of a steady expansion and centralization of EPA's authority. This trend was reversed for a time in the 1980s when President Reagan used the New Federalism to attempt to devolve authority back to states (Lester 1995b), but the basic model of the 1970s remains today.

In 1995, the EPA created the National Environmental Performance Partnership System (NEPPS) in response to state complaints about excessive oversight. The basis for the NEPPS was that the EPA and a state agency would negotiate measures of results that would become the basis for evaluating state performance and grant spending. The goal was to shift from oversight of outputs (i.e., counting such "beans" as permits issued or inspections conducted) to agreed-upon outcomes (such as changes in air quality). The idea was to give states more flexibility in deciding how to allocate their resources and run their programs, so long as they achieved the desired results. Although many states eventually did qualify for the NEPPS model, it never worked entirely as the states hoped. Among the concerns were the unwillingness of some EPA offices to grant as much discretion as states wanted and a lack of flexibility in shifting resources among programs (Copeland 1997; Scheberle 2005; see also NAPA 1997, 143–169, for a case study).

The EPA-state relationship will continue to evolve, depending on the political environment, federal and state resources, executive branch and EPA leadership, and state capabilities. What is clear at this point, however, is that states are no longer the weaker link as they were viewed in the 1970s. Many states today are seen as being more capable, innovative, and adaptable than the federal agency. On some issues, notably climate change and pollution prevention, states are making more progress, although that is a function more of the conditions of national politics than the EPA itself (Rabe 2010).

4.2. Economic and Risk Analysis in Decision Making

To understand the EPA, it is necessary to be aware of the analytical issues that are central to its decision making. Much of the literature on the EPA throughout its history has focused on the role, strengths, and limits of economic and risk analysis. Of the two, economics has probably been more contentious, but the role of risk as a concept and the design and applications of risk assessment also have engendered controversy.

Concern over economic impacts is a fact of life for the EPA. As noted above, a core tension for 40 years has been defining and redefining the balance among economic and environmental goals. This tension is reflected in laws under which the EPA exercises authority as well as in the battles that occur in the process of the issuing regulations. In the National Ambient Air Quality Standards, for example, the EPA is directed to base decisions on health only, without regard for costs. In setting emission standards for major air and water pollution sources, however, it must specify technology standards that are economically feasible. To regulate existing chemicals under the Toxic Substances Control Act, the EPA must establish that benefits exceed risks (Portney and Stavins 2000). Clearly, a lack of political consensus on the role of economics is reflected in the inconsistencies and ambiguities in the EPA's laws and the swings in the pendulum that define its history (Morgenstern 1997).

At the time of the EPA's founding, the Nixon administration was concerned that the new agency would move to control pollution too aggressively (that is, without regard to costs). An Office of Planning and Management, with a mandate to analyze and limit economic impacts, was part of the initial organization. This office played an influential role in regulatory decisions for more than two decades, until it was downgraded in the mid-1990s. Although the EPA still routinely conducts economic analysis of regulations, administrators since have relied less on the policy office. In recent years, the lead for these analyses has shifted to the four major programs for air, water, waste, and chemicals. These analyses are conducted under *Guidelines for Preparing Economic Analyses* (EPA 2010c), which covers three aspects of agency decisions: a *benefit-cost analysis* that considers whether there are net benefits to society; an *analysis of economic impacts* on industry and others; and an *equity or distributional analysis* of the effects of decisions on subpopulations, such as low-income groups, minorities, and children.

These guidelines apply to nearly every policy or regulatory decision the EPA makes. Major decisions (defined as those with annual effects of $100 million or more) typically are the subject of a comprehensive analysis of benefits and costs. Other actions of at least moderate policy significance are evaluated for their economic impacts, such as effects on jobs, prices, plant closings, and so on. Most also are assessed for distributional effects, especially under the Obama administration, for which environmental justice is a priority. Under a series of executive orders, the Office of Information and Regulatory Affairs at OMB reviews and may offer comments on all proposed and final regulations and associated economic analyses. The EPA also is required to examine other economic issues, such as effects on small business and/or state and local governments, under such laws as the Regulatory Flexibility Act and Unfunded Mandates Reform Act. In recent years, the EPA typically is working on some 40–50 cost-benefit analyses at any time.

Like economics, risk analysis has been a foundation of the EPA's analytical agenda. The EPA and other agencies, such as the Food and Drug Administration, began to use risk assessment in the 1970s as a means of quantitatively measuring the harm posed by substances (Andrews 2000, 2005). They used risk assessment to decide whether or not to regulate and, if so, how stringently. Since then, the EPA has used risk assessments for a range of regulatory decisions, such as levels of pesticide residues to allow in food, cleanup standards for abandoned hazardous waste (Superfund) sites, acceptable contaminant levels in drinking water, controls over emissions of air toxics, action levels for radon in homes, and approval of chemicals for distribution in commerce (EPA 2004a). Combining estimates of toxicity and exposure, risk assessments provide a quantitative range of likely hazards; such data are a key input for regulatory decisions.

At times in the EPA's history, the concept of risk has played a role in priority setting as well as regulatory decision making. The use of risk analysis expanded greatly in the mid-1980s when Ruckelshaus returned as administrator. With the EPA's reputation as a science-based agency in tatters and its overall technical competency at a low point, he saw the need for a new decision framework. In doing so, he drew on a distinction proposed by the National Academy of Sciences between risk *assessment* and risk *management*. The first referred to the relatively neutral, technical process of estimating risk; the second was the more political, value-based process of deciding what to do about a risk. This paralleled a dichotomy in administrative theory between fact (assessment) and value (management) premises of decision making (Ruckelshaus 1985). This distinction is easier to maintain in theory than in practice. Risk assessments involve assumptions and uncertainties and thus reflect values. Still, the risk assessment/risk management distinction provided an analytical framework in a time of turmoil and influenced the EPA's approach to decision making (EPA 1987, 1990; Fiorino 1990).

Responsibility for setting standards and improving the quality of risk analyses rests with a Risk Assessment Forum in the EPA's Office of Science Policy. The forum guides risk policy, maintains the EPA's risk assessment guidelines, and advises on risk issues. Among the guidelines it manages are those on ecological risk and kinds of health risks, such as reproductive toxicity, mutagenicity, carcinogens, and exposure assessment.

Economics and risk are the two fundamental analytical tools that underlie EPA policy making. Their role varies based on the legal provisions under which a decision is being made, the quality of data, the political dynamics affecting the issues at hand, and the public visibility and salience of the decision. Although environmentalists have been critical of these tools, especially benefit-cost analysis, their conclusions often have supported environmental programs in the past. A retrospective analysis of the Clean Air Act, for example, concluded that air quality programs had delivered social benefits well in excess of their costs (EPA 1997). Similarly, risk assessments help the EPA set priorities and determine standards. At the same time, opponents of regulation have used both tools in efforts to relax standards and paralyze the regulatory process. Like any tool, these analyses maybe well or poorly designed; they are used constructively or not. Either way, they are an essential part of the EPA's decision making and figure prominently in public debates.

4.3. Environmental Innovation

The chapter opening raised the issue of the EPA's history of and capacity for innovation. As bureaucracies, agencies like the EPA often, by design, face limits when it comes to being innovative. They are designed to embody the strengths of Weber's classic model of bureaucracy, by being predictable, using expertise, organizing complex tasks, acting impersonally, and so on. Add to these characteristics, which are common to all bureaucracies, the contentiousness of the EPA's political environment, historical distrust among various interest groups, and prescriptive nature of its laws, and the barriers to innovation in environmental policy become even more formidable. A critical issue for the future of the agency is its capacity for innovation, not only in its own policies but in the effects that it has on technology and management innovation in entities that it regulates.

The most successful area of policy innovation has been incorporating emissions trading into the regulatory system. The EPA first applied trading in the late 1970s as a way of allowing development in Southern California without exceeding air quality standards more than was already occurring (Andrews 1999, 270–272). With offsets, new sources could expand and increase emissions if they induced existing ones to reduce emissions by a more than equivalent amount. This later evolved into regional trading for several air pollutants. Congress recognized the value of trading by adopting it as a centerpiece of the acid rain strategy in the 1990 Clean Air Act Amendments (Stavins 1998). Trading has been applied in other areas, such as removing lead from gasoline and reducing nonpoint source water pollution. Cap-and-trade programs also have been central to recent proposals for cutting greenhouse gas emissions (Rosenbaum 2010a).

Another area of innovation has been using information disclosure as a means of reducing pollution. Expressed most directly in the Toxics Release

Inventory (TRI), part of the 1986 Superfund amendments, this strategy requires public reporting of chemicals that are released, stored, or otherwise managed at industrial facilities. Rather than direct pollution sources to cut their emissions or install new technology, this approach uses public disclosure to motivate changes in behavior. The theory is that facilities will seek to avoid the negative attention that comes with disclosure. There is at least some empirical support for this theory, although it is subject to many qualifications (Kraft, Stephan, and Abel 2011). Based partly on this experience, reporting and transparency have become major additions to the EPA's portfolio in the last two decades. Both trading and disclosure now are recognized in law. The two differ in that trading began as an EPA initiative that was later incorporated as law, while disclosure began as legislative action.

The EPA's record as an innovator is less impressive in other areas. Permitting, for example, has long been a source of complaints because of processing times and costs, the large number of permits that may be needed, and fragmentation by environmental programs. Yet efforts to streamline, consolidate, or integrate permitting at various times have had little success (Davies 2001). An initiative for flexible air permitting begun in the 1990s has shown some benefit, but large-scale adoption still is uncertain (EPA 2004b).

As part of the reinventing government movement of the 1990s, the Clinton administration launched "streamlining environmental regulation" initiatives that had almost no effect (Fiorino 2006, 121–156; Marcus, Geffen, and Sexton 2002). Among these was a Common Sense Initiative that convened a range of stakeholders in a review of policies affecting several industry sectors. The goal was to reach consensus on policies for achieving "cleaner, cheaper, and smarter" outcomes (Coglianese and Allen 2005). This foundered on disagreements among stakeholders and a flawed process. Another initiative, Project XL, invited regulated entities to propose changes in rules that would allow them to achieve better results at less cost. The EPA approved 50 projects; some led to policy change. However, a goal of using them as the basis for a broader set of regulatory innovations was not met (Marcus and Geffen 2002). The relatively more successful EPA voluntary programs have been those that are not related administratively to the agency's regulatory functions, such as the Energy Star program (for assessments of voluntary programs overall, see Morgenstern and Pizer 2007).

A third area of innovation, integrating collaborative and voluntary programs into the regulatory system, also has had limited success. What voluntary programs exist are limited in number, resources, and influence, and have not been well integrated into the existing system. For those advocating an EPA limited to regulation and enforcement, this is the preferred outcome. For proponents of flexible and adaptable strategies, as is discussed in the next section, the failure to integrate voluntary and collaborative efforts into the policy mix has been a disappointment (Fiorino 2009). In recent years, much of the environmental policy innovation has occurred in states and locally (Steelman 2010).

5. SHOULD THE EPA OF THE PAST DEFINE THE EPA OF THE FUTURE?

A recent dimension of writing on the EPA is the relevance of its past for its future. This affects more than the EPA; the fit between the existing policy system and the needs of a new era based on environmental sustainability is a much larger debate. As the focal point for most nonenergy environmental policy in the United States, however, these debates raise the issue of the EPA's role and whether it should adapt to a new era in environmental problem solving (Aspen Institute 2000; Chertow and Esty 1997; Eisner 2006; Fiorino 2006, 2009; NAPA 1995, 1997, 2000; Ruckelshaus 1998). Much of the literature turns on this question.

Discussions of the EPA's future have typically focused on three questions: (1) What is its role? (2) Should its organizational structure change? (3) Should its strategies change? With respect to its role, much of the debate revolves around whether the EPA should function entirely as a regulator and enforcer or serve more broadly as an environmental problem solver. Under the first conception, the view is that Congress has invested legal responsibilities in the EPA, far more than it can fulfill given available resources, and those should determine its entire portfolio. Any effort to exercise a broader mandate or cultivate other relationships interferes with the EPA's ability to fulfill its regulatory responsibilities. Attempting to build collaborative relationships with regulated firms, this view holds, undermines the EPA's role as a regulator, distracts it from performing core legal functions, and drains precious resources from the core tasks of standard-setting and enforcement.

In contrast, the second view stresses the need for taking a comprehensive and flexible approach to defining the EPA's role. Regulation and enforcement are defining but not necessarily limiting aspects of its activities. Indeed, the EPA's regulatory authority provides a useful basis for leveraging the agency's overall resources to achieve results with flexible and collaborative methods: partnerships, voluntary agreements that complement or expand on regulatory tools, and innovative programs, such as those discussed above. In this conception, an EPA that performs its core regulatory tasks is not inconsistent with the EPA being an adaptable and creative problem-solving organization.

On the second question, that of structure, there are internal and external aspects. Internally, the issue is whether the traditional structure based on environmental medium is sufficient for the challenges of sustainability. As noted above, the fragmentation of EPA's programs has been cited as an impediment to its effectiveness throughout its history (Funke 1993; Haigh and Irwin 1990). The typical response is that an alternative organizational model, based on industry sector, type of contaminant, or geographic area, among others, should be considered (an interesting example is Weiland and Vos 2002). At various times in its history, such options have been proposed or attempted by the EPA (Schmandt 1985). There are two issues with these proposals, however. One is their feasibility. So long as the laws and oversight associated with them are fragmented along current lines, the EPA cannot change. Congressional reform must precede EPA reform. Second, a restructured EPA would substitute one set of problems for another. Having an office focused on the petrochemical industry or on cross-media lead issues, for example, would create a need to coordinate air, water, and waste policies.

The external aspect refers to the options of expanding the EPA's role or creating a new agency. Terry Davies (2009), who was on the staff of the Ash Council, has called for a Department of Environmental and Consumer Protection that consolidates six agencies, among them the EPA, the U.S. Geological Survey, the National Oceanic and Atmospheric Administration, and the Occupational Safety and Health Administration. The basis for this proposal is to develop more effective oversight for new technologies. Another such overhaul would be to link agencies under a theme of environmental sustainability, combining aspects of environmental, energy, resource management, and transportation.

The third issue—of the EPA's strategies—turns on the adequacy and suitability of the EPA's approach to a new generation of problems and a changing policy landscape. To a degree, Congress and the EPA have adjusted by moving from an approach based strictly on administrative rationalism to one based also on democratic pragmatism and economic rationalism (Dryzek 2005). This shift is captured above in the discussion of the three policy epochs and types of learning. Indeed, the incorporation of emissions trading and information disclosure programs constitute the most substantive cases of innovation in the EPA's four decades. They are the foundation of the partial shift from the first to the second epochs. Still, many scholars urge even broader changes in the EPA's regulatory model. These scholars draw on lessons from such countries as Sweden, the Netherlands, and United Kingdom. They argue that the EPA and government generally should pursue flexible, cost-effective, adaptable, and performance-based policies and expand beyond its role as a regulator and enforcer (Durant, Fiorino, and O'Leary 2004; Eisner 2006; NAPA 1997, 2000; Press and Mazmanian 2010). From this perspective, the EPA's role and its strategies become one and the same issue.

Consistent with the definition of an emerging third epoch organized around the concept of sustainability, scholars and the EPA itself have begun to think longer-term and more holistically about its future (Grossarth and Hecht 2007). An example is an essay published by several experts on the approach of the EPA's 40th anniversary. Titled "EPA at 40: Bringing Environmental Protection into the 21st Century," the essay calls for a reorientation of the EPA to make it more an environmental *sustainability* than an environmental *protection* agency (Fiksel et al. 2009). The medium-based, fragmented structure has become outdated and should be replaced with an agency able to respond to the "complex and interrelated nature" of the multiple stresses on the environment that exist today. It calls on the EPA to develop a capacity for "sustainability science" that is "integrated, systems-based, and cross-media," for better metrics that measure progress toward sustainability, and for "cost-effective and innovative solutions consistent with smart economic growth." What this thoughtful essay does not tell us is how an agency with a fragmented legal framework, one that is regularly micromanaged by Congress, with an agenda determined often by lawsuits, and all within a highly decentralized and fragmented political system, will achieve this level of policy and scientific integration.

Given its critical role in U.S. domestic policy and the political attention it has drawn, surprisingly little research has been conducted on the EPA as an institution. Far more scholarly effort has been devoted to its policies than to the factors that explain the behavior and capacities of the agency itself. For example, although there has been considerable analysis of the pros and cons of alternatives to conventional regulation, such as market incentives or information disclosure, there has been limited research on factors that influence the adoption and implementation of such alternatives from an agency perspective. Similarly, the need for incorporating more flexible and adaptable policies within the EPA portfolio has been discussed more than the match between such policies and the agency's organization, staffing, and culture. Similarly, theoretical frameworks used in the public policy field could be applied to study EPA's evolution and behavior. Among these are the punctuated equilibrium (True, Jones, and Baumgartner 1999) and advocacy coalition frameworks (Sabatier and Jenkins-Smith 1999); both have been applied to environmental politics but not specifically to the EPA as an institution.

Among the specific issues that warrant priority attention for further research are the effects of the political oversight system on the agency's strategic performance and capacity for innovation; the implications of the EPA's organization, resource allocations, culture, and staffing for meeting the new and complex challenges of environmental sustainability; the effectiveness of the current patterns in EPA-state relationships, given the shrinking resources; and the relevance of innovations adopted in other countries, such as integrated permitting or national sustainability and planning, for the EPA.

Much has changed about the tasks the EPA has been assigned and the world in which it operates. Among the changes are new types of problems, a far more globally competitive economy, a service- and knowledge-based economy, new technologies, and the emergence of climate change as the preeminent environmental issue of our time. Yet, with some notable exceptions, the EPA still is operating very much with the strategies and tools of the 1970s. This is not necessarily the fault of the agency or its leadership. It is more a result of the atmosphere in which the EPA operates, including a lack of consensus on government's role, high levels of distrust, the complexity of the choices, and a fragmented institutional setting.

After 40 years, the EPA is still a work in progress. As we look to the challenges of a new century, it seems clear that the next 40 years cannot be a mere extension of the last 40. The EPA and other agencies should move from a mind-set of environmental protection to one of environmental sustainability. They will need policies that support long-term technology innovation. They will have to develop integrated strategies, not only across air, water, and land, but across levels of government and among agencies. Without the participation and consent of key political institutions, however—especially Congress—a transition to an epoch of environmental sustainability is not likely to occur.

REFERENCES

Andrews, R. N. L. 1999. *Managing the Environment, Managing Ourselves: A History of American Environmental Policy*. New Haven, CT: Yale University Press.

———. 2000. "Risk-Based Decisionmaking." In *Environmental Policy*, 4th ed., ed. N. J. Vig and M. E. Kraft, 210–231. Washington, DC: CQ Press.

———. 2005. "Risk Based Decision Making." In *Environmental Policy in the Twenty-first Century*, 6th ed., ed. N.J. Vig and M.E. Kraft, 215–238. Washington, DC: CQ Press.

Aspen Institute. 2000. *A Call to Action to Build a Performance-Based Environmental Management System*. Washington, DC: Aspen Institute.

———. 2010. *40 Years: 10 Ways EPA Has Strengthened America*. Washington, DC: Aspen Institute.

Bosso, C. J. 2000. "Environmental Groups and the New Political Landscape." In *Environmental Policy*, 4th ed., ed. N. J. Vig and M. E. Kraft, 55–76. Washington, DC: CQ Press.

Chertow, M., and D. C. Esty. 1997. *Thinking Ecologically: The Next Generation of Environmental Policy*. New Haven, CT: Yale University Press.

Coglianese, C. 2007. "Business Interests and Information in Environmental Rulemaking." In *Business and Environmental Policy: Corporate Interests in the American Political System*, ed. M. E. Kraft and S. Kamieniecki, 185–210. Cambridge, MA: MIT Press.

Coglianese, C., and L. K. Allen. 2005. "Building Sector-Based Consensus: A Review of the US EPA's Common Sense Initiative." In *Industrial Transformation: Environmental Policy Innovation in the United States and Europe*, ed. T. de Bruijn and V. Norberg-Bohm, 65–92. Cambridge, MA: MIT Press.

Copeland, C. 1997. *Environmental Policy: Issues in State-Federal Relations*. Washington, DC: Congressional Research Service.

Crotty, P. M. 1988. "Assessing the Role of Federal Administrative Regions: An Exploratory Analysis." *Public Administration Review*, 48: 642–648.

Davies, J. C. 1970. *The Politics of Pollution*. New York: Pegasus.

———. 2001. *Reforming Permitting*. Washington, DC: Resources for the Future.

———. 2009. "Nanolessons for Revamping Government Oversight of Technology." *Issues in Science and Technology* (Fall): 43–50.

Davies, J. C., and B. S. Davies. 1975. *The Politics of Pollution*. 2nd ed. Indianapolis: Bobbs-Merrill.

Davies, J. C., and J. Mazurek. 1998. *Pollution Control in the United States: Evaluating the System*. Washington, DC: Resources for the Future.

Dryzek, J. S. 2005. *The Politics of the Earth: Environmental Discourses*. 2d ed. Oxford: Oxford University Press.

Durant, R. F. 1993. "Hazardous Waste, Regulatory Reform, and the Reagan Revolution: The Ironies of an Activist Approach to Deactivating Bureaucracy." *Public Administration Review* 53: 550–560.

Durant, R. F., D. J. Fiorino, and R. O'Leary, eds. 2004. *Environmental Governance Reconsidered: Challenges, Choices, and Opportunities*. Cambridge, MA: MIT Press.

Eisner, M. A. 2006. *Governing the Environment: The Transformation of Environmental Regulation*. Boulder, CO: Lynne Rienner.

Environmental Law Institute (ELI). 1998. *Barriers to Environmental Technology and Use. Washington*, DC: ELI.

Fears, D. 2011. "House Readies Bill to Prohibit EPA from Regulating Carbon Emissions." *Washington Post*, February 3.

Fiksel, J., T. Graedel, A. D. Hecht, D. Rejeski, G. S. Sayler, P. M. Senge, and T. L. Theis. 2009. "EPA at 40: Bringing Environmental Protection into the 21st Century." *Environmental Science and Technology* 43: 8716–8720.

Fiorino, D. J. 1990. "Can Problems Shape Priorities? The Case of Risk-Based Environmental Planning." *Public Administration Review* 50: 82–90.

———. 1995. *Making Environmental Policy*. Berkeley: University of California Press.

———. 2001. "Environmental Policy as Learning: A New View of an Old Landscape." *Public Administration Review* 61: 322–334.

———. 2006. *The New Environmental Regulation*. Cambridge, MA: MIT Press.

———. 2009. "Regulating for the Future: A New Approach for Environmental Governance." In *Toward Sustainable Communities: Transition and Transformations in Environmental Policy*, 2nd ed., ed. D. A. Mazmanian and M. E. Kraft, 63–86. Cambridge, MA: MIT Press.

Fraas, A. 1991. "The Role of Economic Analysis in Shaping Environmental Policy." *Law and Contemporary Problems* 54: 113–125.

Funke, O. 1993. "Struggling with Integrated Environmental Policy: The EPA Experience." *Review of Policy Research* 12: 137–161.

Furlong, S. R. 2007. "Business and the Environment: Influencing Agency Policymaking." In *Business and Environmental Policy: Corporate Interests in the American Political System*, ed. M. E. Kraft and S. Kamieniecki, 155–184. Cambridge, MA: MIT Press.

Gaertner, G. H., K. N. Gaertner, and I. Devine. 1983. "Federal Agencies in the Context of Transition: A Contrast between Democratic and Organizational Theories." *Public Administration Review* 43: 421–432.

Graham, M. 1999. *The Morning after Earth Day: Practical Environmental Politics*. Washington, DC: Brookings Institution Press.

Grossarth, S. K., and A. D. Hecht. 2007. "Sustainability at the U.S. Environmental Protection Agency: 1970–2020." *Ecological Engineering* 30: 1–8.

Haigh, N., and F. Irwin, eds. 1990. *Integrated Pollution Control in Europe and the United States*. Washington, DC: Conservation Foundation.

Hobson, M. K. 2009. "The Greenest White House in History." *National Journal*, September 26: 20–29.

Jasanoff, S. 1990. *The Fifth Branch: Science Advisors as Policy Makers*. Cambridge, MA: Harvard University Press.

Kagan, R. A. 1995. "Adversarial Legalism in American Government." In *The New Politics of Public Policy*, ed. M. K. Landy and M. Levin, 23–46. Baltimore: Johns Hopkins University Press.

Kraft, M. E. 1995. "Congress and Environmental Policy." In *Environmental Politics and Policy: Theories and Evidence*, ed. J. P. Lester, 168–205. Durham, NC: Duke University Press.

———. 2000. "Environmental Policy in Congress: From Consensus to Gridlock." In *Environmental Policy*, 4th ed., ed. N. K. Vig and M. E. Kraft, 121–144. Washington, DC: CQ Press.

———. 2010. "Environmental Policy in Congress." In *Environmental Policy: New Directions for the Twenty-First Century*, 7th ed., ed. N. K. Vig and M. E. Kraft, 99–124. Washington, DC: CQ Press.

Kraft, M. E., M. Stephan, and T. D. Abel. 2011. *Coming Clean: Information Disclosure and Environmental Performance*. Cambridge, MA: MIT Press.

Landy, M. K., M. J. Roberts, and S. R. Thomas. 1990. *The Environmental Protection Agency: Asking the Wrong Questions*. New York: Oxford University Press.

———. 1993. *The Environmental Protection Agency: From Nixon to Clinton*. New York: Oxford University Press.

Larson, P. 1998. "A Culture of Innovation." *Environmental Forum* 15: 20–28.

Lazarus, R. J. 2004. *The Making of Environmental Law*. Chicago: University of Chicago Press.

Lester, J. P., ed. 1995a. *Environmental Politics and Policy: Theories and Evidence*, 2nd ed. Durham, NC: Duke University Press.

———. 1995b. "Federalism and State Environmental Policy." In *Environmental Politics and Policy: Theories and Evidence*, 2nd ed., ed. J. P. Lester, 39–60. Durham, NC: Duke University Press.

MacBeth, A., and G. Marchant. 2008. "Improving the Government's Environmental Science." *New York University Environmental Law Review* 17: 134–169.

Marcus, A. A. 1980a. *Promise and Performance: Choosing and Implementing an Environmental Policy*. Westport, CT: Greenwood.

———. 1980b. "Environmental Protection Agency." In *The Politics of Regulation*, ed. J. Q. Wilson, 267–303. New York: Basic Books.

———. 1991. "EPA's Organizational Structure." *Law and Contemporary Problems* 54: 5–40.

Marcus, A. A., D. A. Geffen, and K. Sexton. 2002. *Reinventing Environmental Regulation: Lessons from Project XL*. Washington, DC: Resources for the Future.

Mazmanian, D. A., and M. E. Kraft, eds. 2009. *Toward Sustainable Communities: Transition and Transformations in Environmental Policy*. 2nd ed. Cambridge, MA: MIT Press.

McGarity, T. O. 1991. "The Internal Structure of EPA Rulemaking." *Law and Contemporary Problems* 54: 59–111.

Morgenstern, R. D. ed. 1997. *Economic Analysis at EPA: Assessing Regulatory Impact*. Washington, DC: Resources for the Future.

Morgenstern, R. D., and William A. Pizer, eds. 2007. *Reality Check: The Nature and Performance of Voluntary Environmental Programs in the United States, Europe, and Japan*. Washington, DC: Resources for the Future.

National Academy of Public Administration (NAPA). 1995. *Setting Priorities, Getting Results: A New Direction for the Environmental Protection Agency*. Washington, DC: NAPA.

———. 1997. *Resolving the Paradox of Environmental Protection: An Agenda for Congress, EPA, and the States*. Washington, DC: NAPA.

———. 2000. *environment.gov: Transforming Environmental Protection in the 21st Century*. Washington, DC: NAPA.

National Academy of Sciences. 1983. *Risk Assessment in the Federal Government: Managing the Process*. Washington, DC: National Academy Press.

O'Leary, R. 1993. *Environmental Change: Federal Courts and the EPA*. Philadelphia: Temple University Press.

———. 2010. "Environmental Policy in the Courts." In *Environmental Policy: New Directions for the Twenty-First Century*, 7th ed., ed. N. J. Vig and M. E. Kraft, 125–146. Washington, DC: CQ Press.

O'Leary, R., and S. S. Raines. 2001. "Lessons Learned from Two Decades of Dispute Resolution at the U.S. Environmental Protection Agency." *Public Administration Review* 61: 682–692.

Percival, R. V. 1991. "Checks without Balance: Executive Office Oversight of the Environmental Protection Agency." *Law and Contemporary Problems* 54: 127–204.

Portney, P., and R. Stavins, eds. 2000. *Public Policies for Environmental Protection.* 2nd ed. Washington, DC: Resources for the Future.

Powell, M. 1999. *Science at EPA: Information in the Regulatory Process.* Washington, DC: Resources for the Future.

Press, D., and D. A. Mazmanian. 2010. "Toward Sustainable Production: Finding Workable Strategies for Government and Industry." In *Environmental Policy: New Directions for the Twenty-First Century,* 7th ed., ed. N. J. Vig and M. E. Kraft, 220–243. Washington, DC: CQ Press.

Rabe, B. G. 2010. "Racing to the Top, the Bottom, or the Middle of the Pack? The Evolving State Government Role in Environmental Protection." In *Environmental Policy: New Directions for the Twenty-First Century,* 7th ed., ed. N. J. Vig and M. E. Kraft, 27–50. Washington, DC: CQ Press.

Rosenbaum, W. A. 1995. "The Bureaucracy and Environmental Policy." In *Environmental Politics and Policy: Theories and Evidence,* 2nd ed., ed. J. P. Lester, 206–241. Durham, NC: Duke University Press.

———. 2000. "Escaping the 'Battered Agency Syndrome': EPA's Gamble with Regulatory Reinvention." In *Environmental Policy,* 4th ed., ed. N. J. Vig and M. E. Kraft, 165–189. Washington, DC: CQ Press.

———. 2003. "Still Reforming after All These Years: George W. Bush's 'New Era' at the EPA." In *Environmental Policy: New Directions for the Twenty-First Century,* 5th ed., ed. N. J. Vig and M. E. Kraft, 175–199. Washington, DC: CQ Press.

———. 2010a. "Greenhouse Governance: How Capable Is EPA?" In *Greenhouse Governance: Addressing Climate Change in America,* ed. B. G. Rabe, 286–310. Washington, DC: Brookings Institution Press.

———. 2010b. "Science, Politics, and Policy at the EPA." In *Environmental Policy: New Directions for the Twenty-First Century,* 7th ed., ed. N. J. Vig and M. E. Kraft, 147–170. Washington, DC: CQ Press.

Ruckelshaus, W. D. 1985. "Risk, Science, and Democracy." *Issues in Science and Technology* 1: 19–38.

———. 1996. "Stopping the Pendulum." *Environmental Toxicology and Chemistry* 15: 229–232.

———. 1998. "Stepping Stones." *Environmental Forum* 15: 30–36.

Sabatier, P. A., and H. C. Jenkins-Smith. 1999. "The Advocacy Coalition Framework: An Assessment." In *Theories of the Policy Process,* ed. P. A. Sabatier, 117–166. Boulder, CO: Westview.

Scheberle, D. 2004a. "Devolution." In *Environmental Governance Reconsidered: Challenges, Choices, and Opportunities,* ed. R. F. Durant, D. J. Fiorino, and R. O'Leary, 361–392. Cambridge, MA: MIT Press.

———. 2004b. *Federalism and Environmental Policy: Trust and the Politics of Implementation.* 2nd ed. Washington, DC: Georgetown University Press.

———. 2005. "The Evolving Matrix of Environmental Federalism and Intergovernmental Relationships." *Publius* 35: 69–85.

Schmandt, J. 1985. "Managing Comprehensive Rule Making: EPA's Plan for Integrated Environmental Management." *Public Administration Review* 45: 309–318.

Schreurs, M. 2002. *Environmental Politics in Japan, Germany, and the United States.* Cambridge: Cambridge University Press.

Smith, V. K. 1984. *Environmental Policy under Reagan's Executive Order.* Chapel Hill: University of North Carolina Press.

Stavins, R. N. 1998. "What Can We Learn from the Grand Policy Experiment? Lessons from SO2 Allowance Trading." *Journal of Economic Perspectives* 12: 60–88.

Steelman, T. A. 2010. *Implementing Innovation: Fostering Enduring Change in Environmental and Natural Resource Governance.* Washington, DC: Georgetown University Press.

True, J. L., B. D. Jones, and F. R. Baumgartner. 1999. "Punctuated Equilibrium Theory: Explaining Stability and Change in American Policy Making." In *Theories of the Policy Process,* ed. P. A. Sabatier, 97–115. Boulder, CO: Westview.

U.S. Environmental Protection Agency (EPA). 1987. *Unfinished Business: A Comparative Assessment of Environmental Problems.* Washington, DC: EPA.

——. 1990. *Reducing Risk: Setting Priorities and Strategies for Environmental Protection.* Washington, DC: Science Advisory Board.

——. 1997. *The Benefits and Costs of the Clean Air Act: 1970–1990.* Washington, DC: EPA.

——. 2004a. *Evaluation of Implementation Experiences with Innovative Air Permits.* Washington, DC: Office of Air Quality Planning and Standards and Office of Policy, Economics, and Innovation.

——. 2004b. *An Examination of EPA Risk Assessment Principles and Practices.* Washington, DC: Office of the Science Advisor.

——. 2010a. *FY 2011 EPA Budget in Brief.* Washington, DC: Chief Financial Officer.

——. 2010b. *FY 2011–2015 EPA Strategic Plan: Achieving Our Vision.* Washington, DC: Chief Financial Officer.

——. 2010c. *Guidelines for Preparing Economic Impact Analysis.* Washington, DC: Office of Policy.

Vig, N. J. 2000. "Presidential Leadership and the Environment: From Reagan to Clinton." In *Environmental Policy,* 4th ed., ed. N. J. Vig and M. E. Kraft, 98–120. Washington, DC: CQ Press.

Vogel, D. 1993. "Representing Diffuse Interests in Environmental Policymaking." In *Do Institutions Matter? Government Capabilities in the United States and Abroad,* ed. R. K. Weaver and B. A. Rockman, 237–271. Washington, DC: Brookings Institution Press.

Wallace, D. 1995. *Environmental Policy and Industrial Innovation: Strategies in Europe, the USA, and Japan.* London: Earthscan.

Weiland, P. S. 2007. "Business and Environmental Policy in the Federal Courts." In *Business and Environmental Policy: Corporate Interests and the American Political System,* ed. M. E. Kraft and S. M. Kamieniecki, 213–232. Cambridge, MA: CQ Press.

Weiland, P. S., and R. O. Vos. 2002. "Reforming EPA's Organizational Structure: Establishing an Adaptable Strategy through Eco-Regions." *Natural Resources Journal* 42: 91–131.

CHAPTER 16

BUREAUCRACY AND NATURAL RESOURCES POLICY

CRAIG W. THOMAS

NATURAL resource policy in the United States has changed dramatically since the 1960s. The range of issues has greatly expanded—from debates over resource use versus preservation to uncertainties regarding the impacts of climate change on fire management, biodiversity, and water supply. The locus of policy-making authority has also changed—from relatively closed, issue-specific subsystems composed of congressional committees, public agencies, and resource users, to open systems that cross agency jurisdictions and issue areas. As policy subsystems opened, so did the agencies—from highly centralized bureaucracies managing publicly owned land, to collaborative organizations that include a broad range of public, private, and nonprofit stakeholders. The most recent change has been in the area of accountability relationships, with performance-based accountability challenging the procedural conformism that had been the administrative core of natural resources policy implementation.

This chapter examines the broad range of natural resource policies in the United States, the public agencies that have implemented these policies, and the policy subsystems within which they operate. The chapter also examines how agency cultures have changed as new professions and scientific ideas entered the agencies; and new approaches to natural resources management, such as adaptive management and collaborative governance. Policy topics include traditional resource extraction (such as mining, forestry, and water use), recreational and ascetic uses (such as parks and wilderness), and more contemporary issues (such as biodiversity conservation and climate change impacts). Throughout, the chapter focuses on key directions in theoretical scholarship on natural resource policy and management, while noting potential avenues for future research.

1. Issue Evolution

U.S. natural resource policy began during the Progressive Era (1890–1920), when a diverse range of stakeholders came together to make fundamental changes in electoral and administrative processes at all levels of government. The Progressive coalition included antimonopolists, who sought to distribute public services more equitably across society; Good Government proponents, who sought to reduce corruption and enhance competence within public agencies; and advocates for the efficient use of natural resources (Knott and Miller 1987). With regard to natural resource policy, the Progressives championed a radical shift from laissez-faire markets based on the creation and protection of private property rights with unfettered use of natural resources, to public ownership and centralized management of natural resources by bureaucratic agencies (Andrews 2006).

The Progressive conservationists focused on a few key issues, primarily timber harvesting and water supply. Seeing rapid deforestation on private land throughout the East and Midwest, they established a reform agenda based on the idea of an impending timber famine. Their goal was to maintain a continuing supply of timber for future generations by slowing the rate of timber harvests. Rather than seeking regulation of the private sector, they advocated public ownership and the creation of bureaucratic organizations to manage resource use on public lands. The new agencies would be technocracies employing the principles of scientific management that had been developed in the private sector. It was science not in the sense of biology or the emerging field of ecology, but rather in terms of rational planning (Brunner et al. 2005).

Conservationism was built on a utilitarian philosophy, which historian Samuel Hays (1958) called "the gospel of efficiency." The U.S. Forest Service became the symbol of this conservationist culture. As Gifford Pinchot, the first chief and founder of the Forest Service, famously stated, conservation meant distributing natural resources for "the greatest good for the greatest number in the long run." In terms of timber production, utilitarianism was embodied by the concept of "sustained yield," which treats the management of national forests in terms of long-term crop rotation. In water policy, an engineering culture predominated. The Bureau of Reclamation built dams and water diversion projects in the arid West to use all river water before it reached the sea. The dams would also control floods and serve as "cash registers" in generating electricity, thereby justifying their costs, as they distributed water to farmers and cities at low prices (Reisner 1993). Neither agency advocated preservation in the first half of the twentieth century. To the contrary, conservation meant use in terms of resource extraction; forgone uses, such as wilderness areas in the national forests and undammed rivers in the arid West, were equated with waste (Andrews 2006).

A notable achievement of the Progressive conservationists was reframing debates about economic growth from the private to the public sector. To reduce what they saw as inefficient and inequitable use of natural resources in private markets, conservationists advocated retaining land from the public domain rather than privatizing it under the various settlement acts (Dana and Fairfax 1980). This represented a major shift in the legal basis of resource use in the United States, which had been dominated by John Locke's conception of private property rights (Raymond 2003). The federal government would now retain land rather than privatizing it, and allocate natural resources to the private sector based on utilitarian principles.

The Progressives looked to Prussia as a model for the development of bureaucratic government, particularly with regard to forestry. Woodrow Wilson had been a leading political scientist prior to serving as president, and was one of the founders of the public administration field. He argued that the U.S. government could import the Prussian model of bureaucracy without importing monarchism with it. Accordingly, the Progressives pushed for a functional separation between politics and administration, in which elected officials would adopt policies and bureaucratic agencies would implement them (Knott and Miller 1987). This meant that elected officials would not meddle in administrative matters, and agencies would not create new policies. Instead, the agencies would be staffed by professionals trained in newly established resource management schools. The term "natural resource management" embodied the idea that the agencies merely implemented policies and did not make policies.

By the middle of the twentieth century, academics increasingly rejected the theoretical and empirical premises of the separation of politics from administration; yet the "management" culture continued within the agencies. Changes came slowly, in part through the professional schools, where course content evolved to include a broader range of disciplines. The names of the schools also changed to reflect the broadening curriculum and student interests as the environmental movement expanded. The Yale School of Forestry, for example, which had been founded in 1900 with guidance from Gifford Pinchot, was renamed the School of Forestry and Environmental Studies in 1972. Other schools also subsumed their forestry programs within larger environmental schools or colleges, as at Duke in 1991, and much later at the University of Washington in 2010.

Yet the language of management has continued, as seen in the terms "adaptive management" and "ecosystem management." In adaptive management, agency decisions are guided by findings from the natural sciences rather than by scientific management or public participation (Stankey et al. 2003). In practice, however, adaptive management also includes a political component. Lee (1993) referred to adaptive management as the compass that points technical solutions in a scientifically supported direction, while politics is the gyroscope that defines problems through negotiation and compromise. "Ecosystem management" is more explicitly political, arguing that public land should be managed at the level of ecosystems rather than within agency jurisdictions, while simultaneously considering both scientific and political considerations (Cortner and Moote 1999; Layzer 2008; Weber 2003). By contrast, social scientists have offered the term "adaptive governance," which is explicitly positioned against management through science in favor of public participation at the local level through collaborative processes (Brunner et al. 2005).

Another source of policy change came from the preservationist movement, which had initially been led by the Sierra Club under the leadership of John Muir, who challenged the use-oriented culture advocated by conservationists (Nash 1982). Muir championed the creation of national parks throughout the West until his death in 1914. Congress had already declared Yellowstone as the first national park in 1872, but that was an idiosyncratic event. Muir advocated for national parks as a matter of policy and successfully convinced President Theodore Roosevelt, an avid hunter and wildlife conservationist, to set aside large tracts of public land for recreational and ascetic purposes rather than resource use. Roosevelt did not create the national parks per se, which is the domain of Congress; rather, he used the Antiquities Act (1906), which authorizes presidents to restrict uses of public land as national monuments for historic and scientific purposes. Congress subsequently converted many of these national monuments into national parks (such as the Grand Canyon National Park in 1919) and created the National Park Service (NPS) in 1916 to manage the parks. Presidents have continued to use the Antiquities Act to create national monuments, including Jimmy Carter, who preserved large tracts of land in Alaska, and Bill Clinton, who did so in southern Utah. While conservationists and preservationists differed on issues related to resource use, they both shared a belief that large tracts of land should be held in public ownership and that resource use and access to these lands should be managed by centralized agencies.

While early preservationist policies were driven by ascetic concerns about the enjoyment of nature, a new strand of preservationist philosophy emerged midcentury based on the rights of nature (Nash 1982). Its main advocate was Aldo Leopold, a professional forester trained as a use-oriented conservationist at the Yale School of Forestry. He initially supported extermination of predators on the national forests to enhance the population of game species; but he came to believe this policy was both ecologically and ethically suspect. Exterminating predators led to explosions in browsing species such as deer, followed by overgrazing and starvation. He also came to believe that predators such as wolves have rights to existence, and he advocated for the creation of large wilderness areas within the national forests where hunting and other uses would not be permitted. Leopold's preservationist agenda subsequently emerged in the Wilderness Act of 1964, through which Congress continues to set aside public land in national forests, national parks, and desert range land as restricted use areas.

The key feature of the Wilderness Act is that areas must be roadless to qualify as wilderness. Hence, debates over the designation of wilderness lands have focused on road development, since new roads would disqualify those areas for consideration as wilderness. The Sagebrush Rebellion in the 1970s and the 1980s was a reaction to such restricted-use policies, as ranchers sought to gain more access to rangelands managed by the Bureau of Land Management by arguing that states should have authority over these lands (Cawley 1993). The Sagebrush Rebels were unsuccessful in this regard, and were supplanted by the Wise Use Movement in the 1990s. The Wise Use Movement derived its name from Gifford Pinchot's admonition for the "wise use" of natural resources on public lands. By harking back to conservationist principles, the Wise Use Movement sought to recast the agenda in terms of multiple uses of public land. In other words, it sought to expand the scope of conflict (Pralle 2006), which the preservationists sought to contain in the 1970s and 1980s.

The Endangered Species Act of 1973 also followed from Leopold's preservationist philosophy. Initially focused on well-known species (euphemistically known as "charismatic mega-fauna"), such as the bald eagle, implementation of the ESA by the Fish and Wildlife Service subsequently encompassed all wildlife species, including their habitat, on public and private land (Tobin 1990). By focusing on habitat, not just species, the ESA provided a powerful legal means for preservationists to limit uses of public land beyond areas designated as wilderness and parks. In the 1990s, for example, litigation over the northern spotted owl shut down logging operations on millions of acres of national forests in Washington, Oregon, and California (Yaffee 1994). The ESA also has substantial reach over state and private lands and thus became the most significant regulatory policy in terms of protective (not just procedural) scope.

In the 1990s, the political debates among conservationists and preservationists faded into the background as entirely new issues emerged, such as climate change and invasive species. Climate change impacts, in particular, came to dominate debates about natural resource policy. Preservationist policies seemed increasingly antiquated as scientists argued that entire ecosystems would migrate north and thus out of preserved areas. Climate change thus posed new threats to species, leading to new debates about management practices, including the possibility of transporting some species north as their habitat disappeared. Scientists also predicted that climate change would likely have impacts on the ecosystem services public lands provide, including freshwater, as changes in weather patterns were expected to reduce winter snowpacks needed for summer runoff in parched areas of the West (Karl et al. 2009). Multistate river compacts were typically based on historically high water flows, which increasingly seemed overly optimistic. Wildfires also emerged as an issue of concern, as scientists linked the increasing number of conflagrations to decades of fire suppression, longer fire seasons, and naturally invasive pests such as the mountain pine beetle, which survived warmer winters in greater numbers and decimated millions of acres of forests from Canada to the Mexican border.

Other issues also emerged, including eroded logging roads in the national forests that were silting up rivers due to runoff and landslides, thereby harming fish habitat. River levees managed by the Army Corps of Engineers also appeared insufficient, as storms such as Hurricane Katrina overwhelmed their protective capacity. The once-powerful and bureaucratic Corps of Engineers (Clarke and McCool 1996) increasingly seemed unprepared for addressing the impacts of climate change (Pilkey and Dixon 1996). New approaches to river management also emerged as the era of large dam construction ended in the West, including river restoration (Lowry 2003) and water marketing, in which farmers sell water rights to cities. All of these issues have emerged on the agendas of the resource management agencies in recent decades, particularly those issues related to the impacts of climate change.

2. Policy Arenas

Through the 1970s, the common depiction of natural resource policy making was in terms of subgovernments, or iron triangles, in which the agencies were captured by specific industries at the expense of the public good (Clarke and McCool 1996). In the case of the Forest Service, this meant the timber industry (Hoberg 1997). For river development, it was the Bureau of Reclamation serving local water interests in the arid West, and the Army Corps of Engineers serving the river transportation industry in the East and Midwest (Maass 1951; Reisner 1993). For range land, it was the Bureau of Land Management and ranchers (Calef 1960; Culhane 1981; Klyza 1996). For the National Park Service, it was recreation interests (Andrews 2006). Subgovernments represented the failure of the Progressive movement in that the agencies were supposed to manage for the long-term public interest, not the benefit of specific user groups.

In the 1970s, these subgovernments began to crumble as new legislation opened up decision-making processes within the agencies to public participation (Beierle and Cayford 2002). The bureaucracies themselves changed little at the time, but they were now subject to laws that required them to consider environmental concerns and to follow new procedures that expanded public participation. The first and most important of these laws was the National Environmental Policy Act (NEPA) in 1969. NEPA requires federal agencies to consider the environmental impacts of their activities, such as road building, timber harvests, and issuing permits for mining and other resource extraction purposes. NEPA does not dictate what decisions should be made in terms of resource protection; instead, it mandates that federal agencies weigh the potential environmental impacts of different alternatives, and requires public participation in all stages of the decision-making process (Caldwell 1998). NEPA thereby opened the door for extensive litigation that broke down policy subsystems, as environmental groups now had standing to challenge agency decisions in court, not just in congressional committees and the media. NEPA also became a model for many states, which subsequently adopted their own versions of NEPA, such as the California Environmental Quality Act, which applies to state and local agencies.

Additional federal laws subsequently emerged in the 1970s that focused on specific agencies. The National Forest Management Act (1976) requires the Forest Service to develop management plans that consider a wide range of multiple uses for national forests, while incorporating public participation. The Federal Lands Policy Management Act (1976) similarly requires the Bureau of Land Management, which manages one-eighth of all land in the United States, to consider multiple uses, not just ranching and mining. These new procedural laws also opened up the subgovernments to a wider range of professionals within the agencies to administer these and other laws, including ecologists and hydrologists, who were needed to conduct environmental impact assessments. The so-called "-ologists" gradually replaced the resource conservation professionals that had previously dominated the agencies. This created a conflict between older and newer cultures in these agencies, while increasing the access of a wide range of stakeholders to policy-making processes (Fortmann 1990; Sabatier et al. 1995; Tipple and Wellman 1991).

Some agencies were also given entirely new missions. The Army Corps of Engineers was given authority over wetlands protection under Section 404 of the Clean Water Act (1972), which was ironic in that the Corps was now responsible for issuing permits to dredge or fill wetlands, which it had been doing itself for many decades. Meanwhile, the Fish and Wildlife Service and National Marine Fisheries Service, which were traditionally focused on conserving game and commercial species for user groups, were given authority for implementing the Endangered Species Act (Tobin 1990). The Fish and Wildlife Service and its state counterparts are sometimes derided by environmentalists—with phrases such as "ducks and deer," "fish and feathers," and "moose and goose"—for their tight relationship with hunters and fishers. Under the ESA, a new division within the Fish and Wildlife Service was now responsible for protecting all species and their habitat. Similar changes occurred within state agencies.

Other agencies that had not previously focused on natural resource management also entered the policy arena. The Department of Defense, for example, fell under the requirements of NEPA, the ESA, and other environmental laws (Durant 2007). While it could escape some of these laws in specific circumstances (e.g., through riders to congressional appropriation bills), the DoD culture nonetheless slowly changed to implement these laws. Given that military bases cover large areas of often pristine lands, such as Camp Pendleton Marine Base between Los Angeles and San Diego, and that Congress can transfer these lands to the National Park Service and other agencies, the DoD had a political reason to act as a good steward of natural resources on these bases.

With the weakening of subgovernments and the increasing influence of a wide range of stakeholders, academics developed new theories to explain these expanded policy arenas. The Advocacy Coalition Framework (ACF), for example, was developed to explain long-term policy change for so-called wicked problems, with case studies largely focused on environmental and resource management problems (Sabatier 2005; Weible 2007). Rather than focusing on the power dynamics that held subgovernments together, the ACF focused on the beliefs holding coalitions of agencies and stakeholders together. Punctuated equilibrium theory, by contrast, was developed to explain rapid policy change (Baumgartner and Jones 2003). Unlike the ACF, which grew out of the environmental policy arena, punctuated equilibrium theory is a relatively new entrant to the field of natural resource policy (Repetto 2006), and thus provides an avenue for future research testing this theory.

Other policy-making theories have examined focusing events and scientific ideas as drivers of policy change. Birkland (1998) argued that focusing events, such as natural disasters, can bring rapid change by changing the dominant issues on an agenda and mobilizing interest groups. Focusing events give policy entrepreneurs the opportunity to redefine issues, through the use of causal stories, in ways that enhance the prospects of new policies being adopted in specific venues (Pralle 2006). The 2010 oil spill from the Deepwater Horizon drilling platform in the Gulf of Mexico provided one such focusing event. This highly salient ecological disaster led to reorganization of the Minerals Management Service, which had managed oil, gas, and mineral leases on the outer continental shelf. In a symbolic move, the agency was quickly renamed the Bureau of Ocean Energy Management, Regulation and Enforcement, which suggests a larger enforcement role. However, research is needed on whether management practices within this agency were subsequently changed.

Epistemic community theory, by contrast, argues that scientific ideas bring gradual change as consensus within scientific communities infuses agencies with new problem definitions and solutions (Haas 1990). Epistemic community theory has been applied extensively at the international level and in European cases, but much less so within the United States. An example of epistemic influence at the domestic level is the emergence of conservation biology, which transformed thinking within natural resource agencies by focusing on habitat conservation planning. Though relatively few in number relative to the traditional resource management professions, conservation biologists offered a unified set of planning principles that provided agencies with a means to maintain populations of species before they could be listed under the Endangered Species Act and thus reduce the likelihood of lawsuits (Thomas 2003).

In sum, a wide variety of theories have emerged to explain the transition from subgovernments to broad-based stakeholder participation in the implementation of natural resource policy. The next section focuses on changes in the institutional configurations for policy making within the agencies themselves.

3. PUBLIC AGENCIES

In public discourse, "bureaucracy" has become a pejorative term connoting the negative characteristics of public agencies. Yet in the first half of the twentieth century, bureaucratic organization was viewed as the best means for implementing natural resource policy. The Progressive conservationists believed that procedural conformism would reduce corruption and enhance competence through the systematic application of decision-making principles. Today, by contrast, rule following is viewed by many as "red tape" that slows down action on emerging problems by solidifying the status quo. The creation of bureaucracies also produced a meritocracy in which civil servants were hired from professional schools, took merit exams, and devoted their careers to an agency. But meritocracy also led to the solidification of specific professions within agencies, which narrowed how problems were defined and slowed policy change.

The Forest Service was the epitome of bureaucratic design during the first half of the twentieth century, extolled for its virtues in managing the national forests (Kaufman 1960). As issue agendas evolved to encompass multiple uses after World War II, the Forest Service increasingly came under fire for not responding to these new demands (Tipple and Wellman 1991). The agency's slow response to new issues is not surprising, given that bureaucracies were created to resist change and thereby contain issues. Issue expansion meant giving decision-making power to a broader set of stakeholders (Pralle 2006). Yet resource management agencies have notably varied in their bureaucratization, and thus in how they responded to demands for policy change by external stakeholders and internal professional staff. Some agencies continued to thrive as bureaucracies because their missions remained popular. The national parks were originally managed by military units to remove squatters and Native Americans from the parks. When the NPS was established under the Organic Act (1916), it evolved into a bureaucratic police force of rangers whose jobs were to control the behavior of recreationists in the park, with little training in resource preservation (Lowry 1994). The Park Service thrived in the recreation-oriented era after World War II because managing national parks largely meant policing visitor behavior, which could be done through bureaucratic organization.

The Bureau of Land Management was arguably the least bureaucratized of the natural resource agencies. It had emerged from a 1946 merger of the notoriously corrupt General Land Office, which had authority for privatizing the public domain under the various homestead acts, and the Grazing Service, which allocated grazing permits to private ranchers under the Taylor Grazing Act (1934). Those two agencies had not been bureaucratized, and the merger did little to bureaucratize them. In part, this was because range management was offered at relatively few schools, and the agency hired many ranchers and sons of ranchers (Clarke and McCool 1996). Thus, the BLM remained permeable to local stakeholders, particularly cattle ranchers. The BLM was also underfunded compared to the Forest Service, giving it less capacity to develop administrative infrastructure for planning, managing, and enforcing resource use on the BLM's 270 million acres of land (Culhane 1981). The BLM was also subject to extensive presidential influence, particularly during the Reagan administration (Durant 1992).

An important characteristic of bureaucratic agencies is that they are particularly well suited for addressing narrowly defined problems that have clear technical solutions within bounded agency jurisdictions. This was seen in the concept of sustained yield, where the problem was defined as maintaining timber supply

from national forests over time, with the Forest Service developing a highly technical programming model known as FORPLAN to optimize national forest yields
(O'Toole 1988). Bureaucracies are less suited for addressing complex problems that
require nimble responses to emerging problems that transcend agency jurisdictions. Climate change poses such a challenge because climate change impacts
are uncertain, which means that agencies cannot easily plan for environmental
problems that might occur or proactively develop management practices that will
address these problems. Climate change impacts, including impacts on biodiversity, are also multijurisdictional because they are not confined within the jurisdiction of a single agency. In this regard, agencies governed by fewer rules and norms,
such as the BLM, are better situated for adapting to new problems and coordinating across jurisdictions. This does not mean agencies *will* adapt to new problems
like climate change and other external threats, only that they are more *able* to do so
if agency leaders, Congress, and political appointees provide direction and support
(Freemuth 1991; Jantarasami et al. 2010).

Politically appointed commissions are a hybrid bureaucratic model that has
been used to regulate the use of natural resources in the private sector. Commissions
are composed of two separate bodies: a bureaucratic structure that analyzes problems and recommends solutions, and a politically appointed body that votes on
policy decisions regarding resource use. Unlike the bureaucratic model, with a
single leader at the top who is traditionally promoted from within, commissioners
are appointed for their ties to interest groups and not necessarily based on merit.
Hence, regulatory commissions can incorporate multiple, competing interests
into the highest level of the policy-making process. Some have argued that the
commission model is susceptible to capture by special interests through the political appointment process. For example, the eight Regional Fisheries Management
Councils, which establish marine fishing quotas and allocate resource use among
recreational and commercial fishers within U.S. territorial waters, are dominated
by representatives of those interests, while environmental groups are barely represented (Thomas et al. 2010). Marine preservation, meanwhile, is largely conducted
outside these councils through an interagency framework that creates and manages marine protected areas (Weible 2007).

Collaboration has been a more recent innovation in environmental governance. Collaborative partnerships are voluntary organizations that provide a
venue for bringing public, private, and nonprofit stakeholders together to reach
consensus on transjurisdictional problems (Leach et al. 2002; Sabatier et al. 2005).
Partnerships differ greatly in terms of the scope of participation, issues addressed,
decision-making rules, and the role played by public agencies (Koontz et al. 2004).
Partnerships also differ in scale, ranging from community-level partnerships
(Sabatier et al. 2005; Weber 2003) to regional partnerships (Heikkila and Gerlak
2005; Layzer 2008).

In the 1990s, collaboration was extolled as a means for overcoming judicial gridlock in the courts and for solving local conflicts over resource use. Most of the early
case studies focused on success stories, with a stream of research recommending

best practices for creating and maintaining collaborative partnerships (Wondolleck and Yaffee 2000) and reducing conflicts (O'Leary and Bingham 2003). Subsequent research has been more agnostic, questioning the efficacy of partnerships in producing environmentally protective policies (McKinney and Field 2008).

Collaborative partnerships are in many ways the antithesis of bureaucracy. Membership is open, voluntary, and fluid; decision-making processes are determined by public, private, and nonprofit members; and partnerships rely on their members for operational resources and implementation support. Bureaucratic agencies sometimes participate in collaborative partnerships but are not well suited for doing so. Career mobility within agencies, as individuals move from place to place, means that agency participants in collaborative organizations may come and go, thereby reducing trust, which is an important glue holding collaborative partnerships together (Leach and Sabatier 2005; Thomas 2003). Hierarchical reporting also reduces the likelihood that superiors will sign off on collaborative plans, and bureaucratic rules reduce the discretion of agency participants. Some collaborative partnerships have thus worked around bureaucratic agencies, as occurred when the Quincy Library Group made an end run around the Forest Service by seeking congressional support for their consensus-based plan to change forest management practices in Northern California (Pralle 2006). In 1998, Congress passed the Quincy Library Forest Recovery Act, thereby overriding existing logging activities on three national forests.

Academics have used multiple theories to understand the emergence, stability, and success of collaborative partnerships. One common approach is the advocacy coalition framework, which argues that core beliefs hold partnerships together (Sabatier et al. 2005; Weible 2007). According to this framework, coalition members rarely change core beliefs, which explains why policy change on wicked environmental problems occurs over long time periods. In addition to theories based on individual beliefs, academics have also studied the institutional characteristics of collaborative partnerships, using the institutional analysis and development framework to examine the rule systems that govern their operation (Heikkela and Gerlak 2005; Imperial 1999; Schlager 2004). Others have analyzed partnerships in terms of their stability, developing frameworks to explain why some succeed and others fail (Steelman 2010).

Network theory provides another avenue for understanding partnerships. Policy networks differ from collaboration by focusing on information diffusion and learning within specific policy domains. Lubell and Fulton (2008), for example, have shown that local policy networks substantially increased the likelihood that agricultural producers would adopt best management practices. This is an important finding in that it demonstrates agency participation in local policy networks can lead to environmental improvements through educational processes. The Natural Resources Conservation Service (formerly the Soil Conservation Service) was built on the idea of technical assistance rather than regulation. The agency has long been viewed as relatively weak (Clarke and McCool 1996) and has not been a focus of academic study. But it may have been effectual for decades operating through policy networks, while academics used other theories to analyze the land management and regulatory agencies.

4. ACCOUNTABILITY

A final significant change in natural resource policy has occurred in accountability relationships. Under the bureaucratic model, agencies were held accountable for following procedures, not for results. The bureaucratic model is based on the presumption that rules are designed to achieve intended results. The procedural model of accountability predominated well into the 1990s. Procedural accountability was further strengthened during the 1970s following the emergence of procedural laws such as the National Environmental Policy Act and the procedural components of many other laws (O'Leary 2006). Courts thus became the venue for holding agencies accountable for their decisions.

Yet procedures do not necessarily produce desired outcomes. Procedures are designed, instead, to produce outputs. Outcomes are the social and environmental conditions for which change is desired, such as species populations and forest cover, while outputs are the things agencies produce, such as plans and projects (Koontz and Thomas 2006). Procedural accountability is based on the assumption that following procedures will lead to desired outcomes. This is not necessarily the case, which led to the rise of the performance management movement in the 1990s. Performance management requires entirely new systems to monitor the outputs and outcomes of agencies and the programs within them (May 2007). At the federal level, performance management was embodied by the Performance Assessment Rating Tool (PART), which was created and implemented by the Office and Management and Budget under President George W. Bush. It is not yet clear what effect PART and other performance management systems (such as the Government Performance and Results Act) have had on the implementation of natural resource policies.

5. CONCLUSION

This chapter has covered major trends in U.S. natural resource policy, with a focus on public agencies and their stakeholders. The chapter also covered a wide range of theories that academics have applied to study these trends. Additional research is still needed on these topics, but other theories, methods, and topics remain largely unexplored. For example, the theoretical approaches reviewed in this chapter rely heavily on positivist empirical theories and methods. Interpretive and critical approaches are underrepresented in the field. Jürgen Habermas's theory of communicative action has been applied to the U.S. environmental movement generally (Brulle 2000), but this line of research remains largely unexplored in natural resource policy and management (Parkins and Mitchell 2005). Other critical approaches to policy research are similarly underused. Social construction theory, for example, has been applied primarily to social policies (Schneider and

Ingram 1997), not to natural resource policies. Social construction theory might be a fruitful avenue of research for understanding why some actors are privileged by resource management bureaucracies and how natural resource policies socially construct how society views these actors. Even within the positivist tradition, some research theories and methods remain underexplored, such as agent-based modeling (Gimblett 2002) and principal-agent theory (Waterman et al. 2004).

In terms of understudied topics, a ripe area for research is comparing the performance of public agencies based on their organizational characteristics. Some have argued that different organizational forms, such as centralized bureaucracy or collaborative partnerships, are better suited to different types of problems (Brunner et al. 2005; Lee 1999). But this theoretical argument remains largely untested using comparative case study methods. Devolution is also an understudied topic in natural resource policy. Devolution has often been studied with regard to pollution policy (Scheberle 2004) and "race to the bottom" theories of firm location (Konisky 2007; Potoski 2001), but studies of state versus federal management of natural resources remain relatively rare (Koontz 2002). Studies of state versus federal management of natural resources tend to focus on political movements, such as the Sagebrush Rebellion (Cawley 1993), rather than empirical research comparing the performance of state and federal agencies on specific natural resource issues.

The performance management movement more generally is a ripe area of research in natural resource policy. As a field, natural resource policy has lagged well behind other fields, such as public education and social welfare, in terms of studying the impact of the performance management movement. Research has instead focused on the performance of specific types of management systems, such as ecosystem management (see chapter 27 in this volume), collaborative partnerships (Imperial 2005; McKinney and Field 2008), and policy networks (Lubell and Fulton 2008). Empirical research comparing the performance of different governance systems such as these and comparing performance across natural resource programs is thus far quite limited. Thus, while a large volume of research on natural resource policy has emerged over the last 50 years, there remain many areas of research in terms of theoretical and methodological application in a large number of emerging topical areas, such as climate change impacts.

REFERENCES

Andrews, R. N. L. 2006. *Managing the Environment, Managing Ourselves: A History of American Environmental Policy.* New Haven, CT: Yale University Press.

Baumgartner, F. R., and B. D. Jones. 2003. *Agendas and Instability in American Politics.* Chicago: University of Chicago Press.

Beierle, T. C., and J. Cayford. 2002. *Democracy in Practice: Public Participation in Environmental Decisions.* Washington, DC: Resources for the Future.

Birkland, T. A. 1998. "Focusing Events, Mobilization, and Agenda Setting." *Journal of Public Policy* 18: 53–74.

Brulle, R. J. 2000. *Agency, Democracy, and Nature: The U.S. Environmental Movement from a Critical Theory Perspective.* Cambridge, MA: MIT.

Brunner, R. D., T. A. Steelman, L. Coe-Juell, C. M. Cromley, C. M. Edwards, and D. W. Tucker. 2005. *Adaptive Governance: Integrating Science, Policy and Decision Making.* New York: Columbia University Press.

Caldwell, L. K. 1998. *The National Environmental Policy Act: An Agenda for the Future.* Bloomington: Indiana University Press.

Calef, W. C. 1960. *Private Grazing and Public Lands.* Chicago: University of Chicago Press.

Cawley, R. M. 1993. *Federal Land, Western Anger: The Sagebrush Rebellion and Environmental Politics.* Lawrence: University Press of Kansas.

Clarke, J. Nienaber, and D. C. McCool. 1996. *Staking out the Terrain: Power and Performance Among Natural Resource Agencies.* 2nd ed. Albany: State University of New York Press.

Cortner, H. J., and M. A. Moote. 1999. *The Politics of Ecosystem Management.* Washington, DC: Island.

Culhane, P. J. 1981. *Public Lands Politics: Interest Group Influence on the Forest Service and the Bureau of Land Management.* Baltimore: Resources for the Future.

Dana, S. T., and S. K. Fairfax. 1980. *Forest and Range Policy.* New York: McGraw-Hill.

Durant, R. F. 1992. *The Administrative Presidency Revisited: Public Lands, the BLM, and the Reagan Revolution.* Albany: State University of New York Press.

Durant, R. F. 2007. *The Greening of the U.S. Military: Environment Policy, National Security and Organizational Change.* Washington, DC: Georgetown University Press.

Fortmann, L. 1990. "The Role of Professional Norms and Beliefs in the Agency-Client Relations of Natural Resource Bureaucracies." *Natural Resources Journal* 30: 361–380.

Freemuth, J. C. 1991. *Islands under Siege: National Parks and the Politics of External Threats.* Lawrence: University of Kansas Press.

Gimblett, R. ed. 2002. *Integrating Geographic Information Systems and Agent-Based Modeling Techniques for Simulating Social and Ecological Processes.* Oxford: Oxford University Press.

Haas, P. M. 1990. *Saving the Mediterranean: The Politics of International Environmental Cooperation.* New York: Columbia University Press.

Hays, S. P. 1958. *Conservation and the Gospel of Efficiency.* New York: Atheneum.

Heikkila, T., and A. K. Gerlak. 2005. "The Formation of Large-Scale Collaborative Resource Management Institutions: Clarifying the Roles of Stakeholders." *Policy Studies Journal* 33: 583–612.

Hoberg, G. A. 1997. "From Localism to Legalism: The Transformation Federal Forest Policy." In *Western Lands and Environmental Politics,* ed. C. Davis. Boulder, CO: Westview.

Imperial, M. T. 1999. "Institutional Analysis and Ecosystem-Based Management: The Institutional Analysis and Development Framework." *Environmental Management* 24: 449–465.

———. 2005. "Collaboration and Performance Management in Network Settings: Lessons from Three Watershed Governance Efforts." In *Managing for Results,* ed. J. M. Kamensky and A. Morales. Lanham, MD: Rowman & Littlefield.

Jantarasami, L. C., J. J. Lawler, and C. W. Thomas. 2010. "Institutional Barriers to Climate-Change Adaptation in National Parks and Forests of Washington State." *Ecology and Society* 15 (4). Available at www.ecologyandsociety.org/vol15/iss4/art33.

Karl, T. R., J. M. Melillo, and T. C. Peterson, eds. 2009. *Global Climate Change Impacts in the United States.* New York: Cambridge University Press.

Kaufman, H. 1960. *The Forest Ranger: A Study in Administrative Behavior.* Washington, DC: Resources for the Future.

Klyza, C. M. 1996. *Who Controls Public Lands? Mining, Forestry, and Grazing Policies, 1870–1990.* Chapel Hill: University of North Carolina Press.

Knott, J. H., and G. J. Miller. 1987. *Reforming Bureaucracy: The Politics of Institutional Choice.* Englewood Cliffs, NJ: Prentice-Hall.

Konisky, D. M. 2007. "Regulatory Competition and Environmental Enforcement: Is There a Race to the Bottom?" *American Journal of Political Science* 51: 853–872.

Koontz, T. M. 2002. *Federalism in the Forest: National versus State Natural Resource Policy.* Washington, DC: Georgetown University Press.

Koontz, T. M., T. A. Steelman, J. Carmin, K. S. Korfmacher, C. Moseley, and C. W. Thomas. 2004. *Collaborative Environmental Management: What Roles for Government?* Washington, DC: Resources for the Future.

Koontz, T. M., and C. W. Thomas 2006. "What Do We Know and Need to Know about the Environmental Outcomes of Collaborative Management?" *Public Administration Review* 66 (special issue): 111–121.

Layzer, J. A. 2008. *Natural Experiments: Ecosystem Management and the Environment.* Cambridge, MA: MIT Press.

Leach, W. D., N. W. Pelkey, and P. A. Sabatier. 2002. "Stakeholder Partnerships as Collaborative Policymaking: Evaluation Criteria Applied to Watershed Management in California and Washington." *Journal of Policy Analysis and Management* 21: 645–670.

Leach, W. D., and P. A. Sabatier. 2005. "To Trust an Adversary: Integrating Rational and Psychological Models of Collaborative Policymaking." *American Political Science Review* 99: 491–503.

Lee, K. N. 1993. *Compass and Gyroscope: Integrating Science and Politics for the Environment.* Washington, DC: Island.

———. 1999 "Appraising Adaptive Management." *Ecology and Society* 3(2). Available at www.consecol.org/vol3/iss2/art3.

Lowry, W. R. 1994. *The Capacity for Wonder: Preserving National Parks.* Washington, DC: Brookings Institution Press.

———. 2003. *Dam Politics: Restoring America's Rivers.* Washington, DC: Georgetown University Press.

Lubell, M., and A. Fulton. 2008. "Local Policy Networks and Agricultural Watershed Management." *Journal of Public Administration Research and Theory* 18: 673–696.

Maass, A. 1951. *Muddy Waters: The Army Corps of Engineers and the Nation's Waters.* Cambridge, MA: Harvard University Press.

May, P. J. 2007. "Regulatory Regimes and Accountability." *Regulation and Governance* 1: 8–26.

McKinney, M., and P. Field. 2008. "Evaluating Community-Based Collaboration on Federal Lands and Resources." *Society and Natural Resources* 21: 419–429.

Nash, R. 1982. *Wilderness and the American Mind.* 3rd ed. New Haven, CT: Yale University Press.

O'Leary, R. 2006. "Environmental Policy in the Courts." In *Environmental Policy: New Directions for the Twentieth Century*, ed. N. J. Vig and M. E. Kraft. Washington, DC: CQ Press.

O'Leary, R., and L. B. Bingham, eds. 2003. *The Promise and Performance of Environmental Conflict Resolution*. Washington, DC: Resources for the Future.

O'Toole, R. 1988. *Reforming the Forest Service*. Washington, DC: Island.

Parkins, J., and R. Mitchell. 2005. "Public Participation as Public Debate: A Deliberative Turn in Natural Resource Management." *Society and Natural Resources* 18: 529–540.

Pilkey, O. H., and K. L. Dixon. 1996. *The Corps and the Shore*. Washington, DC: Island.

Potoski, M. 2001. "Clean Air Federalism: Do States Race to the Bottom?" *Public Administration Review* 61: 335–343.

Pralle, S. 2006. *Branching Out and Digging In: Environmental Advocacy and Agenda Setting*. Washington, DC: Georgetown University Press.

Raymond, L. 2003. *Private Rights in Public Resources: Equity and Property Allocation in Market-Based Environmental Policy*. Washington, DC: Resources for the Future.

Reisner, M. 1993. *Cadillac Desert: The American West and Its Disappearing Water*. 2nd ed. New York: Penguin Books.

Repetto, R., ed. 2006. *Punctuated Equilibrium and the Dynamics of U.S. Environmental Policy*. New Haven, CT: Yale University Press.

Sabatier, P. A., W. Focht, M. Lubell, Z. Trachtenberg, A. Vedlitz, and M. Matlock, eds. 2005. *Swimming Upstream: Collaborative Approaches to Watershed Management*. Cambridge, MA: MIT Press.

Sabatier, P. A., J. Loomis, and C. McCarthy. 1995. "Hierarchical Controls, Professional Norms, Local Constituencies and Budget Maximization: An Analysis of U.S. Forest Service Planning Decisions." *American Journal of Political Science* 39: 204–242.

Scheberle, D. 2004. "Devolution." In *Environmental Governance Reconsidered: Challenges, Choices, and Opportunities*, ed. R. F. Durant, D. J. Fiorino, and R. O'Leary. Cambridge, MA: MIT Press.

Schlager, E. 2004. "Common-Pool Resource Theory." In *Environmental Governance Reconsidered: Challenges, Choices, and Opportunities*, ed. R. F. Durant, D. J. Fiorino, and R. O'Leary. Cambridge, MA: MIT Press.

Schneider, A. L., and H. Ingram. 1997. *Policy Design for Democracy*. Lawrence: University of Kansas Press.

Stankey, G. H., B. T. Bormann, C. Ryan, B. Shindler, V. Sturtevant, R. N. Clark, and C. Philpot. 2003. "Adaptive Management and the Northwest Forest Plan." *Journal of Forestry* 101: 40–46.

Steelman, T. A. 2010. *Fostering Enduring Change in Environmental and Natural Resource Governance*. Washington, DC: Georgetown University Press.

Thomas, C. W. 2003. *Bureaucratic Landscapes: Interagency Cooperation and the Preservation of Biodiversity*. Cambridge, MA: MIT Press.

Thomas, C. W., A. B. Soule, and T. B. Davis. 2010. "Special Interest Capture of Regulatory Agencies: A Ten-Year Analysis of Voting Behavior on Regional Fisheries Management Councils." *Policy Studies Journal* 38: 447–464.

Tipple, J. T., and J. D. Wellman. 1991. "Herbert Kaufman's Forest Ranger Thirty Years Later." *Public Administration Review* 51: 421–427.

Tobin, R. 1990. *The Expendable Future: U.S. Politics and the Protection of Biological Diversity.* Durham, NC: Duke University Press.

Waterman, R. W., A. A. Rouse, and R. L. Wright. 2004. *Bureaucrats, Politics, and the Environment.* Pittsburgh: University of Pittsburgh Press.

Weber, E. P. 2003. *Bringing Society Back: Grassroots Ecosystem Management, Accountability, and Sustainable Communities.* Cambridge, MA: MIT Press.

Weible, C. 2007. "An Advocacy Coalition Framework Approach to Stakeholder Analysis: Understanding the Political Context of California Marine Protected Area Policy." *Journal of Public Administration Research and Theory* 17: 95–117.

Wondolleck, J. M., and S. L. Yaffee. 2000. *Making Collaboration Work: Lessons from Innovation in Natural Resource Management.* Washington, DC: Island.

Yaffee, S. L. 1994. *The Wisdom of the Spotted Owl: Policy Lessons for a New Century.* Washington, DC: Island.

CHAPTER 17

··

DEFINING ENVIRONMENTAL RULE MAKING

··

SARA R. RINFRET AND SCOTT R. FURLONG

In *Rulemaking,* Cornelius Kerwin writes, "Rulemaking has something for every key institution and actor in our political system. For this reason alone, we should expect it to be a permanent feature of the way we govern" (2003, 6). This statement is particularly important for students and scholars interested in environmental decision making. We are all familiar with the U.S. environmental policy-making achievements of the past—policy innovations ranging from, but not limited to, the Clean Air Act, the Clean Water Act, the Safe Drinking Water Act, and the Endangered Species Act. But twenty-first-century environmental successes have been slow to follow. Although the U.S. Congress has attempted to modernize environmental policies (e.g., through legislation on energy and climate change), because of sharp partisan differences, environmental policy making has been subject to policy gridlock for some time (Klyza and Sousa 2008). Yet even without major changes in the core statutes, rising concern over environmental problems and new attention to the imperative of sustainable development make it essential to examine the role of environmental rule making and the forces that affect it.

In 2007, Massachusetts and 11 states, several nongovernmental organizations, and local governments sued the Environmental Protection Agency (EPA) for not regulating greenhouse gas emissions under the Clean Air Act. The court ruled in favor of the states, making the EPA the policy-making driver. To move beyond the current congressional environmental policy-making quagmire, we make the argument here that advancement of environmental policy now and in the future depends far more than many people realize about administrative rule making. Hence it is important to improve understanding of the rule-making process. Simply put, we make the case that each stage of the rule-making process provides viable channels for contemporary environmental policy making that can supplement the far more visible legislative process.

In this chapter we explore the underpinnings of the U.S. administrative rule-making process. First we detail the role of the executive branch, the importance of the Administrative Procedure Act (APA), and the stages of the rule-making process. Next we focus on ways in which business and professional groups have influenced the later stages of the rule-making process. From this review, we observe that *ex parte* or off-the-record communications between an agency and interest groups during the preproposal stage is one area to enhance our understanding of environmental rule making. Additional pathways for rule-making research, such as regulatory rooms or rule-making gateways, are particularly fruitful areas of scholarship. Finally, we conclude with a discussion about the most promising paths for future research. Such recommendations may help to uncover additional revelations about the direction of U.S. environmental policy making.

1. The Role of the Executive Branch

1.1. Delegation of Authority

A substantial percentage of environmental policy decisions in the United States take place during the implementation of policies by the executive branch. Implementation of statutory law takes place in a number of ways, but in the case of environmental policy, one of the most important mechanisms is through administrative rule making. Rule making refers to how bureaucratic agencies, such as the U.S. EPA, make policy. It is important at this point to distinguish between congressional or statutory law and regulatory law.

Statutory law is the outcome of the typical lawmaking process within Congress, which includes drafting of legislation, committee actions on it such as hearings and markup or adjustment in language, floor debate and amendment, and votes (by both houses of Congress), and eventually, if successful, approval by the president. The resulting statute or act helps set the direction for the policy actions that will follow. Environmental statutes, such as the Clean Air Act, Clean Water Act, and the Endangered Species Act, are examples of statutory law. Regulatory law, however, consists of the actions and rules undertaken by the executive agencies charged with implementing the congressional statutes. While there is also an extensive process associated with the making of rules, it is generally much less visible to the public than is the legislative process; the press rarely covers the details of administrative proceedings, even those with substantial consequences for public health and the environment. Yet the rules produced by these agencies in many cases have a more direct effect on individuals, businesses, and society than the laws themselves. For example, the Clean Air Act Amendments of 1990, which at the time was one of the most extensive environmental laws ever passed, required over 300 rules to carry out requirements put forth in the law.

Agency regulations have the same legal effect as a statutory law, which raises the question of how agencies acquire the authority to make policy and whether their exercise of that authority meets constitutional requirements. The right to make policy is a result of what is referred to as delegation of authority or power. Delegation of authority is when Congress provides policy-making power to the executive branch. Rule making is the process agencies use to exercise this legislative authority. According to Kenneth Culp Davis (1969), this delegation occurs because programs are necessary and no one (meaning Congress or the president) is willing to set guidelines. Lowi (1979) sees this as potentially problematic in that there may be no constitutional or legal basis for the policies developed, so situations may arise where the regulated are making the policies. Congress may prefer delegation for a number of reasons. For example, the bureaucracy has more expertise in these policy areas and more flexibility to make changes if necessary. Morris Fiorina (1982) argues that Congress delegates in order to "shift the responsibility" of decision making to the agencies: that is, Congress can thereby avoid the controversy and criticism associated with such policies and yet still maintain the ability to oversee the agency activities.

The courts have more or less accepted delegation of authority as constitutional ever since the New Deal era. During the New Deal, the Supreme Court was much more conservative in its interpretation of the delegation doctrine and in three separate cases (*Panama Refining Co. v. Ryan, A.L.A. Schechter Poultry Corp v. United States,* and *Carter v. Carter Coal Co.*) struck down congressional delegations as unconstitutional. Interpretations began to change soon afterward with shifts in the makeup of the Court, the passage of the Administrative Procedure Act (discussed later), and the increasing scope of laws enacted in the 1960s and 1970s. In more recent cases, the Supreme Court has upheld a broader interpretation of delegation and has allowed Congress to provide significant policy-making power to executive agencies (see *Industrial Union Department, AFL-CIO v. American Petroleum Institute* (1980), *American Textile Manufacturers Institute v. Donovan* (1981), and *Whitman v. American Trucking Associations* (2001)). As a result, agencies such as the EPA and Department of the Interior (DOI) have significant discretion in making environmental policy through rule making, but this discretion is not unbridled.

1.2. Limits on Discretion

Agency discretion is limited by a number of tools and processes. Elected officials use these controls to try to influence the decisions of agencies or maintain some level of control over the decision-making process. One of the largest reasons this is necessary is that agencies generally have an information advantage over their political overseers. To partially address this information asymmetry, Congress and the president put different tools in place to try to control agency discretion. This relationship between elected leaders and the bureaucratic agencies is described by the principal-agent model, which refers to the ongoing relationship between the political principal and the bureaucratic agent and how each tries to achieve its sometimes inconsistent goals (see Mitnick 1980; Waterman and Meier 1998). Gary Bryner (1987) characterizes the tools that political principals use as falling into three categories: administrative procedures, economic and scientific decision rules, and political oversight. It is important to recognize in many cases these categories are interrelated. For example, a presidential directive that requires agencies to conduct a cost-benefit analysis of proposed rules is a procedural requirement to use a type of economic analysis or decision rule.

Administrative Procedures. While administrative procedures, or the process of how a rule is developed, may seem innocuous, they can be extremely important in limiting bureaucratic discretion. Procedures can dictate certain activities that must occur prior to a rule's implementation, and these rules are not necessarily neutral (see McCubbins, Noll, and Weingast 1987). In other words, certain organizations may benefit from these seemingly mundane processes.

The primary procedural requirement that affects all agencies is the Administrative Procedure Act (APA), enacted in 1946. This important law established certain minimum procedures for agency rule making to help constrain bureaucratic discretion. Two major components of the law that help control agencies are (1) the granting of the right to seek judicial review to "any person suffering legal wrong because of agency action, or adversely affected or aggrieved by agency action within the meaning of the relevant statute" (Administrative Procedure Act 1946, Section 702), and (2) the setting out of administrative procedures for how agencies would conduct rule making and adjudication. These two parts of the APA limit what agencies can do and allow elected leaders and general citizens to participate in the administrative process. Procedural constraints and the possibility of judicial review affect the decision-making process within an agency. The APA will be discussed in more detail in the next section.

Congress has placed other procedural constraints on agencies as they develop policies, and interestingly, a number of these relate to environmental policy making. The National Environmental Policy Act of 1969, for example, requires environmental impact statements for all major federally funded projects expected to significantly affect the environment. The 1977 amendments to the Clean Water Act allows for a 60-day public comment period on effluent guidelines for toxic water pollutants. Other statutes, such as the Safe Drinking Water Act, require the EPA to allow interested parties to orally present comments and views. Finally, general statutes, such as the Regulatory Flexibility Act and the Small Business Regulatory Enforcement Act, establish procedural requirements to conduct certain types of analyses for all agencies involved in rule making. The Regulatory Flexibility Act, for example, requires agencies to examine the effect of their policies on small businesses and entities.

These procedures may appear to be mundane and neutral, but the writings of McCubbins, Noll, and Weingast (1987) suggest they can be extremely important in shaping policy and controlling agency discretion. Procedures can provide political principals with the necessary tools to help monitor and perhaps influence the activities of bureaucratic agencies. Interest groups with similar parochial interests can also benefit from these procedures. For example, by requiring longer public comment periods, organizations that may be hard-pressed to respond quickly, such as many public interest groups, have the time necessary to get their comments to an agency and potentially affect a policy. Procedures may also set out particular analytical requirements agencies must follow and use in decision making. It is this category of limits on discretion to which we now turn.

Economic and Scientific Decision Rules. These tools have been particularly popular in social regulatory policy areas dependent on substantial technical or economic expertise regarding health, safety, and the environment. There are numerous examples of these tools to limit discretion. According to Bryner (1987), statutory requirements that impose "best available" technology for pollution sources or that require agencies to focus on the hazards at hand regardless of the costs involved are ways technical analyses are used to limit agency discretion. Requiring agencies to collect and use certain types of data and information can force agencies to turn in particular directions or limit their decision-making choices. Another way of limiting discretion is through use of science advisory boards that must review agency decisions prior to issuing policies. For example, OSHA can appoint an ad hoc committee to recommend safety standards (Nichols and Zeckhauser 1977), and per the Clean Air Act a scientific review committee is needed to review new ambient air quality standards (Bryner 1987).

One of the more common forms of analysis used, especially over the past 30 years, has been economic analysis such as cost-effectiveness or cost-benefit analyses. Presidents have issued executive orders requiring agencies to conduct one type of analysis or another to justify the policies at hand. These analyses began in earnest during the Carter administration, which required rule-making processes to include discussion of economic consequences of the alternatives being considered. It was the Reagan administration, though, that took the use of economic analysis to a whole new level with the issuance of Executive Order 12291. Under this order, agencies were required to conduct regulatory impact analyses showing that the potential benefits to society would outweigh the potential costs; that the regulatory objective chosen would maximize net benefits; and that, among a series of alternatives, the one involving the least net cost to society would be chosen. Executive Order 12291 gave OMB the responsibility to oversee this requirement placed upon agencies. Requiring such analyses, and dictating how agencies used them, can limit the agencies' decision-making discretion by dictating the information they had to use when regulating in their policy area. A number of scholars have examined the role of OMB in the rule-making process from a variety of perspectives. Many were conducted during times when the review process was not particularly open to the public view and when the relationship between OMB and many of the regulatory agencies was less than cordial. It is clear from these studies that the role of OMB in the rule-making process could be quite substantial depending on agencies or rules involved (Cooper and West 1988; Berry and Portney 1995; Furlong 1995). More research is needed though in this area. The amount of influence OMB has on agency policy is still not clear. Related to this is the issue of when OMB can insert itself into the process and whether this matters or not. For example, if OMB can get involved at the onset of a rule before an agency can put much time and effort into a policy direction or decision, it may have more influence.

President Clinton replaced Executive Order 12291 with Executive Order 12866 on taking office in 1993. While this executive order potentially provided a bit more latitude to agencies, it is important to note many of the economic analysis requirements remained. The impact of these executive orders really comes down to how individual presidents (and their appointees) determine how stringently or loosely they want to implement them. Executive Order 12886 continued to be used throughout the Clinton terms, the George W. Bush administration, and (as of this writing) the Obama administration. The implementation of these executive orders crosses over to the role presidential oversight plays limiting discretion and, once again, highlights how these different tools overlap.

Oversight. Elected institutions can influence agency policy and limit discretion through a variety of oversight techniques. While often associated with a legislative function performed by Congress to ensure the bureaucracy is following through on congressional intent, presidents also oversee agency behavior and have tools at their disposal to do so. This dual political oversight demonstrates the interesting situation of an agency having multiple principals or, in other words, needing to respond to two different "bosses." On the one hand, Congress provides statutory and budget authority to the agencies; on the other hand, the president is the head of the executive branch and ultimately sits at the top of the bureaucratic hierarchy.

Presidents have both constitutional and implied powers that have evolved to limit agency discretion. The most common and best-known tool a president can use is his appointment power, provided by Article II of the Constitution. Presidents have the power to appoint officials to government offices, such as secretaries to cabinet offices (e.g., secretary of the interior or secretary of state), but also more extensive appointments, such as the EPA administrator and a slew of subcabinet/agency personnel. Presidents will use this power to improve the chances of an agency following his agenda by appointing officials who have similar ideological views. Presidents can remove appointees who fail to follow the presidential agenda and be replaced by another more likely to toe the line (Auer 2008; Daynes and Sussman 2010; also see chapter 14 in this volume). Such appointments have been particularly illustrative in the environmental area over the past few presidencies. President Reagan, who was especially successful in the use of his appointment power, placed conservative and probusiness people, such as James Watt, into the DOI and Ann Gorsuch Burford into the EPA. These individuals shared Reagan's conservative beliefs in regards to the government being too involved in regulating business. George H. W. Bush, a more moderate Republican who wanted to see movement on environmental issues, appointed William Reilly, former president of the World Wildlife Fund, to the EPA administrator post. Democrat Bill Clinton tapped Carol Browner, former legislative aide to Al Gore. President Barack Obama continued this trend with his appointments of Lisa Jackson (a former EPA and New Jersey EPA employee) to the EPA and Ken Salazar (former senator of Colorado) to the Department of Interior. These top-level appointments along with those appointed below can influence agency policy development (Lewis 2008; Moe 1985; Nathan 1983; Waterman 1989; West 1995).

Perhaps one of the most valuable forms of presidential oversight and influence is the actual presidential management of rule making and regulatory policy. As noted earlier, presidential executive orders such as Reagan's EO 12291 play an important role here. In other cases organizational structures within the executive branch have provided presidents (or their designates) with the ability to influence these agency actions (e.g., President Bush's Council on Competitiveness). There have been a number of executive orders issued in recent history directly aimed at influencing agency rule-making behavior and outcomes. Many of these historically have dealt with the economic side of rule-making activities. As part of these efforts, presidents have centralized their management structures in recent history, which has led to their ability to influence agency policy. The OMB and its Office of Information and Regulatory Affairs are the best example of this centralization, theoretically having the ability to review almost any rule making coming out of the executive agencies. Executive review is now an accepted part of the regulatory process, and any president regardless of his or her political leanings is unlikely to eliminate this form of review now that it has been created.

As noted from the above discussion on presidential oversight, presidents have a number of formal and informal tools at their disposal to help influence and control agency policy making. These tools such as appointment power, centralized rule-making management, and the use of executive orders, have become more prevalent during the past 40 years with the growth of the administrative presidency. During this growth, presidents have taken their role as the chief administrative officer very seriously. In many ways, oversight by the president rivals or exceeds, that which occurs by the Congress.

Congressional oversight also occurs as a way to ensure that agency policies are consistent with the statutes passed by Congress. Like the president, members of Congress have a series of tools available to them to influence and control agency policy making. Given other congressional duties, systematic and ongoing oversight of the agencies may not be very prevalent, but a number of scholars nonetheless underscore the considerable power that Congress has to oversee agency activity (Aberbach 1991; Foreman 1989), and they have carefully examined how such oversight occurs (McCubbins and Schwartz 1984).

There are a variety of congressional tools available to oversee agency actions. One of the more common is the use of a committee or subcommittee hearing.

Congress uses hearings to examine a number of different elements regarding agency activity or programs, such as the effectiveness and efficiency of a program. Hearings can occur both prior to implementation to communicate direction or after to discuss outcomes. Congress can also ask for more formal investigations or evaluations of an agency or its programs. The Government Accountability Office is the legislative program evaluation arm often tasked with collecting this kind of information. However, much congressional oversight occurs informally rather than through formal evaluations, and it takes place primarily through telephone calls, meetings, or passing commentary to agency personnel. Of course, these forms of oversight are outside public scrutiny, and Congress can back them up with other, more formal, oversight tools. Congress can also use its budgetary authority as a significant tool to influence agency policy. Increases or decreases in agency budgets can send strong signals to agencies about the way they are implementing environmental policies. Using the EPA as an example, during the early years of the Reagan administration the EPA constant-dollar budget was reduced by 56 percent (Ringquist 1993), which also corresponded to decreased EPA activity. Subsequent years generally saw budget increases as well as increase regulatory activity, particularly during the George H. W. Bush and Clinton eras. Budgets leveled off and eventually decreased a bit during the George W. Bush administration, once again showcasing less interest in environmental policy making.

Of course, the legislative power of Congress provides, in many ways, the ultimate form of oversight. The initial enabling statute that provides agencies with their statutory authority can influence and control agency behavior. Congress also uses statutory deadlines as a way to force agency action by a certain date. In addition, members have used "hammers"—provisions that take effect if an agency fails to act by a certain date. The Resource Conservation and Recovery Act called for a total ban on land disposal if EPA did not publish an alternative rule on this issue (see Kerwin and Furlong 2011). A more specific piece of legislation will also dictate certain policy directions. Theoretically, if Congress is unhappy with an agency policy it can attempt to enact legislation that overrules the agency.

Overruling an agency policy raises a question about one particular tool known as the legislative veto. Legislative vetoes were included in many statutes to allow Congress to veto or disallow an agency action before it went into effect. The Supreme Court in *Immigration and Naturalization Service v. Chadha* (1983) ruled the legislative veto unconstitutional because it violated provisions related to separation of powers and bicameralism. In 1996 Congress passed the Congressional Review Act (CRA) as a way to circumvent some of the concerns included in the *Chadha* ruling. The CRA provides Congress with a "report-and-wait" provision, which gives it the opportunity to review the action before it becomes effective and to pass a joint resolution and present it to the president for his signature barring its final issuance (Korn 1996).

While critics of government often invoke the image of the "runaway bureaucracy" or the "unelected bureaucrat" in describing agency policy-making without limits, it is clear through the mechanisms discussed above that both Congress and the president have the ability to rein in and influence agency policy if they choose. Agencies must walk a tight rope as they serve these two masters and ensure the policies they pursue are acceptable to both or risk being called on the carpet.

2. The Origins and Stages of the Process

We have discussed the role of bureaucratic agencies in the making of public policy and have noted that this often occurs through a process known as rule making. But what are rules and how does this process work? Rules have been part of our nation's policy-making history since the very earliest days of the country (see Kerwin and Furlong 2011). It is fair to say, though, that it became much more prevalent over the past 60 years, particularly after the passage of the APA in 1946. According to the APA, "a rule means the whole or part of an agency statement of general or particular applicability and future effect designed to implement, interpret, or prescribe law or policy" (PL 79-404, Section 551). The APA also discusses three different rule types: legislative, procedural, and interpretive. Legislative or substantive rules are those rules, described in the definition of the rule in Section 551(4) of the APA, that "implement . . . or prescribe law or policy" (Cooper 2007, 145). Procedural, or nonlegislative, rules, represent nonbinding recommendations or advice—such as policy statements made by an agency on a particular issue—that describe the organization, procedure, or practice requirements of an agency. Interpretive rules are statements issued by agencies that present an agency understanding of a rule's meaning, and these do not carry the force of law. Our focus is on legislative rules.

2.1. Rule-Making Process

The APA requires agencies to follow its administrative rule-making guidelines so government entities can carry out congressional statutes through the creation of rules. These guidelines fall into two categories: formal and informal rule making. Formal rule making occurs when agencies issue policies after a hearing is conducted. This process tends to be more procedurally driven and looks much like a trial-type activity.

A large amount of agency policy making occurs through the rule-making process, and specifically through informal or notice-and-comment rule making. The APA requires three minimum steps when agencies conduct informal rule making. First, they must provide notice of a proposed policy. This typically occurs in the *Federal Register.* Second, agencies must provide an opportunity for interested parties to comment on these proposals. Finally, agencies must consider the comments before issuing the final regulation, which is again published in the *Federal Register.* It is this process that agencies such as the EPA and the DOI use in making their policies.

The APA established minimum procedures for notice-and-comment rule making that agencies must follow in developing policies. As noted earlier, Congress has added other administrative requirements for certain areas. In addition, many agencies have taken it upon themselves to add additional procedures in their rule development process. In either case, the procedures required are beyond the minimum provided by the APA but less than those required for a formal rule making. This type of rule-making process is often referred to as hybrid rule making and is not expressly discussed in the APA. Since many of our environmental statutes require additional procedures, such as the opportunity to provide oral comments, one might classify their rule-making process as a hybrid one.

One final rule-making process also related to notice-and-comment and worth noting is negotiated rule making or "reg-neg" (i.e., regulatory negotiation). Reg-neg is a process that tries to develop proposed rules through a consensual process involving the major stakeholders and the agency responsible for developing the rule. Reg-neg recognizes the inherent difficulties in developing rules, including the adversarial conditions and information gaming often associated with traditional informal rule making. Phillip Harter (1982), one of the most influential writers on negotiated rule making, called for a process that recognizes the conflict up front but attempts to resolve that conflict in face-to-face negotiations, with the hope being that ultimately a better proposed rule would result from the negotiated effort. Of course, there are multiple ways to measure better negotiations, and much of the research on this process has focused on the outcomes of rules using reg-neg with some differences of opinion among these studies. It is important to recognize the process involved in a regulatory negotiation typically occurs as a precursor to an actual notice-and-comment process. In other words, the proposal developed during the reg-neg would then go through the APA notice-and-comment process as well (Coglianese 1997; Langbein and Kerwin 2000; Langbein and Freeman 2000; Langbein 2002; O'Leary and Bingham 2003).

2.2. Stages of Rule Making

The APA process for developing rules represents the bare minimum to ensure public notice and participation in rule-making processes. As noted above, most agencies do more than this in developing rules. In addition, there are a number of common internal and external steps that all rules go through during their development. For purposes of this chapter we describe some of the typical stages associated with a notice-and-comment rule.

All rules flow from statutory authority to develop policies in those areas. In other words, an agency must have the policy-making authority granted to them through a law passed by Congress. Once that authority is provided, agencies may have some discretion regarding the setting of priorities (see Kerwin and Furlong 2011). Once selected, development agencies must collect information regarding the problem and potential solution. This often requires informal communication between the relevant stakeholders and agency personnel. A more formal process to collect information is for an agency to issue an Advance Notice of Proposed Rulemaking (ANPRM) in the *Federal Register*. Agencies may use ANPRMs to provide an early alert to stakeholders that they are looking for information and ideas for policy solutions. There is a wide range of information agencies need to collect ranging from technical to economic to political (see Kerwin and Furlong 2011). Once collected, an agency will formulate a proposed rule, which will often go through some type of internal agency review and then, if deemed "significant," will also be reviewed by OMB's Office of Information and Regulatory Analysis. After this review, the proposed rule is published in the *Federal Register*.

This publication is official notice to the general public that the agency is proposing action to address a particular problem. The notice provides information regarding the proposal as well as a period of time in which the agency will take comments. As noted earlier, the agency may also choose (or be required) to conduct public hearings on the proposal. After collecting these comments, the agency will examine them and may make changes to the proposal based on these comments. The final rule will typically go through a similar internal agency and OMB review and is then sent to the *Federal Register* for publication. As noted earlier, as part of the Congressional Review Act passed in 1996, this final rule is also sent to Congress, which may review it and attempt to overrule a regulation with a joint resolution signed by the president (see Kerwin and Furlong 2011).

3. INFLUENCING RULE-MAKING PROCESSES

3.1. Historical Perspectives of Interest Group Power and Influence

One prevalent issue in the rule-making literature is interest group influence, or, more specifically, determining whether interest groups compete in an equitable manner. Scholars such as Mills (1956) and Hunter (1953) posit the elitist perspective—that only a select few, the elite, have the power to influence policy-making in a democratic society. However, postwar American pluralism countered the elitist perspective. Truman (1951) and Dahl (1961) contend that all persons in the United States have some power to influence decision making. Yet other academics, including Olson (1965) and Lindblom (1977), criticize the pluralist framework, asserting that business-oriented groups possess a significant advantage due to their incomparably greater access to resources. Olson argues that groups with many potential members seeking only collective benefits are at a disadvantage because they are unlikely to unite. Lindblom claims that undue influence by businesses was due to their ability to "punish" governments with disinvestment. Through an environmental policy lens, Kraft and Kamieniecki (2007) remind us that despite the ineffective efforts by the business community to repeal major environmental laws, they are successful in getting what they want from policy makers (see Furlong 1997).

Although the pluralist and elitist frameworks are beneficial for rule-making studies, some scholars (Golden 1998; McKay and Yackee 2007) argue that much more is needed to explain interest group influence on the rule-making process. They argue that even though agencies are required by the APA to receive public input during notice-and-comment rule making, business groups dominate the process because they have greater financial resources.

Scholars also utilize the "iron triangle" framework to describe policy-making relationships among and between the legislature, bureaucracy, and interest groups. In this model, agencies are held captive to their clientele. According to Duffy, "The typical iron triangle consists of three parts: the organized groups interested in a particular policy, the congressional committees and subcommittees with jurisdiction of the issue, and the executive agency bureaucrats responsible for that policy" (2003, 19). The iron triangle framework also applies to the field of environmental policy. For example, Defenders of Wildlife president Rodger Schlickeisen (2003) contends that throughout American history, organized private industry groups have persuaded federal bureaucrats and congressional members to promote industry interests as long they received something in return.

Heclo (1978), however, critiques the iron triangle theory because it does not accurately portray the interactions of interest groups, Congress, and bureaucracy. He states that issue networks ("shared knowledge groups that tie together large numbers of participants with common technical expertise") rather than iron triangles are more likely to influence the process (Heclo 1978). Golden (1998) reiterates Heclo's findings in her analysis of agency rule making, noting that the rule-making process is characterized by issue networks with a large number of participants rather than a small number of iron triangles; a focus on this process is needed to enhance our understanding of interest group influence during the proposed and final stages of a rule. This body of literature has guided rule-making scholars to examine interest group influence.

3.2. Examining Interest Group Influence

Recent studies of rule making focus on interest group influence during the proposed and final stages of rule making. This is usually done through examinations of the official rule-making process, including submitted public comments. Several rule-making studies illustrate that business interests dominate this phase. In their seminal work on the EPA's regulatory standards for water pollution, Magat et al. (1986) conclude that industry interest groups participated far more often than any other group in agency rule making. Building on this analysis, Fritschler (1989) analyzes the agency rule to place warning labels on cigarettes, concluding in a case study investigation that business organizations did indeed influence the writing of this final rule. Golden (1998) and West (2004) note that business organizations dominated rule-making processes because they hired consultants to track the *Federal Register* and ensure that their comments conformed to the language of the agency proposing the rule.

Kerwin (2003), in a 1992 survey of Washington lobbyists, questions whether interest group participation influenced the final writing of an agency rule. Using survey data received from all lobbyists listed in the *Government Affairs Yellow Book*, he reviews a representative sample of the organized interests apparent in rule making. He finds that interest groups believe that their primary role—the moment when their ability to influence agency rule making is at its highest—is to participate in public hearings and to informally meet with agencies to discuss rule making.

Additionally, in one of the first empirical studies of the process, Furlong (1993) examines interest group influence on rule making during the later stages of the notice-and-comment process. He employs two surveys to ascertain the relationships between interest groups and bureaucratic processes. In questioning interest groups (i.e., trade associations, business, and advocacy groups), he determines that the top three agencies that stakeholders tried to influence were the Environmental Protection Agency, the Department of Health and Human Services, and the Health Care Financing Administration. Furlong concludes that interest group influence on these agencies is higher because of their intense level of regulatory activity, which made them desirable targets for interest groups. Furlong also finds that although business groups were indeed influential, they did not have distinct advantages over other groups when trying to shape the regulatory process. Last, Furlong concludes, "Evidence from the surveys suggests that participation and influence occurs directly between groups and agencies, just as it does between agencies and congressional committees and between groups and congressional committees" (1993, 230). This study is one of the first to demonstrate that, in terms of influence, interest groups believed agency rule making to be just as important as lobbying members of Congress for legislation.

To delve into how interest groups participate in agency rule making, Golden (1998) questions how much influence such groups exert. She uses the frameworks of iron triangles, agency capture, and issues networks to measure and define influence for a study on notice-and-comment rule making. This examination assesses 11 regulations across three different agencies—the Environmental Protection Agency, the National Highway Traffic and Safety Administration (NHTSA), and Housing and Urban Development (HUD)—to conclude that business groups dominate the notice-and-comment processes for federal rule making. In addition, Golden suggests that when there was a change between the notice of a proposed rule and the final rule, interest group comments during the notice-and-comment period were the primary catalyst for change. For example, in one of her cases, the NHTSA's electric-powered vehicle rule, the agency abandoned its proposed rule altogether because of stakeholder comments. In other cases, however, changes were limited to redefinitions of key terms, or alterations to deadlines for procedural requirements such as record keeping. Agencies are also most likely to change final rules when a general consensus exists among commenters (Golden 1998).

Yackee (2006) reviews Golden's analysis, calling it merely suggestive, and claims that more extensive work is needed to understand the relationship between the behaviors of organized interests and bureaucratic rule making. Yackee develops an empirical framework (2006; 2007 with McKay) grounded in the literature of interest groups, Congress, and competitive lobbying groups (groups that compete to shape government policy outputs) to assess the "direct" influence of interest groups on agency rules. McKay and Yackee qualitatively code over 40 different rules developed by three different agencies to assess the overall impact of interest group influence between the stages of proposing a rule in the *Federal Register* and its final version. Their findings indicate that interest groups do not compete with one another during notice-and-comment rule making because they do not yet know their competitors' lobbying tactics (McKay and Yackee 2007). This research does not specifically focus on environmental decision making, but it does help to explain how interest groups affect a specific stage in the rule-making process.

Kamieniecki's (2006) research, however, does have important implications for environmental policy making. He uses a case study approach to assess the role business plays in salient environmental controversies. This project builds on prior research conducted by Golden (1998). In contrast to her research, Kamieniecki utilizes theories of issue definition, framing, and agenda building to analyze corporate behavior during proposed rules. In using frame analysis (e.g., Goffman 1974), he concludes that the political elite, as well as leaders of interest groups, frame the conflict in order to influence the outcome. In addition, he finds that although business interests had almost no influence over the language of final rules concerning environmental and natural resource issues, they do make a strong effort to define the debate on their terms.

Kamieniecki's findings are important to note because, unlike previous scholarship concluding that business dominated proposed rules (McKay and Yackee 2007; Yackee 2006), Kamieniecki argues that industry interests did not have considerable influence on the notice-and-comment rule-making processes (proposed and final stages) during the creation of specific environmental or natural resource policies. However, like much other work examining the rule-making process, Kamieniecki notes that questions and limitations still remain about the role of interest groups during the preproposal stage. The overwhelming focus to date within the rule-making literature remains on the proposed and final rule-making stages.

3.3. Controversies and New Directions to Analyze Interest Groups and Rule Making

Numerous issues and controversies currently exist within the rule-making literature. Scholars argue over the best methodological approach to measure interest group influence and are divided about which stage in the process is most likely to offer viable findings (e.g., Baumgartner and Leech 1998; Berry 1999). Academics take different approaches toward analyzing public comments made during the proposed stage of rule making. Scholars also debate whether the study of normal rules (those that receive 1,000 or fewer submitted public comments) or contentious rules (those that receive over 1,000 public comments) offer more useful insight on how interest groups influence rule-making outcomes (Golden 1998; Yackee 2008). The major difficulty is that investigations typically focus on either low or high levels of public comments received (Golden 1998; McKay and Yackee 2007), ignoring the large number of more common cases that fall between the two extremes. For example, the U.S. Forest Service's Roadless Rule falls at the high end of the spectrum, with over a million commenters weighing in. In contrast, the Department of Transportation's Medical Waste Rule lacked substantial public comments. Most rule-making scholarship focuses on contentious rules, which is not representative of the broad spectrum of normal notice-and-comment rule making (Yackee 2008).

Another intrinsic concern is whether scholarly findings would differ when reviewed during the preproposal stage of a rule. Research shows that interest groups are informally contacted by agencies during rule development (Lubbers 2002). Furlong (1993) and Kerwin (2003) recognize that interest groups often have access to data or provide technical expertise that agencies need during the preproposal stages of a rule, as agencies are rarely in possession of all the information needed to write a rule. Moreover, Kerwin's (2003) survey of interest groups finds that one of the most effective techniques described by groups working to exercise influence over rule-making processes was to informally contact or meet with an agency before a rule was proposed in the *Federal Register*. Informal techniques such as meetings or telephone calls occur between agency staff and interest groups during the drafting of a rule (Kerwin 2003). The current literature does not, however, explore this process. Baumgartner and Leech (1998) claim that further understanding of the tactics interest groups use to lobby agency personnel at the preproposal stage in policy-making is needed to increase our knowledge of rule making and work since then reinforces this perspective (Kerwin 2003; West 2005; Yackee 2008).

There are only a few recent attempts to analyze the preproposal stage in rule making (Hoefer and Ferguson 2007; Naughton et al. 2009; Rinfret 2009, 2011a, 2011b, 2011c; West 2009; Yackee 2012). Hoefer and Ferguson (2007) develop a regression analysis and argue that interest groups use their resources to give agency decision makers advice during the preproposal stage in exchange for gaining a better idea of what actions an agency is considering taking. Naughton et al. (2009), in contrast to Hoefer and Ferguson's methods, analyze the preproposal stage by using ANPRMs listed in the Unified Agenda (a semiannual report released by the General Services Administration that provides an overview of substantive rules by agency) to analyze the influence of interest groups on the Department of Transportation (DOT).

West's (2009) *Inside the Black Box* suggests that we need to include the preproposal stage to determine the significance of influence at this stage.

Rinfret (2011a, 2011b) offers a different perspective by examining environmental case studies within the U.S. Fish and Wildlife Service (USFWS) and EPA. In her investigation of the USFWS she claims that interest groups that participate during the preproposal phase shape the language of an NPRM. In her most recent study about the EPA (Rinfret 2011c), she demonstrates that the Office of Transportation and Air Quality is using a new approach, shuttle diplomacy, during the the preproposal stage in order to negotiate stakeholder differences prior to the publication of an NPRM (Rinfret 2011c). Yet, what is most important about this informal stage in the rulemaking process is that it is not subject to legal restrictions. Therefore, this is one way for agencies to collect information while mitigating costs. Interactions that take place during agency preproposal development form a pathway for organized interests to influence agency rule making and are therefore important to study (Rinfret 2011c; West 2005 and 2009; Yackee 2008).

3.4. Different Approaches to the Examination of Rule Making and Interest Groups

One complaint about traditional rule-making processes is that agencies should do a better job of encouraging participation (Coglianese et al. 2009). Thus, there are additional outlets for participants interested in becoming involved in environmental rules. These channels include e-rule-making and negotiated rule making.

The origins of e-rule-making date back to the Clinton and George W. Bush administrations. Stated differently, e-rule-making is a flexible document system that allows commenters to see comments submitted for proposed rules. This approach was made possible in 2003 by the Bush administration with the launching of the Regulations.gov website. Regulations.gov is a web portal to "help ensure that the rule-making process is more accessible by making rule-making dockets accessible via the Internet" (Coglianese et al. 2008, 12). Some of the concerns that surround e-rule-making are that it is difficult for the general public to navigate and it does not encourage or increase participation.

In an attempt to understand the legitimacy of e-rule-making, Schlosberg et al. (2009) examined environmental rules within the EPA and DOT. They sought to determine if participation and deliberations increased across commenters. The notion was that since commenters could view the comments that have been submitted, groups would deliberate about the content of the rule by responding to each other. On the contrary, the findings from this study indicate that participation increased, but deliberation between groups did not occur. One reason for this could be that the technology is not user-friendly (Coglianese et al. 2008).

In a response to some of these concerns, under the Obama administration's Open Government Directive, agencies such as the EPA and U.S. Department of Agriculture (USDA) are retooling their e-rule-making efforts. The EPA's new Rule-making Gateway provides specific links to Regulations.gov to streamline their rule-making efforts. The idea is that this is a user-friendly approach. In addition, the USDA is creating a planning rule website as a central hub for all of its rule-making activities, public meetings, and background information. Despite these efforts, a concern remains that there is no uniformity across agencies. However, the Obama administration is dedicated to determining what avenues do work to foster innovation (OMB Watch 2010).

Often, one aspect of environmental rule making is that it attempts to tackle controversial issues (e.g., the U.S. Fish and Wildlife Service's delisting of the northern rocky wolf). And one approach to tackling these concerns is to utilize negotiated rule making (reg-neg). This type of rule making consists of interested parties working with an agency to try to craft the language of a proposed rule. Harter (1982) argues that the traditional form of rule making (submission of comments) invites an adversarial environment because different groups are vying to influence the agency. He suggests that reg-neg is one alternative for addressing adversarial rule makings. In contrast, Coglianese (1997) provides another perception about reg-neg. He questions whether reg-neg increases participation or lessens conflict. His findings indicate that reg-neg does not necessarily reduce conflict. More positively, Langbein and Kerwin (2000) demonstrated that participants involved during reg-neg felt a great involvement in the process.

4. FUTURE RESEARCH

This chapter demonstrates that the study of the rule-making processes is beneficial to understanding interest group influence and more broadly, environmental policy making. While this examination attempts to argue the importance of this scholarship, more work is needed to continue and expand this body of research. This chapter is a stepping-stone to future study.

Ultimately, it is a daunting task for scholars to capture interest group influence during rule-making processes. In particular, the preproposal stage in the rule-making process is difficult to understand because so much informal communication is occurring behind the scenes. To illustrate such communication, future research could take an approach similar to that of Kaufman (1960) and focus exclusively on and provide a more in-depth analysis of an individual agency to give a firsthand account of the impact stakeholders have on the language of a proposed rule. Researchers would immerse themselves within this agency and observe how the preproposal stage unfolds. This way the researcher could report directly on how an agency works with stakeholders during the preproposal stage and their impact on the language of the rule published in the *Federal Register*. Such research could begin to document this informal communication, but possibly at the expense of broader generalizations across agencies (Rinfret 2011a, 2011b).

Additional research should also compare influence during this preproposal stage across presidential administrations. The basic time frame for much recent scholarship is the George W. Bush administration. Future studies could compare, for example, the Obama and Bush administrations. Comparison across presidential administrations would help to explain if stakeholder influence differs between presidencies. Understanding the differences in political influence, especially for agencies such as the U.S. Fish and Wildlife Service, is particularly important. For instance, future inquiries could examine the Department of Interior's recent position that it will depart from the previous administration's decision to vacate revisions of the critical habitat for the spotted owl because of improper political influence (U.S. Department of Interior 2009). Areas of research such as this could expand our understanding of political influence during rule-making processes (Rinfret 2011b).

Other research could compare interview responses from the preproposal stage with comments made by stakeholders once the rule has been published in the *Federal Register*. Rinfret (2009), for example, examined information at Regulations.gov to determine whether the stakeholders she interviewed submitted comments once the rule was published for notice-and-comment. Interestingly, only two or three stakeholders from the 60 who were interviewed submitted comments after publication, with these being nearly verbatim to statements made during the interviews. The fact that many of the interviewees did not submit comments illustrates that there are some limitations in focusing solely on the analysis of submitted comments— those that the literature customarily uses to assess influence. Thus, new studies are needed to compare interest influence exerted during the preproposal stage with that in later stages in the rule-making process. To make this research possible, future projects might need to ask interviewees if their names could be publicized to determine whether statements made about the preproposal stage change once a rule is published and open for comment.

One final future area for research is to determine whether additional factors are influencing the preproposal stage. Employees within the Office and Management and Budget "sign off on" or "approve" the language of an agency rule before publication in the *Federal Register* (Rinfret 2011b). An interesting and important area of research, according to Kargman (1986), is to determine to what extent high-ranking public officials within an agency or employees from an outside source such as OMB are affecting the NPRM on their own.

Much can be learned from the studies reviewed in this chapter. The rule-making scholarship has provided important findings about interest group influence by studying different stages of the rule-making process. This area of research can provide numerous insights for students of political science and public administration as well as for other scholars who study U.S. environmental policy. In all likelihood, Congress will remain politically divided and subject to policy gridlock for years to come. Such a condition reinforces the importance of agency rule making as a viable pathway for policy making. In the absence of congressional action, we may look increasingly to agency decision making for critical and innovative environmental policy making that demands increased attention by scholars.

REFERENCES

Auer, M. R. 2008. "Presidential Environmental Appointments in Comparative Perspective." *Public Administration Review* 68 (1): 68–80.

Auerbach, J. D. 1991. *Keeping a Watchful Eye: The Politics of Congressional Oversight.* Washington, DC: Brookings Institution Press.

Baumgartner, F. R., and B. L. Leech. 1998. *The Importance of Groups in Politics and Political Science.* Princeton, NJ: Princeton University Press.

Berry, J. M. 1999. *The New Liberalism: The Rising Power of Citizen Groups.* Washington, DC: Brookings Institution Press.

Bryner, G. 1987. *Bureaucratic Discretion: Law and Policy in Federal Regulatory Agencies.* New York: Pergamon.

Coglianese, C. 1997. "Assessing Consensus: The Pressure and Performance of Negotiated Rulemaking." *Duke Law Review* 6: 1255–1349.

Coglianese, C., H. Kilmartin, and E. Mendelson. 2009. "Transparency and Public Participation in the Rulemaking Process." *George Washington Law Review* 77: 924–972.

Cooper, J., and W. West. 1988. "The Theory and Practice of OMB Review of Agency Rules." *Journal of Politics* 50: 864–895.

Cooper, P. 2007. *Public Law and Public Administration.* Belmont, CA: Thomson Wadsworth.

Davis, K. C. 1969. *Discretionary Justice: A Preliminary Inquiry.* Urbana: University of Illinois Press.

Dahl, R. A. 1961. *Who Governs? Democracy and Power in an American City.* New Haven, CT: Yale University Press.

Daynes, B. W., and G. Sussman. 2010. *White House Politics and the Environment: Franklin D. Roosevelt to George W. Bush.* College Station: Texas A&M University Press.

Duffy, R. J. 2003. *The Green Agenda in American Politics: New Strategies for the Twenty-First Century.* Lawrence: University Press of Kansas.

Fiorina, M. 1982. "Legislative Choice of Regulatory Forms: Legal Process or Administrative Process." *Public Choice* 39: 33–66.

Foreman, C. J. 1989. *Signals from the Hill: Congressional Oversight and the Challenge of Social Regulation.* New Haven, CT: Yale University Press.

Freeman, J., and L. I. Langbein. 2000. "Regulatory Negotiation and the Legitimacy Benefit." *New York University Environmental Law Journal* 9: 60–151.

Fritschler, A. L. 1989. *Smoking and Politics.* Upper Saddle River, NJ: Prentice Hall.

Furlong, S. R. 1993. "Interest Group Influence on Regulatory Policy." PhD diss., American University.

———. 1995. "The 1992 Regulatory Moratorium: Did It Make a Difference?" *Public Administration Review* 55: 254–262.

———. 1997. "Interest Group Influence on Rulemaking." *Administration and Society* 29: 213–235.

Goffman, E. 1974. *Frame Analysis: An Essay on the Organization Experience*. Boston: Northeastern University Press.

Golden, M. M. 1998. "Interest Groups in the Rule-Making Process: Who Participates? Whose Voices Get Heard?" *Journal of Public Administration Research and Theory* 8 (2): 245–270.

Harter, P. 1982. "Negotiating Regulations: A Cure for the Malaise." *Georgetown Law Journal* 71: 17–31.

Heclo, H. 1978. *A Government of Strangers: Executive Politics in Washington*. Washington, DC: Brookings Institution Press.

Hoefer, R., and K. Ferguson. 2007. "Controlling the Levers of Power: How Advocacy Organizations Affect the Regulation Writing Process." *Journal of Sociology and Social Welfare* 34 (2): 83–108.

Hunter, F. 1953. *Community Power Structure: A Study of Decision Makers*. Chapel Hill: University of North Carolina Press.

Kamieniecki, S. 2006. *Corporate America and Environmental Policy: How Often Does Business Get Its Way?* Stanford, CA: Stanford Law and Politics.

Kargman, S. T. 1986. "OMB Intervention in Agency Rulemaking: The Case for Broadened Review Record." *Yale Law Journal*. 95: 1789–1810.

Kaufman, H. 1960. *The Forest Ranger: A Study in Administrative Behavior*. Washington, DC: Resources for the Future Press.

Kerwin, C. M. 2003. *Rulemaking: How Government Agencies Write Law and Make Policy*. 3rd ed. Washington, DC: CQ Press.

Kerwin, C. M., and S. R. Furlong. 2011. *Rulemaking: How Government Agencies Write Law and Make Policy*. 4th ed. Washington, DC: CQ Press.

Klyza, C., and D. Sousa. 2008. *American Environmental Policy, 1990–2006*. Cambridge, MA: MIT Press.

Korn, J. 1996. *The Power of Separation: American Constitutionalism and the Myth of the Legislative Veto*. Princeton, NJ: Princeton University Press.

Kraft, M. E., and S. Kamieniecki, eds. 2007. *Business and Environmental Policy: Corporate Interests in the American Political System*. Cambridge, MA: MIT Press.

Langbein, L. I. 2002. "Responsive Bureaus, Equity, and Regulatory Negotiation: An Empirical View." *Journal of Policy Analysis and Management* 21: 449–465.

Langbein, L., and C. M. Kerwin. 2000. "Regulatory Negotiation versus Conventional Rulemaking: Claims, Counter Claims and Empirical Evidence." *Journal of Public Administration Research and Theory* 10 (3): 599–632.

Lewis, D. E. 2008. *The Politics of Presidential Appointments: Political Control and Bureaucratic Performance*. Princeton, NJ: Princeton University Press.

Lindblom, Charles. 1977. *Politics and Markets*. New York: Basic Books.

Lowi, T. J. 1979. *The End of Liberalism: The Second Republic of the United States*. New York: Norton.

Lubbers, J. S. 2002. "The Future of Electronic Rulemaking: A Research Agenda." *Administrative and Regulatory Law News* 27 (6–7): 22–23.

Magat, W., A. Krupnick, and W. Harrington. 1986. *Rules in the Making: A Statistical Analysis of Regulatory Agency Behavior*. Washington, DC: Resources for the Future Press.

McCubbins, M. D., R. G. Noll, and B. R. Weingast. 1987. "Administrative Procedures as Instruments of Political Control." *Journal of Law, Economics, and Organization* 3: 243–277.

McCubbins, M. D., and T. Schwartz. 1984. "Congressional Oversight Overlooked: Police Patrols versus Fire Alarms." *American Journal of Political Science* 28 (1): 165–179.

McKay, A., and S. W. Yackee. 2007. "Interest Group Competition on Federal Agency Rules." *American Politics Research* 33 (3): 336–357.

Mills, C. W. 1956. *The Power Elite.* Oxford: Oxford University Press.

Mitnick, B. 1980. *The Political Economy of Regulation.* New York: Columbia University Press.

Moe, T. M. 1985. "The Politicized Presidency." In *New Directions in American Politics*, ed. J. E. Chubb and P. E. Peterson. Washington, DC: Brookings Institution Press.

Nathan, R. 1983. *The Administrative Presidency.* New York: Wiley.

Naughton, K., C. Schmid, S. W. Yackee, and X. Zhan. 2009. "Understanding Commenter Influence during Rule Development." *Journal of Policy Analysis and Management* 28 (2): 258–277.

Nichols, A. L., and R. J. Zeckhauser. 1977. "Government Comes to the Workplace: An Assessment of OSHA." *Public Interest* 49: 39–69.

O'Leary, R., and L. B. Bingham. 2003. *The Promise and Performance of Environmental Conflict Resolution.* Washington, DC: RFF Press.

Olson, Mancur. 1965. *The Logic of Collective Action: Public Goods and the Theory of Groups.* Cambridge, MA: Harvard University Press.

OMB Watch. 2010. "At Agencies, Open Government and E-Rulemaking Go Hand in Hand." http://www.ombwatch.org/node/10935 (accessed April 27, 2010).

Portney, K., and J. Berry. 1995. "Centralizing Regulatory Control and Interest Group Access: The Quayle Council on Competitiveness." In *Interest Group Politics*, 4th ed., ed. A. Cigler and B. Loomis. Washington, DC: CQ Press.

Rinfret, S. R. 2009. "Changing the Rules: Interest Groups and Federal Environmental Rulemaking." PhD diss., Northern Arizona University.

———. 2011a. "Behind the Shadows: Interest Groups and the U.S. Fish and Wildlife Service." *Human Dimensions of Wildlife: An International Journal* 16 (1): 1–14.

———. 2011b. "Frames of Influence: U.S. Environmental Rulemaking Cases." *Review of Policy Research* 28 (3): 231–245.

———2011c. "Cleaning Up the Air: The EPA and Shuttle Diplomacy." *Environmental Practice* 13 (3): 1–8.

Ringquist, E. J. 1993. *Environmental Protection at the State Level: Politics and Progress in Controlling Pollution.* Armonk, NY: M. E. Sharpe.

Schlickeisen, R. 2003. "Earth Day Finds Environment Squeezed by Iron Triangle." Defenders of Wildlife. www.defenders.org/newsroom/press_releases_folder/2003/04_18_2003_earth_day_finds_environment_squeezed_by_iron_triangle.php (accessed April 27, 2012).

Schlosberg, D., S. Zavestoski, and S. Shulman. 2009. "Deliberation in E-Rulemaking? The Problem of Mass Participation." In *Online Deliberation: Design, Research, and Practice*, ed. T. Davies and S. P. Gangadharan, 133–149. Chicago: University of Chicago Press.

Truman, D. 1951. *The Governmental Process.* New York: Alfred A. Knopf.

U.S. Department of Interior. 2009. "Interior Withdraws Legally Flawed Plan for Oregon Forests, Presses for Sustainable Timber Harvests." http://www.fws.gov/home/feature/2009/pdf/07-16-09FINALNorthwestForestPlanAnnouncement.pdf (accessed April 27, 2012)

Waterman, R. W. 1989. *Presidential Influence and the Administrative State.* Knoxville: University of Tennessee Press.

Waterman, R., and K. Meier. 1998. "Principal-Agent Models: An Expansion." *Journal of Public Administration Research and Theory* 8: 197.

West, W. F. 1995. *Controlling the Bureaucracy: Institutional Constraints in Theory and Practice.* Armonk, NY: M. E. Sharpe.

———. 2004. "Formal Procedures, Informal Procedures, Accountability, and Responsiveness in Bureaucratic Policymaking: An Institutional Policy Analysis." *Public Administration Review* 46 (2): 66–80.

———. 2005. "Administrative Rulemaking: An Old and Emerging Literature." *Public Administration Review* 65 (6): 655–668.

———. 2009. "Inside the Black Box: The Development of Proposed Rules and the Limits of Procedural Controls." *Administration and Society* 41 (5): 576–599.

Yackee, S. W. 2006. "Sweet-Talking the Fourth Branch: The Influence of Interest Group Comments on Federal Agency Rulemaking." *Journal of Public Administration Research and Theory* 16: 103–124.

———. 2008. "The Hidden Politics of Regulation: Interest Group Influence during Agency Rule Development." Paper presented at the annual meeting of the Midwest Political Science Association, Chicago, April 3, 2008.

———. 2012. "The Politics of Ex Parte Lobbying: Pre-Proposal Agenda Building and Blocking During Agency Rulemaking." *Journal of Public Administration Research and Theory* 22: 373–393.

CHAPTER 18

ENVIRONMENTAL FEDERALISM AND THE ROLE OF STATE AND LOCAL GOVERNMENTS

DENISE SCHEBERLE

THE casual observer may think that environmental policy is solely the domain of the national government, but state and local governments also play essential roles in protecting the environment. In the simplest terms, environmental laws depend on the national government, state governments, local governments, communities, and citizens to build effective environmental programs. Rather than sharp demarcations of responsibilities, governments interact in mutually dependent ways in the process of implementing environmental laws. However, these interdependencies are often accompanied by friction as policy makers dispute appropriate levels of oversight, support, and involvement.

This chapter begins by providing a brief overview of federalism and intergovernmental relations, focusing particularly on the legal structures for federalism and how these structures play out in the environmental field. Subsequent sections highlight the evolving nature of intergovernmental relationships within environmental programs, including discussions of federal-state working relationships, differences in state capacity and willingness to engage in environmental protection, advocacy by state and local governments, and state and local government innovation. A final section offers some conclusions about environmental federalism.

1. Setting the Context: Federalism and Intergovernmental Relations

1.1. Federalism Defined

Many people look to government to address their concerns, including concerns about protecting the environment. However, which government (national, state, or local), or combination of governments, should address public issues is a subject of much debate today, as it was at the founding of the country. One of the enduring central tensions in the U.S. Constitution involves the appropriate allocation of power between the national and state governments. Federalism describes this allocation of power and is best understood as a system of constitutionally derived and apportioned authority where state and national governments retain sovereignty yet at the same time are interdependent.

State sovereignty is protected, in part, by the Tenth Amendment, which reserves powers not given expressly to the national government to state governments and to the people. The Constitution also restricts the scope of congressional authority. Powers given to Congress are expressly listed in Article I, implying that congressional actions may be limited and must be in conformance with the provisions in Article I. For example, Congress regulates interstate commerce, which has been the main rationale for creating national environmental laws. Congress also makes laws "necessary and proper" to exercise its enumerated powers and provide for the general welfare.

In Article VI, Section 2, referred to as the "national supremacy clause," the Constitution further stipulates that national laws take preeminence over state laws whenever such action is viewed as legitimate and within the scope of enumerated and implied powers. This, too, has come into play as environmental laws passed by Congress and subsequent federal regulations have displaced previous state law and regulations. The Constitution, in short, establishes a system where power is divided between governments and sovereignty is retained by both, but where the national government has the ability to act in traditional state policy domains, including regulating pollution or protecting natural resources, provided that such action is in accordance with constitutional authority.

1.2. Intergovernmental Relations Defined

Local governments do not have constitutionally derived sovereignty as state governments do. Instead, local governments are created by state governments and exercise powers given to them through state constitutions and state laws. States vary in the amount of autonomy they grant to local governments. Thirty-nine states are described by the National League of Cities as "Dillon's Rule" states, after an 1868 court decision that reinforced a strict and narrow construction of the authority of local governments (National League of Cities 2010). In some states, local governments may be granted home rule authority, which give these local governments additional decision-making autonomy.

Local governments play critically important roles in many environmental programs, especially those related to infrastructure and public health. Local governments provide safe drinking water and wastewater treatment, operate recycling programs, protect local watersheds, detect and remove lead-based paint in housing, offer emergency management and response to disasters and chemical spills, and monitor asbestos in schools—just to name a few examples. Local governments may establish building codes, zoning and land use requirements, and incentive programs that lead to more sustainable communities and preserve open spaces (Mazmanian and Kraft 2009; Portney 2003). Environmental programs are implemented by a variety of local governments, including cities, towns, and villages, counties, and special districts. Special districts, sometimes called public authorities, often manage local water and wastewater services in urban and rural communities. Their numbers have tripled in the last 50 years, along with their ability to influence local governance (Mullin 2009). Thus, while it is tempting to judge the quality of U.S. environmental programs by focusing on actions taken at the national or state level, local governments assist in implementing many state environmental programs and are essential actors in their own right in protecting the environment.

The interaction between national, state, and local governments is often referred to as "intergovernmental relations," a broad term that concerns how these governments work together in the daily business of solving public problems. Few would argue that this relationship implies anything other than mutual reliance and shared fate. National, state, and local governments are inextricably linked in most policy situations, and, as alluded to in the above list of local responsibilities, environmental policy is no exception. As President Richard Nixon observed in 1969, "We can no longer have effective government at any level unless we have it at all levels. There is too much to be done for the cities to do it alone, or for Washington to do it alone, or for the states to do it alone" (quoted in Wright 1982, 4). Or, as Terry Sanford, former governor of North Carolina, remarked, "The governments are all in the same boat, tossed by the same waves and dependent on each other's paddles. When any one fails to row, they all move more slowly, and the waves become more dangerous for all" (1967, 97).

Scholars have long emphasized these governmental interdependencies in the U.S. system (Elazar 1962; Grodzins 1966; Kincaid 1990; Sanford 1967; Wright 1982). Nearly 50 years ago, Morton Grodzins suggested that public responsibilities could not be precisely defined among governments but were shared in a kind of "marble-cake federalism" (1966, 80). This "inseparable mingling" of functional administrative responsibilities promoted patterns of negotiated behavior among national, state, and local officials tasked with implementing public policies.

Prominent federalism scholar Daniel Elazar (1962) noted that a cooperative partnership exists among national, state, and local governments, since the administrative functions are shared by officials at all levels of government. He later used the metaphor of a matrix to describe this as collaborative federalism, suggesting that governmental actors engaged in negotiated cooperation within multiple and interdependent networks (Elazar 1984, 3). In a matrix composed of constitutionally and statutorily distributed powers and necessary interdependencies, local, state, and federal actors must bargain and negotiate to run programs and implement laws (Agranoff 2001).

1.3. Collaboration and Frustration in Intergovernmental Relations

Despite these observations of mutual dependence and "rowing together," collaboration may not be the best way to describe federalism or intergovernmental relations. This shared-power arrangement called federalism has also been dubbed "America's endless argument" (Donahue 1997, 18) and "a harmonious system of mutual frustration" (Hofstadter 1948, 9). Frustrations and arguments among intergovernmental actors abound, and they take place in many arenas.

The most obvious arena is the legal one, where questions of appropriate exercise of constitutional authority and statutory requirements are raised. Did Congress exceed its authority in creating the new law or mandating additional state action? Did the U.S. Environmental Protection Agency (EPA) exceed the scope of its authority as described in the law? Has the EPA failed to meet its own obligations to state or local governments under national environmental law? Answers to these questions are often found in court decisions. Take, for example, the responsibility of the EPA under the Clean Air Act to review every five years the standards it sets for ubiquitous air pollutants such as ozone, sulfur dioxide, or lead. The agency is typically "persuaded" to do such reviews only after the American Lung Association and other groups have sued the agency for failure to perform a nondiscretionary duty. In August 2011, the EPA finalized its review of the standard for carbon monoxide as a result of a court order to do so (U.S. EPA 2011). In *Connecticut v. American Electric Power*, a coalition of state attorneys general sought to use federal common law to force power companies to cap and then reduce greenhouse gas emissions. Though the Supreme Court's decision in 2011 held that the Clean Air Act displaced federal common law actions, the case illustrates the ability of states to force the hand of polluting industries, as well as the EPA.

In the political arena, insufficient funding through national grants-in-aid causes frustration on the part of recipient governments (Davis and Lester 1989). State and local governments argue that the national government mandates too much and gives too little to support the implementation of public programs. Between 1960 and 1993, over 60 new federal mandates were enacted, many of them in the field of environmental protection, including requirements under, for example, the Clean Air Act, Safe Drinking Water Act, and Clean Water Act (Conlan 2008). Only two such mandates existed before 1960 (Conlan 2008). Chafing at what they viewed as unfunded responsibilities that they would have to bear, local government officials organized the first "National Unfunded Mandates Day" on October 27, 1993, calling for relief from federal mandates that threatened the intergovernmental partnership. The Unfunded Mandates Reform Act, signed by President Clinton on March 22, 1995, signaled that politicians in Washington recognized the concerns of state and local governments about the increased cost of complying with new federal requirements, many in the field of environmental protection. For example, additional mandates under the Safe Drinking Water Act required local public water supply systems to test for new contaminants. The same law contained provisions that state governments prepare programs to protect wellhead areas but offered no funding to do so. Initial scholarly research suggested that the Unfunded Mandates law did little to decrease federal mandates or costs to state and local governments (Novinson 1995), a conclusion supported by data from the Environmental Council of the States (ECOS), which suggested that federal funding decreased as a portion of the total costs of state and local programs (ECOS 2008).

On a more practical level, oversight by federal environmental agencies has often been criticized as a form of intergovernmental micromanagement. The arena of working relationships among federal, state, and local environmental officials may become strained, even counterproductive, in the face of arguments about funding, programmatic direction, and control. These issues are described in more detail in subsequent sections of the chapter. At the heart of much of this conflict is a complex congressional tool called preemption. Environmental federalism and intergovernmental relations have taken on new dimensions as Congress acted to preempt state environmental laws, as noted in the next section.

2. Preemption and the Evolution of Government Roles

2.1. The Preemption Revolution

As the national government has grown in both size and scope, the courts have interpreted and refereed the boundaries of national and state powers. Until the 1930s, Supreme Court decisions supported a notion of "dual federalism," with a narrower view of the role of the national government in traditional state activities (Wright 1982, 185). States retained significant responsibility for meeting safety and social needs of its citizens, and the national government's role was principally in international, interstate commerce, and economic arenas. This view, however, changed in the twentieth century, due in part to the ills of the Great Depression, which painfully revealed the inability of states to address unilaterally socioeconomic needs.

The balance in the shared-power relationship continued its shift to the national government in the decades following World War II. National action was increasingly viewed by the courts and Congress as appropriate within the constitutionally described federal principle (Zimmerman 2001). National laws that preempted state laws, sometimes referred to as federal supersession, were overwhelmingly supported by the courts as legitimate (Conlan and Dudley 2005). Through the last half of the twentieth century, preemption became a tool of choice for Congress when it decided to act in an area that had previously been the domain of state governments. Of the 522 preemption statutes enacted by Congress between 1790 and 2004, 355 (roughly 68 percent) were passed after 1965 (Zimmerman 2005, 187). Similar to the unfunded mandates issue described earlier, the national government's "preemption revolution" prompted a backlash by state government officials. State officials' displeasure regarding what they viewed as federal encroachment into their policy domains grew considerably in the 1970s, 1980s, and 1990s as Congress acted in the environmental arena.

Environmental laws embodied the preemption revolution. Nearly all major national environmental laws in the first environmental decade, including the Clean Air Act of 1970, the Clean Water Act of 1972, and the Resource Conservation and Recovery Act of 1976 (concerning hazardous waste disposal), followed a pattern of partial preemption (Crotty 1987). Perhaps unsurprisingly, given the host of environmental issues confronting the country at the time, Senator Edmund Muskie (D-ME) and other members of Congress were determined to insert a strong federal regulatory presence in creating new environmental laws. In part, they feared that states were too beholden to industrial interests (Billings 1996; Hays 2000). Lawmakers reasoned that while both state and national governments wanted environmental protection, political and economic forces made it difficult for states to regulate industrial polluters effectively. So bold new pollution-control laws passed beginning in the 1970s changed the landscape of environmental federalism forever, establishing a host of strong command-and-control federal regulatory programs. These programs represented a dramatic departure from the previous approach of the national government to let states take the lead in determining the extent of regulations imposed on industrial polluters.

2.2. The Process and the Politics of Preemption

In order to continue to exercise regulatory authority under these new national laws, states were required to develop standards at least as stringent as those established in the national law or by the federal agency tasked with making the law work (typically the EPA). In most cases the federal standards would operate as a floor, and states remained free to adopt more stringent measures. The assumption of partial or full control by states over one of these environmental programs is known as delegation. In order for delegation to occur, the state legislature must pass authorizing legislation at least as stringent as the federal standard, while also demonstrating that the state has adequate resources to run the program (referred to as state equivalency). Additionally, states had to demonstrate that state agencies had sufficient capacity (staff and expertise) and adequate enforcement mechanisms to run the environmental program. Once the state plan was approved by the oversight agency, delegated regulatory responsibility (primacy) was given to the state.

Delegation often occurs incrementally by section of each environmental law. For example, a state may have primacy for permitting point source discharges under Section 402 of the Clean Water Act (the National Pollution Discharge Elimination System), but not have delegated authority for the pretreatment program that applies to wastewater treatment facilities. While 48 states have primacy for the point-source permitting program, only two states, Michigan and New Jersey, have approval to operate the federal wetlands permitting program under Section 404 of the Clean Water Act. Nonetheless, the trend has been a slow and steady increase in the number of programs delegated to the states. By 2000, states ran about three-fourths of all environmental programs, up from 41 percent in 1993 (ECOS 2000). As of 2010, states had primacy for 96 percent of all delegable programs within environmental laws (ECOS 2010).

Given that these national laws ultimately hold the EPA responsible for successful implementation, states must continue to demonstrate that they are capable of running the delegated program or risk losing it. The EPA may exercise its oversight role and, after following appropriate procedures, reassume regulatory authority should a state fail to implement or enforce program requirements adequately or fail to bring state regulations to new standards set by the federal agency. In practice, this rarely happens. States are typically not eager to cede programs to their federal counterparts. Moreover, the 10 EPA regional offices that have primary contact with state environmental agencies are often reluctant to reassume day-to-day responsibility for state environmental programs, as they lack staff and resources to run operations within state borders (Fiorino 2006; Scheberle 2004).

But it can work the other way, too. On occasion, a state has returned primacy or threatened to do so, especially when federal grant dollars are viewed as inadequate support for the state program (Crotty 1987; Davis and Lester 1987; Davis and Lester 1989). The EPA or other federal agency officials often engage in negotiations with their state counterparts to encourage them to reaccept or to not relinquish primacy. Thus, according to Zimmerman (2005), Posner (2005), and others, partial preemption forges a national-state partnership requiring ongoing negotiation and has had the greatest impact on the nature of the federal system.

Different federal-state arrangements exist as well. For example, states do not have complete delegated authority under the Asbestos Hazard and Emergency Response Act (the law governing the management of asbestos-containing materials in schools), but must apply for a waiver from the EPA to run the inspection, out-reach, and informational components of the program. Enforcement responsibilities reside with the EPA regional offices, and states that want to participate in asbes-tos enforcement activities enter into a cooperative agreement. Another approach to federal-state interactions creates voluntary programs that rely on grant monies for state participation. The Indoor Radon Abatement Act, for example, provides matching funds to states to participate in operating radon awareness programs and residential radon surveys. Sometimes Congress can oblige states to perform cer-tain tasks within environmental laws. The Safe Drinking Water Act mandated that states conduct source water assessments. States that opt not to comply may face sanctions in other programs, most notably reductions in federal highway funding allocated to the state.

However, constitutional protections for state sovereignty ensure that Congress cannot compel states to implement federal regulatory programs (Conlan and Dudley 2005). This "anticommandeering" principle was expressed clearly by the U.S. Supreme Court in *Hodel v. Virginia Surface Mining & Reclamation Association* in 1981, where the Court held that Congress could not "commandeer the legislative processes of the states by directly compelling them to enact and enforce a federal regulatory program" (452 U.S. 264, 288). Congress could certainly act to protect the environment from the consequences of coal mining (as it had in the law under challenge, the Surface Mining Control and Reclamation Act of 1977). It could not, however, force a particular regulatory program on coal mining states.

The Court returned to the "anticommandeering" principle in *New York v. United States* in 1992. New York successfully challenged portions of the Low-Level Radioactive Waste Policy Amendments Act of 1985, which threatened to require states with inadequate waste disposal capacity to take title to, and assume liability for, low-level radioactive waste generated within the state (Adler 2005). In writing the majority opinion, Justice O'Connor laid out simple ground rules for federal efforts to enlist state assistance in regulatory programs:

> The Constitution enables the federal government to preempt state regulation contrary to federal interests, and it permits the federal government to hold out incentives to the states as a means of encouraging them to adopt suggested regulatory schemes. It does not, however, authorize Congress simply to direct the states to adopt Congress's policy prescriptions. In simple terms: "Whatever the outer limits of state sovereignty may be, one thing is clear: The federal government may not compel the states to enact or administer a federal regulatory program." (Quoted in Adler 2005, 398).

In sum, environmental federalism after the preemption revolution is a para-dox. On the one hand, Congress has put federal agencies in the lead by passing laws that enable these agencies to establish regulations governing pollution control and environmental protection. Partial preemption of state laws has consistently been upheld by the courts, though states retain the ability to decide whether to operate environmental programs in the first place, and then how to meet the national stan-dards. State and local governments look to the national government for technical and financial support in implementing national environmental laws and depend on federal grants-in-aid, even if the funding has dwindled (Peterson 1995).

On the other hand, the national government depends on state and local governments for implementation and cannot hope to implement the laws without the participation of state and local governments. Federal agencies are reluctant to reassume regulatory or programmatic control. Thus, the system is cooperative, co-optive, and quarrelsome—guaranteed to evoke images of Sanford's (1967) rowboat while also evoking visions of fisticuffs among intergovernmental officials. This complex arrangement is the essence of the give-and-take tensions of environmental federalism (Scheberle 2005). The next section explores how state and local governments have responded to their evolving roles within environmental programs.

3. Dimensions of Environmental Federalism

Previous sections have briefly described the legal framework for states to run environmental programs under national environmental laws and have provided some context from which to understand environmental federalism and intergovernmental relations. This section provides a glimpse into three areas that will likely shape the contours of environmental federalism in future years: budgetary constraints, working relationships, and ongoing innovation within subnational governments.

3.1. Budgetary Trends for State Environmental Programs

Any serious discussion of environmental federalism must pay some attention to how environmental programs are funded. Federal grant-in-aid support provides a major incentive accompanying state assumption of responsibility for running environmental programs under national environmental laws, whether through partial preemption, mandates, or voluntary programs. To fund environmental programs, Congress provides assistance to states primarily through State and Tribal Assistance Grants (STAG), which are composed of two parts: Categorical Grants (which assist with the operation of delegated programs) and Infrastructure funds (which are used primarily by local governments for water and wastewater programs). Typically, these grants have matching requirements, requiring states to pull from general funds or fees to meet the match.

As noted previously, data suggest that the federal share of funding has not kept up with increased costs of running state environmental programs. ECOS spending data reveal that states have increased their financial obligation to fund environmental programs even as the federal proportional contribution has declined over time (ECOS 2008, 2010a). From 2005 to 2008, total expenditures by states on delegated environmental programs went from approximately $7.5 billion to $12.6 billion (ECOS 2008). However, federal funding did not keep pace, increasing just over $1 billion in the same period. The federal share of the financial burden for operating environmental programs went from 39 percent to just over 23 percent during this time, forcing states to turn to other in-state revenue sources, such as fees, to make up the difference. In contrast, federal funding of state environmental programs averaged 43 percent in the 1980s.

This is a discouraging trend for states, especially given the perilous budget situations faced by many states in the years since this ECOS study and the tsunami of expenses facing state and local governments for water and wastewater infrastructure repair and enhancements. In 2007, EPA conducted its fourth Drinking Water Infrastructure Needs Survey, as required under the Safe Drinking Water Act. Total needs reported by local public water suppliers were $334.8 billion, a finding comparable to the assessment done four years earlier (U.S. EPA 2009). These findings reflect the challenges confronting public water supply systems as they deal with an aging infrastructure network (in many cases, systems that have elements 50 to 100 years old) and increased requirements for contaminant control.

The situation is comparable or worse for wastewater treatment systems. The Congressional Budget Office (CBO) predicts that wastewater systems will need to invest between $13.0 billion and $20.9 billion annually until 2019 to replace degraded systems (this compares to $11.6 billion and $20.1 billion in annual investments for drinking water systems) (CBO 2002, ix). These figures do not include the annual operation and maintenance costs of these systems (which are not eligible for aid under current federal programs). The CBO estimates costs will average between $25.7 billion and $31.8 billion for drinking water systems and between $20.3 billion and $25.2 billion for wastewater systems (using 2001 dollars).

The deep and tenacious economic crisis that began in 2008 eventually prompted congressional attempts to reinvigorate the economy, with deeper support for state and local infrastructure programs. Federal aid to state and local governments reached levels not seen in a decade, and federal grants comprised more than one-third of the funding in the American Recovery and Reinvestment Act (ARRA) (Conlan and Posner 2010, 2, 36). Not surprisingly, ECOS cheered President Obama's 2011 budget proposal, which contained a substantial increase for State and Tribal Assistance Grants and for State Revolving Funds, which support infrastructure investment, reversing a multiyear trend of flat or declining federal support for state environmental agency work. States responded quickly, committing 100 percent of the Safe Drinking Water and Clean Water ARRA funds within the time allotted. Water and wastewater construction programs that were "shovel ready" were allocated an additional $5.8 billion—not nearly enough to meet infrastructure needs as suggested by the CBO and EPA reports, but more than had been allocated in many years.

However, additional stimulus funding will likely not be forthcoming, and substantial increases in other types of federal financial support to state and local environmental programs are unlikely given the political climate in the 112th Congress and a focus on reducing the federal deficit. As a result, local water and wastewater suppliers as well as state environmental regulatory programs will have to fund programmatic needs from in-state sources of revenue. Most states are facing budget shortfalls totaling billions of dollars in upcoming budgets and are ill-equipped to address new costs. An ECOS survey found that state environmental budgets decreased by an average of about $9 million per state in fiscal year 2010 and nearly $12 million per state in fiscal year 2011 (Brown and Fishman 2010, 3).

Local governments fared no better in the aftermath of the 2008 recession. The National League of Cities reported that U.S. cities would likely face an estimated shortfall of $56 billion to $83 billion from 2010 to 2012 (Hoene 2009). Surveys done in 2010 by the league illustrate the continued pressure on local budgets. Nearly 90 percent of city finance officers reported that their cities were less able to meet fiscal needs in 2010 than in the previous year (Hoene and Pagano 2010). Faced with budget shortfalls and declining transfers from state governments, cities were most likely to cut staff and to defer infrastructure projects (Hoene and Pagano 2010).

3.2. Working Relationships

As noted previously, the practical give-and-take of daily intergovernmental relations proved difficult almost immediately after the passage of new national environmental laws. The EPA was slow to delegate programs back to the states. Key obstacles included varying interpretations within the EPA about how to judge the adequacy of state applications for primacy, state concerns about continued federal funding for state environmental programs, perceived inflexibility by the EPA in assessing the equivalency of state programs to the national standards, as well as what state officials perceived as inflexible oversight (U.S. EPA 1984). Improving state-federal relationships within environmental programs would require both a clearer articulation of what was necessary for a state to receive delegated authority and a careful conversation about the nature of federal oversight.

In 1984, the EPA administrator, William Ruckelshaus, issued guidance on delegating programs to state and local governments (U.S. EPA 1984). Recognizing that the agency's intent was to transfer the administration of national programs to state and local governments to the fullest extent possible, Ruckelshaus urged officials at the EPA headquarters and regional offices toward a cooperative working relationship with their state counterparts. While noting that the EPA must carry out its legal obligation to ensure that statutory and regulatory requirements are met, Ruckelshaus declared that the agency would adopt a flexible approach toward approving and then overseeing state programs (U.S. EPA 1984).

Defining the boundaries of this federal-state partnership continued to be a key source of conflict in intergovernmental relations in environmental policy (Gormley 1987; Lowry 1992; Teske 2004; U.S. GAO 1995). State officials chafed at what they saw as a lack of trust from their federal overseers, sometimes to the point that intergovernmental conflict was identified by state environmental program managers as the largest obstacle to implementing environmental programs (Scheberle 2004). A watershed for state-EPA relations was the performance partnership approach developed as part of the National Environmental Performance Partnership System (NEPPS) in the mid-1990s. At the program core was a promise: states would develop key environmental performance indicators under its delegated programs; the EPA, in turn, would adopt a broader view of oversight (NAPA 2000). Details would be worked out in the performance partnership agreements. NEPPS provided another carrot too: states could receive performance partnership grants, which would increase the ability of states to determine how grant funds would be used across environmental programs. Ultimately, NEPPS resulted in 42 performance partnership agreements, performance partnership grants, or both, but did not eliminate intergovernmental tensions over the appropriate scope of federal oversight (Fiorino 2006; Rabe 2003). In some instances, EPA regional officials worried that some states, if given too much flexibility under NEPPS, would bow to major economic and political pressures within the state (Scheberle 2004).

Since NEPPS, EPA administrators have continued to call for improved intergovernmental relationships. In 2011, EPA administrator Lisa Jackson called for stronger partnerships with state environmental agencies and listed this as one of the agency's top seven priorities. However, she also signaled that the agency would not ignore its accountability under the law: "EPA must do its part to support state and tribal capacity and, through strengthened oversight, ensure that programs are consistently delivered nationwide" (U.S. EPA 2011).

3.3. Comparing State Performance and Innovation

Jackson's comment about ensuring that programs are consistently delivered nationwide reveals a fundamental reality about environmental federalism. State governments seldom act in concert or in the same way. Federalism and environmental policy scholars have long pointed to variations in state performance and have sought to explain why some states seem to leapfrog other states in efforts to protect the environment or lead in innovation. Scholars have consistently identified substantial differences among state performance as measured in agency outputs (inspections, enforcement actions) and policy outcomes (cleaner air, water, less waste) (Davis and Lester 1989; Derthick 2010; Koontz 2002; Kraft, Stephan, and Abel 2011; Lowry 1992; Posner 2010; Rabe 2003, 2004, 2010; Ringquist 1993). Such studies reveal that states are uniquely situated in cultural, political, technical, legal, and economic contexts, and these contexts shape state responses to environmental issues as well as their capacity and willingness to regulate industries within their borders.

Davis and Lester (1989, 58) suggested that state's ability to implement environmental programs was based on two complementary dimensions: a state's institutional capacity to absorb new programs and the extent of federal funding available to support state efforts. Variations in capacity helped to explain variations in implementation patterns across the 50 states, a finding supported by implementation research (Goggin et al. 1990; Mazmanian and Sabatier 1983; Miller 1989).

Another common theme explaining state variations in performance rests with the political and economic forces in the states. Kraft, Stephan, and Abel (2011) found that variations in state political forces had a major impact on industrial environmental performance under the Toxics Release Inventory requirements in the Emergency Planning and Community Right to Know Act. Important political factors fostering industrial facilities to become safer and cleaner (that is, to release fewer toxic pollutants) included environmental group strength and an ideologically liberal electorate. Industries that are economic powerhouses within a state may also influence the willingness of states to engage in regulatory enforcement, creating a "race to the bottom" as states seek to foster economic development (Konisky 2007; Potoski and Woods 2002). Similar explanations have been offered in studies of differing efforts among states in hazardous waste programs (Davis 1993; Lester, Franke, O'M. Bowman and Kramer 1983), air programs (Ringquist 1993), environmental justice efforts (Ringquist and Clark 2002), enforcement of coal mining regulations (Hedge, Menzel, and Williams 1988), water pollution (Hoornbeek 2005), information disclosure programs (Abel, Stephan, and Kraft 2007), or state natural resources policy (Koontz 2002a, 2002b).

States should not, however, be seen as reluctant actors in environmental and natural resource protection. Indeed, state and local governments provide venues for innovation, creative use of resources and leadership in environmental programs. While variations in the pace of innovation among state and local governments also exist, it is undeniable that states, local governments, and communities have led in some of the country's thorniest environmental issues, including wetland protection, land conservation, and climate change (Ceplo and Yandle 1997; Lester 1994; Mazmanian and Kraft 2009; Rabe 2010a, 2010b; Steelman 2010; Vig and Kraft 2000). Especially in the area of climate change, states such as California, New York, Maryland, Massachusetts, and Pennsylvania have surged ahead of the national government (Engel and Miller 2009; Rabe 2004). Chapter 8 in this volume explores this phenomenon further.

State and local governments have sued to stop national foot-dragging on environmental issues, as described earlier. Nowhere is this more apparent than in *Massachusetts v. EPA* (2007), the first pronouncement by U.S. Supreme Court on climate change (Engel 2006). As a result of the Court's decision, the EPA was required to take a hard look at greenhouse gases (GHG; in this case, carbon dioxide) as a pollutant under the Clean Air Act, and, more specifically, at regulating emissions from mobile sources on Section 202 of the law.

The decision punctuates the power of environmental federalism in several ways. First, it presents a dramatic picture of the willingness of states to challenge federal reluctance in pursuing the issue of climate change. California passed the Clean Cars Law, the nation's first binding limits on global warming pollution from tailpipes in 2002. Three years later, Governor Arnold Schwarzenegger established bold

GHG emission reduction targets for California (Executive Order S-3–05, June 1, 2005). Assembly Bill 32, the California Global Warming Solutions Act, passed in August 2006, required the state to reduce GHG emissions to 1990 levels by 2020. Controlling emissions from automobiles required a waiver by the EPA under the Clean Air Act (which was initially denied by the agency in 2008 but subsequently granted in 2009 after President Obama asked the EPA to reconsider its decision).

In 2003, the EPA denied a petition from environmental groups and several state and local governments that requested the agency to control GHG emissions from automobiles under the mobile source requirements found in Section 202 (a) (1) of the Clean Air Act. As a result of the agency's decision, 12 states (California, Connecticut, Illinois, Massachusetts, Maine, New Jersey, New Mexico, New York, Oregon, Rhode Island, Vermont, and Washington), three cities (New York, Baltimore, and Washington, DC), two U.S. territories (American Samoa and Northern Mariana Islands), and several environmental groups filed suit. In its decision, the Court recognized that Massachusetts, as a sovereign state, had standing to sue the EPA. The Court found that petitioners had two factors in their favor (Meltz 2007). First, the Clean Air Act specifically authorizes challenges to agency action unlawfully withheld, in this case, the agency's denial of the petition. Second, the Court found that the petitioner injury on which it focused—Massachusetts's loss of shore land from global-warming-induced sea-level rise—was that of a sovereign state rather than a private entity. The relevance here is that states have a special, constitutionally protected right to be heard in federal courts.

A second observation that can be drawn about environmental federalism from this case is that states are increasingly environmental leaders, offering innovative responses to pressing environmental problems. California's emission requirements were subsequently been adopted by other states, representing a large portion of the country and a major market for U.S. automobile manufacturers. In 2009, President Obama announced a first-ever national policy aimed at both increasing fuel economy and reducing GHG pollution for all new automobiles and trucks sold in the United States.

Other state innovations provide evidence of state leadership in climate change. As of 2009, 18 states had a legislated requirement that part of their electricity be generated through renewable energy. Other states are moving in this direction, even in the face of slowing economic growth. The West Coast Governors Global Warming Initiative, approved in 2004, commits California, Oregon, and Washington to targets for state vehicle fleets, hybrid vehicles purchases, new energy efficiency standards, and stringent energy-related building codes. Seven states participate in the Northeastern States Regional Greenhouse Gas Initiative (RGGI), a cap-and-trade system for GHG emissions designed to stabilize emissions by 2015, followed by a 10 percent reduction between 2015 and 2020.

A final observation returns to the beginning of this section. States do not speak with one voice in climate change any more than they do in other environmental programs. While the *Massachusetts v. EPA* case is heralded as a watershed moment for state action to address climate change, not all states were at the party. Seldom discussed is that nearly the same number of states joined the case for the opposition. Ten states (Arkansas, Idaho, Kansas, Michigan, North Dakota, Nebraska, Ohio, South Dakota, Texas, and Utah) were intervenors in the case, supporting the EPA's decision not to regulate carbon dioxide within the Clean Air Act. Like other intervenors from automobile- and truck-related trade groups, these states worried about the costs of complying with new regulations should the EPA choose to move forward in addressing climate change.

4. Conclusion

Environmental federalism is at the crux of environmental protection in the United States. This constitutionally based system provides states and the national government with sovereign positions to address environmental issues. The 40-year history of environmental command-and-control laws and subsequent preemption of state law provides evidence of changing relationships that remain complex, collaborative, and confrontational. At the same time, new partnerships are forged and state and local government innovations remain essential to making progress in environmental protection. Environmental federalism and intergovernmental relations provides resiliency against political pressures, whether they come from the bottom up or the top down, and buffers retrenchment efforts in environmental programs, whether from the states or the national government.

In sum, state and local governments are essential to further progress in environmental protection, but they need the architecture of environmental federalism and national environmental laws. In turn, the implementation of national environmental laws depends on state and local governments as partners, whether reluctant or energetic. State and local governments may bring innovative approaches and on-the-ground wisdom to environmental problem solving. Though federal and state agencies share the goal of protecting the environment, they may not support the same solutions, rate of change, funding levels, or oversight orientation. States and local governments are better equipped to deal with environmental challenges than in the first environmental decade, but individually they operate with unique constraints. Future research can help guide understanding of influences on intergovernmental working relationships and the evolving roles of national, state, and local governments.

REFERENCES

Abel, T. D., M. Stephan, and M. E. Kraft. 2007. "Environmental Information Disclosure and Risk Reduction among the States." *State and Local Government Review* 39 (3): 153–165.

Adler, J. H. 2005. "Judicial Federalism and the Future of Federal Environmental Regulation." *Iowa Law Review* 90 (2): 377–471. Available at SSRN: http://ssrn.com/abstract=690827.

Agranoff, R. 2001. "Managing within the Matrix: Do Collaborative Intergovernmental Relations Exist?" *Publius* 31 (Spring): 31–56.

Billings, L. G. 1996. "The Founder: Why Edmund Muskie Mattered." *Environmental Forum* 13 (May/June): 23–27.

Brown, R. S., and A. Fishman. 2010. "Status of State Environmental Agency Budgets, 2009–2011." *Green Report*. Environmental Council of the States. August. www.ecos.org/files/4157_file_August_2010_Green_Report.pdf (accessed July 15, 2011).

Ceplo, K., and B. Yandle. 1997. "Western States and Environmental Federalism." In *Environmental Federalism*, ed. T. L. Anderson and P. J. Hill. Lanham, MD: Rowman and Littlefield.

Conlan, T. 2008. "Between a Rock and a Hard Place: The Evolution of American Federalism." In *Intergovernmental Management for the 21st Century*, ed. T. Conlan and P. Posner, 26–41. Washington, DC: Brookings Institution Press.

Conlan, T., and R. Dudley. 2005. "Janus-Faced Federalism: State Sovereignty and Federal Preemption in the Rehnquist Court." *PS: Political Science & Politics* 38 (July): 363–366. doi:10.1017/S104909650505002X. Available at http://www.apsanet.org/imgtest/363-366.pdf.

Conlan, T., and P. Posner. 2010. "Inflection Point? Federalism and the Obama Administration." Presented at the annual meeting of the American Political Science Association, September 2–5, Washington, DC.

Crotty, P. 1987. "The New Federalism Game: Primacy Implementation of Environmental Policy." *Publius* 17: 53–67.

Davis, C. E. 1993. *The Politics of Hazardous Waste*. Englewood Cliffs, NJ: Prentice Hall.

Davis, C., and J. P. Lester. 1987. "Decentralizing Federal Environmental Policy: A Research Note." *Western Political Quarterly* 38: 447–463.

———. 1989. "Federalism and Environmental Policy." In *Environmental Politics and Policy: Theories and Evidence*, ed. J. P. Lester. Durham, NC: Duke University Press.

Derthick, M. 2010. "Compensatory Federalism." In *Greenhouse Governance: Addressing Climate Change in America*, ed. B. G. Rabe, 58–73. Washington, DC: Brookings Institution Press.

Donahue, J. 1997. "The Disunited States." *Atlantic Monthly* 279 (May): 18–21.

Elazar, D. J. 1962. *The American Partnership: Intergovernmental Cooperation in the Nineteenth Century United States*. Chicago: University of Chicago Press.

———. 1984. *American Federalism: A View from the States*. 3rd ed. New York: Harper and Row.

Engel, K. H. 2006. "State and Local Climate Change Initiatives: What Is Motivating State and Local Governments to Address a Global Problem and What Does This Say about Federalism and Environmental Law?" Arizona Legal Studies Discussion Paper No. 06-36. *Urban Lawyer* 38: 1015–1033; available at http://ssrn.com/abstract=933712.

Engel, K. H., and M. L. Miller. 2009. "State Governance: Leadership on Climate Change." Arizona Legal Studies Discussion Paper No. 07-37. In *Agenda for a Sustainable America 441*, ed. J. C. Dernbach. Washington, DC: Environmental Law Institute. Available at http://ssrn.com/abstract=1081314.

Environmental Council of the States (ECOS). 2000. *States Protect the Environment*. Washington, DC: ECOS.

———. 2008. *Spending*. www.ecos.org/section/states/spending (accessed December 20, 2010).

———. 2010a. *Annual Report and Almanac*. Washington, DC: ECOS.

———. 2010b. *Delegation by Environmental Act*. Washington, DC: ECOS. Available at www.ecos.org/section/states/enviro_actlist (accessed January 15, 2011).

Fiorino, D. J. 2006. *The New Environmental Regulation*. Cambridge, MA: MIT Press.

Goggin, M. L., A. O'M. Bowman, J. P. Lester, and L. O'Toole. 1990. *Implementation Theory and Practice: Toward a Third Generation*. Glenview, IL: Scott, Foresman and Co.

Gormley, W. 1987. "Intergovernmental Conflict on Environmental Policy: The Attitudinal Connection." *Western Political Quarterly* 40: 285–303.

Grodzins, M. 1966. *The American System*. Ed. D. J. Elazar. Chicago: Rand McNally.

Hays, S. P. 2000. *A History of Environmental Politics since 1945*. Pittsburgh: University of Pittsburgh Press.

Hedge, D. M., D. C. Menzel, and G. H. Williams. 1988. "Regulatory Attitudes and Behavior: The Case of Surface Mining Regulation." *Western Political Quarterly* 41 (2): 323–340.

Hoene, C. W. 2009. "City Budget Shortfalls and Responses: Projections for 2010–2012." *Research Brief on America's Cities, Vol. 4*. Washington, DC: National League of Cities.

Hoene, C. W., and M. A. Pagano. 2010. "City Fiscal Conditions in 2010." *Research Brief on America's Cities* (October). Washington, DC: National League of Cities.

Hofstadter, R. 1948. *The American Political Tradition*. New York: Alfred A. Knopf.

Hoornbeek, J. A. 2005. "The Promises and Pitfalls of Devolution: Water Pollution Policies in the American States." *Publius* 35 (1): 87–114.

Kincaid, J. 1990. "From Cooperative to Coercive Federalism." *Annals of the American Academy of Political and Social Science* 509 (May): 139–152.

Konisky, David. 2007. "Regulatory Competition and Environmental Enforcement: Is There a Race to the Bottom?" *American Journal of Political Science* 51 (4): 853–872.

Koontz, T. M. 2002a. *Federalism in the Forest: National versus State Natural Resource Policy*. Washington, DC: Georgetown University Press.

———. 2002b. "State Innovation in Natural Resources Policy: Ecosystem Management on Public Forests." *State and Local Government Review* 34 (3): 160–172.

Kraft, M. E., M. Stephan, and T. D. Abel. 2011. *Coming Clean: Information Disclosure and Environmental Performance*. Cambridge, MA: MIT Press.

Lester, J. P. 1994. "A New Federalism? Environmental Policy in the States." In *Environmental Policy in the 1990s*, 2nd ed., N. J. Vig and M. E. Kraft. Washington, DC: CQ Press.

Lester, J. P., J. L. Franke, A. O' M. Bowman, and K. Kramer. 1983. "A Comparative Perspective on State Hazardous Waste Regulation." In *The Politics of Hazardous Waste Management*, ed. J. P. Lester and A. O'M. Bowman, 212–231. Durham, NC: Duke University Press.

Lowry, W. R. 1992. *The Dimensions of Federalism: State Governments and Pollution Control Policies*. Durham, NC: Duke University Press.

Mazmanian, D. A., and M. E. Kraft, eds. 2009. *Toward Sustainable Communities: Transition and Transformations in Environmental Policy*. 2nd ed. Cambridge, MA: MIT Press.

Mazmanian, D. A., and P. Sabatier. 1983. *Implementation and Public Policy*. Glenview, IL: Scott Foresman and Co.

Meltz, R. 2007. "The Supreme Court's Climate Change Decision: Massachusetts v. EPA." *Congressional Research Service Report for Congress* RS22665 (May 18).

Miller, R. 1989. "Implementing a Program of Cooperative Federalism in Surface Mining Policy." *Policy Studies Review* 9 (1): 79–87.

Mullin, M. 2009. *Governing the Tap: Special District Governance and the New Local Politics of Water.* Cambridge, MA: MIT Press.

National Academy of Public Administration. 2000. *Environment.gov: Transforming Environmental Protection for the 21st Century.* Washington, DC: NAPA.

National League of Cities. 2010. "Local Government Authority: Home Rule and Dillon's Rule." Available at www.nlc.org/build-skills-networks/resources/cities-101/local-government-authority (accessed May 7, 2012).

Novinson, J. 1995. "Unfunded Mandates: A Closed Chapter?" *Public Management* 77 (7): 16–20.

Peterson, P. 1995. *The Price of Federalism.* Washington, DC: Brookings Institution Press.

Portney, K. E. 2003. *Taking Sustainable Cities Seriously: Economic Development, the Environment, and Quality of Life in American Cities.* Cambridge, MA: MIT Press.

Posner, P. L. 2005. "The Politics of Preemption: Prospects for the States." *PS: Political Science & Politics* 38 (July): 371–374.

———. 2010. "The Politics of Vertical Diffusion: The States and Climate Change." In *Greenhouse Governance: Addressing Climate Change in America*, ed. Barry G. Rabe, 37–100. Washington, DC: Brookings Institution Press.

Potoski, M., and N. D. Woods. 2002. "Dimensions of State Environmental Policies: Air Pollution Regulation in the United States." *Policy Studies Journal* 30 (2): 208–226.

Rabe, B. G. 2003. "The Promise and Pitfalls of Decentralization." In *Environmental Policy: New Directions for the Twenty-First Century*, 5th ed., Norman J. Vig and Michael E. Kraft, 33–57. Washington, DC: CQ Press.

———. 2004. *Statehouse and Greenhouse: The Emerging Politics of American Climate Change Policy.* Washington, DC: Brookings Institution Press.

———. 2010a. "Racing to the Top, the Bottom or the Middle of the Pack: The Evolving State Government Role in Environmental Protection." In *Environmental Policy: New Directions for the Twenty-First Century*, 7th ed., ed. N. J. Vig and M. E. Kraft, 27–50. Washington, DC: CQ Press.

———. 2010b. "Introduction: The Challenges of U.S. Climate Governance." In *Greenhouse Governance: Addressing Climate Change in America*, ed. B. G. Rabe, 3–24. Washington, DC: Brookings Institution Press.

Ringquist, E. J. 1993. *Environmental Protection at the State Level: Politics and Progress in Controlling Pollution.* Armonk, NY: M. E. Sharpe.

Ringquist, E. J., and D. H. Clark. 2002. "Issue Definition and the Politics of State Environmental Justice Policy Adoption." *International Journal of Public Administration* 25 (2–3): 351–389.

Sanford, T. 1967. *Storm over the States.* New York: McGraw-Hill.

Scheberle, D. 2004. *Federalism and Environmental Policy: Trust and the Politics of Implementation*, 2nd ed. Washington, DC: Georgetown University Press.

———. 2005. "The Evolving Matrix of Environmental Federalism and Intergovernmental Relationships." *Publius* 35 (1): 69–86.

Steelman, T. A. 2010. *Implementing Innovation: Fostering Enduring Change in Environmental and Natural Resource Governance.* Washington, DC: Georgetown University Press.

Teske, P. 2004. *Regulation in the States*. Washington, DC: Brookings Institution Press.

U.S. Congressional Budget Office. 2002. "Future Investment in Drinking Water and Wastewater Infrastructure (November)." Available at www.cbo.gov/ftpdocs/39xx/doc3983/11–18-WaterSystems.pdf (accessed January 31, 2011).

U.S. Environmental Protection Agency. 1984. "EPA Policy Concerning Delegation to State and Local Governments." Unpublished document, April 4. Publication Number 230R85001 http://nepis.epa.gov/Exe/ZyPURL.cgi?Dockey=900D0K00.txt (accessed January 31, 2011).

———. 2009. *Drinking Water Infrastructure Needs Survey and Assessment: Fourth Report to Congress*. Office of Water. EPA 816-R-09-001 (March).

———. 2011. "Fact Sheet: National Ambient Air Quality Standards for Carbon Monoxide-Final Rule." August 12. Available at www.epa.gov/airquality/carbonmonoxide/pdfs/COFactSheetAugust12v4.pdf.

U.S. Government Accountability Office. 1995. *EPA and the States: Environmental Challenges Require a Better Working Relationship*. GAO/RCED-95-64 (April). Washington, DC: GAO. Available at http://gao.justia.com/environmental-protectio n-agency/1995/4/epa-and-the-states-rced-95–64/RCED-95-64-full-report.pdf.

Vig, N. J., and M. E. Kraft, eds. 2000. *Environmental Policy: New Directions for the Twenty-First Century*, 4th ed. Washington, DC: CQ Press.

Wright, D. S. 1982. *Understanding Intergovernmental Relations*. 2nd ed. Monterey, CA: Brooks/Cole.

Zimmerman, J. F. 2001. "National-State Relations: Cooperative Federalism in the Twentieth Century." *Publius* 31 (Spring): 15–30.

———. 2005. *Congressional Preemption: Regulatory Federalism*. Albany: State University of New York Press.

CHAPTER 19

....

THE PROMISE AND PERFORMANCE OF COLLABORATIVE GOVERNANCE

....

ANDREA K. GERLAK, TANYA HEIKKILA, AND MARK LUBELL

COLLABORATIVE governance is commonly described as a collective decision-making process that allows diverse sets of actors who share an interest or stake in a policy or management issue to work together toward mutually beneficial outcomes. In the environmental and natural resources management field, collaborative governance has become increasingly more prevalent and visible in recent decades (Durant et al. 2004; Koontz and Thomas 2006; Pretty 2003; Sabatier et al. 2005). It has emerged in diverse arenas, including water management (Born and Genskow 2001; Clark et al. 2005; Imperial 2005; Leach et al. 2002), ecosystem restoration (Heikkila and Gerlak 2005; Karkkainen 2002; Layzer 2008), forest management (Cheng and Mattor 2006; Ebrahim 2004), land use and open-space protection (Frame et al. 2004; Kellogg 2009; Smith 2009), and endangered species protection (Weber et al. 2005). Scholars and practitioners alike view collaborative governance as an alternative to more traditional forms of environmental governance, such as top-down regulatory and technocratic management, as well as an alternative to interest group adversarialism, which often leads to enduring and expensive conflicts (Ansell and Gash 2007; Brunner and Steelman 2005; Margerum and Whitall 2004; Wondolleck and Yaffee 2000).

A key function of collaborative governance in the environmental and natural resource field is addressing collective action problems that cross multiple jurisdictional and functional boundaries (Feiock 2009; Weber 2009). Collective action problems arise in these settings because typically no single actor—at least under traditional administrative structures and arrangements—has the capacity or incentive to develop or sustain a comprehensive approach to solving issues like transboundary water pollution or habitat degradation (Bryson et al. 2006; Kettl 2006; McGuire 2006; Sandström and Carlsson 2008). Many individuals, public agency managers, corporations, nonprofits, and policy makers across scales and levels of authority have overcome these collective action problems by establishing shared agreements, management strategies, programs, and institutions at the scale of the resource dilemma. Collaborative governance arrangements may be formal (e.g., established by statute or an agreement) or informal (e.g., through grassroots dialogue) and may be initiated by any actors with interest or authority in a shared environmental or natural resource problem (Koontz and Thomas 2006; Smith 2009). Collaborative governance in the environmental field is part of a broader trend across the United States and internationally to address complex public sector challenges through networks, interorganizational coordination, and multilevel institutions (Ansell and Gash 2007; Keast et al. 2004; Mandel and Steelman 2003; Sirianni 2009).

Despite the increasing popularity of collaborative governance, some are skeptical as to whether it can deliver on its promise to solve increasingly complex and uncertain environmental challenges. Moreover, data and evidence on the environmental outputs and outcomes of collaborative efforts are weak, or in some cases nonexistent. Thus, given both the growing importance of collaborative governance and the uncertainties surrounding it, this chapter offers an in-depth assessment of both its promise and its possible pitfalls. We first briefly summarize the origins and evolution of collaborative governance and then compare the claims of the proponents and opponents. We next review what is known and what is still uncertain from the growing body of empirical research studying collaborative environmental governance. The conclusion speculates on the future of collaborative governance for both research and practice.

1 .ORIGINS OF COLLABORATIVE GOVERNANCE

Collaborative governance evolved, in part, from a growing recognition of the limitations of traditional policy solutions, particularly command-and-control/state-driven policies and management (Eisner 2007; Klyza and Sousa 2008; Mazmanian and Kraft 2009; Vig and Kraft 2010). National-level policies such as the Clean Air Act (1970), Clean Water Act (1972), Endangered Species Act (1973), Toxic Substances Control Act (1976), and Forest Management Act (1976) proved to be relatively effective at limiting "end of the pipe" pollution, protecting public health, protecting individual species, or sustaining adequate resources for human consumption. Such policies have been arguably less effective at addressing issues that are diffuse, transboundary, and subject to scientific uncertainty, such as nonpoint source pollution, climate change, and the protection of biodiversity. Many such challenges have intensified internationally due to rapid urbanization (80 percent of the United States and 50 percent of the world population now live in cities, compared to 13 percent at the turn of the twentieth century) and the resultant changes in land use and increases in resource consumption needed to support growing populations and economies. Even the primary agencies responsible for implementing regulatory policies, including the U.S. Environmental Protection Agency (EPA), U.S. Bureau of Land Management, and U.S. Forest Service, have recognized the limitations of top-down approaches in dealing with emerging environmental challenges, expressly calling for more collaborative and community-based approaches (Margerum and Whitall 2004).

Another factor driving the emergence of collaborative environmental governance is our expanding knowledge of ecosystems, ecology, and Earth systems. In the 1960s and 1970s, Rachel Carson's (1962) *Silent Spring* and Barry Commoner's (1970) *The Closing Circle* both highlighted the ecological implications of human activities like pesticides and nuclear testing. Since the 1980s, however, scientists, public agencies, and even the lay public have become more cognizant of the interdependencies of the components of ecosystems and the functions and services they provide (Millennium Ecosystem Assessment 2005). Water is no longer viewed as a single resource to manage; the flow of watersheds is intricately coupled with wetlands, groundwater basins, and riparian areas that provide food and habitat for species. Forests are no longer seen as stands of timber to be managed for human consumption; they provide habitat, help regulate and support stream flows, and serve as carbon sinks (among many other functions). Furthermore, society has become attuned to the mounting evidence around the potential vulnerabilities that climate change may impose on various Earth systems (e.g., hydrologic cycles, weather patterns, forests, coral reefs, and glaciers), the species that depend on them, as well as the interactive effects that changes in one of these systems may have on others (IPCC 2007).

Increasing attention to the complexities and interdependencies of the earth's ecological, physical, and social systems has led to growing concerns regarding the inadequacies of existing administrative structures to manage and address environmental problems at the appropriate scale and functional scope (Kenward et al. 2011; Mullner et al. 2001). Collaborative governance efforts have emerged to bring together government actors and other interested stakeholders from different jurisdictions and organizations to help deal with the complex interdependencies of modern environmental problems that emerge at ecosystem scales (e.g., watersheds and forests) and at the scale of specific resource dilemmas (e.g., an area of species habitat that has been impaired by human development), as well as across functional areas (e.g., flood control management and wildlife conservation) (Mullner et al. 2001; Wondolleck and Yaffee 2000).

A third factor that has contributed to the growth of collaborative environmental governance, which is also tied to dissatisfaction with traditional policy tools and to our growing awareness of the Earth's ecological dilemmas, is the rising number and intensity of conflicts over natural resources. Some of these conflicts stem from the increasing competition among the growing urban and industrial sectors that consume natural resources, as well as the externalities their uses impose on others through pollution or resource extraction, especially in rural areas (Emerson et al. 2009). Conflicts also are on the rise as many individuals, communities, and societies come to recognize the intrinsic and "non-use" values of natural resources and environmental services—values that are challenging to sustain when they must compete with economic values and human consumptive needs.

Finally, collaborative governance is part of the worldwide trend toward "New Public Management," which focuses on the efficient delivery of public goods, public-private partnerships for infrastructure, and the use of nonregulatory policy tools like market-based instruments and incentives (Agranoff and McGuire 2003; Kettl 2006; Milward and Provan 2000; Rhodes 1996). Coupled with this trend has been a push toward greater decentralization of environmental governance across the globe, which allows for locally and regionally specific policies and programs that engage with local stakeholders (Jessop 1999; Lemos and Agrawal 2006). Thus, more diverse sets of actors have entered the governance scene from diverse sectors and scales, which can necessitate institutional arrangements that provide coordination and "metagovernance" (Bell and Park 2006), as well as through self-organized partnerships, networks, and regional agreements (Imperial 2005; Scharpf 1994), which typify many collaborative governance institutions.

In the environmental field, scholarship has widely recognized that collaborative governance arrangements among natural resource users, particularly in local, "common pool resource" settings (e.g., fisheries, forests, water), are by no means new (Ostrom 1990; Wade 1994). However, research on these self-organized institutions has proliferated across diverse geopolitical and resource settings (e.g., see Agrawal 2002), and knowledge has been accumulating about the conditions that are likely to spur collective action and promote institutional effectiveness. Recognition of the contributions of this scholarship in both theory and practice came in the form of a Nobel Prize in economics to one of the field's founders, Elinor Ostrom, in 2009.

While the scholarly research on self-governing institutions for managing common pool resources began to flourish during the late 1980s and early 1990s, we also witnessed the proliferation of numerous small-scale collaborative governance efforts in the United States, particularly around watersheds (Lubell et al. 2002; Sabatier et al. 2005). These efforts represent a type of "Tocquevilleian" experiment in local management of environmental issues that were not effectively being addressed by traditional regulatory or agency-centered approaches. These institutions brought together landowners along watersheds, including ranchers and farmers, representatives from local communities, environmental groups, state and federal fish and wildlife managers, departments of environmental quality, and water agencies. Some have argued that the local scale is seen as the key institutional arena for experimenting with nonhierarchical, more networked governance (Brenner and Theodore 2002) and is often where the community conditions exist that can foster collective action, such as trust, clearly defined boundaries around resource issues and actors, local knowledge about the resource, and experience working together (Ostrom 1990).

Collaborative governance efforts in the United States, however, have not been limited to the local scale. Regional collaborative efforts are also on the rise, such as the Montana Forest Restoration Committee and the Cooperative Sagebrush Initiative, which cover 11 states in the western United States (Doyle and Drew 2008; Gerlak and Heikkila 2006; Vigmostad et al. 2005). Some of these regional governance programs have been in place for decades, including the Chesapeake Bay Program, which started in 1983 as a federal-state-local effort to improve water quality and habitat in the bay; the Columbia River Basin's Northwest Power and Conservation Council's Fish and Wildlife Program, which started in 1980 among the four basin states and federal and local stakeholders; and the Quincy Library Group's collaborative management of 2.3 million acres of national forest lands in Northern California, which emerged in 1992 as a way to move beyond conflicts between environmentalists, the timber industry, and public agencies. What is clear is that collaborative governance has spread throughout multiple geographic scales and environmental issues, which makes analyzing its operation and effectiveness all the more important.

2. PROPONENTS OF COLLABORATIVE GOVERNANCE

Many researchers argue that collaborative governance agreements and programs are easier to implement and more durable than traditional command-and-control, regulatory approaches and ultimately can lead to more successful outcomes (Gunton and Day 2003; Innes and Booher 1999; Moote et al. 1997; Susskind and Cruikshank 1987; Wondolleck and Yaffee 2000). Proponents advance a range of arguments for why collaborative governance may be better than regulation for solving environmental problems. At the heart of most of these arguments is the idea that collaborative governance can reduce the transaction costs that arise when actors try to devise shared rules and strategies needed to conserve or maintain a shared resource (Ostrom 1990). Transaction costs include the costs of resources and effort needed for searching for mutually beneficial solutions, bargaining over possible outcomes, and monitoring and enforcing the resulting agreement (North 1990).

In particular, collaborative governance is believed to reduce transaction costs for addressing diffuse, uncertain, and complex problems, such as biodiversity loss

(Thomas 2003). Such actions typically involve multiple actors whose cumulative decisions interact with complex ecological processes. Both the number of relevant stakeholders and the uncertainty inherent in these processes increase the costs of bargaining, monitoring, and enforcement. While collaborative governance may be well suited for the types of problems that have traditionally stymied regulatory approaches, it is not necessarily effective for all kinds of problems. From a transaction costs perspective, in assessing any institutional arrangement, it is crucial to compare performance to other institutional options (Williamson 1985). For example, regulatory approaches have worked fairly well for point sources of water and air pollution (Cohen 2006) and, compared to collaborative approaches, regulatory institutions may have lower transaction costs when addressing point source problems.

Within the context of uncertain and complex environmental problems, proponents of collaborative governance have further articulated some of the mechanisms by which collaborative governance reduces transaction costs. One of most common arguments is that collaborative governance increases the level of social capital among stakeholders (Leach and Sabatier 2005), which is broadly defined as trust, networks of civic engagement, and norms of reciprocity (Putnam 1995). The inclusive nature of collaborative governance increases social capital by allowing stakeholders to interact over time, making new social connections and providing the basis for empathy for other interests. Collaboration contributes to increased trust and improved working relationships essential to cooperation and sustaining engagement (Frame et al. 2004; Leach and Sabatier 2005). Ultimately, these mechanisms can improve policy effectiveness—increasing cooperation theoretically leads to better decisions, reduced conflict, sustained policy implementation, and improved environmental outcomes.

The collaborative governance mechanisms that help reduce the transaction costs of governing complex environmental problems are also valued for their contributions to democratic principles (Leach 2006). Collaborative governance is thought to be more transparent, participatory, and responsive than centralized and hierarchical forms of public management (Bingham et al. 2008; Cooper et al. 2008; Fung 2006; Thomson et al. 2008). Collaborative governance is responsive to citizens because agency experts are no longer making unilateral decisions in closed venues (Futrell 2003; Williams and Matheny 1995). This inclusiveness is believed to increase the procedural and distributive fairness of policy decisions by addressing a diverse set of interests, including groups underrepresented in traditional policy venues (Fawcett et al. 1995; Lasker and Weiss 2003; Merkhofer et al. 1997; Mitchell 2005; Schuckman 2001), or groups such as tribes that have grown accustomed to settling resources disputes in courtrooms (Cronin and Ostergren 2007). Actors are more likely to cooperate when processes are viewed as fair (Tyler 1990), and they are less likely to utilize adversarial venues like the courts to achieve their policy objectives.

Since collaborative governance is considered to be more open and responsive to diverse sets of interests, scholars also argue that it may increase policy learning and innovation, making it more agile and adaptive, and better able to deal with change and uncertainty than state-centric, rigid bureaucracies (Bingham and O'Leary 2008; Connick and Innes 2003; Henton et al. 1991; Pahl-Wostl 2007). Diverse sets of stakeholders often have different types of expertise and information to bring to bear on a problem, which enables the development of "sophisticated forms of collective learning and problem solving" (Ansell and Gash 2007, 19). Many collaborative processes make an explicit effort to increase the level of scientific research on environmental problems, including the integration of a range of informatics and decision-support tools, which can further enhance the capacity for learning (Gerlak and Heikkila 2011). Additionally, the learning that emerges from a single collaborative process can diffuse to other settings or can lead to the scaling up of local approaches to address regional challenges (Goldstein and Butler 2009).

Last, state and federal financial support for collaborative governance can reduce transaction costs at the regional or local level. Many collaborative governance programs are supported by a grant program, legislative earmarks, or some other form of budget allocation that provides financial support for everything from travel to meetings to building major environmental and infrastructure projects. The ebb and flow of these funding sources reflects larger political forces and can directly affect the success of collaborative governance. For example, the George W. Bush administration was widely viewed as reducing support for major ecosystem programs like Everglades restoration, while the Obama administration has worked for increased funding. Such funding is a major incentive for local collaboration and can be used strategically by higher levels of government to achieve or stymie specific policy goals.

3. Criticisms of Collaborative Governance

It is fair to say that the proponents of collaborative governance dominated the early research and dialogue, which began to increase in the early 1990s. However, a range of critics have emerged in the wake of this early enthusiasm, especially as many of the flagship examples of collaborative governance have struggled to solve environmental problems. These critical perspectives continue to expand (McCloskey 1996, 2000, 2001; Moote et al. 1997).

One early criticism was that collaborative governance may be an instance of "symbolic policy" (Edelman 1964; Lubell 2004). Symbolic policy occurs when policy actors accept a policy decision as a symbol of progress, which then deflects their attention from the ongoing problems. As a result, the problems continue without any true solution; people just are not paying as much attention. For example, Lubell's (2004) research indicates that participants in the collaborative National

Estuary Program increased their levels of trust and policy satisfaction (attitudes), but not their overall level of joint policy implementation (behaviors)—all talk, and no action. The argument about collaborative governance has become even more poignant as actors involved with some of the flagship programs have realized that "getting better together" has not fully solved environmental problems.

Collaborative governance may also increase the possibility of "capture" of government agencies by local interest groups (McCloskey 2000). The classic example of capture is how ranchers influenced the rangeland policies of the Grazing Bureau (predecessor to the Bureau of Land Management) in the 1930s, which essentially enabled continued overgrazing despite federal law designed to close the range. Local capture has long been a concern of environmental groups who fear their more diffuse interests are not adequately represented relative to concentrated economic interests. Echeverria (2001), for example, criticizes the Platte River Collaborative Watershed Planning Process because the negotiating table is uneven and is weighted toward development interests. He argues that development interests and environmental advocates have widely different capacities. Because their constituency is so large and diffuse, conservation advocates are routinely at a disadvantage in contests with representatives of relatively more cohesive and more easily organized economic interests. Without strong counter-measures to represent less powerful voices, and without "neutral" agency leadership, Schuckman (2001) argues that collaborative governance is skewed against environmental groups. Collaborative governance raises the fear of capture because it decentralizes policy decisions to be more responsive to political interests in a particular place.

Collaborative governance also endorses (in spirit if not in practice) the idea of consensus decision making, where all stakeholders must agree on a set of policy actions (Kenney 2000). However, this makes it very easy for single actors to veto any particular decision with which they do not agree. Such veto power leads to least-common-denominator decisions, which often cannot address fundamental causes of environmental problems. Consensus building also requires time and cannot be rushed; one of the most common complaints made by policy actors regards the delays caused by collaborative governance (Coglianese and Allen 2003; Gunton and Day 2003; Imperial 2005; Margerum 2002; Roussos and Fawcett 2000; Till and Meyer 2001; Warner 2006; Yaffee and Wondolleck 2003). Such delays may actually increase transaction costs, thus undermining the arguments for many of the advantages of collaborative governance.

A more recent criticism is the lack of analysis of how collaborative governance relates to other policy decisions in a particular geographic region. Collaborative governance does not operate in a policy vacuum; there are many other ongoing decision venues in most contexts. Lubell, Henry, and McCoy (2010) borrow Norton's (1957) "ecology of games" metaphor to analyze the dynamics of multiple policy institutions, and they suggest that collaborative governance can actually have negative feedbacks on the capacity of actors to cooperate in other policy venues. Decisions made in the context of a single collaborative process are very likely to have unintended consequences, and policy analysis that ignores the true complexity of governance is likely to reach the wrong conclusion.

All of these criticisms ultimately boil down to the question of whether collaborative governance delivers its promise of improved environmental outcomes. There remains serious doubt as to whether collaborative governance has met its environmental goals. While the performance of collaborative governance can be directly measured with indicators such as attitude changes and changes in policy outputs like financial expenditures, research, environmental projects, and plans (Leach and Sabatier 2005), observing these policy outputs is not sufficient to achieve environmental outcomes. The best plans may not be implemented, and the environmental projects that are developed may not make significant enough changes in how people use environmental resources. The environmental outcomes criticism remains the most important and difficult challenge to evaluate.

4. What (We Think) We Know about Collaborative Governance

Despite some disagreement surrounding the overall advantages of collaborative environmental governance, the extant literature has produced some agreement on the key sets of variables that affect both the origins and relative success of collaborative governance. In one of the broadest empirical studies, Lubell et al. (2002) analyze the origins of collaborative watershed partnerships across the entire United States. They find that watershed partnerships are more likely to exist in watersheds with high levels of nonpoint source pollution problems and lower levels of regulatory enforcement. Partnerships are also more likely to appear in watersheds with a prior history of collaboration and higher socioeconomic status; these provide social and human capital to overcome organizational costs (Leach and Sabatier 2005). Partnerships are less likely to emerge in watersheds with higher proportions of minority residents, raising questions of environmental justice and unequal access to political resources (Kamieniecki and Below 2008). Other research has pointed to the importance of a "hurting stalemate"—when stakeholders believe that the status quo will benefit no one—as a motivation for collaboration in order to escape the high costs of conflict in ongoing litigation battles or regulatory processes like the Endangered Species Act (Sabatier et al. 2005). In studying large-scale collaborative governance programs in the Columbia River basin, the Chesapeake Bay, the Florida Everglades, and the California Bay-Delta, Heikkila and Gerlak (2005) found that science, leadership, and prior organizational experience played key roles in raising awareness among diverse stakeholders about the unacceptability of the status quo prior to the emergence of collaborative governance.

Research on the variables that affect the performance of collaborative governance is more extensive and investigates a wide range of variables. Clear process rules, open lines of communication, active and sustained stakeholder engagement, mutual learning, and transparent flow of technical information have been identified as factors associated with effective collaborative performance (Ansell and Gash 2007; Bingham et al. 2005; Busenberg 1999; Daniels and Walker 1996; Geoghegan and Renard 2002; Glasbergen and Driessen 2005; Gunton and Day 2003; Imperial 2005; Leach et al. 2002; Murdock et al. 2005; Rogers et al. 1993). Policy entrepreneurs and leaders have been shown to play a key role in bearing some of the organizational costs of collaboration (Ansell and Gash 2007; Heikkila and Gerlak 2005; Kettl 2006; Schneider and Teske 1995; Thomas 2003), along with providing new ideas or shared norms around which participants coalesce (Weber 2009).

Getting the "right" people to the table also matters in collaborative governance (Ansell and Gash 2007; Carlson 2007; Carpenter and Kennedy 2001; Emerson et al. 2009). This typically includes those who will be affected by subsequent actions or decisions, those who have the power to contribute to or to block progress, and those who possess skills, expertise, knowledge, and resources essential to collaborative performance (Beierle and Cayford 2002; Sirianni 2009). Exclusion of critical agents may compromise the process or the outcome of the collaborative effort, including participant commitment and trust (Dietz and Stern 2008; Johnston et al. 2010; Weber 2003). Stakeholders who are committed to the idea of collaboration and who know how to "play well with others" are also a positive influence on success because they are less likely to exit if they are not achieving their policy goals (Gunton and Day 2003; Margerum 2001, 2002; Tett et al. 2003).

Government agencies play a particularly important role for facilitating success (Koontz et al. 2004). Ostrom (1990) argues that higher-level governing authorities must recognize the legitimacy of local institutions for them to be successful. Government agencies can help support collaborative governance by providing funding and encouraging broad stakeholder participation (Schneider et al. 2003). Weak commitment on the part of government agencies, or resistance on the part of stakeholders, can challenge implementation and threaten success (Berardo 2005; Kumar et al. 2007; Weible 2011; Yaffee and Wondolleck 2003). Organizational culture, particularly in traditional land management agencies with a focus on top-down expertise, may serve as a significant barrier to effective collaboration (Carr et al. 1998). Many of the collaborative governance programs in the United States suffered during the George W. Bush administration due to lack of commitment from federal agencies (Lubell and Segee 2010).

How the structure of policy networks influences success is a particularly active area of research. The standard hypothesis is that social capital is enhanced by dense policy networks that span administrative, geographic, and ideological boundaries (Schneider et al. 2003). Dense policy networks with many reciprocal relationships are argued to increase trust and allow the development of norms of cooperation. Boundary-spanning networks are thought to promote greater access to external sources of information and knowledge critical to success (Bodin et al.

2006; Liebskind et al. 1996; Olsson et al. 2004; Pedler et al. 1991). The diversity of information and knowledge that social networks provide, especially citizen and local knowledge, helps to foster learning and broader collaborative success (Keen and Mahanty 2006; Schusler et al. 2003; Weber 2009). However, there still remains an ongoing debate as to exactly which network structures are linked to performance, and under what conditions (Crona and Bodin 2006; Janssen et al. 2007).

5. What (We Think) We Don't Know about Collaborative Governance

Despite more than a decade of intense research on collaborative policy, many knowledge gaps still remain. Here we discuss several issues that require further research including environmental effectiveness, role of political power, linkages to other institutions, spatial and temporal scales, policy learning, and institutional diversity.

We have already alluded several times to the most outstanding knowledge gap in the study of collaborative governance: whether it achieves environmental outcomes (Koontz and Thomas 2006; O'Leary et al. 2006; Smith 2009). Nearly all of the research on effectiveness has measured process factors, such as changes in attitudes and behaviors, or planning outputs (Ansell and Gash 2007; O'Leary and Bingham 2003; Sabatier et al. 2005; Thomson and Perry 2006). A variety of normative goals including fairness, inclusion, participant satisfaction, and representativeness have also been studied (Bingham and O'Leary 2008; Innes and Booher 1999; Meier and O'Toole 2001; O'Leary and Bingham 2003; O'Leary et al. 2006; Sipe and Stiftel 1995). Rogers and Weber (2010, 548) suggest a new distinctive set of outcome categories "affecting and enhancing agencies' and communities' capacity to solve, and otherwise make progress on, interconnected public problems." Yet only a few case studies have extended the analysis of performance to environmental outcomes (for example, see Weber 2009). Much more systematic research is needed on what collaborative governance actually achieves in terms of environmental outcomes.

There are several related reasons for this knowledge gap about environmental effectiveness. It is difficult to find control groups to assess the counterfactual— what would happen without collaborative governance? Lubell's (2003) study of the National Estuary Program is one of the few to compare watersheds with and without collaborative governance, but it did not measure environmental outcomes. The capacity to measure environmental outcomes is also limited by the availability and comparability of environmental data across ecosystems. For example, in watersheds, water quality data are heavily fragmented over space and time. Further, making causal links between collaborative governance and ecological outcomes can be problematic because it is often difficult to isolate variables (Conley and Moote 2003, 380). Last, collaborative governance evolves over long periods of time, and it may be premature to go beyond intermediate changes in attitudes and behaviors.

Collaborative governance is typically studied from an efficiency standpoint, in terms of how to find mutual gains from cooperation. Less is known about how political power influences the collaborative outcomes, or even how to best define political power (Moe 2005). At the very least, political power affects how any gains from cooperation are distributed. Power imbalances between stakeholders are a commonly noted problem in collaborative governance (Gray 1989; Gunton and Day 2003; Imperial 2005; Short and Winter 1999; Susskind and Cruikshank 1987; Tett et al. 2003; Warner 2006). In addition, political power strongly influences and constrains the decision making and actions of resource managers in collaborative arrangements (Raik and Wilson 2006). If some stakeholders do not have the capacity, organization, status, or resources to participate, or to participate on an equal footing with other stakeholders, the collaborative governance process will be prone to manipulation by strong actors. The capacity of different groups to achieve their goals in the context of collaborative governance affects their overall participation. For example, some environmental groups prefer adversarial processes like courts and legislative venues, where they believe they can exert more influence (Gray 1989).

Research on collaborative governance has failed to recognize how individual programs interact with the wide range of other institutional arrangements in a particular system—in what can be called the "ecology of games" (Long 1958; Lubell, Henry, and McCoy 2010). Any particular collaborative process may have positive or negative feedbacks on the performance of other policy decisions. For example, agreements made at the river basin scale across states have direct implications for how the states, as parties to those agreements, then govern the individual water users in their jurisdiction; if the state-level rules are misaligned with basinwide rules, conflicts can ensue (Heikkila et al. 2011). In part this is because a federated system like the United States may feature both horizontal and vertical interdependencies. Within this context, Bardach (2001) argues collaborative activities across scales are evolutionary and emergent. Network analysis is one promising approach for studying the nature and strength of linkages among multiple policy processes, and how those linkages evolve over time.

Vertical and horizontal linkages are related to the overall problem of how spatial and temporal scales influence collaborative governance. One important consideration is how the factors that affect the performance of collaborative governance might vary across spatial scales or might change over time as a particular process evolves (Heikkila and Gerlak 2005). Scale mismatch is another problem that can also affect performance. Cumming et al. (2006) argue that mismatches between institutional and ecological scales reduce the resilience of social ecological systems. There is also often a mismatch in temporal scales, especially with respect to social expectations about performance. Several years may be needed to demonstrate measurable success (Leach et al. 2002), particularly ecological improvement (Doyle and Drew 2008; Layzer 2008), but there is often political pressure to demonstrate short-term outcomes. This creates a great deal of uncertainty about whether to continue investing in an ongoing program.

The problem of temporal mismatch further raises questions about the extent to which collaborative governance can promote learning among the actors involved and interested stakeholders over time. In theory, such learning might help reconcile competing expectations by establishing a shared understanding around the ecosystem or environmental functions. One perspective is that collaborative governance serves as a "boundary" organization around which actors with diverse knowledge and technical skills can develop a common platform for information sharing and ultimately learning (Kallis et al. 2009; Lejano and Ingram 2008). However, network analysts who study stakeholder relationships within collaborative governance continue to debate what types of network structures facilitate learning, and under what conditions (Bodin and Crona 2009; Crona and Bodin 2006; Newig et al. 2010). This literature underscores the fact that both the theories and empirical evidence of how learning emerges in collaborative governance processes are still in their infancy. Part of the challenge stems from a lack of consensus on how learning in collaborative contexts can be operationalized and measured. A recent framework offers researchers guidance in this area, while also drawing out some of the structural, social, and technical features of collaborative governance that might foster learning (Gerlak and Heikkila 2011). Yet both longitudinal and cross-case research on learning within collaborative governance processes is needed to develop this line of research further.

Theoretically grounded cross-case comparisons are needed to extend another area of uncertainty around collaborative environmental governance, which relates to the issue of institutional diversity (Ostrom 2009). Collaborative processes are not all created equal. They exhibit tremendous diversity in their authority, decision rules, mandates, functional processes, and participants. Most collaborative governance research relies on an archetype of institutional rules (i.e., inclusive participation, consensus decisions) to differentiate collaborative governance as a particular class of policy decision process. However, it is also important to understand the institutional diversity within and across collaborative governance processes, and how diverse forms fit into the political niches created by different community and ecological contexts. The framework developed by Ostrom (2009) and colleagues (Janssen et al. 2007) for evaluating the sustainability of social-ecological systems is promising in this regard because it examines how a particular institutional structure operates within ecological, political, and social environments. Such a framework identifies the sets of variables that are essential for exploring the interaction among diverse governance features, types of actors, resources, and resource units, which could ultimately help link the performance of collaborative governance to its "fitness" within a particular social-ecological system.

6. The Future of Collaborative Environmental Governance

One of the critical questions about collaborative governance is whether society should continue to invest in this approach as a solution to environmental problems. If reality is any guide, then the answer is a definite yes because collaborative governance continues to spread to all arenas of public policy, all over the world, despite the lack of consensus regarding performance. We offer more tentative support for continuing the collaborative governance experiment—we are enthusiastic because of its many theoretical benefits, but cautious because of the ongoing scientific debate. But at the time there really are no other policy tools that appear well suited to solving problems on the scale of ecosystems, and we think that collaborative governance should remain a viable member of the policy toolkit, along with command-and control, market-based, and voluntary approaches.

Collaborative governance is clearly not a panacea and should be used where appropriate (Ostrom 2007) and integrated with the other policy tools. From a transaction cost standpoint, the key question is what policy institutions minimize the transaction costs of environmental collective action for different problems. Transaction costs are a function of the ecological, social, and political circumstances in which a policy tool is applied. As previously discussed, collaborative governance might be the right tool for ecosystem management, but other policy tools have lower transaction costs for other types of problems.

However, it would be foolish to continue the collaborative governance experiment without continued research into its effectiveness. We especially need research into environmental performance over time. This requires a long-term investment in research over multiple comparative sites. International comparative research is also needed to investigate how collaborative governance plays out in different social and institutional contexts. Understanding how diverse institutions evolve to solve problems in different types of contexts is ultimately one of the most important questions that remains to be answered: form fits function in policy institutions, but we are not exactly sure how yet.

REFERENCES

Agranoff, R., and M. McGuire. 2003. *Collaborative Public Management*. Washington, DC: Georgetown University Press.

Agrawal, A. 2002. "Common Resources and Institutional Sustainability." In *The Drama of the Commons*, ed. E. Ostrom, T. Dietz, N. Dolsak, P. Stern, S. Stonich, and E. Weber, 41–86. Washington, DC: National Academy Press.

Ansell, C., and A. Gash. 2007. "Collaborative Governance in Theory and Practice." *Journal of Public Administration Research and Theory* 18 (4): 543–571.

Bardach, E. 2001. "Developmental Dynamics: Interagency Collaboration as an Emergent Phenomenon." *Journal of Public Administration Research and Theory* 11 (2): 149–164.

Beierle, T. A., and J. Cayford. 2002. *Democracy in Practice*. Washington, DC: Resources for the Future.

Bell, S., and A. Park. 2006. "The Problematic Metagovernance of Networks: Water Reform in New South Wales." *Journal of Public Policy* 26 (1): 63–83.

Berardo, R. 2005. "The East Central Florida Regional Water Supply Planning Initiative: Creating Collaboration." In *Adaptive Governance and Water Conflict,* ed. J.T. Scholz and B. Stiftel, 64–73. Washington, DC: Resources for the Future.

Bingham, L. B., and R. O'Leary, eds. 2008. *Big Ideas in Collaborative Public Management.* Armonk, NY: M. E. Sharpe.

Bingham, L. B., R. O'Leary, and C. Carlson. 2008. "Frameshifting Lateral Thinking for Collaborative Public Management." In *Big Ideas in Collaborative Public Management,* ed. L. B. Bingham and R. O'Leary, 3–16. Armonk, NY: M. E. Sharpe.

Bingham, L. B., T. Nabatchi, and R. O'Leary. 2005. "New Governance: Practices and Processes for Stakeholder and Citizen Participation in the Work of Government." *Public Administration Review* 65 (5) (September/October 2005): 547–558.

Bodin, Ö., and B. I. Crona. 2009. "The Role of Social Networks in Natural Resource Governance: What Relational Patterns Make a Difference?" *Global Environmental Change* 19: 366–374.

Bodin, Ö., B. Crona, and H. Ernstson. 2006. "Social Networks in Natural Resource Management: What Is There to Learn from a Structural Perspective?" *Ecology and Society* 11 (2): 2.

Born, S. M., and K. D. Genskow. 2001. *Toward Understanding New Watershed Initiatives: A Report from the Madison Watershed Workshop.* Madison: University of Wisconsin—Cooperative Extension.

Brenner, N., and N. Theodore. 2002. "Preface: From the 'New Localism' to the Spaces of Neoliberalism." *Antipode* 34 (3): 341–347.

Brunner, R. D., and T. A Steelman. 2005. *Adaptive Governance: Integrating Science, Policy, and Decision Making.* New York: Columbia University Press.

Bryson, J. M., B. C. Crosby, and M. M. Stone. 2006. "The Design and Implementation of Cross-Sector Collaborations: Propositions from the Literature." *Public Administration Review* 66 (supplement): 11.

Busenberg, G. J. 1999. "Collaborative and Adversarial Analysis in Environmental Policy." *Policy Sciences* 32: 1–11.

Carlson, C. 2007. *A Practical Guide to Collaborative Governance.* Portland, OR: Policy Consensus Initiative.

Carpenter, S. L., and W. J. D. Kennedy. 2001. *Managing Public Disputes: A Practical Guide for Government, Business, and Citizen's Groups.* San Francisco: Jossey-Bass.

Carr, D. S., S. W. Selin, and M. A. Schuett. 1998. "Managing Public Forests: Understanding the Role of Collaborative Planning." *Environmental Management* 22 (5): 767–776.

Cheng, A. S., and K. M. Mattor. 2006. "Why Won't They Come? Stakeholder Perspectives on Collaborative National Forest Planning by Participation Level." *Environmental Management* 38: 545–561.

Clark, B. T., N. Burkardt, and M. D. King. 2005. "Watershed Management and Organizational Dynamics: Nationwide Findings and Regional Variation." *Environmental Management* 36 (2): 297–310.

Coglianese, C., and L. K. Allen. 2003. *Building Sector-Based Consensus: A Review of the EPA's Common Sense Initiative.* Working Paper RWP03. Cambridge, MA: Harvard University, JFK School of Government.

Cohen, S. 2006. *Understanding Environmental Policy.* New York: Columbia University Press.

Conley, A., and M. A. Moote. 2003. "Evaluating Collaborative Natural Resource Management." *Society and Natural Resources* 165: 371–386.

Connick, S., and J. E. Innes. 2003. "Outcomes of Collaborative Water Policy-Making: Applying Complexity Thinking to Evaluation." *Journal of Environmental Planning and Management* 46 (2): 177–197.

Cooper, T. L., T. A. Bryer, and J. W. Meek. 2008. "Outcomes Achieved through Citizen-Centered Collaborative Public Management." In *Big Ideas in Collaborative Public Management,* ed. L. B. Bingham and R. O'Leary, 211–229. Armonk, NY: M. E. Sharpe.

Crona, B., and Ö. Bodin. 2006. "What You Know Is Who You Know? Communication Patterns among Resource Users as a Prerequisite for Co-management." *Ecology and Society* 11 (2): 7. Available at www. ecologyandsociety.org/vol11/iss2/art7/.

Cronin, A. E., and D. M. Ostergren. 2007. "Democracy, Participation, and Native American Tribes in Collaborative Watershed Management." *Society and Natural Resources* 20 (6): 527–542.

Cumming, G. S., D. H. M. Cumming, and C. L. Redman. 2006. "Scale Mismatches in Social-Ecological Systems: Causes, Consequences, and Solutions." *Ecology and Society* 11 (1): 14. Available at www.ecologyandsociety.org/vol11/iss1/art14/.

Daniels, S. E., and G. B. Walker. 1996. "Collaborative Learning: Improving Public Deliberation in Ecosystem-Based Management." *Environmental Impact Assessment* 16: 71–102.

Dietz, T., and P. C. Stern, eds. 2008. *Public Participation in Environmental Assessment and Decision Making.* Washington, DC: National Research Council.

Doyle, M., and C. A. Drew, eds. 2008. *Large-Scale Ecosystem Restoration: Five Case Studies from the United States.* Washington, DC: Island.

Durant, R. F., Y. P. Chun, B. Kim, and S. Lee. 2004. "Toward a New Governance Paradigm for Environmental and Natural Resources Management in the 21st Century?" *Administration and Society* 35: 643–682.

Ebrahim, A. 2004. "Institutional Preconditions to Collaboration: Indian Forest and Irrigation Policy in Historical Perspective." *Administration and Society* 36: 208–242.

Echeverria, J. D. 2001. "No Success Like Failure: The Platte River Collaborative Watershed Planning Process." *William and Mary Environmental Law and Policy Review* 25: 559–604.

Edelman, M. 1964. *The Symbolic Uses of Politics.* Urbana: University of Illinois Press.

Eisner, M. A. 2007. *Governing the Environment: The Transformation of Environmental Regulation.* Boulder, CO: Lynne Rienner.

Emerson, K., P. J. Orr, D. L. Keyes, and K. M. McKnight. 2009. "Environmental Conflict Resolution: Evaluating Performance Outcomes and Contributing Factors." *Conflict Resolution Quarterly* 27 (1): 27–64.

Fawcett, S. B., A. Paine-Andrews, V. T. Francisco, J. A. Schultz, K. P. Richter, R. K. Lewis, and E. L. Williams. 1995. "Using Empowerment Theory in Collaborative Partnerships for Community Health and Development." *American Journal of Community Psychology* 23: 677–697.

Feiock, R. C. 2009. "Metropolitan Governance and Institutional Collective Action." *Urban Affairs Review* 44 (3): 356–377.

Frame, T. M., T. I. Gunton, and J. C. Day. 2004. "The Role of Collaborative Planning in Environmental Management: An Evaluation of Land and Resource Management Planning in British Columbia." *Journal of Environmental Planning and Management* 22: 767–776.

Fung, A. 2006. "Varieties of Participation in Complex Governance." *Public Administration Review* 66: 66–75.

Futrell, R. 2003. "Technical Adversarialism and Participatory Collaboration in the U.S. Chemical Weapons Disposal Program." *Science, Technology, and Human Values* 28: 451–482.

Geoghegan, T., and Y. Renard. 2002. "Beyond Community Involvement: Lessons from the Insular Caribbean." *Parks* 12 (2): 16–25.

Gerlak, A. K., and T. Heikkila. 2006. "Comparing Collaborative Mechanisms in Large-Scale Ecosystem Governance." *Natural Resources Journal* 46 (3): 657–707.

———. 2011. "Building a Theory of Learning in Collaboratives: Evidence from the Everglades Restoration Program." *Journal of Public Administration Research and Theory* 21: 619–644.

Glasbergen, P., and P. J. Driessen. 2005. "Interactive Planning of Infrastructure: The Changing Role of Dutch Project Management." *Environment and Planning C: Government and Policy* 23: 263–277.

Goldstein, B. E., and W. H. Butler. 2009. "The Network Imaginary: Coherence and Creativity within a Multiscalar Collaborative Effort to Reform US Fire Management." *Journal of Environmental Planning and Management* 52 (8): 1013–1033.

Gray, B. 1989. *Collaborating: Finding Common Ground for Multi-Party Problems.* San Francisco: Jossey-Bass.

Gunton, T. I., and J. C. Day. 2003. "The Theory and Practice of Collaborative Planning in Resource and Environmental Management." *Environments* 31 (2): 5–19.

Heikkila, T., and A. K. Gerlak. 2005. "The Formation of Large-Scale Collaborative Resource Management Institutions: Clarifying the Roles of Stakeholders, Science, and Institutions." *Policy Studies Journal* 33 (4): 583–612.

Heikkila, T., E. Schlager, and M. W. Davis. 2011. "The Role of Cross-Scale Institutional Linkages for Common Pool Resource Management: Assessing Interstate Compacts." *Policy Studies Journal* 39 (1): 121–145.

Henton, D., J. Melville, T. Amsler, and M. Kopell. 1991. *Collaborative Governance: A Guide for Grantmakers.* Menlo Park, CA: William and Flora Hewlett Foundation.

Imperial, M. 2005. "Using Collaboration as a Governance Strategy: Lessons from Six Watershed Management Programs." *Administration and Society* 37: 281–320.

Innes, J. E., and D. E. Booher. 1999. "Consensus Building and Complex Adaptive Systems: A Framework for Evaluating Collaborative Planning." *Journal of the American Planning Association* 65 (4): 412–423.

Intergovernmental Panel on Climate Change (IPCC). 2007. *Climate Change 2007: Fourth Assessment Report.* Available at http://www.ipcc.ch/publications_and_data/publications_and_data_reports.shtml#.T6fk86sgrYQ (accessed May 5, 2012).

Janssen, M. A., J. M. Anderies, and E. Ostrom. 2007. "Robustness of Social-Ecological Systems to Spatial and Temporal Variability." *Society and Natural Resources* 20 (4): 307–322.

Jessop, B. 1999. "Narrating the Future of the National Economy and the National State: Remarks on Remapping Regulation and Reinventing Governance." In *State/Culture: State Formation after the Cultural Turn*, ed. G. Steinmetz, 378–405. Ithaca, NY: Cornell University Press.

Johnston, E. W., D. Hicks, N. Nan, and J. C. Auer. 2010. "Managing the Inclusion Process in Collaborative Governance." *Journal of Public Administration Research and Theory* 18 (4): 543–571.

Kallis, G., M. Kiparsky, and R. Norgaard. 2009. "Collaborative Governance and Adaptive Management: Lessons from California's CalFed Water Program." *Environmental Science and Policy* 12 (6): 631–643.

Kamieniecki, S., and A. Below. 2008. "Ethical Issues in Storm Water Policy Implementation: Disparities in Financial Burdens and Overall Benefits." In *Water, Place and Fairness: Tempering Efficiency with Equity*, ed. J. Whiteley, H. Ingram, and R. Perry, 69–94. Cambridge, MA: MIT Press.

Karkkainen, B. C. 2002. "Collaborative Ecosystem Governance: Scale, Complexity, and Dynamism." *Virginia Environmental Law Journal* 21: 1–51.

Keast, R., M. P. Mandell, K. Brown, and G. Woolcock. 2004. "Network Structures: Working Differently and Changing Expectations." *Public Administration Review* 64 (3): 363–371.

Keen, M., and S. Mahanty. 2006. "Learning in Sustainable Natural Resource Management: Challenges and Opportunities in the Pacific Northwest." *Society and Natural Resources* 19 (6): 497–513.

Kellogg, W. A. 2009. "Ohio's Balanced Growth Program: A Case Study of Collaboration for Planning and Policy Design." *Journal of Environmental Planning and Management* 52 (4): 549–570.

Kenney, D. S. 2000. *Arguing about Consensus: Examining the Case against Western Watershed Initiatives and Other Collaborative Groups Active in Natural Resources Management*. Boulder: University of Colorado School of Law, Natural Resources Law Center.

Kenward, R. E., et al. 2011. "Identifying Governance Strategies That Effectively Support Ecosystem Services, Resource Sustainability, and Biodiversity." *PNAS* 18 (13): 5308–5312.

Kettl, D. F. 2006. "Managing Boundaries in American Administration: The Collaborative Imperative." *Public Administration Review* 66 (6): 10–19.

Klyza, C. M., and D. Sousa. 2008. *American Environmental Policy, 1990–2006: Beyond Gridlock*. Cambridge, MA: MIT Press.

Koontz, T. M., T. A. Steelman, J. Carmin, K. S. Korfmacher, C. Moseley, and C. W. Thomas. 2004. *Collaborative Environmental Management: What Roles for Government?* Washington, DC: Resources for the Future.

Koontz, T. M., and C. W. Thomas. 2006. "What Do We Know and Need to Know about the Environmental Outcomes of Collaborative Management?" *Public Administration Review* 66 (6): 111–121.

Kumar, S., S. Kant, and T. L. Amburgey. 2007. "Public Agencies and Collaborative Management Approaches: Examining Resistance among Administrative Professionals." *Administration and Society* 39 (5): 569–610.

Lasker, R. D., and E. S. Weiss. 2003. "Broadening Participation in Community Problem-Solving: A Multidisciplinary Model to Support Collaborative Practice and Research." *Journal of Urban Health: Bulletin of the New York Academy of Medicine* 80: 14–60.

Layzer, J. A. 2008. *Natural Experiments: Ecosystem-Based Management and the Environment*. Cambridge, MA: MIT Press.

Leach, W. D. 2006. "Collaborative Public Management and Democracy: Evidence from Western Watershed Partnerships." *Public Administration Review* 66 (supplement): 100–110.

Leach, W. D., N. W. Pelkey, and P. Sabatier. 2002. "Stakeholder Partnerships as Collaborative Policymaking: Evaluation Criteria Applied to Watershed

Management in California and Washington." *Journal of Policy Analysis and Management* 21 (4): 645–670.

Leach, W. D., and P. A. Sabatier. 2005. "Are Trust and Social Capital the Keys to Success?: Watershed Partnerships in California and Washington." In *Swimming Upstream: Collaborative Approaches to Watershed Management*, ed. P.A. Sabatier, W. Focht, M. Lubell, Z. Trachtenberg, A. Vedlitz, and M. Matlock, 233–258. Cambridge, MA: MIT Press.

Lejano, R. P., and H. Ingram. 2008. "Collaborative Networks and New Ways of Knowing." *Environmental Science and Policy* 12 (6): 653–662.

Lemos, M. C., and A. Agrawal. 2006. "Environmental Governance." *Annual Review of Environment and Resources* 31: 297–325.

Liebeskind, J. P., A. L. Oliver, L. Zucker, and M. Brewer. 1996. "Social Networks, Learning and Flexibility: Sourcing Scientific Knowledge in New Biotechnology Firms." *Organization Science* 7 (4): 429–443.

Long, N. E. 1958. "The Local Community as an Ecology of Games." *American Journal of Sociology* 64: 251–261.

Lubell, M. 2003. "Collaborative Institutions, Belief-Systems, and Perceived Policy Effectiveness." *Political Research Quarterly* 56 (3): 309–323.

Lubell, M. 2004. "Collaborative Environmental Institutions: All Talk and No Action?" *Journal of Policy Analysis and Management* 23 (3): 549–573.

Lubell, M., A. D. Henry, and M. McCoy. 2010. "Collaborative Institutions in an Ecology of Games." *American Journal of Political Science* 54 (2): 287–300.

Lubell, M., M. Schneider, J. T. Scholz, and M. Mete. 2002. "Watershed Partnerships and the Emergence of Collective Action Institutions." *American Journal of Political Science* 46 (1): 148–163.

Lubell, M., and B. Segee. 2010. "Conflict and Cooperation in Natural Resource Management." In *Environmental Policy: New Directions for the Twenty-First Century*, 7th ed., ed. N. J. Vig and M. E. Kraft. Washington, DC: CQ Press.

Mandell, M. P., and T. A. Steelman. 2003. "Understanding What Can Be Accomplished through Interorganizational Innovations: The Importance of Typologies, Context, and Management Strategies." *Public Management Review* 5 (2): 197–224.

Margerum, R. D. 2001. "Organizational Commitment to Integrated and Collaborative Management: Matching Strategies to Constraints." *Environmental Management* 28 (4): 21–31.

———. 2002. "Evaluating Collaborative Planning: Implications from an Empirical Analysis of Growth Management." *Journal of the American Planning Association* 68 (2): 179–193.

Margerum, R. D., and D. Whitall. 2004. "The Challenges and Implications of Collaborative Management on a River Basin Scale." *Journal of Environmental Planning and Management* 47 (3): 409–429.

Mazmanian, D. A., and M. E. Kraft. 2009. "The Three Epochs of the Environmental Movement." In *Toward Sustainable Communities: Transition and Transformation in EnvironmentalPolicy*, 2nd ed., ed. D. A. Mazmanian and M. E. Kraft, 3–42. Cambridge, MA: MIT Press.

McCloskey, M. 1996. "The Skeptic: Collaboration Has Its Limits." *High Country News* 28 (9): 7.

———. 2000. "Problems with Using Collaboration to Shape Environmental Public Policy." *Valparaiso University Law Review* 34 (2): 423–434.

——. 2001. "Is This the Course You Want to Be On?" *Society and Natural Resources* 14 (4): 627–634.

McGuire, M. 2006. "Collaborative Public Management: Assessing What We Know and How We Know It." *Public Administration Review* 66 (supplement): 10.

Meier, K. J., and L. J. O'Toole. 2001. "Managerial Strategies and Behavior in Networks: A Model with Evidence from U.S. Public Education." *Journal of Public Administration Research and Theory* 11: 271–293.

Merkhofer, M. W., R. Conway, and R. G. Anderson. 1997. "Multiattribute Utility Analysis as a Framework for Public Participation in Siting a Hazardous Waste Management Facility." *Environmental Management* 21: 831–839.

Millennium Ecosystem Assessment. 2005. *Ecosystems and Human Well-Being: Synthesis*. Washington, DC: Island.

Milward, H. B., and K. G. Provan. 2000. "How Networks Are Governed." In *Governance and Performance: New Perspectives,* ed. C. K. and L. E. Lynn, 238–262. Washington, DC: Georgetown University Press.

Mitchell, B. 2005. "Participatory Partnerships: Engaging and Empowering to Enhance Environmental Management and Quality of Life?" *Social Indicators Research* 71: 123–144.

Moe, T. 2005. "Power and Political Institutions." *Perspectives on Politics* 3 (2): 217–233.

Moote, M. A., M. P. McClaran, and D. K. Chickering. 1997. "Theory in Practice: Applying Participatory Democracy Theory to Public Land Planning." *Environmental Management* 21 (6): 877–889.

Mullner, S. A., W. A. Hubert, and T. A. Wesche. 2001. "Evolving Paradigms for Landscape-Scale Renewable Resource Management in the United States." *Environmental Science and Policy* 4: 39–49.

Murdock, B., C. Wiessner, and K. Sexton. 2005. "Stakeholder Participation in Voluntary Environmental Agreements: Analysis of 10 Project XL Case Studies." *Science, Technology and Human Values* 30: 223–250.

Newig, J., D. Günther, and C. Pahl-Wostl. 2010. "Neurons in the Network Learning in Governance Networks in the Context of Environmental Management." *Ecology and Society Ecology and Society* 15 (4): 24.

North, D. C. 1990. *Institutions, Institutional Change, and Economic Performance.* New York: Cambridge University Press.

O'Leary, R., and L. B. Bingham, eds. 2003. *The Promise and Performance of Environmental Conflict Resolution*. Washington, DC: Resources for the Future.

O'Leary, R., C. Gerard, and L. B. Bingham. 2006. "Introduction to the Symposium on Collaborative Public Management." *Public Administration Review* 66 (supplement): 111–121.

Olsson, P., C. Folke, and F. Berkes. 2004. "Adaptive Comanagement for Building Resilience in Social-Ecological Systems." *Environmental Management* 34: 75–90.

Ostrom, E. 1990. *Governing the Commons: The Evolution of Institutions for Collective Action.* New York: Cambridge University Press.

——. 2007. "A Diagnostic Approach for Going beyond Panaceas." *Proceedings of the National Academy of Sciences* 104 (39): 15181–15187.

——. 2009. "A General Framework for Analyzing Sustainability of Social-Ecological Systems." *Science* 24: 419–422.

Pahl-Wostl, C. 2007. "Transitions toward Adaptive Management of Water: Facing Climate and Global Change." *Water Resources Management* 21 (1): 49–62.

Pedler, M., J. Burgoyne, and T. Boydell. 1991. *The Learning Company: A Strategy for Sustainable Development*. London: McGraw-Hill.

Pretty, J. 2003. "Social Capital and the Collective Management of Resources." *Science* 302 (5652): 1912–1914.

Putnam, R. 1995. "Bowling Alone: America's Declining Social Capital." *Journal of Democracy* 6 (1): 65–78.

Raik, D. B., and A. L. Wilson. 2006. "Planning in Collaborative Wildlife Management: A Critical Perspective." *Journal of Environmental Planning and Management* 49 (3): 321–336.

Rhodes, R. A. W. 1996. "The New Governance: Governing without Government." *Political Studies* 44 (4): 652–667.

Rogers, E., and E. P. Weber. 2010. "Thinking Harder about Outcomes for Collaborative Governance Arrangements." *American Review of Public Administration* 40 (5): 546–567.

Rogers, T., B. Howard-Pitney, E. C. Feighery, D. G. Altman, J. M. Endres, and A. G. Roeseler. 1993. "Characteristics and Participant Perceptions of Tobacco Control Coalitions in California." *Health Education Research, Theory and Practice* 8: 345–357.

Roussos, S. T., and S. B. Fawcett. 2000. "A Review of Collaborative Partnerships as a Strategy for Improving Community Health." *Annual Review of Public Health* 21: 269–402.

Sabatier, P. A., W. Focht, M. Lubell, Z. Trachtenburg, A. Vedlitz, and M. Matlock, eds. 2005. *Swimming Upstream: Collaborative Approaches to Watershed Management*. Cambridge, MA: MIT Press.

Sabatier, P. A., C. M. Weible, and J. Ficker. 2005. "Eras of Watershed Management in the United States: Implications for Collaborative Watershed Approaches." In *Swimming Upstream: Collaborative Approaches to Watershed Management*, ed. P. A. Sabatier, W. Focht, M. Lubell, Z. Trachtenberg, A.Vedlitz, and M. Matlock, 23–52. Cambridge, MA: MIT Press.

Sandström, A., and L. Carlsson. 2008. "The Performance of Policy Networks: The Relation between Network Structures and Network Performance." *Policy Studies Journal* 36 (4): 497–524.

Scharpf, F. 1994. "Games Real Actors Play: Positive and Negative Coordination in Embedded Negotiations." *Journal of Theoretical Politics* 6: 27–53.

Schneider, M., J. Scholz, M. Lubell, D. Mindruta, and M. Edwardsen. 2003. "Building Consensual Institutions: Networks and the National Estuary Program." *American Journal of Political Science* 47: 143–158.

Schneider, M., P. Teske, and M. Mintrom. 1995. *Public Entrepeneurs: Agents for Change in American Government*. Princeton, NJ: Princeton University Press.

Schuckman, M. 2001. "Making Hard Choices: A Collaborative Governance Model for the Biodiversity Context." *Washington University Law Quarterly* 79: 343–365.

Schusler, T. M., D. J. Decker, and M. J. Pfeffer. 2003. "Social Learning for Collaborative Natural Resource Management." *Society and Natural Resources* 15: 309–326.

Short, C., and M. Winter. 1999. "The Problem of Common Land: Towards Stakeholder Governance." *Journal of Environmental Planning and Management* 42: 613–630.

Sipe, N. G., and B. Stiftel. 1995. "Mediating Environmental Enforcement Disputes: How Well Does It Work?" *Environmental Impact Assessment Review* 25: 18.

Sirianni, C. 2009. *Investing in Democracy Engaging Citizens in Collaborative Governance.* Washington, DC: Brookings Institution Press.

Smith, C. 2009. "Institutional Determinants of Collaboration: An Empirical Study of County Open-Space Protection." *Journal of Public Administration Research and Theory* 19 (1): 1–21.

Susskind, L., and J. Cruikshank. 1987. *Breaking the Impasse: Consensual Approaches to Resolving Public Disputes.* New York: Basic Books.

Tett, L., J. Crowther, and P. O'Hara. 2003. "Collaborative Partnerships in Community Education." *Journal of Education Policy* 18: 37–51.

Thomas, C. W. 2003. *Bureaucratic Landscapes: Interagency Cooperation and the Preservation of Biodiversity.* Cambridge, MA: MIT Press.

Thomson, A. M., and J. Perry. 2006. "Collaboration Processes: Inside the Black Box." *Public Administration Review* 66 (supplement): 20–32.

Thomson, A. M., J. L. Perry, and T. K. Miller. 2008. "Linking Collaboration Processes and Outcomes: Foundations for Advancing Empirical Theory." In *Big Ideas in Collaborative Public Management*, ed. L. B. Bingham and R. O'Leary, 97–120. New York: M. E. Sharpe.

Till, J. E., and K. R. Meyer. 2001. "Public Involvement in Science and Decision Making." *Health Physics* 80: 370–378.

Tyler, T. R. 1990. *Why People Obey the Law.* New Haven, CT: Yale University Press.

Vig, N., and M. E. Kraft, eds.. 2010. *Environmental Policy: New Directions for the Twenty-First Century*, 7th ed. Washington, DC: Congressional Quarterly Press.

Vigmostad, K. E., N. Mays, A. Hance, and A. Cangelosi. 2005. *Large-Scale Ecosystem Restoration: Lessons for Existing and Emerging Initiatives.* Washington, DC: Northeast Midwest Institute.

Wade, R. 1994. *Village Republics: Economic Conditions for Collective Action in South India.* San Francisco: Institute for Contemporary Studies Press.

Warner, J. F. 2006. "More Sustainable Participation? Multi-Stakeholder Platforms for Integrated Catchment Management." *Water Resources Development* 22 (1): 15–35.

Weber, E.P. 2003. *Bringing Society Back In: Grassroots Ecosystem Management, Accountability, and Sustainable Communities.* Cambridge, MA: MIT Press.

Weber, E. P. 2009. "Explaining Institutional Change in Tough Cases of Collaboration: 'Ideas' in the Blackfoot Watershed." *Public Administration Review* 69 (2): 314–327.

Weber, E. P., N. P. Lovrich, and M. Gaffney. 2005. "Collaboration, Enforcement, and Endangered Species: A Framework for Assessing Collaborative Problem-Solving Capacity." *Society and Natural Resources* 18: 677–698.

Weible, C. M. 2011. "Political-Administrative Relations in Collaborative Environmental Management." *International Journal of Public Administration* 34 (7): 424–435.

Williams, B., and A. Matheny. 1995. *Democracy, Dialogue, and Environmental Disputes: The Contested Languages of Social Regulation.* New Haven, CT: Yale University Press.

Williamson, O. E. 1985. *The Economic Institutions of Capitalism: Firms, Markets, Relational Contracting.* New York: Free Press.

Wondolleck, J. M., and S. L. Yaffee. 2000. *Making Collaboration Work: Lessons from Innovation in Natural Resource Management.* Washington, DC: Island.

Yaffee, S. L., and J. Wondolleck. 2003. "Collaborative Ecosystem Planning Processes in the United States: Evolution and Challenges." *Environments* 31 (2): 59–72.

PART V

....

THE ROLE OF
INFORMAL
POLITICAL
ACTORS

....

CHAPTER 20

....

ISSUE FRAMING, AGENDA SETTING, AND ENVIRONMENTAL DISCOURSE

....

DEBORAH LYNN GUBER AND CHRISTOPHER J. BOSSO

IN 1922, in a classic book with the deceptively simple and unassuming title *Public Opinion*, Walter Lippmann proposed that people form a "picture of the world outside" from "the pictures in their heads." Thus, while citizens "live in the same world," they "think and feel in different ones" based on the subjective and necessarily abridged images that they construct and that are created for them by others (Lippmann 1922, 20). In an age between two world wars, with fear of propaganda on the rise, this was an influential if not wholly original idea. As Lippmann reminded his readers, Plato had used the allegory of a cave in *The Republic* to show how human beings, in their quest for understanding, were akin to prisoners who saw not the objects of reality but, rather, in the dim firelight, the shadows they cast as puppets on the wall; the marionettes themselves and the source of their strings were hidden and undiscovered (Plato 1968).

For Lippmann—a pragmatic and largely pessimistic journalist and public intellectual—cognitive shortcuts were as lamentable as they were natural and instinctive, aiding in what he called "the manufacture of consent" (1922, 248).

Average citizens are distracted and inattentive to public affairs, he acknowledged. However, in all fairness, the world about them is a vast place, "altogether too big, too complex, too fleeting for direct acquaintance." Their brains and their dispositions are "not equipped to deal with so much subtlety, so much variety, so many permutations and combinations," so they manage by reconstructing that world on a more modest scale. He believed that to "traverse the world, men must have maps of the world," even if the mental roads and highways on which they rely are but crude representations, drawn in by others with, at times, an intent to mislead and misdirect (Lippmann 1922, 16).

Lippmann had no formal training in the social sciences and no incentive to use or coin the terminology that would later dominate an entire field of academic inquiry. It was Harold Lasswell (1948) who connected the pieces more formally—reimaging them as a sequence of communications in which scholars might identify who said what, to whom, in what channel, and with what effect. Others would settle on the more precise labels of *issue framing* (Goffman 1974) and *agenda setting* (McCombs and Shaw 1972). But at the root of it all are Lippmann's views on cognition. If news media and other political actors could "powerfully direct the play of our attention," he observed, their impacts would be felt both within our heads and in the real world where action and indecision take place, and would become policy (Lippmann 1922, 30).

Today, scholars recognize that difficult conditions become public problems only after citizens and leaders come to see them not as the product of accident or fate, but as something "caused by human actions and amenable to human intervention" (Stone 1989, 281), a process that is often itself an act of social construction (Berger and Luckmann 1966). Perhaps above all, it is this standard that makes the emergence of the U.S. environmental movement in the twentieth century so impressive. Based on intuition and vicarious experience, people tend to accept that events in the natural world—even extreme ones, like droughts, blizzards, and hurricanes—are undirected and largely uncontrollable (Bostrom and Lashof 2007; Goffman 1974; Moser and Dilling 2004). For the environment to generate public concern, and for that concern to move onto the policy agenda, an entirely different "causal story" is required, one that has been both revolutionary and transformative (Gottlieb 2005; Rubin 1994; Stone 1989).

In *Silent Spring* (1962), Rachel Carson argued that the damage she observed to plant and animal species was not an accidental occurrence. Rather, it was human-made, the result of pollution and the overuse of chemical insecticides. At Love Canal in Niagara Falls, New York, activists in the late 1970s insisted that birth defects and other health problems found among local residents were not random chance but, rather, the result of exposure to corroding barrels of toxic waste buried in the landfill on which their homes had been constructed (Brown 1980). More recently, scientists and meteorologists explain rising global temperatures and melting polar ice caps not as mere weather events but as symptoms of a larger, more complex pattern of climate change caused by an accumulation of greenhouses gases released by humans in the daily course of modern life (Weart 2008).

In these cases and more, there are conclusions based on statistical and scientific fact, but their traction and momentum in the political realm owe more to the deliberate use of language and symbols (Edelman 1964). As Stone (1989, 282) points out:

> Problem definition is a process of image making.... Conditions, difficulties, or issues thus do not have inherent properties that make them more or less likely to be seen as problems or to be expanded. Rather, political actors *deliberately portray* them in ways calculated to gain support for their side. And political actors, in turn, do not simply accept causal models that are given from science or popular culture or any other source. They compose stories that describe harms and difficulties, attribute them to actions of other individuals or organizations, and thereby claim the right to invoke government power to stop the harm.

For Stone, and for generations of scholars at work since Lippmann's day, politics and policy making are made up of an amalgam of experiences, motivations, and mediated interactions that push and pull against each other. Nowhere is this struggle more clearly observed than in the field of environmental policy.

To identify a problem, diagnose its cause, attribute blame, and propose a solution is to engage in a long and complex chain of events that lie at the very heart of political life and public affairs. The goal of our chapter—like others in this volume—is to identify key scholarship in the field. We do so by connecting two broad interdisciplinary threads. First, we tackle the subject of *issue framing*, which focuses on the formation of public attitudes and the way in which issues are packaged and presented for mass consumption. Second, we address *agenda setting*, which centers on political elites and the decisions that are made—or deferred— within the policy-making process. Finally, we draw on both to suggest productive avenues for future research.

1. THE PICTURES IN OUR HEADS

When Lippmann (1922) wrote of the "pictures in our heads," his insight into the selective and malleable qualities of public opinion was little more than conjecture (Berinsky and Kinder 2006). Decades later, there is ample evidence of its power across the social sciences, within disciplines as diverse as cognitive psychology, linguistics, sociology, media and communication studies, behavioral economics, and political science. Experiments, surveys, and case studies, to say nothing of real-world events, all demonstrate the ubiquity of *frames*—the modern term scholars use for a concept that can trace its lineage back to Lippmann.

Frames are variously described as "mental boxes" and "interpretative storylines" (Nisbet 2009, 22). When captured by a "deft metaphor, catchphrase, or other symbolic device," frames are thought to give meaning and organization to "an unfolding strip of events," weaving an intricate web of cause and effect that can be used to define problems, diagnose causes, attribute blame and responsibility, make moral judgments, and suggest remedies (Gamson and Modigliani 1989, 3, 143; Entman 1993; Kuypers 2009; Stone 1989). Hence, when politicians defend oil exploration in the Arctic National Wildlife Refuge by reference to national security and energy independence, they promote a frame that supports a particular policy prescription (Guber and Bosso 2007), just as those who emphasize uncertainty and a lack of scientific consensus in the debate over global warming seek to obstruct one (Luntz 2002; McCright and Dunlap 2000; Nisbet 2009). Simply put, issue framing involves the selection of a particular attribute and an effort to make it more salient in the minds of average citizens relative to a host of other considerations that might come to mind (Entman 1993).

Yet despite nearly a century of scholarship, progress on the subject has been slow, much to the frustration of researchers who complain about its fragmentation across the disciplines (Chong and Druckman 2007; Druckman 2001a; Entman 1993). On the one hand, frames are seen as essential to the way individuals come to understand complex issues and events; on the other, there is fear that frames are easily manipulated by elites for political gain. In short, there is both a cognitive process and a communications strategy to uncover and reconnect (Berinsky and Kinder 2006; Druckman 2001a; Kinder and Nelson 2005).

1.1. Frames as Mental Structures

Scientists believe that frames are embedded deep in the synapses of the brain (Lakoff 2004, 2008). Since average citizens can never fully comprehend the world around them, and are often disinterested and discouraged by the effort, they become "cognitive misers" both of choice and of necessity (Fiske and Taylor 1984), dependent on frames, schemas, and other heuristic devices that allow them to process information efficiently and ease its recall from stores of short- and long-term memory (Chong and Druckman 2007; Conover and Feldman 1984; Entman 1993; Goffman 1974; Scheufele and Tewksbury 2007). Indeed, a multitude of studies show that when facts fail to fit existing frames, it is the frames that are stubbornly maintained, while inconvenient facts go ignored (Lakoff 2004).

Zaller and Feldman (1992) believe that on a wide range of issues, people hold in their heads opposing considerations, which under varied circumstances might lead them to one decision or another. When interviewed by pollsters, they call to mind a sample of those ideas: some made salient by recent experiences or events, and others that they have been primed to consider by the questionnaire itself. Most respondents are ambivalent about most issues most of the time, so their answers are particularly vulnerable to framing effects that are created—intentionally or not—by the order in which questions are posed, the language used, the mental associations that are prompted, or the response categories that are offered. In other words, since attitudes are not securely anchored (Converse 1964), they can be "readily blown" from one side of an issue to another, with effects that are both powerful and wide-ranging

(Sniderman and Theriault 2004, 133; see also Citrin, Reingold, and Green 1990; Gamson and Modigliani 1989; Nelson and Kinder 1996; Zaller 1992).

In a classic example of prospect theory for which Kahneman would later win a Nobel Prize in economics, respondents were given a hypothetical scenario involving the outbreak of disease. Defining the issue in terms of lives gained versus lives lost altered the degree of risk people were willing to accept (Kahneman and Tversky 1984; Tversky and Kahneman 1981). Scholars have also discovered framing effects on a host of other issues, from government spending in general (Jacoby 2000), to more specific policy decisions on the war in Iraq (Kull, Ramsay, and Lewis, 2003–2004), poverty and social welfare (Feldman and Zaller 1992; Iyengar 1990), trade and globalization (Hiscox 2006), freedom of speech for hate groups (Druckman 2001b; Nelson, Clawson, and Oxley 1997), affirmative action (Kinder and Sanders 1990, 1996), mandatory AIDS testing (Sniderman, Brody, and Tetlock 1991), and gay marriage (Pan, Meng, and Zhou 2010), to name but a few.

The environment figures prominently within this growing body of literature (Gray 2003) because it is a topic that connects to—and conflicts with—so many other policy arenas, from health and welfare, to national security, to jobs and the economy (Sharp 2008). Polling is difficult when such issues intertwine because Americans genuinely value both sides of the debate (Ladd 1982). Under ideal conditions, they want to preserve and protect sensitive areas like the Arctic National Wildlife Refuge (ANWR) from large-scale human intervention and development. At the same time, they express a desire to strengthen energy security at home, even if it means increasing domestic oil production in regions like ANWR (Guber and Bosso 2007). In struggling through a period of rising gas prices, consumers desire higher fuel economy for their cars, but they also value highway safety and vehicle performance, which some see as compromised by the current generation of hybrids (Noland 2004). They favor the development of alternative energy sources in principle but worry about higher utility bills and about the aesthetic impact of new technologies, such as wind turbines (Farhar 1994). In short, Americans are endlessly conflicted when asked to make hard choices between goals they value equally (Hochschild 1981). Frames, therefore, play a vital role in directing attention and in easing the process of decision making.

1.2. Frames as Narrative Devices

If frames are cognitive structures that help citizens make sense of politics, they also lead "double lives" in that they are equally important components of elite discourse and political rhetoric (Callaghan and Schnell 2005; Kinder and Nelson 2005; Kuypers 2009). As Berinsky and Kinder (2006, 642) remind us, a "good frame is at its heart a good story," so it is no surprise that frames are used by mass media to craft news reports and to develop compelling narratives (Boykoff and Boykoff 2004; Iyengar 1991; Iyengar and Kinder 1987; McComas and Shanahan 1999; Scheufele and Tewksbury 2007). But frames are also employed by political parties, candidates, and consultants to win elections (Lakoff 2004; Luntz 2007), by policy makers to define options and make programmatic decisions (Nisbet 2009), by interest groups and corporations to lobby government officials and manipulate consumer behavior (Guber and Bosso 2007; Pettenger and Plec 2010), and by scientists, even, to simplify and communicate technical details to a lay public (Brittle 2009; Nisbet 2009; Nisbet and Mooney 2007).

In short, the ability to frame an issue for others is one of the most important tools these actors and interests have at their disposal (Jacoby 2000). Yet, observers quickly add, the process is ripe with "nefarious possibilities," since frames can become "freewheeling exercises in pure manipulation" (Kinder and Herzog 1993, 363; Chong and Druckman 2007; Sniderman and Theriault 2004). For example, the George W. Bush administration's touted "Clear Skies" and "Healthy Forests" initiatives of 2003 were derided by environmental activists as little more than cynical efforts to mislead and misdirect voters with soft language and comforting words while quietly catering to the interests of industry (Kennedy 2004; Vaughn and Cortner 2005).

Still, even the most politically motivated frames operate within certain conventional limits. Not all issues are equally susceptible to manipulation from the start. Framing effects are most powerful when directed toward "hard" issues that are unfamiliar and technically difficult to understand, as opposed to "easy" ones made stable by years of familiarity and instinct (Carmines and Stimson 1980; Lau and Redlawsk 2001; Lee and Chang 2010). Frames also falter when they fail to resonate with existing beliefs and cultural values (Chong and Druckman 2007; Gamson and Modigliani 1987), and, at least among the politically aware, conflict with ideological commitments and partisan ties (Lee and Chang 2010). Finally, when measuring audience response, the credibility of a frame's source, its message, and its delivery matter (Callaghan and Schnell 2009; Druckman 2001; Lee and Chang 2010), and the presence of an active and appealing counterframe can do much to neutralize a frame's persuasive impact (Callaghan and Schnell 2005; Druckman 2001a, 2004; Sniderman and Theriault 2004).

When considering the increasingly diverse list of problems environmental activists face—from air and water pollution to the protection of endangered species and the conservation of energy and other natural resources—it is understandable that the choice of a particular frame breeds controversy (Shellenberger and Nordhaus 2004) and that its effects, once communicated, are often messy and unpredictable. Perhaps the evolution of global warming as a public issue illustrates this best of all.

1.3. Framing Global Climate Change

In 2002, Frank Luntz, a pollster and Republican Party strategist, was hired to help the GOP improve its image in time for the upcoming midterm congressional elections. In a lengthy memorandum, later leaked to the media, he advised candidates to assure voters they were committed to "preserving and protecting" the environment but that it could be done "more wisely and effectively" (Luntz 2002, 107; Luntz 2007). The way to win the global warming debate, he said, was to use language that emphasized scientific uncertainty—even where none existed. It was important to make the *right* decision, he said, not simply a quick decision that might harm the economy unnecessarily or put the United States in an unfair position relative to its trading partners worldwide. In the convenient script he provided, if candidates were challenged on the Kyoto Protocol or some similar proposal, they were told to say this:

> We must not rush to judgment before all the facts are in. We need to ask more questions. We deserve more answers. And until we learn more, we should not commit America to any international document that handcuffs us either now or into the future. (Luntz 2002, 138)

While the editors of the *New York Times* mocked the strategy as an "environmental word game" and a "recipe for cynicism and political manipulation," it nevertheless played well within the mainstream media's own bias toward providing "balanced" coverage (Boykoff and Boykoff 2004, 2007). By reinforcing partisan divisions and undermining public confidence in the science (Nisbet and Scheufele 2010), there is little doubt that Luntz contributed to Republican gains in Congress in 2002 (Bosso and Guber 2005; Editorial 2003, A16; McCright and Dunlap 2003).

In the years to follow, environmentalists could point to polls showing widespread support for their proposals, yet time and again found themselves losing politically to savvier opponents who were better at framing issues to their tactical advantage (Shellenberger and Nordhaus 2004, 11–12, 32). What Luntz instinctively understood was that while "global warming" had captured the public's imagination and generated concern (Whitmarsh 2009), under the right circumstances it could also "turn people off, fostering images of shaggy-haired liberals, economic sacrifice and complex scientific disputes" (Broder 2009). Equally important, doomsday scenarios offered by environmentalists too often created "feelings of helplessness and isolation among would-be supporters" (Louv 2005: E1). In contrast to the dire warnings by so-called global warming "alarmists," Luntz (2002, 137) crafted a message focused on "American superiority in technology and innovation," a reassuring frame long used to support nuclear power (Gamson and Modigliani 1987). It was persuasive in its new context because it affirmed—rather than challenged—a long-standing American worldview that valued prosperity, independence, economic development, and self-sufficiency (Smerecnik and Dionisopoulos 2009).

As a matter of public interest and government policy, the issue of global warming stumbled for another reason as well. Since average citizens were likely to estimate its dangers by reference to anecdotal changes in the weather, it became easy to dismiss the problem as temporary, nonurgent, or at the very least intractable (Immerwahr 1999). Even the term itself was problematic (Montenegro 2009), because it seemed to ensure a rise in global temperatures that was "easily discredited" by the next cold spell, including the record snowfalls that fell across the eastern United States during the winters of 2010 and 2011 (Schuldt, Konrath, and Schwarz 2011, 122). During one particularly nasty blizzard that buried the city of Washington, Senator James Inhofe (R-OK) encouraged his grandchildren to build an igloo on Capitol Hill, christening it "Al Gore's new home," while on the social networking site Twitter, Senator Jim De Mint (R-SC) posted, "It's going to keep snowing in D.C. until Al Gore cries 'uncle'" (Milbank 2010, A21). Since people tend to take cues from elites they trust most (Callaghan and Schnell 2009; Krosnick et al. 2006), both efforts were intended to undermine the credibility of global warming's most prominent messenger (see Nisbet 2011).

Still, few frames succeed unfettered without viable and persuasive counterframes (Chong and Druckman 2007; Druckman 2004, 2010; Gamson and Modigliani 1987; Sniderman and Theriault 2004), and climate change is no exception. While the term has long provided an "appealing frame for those who favor the status quo in climate policy," activists have increasingly preferred the phrase "climate change," in part because it can more "easily accommodate unseasonably cold temperatures and record snowfalls" (Schuldt, Konrath, and Schwarz 2011, 116). Some have also begun to emphasize the environmental component of climate policy *less*—for example, by drawing attention to economic opportunities or health effects that may do more to attract and sustain a sympathetic audience (Maibach et al. 2010; Nordhaus and Shellenberger 2007; Rabe 2004; Shellenberger and Nordhaus 2004).

It is tempting to malign any political strategy built around issue frames as based on craven opportunity, not principle. As Zaller (1992, 95) explains, framing by elites is still "discussed in conspiratorial tones, as if, in a healthy democratic polity, [it] would not occur." However, the fact that it regularly occurs means that the impacts of such efforts on the timing and the longevity of policy windows cannot be ignored (Kingdon 1995). In the end, says Luntz, people want to hear about energy independence and job creation, not just "melting glaciers or polar bears" (Zwick 2010). If he is correct—and shifting rhetoric in Washington under the Obama administration suggests as much (Nisbet and Scheufele 2010)—it is a strategy with the potential to build bipartisan support for climate policy and move it onto the public agenda.

2. SETTING THE AGENDA

As the struggle over framing global warming suggests, the process by which problems are defined and get onto the agenda of attention and action powerfully shapes policy making. As Schattschneider (1960, 68) reminds us in *The Semi-Sovereign People*, "The definition of the alternatives is the supreme instrument of power. He who determines what politics is about runs the country, because the definition of alternatives is the choice of conflicts, and the choice of conflicts allocates power."

Within this observation lie profoundly important dynamics that define our politics, our policies, and even democracy itself.

2.1. Conditions versus Problems

What do scholars mean when they refer to a "problem" in the first place? The very notion of problem *definition* suggests its contested nature. There may be an "objective condition"—such as the buildup of carbon dioxide in the atmosphere—that can be observed, measured, and even understood as "bad" in the abstract, without citizens, governments, and vested interests perceiving that it poses undesirable consequences. Insofar as those beliefs hold, there is no "problem" that merits attention, much less action (Jones 1975, 20). There is only a "condition" with which we choose to live (Pralle 2009).

As noted above, Lippmann's (1922, 20) observation about "the pictures in our heads" speaks to a perceptual gap in which many environmental problems reside. In developed countries, at least, comparatively few people have felt the direct impacts of the conditions that characterize different eras in environmentalism. Even first-generation conservation battles reflected an imbalance in incentives between those seeking to exploit a natural resource for material gain and others determined to manage it for use by future generations, or to preserve it entirely for aesthetic or normative reasons (Hays 1959). In this regard, John Muir's fight to protect the Sierra Nevada range in the late nineteenth century, the way Greenpeace mobilized opposition to whaling in the 1970s, and the success of those struggling to keep ANWR free of oil exploration today all depend on their respective abilities to evoke potent images of pristine wilderness or threatened species to sympathetic individuals who may never get to Yosemite, much less to the Arctic, or who may never see a whale.

In the same vein, the power of Rachel Carson's *Silent Spring* (1962), which to many sparked contemporary environmentalism, lay in her ability to paint a chilling image of paradise lost through the rampant use of chemicals, communicated to an attentive public increasingly sensitized to the potential ill effects of post–World War II science and technology. Carson's alarms about pesticides, magnified visually by the increasingly important medium of television, also resonated because she was able to extrapolate harm to birds to potential harm to human health. Other second-generation environmental problems—whether fixed in the public mind by Love Canal or by Chernobyl—reflected growing concerns about possibly irreversible effects of chemicals and radioactivity on ourselves and our children.

Third-generation environmental problems such as climate change pose the greatest challenges for those seeking to define conditions as problems amenable to action (Shellenberger and Nordhaus 2004). Even presuming widespread acceptance of the scientific consensus about the facts of climate change, many in the developed world may have only indirect or peripheral experience with its impacts.

Moreover, those impacts might be decades away, while the costs to stave them off are immediate and tangible.

So not all conditions become *problems*. Factors that play a role in this equation include the *degree of issue saliency* (Downs 1972; Cobb and Elder 1972; Schattschneider 1960); *degree of perceived novelty* (Downs 1972); *degree of perceived complexity* (Nelkin and Pollack 1982); *perceived distribution of costs and benefits* (Wilson 1973); *images of affected populations* (Cobb and Elder 1972; Bosso 1989; Baumgartner 1989; Baumgartner and Jones 1993; Rochefort 1986; Katz 1990); and *values about the proper role of government* (Mucciaroni 1990). In the main, perception that a condition constitutes a "problem" and the probability of its "solution" depends on whether there is consensus that the condition merits attention, that a solution exists, and, more centrally, that the solution lies within the accepted purview of government action.

For example, the classic "moon/ghetto" conundrum of the Great Society Era of the 1960s—"If we can put a man on the moon, why can't we solve the problems of the ghetto?"—stems from divergent views about the goals themselves. Going to the moon was an easy *policy* problem: success was readily judged (i.e., getting there and returning safely), and the goal meshed with dominant social values (e.g., technological innovation, the frontier spirit, competing with the Soviets) and, as Nelson argues, "had the advantage of not threatening significant interests and of promising something to several" (1977, 14). By contrast, solving the "problem" of "environmental justice" (Bullard 1990) is far less consensual because many don't agree that lower-income or racial minority populations suffer disproportionately from environmental harms or, if they admit to such effects, resist acting because solutions require resource redistribution (Ripley and Franklin 1984) or the imposition of new costs on others (Wilson 1973).

So *types of problems* matter (Bosso 1987). Some are "simple" less because of any intrinsic quality but because there exists consensus on ends *and* means. Such problems are rare, as the Apollo project example suggests. Other problems are "technical," characterized by conflict over means. For example, few Americans question the value of economic growth; instead, they argue over means—whether government should boost spending, manipulate the money supply, cut taxes, or do nothing and let the invisible hand of the market operate. While the nascent field of sustainable economics offers a countervailing intellectual paradigm to the standard growth model (Daly 1977), orthodoxy is difficult to dislodge, and most arguments over economic policy still focus on means, not ends.

Other conflicts are more "morally complex." For example, debates over genetically modified organisms typically focus less on technical feasibility than on a fundamental moral question: is it right to "play with nature"? To moral philosophers like Bill McKibben (2003), the central concern is at what point we lose our "human-ness" in our quest to engineer nature, or ourselves. In this view, problems like food availability or species diversity are not "solved" by technology. Instead, they require a profound, perhaps unsettling discussion about the kind of world in which we wish to live.

The most intractable problems lack consensus on goals *or* means, as Bosso suggests in the debate over chemical pesticides:

> With respect to pesticides, it is almost impossible to find agreement on ends because the ends themselves often are clearly incompatible: environmentalists may seek to rid the earth of pesticides at any cost; chemical firms may seek to maximize profits; farmers want inexpensive and effective pesticides to maintain high crop yields at lower costs; public health officials want to eradicate disease. Consumers...want cheap food, which might lead them to support the wide use of pesticides, but they also fear the possibly carcinogenic effects of pesticides residues in that food or in the environment. (1987, xiii)

Most contemporary environmental problems reside within this contested realm. It is one thing to generate support to remediate obvious air pollutants—and even then it is difficult to do so if solutions impose costs that affect local jobs and economies—a far different matter to get consensus on conditions like climate change, endocrine disruptors, loss of biodiversity, or the impacts of emerging technologies. On climate change, for example, success is neither clearly defined nor immediately attainable, and "solving" the problem may require individual and collective sacrifices that clash with long-held beliefs about the "American way of life." As a result, for political leaders inaction on climate is a rational default strategy, at least until some framing event catalyzes popular opinion enough to push it onto the agenda of action. And that is only the start.

2.2. Agendas and Action

Visible framing events like the 2010 Deepwater Horizon oil spill are the exception, not the rule, in political life. Most of the time, as Charles Lindblom argues, policy makers "have to identify and formulate the problem" (1966, 13). Lindblom's observation speaks to a constant struggle among organized interests, political elites, and citizens to get their respective problems onto the agenda of action and, alternatively, keep *other* problems *off* the agenda. Sometimes these struggles reflect the classic pluralist conception of "active and interested interests" openly vying over the agenda (Dahl 1956). At other times, problems never seem to be discussed, perhaps because they are judged to contravene prevailing social values, dominant ideologies, and powerful cultural norms (Bachrach and Baratz 1970; Crenson 1971) or are crowded out by what Cobb and Elder call the "systemic" agenda, those issues "that are commonly perceived by the members of the political community as meriting public attention and...involving matters within the legitimate jurisdiction of existing governmental authority" (1972, 85).

In short, the choices that confront policy makers are situated within broader societal values and priorities. As a result, even deeply felt concerns about the environment compete with other problems. Some, such as the overall state of the economy, dominate the public mind and persistently top the list of "most important problems" in any public opinion poll (Dunlap 1991). The "environment," by contrast, only seems to top the agenda of attention after some framing event, and often only momentarily as more powerfully embedded issue concerns reassert their primacy. For example, for all its potent imagery, the Deepwater Horizon oil spill had no demonstrable impact on U.S. energy policy (Fahrenthold and Eilperin 2010). Instead, the dominant narrative focused on ensuring that British Petroleum cleaned up the spill and indemnified Gulf residents hurt by its immediate effects. Any potential for reframing U.S. energy policy away from environmentally harmful petroleum quickly dissipated amid fears that higher oil prices would exacerbate the lingering economic recession. Indeed, within the year the Obama administration reinstated deepwater drilling in the Gulf of Mexico (Broder and Krauss 2011).

The fleeting attention to and impacts of the Deepwater Horizon incident on energy and environmental policy agendas aptly illustrates the "issue-attention cycle" identified by Anthony Downs, a "systematic cycle of heightening public interest and then increasing boredom with major issues" that is "rooted both in the nature of certain domestic problems and in the way major communications media interact with the public" (1972, 39). Mass public attention to environmental problems is cyclical, Downs argues. Thus, a dire condition may exist long before public attention gets focused on it through some type of "alarmed discovery." What follows is "euphoric" public enthusiasm for problem solution, which wanes with time and with public recognition of the true costs involved. Public boredom or discouragement about the problem's apparent intractability remands the issue into a "limbo" of low saliency and the reassertion of "normal" politics dominated by organized interests with clear economic stakes in the status quo. The issue may reemerge spasmodically, but it is no longer so "new" (Downs 1972, 39–40).

The type of condition likely to go through this cycle, Downs argues, does not affect a majority, emerges out of social conditions providing "significant benefits to a majority or a powerful minority of the population," and no longer has any "intrinsically exciting" quality (1972, 41). Thus, most of us are not affected directly, to solve the problem (or even to address its symptoms) requires a significant redistribution of resources, and it invariably fades from view with continued exposure. Most environmental problems, in particular those affecting low-income communities or people in far-off nations, fit this equation, underscoring the challenge facing environmental advocates on problems of environmental justice, depletion of tropical rainforests, or, most telling, the effects of climate change (Duffy 2003).

2.3. Institutions and Agendas

To focus on agenda setting also prompts us to affirm the essentiality of formal institutions, rules, procedures, and organizational hierarchies. In assessing Kingdon's (1995) pathbreaking work on agendas, Gary Mucciaroni observes that the scholarship at that time failed to appreciate the impacts of system structure on agendas. "Political institutions are structures with perhaps the greatest impact on policy," says Mucciaroni (1992, 466). "[They] make up the topography, the banks and riverbeds that channel and shape participants' behavior." Or, as Schattschneider observed decades earlier, "The function of institutions is to channel conflict; institutions do not treat all forms of conflict impartially" (1960, 71).

Even so, until recently there was little focus in political science on how structural features of the political system independently affected how problems get on the agenda and are addressed by government. Policy entrepreneurs may compete for advantage within respective decision arenas (Cohen 1995; Layzer 2002), and they may even "shop around" for the most sympathetic venues (Baumgartner and Jones 1993; Pralle 2006), but their capacity to maneuver is constrained in part by the system's overall structure. To be sure, the formal design of the political system does not determine agenda setting—the story of environmentalism itself is testimony to the power of ideas (Shabecoff 2000)—but it does induce patterns in how agendas get set.

For example, a defining feature of the U.S. system is federalism, the constitutional apportionment of governing authority among the national government and the respective state governments, each of them dealing with problems within their particular jurisdictions. In a federalist system, problems traditionally seen as within the purview of state government will not automatically migrate to the national agenda. For example, as Charles O. Jones (1975) points out, air pollution policy was a state (if not local) function until the late 1960s, when more expansive interpretations of the Constitution's interstate commerce clause and growing recognition of pollution as a national matter moved the problem onto the agenda of Congress. Indeed, one can argue that the spate of federal environmental laws to erupt between 1967 and 1974 reflected pent-up frustration with the inability and unwillingness of states to act. More recently, as Rabe (2004) shows in studying climate change policy formation, activists are focusing on state agendas out of frustration with inaction at the federal level. While recent decades have witnessed a blurring of jurisdictional lines and creation of many vertical linkages among federal, state, and local officials, the reality of federalism remains, with independent effects on agenda dynamics.

The constitutional separation of powers embedded in the U.S. system also shape how problems are drawn to and dealt with by the national government. The system in many ways is a centrifuge of divided institutional power and fractionated representation that is directed at dissipating temporary policy majorities before they produce rapid and possibly destabilizing change (Nicholas 1981). The already fleeting nature of Downs's "issue-attention cycle" is further blunted by a system that makes it hard to translate majority opinion into action. Yet that same system, particularly through a legislature based on geographical representation, grants to smaller and more localized economic interests a great deal of access. It thus is no surprise, as Mucciaroni suggests, that Kingdon's model of agenda setting—with its focus on the converging "streams" of ideas, actors, and political contexts—is most useful "for describing policy-making in the United States, where the institutional structure is fragmented and permeable, where participation is particularistic and fluid, and coalitions are often temporary and *ad hoc*" (Mucciaroni 1992, 466).

Finally, the constitutional array of checks and balances also means that Congress and the presidency as institutions openly vie for primacy over problem definition and agenda setting in ways rarely seen in more unitary systems. For example, as Harrison and Hoberg find in comparing regulatory styles in the United States and Canada, "conflict between legislative and executive branches in the U.S. often publicizes the regulatory agenda. In contrast, Canadian regulatory agencies and ministers exercise greater discretion with respect to publicizing their agenda" (1991, 6). In Canada, as in parliamentary systems generally, the party in power can typically shape both legislative and executive agendas (see also Montpetit 2003). In the United States, the constitutionally rooted tension between separate and nearly autonomous branches produces fluid agenda dynamics. In the absence of cohesive parties, conflicts between the executive and a bicameral legislature, where divided partisan control is a fact of life, makes agenda dynamics livelier and less predictable.

System structure thus affects agenda formation. In the United States, the competing centers of authority and multiple routes for issue representation provide many venues into which demands can flow (Baumgartner and Jones 1993; Bosso 1987), a permeability that in many ways gives the system resiliency and legitimacy. In a system of fragmented authority, however, problems may never get to the national government, may bounce around within the layers of federalism, or may get mired in conflicts between the branches of government. The system's design militates against a broadly arrayed problem (e.g., climate change) being addressed by the national government unless societal forces can "boost" it with a velocity sufficient to overcome the system's intrinsic inertia. Seen from this perspective, the U.S. system displays tremendous structural friction, such that momentarily important problems can dissipate as they run up against institutional features designed to do as the framers of the Constitution intended: cool the "passions" of the moment and slow down change enough to ensure overall system stability. As such, to echo Downs, any "alarmed enthusiasm" about climate change, or about the nation's reliance on oil in the wake of the Deepwater Horizon accident, can easily fade in the face of structurally induced inertia.

That same systemic inertia also makes it possible to retain gains already made despite concerted efforts by opponents. As students of American political development (e.g., Orren and Skowronek 2004) make clear, policy choices made decades ago—and embedded into laws, regulatory agencies, and webs of organized interests—have profound impacts on the shape and direction of contemporary policy, and even on the choices we argue. This is nowhere more evident than in U.S. environmental politics and policy, both of which continue to be shaped fundamentally by the dramatic policy breakthroughs made during the "environmental era" of the mid-1960s to late 1970s. Klyza and Sousa note the enduring impacts of this American "green state," which go beyond the boundaries imposed by existing laws and agencies:

> When the recent layer of the green state were laid down in the years 1964–1980, it was accompanied by fundamental changes in society that continue—namely the development of a highly professional and relatively well-funded issue advocacy community and widespread—though admittedly shallow public support. This

combination of strong interest groups and broad public support has helped to prevent the kind of rollbacks that occurred in other liberal and progressive policy realms. (2008, 296)

The institutional inertia of the U.S. system, momentarily dislodged, reasserted itself, but along a new axis of discourse that continues to shape environmental politics. As GOP pollster Frank Luntz well understood as he sought to devise conservative talking points on environmental policy, the environmental "frame" had come to be part of the systemic agenda, imposing its constraints on what was deemed legitimate.

2.4. Images, Venues, and Actors

If the intrinsic nature of problems and the formal structure of the political system have independent impacts on agenda formation, such "predecision" factors are not deterministic. *Politics* still matters. In the United States, at least, the standard picture is of multiple actors and interests competing for access and influence from a variety of strategic positions. Given the features of the system and diversity within the nation itself, it is no wonder that studies of agenda setting in the United States tend to take as their points of departure the pluralist image of competition among organized interests in and out of government (Dahl 1956; Walker 1991).

Such competition has a shape. "In a system like the U.S.," argue Milward and Laird, "there are many different access points and one institution or jurisdiction rarely controls a given policy domain. *Policy communities* serve to knit this fragmented system of governance together" (1991, 3). Whether such a community is a "subgovernment" (Freeman 1955), "issue network" (Heclo 1978), or "advocacy coalition" (Sabatier 1988), within each there are, as Sabatier argues, "actors from a variety of public and private organizations at all levels of government who share a set of basic beliefs (policy goals plus causal and other perceptions) and who seek to manipulate the rules of various government institutions in order to achieve those goals over time" (1991, 279). This depiction echoes Schattschneider's (1960) observation that at the core of politics is a conflict between those seeking to expand (or socialize) participation in a policy debate and those working to minimize (or privatize) it. Such a struggle is over both the definition of problems and control over the processes and arenas within which the debates occur.

Longitudinal studies of policy formation bear out this point. Bosso, in examining four decades of U.S. policy toward chemical pesticides, concluded that perhaps "the most powerful change in the pesticides policy case was its being redefined as an environmental matter; *loss of the power to define the issue* was probably the most critical factor causing the decline of the pesticides subgovernment" (1987, 256; emphasis added). Duffy notes similar shifts in U.S. nuclear power policy making: members of the "nuclear subgovernment" have found it increasingly difficult "to maintain their influence within the more open political environment" (1997, 122).

Such single case studies get critical comparative and empirical support in the work of Baumgartner and Jones (1990, 1993), who examine a range of policy areas (e.g., smoking, pesticides, and nuclear power) over time and conclude that "failure to control the images associated with a policy can lead to loss of control over the policy itself, even when it appears to be firmly within the institutional jurisdiction of influential groups all of whom favor the current direction of public policy" (1990, 5).

Taken together, as Baumgartner and Jones (1993) show, these studies reveal similar agenda dynamics. In most cases, policies were formulated originally under conditions of limited participation and mostly positive public perceptions of the issue's "image." The result is subgovernment dominance, often for decades. Over time, however, defenders of the status quo would struggle to maintain their preferred definition of the problem and to control the venues for policy formation as more and ever-diverse interests in and outside government demand to have a say on an increasingly controversial issue (Pralle 2006). In each case, the formerly tight "iron triangle" (Cater 1964) defending the status quo crumbles, replaced by a broader and more permeable "sloppy hexagon" (Jones 1979), "issue network" (Heclo 1978), "policy community" (Milward and Laird 1991), or "advocacy coalition" (Sabatier 1988). The resulting socialization of conflict produces more contested problem definition, greater policy fluidity, and even stalemate, at least until a new consensus emerges (Bosso 1987; Downs 1972; Duffy 1997; Hoberg 1992; Jones 1975; Mucciaroni 1990). Whether it is the "intrusion" of environmental perspectives into the debate over pesticides or nuclear power, the policy community that can define a problem's image also has the edge in setting the agenda of action.

One notes that these studies share a focus on configurations of shared policy interests, not on mass opinion. As Sabatier argues, "Understanding the policy process requires looking at the intergovernmental policy community or subsystem—composed of bureaucrats, legislative personnel, interest group leaders, researchers, and specialist reporters within a substantive policy area—as the basic unit of study" (1991, 269). This perspective has practical and normative implications. For one thing, it helps us to understand why generalized public support for environmental values does not automatically translate into action on problems like energy efficiency, or even climate change. It also explains why policy change nonetheless occurs, and much more than one might assume by looking at class structure, ideologies, or institutions alone. There *is* change amid seeming stability (see also Klyza and Sousa 2008; Layzer 2002). At its core, as Schattschneider (1960) understood, is the capacity to define what politics means.

3. CONCLUSION

"The environment" was not a problem when Lippmann (1922) penned the observation that opens this chapter. Indeed, "the environment" itself is a value frame that emerged in the middle of the twentieth century out of growing scientific under-standing of and concern for the causal connections between the side effects of the techno-industrial age on nature and, perhaps more important, on human health. That frame took root in the overall social upheavals of the 1960s and 1970s and today takes its place as a potent, if diffuse, set of economic, social, and cultural values. In many ways, as Klyza and Sousa (2008) argue, the endurance of the American "green state" itself exemplifies the potency of the environmental frame in the public mind.

Even so, within the "green state" reside an array of meanings, and "the envi-ronment" as such will always remain a contested value system, subject to disputes between "deep greens" at one end of the ideological spectrum to "free-market environmentalists" at the other—and everyone in between. The absence of con-sensus values underscores the centrality of problem definition and agenda setting in environmental politics and reminds us that whoever can define what "the envi-ronment" means has the advantage, even if the room for maneuver is constrained by decades of policy choices.

The absence of consensus about "the environment" also reminds us that envi-ronmental conditions are always refracted through diverse perceptual lenses and accompanied by competing immediate needs. Broad if diffuse general support for the environment will not keep local constituencies from supporting short-term eco-nomic interests in pursuit of jobs, or from voting for candidates with poor environ-mental records. If, as Dunlap observes, few candidates want to be painted as openly anti-environment, "there is as yet little evidence of a 'green bloc' of single-issue voters comparable to the anti-abortion or anti–gun control blocs" (1991, 33). "The environment" still competes with other, often more momentarily pressing priori-ties. Even in the face of disasters like Deepwater Horizon, generalized public con-cern for environmental protection will not translate automatically into support for specific policies. It translates only into *opportunities* to frame problems in ways that propel them onto the agenda of action.

Yet, as seems clear from the endurance of the environmental frame over the past half century, those same debates take place within a systemic agenda of dis-course (Cobb and Elder 1972) where "the environment" is embedded as a legitimate matter of public concern. As Luntz for one recognized, we are all environmentalists now. Our debates are about how—not whether—to translate environmental val-ues into action. Amid laments of the "death" of environmentalism (Shellenberger and Nordhaus 2004), the often-overlooked potency of the environmental frame in American politics merits greater reflection.

REFERENCES

Bachrach, P., and M. Baratz. 1970. *Power and Poverty: Theory and Practice.* New York: Oxford University Press.

Baumgartner, F. R. 1989. *Conflict and Rhetoric in French Policymaking.* Pittsburgh: University of Pittsburgh Press.

Baumgartner, F. R., and B. D. Jones. 1990. "Shifting Images and Venues of a Public Issue: Explaining the Demise of Nuclear Power in the United States." Paper presented at the annual meeting of the American Political Science Association, Atlanta, Georgia, September 1–3.

Baumgartner, F. R., and B. D. Jones. 1993. *Agendas and Instability in American Politics*. Chicago: University of Chicago Press.

Berger, P. L., and T. Luckmann. 1966. *The Social Construction of Reality: A Treatise in the Sociology of Knowledge*. Garden City, NY: Anchor Books.

Berinsky, A. J., and D. R. Kinder. 2006. "Making Sense of Issues through Media Frames: Understanding the Kosovo Crisis." *Journal of Politics* 68 (August): 640–656.

Bosso, C. J. 1987. *Pesticides and Politics: The Life Cycle of a Public Issue*. Pittsburgh: University of Pittsburgh Press.

———. Bosso, C. J. 1989. "Setting the Public Agenda: Mass Media and the Ethiopian Famine." In *Manipulating Public Opinion: Essays on Public Opinion as a Dependent Variable*, ed. M. Margolis and G. Mauser, 153–174. Monterey, CA: Brooks-Cole.

Bosso, C. J., and D. L. Guber. 2005. "Maintaining Presence: Environmental Advocacy and the Permanent Campaign." In *Environmental Policy: New Directions for the Twenty-First Century*, 6th ed., ed. N. J. Vig and M. E. Kraft, 78–66. Washington, DC: CQ Press.

Bostrom, A., and D. Lashof. 2007. "Weather or Climate Change?" In *Creating a Climate for Change: Communicating Climate Change and Facilitating Social Change*, ed. S. C. Moser and L. Dilling, 31–43. Cambridge: Cambridge University Press.

Boykoff, M. T., and J. Boykoff. 2004. "Balance as Bias: Global Warming and the U.S. Prestige Press." *Global Environmental Change* 15: 125–136.

———. 2007. "Climate Change and Journalistic Norms: A Case Study of U.S. Mass-Media Coverage." *Geoforum* 38: 1190–1204.

Brittle, C., and N. Muthuswamy. 2009. "Scientific Elites and Concern for Global Warming: The Impact of Disagreement, Evidence, Strength, Partisan Cues, and Exposure to News Content on Concern for Climate Change." *International Journal of Sustainability Communication* 4: 23–44.

Broder, J. M. 2009. "Another Weapon Emerges in the Combat over Global Warming: A Thesaurus." *New York Times*, May 2.

Broder, J. M., and C. Krauss. 2011. "Oil Drilling to Resume in the Gulf's Deep Waters." *New York Times*, March 1.

Brown, M. H. 1980. *Laying Waste: The Poisoning of America by Toxic Waste*. New York: Pantheon Books.

Bullard, R. D. 1990. *Dumping in Dixie: Race, Class, and Environmental Quality*. Boulder, CO: Westview.

Callaghan, K. J., and F. Schnell. 2005. *Framing American Politics*. Pittsburgh: University of Pittsburgh Press.

———. 2009. "Who Says What to Whom: Why Messengers and Citizen Beliefs Matter in Social Policy Framing." *Social Science Journal* 46: 12–28.

Carmines, E. G., and J. A. Stimson. 1980. "The Two Faces of Issue Voting." *American Political Science Review* 74: 78–91.

Carson, R. 1962. *Silent Spring*. Boston: Houghton Mifflin.

Cater, D. 1964. *Power in Washington*. New York: Random House.

Chong, D., and J. N. Druckman. 2007. "Framing Theory." *Annual Review of Political Science* 10: 103–126.

Citrin, J., B. Reingold, and D. P. Green. 1990. "American Identity and the Politics of Ethnic Change." *Journal of Politics* 52: 1124–1154.

Cobb, R. W., and C. D. Elder. 1972. *Participation in American Politics: The Dynamics of Agenda-Building.* Boston: Allyn and Bacon.

Cohen, R. 1995.*Washington at Work: Back Room and Clean Air.* 2nd ed. Boston: Allyn and Bacon.

Conover, P. J., and S. Feldman. 1984. "How People Organize the Political World: A Schematic Model." *American Journal of Political Science* 28: 95–126.

Converse, P. E. 1964. "The Nature of Belief Systems in Mass Publics." In *Ideology and Discontent*, ed. David E. Apter. New York: Free Press.

Crenson, M. 1971. *The Un-Politics of Air Pollution.* Baltimore: Johns Hopkins University Press.

Dahl, R. A. 1956. *A Preface to Democratic Theory.* Chicago: University of Chicago Press.

Daly, H. 1977. *Steady-State Economics.* Washington, DC: Island.

Downs, A. 1972. "Up and Down with Ecology: The Issue-Attention Cycle." *Public Interest* 28: 38–50.

Druckman, J. N. 2001a. "The Implications of Framing Effects for Citizen Competence." *Political Behavior* 23: 225–256.

———. 2001b. "On the Limits of Framing Effects: Who Can Frame?" *Journal of Politics* 63: 1041–1066.

———. 2004. "Political Preference Formation: Competition, Deliberation, and the (Ir)relevance of Framing Effects." *American Political Science Review* 98: 671–686.

———. 2010. "Competing Frames in a Political Campaign." In *Winning with Words: The Origins and Impact of Framing*, ed. B. F. Schaffner and P. J. Sellers. New York: Routledge.

Duffy, R. J. 1997. *Nuclear Politics in America: A History and Theory of Government Regulation.* Lawrence: University Press of Kansas.

———. 2003. *The Green Agenda in American Politics: New Strategies for the Twenty-First Century.* Lawrence: University Press of Kansas.

Dunlap, R. E. 1991. "Public Opinion in the 1980s: Clear Consensus, Ambiguous Commitment." *Environment* 33: 10–15, 32–37.

Edelman, M. 1964. *The Symbolic Uses of Politics.* Urbana: University of Illinois Press.

Editorial. 2003. "Environmental Word Games." *New York Times*, March 15.

Entman, R. M. 1993. "Framing: Toward a Clarification of a Fractured Paradigm." *Journal of Communication* 43: 51–58.

Fahrenthold, D. A., and J. Eilperin. 2010. "Historic Oil Spill Fails to Produce Gains for U.S. Environmentalists." *Washington Post*, July 12.

Farhar, B. C. 1994. "Trends: Public Opinion about Energy." *Public Opinion Quarterly* 58: 603–632.

Fiske, S. T., and S. E. Taylor. 1984. *Social Cognition.* Reading, MA: Addison-Wesley.

Freeman, J. L. 1955. *The Political Process.* New York: Random House.

Gamson, W. A., and A. Modigliani. 1987. "The Changing Culture of Affirmative Action." In *Research in Political Sociology* 3, ed. R. D. Braungart, 137–177. Greenwich, CT: JAI Press.

———. 1989. "Media Discourse and Public Opinion on Nuclear Power: A Constructionist Approach." *American Journal of Sociology* 95: 1–37.

Goffman, E. 1974. *Frame Analysis: An Essay on the Organization of Experience*. New York: Harper & Row.

Gottlieb, R. 2005. *Forcing the Spring: The Transformation of the American Environmental Movement*. Washington, DC: Island.

Gray, B. 2003. "Framing of Environmental Disputes." In *Making Sense of Intractable Environmental Conflicts: Frames and Cases*, ed. Roy J. Lewicki, Barbara Gray, and Michael Elliot, 11–34. Washington, DC: Island.

Guber, D. L., and C. J. Bosso. 2007. "Framing ANWR: Citizens, Consumers, and the Privileged Position of Business." In *Business and Environmental Policy*, ed. M. E. Kraft and S. Kamieniecki, 35–60. Cambridge, MA: MIT Press.

Harrison, K., and G. Hoberg. 1991. "Setting the Environmental Agenda in Canada and the United States: The Cases of Dioxin and Radon." *Canadian Journal of Political Science* 24: 3–27.

Hays, S. 1959. *Conservation and the Gospel of Efficiency: The Progressive Conservation Movement, 1890–1920*. Cambridge, MA: Harvard University Press.

Heclo, H. 1978. "Issue Networks and the Executive Establishment." In *The New American Political System*, ed. A. King, 87–124. Washington, DC: American Enterprise Institute.

Hiscox, Michael J. 2006. "Through a Glass and Darkly: Attitudes toward International Trade and the Curious Effects of Issue Framing." *International Organization* 60: 755–780.

Hoberg, G. 1992. *Pluralism by Design: Environmental Policy and the American Regulatory State*. New York: Praeger.

Hochschild, J. L. 1981. *What's Fair? American Beliefs about Distributive Justice*. Cambridge, MA: Harvard University Press.

Immerwahr, J. 1999. *Waiting for a Signal: Public Attitudes toward Global Warming, the Environment and Geophysical Research*. American Geophysical Union, Electronic Publication. Available at www.policyarchive.org/handle/10207/bitstreams/5662.pdf.

Iyenhar, S. 1990. "Framing Responsibility for Political Issues: The Case of Poverty." *Political Behavior* 12: 19–40.

———. 1991. *Is Anyone Responsible? How Television Frames Political Issues*. Chicago: University of Chicago Press.

Iyengar, S., and D. R. Kinder. 1987. *News That Matters: Television and American Opinion*. Chicago: University of Chicago Press.

Jacoby, W. G. 2000. "Issue Framing and Public Opinion on Government Spending." *American Journal of Political Science* 44: 750–767.

Jones, C. O. 1975. *Clear Air: The Policies and Politics of Pollution Control*. Pittsburgh: University of Pittsburgh Press.

Jones, C. O. 1979. "American Politics and the Organization of Energy Decision Making." *Annual Review of Energy*, 4: 99–110.

Kahneman, D., and A. Tversky. 1984. "Choices, Values, Frames." *American Psychologist* 39: 341–350.

Katz, M. B. 1990. *The Undeserving Poor: From the War on Poverty to the War on Welfare*. New York: Pantheon Books.

Kennedy, R. F., Jr. 2004. *Crimes against Nature: How George W. Bush and His Corporate Pals Are Plundering the Country and Hijacking Our Democracy*. New York: HarperCollins.

Kinder, D. R., and D. Herzog. 1993. "Democratic Discussion." In *Reconsidering the Democratic Public*, ed. G. E. Marcus and R. L. Hanson. University Park: Pennsylvania State University Press.

Kinder, D. R., and T. E. Nelson. 2005. "Democratic Debate and Real Opinions." In *Framing American Politics*, ed. K. J. Callaghan and F. Schnell, 103–122. Pittsburgh: University of Pittsburgh Press.

Kinder, D. R., and L. M. Sanders. 1990. "Mimicking Political Debate with Survey Questions: The Case of White Opinion on Affirmative Action for Blacks." *Social Cognition* 8: 73–103.

———. 1996. *Divided by Color: Racial Politics and American Ideals*. Chicago: University of Chicago Press.

Kingdon, J. 1995. *Agendas, Alternatives, and Public Policies*. 2nd ed. New York: Longman.

Klyza, C. M., and D. Sousa. 2008. *American Environmental Policy, 1990–2006: Beyond Gridlock*. Cambridge, MA: MIT Press.

Krosnick, J. A., A. L. Holbrook, L. Lowe, and P. S. Visser. 2006. "The Origins and Consequences of Democratic Citizens' Policy Agendas: A Study of Popular Concern about Global Warming." *Climatic Change* 77: 7–43.

Kull, S., C. Ramsay, and E. Lewis. 2003–2004. "Misperceptions, the Media, and the Iraq War." *Political Science Quarterly* 118 (Winter): 569–598.

Kuypers, J. A. 2009. *Rhetorical Criticism: Perspectives in Action*. Lanham, MD: Lexington Books.

Ladd, E. C. 1982. "Clearing the Air: Public Opinion and Public Policy on the Environment." *Public Opinion* 5 (August/September): 16–20.

Lakoff, G. 2004. *Don't Think of an Elephant! Know Your Values and Frame the Debate*. White River Junction, VT: Chelsea Green.

———. 2008. *The Political Mind: Why You Can't Understand 21st Century American Politics with an 18th Century Brain*. New York: Viking.

Lasswell, H. D. 1948. "The Structure and Function of Communication in Society." In *The Communication of Ideas*, ed. Lyman Bryson, 37–51. New York: Harper and Row.

Lau, R. R., and D. P. Redlawsk. 2001. "Advantages and Disadvantages of Cognitive Heuristics in Political Decision Making." *American Journal of Political Science* 45: 951–971.

Layzer, J. 2002. *The Environmental Case: Translating Values into Policy*. Washington, DC: CQ Press.

Lee, Y., and C. Chang. 2010. "Framing Public Policy: The Impacts of Political Sophistication and Nature of Public Policy." *Social Science Journal* 47: 69–89.

Lindblom, C. 1966. *The Policymaking Process*. Englewood Cliffs, NJ: Prentice-Hall.

Lippmann, W. 1922. *Public Opinion*. New York: Harcourt, Brace and Company.

Louv, R. 2005. "Reseeding Environmentalism." *Oregonian*, March 27.

Luntz, F. 2002. *Straight Talk*. Alexandria, VA: Luntz Research.

———. 2007. *Words That Work: It's Not What You Say, It's What People Hear*. New York: Hyperion.

Maibach, E. W., M. Nisbet, P. Baldwin, K. Akerlof, and G. Diao. 2010. "Reframing Climate Change as a Public Health Issue: An Exploratory Study of Public Reactions." *BMC Public Health* 10: 299–309.

McComas, K., and J. Shanahan. 1999. "Telling Stories about Climate Change: Measuring the Impact of Narratives on Issue Cycles." *Communication Research* 26: 30–57.

McCombs, M. E., and D. L. Shaw. 1972. "The Agenda-Setting Function of Mass Media." *Public Opinion Quarterly* 36: 176–187.

McCright, A. M., and R. E. Dunlap. 2000. "Challenging Global Warming as a Social Problem: An Analysis of the Conservative Movement's Counter-Claims." *Social Problems* 47: 499–522.

———. 2003. "Defeating Kyoto: The Conservative Movement's Impact on U.S. Climate Change Policy." *Social Problems* 50: 348–373.

McKibben, B. 2003. *Enough: Staying Human in an Engineered Age*. New York: Holt.

Milbank, D. 2010. "Global Warming's Snowball Fight." *Washington Post*, February 14.

Milward, H. B., and W. Laird. 1991. "Ideas, Agendas and Public Policy." *Policy Currents* 1: 2–3.

Montenegro, M. 2009. "Is There a Better Word for Doom?" *Seed Magazine*, May 21.

Montpetit, É. 2003. *Misplaced Distrust: Policy Networks and the Environment in France, the United States, and Canada*. Vancouver: UBC Press.

Moser, S. C., and L. Dilling. 2004. "Making Climate Hot: Communicating the Urgency and Challenge of Global Climate Change." *Environment* 46 (December): 32–46.

Mucciaroni, G. 1990. *The Political Failure of Employment Policy, 1945–1982*. Pittsburgh: University of Pittsburgh Press.

———.1992. "The Garbage Can Model and the Study of Policy Making: A Critique," *Polity*, 24, 3 (1992): 459–482.

Nelkin, D., and M. Pollack. 1982. *The Atom Besieged: Antinuclear Movements in France and Germany*. Cambridge, MA: MIT Press.

Nelson, R. R. 1977. *The Moon and the Ghetto: An Essay on Public Policy Analysis*. New York: W. W. Norton & Company.

Nelson, T. E., R. A. Clawson, and Z. M. Oxley. 1997. "Media Framing of a Civil Liberties Conflict and Its Effect on Tolerance." *American Political Science Review* 91: 567–583.

Nelson, T. E., and D. R. Kinder. 1996. "Issue Frames and Group-Centrism in American Public Opinion." *Journal of Politics* 58: 1055–1078.

Nicholas, H. G. 1981. *The Nature of American Politics*. New York: Oxford University Press.

Nisbet, M. C. 2009. "Communicating Climate Change: Why Frames Matter to Public Engagement." *Environment* 51: 514–518.

———. 2011. *Climate Shift: Clear Vision for the Next Decade of Public Debate*. Washington, DC: American University School of Communication. Available at climateshiftproject.org/wp-content/uploads/2011/04/Climate-Shift-report-FINAL-4-18-11.pdf.

Nisbet, M. C., and C. Mooney. 2007. "Framing Science: To Engage Diverse Publics Scientists Must Focus on Ways to Make Complex Topics Personally Relevant." *Science* 316: 5821.

Nisbet, M. C., and D. A. Scheufele. 2010. "What's Next for Science Communication? Promising Directions and Lingering Distractions." *American Journal of Botany* 96: 1767–1778.

Noland, R. B. 2004. "Motor Vehicle Fuel Efficiency and Traffic Fatalities." *Energy Journal* 25: 1–22.

Nordhaus, T., and M. Schellenberger. 2007. *Break Through: From the Death of Environmentalism to the Politics of Possibility*. New York: Houghton Mifflin.

Orren, K., and S. Skowronek. 2004. *The Search for American Political Development.* Cambridge: Cambridge University Press.

Pan, P., J. Meng, and S. Zhou. 2010. "Morality or Equality? Ideological Framing in News Coverage of Gay Marriage Legitimization." *Social Science Journal* 47: 630–645.

Pettenger, M., and E. Plec. 2010. "Selling Green: How Green Is ExxonMobil's Framing of Alternative Energy?" Paper presented at the annual meeting of Theory vs. Policy? Connecting Scholars and Practitioners, New Orleans Hilton Riverside Hotel, Loews New Orleans Hotel, New Orleans, LA, February 17.

Plato. 1968. *The Republic.* Translation and commentary by Allan Bloom. New York: Basic Books.

Pralle, S. 2006. *Branching Out, Digging In: Environmental Advocacy and Agenda Setting.* Washington, DC: Georgetown University Press.

Pralle, S. 2009. "Agenda-Setting and Climate Change." *Environmental Politics* 18: 781–799.

Rabe, B. G. 2004. *Statehouse and Greenhouse: The Emerging Politics of American Climate Change Policy.* Washington, DC: Brookings Institution Press.

Ripley, R. B., and Grace A. Franklin. 1984. *Congress, the Bureaucracy, and Public Opinion.* Homewood, IL: Dorsey.

Rochefort, D. A. 1986. *American Social Welfare Policy: Dynamics of Formulation and Change.* Boulder, CO: Westview.

Rubin, C. T. 1994. *The Green Crusade: Rethinking the Roots of Environmentalism.* New York: Rowman & Littlefield.

Sabatier, P. 1988. "An Advocacy Coalition Framework of Policy Change and the Role of Policy-Oriented Learning Therein." *Policy Sciences* 21: 129–168.

Schattschneider, E. E. 1960. *The Semi-Sovereign People: A Realist's View of Democracy in America.* New York: Holt, Rhinehart, and Winston.

Scheufele, D. A., and D. Tewksbury. 2007. "Framing, Agenda Setting, and Priming: The Evolution of Three Media Effects Models." *Journal of Communication* 57: 9–20.

Schuldt, J. P., S. H. Konrath, and N. Schwarz. 2011. "'Global Warming' or 'Climate Change'? Whether the Planet Is Warming Depends on Question Wording." *Public Opinion Quarterly* 75: 115–124.

Shabecoff, P. 2000. *Earth Rising: American Environmentalism in the 21st Century.* Washington, DC: Island.

Sharp, E. L. 2008. "Energy and the Environment: Issue Framing in Presidential Debates." Unpublished manuscript. Available at dukespace.lib.duke.edu/dspace/bitstream/handle/10161/556/sharp_mp_nich.pdf?sequence=1.

Shellenberger, M., and T. Nordhaus. 2004. "The Death of Environmentalism: Global Warming Politics in a Post Environmental World." Available at www.thebreakthrough.org/PDF/Death_of_Environmentalism.pdf (accessed January 1, 2012).

Smerecnik, K. R., and G. N. Dionisopoulos. 2009. "McCain's Issue Framing in 2008: The Environment as Freedom and a Commodity." In *The 2008 Presidential Campaign: A Communication Perspective,* ed. Robert E. Denton Jr., 148–169. Lanham, MD: Rowman & Littlefield.

Sniderman, P. M., R. A. Brody, and P. E. Tetlock. 1991. *Reasoning and Choice: Explorations in Political Psychology.* New York: Cambridge University Press.

Sniderman, P. M., and S. M. Theriault. 2004. "The Dynamics of Political Argument and the Logic of Issue Framing." In *Studies in Public Opinion: Attitudes,*

Nonattitudes, Measurement Error, and Change, ed. Willem E. Saris and Paul M. Sniderman, 133–165. Princeton, NJ: Princeton University Press.

Stone, D. A. 1989. "Causal Stories and the Formation of Policy Agendas." *Political Science Quarterly* 104: 281–300.

Tversky, A., and D. Kahneman. 1981. "The Framing of Decisions and the Psychology of Choice." *Science* 211: 453–458.

Vaughn, J., and H. Cortner. 2005. *George W. Bush's Healthy Forests: Reframing the Environmental Debate.* Boulder: University of Colorado Press.

Walker, J. L., Jr. 1991. *Mobilizing Interest Groups In America: Patrons, Professions, and Social Movements.* Ann Arbor: University of Michigan Press.

Weart, S. R. 2008. *The Discovery of Global Warming.* Cambridge, MA: Harvard University Press.

Whitmarsh, L. 2009. "What's in a Name? Commonalities and Differences in Public Understanding of 'Climate Change' and 'Global Warming.'" *Public Understanding of Science* 18: 401–420.

Wilson, J. Q. 1973. *Political Organizations.* New York: Basic Books.

Zaller, J. 1992. *The Nature and Origins of Mass Opinion.* Cambridge: Cambridge University Press.

Zaller, J., and S. Feldman. 1992. "A Simple Theory of the Survey Response: Answering Questions versus Revealing Preferences." *American Journal of Political Science* 36: 579–616.

Zwick, J. 2010. "Frank Luntz on How to Pass a Climate Bill." *New Republic,* January 21. Available at www.tnr.com/blog/the-vine/frank-luntz-how-pass-climate-bill.

CHAPTER 21

···

PUBLIC OPINION ON ENVIRONMENTAL POLICY IN THE UNITED STATES

···

DAVID P. DANIELS, JON A. KROSNICK,
MICHAEL P. TICHY, AND
TREVOR TOMPSON

In the United States, as in any democracy, scholars believe that public opinion is an important potential determinant of the nation's policy agenda (Kingdon 1995; chapter 20 in this volume). One mechanism for this influence is survey research, which can illuminate the public's views and wishes. Environmental issues were largely overlooked in opinion surveys until 1965, when they began to garner significant media and political attention (Dunlap 1991b). Events such as the inaugural Earth Day in 1970, which had an estimated involvement of 20 million people, received massive exposure that helped consolidate a growing public awareness of the environment and the damage that humans could do to it (Dunlap 1989). As a result, news media and public polling organizations during the last few decades have routinely asked Americans questions about environmental issues. These surveys have received regular news coverage, bringing their results into the set of considerations that could influence American politicians as they crafted and voted on proposed legislation. While this research has been done and disseminated, academic scholars have conducted many other surveys and published their own investigations of the nature, origins, and consequences of public opinion on the environment.

In exploring these issues, pollsters and academics have developed a wide variety of questions to measure environmental attitudes and beliefs. But different studies have used different measures and have made very different assumptions about the underlying structure of these items (for an overview, see Dunlap and Jones 2002). Some research has reported evidence that has been interpreted to indicate that many seemingly dissimilar measures are surface manifestations of just one underlying attitudinal dimension (e.g., Guber 1996; Pierce and Lovrich 1980; Xiao and Dunlap 2007). Other research has suggested that a small set of factors underlie sets of attitudinal measures (e.g., Buttel and Johnson 1977; Carman 1998; Van Liere and Dunlap 1981).

Prominent in the latter group are many studies that have used the New Environmental Paradigm (NEP) Scale (Dunlap and Van Liere 1978), which has sometimes appeared to tap two or more underlying latent factors (Dunlap et al., 2000, 430–431). And still other research has interpreted weak correlations between different measures of environmental attitudes and beliefs as indicating a much larger set of underlying constructs (e.g., Cluck 1998; deHaven-Smith 1988, 1991; Klineberg, McKeever, and Rothenbach 1998). Looking at such data, deHaven-Smith (1991, 97) argued that "researchers should abandon survey designs and statistical techniques that presuppose the existence of a generalized concern for the environment. Survey questions that lump numerous environmental issues together and scales that combine responses to a variety of environmental items are based on faulty premises."

This chapter reviews an array of survey questions that have been employed in past research in the United States, along with evidence addressing the question of whether these items are best thought of as unidimensional or multidimensional. We begin by outlining our main theme: employing different measures of environmental attitudes and beliefs leads to strikingly different conclusions about Americans' commitment to environmental protection. We assess evidence on the measures' trends over time and the measures' correlations with social and political variables. Taken together, this evidence leads us to conclude that each measure has integrity and would be best examined on its own, rather than combined with other measures into indexes seeking to describe higher-order constructs. We then consider evidence on how such environmental attitudes and beliefs may have impacted environmental policy via candidate choice, dynamic representation, and ballot propositions (see chapters 20, 22, and 24 in this volume). Finally, we highlight directions for future research on public opinion and environmental policy.

1. Measures of Environmental Attitudes, Beliefs, and Preferences

A search of questions asked in a wide array of surveys of representative national samples of American adults yielded items that we assigned to 16 categories, which are described in Table 21.1 along with example questions of each type.[1] Viewed from a distance, many of these categories might seem to tap a single underlying construct that could be termed "support for environmental protection" or "concern about the environment." But we believe that this would be a mistake. For policy makers or politicians interested in assessing Americans' preferences on environmental policy, attempting to interpret every environmentally relevant survey question as indicative of general "environmental concern" is likely to be more mystifying than enlightening.

For instance, according to some of these questions, Americans appear to have been overwhelmingly "concerned" about the environment. In Gallup Organization surveys between 1989 and 2011, for example, the vast majority of respondents (between 78 percent and 91 percent) said they worried a "great deal" or a "fair amount" about pollution of rivers, lakes, and reservoirs; similar majorities (between 69 percent and 88 percent) said they worried a "great deal" or a "fair amount" about air pollution.[2] Moreover, most Americans have favored various types of environmental protection efforts. In General Social Survey (GSS) surveys between 1982 and 2010, for example, consistent majorities (between 50 percent and 75 percent) have said we are spending "too little" on "improving and protecting the environment," while small minorities (between 4 percent and 13 percent) have said we are spending "too much."[3]

By other metrics, however, Americans appear to be "unconcerned" with the environment. In March 2010, when Gallup asked the standard open-ended "Most Important Problem" (MIP) question—"What do you think is the most important problem facing this country today?"—just 2 percent of people mentioned the environment or pollution, a rate typical of surveys in recent years. This finding has led some scholars to conclude that the salience of environmental issues was very low (e.g., Bosso and Guber 2006). Yet in the same poll, when Gallup asked a slightly

---

1. We relied on the iPOLL database of survey questions built and maintained by the Roper Center for Public Opinion Research at the University of Connecticut. Included in the database are question wordings and results of surveys conducted by a wide array of academic and nonacademic survey research organizations. We searched for survey questions containing "environment," "air," "water," or "pollution," during a span of two years (1984 to 1986), which represented roughly the midpoint of the years of data available. Each item located in this search was used to construct search terms for additional searches intended to locate all instances of the item for the entire span of dates included in the Roper Center for Public Opinion Research database.
2. The full question wording is: "I'm going to read you a list of environmental problems. As I read each one, please tell me if you personally worry about this problem a great deal, a fair amount, only a little, or not at all. First, how much do you personally worry about...[pollution of rivers, lakes, and reservoirs/air pollution]" (Gallup Organization, various years from 1989 to 2011).
3. The full question wording is: "We are faced with many problems in this country, none of which can be solved easily or inexpensively. I'm going to name some of these problems, and for each one I'd like you to tell me whether you think we're spending too much money on it, too little money, or about the right amount on...improving and protecting the environment" (General Social Survey, various years from 1982 to 2010).

Table 21.1 Sixteen Categories of Survey Items on Environmental Issues

Category	Example Survey Item		
	Question	Response(s)	%
1. Evaluations of past environmental quality	Do you think the overall quality of the environment around here is very much better than it was five years ago, somewhat better than it was five years ago, slightly better than it was five years ago, slightly worse, somewhat worse, or very much worse than it was five years ago? (July 1994, Cambridge Reports/Research International)	Slightly worse, somewhat worse, or very much worse	40
2. Evaluations of present environmental quality	How would you rate the overall quality of the environment in this country today—as excellent, good, only fair, or poor? (March 4–7, 2010, Gallup Organization)	Only fair or poor	53
3. Evaluations of future environmental quality	Looking ahead 10 years, do you think the overall quality of the environment in your area will be very much better than it is today, somewhat better, slightly better, slightly worse, somewhat worse, or very much worse than it is today? (July 1994, Cambridge Reports/ Research International)	Slightly worse, somewhat worse, or very much worse	42
4. Perceived seriousness of environmental problems	How serious a threat to the future well-being of the United States do you consider each of the following—extremely serious, very serious, somewhat serious, not very serious, or not a threat at all? How about...the environment, including global warming? (May 24–25, 2010, Gallup Organization)	Extremely serious or very serious	51
5. Judgments of national and international importance of environmental protection	How important are the following issues to you personally...Not at all important, slightly important, moderately important, very important or extremely important? How about...the environment? (March 3–8, 2010, Associated Press/ GFK)	Extremely important or very important	62

Table 21.1 (Continued)

Category	Example Survey Item		
	Question	Response(s)	%
6. Desired amount of spending to protect the environment	We are faced with many problems in this country, none of which can be solved easily or inexpensively. I'm going to name some of these problems, and for each one I'd like you to tell me whether you think we're spending too much money on it, too little money, or about the right amount. Are we spending too much, too little, or about the right amount on…improving and protecting the environment? (March 15–August 12, 2010, General Social Survey)	Too little	56
7. Desired amount of government effort to protect the environment	Do you think the U.S. government is doing too much, too little, or about the right amount in terms of protecting the environment? (March 4–7, 2010, Gallup Organization)	Too little	46
8. Evaluations of environmentalists and environmentalism	Thinking about the environmental movement, do you think of yourself as—an active participant in the environmental movement, sympathetic toward the movement but not active, neutral, or unsympathetic toward the environmental movement? (March 4–7, 2010, Gallup Organization)	Active or sympathetic	61
9. Evaluations of the handling of environmental issues by specific organizations and political actors	Do you approve or disapprove of the way Barack Obama is handling…environmental policy? (March 19–21, 2010, CNN/Opinion Research Corporation)	Approve	55
10. Perceived political party superiority in handling environmental protection	When it comes to…protecting the environment which party do you think would do a better job—the Democratic Party, the Republican Party, or both about the same? If you think that neither would do a good job, please just say so. (August 5–9, 2010, NBC/Wall Street Journal)	Republican Party	13

(continued)

Table 21.1 (Continued)

Category	Example Survey Item		
	Question	Response(s)	%
11. Reported impact of environmental considerations on voting behavior	How important will each of the following be to your vote for Congress this year—will it be extremely important, very important, moderately important, or not that important?...The environment. (August 6–10, 2010, CNN/Opinion Research Corporation)	Extremely important or very important	58
12. Emotional reactions to environmental issues	I'm going to read you a list of environmental problems. As I read each one, please tell me if you personally worry about this problem a great deal, a fair amount, only a little, or not at all. How much do you personally worry about...pollution of rivers, lakes, and reservoirs? (March 4–7, 2010, Gallup Organization)	A great deal or a fair amount	78
13. Personal interest in, and attention to, news media coverage of the environment	Now I will read a list of some stories covered by news organizations this past month. As I read each item, tell me if you happened to follow this news story very closely, fairly closely, not too closely, or not at all closely....The celebration of Earth Day. (May 3–7, 1990, Times Mirror)	Very closely or fairly closely	68
14. Self-reported activism on environmental issues	Which of these, if any, have you, yourself, done in the past year?...Been active in a group or organization that works to protect the environment. (March 4–7, 2010, Gallup Organization)	Yes, have done	17
15. Trade-offs between environmental protection and other policy goals	Which of these two statements is closer to your opinion? We must be prepared to sacrifice environmental quality for economic growth. We must sacrifice economic growth in order to preserve and protect the environment. (September 1994, Cambridge Reports/Research International)	We must sacrifice economic growth in order to preserve and protect the environment	53

Table 21.1 (Continued)

Category	Example Survey Item		
	Question	Response(s)	%
16. Willingness to pay for environmental protection	How much more per month would you personally be willing to pay for all the goods and services you use as a contsumer, if you knew that as a result of your paying higher prices business and industry would be able to operate in a way that did not harm the environment? (July 1993, Cambridge Reports/Research International)	Over $50	15

different question—"Looking ahead, what do you think will be the most important problem facing our nation 25 years from now?"—the environment and pollution were mentioned second most often (by 11 percent), behind only the federal budget deficit (14 percent), and tied with mentions of the economy in general (11 percent). Experiments embedded in several 2009 surveys replicated this pattern: when people were asked the traditional MIP question, they rarely mentioned the environment or global warming; but when people are asked to identify "the most serious problem facing the world in the future if nothing is done to stop it," the *most* frequent issue domain mentioned was the environment and global warming, cited by over 20 percent of respondents (Yeager et al., 2011).

From the above examples, we conclude that a single survey item can make it appear as if the majority of Americans have been overwhelmingly committed to environmental protection, unconcerned about the environment, or almost anywhere in between. In other words, conclusions about the American public's degree of environmental concern will vary depending on the particular measures employed to operationalize "environmental concern."

2. Multifaceted Environmental Attitudes and Beliefs

2.1. Trends over Time

The same conclusion is supported by past studies of trends over time in environmental beliefs and attitudes. Many claims have been made about these trends. For example, Erskine (1972) described how public concern about the environment quickly became widespread between 1965 and 1970. After the inaugural Earth Day in 1970, concern is said to have declined somewhat during the ensuing 10 years but remained substantial

(Dunlap 1991b). During the 1980s, public support for environmental protection is said to have surged to record-high levels (Dunlap 1991a), reaching a peak with the 20th anniversary of Earth Day in 1990, and then subsided to a more moderate level, where it remained throughout the 1990s (Dunlap 2002). In the early to mid-2000s, environmental concern is said to have declined (Bosso and Guber 2006).

This may not be the most sensible way to characterize public opinion. As just a small set of evidence, consider Figure 21.1, which displays "pro-environmental" trends over time in answers to eight survey questions that were asked frequently

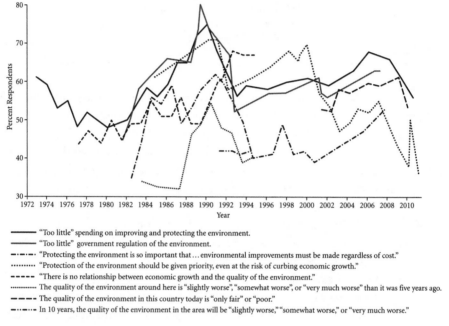

_____ "Too little" spending on improving and protecting the environment.
_____ "Too little" government regulation of the environment.
—·—·— "Protecting the environment is so important that ... environmental improvements must be made regardless of cost."
············ "Protection of the environment should be given priority, even at the risk of curbing economic growth."
— — — — "There is no relationship between economic growth and the quality of the environment."
············ The quality of the environment around here is "slightly worse", "somewhat worse", or "very much worse" than it was five years ago.
— — — — The quality of the environment in this country today is "only fair" or "poor."
—·—·—·— In 10 years, the quality of the environment in the area will be "slightly worse," "somewhat worse," or "very much worse."

Figure 21.1 Trends in Environmental Attitudes and Beliefs over Time [4]

4. The question wordings for Figure 21.1 are as follows (in order of presentation in the legend): "We are faced with many problems in this country, none of which can be solved easily or inexpensively. I'm going to name some of these problems, and for each one I'd like you to tell me whether you think we're spending too much money on it, too little money, or about the right amount on ... improving and protecting the environment" (General Social Survey, various years from 1973 to 2010). "In general, do you think there is too much, too little, or about the right amount of government regulation and involvement in the area of environmental protection?" (Cambridge Reports/Research International, 1982 to 1994; Wirthlin Worldwide, 1996 to 2000 [Wirthlin Worldwide omitted the phrase "In general" from the question wording]; Harris Interactive, 2005 and 2007). "Do you agree or disagree with the following statement? Protecting the environment is so important that requirements and standards cannot be too high, and continuing environmental improvements must be made regardless of cost" (CBS News/*New York Times,* various years from 1981 to 2007). "With which one of these statements about the environment and the economy do you most agree—protection of the environment should be given priority, even at the risk of curbing economic growth, or economic growth should be given priority,

between 1973 and 2010. In fact, only one of these time trends matches the narrative in the previous paragraph:

- The environmental spending item shows the purported decline in the 1970s, the rise in the 1980s, and the decline in the early 1990s, but shows an increase in the early 2000s rather than a decrease.
- The environmental government regulation item shows a different pattern— an increase in the 1980s and a decrease in the early 1990s; but it, too, shows an increase rather than a decrease in the 2000s.
- The environmental protection importance item shows the increase in the 1980s and the decrease in the early 1990s, but it again shows an increase in the 2000s.
- The item trading off the environment against economic growth shows the 1980s increase, but it shows a rise across the 1990s and a series of sharp decreases in the 2000s, broken by an upward spike in 2010.
- The proportion of people denying a trade-off between environmental protection and economic prosperity shows yet another pattern, with a slow increase in denial across the 1980s and a sharp increase in denial in the early 1990s.
- The retrospective environmental quality assessment shows the claimed sharp increase in negative evaluations in late 1980s and a decline in those evaluations in the 1990s.
- The current environmental quality item shows an increase in negative evaluations across the 2000s and a sharp decline in 2010.
- Finally, the prospective environmental quality item shows no change in the early 1990s, even while the other seven items exhibited dramatic changes.

Figure 21.1 suggests that general concern about the environment is not manifested equivalently by the array of measures illustrated there. Instead, the various measures all appear to have integrity and to tap distinct judgments.

even if the environment suffers to some extent?" (Gallup Organization, various years from 1984 to 2011). "Which of these two statements is closer to your opinion? 1. There is no relationship between economic growth and the quality of the environment— indeed, we can have more and more goods and services and also a clean world. 2. We cannot have both economic growth and a high level of environmental quality, we must sacrifice one or the other" (Cambridge Reports/Research International, 1977 to 1994). "Do you think the overall quality of the environment around here is very much better than it was five years ago, somewhat better than it was five years ago, slightly better than it was five years ago, slightly worse, somewhat worse, or very much worse than it was five years ago?" (Cambridge Reports/Research International, 1983 to 1994). "How would you rate the overall quality of the environment in this country today—as excellent, good, only fair, or poor?" (Gallup Organization, 2001 to 2010). "Looking ahead 10 years, do you think the overall quality of the environment in your area will be very much better than it is today, somewhat better, slightly better, slightly worse, somewhat worse, or very much worse than it is today?" (Cambridge Reports/ Research International, 1991 to 1994).

What factors might explain these many variations in the public's environmental attitudes and beliefs over time? First, support for environmental protection is thought to be contingent on favorable economic conditions (Elliott, Regens, and Seldon 1995). As one journalist noted in the wake of the 2008 election: "Concern for the environment is traditionally the first thing thrown overboard when economic seas get rough" (Walsh 2008).

Second, public opinion may react to changes in the condition of the natural environment. In particular, dramatic events such as the 1979 Three Mile Island nuclear accident or the 1989 *Exxon Valdez* oil spill may have played key roles in affecting public thinking (Leiserowitz, Kates, and Parris 2006). In Figure 21.1, for instance, the 2010 spike in the item trading off the environment against economic growth coincided with widespread media coverage of the *Deepwater Horizon* oil spill in the Gulf of Mexico.

Third, some changes in opinion may be attempts to minimize social change. Specifically, when government policy moves in one direction, the public may move in the opposite direction to restrain government's movement. For example, growth during the 1980s in some pro-environmental attitudes has sometimes been viewed as a reaction against the Reagan administration's opposition to environmental regulation (Dunlap 1991a, 1995). Although public attitudes do not appear to respond in this manner to levels of federal spending on the environment (Wlezien 1995), some evidence suggests that such "thermostatic" adjustment has occurred in response to changes in state-level funding of environmental programs (Johnson, Brace, and Arceneaux 2005).

Fourth, public opinion on environmental issues may be shaped by advocacy efforts from the environmental movement. Strong public support for environmental protection increases the credibility of pro-environmental groups (Mitchell 1984), so it is not surprising that efforts to spur public concern are common activities for such organizations (Brulle 2010). Advocacy by organizations opposed to the environmental movement, such as trade associations, could be similarly influential (see chapter 23 in this volume).

Finally, cohort replacement may generate compositional changes in the environmental attitudes held by the public (Kanagy, Humphrey, and Firebaugh 1994). As we will discuss shortly, the impact of these and other forces on public opinion appear to be different for different beliefs and attitudes, the investigation of which will be a useful agenda for future research.

2.2. Social and Political Correlates

If the various environmental attitude and belief measures described above tap a single underlying construct (e.g., "concern about the environment"), they should be similarly associated with other social and political variables. But as our review below illustrates, and as several scholars have suggested (e.g., deHaven-Smith 1988;

Klineberg, McKeever, and Rothenbach 1998), such uniformity does not appear to be the case (see also Diamantopoulos et al. 2003).[5]

Age. Scholars have argued that age should be negatively related to pro-environmental attitudes. One possible reason is cohort effects: younger birth cohorts, born after the 1970s surge in environmental concern, may have experienced more "pro-environmental" socialization (Hays 1987; Kanagy, Humphrey, and Firebaugh 1994). Another possible reason is life-cycle effects: younger adults may be more open to social change generally and therefore more accepting of arguments made in favor of protecting the environment (Van Liere and Dunlap 1980). Consistent with this logic, younger Americans have been more likely to support increased spending on "improving and protecting the environment" (Jones and Dunlap 1992). Most studies have also found a negative relation between age and the NEP (Dunlap et al. 2000). However, Samdahl and Robertson (1989) reported a *positive* association between age and a composite gauging support for five specific environmental regulations—for example, implementing "stronger laws to control transportation and dumping of hazardous waste."

Income. Some researchers have suggested that pro-environmental attitudes should be concentrated among wealthy Americans, since poorer Americans must be more concerned with meeting their basic economic needs, whereas wealthy Americans can afford the "luxury" of concern for the natural environment (for a review, see Van Liere and Dunlap 1980). Yet income has proven to be an inconsistent and typically a poor predictor of support for increased spending on the environment (Jones and Dunlap 1992). Moreover, Uyeki and Holland (2000) found that income was *negatively* associated with a scale they labeled "Pro-environment," composed of items measuring agreement with three assertions: "Economic growth always harms the environment," "Almost everything we do in modern life harms the environment," and "Nature would be at peace and in harmony if only human beings would leave it alone."

Education. Scholars have argued that educational attainment should be positively related to environmental attitudes, since more education is likely to facilitate awareness and understanding of complex environmental problems (Howell and Laska 1992; Van Liere and Dunlap 1980). In line with this reasoning, more educated respondents have been more likely to support increased environmental spending (Jones and Dunlap 1992). Also, studies have typically found a positive relation between education and the NEP (Dunlap et al. 2000). However, Buttel and Johnson (1977) found no significant association between education and an index of three items that gauged the urgency respondents felt for dealing with local environmental problems, support for more government effort to curb air and water pollution, and support for the creation of more parks. Samdahl and Robertson

---

5. Although the rest of this chapter focuses on survey questions asked of national samples, most work in this section studies subnational samples. Therefore, dissimilar associations of environmental measures with social and political variables might stem from differences in populations instead of, or in addition to, differences in measures.

(1989) reported that education was *negatively* associated with a composite measuring support for environmental regulations. And Uyeki and Holland (2000) found that education was negatively associated with their scale of pro-environmental attitudes.

Party Identification and Political Ideology. In the early 1970s, the environment was a relatively nonpartisan issue, and the Republican and Democratic Parties were seen as about equally likely to favor environmental protection (Ogden 1971). During the past 30 years, however, Democrats (and liberals) and Republicans (and conservatives) have been modestly differentiated in at least some environmental beliefs and attitudes (e.g., Kamieniecki 1995). For example, Democrats and liberals have been more likely than Republicans and conservatives to endorse the goals of the environmental movement, to think of themselves as active in or sympathetic toward the movement, and to believe that environmental organizations have done more good than harm (chapter 24 in this volume; Dunlap, Xiao, and McCright 2001). Most studies have found the NEP to be positively associated with liberalism (Dunlap et al. 2000). Party identification and ideology measures have been significant predictors of preferences regarding environmental spending, with Democrats and liberals more likely to support increased spending (Jones and Dunlap 1992), as well as "feeling thermometer" ratings of environmentalists, with Democrats and liberals more likely to say they felt warmly toward environmentalists (Guber 2003, chap. 4).

However, it is important not to exaggerate the magnitude of these partisan and ideological divides: majorities of both Democrats (74 percent) and Republicans (51 percent) reported being either active in or sympathetic to the environmental movement in a March 2010 Gallup poll. Thus, while clear partisan differences over the environment exist, it is not true that a majority of Republican citizens disagrees with the majority of Democratic citizens on this issue (though partisan elites, such as members of Congress, appear to be much more polarized, at least as judged by their voting records; see chapter 13 in this volume). Along these lines, some studies have found that partisan differences on environmental attitudes, even when statistically significant, are small in magnitude compared to ideological differences (Howell and Laska 1992, Jones and Dunlap 1992). Accordingly, Pierce and Lovrich (1980) found that ideology, but *not* party identification, was significantly associated with one's orientation toward a "preservationist" identification versus a "developmentalist" identification. In contrast, Uyeki and Holland (2000) found that party identification, but *not* ideology, was significantly associated with their scale of pro-environmental attitudes, with Democrats being more pro-environmental (see chapter 24 in this volume).

Race and Ethnicity. Whites and blacks have not differed in consistent ways across a broad range of environmental attitudes and beliefs (Mohai 2003), despite several theoretical arguments suggesting that racial differences might be expected in one direction or another (Mohai and Bryant 1998). Jones and Dunlap (1992) reported that race was a poor predictor of support for environmental spending, but when differences existed, nonwhites were more likely than whites to support increased spending. Mitchell (1980) found that blacks were less likely than whites to describe themselves as sympathetic to, or active in, the environmental movement. Mohai and Bryant (1998) found few differences between black and white respondents' ratings of the seriousness of various environmental problems, although whites were more likely to describe depletion of the ozone layer as a "very serious" problem, and blacks were more likely to describe air pollution and water pollution as "very serious." Whittaker, Segura, and Bowler (2005) found that Hispanics were more likely than non-Hispanic whites to support increased state-level spending on environmental regulations and to express concern about protecting the state's environment but were no more likely to describe themselves as environmentalists. Thus, different environmental attitudes have correlated differently with race and ethnicity.

Gender. Scholars have suggested that women should be more pro-environmental than men, owing to more socialization as nurturers (Davidson and Freudenburg 1996), greater perceived vulnerability to risk (Bord and O'Connor 1997), and/or higher levels of altruism (Dietz, Kalof, and Stern 2002). Gender has usually been unrelated to support for increased spending on the environment; when a gender difference has appeared, women have been more likely than men to support increased spending (Jones and Dunlap 1992). Blocker and Eckberg (1989) found that women expressed more concern than men about local environmental problems (e.g., local water or air pollution), but women and men did not differ in their answers to questions about trade-offs, such as agreeing that "we should maintain our efforts to control pollution, even if this slows down the economy and increases unemployment." Mohai (1992) found that women were more likely than men to view six out of six specific environmental problems as serious but were less likely than men to report membership in environmental organizations.

Stern, Dietz, and Kalof (1993) found that women were more willing than men to pay higher income taxes and gasoline prices to accomplish environmental protection. Blocker and Eckberg (1997) reported that women were more pro-environmental than men in their "environmental fears" about, for example, pollution, nuclear power, pesticides, and the greenhouse effect, but these investigators found no gender difference regarding whether government should require people and businesses to protect the environment. Thus, the existence and extent of gender differences in environmental attitudes appear to vary depending on which environmental attitude is being measured.

2.3. Our Investigation

To further investigate the relations of different environmental attitudes with demographics and political variables, we analyzed data from the 1996 American National Election Studies (ANES) survey, which included a rich battery of 10 environmental items. These questions asked about government effort toward environmental protection, reducing air pollution, managing natural resources, cleaning up lakes and parks, cleaning up hazardous or toxic waste, reducing solid waste and garbage, and addressing global warming; federal spending on environmental protection; trade-offs between environmental protection and jobs; and environmental regulation of business.

We estimated the parameters of 10 OLS regression equations gauging the associations of various demographic and political variables with the 10 environmental items above.[6] We found only one consistent pattern across the 10 items: Republicans were significantly less pro-environmental than Independents on 9 out of 10 measures. No other demographic or political variable had a similarly uniform effect across all 10 environmental questions. Liberals were more pro-environmental than moderates according to 5 of the measures, but not according to the other 5. Blacks were more likely than whites to prefer increased government effort on addressing global warming and reducing solid waste, but did not differ on any of the other 8 measures. Most strikingly, women were *more* likely than men to support environmental regulation of business, but *less* likely to support increased spending on the environment. These are all instances confirming Van Liere and Dunlap's (1981, 669) observation that "a composite scale including diverse dimensions of environmental concern might 'mask' the true relationships between the dimensions and, for example, selected demographic variables." Depending on which measure of environmental attitudes a researcher uses, he or she could reach different conclusions about the correlates of pro-environmental attitudes.[7]

---

6. See Table A1 in the online appendix.
7. Reinforcing the same conclusion, factor analyses of the 10 environmental items on the 1996 ANES indicate that they do not appear to measure the same construct. An iterated principal factor analysis with varimax rotation on the unweighted data yielded three distinct factors with eigenvalues greater than 1, plus two additional items that each loaded on their own factors. However, the first three of these factors did not have completely clear and distinct conceptual definitions. Loading on the first factor was support for government effort to protect the environment, to reduce air pollution, and to manage natural resources. Loading on the second factor was support for government effort to clean up lakes and parks, to clean up hazardous waste, and to reduce garbage. Loading on the third factor were support for environmental spending even at the expense of jobs and support for government regulation of business to protect the environment. Support for government spending to protect the environment and for government effort to address global warming did not load on any of the three factors. For this factor structure, a confirmatory factor analysis indicated acceptable fit (CFI = .978, TLI = .965, RMSEA = .055, and SRMR = .024; see Hu and Bentler 1998), whereas models positing fewer factors did not adequately account for the covariances among the indicators.

3. IMPLICATIONS FOR ENVIRONMENTAL POLICY

Scholars of public policy often refer to the policy process model to help understand the dynamics of policy making (Kraft 2011, chap. 3). In brief, the model consists of six stages: *agenda setting*, in which issues are recognized as problems worthy of government attention (Kingdon 1995); *policy formulation*, in which solutions are proposed; *policy legitimation*, in which policy action is authorized by law or other means; *policy implementation*, in which resources are deployed to put programs into effect; *policy evaluation*, in which success is measured relative to objectives and costs; and *policy change*, in which programs are revised or even terminated. In the United States, environmental policy making over time has been highly discontinuous, marked by long periods of stability with occasional bursts of rapid change (Repetto 2006).

The policy-making process emphasizes that the impact of voters' environmental attitudes on governmental action is felt largely, though not entirely, through the politicians they elect. In fact, public opinion on the environment can shape environmental policy in at least three distinct ways. First, citizens' environmental attitudes may influence their votes in elections when candidates are perceived to favor different approaches to environmental policies, sweeping into office those legislators who hold the preferences of the majority of their constituents. Second, officeholders may choose to vote on pieces of environmental legislation in ways that anticipate the likely electoral consequences of voters' environmental attitudes. Third, voters may choose to support or not support statewide ballot propositions focusing on environmental policies. We discuss each of these next.

3.1. Candidate Choice and the Environment

Many scholars have observed that environmental issues have not seemed to substantially impact citizens' voting behavior. For example, Ladd and Bowman (1995, 44) said that "election results seem to suggest that the issue is not a significant one for most voters." Repetto (2006, 3) remarked that "environmental causes seem to have won people's support but not strongly enough to change their buying behaviors or their votes." Correspondingly, Guber (2001b) found that preferences for protecting the environment over protecting jobs had only a minimal association with voter choice in the 1996 presidential election.

However, other studies suggest that different environmental attitudes *have* been important drivers of many election outcomes. Davis and Wurth (2003) studied the 1996 presidential election using the same data and control variables as Guber (2001b) and found that attitudes toward spending on environmental protection were significant predictors of vote choice, advantaging Bill Clinton over Bob Dole. Extending this work, Davis, Wurth, and Lazarus (2008) found that attitudes toward environmental spending were significantly associated with presidential candidate evaluations in every presidential election between 1984 and 2000 and that environmental spending preferences were significantly related to presidential vote choice in 1984, 1988, 1992, and 1996, though not in 2000. In each case, people more supportive of spending to protect the environment were more supportive of the Democratic Party's candidate. Alvarez and Nagler (1998) found that voters were less likely to support presidential candidates in the 1996 election whose views on environmental regulation were distant from their own.

We examined this issue further by gauging the relations between presidential candidate choice and all 10 environmental attitude measures included in the 1996 ANES survey. Candidate choice was operationalized in two different ways: (1) vote choice, reported after the election, and (2) the difference between feeling thermometer ratings of Clinton and Dole, following Davis, Wurth, and Lazarus (2008). In each model specification, we controlled for a standard array of political and demographic covariates.[8]

When all 10 environmental items were considered individually in logistic regressions, more pro-environmental attitudes were positively associated with the likelihood of voting for Clinton over Dole, but only one item reached conventional levels of statistical significance, while two others were marginally significant.[9] When we conducted OLS regressions predicting the difference between Clinton and Dole feeling thermometer ratings, we found stronger and more consistent relations: for 9 of the 10 environmental attitude measures, more pro-environmental attitudes were associated with significantly more support for Clinton, though this was not true for the 10th.[10] Thus, although more pro-environmental stances may have yielded more positive evaluations of Clinton and/or more negative evaluations of Dole, only a few of these attitudes appeared to benefit Clinton in terms of actual votes.

3.2. Dynamic Representation and the Environment

Elected officeholders may adjust public policy in anticipation of the possible electoral consequences of public opinion (Stimson, MacKuen, and Erikson 1995). Even entrenched incumbents might nevertheless feel duty-bound to give some weight to their constituents' opinions (Bartels 1991). Accordingly, Weaver's (2008) cross-

---

8. Our model specifications differ somewhat from those of Guber (2001b) and Davis and Wurth (2003), whose independent variables included not only political and demographic variables but also nonenvironmental issue positions (e.g., defense spending, abortion rights). We omitted this latter group of variables, opting to focus on the estimation of a larger number of political and demographic coefficients, including party identification, ideology, education, income, gender, race, ethnicity, and age. Full details are in the online appendix.
9. See Table A2 in the online appendix.
10. See Table A3 in the online appendix.

national study found that people's willingness to make economic sacrifices for the environment (e.g., by paying higher prices) was often positively associated with measures of environmental governance (e.g., stringency of environmental regulations). Agnone (2007) found that an index of environmental attitudes (consisting mostly of preferences on environmental spending) was positively associated with the number of pro-environmental laws passed by Congress each year. In contrast, however, Olzak and Soule (2009) found that the percentage of the public saying that the environment is the "most important problem" had no significant relation with the number of congressional hearings on the environment or pro-environmental laws passed each year. Clearly, more of this type of work is merited to illuminate how and when public opinion on the environment directs or limits public policy.[11]

3.3. Direct Democracy and the Environment

Ballot propositions on environmental issues present opportunities for the American public to participate directly in the process of creating environmental policy at the state level. Lake (1983, 222) found that California environmental ballot measures between 1970 and 1980 "met with the same or slightly better rates of approval than their non-environmental counterparts." Guber (2003, chap. 7) found that, in elections between 1964 and 2000, 62 percent of legislative referenda and 40 percent of citizen-initiated ballot measures were approved—a success rate at least as strong as that of propositions in general (cf. Magleby 1994, 251). Some scholars have speculated that the success of environmental ballot propositions is a function of the extent of "negative or positive connotations of the wording" (Lutrin and Settle 1975, 371) and the impact of negative advertising that emphasizes their potential economic costs, with success more likely in "simple, inexpensive, and low-key campaigns" (Guber 2001a, 130). In a broader sense, these election outcomes imply that the public is not uniformly "for" or "against" environmental protection. Public attitudes depend on the particular environmental issue in question.

4. CONCLUSION

Three decades ago, Van Liere and Dunlap (1980, 193–194) proposed that researchers should avoid "lumping" together measures of public concern about various types

---

11. Of course, political elites make policy and may also drive public opinion, so any observed congruence between public opinion and policy may be attributable to the influence of elites rather than to the influence of the public.

of environmental damage, noting that "it is unclear whether persons concerned about one of these issues will be equally concerned about the others." We endorse this viewpoint and suggest that it should be applied beyond simply measures of concern. We have reviewed an array of evidence which suggests that scholars should treat each measure as independent, with integrity of its own. Certainly, this conclusion is not one that advocates parsimony, but parsimony at the expense of validity hardly seems to be a worthwhile goal.

Of course, single items have drawbacks of their own, and we would prefer to use multiple indicators—*if* they measured the same construct. Admittedly, we have not proposed multiple indicators in this chapter (but see Carman 1998; Guber 1996; and Xiao and Dunlap 2007). Instead, we have suggested a simple framework for studying Americans' environmental attitudes that can naturally accommodate, for example, evidence suggesting that some environmental items predict presidential vote choice while others do not.

Going forward, we recommend that future survey designers include a wide array of existing measures. Items could be drawn from Table 21.1, to allow for over-time comparison with prior surveys. But another approach would be to borrow items from "America's Report Card on the Environment" (ARCE), a battery of questions designed to tap a range of environmental topics and administered by Stanford University and the Associated Press in national surveys in 2006 and 2007 (Krosnick, Bannon, and DeBell 2007). As Table 21.2 shows, the first questions on the ARCE asked respondents to make current, retrospective, and prospective evaluations of environmental quality. In 2007, 42 percent of respondents rated the current condition of the world environment as very poor or poor. Fifty-three percent of respondents said that, relative to 10 years ago, the environment today is somewhat worse or much worse. And 52 percent of respondents said that 10 years from now, the world environment will be somewhat worse or much worse. Thus, about half of Americans provided negative evaluations of environmental quality.

A second set of questions (again, see Table 21.2) asked respondents to evaluate how the president, Congress, and American businesses were handling environmental issues. In 2007, only 20 percent of respondents approved of President Bush's handling of the environment. Similarly low percentages approved of handling of the environment by Congress (15 percent) and American businesses (22 percent). A third set of questions asked respondents how much they wanted the president, Congress, and American businesses to do to protect the environment. Two-thirds of respondents wanted President Bush to do a "great deal" or "a lot" to help the environment in the coming year. Large majorities of respondents also desired a great deal or a lot of action from Congress (71 percent) and American businesses (72 percent).[12]

---

12. The first survey was conducted by telephone March 9–14, 2006, with a random national sample of 1,002 adults. Sampling and data collection were done by TNS of Horsham, PA. The second survey was conducted by telephone September 21–23, 2007, with a random national sample of 1,001 adults. Sampling and data collection were conducted by Ipsos Public Affairs.

Table 21.2 "America's Report Card on the Environment"

Question	Responses Suggesting Environmental Concern	Year (%)	
		2006	2007
1. How would you rate the condition of the natural environment in the world today? Excellent, good, fair, poor, very poor	Poor or very poor	33	42
2. Compared to 10 or so years ago, do you think the natural environment in the world today is…much better, somewhat better, about the same, somewhat worse, much worse?	Somewhat worse or much worse	60	56
3. Thinking ahead to 10 or so years from now, do you think the natural environment in the world will be…much better, somewhat better, about the same, somewhat worse, much worse?	Somewhat worse or much worse	55	52
4. Thinking about the way President Bush is handling issues involving the natural environment, do you…strongly approve, somewhat approve, neither approve nor disapprove, somewhat disapprove, strongly disapprove?	Somewhat disapprove or strongly disapprove	53	53
5. Thinking about the way American businesses are handling issues involving the natural environment, do you…strongly approve, somewhat approve, neither approve nor disapprove, somewhat disapprove, strongly disapprove?	Somewhat disapprove or strongly disapprove	47	45
6. Thinking about the way the U.S. Congress is handling issues involving the natural environment, do you…strongly approve, somewhat approve, neither approve nor disapprove, somewhat disapprove, strongly disapprove?	Somewhat disapprove or strongly disapprove	53	50
7. During the past year, how much did President Bush's policies do to help the natural environment? A great deal, a lot, a moderate amount, a little, nothing	A little or nothing	66	75

(continued)

Table 21.2 (*Continued*)

Question	Responses Suggesting Environmental Concern	Year (%) 2006	Year (%) 2007
8. During the past year, how much did American businesses do to help the natural environment? A great deal, a lot, a moderate amount, a little, nothing	A little or nothing	54	62
9. During the past year, how much did President Bush's policies do to harm the natural environment? A great deal, a lot, a moderate amount, a little, nothing	A great deal or a lot	28	29
10. During the past year, how much did American businesses do to harm the natural environment? A great deal, a lot, a moderate amount, a little, nothing	A great deal or a lot	29	34
11. During the next year, how much do you want President Bush to do to help the natural environment? A great deal, a lot, a moderate amount, a little, nothing	A great deal or a lot	72	67
12. During the next year, how much do you want the U.S. Congress to do to help the natural environment? A great deal, a lot, a moderate amount, a little, nothing	A great deal or a lot	76	71
13. During the next year, how much do you want American businesses to do to help the natural environment? A great deal, a lot, a moderate amount, a little, nothing	A great deal or a lot	76	72
14. During the next year, how much do you want the American public to do to help the natural environment? A great deal, a lot, a moderate amount, a little, nothing	A great deal or a lot	77	75

In light of our review of past surveys' measures of environmental attitudes and beliefs, it is obvious that the battery of questions in the ARCE could be expanded to cover more content domains, ideally by following principles of optimal questionnaire design (Krosnick and Presser 2010). Possible additions could include the following:

"How important are environmental issues to you personally? Extremely important, very important, moderately important, slightly important, or not important at all?"

"How important is it that the United States works to protect the environment? Extremely important, very important, moderately important,
slightly important, or not important at all?"

"How important is it that other countries around the world work to protect the environment? Extremely important, very important, moderately
important, slightly important, or not important at all?"

"Would you like the federal government to spend more money on protecting
the environment, spend less money on this, or spend about the amount of
money it's spending now for this purpose? A great deal more/less or somewhat more/less?"

"Would you like the federal government/the president/the U.S. Congress to
work harder on protecting the environment, work less hard on protecting
the environment, or work about as hard as he/she/it is now to protect the
environment? A great deal harder/less hard or somewhat harder/less hard?"

"Do you personally favor, oppose, or neither favor nor oppose the federal
government doing things to protect the environment? Do you favor/oppose
this a great deal or a moderate amount?"

"How closely do you pay attention to news stories about the environment?
Extremely closely, very closely, moderately closely, slightly closely, or not at all?"

Measuring a wide array of environmental beliefs and attitudes allows researchers to explore many important questions that presently remain unanswered. What
are the impacts of environmental attitudes on presidential primary elections, congressional elections, state elections, and local elections? Beyond candidate choice,
do voters' environmental attitudes affect their decisions to turn out in the first
place? More specifically, what are the ramifications of *different* environmental attitudes held by the public for environmental policy making? Do the impacts of environmental attitudes on public policy vary depending on how much media attention
is paid to surveys measuring each opinion?

We end with two final recommendations for future research. First, we suggest
avoiding the use of batteries that combine disparate items (e.g., across multiple categories in Table 21.1). The fact that a number of items may all be facially relevant to
environmental concern in general should not be enough to warrant their inclusion
on the same index. Along these lines, researchers should view factor analysis results
cautiously. For example, Mohai (1985) and Mohai and Twight (1987) labeled one of
their scales as measuring "intensity" of "environmental concern." Their measures
of this construct included items asking the respondent to indicate the seriousness of
various problems (e.g., "water pollution") and items asking respondents how much
they agreed with various "prodevelopment" statements (e.g., "economic growth is
more important than protecting the environment"). We believe it does not make
much sense to describe a person who is optimistic about future water quality, yet
eager to make economic sacrifices to prevent water pollution, as having a mediocre
or middling level of environmental concern. The "failure" of this person to show one
type of concern takes nothing away from "successful" exhibition of another type.

Second, taking the multifaceted nature of environmental attitudes seriously requires us to recognize that our ability to generalize individual findings may be limited. We therefore suggest avoiding the interpretation of any single question as broadly indicative of an underlying "generalized environmental concern." Similarly, we recommend using caution in characterizing subgroups as having uniformly "higher" or "lower" level of concern than other subgroups. Given that environmental problems and policies are inherently multidimensional, we should not be surprised that public opinion on the environment is often expressed in complex and heterogeneous ways. Although the "dimensionality debate" is certainly not over, we believe that a focus on single items will accelerate progress toward a better understanding of public opinion on the environment and its potential consequences for public policy.

ACKNOWLEDGMENT

Jon Krosnick is University Fellow at Resources for the Future. This research was supported by a grant from Resources for the Future. The authors thank Shanto Iyengar and Riley Dunlap for very helpful comments, and Ray Kopp for his help and collaboration. David Daniels was supported by a National Science Foundation Graduate Research Fellowship under Grant DGE-0645962. Address correspondence to David Daniels or Jon Krosnick, Department of Political Science, Stanford University, Stanford, CA 94305 (email: ddaniels@stanford.edu or Krosnick@stanford.edu). The online appendix is available at http://comm.stanford.edu/faculty/krosnick/docs/2011/Environmental%20Attitudes%20Lit%20Review%20-%20online%20appendix.pdf.

REFERENCES

Agnone, J. M. 2007. "Amplifying Public Opinion: The Policy Impact of the U.S. Environmental Movement." *Social Forces* 85 (4): 1593–1620.

Alvarez, R. M., and J. Nagler. 1998. "Economics, Entitlements, and Social Values: Voter Choice in the 1996 Presidential Election." *American Journal of Political Science* 42: 1349–1363.

Bartels, L. M. 1991. "Constituency Opinion and Congressional Policy Making: The Reagan Defense Build Up." *American Political Science Review* 85 (2): 457–474.

Blocker, T. J., and D. L. Eckberg. 1989. "Environmental Issues as Women's Issues: General Concerns and Local Hazards." *Social Science Quarterly* 70: 586–593.

———. 1997. "Gender and Environmentalism: Results from the 1993 General Social Survey." *Social Science Quarterly* 78: 841–858.

Bord, R. J., and R. E. O'Connor. 1997. "The Gender Gap in Environmental Attitudes: The Case of Perceived Vulnerability to Risk." *Social Science Quarterly* 78: 830–840.

Bosso, C. J., and D. L. Guber. 2006. "Maintaining Presence: Environmental Advocacy and the Permanent Campaign." In *Environmental Policy: New Directions for the Twenty-First Century*, 6th ed., ed. N. Vig and M. Kraft, 78–99. Washington, DC: CQ Press.

Brulle, R. J. 2010. "Politics and the Environment." In *The Handbook of Politics: State and Civil Society in Global Perspective*, ed. K. Leicht and J. C. Jenkins, 385–406. New York: Springer.

Buttel, F. H., and D. E. Johnson. 1977. "Dimensions of Environmental Concern: Factor Structure, Correlates, and Implications for Research." *Journal of Environmental Education* 9: 49–64.

Carman, C. J. 1998. "Dimensions of Environmental Policy Support in the United States." *Social Science Quarterly* 79 (4): 717–733.

Cluck, R. 1998. "The Multi-Dimensional Basis of Environmental Attitudes." PhD diss., Mississippi State University.

Davidson, D. J., and W. R. Freudenberg. 1996. "Gender and Environmental Risk Concerns: A Review and Analysis of Available Research." *Environment and Behavior* 28: 302–339.

Davis, F. L., and A. H. Wurth. 2003. "Voting Preferences and the Environment in the American Electorate: The Discussion Extended." *Society and Natural Resources* 16 (8): 729–740.

Davis, F. L., A. H. Wurth, and J. C. Lazarus. 2008. "The Green Vote in Presidential Elections: Past Performance and Future Promise." *Social Science Journal* 45 (4): 525–545.

deHaven-Smith, L. 1988. "Environmental Belief Systems: Public Opinion on Land Use Regulation in Florida." *Environment and Behavior* 20: 76–99.

———. 1991. *Environmental Concern in Florida and the Nation*. Gainesville: University of Florida Press.

Diamantopoulos, A., B. B. Schlegelmilch, R. R. Sinkovics, and G. M. Bohlen. 2003. "Can Socio-Demographics Still Play a Role in Profiling Green Consumers? A Review of the Evidence and an Empirical Investigation." *Journal of Business Research* 56 (6): 465–480.

Dietz, T., L. Kalof, and P. C. Stern. 2002. "Gender, Values, and Environmentalism." *Social Science Quarterly* 83 (1): 353–364.

Dunlap, R. E. 1989. "Public Opinion and Environmental Policy." In *Environmental Politics and Policy*, ed. J. P. Lester, 87–134. Durham, NC: Duke University Press.

———. 1991a. "Public Opinion in the 1980s: Clear Consensus, Ambiguous Commitment." *Environment* 33 (8): 10–37.

———. 1991b. "Trends in Public Opinion toward Environmental Issues: 1965–1990." *Society and Natural Resources* 4: 285–312.

———. 1995. "Public Opinion and Environmental Policy." In *Environmental Politics and Policy*, 2nd ed., ed. J. P. Lester, 63–114. Durham, NC: Duke University Press.

———. 2002. "An Enduring Concern: Light Stays Green for Environmental Protection." *Public Perspective* (September/October): 10–14.

Dunlap, R. E., and R. E. Jones. 2002. "Environmental Concern: Conceptual and Measurement Issues." In *Handbook of Environmental Sociology*, ed. R. Dunlap and W. Michelson, 482–524. Westport, CT: Greenwood.

Dunlap, R. E., and K. D. Van Liere. 1978. "The 'New Environmental Paradigm': A Proposed Measuring Instrument and Preliminary Results." *Journal of Environmental Education* 9 (4): 10–19.

Dunlap, R. E., K. D. Van Liere, A. G. Mertig, and R. E. Jones. 2000. "Measuring Endorsement of the New Ecological Paradigm: A Revised NEP Scale." *Journal of Social Issues* 56 (3): 425–442.

Dunlap, R. E., C. Xiao, and A. M. McCright. 2001. "Politics and Environment in America: Partisan and Ideological Cleavages in Public Support for Environmentalism." *Environmental Politics* 10: 23–48.

Elliott, E., J. L. Regens, and B. J. Seldon. 1995. "Exploring Variation in Public Support for Environmental Protection." *Social Science Quarterly* 76 (1): 41–52.

Erskine, H. 1972. "The Polls: Pollution and Its Costs." *Public Opinion Quarterly* 35 (1): 120–135.

Guber, D. L. 1996. "Environmental Concern and the Dimensionality Problem: A New Approach to an Old Predicament." *Social Science Quarterly* 77 (3): 644–662.

———. 2001a. "Environmental Voting in the American States: A Tale of Two Initiatives." *State and Local Government Review* 33 (2): 120–132.

———. 2001b. "Voting Preferences and the Environment in the American Electorate." *Society and Natural Resources* 14: 455–469.

———. 2003. *The Grassroots of a Green Revolution: Polling America on the Environment.* Cambridge, MA: MIT Press.

Hays, S. P. 1987. *Beauty, Health, and Permanence: Environmental Politics in the United States, 1955–1985.* Cambridge: Cambridge University Press.

Howell, S. E., and S. B. Laska. 1992. "The Changing Face of the Environmental Coalition: A Research Note." *Environment and Behavior* 24: 134–144.

Hu, L., and P. M. Bentler. 1998. "Fit Indices in Covariance Structure Modeling: Sensitivity To Underparameterized Model Misspecification." *Psychological Methods* 3 (4): 424–453.

Johnson, M., P. Brace, and K. Arceneaux. 2005. "Public Opinion and Dynamic Representation in the American States: The Case of Environmental Attitudes." *Social Science Quarterly* 86 (1): 87–108.

Jones, R. E., and R. E. Dunlap. 1992. "The Social Bases of Environmental Concern: Have They Changed over Time?" *Rural Sociology* 57 (1): 28–47.

Kamieniecki, S. 1995. "Political Parties and Environmental Policy." In *Environmental Politics and Policy*, 2nd ed., ed. J. P. Lester, 146–167. Durham, NC: Duke University Press.

Kanagy, C. L., C. R. Humphrey, and G. Firebaugh. 1994. "Surging Environmentalism: Changing Public Opinion or Changing Publics?" *Social Science Quarterly* 75 (4): 804–819.

Kingdon, J. W. 1995. *Agendas, Alternatives, and Public Policies.* 2nd ed. New York: HarperCollins.

Klineberg, S. L., M. McKeever, and B. Rothenbach. 1998. "Demographic Predictors of Environmental Concern: It Does Make a Difference How It's Measured." *Social Science Quarterly* 79: 734–753.

Kraft, M. E. 2011. *Environmental Policy and Politics.* 5th ed. Boston: Longman.

Krosnick, J. A., B. Bannon, and M. DeBell. 2007. "The Second Annual 'America's Report Card on the Environment' Survey." Release by the Woods Institute for the Environment at Stanford University. Available at http://woods.stanford.edu/docs/surveys/Global-Warming-200709-AP-survey.pdf.

Krosnick, J. A., and S. Presser. 2010. "Questionnaire Design." In *Handbook of Survey Research*, 2nd ed., ed. J. D. Wright and P. V. Marsden. West Yorkshire, UK: Emerald Group.

Ladd, E. C., and K. H. Bowman. 1995. *Attitudes toward the Environment: Twenty-Five Years after Earth Day.* American Enterprise Institute for Public Policy Research. Washington, DC: AEI Press.

Lake, L, M. 1983. "The Environmental Mandate: Activists and the Electorate." *Political Science Quarterly* 98 (2): 215–233.

Leiserowitz, A. A., R. W. Kates, and T. M. Parris. 2006. "Sustainability Values, Attitudes, and Behaviors: A Review of Multinational and Global Trends." *Annual Review of Environment and Resources* 31: 413–444.

Lutrin, C. E., and A. K. Settle. 1975. "The Public and Ecology: The Role of Initiatives in California's Environmental Politics." *Western Political Quarterly* 28 (2): 352–371.

Magleby, D. B. 1994. "Direct Legislation in the American States." In *Referendums around the World: The Growing Use of Direct Democracy*, ed. D. Butler and A. Ranney, 218–257. Washington, DC: AEI Press.

Mitchell, R. C. 1980. "Public Opinion on Environmental Issues: Results of a National Public Opinion Survey." In *Environmental Quality*, 401–425. Washington, DC: Council on Environmental Quality.

——. 1984. "Public Opinion and Environmental Politics in the 1970s and 1980s." In *Environmental Policy in the 1980s*, ed. N. Vig and M. Kraft, 51–74. Washington, DC: CQ Press.

Mohai, P. 1985. "Public Concern and Elite Involvement in Environmental-Conservation Issues." *Social Science Quarterly* 66 (4): 820–838.

——. 1992. "Men, Women, and the Environment: An Examination of the Gender Gap in Environmental Concern and Activism." *Society and Natural Resources* 5 (1): 1–19.

——. 2003. "Dispelling Old Myths: African American Concern for the Environment." *Environment* 45: 18.

Mohai, P., and B. Bryant. 1998. "Is There a 'Race' Effect on Concern for Environmental Quality?" *Public Opinion Quarterly* 62 (4): 475–505.

Mohai, P., and Ben W. Twight. 1987. "Age and Environmentalism: An Elaboration of the Buttel Model Using National Survey Evidence." *Social Science Quarterly* 68: 798–815.

Ogden, D. M. 1971. "The Future of Environmental Struggle." In *The Politics of Neglect: The Environmental Crisis*, ed. R. Meek and J. Straayer. Boston: Houghton Mifflin.

Olzak, S., and S. A. Soule. 2009. "Cross-Cutting Influences of Environmental Protest and Legislation." *Social Forces* 88 (1): 201–225.

Pierce, J. C., and N. P. Lovrich Jr. 1980. "Belief Systems Concerning the Environment: The General Public, Attentive Publics, and State Legislators." *Political Behavior* 2 (3): 259–286.

Repetto, R. 2006. Introduction to *Punctuated Equilibrium and the Dynamics of U.S. Environmental Policy*, ed. R. Repetto, 1–23. New Haven, CT: Yale University Press.

Samdahl, D. M., and R. Robertson. 1989. "Social Determinants of Environmental Concern." *Environment and Behavior* 21 (1): 57–81.

Stern, P. C., T. Dietz, and L. Kalof. 1993. "Value Orientations, Gender, and Environmental Concern." *Environment and Behavior* 25 (3): 322–348.

Stimson, J. A., M. B. Mackuen, and R. S. Erikson. 1995. "Dynamic Representation." *American Political Science Review* 89 (3): 543–565.

Uyeki, E. S., and L. J. Holland. 2000. "Diffusion of Proenvironment Attitudes?" *American Behavioral Scientist* 43: 646–662.

Van Liere, K. D., and R. E. Dunlap. 1980. "The Social Bases of Environmental
    Concern: A Review of Hypotheses, Explanations and Empirical Evidence." *Public
    Opinion Quarterly* 44: 181–199.
———. 1981. "Environmental Concern: Does It Make a Difference How It's
    Measured?" *Environment and Behavior* 13 (6): 651.
Walsh, B. 2008. "Despite the Economy, Obama Vows to Press Green Agenda." *Time*,
    November 19. Available at www.time.com/time/health/article/0,8599,1860431,00.
    html.
Weaver, A. A. 2008. "Does Protest Behavior Mediate the Effects of Public Opinion
    on National Environmental Policies?" *International Journal of Sociology* 38 (3):
    108–125.
Whittaker, M., G. M. Segura, and S. Bowler. 2005. "Racial/Ethnic Group Attitudes
    toward Environmental Protection in California: Is 'Environmentalism' Still a
    White Phenomenon?" *Political Research Quarterly* 58 (3): 435–447.
Wlezien, C. 1995. "The Public as Thermostat: Dynamics of Preferences for
    Spending." *American Journal of Political Science* 39 (4): 981–1000.
Xiao, C., and R. E. Dunlap, 2007. "Validating a Comprehensive Model of
    Environmental Concern Cross-Nationally: A U.S.-Canadian Comparison." *Social
    Science Quarterly* 88 (2): 71–93.
Yeager, D. S., S. B. Larson, J. A. Krosnick, and T. Tompson. 2011. "Measuring
    Americans' Issue Priorities: A New Version of the Most Important Problem
    Question Reveals More Concern about Global Warming and the Environment."
    Public Opinion Quarterly 75 (1): 125–138.

CHAPTER 22

PUBLIC PARTICIPATION, CITIZEN ENGAGEMENT, AND ENVIRONMENTAL DECISION MAKING

DOROTHY M. DALEY

PUBLIC participation is a basic tenet of American democracy. It is widely viewed as a necessary component of decision making at all levels of government. There is, however, less agreement regarding the appropriate form and extent of public involvement in decision making. Public participation or civic engagement includes a variety of activities. For example, voting, letter writing, attending public meetings, becoming involved in collaborative decision making processes, sitting on a community advisory board, or even using legal mechanisms to challenge government decisions are all forms of public participation. While overall levels of civic engagement in the United States have declined in the last two to three decades (Macedo et al. 2005; Putnam 2000), opportunities for public participation have increased substantially (ACIR 1979; Beierle and Cayford 2002; Dietz et al. 2008).

In environmental and natural resource policy, most major pieces of legislation mandate some form of public participation. And in recent years, environmental and natural resource agencies have gone beyond legislatively mandated public participation provisions to engage citizens actively in novel and creative ways. As opportunities for civic engagement in environmental decision making have increased, so, too, has scholarship examining the nature and consequences of increased public participation.

In keeping with the editorial charge, this chapter takes stock of the scholarly literature that explores civic engagement and environmental decision making in American politics. This is a tremendously broad literature that ranges from philosophical arguments on the nature and scope of participation to theoretically grounded social science research evaluating the ways in which participation changes decision processes and outcomes. This chapter reviews this expansive literature, assesses its strengths and weaknesses, identifies broad areas of agreement and divergence, and pinpoints knowledge gaps that future research should address. Specifically, this chapter examines the background and history of public participation and environmental policy, emphasizing the tension between scientifically informed decision making, democratic ideals, and broad changes in environmental policy. This study also outlines the arguments for and against widespread participation in environmental decision making. It explores the notion of what constitutes a community and the challenges inherent in identifying and defining "the public" in a decentralized political system. In addition, the study describes and assesses different decision-making approaches that utilize public participation, ranging from traditional public hearings and comments to more involved collaborative decision processes. Finally, the chapter includes a discussion of the ways in which public participation influences environmental decision making and suggests areas of inquiry for future research.

1. Background and History

Public participation in environmental and natural resource decision making is, in part, a response to Progressive Era reforms of administrative structure (Beierle and Cayford 2002). In the late nineteenth and early twentieth centuries, these reforms professionalized American civil service, insulating bureaucrats from the vagaries of politics and corruption. With political pressure at bay, reformers believed civil servants could make efficient decisions advancing the greater good and relying on the best scientific and technological knowledge to solve public problems (Brehm and Gates 1997; Fine and Owen 2005; Irvin and Stansbury 2004). While these reforms separated politics and professional administration within government, they also created barriers between citizens and bureaucrats. Avenues for citizen input were limited to the ballot box, and although the Administrative Procedure Act of 1946 established general provisions increasing participation in government decision making, professional discretion within administrative settings was emphasized (Bingham, Nabatchi, and O'Leary 2005; Cooper, Bryer, and Meek 2006; Dietz et al. 2008; Fine and Owen 2005).

Administrative discretion, however, can conflict with democratic ideals of accountability and transparency, particularly when addressing environmental and natural resources issues that are technically complex and value laden. As environmental and natural resource policy has evolved and grown, there has been considerable tension between technical expertise and democratic ideals advancing citizen engagement (Dietz et al., 2008; Dryzek 2005; Fine and Owen 2005; Irvin and Stansbury 2004). Indeed, this tension is codified in most major environmental legislation. For example, the National Environmental Policy Act, the Clean Air Act, the Endangered Species Act, and the Clean Water Act all emphasize scientific decision making while requiring some form of public participation. Administrators are directed to base regulatory standards on best available scientific and technical evidence, as well as to provide affected stakeholders opportunities to engage in planning and decision-making processes (Dietz et al. 2008; Fine and Owen 2005). In theory, these approaches do not have to come into conflict; in practice, however, research suggests conflict, dissatisfaction, and gridlock have been all too common across a range of environmental and natural resource decision making (Innes and Booher 2004; Reed 2008).

This interplay between technical expertise and public participation in environmental and natural resource decision making reflects Americans' faith in general scientific and technological approaches, as well as an abiding distrust of government institutions. Most environmental problems are technically complex, value-laden, and difficult and costly to address. When the majority of federal environmental legislation was passed in the late 1960s and 1970s, Congress was optimistic that scientific information could unlock the keys to solve environmental problems. In addition, legislators assumed we could improve air and water quality and reduce hazardous and solid waste contamination with limited costs and in a timely fashion (Fine and Owen 2005; Lazarus 1991). Despite this optimism, legislatively mandated forms of public participation provide an additional "check" to ensure that agencies are responsive to local concerns. Public notice and comment processes, public hearings, citizens' right to sue, and negotiated rule making can institutionalize responsiveness to the general public within environmental and natural resource agencies. Granting citizens the right to file suit in many environmental situations has fostered increased collaborative decision making early in the planning process as a means to sidestep costly litigation (Fine and Owen 2005). However, federal and state agencies have not uniformly embraced early and increased collaborative planning; for example, state environmental agencies vary considerably in how they incorporate public participation in the creation of their State Implementation Plans necessary under the Clean Air Act. The complex technical modeling needed to identify air quality improvements often constricts the public's ability to contribute to planning decisions (Fine and Owen 2005).

Widespread devolution of implementation authority to state and local governments directly influences public participation and environmental decision making. Devolution of authority to subnational governments should—in practice—ease burdens on participation. State and local governments may be more accessible to the general public, and this accessibility could increase both the level and the impact of participatory activity (Macedo et al. 2005). In other words, subnational governments may be more equipped to respond to its citizens' demands. Ironically, the early literature on devolution and environmental decision making theorized that state environmental agencies would be unable to resist bureaucratic capture and that state regulators would become subservient to industrial interests. More recent scholarship suggests that states have adequate capacity to balance competing interests. In fact, some state and local governments have been more successful than the federal government in tackling environmental challenges like climate change—a transboundary issue usually best addressed by national governments (Rabe 2004, 2010). While the literature suggests that subnational governments are more accessible and that public demands may be more easily translated into decision making, empirical research is needed to compare and contrast public participation at different levels of decision making. There are, however, considerable difficulties in constructing a research design to evaluate the relationships between devolution, public participation, and environmental decision making. Part of this challenge stems from the diversity of 50 different state governments and thousands of local governments within the states. It would take considerable resources to identify comparable participatory activity at all levels of government in as many settings as possible and to track these cases over time to distinguish the influence of devolution on participation.

Finally, the growing interest in nonregulatory decision making, including incentive-based programs, may involve increased opportunity for public participation. The interest in nonregulatory approaches underscores a growing emphasis on efficiency in government decision making. In environmental and natural resource policy, this shift has roughly coincided with a transition to "New Public Administration," which encourages the use of corporate strategies in the public sector. Environmental decision makers are not only considering the use of incentive-based programs to achieve environmental improvements; they are also increasingly emphasizing performance management within the civil sector (Cooper et al. 2006). This managerial approach can include increased stakeholder participation as agencies aim to achieve environmental goals at reduced costs while balancing "client" satisfaction. Environmental and natural resource agencies are keenly aware that they have multiple "clients," including the general public (Ansell and Gash 2008; Irvin and Stansbury 2004; Rosenbaum 2010).

2. Environmental Protection, Democracy, and Public Participation

The relationship between public participation and scientific and technical decision making has changed over time. As the complexity and challenge of addressing environmental issues comes into sharper focus, there has been a consistent effort to insert more public values into technical aspects of environmental decision making. Much of the scholarship advocating a better balance between technical decision making and public participation rests on normative arguments rooted in democratic principles. Environmental decisions must be informed by solid scientific information. However, these decisions cannot rest solely on scientific and technical expertise. Environmental policy reflects value preferences regarding the nature and distribution of environmental risks, costs, and benefits (Coenen, Huitema, and O'Toole 1998; Dietz et al. 2008; Weber 2003).

A democratic society should reflect the will of the public, and widespread public participation in decision making is one consistent mechanism to ensure an accurate reflection of public preferences. While this broad argument underpins much of the normative scholarship on public participation and environmental decision making, there is no single or dominant theoretical focus (Dietz et al. 2008). Conceptual issues of advancing equality, self-governance, and civic capacity are consistent themes used to advocate public participation as a general principle (Coenen, Huitema, and O'Toole 1998; Dietz 2008; Macedo et al. 2005; Reed 2008; Sirianni 2009).

Not all arguments for increased participation rest on ideals of democratic self-governance. From a practical standpoint, the general public in an affected community is likely to have specific contextual information about the nature of the problem, as well as insight into local norms and behavior that could be invaluable in tailoring policy implementation to favor success (Becker and Ostrom 1995; Dietz et al. 2008; Ostrom 2007).

Ultimately, increased participation is heralded as a mechanism that can (1) empower citizens, increase equity, and advance education by providing information; (2) resolve conflict and gridlock; (3) avoid legal battles; (4) improve overall legitimacy and support for decisions; and, finally, (5) increase the quality of decisions, a point that I will return to later in this chapter (Bulkeley and Mol 2003; Dryzek 2005; Dietz et al. 2008; Irvin and Stansbury 2004; Reed 2008). This is a daunting list of potential accomplishments, and—as with many aspects of environmental politics—the devil is in the details. A recent National Research Council report on public participation and environmental decision making (Dietz et al. 2008) suggests that participation can deliver on many, if not all, of these challenges, but *only* when it is done well.

Successful participatory mechanisms tend to have a clear purpose, institutional commitment, and adequate financial and human capital; to integrate the timing of participatory activities and decision-making processes; to ensure the ability of participation to effect change; and to emphasize implementation and evaluation (Beierle and Cayford 2002; Charnley and Engelbert 2005; Chase et al. 2004; Dalton 2005; Dietz et al. 2008; Leach 2006; Reed 2008; Sirianni 2009; Tuler and Webler 2010). This is a nontrivial list of characteristics that can be difficult to achieve, particularly when governments are facing resource constraints. Some scholars suggest that dramatic institutional changes are necessary to adequately incorporate all stakeholders, including the public, in environmental decision making (Weber 2003; Booher and Innes 2010). Others contend that advancing the practice of deliberative democracy is needed to improve the balance between technical expertise and public preferences (Meadowcroft 2004). Thoughtful deliberation and the meaningful exchange of ideas throughout a decision-making process enhances the overall value of a decision and the civic and intellectual capacity of a citizenry (Dietz et al. 2008; Dryzek 2005; Meadowcroft 2004).

Opponents to increased public participation in environmental decision making suggest that extensive civic engagement in environmental policy may do more
harm than good. This argument stems from a rational/economic perspective; the
costs of widespread deliberative democracy in decision making are likely to outweigh the benefits of participation (Coglianese 1997; Sunstein 2006). There are several components to this argument. The most basic aspect of opposition to more
public participation stems from a healthy respect for the transaction costs associated with a diverse public (Bingham, Nabatchi, and O'Leary 2005). As diversity
across the country increases, understanding and balancing competing demands in
the decision-making process will become more and more challenging.

The complex nature of environmental problems can also hinder effective public
engagement (Fine and Owens 2005). Considerable investment on the part of the public is necessary to understand the scientific and technical components of environmental decision making. While the public need not become experts, it is likely that
some education will be important. If this commitment is lacking, then the implicit
consequence is haphazard or even poor-quality decisions (Alberts 2007; Arvai and
Froschauer 2010). In one sense, this argument is a counterpoint to the notion that
when done well, public participation adds considerable value to the decision-making
process. Critics suggest that many of our standard participatory mechanisms do not
come close to satisfying the definition of "successful"—meaning participation that
has a clear purpose; an institutional commitment; adequate financial and human
capital; the ability to change decision making; and a focus on implementation and
evaluation. As a result, standard participatory processes add time, cost, and conflict
to any situation, possibly increasing rather than reducing overall polarization and
putting viable solutions out of reach (Innes and Booher 2004).

While opportunities for public participation in environmental decision making have increased, the overall uptake of these decision strategies remains uneven
(Carmin, Darnall, and Mil-Homens 2003; Coglianese 2006). More participatory
opportunities do not necessarily equate with increased levels of participation.
The literature seems to reflect an "all or nothing" approach to public participation; broad public representation in all stages of decision making is critical, or
such widespread participation is not feasible and it will render our institutions
ineffective in practice. Comparatively, there is less emphasis on trying to discern
when an agency needs to engage in participatory approaches to decision making
and when delegation is an effective approach to environmental problem solving.
Research is needed to characterize what types of decisions will benefit from public deliberation and also to identify the optimal mix of participatory strategies
needed to address environmental problems efficiently. Case study research indicates that the costs and challenges of participation increase significantly when
(1) the spatial scale of the problem is large; (2) low-income residents are affected
by the situation, but there are considerable barriers for their participation;
(3) the community is diverse; (4) complex technical information is required; and
(5) there are competing views on the nature and definition of the problem (Irvin
and Stansbury 2004).

Interestingly, these are also the characteristics that elicit normative arguments for increased participation. More research is needed to advance our general understanding of how and when an agency should delegate versus engage participatory mechanisms. While the quantity and quality of scholarship exploring public participation and environmental decision making has increased over time, its generalizability has been limited (Dietz et al. 2008). As the field advances, it should benefit from creative research designs that identify an appropriate counterfactual. Some of the case study research in this area relies on a counterfactual to characterize important relationships. However, the majority of the work exploring public participation and decision making has relied on stand-alone case studies with no clear comparison or control group. While this provides fertile ground for inductive research and theory building, it limits our ability to draw inferences from the research. Without a solid research design, scholarship in this field can provide only limited guidance as to the optimal mix of decision-making tools.

Finally, many agree that while participation can facilitate equality and improve enfranchisement in a decision-making process, representation in participatory activities is a persistent challenge (Macedo et al. 2005). Often, participatory processes reflect systemic disparities in society; well-educated and wealthy individuals are more likely to engage, regardless of the participatory outlet (Dietz et al. 2008; Macedo et al. 2005). This trend may be exacerbated in highly decentralized systems where some local communities are more likely to mobilize and exert influence in the decision-making process than other communities. In the American context, siting decisions for power plants, manufacturing facilities, landfills, or any "locally unwanted land use" (LULU) often elicits a "Not in My Backyard" (NIMBY) response. One community may be able to block siting successfully, and this can create pressure on other communities that cannot, or do not, engage in participatory activities. Because low-income and minority communities with lower educational attainment have historically mobilized less than wealthy, white, and highly educated communities, equity and distribution of environmental risks and benefits has become a prominent area of inquiry in environmental politics (Brulle and Pellow 2006; Noonan 2008; Ringquist 2005). In the American context, NIMBY reactions can exacerbate the distribution of environmental risks across low-income and minority communities (Foreman 1998; Munton 1996).

3. COMMUNITIES AND ENVIRONMENTAL PROTECTION—IDENTIFYING STAKEHOLDERS

On the one hand, it seems like a relatively straightforward task to identify who will be affected by an environmental problem or policy. In practice, however, it remains challenging. Environmental problems operate on multiple temporal and spatial scales. To add to the complexity, these spatial and temporal scales do not usually coincide with political boundaries and planning horizons. When environmental problems have large spatial scales and long temporal scales, it is more difficult to identify "the affected community" (Dietz et al. 2008). As the scale increases, the sheer number and diversity of stakeholders also increase. Participants with dramatically differing values and goals challenge the participatory process (Sabatier et al. 2005); while there can be considerable benefit to additional perspectives, it can also create conflict and gridlock in decision making (Dietz et al. 2008). The view that participatory mechanisms can insert "public values" begs the question: which public? As noted above, participatory processes can—and sometimes do—reinforce existing social and political disparities.

Often, for environmental issues, the regulated private sector is well resourced, well organized, and motivated to influence decision making. Environmental interest groups tend to be well organized and motivated to participate in decision making, but with fewer financial resources these groups cannot afford to become involved in every major environmental decision. Even when environmental groups participate in decision making, it remains unclear when an interest group represents "the community." When citizens participate—in the absence of a group affiliation—it is a challenge to determine the extent to which these citizens represent broader community interest (Irvin and Stansbury 2004). Research suggests that individuals try to influence or change environmental decision making to achieve their goals (Dietz et al. 2008; Lubell et al. 2005). These are individuals that are motivated enough to overcome a collective action dilemma and dedicate time and energy in some sort of participatory activity. It is not at all clear if or when the goals of motivated individuals who participate reflect broader community interests and align to provide collective benefits.

The nebulous concept of "community" is an additional challenge facing administrators and researchers who work in this area. Community is a widely used term, yet there is considerable variation in how administrators and researchers measure or operationalize community. Diversity and complexity of community measurements are likely to increase as technology increases connectivity between individuals: are communities defined solely by geography, or is it appropriate to employ a more complex notion of a social network?

While this critique aimed at the measurement validity of different ways to operationalize community may seem to be purely methodological, it also has practical implications. As environmental and natural resource agencies utilize more intensive participatory mechanisms to improve the balance of technical expertise and lay knowledge, it will be important to have clear definitions regarding the scope of the community of concern. Some argue that communities should have a central role in defining environmental problems and setting the agenda (Landy, Roberts, and Thomas 1994), and this argument has been institutionalized in certain areas of environmental decision making. The Environmental Protection Agency promotes the notion of "accountable devolution" (Sirianni 2009) or working with local stakeholders to improve environmental protection. For example, the

EPA's Community Action for a Renewed Environment (CARE) is a competitive grants program designed to empower local communities to address environmental health priorities as defined by the community. This flexible approach to empowering communities has been largely viewed as successful (Hansell, Hollander, and John 2009; Sirianni 2009). However, given the broader theme in the literature suggesting that participation often reproduces existing disparities, the success of these local, grassroots initiatives is likely to hinge on the ability of limited activists to represent accurately a broader cross-section of the community.

When pieced together, the literature paints a rather dismal picture: participation is critically important to instill public values into environmental decision making. Yet, overall levels of civic engagement and participation are declining (Macedo et al. 2005), and patterns of participation tend to re-create existing cleavages in society, leading to concerns that persistently disadvantaged stakeholders and communities will remain external to decision making. There are, of course, exceptions to this pattern, many of which are documented in the environmental justice literature discussed in the introductory chapter. Eliminating or reducing barriers to participation remains a critical task, as is ensuring diversity of representation.

4. Models of Decision Making: Traditional, Collaborative, and Consensus-Based Participatory Approaches

Traditional models of environmental decision making tend to be regulatory in nature. A legislative branch crafts and passes environmental law addressing a particular problem, such as air or water quality degradation. Implementation is delegated to an agency, which must translate legislative intent into detailed regulatory decisions. The type of compromise needed to build a legislative coalition and the complex technical aspects of environmental problems often contribute to considerable administrative discretion as agencies work to determine how exactly the implementation process can be structured to achieve legislative goals. While the interest in nonregulatory approaches to environmental problems may limit the sheer volume of regulatory decisions needed, incentive-based policies, such as tradable permits in the 1990 Clean Air Act Amendments, still require considerable regulatory guidance.

Federal and state environmental agencies utilize several standard public participation approaches during the process of setting standards, drafting specific language to provide guidance in meeting those standards in diverse economic settings, and articulating enforcement and compliance provisions. Public notice and written comment periods, public hearings, and negotiated rule making are widely used as this regulatory process unfolds. These participatory mechanisms are based on limited communication and contact between administrators and the affected public. More often than not, administrators have already made a set of fundamental decisions regarding the nature of a problem and an appropriate solution (Innes and Booher 2004); participation serves to appraise the public about the internal decision making within an agency. This approach to public participation and environmental decision making does not emphasize the public's ability to affect change in the government's decision, and it can create an adversarial relationship between the agency personnel and the public.

In the last 20 years, environmental and natural resource agencies have made considerable efforts to expand opportunities for citizen engagement (Daley 2007, 2008; Dietz et al. 2008; Sabatier et al. 2005). In addition to holding public hearings on environmental and natural resource issues and relying on negotiated rule making, agencies have been actively stimulating the formation of Community Advisory Boards (CABs) and relying on these boards to contribute to both environmental assessment and decision making. Agencies have also invested resources in advancing technical expertise within a community by providing direct grants to community organizations (Daley 2007; Sirianni 2009).

These public participation mechanisms represent a shift in approach from simple communication between administrators and the affected public to a nuanced relationship engaging the public in the decision-making process. Advisory boards have been widely used to help facilitate decision making at hazardous waste sites by the EPA and the military sector as well. In the Superfund program, the EPA has created community outreach offices in each of the agency's 10 regional offices. And outreach staff facilitate the formation of CABs at hazardous waste sites to ensure that the public is represented in decision making. The Department of Defense has fostered the creation of Restoration Advisory Boards (RABs) to advance decision making under the Base Realignment and Closure Commission (BRAC) and other military sites that are contaminated (Laurian 2007). Ideally, CABs and RABs are small groups of diverse stakeholders that reside near a contaminated site. Because addressing hazardous waste contamination can take a decade or more, CABs and RABs commit to meet for an extended period of time to advise the government on decision making for the site. The EPA, the Department of Defense, and the Department of Energy, the main agencies that rely on CABs and RABs, often provide direct support in terms of advancing technical capacity. Technical assistance grants may be available to help ensure that participants have an adequate understanding of the nature of the contamination and potential trade-offs in different decision-making strategies.

This nuanced approach to participation and decision making has the capacity to be successful. CABs and RABs are usually dedicated to a specific geographic area—a hazardous waste site—and have the distinct overarching purpose of cleaning up a contaminated property. If CABs and RABs are formed early in the decision-making process, then they may have the ability to affect decision making.

The provision of financial resources to advance technical capacity can go a long way toward empowering the participants to contribute meaningfully to the process. The extended timeline can also be beneficial. If a CAB or RAB does not experience too much attrition in membership, then there is time to develop trust among stakeholders and trust between stakeholders and the agency decision makers. Trust among participants in a decision-making process can reduce overall conflict and gridlock (Lubell et al. 2005). Despite their promise, CABs and RABs can be one-way risk communication disguised as a conciliatory decision-making process (Laurian 2007). More research is needed to understand the extent of stakeholder diversity on these boards, along with understanding when they are genuinely used to engage the public as opposed to simply being the recipients of one-way agency communication.

Compared to traditional participatory mechanisms, advisory boards have more of the characteristics that are affiliated with the promise of public participation and environmental decision making (Dietz et al. 2008). Collaborative decision-making approaches that emerged from watershed partnerships in the 1990s are also promising. Collaborative decision making entails a diverse set of government and nongovernment actors focused on the spatial, as opposed to political, boundaries of an environmental problem, most often a watershed. They tend to emphasize broad engagement of stakeholders including the public, businesses or regulated entities, researchers, and multiple local, state, and federal government agencies. These stakeholder networks could be formalized arrangements that focus on conflict resolution or decision making, or they could be an informal partnership engaged in consensus-based decision making, voluntary implementation of decisions, and a broader eye toward adaptive management within a watershed (Sabatier et al. 2005). This type of collaborative decision making rejects the typical single-agency approach that "stovepipes" water management while neglecting the complex connections between critical areas contributing to water supply or quality issues, such as agriculture, flood control, species management, and urban growth. Collaborative approaches to environmental decision making are predicated on a process that allows competing demands to be explicitly evaluated. While grassroots collaborative approaches have taken root in watershed planning, other areas of environmental decision making are experimenting with collaborative approaches to expand the public's role in technical decision making. Mediated modeling, a structured process that enables diverse stakeholders to engage in systems-based modeling to understand better air quality decision making, has been used in some urban areas to advance technical expertise in stakeholder communities (Thompson et al. 2010).

Finally, in addition to collaborative decision-making mechanisms, there are also collaborative research mechanisms that engage the public. Community-based participatory research (CBPR) has an established history in public health, and it is becoming prominent in environmental assessment and decision making (Israel et al. 2010). CBPR is an intensive collaborative effort that engages the community in the research process. It is distinct from community-based research that emphasizes conducting research in a particular location but does not actively engage community residents as part of the research team. CBPR as a method is rooted in critical theory and constructivism, which both suggest that researchers should not discount public knowledge (Israel et al. 1998). Core principles of this approach resemble the characteristics of successful public participation articulated by Dietz et al. (2008): CBPR is based on a collaborative relationship where community members and researchers are equal partners in assessing the problem, formulating the research questions, data collection and analysis, and dissemination of results. Ultimately, the goal is to forge a win-win relationship where all participants directly benefit from the applied nature of the research endeavor (Israel et al. 1998).

While CBPR has not been as widely used in environmental research and decision making, it is becoming prominent, and federal funding agents are committed to advancing these partnerships (O'Fallon and Dearry 2002; O'Fallon et al. 2003). The National Institute for Environmental Health Sciences is an avid proponent of community-university partnerships to produce grounded knowledge advancing decision making. Many of these partnerships have developed around issues of environmental justice and health disparities.[1]

5. Public Participation and Environmental Outcomes

Proponents of increased public participation contend that it has democratic and substantive benefits. When done well, public participation in environmental decision making can improve both the decision-making process and its outcomes. It has the ability to advance democratic ideals by empowering citizens and expanding overall intellectual capacity within a citizenry. Public participation legitimizes environmental decisions and can increase or solidify trust among participants. In doing so, participation can avoid or resolve entrenched conflict between stakeholders (Dietz et al. 2008; Irvin and Stansbury 2004; Reed 2008). And, finally, when public participation is done well, it can improve the overall quality of public environmental decision making (Bulkeley and Mol 2003; Dryzek 2005; Dietz et al. 2008; Irvin and Stansbury 2004; Reed 2008).

There is considerable variation in how research measures the quality of an environmental decision. Environmental decisions have multiple dimensions, and often researchers explore the impact of environmental decisions on social and political outcomes while wrestling with how best to understand the impact of participation on environmental quality. Typically, when researchers suggest that participation improves environmental decision making, they are actually contending

---

1. See http://www.niehs.nih.gov/research/supported/programs/justice/index.cfm for a list of externally funded CBPR projects.

that participants are more satisfied with decision-making processes and outcomes. While improved participant satisfaction could be important elements of social and political outcomes, such as improved trust and social capital, increased partici- pant satisfaction does not necessarily translate into an improved environmental outcome. In fact, some argue that increased participant satisfaction is a flawed measure of social welfare; patterns of representation in participatory activities are skewed, suggesting relying on participant satisfaction will result in considerable bias (Coglianese 2003).

The relationship between decision-making processes, including the participa- tory process, and environmental outcomes has been far more challenging to under- stand. The diverse nature of factors that shape changes in air or water quality, for example, make it exceedingly difficult to determine whether decisions stem- ming from the participatory processes translate into environmental improvements (Koontz and Thomas 2006). Several factors contribute to this challenge. First, the lag effect between policy and environmental change is considerable. It can take up to a decade to implement a policy change, and this, combined with the longer time horizons inherent in environmental processes, suggests that discerning the signal between a decision process and environmental change will remain difficult. Second, controlling for important additional causal variables in a complex and dynamic system is difficult. Political decisions are not the only factor contributing to environmental change. Therefore, the research design hurdles and data collec- tion challenges are nontrivial (Koontz and Thomas 2006).

While direct measures of change in environmental quality stemming from participatory activities would be ideal, they are likely to remain elusive. Instead, researchers rely on measures of agreement among stakeholders and overall levels of satisfaction. Bierele and Cayford (2002) advance the field considerably by aggre- gating across multiple existing cases to determine the impact of variation in partic- ipatory practice on environmental decision making. Moreover, they attempt to use multiple measures of substantive decision quality to determine how different levels of participation may be connected to different levels of quality in decisions. These include, among other things, cost-effectiveness, joint gains, and innovations. Their large-N case study analysis suggests that public participation tends to improve sub- stantive decision quality in at least one of the dimensions they measured.

In much of the literature (Beierle and Cayford 2002; Dietz et al. 2008; Innes and Booher 2004; Meadowcroft 2004; Reed 2008), the assumption seems to be that a "good" decision-making process—that is, one that blends public values with tech- nical information—will more likely than not benefit the environment over time. That benefit may stem from an improved implementation process as a wider range of stakeholders perceive the decision as legitimate. The benefit may stem from a clear and correct identification of the underlying elements of the nature of the problem. Blending the art of participation with the science of environmental prob- lems is more likely to produce a decision that reflects both the technical details on the nature of the problem and the value preferences regarding the distribution of risks and rewards (Dietz et al. 2008).

While the literature (Bingham, Nabatchi and O'Leary 2005; Booher and Innes 2010; Dietz at al. 2008; Reed 2008; Sirianni 2009) highlights the remarkable promise of public participation in advancing environmental decision making, it also suggests important caveats in at least two regards. First, the promise of public participation is contingent on the quality of the participatory process and the willingness of participants to engage. If the process is flawed or the participants are not broadly representative, then the participation could actually detract from the quality of environmental decision making and undermine trust in government. Second, while the research in this area has advanced over time, the field is limited by extensive reliance on case studies (see Dietz et al. 2008, 76–80, for a compelling discussion highlighting the need to, at a minimum, rely on comparison cases, and, ideally, broaden research designs with an eye toward stronger internal validity). Case studies are valuable and should not be abandoned. However, we need to augment case study research with different research designs to test the quality of existing inferences and expand the set of questions that could be tackled.

Future research in this area would benefit considerably from a serious treatment of counterfactual or comparison cases whenever possible. Research that strives to understand the impact of participation on decision making should pay particular attention to internal validity in research design. Is decision making significantly different in the absence of a participatory process? Research that continues to refine our understanding of the relationship between participatory approaches and multi-dimensional markers of successful outcomes is also needed. Agencies would benefit from research regarding what factors should guide their choice of participatory process. Finally, there is very limited information regarding how some of the more creative collaborative forms of decision making should be institutionalized in an existing federalist system. Research is needed to understand the ways in which successful collaborative approaches might be best scaled up and applied in diverse settings.

REFERENCES

Advisory Commission on Intergovernmental Relations. 1979. *Citizen Participation in the American Federal System*. Washington: Advisory Commission on Intergovernmental Relations.

Alberts, D. J. 2007. "Stakeholders or Subject Matter Experts, Who Should Be Consulted?" *Energy Policy* 35 (4): 2336–2346.

Ansell, C., and A. Gash. 2008. "Collaborative Governance in Theory and Practice." *Journal of Public Administration Research and Theory* 18 (4): 543–571.

Arvai, J. L., and A. Froschauer. 2010. "Good Decisions, Bad Decisions: The Interaction of Process and Outcome in Evaluations of Decision Quality." *Journal of Risk Research* 13 (7): 845–859.

Becker, C. D., and E. Ostrom. 1995. "Human-Ecology and Resource Sustainability— the Importance of Institutional Diversity." *Annual Review of Ecology and Systematics* 26: 113–133.

Beierle, T. C., and J. Cayford. 2002. *Democracy in Practice: Public Participation in Environmental Decisions.* Washington, DC: Resources for the Future.

Bingham, L. B., T. Nabatchi, and R. O'Leary. 2005. "The New Governance: Practices and Processes for Stakeholder and Citizen Participation in the Work of Government." *Public Administration Review* 65 (5): 547–558.

Booher, D. E., and J. E. Innes. 2010. "Governance for Resilience: CALFED as a Complex Adaptive Network for Resource Management." *Ecology and Society* 15 (3): 35.

Brehm, J., and S. Gates. 1997. *Working, Shirking, and Sabotage: Bureaucratic Response to a Democratic Public, Michigan Studies in Political Analysis.* Ann Arbor: University of Michigan Press.

Brulle, R. J., and D. N. Pellow. 2006. "Environmental Justice: Human Health and Environmental Inequalities." *Annual Review of Public Health* 27: 103–124.

Bulkeley, H., and A. P. J. Mol. 2003. "Participation and Environmental Governance: Consensus, Ambivalence and Debate." *Environmental Values* 12 (2): 143–154.

Carmin, J., N. Darnall, and J. Mil-Homens. 2003. "Stakeholder Involvement in the Design of US Voluntary Environmental Programs: Does Sponsorship Matter?" *Policy Studies Journal* 31 (4): 527–543.

Charnley, S., and B. Engelbert. 2005. "Evaluating Public Participation in Environmental Decision-Making: EPA's Superfund Community Involvement Program." *Journal of Environmental Management* 77 (3): 165–182.

Chase, L. C., D. J. Decker, and T. B. Lauber. 2004. "Public Participation in Wildlife Management: What Do Stakeholders Want?" *Society and Natural Resources* 17 (7): 629–639.

Coenen, F. H. J. M., D. Huitema, and L. J. O'Toole. 1998. "Participation and the Quality of Environmental Decision Making: An Assessment." In *Participation and the Quality of Environmental Decisionmaking*, ed. F. Coenen, D Huitema, and L O'Yoole Jr. Norwell, MA: Kluwer Academic Publishers

Coglianese, C. 1997. "Assessing Consensus: The Promise and Performance of Negotiated Rulemaking." *Duke Law Journal* 46 (6): 1255–1349.

———. 2003. "Is Satisfaction Success? Evaluating Public Participation in Regulatory Policymaking." In *The Promise and Performance of Environmental Conflict Resolution*, ed. R. O'Leary and L. B. Bingham. Washington DC: Resources for the Future.

———. 2006. "Citizen Participation in Rulemaking: Past, Present, and Future." *Duke Law Journal* 55 (5): 943–968.

Cooper, T. L., T. A. Bryer, and J. M. Meek. 2006. "Citizen-Centered Collaborative Public Management." *Public Administration Review* 66 (Supplement S1): 76–88.

Daley, D. M. 2007. "Citizen Groups and Scientific Decisionmaking: Does Public Participation Influence Environmental Outcomes?" *Journal of Policy Analysis and Management* 26 (2): 349–368.

———. 2008. "Public Participation and Environmental Policy: What Factors Shape State Agency's Public Participation Provisions?" *Review of Policy Research* 25 (1): 20–34.

Dalton, T. M. 2005. "Beyond Biogeography: A Framework for Involving the Public in Planning of US Marine Protected Areas." *Conservation Biology* 19 (5): 1392–1401.

Dietz, T., P. C. Stern, U.S. National Research Council Panel on Public Participation in Environmental Assessment and Decision Making, and U.S. National Research Council Committee on the Human Dimensions of Global Change. 2008. *Public*

Participation in Environmental Assessment and Decision Making. Washington, DC: National Academies Press.

Dryzek, J. S. 2005. *The Politics of the Earth: Environmental Discourses.* 2nd ed. New York: Oxford University Press.

Fine, J. D., and D. Owen. 2005. "Technocracy and Democracy: Conflicts between Models and Participation in Environmental Law and Planning." *Hastings Law Journal* 56 (5): 901–981.

Foreman, C. H. 1998. *The Promise and Peril of Environmental Justice.* Washington, DC: Brookings Institution Press.

Hansell, W. H., E. Hollander, and D. John. 2009. *Putting Community First: A Promising Approach to Federal Collaboration for Environmental Improvement.* Washington. DC: National Academy of Public Administration.

Innes, J. E., and D. E. Booher. 2004. "Reframing Public Participation: Strategies for the 21st Century." *Planning Theory and Practice* 5 (4): 419–436.

Irvin, R. A., and J. Stansbury. 2004. "Citizen Participation in Decision Making: Is It Worth the Effort?" *Public Administration Review* 64 (1): 55–65.

Israel, B. A., C. M. Coombe, R. R. Cheezum, A. J. Schulz, R. J. McGranaghan, R. Lichtenstein, A. G. Reyes, J. Clement, and A. Burris. 2010. "Community-Based Participatory Research: A Capacity-Building Approach for Policy Advocacy Aimed at Eliminating Health Disparities." *American Journal of Public Health* 100 (11): 2094–2102.

Israel, B. A., A. J. Schulz, E. A. Parker, and A. B. Becker. 1998. "Review of Community-Based Research: Assessing Partnership Approaches to Improve Public Health." *Annual Review of Public Health* 19: 173–202.

Koontz, T. M., and C. W. Thomas. 2006. "What Do We Know and Need to Know about the Environmental Outcomes of Collaborative Management?" *Public Administration Review* 66: 111–121.

Landy, M. K., M. J. Roberts, and S. R. Thomas. 1994. *The Environmental Protection Agency: Asking the Wrong Questions from Nixon to Clinton.* Expanded ed. New York: Oxford University Press.

Laurian, L. 2007. "Deliberative Planning through Citizen Advisory Boards—Five Case Studies from Military and Civilian Environmental Cleanups." *Journal of Planning Education and Research* 26 (4): 415–434.

Lazarus, R. J. 1991. "The Tragedy of Distrust in the Implementation of Federal Environmental Law." *Law and Contemporary Problems* 54: 311–374.

Leach, W. D. 2006. "Collaborative Public Management and Democracy: Evidence from Western Watershed Partnerships." *Public Administration Review* 66 (Supplement S1): 100–110.

Lubell, M., P. A. Sabatier, A. Vedlitz, W. Focht, Z. Trachtenberg, and M. Matlock. 2005. "Conclusions and Recommendations." In *Swimming Upstream: Collaborative Approaches to Watershed Management*, ed. P. A. Sabatier, W. Focht, M. Lubell, Z. Trachtenberg, A. Vedlitz, and M. Matlock. Cambridge, MA: MIT Press.

Macedo, S., et al. 2005. *Democracy at Risk: How Political Choices Undermine Citizen Participation and What We Can Do about It.* Washington, DC: Brookings Institution Press.

Meadowcroft, J. 2004. "Deliberative Democracy." In *Environmental Governance Reconsidered: Challenges, Choices, and Opportunities*, ed. R. F. Durant, D. J. Fiorino, and R. O'Leary. Cambridge, MA: MIT Press.

Munton, D., ed. 1996. *Hazardous Waste Siting and Democratic Choice.* Washington DC: Georgetown University Press.

Noonan, D. S. 2008. "Evidence of Environmental Justice: A Critical Perspective on the Practice of EJ Research and Lessons for Policy Design." *Social Science Quarterly* 89 (5): 1154–1174.

O'Fallon, L. R., and A. Dearry. 2002. "Community-Based Participatory Research as a Tool to Advance Environmental Health Sciences." *Environmental Health Perspectives* 110: 155–159.

O'Fallon, L. R., G. M. Wolfle, D. Brown, A. Dearry, and K. Olden. 2003. "Strategies for Setting a National Research Agenda That Is Responsive to Community Needs." *Environmental Health Perspectives* 111 (16): 1855–1860.

Ostrom, E. 2007. "Institutional Rational Choice: An Assessment of the Institutional Analysis and Development Framework." In *Theories of the Policy Process*, ed. P. A. Sabatier. Boulder, CO: Westview.

Putnam, R. D. 2000. *Bowling alone: The Collapse and Revival of American Community.* New York: Simon & Schuster.

Rabe, B. G. 2004. *Statehouse and Greenhouse: The Emerging Politics of American Climate Policy.* Washington, DC: Brookings Institution Press.

——, ed. 2010. *Greenhouse Governance: Addressing Climate Change in America.* Washington, DC: Brookings Institution Press.

Reed, M. S. 2008. "Stakeholder Participation for Environmental Management: A Literature Review." *Biological Conservation* 141 (10): 2417–2431.

Ringquist, E. J. 2005. "Assessing the Evidence of Regarding Environmental Inequities: A Meta-Analysis." *Journal of Policy Analysis and Management* 24 (2): 223–247.

Rosenbaum, W. A. 2010. "Science, Politics, and Policy at the EPA." In *Environmental Policy: New Directions for the Twenty-First Century*, ed. N. J. Vig and M. E. Kraft. Washington, DC: CQ Press.

Sabatier, P. A., W. Focht, M. Lubell, Z. Trachtenberg, A. Vedlitz, and M. Matlock. 2005. "Collaborative Approaches to Watershed Management." In *Swimming Upstream: Collaborative Approaches to Watershed Management*, ed. P. A. Sabatier, W. Focht, M. Lubell, Z. Trachtenberg, A. Vedlitz, and M. Matlock. Cambridge, MA: MIT Press.

Sirianni, C. 2009. *Investing in Democracy: Engaging Citizens in Collaborative Governance.* Washington, DC: Brookings Institution Press.

Sunstein, C. R. 2006. *Infotopia: How Many Minds Produce Knowledge.* New York: Oxford University Press.

Thompson, J. L., C. B. Forster, C. Werner, and T. R. Peterson. 2010. "Mediated Modeling: Using Collaborative Processes to Integrate Scientist and Stakeholder Knowledge about Greenhouse Gas Emissions in an Urban Ecosystem." *Society and Natural Resources* 23 (8): 742–757.

Tuler, S., and T. Webler. 2010. "How Preferences for Public Participation Are Linked to Perceptions of the Context, Preferences for Outcomes, and Individual Characteristics." *Environmental Management* 46 (2): 254–267.

Weber, P. 2003. *Bringing Society Back In: Grassroots Ecosystem Management, Accountability, and Sustainable Communities.* Cambridge, MA: MIT Press.

....

CHAPTER 23

ORGANIZED INTERESTS AND ENVIRONMENTAL POLICY

....

ROBERT J. DUFFY

POLITICAL scientists have long recognized the central role of interest groups in politics and policy making and have written extensively about their implications for representation and democratic governance. Indeed, the already voluminous interest group literature has grown significantly in recent decades and has also become more theoretically sophisticated. A field once criticized for being narrow and theoretically challenged has grown to include rich case studies of single groups and of particular policy decisions, as well as some excellent large-scale empirical studies of group lobbying. Although the field continues to be marked by a diversity of theoretical approaches, methodological choices, and research questions, we now know much more about group mobilization and the forces that affect it, what groups do to influence policy making, the breadth and diversity of the interest group system, and how it has changed over time (Baumgartner and Leech 1998). The literature on organized interests in environmental policy making is more modest, but it has been influenced by the broader interest group research and thus reflects many of its defining traits, including greater theoretical and methodological sophistication.

This chapter provides an overview and assessment of the research on organized interests in environmental and natural resource policy making, with an eye toward identifying the most significant contributions. We begin by considering the question of how groups mobilize and maintain themselves, followed by a discussion of some of the key debates in the literature: efforts to map the contours, composition, and evolution of the environmental group system, what groups do to influence policy making, and how to assess group influence in policy making. The chapter concludes with suggestions for future research.

In seeking to explain the dramatic increase in both the number and size of environmental organizations that began in the 1960s, researchers have built on the work of David Truman, Mancur Olson, Robert Salisbury, and others. Truman (1950) argued that groups form when people who share similar concerns or interests decide to come together; group mobilization is a spontaneous response to economic or social disturbances. Truman also suggested that mobilization by one set of interests would spur a countermobilization by others who felt threatened. Olson (1965) rejected Truman's assumption that common interests were enough to explain group mobilization; on the contrary, he argued that there were significant barriers to group formation and maintenance, especially for those seeking collective goods. Perhaps most important, as long as individuals received the collective goods that interest groups were working to obtain, regardless of whether they contributed to the effort, it would be difficult to spur many people into action. For Olson, in the absence of groups offering selective, material benefits, rational individuals would decide not to join such organizations, therefore large groups devoted to the pursuit of collective goods would be in short supply. The problem for Olson, of course, is that he made his argument at precisely the time that citizen groups were increasing in size and number.

Salisbury's exchange theory (1969) sought to resolve this puzzle by highlighting the entrepreneurship role of group leaders, arguing that potential members could be enticed by a mix of material and nonmaterial benefits. For Salisbury and Olson, individuals joined groups for the benefits they received, not for ideological or policy reasons. Both were skeptical of the notion that the leaders of public interest groups were committed to the pursuit of expressive goals; indeed, for Salisbury, group leaders were primarily concerned with maintaining the group, not with influencing public policy. Echoing Salisbury's emphasis on the importance of leadership, Walker (1983) argued that patrons of political action played a key role in the formation and maintenance of citizen groups. He stressed the importance of private sector actors, such as foundations, and government as sources of financial support for such groups.

The literature on environmental organizations has also been concerned with questions of mobilization and maintenance. Shaiko (1999), for example, examines how the dramatic increase in membership rolls and budgets that began in the 1960s affected five national environmental groups (the Environmental Defense Fund, the National Wildlife Federation, the Sierra Club, the Wilderness Society, and Environmental Action), focusing on how they tried to balance organizational maintenance and political representation. More specifically, Shaiko (1999, 4) analyzes the relationship between group leaders and rank-and-file members and claims that "the messages sent directly to policy makers from organization leaders and their lobbyists—the 'voices'—must be supported by similarly informed messages from the grassroots memberships—the 'echoes.'" Although the five groups he examines are different in many ways, as national membership groups they are not really representative of the full range of environmental organizations in the United States. And the focus on congressional policy making provides at best an incomplete picture of the advocacy efforts of even the national groups, who are also involved in agency rule making, legal action, and more.

Whereas Shaiko examines the connections between group leaders and grass-roots members, Bosso (2005) focuses on the evolution of organized environmental advocacy in the United States, especially since the early 1970s, and argues that the ability to adapt is critical to group survival. Using as his theoretical base the population ecology model developed by Gray and Lowery (1996), Bosso (2005, 11) examines the major environmental organizations "as constituent parts of a singular entity, a specific advocacy community." It is this focus on a single advocacy community over time that distinguishes his analysis from other work on environmental organizations. Bosso focuses on the adaptation of the environmental advocacy community to changes in external societal, political, and economic conditions and internal maintenance needs. In addition, he evaluates the processes by which organizations are moved into distinct policy or tactical niches, where they can operate mainly on their own, and suggests that niche seeking is critical to the survival of the individual organization and the overall dimensions of the national environmental advocacy community. He argues that the transformation of environmental advocacy from the relatively inchoate movement of the late 1960s to the more professionalized organizations we see today was "necessary for the long-term success of environmental policy in the United States" (Bosso 2005, 8).

1. THE EVOLUTION OF THE ENVIRONMENTAL GROUP SYSTEM

Today, there are perhaps tens of thousands of organized interests active in environmental and natural resource policy making across all levels of government. These organizations vary widely in their heritage, structure, size, budgets, issue orientations, degree of professionalization, and level of political engagement. Environmental groups differ in their passion and level of support for environmental and natural resource protection. Even among those who might be considered part of the environmental movement, there is a great deal of diversity with respect to goals and strategies; some utilize traditional lobbying methods, while others employ more confrontational, direct action (Audley 1997; Bosso 1994; Mitchell 1989; Snow 1992). Indeed, groups ostensibly on the same side of issues often compete with one another for members, attention, and funding (Bosso 2005). Diversity is also the norm among the many business groups that are active in environmental and natural resource policy making—they are anything but monolithic.

Given the many organizations active in environmental policy making, it is useful to establish some general categories. Perhaps most familiar are the national "mainstream" environmental organizations like the Sierra Club, the Wilderness Society, the National Wildlife Federation, the Audubon Society, and others that Chris Bosso (2005) labels "the immortals." This category also includes the many well-known national organizations established in the 1960s and 1970s, including the Environmental Defense Fund (EDF), the Natural Resources Defense Council (NRDC), Friends of the Earth, Greenpeace, and the League of Conservation Voters (LCV). Most of these groups engage in one or more of the typical advocacy activities: lobbying, testifying, conducting and disseminating research, litigating, electioneering, and so on. There are also a number of more radical green groups like Earth First!, Earth Liberation Front, and Sea Shepherds who reject conventional "inside" politics and instead emphasize direct action and fundamental social change, although most observers have concluded that they have little political influence (Kamieniecki, Coleman, and Vos 1995; Kraft and Wuertz 1996; Manes 1990).

The environmental advocacy community also includes thousands of less well-known regional and local grassroots organizations. As with the national groups, there is a great deal of diversity within this segment of the advocacy community; some are membership organizations, but others are not. Some have professional leadership, while others are largely driven by volunteers. Many of these organizations are primarily concerned with specific local environmental threats, such as hazardous waste or toxics releases, and land use issues. Some observers see in these groups the potential for a broadly supported civic environmentalism organized around local and regional environmental issues, especially if such groups can blend environmental, social, and economic concerns in an urban setting (Gottlieb 2001; Kraft 2011; Mazmanian and Kraft 2009; Paehlke 2010).

Business groups are, of course, also very active in environmental and natural resource policy making. Automobile manufacturers, chemical companies, and energy firms are the most familiar, but the list is much longer and includes trade associations like the Chamber of Commerce and the National Association of Manufacturers. Within the last 10 years, the number of 501c organizations funded by corporate money has also exploded, with some focusing on public education campaigns aimed at influencing debate over energy and climate change policies. Finally, there are the "wise-use" and property rights organizations that are opposed to much federal environmental regulation, most notably on public land issues in the West (Brick and Cawley 1996; Helvarg 1997; Switzer 1997).

The general consensus is that environmental advocacy has evolved in stages, with distinct periods of group formation (Ingram 1995; Shabecoff 2000). The first wave began with the formation of a number of conservation groups such as the Sierra Club, the Audubon Society, and the Izaak Walton League, who were primarily interested in the protection of forests and other natural resources, including wildlife. Even at this early stage, environmentalists debated the relative merits of conservation and preservation (Miller 2001; Nash 2001).

The second wave of group mobilization began in the 1960s and 1970s, the so-called golden age of environmentalism, when Congress adopted many new environmental laws. Many of these groups, including NRDC, EDF, and Greenpeace, organized because of concerns about the effects of air and water pollution. Groups born in this era tended to be engaged in politics from the outset and used tactics, including litigation, that were then novel to the movement (Gottlieb 1993).

Baumgartner and Jones (1993, 186) claim that the environmental movement was the "largest, most visible, and fastest growing part" of the citizen group sector from 1960 to 1980, with the number of groups listed in the *Encyclopedia of Associations* growing from 119 to 380. Not only did the number of groups increase, but their membership ranks swelled as well, leading to a dramatic increase in their budgets, which in turn allowed them to hire more staff and lobbyists. By the early 1970s, 70 environmental organizations had opened offices in Washington, DC, and the number of full-time environmental lobbyists increased from two in 1969 to 88 by 1985 (Mitchell, Mertig, and Dunlap 1992). Berry (1999) argues that environmental group leaders consciously built their organizations, hiring more lawyers, economists, scientists, and policy analysts in order to enhance the groups' expertise and credibility, and thus their policy influence. This decision facilitated greater access to congressional policy making; indeed, Berry argues that citizen groups represented a disproportionate share of those testifying before Congress.

The business community and conservative organizations responded to these developments by countermobilizing in an effort to restrict the economic impact of the new environmental laws and rules (see chapter 1 in this volume). Smith (2000), for example, documents a significant increase in business lobbying activity, campaign spending, and support for policy research and think tanks highlighting the cost of new laws. Others noted a countermobilization by a grassroots "backlash" movement of outdoor recreationists, ranchers, farmers, property rights advocates, and wise-use organizations upset about federal management of public and private lands (Helvarg 1997; Switzer 1997).

A third wave of mobilization within the environmental community occurred in the 1980s, marked by a dramatic increase in the number of local and regional grassroots organizations. Although these groups varied in issue orientation, they tended to be community-based and motivated by a desire to shift the focus of policy to the local level (Bosso 1994; Ingram, Colnic, and Mann 1995). Many of the groups formed in response to specific local hazards, so health concerns were often at the core of their mission. Because of differences in goals and strategies, many of these groups had a complicated relationship with the national groups, thinking them more interested in protecting endangered species than in protecting poor people, and too willing to compromise (Freudenberg and Steinsapir 1991).[1] In fact, by the 1990s mainstream environmental groups were often attacked as being too

---

1. Collaborative resource management also emerged as a point of contention between local environmentalists and national organizations, with the latter arguing that such efforts often resulted in less effective natural resource policies.

timid; critics were claiming that the tendency to compromise had pushed the environmental movement to the brink of irrelevance (Dowie 1995; Sale 1993; Shabecoff 1993; Shellenberger and Nordhaus 2004). Others suggested that the mainstream groups had moderated their stances because they had become too professionalized, citing an inevitable tendency of organizations to become more risk-averse over time and less willing to assume controversial positions (Bevington 2009).

Although there is widespread agreement that the environmental policy making arena has become more crowded over time, there is little consensus as to why. Some have argued (Ingram, Colnic, and Mann 1995; Klyza and Sousa 2008) that pluralism, with its emphasis on waves of mobilization and countermobilization in response to perceived disturbances or threats to group interests, offers the best explanation. In this view, environmental organizations did not rely on the provision of selective, material benefits to attract and retain members; on the contrary, individuals joined groups because they wanted to protect the environment. The increase in the number of environmental groups between 1960 and 1980 corresponds with the dramatic mobilization shifts among citizen groups in that same time frame. For example, EDF mobilized in response to concerns over the health effects of DDT, while Environmental Action formed in response to the first Earth Day (Ingram, Colnic, and Mann 1995). Also cited are the spikes in group membership that coincided with perceived threats to the environment in the 1960s, and with the Reagan and George W. Bush administrations.

Others have attributed the rise of environmentalism and environmental organizations to the prosperity of the postwar era, when Americans had more leisure time, more disposable income, and opportunities to partake in outdoor recreation (Hays 1987). Walker (1983) noted the importance of patrons from the private sector and government as critical in the formation of public interest organizations, including environmental groups. Brulle and Jenkins (2005) identified environmental groups as particular beneficiaries of the patronage of funders, including the Ford Foundation, which provided substantial support for EDF and NRDC (Berry 1999; Ingram, Colnic, and Mann 1995). Although external funding certainly facilitated the creation of many groups in the 1960s, it cannot explain the creation of others or the increase in grassroots organizations.

Still others have argued that structural changes in government spurred the growth in citizen groups and their incorporation into the political process. The growing federal role in environmental and natural resource policies in the 1960s and 1970s, as manifested in the many new programs and agencies, helped create new constituencies for government action. In general, the advent of the "new social regulation" resulted from, and facilitated, participation in administrative matters by citizen groups, including environmental organizations (Harris and Milkis 1996). Gray and Lowery (1996) also show that the formation of groups follows the growth of available resources and expanded government activity. Simply put, the new programs and agencies created more points of access to government.

Changes within government also spurred group formation and participation. A number of the new environmental laws required public involvement of groups through hearings and notice and comment rule makings, and in some cases direct funding of intervenor groups as well. Congressional decentralization resulted in the proliferation of subcommittees, which offered environmental groups greater access to policy makers. By the end of the 1970s, an incredible 110 subcommittees had some jurisdiction over the EPA. In addition, the federal courts liberalized standing rules, granting environmental organizations greater access to the courts (Melnick 1983).

Clearly, the environmental and natural resource policy making arenas are, in the words of Klyza and Sousa (2008, 287), "thick with contending interests." The question is to what effect. Some have argued that despite the shift in mobilization patterns over the last 30 years, business groups are still dominant (Dowie 1995; Shabecoff 1993; Shellenberger and Nordhaus 2004). Others have suggested that environmental groups have leveled the playing field and now win more often than in the past (Baumgartner et al. 2009; Berry 1999). Still others contend that all of the interest group mobilization has contributed to legislative gridlock on environmental issues; business organizations are unable to repeal or significantly weaken existing laws, while environmental organizations are not powerful enough to enact tough new laws or ensure faithful implementation of existing ones (Bosso 1994).

Klyza and Sousa (2008) argue that we should not confuse legislative gridlock with policy gridlock or stasis. There is, they acknowledge, legislative gridlock on the keystone environmental laws, with neither side able to achieve a policy breakthrough. But they argue that environmental policy making is dynamic, not static, and they suggest that the stalemate in Congress has shifted policy choices to non-legislative venues, such as the executive branch, the courts, and state and local governments.[2] "Intense mobilization on all sides of issues," they argue, "coupled with policy-making processes that offer multiple points of access to competing interests, create considerable instability in the policymaking process" (Klyza and Sousa 2008, 33). In fact, they argue that the larger pattern of environmental policy making is of a slow, uneven movement in directions generally favored by greens. The primary reason for this is the considerable strength of the policy status quo, embodied in the "green state"—the accumulated environmental laws, rules, and court decisions constructed during the last century, including many "first-generation" laws enacted during the 1970s. The mobilization of environmental organizations and strong public support for the cause of environmental protection also make it exceedingly difficult for opponents to redirect policy.

It is clear that we know much more about group mobilization in this policy domain than we used to, although we know more about the large national groups than we do about those operating at the local, state, or regional levels, or about those operating outside the mainstream. Similarly, the relationships between the grassroots and national organizations remains an understudied topic (Ingram,

---

2. Democratic control can explain why some cities (New York, Los Angeles, Portland) and states (New York, California, Colorado) have adopted ambitious climate and sustainability programs.

Colnic, and Mann 1995), especially in light of some of the recent capacity-building efforts undertaken by foundations and national groups.

2. Group Lobbying Tactics and Strategies

Large-scale empirical surveys of group behavior have taught us a great deal about what organized interests do to influence policy (Berry 1999; Gray and Lowery 1996; Heinz et al. 1993; Schlozman and Tierney 1986; Walker 1991). Interest group strategies on any given issue are a function of many contextual factors: group resources (budgets, staff size, number of lobbyists, number of members, status, etc.), group goals (long-term and short-term, including whether the group is seeking to defend or challenge the status quo); the political opportunity structure (partisan control of Congress and the White House; the support or opposition of other groups; relationships with key gatekeepers inside government); the target of lobbying (Congress, the White House, federal agencies, the courts, the public); public opinion; and the stage of the policy process (issue framing, policy formulation, implementation, etc.).

Group strategies are often divided into two categories. Direct, or inside lobbying, typically involves formal or informal face-to-face meetings between group representatives and public officials or their staffs, testimony in hearings, written comments on proposed rules or laws, the provision of research, and other direct information exchanges. Indirect or outside lobbying, however, typically involves group leaders trying to mobilize members or the general public and to have them contact public officials. This can take the form of letter-writing or email campaigns, print or broadcast advertising, or less traditional actions such as demonstrations or protests. The conventional wisdom is that inside lobbying is the province of groups with the resources to hire paid lobbyists, or with the connections and status that yield access to public officials. Outside lobbying, by contrast, is thought to be the refuge of those who are excluded from the inside game.

E. E. Schattschneider once suggested (1960, 2) that "the outcome of all conflict is determined by the scope of its contagion. The number of people involved in any conflict determines what happens; every change in the number of participants affects the result." In addition, he observed that the scope of conflict over an issue influences the type of political activity characteristic of that policy area; as a result, the politics of controversial issues will differ from those with a narrow scope. Following Schattschneider, many have argued that most policy conflicts involve one set of actors seeking to expand conflict and another set seeking to restrict it. More specifically, it was assumed that the losers in any given conflict would seek to expand participation, usually by trying to reframe the issue and show that it had broader implications, while those who were winning would seek to restrict participation by arguing that others were unaffected.

But Pralle (2006) has argued that this conflict expansion/containment model
assumes a static structure of competition and is thus accurate for only some conflicts. She notes that the incentives of players necessarily change as the nature
of a conflict shifts. In relatively new policy conflicts, competing interest groups
are typically not equally matched: one side enjoys greater resources and access to
policy making. Consequently, groups behave as Schattschneider predicted, with
one side seeking to expand the conflict and the other to limit it. But as the relative
difference in group resources and access diminishes, groups may reassess their
strategic choices. As an issue becomes more salient, more actors, including policy
makers, have incentives to become involved. Defenders of the policy status quo
may no longer be able to rely on superior resources and access to maintain their
preferred policy and may thus seek to expand participation by recruiting allies.
Even groups that are accustomed to using inside strategies may mimic their oppo-
nent's strategies and seek to expand the conflict when an issue becomes highly
salient.

A study of interest groups by Baumgartner et al. (2009) confirms that those
challenging the status quo are more likely to try to expand the scope of conflict
and are more likely to engage in outside tactics. Compared to those defending the
status quo, challengers are more likely to organize public relations campaigns and
adopt other tactics designed to mobilize the public. Defenders of the status quo,
however, have little reason to engage in conflict expansion except in response to a
viable challenge.

This shows that group strategies are situational, not fixed according to group
type. Much of the early literature on group advocacy in environmental and natural
resource policy making showed that environmental organizations behaved as classic outsiders, trying desperately to expand the scope of the conflict. But as circumstances shifted, group strategies did as well. Groups that were once resource-poor
and had few alternatives to outside lobbying changed their approach as their membership rolls and balance sheets grew. Similarly, groups that were once upstarts
behaved differently once they were viewed as regular, legitimate participants by
policy makers. And more to the point, in seeking to defend environmental laws
adopted decades ago, environmental organizations now find themselves in the
position of defending the status quo, while business groups are in the unenviable
position of challenging it, which is a more daunting task.

A review of group advocacy in the environmental policy arena suggests that
Pralle and Baumgartner are correct. Until the 1970s, most environmental organizations had very few members and financial resources, and the issue had not yet
become salient nationally. Aside from some low-key, personal appeals by a handful
of group leaders on wilderness issues in the 1950s and 1960s (Allin 1982), most of
the environmental community's biggest policy victories during that period came
from outside lobbying. One notable example was the controversy over a proposed
dam in Echo Park in Dinosaur National Monument, Colorado. The Sierra Club, the
Izaak Walton League, and the Wilderness Society opposed construction of the dam
and conducted a highly effective public education campaign (Harvey 1994). In fact,

Andrews (1999) argued that the Echo Park experience taught environmental groups new tactics for using mass media to mobilize broad-based political opposition.

By the 1960s, when the groups had more members, money, and professional staff, they devoted more resources and energy to direct lobbying. A number of studies suggest that mainstream groups played important roles in the passage of environmental laws, including the National Environmental Policy Act (NEPA), the Clean Air and Water Acts, and the Endangered Species Act (Ackerman and Hassler 1981; Cohen 1995). The national groups also played a key role in adding right-to-know provisions to the Superfund Amendments and Reauthorization Act in the 1980s (Gottlieb 2001). Lowry (1997) shows that the national groups reinvested much of their new wealth into building their organizations and devoted more than 43 percent of their expenditures to lobbying and other advocacy activities.

In general, most of the mainstream national environmental organizations engage in the "standard American political practices" of lobbying, electioneering, litigation, coalition building, and public mobilization (Ingram, Colnic, and Mann 1995). A few mainstream groups act directly in pursuit of their goals; the Nature Conservancy, for example, buys land in order to protect it. Groups that are not part of the mainstream, such as Earth First!, the Earth Liberation Front, and Sea Shepherds, use nontraditional, sometimes confrontational approaches, such as the disruption of Japanese whaling operations (Kamieniecki, Coleman, and Vos 1995). For the most part, though, these groups do not command a large public following and do not have many policy victories to claim as their own.

Outside the mainstream, local and regional grassroots organizations utilize different tactics than pragmatic or incremental groups (Bevington 2009; Zakin 1993; Zisk 1992). Zisk's study comparing mainstream "pragmatic" groups with "transformational" local grassroots groups shows that the latter relied less on professional staff, were more likely to base decisions on majority rule, were unlikely to compromise, and were thus more prone to membership instability and low institutional capacity (Zisk 1992). Bevington (2009) disagrees, citing the success of small, radical groups using outside tactics, mainly litigation. According to Bevington, grassroots biodiversity organizations used an outsider strategy for social change that did not depend on appealing to politicians and avoiding controversy. Relying on ESA citizen suit provisions that mandated reimbursement of attorneys successfully suing for enforcement, the groups litigated to force federal agencies to enforce the law.

Advocacy by the large national environmental groups began to change in the early 1990s. Indeed, Mitchell, Mertig, and Dunlap (1992, 21) suggest that "the scale of the environmental movement's advocacy, its sophistication, and especially its continuity," was new, as groups sought to be involved in all stages of policy making. Duffy (2003) argues that in the 1990s, after the Republican takeover of Congress, environmental groups experimented with new methods of issue definition and agenda setting and placed more emphasis on this task than in previous years. Compared to earlier periods, scholars noted several new dimensions of environmental advocacy; perhaps most notably, lobbying efforts are more professional and strategic. Similarly, Kraft and Wuertz (1996) claim that environmental groups increased the frequency and sophistication of their indirect lobbying when they discovered that direct lobbying was becoming less effective in a changed political environment. Shaiko (1999) argues that more frequent grassroots campaigns helped generate public pressure for the policy agendas of various groups and, as the messages from the grassroots echoed the sentiments of group leaders, helped reinforce and legitimize the arguments of the lobbyists for groups.

The methods of generating and coordinating grassroots campaigns also changed, thanks largely to advances in communication technology, which made messaging quicker and cheaper. The use of email, websites, and social networking sites now plays a key role in group communications, allowing groups to educate and mobilize members quickly and cheaply, generating tens of thousands of telephone calls and emails within hours. Environmental activists have embraced the value of strategic communications and are putting a higher priority on gaining and holding public attention, an important factor as they try to define environmental issues and shape the public agenda (Duffy 2003; Guber and Bosso 2007; Merry 2010).

Business groups have shifted gears as well. Layzer (2007) shows how business groups resort to outside lobbying to raise doubts among the public as to the causes and consequences of climate change. The goal is to suggest that there is a great deal of scientific uncertainty about the matter so that Congress will postpone action on the issue. The efforts, funded by Koch Industries and others, also raise questions about the potential cost of any climate change policies—a classic strategy of those defending the status quo (Baumgartner et al. 2009).

In many ways, then, environmental advocacy is in flux. Environmental groups are not doing anything completely new; rather, they continue to do many of the same things they have always done, but in different ways and with more intensity. Depending on their own particular expertise, some environmental groups seek to educate and mobilize the public, others engage in policy analysis and research, and still others litigate. A few groups try to do it all. Today, there is also a growing awareness that these tasks are inextricably linked.

A number of opportunities exist for future research. For example, what tactics and strategies do organized interests use when seeking to influence state and local governments? Do they mirror those used by the Sierra Club and others when lobbying in Washington, or are they different? What internal factors influence group lobbying activities? Are certain types of environmental organizations, or businesses, more or less likely to participate in certain ways? And how does context influence the choice of lobbying activities—when do groups use certain strategies, and why?

3. Assessing Access and Influence

Although most scholars suggest that organized interests are actively involved in trying to shape and influence environmental policy, there is no consensus as to how effective they are (Vogel 1989; Kraft and Kamieniecki 2007a). Some have argued that environmental organizations have succeeded in influencing policy outcomes, while others counter that business organizations have been far more influential. A third camp finds policy stalemate. Some of the disagreement may result from observers confusing access with influence, while some may stem from scholars using different methods of measuring influence, a notoriously difficult task. Case studies of individual policy decisions, for example, may yield different perspectives on the "who wins" question. As a result, it is not surprising that observers cannot agree on what they have found and what it means for environmental policy.

Scholars have long pondered the relative influence of interest groups over policy outcomes; some note that group access and influence are significantly affected by changes in the political opportunity structure. For example, elections and shifts in partisan control of Congress and the White House can profoundly alter long-standing relationships. The Republican Party takeover of Congress in 1995 ended decades of Democratic Party control and ushered in a wholesale replacement of committee and subcommittee chairs. Control of the agenda thus shifted to new gatekeepers who were decidedly less sympathetic to environmental groups (Kraft 2006). With limited access to the new majority, environmental groups were forced to reconsider the inside lobbying strategies they had long relied on, putting more emphasis on playing defense to protect existing laws (Ingram, Colnic, and Mann 1995). Republicans regained control of the House in 2011, so now environmental organizations find themselves in a similar defensive posture, fighting to prevent budget cuts to key programs and efforts to curtail the EPA's regulatory capacities.

Partisan change in the White House has similarly affected group access. Presidents Carter and Clinton were generally more sympathetic to environmental organizations than were their Republican counterparts. Carter, for example, appointed a number of environmentalists to key positions in EPA and the Department of Interior, while Reagan appointees generally shared his skepticism of environmental regulations. Although not always thrilled with the Clinton administration, environmental group leaders surely were more welcome there than in George W. Bush's White House. This is best illustrated by the Energy Task Force headed by Vice President Cheney, which met regularly with industry officials to develop an energy policy but only belatedly invited the leaders of environmental groups to a photograph session just days before announcing their plan.

A number of observers (e.g., Kamieniecki 2006) have argued that whether it is because of unequal resources, a political culture that favors business, or strategic or tactical missteps by environmental organizations themselves, the bottom line is the same—business gets what it wants more often than not. To cite one example, Bosso (1994, 40) suggests that environmentalists cannot compete in the politics of interests, noting that "fighting the moneyed lobbyists is a futile proposition." In perhaps the most systematic assessment of the relative influence of organized interests in environmental policy, Kraft and Kamieniecki (2007b) suggest that business has the flexibility and resources to choose at which stages of the policy process to fight. In their view, business does not challenge environmental rules and laws when the particular issues are salient; instead, business mounts limited opposition in Congress and challenges the decisions in venues (regulatory agencies and the courts) that are less visible to media and public scrutiny. Rule making involves specific policy issues, and this typically gives an edge to actors with detailed information and knowledge of the policy in question. In many cases this means business groups, although a number of the mainstream national environmental groups have large and capable staff.

Furlong's (2007) study of business involvement in rule making concludes that business interests are significantly more active in the administrative process, comprising 94 percent of all the registered lobbyists on environmental issues, compared to just 3 percent for public interest groups. In addition, individual businesses participated in twice the number of rule makings than did public interest groups and were similarly overrepresented in informal lobbying, especially in the executive branch. The evidence, he suggests, is that informal, off-the-record participation prior to rule making is especially important in affecting agency decisions. In the end, Furlong concludes that business interests have significantly more access in environmental policy and notes that although access does not guarantee influence, it is a necessary condition for influence to occur.

With respect to the courts, Weiland (2007) and McSpadden (2007) argue that business groups have prevailed more often than they have lost, particularly after the 1980s, when conservative judges, appointed by Republican presidents, became the majority. Superior financial and legal resources again seem to be the primary explanation for business success. Using empirical data, McSpadden contends that business use of the courts has increased over time in both pollution control and land use cases and that business is now the dominant force in environmental and natural resource litigation in the federal courts. This was not always the case; a number of the 1960s- and 1970s-era environmental laws contained citizen suit provisions that opened a door to litigation by public interest groups. When environmental groups had some success using this route, business responded by adding legal staff and creating environmental departments to defend against government and citizen suits. It was during this same period that a number of conservative legal foundations, such as the Mountain States Legal Foundation, were formed and began challenging the new laws. McSpadden (2007) documents how business groups have challenged new rules in court, citing excessive costs, allowing them to avoid compliance during litigation and thus saving money. Business also became more adept at shopping for the most sympathetic courts, and changes in the political opportunity structure also benefited business interests, as Democratic judges were replaced by Reagan and Bush appointees.

Some have suggested that environmental organizations are their own worst enemies and that self-inflicted wounds explain their relative lack of influence. In his stinging critique of the national groups, Dowie (1995, xii) argues that although the environment is in better shape now than in earlier decades, it would be "in better condition had environmental leaders been bolder; more diverse in class, race, and gender; less compromising in battle; and less gentlemanly in the day-to-day dealings with adversaries." Shabecoff (1993, 113) echoes that claim, saying that the environmental movement "has been a minor, rather ineffectual player in the political process. Its engagement has been tentative and diffident—it plays at politics rather than going to war." Similarly, in what is perhaps the most noteworthy example of this thinking, Shellenberger and Nordhaus (2004) indict the mainstream groups for a lack of vision, for embracing an overly narrow agenda, and for failing to capture the public's imagination. Although one may argue with their conclusions, it is clear that Shellenberger and Nordhaus (2004, 11) believe that environmental groups need to reexamine themselves if they want to understand why it had been "easy for anti-environmental interests to gut 30 years of environmental protections."

Some, noting that interest groups operate in a pluralist system, have argued that corporate power has limits (Vogel 1989; Baumgartner and Leech 1998; Berry 1999; Smith 2000; Baumgartner et al. 2009). Instead of finding that business groups have dominated environmental policy making, these scholars depict a more nuanced state of affairs, with environmental groups finding a fair measure of success, despite having fewer resources. In the same vein, Kamieniecki (2006) and Kraft and Kamieniecki claim (2007b) that business groups tend to lose when issues are salient to the public and environmental groups have gained media attention.

Berry (1999) has argued that beginning in the 1960s, citizens groups, especially liberal ones, were responsible for moving the congressional agenda to postmaterial concerns, including the environment. Building on the argument by Baumgartner and Jones (1993) that changes in mobilization patterns can reorient the congressional agenda, Berry shows that citizen groups interested in quality-of-life issues were major actors in policy debates and actively involved in initiating agenda items; he concludes that the increase in postmaterial issues on the congressional agenda was linked to citizen group advocacy. In this view, value change by itself did not automatically result in new policies; rather, political organizations, many of them newly formed in the public lobby era, actively worked to mobilize those who shared their values and set out to influence policy makers. A dramatic shift in the mobilization of bias meant that citizen groups, including those focused on the environment, were effective in shaping the congressional agenda and in influencing legislation once Congress took up the issue (Berry 1999). Berry's argument is not that environmentalists have been dominant in congressional policy making; in fact, he notes that business groups prevailed more often than other groups, but not as often as in earlier periods. Simply put, the policy making arena became more challenging for business as citizen groups grew in number and became more active.

Similarly, Baumgartner et al. (2009, 193) contend that there are "many complications to the rich-get-richer story as it relates to the policy process." Indeed, after comparing organizations on a wide range of resources (lobbying expenditures, number of former government officials employed by the organization as lobbyists, campaign contributions, allies within government, membership size, and overall financial resources), they find that although business groups typically have greater resources, there are "surprisingly weak links" between material resources and the ability to move policy in one's preferred direction. In fact, they conclude, "For the most part, resources have no significant correlation with a positive policy outcome" (Baumgartner et al. 2009, 203). In part, this is because organizations rarely lobby alone; more typical is that groups lobby in coalitions with other allies who have their own resources. As a result, opposing sides in policy conflicts are often diverse in composition and relatively evenly matched in resources. So although environmental organizations cannot match the financial resources of many business groups, they rarely lobby alone and often have business groups as allies, thereby minimizing resource inequalities.

The single best predictor of success in the lobbying game, Baumgartner et al. (2009) suggest, is not how much money an organization has but simply whether it is attempting to protect or challenge the policy that is already in place. As students of American politics know, it is exceedingly difficult to change the status quo—the constitutional system of checks and balances fragments and decentralizes power, making it hard to reorient public policy. In addition to the factors cited above, Baumgartner and his coauthors (2009) believe that the status quo on any given policy area is protected by a stable set of advocates within that policy community. The advocates on each side of the issue are intimately familiar with both the policy and the arguments used to defend and attack it, and this shared knowledge among actors in the policy community provides structure and continuity to the policy conflict. Because powerful institutional and social forces protect the status quo, it takes an even more powerful set of pressures to produce change. This can explain why resource inequalities and shifts in partisan control of Congress and the White House have not allowed business to redirect environmental policy—environmental laws are now the status quo, and their defenders have been able to protect the laws from efforts to weaken them. As Klyza and Sousa (2008) have argued, the green state has proven to be remarkably resilient and has frustrated those seeking to undo it.

Others have argued that mainstream environmental organizations have been influential. Libby (1998), for example, argues that groups that are based in social movements, like environmental organizations, function both as conventional interest groups and as organizers of citizen protest and concludes that they have been effective counterweights to business. Ingram, Colnic, and Mann (1995, 115) claim that "environmental interest groups have become major forces in the political system, capable of altering the political agenda and winning significant victories against the usually dominant industrial and commercial interests of the United States." Indeed, they claim that the groups have "institutionalized" concern with environmental issues. Similarly, Kamieniecki (1991) and others (Cawley 1993; Pierce et al. 1992; Scheberle 1994; Bosso and Guber 2007) have cited examples of effective agenda setting and issue framing by environmental groups, including efforts to frame the debate over wilderness as a choice between preserving or destroying unique areas. In his study of the Clean Air Act Amendments of 1990, Cohen

(1995) argues that although the organizations comprising the National Clean Air Coalition were major actors in the debate, their influence peaked after President George H. W. Bush announced his support for a bill. Once passage of a law came to be seen as inevitable, the groups were pushed to the sideline and were locked out of the actual drafting of the law.

Although it may be a fool's errand given the inherent difficulty of the task, additional research into the influence question is warranted. The contribution by Baumgartner et al. (2009) in this area is a welcome addition to the general question of the link between material resources and policy outcomes, and further work of this type in the environmental arena may yield fresh insights. We know that business groups typically have more resources and greater access to policy makers than environmental organizations, but we still do not have a good handle on how those advantages translate, or fail to translate, into influence over policy decisions, or whether those advantages matter more at certain stages of the policy process than at others. Cohen (1995) and others have argued, for example, that although the mainstream environmental organizations have succeeded in framing issues and setting the agenda, they have been much less effective in shaping the substance of legislation and rule making, and in the implementation phase, all of which are critically important for improving environmental quality.

4. CONCLUSIONS

What do we know after 30 years of research into group activity in this policy area? Perhaps most important, we know that organizations involved in environmental policy issues mirror broader trends in American politics. It is thus helpful to understand these trends and to not assume that these policy arenas, or the groups active in them, are somehow unique. We also know that there are more organized interests today than there were 30 or 40 years ago, and this has yielded more crowded and complex policy making spheres. It is also widely acknowledged that it is misleading to speak of either "environmentalists" or "business" as if they were monolithic blocs, sharing the same policy preferences. The real world is not that simple; indeed, there is great diversity among both environmental organizations and those representing business, and sometimes environmental organizations find themselves allied with business groups.

Similarly, it seems clear that in the last 15 to 20 years, advocacy by organized interests generally has increased in scale, sophistication, and intensity. As Baumgartner et al. have shown (2009), getting attention is perhaps the biggest obstacle facing advocates in Washington, and the stepped-up lobbying efforts have made it even more daunting. Like organizations in other policy arenas, environmental and business groups now devote more time and resources to issue framing and agenda setting, hoping to advance their policy preferences.

Moreover, advances in technology have reduced the cost of communication, allowing groups with meager financial resources to have a shot at breaking through the noise. The same technology also means that grassroots campaigns are no longer conducted only by membership groups, as the fossil fuel industry's efforts to muddy the waters on climate change attest. The proliferation of multiple organizational entities (501c3, 501c4, 527, etc.), each designed for different ends, also reflects this trend. "All-directional lobbying," as Browne (1998) notes, is now commonplace, with organized interests reaching out to everyone in a never-ending cycle of advocacy.

A number of opportunities exist for future research. Despite some notable recent efforts, there is a veritable laundry list of things we do not know about the role of business organizations in environmental policy, including what they try to do to influence policy decisions and how successful they are. Most of the research questions identified by Kraft and Kamieniecki (2007b) in their study of business and environmental policy remain. There has been, for example, little systematic research into whether the strategies and tactics used by business differ between federal and state and local levels, as well as among states and cities. In light of Rabe and Mundo's (2007) claim that we can no longer predict the role of business interests in state and local policy making, additional empirical research into the factors that influence those decisions would be useful. In short, although we have learned a great deal about environmental advocacy in recent years, there is still much we can learn.

REFERENCES

Ackerman, B., and Hassler, W. 1981. *Clean Coal/Dirty Air.* New Haven, CT: Yale University Press.

Allin, C. 1982. *The Politics of Wilderness Preservation.* Westport, CT: Greenwood.

Andrews, R. N. L. 1999. *Managing the Environment, Managing Ourselves: A History of American Environmental Policy.* New Haven, CT: Yale University Press.

Audley, J. J. 1997. *Green Politics and Global Trade: NAFTA and the Future of Environmental Politics.* Washington, DC: Georgetown University Press.

Baumgartner, F., and B. Jones. 1993. *Agendas and Instability in American Politics.* Chicago: University of Chicago Press.

Baumgartner, F., and B. Leech. 1998. *Basic Interests: The Importance of Groups in Politics and in Political Science*: Princeton: Princeton University Press.

Baumgartner, F., et al. 2009. *Lobbying and Policy Change: Who Wins, Who Loses, and Why.* Chicago: University of Chicago Press.

Berry, J. 1999. *The New Liberalism: The Rising Power of Citizen Groups.* Washington, DC: Brookings Institution Press.

Bevington, D. 2009. *The Rebirth of Environmentalism: Grassroots Activism from the Spotted Owl to the Polar Bear.* Washington, DC: Island.

Bosso, C. J. 1994. "After the Movement: Environmental Activism in the 1990s." In *Environmental Policy in the 1990s*, 2nd ed., ed. N. J. Vig and M. E. Kraft. Washington, DC: CQ Press.

————. 2005. *Environment, Inc: From Grassroots to Beltway.* Lawrence: University Press of Kansas.

Brick, P., and R. M. Cawley, eds. 1996. *A Wolf in the Garden: The Land Rights Movement and the New Environmental Debate.* Lanham, MD: Rowman and Littlefield.

Browne, W. P. 1998. "Lobbying the Public: All Directional Lobbying." In *Interest Group Politics*, 5th ed., ed. A. Cigler and B. Loomis. Washington, DC: CQ Press.

Brulle, R., and J. Jenkins. 2005. "Foundations and the Environmental Movement: Priorities, Strategies and Impact." In *Foundations For Social Change: Critical Perspectives on Philanthropy and Popular Movements*, ed. D. Faber and D. McCarthy. New York: Rowman & Littlefield.

Cawley, R. M. 1993. *Federal Land, Western Anger: The Sagebrush Rebellion and Environmental Politics.* Lawrence: University Press of Kansas.

Cohen, Richard E. 1995. *Washington at Work: Back Rooms and Clean Air.* 2nd ed. New York: Allyn & Bacon.

Dowie, M. 1995. *Losing Ground: American Environmentalism at the Close of the Twentieth Century.* Cambridge, MA: MIT Press.

Duffy, R. J. 2003. *The Green Agenda in American Politics: New Strategies for the Twenty-First Century.* Lawrence: University Press of Kansas.

Freudenberg, N., and C. Steinsapir. 1991. "Not in Our Backyards: The Grassroots Environmental Movement." *Society and Natural Resources* 4: 235–245.

Furlong, S. R. 2007. "Businesses and the Environment: Influencing Agency Policymaking." In *Business and Environmental Policy: Corporate Interests in the American Political System*, ed. M. Kraft and S. Kamienicki. Cambridge, MA: MIT Press.

Gottlieb, R. 1993. *Forcing the Spring: The Transformation of the American Environmental Movement.* Washington, DC: Island.

————. 2001. *Environmentalism Unbound: Exploring New Pathways for Change.* Cambridge, MA: MIT Press.

Gray, V., and D. Lowery. 1996. *The Population Ecology of Interest Representation: Lobbying Communities in the American States.* Ann Arbor: University of Michigan Press.

Guber, D. L., and C. J. Bosso. 2007. "Framing ANWR: Citizens, Consumers, and the Privileged Position of Business." In *Business and Environmental Policy: Corporate Interests in the American Political System*, ed. M. Kraft and S. Kamienicki. Cambridge, MA: MIT Press.

————. 2010. "Past the Tipping Point? Public Discourse and the Role of the Environmental Movement in a Post-Bush Era." In *Environmental Policy*, 7th ed., ed. N. J. Vig and M. E. Kraft. Washington, DC: CQ Press.

Harris, R. A., and S. M. Milkis. 1996. *Remaking American Politics*, 2nd ed. Boulder, CO: Westview.

Harvey, M. 1994. *A Symbol of Wilderness: Echo Park and the American Conservation Movement.* Seattle: University of Washington Press.

Hays, S. P. 1987. *Beauty, Health, and Permanence: Environmental Politics in the United States, 1955–1985.* New York: Cambridge University Press.

Heinz, J. P., E. O. Laumann, R. L. Nelson, and R. H. Salisbury. 1993. *The Hollow Core: Private Interests in National Policymaking.* Cambridge, MA: Harvard University Press.

Helvarg, D. 1997. *The War against the Greens: The "Wise-Use" Movement, the New Right, and Anti-Environmental Violence.* San Francisco: Sierra Club Books.

Ingram, H. M., D. H. Colnic, and D. E. Mann. 1995. "Interest Groups and Environmental Policy." In *Environmental Politics and Policy: Theories and Evidence*, 2nd ed., ed. J. P. Lester. Durham, NC: Duke University Press.

Kamieniecki, S. 1991. "Political Mobilization, Agenda Building, and International Environmental Policy." *Journal of International Affairs* 44: 339–358.

———. 2006. *Corporate America and Environmental Policy: How Often Does Business Get Its Way?* Palo Alto, CA: Stanford University Press.

Kamieniecki, S., S. D. Coleman, and R. O. Vos. 1995. "The Effectiveness of Radical Environmentalists." In *Ecological Resistance Movements: The Global Emergence of Radical and Popular Environmentalism*, ed. B. R. Taylor. Albany: State University of New York Press.

Klyza, C. M., and D. Sousa. 2008. *American Environmental Policy, 1990–2006: Beyond Gridlock.* Cambridge, MA: MIT Press.

Kraft, M. 2006. "Environmental Policy in Congress." In *Environmental Policy: New Directions for the Twenty-First Century*, 7th ed., ed. N. J. Vig and M. E. Kraft. Washington, DC: CQ Press.

———. 2011. *Environmental Politics and Policy.* 5th ed. New York: Pearson Longman.

Kraft, M., and S. Kamieniecki, eds. 2007a. "Analyzing the Role of Business in Environmental Policy." In *Business and Environmental Policy: Corporate Interests in the American Political System*, ed. M. Kraft and S. Kamieniecki. Cambridge, MA: MIT Press.

Kraft, M., and S. Kamieniecki, 2007b. "Conclusions: The Influence of Business on Environmental Politics and Policy." In *Business and Environmental Policy: Corporate Interests in the American Political System*, ed. M. Kraft and S. Kamieniecki. Cambridge, MA: MIT Press.

Kraft, M., and D. Wuertz. 1996. "Environmental Advocacy in the Corridors of Government." In *The Symbolic Earth*, ed. J. G. Cantrill and C. L. Oravec. Lexington: University of Kentucky Press.

Layzer, J. A. 2007. "Deep Freeze: How Business Has Shaped the Global Warming Debate in Congress." In *Business and Environmental Policy: Corporate Interests in the American Political System*, ed. M. Kraft and S. Kamieniecki. Cambridge, MA: MIT Press.

Libby, R. T. 1998. *Eco-Wars: Political Campaigns and Social Movements.* New York: Columbia University Press.

Lowry, R. C. 1997. "The Private Production of Public Goods: Organizational Maintenance, Managers' Objectives, and Collective Goals." *American Political Science Review* 92: 308–323.

Manes, C. 1990. *Green Rage: Radical Environmentalism and the Unmaking of Civilization.* Boston: Little, Brown.

Mazmanian, D. A., and M. E. Kraft, eds. 2009. *Toward Sustainable Communities: Transition and Transformation in Environmental Policy.* 2nd ed. Cambridge, MA: MIT Press.

McSpadden, L. 2007. "Industry's Use of the Courts." In *Business and Environmental Policy: Corporate Interests in the American Political System*, ed. M. Kraft and S. Kamienicki. Cambridge, MA: MIT Press.

Melnick, R. S. 1983. *Regulation and the Courts: The Case of the Clean Air Act.* Washington, DC: Brookings Institution Press.

Merry, M. K. 2010. "Emotional Appeals in Environmental Group Communications."
In *American Politics Research* 38 (5): 862–889.

Miller, C. 2001. *Gifford Pinchot and the Making of Modern Environmentalism.*
Washington, DC: Island.

Mitchell, R. C. 1989. "From Conservation to Environmental Movement: The
Development of the Modern Environmental Lobbies." In *Government and
Environmental Politics*, ed. Michael Lacey. Baltimore: Johns Hopkins University
Press.

Mitchell, R. C., A. G. Mertig, and R. E. Dunlap. 1992. "Twenty Years of
Environmental Mobilization: Trends among National Environmental
Organizations." In *American Environmentalism: The U.S. Environmental
Movement, 1970–1990.* Philadelphia: Taylor and Francis.

Nash, R. F. 2001. *Wilderness and the American Mind.* 4th ed. New Haven, CT: Yale
University Press.

Olson, M. 1965. *The Logic of Collective Action: Public Goods and the Theory of
Groups.* Cambridge, MA: Harvard University Press.

Paehlke, R. C. 2010. "Sustainable Development and Urban Life in America." In
Environmental Policy, 7th ed., ed. N. J. Vig and M. E. Kraft. Washington, DC: CQ
Press.

Pierce, J. C., et al. 1992. *Citizens, Political Communication, and Interest Groups:
Environmental Organizations in Canada and the United States.* New York: Praeger.

Pralle, S. B. 2006. *Branching Out, Digging In: Environmental Advocacy and Agenda
Setting.* Washington, DC: Georgetown University Press.

Rabe, B. G., and P. A. Mundo. 2007. "Business Influence in State-Level Environmental
Policy." In *Business and Environmental Policy: Corporate Interests in the American
Political System*, ed. M. Kraft and S. Kamienicki. Cambridge, MA: MIT Press.

Sale, K. 1993. *The Green Revolution: The American Environmental Movement, 1962–
1992.* New York: Hill and Wang.

Salisbury, R. H. 1969. "An Exchange Theory of Interest Groups." *Midwest Journal of
Political Science* 13 (1): 1–32.

Schattschneider, E. E. 1960. *The Semi-Sovereign People: A Realist's View of
Democracy in America.* New York: Holt, Rinehart, and Winston.

Scheberle, D. 1994. "Radon and Asbestos: A Case Study of Agenda-Setting and
Causal Stories." *Policy Studies Journal* 22 (1): 74–86.

Schlozman, K. L., and J. T. Tierney. 1986. *Organized Interests and American
Democracy.* New York: Harper and Row.

Shabecoff, P. 1993. *A Fierce Green Fire: The New American Environmental Movement.*
New York: Hill and Wang.

———. 2000. *Earth Rising: American Environmentalism in the 21st Century.*
Washington, DC: Island.

Shaiko, R. G. 1999. *Voices and Echoes for the Environment: Public Interest
Representation in the 1990s and Beyond.* New York: Columbia University Press.

Shellenberger, M., and T. Nordhaus. 2004. "The Death of Environmentalism: Global
Warming Politics in a Post-Environmental World." October. Available at www.
thebreakthrough.org/pdf/Death_of_Environmentalism.pdf.

Smith, M. A. 2000. *American Business and Political Power: Public Opinion, Elections,
and Democracy.* Chicago: University of Chicago Press.

Snow, D. 1992. *Inside the Environmental Movement: Meeting the Leadership
Challenge.* Washington, DC: Island.

Switzer, J. V. 1997. *Green Backlash: The History and Politics of Environmental Opposition in the U.S.* Boulder, CO: Lynne Rienner.

Truman, D. 1971. *The Governmental Process*, 2nd ed. New York. Knopf.

Vogel, D. 1989. *Fluctuating Fortunes: The Political Power of Business in America*. New York: Basic Books.

———. 2005. *The Market for Virtue: The Potential and Limits of Corporate Social Responsibility*. Washington, DC: Brookings Institution Press.

Walker, J. L. 1983. "The Origins and Maintenance and Interest Groups in American." *American Political Science Review* 63 (3): 390–406.

———. 1991. *Mobilizing Interest Groups in America*. Ann Arbor: University of Michigan Press.

Weiland, P. S. 2007. "Business and Environmental Policy in the Federal Courts." In *Business and Environmental Policy: Corporate Interests in the American Political System*, ed. M. Kraft and S. Kamieniecki. Cambridge, MA: MIT Press.

Zakin, S. 1993. *Coyotes and Town Dogs: Earth First! and the Environmental Movement*. New York: Viking.

Zisk, B. H. 1992. *The Politics of Transformation: Local Activism in the Peace and Environmental Movements*. Westport, CT: Praeger.

CHAPTER 24

....

PARTIES, CAMPAIGNS, AND ELECTIONS

....

AMY BELOW

An extremely broad category of concerns, environmental policies can cover issues from species and ecosystem preservation to the protection of human health, and they can be as targeted as requiring specific technologies be used in specific industries or as general as setting national targets for greenhouse gas emission reductions. Key to what decisions get made and how they are made is *who* is making these decisions. As described in many of the chapters in this book, a variety of formal and informal actors participate in environmental policy making at all levels of government. This chapter focuses on these actors, with specific attention to their role in electoral processes. Environmentalists have been active participants in electoral processes since the beginning of the modern environmental era in the 1960s and 1970s, particularly by campaigning for candidates likely to favor their position on public policies and working to approve legislation directly via state and local ballot initiatives referenda. Research on these efforts shows that while many environmental initiatives and referenda have been approved and green candidates elected at the local and state level, the environmental movement has had much less of an impact on national campaigns and elections (Bosso and Guber 2006).

This chapter reviews existing literature concerning the relationships between parties, campaigns, and elections and environmental politics and policy. The following pages review studies conducted on the ability of political parties (the Democratic, Republican, and Green Parties, specifically) to represent environmental interests and win elections, the impact environmental issues have on campaigns and elections, and how well elected representatives carry out their pro- or anti-environmental campaign pledges once in office. The chapter then reviews the role of direct democracy and the evolution of environmentally related initiatives and referenda and their success at the polls. The last section concerns the role of the media in environmental politics and policy. One of the largest impacts the media have on the electoral process is their ability to craft the agenda for political candidates and policy makers. Another aim of this chapter is to highlight gaps in knowledge and suggest areas for future research. The chapter concludes with suggestions for research that can help us better understand the relationships between parties, campaigns, and elections and environmental politics and policy, and the role of formal and informal actors in electoral processes.

1. REPRESENTATIVE DEMOCRACY

1.1. Political Parties

In the U.S. form of representative democracy, the electorate chooses who they wish to represent them in government. The victors, whether presidents, members of Congress, or state and local representatives, become the official policy makers responsible for representing the desires of their constituents in governance. For decades, scholars have studied how well the concerns of the public are manifest in their democratically elected representatives and their behavior in office (Clinton 2006; Erikson 1978; Glazer and Robbins 1985; Miller and Stokes 1963). One way Americans have attempted to ensure that their voices are heard is by forming and supporting political parties and electing party members to office. They hope, of course, that candidates from their own party would best represent their policy preferences. Though not mentioned in the Constitution (in fact, they were intentionally omitted from it), political parties have become significant actors in U.S. politics and thus have played an active role in environmental policy making.

The United States party system has evolved into one dominated by two parties: Democrats and Republicans. Despite long-standing criticism that the two parties have become indistinguishable from each other on a number of issues (Herrington 2010), consensus has emerged that over time the Democratic Party has come to better represent environmental interests. The Green Party has emerged as an alternative for those who believe the traditional parties do not sufficiently focus on environmental issues or who are critical of the policies they implement. While the Green Party has had little impact on environmental policy making, it has had a substantial impact on two presidential elections.

1.1.1. *Democrats versus Republicans*

In the early decades of the movement in the United States, environmentalism was commonly considered a nonpartisan issue (Ogden 1971), as it was thought that concern for environmental protection transcended political ideology and partisan loyalties. Environmental well-being was a universal concern. However, it did not take long for a division to emerge—a relatively distinct division—between Democrats and Republicans based on political ideology. Republican ideology argues for individual liberty as opposed to government interference. Its preference for small government coincides with a probusiness, free-market attitude and thus an aversion to government control, especially when it imposes perceived high economic costs through adoption of environmental and other regulations (Dunlap and Gale 1974; Kraft 2011; Rosenbaum 2011). Democratic ideology is more commonly associated with liberalism and an acceptance of government involvement in the political, economic, and social lives of the people. As Field (2007, 80) summarizes the differences, "Democrats are usually thought to favor greater reliance on statutory pollution-control regulations as a way to improve environmental quality; Republicans are more inclined to stress the economic costs of pollution control and to tout the advantages of voluntary approaches to improving the environment." As a result, individuals who favor the creation of government policies to protect the environment, even if it means curtailing some individual (or corporate) liberties, are more likely to align themselves with the Democratic Party. Those against imposing environmental regulations more commonly ally with the Republican Party.

When asked whom they trusted to best protect the environment, the public generally has more faith in Democrats than Republicans. Voters polled in 2002 preferred Democratic congressional representatives over Republicans 49 to 28 percent (Kriz 2002). Kamieniecki (1995) found that the strength of party identification affects how voters responded to such a question. The stronger individuals' party identification, the more they believed their own party better protects the environment. He also found that a larger number of Republicans than Democrats believed that the other party was a better protector. In other words, a number of self-identifying Republicans felt that Democrats would be better environmental stewards. This phenomenon was particularly prominent during the Reagan and George H. W. Bush presidencies.

Voters often use a party's platform to help them decide which party to join or for whom to vote. Platforms are intended to reflect the principles and policies that a party espouses. While the environment has not been significantly salient in either party's platform compared to other policy areas, how each has addressed environmental issues when mentioned corroborate the Democrat/Republican divide. In similar studies of party platforms, Kamieniecki (1995) and Tatalovich and Wattier (1999) found clear differences in party stances on the environment. Republican platforms have generally pitted environmental protection against economic development and well-being, maintaining that environmental regulations and associated wasteful spending should be avoided in order to ensure a healthy economy. In a study of party platforms in 1980, Kraft (1984) similarly noted how the Republican platform defined environmental quality in terms of economic well-being: environmental policies are justified only if they do not impose economic costs. Democratic platforms have typically not presented environmentalism and a strong economy as mutually exclusive concerns and have argued that environmental protection "can create job opportunities," as stated in its 1972 platform (Tatalovich and Wattier 1999, 155) and in both party platforms and presidential pronouncements during Bill Clinton's and Barack Obama's presidencies.

An important point, however, is that while generalizations can be made about the two dominant parties and their platforms, they are not homogenous units. Variations of "environmentalism" do exist within parties, particularly with moderates and independent voters. For example, moderate Republicans have commonly spoken out against some of their more conservative counterparts and their "anti-environment" statements and/or policies. The national nonprofit organization Republicans for Environmental Protection (now called ConservAmerica), for instance, advocates conservation and environmental stewardship. Its members promote environmental protection (and a healthy economy) and endorse environmentally friendly Republican candidates. The organization's website publicizes the environmental voting records of Republican members of Congress. There are also divides along gender lines (Baker 1996), between urban and rural communities (Baker 1996; Burns 2008), and between coastal and noncoastal urban centers (Burns 2008).

While such variables have a cumulative effect on a voter's environmental values, scholars continue to find support for a divide along party lines. Riley Dunlap and his coauthors conducted a series of studies to test the partisanship hypothesis. The first, a case study of the Oregon state legislature (Dunlap and Gale 1974), revealed a strong relationship between party identification and pro-environment voting. A follow-up study of pro-environment voting in the 92nd Congress provided similar support for partisanship at the national level (Dunlap and Allen 1976).

A number of subsequent studies have shown not only that partisanship has an influence but also that the influence has increased over time. For example, in a study spanning data over a 30-year period, Shipan and Lowry (2001) found that the voting difference on environmental legislation between Democrats and Republicans in both houses of Congress has increased progressively since the 1970s. The authors argue that regional differences, factions within parties, and changes in individual preference account for the change over time. Sussman et al. found that the divide began to take shape in the mid- to late 1970s and "by the late 1990s, 'green' voting among Republicans was becoming a rare event" (2002, 96).[1] They found similar results in state legislatures, though with regional variation. Dunlap, Xiao, and McCright (2001) came to a similar conclusion regarding divergences in both Congress and the general public, concluding that partisanship has been increasing over time. The authors argue that "it is not an exaggeration to say that the Democrats have become the 'environmental party,' and Republicans the 'anti-environmental party'" (30). Such a conclusion lends credence to Dunlap, Xiao, and McCright's observation that "the

---

1. More specifically, Rosenbaum (2011) argues that a lull in partisanship in the 1970s was renewed in the 1980s as a response to the Reagan administration's weakening of environmental regulation and preference for free market policies. Partisanship again waned in the 1990s but was again awakened just after the turn of the century when Republican George W. Bush took office.

time has finally come to give up the image of environment as a 'motherhood' issue once and for all" (2001, 45). In contrast, many voters fail to see a difference between the two main parties on environmental issues. Similarly, even though there are distinctions between how Democrats and Republicans in Congress vote on environmental legislation, very few accentuate these differences during their campaigns. Additional research into this disconnect could be illuminating.

Burns (2008), however, notes that climate change seemed to be an area that could overcome the pronounced partisan cleavages. He argues that a nonpartisan political consensus to take action has emerged. Opinions on the topic do not seem to rely strictly on party allegiance. A prominent 2008 advertising campaign sponsored by the nonpartisan group We Can Solve It calling for bipartisan support of the issue provides evidence of this.[2] Since that time, however, the partisan divide has seemed to grow increasingly pronounced as congressional discussions of specific policies, including cap-and-trade legislation, have taken center stage and emphasized contentious perspectives on government regulation. In fact, today the partisan divide over climate change legislation is perhaps the most contentious of all environmental issues (Dunlap and McCright 2008). For example, a 2010 Yale Project on Climate Change Communication survey found that Democrats were considerably more likely to view global warming as an important policy area than Republicans (Leiserowitz 2010).

Such divisions suggest that observed environmental partisanship rests on a more fundamental disagreement between competing political ideologies. Scholars (such as Dunlap, Xiao, and McCright 2001) point out that environmental sensitivity and the acceptance of environmental regulation correspond to a "liberalness" or "conservativeness" more than to party identification. In principle, individuals are not opposed to protecting the environment and do not harbor "anti-environment" sentiments. However, there are distinctions in how people believe the environment should be managed. In other words, there are disagreements over how much the government should regulate behavior in order to protect the environment. Kamieniecki (1995) also acknowledges the role of ideology. He found that it is more associated with voters' views on regulating business and imposing taxes in order to protect the environment than partisanship but found that partisanship is more closely associated with voters' evaluations of an individual politician's handling of environmental issues than ideology. He thus concludes that both are associated with environmentalism. Political ideology is important, but it "does not cancel out the relationship between partisanship and environmentalism" (Kamieniecki 1995, 165).

1.1.2. Third Parties

For those who are not satisfied by either the Democratic or Republican Parties, another option is to join a third party. Over the years, a number of parties have

---

2. One commercial highlighted former Speaker of the House Democrat Nancy Pelosi and former Speaker Republican Newt Gingrich. Another featured liberal Democrat Reverend Al Sharpton and Republican Christian conservative Pat Robertson.

concentrated on environmental issues, including Theodore Roosevelt's Bull Moose Party, which espoused a platform of natural resource conservation (Field 2007). The most common option today is the Green Party. Although the Green Party is concerned with a number of social and economic issues (including living wages for workers, universal health care, and reform of the civil justice system), it focuses significant attention on environmental protection and ecological sustainability.[3] It is commonly considered the "greenest" of the political parties in the United States. Unlike the two dominant parties, the Green Party does not claim to represent a particular political ideology. Nonetheless, party members are likely to self-identify as liberal.

The origins of the Green Party in the United States can be traced back to 1984 and a meeting of environmental activists in St. Paul, Minnesota, that became known as the Green Committees of Correspondence. Beginning in 1990 with Alaska and California, states began forming their own green parties, and the name of the national organization changed to The Greens, or Green Party USA. Beginning in 1996, another grouping of states combined to form the Association of State Green Parties. To this day, the two strains of green parties exist simultaneously. In 2001, the Association of State Green Parties became the Green Party of the United States (the party that nominated Ralph Nader to run for president in 2000; see Green Party of the United States 2004). In terms of representation in government, Green Party candidates have not been very successful on the national level; most Green Party officials hold positions at state or local levels. As of the beginning of 2011, there were 120 Green officeholders, including six city mayors.[4]

Though few Green Party members have been elected to national office, the American electorate does care about environmental protection. As the studies discussed above suggest, environmentally-minded voters tend to align themselves not with the Green Party but with the Democratic Party. Studies of survey data, party platforms, and legislative roll-call voting suggest that party identification can be a good indicator of how a voter feels about environmental issues. In fact, party identification has become an even stronger indicator as the partisan divide over environmental issues has grown over time.

However, partisanship is not a foolproof indicator, since the Democratic and Republican parties are not homogenous. Variations exist within each party. What may be an even stronger indicator of a voter's environmental feelings is political ideology. How an individual feels about government regulation is commonly associated with how that person feels about environmental policy and how she or he

3. The Green Party's Ten Key Values are 1) grassroots democracy, 2) social justice and equal opportunity, 3) ecological wisdom, 4) nonviolence, 5) decentralization, 6) community-based economics and economic justice, 7) feminism and gender equity, 8) respect for diversity, 9) personal and global responsibility, and 10) future focus and sustainability (Green Party of the United States).

4. Lem and Dowling (2006) record that there were 205 Green public officeholders in 2003, though mostly at lower levels of government.

votes for political candidates. It is to the role of the environment in political campaigns and elections that the chapter now turns.

1.2. Campaigns and Elections

1.2.1. *The Role of Environmentalists*

One way that environmentalists can have a large impact on environmental policy and insert themselves into the democratic process is via their participation in political campaigns and elections. They can push to make sure environmentalism is on the campaign agenda and thus is considered by all candidates. In this way they can give prominence to environmental issues in hopes that policies will eventually be enacted that protect environmental resources. They can also elect candidates who have, or they anticipate will have, the best environmental record, candidates who will enact necessary environmental legislation. Unfortunately, environmentalists have not been very successful at agenda setting. Environmental issues have rarely been a significant campaign issue and have rarely affected election outcomes (Bosso and Guber 2006; Kraft 2011). However, environmentalism has slowly become a more prominent issue over time; it achieved its most dominant presence thus far in the 2008 presidential campaign between candidates John McCain and Barack Obama.

Traditionally, however, environmental issues have been noticeably absent from national campaigns, particularly presidential campaigns (Vig 2010). Steven Burns (2008) analyzed how much environmentalism permeates the public consciousness, particularly in national elections. His conclusion was "not much" (Burns 2008, 8). The majority of political discussions around the environment are among specialists (mainly environmental advocates, interested industry representatives, and representatives of specific government agencies) rather than among the general electorate. Besides, most environmental issues are too scientific and technical to hold voters' attention long enough to make an impact. A contemporary exception is climate change. Though the scientific underpinnings are quite complex, the issue itself has evolved from a purely environmental issue to an economic, public health, and national security issue that has had a unique ability to capture and thus far maintain the public's attention. Additionally, climate change has been framed by many as a "crisis," and crises attract political attention. However, climate change has been a political issue in the United States for decades and has only recently become a serious policy concern and a part of national campaign rhetoric. Other environmental issues have been even less prominent.

According to Guber (2001b), this is the result of three factors. First, environmentalism has low issue salience. Many voters are concerned about the environment, but when forced to prioritize, the environment is rarely near the top of the list. Citing analysis of National Election Survey (NES) data compiled for the 1996 presidential campaign between Democrat Bill Clinton and Republican Bob Dole, Guber writes that "environmental preferences all but disappear among a sea of competing influences, including controls for partisan identification and political ideology" (2001, 459). Bomberg (2001) points out, however, that low issue salience in elections does not suggest a complete lack of public concern for the environment. In fact, polls reveal a consistent preference for stronger environmental policies. Nonetheless, when voters are faced with prioritizing a list of issues or when they must face what they perceive to be economic versus environment trade-offs, the environment traditionally takes a backseat.

Second, when it comes to environmental issues most voters do not discern a noticeable difference between candidates. Even though polling data show that the Democratic Party and its candidates are thought to be stronger on environmental issues, the difference is muted in campaigns, particularly presidential campaigns (Bosso and Guber 2006). As a result, voters use other policy markers to help them decide who gets their vote. Environmental issues lose their relevance in the voting booth as other policy areas overpower them; candidates know this and run their campaigns accordingly.

Third, Guber (2001b) points to partisan loyalty. Partisan voters are rarely willing to cross party lines because of disagreements in one policy area (especially one with such low issue salience); their long-held beliefs and ideological ties are not easily severed. For instance, for a Republican to vote green they would likely have to cast a vote for a more liberal Democratic candidate or in favor of strict government regulation. Such a shift is not likely. For independent voters, however, the environment is more likely to be a distinguishing factor. Without deep allegiances to either main party or political ideology, independents with environmental concerns are more likely to be swayed by a candidate's environmental record.

Case studies of recent presidential campaigns and elections and the environment's impact on them provide contrasting perspectives. Scholars disagree as to whether the environment has been a factor in presidential campaigns and elections. For example, results from an analysis of campaign media coverage led Tatalovich and Wattier (1999) to conclude that the environment was not a salient issue in presidential campaigns from 1972 to 1992. A subsequent study during the same time period found that environmental issues were of little concern to voters, as less than 4 percent of respondents mentioned that environmental concerns were important to them, as compared to no fewer than 12 percent who mentioned economic issues (Wattier and Tatalovich 2000). Taken together, the two studies suggest the public was not attentive to environmental issues and, as a result, neither were candidates and their campaigns. Bosso and Guber (2006) similarly argue that the environment was not a factor in both the 1996 and 2000 presidential campaigns. (See the discussion below for how these results compare with the recent 2008 presidential campaign.) Due to the aforementioned deterrents of issue salience and a lack of differences between candidates and partisan loyalty, the environment failed to place among voters' priorities.

In comparison, it was anticipated that the environment might play a larger role in national congressional campaigns in the mid-1990s than it had in the past. As a result of the 1994 midterm elections and the "Republican Revolution," the Republican Party gained control of both the House and the Senate. According to the League of Conservation Voter's (LCV) Scorecard, Republicans in the 104th Congress, including newly elected members, had a distinctly poor environmental voting record. It was anticipated that environmentalists would use this record against Republicans during the 1996 campaign season (Baker 1996). Voters would express their displeasure with the newly elected officials, elect more Democrats, and return control of at least one branch to the Democrats. In the end, Democrats were able to narrow the lead in the House by a few seats, but the Republicans maintained control of both chambers. The Republican Party's poor environmental record in Congress did not appear to affect the outcome of these elections. Presidential candidate Senator Bob Dole had the worst voting record of all: from 1970 to 1995 he supported environmental legislation 20 percent of the time, lower than the Republican average. While Dole was not elected president in 1996, it is not likely that his environmental record explains why he lost his presidential bid. Environmental issues were not a significant topic throughout the campaign.

Focusing attention on the 2000 presidential campaign between Democrat Al Gore and Republican George W. Bush, Bomberg (2001) argues that, just as with the 1996 congressional election, there was potential for the environment to be a factor but in fact it was not. This was the first campaign with a prominent environmental activist as a candidate. Gore had championed environmental issues during his vice presidency and had even written a book, *Earth in the Balance* (1993), arguing for the necessity of an urgent and radical rethinking of our relationship with the planet and its ecosystems. This made for an obvious difference between the two candidates of which voters would surely take note. In addition, this was the first year that a Green Party candidate would run, ideally making the environment a campaign issue. Coupled with the mass mobilization of environmental groups (like the Sierra Club and the LCV) and their major financial contributions, 2000 looked to be the year the environment would finally gain national attention. In the end, the 2000 campaign unfolded as all campaigns before it; environmental issues garnered little attention and the environment had little effect on voter choice. Neither Gore nor Green Party candidate Ralph Nader made the environment a prominent campaign issue.

Bosso and Guber (2006) make similar observations about the 2004 presidential campaign. They note that Democrats failed to take advantage of the difference between Republican incumbent George W. Bush's and Democrat John Kerry's environmental positions and make the environment a strategic and prominent campaign issue. Campaign debate and rhetoric instead focused mainly on defense and the war in Iraq (which overshadowed most domestic and social issues).

However, not everyone agrees that the environment is ineffectual when it comes to national campaigns and elections. For example, Davis and Wurth (2003) directly counter Guber's (2001b) conclusions about voter choice and the 1996 presidential election. Using the same NES data as a starting point, Davis and Wurth use a different variable to measure environmental support.[5] As a result, they found confirmation that the environment did affect voters' evaluations of candidates and, ultimately, how they cast their final vote. The authors acknowledge that the environment was not one of the top concerns, but "there are indications that the environment is relevant and visible" (Davis and Wurth 2003, 729). Alvarez and Nagler (1998) draw similar conclusions about the 1996 election, finding that the relationship between voters' and candidates' environmental preferences (how closely they are aligned) was a significant predictor of how voters cast their ballot.

Davis, Wurth, and Lazarus (2008) took the analysis a step further by conducting a study of five presidential elections from 1984 to 2000. They found the environment had a significant impact on four out of five elections. (It did not significantly impact the 2000 election.)

The greatest perceived difference occurred in the 1996 campaign between Democrat Bill Clinton and Republican Bob Dole. Clinton continued to pledge his support for environmental regulation, while Dole threatened to cut spending for environmental protection. Davis, Wurth, and Lazarus argue that although the environment did not determine the outcome of this election, it did have an impact on voters' decisions. Only the economy and abortion were more influential.

Compared to previous campaigns, the environment played a much larger role in the 2008 competition between Democrat Barack Obama and Republican John McCain. As Michael Gerrard wrote, "For the first time in living memory, the environment is receiving significant attention in a presidential election" (2008). Both candidates publicized their views on a number of environmental issues, particularly those relating to energy and climate change. McCain even made a public effort to distinguish himself from George W. Bush's poor environmental record in an effort to avoid being targeted as the "anti-environment" candidate and possibly to hide his own poor congressional record.

Nonetheless, their views as publicized on the campaign trail were not markedly distinct on a number of environmental issues. For example, both supported efforts to address climate change, including supporting cap-and-trade legislation. Both were in favor of reducing the country's dependence on foreign oil and encouraging the use of renewable energy. What separated the candidates was mainly the role they felt the government should play (versus relying on market incentives and individual initiative). Because the differences were based on clear divides in political ideology, any distinctions between candidates were likely not enough to entice voters to cross party lines. In addition, a number of other issues, including economic recovery, employment, and the wars in Iraq and Afghanistan, likely played a more influential role in voter preference. Thus, while the environment was more

---

5. The authors argue that the wording of Guber's questions force respondents to make a decision between jobs and the environment, to make a trade-off. The authors believe that most people do not conceive of environmental protection in a zero-sum way and instead formulated questions to avoid a falsely-conceived choice for respondents.

prominent in the 2008 campaign than in previous elections, it is not clear whether the issue affected voter preference or election results.[6]

Although existing literature does not provide conclusive support that the environment has a strong effect on campaigns and election outcomes, it would be wrong to conclude that environmental issues are of little or no political consequence. It would be similarly remiss to assume that the environment has a uniform impact on all voters (and candidates). The environment's influence varies by individual voter and by context. For some voters, under particular circumstances (especially those at the political margins), the environment can be quite influential, even in national elections (Guber 2001b). The same can be said of voters unaligned with either dominant party. Independents are thought to be "swing" voters when it comes to environmental concerns. Moreover, if the role environmental issues played in the 2008 campaign represents the beginning of a new trend, it is possible that the environment will have even greater influence on campaigns and elections in the future.

1.2.2. Postelection Environmentalism

The study of environmentalism and campaigns and elections does not end when the polls close. When the campaigns end, what happens once the victors take office? Do they keep their campaign promises? Studies have shown that presidential candidates tend to keep their environmental campaign promises more often than not. One investigation shows that 64 percent of presidents studied from 1932 to 1996 kept their environmental pledges, both Democrat and Republican (Sussman et al. 2002). In a comparison of State of the Union speeches and party platforms, Wattier and Tatalovich (2000) find that presidents pay more attention to environmental issues in their speeches than in their campaigns. Their findings suggest that presidents are more hesitant to broadcast their views during a campaign than on taking office, thus reinforcing arguments about the lack of saliency of environmental issues in presidential elections.

Wattier and Tatalovich (2000) similarly point out that presidential agendas do not always reflect party platforms. The campaigns and presidencies of Richard Nixon, Ronald Reagan, and Jimmy Carter are good examples. Nixon's campaign did not devote much time to environmental issues, but his legislative record has made him one of the most environmental presidents in recent history. Reagan made it a top priority of his presidency to do away with costly and onerous environmental legislation, even though his 1980 campaign would never have predicted

---

6. A similar conclusion could be made about the 2010 mid-term election wherein republicans regained control of the House. Environmental issues such as off-shore oil drilling, renewable energy and carbon taxes were common campaign topics and, although they can be related to economic issues, they were overshadowed by concern for the harsh economic conditions the country was facing as a result of the Great Recession. A number of fiscally conservative republicans and Tea Party candidates were elected to seats previously controlled by democrats.

it. In contrast, Carter campaigned in 1984 against Reagan's anti-environmental policies yet did not make it a presidential priority. Discrepancies in the previous case studies are likely due to changing political contexts on taking office, not necessarily misleading campaign rhetoric.

Congressional representatives have also been good at keeping their promises. A study by Ringquist and Dasse found that members of the 105th Congress kept their environmental campaign promises 73 percent of the time (2004). However, there are variations among individual legislators. Long-term representatives are more likely to keep their promises, while representatives from southern states are more likely to break theirs. Republicans are also more likely to break their promises. Perhaps this is because, as mentioned earlier, no one claims to be against the environment, and no candidate claims to be the "anti-environment" candidate. Even Republican candidates express support for a clean and healthy environment. However, on taking office, political ideology related to beliefs about the proper size and role of government and government regulation generally determines their voting behavior. Their votes for deregulation and budget cuts can be interpreted as anti-environmental votes and thus breaking environmental promises. It is also possible that environmental campaign promises are made under the assumption that voters will not pay close attention to their behavior (especially on votes on specific pieces of legislation) once they take office due to the low salience of environmental issues. Perhaps most interesting for environmentalists, the Ringquist and Dasse (2004) study reveals that pro-environmental promises are more likely to be broken than anti-environmental ones. These results suggest that when pro-environment representatives are elected, they find it difficult to keep their promises once in office. Again, these results suggest not that candidates engage in deceit or trickery on the campaign trail but, rather, that campaigning and governing on environmental issues can be two very different processes.

1.2.3. *The Role of the Green Party*

Another way that environmentalists can influence campaigns and elections is by running their own candidates—Green Party candidates. Although the Green Party is one of the largest third parties in the United States (along with the Libertarian and Constitution Parties) as it is recognized by a majority of U.S. states, it has not been successful at electing Green Party candidates at the national level. However, this is not to say that the party has not had any effect on the outcome of national elections. Ralph Nader's campaign for president in 2000 arguably played a pivotal role in the election of George W. Bush.

In addition to the fact that the Green Party has not gained equal popularity across all regions of the country (Kraft 2011) and that it cannot compete with the two dominant parties in terms of sheer numbers, structural constraints built into the U.S. electoral system have prevented any measurable success at the national level. For example, in many cases, while Democratic and Republican candidates are automatically allowed on ballots, third parties must secure a spot by collecting vast numbers of signatures. This sometimes requires months of volunteer hours and extensive resources. Funding is also an obstacle for third parties. Aside from the difficulty in obtaining private funds for a third party that is not expected to be a serious contender, public funds are difficult to secure. Again, whereas the two main parties already have access to public funds as soon as they nominate their candidates, third parties must win at least 5 percent of the vote in a national election to ensure public funds are available for the following year. If they can do this, they are still only guaranteed money proportionate to the percentage of the vote won (Doyle and McEachern 2008). This would be a relatively small number.

Perhaps the biggest obstacle to a Green Party candidate winning many state and national elections is the "first past the post" or "winner take all" system. The United States electoral system is structured such that the candidate with the most votes wins. Even if candidates only receive 25 percent of the vote (meaning 75 percent voted for other candidates), they can win the election. This is particularly important in presidential elections, which are decided by the Electoral College: the candidate with the most votes in a state wins all of the state's electoral votes. A candidate coming in a close second wins none. Aware of how the system functions, many voters view a vote for a third-party candidate as a wasted vote (Bosso and Guber 2006; Duffy 2003). Thus, even if they would prefer, for example, the Green Party candidate, voters with environmental values often cast their ballots for Democratic candidates instead to ensure that their vote "counts."

Some of the most prominent examples of Green Party candidates on a national level are the presidential campaigns of Ralph Nader. Nader first ran in 1996 as a presidential candidate on the ballot in a number of states. While Nader was not successful in wining electoral votes in these states, he was able to influence the campaign agenda in some states, particularly in California.

Nader's presidential run in 2000 was significantly more consequential and controversial.[7] In one of the closest presidential elections in U.S. history, Republican candidate George W. Bush narrowly defeated Democratic candidate Al Gore. While Gore won a slightly bigger percentage of the popular vote (48.4 percent to 47.9 percent), thanks to the ruling in *Bush v. Gore* and the decision on Florida's electoral votes, Bush won 271 to Gore's 266 electoral votes and thus became president.[8] Many Democrats blamed Bush's win on Nader. They believe Nader "stole" votes in a number of key states that would have otherwise gone to Gore. As evidence, Nader received almost 3 million votes, while only 500,000 votes separated Bush and Gore (Burden 2005a).

While many Democratic Party voters called Nader a "spoiler" in search of attention and blamed Gore's loss on him, others saw Nader's candidacy as a strategic move for the benefit of the future of the Green Party. Burden (2005b) studied

---

7. Nader also ran for president in 2004 and 2008, but as an Independent.
8. Bush's 271 electoral votes represented 50.4 percent of all possible votes while Gore's 266 represented a close 49.4 percent.

Nader's campaign to determine which argument was most plausible. He concluded that Nader's true objective was to earn 5 percent of the popular vote, enough to ensure the Green Party matching funds in the next presidential election, not to steal votes from the Democrats. If Nader "stole" votes from the candidate that may have won in his absence, it was unintentional. Regardless, in the end Nader failed to reach the 5 percent threshold.[9]

Green Party candidates had a similar impact on congressional elections in 2000. Though 40 candidates ran for office, none were successful. A number did, however, win enough votes to affect the outcomes of elections, winning enough votes to help Republican candidates win or make elections uncomfortably close for Democratic candidates (Duffy 2003).[10]

After the 2000 election, the Green Party fell out of favor with a number of voters who support environmental protection. While the party remained successful in some state and local elections, it has received less attention on the national level since 2000. In the next election (2004), Ralph Nader was replaced on the presidential ticket by David Cobb. It is alleged that party leaders instructed members to vote for the Green ticket "only in states where their vote doesn't matter," believing that electing any challenger would be better than reelecting Bush for another term (Doyle and McEachern 2008, 182). This request likely raised huge questions for environmentalists, as many were forced to either cast their vote on principle (and for the Green Party candidate) or forgo their environmental beliefs and cast a compromise vote or a "lesser of two evils" vote in hopes that the candidate least supportive of environmental protection did not get elected.[11] Perhaps as a result of this type of voting, the Green Party won just under 120,000 votes in 2004 (compared to more than 2,880,000 in 2000). The Green Party maintained its small presence in the 2008 presidential election, with candidate Cynthia McKinney winning just over 160,000 votes. As the Democratic and Republican candidates focused on the environment more in 2008 than in years past, voters relied on traditional partisanship rather than issue voting. Additional research into how Green Party members have voted in recent elections (either along party lines/issue voting or strategic voting) could provide greater insight into how Green Party candidates affect elections.

9. The argument that Nader cost Gore the election is weakened somewhat by the uncertainty of whether those that voted for Nader would have voted in the election at all had Nader not been a candidate. If they would not have voted, their votes cannot be considered "stolen" from Gore and the divide between Gore and Bush would have remained the same.

10. Duffy (2003) lists this phenomenon as happening in Michigan's Eighth District (providing a 151 vote victory for the republican candidate) and in New Jersey's Twelfth District (causing the democrat incumbent to win by less than 300 votes).

11. For example, in 2000 an environmentalist would forego voting for Nader and, instead, cast an "anti-Bush" vote for Gore.

2. DIRECT DEMOCRACY

Environmentalists can also participate in the democratic process and affect policy making by voting for legislation directly via state and local level initiatives and referenda. Even though political parties and other interest groups often play highly influential roles in the life cycle of these political instruments (discussed in greater detail in chapters 20 and 23 in this volume), including how they get on the ballot and whether they pass, the intention behind these measures is to give the people a direct voice in the democratic process. Given that environmental issues have low salience in the national agenda and are not awarded notable time in national campaigns, state and local politics can provide a different perspective on the public's sense of environmentalism. At this level, "environmental issues seem to enjoy greater salience and less competition for room on a crowded political agenda" (Guber 2001a, 466). As a result, initiatives and referenda provide great insight into how voters feel about environmental policy and reveal a voter's willingness to pay for it.

Initiatives and referenda provide great insight because they give the public direct legislative powers. In addition, most varieties of referenda and initiatives reach the ballot due to popular demand. Although rules vary by state, in general initiatives and referenda qualify for the ballot once they receive a set number of registered voter signatures. With direct initiatives, citizen groups work to place a piece of legislation on the ballot and the public votes it up or down. With indirect initiatives, proposals still originate with the public but are prescreened by the legislature before reaching the ballot. Twenty-four states have the initiative process. Referenda refer more specifically to existing legislation that the public votes to enact or repeal. For example, some state legislatures are required by law to obtain public approval on certain budgetary items. All states but Delaware also require a popular vote to approve constitutional amendments. These must be placed on the ballot by the legislature. A different variant, a popular referenda, is placed on the ballot by the public (and still refer to existing legislation). Twenty-four states have some form of referendum process. A number of states use both tools (initiatives and referenda), though not all.

As Dell (2009) found in a recent study of democratic participation in state-level environmental policy making, there has been a dramatic increase in the use of initiatives and referenda. Since the 1950s, the use of both approaches has increased 24-fold; the use of initiatives alone has increased 15-fold. Each state's use of these tools varies considerably, however. Totals from 1900 to 2000 show that California and Maine had 90 and 67 propositions on the ballot, respectively, while Iowa, Utah, and Wyoming had only one each. The passage rate of these propositions is perhaps more telling as it is a better measure of public support. Dell (2009) found that the average passage rate for environmental propositions over the last four decades never fell below 60 percent (as compared to a passage rate of around 40 percent for all ballot issues combined). In addition, those that passed did so comfortably.

While the amount of money and, thus, media time available in support of or against a measure is a common predictor of its success (David and Kelly 1998; Guber 2001a), it is not the only factor determining a proposition's future. For example, issue framing is crucial. As Guber writes, "What is most important is the ability of savvy political campaigns to define the terms of debate in ways favorable to their case" (2001a, 122). Grassroots support and a developing environmental ethos have also supported the passage of environmental initiatives and referenda. Confusing language (especially for nonbond and nontax measures) and a low level of public understanding of environmental problems can be formidable obstacles, but grassroots mobilization (Lake 1983) and a growing environmental ethos (Dell 2009) have proven to provide substantial support among the general public for environmental measures.

This expanding support could help explain the growing spectrum of environmental issues that propositions have covered over the years (and the corresponding increase in environmental group activity related to these propositions). Initiatives and referenda commonly focus on traditional environmental issues such as fisheries and wildlife, pollution, and transportation. Land conservation has also been a popular focus even in strongly Republican-leaning states and localities (Kraft 2011). For example, the 1990s saw the popularization of various "smart growth" measures to implement sustainable development and urban growth boundaries and to preserve green spaces. In the twenty-first century, climate change and energy-related propositions have become increasingly popular, though they were less successful in 2008, possibly because of poor economic conditions (Kraft 2011).

A prominent example of citizen-led support for climate change legislation is California's Proposition 23, on the ballot in 2010. The proposition was intended to suspend (some argue the "suspension" was meant to be indefinite) the implementation of Assembly Bill 32, the "Global Warming Solutions Act of 2006." In spite of exceedingly harsh economic conditions in the state and the complexity of the proposition (a "yes" vote for Proposition 23 was a "no" vote on AB 32), Californians voted down the proposition with over 60 percent of the vote. Also meaningful is the fact that the public voted down this proposition despite the approximately 9 million dollars donated by supporters of the measure. The donations were controversial because the majority of the money came from out-of-state interests and oil and gas companies, including the Texas-based Valero Energy Corporation and Tesoro Corporation, which together donated a cumulative total of over $5 million.[12] Opponents donated a total of approximately $34 million to the campaign, an amount that likely helped defeat the proposition.[13]

---

12. Estimates range from a total of 5.5 to 7.4 million dollars.
13. A number of studies have focused on the use of the initiative and referendum process in California and Oregon for environmental policy making. See, for example, Kahn (1997), Lake (1983) and Lutrin (1975) on California and Ellis (2005) on Oregon.

3. THE ROLE OF MEDIA

In addition to voters, parties, and candidates (as well as other actors discussed in this volume), the media (including television, radio, Internet, and print outlets) also play a number of important roles in the democratic process, including covering news events, educating the public, and serving as a medium for campaign publicity. Perhaps the media's most important role (encompassing the aforementioned) is as an agenda setter (McCombs 2004; Switzer 2004; Wood and George 1999). Media help determine what issues and debates become part of public discourse and to what voters, candidates, and policy makers devote attention. In this way, media's role is not necessarily to tell the public what to think, but what to *think about* (Cohen 1963). Although, as discussed above, environmental issues have little political salience, the media help to raise their social (and in some cases political) salience by bringing them to the public's attention.

The frequency with which the media have placed environmental issues on the public and political agenda has increased over time. In the early twentieth century, environmental issues of preservation and conservation rarely received coverage, as they were not "mediagenic" and lacked "televisuality" (Cracknell 1993). When environmentalism expanded to include air and water pollution and environmentalists began making links between environmental health and human health, coverage (especially television) increased. Environmental problems became human problems; they became salient and thus newsworthy. In the 1970s, coverage increased due to large-scale environmental disasters such as Love Canal, Three Mile Island, and the Santa Barbara oil spill. These were media-ready events ripe for coverage. Largely as a result of these crises events, in the 1980s a number of popular magazines, including *Time, National Geographic,* and *Scientific American*, devoted cover pages and lead stories to impending environmental threats.[14] Today environmental crises continue to garner considerable media attention. A case in point was the 24/7 coverage of the 2010 BP oil spill in the Gulf of Mexico. Every major television network (including cable news channels) covered the event for weeks. Coverage included interviews with scientists, politicians, local people, and even live footage of the leak (provided by an underwater camera).

While media often cover environmental crises, a number of less "mediagenic" environmental problems go unnoticed or "undernoticed." This is because many environmental problems "do not fall neatly into an 'event centered' framework" (Sussman et al. 2002, 73). Many are related to environmental risks (meaning that an event has yet to take place) and are abstract ideas that are difficult to encapsulate

---

14. *Time* featured a cover story "The Poisoning of America" in 1980 and "Endangered Earth in 1989. *National Geographic* published its cover story "Can Man Save This Fragile Earth?" in 1989 and *Scientific American* ran the lead story "Managing Planet Earth" in 1989 (Miller 2002).

in a short news segment or in a brief newspaper or magazine article. These same environmental problems are also highly complex scientific issues that evolve slowly over time. The lay public often relies on journalists to explain complex scientific concepts, yet journalists commonly do not have the scientific background and training to thoroughly understand the problem, let alone succinctly explain it (Dennis 1991; Sussman et al. 2002). In many cases, the amount of time necessary to conduct even background research on the topic is prohibitive. Adequate coverage of such issues would also necessitate lengthy features and/or iterative episodes as some problems develop over months, years, or decades. In the end, many environmental problems receive relatively little coverage; they do not end up on anyone's agenda.

Just as the nature of most environmental problems is not often conducive to media attention, the nature of media as an industry places several limitations on what it can cover and how it is covered. While one of media's objectives is to inform the public, its dual objective is to make a profit (Harper and Yantek 2003; Miller 2002). Media is an industry, an industry that is controlled by large financial corporations who dictate operations *and* message (Sussman et al. 2002). Thus, the decision whether to cover environmental issues and how to cover them does not always reside with journalists; at least as often it resides with media moguls and CEOs. The fact that such decisions are made by a select few sheds doubt on how democratic the media truly are (Parenti 2002). Media coverage is determined not by public interest and demand, but by which stories will attract the most viewers. As a result, as Graber (1997) writes, sometimes journalists manipulate stories and sensationalize the news. Environmental problems can be blown out of proportion or misrepresented in order "make a story."

As shown by Guber and Bosso in chapter 20, the media do this by framing. According to Entman, framing is the selection "and highlighting [of] some facets of events or issues, and making connections among them so as to promote a particular interpretation, evaluation, and/or solution" (2004, 5). Journalists have the ability to select the frame to suit their objective, whether to educate or to entice viewers. Journalists can also present environmental problems in such a way as to provoke fear in their audience. Writing about climate change, Ungar discussed how media coverage of record-setting heat and drought in 1988 mobilized the latent dread in global climate change (and inherent in many environmental threats) and wrote that "media packages [now] focused on the fear of impending ecological collapse" (1992, 492). Media coverage took advantage of the social scare induced by extreme weather, creating a frame of fear. As a result, climate change was elevated in public concern and in the political agenda.

Another characteristic of media that affects coverage is the industry's objective to be (or at least appear to be) unbiased. As Miller writes, "Reporters are obliged to seek out and publicize the views of people on both sides of the issue...however responsible or irresponsible—or isolated—a particular spokesperson may be" (2002, 60). For example, even if an overwhelming majority of scientists have reached consensus on an issue, the media often award the majority the same amount of attention as a small handful of dissenters. As a result, coverage of environmental issues (e.g., climate change) tends "to represent opposing views rather than truths" (Miller 2002, 60). In this way, the media have become an interest group of their own (Miller 2002) and are not neutral actors (Sussman et al. 2002).

If media outlets can place environmental issues on the political agenda (either by providing accurate or inaccurate coverage), does it follow that they can also affect environmental policy making? A number of scholars have studied whether and, if so, how and to what extent media affect public policy.[15] One way scholars have found media to impact policy making is by affecting the public opinion to which policy makers respond. By providing media coverage they give environmental issues salience. The public then pressures policy makers to adjust policies according to their new desires. Even if there is no public consensus, policy makers can be cued into public debate and devote attention to the issue. Extremely visible policy makers such as presidents and members of Congress are most likely to be indirectly affected by media coverage in this way (Wood and George 1999). Policy makers can also be affected by media directly. Cook et al. (1983) found that when exposed to media reporting on a particular issue, government policy makers changed their attitudes on that issue. In this scenario, "the public was almost completely bypassed" (30) as policy makers' views were directly impacted by news coverage.

The media also play a critical role in campaigns and elections both as they publicize candidates' rallies, speeches, and photo opportunities and as they air and publish campaign advertisements. A number of scholars have also studied these phenomena, including Brians (1996), Jamieson (1984), Kim (2005), Min (2004), and Sigelman (1991). Two prominent examples illustrate media's role in presidential campaigns. The first was candidate George H. W. Bush's claim to become the "environmental president." At a speech in Erie Metropark, Michigan, Bush said, "Those who think we're powerless to do anything about the 'greenhouse effect' are forgetting about the 'White House effect'" (*New York Times* 1988). His quote was quickly picked up by numerous television and print outlets across the country (Sussman et al. 2002) and became a prominent sound bite in the campaign. Media also played the role of conduit in this election when it aired a negative Bush campaign ad blaming candidate Michael Dukakis for the horrific pollution in Boston Harbor. Because Democratic candidate Dukakis was promoting himself as an environmental candidate, the commercial had a large impact. Many, however, criticized the controversial ad for being misleading in message and visuals.[16]

---

15. For examples, see Shanahan (2008) for a discussion of coverage of policy decisions in the Greater Yellowstone area, Tan (2009) for discussion of media's role in state level policy making and Yates (2000) for analysis of media's role in EPA policy making.

16. The Dukakis campaign was likely hurt more by the controversial "Willie Horton" commercial about convicted felon Horton who, while out on a weekend furlough program supported by then Massachusetts governor Dukakis, committed assault, armed robbery and rape. It is likely, however, that the commercials had a cumulative effect on Dukakis's unsuccessful campaign.

A number of environmental nongovernmental organizations, corporations, and citizens' groups have also utilized media outlets to influence campaigns and policy making, and even for PR. Some notable examples include LCV commercials targeting "Dirty Dozen" candidates in national and state elections and campaigns by companies like General Electric, BP, and Honda to promote themselves as green companies with environmentally sensitive objectives and products.

4. CONCLUSION

The democratic process in the United States is complex. It allows a number of actors access to the system, both directly and indirectly, and it involves a number of different political and policy-making processes. Environmentalists have access to the democratic process at a number of different points and in a number of different ways. They have the opportunity to join the Green Party and express their concerns via its party platform and its political candidates as they run for office. Though Green Party candidates have yet to be elected to high-profile national posts, they have not been inconsequential in affecting campaign rhetoric and the outcome of elections and have been elected to a number of state and local posts. Environmentalists who do not wish to join the Green Party or vote for its candidates have often found the Democratic Party to represent environmental interests relatively well, at least in comparison to the Republican Party (though this distinction is not infallible). The Democratic Party platform has generally had a more pro-environment and liberal ideological focus advocating for tougher regulations and government intervention. However, both Democratic and Republican policy makers have been largely successful at keeping their campaign pledges regarding environmental legislation, though pro-environment promises are kept less frequently than anti-environmental ones (Ringquist and Dasse 2004). Environmentalists can also affect policy making by exercising their rights of direct democracy and supporting environmentally-sensitive initiatives and referenda on state or local level ballots. The number and scope of such measures has grown over time, and they have met with notable success at the polls. Journalists, candidates, corporations, and environmentalists have also utilized media as a way to affect environmental policy making. As media help give some environmental issues salience (or ignore others, denying them salience), they help set the political agenda and influence to which issues policy makers pay attention.

As this chapter illustrates, environmentalists have been able to influence successfully political processes and policy makers. However, this influence may not be sufficient for some. Many obstacles (such as the dominant two-party system, comparatively weak political saliency and media biases) remain. In order to facilitate a better understanding of the relationship between democracy and environmental politics and policy, this chapter ends with recommendations for future research. First, in relation to political parties and the democratic process it may prove insightful to understand whether those who are most or least supportive of environmental protection are more active. Findings from such research could be beneficial both from a theoretical and an empirical perspective. A similar question worth addressing is whether moderates (both Democrats and Republicans) are more protective of the environment than others in the electorate. If this is the case, does this view affect their vote? Another intriguing question to ask is what effect the Tea Party will have on environmental voters and elections. Will the Tea Party's effect on elections be similar to that of the Green Party? There is also the question of proxy voting in elections. As this chapter has shown, the environment has frequently not been a top priority in elections, and candidates have rarely addressed environmental issues in their campaigns. At the same time, the public consistently shows general concern for environmental protection. Is it possible that voters use candidates' views on other related issues—such as abortion or civil rights—as a cue for their views on the environment? Positions on these issues may be closely associated with the more general dimension of support for government intervention.

Another set of potential research questions stems from recent changes in technology and the economy. For example, future research into the changing role of the media in the electoral process should analyze how the surge in social media and other Internet and cell phone–related outlets are influencing public attitudes and beliefs and electoral outcomes. Have these new media allowed for more access to the electorate? Who has utilized them the most and with what effect? Has their use made an impact on voters, elections, and policy makers? In terms of economic changes, new research should (re)consider the "jobs versus the environment" debate, particularly in light of the severe and lengthy economic crisis in the late 2000s. Has the electorate's views on the issue changed? An updated investigation should consider green technology and green jobs, two issues that President Obama strongly advocated for in his State of the Union address in January 2011. Another line of research, and one that links technology and economics, is that of energy. With higher gasoline prices, increasing unrest in the Middle East, the BP oil spill in the Gulf of Mexico, and the meltdown of the Fukushima nuclear power plant in Japan, energy has become a salient political issue. Could energy be the new environmental issue that finally becomes a prominent and long-lasting campaign issue? Or will it rise and fall in prominence, as it has before, once these events are significantly behind us? Answers to these and other related questions will provide researchers a fuller picture of the nexus between democracy and environmental politics and policy.

REFERENCES

Alvarez, M. R., and J. Nagler. 1998. "Voter Choice in the 1996 Presidential Election." *American Journal of Political Science* 42 (4): 1349–1363.

Baker, B. 1996. "The Environment as Election Issue." *BioScience* 46 (8): 574.

Bomberg, E. 2001. "Profile—The US Presidential Election: Implications for Environmental Policy." *Environmental Politics* 10 (2): 115–121.

Bosso, C. J., and D. L. Guber. 2006. "Maintaining Presence: Environmental Advocacy and the Permanent Campagin." In *Environmental Policy: New Directions for the Twenty-First Century*, ed. N. J. Vig and M. E. Kraft, 78–99. Washington, DC: CQ Press.

Brians, C. L., and M. P. Wattenberg. 1996. "Campaign Issue Knowledge and Salience: Comparing Reception from TV Commercials, TV News and Newspapers." *American Journal of Political Science* 40 (1): 172–193.

Burden, B. C. 2005a. "Minor Parties and Strategic Voting in Recent U.S. Presidential Elections." *Electoral Studies* 24 (4): 603–618.

———. 2005b. "Ralph Nader's Campaign Strategy in the 2000 U.S. Presidential Election." *American Politics Research* 33 (5): 672–699.

Burns, S. 2008. "Environmental Policy and Politics: Trends in Public Debate." *Natural Resources and Environment* 23 (2): 8–12.

Clinton, J. D. 2006. "Representation in Congress: Constituents and Roll Calls in the 106th House." *Journal of Politics* 68 (2): 397–409.

Cohen, B. C. 1963. *The Press and Foreign Policy*. Princeton, NJ: Princeton University Press.

Cook, F. L., T. R. Tyler, E. G. Goetz, M. T. Gordon, D. Protess, D. R. Leff, and H. L. Molotch. 1983. "Media and Agenda Setting: Effects on the Public, Interest Group Leaders, Policy Makers, and Policy." *Public Opinion Quarterly* 47 (1): 16–35.

Cracknell, J. 1993. "Issue Arenas, Pressure Groups and Environmental Agendas." In *The Mass Media and Environmental Issues*, ed. A. Hansen, 3–21. New York: Leicester University Press.

David, B. M., and D. P. Kelly. 1998. "Consultants and Direct Democracy." *PS, Political Science and Politics* 31 (2): 160–169.

Davis, F. L., and A. H. Wurth. 2003. "Voting Preferences and the Environment in the American Electorate: The Discussion Extended." *Society and Natural Resources* 16: 729–740.

Davis, F. L., A. H. Wurth, and J. C. Lazarus. 2008. "The Green Vote in Presidential Elections: Past Performance and Future Promise." *Social Science Journal* 45: 525–545.

Dell, K. D. 2009. "The Grassroots Are Greener: Democratic Participation and Environmental Policies in State Politics." *Review of Policy Research* 26 (2): 699–727.

Dennis, E. E. 1991. "In Context: Environmentalism in the System of the News." In *Media and the Environment*, ed. C. LaMay and D. E. Everette, 55–64. Washington, DC: Island.

Doyle, T., and E. McEachern. 2008. *Environmental Politics*. 3rd ed. New York: Routledge.

Duffy, R. J. 2003. *The Green Agenda in American Politics: The Strategies for the Twenty-First Century*. Lawrence: University Press of Kansas.

Dunlap, R. E., and M. P. Allen. 1976. "Partisan Differences on Environmental Issues: A Congressional Roll-Call Analysis." *Western Political Quarterly* 29 (3): 384–397.

Dunlap, R. E., and R. P. Gale. 1974. "Party Membership and Environmental Politics: A Legislative Roll-Call Analysis." *Social Science Quarterly* 55 (3): 670–690.

Dunlap, R. E., and A. M. McCright. 2008. "A Widening Gap: Republican and Democratic Views on Climate Change." *Environment* 50 (5): 26–35.

Dunlap, R. E., C. Xiao, and A. M. McCright. 2001. "Politics and Environment in America: Partisan and Ideological Cleavages in Public Support for Environmentalism." *Environmental Politics* 10 (4): 23–48.

Ellis, R. J. 2005. "Direct Democracy." In *Oregon Politics and Government: Progressives versus Conservative Populists*, ed. R. A. Clucas, M. Henkels, and B. S. Steel. Lincoln: University of Nebraska Press.

Entman, R. M. 2004. *Projections of Power: Framing News, Public Opinion, and U.S. Foreign Policy*. Chicago: University of Chicago Press.

Erikson, R. S. 1978. "Constituency Opinion and Congressional Behavior: A Reexamination of the Miller-Stokes Representation Data." *American Journal of Political Science* 22 (3): 511–535.

Field, B. C. 2007. *Environmental Policy: An Introduction*. Long Grove, Ill.: Waveland Press.

Gerrard, M. B. 2008. "McCain vs. Obama on the Environment, Energy, and Resources." *Natural Resources and Environment* 23: 3.

Glazer, A., and M. Robbins. 1985. "Congressional Responsiveness to Constituency Change." *American Journal of Political Science* 29 (2): 259–273.

Gore, A. 1993. *Earth in the Balance: Ecology and the Human Spirit*. New York: Penguin Books.

Graber, D. A. 1997. *Mass Media and American Politics*. Washington, DC: CQ Press.

Green Party of the United States. 2000. *Ten Key Values of the Green Party*. Available at www.gp.org/tenkey.shtml (accessed February 2, 2011).

——. 2004. *Twentieth Anniversary of the American Green Movement*. Available at www.greenparty.org/intro.php (accessed February 2, 2011).

Guber, D. L. 2001a. "Environmental Voting in the American States: A Tale of Two Initiatives." *State and Local Government Review* 33 (2): 120–132.

——. 2001b. "Voting Preferences and the Environment in the American Electorate." *Society and Natural Resources* 14: 455–469.

Harper, J. and Yantek, T. 2003. *Media, Profit, and Politics: Competing Priorities in an Open Society*. Conference Proceedings. Kent State University Symposium on Democracy. Kent, Ohio: Kent State University Press.

Herrington, S. 2010. "There's No Difference between Democrats and Republicans." *Huffington Post*, September 7. Available at www.huffingtonpost.com/stephen-herrington/theres-no-difference-betw_b_706364.html.

Jamieson, K. H. 1984. *Packaging the Presidency: A History and Criticism of Presidential Campaign Advertising*. New York: Oxford University Press.

Kahn, M. E., and J. G. Matsusaka. 1997. "Demand for Environmental Goods: Evidence from Voting Patterns on California Initiatives." *Journal of Law and Economics* 40: 137–173.

Kamieniecki, S. 1995. "Political Parties and Environmental Policy." In *Environmental Politics and Policy: Theories and Evidence*, ed. J. P. Lester, 146–157. Durham, NC: Duke University Press.

Kim, S., D. A. Scheufele, and J. Shanahan. 2005. "Who Cares about the Issues? Issue Voting and the Role of News Media during the 2000 U.S. Presidential Election." *Journal of Communication* 55 (1): 103–121.

Kraft, M. E. 1984. "A New Environmental Policy Agenda: The 1980 Presidential Campaign and Its Aftermath." In *Environmental Policy in the 1980s: Reagan's New Agenda*, ed. N. J. Vig and M. E. Kraft, 29–50. Washington, DC: CQ Press.

——. 2011. *Environmental Politics and Policy*. 5th ed. New York: Pearson.

Kriz, M. 2002. "In Voters' Eyes, This Bush Isn't Green." *National Journal* 34: 25.

Lake, L. M. 1983. "The Environmental Mandate: Activists and the Electorate." *Political Science Quarterly* 88 (2): 215–233.

Leiserowitz, A., N. Smith, and J. R. Marlon. 2010. *Americans' Knowledge of Climate Change*. New Haven, CT: Yale University Press.

Lem, S. B., and C. M. Dowling. 2006. "Picking Their Spots: Minor Party Candidates in Gubernatorial Elections." *Political Research Quarterly* 59 (3): 471–480.

Lutrin, C. E. 1975. "The Public and Ecology: The Role of Initiatives in California's Environmental Politics." *Western Political Quarterly* 28 (2): 352.

McCombs, M. E. 2004. *Setting the Agenda: The Mass Media and Public Opinion*. Malden, MA: Blackwell.

Miller, N. 2002. *Environmental Politics: Interest Groups, the Media, and the Making of Policy*. Boca Raton, FL: Lewis.

Miller, W. E., and D. E. Stokes. 1963. "Constituency Influence in Congress." *American Political Science Review* 57 (1): 45–56.

Min, Y. 2004. "News Coverage of Negative Political Campaigns—an Experiment of Negative Campaign Effects on Turnout and Candidate Preference." *Harvard International Journal of Press-Politics* 9 (4): 95–111.

New York Times. 1988. "From Afar, Both Candidates Are Environmentalists." *New York Times*, September 24.

Ogden, D. 1971. "The Future of Environmental Struggle." In *The Politics of Neglect: The Environmental Crisis*, ed. R. L. Meek and J. A. Straayer. Boston: Houghton Mifflin, 243–250.

Parenti, M. 2002. *Democracy for the Few*. Boston: Bedford/St. Martin's.

Ringquist, E. J., and C. Dasse. 2004. "Lies, Damned Lies, and Campaign Promises? Environmental Legislation in the 105th Congress." *Social Science Quarterly* 85 (2): 400–419.

Rosenbaum, W. A. 2011. *Environmental Politics and Policy*. 8th ed. Washington, DC: CQ Press.

Shanahan, E., M. McBeth, P. Hathaway, and R. Arnell. 2008. "Conduit or Contributor? The Role of Media in Policy Change Theory." *Policy Sciences* 41 (2): 115–138.

Shipan, C. R., and W. R. Lowry. 2001. "Environmental Policy and Party Divergence in Congress." *Political Research Quarterly* 54 (2): 245–263.

Sigelman, L., and D. Bullock. 1991. "Candidates, Issues, Horse Races, and Hoopla." *American Politics Research* 19 (1): 5–32.

Sussman, G., B. W. Daynes, and J. P. West. 2002. *American Politics and the Environment*. New York: Longman.

Switzer, J. V. 2004. *Environmental Politics: Domestic and Global Dimensions*. Belmont, CA: Thomson/Wadsworth.

Tan, Y., and D. H. Weaver. 2009. "Local Media, Public Opinion, and State Legislative Policies Agenda Setting at the State Level." *International Journal of Press-Politics* 14 (4): 454–476.

Tatalovich, R., and M. J. Wattier. 1999. "Opinion Leadership: Elections, Campaigns, Agenda Setting, and Environmentalism." In *The Environmental Presidency*, ed. D. L. Soden. Albany: State University of New York Press.

Ungar, S. 1992. "The Rise and (Relative) Decline of Global Warming as a Social Problem." *Sociological Quarterly* 33 (4): 483–501.

Vig, N. J. 2010. "Presidential Powers and Environmental Policy." In *Environmental Policy: New Direction for the Twenty-First Century*, ed. N. J. Vig and M. E. Kraft, 75–98. Washington, DC: CQ Press.

Wattier, M. J., and R. Tatalovich. 2000. "Issue Publics, Mass Publics, and Agenda Setting: Environmentalism and Economics in Presidential Elections." *Environment and Planning C: Government and Policy* 18: 115–126.

Wood, B. D., and C. E. George. 1999. "Who Influences Whom? The President, Congress, and the Media." *American Political Science Review* 93 (2): 327–344.

Yates, A. J., and R. L. Stroup. 2000. "Media Coverage and EPA Pesticide Decisions." *Public Choice* 102 (3): 297–312.

PART VI

POLICY
APPROACHES AND
ANALYTIC TOOLS

CHAPTER 25

THE ROLE OF MARKET INCENTIVES IN ENVIRONMENTAL POLICY

SHEILA M. OLMSTEAD

1. INTRODUCTION

The bedrock principle of economics is that competitive markets give rise to efficient outcomes. This principle underlies the "first fundamental welfare theorem," the analytical expression of Adam Smith's theory of the "invisible hand," which supports a presumption of nonintervention in markets (Smith 1776). Like many economic theories, however, it comes packaged with several conditions. Only complete markets can be presumed efficient—the costs of producing goods and services must be borne fully by suppliers, while the benefits from consuming them accrue entirely to the buyers. But economic activity often creates unwanted by-products, such as water and air pollution, that impose costs on consumers or firms downstream or downwind. These costs are not usually captured in markets. In other cases, providing a good or service such as clean water and sanitation may generate indirect benefits for populations other than those paying for services. These two simple but ubiquitous examples demonstrate that, for many environmental goods and services, markets are incomplete and thus inefficient. Economic theory suggests that the way to deal with market failures is to fill in the incomplete nature of the market by providing price signals, assigning private property rights, or creating a market in environmental goods and services.

This chapter surveys the framework that economics brings to environmental policy and, in particular, the use of market incentives in relation to conventional approaches to regulating environmental quality. I begin by considering why and how markets fail to result in the optimal level of environmental quality, and end by considering how they might be induced to do so. Section 2 defines market failure more precisely in the context of environmental problems. Section 3 considers what economic theory has to say about solutions to market failure in the environmental realm. Section 4 compares and contrasts market-based environmental policies with more traditional, prescriptive approaches. Section 5 offers a closer focus on market-based policy instruments themselves, comparing and contrasting the two most common approaches, taxes and tradable permits. Section 6 summarizes the experience with selected market-based environmental policies in practice. Conclusions and possible areas for future research are offered in section 7.

2. Market Failure and the Environment

Three classes of market failure are particularly relevant to environmental management: externalities, public goods, and the "tragedy of the commons."[1] This section defines each of these market failures and illuminates their relevance to environmental policy.

2.1. Externalities

An externality results when the actions of one individual (or firm) have a direct, unintentional, and uncompensated effect on the well-being of other individuals or the profits of other firms (Baumol and Oates 1988). In the presence of an externality, the private and social net benefit of an economic activity diverge, and government intervention to correct this divergence can increase total economic welfare (Pigou 1920). While environmental problems are typically framed as negative externalities, positive externalities are also common. For example, a firm that carries out research and development produces knowledge that its rivals can use—a positive externality, since some of the benefits from the research are captured by firms who do not contribute to its expense. The optimal level of an externality is the level at which the marginal benefit of providing it (or reducing it, in the case of a negative externality) is exactly equal to the marginal cost.

---

1. Markets also fail when they are not competitive (one or more firms have market power), or when information is asymmetrical (sellers have more or better information than buyers, or vice-versa). These market failures do have some relevance to environmental policy, but a full treatment is beyond the scope of this chapter.

2.2. Public Goods

A second type of market failure in the environmental realm arises with public goods—goods that are shared by all and owned by no one. Biodiversity is an example of an environmental public good. Among other benefits, greater genetic diversity makes the food supply more robust to threats from parasites and disease and offers the potential for new medicines or industrially useful chemicals. Everyone enjoys the benefits of biodiversity (they are "nonexcludable"), and no one person's enjoyment reduces the amount available to others (they are "nonrival").

The joint characteristics of nonrivalry and nonexcludability ensure that private markets will undersupply public goods. The economic theory of efficient public goods provision was formalized by Lindahl (1985).[2] In a "Lindahl equilibrium," a public good is provided at the level at which the marginal social benefit of the good is exactly equal to the marginal social cost, and each consumer of the good pays a total tax for provision equal to the value of the public good she or he receives.[3] Private markets do not result in this efficient level of provision, due to the incentive to free ride on what is provided by others. The dual problems of eliciting consumers' true willingness to pay for public goods and developing social choice mechanisms that actually provide public goods through central taxation, private donations, or other means have given rise to very large literatures in economics and political science (see, for example, Andreoni 1988; Arrow 1951; Buchanan 1968; Olsen 1965).

2.3. Tragedy of the Commons

The third category of environmental market failures, the "tragedy of the commons," suggests that people sharing common access to a natural resource will tend to overexploit it unless they can develop effective government institutions (or social norms) to regulate its use (Hardin 1968). Hardin used the metaphor of an English pasture, or "commons." The more sheep graze the commons, the less food is available for each of them. Each shepherd bears only a portion of the costs from an additional animal (since those are spread over the herd as a whole)—but she receives the entire gain from increasing her private flock. The result is that each shepherd puts too many sheep to pasture, from the point of view of the commons as a whole. The "tragedy" is that the resulting overgrazing reduces the pasture's productivity. As a result, every shepherd would be better off if all could agree to restrict their flocks—but none has an incentive to do so on his own. If one shepherd pares down his flock, another may respond by adding a sheep to his own.

This metaphor of the "commons" applies to many natural resources, but only under two important conditions (Hardin 1968). First, access to the resource must be unrestricted. Economists describe such resources as open-access resources. An

---

2. Lindahl's original contribution, printed in German, was published in 1919.
3. The theory of estimating this efficient level of provision was further developed by Samuelson (1954, 1955).

open-access resource is nonexcludable (like public goods) but rival, rather than nonrival, in consumption. The lack of exclusion usually stems from a combination of institutional and physical factors. The second important condition is diminishing marginal returns. As the number of people using the resource grows, the benefits from the resource must increase at a slower rate.

Note that economists typically distinguish open-access resources from true common property, to which access is nonexcludable only within a limited, well-defined group. In true "commons," social norms and other institutions often successfully limit resource extraction, and while they may not achieve efficient levels of resource use, they may prevent the full tragedy of overuse and eventual collapse (Ostrom 1990).

3. USING MARKET PRINCIPLES TO CORRECT MARKET FAILURES

3.1. Legal Liability Regimes

One obvious route to correcting environmental market failures is the legal system. For example, if a timber company will be held liable for negative environmental consequences of poor harvesting practices, it may be forced to internalize the costs of those damages (turning them into private costs), or face the risk of high-cost legal settlements. Liability rules that internalize the external costs of pollution are quite common; in the United States, two examples are the compensation of victims of environmental pollution through the common law tort system, and the federal Superfund legislation, which assigns liability through the court system for hazardous waste cleanup (Menell 1991). Much work has been done in the area of law and economics on the effects of liability rules under Superfund and related state laws (Alberini and Austin 2002; Chang and Sigman 2000 and 2007; Kornhauser and Revesz 1994; Sigman 1998). There is some evidence that strict liability regimes reduce unexpected pollution releases to the environment. But relying on court systems alone to correct environmental market failures is inefficient. Courts consider such problems on a case-by-case basis, and, even allowing for class-action lawsuits, the costs of such an approach are extremely high (Menell 1991).

3.2. Legislative and Administrative Environmental Regulation

The high cost of relying on liability regimes, alone, as a disincentive for environmental harm, suggests that it may be optimal for governments to intervene to correct market failures in the environmental realm through legislative and administrative regulation.[4] I focus here on describing the economic theory related to the design of cost-effective administrative regulation.

3.2.1. Prescriptive Environmental Policy Instruments

Until the 1990s, the standard approach to environmental regulation relied almost exclusively on an array of policy instruments that economists refer to as "command-and-control" (CAC) or prescriptive approaches, which focus on regulating the behavior or performance of individual factories, power plants, and other commercial and industrial facilities. While there are many such approaches, they fall into two general classes: technology standards and performance standards. A technology standard requires firms to use a particular pollution abatement technology. For example, the 1977 Clean Air Act Amendments required new power plants to install large flue-gas desulfurization devices ("scrubbers") to remove sulfur dioxide from stack gases. A performance standard allows polluters more leeway in the choice of control technology, imposing a ceiling on total emissions in a period (for example, tons per year), or a maximum allowable emissions rate (for example, pounds of pollution per unit of output produced, or per unit of fuel consumed). Hybrid approaches are also common. For example, in the United States, the Clean Water Act requires individual point sources of pollution to meet emissions limitations based on "best available" technology, which tends to include a single technology, or a small number of related technologies. In theory, regulators can vary technology or performance standards across regulated firms, but in practice they have tended to implement uniform standards.

CAC policy instruments are not all equal in economic terms. For example, performance standards are generally better than technology standards at minimizing the sum of emissions control costs and pollution damages (Besanko 1987). Even within the category of performance standards, some are better than others in terms of their effectiveness and cost-effectiveness (Helfand 1991). For reasons discussed throughout the rest of this chapter, however, economic theory strongly favors market-based over CAC policy instruments.

3.2.2. Market-Based Environmental Policy Instruments

In contrast to the prescriptive approaches described above, market-based policy instruments (MBIs) are decentralized, focusing on aggregate or market-level outcomes, such as total pollution levels or total emissions, rather than the activities of individual facilities. The classic economic prescription is to tax negative externalities and subsidize positive externalities, with the efficient tax (subsidy) equal to the marginal damages (benefits) at the efficient level of the externality (Baumol 1972;

---

4. From the perspective of efficiency, a mix of administrative regulation and liability rules for pollution control may be optimal (Shavell 1984; Kolstad et al. 1990).

Pigou 1920; Sandmo 1975).[5] In response to a tax, regulated firms have two choices for each unit of pollution they would have emitted in the absence of regulation—they can continue to emit that unit, paying the tax, or they can abate that unit, incurring costs to do so. Thus, each firm will reduce emissions just to the point at which the marginal cost of emissions abatement is equal to the unit tax on emissions. Since each firm equates the cost of abatement with the tax, marginal abatement costs are equal across firms, generating the least-cost allocation of emissions reductions.

While environmental taxation had been proposed since the early part of the last century, a seminal but much later contribution by Ronald Coase recognized the fundamental symmetry of externalities, giving rise to another set of approaches. Coase (1960) noted that the direction of compensation was not prescribed by the efficiency criterion and that the mere existence of externalities in a market could, under certain very restrictive conditions, induce private negotiation of efficient outcomes.[6] Coase was quite clear that such outcomes would be hindered in the real world by transaction (bargaining) costs and other barriers, especially with a large number of parties involved. Nonetheless, his contribution provided a new touchstone for the theory of efficient environmental regulation and highlighted the importance of property rights in the question of how private markets will tend to resolve environmental problems, if at all.

Coase's focus on property rights is linked to the development of systems of marketable pollution permits, known as "cap-and-trade" systems (though there are other variations on the same theme). In order for Coasian bargaining to occur, the government must assign and enforce property rights to pollution, or pollution abatement (Dales 1968; Montgomery 1972).[7] The conceptual framework of emissions trading programs arising from these early contributions is well described in Tietenberg (2006). The regulator sets an aggregate cap on pollution and allocates the implied number of pollution permits to the regulated community, either by auction or some system of free allocation or "grandfathering," generally based on past polluting behavior. The pollution permits are transferable, and each firm will buy and sell permits based on a comparison of market permit prices with its own marginal abatement costs (in the same way that a firm reacts to an emissions tax, except that the price is set by the market, rather

---

5. Note that, in the dynamic context, subsidies can lead to excessive entry into the subsidized industry, and are, thus, not truly equivalent to taxes in their ability to achieve efficient externality management (Baumol and Oates 1988).

6. Of course, the outcome of Coasian bargaining—who compensates whom—has important distributional implications, even if it does not affect efficiency.

7. Dales (1968) refers to a system of tradable permits for *emissions*; Montgomery (1972) refers to a system of tradable permits for pollution *concentrations* in an airshed or waterbody. Most existing tradable permit systems are modeled on the former.

than the regulator, who focuses, instead, on the quantity of allowable emissions). When the permit market clears, each firm has equated its own marginal pollution abatement cost with the prevailing permit price, resulting in equal marginal costs across firms, and the least-cost allocation of control responsibility to meet the aggregate cap.

One of the most appealing aspects of cap-and-trade is that, in theory, the ability of such a policy to arrive at the least-cost allocation of responsibility for emissions abatement across regulated firms is independent of the initial allocation of permits. This means that initial permit allocations may be manipulated to accomplish distributional outcomes that build sufficient political support for new or more stringent environmental regulations, as seen in the establishment of the Acid Rain Program in the negotiation of the Clean Air Act Amendments of 1990 (Joskow and Schmalensee 1998); or to meet income redistribution goals or exogenous "fairness" criteria, as has been suggested for the establishment of an international carbon emissions trading regime (Olmstead and Stavins 2011).

There are some important exceptions to this general rule. First, market power in the permit market (a small number of permit sellers) can lead permit sellers to withhold permits and drive up permit prices, establishing a correlation between initial permit allocation and the ability of the cap-and-trade system to achieve least-cost aggregate abatement (Hahn 1984).[8] Marginal transactions costs that increase or decrease with the size of permit trades may also establish such a correlation (Stavins 1995). In most cases, however, permits can be freely distributed in any fashion without interfering with the efficient functioning of emissions markets. The economic theory of cap-and-trade has not only impacted the way in which governments regulate pollution, but has also contributed to several important natural resource policy problems, including fisheries management and land preservation.

A wide array of other policy instruments fall within the category of MBIs. For example, the reduction or elimination of environment-damaging subsidies is a market-based approach to environmental policy, as are deposit-refund systems (Stavins 2003). Mandatory information disclosure policies may correct a type of market failure relevant to the environment not discussed earlier—information asymmetry—or may simply provide information that allows consumers to express more effectively their preferences over how their consumption choices affect the provision of public goods in the marketplace (see, for example, chapter 26 in this volume). To minimize overlap with other chapters, I focus only on taxes and permits in the discussion of MBIs in the remainder of the chapter.

---

8. Small trading volume in at least one permit market, that for total suspended particulates in Santiago, Chile, has been attributed to market concentration (Montero et al. 2002).

4. Comparing and Contrasting Market-Based Environmental Policy Instruments with Prescriptive Approaches

This section compares CAC policies with MBIs in terms of short- and long-run cost-effectiveness, monitoring and enforcement, and distributional implications. While MBIs are generally preferable from an economic perspective, the section ends with a discussion of the conditions under which CAC environmental policies may be preferred.

4.1. Short-Run Cost-Effectiveness

Economic efficiency prescribes the adoption of policies that maximize net social benefits—setting the optimal standard for allowable pollution levels, for example. However, economists' goal of maximizing net benefits is one of many competing goals in the policy process. Even when an environmental standard is inefficient (too stringent, or not stringent enough to maximize net benefits), economic analysis can still help to select the particular policy instruments used to achieve that standard (Baumol and Oates 1971). A cost-effective environmental policy instrument is one that can achieve a given environmental standard at least cost.

The principle that MBIs are more cost-effective than CAC policies in the short run is well developed in economic theory (Baumol and Oates 1971; Bohm and Russell 1985; Crocker 1966; Hahn and Stavins 1992; Stavins 2003; Tietenberg 1990). MBIs have this advantage over CAC policies because the former take advantage of abatement cost differences across regulated firms. The firms with the lowest abatement costs exercise the most control, and those with the highest costs control less (paying more for permits or higher tax bills). In fact, the magnitude of the short-run cost advantage of MBIs over a uniform performance standard is directly correlated with the degree of abatement cost heterogeneity across regulated firms—if firms' abatement costs are homogeneous, this advantage disappears (Newell and Stavins 2003).

4.2. Long-Run Cost-Effectiveness: Incentives for Technological Change

The short-run cost-effectiveness of market-based approaches to environmental policy tend to be emphasized in public policy debates; this is a critical argument in favor of MBIs. However, the greatest potential cost savings from these types of environmental policies may be achieved in the long run. In the long run, firms' abatement technologies are not fixed. Because they require firms to pay to pollute, MBIs provide strong incentives for regulated firms to invest in new technologies that reduce pollution abatement costs over time by either creating these innovative technologies themselves or adopting cheaper pollution control technologies developed by other firms (Downing and White 1986).

This effect is strongest and most intuitive under a pollution tax. When regulated by a unit tax on emissions, firms' compliance costs are the sum of abatement costs (for units of pollution they choose to reduce) and their tax bill (for each unit they continue to emit). A technology that reduces their marginal abatement costs thus has two effects: (1) it reduces the abatement cost for each unit they chose to abate with the old technology; and (2) it reduces the firm's total tax bill—the firm will now abate additional units, for as long as the unit tax is unchanged, abatement now compares favorably with paying the tax over a greater range of abatement opportunities than it did before the cheaper technology was introduced.[9] This extra savings associated with the reduced tax bill is absent under a performance standard.

The incentive for long-run technological change under a tradable permit policy is also stronger than under a performance standard, but not as strong as under the tax (Milliman and Prince 1989). Since firms must pay the permit price for every unit of pollution they continue to emit (as well as abatement costs for those they eliminate), there is some extra incentive for innovation or adoption of new, lower-cost abatement technologies, though the magnitude of the incentive depends on whether a firm is a buyer or seller in the permit market, before and after the technology is adopted (Jung et al. 1996; Malueg 1989). However, as more firms adopt the new technology, reducing demand for permits, the market permit price will fall (abatement is now cheaper, on the margin). This effect on permit prices dampens the extra incentive for innovation, relative to the tax.[10]

How do market-based policies compare with technology standards in terms of the incentive provided for long-run technological change (and the resulting improvements in costs and environmental quality)? Outside economics, belief in the power of the "technology-forcing standard" to promote innovation is strong. History suggests, however, that regulators have little talent for knowing how much improvement over existing technology is actually feasible for private firms, and by when, resulting in technology standards that are either unambitious or too ambitious (Jaffe and Stavins 1995). Even if regulators get it right in a static setting, such approaches lock in the current "best available technology" and, by definition,

9. Note that this means that total abatement will also increase under the tax, increasing the environmental benefits of the tax relative to a CAC policy. This effect of the tax on abatement will be important in the comparison of taxes and tradable permits in Section 5.

10. If permits are auctioned rather than distributed freely to polluting firms, this difference in long-run incentives for technological change between taxes and tradable permit systems disappears, since government revenues, rather than firm profits, absorb the impact of reduced permit prices (Milliman and Prince 1989).

constrain the approaches firms may take toward reducing pollution—removing any dynamic incentive to develop new, better-performing technologies, which may simply result in a tightened standard (Jaffe and Stavins 1995).

4.3. Monitoring and Enforcement

Abatement costs comprise the lion's share of total environmental regulatory costs. Monitoring and enforcement costs are often the second-largest class of costs, though they are much smaller.[11] Nonetheless, these costs should be included in a careful comparison of alternative policies, especially in developing countries, where monitoring and enforcement institutions may be weak (Eskeland and Jimenez 1992).

Unlike the dimension of short- and long-run cost-effectiveness, there is no general rule about whether MBIs or CAC policies are more costly to monitor and enforce.[12] The lower compliance costs associated with market-based policies would suggest intuitively that firms are more likely to comply, lowering monitoring and enforcement costs relative to CAC approaches. But in fact, depending on the shape of firms' abatement cost functions, performance standards can be less costly to monitor and enforce than tradable permit policies (Malik 1992).

Diffuse pollution problems, such as emissions from home heating or automobiles, tend to be regulated using CAC in part because monitoring and enforcement costs are high. There are important exceptions. For example, using prices to induce household water conservation may have lower monitoring and enforcement costs than prescriptive policies, where household water use is already metered (Mansur and Olmstead 2007). In addition, MBIs can be adapted to some such situations; input or output taxes may be good substitutes for emissions taxes (Schmutzler and Goulder 1997). Similarly, for nonpoint source pollution, taxes on inputs and other emissions proxies, and charges based on ambient environmental quality may be acceptable alternatives (Griffin and Bromley 1982; Segerson 1988).

4.4. Distributional Implications

The discussion thus far has implicitly assumed that the damages from a unit of pollution are constant over space and time—that a unit of abatement from a firm

---

11. For example, in the U.S. regulation of sulfur dioxide (SO_2) from power plants under the Acid Rain Program, a scrubber to remove SO_2 at an individual power plant costs tens or hundreds of millions of dollars to install, and several million dollars per year to operate. Continuous emissions monitoring at each plant, required to enforce the regulation, costs a few hundred thousand dollars to install, and about fifty thousand dollars per year to operate (Keohane and Olmstead 2007).

12. The significant economic literature on monitoring and enforcement of environmental policies is summarized in Cohen (1999).

in approximately any location, at approximately any time, is equivalent to a unit from any other firm. This spatial and temporal "uniform mixing" of pollution is relevant to some environmental problems (e.g., greenhouse gas emissions), at least to a first approximation. However, many pollutants are nonuniformly mixed in the environment—hazardous waste may poison soil or groundwater at a specific site but have no effects outside a well-defined region. Between greenhouse gas emissions (almost perfectly uniformly mixed) and hazardous waste (highly non-uniformly mixed) lies a wide array of pollution problems for which nonuniform mixing may be an important issue.

MBIs, by construction, result in different quantities of abatement by different firms (low-abatement-cost firms reduce pollution more than high-abatement-cost firms). For nonuniformly mixed pollutants, MBIs that do not account for locational differences in the marginal damages from pollution may create pollution "hot spots," relative to CAC approaches that require equivalent reductions from all sources. This challenge has been carefully addressed in the environmental and resource economics literature. Establishing trading ratios that vary by each potential trading partner pair, in the manner of exchange rates, is an efficient approach (Farrow et al. 2005; Hung and Shaw 2005; Oates et al. 1983; Rodríguez 2000; Tietenberg 1985). Spatially or temporally differentiated taxes can also be designed in this context, and in some cases, zoning approaches, in which the value of abatement by different polluters is weighted by geographic region, but not differentially for each firm, can be reasonable solutions (Boyd 2003).

The key, however, is to realize that implementing a market-based approach that does *not* account for the location of emissions in such cases may result in social outcomes that are worse than those achievable using CAC, if the high-damage firms also have high abatement costs. In addition, the abatement cost savings achievable using market-based approaches will generally be less than what could be achieved without accounting for spatial heterogeneity in the impact of emissions, since trading ratios restrict trading. In these cases, the cost-effectiveness advantage of MBIs over CAC approaches may be reduced.

4.5. Are Prescriptive Approaches Ever Preferable from an Economic Perspective?

MBIs are, for many environmental policy problems, the economically preferable choice. However, in some cases CAC approaches may be preferable (Rose-Ackerman 1973). When nonuniform mixing is severe, MBIs are simply not feasible—this would be the case, for example, for arsenic and other contaminants in piped drinking water (Niskanen 2001), or for nuclear waste disposal. In other cases, abatement costs may differ so little across regulated entities (in the case where a single control technology is universally effective, for example), that a technology standard is cost-effective relative to a market-based policy, given lower monitoring and enforcement costs. Requiring double hulls on large, oceangoing oil tankers to reduce the risk of unintended spills is a good example. For some nonuniformly mixed pollution problems, differentiated taxes or tradable permit systems using trading ratios, while feasible, will result in small abatement cost reductions relative to CAC policies, and these small gains may not be enough to justify an MBI with higher monitoring and enforcement costs. This may also be true for diffuse pollution problems with a large number of regulated entities, even if pollutants are uniformly mixed.

5. COMPARING AND CONTRASTING TWO MARKET-BASED INSTRUMENTS: TAXES AND PERMITS

Section 4 considered some of the many differences between CAC and MBI approaches to environmental policy problems. But there are also important differences between the two major MBIs—taxes and tradable permit systems. These differences are the focus of this section.

5.1. Uncertainty and Efficiency: The Weitzman Rule

Taxes and tradable permits are, in some senses, opposite sides of the same coin. Tax policies ("price instruments") implement a price on pollution, and firms react by reducing emissions just to the point at which their own marginal abatement costs are equal to the tax, minimizing total abatement costs. Tradable permit systems ("quantity instruments") implement an aggregate cap on pollution, trading among regulated firms determines the market permit price, and firms reduce emissions just to the point at which their own marginal abatement costs are equal to that price, minimizing total abatement costs. Moreover, the equilibrium allocation of emissions control across regulated firms will be the same under a permit system and a tax set to achieve the same aggregate quantity of control.

This theoretical equivalence of taxes and tradable permit systems relies on an important assumption, however. In order for regulators to set a tax that achieves the same level of aggregate control implied by a permit policy, they must have a good deal of knowledge about the regulated industry's marginal control costs. Regulators will usually have some pollution target in mind, but aggregate emissions after the tax will hit that target only if they "guess" correctly about how abatement costs vary with pollution levels. The permit system, in contrast, offers relative certainty over the aggregate quantity of pollution (the regulator sets the cap), but the cost of control will be uncertain unless regulators have very precise information about abatement costs.

When abatement costs are uncertain, whether taxes or permits are preferred depends on the size of the economic loss from not knowing costs precisely when the policy is set, which itself depends on the relative slopes of the marginal cost and marginal benefit curves for pollution abatement (Weitzman 1974). The rule of thumb to apply in these cases, known as the "Weitzman Rule," is that a tax (price) is preferable when marginal benefits are flat relative to marginal costs, and a permit policy (quantity) is preferable when the reverse is true.[13]

This rule has an intuitive feel when we consider the implications of "steepness" on the benefits side, as well as the cost side. A steep marginal benefit curve suggests large gains in the benefits of abatement (the avoided damages from pollution), even for small changes in abatement levels. Because taxes pin down the price of pollution and allow the quantity to vary, they are less desirable in such settings, where large damages may be incurred from small changes in the quantity of pollution. A steep marginal cost curve suggests large increases in the costs of abatement, even for small changes in abatement levels. Because permits allow costs to vary, they are less desirable in such settings.

This concept has given rise to many extensions.[14] Economists have also considered hybrid MBIs that have some of the advantages of both approaches. For example, a "safety valve" system would combine tradable permits with a government promise to sell additional permits at a specified price, effectively placing a ceiling on abatement costs (Jacoby and Ellerman 2004; Pizer 1999). A "price collar" would simultaneously implement a permit price floor (Burtraw et al. 2010).

5.2. Raising Public Revenues and Interaction with Existing Taxes

Taxes and auctioned permit systems raise public revenues, while grandfathered permit policies do not. The revenue raised with such policies is not an economic cost, but a transfer from affected firms to the government. However, from a distributional perspective, firms surely view tax payments and permit bills as costs—this may be one of the reasons that tax approaches are so uncommon and that almost all applications of tradable permit policies have freely allocated permits, rather than auctioning them (Keohane et al. 1998).

---

13. In contrast to cost uncertainty, uncertainty over the marginal benefits of pollution abatement does not have implications for the relative efficiency of taxes and tradable permit policies, unless benefits and costs are correlated (Stavins 1996).

14. For generalizations of the basic model see, for example, Roberts and Spence (1976) and Yohe (1976). For the application to stock pollutants, like CO_2 in the upper atmosphere, see Hoel and Karp (2001) and Newell and Pizer (2003).

The revenue-raising capability of taxes and auctioned permits has caused many to suggest that the replacement of existing taxes on labor and capital with taxes on environmental externalities could create a "double dividend," simultaneously correcting a market failure and reducing the market distortion introduced by existing taxes (Repetto et al. 1992). However, in the presence of other distortions in the general economy, the implementation of what would be efficient policies in the absence of such constraints may not actually improve social welfare. This issue is often termed the "theory of the second-best" (Lipsey and Lancaster 1956), and it is relevant to the comparison of taxes and permits.

Using revenues from taxes on environmental externalities to replace or reduce taxes on capital and labor does produce a first-order efficiency gain, known as the "revenue recycling effect." However, environmental taxes raise consumer prices and act as implicit taxes on capital and labor, reducing real returns and depressing factor supply—an efficiency loss known as the "tax interaction effect" (Bovenberg and deMooij 1994; Bovenberg and Goulder 1996; Parry 1995). The net effect of an environmental policy depends on which effect dominates. Freely allocated permits have only tax interaction effects (they collect no revenues to recycle)—thus, environmental taxes and auctioned permits are preferred, in comparison to these policies, all else being equal (Goulder et al. 1997; Goulder et al. 1999).[15]

However, even among policy instruments that do take advantage of the revenue recycling effect, this effect can offset some, but not all, of the costs of pollution control—the net effect of the policy on social welfare depends on the relative size of this effect and the tax interaction effect. Under some reasonable conditions, the tax interaction effect may outweigh the revenue recycling effect, implying a net social loss from environmental taxation (Goulder and Parry 2008). These analyses also suggest that the optimal environmental tax in the presence of preexisting distortionary taxes will be less than the Pigouvian rate assuming no such distortions (Bovenberg and Goulder 1996; Parry 1995).

5.3. Responsiveness to Changes in the Economy

Recall the most important difference between taxes and tradable permits, highlighted in the discussion of abatement cost uncertainty in section 5.1—taxes hold constant the price of pollution (allowing the aggregate control quantity to vary), and permits hold constant the aggregate quantity of pollution (allowing the price

---

15. Technology and performance standards also have no revenue-recycling effect, and thus compare poorly with taxes and auctioned permits along these lines. However, under some conditions these CAC approaches may have smaller tax interaction effects than grandfathered permit policies—this, along with monitoring and enforcement costs and other considerations, should be considered in a full cost-benefit comparison of policies (Goulder et al. 1999).

to vary). This distinction is also important in understanding the ways that each of these market-based policy instruments respond to changes in the general economy, including economic growth, inflation, and technological progress.

If economic growth results in more and larger sources of pollution over time, an environmental tax will allow an increase in aggregate emissions; aggregate emissions under a permit policy will remain unchanged, though permit prices will rise (with demand). Under general price inflation, the real value of a unit tax on pollution will decrease, and pollution levels will increase; aggregate emissions will not change under a permit policy in the face of inflation, and permit prices, while higher nominally, will be unchanged in real terms. In response to technological change that reduces the cost of pollution abatement, taxes will result in increased abatement by regulated firms; permit prices will fall, but aggregate abatement will be unchanged.

These may be second-order considerations, relative to the issues raised in sections 5.1 and 5.2. However, in some settings, the distinctions can be very important. For example, environmental taxes in Central and Eastern European countries were significantly eroded by the inflation that accompanied their economic transition in the 1990s.

6. Analyses of Selected Market-Based Environmental Policies in Practice

This section discusses several examples of market-based environmental policies in practice, assessing performance along selected dimensions from sections 4 and 5. This discussion of existing policies is by no means exhaustive. For comprehensive reviews of market-based policy applications, see Stavins (2003), Sterner and Coria (2011), and Kolstad and Freeman (2007).

6.1. Reducing Sulfur Dioxide Emissions from U.S. Power Plants

Many countries regulate the emission of sulfur dioxide (SO_2), an air pollutant that can damage human health and also causes acid rain, which harms forests and aquatic ecosystems. Power plants are a major source of U.S. SO_2 emissions. The 1990 Clean Air Act (CAA) Amendments set a new goal for SO_2 emissions reductions from older power plants not regulated under the original CAA. The amendments required 10 million tons of SO_2 emissions abatement, roughly a 50 percent reduction in emissions by covered plants. The U.S. government chose to achieve this reduction in emissions using a tradable permit policy, freely allocating permits to power plants and allowing them to trade.[16] The result was an active market for SO_2 emissions permits.

Recent regulatory events have effectively dismantled the U.S. SO_2 market. In 2005, the EPA's proposed Clean Air Interstate Rule (CAIR) would have further reduced SO_2 emissions in the 28 eastern states by one-half, beginning in 2010, halving the value of SO_2 allowances in the market (resulting in increased allowance prices) (Palmer and Evans 2009). Several states and industry filed suit, challenging the agency's authority to reduce the value of permits in this way. A federal court initially vacated the CAIR in July 2008, then reversed itself in December 2008, asking that the EPA rewrite the rule—and both events caused significant volatility in SO_2 market prices (ICAP Energy 2009). By mid-2009, SO_2 allowances were trading at record low prices, well below marginal abatement costs. In July 2010, the EPA issued the Transport Rule, to replace the CAIR in 2012. Under both rules, allowances cannot be banked but will instead be issued once every three years. As a result, firms holding the estimated 12 to 14 million SO_2 permits from the Acid Rain Program, which issued permits out to 2039, sought to use as many as possible before 2011, driving permit prices to zero (Hart 2010).

While it operated, the U.S. SO_2 trading program produced cost savings of about $1.8 billion annually, compared with the most likely alternative policy considered during deliberations over the 1990 CAA Amendments, which would have required each firm to install the same technology to reduce emissions (Keohane 2007). Early evidence of the policy's incentive for long-run, cost-reducing technological change is also available. Allowance trading seems to have boosted the incentive for electric utilities to adopt lower-cost technologies (Keohane 2007). Evidence from patent data suggests also that allowance trading spurred firms that design and build scrubbers to raise removal efficiency (Popp 2003). Monitoring and enforcement costs were roughly two orders of magnitude less than abatement costs, and the policy had very high rates of compliance, perhaps due in part to fines for noncompliance ($2,000/ton), well above prevailing permit prices.

SO_2 is not uniformly mixed, raising two distributional concerns. First, emissions in the Midwest blow to the Northeast, affecting populations and ecosystems there, while emissions from states like Maryland and Delaware blow out over the Atlantic Ocean. If trading had moved emissions from Delaware to Ohio, this would have been counter to the policy's goals. In fact, the opposite seems to have occurred. The largest reductions were achieved in Ohio, Indiana, and other midwestern states (Ellerman et al. 2000). However, nothing in the design of the market itself determined that this would be the case. An additional distributional concern with potentially significant consequences is the movement of SO_2 emissions from rural to urban areas caused by trading. The evidence suggests that trading did shift emissions from rural to urban areas, relative to either a uniform performance standard or a permit system with trading ratios that adjust for the relative damages

---

16. The definitive reference on the U.S. SO_2 market is Ellerman et al. (2000).

from emissions (Henry et al. 2011). Depending on what is assumed about the monetized value of changes in human health risk, the increase in damages from trading SO_2 as if it were uniformly mixed may even have exceeded the abatement cost savings attributed to trading (Henry et al. 2011).

The U.S. SO_2 market is the longest-running significant experiment with an MBI for pollution control thus far, and much has been learned about the promise and problems of market-based instruments, in practice, from studying this market. The collapse of the SO_2 market due to regulatory changes represents a failed opportunity to continue reaping the rewards of the policy in terms of short- and long-run cost-effectiveness. The policy instruments that replace it are likely to generate abatement costs significantly higher than what could have been achieved by adapting the SO_2 permit market's design to meet new regulatory goals (Palmer and Evans 2009).

6.2. Regulating Global Carbon Dioxide Emissions Using Tradable Permits

The Kyoto Protocol, the 1997 international climate change treaty eventually signed by more than 180 countries, included emissions trading as a mechanism for achieving national carbon dioxide (CO_2) emissions reduction targets. Among industrialized countries that took on emissions reduction targets under the Kyoto Protocol, the countries of the European Union (EU) opted to use an emissions trading system (ETS), established in 2005, to meet their targets. The Protocol sets a cap on CO_2 emissions for the EU as a whole, allocated by the EU to member countries. Member countries then divide emissions allotments among several industries: electric power generation; refineries; iron and steel; cement, glass, and ceramics; and pulp and paper.

The EU ETS is the world's largest emissions trading system, covering almost 12,000 facilities in 27 countries in 2008, and accounting for nearly one-half of EU CO_2 emissions (Ellerman and Buchner 2007; Ellerman and Joskow 2008). The Kyoto Protocol's emissions caps did not begin to bind until 2008, so the pilot phase of the EU ETS (2005–2007) was designed to set up the institutional and operating structures necessary for trading. The cap in the EU system in this pilot phase was a small reduction (a few percentage points) below expected emissions in the absence of the policy. The binding of caps in 2008 coincided with a global economic recession (and hence falling CO_2 emissions), and market participants' emissions were below the aggregate cap in 2009 and 2010; it is too soon to predict the potential impact of the EU ETS on emissions or compliance costs.

The United States did not ratify the Kyoto Protocol, and it has not adopted a binding national greenhouse gas (GHG) emissions reduction target. Nonetheless, support for action on climate change has led some states to enact policies to reduce GHG emissions. The largest U.S. market-based initiative is the Regional

Greenhouse Gas Initiative (RGGI), a cap-and-trade system among electricity generators in 10 northeastern states, which began in earnest in 2009. Allowances under RGGI are auctioned, and firms trade allowances and various financial derivatives (including futures and options contracts) in a secondary market. The program's CO_2 emissions cap for 2009–2014 roughly equals the sum of recent emissions among covered generators, then declines by 2.5 percent per year from 2015 through 2018.[17] California continues to take serious steps toward the planned 2012 launch of its own cap-and-trade system for CO_2 emissions to meet the goal of its Global Warming Solutions Act of 2006—achieving emissions in 2020 equal to those of 1990 (Jaffe and Stavins 2010).

In June 2009, the U.S. federal government appeared to be taking significant steps toward putting in place a national cap-and-trade policy to reduce CO_2 emissions, with the passage in the House of Representatives of the American Clean Energy and Security Act, also known as the Waxman-Markey bill. The legislation would have capped national GHG emissions by nearly all significant sources, including coal-fired power plants, factories, natural gas suppliers, and fuels, setting up an economywide cap-and-trade system to achieve emissions reductions. In May 2010, companion legislation was introduced in the U.S. Senate by Senators John Kerry and Joseph Lieberman—the American Power Act. Like the House legislation, this proposal featured a cap-and-trade system. The Senate abandoned its effort to pass the Kerry-Lieberman bill or any competing proposal in July 2010 as economic concerns eclipsed the goal of passing comprehensive climate legislation. In the process, cap-and-trade was demonized by conservatives in both houses as "cap-and-tax," making it unlikely, at least in the short run, that a meaningful price on carbon will be a component of any approach the United States does adopt.

A number of other major countries in the industrialized world are considering the adoption of national cap-and-trade systems to reduce CO_2 emissions, including Australia, Canada, Japan, and New Zealand (Jaffe and Stavins 2010). China's 12th Five-Year Plan, adopted in the spring of 2011, incorporates market mechanisms (along with other approaches) to achieve domestic carbon-intensity reduction goals, though it is not yet clear how these will play out.

That GHG emissions markets have been discussed and initiated in so many countries and regions stems in part from the realization that market-based approaches hold the potential to decrease very significantly the aggregate costs of reducing the GHG emissions that are changing the global climate (Olmstead and Stavins 2011). Estimates suggest that a system of international tradable permits—even if implemented only for the industrialized countries (as under the Kyoto Protocol)—could reduce costs by 50 percent relative to a system of emissions caps with no trading. If such a system also included major developing countries,

---

17. The combination of reduced electricity demand due to the economic recession of 2008–2009 and lower natural gas prices (due partly to increased U.S. supplies of shale gas) has resulted in the RGGI emissions cap being non-binding and likely to remain so unless participating states reduce the cap, making the program more stringent.

costs could be lowered again by one-half (Blanford et al. 2010; Edmonds et al. 1997; Jacoby et al. 2010).

6.3. Air Pollution Taxes

Taxes have also been used to address air pollution, though in essentially all cases, they have been lower than true Pigouvian taxes (Stavins 2003). Nonetheless, such taxes can be expected to reduce emissions if they are above marginal abatement costs for some firms. There are a small number of empirical economic analyses of air pollution taxes in the literature.

Since 1992, Sweden has charged a unit tax on nitrogen oxide (NOx) emissions to power plants producing above threshold annual output (which has changed over time), rebating revenues, less administrative costs, to payees in proportion to their energy output (Sterner and Coria 2011). While the tax covers only a small percentage of Sweden's domestic NOx emissions, estimates suggest that it has reduced emissions by regulated firms (Blackman and Harrington 2000).

France has imposed a tax on air pollutants from large power plants, adding pollutants over time—SO_2 since 1985, NOx and hydrochloric acid since 1990, and volatile organic compounds since 1995 (Millock and Nauges 2006). Most revenues are rebated as subsidies for innovation and adoption of pollution control technologies. While the tax may have reduced emissions of SO_2 and, to a smaller extent, NOx, the subsidy appears to have increased emissions by an amount that more than offsets the effect of the tax; the tax level is not the only important design component of environmental tax systems (Millock and Nauges 2006).

Several European nations taxed carbon emissions prior to the establishment of the EU ETS. In most of these countries, significant tax exemptions made effective tax rates much lower than nominal rates (Ekins and Speck 1999). For example, Norway has taxed CO_2 since 1991, at tax levels among the world's highest. Between 1991 and 1999, the tax reduced Norwegian CO_2 emissions by just over 2 percent (Bruvoll and Larsen 2004). The modest effect of the tax is due in part to extensive exemptions, including cement production, air and ocean transport, use of coal and coke in metals production (e.g., aluminum and carbide), fishing, and other sectors; all told, about 36 percent of Norwegian CO_2 emissions are exempted (Bruvoll and Larsen 2004).

China has assessed fees on air and water pollution and solid waste through its pollution levy system since the early 1980s. Fees are levied only for pollution exceeding national uniform standards, and there is debate about whether the fees lie above or below abatement costs (Florig et al. 1995; Wang and Wheeler 2000). The most careful estimate of the impacts of the Chinese pollution levy system suggests that it has reduced pollution emissions to both air (total suspended particulates) and water (chemical oxygen demand) (Wang and Wheeler 2000).

Some revenue-raising taxes may have significant environmental cobenefits. For example, most countries tax gasoline, which reduces driving and provides an incentive to purchase fuel-efficient vehicles. In the United States, as in many other countries, the revenues from most state gasoline taxes are used to maintain and expand transportation infrastructure; U.S. gasoline taxes are not explicit pollution control policies. Economists have, however, estimated the optimal U.S. gasoline tax ($0.83/gallon), taking into account the most significant externalities: emissions of local pollutants (particulate matter and nitrous oxides), carbon dioxide emissions, traffic congestion, and the accident costs not borne by drivers (Parry and Small 2005).

6.4. Individual Tradable Fishing Quotas

Market-based approaches can be designed to "get the prices right" in natural resource management problems other than pollution control. The classic economic case of an open-access resource characterized by the tragedy of the commons is a deep-sea fishery. As long as there are positive economic profits to fishing in a particular region, capital and labor (fishers) continue to enter, with fishers considering their own marginal benefit and cost but not considering scarcity in the fishery as a whole. Because no individual fisher can capture the asset value of the fishery, it is ignored, and rents are dissipated (Gordon 1954).

An increasingly common MBI for fisheries management assigns tradable property rights to deal with this problem. The world's largest market for tradable individual fishing quotas (IFQs), created in 1986, is in New Zealand. By 2004, it covered 70 different fish species. The government of New Zealand has divided coastal waters into "species-regions," generating 275 separate markets that cover more than 85 percent of the commercial catch in the area extending 200 miles from New Zealand's coast (Iudicello et al. 1999).

A market for fishing quota works similarly to a market for pollution permits. The government establishes a total allowable catch (TAC), distributing shares to individual fishers. Fishers can trade their assigned quota, which represents a percentage of the TAC for a particular species-region. Have the IFQ markets in New Zealand helped reduce overfishing and restore fish stocks? This question is much harder to answer than it was in the world of pollution control. Fish populations are hard to measure, and they depend critically on many things other than human fishing effort. But few, if any, species populations covered by New Zealand's extensive IFQ markets are worse off under the policy, and some show significant signs of recovery (Newell et al. 2005), in sharp contrast to the crashes of fish stocks in other parts of the world during this same time period. In the United States, Pacific halibut and sablefish off the coast of Alaska, mid-Atlantic surf clams and ocean quahogs, South Atlantic wreckfish, and red snapper in the Gulf of Mexico are all regulated using IFQ markets. Iceland manages stocks of 20 fish and shellfish species using IFQ markets in a system established in 1990.

Economists have begun to consider the impacts of these many applications of market-based policy to fisheries management on a global scale. An analysis of catch statistics from 11,315 global fisheries between 1950 and 2003 provides the first large-scale empirical evidence for the effectiveness of these approaches in halting and even reversing the global trend toward fisheries collapse. Researchers empirically estimate the relative advantage of IFQ fisheries over non-IFQ fisheries in terms of a lower probability of collapse, and their results suggest that, had all non-IFQ global fisheries switched to management through tradable quotas in 1970, the percentage of collapsed global fisheries by 2003 could have been reduced from more than 25 percent, to about 9 percent (Costello et al. 2008).

6.5. Municipal Solid Waste Management

Market-based approaches have also been used to manage solid waste. Some waste products have high recycling value. But most household waste ends up as trash, disposed of legally in landfills or incinerators or illegally dumped. The marginal cost of public garbage collection and disposal for an American household has been estimated at $1.03 per trash bag, but until recently, the marginal cost of disposal borne by households was approximately zero (Repetto et al. 1992).

An increasingly common waste management policy is the "pay as you throw" system, a volume-based waste disposal charge often assessed as a requirement for the purchase of official garbage bags, stickers to attach to bags of specific volume, periodic disposal charges for official city trash cans of particular sizes, and (rarely) charges based on the measured weight of curbside trash. These are environmental taxes, internalizing the costs of disposing of household waste. In 2006, more than 7,000 U.S. communities had some form of pay-as-you-throw disposal (Skumatz Economic Research Associates 2006).

Charlottesville, Virginia, imposed a charge of 80 cents per trash bag in the mid-1990s. This tax was estimated to have reduced the number of bags thrown out by about 37 percent (Fullerton and Kinnaman 1996). However, the effect was offset by two factors that have proven to be common problems with such programs. First, the reduction in the total weight of trash thrown away was much smaller, since consumers compacted trash in order to reduce the number of bags they used. Second, illegal disposal increased. In Marietta, Georgia, a fee-per-bag program (set at 75 cents) reduced the total weight of waste setouts (including both reductions in trash and increased recycling) by 36 percent, and requiring households to purchase a reusable plastic trash can reduced them by about 14 percent (Van Houtven and Morris 1999). Using telephone survey data from 21 cities in which unit pricing of solid waste had been implemented in some form, Miranda et al. (1994) find that the policies reduced waste taken to landfills in all of the cities, with an average reduction in tonnage of 40 percent.

6.6. Land and Habitat Preservation

Tradable development rights (TDRs) have been applied to solve problems as diverse as deforestation in the Brazilian Amazon and the disappearance of farmland near U.S. urban areas. The program in Calvert County, Maryland, in the far suburbs of Washington, DC, preserved an estimated 13,000 acres of farmland between 1978 and 2005 (McConnell et al. 2006). In Brazil, TDRs have been used to slow the conversion of ecologically valuable lands to agriculture since 1998; each parcel of private property that is developed must be offset by preserving a forested parcel (within the same ecosystem and with land of greater or equal ecological value) elsewhere. Simulations of the Brazilian policy for the state of Minas Gerais suggest that TDRs lower the cost to landowners of protecting a unit of forested land (Chomitz 2004). Landowners can develop the most profitable land and preserve less profitable land.

There are several challenges to using MBIs for land preservation.[18] For example, how can land developers prove (and regulators ensure) that a preserved parcel is really "additional"—that it would not have remained in the desired land use without the developer's efforts? How can we measure the ecological "equivalence" of two land parcels? Land preservation policy is a new and important application of MBIs, and important questions like these will be addressed by economists, working with natural and physical scientists, as experimentation continues.

7. CONCLUSIONS

As I write this chapter, many countries are still mired in a global economic crisis, and fiscal concerns are likely to dominate both domestic and international discussions of environmental issues for several years. In this context, continued research on market-based environmental policy is critical. Both economic theory and empirical evidence suggest that market-based environmental policy instruments are more cost-effective than prescriptive policies in the short run and that they provide strong incentives for cost-reducing technological change in the long run. The growing number of cap-and-trade policies (and, to a much smaller extent, taxes) in environmental regulation suggests that at least some governments recognize the advantages of MBIs. This, in itself, represents significant progress—30 years ago, a chapter like this could have discussed much, though not all, of the theory contained herein, but could have included no meaningful assessment of how these policies perform in practice.

---

18. A related policy, wetlands mitigation banking, holds similar promise and faces similar challenges. See National Research Council (2001) and Salvesen et al. (1996).

But empirical analysis of current and future environmental applications of taxes and tradable permits is not all that future scholarly research in economics has to contribute to the policy process. Economists have now moved on to confronting some of the biggest challenges to expanding market-based approaches to environmental policy. Chief among these is the concern about developing truly tradable commodities, since many environmental problems have important spatial and temporal components. The development of differentiated taxes and trading ratio regimes for permit systems often requires that economists work in partnership with natural and physical scientists to ensure that the cost savings achievable from MBIs is not eroded by an increase in damages from undesirable changes in the distribution of pollution or the biophysical services provided by wetlands, fisheries, and other critical natural resources.

The political economy of policy instrument choice in environmental regulation is an additional area of research that will have much to offer to future policy makers seeking to tap many of the potential advantages of MBIs. The recent collapse of the U.S. SO_2 trading market, resulting directly from new regulatory requirements that might have been accommodated in a redesigned market, is an important reminder that the gains from MBIs may be fleeting if economists fail to convince important stakeholders of their advantages (repeatedly, and over time). Those who would support the application of cap-and-trade or other MBIs to the control of carbon emissions in the United States and elsewhere could likewise benefit from a deeper understanding of how economic concepts are translated in the policy context. Without MBIs, the costs of meaningful GHG emissions reductions, and many other environmental management goals, may be a very substantial barrier to achieving any policy at all.

REFERENCES

Alberini, A., and D. Austin. 2002. "Accidents Waiting to Happen: Liability Policy and Toxic Pollution Releases." *Review of Economics and Statistics* 84: 729–741.

Andreoni, J. 1988. "Privately Provided Public Goods in a Large Economy: The Limits of Altruism." *Journal of Public Economics* 35: 57–73.

Arrow, K. J. 1951. *Social Choice and Individual Values*. New York: Wiley.

Baumol, W. J. 1972. "On Taxation and the Control of Externalities." *American Economic Review* 62: 307–322.

Baumol, W., and W. Oates. 1971. "The Use of Standards and Prices for Protection of the Environment." *Swedish Journal of Economics* 73: 42–54.

———. 1988. *The Theory of Environmental Policy*. 2nd ed. New York: Cambridge University Press.

Besanko, D. 1987. "Performance versus Design Standards in the Regulation of Pollution." *Journal of Public Economics* 34: 19–44.

Blackman, A., and W. Harrington. 2000. "The Use of Economic Incentives in Developing Countries: Lessons from International Experience with Industrial Air Pollution." *Journal of Environment and Development* 9 (1): 5–44.

Blanford, G. J., R. G. Richels, and T. F. Rutherford. 2010. "Revised Emissions Growth Projections for China: Why Post-Kyoto Climate Policy Must Look East." In *Post-Kyoto International Climate Policy: Implementing Architectures for Agreement*, ed. J. E. Aldy and R. N. Stavins. New York: Cambridge University Press.

Bohm, P., and C. F. Russell. 1985. "Comparative Analysis of Alternative Policy Instruments." In *Handbook of Natural Resource and Energy Economics*, vol. 1, ed. A. V. Kneese and J. L. Sweeney. Amsterdam: North-Holland.

Bovenberg, A. L., and R. A. de Mooij. 1994. "Environmental Levies and Distortionary Taxation." *American Economic Review* 84: 1085–1089.

Bovenberg, A. L., and L. H. Goulder. 1996. "Optimal Environmental Taxation in the Presence of Other Taxes: General Equilibrium Analyses." *American Economic Review* 86: 985–1000.

Boyd, J. 2003. "Water Pollution Taxes: A Good Idea Doomed to Failure?" *Public Finance and Management* 3: 34–66.

Bruvoll, A., and B. M. Larsen. 2004. "Greenhouse Gas Emissions in Norway: Do Carbon Taxes Work?" *Energy Policy* 32: 493–505.

Buchanan, J. M. 1968. *The Demand and Supply of Public Goods*. Chicago: Rand-McNally.

Burtraw, D., K. L. Palmer, and D. B. Kahn. 2010. "A Symmetric Safety Valve." *Energy Policy* 38: 4921–4932.

Chang, H. F., and H. Sigman. 2000. "Incentives to Settle under Joint and Several Liability: An Empirical Analysis of Superfund Litigation." *Journal of Legal Studies* 29: 205–236.

———. 2007. "The Effect of Joint and Several Liability under Superfund on Brownfields." *International Review of Law and Economics* 27: 363–384.

Chomitz, K. M. 2004. "Transferable Development Rights and Forest Protection: An Exploratory Analysis." *International Regional Science Review* 27 (3): 348–373.

Coase, R. H. 1960. "The Problem of Social Cost." *Journal of Law and Economics* 3: 1–44.

Cohen, M. A. 1999. "Monitoring and Enforcement of Environmental Policy." In *International Yearbook of Environmental and Resource Economics 1999/2000*, ed. T. Tietenberg and H. Folmer. Cheltenham, UK: Edward Elgar.

Costello, C., S. Gaines, and J. Lynham. 2008. "Can Catch Shares Prevent Fisheries Collapse?" *Science* 321: 1678–1681.

Crocker, T. 1966. "The Structuring of Atmospheric Pollution Control Systems." In *The Economics of Air Pollution*, ed. H. Wolozin. New York: Norton.

Dales, J. H. 1968. *Pollution, Property and Prices*. Toronto: University of Toronto Press.

Downing, P. B., and L. J. White. 1986. "Innovation in Pollution Control." *Journal of Environmental Economics and Management* 13: 18–27.

Edmonds, J., S. H. Kim, C. N. McCracken, R. D. Sands, and M. A. Wise. 1997. *Return to 1990: The Cost of Mitigating United States Carbon Emissions in the Post-2000 Period*. Washington, DC: Pacific Northwest National Laboratory, operated by Battelle Memorial Institute.

Ekins, P., and S. Speck. 1999. "Competitiveness and Exemptions from Environmental Taxes in Europe." *Environmental and Resource Economics* 13: 369–396.

Ellerman, A. D., and B. K. Buchner. 2007. "The European Union Emissions Trading Scheme: Origins, Allocation, and Early Results." *Review of Environmental Economics and Policy* 1 (1): 66–87.

Ellerman, A. D., and P. L. Joskow. 2008. *The European Union's Emissions Trading System in Perspective.* Washington, DC: Pew Center on Global Climate Change.

Ellerman, A. D., P. J. Joskow, R. Schmalensee, J.-P. Montero, and E. M. Bailey. 2000. *Markets for Clean Air: The U.S. Acid Rain Program.* New York: Cambridge University Press.

Eskeland, G. S., and E. Jimenez. 1992. "Policy Instruments for Pollution Control in Developing Countries." *World Bank Research Observer* 7 (2): 145–169.

Farrow, R. S., M. T. Schultz, P. Celikkol, and G. L. Van Houtven. 2005. "Pollution Trading in Water Quality Limited Areas: Use of Benefits Assessment and Cost-Effective Trading Ratios." *Land Economics* 81: 191–205.

Florig, H. K., W. O. Spofford, Jr., X. Ma, and Z. Ma. 1995. "China Strives to Make the Polluter Pay." *Environmental Science and Technology* 29 (6): 268–273.

Fullerton, D., and T. C. Kinnaman. 1996. "Household Responses to Pricing Garbage by the Bag." *American Economic Review* 86 (4): 971–984.

Gordon, H. S. 1954. "The Economic Theory of a Common Property Resource: The Fishery." *Journal of Political Economy* 62: 124–142.

Goulder, L. H., and I. W. H. Parry. 2008. "Instrument Choice and Environmental Policy." *Review of Environmental Economics and Policy* 2 (2): 152–174.

Goulder, L. H., I. W. H. Parry, and D. Burtraw. 1997. "Revenue-Raising vs. Other Approaches to Environmental Protection: The Critical Significance of Pre-existing Tax Distortions." *RAND Journal of Economics* 28 (4): 708–731.

Goulder, L. H., I. W. H. Parry, R. C. Williams, III, and D. Burtraw. 1999. "The Cost-Effectiveness of Alternative Instruments for Environmental Protection in a Second-Best Setting." *Journal of Public Economics* 72 (3): 329–360.

Griffin, R. C. and D. W. Bromley. 1982. "Agricultural Runoff as a Nonpoint Externality: A Theoretical Development." *American Journal of Agricultural Economics* 64: 547–552.

Hahn, R. W. 1984. "Market Power and Transferable Property Rights." *Quarterly Journal of Economics* 99: 753–765.

Hahn, R. W., and R. N. Stavins. 1992. "Economic Incentives for Environmental Protection: Integrating Theory and Practice." *American Economic Review, Papers and Proceedings* 82 (2): 464–468.

Hardin, G. 1968. "The Tragedy of the Commons." *Science* 162 (3859): 1243–1248.

Hart, G. 2010. "Are SO_2 Markets Doomed? Interview with Gary Hart, a Market Analyst for ICAP Energy." *Environmental Markets Newsletter,* July 14. Available at www.jlnenvironmental.com/2010/07/are-so2-markets-doomed_14.html.

Helfand, G. E. 1991. "Standards versus Standards: The Effects of Different Pollution Restrictions." *American Economic Review* 81 (3): 622–634.

Henry, D., N. Z. Muller, and R. Mendelsohn. 2011. "The Social Cost of Trading? Measuring the Increased Damages from Sulfur Dioxide Trading in the United States." *Journal of Policy Analysis and Management* 30 (3): 598–612.

Hoel, M., and L. S. Karp. 2001. "Taxes and Quotas for a Stock Pollutant with Multiplicative Uncertainty." *Journal of Public Economics* 82: 91–114.

Hung, M.-F., and D. Shaw. 2005. "A Trading-Ratio System for Trading Water Pollution Discharge Permits." *Journal of Environmental Economics and Management* 49: 83–102.

ICAP Energy. 2009. "CAIR Litigation Has Shot an Arrow through the Heart of the SO_2 Trading Market." *Environmental Markets Brief* 1 (2): 1–4.

Iudicello, S., M. Weber, and R. Wieland. 1999. *Fish, Markets and Fishermen: The Economics of Overfishing.* Washington, DC: Island.

Jacoby, H. D., and D. A. Ellerman. 2004. "The Safety Valve and Climate Policy." *Energy Policy* 32 (4): 481–491.

Jacoby, H. D., M. H. Babiker, S. Paltsev, and J. M. Reilly. 2010. "Sharing the Burden of GHG Reductions." In *Post-Kyoto International Climate Policy: Implementing Architectures for Agreement*, ed. J. E. Aldy and R. N. Stavins. New York: Cambridge University Press.

Jaffe, A. B., and R. N. Stavins. 1995. "Dynamic Incentives of Environmental Regulations: The Effects of Alternative Policy Instruments on Technology Diffusion." *Journal of Environmental Economics and Management* 29: S43–63.

———. 2010. "Linkage of Tradable Permit Systems in International Climate Policy Architecture." In *Post-Kyoto International Climate Policy: Implementing Architectures for Agreement*, ed. J. E. Aldy and R. N. Stavins. Cambridge: Cambridge University Press.

Joskow, P., and R. Schmalensee. 1998. "The Political Economy of Market-Based Environmental Policy: The U.S. Acid Rain Program." *Journal of Law and Economics* 41: 89–135.

Jung, C., K. Krutilla, and R. Boyd. 1996. "Incentives for Advanced Pollution Abatement Technology at the Industry Level: An Evaluation of Policy Alternatives." *Journal of Environmental Economics and Management* 30: 95–111.

Keohane, N. O. 2007. "Cost Savings from Allowance Trading in the 1990 Clean Air Act." In *Moving to Markets in Environmental Regulation: Lessons from Twenty Years of Experience*, ed. C. E. Kolstad and J. Freeman. New York: Oxford University Press.

Keohane, N. O., and S. M. Olmstead. 2007. *Markets and the Environment*. Washington, DC: Island.

Keohane, N. O., R. L. Revesz, and R. N. Stavins. 1998. "The Choice of Regulatory Instruments in Environmental Policy." *Harvard Environmental Law Review* 22 (2): 313–367.

Kolstad, C., and J. Freeman, eds. 2007. *Moving to Markets in Environmental Regulation: Lessons from Twenty Years of Experience*. New York: Oxford University Press.

Kolstad, C., T. Ulen, and G. Johnson. 1990. "Ex Post Liability for Harm vs. Ex Ante Safety Regulation: Substitutes or Complements?" *American Economic Review* 80: 888–901.

Kornhauser, L. A., and R. L. Revesz. 1994. "Multidefendant Settlements under Joint and Several Liability: The Problem of Insolvency." *Journal of Legal Studies* 23: 517–542.

Lindahl, E. 1985. "Just Taxation: A Positive Solution." In *Classics in the Theory of Public Finance*, ed. R. A. Musgrave and A. Peacock. London: Macmillan.

Lipsey, R. G. and K. Lancaster. 1956. "The General Theory of Second Best." *Review of Economic Studies* 24 (1): 11–32.

Malik, A. S. 1992. "Enforcement Costs and the Choice of Policy Instruments for Controlling Pollution." *Economic Inquiry* 30: 714–721.

Malueg, D. A. 1989. "Emission Credit Trading and the Incentive to Adopt New Pollution Abatement Technology." *Journal of Environmental Economics and Management* 16: 52–57.

Mansur, E. T., and S. M. Olmstead. 2007. "The Value of Scarce Water: Measuring the Inefficiency of Municipal Regulations." National Bureau of Economic Research Working Paper No. 13513. Cambridge, MA: NBER.

McConnell, V., M. Walls, and E. Kopits. 2006. "Zoning, Transferable Development Rights and the Density of Development." *Journal of Urban Economics* 59: 440–457.

Menell, P. S. 1991. "The Limitations of Legal Institutions for Addressing Environmental Risks." *Journal of Economic Perspectives* 5 (3): 93–113.

Milliman, S. R., and R. Prince. 1989. "Firm Incentives to Promote Technological Change in Pollution Control." *Journal of Environmental Economics and Management* 17: 247–265.

Millock, K., and C. Nauges. 2006. "Ex Post Evaluation of an Earmarked Tax on Air Pollution." *Land Economics* 82 (1): 68–84.

Miranda, M. L., J. W. Everett, D. Blume, and B. A. Roy, Jr. 1994. "Market-Based Incentives and Residential Municipal Solid Waste." *Journal of Policy Analysis and Management* 13: 681–698.

Montero, J.-P., J. M. Sanchez, and R. Katz. 2002. "A Market-Based Environmental Policy Experiment in Chile." *Journal of Law and Economics* 45: 267–287.

Montgomery, W. D. 1972. "Markets in Licenses and Efficient Pollution Control Programs." *Journal of Economic Theory* 5: 395–418.

National Research Council. 2001. *Compensating for Wetland Losses under the Clean Water Act*. Washington, DC: National Academy Press.

Newell, R. G., and W. A. Pizer. 2003. "Regulating Stock Externalities under Uncertainty." *Journal of Environmental Economics and Management* 45: 416–432.

Newell, R. G., J. N. Sanchirico, and S. Kerr. 2005. "Fishing Quota Markets." *Journal of Environmental Economics and Management* 49 (3): 437–462.

Newell, R. G., and R. N. Stavins. 2003. "Cost Heterogeneity and the Potential Savings from Market-Based Policies." *Journal of Regulatory Economics* 23: 43–59.

Niskanen, W. A. 2001. "Arsenic and Old Facts." *Regulation* 24 (3): 54.

Oates, W. E., A. J. Krupnick, and E. Van de Verg. 1983. "On Marketable Air-Pollution Permits: The Case for a System of Pollution Offsets." *Journal of Environmental Economics and Management* 10: 233–237.

Olmstead, S. M., and R. N. Stavins. 2012. "Three Key Elements of Post-2012 International Climate Policy Architecture." *Review of Environmental Economics and Policy* 6 (1): 65–85.

Olsen, M. 1965. *The Logic of Collective Action*. Cambridge, MA: Harvard University Press.

Ostrom, E. 1990. *Governing the Commons: The Evolution of Institutions for Collective Action*. Cambridge: Cambridge University Press.

Palmer, K., and D. A. Evans. 2009. "The Evolving SO_2 Allowance Market: Title IV, CAIR, and Beyond." Policy Commentary, July 13. Washington, DC: Resources for the Future. Available at www.rff.org/Publications/WPC/Pages/090713-Evolving-SO$_2$-Allowance-Market.aspx.

Parry, I. W. H. 1995. "Pollution Taxes and Revenue Recycling." *Journal of Environmental Economics and Management* 29: S64–77.

Parry, I. W. H., and K. Small. 2005. "Does Britain or the United States Have the Right Gasoline Tax?" *American Economic Review* 95: 1276–1289.

Pigou, A. C. 1920. *The Economics of Welfare*. London: Macmillan and Co.

Pizer, W. A. 1999. "Combining Price and Quantity Controls to Mitigate Global Climate Change." *Journal of Public Economics* 85: 409–434.

Popp, D. 2003. "Pollution Control Innovations and the Clean Air Act of 1990." *Journal of Policy Analysis and Management* 22 (4): 641–660.

Repetto, R., R. C. Dower, R. Jenkins, and J. Geoghegan. 1992. *Green Fees: How a Tax Shift Can Work for the Environment and the Economy*. Washington, DC: World Resources Institute.

Roberts, M. J., and M. Spence. 1976. "Effluent Charges and Licenses under Uncertainty." *Journal of Public Economics* 5: 193–208.

Rodríguez, F. 2000. "On the Use of Exchange Rates as Trading Rules in a Bilateral System of Transferable Discharge Permits." *Environmental and Resource Economics* 15: 379–395.

Rose-Ackerman, S. 1973. "Effluent Charges: A Critique." *Canadian Journal of Economics* 4: 512–528.

Salvesen, D., L. L. Marsh, and D. R. Porter, eds. 1996. *Mitigation Banking: Theory and Practice.* Washington, DC: Island.

Samuelson, P. A. 1954. "The Pure Theory of Public Expenditure." *Review of Economics and Statistics* 36 (4): 387–389.

———. 1955. "Diagrammatic Exposition of a Theory of Public Expenditure." *Review of Economics and Statistics* 37 (4): 350–356.

Sandmo, A. 1975. "Optimal Taxation: An Introduction to the Literature." *Journal of Public Economics* 6: 37–54.

Schmutzler, A., and L. H. Goulder. 1997. "The Choice between Emission Taxes and Output Taxes under Imperfect Monitoring." *Journal of Environmental Economics and Management* 32: 51–64.

Segerson, K. 1988. "Uncertainty and Incentives for Nonpoint Pollution Control." *Journal of Environmental Economics and Management* 15: 87–98.

Shavell, S. 1984. "A Model of the Optimal Use of Liability and Safety Regulation." *RAND Journal of Economics* 15: 271–280.

Sigman, H. 1998. "Liability Funding and Superfund Clean-up Remedies." *Journal of Environmental Economics and Management* 35: 205–224.

Skumatz Economic Research Associates, Inc. 2006. "Pay As You Throw (PAYT) in the U.S.: 2006 Update and Analyses. Final Report to the U.S. EPA Office of Solid Waste." December 30. Superior, CO. Available at www.epa.gov/osw/conserve/tools/payt/pdf/sera06.pdf.

Smith, A. 1776. *The Wealth of Nations.* London: W. Strahan and T. Cadell.

Stavins, R. N. 1995. "Transaction Costs and Tradeable Permits." *Journal of Environmental Economics and Management* 29: 133–148.

———. 1996. "Correlated Uncertainty and Policy Instrument Choice." *Journal of Environmental Economics and Management* 30: 218–232.

———. 2003. "Experience with Market-Based Environmental Policy Instruments." In *Handbook of Environmental Economics,* vol. 1, ed. K.-G. Mäler and J. Vincent. Amsterdam: Elsevier Science.

Sterner, T., and J. Coria. 2011. *Policy Instruments for Environmental and Natural Resource Management.* 2nd ed. Washington, DC: Resources for the Future.

Tietenberg, T. H. 1985. *Emission Trading: An Exercise in Reforming Pollution Policy.* Washington, DC: Resources for the Future.

———. 1990. "Economic Instruments for Environmental Regulation." *Oxford Review of Economic Policy* 6 (1): 17–33.

———. 2006. *Emissions Trading: Principles and Practice.* 2nd ed. Washington, DC: Resources for the Future.

Van Houtven, G. L., and G. E. Morris. 1999. "Household Behavior under Alternative Pay-as-You-Throw Systems for Solid Waste Disposal." *Land Economics* 75: 515–537.

Wang, H., and D. Wheeler. 2000. "Endogenous Enforcement and Effectiveness of China's Pollution Levy System." World Bank Policy Research Working Paper No. 2336. Washington, DC: World Bank Development Research Group.

Weitzman, M. L. 1974. "Prices vs. Quantities." *Review of Economic Studies* 41: 477–491.

Yohe, G. W. 1976. "Towards a General Comparison of Price Controls and Quantity Controls under Uncertainty." *Review of Economic Studies* 45: 229–238.

CHAPTER 26

....

FLEXIBLE APPROACHES TO ENVIRONMENTAL REGULATION

....

LORI S. BENNEAR AND CARY COGLIANESE

"FLEXIBLE regulation" might sound like an oxymoron, but it has actually become a widely accepted catchphrase for a pragmatic approach to regulation. The phrase stakes out a middle ground between regulation's defenders and its critics, promising the achievement of important health, safety, and environmental objectives while also minimizing costs and preserving liberty. For over 30 years, the ideal of "regulatory flexibility" has been embedded in federal law in the United States, with legislation requiring administrative agencies "to solicit and consider flexible regulatory proposals" when contemplating new requirements that would affect small businesses (Regulatory Flexibility Act 1980). In early 2011, President Obama adopted a more general order to agencies to pursue "flexible approaches" whenever "relevant, feasible, and consistent with regulatory objectives, and to the extent permitted by law" (Obama 2011). Agencies are now required to "identify and consider regulatory approaches that reduce burdens and maintain flexibility and freedom of choice for the public" (Obama 2011).

In response to demands for greater flexibility, environmental regulators have implemented a "varied basket of more flexible regulatory strategies" (Karkkainen 2006). These strategies—which range from performance and market-based standards to requirements for information disclosure or pollution prevention planning—have also fueled a corresponding effort by scholars in the social and policy sciences to refine the theoretical expectations for flexible approaches to regulation and to test these expectations empirically. Research has confirmed that flexible approaches can sometimes result in the very kinds of improvements in environmental conditions that traditional forms of regulation seek to obtain. However, not all flexible approaches result in significant improvements, and some have been linked, on occasion, with unintended adverse outcomes. This chapter assesses what we know about flexible approaches to environmental regulation. We begin by defining more precisely what we mean by flexible regulation, placing the concept within a general framework of regulation. Adhering to this framework, we proceed in each subsequent part of this chapter to show the role that flexible regulation can play in environmental protection and to assess what we know about flexible regulation's impacts on business behavior and environmental quality.

1. Framework of Flexible Regulation

Flexibility and regulation exist in tension because flexibility implies choice, while regulation limits choice. Two different regulations addressing the same problem and targeting the same individuals or businesses may nevertheless permit different degrees of choice in how to act. The regulation that affords the greater degree of choice can be said to be more flexible. If two regulations are equally effective (that is, achieve the same results) and differ only in that one provides greater flexibility than the other, the more flexible one would be clearly better to adopt because the choice afforded either is intrinsically valuable or allows regulated targets to choose less costly ways to comply. Of course, regulatory flexibility can come at a price if regulated targets use it to choose actions that comply with the regulation but that prove less effective at solving the social problem motivating the regulatory intervention.

Different regulatory approaches can yield different degrees of flexibility because they vary in how they are structured. The broad literature on regulation contains numerous taxonomies of regulatory structures (Richards 2000), but all variants of regulation can be distilled down to the four components inherent in any regulatory scheme: (1) the command embedded in the regulation, (2) the target of the regulation, (3) the consequences associated with compliance or noncompliance with the command, and (4) the regulator (Coglianese 2010a, 2010b). The *regulator* is the entity that creates and enforces the regulation. The *target* refers to the entity or entities to which the regulation applies. The *command* refers to what the regulator instructs the target to do or to refrain from doing. The regulatory *consequences* are what the regulator imposes on the target for complying or failing to comply; they can be positive or negative, large or small, certain or uncertain.

To see how these differences affect flexibility, consider first the regulatory command. The command can affect flexibility by its stringency, its structure, and its specificity. Stringency—or how much pollution reduction is commanded—affects both costs and flexibility, two related but distinct concepts. Flexibility relates to costs because regulated targets that have a greater range of choice—more flexibility—will be able to select lower-cost ways of complying. However, not all differences in cost derive from flexibility. Two regulations addressing the same problem might well each afford a regulated target only one way to comply, but the single action compelled by the less stringent of the two may simply cost less.

Commands vary by more than just their stringency; they also differ in terms of their structure, or *what* they direct targets to do or achieve. Some commands direct targets to take or refrain from actions, while others only prescribe or proscribe specified end-states that are caused by actions. The former we call *means* standards, although they are also sometimes called technology, design, or specification standards. By contrast, commands commonly called *performance* standards do not mandate any particular action or installation of technology, only the attainment or avoidance of an end-state such as a specified level of emissions from a smokestack (Coglianese, Nash, and Olmstead 2003; May 2011).

These two types of standards—*means* and *performance*—can be distinguished further based on where they intervene in the causal chain leading up to the problem that the standard is supposed to help solve, something which in turn affects the amount of flexibility for regulated targets. To illustrate, consider a highly stylized causal chain that leads to sickness—say, asthma—from industrial air pollution. As shown in Figure 26.1, the causal chain begins with (A) business decision making that leads to (B) manufacturing operations or other behaviors that generate (C) emissions of pollutants that ultimately lead to (D) cases of asthma. Regulatory commands can be situated at any one of these steps in the causal chain.

A means standard might fall along the chain at step (B), mandating the installation of emissions control technology to reduce levels of a pollutant. As Figure 26.1 shows, in such a case the regulatory standard would foreclose other choices, such as changing to a cleaner input. A performance standard situated at step (C), by contrast, would specify the permissible level of a pollutant but would allow the regulated target the choice of how to reduce emissions of that pollutant, either changing to a cleaner input or installing emissions control technology. A target would have still greater choice if the standard were situated at step (D), which we call a *meta-performance* standard. For example, a regulation that simply imposed a general duty of care to reduce the risk of asthma cases would allow the regulated target to choose to reduce either of the precursor pollutants in Figure 26.1 and to choose, for each of these pollutants, which way to reduce it.

Another regulatory approach would be to focus on the first step, (A), such as by requiring targets to engage in information gathering, planning, and other management practices that should enable them to make better decisions about reducing the environmental impacts of their operations (Coglianese and Lazer 2003; Hutter 2001). Management-based regulation and information disclosure laws are examples of this approach, which we generalize here under the label of *meta-means* standards. Meta-means standards are means standards in that

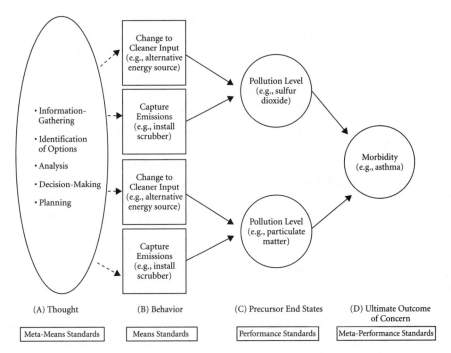

Figure 26.1 Choice Structure, Regulatory Intervention Points, and
Types of Regulatory Commands

they do mandate some action, but the actions they compel lie at a very early stage of a causal chain leading to a problem. In our stylized example, the regulator could require a target to identify pollutants it generated that contribute to asthma levels and then to develop its own plan of action aimed at reducing that risk, an example of a management-based regulation (Bennear 2006). The range of behavioral choices available to the target with such a meta-means standard would be the same as with a meta-performance standard. In our example, the target could choose to focus on either of the precursor pollutants and then on either of the two means of reducing those pollutants. The main difference is that under a meta-means standard the target has no choice but to engage in the required information gathering and plan development, whereas under the meta-performance standard such planning would occur only as the outgrowth of the mandated performance.

Of course, not all commands targeting the same link on the causal chain will promise an equal degree of flexibility. Even when addressing the same link, standards can be written with different levels of *specificity*. For example, a means standard that requires the installation of technology might require either the "installation of reasonably available control technology" or the "installation of a dry scrubber." Both are means standards intervening at the same step on the causal chain, and hence they both preclude targets from meeting their legal obligation by, say, changing to cleaner inputs; however, the first standard would obviously give more flexibility than the second, assuming that both a dry scrubber and a wet scrubber are "reasonably available." In a similar way, performance standards can vary in their specificity. A command that requires facilities to reduce emissions of a pollutant to a "reasonable level" will undoubtedly permit greater flexibility than a more specific standard that requires reductions to "0.05 parts per million," even though both are performance standards.

Just as variation in the specificity, structure, and stringency of commands affects flexibility, so too can variation in regulations' targets. All other things equal, the broader the target, the greater the flexibility. For example, an automobile emissions standard could target either individual automobiles or a manufacturer's entire fleet. If the regulation imposes an emissions limit on each and every car (a narrow target), it will give the manufacturer much less flexibility than would a fleetwide average emissions limit (a broad target), even though both are performance standards.

The expected consequences of regulation can also affect flexibility. A highly specific means standard backed up with no consequences for noncompliance would, in reality, afford a target more flexibility than a general meta-performance backed up with strict oversight and significant penalties. Similarly, when positive consequences are offered for compliance, targets may not see themselves as constrained if these rewards are modest or trivial. However, if a positive consequence is substantial, such as the granting of a license to operate a business, targets will be much more constrained to do what is needed to earn the "reward."

Finally, the identity of the regulator can affect flexibility as well. Although typically the regulator is a governmental entity, a variety of nongovernmental entities can impose commands that are backed up with consequences, including insurance companies, customers, industry trade organizations, and private standard-setting entities such as the International Organization for Standardization (ISO) or the International Electrotechnical Commission (Gunningham and Rees 1997). A target can even "regulate" itself by imposing commands on its own members or employees. To account for self-regulation, we posit that the closer the connection between the regulator and the target, the greater the flexibility the target will have, all else being equal.

Flexibility in the case of self-regulation, though, does not necessarily mean that the command adopted will actually afford, by its terms, greater choice. A private or self-regulatory entity can adopt just as constraining a means standard as any government regulator can. However, when there is a degree of unity between the regulator and the target, any behavior demanded by a regulatory command will more likely reflect the very choices the targeted entity would have made. In situations of complete self-regulation, the slate of options a target has to require of itself is, at least in principle, wide open.

In the end, the actual level of flexibility afforded by any regulation will be a function of its four elements—regulator, target, command, and consequences—*combined with* the specific set of choices available to the regulated entity in each particular circumstance in which it finds itself. Flexibility is, after all, also a function of the underlying behavioral (physical, economic, or technological) choices available to an entity. At the limit, if there is only one way to reduce emissions of a certain pollutant, then in practice it does not matter whether the regulator adopts a means standard or a performance standard.

What can be said, then, as a general matter about flexible approaches to regulation? Answering that question is the purpose of the remainder of this chapter. Having elucidated the range of flexible approaches to regulation, we now focus on the role and impacts of actual flexible approaches. Does flexible regulation yield some positive environmental impact? If so, when? Although we track here the existing research literature in emphasizing the question of whether flexible regulation can yield at least some environmental benefits, we acknowledge that this emphasis offers but a partial evaluation of flexible regulation. We note that any number of alternative policy approaches might also be *effective* in the sense of yielding at least some environmental benefits. A more complete evaluation of any regulatory approach would consider how well the full effects of that approach—benefits *and* costs—compares with the full effects of other approaches. Furthermore, any policy approach may be evaluated on a variety of policy criteria, whether economic (e.g., cost-effectiveness, efficiency, and incentives for technological innovation), political (e.g., political feasibility and transparency), or distributional (e.g., equity and justice). Naturally, different criteria are likely to yield different judgments about the desirability of any approach to environmental regulation in different circumstances.

2. FLEXIBLE COMMANDS

We focus first on flexible commands: performance standards, information disclosure, and management-based regulation. The flexibility of these commands derives from the ways that they permit a regulated target to choose from among a range of actions in order to reduce the environmental impacts of their behavior.

2.1. Performance Standards

Performance standards command the avoidance or attainment of an end-state, giving individuals and businesses subject to regulation the opportunity to choose their own concrete actions, provided that the end-state commanded is satisfied (May 2011). By focusing on an end-state and giving the targets of the regulation choice in how to achieve that end-state, performance standards allow targets to select the least costly means of meeting the commanded level of performance. Performance standards also allow for innovation and technological development in ways that means standards cannot typically accommodate (Jaffe, Newell, and Stavins 2004).

For these reasons, performance standards have been widely lauded by academics and policy makers (Coglianese, Nash, and Olmstead 2003). Since the early 1990s, federal agencies in the United States have operated under a presidential order that admonishes them whenever feasible to "specify performance objectives, rather than specifying the behavior or manner of compliance that regulated entities must adopt" (Clinton 1993). The White House Office of Management and Budget (OMB) has elaborated that "performance standards are generally to be preferred to engineering or design standards because performance standards provide the regulated parties the flexibility to achieve the regulatory objective in a more cost-effective way" (OMB 1996). More recently, President Obama's 2011 executive order on regulation likewise stated that agencies "must" use performance standards whenever feasible (Obama 2011).

As favorably as performance standards have been viewed, these standards also can pose real challenges. For one thing, regulators and inspectors need a way of measuring performance (OMB 1996, 2003). Yet sometimes measurement can be difficult because of the highly distributed nature of the problem, such as when ensuring compliance with emissions limits requires continuous monitoring of hundreds of thousands of smokestacks and pipes.

In addition, if performance standards are so narrowly defined that they permit regulated entities only one realistic option of what action to take, they provide no advantage over a means standard that compels that same action. As OMB has noted, it is "misleading and inappropriate to characterize a standard as a performance standard if it is set so that there is only one feasible way to meet it" (OMB 1996).

Finally, performance standards may be somewhat more susceptible to the law of unintended consequences. For example, one study of performance-based building standards in New Zealand has suggested that the flexibility they afforded led to a major national "leaky building" crisis, with as many as tens of thousands of homes afflicted with extensive rotting (May 2003). The building standards commanded performance in terms of durability and stability but not weatherproofing, which allowed builders to meet code using cheaper materials that met the performance requirements but did not adequately resist rain.

Another consideration with performance standards is that even though they provide individual regulated targets with flexibility needed to achieve cost savings, they often still treat all targets equally, meaning that every target has to meet the same level of allowable emissions. Since the marginal costs of controlling emissions can vary across different businesses, such uniform performance standards can miss opportunities for greater flexibility and cost savings. When only the marginal abatement costs, and not the marginal benefits of abatement, vary over space, a more cost-effective way to attain the same level of overall pollution control would be to allow the end-state to vary from target to target, keeping the aggregate level of allowable pollution the same. In theory, one way to do this would be to set performance standards on an individualized basis for each regulated entity, so that those businesses with lower costs of control would be asked to reduce more pollution than firms with higher costs of control. As long as the average level of emissions remained the same, such a case-by-case approach would be superior to uniform performance standards because the same ambient environmental quality would be achieved at lower overall costs.

The obvious problem with this approach is the practical infeasibility of setting individualized standards when dealing with pollutants emitted from thousands of dispersed sources. One way to overcome this problem would be through a per-unit pollution tax that sets a price on each unit of pollution emitted by each source (Pigou 1932). Under a pollution tax, which is a type of performance standard because the consequences are triggered by an end-state (i.e., the level of emissions), the command changes from the conventional one, which tells targets to keep their emissions below an aggregate level in order to avoid large financial consequences, to one that tells them they will incur smaller financial consequences for every incremental unit of pollution they emit (Dales 1968). Under the latter approach, targets can choose to abate pollution using any means they see fit—or to pay the tax. The tax would be the same for each targeted firm, but they would have greater flexibility because each firm would be allowed to respond to the tax according to its own marginal abatement costs (see chapter 25 for more details).

2.2. Information Disclosure

Although requirements to disclose information are inflexible with respect to the information they mandate be disclosed, they leave regulated firms with total flexibility about whether and how to address the environmental conditions that must be reported. Two major federal regulations in the United States—the Toxics Release Inventory (TRI) and the Consumer Confidence Reports (CCR)—require the disclosure of environmental information. EPA's TRI program, established under the 1986 Emergency Planning and Community Right to Know Act, requires facilities from several industrial sectors to report publicly the amount of toxic chemicals they release into the environment, provided they manufacture or use more than a specified amount of those chemicals (Kraft, Stephan, and Abel 2011). Amendments made in 1996 to the Safe Drinking Water Act led to the CCR rule that requires community water systems to report annually to their customers on the quality of the water supplied (Bennear and Olmstead 2008). Both TRI and CCR had been conceived initially as primarily advancing citizens' "right to know," but over the years they have come to be considered flexible approaches for achieving traditional environmental regulatory goals (Kraft, Stephan, and Abel 2011). For example, according to one recent account, the TRI "may be the most unambiguous success story in all of environmental law" (Thaler and Sunstein 2008, 192). Clearly, some analysts believe that mandated information disclosure can serve as a flexible type of pollution regulation (Fung and O'Rourke 2000).

Empirical analysis of information disclosure regulations in the United States has suggested that they can be at least moderately effective in inducing some behavioral change, if not even some improvement in terms of the ultimate outcome of environmental quality (Kraft, Stephan, and Abel 2011). Research has found that the CCR lowered violations among community water systems that were required to disclose these violations to the public (Bennear and Olmstead 2008).

Empirical evidence of the effectiveness of information disclosure programs, particularly the TRI, has been tempered by analyses demonstrating that at least some of the apparent reductions in emissions are likely spurious, resulting from changes in reporting requirements (Poje and Horowitz 1990), changes in categorizations of release data (Natan and Miller 1998; Poje and Horowitz 1990), changes in reporting behavior among firms (Bennear 2008), changes in firm organization (Grant and Jones 2003), and other traditional regulatory approaches (de Marchi and Hamilton 2006). Because of the difficulty in separating the causal impact of information disclosure from other correlated activities, one of the most extensive studies of TRI has concluded that "the separate and exact impacts that the provision of information has on toxic emissions are, to date, unknown" (Hamilton 2005, 242).

The impact of information programs may be hampered by the lack of public awareness of the data despite mandates for data provision (Atlas 2007; Ben-Shahar and Schneider 2011). Nevertheless, researchers have offered four main theoretical explanations—market, legal, political, and internal—for why information disclosure might lead to improved environmental performance (Sunstein 1999; Tietenberg 1998).

First, disclosure of information may generate *market* pressures for environmental improvements if consumers, investors, or employees have preferences about environmental performance. Studies of stock market reactions to TRI data have suggested that investors take note (Hamilton 1995; Khanna, Quimio, and Bojilova 1998; Konar and Cohen 1997), with the largest reported reductions in TRI emissions coming at companies with the largest negative stock market reactions (Khanna, Quimio, and Bojilova 1998; Konar and Cohen 1997). Studies of housing market responses have exhibited mixed results (Bui and Mayer 2003; Oberholzer-Gee and Mitsunari 2006).

Second, mandated information disclosure may induce *legal* pressures for environmental improvements, particularly to avoid tort liability (Tietenberg 1998). Environmental right-to-know data may serve as proxies for liability risks, the management of which may lead to improvements in environmental performance.

Third, disclosed information may generate *political* pressures that motivate environmental improvements. Revelations about environmental performance may influence future regulatory efforts (Bennear and Olmstead 2008; Helland and Whitford 2003; Karkkainen 2001; Sunstein 1999).

Finally, independent of disclosure's effects on market, legal, and political factors, the collection and release of information may otherwise affect the *internal* decision making of an organization. Measuring and reporting data on environmental performance may itself lead to internal changes at the firm that improve environmental performance, perhaps to fulfill the environmental preferences of managers (Karkkainen 2001).

Regardless of the particular mechanism, theory suggests that disclosure mandates will be more effective when the information disclosed becomes more embedded in the decisions of both disclosers and users (Weil et al. 2006). For example, disclosure of drinking water pollutant and violation information under CCR appears associated with reduced regulatory violations—but only among suppliers that were required to mail their reports directly to consumers, not among those that posted the notification in a newspaper or made it available on request (Bennear and Olmstead 2008). If disclosure regulations are more effective when information becomes embedded in decision making, this may help explain why such disclosure appears to lead to greater environmental protection in communities where educational levels are generally higher (Shapiro 2005; Shimshack, Ward, and Beatty 2007).

2.3. Management-Based Regulation

Like information disclosure, management-based regulation does not mandate specific means for achieving regulatory ends but instead mandates what we have called "meta-means." Some regulations are considered management-based because they require businesses to conduct planning designed to foster attention to ways of improving their environmental performance. For example, the Massachusetts Toxics Use Reduction Act (TURA) requires businesses that use a large quantity of toxic chemicals to develop a pollution prevention plan that identifies ways to reduce their use of toxics. TURA does not require businesses to undertake any pollution control measures or even to implement their pollution prevention plans; it only requires they develop plans.

The first way management-based regulation may improve environmental quality is through changes in internal decision making at the regulated entities. In order for management-based regulation to be effective through this channel, it must be the case that the businesses are not already voluntarily engaging in the level of environmental management prescribed by the regulation and that there is a strong complementarity between management effort and planning and environmental quality (Bennear 2006). The second way management-based regulation may be effective is through information sharing between the regulated entities and the regulator. The information generated through the development of required plans may reveal something important to regulators about the costs and benefits of environmental improvements. Information sharing can also allow for comparison across regulated entities, which can in turn improve performance through targeted inspections or technical assistance (Bennear 2006; Karkkainen 2001).

Drawing on the concept of transactions costs, Coglianese and Lazer (2003) have argued that management-based regulation is preferable when there is significant heterogeneity among regulated entities and measuring and regulating outputs is difficult. The heterogeneity makes technology standards costly and inefficient, while the difficulty in measuring outputs makes performance standards infeasible. Bennear (2006) extended this theoretical argument to include the degree of uncertainty about the nature of the risk being regulated, arguing that if the risk is highly uncertain, management-based regulation may be less costly than command-and-control regulations and may provide regulators with information on the cost and benefits of risk reduction that can then inform future regulatory efforts.

The primary empirical analyses of management-based regulation in environmental policy have come from states that have adopted management-based programs like the Massachusetts TURA (Bennear 2006, 2007; Coglianese and Lazer 2003). Studies of individual state programs—such as those in New Jersey (Natan et al. 1996) and Massachusetts (Keenan, Kanner, and Stoner 1997)—have found that businesses view the required planning as beneficial. In one survey, 81 percent of Massachusetts business respondents reported an intention to implement at least some of the pollution prevention activities identified in their mandated plans, although smaller plants were less likely to view the program as beneficial (Keenan, Kanner, and Stoner 1997). Analysis of panel data covering 31,000 manufacturing plants in 49 U.S. states has indicated that management-based regulation significantly lowered toxic emissions and increased source reduction activities, but had no impact on the number of chemicals reported (Bennear 2007). However, the observed reductions in emissions appeared not to persist at statistically significant levels longer than a half-dozen years past the adoption of the regulation, which may suggest that over time management-based regulation loses its effectiveness because the required planning at the outset enables businesses to discover and undertake relatively easy corrective actions while further planning does not reveal additional "low-hanging fruit."

3. FLEXIBLE TARGETS

Given that abatement costs vary across different sources of pollution, pollution control can be achieved more cost-effectively by varying the desired end-state imposed on these different sources. This could be done by specifying a different performance standard for each source, but, as noted earlier, this is generally infeasible as a practical matter. However, it is possible to achieve the same effect by varying the target. Target flexibility occurs when regulations define the target to include (1) multiple sources, (2) one source over time, or (3) both.

Regulatory flexibility achieved by broadening the definition of the target dates back at least to the mid-1970s in the United States, with the inclusion of the "offset" policy in the 1977 amendments to the Clean Air Act (U.S. EPA 2001). The offset policy allowed for new polluting facilities to locate in nonattainment areas provided that they, among other things, offset resulting increases in pollution with reductions at other facilities. The offset policy also redefined the regulatory target by allowing for averaging of emissions reductions over time, a process known as banking. A facility that decreased emissions more than required in one period was allowed to bank credits for those emissions reductions to apply in later periods (U.S. EPA 2001).

In subsequent years, EPA extended target flexibility by promulgating "bubble" and "netting" policies. The EPA announced its bubble policy in 1979, allowing emissions averaging among regulated sources within the same plant as long as the aggregate emissions in the imaginary "bubble" around the plant remained constant (U.S. EPA 2001). In 1986, EPA also allowed for additional target flexibility through "netting," a policy that allowed a facility to be expanded or modified without triggering an extensive and expensive "New Source Review," provided it demonstrated that any increases in emissions from the changes were matched with decreases from other units in the plant (U.S. EPA 2001). Both the bubble and netting policies were a clear extension of the concept underlying the offset policy, offering target flexibility to even more facilities.

All such policies—offsets, bubbles, banking, and netting—are variants of a so-called market-based approach that relies on emissions credits or allowances that are allocated across different firms (Tietenberg 1985). Firms must meet an emissions level equal to the credits they possess, but they can free up credits at some sources by doing more than required and then can "spend" those credits by doing less than required at other sources or at a later date. Under emissions trading systems, also known as cap-and-trade, firms with excess credits can also freely sell them to other businesses that face higher costs of pollution control. In this way, emissions trading and credit systems are designed to achieve a fixed level of pollution control—the level determined by total number of credits allocated—but at a lower overall cost.

An extensive body of research on these market-based approaches has generally confirmed that they can achieve more cost-effective outcomes than uniform performance standards (Cropper and Oates 1992; Stavins 2000, 2007) (also see chapter 25 in this volume). For example, in the United States a credit program was used successfully in phasing out the use of lead as a gasoline additive (Newell and Rogers 2004; Nichols 1997; Nussbaum 1992), and a cap-and-trade program was used in controlling sulfur dioxide pollution from coal power plants (Stavins 1998). One additional advantage of tradable permit or credit programs is that they provide incentives for firms to find innovative ways to reduce their pollution, as they allow firms to sell excess permits or credits (Newell, Jaffe, and Stavins 1999).

As with uniform performance standards, however, market-based standards have raised concerns about unintended side effects from the flexibility they give to regulated targets. In particular, tradable permits may lead to so-called hot spots if trading results in pollution permits that are concentrated in one proximate area. Banking of permits can result in earlier achievement of environmental goals, but at the expense of reductions in environmental standards at a later date. There are also concerns that trading will disproportionately harm small businesses.

Evidence from the SO_2 trading program has indicated that hot spots resulting from trading never became a significant issue, but that the banking allowed under that program did result a much faster reduction of SO_2 in the early period followed by slower reductions in later periods (Burtraw and Mansur 1999). During the lead phaseout from gasoline, large refiners were typically sellers of credits, while small refiners were typically buyers. Some small refiners did go out of business, yet the evidence has suggested that small refiners were still better off than they would have been under a uniform performance standard (Newell and Rogers 2003).

4. FLEXIBLE CONSEQUENCES

Environmental regulators can also promote flexibility by relying on modest rewards, rather than the threat of punishment, to try to encourage environmentally responsible behavior. In what have become known as voluntary environmental programs, government threatens no penalties—not even a taint of lawbreaking—for failing to meet the eligibility criteria established for membership in these programs. They do, however, offer various forms of rewards and recognition to those firms that meet the criteria and apply for membership.

Researchers sometimes distinguish voluntary *programs*, through which the government sets general eligibility parameters, from voluntary *agreements*, through which the government negotiates with individual businesses or other targets to provide case-specific rewards or incentives in exchange for individual commitments to exceed the performance required by law. In both cases, the flexibility comes from the voluntary nature of the program or agreement. However, in either case if no negative consequences exist for failing to meet government's demands, the question arises of why businesses would voluntarily make presumably costly improvements in their environmental performance (Carraro and Siniscalco 1996; Lyon and Maxwell 2003; Maxwell, Lyon, and Hackett 2000; Segerson and Miceli 1998; Wu and Babcock 1999).

Researchers have emphasized two primary motivations. The first is the threat of regulation, suggesting that voluntary participation may at times be less voluntary than it seems. When the option to take voluntary action arises against a background threat of inflexible regulation, firms are more likely to take such action (even if they still do not control as much pollution as would be socially desirable) (Maxwell, Lyon, and Hackett 2000; Segerson and Miceli 1998). The second motivation derives from the rewards offered by government. If these rewards are substantial enough, such as if government can provide distinctive technical support to help companies identify both environmental and economic gains, then voluntary approaches might yield results comparable to those from conventional regulation

(Wu and Babcock 1999). However, because subsidies or rewards are costly for government to provide, the "carrot" approach typically will not be expected to lead to a socially optimal level of pollution control. If rewards offered as part of voluntary programs or agreements are modest, they may only entice firms to capture the "low-hanging fruit," at most prompting inexpensive action that firms might have eventually taken anyway.

Empirical analyses of voluntary programs have sought to determine whether these programs yield improvements in environmental performance relative to what would have happened in the absence of the programs. Most studies have compared performance of participants to nonparticipants and have attempted to control for differences in baseline performance of facilities that choose to participate. For example, the most widely studied voluntary program has been the EPA's 33/50 program. Launched in 1991 with a goal of reducing releases of 17 high-priority toxic chemicals among participating facilities by 33 percent by 1992 and 50 percent by 1995, the 33/50 program required participating businesses to commit to reducing emissions of one of the targeted chemicals. In exchange, EPA would send participants a certificate and provide positive publicity for them.

Early studies of the 33/50 program found that participants in the program decreased releases of the targeted chemicals to all media relative to nonparticipants when controlling for differences in the types of participating firms and that participants decreased releases on nontargeted toxic chemical more than nonparticipants, implying a potential spillover effect from the program (Khanna and Damon 1999). Although the positive impact of 33/50 has been reported in other research (e.g., Sam, Khanna, and Innes 2009), other subsequent analysis has indicated that the 33/50 program did not cause meaningful reductions in toxic releases (e.g., Gamper-Rabindran 2006; Vidovic and Khanna 2007). For example, decreases in participant releases may have been due to the fact that participating facilities increased *off-site* transfers of targeted chemicals, which lowered total releases but may not have reflected significant improvements in waste management or environmental performance (Gamper-Rabindran 2006).

Government has created many other voluntary initiatives beyond the 33/50 program, particularly in an effort to reduce greenhouse gas emissions. For example, the Department of Energy's Climate Challenge program, which emerged from a voluntary agreement between DOE and the electric utility industry, sought to reduce, avoid, or sequester greenhouse gas emissions. Welch, Mazur, and Bretschneider (2000) found that participants did decrease their emissions of greenhouse gases—but that nonparticipants actually decreased emissions by even more. Delmas and Montes-Sancho (2010) found that early participants decreased GHG emissions by more than nonparticipants but that these early successes were more than offset by the poor performance of late joiners. They argued, consistent with Lyon and Kim (2006), that this may be evidence that late joiners are engaging in "greenwashing" and attempting to free-ride off the success of early joiners.

By contrast, the EPA's ClimateWise program, launched by EPA in 1993, appears to have had at least some modest effects (Pizer, Morgenstern, and Shih 2010). ClimateWise asked participants to develop a baseline inventory of greenhouse gas emissions and pledge to reduce these emissions. In exchange, participants were offered technical assistance and public recognition of their efforts. Using propensity score matching to control for differences between participants and nonparticipants, Pizer, Morgenstern, and Shih (2010) found that participation in ClimateWise had small effects on fuel and electricity expenditures—generally less than 10 percent—but no effect on fuel cost.

At best, it appears that voluntary programs sometimes lead to improvements in energy use and perhaps environmental quality, above and beyond what businesses might have achieved anyway. However, even when they do, the effects are still generally modest (Borck and Coglianese 2009; Koehler 2007; Morgenstern and Pizer 2007).

5. FLEXIBLE REGULATORS

Finally, we turn to the identity of the regulator as a final source of flexibility. As noted in part 1, the regulator need not always be a governmental entity or official. Sometimes industry can set its own rules, and government at times may even encourage such self-regulation in lieu of governmental action. In addition, government can seek to encourage businesses to do their own inspections, even providing limited forms of immunity for legal violations that are discovered through such self-auditing practices.

5.1. Industry as Regulator

Self-regulation seeks to accomplish flexibility by allowing regulated entities to choose the least-costly means of reducing environmental damages. By having industry groups, even business firms themselves, set their own rules for environmental performance, presumably they will adopt rules that call for the very practices that they would choose under a flexible command or a flexible consequence. Sometimes nongovernmental organizations, such as the International Organization for Standardization (ISO), can also provide standards which businesses can opt voluntarily to follow (Prakash and Potoski 2006).

As with flexible consequences, it might initially be unclear why industry groups would voluntarily establish or comply with standards that presumably would be costly for their members. One reason may be that poor environmental performance at one firm or facility creates negative spillover effects on other firms or facilities, at least in some industrial sectors (Barnett and King 2008; King, Lenox, and Barnett 2002).

A problem that can theoretically arise with self-regulatory initiatives is that the firms that have the most to gain from self-regulatory "protection" may be the firms with the worst environmental performance—a concept known as adverse selection (Lenox and Nash 2003). Adverse selection is likely to be a larger problem when the self-regulatory initiative has low standards for membership and weak monitoring of members' compliance (Lenox and Nash 2003; Prakash and Potoski 2006).

The most frequently studied industry self-regulatory environmental program is the Responsible Care program developed by the American Chemistry Council (ACC) (formerly the Chemical Manufacturers Association). Under Responsible Care, chemical companies make commitments to a series of practice codes governing manufacturing, distribution, and community relations (Nash and Ehrenfeld 1997). The practice codes are generally quite broad and offer partici-pating firms significant discretion in establishing their own performance stan-dards and determining how best to meet these standards (Nash and Ehrenfeld 1997). Initially, the ACC did not require third-party certification of members' activities, did not disclose members' compliance (or noncompliance), and did not remove members that were noncompliant; however, over time the trade asso-ciation has added stronger membership requirements (Coglianese 2010a; Nash 2002). Perhaps because of its initially rather lax standards, Responsible Care has yielded at best only mixed results. Member firms' compliance has been shown to vary widely (Howard, Nash, and Ehrenfeld 1999), and some research has indi-cated that members decreased their toxic releases at a slower rate than nonmem-bers (King and Lenox 2000).

Another leading example of a self-regulatory program is the ISO 14000 series of environmental management standards. Unlike Responsible Care, ISO 14000 standards originate outside of both government and industry, emanating from the nongovernmental International Organization for Standardization. Hundreds of thousands of facilities worldwide have developed environmental management systems that meet ISO standards. These management systems are similar to the pollution prevention plans required under management-based regulation, but the ISO standards are adopted on a nonbinding basis by a transnational, nongovern-mental organization. Perhaps due to their widespread adoption, the ISO standards' impact on environmental performance has been extensively analyzed. The most systematic empirical research to date has found that ISO-certified businesses did report lower emissions and better regulatory compliance than noncertified busi-nesses, but these effects were substantively quite modest even though statistically significant (Prakash and Potoski 2006).

5.2. Industry as Inspector

In addition to the flexibility afforded by having industry set its own standards, industry can be encouraged to police itself, introducing a degree of flexibil-ity through the discretion inherent in any street-level inspector. Given the vast number of regulated entities in a developed economy, government may find it more budget-friendly if these entities can be induced to audit themselves, correcting and reporting any violations they discover (Friesen 2006; Innes 2001). Reducing fines when these entities identify and disclose their own violations may help create the proper incentives for firms to self-audit (Pfaff and Sanchirico 2000). For example, the U.S. EPA Audit Policy, adopted in 1995, removes the punitive component of fines if the firm discovers a violation through an environmental self-audit, promptly discloses the violation, corrects the violation, and prevents recurrence.

As with other flexible approaches, the evidence on the effectiveness of self-auditing incentives is mixed. Interestingly, about 90 percent of violations reported voluntarily under the EPA's Audit Policy are reporting or recordkeeping violations (as opposed to substantive environmental violations), whereas only about 15 percent of violations uncovered during routine governmental audits are reporting or recordkeeping violations (Pfaff and Sanchirico 2004). Nevertheless, businesses are apparently more likely to self-report violations if they are inspected frequently or subject to a targeted compliance initiative by EPA, suggesting some complementarity between government enforcement and self-enforcement actions (Short and Toffel 2008).

The key question, of course, is whether disclosure of violations under the Audit Policy results in improved compliance performance. At least one study found that facilities that self-disclose were twice as likely to have a clean inspection in the future and have a 20 percent reduction in the number of abnormal releases of toxics (Toffel and Short 2011).

6. CONCLUSION

The great appeal of a flexible approach to environmental protection stems from a worthy desire to achieve regulatory goals while still preserving much-cherished freedom of choice. We have shown how this desire manifests itself in flexible approaches that come in many forms, varying in what they command and target, what consequences they impose, and who creates and enforces them. Some flexible approaches can and do achieve demonstrable, positive environmental outcomes. But results vary. Some flexible approaches, like performance and market-based standards, can sometimes result in significant environmental gains and cost savings, while others, like voluntary programs and self-regulation, present more mixed records of achievement.

Notwithstanding the great interest in flexible approaches by environmental policy makers, the existing research has only scratched the surface in what needs to be known in order to use these approaches in appropriate circumstances with intended results. In particular, more research is needed to measure a broader range of effects from these approaches and then to compare the results with similar full accountings across the range of all regulatory approaches. We know of no systematic analysis, for example, of flexible approaches that have fully assessed both their benefits as well as their costs, or that has compared these benefits and costs to those of other policy approaches. Admittedly, such comparisons are more difficult for researchers to make, and there have been sensible reasons for researchers to focus first on whether flexible approaches can yield any positive environmental impacts at all. Especially for those approaches that mandate no specific environmental improvement, it is hard to fathom why businesses might otherwise invest in making such improvements when not required to do so. Furthermore, it has been reasonable to assume, even implicitly, that a focus on costs is less important given that flexibility will undoubtedly be exploited by regulated entities to achieve cost savings. But now that the first wave of research has shown that many flexible approaches can sometimes work—even if at times only rather tepidly—the next frontier will be to discern whether the marginal gains from flexible approaches are enough to justify whatever costs they impose, especially for approaches like information disclosure and management-based standards that can impose extensive paperwork burdens.

REFERENCES

Atlas, M. 2007. "TRI to Communicate: Public Knowledge of the Federal Toxics Release Inventory." *Social Science Quarterly* 88: 555–572.

Barnett, M. L., and A. A. King. 2008. "Good Fences Make Good Neighbors: A Longitudinal Analysis of an Industry Self-Regulatory Institution." *Academy of Management Journal* 51: 1150–1170.

Bennear, L. S. 2006. "Evaluating Management-Based Regulation: A Valuable Tool in the Regulatory Toolbox?" In *Leveraging the Private Sector: Management-Based Strategies for Improving Environmental Performance*, ed. C. Coglianese and J. Nash. Washington, DC: Resources for the Future.

———. 2007. "Are Management-Based Regulations Effective? Evidence from State Pollution Prevention Programs." *Journal of Policy Analysis and Management* 26: 327–348.

———. 2008. "What Do We Really Know? The Effect of Reporting Thresholds on Inferences Using Environmental Right-to-Know Data." *Regulation & Governance* 2: 293–315.

Bennear, L. S., and S. M. Olmstead. 2008. "The Impacts of the 'Right to Know': Information Disclosure and the Violation of Drinking Water Standards." *Journal of Environmental Economics and Management* 56: 117–130.

Ben-Shahar, O., and C. E. Schneider. 2011. "The Failure of Mandated Disclosure." *University of Pennsylvania Law Review* 159: 647–749.

Borck, J. C., and C. Coglianese. 2009. "Voluntary Environmental Programs: Assessing their Effectiveness." *Annual Review of Environment and Resources* 34: 305–324.

Bui, L. T. M., and C. J. Mayer. 2003. "Regulation and Capitalization of Environmental Amenities: Evidence from the Toxic Release Inventory in Massachusetts." *Review of Economics and Statistics* 85: 693–708.

Burtraw, D., and E. Mansur. 1999. "Environmental Effects of SO$_2$ Trading and Banking." *Environmental Science and Technology* 33: 3489–3494.

Carraro, C., and D. Siniscalco. 1996. "Voluntary Agreements in Environmental Policy: A Theoretical Appraisal." In *Economic Policy for the Environment and Natural Resources: Techniques for the Management and Control of Pollution*, ed. A. Xepapadeas. Cheltenham, UK: Edward Elgar.

Clinton, W. 1993. Executive Order No. 12866 of September 30, "Regulatory Planning and Review." *Federal Register* 58, September 30, pp. 51735, 51736. Available at www.epa.gov/fedreg/eo/eo12866.htm.

Coglianese, C. 2010a. "Engaging Business in the Regulation of Nanotechnology." In *Governing Uncertainty: Environmental Regulation in the Age of Nanotechnology*, ed. C. Bosso. Washington, DC: Resources for the Future.

———. 2010b. "Management-Based Regulation: Implications for Public Policy." In *Risk and Regulatory Policy: Improving the Governance of Risk*, ed. G. Bounds, N. Malyshev, and J. Konvitz. Paris: Organisation for Economic Co-operation and Development.

Coglianese, C., and D. Lazer. 2003. "Management-Based Regulation: Prescribing Private Management to Achieve Public Goals." *Law & Society Review* 37: 691–730.

Coglianese, C., J. Nash, and T. Olmstead. 2003. "Performance-Based Regulation: Prospects and Limitations in Health, Safety, and Environmental Protection." *Administrative Law Review* 55: 705–729.

Cropper, M. L., and W. E. Oates. 1992. "Environmental Economics: A Survey." *Journal of Economic Literature* 30: 675–740.

Dales, J. H. 1968. *Pollution, Property and Prices: An Essay in Policy-Making and Economics*. Toronto: University of Toronto Press.

Delmas, M. A., and M. Montes-Sancho. 2010. "Voluntary Agreements to Improve Environmental Quality: Symbolic and Substantive Cooperation." *Strategic Management Journal* 31: 575–601.

de Marchi, S., and J. T. Hamilton. 2006. "Assessing the Accuracy of Self-Reported Data: An Evaluation of the Toxics Release Inventory." *Journal of Risk and Uncertainty* 32: 57–76.

Friesen, L. 2006. "The Social Welfare Implications of Industry Self-Auditing." *Journal of Environmental Economics and Management* 51: 280–294.

Fung, A., and D. O'Rourke. 2000. "Reinventing Environmental Regulation from the Grassroots Up: Explaining and Expanding the Success of the Toxics Release Inventory." *Environmental Management* 25: 115–127.

Gamper-Rabindran, S. 2006. "Did the EPA's Voluntary Industrial Toxics Program Reduce Emissions? A GIS Analysis of Distributional Impacts and By-Media Analysis of Substitution." *Journal of Environmental Economics and Management* 52: 391–410.

Grant, D., and A. W. Jones. 2003. "Are Subsidiaries More Prone to Pollute? New Evidence from the EPA's Toxics Release Inventory." *Social Science Quarterly* 84: 162–173.

Gunningham, N., and J. Rees. 1997. "Industry Self-Regulation: An Institutional Perspective." *Law & Policy* 19: 363–414.

Hamilton, J. T. 1995. "Pollution as News: Media and Stock Market Reactions to the Toxics Release Inventory Data." *Journal of Environmental Economics and Management* 28: 98–113.

———. 2005. *Regulation through Revelation: The Origin, Politics and Impacts of the Toxics Release Inventory Program*. New York: Cambridge University Press.

Helland, E., and A. B. Whitford. 2003. "Pollution Incidence and Political Jurisdiction: Evidence from the TRI." *Journal of Environmental Economics and Management* 46: 403–424.

Howard, J., J. Nash, and J. Ehrenfeld. 1999. "Industry Codes as Agents of Change: Responsible Care Adoption by U.S. Chemical Companies." *Business Strategy and the Environment* 8: 281–295.

Hutter, B. 2001. *Regulation and Risk: Occupational Health and Safety on the Railways.* Oxford: Oxford University Press.

Innes, R. 2001. "Violator Avoidance Activities and Self-Reporting in Optimal Law Enforcement." *Journal of Law, Economics, and Organization* 17: 239–256.

Jaffe, A. B., R. G. Newell, and R. N. Stavins 2004. "Technology Policy for Energy and the Environment." In *Innovation Policy and the Economy*, vol. 4, ed. A. B. Jaffe, J. Lerner, and S. Stern. Cambridge, MA: MIT Press.

Karkkainen, B. C. 2001. "Information as Environmental Regulation: TRI and Performance Benchmarking, Precursor to a New Paradigm?" *Georgetown Law Journal* 89: 257–370.

——. 2006. "Information-Forcing Environmental Regulation." *Florida State University Law Review* 33: 861–902.

Keenan, C., J. L. Kanner, and D. Stoner. 1997. *Survey Evaluation of the Massachussets Toxics Use Reduction Program.* TURI Methods and Policy Report No. 14. Lowell: he Massachusetts Toxics Use Reduction Institute, University of Massachusetts, Lowell.

Khanna, M., and L. A. Damon. 1999. "EPA's Voluntary 33/50 Program: Impact on Toxic Releases and Economic Performance of Firms." *Journal of Environmental Economics and Management* 37: 1–25.

Khanna, M., W. R. H. Quimio, and D. Bojilova. 1998. "Toxics Release Information: A Policy Tool for Environmental Protection." *Journal of Environmental Economics and Management* 36 (3): 243–266.

King, A. A., and M. J. Lenox. 2000. "Industry Self-Regulation without Sanctions: The Chemical Industry's Responsible Care Program." *Academy of Management Journal* 43: 698–716.

King, A. A., M. Lenox, and M. L. Barnett. 2002. "Strategic Responses to the Reputation Commons Problem." In *Organizations, Policy, and the Natural Environment: Institutional and Strategic Perspectives*, ed. A. J. Hoffman and M. J. Ventresca. Stanford, CA: Stanford University Press.

Koehler, D. A. 2007. "The Effectiveness of Voluntary Environmental Programs: A Policy at a Crossroads?" *Policy Studies Journal* 35: 689–722.

Konar, S., and M. A. Cohen. 1997. "Information as Regulation: The Effect of Community Right to Know Laws on Toxic Emissions." *Journal of Environmental Economics and Management* 32: 109–124.

Kraft, M. E., M. Stephan, and T. D. Abel. 2011. *Coming Clean: Information Disclosure and Environmental Performance.* Cambridge, MA: MIT Press.

Lenox, M. J., and J. Nash. 2003. "Industry Self-Regulation and Adverse Selection: A Comparison across Four Trade Association Programs." *Business Strategy and the Environment* 12: 343–356.

Lyon, T. P., and E.-H. Kim. 2006. "Greenhouse Gas Reductions or Greenwash?: The DOEs 1605b Program." November 2006. Available at SSRN: http://papers.ssrn.com/sol3/papers.cfm?abstract_id=981730 (accessed May 6, 2012).

Lyon, T. P., and J. W. Maxwell. 2003. "Self-Regulation, Taxation, and Public Voluntary Environmental Agreements." *Journal of Public Economics* 87: 1453–1486.

Maxwell, J. W., T. P. Lyon, and S. C. Hackett. 2000. "Self-Regulation and Social Welfare: The Political Economy of Corporate Environmentalism." *Journal of Law and Economics* 43: 583–617.

May, P. J. 2003. "Performance-Based Regulation and Regulatory Regimes: The Saga of Leaky Buildings." *Law and Policy* 25: 381–401.

———. 2011. "Performance-Based Regulation." In *Handbook on the Politics of Regulation*, ed. D. Levi-Faur. Northampton, MA: Edward Elgar.

Morgenstern, R. D., and W. A. Pizer, eds. 2007. *Reality Check: The Nature and Performance of Voluntary Environmental Programs in the United States.* Washington, DC: Resources for the Future.

Nash, J. 2002. "Industry Codes of Practice: Emergence and Evolution." In *New Tools for Environmental Protection: Education, Information, and Voluntary Measures*, ed. T. Dietz and P. C. Stern. Washington, DC: Resources for the Future.

Nash, J., and J. Ehrenfeld. 1997. "Codes of Environmental Management Practice: Assessing their Potential as a Tool for Change." *Annual Review of Energy and the Environment* 22: 487–535.

Natan, T. E., Jr., and C. G. Miller. 1998. "Are Toxics Release Inventory Reductions Real?" *Environmental Science and Technology* 32: 368A–374A.

Natan, T. E., Jr., C. G. Miller, B. A. Scarborough, and W. R. Muir. 1996. "Evaluation of the Effectiveness of Pollution Prevention Planning in New Jersey." Alexandria, VA: Hampshire Research Associates Inc. May 1996. Available at www.nj.gov/dep/opppc/reports/hamp1.htm (accessed May 6, 2012).

Newell, R. G., A. B. Jaffe, and R. N. Stavins. 1999. "The Induced Innovation Hypothesis and Energy-Saving Technological Change." *Quarterly Journal of Economics* 114: 941–975.

Newell, R. G., and K. Rogers. 2003. *The Market-Based Lead Phasedown.* RFF Discussion Paper 03-37. Washington, DC: Resources for the Future.

———. 2004. "Leaded Gasoline in the United States: The Breakthrough of Permit Trading." In *Choosing Environmental Policy: Comparing Instruments and Outcomes in the United States and Europe*, ed. W. Harrington, R. D. Morgenstern, and T. Sterner. Washington, DC: Resources for the Future.

Nichols, A. L. 1997. "Lead in Gasoline." In *Economic Analyses at EPA: Assessing Regulatory Impact*, ed. R. D. Morgenstern. Washington, DC: Resources for the Future.

Nussbaum, B. D. 1992. "Phasing Down Lead in Gasoline in the U.S.: Mandates, Incentives, Trading, and Banking." In *Climate Change: Designing a Tradable Permit System*, ed. T. Jones and J. Corfee-Morlot. Paris: Organisation for Economic Co-operation and Development.

Obama, B. 2011. Executive Order No. 13563 of January 18, "Improving Regulation and Regulatory Review." *Federal Register* 76, no. 2, p. 3821. Available at www.gpo.gov/fdsys/pkg/FR-2011-01-21/pdf/2011-1385.pdf.

Oberholzer-Gee, F., and M. Mitsunari. 2006. "Information Regulation: Do the Victims of Externalities Pay Attention?" *Journal of Regulatory Economics* 30: 141–158.

Pfaff, A., and C. W. Sanchirico. 2000. "Environmental Self-Auditing: Setting the Proper Incentives for Discovery and Correction of Environmental Harm." *Journal of Law, Economics and Organization* 16: 189–208.

———. 2004. "Big Field, Small Potatoes: An Empirical Assessment of EPA's Self-Audit Policy." *Journal of Policy Analysis and Management* 23: 415–432.

Pigou, A. C. 1932. *The Economics of Welfare.* London: Macmillan and Co.

Pizer, W. A., R. Morgenstern, and J.-S. Shih. 2010. "The Performance of Voluntary Climate Programs: Climate Wise and 1605(b)." Discussion Paper No. 08–13-REV. Washington, DC: Resources for the Future.

Poje, G. V., and D. M. Horowitz. 1990. *Phantom Reductions: Tracking Toxic Trends.* Washington, DC: National Wildlife Federation.

Prakash, A., and M. Potoski. 2006. *The Voluntary Environmentalists: Green Clubs, ISO 14001, and Voluntary Environmental Regulations.* Cambridge: Cambridge University Press.

Regulatory Flexibility Act. 1980. 5 U.S. Code, sec. 601–12.

Richards, K. R. 2000. "Framing Environmental Policy Instrument Choice." *Duke Environmental Law and Policy Forum* 10: 221–285.

Sam, A. G., M. Khanna, and R. Innes. 2009. "Voluntary Pollution Reduction Programs, Environmental Management, and Environmental Performance: An Empirical Study." *Land Economics* 85: 692–711.

Segerson, K., and T. J. Miceli. 1998. "Voluntary Environmental Agreements: Good or Bad News for Environmental Protection?" *Journal of Environmental Economics and Management* 36: 109–130.

Shapiro, M. D. 2005. "Equity and Information: Information Regulation, Environmental Justice, and Risks from Toxic Chemicals." *Journal of Policy Analysis and Management* 24: 373–398.

Shimshack, J., M. Ward, and T. Beatty. 2007. "Mercury Advisories: Information, Education, and Fish Consumption." *Journal of Environmental Economics and Management* 53: 158–179.

Short, J. L., and M. W. Toffel. 2008. "Coerced Confessions: Self-Policing in the Shadow of the Regulator." *Journal of Law, Economics, and Organization* 24: 45–71.

Stavins, R. N. 1998. "What Can We Learn from the Grand Policy Experiment? Lessons from SO_2 Allowance Trading." *Journal of Economic Perspectives* 12: 69–88.

———. 2000. "Market-Based Environmental Policies." In *Public Policies for Environmental Protection,* ed. P. R. Portney and R. N. Stavins. Washington, DC: Resources for the Future.

———. 2007. "Market-Based Environmental Policies: What Can We Learn from U.S. Experience (and Related Research)?" In *Moving to Markets in Environmental Regulation: Lessons from Twenty Years of Experience,* ed. J. Freeman and C. D. Kolstad. New York: Oxford University Press.

Sunstein, C. R. 1999. "Informational Regulation and Informational Standing: Akins and Beyond." *University of Pennsylvania Law Review* 147: 613–675.

Thaler, R. H., and C. R. Sunstein. 2008. *Nudge: Improving Decisions about Health, Wealth, and Happiness.* New Haven, CT: Yale University Press.

Tietenberg, T. H. 1985. *Emissions Trading: An Exercise in Reforming Pollution Policy.* Washington, DC: Resources for the Future.

———. 1998. "Disclosure Strategies for Pollution Control." *Environmental and Resource Economics* 11: 587–602.

Toffel, M. W., and J. L. Short. 2011. "Coming Clean and Cleaning Up: Does Voluntary Self-Reporting Indicate Effective Self-Policing?" *Journal of Law and Economics* 54: 609–649.

U.S. Environmental Protection Agency (U.S. EPA). 2001. *The United States Experience with Economic Incentives for Protecting the Environment.* Washington, DC: U.S. EPA, National Center for Environmental Economics. Available at yosemite.epa.gov/ee/epa/eerm.nsf/vwAN/EE-0216B-13.pdf/$file/EE-0216B-13.pdf.

U.S. Office of Management and Budget (OMB). 1996. "Economic Analysis of Federal
     Regulations under Executive Order 12866 (January 11, 1996)." Available at www.
     whitehouse.gov/omb/inforeg_riaguide.
———. 2003. "Circular A-4 (September 17, 2003)." Available at www.whitehouse.gov/
     omb/circulars_a004_a-4.
Vidovic, M., and N. Khanna. 2007. "Can Voluntary Pollution Prevention Programs
     Fulfill Their Promises? Further Evidence from the EPA's 33/50 Program." *Journal
     of Environmental Economics and Management* 53: 180–195.
Weil, D., A. Fung, M. Graham, and E. Fagotto. 2006. "The Effectiveness of
     Regulatory Disclosure Policies." *Journal of Policy Analysis and Management* 25:
     155–181.
Welch, E., A. Mazur, and S. Bretschneider. 2000. "Voluntary Behavior by Electric
     Utilities: Levels of Adoption and Contribution of the Climate Challenge Program
     to the Reduction of Carbon Dioxide." *Journal of Policy Analysis and Management*
     19: 407–425.
Wu, J. J., and B. A. Babcock. 1999. "The Relative Efficiency of Voluntary vs.
     Mandatory Environmental Regulation." *Journal of Environmental Economics and
     Management* 38: 158–175.

CHAPTER 27

··

ECOSYSTEM-BASED MANAGEMENT AND RESTORATION

··

JUDITH A. LAYZER

THE concept of ecosystem-based management (EBM) emerged in the 1980s and came into its own in the 1990s. EBM is a reaction to the expert-driven, single-focus, jurisdiction-by-jurisdiction approach to natural resource management that prevailed during the latter half of the twentieth century. It is an integrative approach that aims to restore ecological—as well as social and economic—resilience across whole landscapes. Although EBM experiments have been undertaken around the world, systematic assessments of their results remain sparse; more common are detailed descriptions of individual projects (see, for example, Clark et al. 1991; Doyle and Drew 2008; Keiter 2003; Pirot, Meynell, and Elder 2000; Rabe 1999; UNCB 2003; UNDP et al. 2003). To date, research suggests that EBM has yielded important environmental benefits, including land acquisition and protection of marine reserves (see, for example, Layzer 2008; Ruckelshaus et al. 2008). EBM has also generated improvements in scientists' understanding of large-scale ecosystems (Doyle and Drew 2008; Layzer 2008; Tallis et al. 2010). But those scientific advances have not necessarily translated into the kinds of political and policy changes that proponents of EBM had hoped. Instead, the pursuit of multiple goals simultaneously—often the result of stakeholder collaboration—has led to solutions that are environmentally risky and unlikely to bring about resilient landscapes. In fact, the environmental effectiveness of EBM appears to depend heavily on the exercise of political leadership and the existence of a precautionary legal framework (Layzer 2008).

This chapter begins by recounting the origins of EBM and describing early efforts to implement an ecosystem-based approach. After detailing the theoretical benefits of EBM and the criticisms leveled against it, the chapter summarizes the results of recent assessments, noting the strengths and weaknesses of these analyses. It concludes by articulating several unanswered questions and offering suggestions for further research.

1. The Origins of EBM

EBM was originally the brainchild of natural resource managers and members of the applied biology community who were concerned about the deterioration of natural systems. By the 1970s, decades of ecological research had discredited the equilibrium-based paradigm, according to which ecosystems are closed, self-regulating, and subject to a single, stable equilibrium. In its place, ecologists were gravitating toward a "flux of nature" paradigm in which ecosystems experience important limits from external sources; disturbances—such as fire, floods, droughts, and storms—play a central role in shaping ecosystem dynamics; and humans are an inextricable part of natural systems (Perry and Amaranthus 1997; Pickett and Ostfelt 1995). From this perspective, ecosystems are open and unpredictable, rather than closed and comprehensible; process, dynamics, and context are more important than end-point stability (Meffe and Carroll 1994). Parallel to these developments in ecology was the emergence of a new discipline, conservation biology, whose practitioners focus on conserving biological diversity and ecological integrity, not maximizing commodity production (Noss and Cooperrider 1994).[1]

Ecologists and conservation biologists charged that the conventional management paradigm, with its emphasis on controlling natural variation, was producing brittle ecosystems that were unable to deal with external shocks (Holling and Meffe 1996). "The command-and-control approach," wrote Holling and Meffe (1996, 329), "implicitly assumes that the problem is well-bounded, clearly defined, relatively simple, and generally linear with respect to cause and effect." But in a complex, nonlinear, and poorly understood world, such an approach could have disastrous ecological, social, and economic consequences. Benign neglect, an alternative approach to management that was also rooted in the equilibrium-based paradigm, was untenable as well: often practiced in nature preserves, benign neglect led to

---

1. According to both environmental educator Edward Grumbine (1994) and policy analyst Richard Haeuber (1998), the EBM concept has historical roots that predate the "flux of nature" paradigm in ecology: in the early 1930s the Ecological Society of America's Committee for the Study of Plant and Animal Communities recommended protecting ecosystems, not just species; incorporating natural disturbance regimes into management; and using a core reserve/buffer design approach for natural area protection.

increasing populations of wildlife that, when confined within park boundaries, first decimated vegetation and then declined precipitously (Botkin 1990).

Even as scientists were expressing dismay about the results of conventional natural resource management, environmentalists and environmentally oriented policy scholars and practitioners were disparaging the approach to policy making that prevailed in the 1970s and early 1980s. Drawing on the philosophies articulated by George Perkins Marsh in the 1800s and Aldo Leopold in the early 1940s, environmentalists had long insisted that planning should conform to ecological boundaries rather than political jurisdictions and that policy making should address environmental problems in a comprehensive and holistic fashion. They had hoped that the environmental laws passed in the 1960s and 1970s would transform resource management agencies from commodity maximizers into defenders of forest, range, and coastal lands. Yet despite new, environmentally protective mandates, those agencies' institutionalized emphasis on commodity extraction and commercial development proved resistant to change. Rather than fundamentally altering their practices, public officials simply tried to accommodate environmental demands within the existing multiple-use framework. The typical result was perpetual conflict over rules and decisions, with development interests defending their historical prerogatives and environmentalists seeking to enforce new statutory mandates through administrative challenges and litigation.

Further complicating matters was the fact that in many large-scale ecosystems multiple entities had jurisdiction over land and natural resources, creating an incoherent mix of rules and practices. The U.S. Forest Service and the Bureau of Land Management (BLM) tried to balance demands for commodity production, recreation, and wilderness preservation on the tracts they controlled. On adjacent property managed by the Fish and Wildlife Service (FWS) or the National Park Service (NPS), public officials aimed to conserve habitat for wildlife and protect scenic vistas. Meanwhile, the Bureau of Reclamation and the Army Corps of Engineers operated federal irrigation and flood-control projects, both of which affected surrounding lands. Although their jurisdictional boundaries were ecologically meaningless, these various agencies made little effort to coordinate their activities. Exacerbating the management challenge, state- and privately owned parcels— often the most valuable ecologically—were scattered among the federally owned land but were subject to their own regulations, including local zoning ordinances, property tax laws, and state forestry and wildlife rules.

Critics from a variety of disciplines charged that the combination of perpetual conflict, complex landownership and land-use patterns, and an overwhelming focus on individual resources or species had caused the rapid decline of wildlife and vital ecological services. To remedy these deficiencies, they proposed an approach originally known as "ecosystem management," in which planning would be comprehensive and integrative, focusing on interactions among ecosystem elements, and implementation would be responsive to new scientific information (Christensen et al. 1996; Grumbine 1994; IEMTF 1995). (Over time, EBM became the preferred label because it better conveys the idea of managing the activities of humans within ecosystems, not the ecosystems themselves.) The overriding goal of this new approach, according to its proponents, was ecological restoration—that is, the recovery of an ecosystem that has been degraded, damaged, or destroyed.[2]

2. EARLY EFFORTS AT EBM

Some of the earliest U.S. examples of EBM actually preceded efforts to define the approach formally. For example, although not explicitly identified as EBM, multi-state efforts to restore the Great Lakes and the Chesapeake Bay initiated in the late 1970s and early 1980s adopted an ecosystem-based approach (Ernst 2003; Slocombe 1998). But two events in the late 1980s underscored the need for and catalyzed high-level interest in EBM: the controversy surrounding efforts to conserve grizzly bear habitat in the Greater Yellowstone region, and the fight to save the northern spotted owl and its old-growth forest habitat in the Pacific Northwest.

The Greater Yellowstone Ecosystem (GYE) initiative was the first widely touted attempt at EBM in the United States. The GYE, which is the largest nearly intact natural ecosystem in the temperate zone, includes more than 18 million acres of land in the states of Wyoming, Montana, and Idaho. The world's biggest elk herds reside in Greater Yellowstone, as does one of the few remaining free-roaming bison herds; the region contains critical habitat for the grizzly bear, whooping crane, bald eagle, peregrine falcon, and trumpeter swan (Keiter 1991). The GYE is also a "complex patchwork of management and ownership" (Goldstein 1991), including 28 different political units. It contains two national parks (Yellowstone and Grand Teton), portions of six national forests, three national wildlife refuges, BLM land-holdings, and state and private lands. National Park Service and Forest Service wilderness lands total about 6 million acres; Forest Service multiple-use lands comprise another 6 million acres. State and private lands occupy only 7 percent to 30 percent of the GYE, depending on where the boundary is drawn, but are extremely important because many are in river valleys or lower-elevation areas that are critical to migrating wildlife (Goldstein 1991).

Historically, the lack of shared conservation goals among the region's many stakeholders led to habitat fragmentation, disruption of ecological processes, and human-wildlife confrontations (Glick and Clark 1998). Activity on surrounding land encroached on pockets of wilderness, undermining efforts to maintain the area's natural ecosystems. For environmentalists and environmentally oriented scientists, these problems suggested the need for more integrated land management. Biologists Frank and John Craighead coined the term Greater Yellowstone Ecosystem in the late 1970s, when they discovered that the grizzly bear roamed far

---

2. Scholars and practitioners have long debated the definition of "restoration." This definition follows that of the Society for Ecological Restoration (SER).

beyond the boundaries of Yellowstone National Park. They proceeded to advocate for a single bear management scheme for the entire GYE. Drawing on their work, the Greater Yellowstone Coalition, an umbrella organization for the region's environmental groups, began advocating a comprehensive ecosystem management strategy for the GYE (Fitzsimmons 1999).

In the mid-1980s, after a hearing in the House of Representatives where legislators castigated the NPS and Forest Service for failing to coordinate their planning and management activities, the two agencies reinvigorated the Greater Yellowstone Coordinating Committee (GYCC), an interagency group created in the 1960s. In June 1990 the GYCC issued a draft vision document that called for ecosystem management and conjured a landscape that was largely wild. The vision document stated:

> The overall mood of the GY[E] will be one of naturalness, a combination of ecological processes operating with little restraint and humans moderating their activities so that they become a reasonable part of, rather than encumbrances upon, those processes.... The overarching goal is to conserve the sense of naturalness and maintain ecosystem integrity in the GY[E] through respect for ecological and geological processes and features that cross administrative boundaries. (Quoted in Fitzsimmons 1999, 78)

Environmentalists, though skeptical that real change would ensue, were pleased with the document's emphasis on preservation. But local politicians and economic interests were outraged by the draft, which they claimed would threaten private property rights and cripple the region's economy. The final document, released after a year of negotiations, was a pale version of the original: it was 10 pages long, rather than the initial 60; the GYE itself had shrunk from 19 million acres in multiple ownerships to 11.7 million acres of national forest and national park lands; and the overarching goal of conserving "naturalness" and ecological integrity was nowhere to be found. In its bland new incarnation, the vision statement was largely ignored by politicians and the public (Keiter 2003).

A more successful EBM initiative was the Northwest Forest Plan crafted in response to the spotted owl crisis in the Pacific Northwest. In the early 1970s, Eric Forsman, a graduate student in biology, began to suspect that clear-cutting of old-growth trees in the region was endangering the northern spotted owl. He and his adviser alerted local and state officials in Oregon, as well as the Forest Service and the BLM, both of which controlled substantial portions of owl habitat in Oregon, Washington, and Northern California. Loath to antagonize the region's timber industry, federal land managers reluctantly agreed to adopt minimal measures to protect the owl. Emerging science made clear that these steps were inadequate, however, and environmentalists pressed the agencies to do more. Increasingly visible disputes over preserving the owl and its old-growth forest habitat erupted throughout the 1980s but did not come to a head until 1988, when federal courts in Portland and Seattle virtually halted logging in federally owned old-growth forests. Unable to devise a scientifically defensible solution, the George H. W. Bush administration left office with the issue unresolved (Layzer 2012b; Yaffee 1994).

In the spring of 1993, only months into his first term, President Bill Clinton convened a forest summit and invited all the major stakeholders. He subsequently charged a team of experts with crafting a forest management plan that would end the stalemate in the region. The resulting Northwest Forest Management Plan, formally adopted in 1994, was not a perfect example of EBM; in particular, it was the product of only minimal stakeholder engagement. But it did embody other important EBM attributes. It was a large-scale plan whose boundaries were defined not by political jurisdictions but by the spotted owl's range—including federal, state, and private lands. Moreover, it sought to protect not only owls but also salmon and other native species. Based on a comprehensive, state-of-the-art scientific assessment, it prescribed creating a network of interconnected reserves that would facilitate dispersal of old-growth species and would reestablish disturbance regimes. And it proposed creating 10 adaptive management areas where land managers could experiment with novel interventions. Because the plan reduced logging to well below historical levels, it also included measures such as job retraining to help dislocated timber workers and their communities adjust to the new regime (Layzer 2012b).

3. Theoretical Benefits of EBM

By the mid-1990s, in the wake of the spotted owl controversy, the ecosystem-based approach had crystallized and become the preferred strategy of many professional societies and the dominant paradigm—at least rhetorically—governing the nation's land management agencies (see, for example, Beattie 1996; Christensen et al. 1996; Dombeck 1996; IEMTF 1995; NAPA 1995; PCSD 1996; Society of American Foresters 1993; Thomas 1996; U.S. EPA 1994; Western Governors' Association 1998). Scholars and practitioners offered a variety of definitions that consistently emphasized a handful of elements that, taken together, would lead to more comprehensive management at larger spatial scales on a longer time frame than conventional management and would therefore lead to more resilient natural systems (see Table 27.1) (Browman et al. 2004; Brussard, Reed, and Tracy 1998; Christensen et al. 1996; Clark 1999; GAO 1994; Gordon and Coppock 1997; Franklin 1997; Grumbine 1994; Keiter 1998, 2003; Lamont 2006; Lee 1993; Meffe et al. 2002; Wallace et al. 1996; Yaffee 1999, 2002).

3.1. Landscape-Scale Planning

First and foremost, according to its proponents, EBM involves holistic planning at a landscape scale—that is, planning across a mosaic of ecosystems (Forman 1995). As forest ecologists David Perry and Michael Amaranthus explain, "The critical role of landscapes and regions in buffering the spread of disturbances,

Table 27.1 Traditional Natural Resource Management versus Ecosystem-Based Management

Attribute	Traditional Natural Resource Management	Ecosystem-Based Management
Underlying View of Nature	A collection of resources to control	Complex, dynamic, interrelated, and inherently unpredictable systems
Relevant Science	Equilibrium perspective: succession leads to stable climax communities; reductionist methods; goal is predictability	"Flux of nature" perspective: disturbance is normal; holism; embrace of uncertainty and surprise
Goal(s) of Management	Maximum sustainable yield of commodities	Sustainable ecosystems, ecological integrity or balance between commodity production, amenities, and ecological integrity
Scale of Planning and Management	Defined by political jurisdiction	Defined by ecology of the landscape and problems to be solved
Decision-making approach	Centralized, top-down, expert-driven	Decentralized, participatory, collaborative
Implementation/Solutions	Prescriptive, uniform, piecemeal, technology-based; emphasis on control and remediation of damage	Incentive-based or voluntary, locally tailored, holistic, and performance-based; emphasis on prevention
	Management that is rigid and aims for control	Management that is experimental, adaptive

Source: Adapted from Cortner and Moote 1999; Meffe et al. 2002.

providing pathways of movement for organisms, altering climate, and mediating key processes such as the hydrologic cycle means that the fate of any one piece of ground is intimately linked to its larger spatial context" (1997, 49). Ecologists acknowledge that there is no single, accepted scientific definition of an ecosystem (Szaro, Sexton, and Malone 1998). But there are distinctive landscapes, such as watersheds, that are widely recognized as meaningful. The essential points are that planning, and therefore management, should (1) be organized around the problem(s) to be solved, not political units or property lines; (2) address concerns across a full range of spatial scales; and (3) focus on the relationships among landscape elements rather than simply addressing each element in isolation (Brussard, Reed, and Tracy 1998).

In theory, landscape-scale planning yields several environmental benefits. It requires scientists to develop integrative assessments that illuminate the relationships among ecosystem components, as well as the ecological structures and functions that are critical to a system's long-term resilience; it also requires them to incorporate multiple scales and the dynamic character of ecosystems. Such assessments should raise policy makers' and stakeholders' awareness and knowledge of critical ecological processes. As a result, they should be more likely to design solutions that are holistic and comprehensive—and therefore more effective at conserving and restoring biological diversity than are uniform, national-level policies (Christensen et al. 1996; Meffe and Carroll 1994; Murphy 1999). In addition, landscape-scale planning and implementation require coordination among the numerous entities with jurisdiction over a given region. Such coordination, in turn, ought to alleviate the problems that arise when federal and state agencies within a single ecosystem pursue inconsistent policies. It should also avert the "death by a thousand cuts" that occurs when localities make decisions that disregard spillovers across jurisdictions and facilitate urban sprawl (Beatley and Manning 1997).

3.2. Stakeholder Collaboration

A second critical feature of EBM is collaboration among stakeholders—an attribute that gained prominence as proponents contemplated the challenges of implementation (Duane 1997). In particular, proponents contend that stakeholders ought to select the desired states of the landscape and formulate the means to achieve those states. In most collaborative planning processes, participants deliberate with the aim of reaching consensus, generally defined as willingness by all to accept the decisions of the group. When properly structured, consensus-based problem solving identifies solutions that promise gains for all the participants—although no one group is likely to get everything it wants.

In theory, engaging stakeholders in a collaborative process of defining the goals, objectives, and outputs of EBM will produce several environmental benefits. Over time, repeated interactions among stakeholders are likely to increase their knowledge and understanding of one another's interests, eventually fostering trust among the participants (Axelrod 1984; Dryzek 1990; Innes and Booher 1999; Susskind and Cruikshank 1987). Trust, in turn, generates creative interactions, which can yield innovative solutions (Dryzek 1990; Innes 1996; Wondollek and Yaffee 2000). As political scientists Philip Brick and Edward Weber (2001, 18) explain: "Instead of a system premised on hierarchy, collaboratives devolve significant authority to citizens, with an emphasis on voluntary participation and compliance, unleashing untapped potential for innovation latent in any regulated environment."

Proponents of collaboration also anticipate solutions that are more effective at solving environmental problems because the process incorporates more and better information, and does so more thoroughly, than top-down approaches. Collaboration ought to engage scientists more productively than adversarial approaches because in a deliberative forum, reasoning rather than tactics is paramount (Andrews 2002; Ozawa 1991). Moreover, unlike decision making by narrowly trained experts, collaboration incorporates local knowledge, which is based on extended, close observation of how an ecosystem behaves (Berkes 1999; Brunner et al. 2005; Fischer 2000). In the process, it filters out the biases and broadens the perspectives of experts (Brick and Weber 2001; Susskind and Cruikshank 1987).

As important, involving all interested parties can ease implementation, since everyone who might obstruct the implementation of a solution will have participated in formulating it (Blumenthal and Jannink 2000; Meffe et al. 2002). As forestry scientist John Gordon and environmental writer Jane Coppock point out: "The inclusiveness of the process broadens the base of support, making it harder for die-hard opponents to overturn agreements as soon as they see a political advantage" (1997, 44). By contrast, locals tend to perceive mandates issued by federal officials as unfair and illegitimate, and therefore to resent and resist them (Susskind and Cruikshank 1987). In short, according to marine scientists Heather Leslie and Karen McLeod, "meaningful engagement with stakeholders is needed to create management initiatives that are credible, enforceable, and realistic" (2007, 542).

3.3. Flexible, Adaptive Implementation

The third element of EBM is implementation that is flexible and adaptive. A flexible implementation strategy employs information, incentives, performance standards, and voluntarism, rather than prescriptive rules and deterrence. According to its proponents, such flexibility is essential because next-generation environmental problems are fundamentally different from those tackled in the 1970s; whereas centralized rules may have been appropriate for problems caused by large factories, they are inadequate for dealing with suburban sprawl, agricultural runoff, and other problems caused by myriad individual decisions (Esty and Chertow 1997; Graham 1999; Mazmanian and Kraft 1999). Adaptive management entails designing interventions to illuminate ecosystem responses and adjusting management to reflect new scientific knowledge. In its ideal form, adaptive management begins with the establishment of baseline conditions and the identification of gaps in knowledge about a system; next, scientists devise management interventions as experiments that test hypotheses about the behavior of the system and monitor the results of those interventions; finally, managers modify their practices in response to information gleaned from monitoring (Holling 1978).

Flexible, adaptive implementation promises at least two major environmental benefits. In theory, flexibility fosters a sense of stewardship among regulated entities, increasing the likelihood they will take protective measures that exceed minimal legal requirements (Fiorino 2004). By contrast, say critics of the status quo, traditional regulatory approaches appear unreasonably burdensome and arbitrary, so they provoke resistance or efforts to circumvent the rules. Those who do comply are likely to engage in the minimum legally required behavior change (Fiorino 2004; Freeman 1997). According to its proponents, adaptive management promotes continuous learning, which is essential because both ecological and social systems are complex, dynamic, and inherently unpredictable (Cortner and Moote 1999; Holling 1995, 1996; Karkkainen 2002; Lee 1993). Adjustment in response to new information can, in theory, result in management practices that reflect the best scientific understanding of ecosystem process and function.

4. Critiques of EBM

Despite great enthusiasm about the potential benefits of EBM, critics feared the concept was too ambiguous to bring about genuine environmental protection, and that absent a shift in values, EBM would yield more of the same while breeding complacency (Lackey 1998; Ludwig et al. 1993; Stanley 1995). Some critics suggested that existing statutory frameworks that give precedence to commodity production or species-level obligations might impede ecosystem-based approaches (Keiter 1998; Tarlock 2003). Others worried that institutional factors—particularly longstanding agency missions and standard operating procedures—would obstruct EBM initiatives (Cortner and Moote 1999; Keiter 1998). Still others argued that flexible implementation would allow evasion of protective measures by recalcitrant managers and stakeholders (Lowi 1999; Steinzor 2000), while adaptive management, although desirable in theory, would encounter resistance in practice (Johnson 1999; Stankey et al. 2003; Walters 1997).

But the gravest concerns about EBM focused on stakeholder collaboration. Critics argued that collaboration aimed at consensus would yield lowest-common-denominator solutions rather than environmentally protective ones. According to this logic, collaboration undermines efforts to depart dramatically from the status quo because, in an effort to attain consensus, planners exclude or marginalize those with "extreme" views, skirt contentious issues, focus on the attributes of the ecosystem that are easiest to control, and avoid considering solutions that impose costs on participating stakeholders (Beierle and Cayford 2002; Coglianese 2001; Eckersley 2002; Peterson, Peterson, and Peterson 2005; Stanley 1995). Some skeptics charged that collaboration actually exacerbates the power imbalance between environmental and development interests, and therefore generates *worse* outcomes than the traditional regulatory approach (Amy 1990; Coggins 2001; McCloskey 1996; Stahl 2001; Steinzor 2000).

Disagreements over the likely consequences of stakeholder collaboration were rooted in differences in the extent to which proponents believed that restoring ecological integrity and biological diversity should constrain human activity—that is, whether they adopted an ecocentric or anthropocentric point of view. Some proponents of EBM, many of them scientists, emphasized restoring and sustaining healthy ecosystems and moderating human behavior to accommodate natural constraints (Callicott 2000; Christensen et al. 1996; Grumbine 1994; Lamont 2006; Noss and Scott 1997; Wood 1994). For example, environmental policy analyst Christopher Wood argued that "to embrace the ecosystem management concept is to accept that ecological factors such as maintaining biological diversity, ecological integrity, and resource productivity dictate strict limits on social and economic uses of the land" (1994, 7). Similarly, environmental educator Edward Grumbine contended that "ecosystem management integrates scientific knowledge of ecological relationships within a complex sociopolitical and values framework toward the general goal of protecting native ecosystem integrity over the long term" (1994, 31). And ecologist Hal Salwasser argued: "The aim of ecosystem management on national forests should be to sustain healthy land first, then to provide people with the variety of benefits and options they need and want, consistent with basic land stewardship" (1998, 90).

By contrast, many others proffered a view of sustainability in which social, economic, and ecological systems are pursued simultaneously. For example, in 1996 the Keystone Center defined ecosystem management as "a collaborative process that strives to reconcile the promotion of economic opportunities and livable communities with the conservation of ecological integrity and biological diversity" (quoted in Fitzsimmons 1999, 6). For planners Robert Szaro, William Sexton, and Charles Malone, "The mandate [of EBM] should be to protect environmental quality while also producing the resources that people need. Therefore, ecosystem management cannot simply be a matter of choosing one over the other" (1998, 3). And according to the Ecosystem-Based Management Tools Network, a web-based alliance of EBM researchers and practitioners seeking to promote EBM for coastal and marine environments, EBM "is concerned with the ecological integrity of coastal-marine systems and the sustainability of both human and ecological elements."

President Clinton's Interagency Ecosystem Management Task Force issued perhaps the consummate statement of the multiple-goals perspective. According to the task force:

> The goal of the ecosystem approach is to restore and sustain the health, productivity, and biological diversity of ecosystems and the overall quality of life through a natural resource management approach that is fully integrated with social and economic goals. This is essential to maintain the air we breathe, the water we drink, the food we eat, and to sustain natural resources for future populations. The ecosystem approach recognizes the interrelationship between natural systems and healthy, sustainable economies. It is a common sense way for public and private managers to carry out their mandates with greater efficiency. (1995, 3)

Cortner and Moote acknowledged the tension that pervaded definitions of EBM. "While ecosystem management explicitly recognizes that social goals and objectives play a central role in framing management direction," they noted, "it also presumes that humans will decide to make protection of ecological processes their overriding social objective" (1999, 42). Similarly, the U.S. Government Accountability Office (GAO) observed: "Proponents of ecosystem management believe that coordinating human activities across large geographic areas to maintain or restore healthy ecosystems…would, among other things, better address declining ecological conditions and ensure the sustainable long-term use of natural resources, including the production of natural resource commodities" (U.S. GAO 1994, 4). The GAO also recognized, however, that "in the absence of a clear statement of federal priorities for sustaining and restoring ecosystem and the minimum level of ecosystem health needed to do so, ecosystem management has come to represent different things to different people" (ibid., 38).

In sum, critics worried that EBM would yield insufficiently protective solutions by empowering development interests and disadvantaging environmentalists. In particular, those with an ecocentric perspective suspected that stakeholder collaboration would generate a combination of social, economic, and environmental goals, rather than making the resilience of natural systems paramount. Such a result, they worried, would inevitably undermine efforts at ecological restoration.

5. EBM IN PRACTICE

Despite its ambiguities and disagreements over its effectiveness, EBM has become the dominant approach to natural resource management. By 1999 federal officials in the United States had stopped referring to ecosystem management, retreating in the face of vitriolic reactions from commodity interests and western wise-use advocates.[3] Yet the concepts that underpin EBM persisted, and initiatives continued under different names. Under the conservative Bush administration, "collaborative conservation" became the watchword, but the approach to biodiversity conservation resembled EBM. For example, in 2006 the Cooperative Sagebrush Initiative began engaging stakeholders across eleven western states in an effort to reconcile resource use with conservation of the sage grouse, whose numbers were dwindling as a result of habitat fragmentation.

Moreover, even as the term fell out of favor among U.S. land managers, enthusiasm grew for applying EBM principles to the management of marine ecosystems (Browman et al. 2004; McLeod et al. 2005; Rosenberg and McLeod 2005; Ruckelshaus et al. 2008; UNEP and GPA 2006). California's 1999 Marine Life

---

3. While environmentalists feared that EBM would yield insufficiently protective solutions, conservatives argued that EBM was a vehicle of nature-worshipping environmentalists to elevate protection of ecosystems above all else (see, for example, Fitzsimmons 1999).

Management Act required EBM for managing all marine wildlife in the state's waters. Two prestigious scientific panels—the Pew Oceans Commission (2003) and the U.S. Commission on Ocean Policy (2004)—recommended taking an ecosystem-based approach to managing marine systems. In fact, by the early 2000s EBM had become the dominant paradigm for managing natural resources around the world, and several international organizations—including the United Nations (UNCB 2003; UNDP et al. 2003), the World Conservation Union (Pirot, Meynell, and Elder 2000), and the Millennium Ecosystem Assessment (MEA 2003)—had developed case studies and principles for successful implementation of EBM.[4]

Although enthusiasm for EBM has been widespread and sustained, systematic assessments of its efficacy have been few and far between. In part this is because, until recently, few initiatives had existed long enough for evaluators to assess their substantive benefits. Of those few, their complexity and heterogeneity made evaluation particularly challenging. Since the mid-2000s, however, scholars have sought to document the results of EBM and, to the extent possible, analyze the reasons for its success or failure.

5.1. A Comparative Assessment

One analysis completed in the late 2000s sought to discern the mechanisms by which EBM produces results by comparing seven cases, four involving aquatic ecosystems and three involving terrestrial ecosystems (Layzer 2008). All seven initiatives yielded concrete policies and practices that appeared likely, over time, to produce environmental benefits. Each prompted the creation of a deeper and more holistic understanding of how specific ecosystems work, which in turn fostered widespread recognition among policy makers and stakeholders of the relationships among the landscape's ecological elements and functions. Without exception, the programs furnished participants with a rationale for raising large sums of money that were used to acquire ecologically valuable land or undertake activities aimed at restoring ecological functions. And each empowered environmentally oriented personnel within agencies and jurisdictions, some of whom tried to institutionalize environmentally beneficial practices. Only those initiatives that did *not* rely on collaborative planning, however, generated policies and practices that appeared likely to conserve and restore biological diversity and, therefore, ecological resilience.

A comparison among the seven cases revealed that a landscape-scale focus was an important catalyst for the adoption of protective policies and practices. In each of the cases, scientists described a defining "moment" when, for the first time, they saw the system as a whole, not just a set of parts. In addition, scientists identified key drivers of ecological damage and documented the mechanisms by which that damage was occurring. And they recommended measures for conserving key

4. Elsewhere, EBM goes by other names, including Integrated Coastal Management, Integrated Water Resources Management, and Integrated River Basin Management.

species and the ecological processes they depend on. Moreover, in every case, trying to address problems at a landscape scale prompted planners to adopt comprehensive approaches to environmental problem solving and led to new forms of
coordination among disparate agencies and jurisdictions.

The beneficial effects of collaborating with stakeholders were more elusive,
however. In the four cases where policy makers deferred to stakeholders to set
goals, the policies and practices that emerged appeared unlikely to conserve or
restore ecological health because, to gain consensus, planners skirted trade-offs
and opted instead for solutions that promised something for everyone. The resulting plans typically featured management-intensive approaches with little buffering.
As a result, they imposed the risk of failure on the natural system. There are several
explanations for this finding. First, although collaboration did enhance trust, there
is little evidence that stakeholders' interests were genuinely transformed or that their
interactions generated innovative solutions. Instead, consensus-oriented groups
tended to marginalize advocates who espoused "extreme" views. Negotiations
often resembled bargaining more than deliberation, particularly as plans became
increasingly specific. And stakeholder groups tended to avoid the most difficult
issues or paper over differences by using vague language—a practice that ultimately haunted implementation.

Stakeholder collaboration also did not ensure that the best available information
would prevail. The four initiatives that involved stakeholder collaboration created
scientific enterprises that were difficult to penetrate, so local knowledge was often
ignored. Nor did collaboration put an end to bickering among stakeholders over
science. The evidence also failed to support the notion that collaboration ensures
durable implementation. Instead, implementation exposed many of the differences
papered over during the collaborative planning processes, as stakeholders sought
to prevent or modify projects that threatened their short-term interests.

A commitment to flexible, adaptive implementation did not compensate for
the failings of environmentally risky plans and, in fact, sometimes exacerbated
them. Flexible implementation allowed managers with missions that were incompatible with ecological restoration to resume user-friendly practices when political conditions shifted. The rhetoric of adaptive management did not automatically
create a willingness to alter policies in the face of new information. There were
a variety of reasons for this: minimalist plans actually provided little room for
adjustment; management and monitoring were insufficiently funded; and there
were inadequate mechanisms for translating learning by scientists into management changes.

By contrast, when policy makers—elected officials, administrators, or judges—
endorsed an environmentally protective goal and used regulatory leverage to prevent development interests from undermining that objective, as they did in the three
comparison cases, the resulting policies and practices were more likely than their
counterparts to conserve or restore ecological integrity. In these cases, a willingness
among political leaders to make ecological health the preeminent goal changed the
balance of power and altered perceptions of what was politically feasible. When

restoring ecological health was the paramount goal, planners were more likely to approve, and managers to implement, approaches that relied less on energy-intensive manipulation and more on enhancing the ability of natural processes to sustain themselves—even if doing so imposed costs on some stakeholders.

5.2. Analyses of Individual Cases

The insights generated by this comparative analysis should be taken as cautionary rather than definitive. In particular, it is important to note that the four cases of genuine EBM were more complex, both geographically and organizationally, than the comparison cases. That said, the findings were consistent with the results of other research into EBM or its components. For example, detailed examinations of the Chesapeake Bay Program yielded comparable results. Established in 1983, the Chesapeake Bay Program aimed to restore the resilience of the nation's largest and most productive estuary. But on January 5, 2010, the 26-year-old program missed yet another cleanup deadline: efforts to reduce pollution in the bay had fallen more than 40 percent short of the program's goals, and—with nearly $6 billion spent—monitoring data suggested that the impacts of relentless growth were overwhelming pollution control efforts (Fahrenthold 2010).

Most observers attributed the program's failures to its reliance on collaborative planning and flexible implementation (Ernst 2003; Horton 2003; Layzer 2012a). Historically, the bay program operated as a multistate cooperative, with the Environmental Protection Agency (EPA) in a supporting role and the bay states following different paths depending on their political culture and proximity to the bay. While the state of Maryland typically adopted more stringent measures, Virginia and Pennsylvania took advantage of the program's flexibility to adopt minimally restrictive policies and practices. Furthermore, the states' heavy reliance on nonregulatory approaches—such as educational programs, incentives, and non-regulatory stewardship initiatives—yielded little in the way of results. In fact, the single most effective measure taken in the watershed was the ban on phosphate detergent adopted by the bay states in the 1980s and 1990s (Boesch and Greer 2003; Cohn 1989).

Similarly, scholars reported that a decades-long, multibillion-dollar international effort to restore ecological integrity in the Great Lakes "remain[ed] vulnerable to uneven and ever-changing levels of commitment from its respective jurisdictions" (Rabe 1999, 251). By the mid-2000s there were signs of progress in the Great Lakes: phosphorus inputs had declined; the walleye had recovered dramatically, as a result of fishing limits and phosphorus controls; and the population of the burrowing mayfly, historically the dominant benthic invertebrate in the lakes, rebounded between 1990 and 2001 (Shear 2006). The available data suggested, however, that wetland-dependent birds were static or declining, non-native fish dominated prey fish in most areas, and native freshwater mussel communities had been decimated by invasive zebra mussels (Shear 2006). Moreover, progress was likely to be negated by population growth and urban sprawl, the effects of which would be exacerbated by global warming (Shear 2006).

In his impressionistic account of his experiences with collaborative watershed-scale planning for the Platte River, legal scholar John Echeverria argued that from the outset, planning was "heavily weighted in favor of parochial economic interests" (2001, 560). He noted that the inhospitable political context in which the process began largely determined the extent to which protective measures were possible. He speculated that water users and political leaders in the river-basin states embraced the Platte program because it gave them more say than a purely federal program would have, and because it created opportunities to argue for taxpayer help in paying project mitigation costs. Echeverria concluded that the negotiated solution would almost certainly be a failure, both in absolute terms and relative to what could have been accomplished through the exercise of regulatory muscle.

Some other, less prominent initiatives also fell short of restoring ecological resilience because planners were unwilling to tackle thorny issues. For example, Arizona's collaborative Upper San Pedro Partnership (USPP), formed in 1998, failed to prevent the San Pedro River from running dry for the first time in 2005. Although the partnership generated and disseminated an impressive amount of information to stakeholders, and local governments took several steps to reduce water consumption in the region, there was no consensus on the ultimate issue: growth control. According to environmental planners George Saliba and Katharine Jacobs, "Perhaps the largest criticism leveled against the USPP is its inability to make difficult decisions regarding growth.... The politics and economics of growth in Arizona make this conversation very difficult" (2008, 41).

5.3. Studies of Marine EBM

Scholars investigating marine EBM also discerned pallid results. In a review of EBM in fisheries management around the world, fisheries scientist Tony Pitcher and his colleagues found that while many countries had articulated EBM principles, few had actually taken the steps to achieve effective implementation. Only a handful of countries in the developed world were clearly moving toward EBM, and even many European countries received dismal ratings. The authors concluded that "whilst the late nineties...saw the blossoming of 'Oceans' approaches aimed at developing and applying EBM principles to multiple sectors in multi-stakeholder processes, the gradual pace of these reforms and their perceived expense has meant that few have been implemented" (2009, 231).

Similarly, ecologists Katie Arkema, Sarah Abramson, and Bryan Dewsbury (2006) investigated 49 management plans for eight large marine and coastal ecosystems to assess the extent to which managers were actually practicing EBM.

They found that implementation of EBM principles was lagging. In particular, management objectives included more detailed human criteria than ecological and management criteria; for example, many of the plans were dominated by objectives that focused on promoting commercial and recreational uses compatible with resource protection, such as maintaining public access and rebuilding depleted fisheries.

5.4. Studies of Collaborative Planning

Other studies supported claims about the propensity of collaborative planning, in particular, to yield environmentally risk-tolerant solutions. For example, in her detailed analysis of the Quincy Library Group (QLG), political scientist Sarah Pralle found that the decision by key activists to plan collaboratively in a local forum led planners to redefine the problem as forest fires, rather than as excessive logging. Doing so defused conflict and allowed for a solution that gave something to everyone without necessarily addressing the root cause of the region's environmental degradation. Pralle noted that the focus on process disarmed environmental challengers, who found it difficult to combat the "overwhelmingly positive characterization" of local, collaborative decision making. She observed: "In a world of polarized interest groups and partisan gridlock, policymakers may be more than willing to settle for outward signs of consensus rather than true political compromises" (2006, 202).

Similarly, in her study of two collaborative projects within the broader Everglades restoration in South Florida, political scientist Kathryn Frank found that collaboration was better at resolving conflict than at problem solving, which tended to be a subordinate objective. She concluded that

> since collaborative processes did not significantly change power relations, collaborative outputs and the political capital upon which they depended were largely transient. Collaboration produced a delicate balancing act of aligned interests in keeping with the rhetoric of win-win and sustainability. Collaborative recommendations appeared highly integrated, yet under the surface there were strategic motivations and shallow commitments. The agreements began to unravel when system dynamics of technical shortcomings changed the conditions upon which the agreements depended. Combine this with the long-range dominance of economic interests, and the result was poorer implementation performance for environmental plan features. (Frank 2009, 238)

More generally, scholars have ascertained that collaborative problem solving appears to increase human and social capital (Beierle and Cayford 2002; Gunton, Day, and Williams 2003; Innes et al. 1994; Leach, Pelkey, and Sabatier 2002; Lubell 2005; Weber 2003). But they have struggled to document a causal link between social capital and improved environmental outcomes (Leach, Pelkey, and Sabatier 2002; Leach and Sabatier 2005; Lubell 2004; Raymond 2006).

5.5. Examples of Success

Observers identified examples of EBM that incontrovertibly resulted in environmental improvements, including the Malpai Borderlands Group on the New Mexico–Arizona border (Sayre 2005) and the Applegate Partnership in Oregon (Weber 2003). Such projects tended to feature the characteristics posited by political scientist Elinor Ostrom (1990) and her colleagues as essential to effective local, collaborative management of common pool resources: appropriators (1) believe they will be harmed if they do not adopt rules to govern use of the resource; (2) are affected in similar ways by the proposed rules; (3) value the continued use of the common property resource (discount rates are low); (4) face low information, transformation, and enforcement costs; (5) share generalized norms of reciprocity and trust; and (6) constitute a relatively small and stable group. In addition, the target resource must be in sufficiently good shape that efforts to protect it will confer benefits, there are valid and reliable indicators of system health, the flow of resources is relatively predictable, and the system is sufficiently small to allow knowledge of external boundaries and internal microenvironments (Ostrom 2001). Unfortunately, such conditions hold in a dwindling number of places and rarely obtain at larger scales.

Furthermore, in many cases, evaluators who have discerned positive results relied on the testimony of participants, rather than on actual evidence of ecological improvement. For example, planning scholar Steven Yaffee (2002) followed 105 partnerships throughout the United States. According to surveys of those initiatives, a majority not only produced better relationships and greater awareness of the ecosystem but also improved scientific understanding, brought about ecological restoration, increased native species populations, and made improvements in "overall ecosystem integrity." Similarly, in a survey by the U.S. GAO (2008) of seven collaborative initiatives, participants claimed they had improved natural resource conditions—although none had collected any data to show their actual impact at a landscape scale. Alternatively, analysts held EBM to process standards, but not to outcome standards. For example, zoologist Heather Tallis and her colleagues (2010) proffered two case studies of "successful" EBM—one in Raja Ampat, Indonesia, and the other in Washington's Puget Sound, Washington—even though neither had demonstrated actual ecological results.

6. CONCLUSIONS

Overall, the evidence suggests that the theoretical benefits of EBM, although widely touted, do not always materialize in practice. In cases where EBM has been fully implemented, landscape-scale planning has yielded discernible benefits, but the effects of collaboration with stakeholders and flexible, adaptive implementation have been more ambiguous. This is not entirely surprising: proponents of EBM often gloss over the potential trade-offs among environmental, economic, and social considerations, particularly in the short run. They assume that a preoccupation with long-term ecological restoration will somehow emerge from a collaborative process. For this to happen, however, participants must be convinced that healthy, functioning ecosystems are essential to human well-being; they must embrace a land ethic and eschew a short-term economic point of view.

Such a transformation is unlikely under any circumstances but, counterintuitively, may be facilitated by the exercise of political leadership and regulatory leverage. That is why, as legal scholar Bradley Karkkainen observes, the federal government plays a critical role in EBM. He argues that productive collaboration is most likely when the most powerful actors have their backs against the wall—usually as a result of a stringent federal law that is likely to be enforced. Mobilization and litigation by environmental advocates can also generate the kind of "pervasive, persistent, and profound uncertainty, and the associated recognition of mutual dependence" necessary to bring about fundamental shifts in the balance of power (Cohen and Rogers 2003, 252).

Given the increasing pressure on already stressed natural systems and the evidence that most existing projects are not likely to yield ecological resilience, scholars should focus on contributing insights that can help practitioners devise more effective, landscape-scale restoration initiatives. In particular, scholars should investigate when and how national-level policies alter the playing field for local and regional entities. Specifically, how and under what circumstances do federal rules and practices empower environmentalists vis-à-vis development interests? What form should federal regulations take to be most potent? Planners would also benefit from systematic assessments of when and how collaboration leads to more environmentally protective outputs over time. What are the most effective collaborative mechanisms? Is it essential to seek consensus? At what scales is collaboration more or less likely to generate environmentally beneficial plans? Finally, given the evidence that apparently beneficial plans do not always lead to environmental improvements (Kondolf and Micheli 1995), scholars should continue to refine and deploy the models and monitoring tools that enable us to link environmental outcomes to the policies and practices generated under the rubric of EBM (Koontz and Thomas 2006).

REFERENCES

Amy, D. J. 1990. "Environmental Dispute Resolution: The Promise and the Pitfalls." In *Environmental Policy in the 1990s*, ed. N. J. Vig and M. E. Kraft. Washington, DC: CQ Press.

Andrews, C. J. 2002. *Humble Analysis: The Practice of Joint Fact-Finding*. Westport, CT: Praeger.

Arkema, K. K., S. C. Abramson, and B. M. Dewsbury. 2006. "Marine
    Ecosystem-Based Management: From Characterization to Implementation."
    Frontiers in Ecology and the Environment 4 (10): 525–532.
Axelrod, R. M. 1984. *The Evolution of Cooperation.* New York: Basic Books.
Beatley, T., and K. Manning. 1997. *The Ecology of Place: Planning for the
    Environment, Economy, and Community.* Washington, DC: Island.
Beattie, M. 1996. "An Ecosystem Approach to Fish and Wildlife Conservation."
    Ecological Applications 6 (3): 696–699.
Beierle, T. C., and J. Cayford. 2002. *Democracy in Practice: Public Participation in
    Environmental Decisions.* Washington, DC: Resources for the Future.
Berkes, F. 1999. *Sacred Ecology.* Philadelphia: Taylor & Francis.
Blumenthal, D., and J. Jannink. 2000. "A Classification of Collaborative Management
    Methods." *Conservation Ecology* 4 (2): 13.
Boesch, D. F., and J. Greer. 2003. *Chesapeake Futures: Choices for the 21st Century.*
    Chesapeake Bay Program Science and Technical Advisory Committee Publication
    No. 03–001, Annapolis, MD: Chesapeake Bay Program.
Botkin, D. 1990. *Discordant Harmonies: A New Ecology for the Twenty-First Century.*
    New York: Oxford University Press.
Brick, P., and E. P. Weber. 2001. "Will the Rain Follow the Plow? Unearthing a
    New Environmental Movement." In *Across the Great Divide: Explorations in
    Collaborative Conservation and the American West,* ed. P. Brick, D. Snow, and S.
    Van De Wetering. Washington, DC: Island.
Browman, H. I., P. M. Cury, R. Hilborn, S. Jennings, H. K. Lotze, P. M. Mace,
    S. Murawski, D. Pauly, M. Sissenwine, K. I. Stergiou, and D. Zeller. 2004.
    "Perspectives on Ecosystem-Based Approaches to the Management of Marine
    Resources." *Marine Ecology Progress Series* 274: 269–303.
Brunner, R. D., T. A. Steelman, L. Co-Juell, C. M. Cromley, C. M. Edwards, and D.
    W. Tucker. 2005. *Adaptive Governance: Integrating Science, Policy, and Decision
    Making.* New York: Columbia University Press.
Brussard, P. F., J. M. Reed, and C. R. Tracy. 1998. "Ecosystem Management: What Is
    It Really?" *Landscape and Urban Planning* 40 (1–3): 9–20.
Callicott, J. B. 2000. "Harmony between Man and Land: Aldo Leopold and the
    Foundations of Ecosystem Management." *Journal of Forestry* 98 (5): 4–13.
Christensen, N. L., A. M. Bartuska, S. Carpenter, C. D'Antonio, R. Francis, J. F.
    Franklin, J. A. MacMahon, R. F. Noss, D. J. Parsons, C. H. Peterson, M. G. Turner,
    and R. G. Woodmansee. 1996. "The Report of the Ecological Society of America
    Committee on the Scientific Basis for Ecosystem Management." *Ecological
    Applications* 6 (3): 665–691.
Clark, Jamie Rappaport. 1999. "The Ecosystem Approach from a Practical Point of
    View." *Conservation Biology* 13 (3): 679–681.
Clark, T. W., E. D. Amato, D. G. Whittemore, and A. H. Harvey. 1991. "Policy and
    Programs for Ecosystem Management in the Greater Yellowstone Ecosystem: An
    Analysis." *Conservation Biology* 5: 412–422.
Coggins, G. C. 2001. "Of Californicators, Quislings, and Crazies: Some Perils of
    Devolved Collaboration." In *Across the Great Divide: Explorations in Collaborative
    Conservation and the American West,* ed. P. Brick, D. Snow, and S. Ven de
    Wetering. Washington, DC: Island.
Coglianese, C. 2001. "Is Consensus an Appropriate Basis for Regulatory Policy?" In
    Environmental Contracts, ed. E. W. Orts and K. Deketelaere. Boston: Kluwer Law
    International.

Cohen, J., and J. Rogers. 2003. "Power and Reason." In *Deepening Democracy: Institutional Innovations in Empowered Participatory Governance*, ed. A. Fung and E. Olin Wright. New York: Verso.

Cohn, D. 1989. "Bans on Phosphates Said to Aid Bay Cleanup." *Washington Post*, January 23.

Cortner, H. J., and M. A. Moote. 1999. *The Politics of Ecosystem Management*. Washington, DC: Island.

Dombeck, M. P. 1996. "Thinking Like a Mountain: BLM's Approach to Ecosystem Management." *Ecological Applications* 6 (3): 699–702.

Doyle, M., and C. A. Drew. 2008. *Large-Scale Ecosystem Restoration: Five Case Studies from the United States*. Washington, DC: Island.

Dryzek, J. 1990. *Discursive Democracy: Politics, Policy, and Political Science*. New York: Cambridge University Press.

Duane, T. P. 1997. "Community Participation in Ecosystem Management." *Ecology Law Quarterly* 24: 771–797.

Eckersley, R. 2002. "Environmental Pragmatism, Ecocentrism, and Deliberative Democracy: Between Problem-Solving and Fundamental Critique." In *Democracy and the Claims of Nature: Critical Perspectives for a New Century*, ed. B. Minteer and B. Pepperman Taylor. Lanham, MD: Rowman & Littlefield.

Ernst, H. R. 2003. *Chesapeake Bay Blues: Science, Politics, and the Struggle to Save the Bay*. Lanham, MD: Rowman & Littlefield.

Esty, D. C., and M. R. Chertow. 1997. "Thinking Ecologically: An Introduction." In *Thinking Ecologically*, ed. M. R. Chertow and D. C. Esty. New Haven, CT: Yale University Press.

Fahrenthold, D. A. 2010. "Efforts to Clean Up Bay off to Another Fresh Start." *Washington Post*, January 6.

Fiorino, D. J. 2004. "Flexibility." In *Environmental Governance Reconsidered: Challenges, Choices, and Opportunities*, ed. R. F. Durant, D. J. Fiorino, and R. O'Leary. Cambridge, MA: MIT Press.

Fischer, F. 2000. *Citizens, Experts, and the Environment*. Durham, NC: Duke University Press.

Fitzsimmons, A. K. 1999. *Defending Illusions: Federal Protection of Ecosystems*. Lanham, MD: Rowman & Littlefield.

Forman, R. T. T. 1995. *Land Mosaics: The Ecology of Landscapes and Regions*. New York: Cambridge University Press.

Frank, K. 2009. "The Role of Collaboration in Everglades Restoration." Ph.D. diss., Georgia Institute of Technology.

Franklin, J. 1997. "Ecosystem Management: An Overview." In *Ecosystem Management: Applications for Sustainable Forest and Wildlife Resources*, ed. A. Haney and M. S. Boyce. New Haven, CT: Yale University Press.

Freeman, J. 1997. "Collaborative Governance in the Administrative State." *UCLA Law Review* 45: 1–98.

Glick, D. A., and T. W. Clark. 1998. "Overcoming Boundaries: The Greater Yellowstone Ecosystem." In *Stewardship across Boundaries*, ed. R. L. Knight and P. B. Landres. Washington, DC: Island.

Goldstein, B. 1991. "The Struggle over Ecosystem Management at Yellowstone." *Bioscience* 42 (3): 183–187.

Gordon, J., and J. Coppock. 1997. "Ecosystem Management and Economic Development." In *Thinking Ecologically: The Next Generation of Environmental Policy*, ed. M. R. Chertow and D. C. Esty. New Haven, CT: Yale University Press.

Graham, M. 1999. *The Morning after Earth Day*. Washington, DC: Brookings Institution Press.

Grumbine, R. E. 1994. "What Is Ecosystem Management?" *Conservation Biology* 8 (1): 27–38.

Gunton, T. I., J. C. Day, and P. W. Williams. 2003. "Evaluating Collaborative Planning: The British Columbia Experience." *Environments* 31 (3): 1–11.

Haeuber, R. 1998. "Ecosystem Management and Environmental Policy in the United States: Open Window or Closed Door?" *Landscape and Urban Planning* 40: 221–233.

Holling, C. S., ed. 1978. *Adaptive Environmental Assessment and Management*. New York: Wiley.

———. 1995. "What Barriers? What Bridges?" In *Barriers and Bridges to the Renewal of Ecosystems and Institutions*, ed. L. H. Gunderson, C. S. Holling, and S. S. Light. New York: Columbia University Press.

———. 1996. "Surprise for Science, Resilience for Ecosystems, and Incentives for People." *Ecological Applications* 6 (3): 733–735.

Holling, C. S., and G. K. Meffe. 1996. "Command and Control and the Pathology of Natural Resource Management." *Conservation Biology* 10 (2): 328–337.

Horton, T. 2003. *Turning the Tide: Saving the Chesapeake Bay*. Washington, DC: Island.

Innes, J. E. 1996. "Planning through Consensus Building." *Journal of the American Planning Association* 62 (4): 460–472.

Innes, J. E., and D. Booher. 1999. "Consensus Building and Complex Adaptive Systems: A Framework for Evaluating Collaborative Planning." *Journal of the American Planning Association* 65 (4): 412–423.

Innes, J. E., J. Gruber, M. Neuman, and R. Thompson. 1994. *Coordinating Growth and Environmental Management through Consensus Building*. Berkeley: California Policy Seminar, University of California.

Interagency Ecosystem Management Task Force (IEMTF). 1995. *The Ecosystem Approach: Healthy Ecosystems and Sustainable Economies*. Vol. 1, Washington, DC: White House Office of Environmental Policy.

Johnson, B. L. 1999. "Introduction to the Special Feature: Adaptive Management—Scientifically Sound, Socially Challenged?" *Conservation Ecology* 3 (1). Available at www.ecologyandsociety.org/vol3/iss1/art10 (accessed January 11, 2011).

Karkkainen, B. C. 2002. "Collaborative Ecosystem Governance: Scale, Complexity, and Dynamism." *Virginia Environmental Law Journal* 21: 189–243.

Keiter, R. B. 1991. "An Introduction to the Ecosystem Management Debate." In *The Greater Yellowstone Ecosystem: Redefining America's Wilderness Heritage*, ed. R. B. Keiter and M. S. Boyce. New Haven, CT: Yale University Press.

———. 1998. "Ecosystems and the Law: Toward an Integrated Approach." *Ecological Applications* 8 (2): 332–341.

———. 2003. *Keeping Faith with Nature: Ecosystems, Democracy, and America's Public Lands*. New Haven, CT: Yale University Press.

Kondolf, G. M., and E. R. Micheli. 1995. "Evaluating Stream Restoration Projects." *Environmental Management* 19 (1): 1–15.

Koontz, T. M., and C. W. Thomas. 2006. "What Do We Know and Need to Know about the Environmental Outcomes of Collaborative Management?" *Public Administration Review* 66 (December, Special Issue on Collaborative Public Management): 111–121.

Lackey, R. T. 1998. "Seven Pillars of Ecosystem Management." *Landscape and Urban Planning* 40 (1–3): 21–30.

Lamont, A. 2006. "Policy Characterization of Ecosystem Management." *Environmental Monitoring and Assessment* 113: 5–18.

Layzer, J. A. 2008. *Natural Experiments: Ecosystem-Based Management and the Environment.* Cambridge, MA: MIT Press.

———. 2012a. "Ecosystem-Based Management in the Chesapeake Bay." In *The Environmental Case*, 3rd ed. Washington, DC: CQ Press.

———. 2012b. "Jobs vs. the Environment: Saving the Northern Spotted Owl." In *The Environmental Case*, 3rd ed. Washington, DC: CQ Press.

Leach, W. D., N. W. Pelkey, and P. A. Sabatier. 2002. "Stakeholder Partnerships As Collaborative Management: Evaluation Criteria Applied to Watershed Management in California and Washington." *Journal of Policy Analysis and Management* 21 (4): 645–670.

Leach, W. D., and P. A. Sabatier. 2005. "Are Trust and Social Capital the Keys to Success?" In *Swimming Upstream: Collaborative Approaches to Environmental Management*, ed. P. Sabatier, W. Focht, M. Lubell, A. Vedlitz, and M. Matlock. Cambridge, MA: MIT Press.

Lee, K. N. 1993. *Compass and Gyroscope: Integrating Science and Politics for the Environment.* Washington, DC: Island.

Leslie, H. M., and K. L. McLeod. 2007. "Confronting the Challenges of Implementing Marine Ecosystem-Based Management." *Frontiers in Ecology and the Environment* 5 (10): 540–548.

Lowi, T. J. 1999. "Frontyard Propaganda." *Boston Review* 24 (5): 17–18.

Lubell, M. 2004. "Collaborative Environmental Institutions: All Talk and No Action." *Journal of Policy Analysis and Management* 23 (3): 549–573.

———. 2005. "Do Watershed Partnerships Enhance Beliefs Conducive to Collective Action?" In *Swimming Upstream: Collaborative Approaches to Environmental Management*, ed. P. Sabatier, W. Focht, M. Lubell, A. Vedlitz, and M. Matlock. Cambridge, MA: MIT Press.

Ludwig, D., R. Hilborn, and C. Walters. 1993. "Uncertainty, Resource Exploitation, and Conservation: Lessons from History." *Science* 260: 17, 36.

Mazmanian, D. A., and M. E. Kraft. 1999. "The Three Epochs of the Environmental Movement." In *Toward Sustainable Communities: Transition and Transformations*, ed. D. A. Mazmanian and M. E. Kraft. Cambridge, MA: MIT Press.

McCloskey, M. 1996. "The Skeptic: Collaboration Has Its Limits." *High Country News*, May 13.

McLeod, K. L., et al. 2005. "Scientific Consensus Statement on Marine Ecosystem-Based Management." Available at www.compassonline.org/sites/all/files/document_files/EBM_Consensus_Statement_v12.pdf (accessed January 4, 2011).

Meffe, G. K., and C. R. Carroll. 1994. *Principles of Conservation Biology.* Sunderland, MA: Sinauer Associates.

Meffe, G. K., L. A. Nielsen, R. L. Knight, and D. A. Schenborn. 2002. *Ecosystem Management: Adaptive, Community-Based Conservation.* Washington, DC: Island.

Millennium Ecosystem Assessment (MEA). 2003. *Ecosystems and Human Well-Being.* Washington, DC: Island.

Murphy, D. 1999. "Case Study." In *Bioregional Assessments*, ed. K. N. Johnson, F. Swanson, M. Herring, and S. Greene. Washington, DC: Island.

National Academy of Public Administration (NAPA). 1995. *Setting Priorities, Getting Results: A New Direction for the U.S. Environmental Protection Agency.* Washington, DC: National Academy of Public Administration.

Noss, R. F., and A. Y. Cooperrider. 1994. *Saving Nature's Legacy.* Washington, DC: Island.

Noss, R. F., and J. M. Scott. 1997. "Ecosystem Protection and Restoration: The Core of Ecosystem Management." In *Ecosystem Management: Applications to Sustainable Forest and Wildlife Resources*, ed. M. Boyce and A. Hanley. New Haven, CT: Yale University Press.

Ostrom, E. 1990. *Governing the Commons: The Evolution of Institutions for Collective Action.* New York: Cambridge University Press.

———. 2001. "Reformulating the Commons." In *Protection the Commons: A Framework for Resource Management in the Americas*, ed. J. Burger, E. Ostrom, and R. Norgaard. Washington, DC: Island.

Ozawa, C. 1991. *Recasting Science: Consensual Procedures in Public Policy Making.* Boulder, CO: Westview.

Perry, D. A., and M. P. Amaranthus. 1997. "Disturbance, Recovery, and Stability." In *Creating a Forestry for the 21st Century*, ed. K. A. Kohm and J. Franklin. Washington, DC: Island.

Peterson, M. N., M. J. Peterson, and T. R. Peterson. 2005. "Conservation and the Myths of Consensus." *Conservation Biology* 19 (3): 762–767.

Pew Oceans Commission. 2003. *America's Living Oceans: Charting a Course for Sea Change.* Arlington, VA: Pew Oceans Commission.

Pickett, S. T. A., and R. S. Ostfeld. 1995. "The Shifting Paradigm in Ecology." In *A New Century for Natural Resources Management*, ed. R. L. Knight and S. F. Bates. Washington, DC: Island.

Pirot, J., P. Meynell, and D. Elder. 2000. *Ecosystem Management: Lessons from around the World.* Cambridge, UK: World Conservation Union.

Pitcher, T. J., D. Kalikoski, K. Short, D. Varkey, and G. Pramod. 2009. "An Evaluation of Progress in Implementing Ecosystem-Based Management in Fisheries in 33 Countries." *Marine Policy* 33: 223–232.

Pralle, S. B. 2006. *Branching Out, Digging In: Environmental Advocacy and Agenda Setting.* Washington, DC: Georgetown University Press.

President's Council on Sustainable Development (PCSD). 1996. *Sustainable America: New Consensus for Prosperity, Opportunity, and a Healthy Environment for the Future.* Washington, DC: U.S. Government Printing Office.

Rabe, B. G. 1999. "Sustainability in a Regional Context: The Case of the Great Lakes Basin." In *Toward Sustainable Communities: Transition and Transformations*, ed. D. Mazmanian and M. E. Kraft. Cambridge, MA: MIT Press.

Raymond, L. 2006. "Cooperation without Trust: Overcoming Collective Action Barriers to Endangered Species Protection." *Policy Studies Journal* 34 (1): 37–57.

Rosenberg, A. A., and K. L. McLeod. 2005. "Implementing Ecosystem-Based Approaches to Management for the Conservation of Ecosystem Services." In *Politics and Socioeconomics of Ecosystem-Based Management of Marine Resources*, ed. H. I. Browman and K. I. Stergio. *Marine Ecology Progress Series* 300: 270–274.

Ruckelshaus, M., T. Klinger, N. Knowlton, and D. P. DeMaster. 2008. "Marine Ecosystem-Based Management in Practice: Scientific and Governance Challenges." *Bioscience* 58 (1): 53–63.

Saliba, G., and K. L. Jacobs. 2008. "Saving the San Pedro River." *Environment* 50 (6): 30–43.

Salwasser, H. 1998. "Ecosystem Management: A New Perspective for National Forest and Grasslands." In *Ecosystem Management: Adaptive Strategies for Natural Resources Organizations in the 21st Century*, ed. J. Aley, W. R. Burch, B. Conover, and D. Field. Philadelphia: Taylor & Francis.

Sayre, Nathan F. 2005. *Working Wilderness: The Malpai Borderlands Group and the Future of the Western Range.* Tucson: Rio Nuevo.

Shear, H. 2006. "The Great Lakes, an Ecosystem Rehabilitated, but Still under Threat." *Environmental Monitoring and Assessment* 113: 199–225.

Slocombe, D. S. 1998. "Lessons from Experience with Ecosystem-Based Management." *Landscape and Urban Planning* 40 (1–3): 31–39.

Society of American Foresters (SAF). 1993. *Sustaining Long-Term Forest Health and Productivity.* Bethesda, MD: Society of American Foresters.

Stahl, A. 2001. "Ownership, Accountability, and Collaboration." In *Across the Great Divide: Explorations in Collaborative Conservation and the American West*, ed. P. Brick, D. Snow, and S. Van de Wetering. Washington, DC: Island.

Stankey, G. H., B. T. Bormann, C. Ryan, B. Shindler, V. Sturtevant, R. N. Clark, and C. Philpot. 2003. "Adaptive Management and the Northwest Forest Plan." *Journal of Forestry* 101 (1): 40–46.

Stanley, T. R., Jr. 1995. "Ecosystem Management and the Arrogance of Humanism." *Conservation Biology* 9 (3): 255–262.

Steinzor, R. I. 2000. "The Corruption of Civic Environmentalism." *Environmental Law Reporter* 30: 10909–10921.

Susskind, L., and J. Cruikshank. 1987. *Breaking the Impasse: Consensual Approaches to Resolving Public Disputes.* New York: Basic Books.

Szaro, R. C., W. T. Sexton, and C. R. Malone. 1998. "The Emergence of Ecosystem Management as a Tool for Meeting People's Needs and Sustaining Ecosystems." *Landscape and Urban Planning* 40 (1–3): 1–7.

Tallis, H., P. S. Levin, M. Ruckelshaus, S. E. Lester, K. McLeod, D. L. Fluharty, and B. S. Halpern. 2010. "The Many Faces of Ecosystem-Based Management: Making the Process Work Today in Real Places." *Marine Policy* 34: 340–348.

Tarlock, A. D. 2003. "Slouching toward Eden: The Eco-pragmatic Challenges of Ecosystem Revival." *Minnesota Law Review* 87: 1173–1208.

Thomas, J. W. 1996. "Forest Service Perspectives on Ecosystem Management." *Ecological Applications* 6 (3): 703–705.

United Nations Convention on Biological Diversity (UNCB). 2003. *Ecosystem Approach: Further Elaboration, Guidelines for Implementation and Relationship with Sustainable Forest Management.* Report of the Expert Meeting on the Ecosystem Approach. Montreal: United National Environment Programme.

United Nations Development Programme (UNDP), United National Environmental Programme, World Bank, and World Resources Institute. 2003. *A Guide to World Resources 2002–2004—Decisions for the Earth—Balance, Voice, and Power.* Washington, DC: World Resources Institute.

United Nations Environment Programme (UNEP) and Global Programme of Action for the Protection of the Marine Environment from Land-Based Activities (GPA). 2006. *Ecosystem-Based Management: Markers for Assessing Progress.* The Hague, Netherlands: United Nations Environment Programme and Global Programme of Action. Available at http://www.unep.org/pdf/ GPA/Ecosystem_based_Management_Markers_for_Assessing_Progress.pdf (accessed June 4, 2012).

United States (U.S.) Commission on Ocean Policy. 2004. *An Ocean Blueprint for the 21st Century*. Washington, DC: U.S. Commission on Ocean Policy.

United States Environmental Protection Agency (U.S. EPA). 1994. *The New Generation of Environmental Protection*. Washington, DC: U.S. EPA.

United States General Accounting Office (U.S. GAO). 1994. *Ecosystem Management: Additional Actions Needed to Adequately Test a Promising Approach*. GAO/RCED-94-111. Washington, DC: U.S. General Accounting Office.

United States Government Accountability Office (U.S. GAO). 2008. *Opportunities Exist to Enhance Federal Participation in Collaborative Efforts to Reduce Conflicts and Improve Natural Resource Conditions*. GAO-08-262. Washington, DC: U.S. Government Accountability Office.

Wallace, M. G., H. J. Cortner, M. A. Moote, and S. Burke. 1996. "Moving toward Ecosystem Management: Examining a Change in Philosophy for Resource Management." *Journal of Political Ecology* 3: 1–36.

Walters, C. 1997. "Challenges in Adaptive Management of Riparian and Coastal Ecosystems." *Conservation Ecology* 1 (2): 1. Available at www.consecol.org/vol1/iss2/art1 (accessed January 11, 2011).

Weber, E. P. 2003. *Bringing Society Back In: Grassroots Ecosystem Management, Accountability, and Sustainable Communities*. Cambridge, MA: MIT Press.

Western Governors' Association. 1998. "Principles for Environmental Management in the West." Resolution 98–001. Denver, CO. Available at http://www.policyconsensus.org/tools/resolutions/western_govs_association_98.html (accessed January 11, 2011).

Wondollek, J. M., and S. L. Yaffee. 2000. *Making Collaboration Work: Lessons From Innovation in Natural Resource Management*. Washington, DC: Island.

Wood, C. A. 1994. "Ecosystem Management: Achieving the New Land Ethic." *Renewable Resources Journal* 12 (1): 6–12.

Yaffee, S. L. 1994. *Wisdom of the Spotted Owl: Policy Lessons for a New Century*. Washington, DC: Island.

———. 1999. "Three Faces of Ecosystem Management." *Conservation Biology* 13 (4): 713–725.

———. 2002. "Ecosystem Management in Policy and Practice." In *Ecosystem Management: Adaptive, Community-Based Conservation*, ed. G. Meffe, L. A. Nielsen, R. L. Knight, and D. A. Schenborn. Washington, DC: Island.

CHAPTER 28

....

THE USE OF STRATEGIC PLANNING, INFORMATION, AND ANALYSIS IN ENVIRONMENTAL POLICY MAKING AND MANAGEMENT

....

STEVEN COHEN

ENVIRONMENTAL policy and management is typically incremental and remedial in nature, but efforts at strategic planning, management analysis, impact projections, and impact analyses have been undertaken with varying success over the past four decades. A remedial approach to policy making seems to be a better fit than a planned approach, especially in America's federal and geographic-centric system, which is most receptive when impacts are tangible and local (e.g., an oil spill or toxic waste leak). Projected or relatively less visible global environmental problems like climate change and marine debris tend to be less successful at translating information about problems and proposed solutions into effective policies. Once environmental problems achieve institutional agenda status, their sheer complexity

I am grateful for the research and editorial assistance of Eve Solomon of the Earth Institute and the editorial assistance of Eve Warburton, a graduate student at Columbia University.

can require us to utilize carefully planned, comprehensive approaches, as we see in the cases of leaking underground storage tanks and sewage treatment.

As Sheldon Kamieniecki and Michael Kraft describe in the introduction, this volume covers the most important research areas in the literature on environmental policy. This chapter focuses on strategic planning and environmental impact assessments, two essential policy-making devices. Other chapters in this section explain the use of additional analytic policy-making tools, and the rest of this volume demonstrates how policy-making tools fit into the greater context of the United States political structure. This chapter provides an understanding of the characteristics and use of strategic planning, information, and analysis as they play out in the greater environmental-policy-making system in the United States.

More specifically, this chapter discusses the use of environmental planning and analysis efforts in the U.S. policy-making system. The chapter begins with an examination of the incremental nature of environmental policy development and describes how the complexity and scientific uncertainty of environmental problems influences policy formulation and implementation. Next, it addresses two important policy-making tools: strategic planning and environmental impact assessment. I then use a series of case studies to illustrate the factors that condition the success and failure of analysis in environmental policy and administration. In some instances these analytic tools contribute to success, and in other cases they are largely irrelevant. Throughout the chapter I discuss what we know and do not know about environmental planning and analysis. Additionally, I identify potential directions for future research.

1. The Incremental Development of Environmental Policy

Even in a complex problem area like environmental protection, where information is critical, there are limits to our ability to collect, analyze, and especially utilize information in policy making. In most places, and certainly in the United States, environmental policy rarely follows a trajectory from values-based goal to implemented policy; at times it looks more like a meandering series of incremental steps that vacillate between contradictory goals. The linear "rational-comprehensive" decision-making process is unrealistic in its assumption that policy makers possess intellectual capacities and sources of information that allow them to consider every policy option and its potential outcome (Lindblom 1959, 80). Offering an alternative, Braybrooke and Lindblom describe most policy making as "decision-making through small or incremental moves on particular problems rather than through a comprehensive reform program" (1963, 71). Incremental policy theory characterizes policy making as "serial," "remedial," and "exploratory," moving *"away* from social ills rather than moving *toward* a known and relatively stable goal" (Braybrooke and Lindblom 1963, 71). Incremental decisions are made in a piecemeal fashion that avoids revolutionary large-scale change and allows the policy maker to minimize risk by taking many tentative small steps instead of a few deliberate large leaps. In this sense, policy does not solve problems; it simply ameliorates them. For example, New York City had over 2,000 homicides in 1992 and around 500 homicides in 2010. Obviously, this problem is less serious today than it was 20 years ago. But for 500 dead people and their families, the problem of homicide has not been solved. Similarly, environmental policy reduces but never eliminates pollution and other forms of environmental degradation.

Some scholars argue that incrementalism is too messy to accomplish certain types of policy change. Dror claims that incremental policy theory does not apply to three typical scenarios: (1) when a change in social values invalidates formerly accepted policy, such as women's suffrage laws; (2) when there are no past policies to work from, as was the case with many 2010 financial reform laws; and (3) when societal technology or knowledge advances beyond current policy constrictions, as in the case of laws that were created when it was first understood that smoking is unhealthy (1964, 154). Further, Dror (1964) argues that incremental policy making functions well only when there is a high level of political stability, continuity, and public satisfaction with current policies. Other critics claim that incremental policies lack a society wide regulatory center or guidance and often reflect consent among partisans rather than popular interest (e.g., Etzioni 1967, 387).

Many environmental advocates claim that interrelated environmental protection issues require sweeping revolutionary change, not small uncoordinated steps. Incremental policy making is spatially fragmented due to the different jurisdictions of city or state government, and spatial fragmentation creates obstacles for policy makers addressing a ubiquitous problem with many sources, such as climate change. According to Coglianese and D'Ambrosio, employing incremental policy to address large-scale environmental problems like climate change, air quality, and water quality can result in the following six outcomes:

1. Non-effect: incremental state and federal policies are not coordinated enough to be effective.
2. Leakage: a climate change policy in one jurisdiction makes pollution in an adjacent jurisdiction worse.
3. Climate Side Effects: hastily adopted policies carry the risk of unintended consequences that exacerbate climate change.
4. Other Side Effects: unintended human or environmental health risks.
5. Lock-In: dependence on one policy prevents or inhibits superior alternatives.
6. Lulling: incremental improvements can lull the public into thinking that climate change is being addressed when it is actually being addressed inadequately. (Coglianese and D'Ambrosio 2008, 1418–1425)

While some believe that incremental policy is inadequate to deal with climate change and other environmental problems, its critics present few viable alternatives. It is unlikely that people will reduce their resource consumption automatically and without incentive. A system of benign totalitarianism, in which environmental priorities reign above all other societal needs, is not a viable alternative; and a system of mass participatory democracy, in which a society might unite to support a single cause, seems equally unlikely. For the most part, we are stuck with the muddled, partial, and incremental politics that define U.S. politics. As Lindblom (1979) writes, it is more promising to work within the preexisting incremental policy framework than it is to turn away from it completely. Protecting the environment and promoting sustainable development will require incremental policy making (Cohen 2006, 18). In the end, we need to ensure that the perfect does not become the enemy of the good. Incrementalism describes how policy tends to be made. It is reality, it is not an ideal.

The major exception to incrementalism takes place during emergencies, crises, and what Braybrooke and Lindblom call "grand opportunities." During these periods, people and institutions are capable of nonincremental leaps and impressive feats of innovation and change. The transition of America's wartime economy in the early 1940s is an example of such a period of time. The immediate aftermath of the 2001 attack on New York's World Trade Center provides another example. The difficulty with these crisis mobilizations is that they exhaust people and organizations and cannot be sustained. Charles O. Jones (1974, 438–464) observes that the 1970 Clean Air Act was a nonincremental leap over previous air legislation. In his view, the extent of public concern regarding air quality created a "grand opportunity" for change and for successful problem solving. He termed this process "speculative augmentation." What had been a poorly understood issue was transformed by popular awareness into a solvable problem. While we saw this with the 1970 clean air legislation, we did not see it in 2010 when the U.S. Senate considered enacting climate change legislation. Scholars interested in this field should consider researching the ways in which current energy crises such as the oil spill in the Gulf of Mexico and the nuclear crisis in Japan affect policy makers' reliance on the use of incrementalism.

Despite its limits, incrementalism should be seen as the default position for environmental policy making. Strategic planning and environmental impact assessments must be grafted onto this incremental framework. The ability of the system to collect, analyze, and absorb scientific and other information is a major limitation on the use of analytic methods in environmental policy making.

2. COMPLEXITY, UNCERTAINTY, AND SOCIAL LEARNING IN ENVIRONMENTAL POLICY

Environmental policy problems differ from traditional scientific problems because they are complex, variable, and uncertain (Funtowicz and Ravetz 2011, paragraph 1). When searching for the key to a traditional scientific puzzle, a researcher uses the scientific method, holding some variables equal while manipulating others in order to reveal a causal relationship. However, the reductionist scientific method does not work well for holistic, interconnected ecological systems. Environmental issues have many inputs and interdependencies, are global or multinational in scale, and have long-term, unforeseeable impacts (Jager 1998, 143). As Arrow et al. explain, "We are relatively ignorant concerning relationships in ecosystems and are likely to underestimate the list of services they provide" (2000, 1402). When studying environmental issues, it is nearly impossible to isolate one variable or reduce an environmental system to a form simple enough to uncover causality. As a result, quantitative data regarding "baselines" of undisturbed systems, changes in disturbed systems, and environmental effects is typically inaccurate, if it exists at all (Leinfelner 1990, 7).

Policy makers sometimes rely on results produced in controlled experiments to help decide which technologies are dangerous and should be regulated. Scientists and policy makers must use methods of simplification to make sense of data and must choose scales of space, time, and organization to minimize complexity (Arrow et al. 2000, 1403). The most reliable environmental evidence is based on controlled experiments and mathematical models. The experiments are specific, reductionist, and replicable. Mathematical models are also replicable, but due to their assumptions, they often have a high level of uncertainty.

The level of scientific uncertainty influences how information is used to address environmental issues (Layzer 2002, 230). When harm cannot be proven, a lack of certainty often inhibits environmental protection policy. During the George W. Bush administration, his top political people perceived a lack of scientific certainty about the realities and causes of global warming. As scientific consensus emerged and uncertainty was reduced, the government had more incentive to address global warming (Cohen 2006, 30). According to William D. Ruckelshaus, former administrator of the U.S. Environmental Protection Agency (EPA), "EPA's laws often assume, indeed demand, a certainty of protection greater than science can provide with the current state of knowledge" (1983, 1026). Environmental risk managers often must make decisions with incomplete knowledge and sometimes great uncertainty (Chapman et al. 1998, 99). The high level of complexity is such that "environmental policy can not be shaped around the idealized linear path of the gathering and then the application of knowledge" (Funtowicz and Ravetz 2011, paragraph 14).

There has been increased pressure for policy makers to switch from an "end of pipe" environmental regulation style to "upstream" environmental regulation—to prevent problems rather than fix them once they already exist (Wynne 1992, 111). One upstream policy strategy is the precautionary principle, generally defined as "preventative action in the face of uncertainty and reversing the burden of proof" (Tickner and Geiser 2004, 803). While environmental agencies in the United States tend to focus on risk analysis and have not widely adopted the precautionary principle, it was internationally declared in the Rio Declaration on Environment and Development as a means of coping with the setbacks caused by uncertainty:

> In order to protect the environment, the precautionary approach shall be widely applied by States according to their capabilities. Where there are threats of serious or irreversible damage, lack of full scientific certainty shall not be used as a reason for postponing cost-effective measures to prevent environmental degradation. (United Nations Conference on Environment and Development 1992, 879)

This is, of course, the method used to license new drugs, which are tested in laboratories and on animals before being introduced for human use. Our economy is run a little differently. We are all canaries in the mine shaft. This is an old story. The mine boss drops a cage holding the live canary into the coal mine and then hoists it back up a few minutes later. If the canary lives, it is assumed it is safe to send the miners into the mine. If the canary dies, we assume the mine is leaking poison gas. We do not use the precautionary principle to regulate the environment; instead, we wait until the canary dies, until harm is proven, before we act to ameliorate harm. Environmental impact assessments project the impact before action is taken, but they are often ignored. Generally, only proven impacts have the political potency required to modify economic activity.

Social learning is another strategy for dealing with the inevitability of uncertainty; social learning involves strategies of flexibility, decentralization, and opening up to many stakeholders (Arentsen et al. 2000, 599). Popular consensus for protecting the environment is strong in the United States. This type of consensus facilitates social learning and allows policy makers to make decisions that override doubts about scientific uncertainty. Daniel Fiorino (2006) argues that U.S. environmental policy has shifted from technical policy learning, in which policy makers respond to environmental problems with more regulation, oversight, and enforcement; to conceptual learning, in which policy objectives are debated, perspectives are shifted, and strategies are reformatted; to social learning, an inclusive and open way of learning from others in order to deal with environmental uncertainty. Social learning involves open relationships between industry and government, as well as recognition of uncertainty in our knowledge of problems and capacity for dealing with them (Fiorino 2006). In many respects the emerging field of sustainability management is built on the social learning success of the environmental movement. The idea that ecosystems are our source of wealth and must be carefully managed is a direct result of a half century of environmental education and social learning. Chapter 9 elaborates on this idea, addressing the societal shift in environmental concerns from the 1970s epoch of clean air and water to a second epoch defined by a push for regulatory reform to the modern epoch of moving toward sustainable communities.

3. Standard Operating Procedures and Analytic Tools for Dealing with Complexity and Uncertainty

In an incremental-policy-making environment, which, if any, analytic tools can environmental regulators use to increase the speed of incremental steps or even achieve rational, comprehensive goals? In this section, I discuss two types of tools that environmental policy makers employ to enhance environmental policy making and implementation: strategic regulatory planning and environmental impact statements.

3.1. Strategic Regulatory Planning

Strategic regulatory planning is an effort by government to develop a comprehensive strategy for influencing behavior (Cohen and Kamieniecki 1991, 12–13). Mintzberg synthesizes the many definitions of "strategy" to formulate this one: "a deliberate conscious set of guidelines that determines decisions into the future" (1978, 935). Strategic planning allows environmental regulators to "place the promulgation of formal regulations within the context of other tools available to affect behavior" of regulated parties (Cohen, Kamieniecki, and Cahn 2005, 26). A strategic plan projects the ways in which the government will influence regulated parties, and the strategies—such as funding, penalties, technical assistance, exhortation, and publicity—that it will use to do so.

Strategic planning can be very effective when it is properly implemented. Cohen, Kamieniecki, and Cahn (2005) present a model for successful strategic regulatory planning, as based on a schematic outline of political strategy formulations developed by MacMillan and Jones (1986) and research by Hoffer and Schendel (1978). According to these analysts, policy makers should follow seven steps when developing a strategic plan:

1. Problem Recognition: What issue are we trying to solve?
2. Identification of Parties: Who does the problem affect and who will help solve it?
3. Historical Analysis: How have different levels of government and other involved parties responded to this issue in the past? Why?
4. Situational Analysis: What are the desired outcomes? What are each party's motivations and goals?
5. Strategic Regulation Formulation: What are the conditions in the regulated community, regulating agency, and outside community? How will these conditions affect alternative regulatory devices, and which regulatory devices are most appropriate in this case?
6. Perform an Ex Ante Review to address the appropriateness and feasibility of the regulatory plan before implementation.
7. Perform an Ex Post Review/Revision to assess how successful the regulatory plan has been at modifying behavior.

Regulation works best when it draws from knowledge of the firms that are being regulated and the communities within which those firms operate. With this knowledge in hand, environmental policy makers can create dynamic strategies that are appropriate for the community they regulate. These seven steps can help policy makers develop strategic plans that are well suited to the regulated party and regulatory agency.

Strategic planning is grafted onto an incremental policy and decision-making process by focusing on near-term plans as well as longer-term goals. The strategic planning processes that are most successful are fully integrated, routine elements of an organization's management system. An organization should update its strategy in light of changing internal and external conditions every 3, 6, or 12 months. The key is to incorporate analytic and thought processes into organizational standard operating procedures. A standard operating procedure (SOP) is a preformed response to a particular stimulus that the organization frequently confronts. A well-functioning strategic planning process is a macro-level SOP that is a routine response to frequent external or interorganizational change. Strategic Planning is a process for changing the micro-level day-to-day SOPs of the organization.

3.2. Environmental Impact Analysis

A second analytic tool that is often used is the environmental impact statement (EIS). In the press release on November 23, 2010, *White House Council on Environmental Quality Issues Guidance to Help Federal Agencies Ensure the Integrity of Environmental Reviews*, the Executive Office of the President's Council on Environmental Quality explains that the National Environmental Policy Act of 1969 (NEPA) "requires Federal agencies to analyze their proposed actions to determine if they could have significant environmental effects." The act uses environmental impact statements as a tool to assess the environmental impact of actions taken by government or by private organizations working with government. Agencies must file an environmental impact statement for any proposed development that significantly affects the environment. When federal actions do not necessarily have a significant environmental impact, an environmental assessment (EA) is required to provide evidence and analysis for exemption from the preparation of an EIS. If government determines that an action will have a significant environmental impact during the environmental assessment process, the federal agency must perform an EIS. Agencies can also grant a categorical exclusion exempting categories of activities that are known not to affect the human environment. The U.S. EPA defines an environmental impact statement as "a detailed analysis that serves to insure that the policies and goals defined in NEPA are infused into the ongoing programs and actions of the federal agency.... The EIS should provide a discussion of significant environmental impacts and reasonable alternatives" (U.S. EPA 2010a). The act decrees that the federal agencies must use every means possible to maintain human environmental health. In order to accomplish this goal, NEPA requires that all federal government agencies use a "systematic, interdisciplinary approach which will insure the integrated use of the natural and social sciences and the environmental design arts in planning and in decision making which have an impact on man's environment" (42 USC § 4332). In other words, environmental impact statements should be scientific evaluations. The creation of an environmental impact statement forces parties to take responsibility for how their actions affect the environment, to create alternatives to the proposed action, to acknowledge any adverse environmental effects necessary to the proposal, and to recognize the short-term and long-term effects as well as any irreversible commitments of resources that an action may necessitate. By attaining scientific knowledge, government agencies can make informed environmental decisions and lessen the chance of damaging the environment.

Environmental impact statement results are published in a Record of Decision (ROD), which also explains any practical means taken to avoid or minimize environmental harm in each case. RODs are published in the Federal Register or on the agency's website (Council on Environmental Quality 2007, 19). However, NEPA's power to prevent environmental harm is limited. As Coggins and Wilkinson observe, "Even if the EIS reveals that a proposed action could be disastrous environmentally, the statute imposes no obligation on the agency to act differently—or at least no obligation that a court will enforce" (1987, 335).

While NEPA only governs the actions of government agencies, the website of Beveridge and Diamond, one of the most prominent environmental law firms in the United States, explains why private companies too must develop environmental impact statements:

> Because of the need to obtain permits or approvals from federal agencies, private developers, natural resources companies, and transportation agencies often must get through a lengthy and costly NEPA process before they can even think about turning dirt.... Over thirty years ago, Congress passed landmark legislation that ordered federal government agencies to consider the impacts to the environment of all proposals for "major federal action." The National Environmental Policy Act (NEPA) is considered the father of all environmental statutes, and it led to the passage of analogous state and local statutes that require government agencies to consider the environmental impacts of various types of development projects.... Private development often requires government approval, and the preparation of an environmental impact review document. The environmental impact review process frequently covers the full spectrum of natural resource issues and socio-economic impacts. (Beveridge and Diamond 2001, paragraph 1)

Scholars identify a number of ways in which environmental impact statements fall short of their goals. Steinemann (2001) claims that environmental impact assessment suffers from a lack of alternatives development; policy makers analyze developed alternatives instead of generating new alternatives and therefore fail to "illuminate crucial tradeoffs, incorporate public values, and explore more environmentally sound approaches" (2001, 4). Phillips and Randolph (2000) identify three main critiques of NEPA in the literature: (1) agencies do not engage the NEPA process early enough in their planning process; (2) there is a lack of rigorous science and use of ecological principles in the analysis of ecological systems and natural resources; and (3) there is little emphasis on the NEPA's original goals, which are often ignored by federal agencies or overturned by U.S. Supreme Court decisions (2000, 1). Friesema and Culhane (1976) also argue that when viewed from a rational decision-making perspective, environmental impact statements fail because they do not produce the best possible scientific results.

In my view, these critiques somewhat miss the mark. Public administrative behavior closely resembles political rather than scientific management, and when viewed from an incremental policy perspective, NEPA has created an effective way to improve policy makers' social and environmental sensitivity. The point of the requirement, as indicated in the title of Serge Taylor's (1984) history of environmental impact statements, is to "make bureaucracies think." It requires agencies and, in the case of large-scale land developers, some private firms to step back for a few months or years and consider the environmental impacts of their actions. It also allows the views of political opponents to gain some legitimacy on the political agenda. The Environmental Impact Statement is a process requirement, not a substantive requirement. While the Environmental Impact Statement does not assure that environmental impacts will have the proper influence in a decision-making process, it does assure that environmental impacts cannot be completely ignored. The Environmental Impact Statement falls short of the rational ideal, yet it is a useful comprehensive policy tool that can influence standard incremental policy processes. It can cause a developer or an agency to modify a project in order to reduce its impact, and in some cases to end a project entirely. An interesting direction for further research might explore policy alternatives to Environmental Impact Assessments and what the success rates of these alternatives have been in protecting ecologically vulnerable land from development.

4. Applying Analytical Tools to Deal with Complex Environmental Decisions: Case Studies

This section presents case studies demonstrating how analytic tools have been used to address environmental problems. I will analyze each case in terms of its overall environmental results and then discuss how analytic tools were used, misused, or ignored during the case. The case of nonpoint source water pollution demonstrates how a lack of federal oversight and planning can impair the cost-effectiveness of environmental infrastructure. The case of technology regulation and industry partnership in the Minerals Management Service demonstrates how economic interests can distort information in decision making. Here, we must pay attention to the institutional arrangements within which analytic information is provided. In contrast, relatively successful cases, such as the EPA's handling of underground storage tanks and sewage treatment, demonstrate conditions under which planning can have an impact (tanks), while indicating how the lack of planning can distort the cost-effectiveness of policy outcomes (sewage).

4.1. Nonpoint Source Pollution

Before the environmental movement, the waterways in the United States were heavily polluted. In New York City in the 1960s, the Hudson River was one of the most polluted rivers in the United States. In Cleveland, the Cuyahoga River actually caught fire. When the nation finally decided that something had to be done about water pollution, a number of laws were passed to address the problem, and while the laws dealt well with point source pollution, the pollution that for the most part came out of pipes, the approach to ameliorating nonpoint source pollution was more complicated and has been less successful.

Water pollution in the United States is primarily regulated by the Clean Water Act (CWA), which was passed in 1972, "to restore the nation's waters to their natural chemical, physical and biological state" (33 USC § 1251). The Clean Water Act does a decent job regulating point source water pollution, which it defines as "any discernible, confined and discrete conveyance, including but not limited to any pipe, ditch, channel, tunnel, conduit, well, discrete fissure, container...from which pollutants are or may be discharged" (33 USC § 1362(14)). The Clean Water Act regulates point source polluters by requiring that any facility intending to discharge into the nation's waters must obtain a permit before beginning its operations, and must comply with federal or state water quality limits or industry-specific, technology-based limits on the discharged pollutant (U.S. EPA 2010b).

Nonpoint source pollution is also subject to the Clean Water Act but is more difficult to regulate because it comes from many diffuse sources, is carried by surface or underground waterways, and includes a number of different pollutants, including fertilizer, grease, waste from livestock, and urban discharge. Because there is no easily identified source, nonpoint source pollution cannot be regulated by giving specific polluters discharge permits. Instead, states must regulate nonpoint source polluters, such as agricultural farms, based on water quality in the area.

Nonpoint source pollution was originally addressed in section 208 of the Clean Water Act, which allows states to set their own water quality limits, and gives them tools and funds to employ general land use regulations and Best Management Practices (BMPs). Under section 208, states and localities were required to identify nonpoint sources and to control them through land use regulation and other means. One scholar explains, "the states had adopted a variety of nonpoint source control programs, but...the programs were erratic and success marginal" (Mandelker 1989, 495). When states failed to identify and regulate nonpoint sources systematically, Congress added section 319 of the Clean Water Act in 1979. Section 319 addresses the need for greater federal leadership to focus the state and local nonpoint source efforts by offering federal grant money for assistance with monitoring and regulating nonpoint source pollution. Despite the provision of federal funds, section 319 still leaves most of the regulatory responsibility up to the states.

A number of other statutes regulate nonpoint source pollution, including the National Forest Management Act (NFMA) of 1976, which requires that the Forest Service use Best Management Practices to protect bodies of water from pollutants.

However, the Forest Management Act does not require the Forest Service to monitor best management practices and lacks enforceable standards (Styron 1993, 101).
The Federal Land Policy and Management Act of 1976 and the Wild and Scenic
Rivers Act of 1968 also include measures to protect water systems from pollution.
The Environmental Protection Agency admits, "We did not do enough to control
pollution from diffuse, nonpoint, sources. Today, nonpoint source (NPS) pollution
remains the Nation's largest source of water quality problems. It is the main reason
that approximately 40 percent of our surveyed rivers, lakes, and estuaries are not
clean enough to meet basic uses such as fishing or swimming" (U.S. EPA 2009a, 1).

Nonpoint sources are difficult to regulate and require the type of large-scale
behavioral change that typically the EPA has not been able to accomplish. Runoff
from our highways can be collected and treated, but secondary roads often lack the
adequate drainage systems they need to be effective. Even worse, the EPA's regulatory
structure and standard procedures promote easier-to-monitor regulation of point
sources through requirements for "gray infrastructure," instead of potentially more
cost-effective "green infrastructure" that reduces nonpoint sources of pollution.

Westchester County, New York, provides a case in point. The county was mandated by the state and federal governments to upgrade their sewer treatment plants
to reduce pollutant discharges into Long Island Sound. As a lower-cost alternative,
the county proposed an imaginative series of ecosystem restorations to reduce nonpoint discharges in the same body of water. The green infrastructure investment
cost less and produced more pollution reduction but was rejected by the state and
federal government. They considered the impact of the ecosystem restoration project to be too uncertain and difficult to measure. In 2011, New York City received a
similar reaction to its "green infrastructure" plan, which provided a lower-cost but
more effective approach to controlling combined sewage overflow. During 2012,
EPA's resistence to green infrastructure eased a bit and New York City was allowed
to pursue a combined green and gray strategy on combined sewage overflow.

The historic bias toward gray infrastructure is not based on hard information
that enhanced sewage treatment works better than ecosystem restoration. Rather, it
reflects the government's political and institutional history of water management
planning and sewage treatment construction. In 1972, the Federal Water Pollution
Control Act was enacted over President Richard Nixon's veto. While the president
could not stop the bill, he worked hard to impair its implementation. Initially, he
impounded all of the environmental planning funds that were to be spent developing areawide water quality management plans under section 208 of the act.[1] These
regional plans were designed to control nonpoint sources and also to decide where
to locate sewage treatment grants funded under section 201 of the act. However,
due to the influence of contractors and construction trade unions, Nixon did not
impound the billions of dollars allocated to build new treatment plants. A great
tragedy of many of those decisions is that the early plants were built without careful

---

1. The Supreme Court eventually forced President Nixon to release the funds that he had
   impounded.

environmental planning. For the most part, they were funded and sited in response to political rather than environmental criteria. While sewage treatment has successfully reduced water pollution in the United States, a carefully planned and integrated water management system could have produced more cost-effective reductions in pollution. This case illustrates the resistance of policy processes to new information—particularly that which is deemed uncertain—and new practices and, therefore, the limits of analysis in incremental environmental policy processes.

4.2. Sewage Treatment

While one might assume that the program to provide federal funding for sewage treatment was a response to data on the health effects of raw sewage, in all likelihood the program was seen as a way to generate political support by funding the construction of a public works project. The government began subsidizing publicly owned treatment works (POTW) after World War II, when the Water Pollution Control Act of 1948 appropriated $22.5 million annually for loans to states for treatment plant construction. By 1968, funding increased to $3.4 billion and municipalities could obtain federal grants that covered up to 55 percent of their treatment plant construction costs. In the 1970s, two important pieces of legislation addressed the issue of water pollution: the Federal Water Pollution Control Act of 1972 and the Clean Water Act (CWA) amendments of 1977 (US EPA 2009b).

During the 1970s, the federal share increased to 75 percent, plants could receive retroactive payments, and grants of up to $9.75 billion were authorized (Bhansali et al. 1992, 175). In 1972, legislation imposed fees on industrial wastewater dischargers. As the government imposed fees on violators, it also continued to fund wastewater treatment plants through the 1977 Clean Water Act Amendments and the 1987 Clean Water Act reauthorization. During the 1970s and 1980s the federal government funded the construction of wastewater treatment facilities throughout the country (Spellman 2009, 9). During those two decades, the federal government distributed more than $60 billion to cities to make sure that wastewater would not affect human health (Duhigg 2009, 1). In recent years these grant programs have been eliminated and replaced by low-interest loan programs.

While waste treatment is a major environmental regulation success story, problems remain. First, plant capacity is not always well planned to meet needs. Some communities have too much capacity, and some have too little. Moreover, many of the country's sewer systems were built over a century ago and often cannot handle the large amount of sewage produced by today's populations, especially when the sewage combines with rainwater to result in what are known as "combined sewer overflows." Combined sewage overflows (CSOs) happen in sewers that are designed to collect rainwater runoff, domestic sewage, and industrial wastewater in the same system of pipes. Combined sewer systems usually transport waste and excess water to a treatment plant, but during periods of heavy rain or snowmelt, these old sewer systems often overflow, spilling untreated waste into surrounding waterways including groundwater that people drink or rivers they use for recreation (U.S. EPA 2011).

The National Pollutant Discharge Elimination System (NPDES) program established by the Clean Water Act issues federal permits that control the discharges from wastewater treatment plants. The EPA's Combined Sewer Overflow Control Policy provides guidance to municipalities and state and federal permitting authorities on how to meet water pollution control goals effectively. This Combined Sewer Overflow Control Policy uses four principles to ensure effectiveness on the local level: (1) clear levels of control; (2) flexibility based on the site; (3) sensitivity to community's financial capability; and (4) review and revision of water quality standards (U.S. EPA 2002).

As noted above, in the United States, federal funding provides essential aid to jurisdictions that cannot afford to develop their own wastewater treatment plants independently. However, in 2011, combined sewer overflows remain a prominent problem, and there is still a need for further mitigation. For example, New York City estimates that it requires over $50 billion to prevent the sewer overflows that occur approximately every other time the city sees rain. The traditional approach to dealing with pollution control is not the entire solution: American cities and the federal government should look to green, as well as gray, infrastructure. Green infrastructure includes porous concrete and green medians that absorb rainfall instead of sending it into the sewers, preventing overflow without the need to fund major sewage system reconstruction.

In the case of sewage treatment, success is due not to sophisticated use of analysis, strategic planning, and environmental information, but to old-fashioned pork-barrel politics. Interest groups and construction firms make money and get jobs from pouring concrete and building facilities. Cost-effectiveness is not sought or achieved; in essence, the problem is bludgeoned into submission. One could argue that this type of solution is a good match for the institutional arrangements and organizational capacities of America's federal system. It takes its place as one of hundreds of federal grant-in-aid programs for infrastructure, similar to aid provided for roads, rails, and ports. But as we see in the case of water quality planning under section 208 of the 1972 Water Pollution Control Act and today's rejection of green infrastructure by EPA lawyers and bureaucrats, the sewage treatment program is almost designed to resist sophisticated planning and environmental impact assessment.

4.3. Regulating Technologies in the Minerals Management Services

The 2010 BP oil spill in the Gulf of Mexico provides an example of the impact of entrenched economic interests on the use of information in policy making. The economic value of oil leases and the need to regulate the drilling process creates a conflict of interest if both processes are managed by the same organization.

Information about the failed safety equipment on the oil rig that was drilling for oil in the Gulf of Mexico that either was not received or was ignored by regulators in the Department of Interior. Economic interests captured the agency empowered to regulate their activities, leaving the drilling contractors and oil companies to self-regulate. While self-regulation worked in many cases, it failed spectacularly during the 2010 BP Gulf oil spill.

In 1982, the Commission on Fiscal Accountability passed the Oil and Gas Royalty Management Act in order to fix the broken system of collecting oil and gas royalties. The Minerals Management Service (MMS) would implement the new act and help meet the nation's energy needs. The Minerals Management Service had two conflicting responsibilities: (1) to collect royalties from oil companies operating within the United States, and (2) to protect United States lands and waters from the companies operating on them. Its dual purpose put the Minerals Management Service in a difficult position, especially as its revenues from collecting royalties on oil and gas soared.

The Minerals Management Service was created by James G. Watt, secretary of the interior under President Reagan. Watt was concerned with the availability of oil in the United States and wanted to make sure that the agency provided enough energy resources for the country. The first director of MMS was William D. Bettenberg. Setting up the agency, Bettenberg relied heavily on industry standards simply because few people besides industry engineers understood drilling technology. As the technology evolved, the agency struggled to keep up, and it continued to create regulations based on industry standards. The Clinton administration reduced regulations and worked to form stronger ties between industry and government; as a result, the Minerals Management Service lost one-tenth of its staff during a time when it was under pressure to increase royalty collection.

In 1995, the Interior Department began to emphasize a system of royalty collection called performance-based regulation, using "any mechanism which attempts to link rewards (generally funding) to desired performance" (Austin 1994, 2). In the Minerals Management Service, rewards were the royalties flowing from oil and gas companies to the federal government. The desired performance was twofold: good drilling practice and the maximization of revenues. The Minerals Management Service used "performance goals" instead of "prescriptive rules" to regulate oil and gas agency actions; according to Blumenthal and Bolstad, "Performance goals leave it to the offshore drilling industry to prevent blowouts....Prescriptive rules detail how it's supposed to go—and hold the industry accountable if it doesn't" (2010, 1). Performance regulation hands the means of disaster prevention over to the industry, which must then regulate itself. Evidence of inadequate regulatory practice is apparent. In 1997 the Minerals Management Service granted three categorical exclusions; by 2000 these exceptions numbered 765.

In 1995, the Deep Water Royalty Relief Act increased the amount of deepwater drilling ventures. It was followed by deepwater royalty relief in 2002 and 2004. During the George W. Bush administration, studies funded in part by the Minerals Management Service indicated that certain technological advances were not being adequately regulated. Two studies revealed the frequent failure of the blind shear ram, the piece of equipment that caused the blowout of the Macondo well in the Gulf of Mexico in 2010 (Urbina et al. 2010). In 2003, MMS had decreed that companies would not be granted deepwater drilling privileges unless they first demonstrated the functionality of blind shear rams, but the industry engineer who approved BP's Macondo well admitted that he never had to look for proof of blind shear ram functionality during his three decades of service (Urbina et al. 2010). The neglected blind shear ram is one of many examples of the ways in which the Minerals Management Service failed to regulate oil extraction technologies. It is now clear that adopting industry standards did not provide the agency with strong enough regulatory tools to prevent environmental disaster effectively.

The well explosion and blowout killed 11 people and significantly damaged ecosystems in the Gulf of Mexico. While information about the unsafe practices aboard the rig was available and known to corporate decision makers, it appears that government regulators were unaware of these issues and therefore unable to regulate. The extreme bias toward the economic benefits of oil drilling dominated the decision-making process and had the effect of screening out information about potential risks. These types of institutional biases provide a major constraint on the use of analytic information in decision making.

4.4. Leaking Underground Storage Tanks

While the Minerals Management Services and the treatment of nonpoint source pollution provide examples of unsuccessful regulation, a more promising view of our government's regulatory success is apparent in the case of the EPA's regulation of leaking underground storage tanks. During the 1970s, environmental regulation in the United States focused on visible pollution—discolored rivers and smoggy skies. In the 1980s, cleanup initiatives shifted toward less obvious polluted resources, such as groundwater, which was found to be polluted by leaking underground storage tanks.

Underground storage tanks are the preferred method of gasoline storage at gasoline stations because they save surface space and are less prone to explosion than above-ground storage. In the early 1980s, the EPA discovered that a substantial portion of underground gasoline storage tanks were leaking and were contaminating groundwater, creating a serious public health risk. The EPA estimated that more than a quarter of underground tanks were leaking into drinking water. In addition, the potentially contaminated groundwater was also used for irrigation, livestock, aquaculture, manufacturing, mining, thermoelectric power generation, and domestic purposes (Kenny et al. 2009, 4).

Prior to 1984, federal legislation did not regulate underground storage tanks—the Resource Conservation and Recovery Act of 1976 only regulates wastes, and petroleum was not considered a waste because it is a useful product. The Clean Water Act of 1972 only required owners of very large tanks to take measures to prevent corrosion. The act also applied only to tanks that served as a direct source of pollution into navigable waters; because underground storage containers are classified as nonpoint pollution sources, the act had no regulatory power over them.

Title 1 of the 1984 Hazardous and Solid Waste Amendments to the Solid Waste Disposal Act of 1976 initiated the regulation of underground gasoline and chemical storage tanks. The Superfund Amendments and Reauthorization Act of 1986 provided cleanup funds when tank owners could not afford a cleanup or when no tank owners could be found. The problem of underground storage tanks had three dimensions that reached the political agenda: (1) developing standards for new and existing tanks to prevent future leaks; (2) clarifying the liability incurred by tank owners; and (3) how to assign responsibility for the payment and execution of cleaning up the damage (Cohen 2005, 66). The diversity of gasoline distributors (tanks belonged to gasoline retail facilities, wholesalers, truck and automobile rental companies, and agencies of government) complicated tank management, and it took the EPA until 1998 to finalize their regulatory strategy.

The EPA approached the problem of leaking storage tanks by working closely with industry and state and local governments to ensure the setting of tank standards, to require tank owners to implement a method of detecting leaks, and to force tank owners to demonstrate their financial capacity to clean up the tanks. First, it commissioned the National American Academy of Public Administration to do a study of the tank issue. The academy worked with the EPA to develop a strategic regulatory plan for regulating underground tanks. The EPA created the Office of Underground Storage Tanks to focus exclusively on the leaking tank issue, and a $100 million trust fund created by Congress in 1986 facilitated the success and expansion of the regulatory program. In implementing the regulation of new tanks and the cleanup of old ones, the EPA adhered to the principles of strategic planning and implemented a far-reaching and cost-effective tank regulation program.

Each state was required to create or designate an agency that would receive notification forms from tank owners, under section 9002(b) of Subtitle 1, Regulation of Underground Storage Tanks. Section 9003(g) prohibits the installation of new tanks unless they prevent corrosion and leaking. The EPA also issued performance standards for every element of underground tank systems. Tank owners were required to implement a leak-detection system and report any detected releases, as well as any corrosion (9003(c); 9003(c) (4)). The EPA was responsible for assigning parties financial responsibility for bodily injury and property damage due to releases from an underground tank; they also had the right to inspect facilities and enforce the provisions of the legislation.

Prior to underground tank regulation, approximately 46,000 tanks leaked each year. By 2009, two-thirds of active underground storage tanks were fully complying with the EPA's leak-prevention and -detection requirements. Of the 488,000 toxic waste releases reported at the beginning of the program, more than 388,000, or approximately 80 percent have been cleaned up (U.S. EPA 2010c). While tanks continue to leak in the United States, the rate of leakage has declined significantly over the past quarter century, in part due to the use of strategic planning in the formulation of this program in the late 1980s and early 1990s.

There are several reasons for this success. One is that the economic interest of tank owners in retaining their products for sale was obvious. A second reason is the superior leadership provided by the EPA's first tank office director, Ron Brand. Finally, the EPA had absorbed a number of lessons provided by previous regulatory failures.

5. CONCLUSIONS

This chapter examined two forms of environmental analysis and planning: strategic planning and environmental impact assessments. It sought to analyze the utilization of these and other less formal methods of information collection and analysis in environmental policy making and implementation. While the complexity of environmental issues makes clear the need for information, planning, and analysis, a number of political, procedural, and structural factors inhibit the use of analysis in environmental decision making. The incremental nature of policy making provides a limit on the amount of information that can be absorbed in policy making by limiting the agenda to issues of short-term immediacy. The tendency of the political process to reflect the power and interests of those with economic resources can also distort the receptivity of decision makers to certain types of information. The nature of the American political structure results in an extreme bias toward problems that are geographic in nature and can be addressed at the local level. The persistence of national sovereignty tends to reduce the political saliency of cross-border environmental issues like climate change and marine debris. Information about these issues is frequently ignored.

In the light of these constraints, how can we improve the quality of environmental policy making and management? Can it be improved? I believe it can, although the information and analysis must be designed to accommodate the constraints that incremental policy making places on our political system. An awareness of the factors that condition the acceptance of new information should inform the format, style, comprehensiveness, and detail of the analytic products provided to decision makers. For example, in assessing the risks of safety practices in deep-sea oil drilling, an emphasis on BP's potential liability for damage (now estimated to exceed $20 billion) might have been more effective than appeals to ethics or environmental stewardship. Additional research on the effective use of analysis and information in policy making is clearly called for. If we knew more about what it takes to bring information and analysis into decision making, we could improve the sophistication and quality of management decisions. Aaron Wildavsky once observed that the objective of policy analysis was to speak truth to power. That remains our objective, no matter how difficult it may be to achieve it.

REFERENCES

Arentsen, M. J., H. T. A. Bressers, and L. O'Toole. 2000. "Institutional and Policy Responses to Uncertainty in Environmental Policy: A Comparison of Dutch and U.S. Styles." *Policy Studies Journal* 28 (3): 597–611.

Arrow, K., G. Daily, P. Dasgupta, S. Levin, K. G. Maler, D. Starrett, T. Sterner, and T. Tietenberg. 2000. "Managing Ecosystem Resources." *Environmental Science and Technology* 34 (8): 1401–1406.

Austin, T. 1994. "Performance Based Regulation: A Discussion Paper." September. www.raponline.org/docs/RAP_Austin_PerformanceBasedRegulation_1994_09. pdf (accessed January 25, 2011).

Bhansali, A., C. Diamond, and B. Yandle. 1992. "Sewage Treatment as an Industry Subsidy." *Economic Geography* 68 (2): 174–187.

Beveridge and Diamond. 2001. "NEPA and State NEPA—Land Use." Available at www.bdlaw.com/practices-71.html (accessed January 25, 2011).

Blumenthal, L., and E. Bolstad. 2010. "U.S. Agency Let Oil Industry Write Offshore Drilling Rules." McClatchy, May 10. Available at http://www.mcclatchydc. com/2010/05/10/93859/us-agency-lets-oil-industry-write.html (accessed January 25, 2011).

Braybrooke, D., and C. E. Lindblom. 1963. *A Strategy of Decision.* New York: Free Press of Glencoe.

Chapman, P. M., A. Fairbrother, and D. Brown. 1998. "A Critical Evaluation of Safety (Uncertainty) Factors for Ecological Risk Assessment." *Environmental Toxicology and Chemistry* 17: 99–108.

Coggins, G. C., C. F. Wilkinson, and J. D. Leshy. *Federal Public Land and Resources Law.* 4th ed. New York: Foundation.

Coglianese, C., and J. D'Ambrosio. 2008. "Policymaking under Pressure: The Perils of Incremental Responses to Climate Change." *Connecticut Law Review* 40 (5): 1411–1429.

Cohen, S. A. 2006. *Understanding Environmental Policy.* New York: Columbia University Press.

Cohen, S. A., and S. Kamieniecki. 1991. *Strategic Planning in Environmental Regulation.* Boulder, CO: Westview.

Cohen, S. A., S. Kamieniecki, and M. A. Cahn. 2005. *Strategic Planning in Environmental Regulation.* Cambridge, MA: MIT Press.

Dror, Y. 1964. "Muddling Through—'Science' or Inertia?" *Public Administration Review* 24 (3): 153–157.

Duhigg, C. 2009. "As Sewers Fill, Waste Poisons Waterways." *New York Times,* November 22.

Etzioni, Amitai. 1967. "Mixed-Scanning: A 'Third' Approach to Decision-Making." *Public Administration Review* 27 (5): 385–392.

Fiorino, D. J. 2006. *The New Environmental Regulation.* Cambridge, MA: MIT Press.

Friesema, P. H., and P. J. Culhane. 1976. "Social Impacts, Politics, and the Environmental Impact Statement Process." *Natural Resources Journal* 16: 339–356.

Funtowicz, S., and J. Ravetz. 2011. "Post-Normal Science: Environmental Policy under Conditions of Complexity." NUSAP.net. Available at www.nusap.net/sections.php?op=viewarticle&artid=13 (accessed January 25, 2011).

Hoffer, C. W., and D. E. Schendel. 1978. *Strategy Formulation: Analytic Concepts.* St. Paul: West.

Jager, J. 1998. "Current Thinking on Using Scientific Findings in Environmental Policy Making." *Environmental Modeling and Assessment* 3 (3): 143–153.

Jones, C. O. 1974. "Speculative Augmentation in Federal Air Pollution Policy-Making." *Journal of Politics* 36 (2): 438–464.

Kenny, J. F., N. L. Barber, S. S. Hutson, K. S. Linsey, J. K. Lovelace, and M. A. Maupin. 2009. *Estimated Use of Water in the United States in 2005.* Reston, VA: U.S. Geological Survey.

Layzer, J. 2002. *The Environmental Case: Translating Values into Policy.* Washington, DC: CQ Press.

Leinfelner, W., ed. 1990. *Uncertainty and Quality in Science for Policy.* Dordrecht, The Netherlands: Kluwer Academic.

Lindblom, C. E. 1959. "The Science of Muddling Through." *Public Administration Review* 19 (2): 79–88.

———. 1979. "Still Muddling, Not Yet Through." *Public Administration Review* 39 (6): 517–526.

MacMillan, I. C., and P. E. Jones. 1986. *Strategy Formulation: Power and Politics.* 2nd ed. St. Paul: West.

Mandelker, D. R. 1989. "Controlling Nonpoint Source Water Pollution: Can It Be Done?" *Chicago Kent Law Review* 65: 479–502.

Mintzberg, H. 1978. "Patterns in Strategy Formation." *Management Science* 24 (9): 934–948.

Phillips, C. G., and J. Randolph. 2000. "The Relationship of Ecosystem Management to NEPA and Its Goals." *Environmental Management* 26 (1): 1–12.

Ruckelshaus, W. D. 1983. "Science, Risk, and Public Policy." *Science* 221 (4615): 1026–1028.

Spellman, F. R. 2009. *Handbook of Water and Waste Water Treatment Plant Operations.* 2nd ed. Boca Raton: Taylor & Francis Group.

Steinemann, A. 2001. "Improving Alternatives for Environmental Impact Assessment." *Environmental Impact Assessment Review* 21 (1): 3–21.

Styron, J. W. 1993. "Regulation of Nonpoint Sources of Water Pollution on Public Lands." *Naval Law Review* 41: 97–114.

Tickner, J. A., and K. Geiser. 2004. "The Precautionary Principle Stimulus for Solutions- and Alternatives-Based Environmental Policy." *Environmental Impact Assessment Review* 24 (7–8): 801–824.

United Nations Conference on Environment and Development. 1992. "Rio Declaration on Environment and Development." *International Legal Materials* 31 (4): 874–880.

U.S. Council on Environmental Quality, Executive Office of the President. 2007. *A Citizen's Guide to the NEPA: Having Your Voice Heard.* Washington, DC. Available at http://ceq.hss.doe.gov/nepa/Citizens_Guide_Dec07.pdf (accessed January 25, 2011).

———. 2010. *White House Council on Environmental Quality Issues Guidance to Help Federal Agencies Ensure the Integrity of Environmental Reviews.* Press Release.

Available at www.whitehouse.gov/administration/eop/ceq/Press_Releases/
November_23_2010 (accessed January 25, 2011).

U.S. Environmental Protection Agency. 2002. *Combined Sewer Overflows CSO
Control Policy.* Available at cfpub.epa.gov/npdes/cso/cpolicy.cfm?program_id=5
(accessed January 19, 2011).

———. 2009a. *Non-Point Source Pollution: The Nation's Largest Water Quality
Problem.* Available at www.swcd.org/YoungsCreekWatershed/ycfactsheet/
Nonpoint%20Source%20Pollution.pdf (accessed January 20, 2011).

———. 2009b. *Water.* August 12. Available at http://www.epa.gov/aboutepa/history/
topics/cwa/index.html (accessed January 19, 2011).

———. 2010a. *Environmental Assessments and Environmental Impact Statements.*
Available at www.epa.gov/reg3esd1/nepa/eis.htm (accessed January 24, 2011).

———. 2010b. Section—Agriculture. Clean Water Act (CWA). October 20. Available
at www.epa.gov/oecaagct/lcwa.html#Summary (accessed January 25, 2011).

———. 2010c, March. *FY 2009 Annual Report on the Underground Storage Tank
Program.* Available at www.epa.gov/oust/pubs/fy09_annual_ust_report_3–10.pdf
(accessed January 26, 2011).

———. 2011. *Combined Sewer Overflows.* Available at cfpub.epa.gov/npdes/home.
cfm?program_id=5 (accessed January 19, 2011).

Urbina, I., D. Barstow, L. Dodd, D. Glanz, and S. Saul. 2010. "Regulators Failed to
Address Risks in Oil Rig Fail-Safe Device." *New York Times*, June 20.

Wynne, B. 1992. "Uncertainty and Environmental Learning: Reconceiving Science
and Policy in the Preventative Paradigm." *Global Environmental Change* 2 (1):
111–127.

CHAPTER 29

ENVIRONMENTAL POLICY AND SCIENCE

WILLIAM ASCHER AND TODDI A. STEELMAN

1. THE PROBLEMS OF SCIENCE AND ENVIRONMENTAL POLICY

Few would dispute that we are faced with pressing environmental challenges. Oceans are under assault, our climate is changing in unprecedented ways, and biodiversity loss is at historic levels. Science clearly has an important role to play in helping us understand these problems and what we might do about them. After all, who could be against science-based decision making or using the best available science? Despite its appeal, however, enormous controversy surrounds the use of science in environmental policy.

Consider, for instance, the debate that has taken place not only in the United States but in other countries throughout the 2000s to place science at the heart of decision making. The European Union (Holmes and Savgard 2008), United Kingdom (Holmes and Clark 2008), Australia (Marston and Watts 2003), Canada (Bielak et al. 2008), and New Zealand (Parliamentary Commissioner for the Environment 2004) pushed reforms so that policy would be driven by science and evidence of what is effective instead of ideologically driven politics (Holmes and Clark 2008; Nutley 2003). "Data rather than dogma," it was argued, is needed to shape policy (Shaxon 2005). These moves mirrored efforts advanced in the United States by the Barack H. Obama administration in 2009. Under the George W. Bush administration (2001–2008), science was believed to have played "second fiddle" to politics (Becker and

Gellman 2007; Grifo 2007; Union of Concerned Scientists 2008). Obama issued a memorandum about the importance of restoring scientific veracity to the White House shortly after taking office. In December 2010 this memorandum was followed by a directive outlining the administration's formal policy on "the preservation and promotion of scientific integrity" in policy making (Holdren 2010, 1).

Understanding the complex relationship between science and environmental policy is crucial for bringing the broadest range of sound science and related considerations to policy makers. In this chapter, we cover the intellectual traditions that have shaped how we view science, current controversies related to science and environmental policy, and some alternatives to deal with the complexities of science and environmental policy making. We suggest along the way that science ought to be seen as one form of knowledge that can inform policy and that understanding the role of science and these other types of knowledge within the distinct phases of the policy process can provide greater insight into how we might think about and use science more constructively.

We touch only on the broadest themes due to space considerations. These themes point to a larger research agenda dealing with the complex relationship between science and policy. To address this complex relationship, future research on the roles of knowledge in the environmental policy process ought to focus on how to uncover the largely unexamined biases embedded in how science is currently incorporated into the policy process. Research should also be devoted to refining the criteria for evaluating the generation, transmission, and use of science, by examining case studies to determine what is most important for a healthy relationship between science and policy. In a more prescriptive vein, research should explore how to overcome the obstacles to providing policy makers with a more balanced set of considerations for their deliberations. Finally, we suggest that case studies could be constructive ways to shed light on how and why knowledge hybrids succeed and fail.

We offer our own outlook, focusing on the combination of technical and political considerations responsible for privileging particular types of knowledge over others and consequently privileging, often unfairly, the considerations conveyed by those types of knowledge. Our premise is that technical constraints, institutional interests, and broad value commitments all shape the effective criteria that elevate particular efforts and outcomes of knowledge processes over other knowledge elements.

2. INTELLECTUAL TRADITIONS IN SCIENCE AND ENVIRONMENTAL POLICY

A well-developed, lengthy discourse has shaped current debates about the role of science in environmental policy, and several threads are relevant to current controversies. We elaborate on five of these threads and demonstrate how they weave together to create a complicated tapestry for interpreting how science relates to policy.

While the early intellectual history of science and policy could be traced back to Aristotle, Sir Francis Bacon, and René Descartes, the intellectual traditions most relevant for our purposes start with the Progressive movement in the late nineteenth century, with its faith in a technocratic approach to management efficiency. Comprehensive rationality and objective technical approaches were proposed as the solution to the pervasive influence of corruptive local politics of the time (Hays 1959). These beliefs shaped the nascent institutions that came to govern natural resources management agencies. Over time, these Progressive assumptions extended to the environmental and health agencies as well.

The second intellectual thread that influences current beliefs about science is positivism. The hallmarks of positivist knowledge are that "facts can be pursued independently of values, only information subject to empirical verification counts as fact, and the goal of policy research is to discover universal laws that can then be applied to all policy problems" (Shapiro and Schroeder 2008, 435). Positivists believe that there is an objective, knowable reality that can be revealed through the scientific process. Karl Popper (1968) advocated the idea that empirical falsification and rigorous hypothesis testing led by deductive reasoning was a better alternative to knowledge generation than an observational, inductive approach. Facts are separable from values, according to positivists; consequently, it is important for researchers to be neutral or unbiased in how they conduct research.

A belief in a linear model of how science influences policy makes up the third thread. In the postwar period, Vannevar Bush, an engineer and the first presidential science adviser, reemphasized the role of science and how it could contribute to the betterment of society in the twentieth century. Based on his experience leading some 6,000 scientists during World War II to leverage the application of science to warfare, Bush wanted to see the same structure applied to peacetime activities (Zachary 1997). With the publication of *Science: The Endless Frontier* in 1945, Bush advocated the creation of the National Science Foundation and laid out a process—a fundamental social contract—by which basic science would inform policy making. The assumptions that drove Bush included a belief that knowledge passed from basic research to applied research and that the benefits ultimately trickled down to society (Byerly and Pielke 1995). This linear model implied that science could inform policy and benefit society simply by unearthing truth, setting it free, and allowing it to wind its way into practical applications.

A fourth thread challenges the linear-model view and calls for a new relationship between scientists and society. These critiques question the practical relevance of the linear-rational model whereby science directly influences policy (Brunner and Ascher 1992; Funtowicz and Ravetz 2001; Owens, Petts, and Bulkeley 2006). Some have called for the social contract for science outlined by Bush in 1945 to be replaced with a new social contract (Byerly and Pielke 1995;

Lubchenko 1998; Stokes 1997). This new social contract would have scientists serve society directly by encouraging them to be more responsive to pressing societal problems, rather than work on basic, purely theoretical problems defined by scientists in the absence of greater input from the nonscientific community. In other words, the linearity of the model would be changed to have society influence science and have scientists work more collaboratively with those whom science ultimately serves.

The final thread in this intellectual tapestry involves science as social construction. Conventional framing suggests that politics is separate from science. The academic field known as Science and Technology Studies (STS) questions this view. Scientists are not godlike generators of pure knowledge. Rather, they are subjected to a variety of influences and biases that affect what they produce and how they produce it. In the 1960s and 1970s, STS scholars characterized science as a social institution (Kuhn 1962; Latour and Woolgar 1979; Merton 1973; Nelkin 1979; Ziman 1978). Challenges to the objectivity and neutrality of science reemerged in the 1990s (Beck 1992; Fischer 1990, 2000; Forsythe 2002; Jasanoff and Wynne 1998; Jasanoff 1990, 1995, 1996, 2003; Latour 1987; Wynne 1996). Even if some scientists conceive of their role as providing values-free analysis, there are fundamental limitations in the concept of scientists' neutrality. Scientists are part of a process in which they interact with political actors and respond to institutional interests and forces. These institutional interests are not necessarily selfish—they include strengthening the respect for the overall scientific enterprise, filtering out what scientists regard as "questionable knowledge," and securing more funding for what the scientists view as compelling. Yet their actions, either as individuals or within scientific institutions, shape what values will be furthered by the science that emerges from these processes.

This history of thought creates a complex context into which the rest of this chapter is situated. The first three threads are mutually reinforcing, while the last two threads challenge this prevailing view. Progressive beliefs resulted in the creation of long-lasting institutions that emphasized the bureaucratic ideal of efficiency guided by expertise. Often these institutions excluded non-experts. Faith in positivism reinforced the status of scientific expertise within these institutions and within society at large. Science was generated using clear protocols that privileged it above other types of knowledge. Finally, the linear model of how science influenced society, and hence policy, maintained a clear distinction between science and society and the status of scientists in driving this process. Challenging this cumulative view of science, STS scholars question positivistic beliefs that the process and outputs of science are objective and unbiased and call for new institutions that can readily accommodate other types of knowledge or information that is equally legitimate for informing policy. Those who critique the linear-rational model call for new institutional structures that reorder how science could play a role in influencing the scientific process and outputs to better serve society at large. Our own beliefs about science and policy align more closely with these last two threads of thought than the first three.

3. Controversies and Shortcomings Related to Science and Environmental Policy

Science has not always been able to deliver what it has promised, leading to disappointment over what science can do for environmental policy. These shortcomings, on which we elaborate below, are indicative of long-standing controversies related to the use of science. These controversies include the politicization of science and the inherent challenges associated with complexity and uncertainty.

3.1. Politicization of Science

Science—that is, the science of conventionally credentialed scientists operating within the mainstream scientific protocols—is widely seen as the source of rationality and efficiency. In contrast, politics is often seen as, at best, a necessary evil, leading to inferior choices and delay. However, politics infuses all aspects of these controversies, because the boundary between science and politics is permeable and indistinct throughout the policy process. Scientific knowledge is used politically; and science itself is often driven by institutional interests and other manifestations of politics.

The politicization of science highlights several shortcomings associated with science and policy. First, whose science do we use as "the best available science"? Different sides in a debate may leverage their own science to advance their own position (Service 2003). Second, there may be legitimate disagreements about what "the best available science" is, as in the cases of the debates over the health risks of the plastics additive bisphenol A (Ascher, Steelman, and Healy 2010, 145–152) and the environmental risks of genetically engineered grains (Sarewitz 2004). In both of these cases, scientists interpret data differently. Contextual differences between studies that are carried out can produce inconsistencies in data. What may constitute the best science in one place may not be the best in another. These differences can be used to exploit the process for political ends (Ascher 2004; Davis 2007). For example, the high-stakes game of continuing the development of Yucca Mountain as the central depository for spent nuclear fuel has been fought in large part over different scientific approaches to address the technical question of whether and how precipitation would percolate through the rock shielding the nuclear waste buried under the mountain (Metlay 2000). Third, different sides in a debate may disagree over the levels of certainty or uncertainty associated with data. Scientists and politicians have different levels of tolerance for uncertainty (Pouyat 1999). As in the case addressing global climate change, decision makers may exploit uncertainty to delay a decision, which inherently advantages the side that would prefer inaction on an issue. In all of these instances, science is marginalized or devalued because it is subjected to unrealistic expectations.

In addition to these challenges, there is a highly optimistic outlook that science leads to greater consensus among stakeholders; greater certainty about trends, conditions, and the potential impact of alternative policies clarifies the common interest; and sound science discredits the special-interest proposals based on unsound knowledge (Sarewitz 2004). While in some cases additional scientific knowledge can create consensus, as in the Montreal Protocol on chlorofluorocarbons in the 1980s, we should calibrate our optimism about what science can do. More and better science alone does not necessarily lead to improved environmental decision making. New knowledge does not necessarily induce contending groups to converge toward a science-based agreement. The gulf between European and American perspectives on whether to permit genetically engineered organisms into agricultural production and food consumption has persisted despite large amounts of research on health and environmental risks. Despite spending $40 billion on climate change research since the 1990s, there is arguably less consensus now in the United States around the topic of climate change than in previous decades. As long as people have different goals, additional scientific information that clarifies the stakes and who the winners and losers will be for each policy option may consequently reinforce value disputes and competing interests rather than harmonize them (Healy and Ascher 1995).

Sabatier (1988) focuses on the interpretations and differential acceptability of the content of science, according to whether data conform to the positions and preferences of each "advocacy coalition" involved in the environmental policy debates. The premise is that information that runs counter to what a particular group wants to believe will be rejected, unless and until the evidence supporting the data is extremely strong. Thus, the reception of science is politicized. Sabatier's outlook also reinforces the skepticism that additional science, even if sound, would lead to the convergence of policy views. The science on a host of issues, ranging from genetically engineered organisms and childhood vaccinations to nuclear risks and global climate change, encounters deeply entrenched skepticism born of suspicion of political or economic motivations.

In fact, politics, as contestation over the outcomes that a society generates and how they will be shared, is inevitable; fair politics that permits the full range of interests to be taken into account is an essential mechanism required to pursue the public interest, as is science. Sound environmental policy—based on constructive public involvement, balanced weighing of interests, relevant science, pertinent local information, and fair mechanisms of conflict resolution—can serve to clarify and secure the common interest. Yet unless a constructive and open synthesis of science and politics can be established, political factors will continue to be seen as illegitimate in orienting science, or will be embedded in implicit forms that distort the roles or functions that science can play. In contrast, science and politics have been merged constructively in a number of cases: the work of the Intergovernmental Panel on Climate Change has recently brought more coherence to the deliberations over cutting greenhouse gas emissions; the science shops in Denmark have been able to provide local communities with contextually relevant science in deliberations over water pollution, organic farming, and energy-saving transportation (Brodersen, Jorgenson, and Hansen 2006).

3.2. Inherent Challenges of Complexity and Uncertainty

A key belief in the science-policy process is that the role of science is to reduce uncertainty and, once uncertainty is addressed, policy solutions will easily follow (Sarewitz 2004). However, two challenges to this view highlight the limitations of science to fulfill these expectations.

First, complexity itself is a barrier to resolving uncertainty. Environmental problems are problems of socio-ecological systems, and the sheer complexity of socio-ecological systems calls into question the ability of science to fully reduce uncertainties associated with understanding them (Gallopìn 2004). Complex natural and social systems inescapably involve uncertainty because they are coevolving systems (Gunderson 1999). Surprises are inevitable. Ecological theory has changed since the 1960s to recognize the randomness of events that cause unique path dependencies rather than tending toward more uniform climax states (Botkin 1990; Gunderson and Holling 2002; Holling 1978). Under these ever-changing conditions, more scientific information will not necessarily lead to better understanding as the system continues to evolve. Confidence in science may even contribute to a misguided sense of certainty in such dynamic systems. The main point in appreciating the role of complexity is that there is a big difference between the view that nature is not in equilibrium and is inherently unpredictable and the view that if we know enough we can clarify uncertainties and move forward (Berkes, Colding, and Folke 2003). As complexity increases, our confidence in what we know ought to be more modest.

Second, the political implication of the dynamics of complexity and uncertainty is that science may raise new questions, making agreement less likely, rather than more likely (Rayner 2006; Sarewitz 2004). In the protracted debate over the siting of the high-level radioactive waste site at Yucca Mountain, Nevada, more science actually led to greater disagreement over whether and how to store radioactive waste at this location (Sarewitz 2004). Additional scientific studies may aggravate rather than alleviate problems in environmental policy making. More science means what, exactly?

These limitations of science related to complexity and uncertainty rest in part with societal expectations about science. Gallopín et al. (2001) question the "existing rules of enquiry" of conventional science. Importantly, they do not lay all the blame on the scientists, in that they argue that society has thus far not questioned the inability of what they call the "classical science project" of conventional, nonintegrative science to address complex socio-ecological interactions. They assert that the prevailing proscience ideology interprets the limitations of the science and/ or its application. The presumption on behalf of society is "that more knowledge will reduce uncertainties, increase capacity for control, and permit the remedying of past mistakes" (Gallopín et al. 2001, 227). As such, Gallopín et al. (2001) suggest that it is important to distinguish the nonapplication or misapplication of what science can do from the need to actually change the processes of science.

Despite the challenges that complexity and uncertainty impose on science, Sarewitz (2004, 393) suggests that "uncertainty about facts need not be an impediment to political resolution of heated controversy." Scientific uncertainty does not have to be resolved before taking action, because no amount of data or theory can eliminate all uncertainty. Policy can and does proceed under uncertainty. Given the complexities inherent in environmental policy, uncertainty will always be prevalent. The real challenge is in how to proceed in light of these inevitable uncertainties.

4. KNOWLEDGE IN THE ENVIRONMENTAL POLICY PROCESS

Given the significant challenges posed in the previous section, how do we proceed to make sense of science and environmental policy? To make sense of this complexity, it is useful to make two distinctions. First, environmental policy making is potentially responsive to three broad knowledge types, not just conventional science (Ascher, Steelman, and Healy 2010). Conventional science, as one subset of knowledge, includes biophysical data as well as effects on human health, ecosystem health, and natural resources. It is incomplete unless it also includes understanding of social, political, and economic aspects of human behavior. For example, predictions of pollution levels that would result from a more stringent regulation depend not only on the biophysical changes that would occur *if* affected actors comply with the regulations, but also on the economic and social factors that determine the degree of compliance. As broad as this seems to be, other types of knowledge are also crucial in informing policy. These additional knowledge types include local knowledge and public preferences. Local knowledge includes information and insights about contextual and practical environmental conditions, insights into environmental patterns and management derived from practice, and awareness of political relationships within a community or patterns of interaction. Knowing whether the migratory waterfowl passing through a particular locality use the natural ponds or reservoirs may be critical for deciding how much water to release from dams during droughts, yet this knowledge cannot be found in scientific journals. Public preferences, beliefs, and priorities provide insight into various individuals' or groups' support of or opposition to a given position or outcome. For example, the public's concern over nuclear reactor meltdowns is a crucial factor in the halt to expanding nuclear energy in the United States following Chernobyl, Three Mile Island, and Fukushima Daiichi, regardless of whether the likely number of deaths is far greater from coal-fired electricity generation.[1] Policy makers need to be exposed to all three of these forms of knowledge about how natural systems work, how people interact with ecosystems, what the citizenry prefers in terms of policies and outcomes, and what effects conceivable policy alternatives would have.

Second, conceptualizing how knowledge is influenced in different phases of the policy process provides greater opportunities for understanding the limitations and opportunities for science, as well as other types of knowledge. The straightforward distinction among the knowledge processes of generation, transmission, and use is helpful in this respect (Ascher, Steelman, and Healy 2010). Knowledge *generation* involves six aspects: gathering, interpreting, theorizing, modeling, endorsing, and synthesizing information and insights. Knowledge *transmission* may take place among a variety of pathways, including the scientific literature, the minds of experts, or those who support or oppose a given policy. Knowledge may be transmitted through an equally diverse set of channels—technical journal articles, popular media, congressional testimony, or word of mouth at the hairdresser or local barber shop. The *uses* of knowledge are also varied, from bringing an issue onto the active policy agenda to helping formulate policy options to choosing and enacting or evaluating a particular policy. Each of these generation, transmission, and use processes entails distinctive actors, technical challenges, and political issues.

In one respect, generation, transmission, and use comprise a linear sequence in that one can trace any element of generated knowledge to determine whether it is or is not transmitted, and whether or not the transmitted knowledge is used. However, this straightforward analytic distinction among the knowledge processes disguises the processes' intricate interactions, which are by no means simply sequential. This "ecology" of knowledge processes begins with the fact that the transmission of particular knowledge elements tends to enhance their standing, often encouraging support for those who created them: transmission not only transforms and gives additional meaning to generated knowledge, but also stimulates knowledge generation. By the same token, the use of knowledge can stimulate knowledge generation and transmission through both demand and rewards: by the gratification that knowledge generators derive from knowing that their work is heeded, by the grants and contracts that government agencies or other interested parties provide to generate knowledge, and by the requirements for information and analysis that new laws and regulations impose.

The twin conceptual lenses of knowledge (science, local knowledge, and public preferences) and the policy process (generation, transmission, and use) provide insight into further dysfunctions related to science and policy.

- Some forms of knowledge are inappropriately privileged, at the expense of other forms.
- Local, practical knowledge is frequently given short shrift in favor of more abstract science developed in laboratories, simulation modeling efforts,

---

1. See Dunlap, Kraft, and Rosa 1993 for analyses of public attitudes and their importance.

or straightforward theorizing. The disastrous water management of the Klamath River Basin, stemming from the neglect of farmers' long experience with rain and flooding cycles related to the endangered suckerfish, is a sad case in point. The ostensibly scientific "biological opinions" of the U.S. Fish and Wildlife Service disregarded decades of experience of the region's farmers, leading to years' worth of battle over the regions resources that was hard on the farmers, Native Americans, and endangered species alike (Brunner and Steelman 2005).

- Public preferences, an obviously important form of knowledge in democratic systems, are frequently poorly incorporated into planning and policy making. For example, although the U.S. National Forest Management Act requires public input, the U.S. Forest Service officials have minimal guidance for using this input (Steelman and Ascher 1997).

- Progress in formulating environmental regulations is sometimes stymied by "quality-control" watchdogs, such as the U.S. Office of Information and Regulatory Affairs (OIRA), through their claims that analysis about the benefits of environmental protection and conservation fails the standards of rigor. This became a highly politicized issue during the George W. Bush administration, as critics of OIRA accused it of using its authority as part of an antiregulation campaign by unjustifiably claiming that regulatory impact analyses were not of high enough quality to proceed through the approval process. OIRA officials claimed that they were merely upholding scientific standards (Adams 2002, 525; Heinzerling 2006).

- Whereas in some nations the suspicion of environmental risks is enough to prompt regulation in keeping with some version of the Precautionary Principle, in the United States the invocation of uncertainty of knowledge often allows potentially hazardous conditions to persist (Vig and Faure 2004). Many examples can be found beyond the well-known tactic of delaying action on global climate change on the absurd grounds that it is better to wait until all uncertainty is resolved. For instance, the delay in the U.S. government's actions to regulate the chemical BPA, a known endocrine disruptor present in a wide range of plastics, reflects the ease with which the opponents of regulation can paralyze progress by invoking scientific uncertainty. While the Canadian government banned BPA, the governments of the United States, Germany, and Japan simply called for more studies, and the U.S. chemical industry association denounced all the studies linking BPA to the potential for health problems, including a report by an expert panel convened by the Center for Evaluation of Risks to Human Reproduction of the National Institute of Environmental Health.

- Existing data-gathering efforts are often slow to give way to gathering newly relevant data. For instance, wildfire managers continue to collect data on the number of acres treated to reduce wildfire threats, even when they are in wilderness areas completely removed from their ability to affect human communities. The more relevant data would be the number of acres treated near human communities where the needs are greatest to mitigate the effects from catastrophic wildfires (Steelman and Burke 2007). Obsolete or otherwise questionable knowledge sometimes takes on iconic status, insulating questionable understandings from proper scrutiny. The severely flawed research on the so-called resource curse published in the mid-1990s continues to be cited as gospel (Banks 2005; Bravo-Ortega and De Gregorio 2006; Matsen and Torvik 2005). The outdated early-1990s estimates of benefits accruing from better water quality were still used in assessing these benefits in the mid-2000s (U.S. Environmental Protection Agency 2009).

• Existing laws, regulations, and executive orders often restrict the decision-aiding analysis that is generated, transmitted, or used in environmental policy making. For example, although presidential executive orders require that the formal benefit-cost analysis be conducted in assessing air quality and water quality regulations, the U.S. Clean Air and Clean Water Acts forbid the explicit application of the benefit-cost analysis in determining the outcome. While the benefit-cost analysis can add to the understanding of the stakes, these analyses are often incomplete. Professional and institutional disincentives are often at play to limit analysts' ability to conduct a comprehensive analysis. The benefits that are the most difficult to monetize are often underinvestigated because they may expose the analyst to professional ridicule. Consequently, the easily monetizable benefits, and most professionally defendable, are most likely to be included. The result is that additional information is considered, even though by law it is prohibited. This more than likely would reduce the impetus for stronger environmental regulations in future rounds of rule making. By the same token, the 1973 U.S. Endangered Species Act narrows data collection to only the listed species and their habitats, excluding other relevant information. This is an impediment to adopting policies that would protect land containing not only the target species, but others, listed and unlisted, as well.

When laws or regulations formally prohibit the consideration of relevant knowledge, these laws or regulations may be subverted to adjust decisions to take the knowledge into account. For example, when the operation of the $100 million Tellico Dam in Tennessee was stalled because of the potential extinction of the snail darter fish, Congress amended the Endangered Species Act to permit a cabinet-level committee to decide whether an exemption should be permitted; when the committee denied the exemption, Congress gave the dam the go-ahead anyway (Wheeler and McDonald 1986).

The potential of sound knowledge to reveal the weaknesses of unsound proposals pushed by special interests is frequently compromised by uncertainty about what criteria ought to be applied to judge the quality of knowledge inputs. In the United Kingdom, local sheep herders' concerns about the Chernobyl disaster's impact on their flocks were ignored because they "merely" had local historical knowledge of the soils where radioactive disposition landed. Scientists' confidence in their models led to the loss of entire flocks of sheep (Wynne 1996). U.S. nuclear policy has foundered in no insignificant part because federal officials dismissed public anxieties over nuclear risks as scientifically naive, although the key political fact has been the anxieties themselves (Dunlap, Kraft, and Rosa 1993).

5. Privileged Knowledge

A broad conclusion covering all three of the knowledge processes and knowledge types is the abundance of possibilities of privileging some forms of knowledge over others. This often creates self-reinforcing patterns that shape the very processes by which future knowledge is produced and applied. Interactive effects among the generation, transmission, and use of knowledge result in changes in the institutions that shape policy making. The adverse consequence is that important knowledge, like local knowledge and public preferences, receives insufficient standing because certain methods of analysis and certain types of scientists are privileged over others. The relative power and status of certain participants in the policy-making process are elevated, while others are diminished. For instance, misconceptions about what constitutes "scientific rigor" often elevate quantification over genuine relevance (Majone 1989). Easily measurable aspects that can be captured with apparent rigor are privileged over less tangible aspects of equal or greater importance. For example, estimates of the economic costs of stringent environmental protection are typically regarded as straightforward and reliable. In contrast, estimates of less tangible environmental amenities such as aesthetics and ecosystem persistence are typically regarded as shakier, and, therefore, are often deemphasized in the benefit-cost analyses conducted by environmental agencies such as the U.S. Environmental Protection Agency. These same biases are prevalent given the reputation for rigor of simulation models, regression analysis, and controlled laboratory experiments. Simulation models may have hundreds of equations, but they cannot represent anything beyond the modeler's theoretical understanding of the dynamics of the modeled systems, with parameters that are estimated on the basis of past data that may or may not be relevant in projecting future trends. By the same token, regression models used to assess the value of environmental amenities are vulnerable to model mis-specification, omitted variables, and inaccurate or missing data. Laboratory experiments appear rigorous by virtue of their capacity to include controls, but their correspondence with real behavior is beyond the ability of the experiments to confirm. Despite these vulnerabilities, such methods are typically presumed to be rigorous and reliable.

Previously generated knowledge is endorsed by the very act of using it, or even simply citing it. This influences the standing of different elements of knowledge. For example, as environmental agencies assess toxicity risks, they necessarily highlight some dosage-response studies over others. Going further, they may decide to require reportage of a broader range of discharges, generating more knowledge about toxic releases. They may also call for more laboratory studies, thereby stimulating (and perhaps funding) knowledge generation.

Institutional interests come into play in the efforts to secure higher standing for particular knowledge generation efforts by particular institutions, such as university labs or independent think tanks; or by particular sets of people with specific credentials of expertise such as people with doctorates in biology or economics. Institutional interests are also reflected in the reliance on particular transmission mechanisms, ranging from the highly technical, such as biochemical engineering journals, to the highly popular, such as *USA Today*. They also play a role in efforts to secure decision-making routines that take up particular types of knowledge, ranging from the species-population inventories that drive the application of the U.S. Endangered Species Act to the admissibility of expert evidence in the courts.

Broader value orientations shape the formulation of the laws, regulations, and processes that use knowledge—and thereby create demand for particular forms of knowledge. The most striking example is the range of principles that underlie the most important U.S. environmental laws. The 1970 Clean Air Act and the 1972 Federal Water Pollution Control Act enshrine the rights of Americans to "clean" air and water—though how clean is unclear. The Endangered Species Act indirectly enshrines the rights of nonhuman species—though its rhetoric is couched in terms of benefits for citizens. The National Forest Management Act calls for the systematic incorporation of public input—though what to make of that input is also unclear. The Clean Water Act requires the best available *economically achievable* technology to reduce toxic emissions, which entails balancing benefits and costs, but is not a full societal benefit-cost analysis because the social benefits of controlling some discharges may still exceed control costs even if economically achievable.

Broad value orientations also shape how different forms of knowledge inputs are received. For example, a high societal priority for wealth will predispose society to demand economic analyses. The risk-averse will favor the Precautionary Principle and will be more responsive to knowledge about risks than about opportunities. Scientific inputs will be more acceptable to those who have high levels of technological optimism.

In addition, assuming a distinct boundary between science and the expression of policy preferences, with the implication that science must be given precedence, leads to the neglect of other types of knowledge in decision making and filters out important considerations in formulating environmental policy. People want both their preferred policies and particular processes for coming up with these preferences (Sagoff 1994). Because of these filterings and attributions of standing that occur in both generating and transmitting knowledge, the knowledge that policy makers come to regard as reliable overly narrows the range of considerations that they take into account. There are limitations on the capacity to convey the full set of sound, relevant knowledge or to filter out unsound knowledge. On the one hand, some limits to generated and transmitted knowledge are inevitable; on the other hand, some unsound knowledge will inevitably escape the filter. In short, the culture, institutions, and rules that shape the filtering of knowledge run the risk of limiting comprehensiveness, jeopardizing dependability, and inappropriately bounding selectivity for knowledge transmitted in policy making.

Yet we cannot regard these problems as arising from merely technical constraints. The filtering, attributions of standing, invocations of some knowledge inputs over others, and the treatment of uncertainty all present opportunities and vehicles for politics at several levels. Control over the generation and dissemination of knowledge is a key resource of the bureaucratic politics that pits one agency against another for standing, jurisdiction, and budget. Consider the proposed building of a cement plant that pits a state-level Department of Commerce against the Department of Environment and Natural Resources. The Commerce Department will argue for the jobs the plant will bring and suggest that the state provide incentives to locate the plant. The Environment and Natural Resources Department will counter that mercury emissions will exceed regulatory standards and that the state should encourage cleaner economic options. The Commerce Department may present its own analysis of environmental impacts, find existing studies with lower predictions of environmental damage, or cite the analysis generated by the cement industry. The "politics of expertise" is employed by agencies; they play the card of expertise, given their respective perspectives in the broader game of bureaucratic politics (Benveniste 1977; Fischer 1990, 2003).

6. Opportunities for Science, Politics, and Policy

The intertwining of knowledge processes, science, policy making, and politics should not be viewed as an alarming sign that science has been inappropriately infiltrated by politics, nor that the environmental policy process is incapable of making the best of the various forms of knowledge (Brown 2009). Yet finding better ways to integrate science, politics, and policy requires exploring new relationships and new institutions.

The overarching thrusts of our specific recommendations are to

- Redefine the boundaries between science and politics. This includes moving beyond the misguided mind-set that conveying values undermines knowledge. In doing so, we prescribe a greater role for alternative forms of knowledge, including increasing the participation of stakeholders in shaping the generation, transmission, and use of knowledge. Counterintuitively, this also means defending the integrity of science.
- Deal constructively with complexity and uncertainty. This includes confronting and overcoming the paralysis that often emerges from the recognition that environmental effects are subject to uncertainty.

• Improve knowledge integration, synthesis, and communication between knowledge generators, transmitters, and users, especially policy makers. This includes ensuring that a broad range of considerations can move through the gauntlet of filtering to the policy makers, while still applying a sufficient degree of quality control.

6.1. Redefining the Boundaries between Science and Politics

We cannot depoliticize science, nor would we want to. The challenge is not to eradicate politics or interest groups from the process but, rather, to build constructive roles for them. Current knowledge processes are principally structured to separate politics from science—a futile effort because science is thoroughly enmeshed in social and political practices. This is not to say that science is unimportant—it is essential. The goal is to acknowledge openly the social and political influences on science, while doing a better job of integrating the knowledge about the biophysical world into the policy process. Additionally, we need to improve on the legitimacy of all types of knowledge, including local knowledge and public preferences. These alternative knowledge types are often unjustifiably regarded as flawed because of their explicit social and political connection.

Our world is too complex to ever have perfect, comprehensive knowledge within the policy-making process. Since the universe of knowledge brought to bear on a policy issue is impossible to bound, this means that we must be selective in which knowledge we choose to use. Being selective means we are employing biases, either implicitly or explicitly. Given this reality, being clear about what influenced the generation and transmission of the knowledge is crucial. We need to make science more transparent, including clarifying the assumptions behind the generation, transmission, and use of science. A whole range of institutional, professional, and personal interests influence how knowledge is created, passed on, and used. Simply ignoring that these interests exist may help perpetuate the myth of objective science and neutral scientists. Science is not values-free. In the long run the effort to develop values-free knowledge generation is counterproductive if we want to restore confidence in science. As Rykiel (2001, 435) observes, "Scientific procedures are aimed at minimizing subjectivity, not at the unattainable goal of eliminating it." Awareness of values positions of scientists, other knowledge generators, and knowledge users allows us to confront those biases that are inappropriate. This will entail restructuring incentives and accountability structures throughout our social institutions such as universities, peer-reviewed publications, grant-making organizations and agencies, repositioning professional reward systems, and encouraging personal change in behavior.

The environmental policy process requires more space for forms of knowledge beyond conventional science, without undermining science. Science and the scientific process are already in a state of crisis. Increasingly, science as an enterprise is castigated in debates ranging from climate change to BPA to the listing of endangered species. This creeping cynicism about the scientific process undermines its long-term legitimacy among policy makers and the public alike.

How then do we defend the integrity of formal science? The Union of Concerned Scientists has suggested several ways to restore the integrity of science. These reforms include legislating whistle-blower rights, enforcing whistle-blower protection, and making government more transparent. Specific policies include giving the public better access to federal science, reforming agency media policies, reforming the Freedom of Information Act, ending overclassification of documents as secret, and disclosing and mitigating conflicts of interest (Union of Concerned Scientists 2008).

Scientists should be allowed to be advocates, and in fact have to be. But this requires transparency in the process. Consequently, it is important to partition the work of sciences from the advocacy of the science. Science has an important role to play in the policy-making process: to help define problems, identify key trends as they relate to problems, inform debate, and educate (Karl, Susskind, and Wallace 2007). However, science cannot provide objective answers to policy questions that inherently involve values. Science is better at identifying the problems than it is in providing clear-cut solutions to those problems (Pouyat 1999). Scientists can defend their findings, but this is an explicitly values-laden process. The peer review process exists to provide a set of methodological protocols, including checks and balances, to create legitimacy in the science that can be used to inform policy. It is imperative that these processes be maintained, albeit with opportunities to make explicit the biases that go into these processes.

Science has often been privileged because it has been seen as a more dependable form of knowledge relative to local knowledge and public preferences. Local knowledge and public preferences are more explicitly influenced by political and social processes, though conventional science is influenced more implicitly by these values. Recognizing that these social and political influences are prevalent in all knowledge generation, transmission, and use is the first step to leveling the playing field for these different knowledge types. To do so, we need to make better progress in the processes that can render local knowledge and public preferences more dependable for specific decision processes. A strictly science-based policy process will be inadequate for the demands of policy makers. Nutley (2003) suggests that strictly evidence-based approaches are naive given the practicalities of policy making and suggests the need for "evidence-informed" or "evidence-aware" policy making. The idea here is that the evidence is clearly important but needs to be tempered by other considerations in the policy process. In the United Kingdom, this has come to mean evidence from stakeholders, experts, departmental staff, street-level bureaucrats, and agencies that will be affected by the policy (United Kingdom Cabinet Office 1999). The inclusion of local knowledge and policy preferences, however, raises the discomfort level of those who want to rely on evidence-only approaches. Beierle and Cayford's (2002) meta-analysis of 237 case studies of stakeholder-based decision-making processes indicated that the quality of the decisions was not compromised and that greater participation had a positive effect on the outcomes of the decision.

Science can be useful, but it depends on how credibility and legitimacy are created. According to Karl, Susskind, and Wallace (2007, 23), "The credibility and legitimacy of science depend upon how and by whom information is gathered and the process by which scientific inquiry is conducted." In part, the processes we utilize are what politicizes science. Our constitutional and administrative systems are based on a model of conflict envisioned by the founding fathers such that no one group or branch of government should dominate another. Within this model one side does battle with the other with the belief that interest groups and different branches of government will check and balance each other—the outcome of which will best serve the best interests of society at large. The role for science in this system is less to inform decision making than to be used as a weapon in a political process to advance one's agenda (Karl, Susskind, and Wallace 2007). Science becomes a casualty in the process, collateral damage within a system that unintentionally devalues what science can deliver. If we restructure our processes to be less intentionally conflictual, then we open up opportunities for science to be more constructive. These opportunities include providing a greater role for collaboration between scientists and nonscientists in the generation, transmission, and use of "knowledge hybrids" (Ascher, Steelman, and Healy 2010). Creating the appropriate incentive structures will be important in moving these visions forward. This will include creating consistent institutional and professional incentives within educational and research-based institutions to encourage rather than discourage the inclusion of nonscientists in these processes.

Many models have been proposed to enhance collaboration among scientists from different disciplines and scientists and nonscientists in the generation, transmission, and use of knowledge. Knowledge hybrids integrate science, local knowledge, and public preferences in different combinations. The intention is to preserve the usefulness of formal science while embracing the benefits of other knowledge forms, including citizen-scientist collaboration, joint fact-finding, and stakeholder-based decision making, among others.

Two scenarios call for different types of knowledge hybrids. One scenario entails employing technical knowledge to implement policies that have been established in broad outline through a participatory process. For example, if the policy emerging from a participatory process is to consolidate nuclear waste in one location, external reviewers should be given authority to undertake their assessments insulated from political pressures. The methodologies to pursue this approach are well developed through advances in expert elicitation, modeling, and forecasting (Arkes et al. 1997; Armstrong 2001; Brewer 2007). The other scenario pertains to situations in which technical issues exist alongside of still-unresolved questions of goals and priorities. Some form of public participation is necessary, but it has to be integrated with systematic assessment of information and theory.

A host of approaches has been offered—and tested in various contexts—to effect this integration. Numerous design dimensions exist to structure interaction between experts and the public.[2] Understanding these design advantages and limitations can help facilitate choosing the right hybrid for the right problem under the right political and technical conditions. For instance, in choosing between a joint fact-finding process and an initiative process, one might want to consider how they differ on the dimensions of representation and the centrality of science. Representation of participants in the initiative process is high, but the centrality of science is low. Conversely, the joint fact-finding process compares less well on representation, but the centrality of science is much higher. Additional design dimensions that are important, but are not covered here due to space limitations, include the role of the convener, independence of participants, early involvement of the public, public influence on final policy, process transparency, resource accessibility, task definition, structured decision making, potential for local knowledge to influence, resource demands, cost-effectiveness, potential for the expression of preferences, the public's role in framing the problem, and the public's role in framing alternatives (Ascher, Steelman, and Healy 2010, 190–201; Rowe and Frewer 2000).

A challenge remains in terms of what standards can be applied to these approaches. Norms are beginning to emerge to assess the effectiveness of the integration of local knowledge and public-preference knowledge into decision making. This is necessary to identify best practices in the form of processes (citizen-science collaboration, joint fact-finding, citizen advisory councils, etc.) and outcomes in such areas as soil management, watershed buffers, and so on. Best practices derived from practical knowledge are inherently localized and contextual. An implication is that decision aids that leverage these best practices must include direction about whether and when the practices are applicable to their particular situations.

6.2. Dealing Constructively with Complexity and Uncertainty

One approach to dealing constructively with complexity and uncertainty is to use scientific conventions to reveal sciences' own limitations. This could be done by demanding that conventional science be explicit about the assumptions, incompleteness, and legitimate disagreements, rather than burying them under arcane formulas or ignoring them altogether. One path forward is to encourage standardized reporting for expressing uncertainty in peer-reviewed work (Moss and Schneider 2000). These standards could be enforced by journal editors and government agencies as criteria for publication. The straightforward acts of expressing uncertainty explicitly, and explaining how conventional models do not eliminate

---

2. For a comprehensive list and evaluation of trade-offs see Rowe and Frewer 2000 as well as Ascher, Steelman, and Healy 2010, 190–201.

all uncertainty, go a long way in sensitizing policy makers and the public of science's strengths as well as limitations.

Another approach to uncertainty and complexity is to make policy more flexible. Adaptive management, an approach that focuses on monitoring, analysis, and adjustment of policy in light of new information, has received great attention since the early 1990s for being able to deal more realistically with the uncertainties inherent in environmental policy (Holling 1978, 1995, 1997). Iterative feedback loops that facilitate social learning among diverse participants are key for making midcourse corrections if the management action is not meeting specified goals. Given the great uncertainties inherent in socio-ecological systems, these feedbacks can detect problems and rectify the situation without having to wait lengthy time periods for comprehensive policy appraisals (Lasswell 1971).

6.3. Improve Knowledge Integration, Synthesis, and Communication

If knowledge is to be used by policy makers, then it is incumbent on scientists and other knowledge producers and transmitters to integrate and synthesize findings so they can be communicated better to those who will ultimately use the information. Scientists think they know how to communicate, when often they do not (Pouyat 1999). Conversely, scientists believe nonscientists need to be better educated to understand what scientists have to say. The responsibility rests on both sides.

On one side, scientists plead that they are misunderstood. Policy makers often have unrealistic expectations about what science can deliver (Pouyat 1999). Scientists commonly believe that policy makers think science can provide values-free, universal "truths" to guide the "right" answer for policy decisions (Herrick and Jamieson 1995; Pouyat 1999). Conveniently for policy makers, if scientists can provide the right answer, then this exculpates policy makers from having to make tough values-based decisions. Pouyat (1999, 282) suggests that what policy makers want is a "bright line" to guide their decision making. Revising and clarifying expectations is a first step in defending the integrity of formal science, as we mention above, and can also help facilitate better communication.

Improving the overall knowledge that will inform policy will come with better attempts to integrate science, local knowledge, and public preferences. After all, the knowledge base is more dependable if both science and experience reinforce each other. The challenge is to discover how to organize and integrate the interactions among knowledge generators operating within different paradigms, knowledge transmitters applying different standards, and knowledge users employing knowledge to pursue different values. Knowledge needs to be integrated among the many different disciplines that are relevant to environmental policy. Several factors have led to the increasingly specialized and esoteric output of professional scientists. This reflects the expansion of foci and scientific personnel as well as a reward structure within professional science that still favors specialization. Because in most fields publishing in disciplinary journals is still a more secure path to promotion and prestige, scientists have incentives to conduct their research and couch their findings to meet specialized disciplinary criteria. Skills for integration across these disciplines is valued less within the culture of science than is specialized knowledge generation. Government and research agencies that receive government funding might be required to hire technical writers to synthesize and translate findings into usable formats.

Because greater interaction among those who generate, transmit, and use knowledge is essential both for maintaining the relevance of knowledge inputs and their responsible use, boundary-spanning organizations and individuals are known to play key roles in bringing their knowledge closely to bear on policy questions (Guston 2001). Haas (2004) suggests the need to create "usable knowledge" that transforms "raw" science into a usable form for policy makers as well as a mechanism for transferring that knowledge to the policy world from scientists. The boundary manager has been described by Pielke (2007) as a "science arbiter" and "honest broker"of policy alternatives. "Boundary organizations produce boundary objects, such as reports, conferences, and the like" (McNie 2007, 28). Cooperative state research, education and extension services, U.S. Sea Grant, the Consultative Group on International Agricultural Research, the Institute for Applied Systems Analysis, the U.S. National Research Council, the now-defunct Congressional Office of Technology Assessment, the Health Effects Institute, the European Environment Agency, and NOAA's Regional Integrated Sciences and Assessments Program are all examples of boundary organizations. However, organizational innovation is needed to entice scientists into these potentially uncomfortable interactions and to induce policy makers to accept the knowledge generated or transmitted by boundary organizations.

7. CONCLUSIONS

In conclusion, we note two paths that the future of science and environmental policy may follow. For the first path, the prospect of broader knowledge incorporation into environmental policy making threatens conventional science institutions, which respond by becoming more rigid, insular, and confined to conventional protocols. In essence, scientists and those who support science would attempt to assert the institution of science as the best and exclusive option for informing policy. This path would devalue other forms of knowledge in the policy process. The consequence of this path would be to drive politics underground so that values-based disputes would be hammered out within the practices of formalized science without participants knowing the value consequences of what appear to be the "scientifically sound" policies.

The second option entails embracing politics and other forms of knowledge to create a constructive role for all knowledge types and how they come to bear on contested claims. This path includes explicit acknowledgement of bias and distributional effects associated with science, local knowledge, and public preferences in the generation, transmission, and use of knowledge. In a democratic society, the common good is most likely served by moving toward this path of openness, inclusion, and greater participation. It is unlikely that greater focus on science only as a privileged source of knowledge will serve the common interest. Maintaining strict boundaries between science and politics in a "science-centric" world is increasingly unrealistic given the diversification in participants, arenas, and resources associated with knowledge generation, transmission, and use. We encourage movement toward the second path for the many reasons laid out in this chapter. This is why further research needs to focus on the biases lurking in the protocols of the generation and transmission of conventional science, as well as on how to improve the evaluation of how knowledge is used or abused in an inevitably politicized policy process. By making our perspectives explicit and our logic clear, we hope to encourage others to debate, argue, or follow our lead in reimagining these boundaries between science, policy, and politics.

REFERENCES

Adams, R. 2002. "Regulating the Rule-Makers: John Graham at OIRA." *Congressional Quarterly Weekly Report* 23 (February): 520–526.

Arkes, H. R., J. L. Mumpower, and T. R. Stewart. 1997. "Combining Expert Opinions." *Science* 275: 461–465.

Armstrong, J. S. 2001. *Principles of Forecasting: A Handbook for Researchers and Practitioners*. Dordrecht, The Netherlands: Kluwer Academic.

Ascher, W. 2004. "Scientific Information and Uncertainty: Challenges for the Use of Science in Policymaking." *Science and Engineering Ethics* 10: 437–455.

Ascher, W., T. Steelman, and R. Healy. 2010. *Knowledge and Environmental Policy: Re-imagining the Boundaries of Science and Politics*. Cambridge, MA: MIT Press.

Banks, G. 2005. "Linking Resources and Conflict the Melanesian Way." *Pacific Economic Bulletin* 20 (1) (May): 185–191.

Beck, U. 1992. *Risk Society: Towards a New Modernity*. London: Sage.

Becker, J., and B. Gellman. 2007. "Leaving No Tracks." *Washington Post*, June 27. Available at blog.washingtonpost.com/cheney/chapters/leaving_no_tracks/index.html (accessed April 15, 2009).

Beierle, T., and J. Cayford. 2002. *Democracy in Practice: Public Participation in Environmental Decisions*. Washington, DC: Resources for the Future.

Benveniste, G. 1977. *The Politics of Expertise*. 2nd ed. San Francisco: Boyd & Fraser.

Berkes, F., J. Colding, and C. Folke, eds. 2003. *Navigating Social-Ecological Systems: Building Resilience for Complexity and Change*. Cambridge: Cambridge University Press.

Bielak, A., A. Campbell, S. Pope, K. Schaefer, and L. Shaxon. 2008. "From Science Communications to Knowledge Brokering: The Shift from 'Science Push' to 'Policy Pull.'" In *Communicating Science in Social Contexts: New Models, New Practices*, ed. D. M. Cheng, D. M. Claessens, T. Gascoigne, J. Metcalfe, and B. Schiele, 201–226. Dordrecht, The Netherlands: Springer.

Botkin, D. B. 1990. *Discordant Harmonies: A New Ecology for the Twenty-First Century*. New York: Oxford University Press.

Bravo-Ortega, C., and J. De Gregorio. 2006. "The Relative Richness of the Poor? Natural Resources, Human Capital and Economic Growth." In *Natural Resources, Neither Curse nor Destiny*, ed. D. Lederman and W. F. Maloney, 71–99. Washington, DC: World Bank.

Brewer, G. D. 2007. "Inventing the Future: Scenarios, Imagination, Mastery, and Control." *Sustainability Science* 2 (1): 159–177.

Brodersen, S., M. S. Jorgensen, and A. Hansen. 2006. "Environmental Empowerment: The Role of Co-operation between Civil Society, Universities, and Science Shops." PATH Conference Proceedings, Scotland. Available at http://www.macaulay.ac.uk/PATHconference/outputs/PATH_abstract_3.2.3.pdf (accessed April 20, 2007).

Brown, M. B. 2009. *Science in Democracy: Expertise, Institutions, and Representation*. Cambridge, MA: MIT Press.

Brunner, R. D., and W. Ascher. 1992. "Science and Social Responsibility." *Policy Sciences* 25 (3): 295–331.

Brunner, R. D., and T. A. Steelman. 2005. "Toward Adaptive Governance." In *Adaptive Governance: Integrating Science, Policy, and Decision-Making*, ed. R. D. Brunner, T. A. Steelman, L. Coe-Juell, C. Cromley, C. Edwards, and D. Tucker, 268–304. New York: Columbia University Press.

Bush, V. 1945. *Science: The Endless Frontier*. Washington, DC: U.S. Government Printing Office. Available at www.nsf.gov/about/history/vbush1945.htm (accessed December 28, 2010).

Byerly, R., and R. Pielke Jr. 1995. "The Changing Ecology of United States Science." *Science* 269: 1531–1532.

Davis, D. 2007. *The Secret History of the War on Cancer*. New York: Basic Books.

Dunlap, R. E., M. E. Kraft, and E. A. Rosa, eds. 1993. *Public Reactions to Nuclear Waste: Citizens' Views of Repository Siting*. Durham, NC: Duke University Press.

Fischer, F. 1990. *Technocracy and the Politics of Expertise*. Newbury Park, CA: Sage.

———. 2000. *Citizens, Experts, and the Environment: The Politics of Local Knowledge*. Durham, NC: Duke University Press.

———. 2003. *Reframing Public Policy: Discursive Politics and Deliberative Practices*. Oxford: Oxford University Press.

Forsyth, T. 2002. *Critical Political Ecology: The Politics of Environmental Science*. London: Routledge.

Funtowicz, S., and J. Ravetz. 2001. "Global Risk, Uncertainty, and Ignorance." In *Global Environmental Risk*, ed. J. Kasperson and R. Kasperson, 173–194. London: Earthscan.

Gallopín, G. C. 2004. "What Kind of System of Science (and Technology) Is Needed to Support the Quest for Sustainable Development?" In *Earth Systems Analysis for Sustainability*, ed. H. J. Schellnhuber, P. J. Crutzen, W. C. Clark, and H. Held, 367–386. Cambridge, MA: MIT Press.

Gallopín, G. C., S. Funtowicz, M. O'Connor, and J. Ravetz. 2001. "Science for the Twenty-First Century: From the Social Contract to the Scientific Core." *International Social Science Journal* 53 (168): 219–229.

Grifo, F. T. 2007. "Senior Scientist with Union of Concerned Scientists Scientific Integrity Program." Written Testimony before the Committee on Oversight and Government Reform, U.S. Congress, House of Representatives, 110th Cong., 1st sess., January 30.

Gunderson, L. 1999. "Resilience, Flexibility, and Adaptive Management—Antidotes for Spurious Certitude?" *Conservation Ecology* 3 (1). Available at www.consecol. org/vol3/iss1/art7/ (accessed July 10, 2009).

Gunderson, L. H., and C. S. Holling. 2002. *Panarchy: Understanding Transformations in Human and Natural Systems.* Covelo, CA: Island.

Guston, D. 2001. "Boundary Organizations in Environmental Policy and Science: An Introduction." *Science, Technology, and Human Values* 26 (4): 399–408.

Haas, P. 2004. "When Does Power Listen to Truth? A Constructivist Approach to the Policy Process." *Journal of European Public Policy* 11 (August): 569–592.

Hays, S. 1959. *Conservation and the Gospel of Efficiency: The Progressive Conservation Movement, 1890–1920.* Cambridge, MA: Harvard University Press.

Healy, R., and W. Ascher. 1995. "Knowledge in the Policy Process: Incorporating New Environmental Information in Natural Resources Policy Making." *Policy Sciences* 28: 1–19.

Heinzerling, L. 2006. "Statutory Interpretation in the Era of OIRA." *Fordham Urban Law Journal* 33: 101–120.

Herrick, C., and D. Jamieson. 1995. "The Social Construction of Acid Rain: Some Implications for Science/Policy Assessment." *Global Environmental Change* 5: 105–112.

Holdren, J. P. 2010. "Scientific Integrity: Memorandum for the Heads of Executive Departments and Agencies." Available at www.whitehouse.gov/sites/default/files/ microsites/ostp/scientific-integrity-memo-12172010.pdf (accessed January 2, 2010).

Holling, C. S., ed. 1978. *Adaptive Environmental Assessment and Management.* New York: John Wiley.

———. 1995. "What Barriers? What Bridges?" In *Barriers and Bridges to the Renewal of Ecosystems and Institutions,* ed. L. H. Gunderson, C. S. Holling, and S. S. Light, 1–34. New York: Columbia University Press.

———. 1997. "Two Cultures of Ecology." *Conservation Ecology* 2 (2). www.consecol. org/vol2/iss2/art4 (accessed March 4, 2009).

Holmes, J., and R. Clark. 2008. "Enhancing the Use of Science in Environmental Policy-Making and Regulation." *Environmental Science and Policy* 11: 702–711.

Holmes, J., and J. Savgard. 2008. "Dissemination and Implementation of Environmental Research." Swedish Environmental Protection Agency Report 5681, February. www.skep-era.net/site/files/WP4_final%20report.pdf (accessed January 2, 2010).

Jasanoff, S. 1990. *The Fifth Branch: Science Advisors as Policymakers.* Cambridge, MA: Harvard University Press.

———. 1995. *Science at the Bar: Law, Sciences, and Technology in America.* Cambridge, MA: Harvard University Press.

———. 1996. "Beyond Epistemology: Relativism and Engagement in the Politics of Science." *Social Studies of Science* 26 (2): 393–418.

———. 2003. "Breaking the Waves in Science Studies: Comment on H. M. Collins and Robert Evans, the Third Wave of Science Studies." *Social Studies of Science* 33 (3): 389–400.

Jasanoff, S., and B. Wynne. 1998. "Science and Decision Making." In *Human Choice and Climate Change.* Vol. 1, *The Societal Framework,* ed. S. Raynor and E. L. Malone, 1–87. Columbus, OH: Battelle Institute.

Karl, H., L. Susskind, and K. Wallace. 2007. "A Dialogue, Not a Diatribe: Effective Integration of Science and Policy through Joint Fact Finding." *Environment: Science and Policy for Sustainable Development* 49 (1): 20–34.

Kuhn, T. 1962. *The Structure of Scientific Revolutions.* Chicago: University of Chicago Press.

Lasswell, H. D. 1971. *A Pre-View of Policy Sciences.* New York: American Elsevier.

Latour, B. 1987. *Science in Action: How to Follow Scientists and Engineers through Society.* Cambridge, MA: Harvard University Press.

Latour, B., and S. Woolgar. 1979. *Laboratory Life: The Social Construction of Scientific Facts.* Beverly Hills, CA: Sage.

Lubchenko, J. 1998. "Entering the Century of the Environment: A New Social Contract for Science." *Science* 279: 491–497.

Majone, G. 1989. *Evidence, Argument and Persuasion in the Policy Process.* New Haven, CT: Yale University Press.

Marston, G., and R. Watts. 2003. "Tampering with the Evidence: A Critical Appraisal of Evidence-Based Policy Making." *The Drawing Board: An Australian Review of Public Affairs* 3 (3): 143–163.

Matsen, E., and R. Torvik. 2005. "Optimal Dutch Disease." *Journal of Development Economics* 78: 494–515.

McNie, E. 2007. "Reconciling the Supply of Scientific Information with User Demands: An Analysis of the Problem and Review of the Literature." *Environmental Science and Policy* 10 (1): 17–38.

Merton, R. K. 1973. "The Normative Structure of Science." In *The Sociology of Science: Theoretical and Empirical Investigations*, ed. N. W. Storer, 267–278. Chicago: University of Chicago Press.

Metlay, D. 2000. "From Tin Roof to Torn Wet Blanket: Predicting and Observing Groundwater Movement at a Proposed Nuclear Waste Site." In *Prediction: Science, Decision Making, and the Future of Nature*, ed. D. Sarewitz, R. Pielke, and R. Byerly, 199–227. Washington, DC: Island.

Moss, R. H., and S. H. Schneider. 2000. "Uncertainties in the IPCC TAR: Recommendations to Lead Authors for More Consistent Assessment and Reporting." In *Guidance Papers on the Cross Cutting Issues of the Third Assessment Report of the IPCC*, ed. R. Pachauri, T. Taniguchi, and K. Tanaka, 33–51. Geneva: World Meteorological Organization.

Nelkin, D. 1979. *Controversy: Politics of Technical Decisions.* London: Sage.

Nutley, S. 2003. "Bridging the Policy/Research Divide. Reflections and Lessons from the UK." Keynote Paper, Facing the Future: Engaging Stakeholders and Citizens in Developing Public Policy. NIG Conference. Canberra, New Zealand, April 28.

Owens, S., J. Petts, and H. Bulkeley. 2006. "Boundary Work: Knowledge, Policy and the Urban Environment." *Environment and Planning C: Government and Policy* 24 (5): 633–643.

Parliamentary Commissioner for the Environment. 2004. "Missing Links: Connecting Science with Environmental Policy." Wellington, New Zealand, September.

Pielke, R., Jr. 2007. *Honest Broker: Making Sense of Science in Policy and Politics.* New York: Cambridge University Press.

Popper, K. 1968. *The Logic of Scientific Discovery.* London: Hutchinson.

Pouyat, R. 1999. "Science and Environmental Policy—Making Them Compatible." *Bioscience* 49 (4): 281–286.

Rayner, S., 2006. "What Drives Environmental Policy?" *Global Environmental Change* 16: 4–6.

Rowe, G., and L. Frewer. 2000. "Public Participation Methods: A Framework for Evaluation." *Science, Technology, and Human Values* 25 (1): 3–29.

Rykiel, E. 2001. "Scientific Objectivity, Value Systems, and Policymaking." *BioScience* 51 (6): 433–436.

Sabatier, P. 1988. "An Advocacy Coalition Framework of Policy Change and the Role of Policy-Oriented Learning Therein." *Policy Sciences* 21 (Fall): 129–168.

Sagoff, M. 1994. "Should Preferences Count?" *Land Economics* 70: 127–144.

Sarewitz, D. 2004. "How Science Makes Environmental Controversies Worse." *Environmental Science and Policy* 7: 385–403.

Service, R. F. 2003. "'Combat Biology' on the Klamath." *Science* 300: 36–39.

Shapiro, S. A., and C. H. Schroeder. 2008. "Beyond Cost-Benefit Analysis: A Pragmatic Reorientation." *Harvard Environmental Law Review* 32: 433–502.

Shaxson, L. 2005. "Is Your Evidence Robust Enough? Questions for Policy Makers and Practitioners." *Evidence and Policy* 1 (1): 101–111.

Steelman, T. A., and W. Ascher. 1997. "Public Involvement in Natural Resource Policymaking." *Policy Sciences* 30: 71–90.

Steelman, T. A., and C. Burke. 2007. "Is Wildfire Policy in the United States Sustainable?" *Journal of Forestry* 105 (2): 67–72.

Stokes, D. 1997. *Pasteur's Quadrant: Basic Science and Technological Innovation.* Washington, DC: Brookings Institution Press.

Union of Concerned Scientists. 2008. *Interference at the EPA: Science and Politics at the US Environmental Protection Agency.* Cambridge, MA: Union of Concerned Scientists, April. Available at www.ucsusa.org/scientific_integrity/interference/interference-at-the-epa.html (accessed April 5, 2008).

United Kingdom Cabinet Office. 1999, March. *Modernising Government.* London: Prime Minister and the Minister for the Cabinet Office.

U.S. Environmental Protection Agency, Scientific Advisory Board. 2009, May. *Valuing the Protection of Ecological Systems and Services.* Washington, DC: U.S. Environmental Protection Agency.

Vig, N. J., and M. G. Faure, eds. 2004. *Green Giants? Environmental Policies of the United States and the European Union.* Cambridge, MA: MIT Press.

Wheeler, W. B., and M. J. McDonald. 1986. *TVA and the Tellico Dam 1936–1979: A Bureaucratic Crisis in Post-Industrial America.* Knoxville: University of Tennessee Press.

Wynne, B. 1996. "May the Sheep Safely Graze? A Reflexive View of the Expert-Lay Knowledge Divide." In *Risk, Environment, and Modernity: Towards a New Ecology,* ed. S. Lash, B. Szerszynski, and B. Wynne, 44–83. London: Sage.

Zachary, G. P. 1997. *Endless Frontier: Vannevar Bush, Engineer of the American Century.* New York: Free Press.

Ziman, J. 1978. *Reliable Knowledge: An Exploration of the Grounds for Belief in Science.* Cambridge: Cambridge University Press.

CHAPTER 30

ENVIRONMENTAL POLICY EVALUATION AND THE PROSPECTS FOR PUBLIC LEARNING

LAWRENCE SUSSKIND AND ALEXIS SCHULMAN

1. INTRODUCTION

In most models of public policy making, the evaluation stage comes after implementation, but before reconsideration of goals, objectives, and policy designs. Evaluation is supposed to facilitate improvements and corrections. The tools and techniques of policy evaluation have received a great deal of attention in the public policy literature, including quantitative tools like cost-benefit analysis and multivariate analysis of large data sets, as well as qualitative tools such as case studies and ethnographic accounts of the results of new programs or policy ideas (Cook and Campbell 1979; Patton 1980; Stokey and Zeckhauser 1978; Yin 1994, 2002). Most accounts of environmental policy making and implementation take the same approach to evaluation: (1) it is in the public interest to determine whether environmental policies, at every level, and the programs designed to implement them, have worked; (2) this can be accomplished by studying the intended and unintended effects of environmental policies using appropriate social science research tools;

and (3) the results of such studies should allow us to "do better" the next time around.

This presumes a number of things. First, it presumes that environmental policy analysts can sort out the effects or impacts of new environmental policies and programs from the effects of everything else that has happened at the same time. That is a heroic assumption. Second, it presumes that these same policy analysts will be able to tally the impacts or effects of the environmental policy they want to study, in light of some agreed-upon benchmarks. This will make clear whether the results were "worth it." Third, it presumes that these studies will allow policy makers to see clearly what they ought to do differently the next time around. All three presumptions have been strongly contested (Fischer 1980, 1995; Ingram and Mann 1980; Manzer 1984; Packwood 2002).

This chapter reviews conventional approaches to environmental policy evaluation, outlines their presumed relevance to policy making and implementation, and points out the main reasons why they have been subject to challenge. Then we contrast the conventional approach to environmental policy evaluation— which presumes the identity of the policy analyst is unimportant—with what we call the "collaborative approach," which emphasizes the need to engage relevant stakeholders (i.e., the users of policy analyses and those affected by them) in the process of environmental policy evaluation. We also describe the emergence of "adaptive" approaches to resource management and sustainable development and explain why they represent an important shift away from emphasizing "success" and "failure" in environmental policy making and toward ongoing public learning for purposes of improvement. "Collaborative adaptive management," the name now given to this new approach, is one of most important developments in environmental policy making. It represents a shift away from the assumption that our scientific understanding of complex socio-ecological systems is sufficient to justify setting precise standards and long-term goals. Rather, it assumes that the complexity and uncertainty surrounding the search for sustainable ways of managing resources and directing growth require us to move more slowly and carefully, with an emphasis on continuous monitoring and step-by-step adjustment.

2. THE DOMAINS OF EVALUATION

Most of the time, policy evaluation has been focused on whether particular environmental policies achieved their intended goal(s). For example, did the federal government's efforts to reduce lead levels in ambient air achieve that result? We call this the first domain of evaluation. Analysts doing policy evaluation in this domain try to measure the impacts or results of policies and programs in light of what was intended. This is not, however, the only way to frame a policy or program evaluation. For example, analysts working in what we call the second domain of evaluation ask, "What positive and negative impacts, in the long and short term, did lead-reduction levels have, regardless of what was intended?" They focus on unintended consequences, which sometimes turn out to be very important. Analysts working in the third domain of evaluation ask, "In light of what we now know, do the original goals or objectives of federal lead-reduction policies still make sense?" Evaluation in the third domain questions the original intent or objectives. As time goes on, it may turn out that even policies and programs that were entirely successful no longer merit support. Finally, evaluators working in the fourth domain ask, "What other policies or policy approaches, advanced in different ways, might be more beneficial (and to whom) than the policy or program we were initially asked to evaluate?" This requires comparing something that has happened with alternatives that have not yet been tried, or at least not implemented in the same locale(s) in the same time period. The tools and techniques needed to answer these four kinds of questions, and the problems they raise, are quite different (Bardach 2012; Haas and Springer 1998; Hogwood and Gunn 1984; Weimer and Vining 2011).

Most environmental policy evaluation begins in the first domain. Congress, state legislators, and city councils want to know whether the laws and regulations they enacted are working. Very quickly, though, evaluation in the first domain leads curious or self-interested researchers to ask second-, third-, and fourth-domain questions. Were there unintended effects? Are there other ways to achieve the same objectives that might be more effective? Are the original policy objectives still relevant? It is difficult to cumulate research on the effectiveness of an environmental policy if all the available evaluative studies begin with different questions and use different methods to answer them.

3. THE CONVENTIONAL APPROACH TO PUBLIC POLICY EVALUATION

By the 1960s and 1970s, systematic and empirically grounded evaluation and research were widely viewed as the "proper basis for decision-making in public policy" (Fischer 1995, 4). For the first time, analysts were directly responsible for the development of public programs, such as those spearheaded under Lyndon Johnson's "Great Society"; public agencies were retooled to expand their research capacities; and by the 1970s, Congress had turned its sights on evaluation, creating the Congressional Budget Office and Office of Technology Assessment and promoting the use of evaluation in a suite of laws (Fischer 1995). Policy professionals were optimistic that by applying quantitative tools and "scientific" methods they would be able to figure out what was working, what needed improvement, and what else might be tried.

However, as the field evolved, it ended up adopting a limited perspective, confining itself to the task of answering questions in the first domain—narrowly defined actual or expected empirical outcomes of given policy goals (Fischer 1995). This focus was coupled with a rigid "scientific approach," which assumed that any qualified expert using prescribed (quantitative) methods would get replicable results. Criticism of this rationalist, expert-guided approach gave rise to other (more relativistic) schools of evaluative theory and practice, variously entitled "postpositivist" or "argumentative/deliberative."[1] However, a great deal of environmental policy evaluation, whether before-the-fact assessments of policies or programs, or after-the-fact analyses of outcomes, still remains grounded in the positivist optimism of the 1960s and 1970s.

Contemporary policy evaluations are undertaken for many reasons by various administrative, legislative, and advocacy organizations. They may be required by law, requested by decision makers, initiated by various stakeholders or demanded by the public at large. They can be completed by a range of actors in different institutional settings, from think tanks, to academic research centers to political oversight bodies. Even given these different starting points, most environmental policy evaluations in the public arena follow a general six-step process:

1. Define the issue and suggest a method of evaluation.
2. Choose a consultant or a study team.
3. Write a contract spelling out the obligations of the evaluators.
4. Perform the evaluation.
5. Submit a draft report for comment.
6. Produce and disseminate findings and recommendations. (Susskind, Jain, and Martyniuk 2001, 10)

This approach presumes that these six steps can and should involve a purely rational process, separating fact (analysis) from values (politics). The feasibility of this enterprise, however, rests on several key assumptions (Bovens, Hart, and Kuipers 2006). It requires (1) that the goals and objectives of particular environmental policies are clear at the outset; (2) that there is agreement on which indicators should be used to gauge policy outputs and outcomes; and (3) that the views and loyalties of the analyst (aside from their technical competence) should have no impact on the outcome, as long as the right methods are used in the right way. However, the goals of specific environmental policies are almost always murky, in part because of the need to satisfy a sufficient number of stakeholders to win political support. And the choice of evaluative criteria, or benchmarks of success, is contested as part of ongoing disciplinary and ideological battles. What gets measured is based on underlying causal models favored by some researchers but rejected by others.

Thus, in practice, there are too many nonobjective judgments that must be made along the way for the outcome not to reflect, at least in part, the biases or

---

1. For a discussion of these schools of evaluation, see Bovens, Hart, and Kuipers 2006.

ideological predispositions of the evaluators and their clients. Value-laden decisions must be made at each step in the process. For example, study sponsors, more
often than not, have a specific desired outcome in mind. By hiring a consultant
who shares the sponsor's bias and defining the scope of their evaluation (steps 1–3),
it is possible for sponsors to obtain evaluation results that are largely preordained
(Susskind, Jain, and Martyniuk 2001).

Furthermore, the decisions and trade-offs made during analysis (step 4),
regardless of the methodological approach selected, have a major impact on findings. Quantitative approaches, seeking to simulate controlled experimental designs,
dominate the field. The benefits of these methods are well recognized. They allow
analysts to draw generalizations about populations from smaller, statistically chosen samples, and to establish the relationship of chosen variables to policy outcomes, and they make it possible to speculate on the relationship between causes
and effects. In theory, the findings of such evaluations are replicable, meaning they
should not hinge on the background of the evaluator.

Since the 1980s, qualitative methods, like case studies and participant observation, have gained in popularity in the environmental policy field because they
provide unique, if not complementary, policy knowledge (Sadovnik 2007; Yanow
2007). While these methods may be weak where quantitative methods are strong—
generalizability, verification, and reliability—they can enrich our understanding
of how environmental policies are working by providing detailed accounts that
pay attention to context, revealing why and how certain policy outcomes may have
occurred (Sadovnik 2007). Since policy makers and stakeholders may be more interested in causation than correlation, qualitative analyses may be the most effective
means of enabling evaluators to make convincing causal arguments.

Although proponents of quantitative approaches have long argued that their
methods are inherently more objective than qualitative ones, requiring less interpretive work (Campbell and Stanley 1963; Page and Stake 1979), both hinge on nonobjective judgments. At various points in a quantitative analysis, for example, it is
necessary to limit the time and geographic scope of an investigation, choose indicators and set discount rates, and integrate or sum up across multiple dimensions
of analysis. As we discuss further in the following sections of this chapter, there
are no objectively correct ways of doing these things. Resource or time limitations
increase the likelihood that evaluators will make arbitrary choices that affect their
findings.

Finally, interpreting study findings, drawing conclusions, and making recommendations (steps 5 and 6) involve what has been called the "normative leap."
Moving from what has been found to what ought to be done requires evaluators
to make still more nonobjective judgments (Schön and Rein 1994). At the point
where conclusions and recommendations must be drawn, study sponsors typically
exercise significant discretion, "softening" findings that do not comport with their
expectations, reframing conclusions, and deciding what to make public.

This inherently political and value-laden process "virtually guarantees controversy," particularly when multiple evaluations are commissioned of the same

policy initiative (Susskind, Jain, and Martyniuk 2001, 7). Not surprisingly, evaluators drawing on different methods and findings rarely come to the same conclusion, leaving policy makers no better positioned to make a wise decision:

> In the ideal world of the positivist social scientist, we stand to gain from this multiplicity: presumably it results in more facts getting on the table. . . . In the real world, multiple evaluations of the same policy tend to be non-cumulative and non-complementary. (Bovens, Hart, and Kuipers 2006, 321)

The obstacles facing decision makers who make use of environmental policy analyses are not limited to having to reconcile contradictory findings. In an effort to understand why so few evaluations actually produce better policy results and are instead ignored by decision makers (Webber 1992; Weiss 1979), researchers have zeroed in on the dynamics of how knowledge is received and disseminated (Kraft 1998). Knott and Wildavsky (1980) proposed "seven standards of utilization" that affect how the results of policy evaluations are interpreted:

1. *Reception*, which occurs when results reach the decision maker.
2. *Cogitation*, which occurs when the decision maker reads, digests, and otherwise thinks about the findings.
3. *Reference*, which occurs if the study has somehow changed the decision maker's preference or worldview.
4. *Effort*, which occurs if and when the study influences the action of the decision maker.
5. *Adoption*, which occurs when the study actually influences policy outcomes.
6. *Implementation*, which occurs when adopted policy becomes practice.
7. *Impact*, which occurs when tangible benefits to society have been realized.

Although the first standard is usually met, there are a number of factors that routinely impede the achievement of the others. First, *cogitation*, *reference*, and *effort*, the standards most influenced by the characteristics of environmental policy evaluations as opposed to the determination and resources of the decision maker, are unlikely to be met if the wrong questions were asked—that is, if the policy evaluation framed the issue in an unhelpful manner, given the concerns of the decision maker. Second, if the study results are not understandable because of the complexity of the methods used, for example, the chances that a decision maker will actually read and comprehend a study are significantly reduced. Third, if the findings of an evaluation are not convincing, providing a new frame of reference, the study is unlikely to meet standards 5–7 (adoption, implementation, and impact). Whether this is the case is a product of the reputation and credibility of the analysts and sponsor (for example, is there a clear bias, and was the study politicized?) and the manner in which the study was conducted.

The conventional approach to environmental policy evaluation frequently fails to produce evaluations that meet all the standards for effective knowledge utilization listed above. The unfortunate result is that while many analyses are conducted, few actually produce wiser policy decisions.

4. Conventional Approaches to Policy Evaluation Are Not Well Suited to the Environmental Policy Field

Because of the complexity of the socio-ecological systems involved, the conventional ways of gauging the success of public policies and programs are not entirely applicable in the environmental policy field. The usual assumptions about measuring costs and benefits create special difficulties for environmental policy evaluators. It is hard to know how to conceptualize gains and losses, for example, when we are trying to study the effectiveness of policies aimed at protecting endangered species or restoring damaged ecosystems. The amount of money saved or spent is hardly relevant to the primary goal of ensuring that natural systems are functioning properly.

Although many environmental policy evaluations do incorporate the monetary valuation of costs and benefits, multiple values are almost always at stake. For example, issues of endangered species conservation invariably involve concerns that go well beyond utilitarian considerations. Environmental issues are ineluctably linked to questions of equity, governance, and even spirituality. The multidimensionality of environmental issues means that a "plurality of legitimate perspectives" can surround the same problem (Funtowicz and Ravetz 1993, 739). Although the core values, interests, and assumptions that result from these disparate positions are often taken for granted, they really ought to be factored into environmental policy evaluation. So, efforts to rely on a unitary measure of value are not only misleading, but also bound to incite conflict.

Further complicating efforts at environmental policy evaluation is the matter of data. For many environmental processes, there are large data gaps. In some instances, operational criteria are not clear and there are no records of continuous performance—all of which are crucial to ex-post evaluation. For example, while solid waste management at the local level is generally well monitored by government agencies, data on recycling streams are still scarce (Crabbé and Leroy 2008). In some instances data exist but cannot be shared because of proprietary or legal restrictions. Even when relevant data can be located, inconsistencies in terminology, collection methods, and questions of reliability present further challenges (Solomon 1998). Data overload can be just as problematic. Mining for relevant data, patching together data sets, or performing comparative analyses with incongruent sources is more of an art than a science, and leaves considerable discretion to the analyst.

Even with high-quality data, the complexity of the socio-ecological systems—composed of a vast number of interacting variables through both space and time—makes it particularly difficult to model the dynamics involved. Without reliable models, it is hard to analyze whether particular policy interventions will or have produced the desired results. Setting the time frames for environmental policy evaluation is also problematic, raising questions about when we can reliably see intended results or judge a policy to be successful. For example, a great many environmental impact assessments of proposed new hydroelectric plants failed to consider the long-term buildup of mercury in aquatic life and the effects of such changes on the well-being of children (Rosenberg, Bodaly, and Usher 1995).

This system complexity also embeds a great deal of uncertainty in environmental policy evaluations. Policy evaluators attempting to assess the desirability of various environmental policy options before or after the fact face uncertainty about the likelihood that particular outcomes will occur, as well as uncertainty regarding the actual characteristics of the outcomes that have transpired. In environmental policy analysis, there are tools like risk assessment, scenario analysis, and sensitivity analysis that can be used to hedge against uncertainty; however, in the environmental policy evaluation field there are no agreed-upon rules about how these techniques, and others like them, should be used (meaning that they are interpreted quite differently by individual evaluators).

To cope with data gaps, system complexity, and the resulting uncertainty, evaluators must make numerous simplifying assumptions. These are inherently political and subjective. For example, no scientific procedure specifies, a priori, a problem definition or a proper scope of analysis. Setting an analytical frame—the description of the system, how it should be bounded in space and time, and what variables should be considered important—introduces all kinds of bias, particularly epistemological bias (Munda 2000). Indeed, different problem framing can yield vastly different results. For example, between 1979 and 2003, evaluations of the environmental costs of new coal power plants varied by a factor of 50,000—a result of the way scientific models were developed and integrated into the evaluation process (Stirling 1997, as cited in Munda 2000).

5. COLLABORATIVE APPROACHES TO ENVIRONMENTAL POLICY EVALUATION

One way, and perhaps the best way, of defending the subjective judgments that are an inevitable part of environmental policy evaluation is to adopt a collaborative or participatory approach to making such assumptions. That is, by involving the relevant stakeholders or their representatives in reviewing the nonobjective judgments essential to environmental policy evaluation (what indicators of impact to use, what geographic scope to set for an evaluative study, or what time frame to specify), it is possible to avoid many, if not all, of the challenges that undermine the political credibility and stymie the use of environmental policy evaluations done in the conventional way. Frequently bundled with "participatory policy analysis" in the evaluation literature, the collaborative approach can be understood as both a strategy for dealing with conflict and a "societal response to changing conditions in increasingly networked societies…where differences in knowledge and values among individuals and communities is growing" (Innes and Booher 1999, 412). Collaborative approaches to environmental policy evaluation are particularly well suited to the type of "socio-technical" (Fischer 1995, 222) or "wicked"[2] problems characteristic of environmental policy dilemmas.

Collaborative evaluation shares a common history with other types of post-positive approaches to public decision making. All were developed in response to perceived flaws in positivist, expert-driven methodologies. They reject the fact/value dichotomy inherent in rationalist evaluation. Postpositivists view evaluation as the continuation of politics by "other means" and note how bias is mobilized even within its initial stages. As Bovens, Hart, and Kuipers (2006, 327) write, "Evaluation simply mirrors the front end of the policy process (agenda setting and problem definition): some group's interests and voices are organized 'in,' whereas other stakeholders are organized 'out.'" The mission of evaluation, then, is not to provide the one best policy choice or final judgment but, rather, to develop knowledge and come to decisions through argumentation among apparently contradictory perspectives (Bovens, Hart, and Kuipers 2006; Fischer 1998). Drawing on the work of deliberative democrats and theories of communicative rationality,[3] the "argumentative" turn in evaluation cites the transformative role of rational discourse. As Innes and Booher explain, "The basic idea of communicative rationality is that emancipatory knowledge can be achieved through dialogue that engages all those with differing interests around a task or problem" (1999, 6).

Collaborative evaluation embraces the theory of communicative rationality, but elaborates a specific *process* of knowledge development and decision making that is drawn from the fields of consensus building and dispute resolution. This approach diverges from other participatory evaluation methods, such as deliberative polling (Fishkin 1991), in that the goal is to build an informed consensus by engaging all relevant stakeholders—representing both majority and minority interests—in joint decision making. By involving all interested parties (including decision makers, analysts, and the stakeholding public) in a fair and transparent way, environmental policy evaluations prepared in this fashion are far more likely to minimize the conflict that surrounds "expert" assessments, increase the perceived legitimacy of the outcome, and produce salient assessments that facilitate

2. Of wicked problems, Ludwig (2001, 759) writes that they "have no definitive formulation, no stopping rule, and no test for final solution."
3. For the development of this theory, see Habermas 1984.

public learning and wise decisions (Innes 1999; Scher 1999; Susskind, Jain, and Martyniuk 2001).

Although there are many ways to undertake a collaborative environmental policy evaluation, there are three key conditions that must be met. First, any group that believes it is a stakeholder should be consulted about the design of the process and the selection of actual participants. Second, a professional facilitator who does not represent the sponsoring agency or organization should be selected to manage the work. Last, all participants in the process should provide written comments on any interim products of any evaluation. The following elaborates further on the basic steps in collaborative evaluation: convening; assigning roles and responsibilities; facilitating group problem solving; reaching agreement; and holding parties to their commitments (Susskind, McKearnan, and Thomas-Larmer 1999).

A collaborative assessment process needs to be convened by someone with the authority to do so. Once a convener, usually a public agency, decides to proceed, the first steps in a collaborative evaluation include identifying the relevant stakeholders and assessing their concerns. When a decision is made to begin a policy evaluation formally, roles and responsibilities are assigned.

The bulk of a collaborative assessment process is typically spent in group work. How this is undertaken is unique to each group. However, the basic principles include these: strive for transparency; seek expert input when engaging in joint fact-finding (see below for more details); create working subcommittees if appropriate; use the help of a skilled facilitator; and use a single-text procedure.

The final stages of a collaborative evaluation include seeking unanimity on a final report, checking back with each participant's constituents, and producing a written record of the understandings that have been reached (Susskind and Cruikshank 2006).

Given the technical nature of most environmental policy issues, joint fact-finding (JFF) may be an integral part, or even primary focus, of a collaborative policy evaluation. JFF is a procedure for involving those affected by policy decisions in the process of generating and analyzing the scientific and technical information that will be used to inform value-laden decisions. The goal is to produce scientific and technical information that is salient, credible, and legitimate through a process that produces shared learning, trust, creative problem solving, and shared ownership (Erhmann and Stinson 1999). As noted, JFF can be embedded in a larger evaluation process, particularly when there is disagreement over the scientific and technical information that ought to be included. The principles of JFF are similar to those of consensus building more generally. That is, stakeholder groups should be fully represented and self-selected; stakeholders should specify the research protocol together (including technical advisors); and a neutral facilitator is usually required to help the group reach a formal, written agreement.

JFF brings stakeholders together with technical experts to refine the questions that will be asked and select the most appropriate methods of answering them. The participants in JFF assess information and data gaps, reframe general questions as specific ones, determine the strengths and shortcomings of various analytic tools, and gather and analyze chosen data. Once an analysis is complete, the group comes to an agreement on how to use the results—how to deal with conflicting interpretations and how to clarify remaining uncertainties and possible contingent responses. Finally, before results are communicated to constituencies and decision makers, stakeholders jointly review final drafts and studies, determine whether further JFF is necessary, and integrate findings into final recommendations.

JFF has been used successfully to evaluate environmental policy options in complex and often volatile political contexts. For example, such a process was used to generate policy recommendations on how water delivery commitments along the Columbia River basin could be met with minimum impact on Glen Canyon National Recreation Area and Grand Canyon National Park. Stakeholders and experts jointly scoped and conducted research with the help of a neutral facilitator and reached consensus on a "single text" that included findings and recommendations (Council on Environmental Quality 2007). JFF may take more time, cost a bit more, and put policy evaluators in what, for some, will be the uncomfortable position of having to interact with nonexperts. But when recent evaluation efforts have been unsuccessful and policy makers want to be sure that "local knowledge" is incorporated into subsequent rounds of decision making, JFF—and more collaborative assessments in general—make sense.

6. ADAPTIVE MANAGEMENT: A GOOD REASON FOR EVALUATION

While collaboration, including joint fact-finding, is an approach to ensuring transparency and enhancing the legitimacy and political credibility of environmental evaluation studies, collaboration in and of itself will not ensure good results. In our view, collaborative approaches to environmental policy evaluation need to be tied to an adaptive approach to environmental management to increase the chances that an evaluation will have a significant impact on decision making (Susskind, Camacho, and Schenk 2010). Given the complexity of environmental systems, and the uncertainties that surround most socio-ecological interactions, almost all environmental policy making is likely to be off the mark, at least at the outset. It makes more sense to think of environmental evaluation as a means of supporting ongoing adjustments or what might be called public or social learning.

From the beginning of each environmental-policy-making effort, attention should be paid to how implementation will be monitored, who will have responsibility for making sense of the findings, and how both ends and means can be continuously adjusted in light of what is learned.

Adaptive management imagines evaluation as something that happens during rather than after policy objectives have been set. For example, objectives like the achievement of "fishable" or "swimmable" water, reductions in greenhouse gas emissions, or the restoration of contaminated areas to their "original" state are general goals that typically need to be recalibrated as more is learned—in order to reshape ongoing programmatic efforts.

7. THE DYNAMICS OF PUBLIC LEARNING

For the results of environmental policy evaluations to have an impact on public decision making, some degree of learning is necessary. "Perfunctory" or "technical" learning is, unfortunately, the most common. Because it seeks only to validate existing policy or consider alternative means within the same goal structure, it is not likely to lead to substantial improvement (Howlett, Ramesh, and Perl 2009). "Contested" learning or social learning that seeks to harmonize competing evaluations by multiple stakeholders and confronts radically different ways of doing things is more likely to lead to marked improvements in environmental outcomes, but this is much less common.

It is quite possible for "nonlearning" (i.e., no learning at all) and other forms of "limited learning" to occur in environmental-policy-making and environmental management situations. Nonlearning involves a failure to undertake a serious review of the results when specific means are used to achieve various desired ends. Limited learning occurs when lessons of only a very restricted sort are drawn during the evaluation process (Howlett, Ramesh, and Perl 2009). Moreover, what individuals learn is one thing; what organizations or networks learn—social learning—is something quite different. The more "open" a policy network is, the greater the extent to which a wide range of stakeholders will have a chance to participate fully in an assessment process. The more fully a wide range of stakeholders participates, the more likely it is that social learning can occur. Of course, when a broader set of assessment techniques is embraced by policy actors with a wide range of viewpoints, there is a possibility that "contestation" will lead to nothing more than stalemate. Contested learning is more likely to produce social learning and not stalemate when a collaborative approach is used to facilitate the emergence of an informed consensus.

Thus, there are two key obstacles to social learning. One is the willingness and capacity of government employees to engage in joint fact-finding and collaborative assessment with a wide range of stakeholders who may be critical of existing policies and programs. The second is the "the nature of the policy sub-system," that is, the extent to which it is open or closed (Howlett, Ramesh, and Perl 2009). In open subsystems, stakeholder elites and government officials are willing to consider modifications in what they are doing (if only to prove their worth). In closed subsystems they are not. Only if these obstacles to social learning can be removed, usually through the leadership of a few key individuals, will the promise of adaptive management, and the challenge to conventional notions of environmental policy evaluation it represents, be realized.

8. CONCLUSIONS

The evolution of environmental policy evaluation should be viewed within the larger context of public policy making or policy science, relatively new fields with a strong commitment to rational analysis. Unfortunately, the unique aspects of environmental systems, particularly their complexity and the uncertainty it creates, make the conventional approach to public policy evaluation particularly difficult in the environmental field. Almost all environmental policy evaluation begins in the first domain, focusing on whether particular targets, such as ensuring "fishable" or "swimmable" water quality, reducing greenhouse gas emissions to pre-1992 levels, or restoring contaminated rivers to their "original" state have been met. However, the unintended or second-order effects soon attract attention. For example, how have attempts to achieve these targets shortchanged other important goals? Then, too, radically different ways of achieving the same objectives—by using new pricing strategies rather than mandating the use of best available technologies—emerge and there is pressure to figure out which will be the most cost-effective or sustainable strategy. Eventually, someone asks whether we really need to keep worrying about these objectives, or whether different problems deserve our attention. The work of environmental policy evaluators in all four domains requires them to make a great many nonobjective judgments so they can delimit what they are evaluating. The only way these judgments, and the results they produce, can be credible is if the relevant stakeholders are involved in specifying what questions need to be answered, which methods of evaluation should be used, how gaps in the data and uncertainties of various kinds should be handled, and how the findings should be interpreted. Such a collaborative approach makes sense, especially in a context in which incremental approaches to management—that stress monitoring and careful adjustments in both means and ends—seem like the most sensible way of proceeding given our inability to model the complexities of the natural-societal systems involved. Incremental approaches, like adaptive management, assume that environmental policies and programs need to be adjusted continuously, creating a demand for social learning. This is an approach to environmental policy evaluation that puts a premium on how to do better, rather than on what has succeeded and who has failed.

Environmental policy analysis, as a field, depends on careful reviews of the ways in which specific evaluation studies are used, or not, in actual policy making. It would help if one or more research centers dedicated its efforts to compiling such reviews and offering periodic summaries of its findings. This could be done online by creating a "wiki" that encourages environmental policy evaluators to report their findings in a consistent format. Those who track the impact of evaluations, done in different ways, on decision making should make special efforts to highlight the assumptions that evaluators are making when nonobjective judgments come into play. Finally, in terms of a substantive research agenda, it would be helpful to know more about the added value that collaboration in environmental policy evaluation yields.

REFERENCES

Bardach, E. 2012. *A Practical Guide for Policy Analysis: The Eightfold Path to More Effective Problem Solving*. 4th ed. Washington, DC: CQ Press.

Bovens, M., P. T. Hart, and S. Kuipers. 2006. "The Politics of Policy Evaluation." In *The Oxford Handbook of Public Policy*, ed. M. Moran, M. Rein and R. E. Goodin. New York: Oxford University Press.

Campbell, D. T., and J. Stanley. 1963. *Experimental and Quasi-experimental Designs for Research*. Boston: Houghton Mifflin.

Cook, T. D., and D. T. Campbell. 1979. *Quasi-experimentation: Design and Analysis Issues for Field Settings*. Chicago: Rand McNally College.

Council on Environmental Quality. 2007. *Collaboration in NEPA: A Handbook for NEPA Practitioners*. Available at ceq.eh.doe.gov/ntf/Collaboration_in_NEPA_Oct_2007.pdf (accessed January 2011).

Crabbé, A., and P. Leroy. 2008. *The Handbook of Environmental Policy Evaluation*. Sterling, VA: Earthscan.

Erhmann, J. R., and B. L. Stinson. 1999. "Joint Fact-Finding and the Use of Technical Experts." In *The Consensus Building Handbook: A Comprehensive Guide to Reaching Agreement*, ed. L. Susskind, S. McKearnan, and J. Thomas-Larmer. Thousand Oaks, CA: Sage.

Fischer, F. 1980. *Politics, Values, and Public Policy: The Problem of Methodology*. Boulder, CO: Westview.

———. 1995. *Evaluating Public Policy*. Chicago: Nelson-Hall.

———. 1998. "Beyond Empiricism: Policy Inquiry in Postpositivist Perspective." *Policy Studies Journal* 26 (1): 129.

Fishkin, J. S. 1991. *Democracy and Deliberation: New Directions for Democratic Reform*. New Haven, CT: Yale University Press.

Funtowicz, S. O., and J. R. Ravetz. 1993. "Science for the Post-Normal Age." *Futures* 25 (7): 739–755.

Haas, P. J., and J. F. Springer. 1998. *Applied Policy Research: Concepts and Cases*. New York: Garland.

Habermas, J. 1984. *The Theory of Communicative Action*. London: Heinemann.

Hogwood, B. W., and L. A. Gunn. 1984. *Policy Analysis for the Real World*. Oxford: Oxford University Press.

Howlett, M., M. Ramesh, and A. Perl. 2009. *Studying Public Policy: Policy Cycles and Policy Subsystems*. New York: Oxford University Press.

Ingram, H. M., and D. E. Mann. 1980. *Why Policies Succeed or Fail*. Beverly Hills, CA: Sage.

Innes, J. E. 1999. "Evaluating Consensus Building." In *The Consensus Building Handbook: A Comprehensive Guide to Reaching Agreement*, ed. L. Susskind, S. McKearnan, and J. Thomas-Larmer. Thousand Oaks, CA: Sage.

Innes, J., and D. E. Booher. 1999. "Consensus Building and Complex Adaptive Systems: A Framework for Evaluating Collaborative Planning." *Journal of the American Planning Association* 65 (4): 412–423.

Knott, J., and A. Wildavsky. 1980. "If Dissemination Is the Solution, What Is the Problem?" *Knowledge: Creation, Diffusion, Utilization* 1 (4): 537–578.

Kraft, M. E. 1998. "Using Environmental Program Evaluation: Politics, Knowledge, and Policy Change." In *Environmental Program Evaluation: A Primer*, ed. G. J. Knaap and J. K. Tschangho. Urbana: University of Illinois Press.

Ludwig, D. 2001. "The Era of Management Is Over." *Ecosystems* 4 (8): 758–764.

Manzer, R. 1984. "Policy Rationality and Policy Analysis: The Problem of the Choice of Criteria for Decision-Making." In *Public Policy and Adminstrative Studies*, ed. O. P. Dwivedi. Guelph, ON: University of Guelph.

Munda, G. 2000. *Conceptualising and Responding to Complexity*. Cambridge, UK: Cambridge Research for the Environment.

Packwood, A. 2002. "Evidence-Based Policy: Rhetoric and Reality." *Social Policy and Society* 1 (3): 267–272.

Page, E. B., and R. E. Stake. 1979. "Counterpoint: Should Educational Evaluation Be More Objective or More Subjective?" *Educational Evaluation and Policy Analysis* 1 (1): 45–47.

Patton, M. Q. 1980. *Qualitative Evaluation Methods*. Beverly Hills, CA: Sage.

Rosenberg, D. M., R. A. Bodaly, and P. J. Usher. 1995. "Environmental and Social Impacts of Large Scale Hydroelectric Development: Who Is Listening?" *Global Environmental Change: Human and Policy Dimensions* 5 (2): 127–148.

Sadovnik, A. R. 2007. "Qualitative Research and Public Policy." In *Handbook of Public Policy Analysis: Theory, Politics, and Methods*, ed. F. Fischer, G. Miller, and M. S. Sidney. Boca Raton, FL: CRC/Taylor & Francis.

Scher, E. 1999. "Negotiating Superfund Cleanup at the Massachusetts Military Reservation." In *The Consensus Building Handbook: A Comprehensive Guide to Reaching Agreement*, ed. L. Susskind, S. McKearnan, and J. Thomas-Larmer. Thousand Oaks, CA: Sage.

Schön, D. A., and M. Rein. 1994. *Frame Reflection: Toward the Resolution of Intractable Policy Controversies*. New York: Basic Books.

Solomon, L. S. 1998. "Evaluation of Environmental Programs: Limitations and Innovation." In *Environmental Program Evaluation: A Primer*, ed. G. J. Knaap and J. K. Tschangho. Urbana: University of Illinois Press.

Stirling, A. 1997. "Limits to the Value of External Costs." *Energy Policy* 25 (5): 517.

Stokey, E., and R. Zeckhauser. 1978. *A Primer for Policy Analysis*. New York: W. W. Norton.

Susskind, L., A. E. Camacho, and T. Schenk. 2010. "Collaborative Planning and Adaptive Management in Glen Canyon: A Cautionary Tale." *Columbia Journal of Environmental Law* 35 (1): 1–56.

Susskind, L., and J. L. Cruikshank. 2006. *Breaking Robert's Rules: The New Way to Run Your Meeting, Build Consensus, and Get Results*. Oxford: Oxford University Press.

Susskind, L., R. K. Jain, and A. O. Martyniuk. 2001. *Better Environmental Policy Studies: How to Design and Conduct More Effective Analysis*. Washington, DC: Island.

Susskind, L., S. McKearnan, and J. Thomas-Larmer, eds. 1999. *The Consensus Building Handbook: A Comprehensive Guide to Reaching Agreement*. Thousand Oaks, CA: Sage.

Webber, D. J. 1992. "The Distibution and Use of Policy Knowledge in the Policy Process." In *Advances in Policy Studies since 1950*, ed. W. N. Dunn and R. M. Kelly. New Brunswick, NJ: Transaction.

Weimer, D. L., and A. R. Vining. 2011. *Policy Analysis: Concepts and Practice.* 5th ed. New York: Pearson Longman.

Weiss, C. H. 1979. "The Many Meanings of Research Utilization." *Public Administration Review* 39 (5): 426–431.

Yanow, D. 2007. "Qualitative-Interpretive Methods in Policy Research." In *Handbook of Public Policy Analysis: Theory, Politics, and Methods*, ed. F. Fischer, G. Miller, and M. S. Sidney. Boca Raton, FL: CRC/Taylor & Francis.

Yin, R. K. 2002. *Case Study Research: Design and Methods.* Thousand Oaks, CA: Sage.

PART VII

CONCLUSION

CHAPTER 31

RESEARCH ON U.S. ENVIRONMENTAL POLICY IN THE NEW CENTURY

MICHAEL E. KRAFT AND SHELDON KAMIENIECKI

As the introductory chapter of this volume explains, since the late 1960s studies on various aspects of environmental politics and policy have increased dramatically. Today we have a far-ranging literature on the strengths, weaknesses, and potential of policy alternatives. As the first chapter notes, this is especially the case for environmental protection policy, long dominated by direct command-and-control regulation, where researchers have studied different approaches, including the use of market incentives, flexible regulation, public-private partnerships, and stakeholder collaboration (e.g., Cohen, Kamieniecki, and Cahn 2005; Durant, Fiorino, and O'Leary 2004; Eisner 2007; Fiorino 2006; Kraft, Stephan, and Abel 2011; Press and Mazmanian 2013; Rosenau 2000). This also is generally true for natural resource policy, where new alternatives have been praised and, to some extent, have become the focus of scholarly investigation (Fairfax et al. 2005; Layzer 2008; Lubell and Segee 2013; Sabatier et al. 2005; Weber 2003; Whiteley, Ingram, and Perry 2008).

In particular, political scientists and policy scholars have written a great deal about various aspects of the environmental policy-making process and the role of a diverse set of policy actors and institutions—from organized interest groups and the media to government policy makers and the role of both natural and social scientists in the policy process (e.g., Durant, Fiorino, and O'Leary 2004; Klyza and Sousa 2008; Kraft 2011; Miller 2002; Vig and Kraft 2013). Scholars have greatly expanded the scope and sophistication of research and increasingly have relied on major theoretical concepts and analytic frameworks from the discipline (for example, related to agenda setting, interest group lobbying, policy-making processes, and compliance behavior) and have used the full range of social science research methods commonly employed today. As a consequence, we now have a much deeper and broader understanding as to why certain environmental controversies are addressed by government leaders and institutions and others are ignored, why certain programs are well funded and others are not, why regulations are strict in some areas and weak in other areas, and which regulatory tools and approaches work well and which do not.

As indicated in the first chapter, most of the literature on U.S. environmental policy and politics addresses major issues of concern at the federal level. Increasingly, however, research is being conducted on state and local issues, policy processes, and institutions. This is evident in, for instance, chapters 9, 18, and 19 in this volume. There also has been increased attention paid to international environmental problems and policy issues over the past two decades, and we expect the size of this literature to expand significantly in the coming years. While we included two chapters (10 and 11) on international environmental issues, the literature has already grown so large that a separate comprehensive volume on global environmental policy is now warranted.

This book has provided a broad and detailed review and assessment of the literature on U.S. environmental policy and politics. As the chapters in the book have shown, numerous studies on this topic have been conducted in response to the changing nature of environmental politics and increased federal government intervention. Even so, until now there has been no single volume or edited collection that brings together this impressive body of work in a way that effectively introduces to those entering the field the most important subjects that have been explored, reviews the most significant scholarship that has been produced, and recommends paths for future research. This book fills that gap by providing a comprehensive, in-depth investigation of the central research issues and concerns in environmental policy and politics, primarily within the U.S. political system.

This last chapter of the book offers a general summary of the sections and chapters in the volume, including recommendations for future research by the contributors. This summary will closely follow the organization of the book. At the end of the chapter we provide our own ideas concerning where the literature should be headed in the coming years.

1. SUMMARY OF THE SECTIONS
AND CHAPTERS

This book contains five major sections and 29 individual chapters (plus an introduction and conclusion) that address important topics found in the literature on environmental policy and politics. The chapters explain and evaluate the evolution of studies conducted in the fields of expertise of the contributors. Authors were able to integrate a large body of scholarship that deals with a variety of substantive environmental problems, from pollution control and public lands to energy and renewable resources. We emphasized governing capacity, major theoretical ideas, political processes and institutions, and policy approaches and analytic methods as the best way to identify fruitful areas of scholarship within the discipline. Contributors have illustrated their arguments with examples of substantive policy issues at appropriate points in their chapters. The chapters included in this volume have produced a clear, comprehensive, and valuable assessment of important previous research on U.S. environmental policy as well as opportunities to expand this research in new directions in the years ahead. In the following paragraphs we offer a general overview of the major sections of the book and explain how certain chapters within these sections, by example, further our understanding of the literature on significant topics.

1.1. The Evolution of Environmental Policy: Major Concepts, Ideas, and Movements

The first major section of the volume focuses on the evolution of environmental policy and the political processes associated with it, and it covers major concepts, theoretical ideas, and policy changes that have been analyzed in the literature. The chapters provide a historical overview of the environmental movement and the development of public policies. They address the rise of green ideas in relation to politics and governing, including environmental ethics, sustainability, and environmental security.

Chapter 2, for example, by Richard Andrews, provides a historical overview of the foundations and changing nature of U.S. environmental policy and politics. Andrews's chapter offers an analysis of critical studies appearing in the literature, from their early foundations through the parallel and intersecting histories of natural resource development and conservation, environmental health, and other policies that ultimately have shaped contemporary environmental policy issues. He concludes by observing that the history of environmental policies reveals a broad range of policy instruments that have been used at different times and to address different problems. Environmental policy history is suffused with complex research questions of administrative discretion and environmental federalism, and it cannot be held up as a story of great progress and gradual victory of environmental sustainability over past practices. Instead, according to Andrews, U.S. environmental policy to date is primarily a story of perennial conflicts among organized advocates of various commercial versus appreciative uses of natural assets, often pitting short-term private extractive benefits against damage to long-term ecological sustainability. Effective solutions to environmental policy problems, in his view, are stalemated by the political dominance of these frames and of the "half-truths" that they each contain, in the hands of leaders on each side.

Andrews believes that the central issue for future environmental policy is how to achieve an environmentally sustainable society that is resilient to the increasing pressures and threats to it, both at the micro level of individuals and businesses and at the macro level of aggregate extraction of materials and energy from the environment and aggregate transformation of ecosystems. Understanding these political forces warrants careful reading of the insights of key political theorists and the rich body of research that now exists on the tragedies and management of open-access resources. Far more research needs to be done on the social and behavioral influences driving both individual and business behavior that affects the environment, and on how different policy incentives influence both the external barriers (costs, availability, etc.) and the internal barriers (e.g., values, attitudes, beliefs, assumptions, and social norms) that drive behavioral choices both favorable and harmful to the environment.

Chapter 4, by Lamont Hempel, explores the development and application of sustainability concepts in environmental policy and politics, paying particular attention to the challenges of operationalizing and measuring sustainability in the dynamic environment of twenty-first-century politics and policy. After surveying the historical roots of the concept, Hempel examines the struggle to refine and apply the concept in contemporary policy analysis. He then reviews the key policy initiatives that have incorporated sustainability language or contributed to its development within each branch of government. Attention is focused on the pragmatic adoption of sustainability principles in policy making at the end of the chapter.

Hempel believes that sustainability, as a primary concept, has major implications for policy specialists in environmental, social welfare, and economic development areas. In effect, policy experts will now be expected to transcend their narrow interest and training for the sake of an integrative and synergistic idea. Environmental analysts will need to probe the social and economic meaning of environmental policies over an indefinite period of time and across a multijurisdictional range of space. This is not only demanding and daunting; it also suggests that depth of knowledge must be sacrificed for breadth. As a consequence, a focus on sustainability will reduce the power and authority of narrow technical specialists and the long-standing political, academic, and professional organizations that support them.

Other chapters in this section touch on green political ideas, ethical challenges, and environmental security. Chapters 3, 5, and 6 further contribute to our understanding of today's major concepts, ideas, and movements in environmental policy making. The chapters in this early part of the book, therefore, provide readers with a foundation to analyze and comprehend topics covered in chapters in subsequent parts of the volume.

1.2. Governing Capacity and Environmental Challenges

The second section contains chapters on a set of macro-level questions about governing capacity in relation to the magnitude and urgency of global environmental challenges, particularly those concerning a third generation of environmental problems, such as climate change and the quest for sustainable development. The chapters in this section present a broad discussion of how governments can respond and have responded to these challenges at the appropriate scale and in a timely manner. Contributors also examine how governments have addressed sustainability challenges, and what we know and what we need to learn about such challenges. Within this context, various writings offer an assessment of the U.S. leadership role past and present, notable actions and challenges, and the factors that affect U.S. policy making on global environmental issues.

In chapter 7, for instance, Rosenbaum analyzes four of the most significant domestic innovations in environmental governance since 1970. He begins by placing these important innovations in the context of major challenges posed to domestic environmental governance by the Third Environmental Era (explained in the introductory chapter). The narrative then turns to the research contributions of these innovations and examines critical research issues now posed by continuing experience with this domestic governance. This chapter illustrates the broad purpose of this volume to provide a comprehensive review and assessment of the literature of environmental policy and politics by examining the important current literature about environmental governance and its implications for a future research agenda, issues fundamental to any examination of environmental policy and politics, past and future. From the author's perspective, environmental governance is an ongoing preoccupation, constantly emerging at the strategic core of all environmental policy research, and is continually compelling because environmental governance is inherently vulnerable to unexpected social change and scientific discovery.

Rosenbaum argues that many of the significant challenges confronting the nation's environmental governance have become readily apparent, while some are still implicit; and both the apparent and the implicit constitute a priority list for continuing policy research and policy innovation. These are especially relevant for four governance institutions that serve as a vital foundation for current environmental policy making and are in need of improvement, reconsideration, and expansion: the National Environmental Policy Act, common pool resources, the Clean Air Act (CAA), and the use of sustainability in policy making. For example, in terms of rethinking the CAA, Rosenbaum believes that the most compelling research priorities include (1) creation of scientifically credible and administratively practical methods for characterizing the human health impacts of climate change in terms relevant to the regulatory criteria required by the CAA; (2) creation of procedures for characterizing the domestic ecological and socioeconomic consequences of climate warming in terms relevant for the CAA; (3) development and evaluation of alternative regulatory strategies to address the predicted national impact of climate change; and (4) assessment of current institutional capacities for regulatory management of climate change across domestic governmental scales and investigation of alternative and innovative approaches to multilevel governance.

In contrast to Rosenbaum's exclusive focus on governance issues at the federal level, chapter 9, by Daniel Mazmanian and Laurie Nijaki, addresses issues primarily at the community and local level of governance. In doing so, they address the question, "How can and should environmental and economic resources be governed given the objectives of sustainability?" As they maintain, the answer is not simple, although we are beginning to see efforts at reaching across the three E's of equity, environmental, and economically driven values that will underlie any governing system worthy of the label, "governance commensurate with sustainable development." Following a brief overview of the rationale for sustainability, they explore the requisite features of society and governance system in a sustainability epoch, along with recognition of several critical barriers to attaining it today. They argue that experimentation and policy entrepreneurship should be undertaken at the community and local level, from which we can all learn. Finally, they discuss several of the major features or criteria of governing in an epoch of sustainable development that they believe are prerequisites and indicative of the changes to come, which they believe helps to identify critical research needs as we move forward.

Mazmanian and Nijaki conclude that addressing environmental degradation and fostering a sense of sustainability in cities and regions will require bringing together a multitude of urban policies—everything from housing and transportation planning to tourism and economic development—all of which have environmental consequences. For policy makers, understanding the interconnectedness at the level of the city and the region will presumably show the way to doing the same at the level of the state, nation, and, where need be, the planet, to achieving the ultimate transformation to sustainable development. They maintain that this will require nothing short of ecosystem management types of approaches that assume complexity, involvement of actors and arenas of activity from local up through global arenas, and an ability to adapt as the human and environmental conditions evolve over time. In other words, we need to craft approaches that bring together dynamic "living" systems that incorporate economic, environmental, social, and cultural factors. Research is needed that will enhance our understanding of the primary causes of environmental degradation and an evaluation of the cost and benefits of the myriad of possible policy approaches. Uncertainties around these costs and benefits also must be explored. The focus is on addressing problems comprehensively—taking environmental governance out of a vacuum in a manner that understands vital policy interconnections. As we continue to see progress in this direction in the third environmental epoch, they suggest that ecosystems thinking and approaches will guide the way in which governmental entities understand their challenges and implementation of their plans, programs, and policies.

Other chapters in this section tackle governing capacity and environmental challenges in other different ways. In chapter 8, for instance, Selin and VanDeveer analyze federal and international aspects of U.S. climate change politics and policy making. Specifically, they examine American climate change politics at federal and subnational governance levels, involving a multitude of legal and political activities and interactions by a large number of actors from the public and private sectors and from civil society. At the same time, chapter 10, by Elizabeth DeSombre, and chapter 11, by Kate O'Neill, analyze the U.S. role in international environmental policy and global environmental management, respectively.

1.3. Government Institutions and Policy Making

The next part of the book examines U.S. political institutions and policy-making processes, with special attention paid to institutional capacity, institutional development and adaptation over time, and policy innovation. More specifically, the chapters in this segment of the volume analyze the courts, legal issues, and environmental policy; Congress and environmental policy, including distinctive legislative processes and actors, and constraints and opportunities for policy making; the American presidency, leadership, and environmental policy; the bureaucracy and environmental and natural resource policy; rule-making processes and public management, including deregulation and its effects on regulatory reform; state and local government and federalism; and multilevel governance and collaborative decision making.

In chapter 14, Norman Vig investigates the role of the American presidency in environmental policy making over time. He points out that while a large environmental policy literature has developed over the past four decades, as summarized in this volume, at the same time presidential studies have emerged as a major subfield in political science. Yet there are still very limited overlaps between the literatures in the two subfields. Few presidential scholars have devoted much attention to environmental policy, and, conversely, environmental policy scholars have been slow to integrate the increasingly sophisticated literature on the presidency into their analyses. When the first academic conference on the "environmental presidency" was held in 2000, only a handful of political scientists had published in the field. Nevertheless, since the mid-1980s a new focus on the use of presidential powers in this area has slowly emerged. Vig's chapter traces some of these developments and discusses the use of presidential powers in detail. He summarizes emerging perspectives on the president's role in environmental policy making and suggests further avenues for research at the end of the chapter. He believes that presidents will play a central role in the future of American environmental policy—though not necessarily a dominant one.

Following a brief discussion about the important role power and influence play in presidential politics, Vig suggests that we need to learn a great deal more about the involvement of the presidency in policy implementation. More specifically, he recommends that researchers address the following questions in the future: How are executive orders carried out? How much bureaucratic resistance is there? How many and what kinds of proposed regulations are blocked by the Office of Information and Regulatory Affairs (OIRA, which oversees regulation), and on what grounds? How much political control is there over scientific research and analysis used in policy making? How has the use of presidential policy instruments changed over time? Is the administrative presidency model still useful, or is it more productive to focus on the larger context of policy making, including the role of public opinion and the media? Should we pay more attention to presidential rhetoric? How has the growing polarization between parties over environmental issues in the past two decades affected the scope for presidential action? A major challenge for future researchers in this area is the clandestine context in which decisions are made in the White House and, to a somewhat lesser extent, in the executive branch. Chapters 12, by Timothy Duane, and 13, by Michael Kraft, examine the literature on the involvement of the two other branches of government, the courts and Congress, respectively, in environmental policy making.

Vig's chapter on the involvement of the president in environmental policy is followed, accordingly, by chapters that examine the literature on different aspects of the bureaucracy. In chapter 15, Daniel Fiorino presents an analysis of the U.S. Environmental Protection Agency (EPA) and the administrative and policy literature associated with it under three headings: relationships with state agencies; the role of economic and risk analysis in decision making; and the capacity for innovation. Chapter 16, by Craig Thomas, follows with an examination of the broad range of natural resource policies in the United States, the public agencies that have implemented these policies, and the policy subsystems within which they operate. His chapter also investigates how agency cultures have changed as new professions and scientific ideas entered the agencies and new approaches to natural resources management, such as adaptive management and collaborative governance. Finally, in chapter 17 Rinfret and Furlong explore the underpinnings of the U.S. administrative rule-making process in environmental policy making, with special attention to the U.S. EPA and other federal agencies.

In chapter 18, Denise Scheberle provides an overview of federalism and intergovernmental relations, focusing particularly on the legal structures for federalism and how these structures play out in environmental policy. She also highlights the evolving nature of intergovernmental relationships within environmental programs, including discussions of federal-state working relationships, differences in state capacity and willingness to engage in environmental protection, advocacy by state and local governments, and state and local government innovation. She concludes by saying that state and local governments are essential to further progress in environmental protection but need the architecture of environmental federalism and national environmental laws. In turn, the implementation of national environmental laws depends on state and local governments as partners, whether they are reluctant or supportive. State and local governments may bring innovative approaches and on-the-ground wisdom to environmental problem solving.

In chapter 19, Andrea Gerlak, Tanya Heikkila, and Mark Lubell analyze previous studies on collaborative governance and environmental policy at the end of this section. Despite the increasing popularity of collaborative governance, some are skeptical as to whether it can deliver on its promise to solve increasingly complex and uncertain environmental challenges. Furthermore, data and evidence on the environmental outputs and outcomes of collaborative efforts are weak, or in some cases nonexistent. Thus, given both the growing importance of collaborative governance and the uncertainties surrounding it, their chapter offers an in-depth assessment of both its promise and its possible pitfalls. They explain the origins and evolution of collaborative governance and then compare the claims of the proponents and opponents. They next review what is known and what is still uncertain from the growing body of empirical research studying collaborative environmental governance. Gerlak and her colleagues call for continued research into the environmental policy effectiveness of collaborative governance. In particular, research into environmental performance over time is greatly needed. International comparative research is also needed to investigate how collaborative governance plays out in different social, cultural, political, and institutional contexts.

1.4. The Role of Informal Political Actors

The fourth major section of the book evaluates the role of informal political actors, especially in regards to their participation in policy making and public education. Thus, contributors analyze the role of public opinion, public participation, interest groups, campaigns, elections, and the media in educating Americans and in the policy-making process. Here, too, attention is paid to the implications for governing capacity and conflict resolution.

In this vein, researchers recognize that certain conditions become public issues only after leaders and citizens come to see them not as the product of accident or fate, but as something that is caused by human behavior and amenable to human intervention, a process that is often itself an act of social construction. As Deborah Guber and Christopher Bosso observe in chapter 20, nowhere is this struggle more clearly observed than in the environmental policy-making area. For an environmental problem to generate public concern, and for that concern to move onto the

policy agenda, an entirely different "causal story" is required, one that is both revolutionary and transformative. To identify a problem, diagnose its cause, attribute
blame, and propose a solution is to engage in a long and complex chain of events
that lie at the heart of political life and public affairs. In order to explain this phenomenon, their chapter connects two broad interdisciplinary threads. First, they
address *issue framing*, which focuses on the formation of public attitudes and the
way in which issues are packaged and presented for mass consumption. Second,
they analyze *agenda setting*, which centers on political elites and the decisions that
are made—or deferred—within the policy-making process. They conclude that,
within the current discourse involving environmental policy issues and problems,
an array of meanings exist. The environment, therefore, will always remain a contested value system, subject to disputes between "deep greens" at one end of the
ideological spectrum to "free-market" environmentalists at the other—and everyone in between. The absence of consensus values and preferences underscores the
centrality of problem definition and agenda setting in environmental politics and
policy and reminds us that whoever can define what "the environment" means has
the advantage, even if the room for maneuvering is constrained by decades of policy choices. They conclude by arguing for more research on the interrelationships
between issue framing, agenda building, and environmental discourse.

In chapter 22, Dorothy Daley explores the vast literature on civic engagement
and environmental decision making in American politics. She notes that this is
a broad literature that ranges from philosophical arguments on the nature and
scope of participation, to theoretically grounded social science research evaluating the ways in which participation influences decision processes and outcomes.
More specifically, she assesses the strengths and weaknesses of previous studies,
identifies broad areas of agreement and divergence, and pinpoints knowledge
gaps that future research should address. She examines the background and history of public participation and environmental policy, emphasizing the strain
between scientifically informed decision making, democratic ideals, and broad
changes in environmental policy. Daley's study also assesses the arguments for
and against widespread participation in environmental decision making. She
explores the notion of what constitutes a community and the challenges inherent in identifying and defining "the public" in a decentralized political system. In addition, her chapter describes and evaluates different policy-making
approaches that utilize public participation, ranging from traditional public
hearings and comments to more involved collaborative decision processes. She
includes a discussion of the ways in which public participation influences environmental policy making, and she suggests areas of inquiry for future research
at the end of the chapter.

Other contributors also examine the role of informal political actors, especially in regard to their participation in policy making and public education. While
David Daniels and his three collaborators (chapter 21) investigate the role of public
opinion in environmental policy making, Robert Duffy (chapter 23) explores the
role of organized interests in shaping environmental decision making. The section

concludes with a chapter by Amy Below (chapter 24) on how political parties, campaigns, and elections affect environmental politics and policy.

1.5. Policy Approaches and Analytic Tools

The last section provides an in-depth review of a diversity of policy approaches and analytic tools and determines their potential contributions to policy making. As these tools continue to evolve, they merit careful appraisal in relation to governing capacity, their contribution to understanding the consequences of policy choices, and their capacity to address questions of policy effectiveness, efficiency, and equity. In response to this challenge, the chapters in this segment of the book address the role of science, political economy, market incentives, ecosystem management and restoration, environmental planning and impact assessments, privatization, self-regulation, and information disclosure, and other voluntary programs in environmental policy making.

Sheila Olmstead (chapter 25), for example, investigates the use of market incentives in environmental policy. Her chapter discusses the framework that economics brings to environmental policy and, in particular, the use of market incentives in relation to traditional approaches to regulating environmental quality. She begins by considering why and how markets fail to result in the optimal level of environmental quality and ends by considering how they might be induced to do so. She then defines market failure more precisely in the context of environmental problems, and she considers what economic theory has to say about solutions to market failure in the environmental realm. Olmstead next compares and contrasts market-based environmental policies with more traditional, prescriptive approaches. She provides a closer focus on market-based policy instruments themselves, comparing and contrasting the two most common approaches, taxes and tradable permits. She discusses the experience with selected market-based environmental policies in practice near the end of the chapter.

Olmstead concludes that continued research on market-based environmental policy is critical. According to her, economic theory and empirical evidence show that market-based environmental policy instruments are more cost-effective than prescriptive policies in the short run and that they provide strong incentives for cost-reducing technological solutions in the long run. The growing number of cap-and-trade policies (and, to a much smaller extent, taxes) in environmental regulation indicates that at least some governments recognize the advantages of market-based policy instruments (MBIs). Empirical assessment of current and future environmental applications of taxes and tradable permits, however, is not all that research in economics has to contribute to the policy process. In her view, economists have now moved on to confronting some of the most critical challenges to expanding market-based approaches to environmental policy. Chief among these is the concern about developing truly tradable commodities, since many environmental problems have significant spatial and temporal components. She notes that the development of differentiated taxes and trading ratio regimes for permit systems often requires economists to work in partnership with natural and physical scientists, so as to ensure that the cost savings achievable from MBIs is not eroded by an increase in damages from undesirable changes in the distribution of pollution or the biophysical services provided by wetlands, fisheries, and other critical natural resources.

In chapter 29, William Ascher and Toddi Steelman examine the role and use of science in environmental policy. As they maintain, understanding the complex relationship between science and environmental policy is crucial for bringing the broadest range of sound science and related considerations to policy makers. Accordingly, their chapter covers the intellectual traditions that have shaped how science is viewed, current controversies related to science and environmental policy, and some alternatives to deal with the complexities of science and environmental policy making. They suggest that science ought to be seen as one form of knowledge that can inform policy and that understanding the role of science and these other types of knowledge within the distinct stages of the policy process can provide greater insight into how one might think about and use science more constructively.

Their discussion points to a broader research agenda involving the complex relationship between science and policy. To address this complex relationship, Ascher and Steelman recommend that future research on the roles of knowledge in the environmental policy process should focus on how to uncover the largely unexamined biases embedded in how science is currently incorporated into the policy-making process. In their opinion, research should also be devoted to refining the criteria for evaluating the generation, transmission, and use of science by examining case studies to determine what is most important for a healthy relationship between science and policy. In a more prescriptive vein, research should explore how to overcome the barriers to providing policy makers with a balanced set of considerations for their deliberations. Finally, they suggest that case studies could be constructive to understanding how and why knowledge hybrids succeed and fail.

Other important chapters are also included in this section of the book. Lori Bennear and Cary Coglianese (chapter 26), for instance, examine privatization and self-regulation, while Judith Layzer (chapter 27) analyzes the success of ecosystem-based management and restoration. Layzer's study of ecosystem-based management and restoration yields mixed results. Sometimes these efforts work very well and sometimes they do not. Hence, much like studies of collaborative decision making and governance, it is important to understand the conditions under which ecosystem-based management is likely to be successful. Steven Cohen (chapter 28) writes about the use of strategic planning, among other approaches, in environmental policy making. Although such an approach is not commonly pursued for reasons he explains, it can be effective when it is used. Finally, Lawrence Susskind and Alexis Schulman (chapter 30) assess the best ways to approach policy evaluation in environmental policy making, underscoring the continuing value of qualitative approaches that complement the more common calls for rigorous quantitative research.

2. FUTURE DIRECTIONS FOR RESEARCH

The chapters in this book identify numerous possible avenues for future research, and space limitations prevent us from discussing every one. Readers interested in a specific field or particular line of inquiry should consult the appropriate section(s) in the volume and review the parts of the chapters that discuss suggested areas of investigation. The last section of this chapter highlights, as examples, potential new research paths mentioned at various points in this volume.

To a large extent, environmental policy involves competing values and difficult trade-offs for decision makers. How this has played out in American politics is discussed in primarily theoretical chapters by Richard Andrews (chapter 2), Lamont Hempel (chapter 4), Robert Paehlke (chapter 5), and Walter Baber and Robert Bartlett (chapter 3). David Daniels and his three colleagues (chapter 21) to a certain extent empirically explore values and trade-offs in their extensive examination of public opinion on environmental policy in the United States. Dorothy Daley (chapter 22) and Amy Below (chapter 24) separately touch on the important role of citizen involvement and democracy and the values associated with these concepts. What is clear from the literature reviewed by all of these authors is that Americans take strong and often contradictory positions on major environmental ideas, issues, and policies. Future researchers should make a greater effort to integrate more closely the question of values and trade-offs with positions that citizens actually take on vital environmental issues. Such studies can pinpoint exactly where conflicts and contradictions exist, increase our understanding of the values and policy positions Americans hold, and identify areas requiring more education.

Michael Kraft (chapter 13) provides an in-depth analysis of the important role of the U.S. Congress in environmental policy making. His chapter helps to explain why Congress has passed certain landmark pieces of legislation while at the same time has failed to adopt other essential legislation in areas where science has clearly identified acute environmental and natural resource problems (e.g., climate change and hard-rock mining). (Ascher and Steelman also discuss the role science and knowledge play in environmental policy making in chapter 29.) As he points out, previous studies have investigated the evolution of individual bills through the different stages of legislative enactment. However, in addition to studying committee or subcommittee hearings on proposed legislation, researchers also should closely study how the ideas for such bills are formulated from the outset and the manner in which they are drafted prior to submission. For that matter, we should also study how ideas and legislative proposals make it onto the political agenda in the first place, such as through the persistent efforts of key policy entrepreneurs and interest groups. This represents a critical phase in the legislative process, one that is generally ignored in the literature. Collecting data on what groups and individuals participate in and shape the initial writing of legislation, often behind the scenes, may be difficult given the hidden nature of the process, but it is nonetheless important to try to shed more light on these activities.

This book focused almost exclusively on issues at the federal level, and future researchers might want to adopt the theoretical and analytic approach employed here to explore environmental policy and politics at the state and local level as well. Chapter 18, by Denise Scheberle, is a good starting point for those who wish to conduct such research. Thus, for example, it would be fruitful to examine issue identification and framing, agenda setting, and policy making in the judicial, legislative, and executive branches of state and local governments. To what extent do the observations in chapter 23 (Duffy) and chapter 20 (Guber and Bosso) pertain to agenda building at the state and local level? Almost no research has been pursued along these lines, and an exploration of government institutions below the national level could further understanding of interest group politics and environmental policy making. Furthermore, states (and localities) represent a venue to try new and creative policy approaches. For instance, research on California's approach to reducing air pollution emissions has provided the federal government with possible ways to tackle this issue at the national level.

More work also needs to be done on theory development, particularly in the areas of issues definition, framing, and agenda building, but also on the politics of policy making and policy change. Political scientists can contribute a great deal to the literature in sociology and communications on issue definition and framing processes. Moreover, the existing literature on agenda denial is quite thin, which is surprising given the frequency with which it occurs and its importance in policy making. A clearer picture must be developed on interest group tactics and strategies and on the political dynamics underlying agenda blocking if researchers are ever to develop a full understanding of agenda formation and policy making. Similarly, it would be helpful to improve our understanding of how major policy change comes about, especially given the considerable obstacles today in addressing third-generation environmental problems. Looking back to previous policy change, for example, in the 1970s, what can we say about the conditions for successful policy making at that time, and what are the implications for comparable policy change over the next few decades?

In chapter 17, Rinfret and Furlong analyze rule making involving environmental and natural resource policy and what tends to influence the rule-making process. Their review of the literature underscores the need to examine how approaches to rule making differ across presidential administrations. There is ample evidence to suggest that the political and ideological orientation of the president and his agency appointees, along with other factors, dictate the content of rules initially proposed. Additional data should therefore be collected on the nature and contents of rules that have been proposed and implemented by various administrations. Clearly, which interest groups and individuals participate in the initial selection and formulation of rules prior to regulatory negotiations taking place is likely to affect rule making greatly. Other factors such as types of legislative mandates, input from the scientific community, and media involvement may also play a part in an administration's decision to promulgate particular new rules and change existing rules.

Steven Cohen (chapter 28), Sheila Olmstead (chapter 25), Judith Layzer (chapter 27), and Andrea Gerlak and her collaborators (chapter 19) examine how particular policy tools and approaches can be successful or unsuccessful in environmental policy making. While Cohen points to the need for greater use of strategic regulatory planning, Olmstead tends to embrace the value of market incentives in environmental policy. Both Layzer and Gerlak and her colleagues are supportive of the use of collaborative management approaches to environmental protection, yet they also voice concern about the overall level of effectiveness of these approaches. A great deal more research needs to be pursued regarding under what conditions certain policy tools are most likely to succeed and fail. Although there is much literature on this general topic, there is no systematic, rigorous study that outlines the specific circumstances that promote or hinder the effectiveness of particular policy tools and instruments.

While the United States was able to take swift action to protect the ozone layer (Benedick 1998; Litfin 1994), it has been largely unable to take action on climate change policy, particularly at the federal level. Despite pressure from a certain sector of the chemical industry, the government played a leadership role in forging a series of successful international agreements to reduce chlorofluorocarbons (CFC) emissions and to shield the ozone layer. In contrast, the U.S. government has been roundly criticized by environmental groups and nearly all advanced industrialized and developing nations for doing too little to reduce greenhouse gas emissions, principally carbon dioxide (CO_2) emissions, which is necessary to halt the continued warming of the Earth's atmosphere. As Selin and VanDeveer (chapter 8) point out, the United States is the largest emitter of CO_2 in the world. Nevertheless, American energy companies, led by the fossil fuel industry, have been quite successful in blocking government action on this issue. As a consequence, the federal government has neither signed the Kyoto climate change treaty nor formulated and implemented a comprehensive plan of its own. Of course, the economic impact of reducing greenhouse gases will be broader and deeper on industry, consumers, and the nation than the economic impact of reducing CFC emissions has been. As Selin and VanDeveer correctly note, the climate change policy issue is extremely complex, and more empirical research needs to be conducted on the factors that influence U.S. involvement in international regimes, such as climate change.

3. Conclusions

This concluding chapter and the other chapters in the volume have offered a large and diversified set of suggestions for future research. In many ways, the book itself reflects the growth and maturation of the study of U.S. environmental policy and politics over the past four decades. All of the chapters point to significant advancements in what we know even while their authors point to remaining gaps in our knowledge. Of particular importance is the way in which students of environmental politics and policy now recognize the need to anchor their work in a literature that is now far more theoretically informed and grounded in solid empirical study. That is, in comparison to previous years, scholars today recognize the value of cumulating knowledge and building on what has been done before. Some topics are so new that even basic descriptions and speculation about, for example, the promise of new governance mechanisms can be valuable. Yet for topics that have already been carefully studied but where approaches, methods, and findings differ, one needs to begin with a summary and integration of that prior work as new studies are designed and conducted to build on that foundation.

The research summarized in this book focuses on political science and to some extent policy studies, and, within these fields, the authors have concentrated on U.S. environmental policy and politics. As we have noted, however, the related fields of comparative and international environmental policy and politics have grown as well and fully merit their own comparable volumes. Much the same might be said for work in normative political theory. There will surely be such efforts in the future.

Finally, it must be said that the study of environmental policy and politics would be incomplete without acknowledging and taking seriously the advice from the National Science Foundation (NSF) that we noted in chapter 1. This concerns the need for interdisciplinary study of environmental problems and how to respond to them. As the Advisory Committee for Environmental Research and Education (2009) observed, "The world is at a crossroads," and humans are stressing natural as well as social systems beyond their capacity. The problems that we face—most notably, but not only, climate change—are enormously complex, and our knowledge is understandably limited, fragmented, and contentious. We believe political science and policy studies have much to contribute to the way we confront these kinds of problems. At the same time, we believe that other social science disciplines (e.g., sociology and economics) have much to contribute as well and that interdisciplinary study also must receive increased recognition and support if we are to understand the multiple and interrelated causes of environmental problems and the likely effect of a diversity of possible policy actions on those problems.

Interdisciplinary study that seeks to integrate social science disciplines is difficult enough and not widely embraced for a variety of reasons related to the conventional ways in which we define legitimate research and the effects of professional reward systems. But what we need goes well beyond the crossing of social science disciplinary boundaries. Solving environmental problems clearly requires the integration of knowledge from a range of disciplines, particularly the natural and social sciences, but also including the humanities, as well as discovery and promotion of new ways to encourage the use of such knowledge in policy making and in building public understanding. No one would argue that such ambitious goals can be easily achieved, but that does not diminish the need to try. Thus, we hope that the chapters included here are of interest to students within political science and policy studies. We also hope they can spark creative research that cuts across conventional disciplinary study and contributes to the vision set out by the NSF committee in 2009 that we significantly improve our capacity to respond effectively to the unprecedented environmental challenges of the twenty-first century.

REFERENCES

Advisory Committee for Environmental Research and Education. 2009. *Transitions and Tipping Points in Complex Environmental Systems*. Washington, DC: National Science Foundation.

Benedick, R. E. 1998. *Ozone Diplomacy: New Directions in Safeguarding the Planet*. Enlarged ed. Cambridge, MA: Harvard University Press.

Cohen, S., S. Kamieniecki, and M. A. Cahn. 2005. *Strategic Planning in Environmental Regulation: A Policy Approach That Works*. Cambridge, MA: MIT Press.

Durant, R. F., D. J. Fiorino, and R. O'Leary, eds. 2004. *Environmental Governance Reconsidered: Challenges, Choices, and Opportunities*. Cambridge, MA: MIT Press.

Eisner, M. A. 2007. *Governing the Environment: The Transformation of Environmental Regulation*. Boulder, CO: Lynne Rienner.

Fairfax, S. K., L. Gwin, M. A. King, L. Raymond, and L. A. Watt. 2005. *Buying Nature: The Limits of Land Acquisition as a Conservation Strategy: 1780–2004*. Cambridge, MA: MIT Press.

Fiorino, D. J. 2006. *The New Environmental Regulation*. Cambridge, MA: MIT Press.

Klyza, C. M., and D. Sousa. 2008. *American Environmental Policy, 1990–2006: Beyond Gridlock*. Cambridge, MA: MIT Press.

Kraft, M. E. 2011. *Environmental Policy and Politics*. 5th ed. New York: Pearson Longman.

Kraft, M. E., M. Stephan, and T. D. Abel. 2011. *Coming Clean: Information Disclosure and Environmental Performance*. Cambridge, MA: MIT Press.

Layzer, J. A. 2008. *Natural Experiments: Ecosystem-Based Management and the Environment*. Cambridge, MA: MIT Press.

Litfin, K. T. 1994. *Ozone Discourses: Science and Politics in Global Environmental Cooperation*. New York: Columbia University Press.

Lubell, M., and B. Segee. 2013. "Conflict and Cooperation in Natural Resource Management." In *Environmental Policy: New Directions for the Twenty-First Century*, 8th ed., ed. N. J. Vig and M. E. Kraft. Washington, DC: CQ Press.

Miller, N. 2002. *Environmental Politics: Interest Groups, the Media, and the Making of Policy*. Boca Raton, FL: Lewis.

Press, D., and D. A. Mazmanian. 2013. "Toward Sustainable Production: Finding Workable Strategies for Government and Industry." In *Environmental Policy: New Directions for the Twenty-First Century*, 8th ed., ed. N. J. Vig and M. E. Kraft. Washington, DC: CQ Press.

Rosenau, P. V. 2000. *Public-Private Policy Partnerships*. Cambridge, MA: MIT Press.

Sabatier, P. A., W. Focht, M. Lubell, Z. Trachtenberg, A. Vedlitz, and M. Matlock, eds. 2005. *Swimming Upstream: Collaborative Approaches to Watershed Management.* Cambridge, MA: MIT Press.

Vig, N. J., and M. E. Kraft, eds. 2013. *Environmental Policy: New Directions for the Twenty- First Century.* 8th ed. Washington, DC: CQ Press.

Weber, E. P. 2003. *Bringing Society Back In: Grassroots Ecosystem Management, Accountability, and Sustainable Communities.* Cambridge, MA: MIT Press.

Whiteley, J. M., H. Ingram, and R. W. Perry, eds. 2008. *Water, Place, and Equity.* Cambridge, MA: MIT Press.

INDEX

....